Principles of ECONOMICS

Principles of ECONOMICS

Robert Haney Scott
UNIVERSITY OF WASHINGTON

Nic Nigro
SEATTLE CENTRAL
COMMUNITY COLLEGE

Macmillan Publishing Co., Inc.
New York

Collier Macmillan Publishers
London

Dedicated to my parents
N.N.

Dedicated to my family
R.H.S.

Printed in the United States of America

Macmillan Publishing Co., Inc.
866 Third Avenue, New York, New York 10022

Collier Macmillan Canada, Ltd.

Library of Congress Cataloging in Publication Data

Scott, Robert Haney.
Principles of economics.

Includes index.
1. Economics. I. Nigro, Nic. II. Title.
HB171.5.S2994 330 81-8409
ISBN 0-02-408360-7 AACR2

Cover and Interior Design: Natasha Sylvester

Printing: 1 2 3 4 5 6 7 8 Year: 2 3 4 5 6 7 8

Preface

The new developments that have occurred in economic theory over the last two decades represent an effort to place macroeconomics on a firmer microeconomic foundation. This means focusing on those microeconomic concepts that motivate individual choices. The cumulative effect of such choices influences and directs the larger economy. Thus, in our text, we start by introducing the fundamental notions of property rights, opportunity cost, transaction costs, and relative prices—the intuitive guts of microeconomic—to bind micro- and macroeconomic theory into a more coherent study.

We recognize that most students do not find economic theory easy. Students coming to it for the first time can be amazed at its level of abstraction. So we have tried to introduce the theory gently, yet avoid triviality. To do so, we introduce property rights, transactions costs, and exchange in Chapter 2 before supply and demand appears in Chapter 3; and Chapter 3 introduces transactions costs as a shift parameter in the supply and demand functions. In Chapter 5, we take a closer look at costs than is usual because basic cost concepts are often deceptively simple in statement but just as often difficult in application. Transactions costs and their role in the analysis of the firm reappear in Chapter 7. And Chapter 19 provides an economic analysis of the democratic political process from a microeconomic point of view.

These basic concepts are carried into macroeconomics to the extent they contribute a better appreciation of macroeconomic functions. Thus Chapter 21 on government shows how the emergence of government can be explained as a logical extension of a few microeconomic principles: namely, scarcity, property rights, transactions costs, and rational choice and the economic efficiency it implies. To put meat on the bare bones of theory, we also employ these concepts to explain the effects on the economy of society's other institutional arrangements. Consequently, there is a full chapter on employment and the labor market. Search and transactions costs help to interpret firm and worker behavior, notably downward money wage inflexibility: while a sense of institutional constraints permeating labor markets is, we believe, essential to understanding today's stubborn inflation.

For its part, the chapter on inflation offers more than the casual, shallow explanations of demand-pull and cost-push inflation. Microeconomic foundations are again summoned to explain new perceptions in macroeconomics such as rational expectations and supply side economics, with its emphasis on the influence of taxes and government regulations on relative prices—hence on work and investment incentives.

Chapter 29 discusses the monetarist–Keynesian controversy over stabilization policy to show that the technical differences between the two viewpoints are subtle rather than dramatic but that their respective implications as to what policy ought to be differ substantially.

To place macroeconomic theory in perspective, we unfold it in historic sequence, following the transition from classical theory to Keynesian theory to the resurrected, but now more sophisticated, classical formulation. To economists it is a fascinating story, and we believe students will find it interesting too. All our lives will be affected by the future application of economic theories developing today.

Each chapter, after the first, starts with a three-part Progress Report which reviews the main concerns of the previous chapter, the highlights of the current chapter, and concepts that will be explored in the following chapter.

Marginal Comments reinforce important concepts and terms. They provide a useful tool for chapter review and comprise a running glossary.

Interesting applications of economic theory are presented in Boxes throughout the text.

Graphs, Charts, and Tables have been carefully designed to be clearly understood.

Chapter Summaries itemize major concepts, and the extensive End-of-Chapter Questions are a useful self-assessment tool for the student of economics, or can be used as starting points for lectures.

The sequence of the text is optional, but any alternative sequence should begin with the introductory section, "Tools of Economics," which includes exchange, transactions costs, and property rights, as well as an appendix explaining such tools as variables and functions, stocks and flows, graphs, equations, and identities. The following chart illustrates possible chapter orders for microeconomics first, macroeconomics first, and a one-semester course.

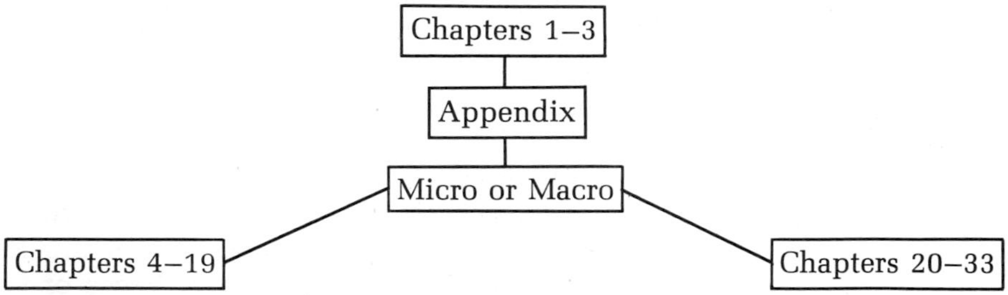

One Semester Course

Micro				Macro		
1	6	12	– – – – – – – Appendix – – – – – – –	20	26	30
3	7	17		24	27	31
4	9			25	29	32

Acknowledgments

We are indebted to the following people for incisive comments and assistance. Chris Hall (University of California at Los Angeles) patiently spent many hours discussing the power—and the weakness—of economic theory. Mack Ott (Pennsylvania State University) and Donald Farness (Oregon State University) were particularly helpful in their thoroughness. The many reviewers to whom we are indebted for their unflagging efforts and insightful suggestions are:

Robert Barckley (San Diego State University)
Larry Beall (Virginia Commonwealth University)
Edward Day (University of Louisville)
Richard Froyen (University of North Carolina)
Paul F. Haas (Bowling Green State University)
David Kemme (University of North Carolina)
Charles Knapp
Roger McCain (Temple University)
Nicholas R. Noble (Miami University)
Kent W. Olson (Oklahoma State University)
Jonas Prager (New York University)
Robert Pulsinelli (Western Kentucky University)
Cadwell L. Ray (University of Tulsa)
Ronald G. Reddall (Allan Hancock Junior College)
David H. Resler
Dennis H. Sullivan (Miami University)
Frank D. Tinari (Seton Hall University)
John A. Tomaske (California State University-Los Angeles)

They are, of course, absolved of any errors. We also express our gratitude to Guenter Conradus for his comments and Phillip Bourque and Barney Dowdle for some of the chapter questions.

Also, a special thanks to our editors, Charles Place and Kate Moran, and our production supervisor, John Travis.

We would also like to thank Carolyn Richardson for typing a manuscript she thought would never end. In addition, we gratefully acknowledge typing assistance from Bonnie Labrec.

Nic Nigro
Robert Haney Scott

Seattle, Washington
1981

Contents

TOOLS OF ECONOMICS

31 Inflation 777

32 International Trade and Exchange Rates 819

33 Economic Growth 853

Index 873

TOOLS OF ECONOMICS

Chapter 1

Economics: Getting Started

If language is not correct, then what is said is not meant. If what is said is not meant, then what ought to be done remains undone.

– Confucius

INTRODUCTION

Individuals in all societies are beset by fundamental problems of physical survival. Mere subsistence requires that they have minimal levels of food, clothing, and shelter. These necessities are extracted from the earth's environment by the application of human effort.

Economics has to do with understanding how men and women provide for their necessities, but it goes beyond concern for necessities. Even if all human necessities are provided, many human wants remain unsatisfied. If wants are unsatisfied, we say that scarcity exists. **Scarcity** means that wants exceed the supply of goods available to satisfy them. If there are not enough goods to go around—not enough to satisfy everyone's wants—then some means must be found to allocate what goods there are among the various uses to which they could be put. Economics is thus concerned with the allocation of scarce goods, and with two questions: What is the best way to provide goods and services to the people, and who will receive these goods and services once they are provided?

Scarcity **means that wants are greater than the goods available to satisfy them.**

The **allocation problem** involves how to produce, what to produce, who is to produce what, and who is to receive what is produced. A closely related yet separate problem is how much of these goods and services particular individuals should receive. This is the **distribution problem**, and it involves the issue of equity or fairness.

The ***allocation problem*** **involves how to produce, what to produce, who is to produce what, and who is to receive what is produced.**

The ***distribution problem*** **involves how much of goods and services particular individuals receive.**

While economics is the study of allocation problems, it is also a science in the full sense of that word. As a science, it rests on a system of logic. In the science of mechanics, for example, formulas have been developed to help engineers solve mechanical problems. These formulas apply to many different kinds of problems. The same is true of economics. As economist John Maynard Keynes once wrote,

> The theory of economics does not furnish a body of settled conclusions immediately applicable to policy. It is a method rather than a doctrine, an apparatus of the mind, a technique of thinking which helps its possessor to draw correct conclusions.

Thus, economics can be seen as a way of thinking about things systematically so that one may understand and interpret economic events.

The study of economics can get us started in solving allocation and distribution problems by asking appropriate questions and avoiding what is irrelevant. In this chapter we are going to talk about the economist's technique of analysis. It is scientific, just as physics and chemistry are scientific. This may surprise you because it is widely believed that since economics, sociology, psychology, and other social sciences deal with human behavior, it is not possible to treat these subjects in a scientific way. As we shall see, this is not true.

The attitude that economics is unscientific may be reinforced, however, because economists often draw conclusions that seem to conflict with common sense—for instance, "some pollution is better than none" or "unbalanced federal budgets can help the economy."

POSITIVE AND NORMATIVE STATEMENTS

Statements about how things are related to each other are called *positive statements;* statements about how things ought to be are called *normative statements.*

There are two fundamental types of issues that human beings are interested in: how things *are,* and how things *ought to be.* Statements about how things are related to each other are called **positive statements**. Statements about how things ought to be are called **normative statements**.

Let us take an example from physics. If you drop a brick out the window, a physicist can tell you how long it will take to reach the ground. Formulas in physics can describe how a falling object behaves: "If you drop a brick from this window, then it will reach the ground three seconds later." This is a prediction, a statement about a relation between what you do and what happens if you do it. It is a statement about the relation between the instant that you let go of the brick and the instant that it reaches ground. It is about how falling bricks behave. All scientific statements, including those in the science of economics, are statements about how things are related to each other.

Normative statements are about how things ought to be: "You should drop the brick out the window." "It is wrong to drop the brick." "I would like to drop the brick." When statements include words such as ought, should, wrong, right, desire, fair, they are almost always normative statements.

A positive statement may tell you something about what will happen if you do drop the brick, but it cannot tell you whether or not you ought to drop it. If there is a child playing in the garden below the window, then certainly people would agree you ought not to drop it, for it may harm the child. On the other hand, if there is a thief or gunman about to do harm then perhaps you ought to drop it in hopes of preventing harm. Science alone does not answer normative questions. Human feelings and attitudes must be added to science in order to answer them.

Normative statements may be concerned with whether buying or producing *Playboy* magazine rather than the *New Yorker* magazine is wrong or right or the best reading material for society. Positive economics, on the other hand, will only record and analyze whether people do buy more (or less) of one kind of magazine than another in response to some change. For example, the magazine's price may change or costs of production change, or another magazine may appear on the market with a slightly different format—like *Ms.* Positive economics is concerned with predicting whether people will buy more magazines in response to these changes. It predicts how people will behave in certain circumstances in the same way the physicist predicts how bricks will behave if you drop them.

It must be noted that economists do not seek to determine why some people have the tastes and preferences they do. They are not specifically interested in the psychology of choice—the subconscious reasons that you buy *Ms.* instead of *Playboy*. Positive economics simply studies and tries to predict the economic choices people will make under certain assumed conditions. It predicts what behavior people will display when these conditions change. As with all science, positive economics attempts to be objective, and to do so it uses the scientific method.

THE SCIENTIFIC METHOD

The *scientific method* involves the sequence of formulating the question, conducting the investigation, and drawing a conclusion.

In simple terms, the scientific method involves the sequence of formulating the question, conducting the investigation, and drawing a conclusion. The sequence can be elaborated upon and the details made more specific. It is outlined in Figure 1-1.

Definitions In forming an awareness and in making up questions one is using definitions. Often these are implicitly understood. Parties to an investigation must agree on what it is they are dealing with. This is fundamental. Terms and concepts employed must mean the same thing in a given experiment. A definition is neither true nor false, but it can be inconsistent. For example, if we speak of a man's tie we have to define it either to include or to exclude things that could arbitrarily be defined as ties, such as a handkerchief stuffed between the shirt collar and the neck, or an ascot.

Hypotheses A hypothesis is a statement about a relation between two events. For example, "When event *A* occurs, then event *B* will occur." This is a hypothesis—a statement about the relation between *A* and *B*. It predicts that *B* will occur if *A* occurs, given certain assumptions. Notice that we did not say that *A caused B*. All we said was that the events are related. In everyday language we often use the word *cause*, or *because*, and slip into the habit of saying that *A* caused *B*, or that *B* was caused by *A*. But in science we should interpret the statement as one about *how* events *A* and *B* are related, and not about *A* causing *B*.

Testing the Hypothesis Does the hypothesis hold or not? To find out if it holds, we cause event *A* to occur, and see if *B* follows. This is called an experiment, and we do it repeatedly to see if we can count on *B* following *A*.

A hypothesis must be formulated in such a manner that its prediction can be tested. For example, let our hypothesis be "People buy more ties when the price of men's ties falls." In constructing this hypothesis we made several implicit assumptions. We assumed certain conditions under which the original hypothesis is to be tested. Our assumptions are that income, tastes, and the prices of other goods are constant during the experiment. Keeping these variables as constant as possible, we can lower the price of ties and record the number of ties sold. If the number sold increases, we can say that our experiment has supported our hypothesis.

It is important to note two things: (1) The experiment can be *repeated* again and again. It takes repeated experiments for us to believe that the quantity bought did not just happen to rise by chance as we lowered the price. (2) The statement must be *refutable*. The lower price could, in fact, be followed either by greater sales *or by fewer sales of ties*. That is, it is possible that our hypothesis could be refuted by the experiment. Every scientific hypothesis must be stated in such a way that an experiment is *capable* of *refuting* its prediction. If you state a hypothesis that is incapable of being refuted by an

Figure 1-1

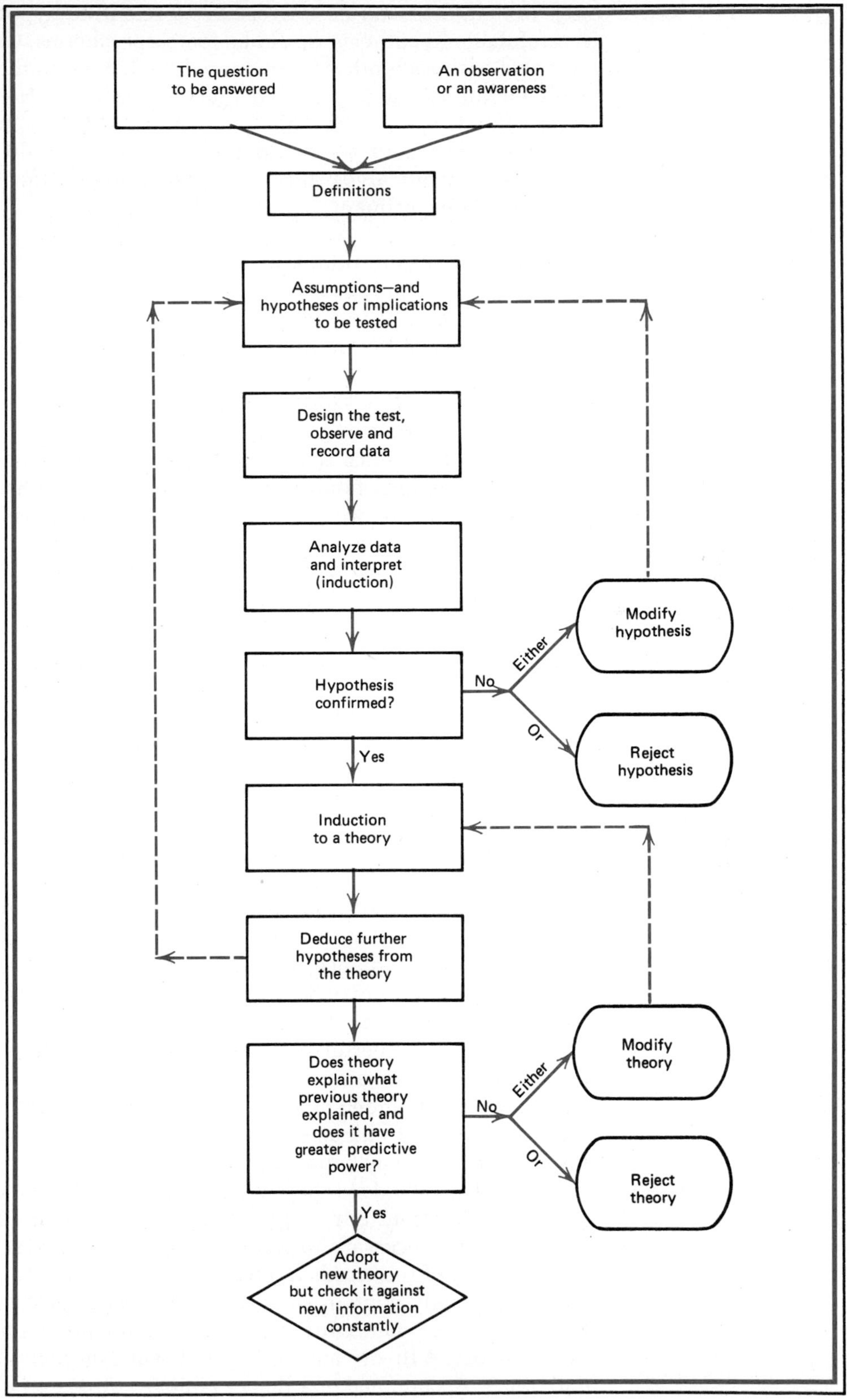
The question to be answered
An observation or an awareness
Definitions
Assumptions—and hypotheses or implications to be tested
Design the test, observe and record data
Analyze data and interpret (induction)
Hypothesis confirmed?
No
Either
Modify hypothesis
Or
Reject hypothesis
Yes
Induction to a theory
Deduce further hypotheses from the theory
Does theory explain what previous theory explained, and does it have greater predictive power?
No
Either
Modify theory
Or
Reject theory
Yes
Adopt new theory but check it against new information constantly

experiment, then you no longer have a scientific hypothesis. An example of a nonrefutable hypothesis would be that Leprechauns, Gnomes, and Hobgoblins compete with each other in an annual track meet in the forest—the Little People's Olympics. (It is reported that last year the Hobgoblins boycotted the meet.) Because we define all types of elves to be unobservable, there is no possible experiment we could undertake that would refute their existence. Statements about elves are, therefore, nonscientific because they are nonrefutable by experiment.

Assumptions Assumptions are really untested hypotheses that are accepted as ground rules for purposes of testing the main hypothesis. One or more of the assumptions may be incorrect without necessarily invalidating the hypothesis. It is the ability of the original hypothesis to predict that is in question.

Observation and Recording of Data Experiments require sensory recognition of data and the recording of data by taste, smell, touch, or sight using pencils, computers, or cameras. Data must be put into a workable, useful form so as to facilitate the design of the study. It is also important that we can verify to others that what we think we see, feel, or measure is what we really see, feel, or measure. For example, we must carefully rule out illusions such as optical illusions. Is the zebra black with white stripes or white with black stripes? We must make sure that our senses are not deceiving us. Data must be accessible to other researchers, and experiments must be designed so that others can undertake them. Otherwise we may just be deluding ourselves.

Analysis and Interpretation of Data Data must be carefully sorted and studied to ensure that they do not systematically and misleadingly bias the results toward an incorrect interpretation of events. Some data may not support the theory at all. But these data may be poor data and unreliable. Repeated experiments may be necessary to ensure that we will reject poor data before rejecting the theory itself.

Conclusion and Generalization If the hypothesis and the data are consistent with each other so that the data support the hypothesis, then the hypothesis is accepted. The acceptance is only tentative, because it is always possible that future experiments may not support it. If the hypothesis is repeatedly supported by the evidence and repeatedly accepted, it may be called a law. Having been led by our experiments to accept a single hypothesis, we may decide to generalize. In our example, observations about the relation between the price and quantity demanded of men's ties may be extended to other economic goods with well-defined characteristics. After finding that people buy more ties at lower prices, we may believe that they will buy more meat at lower prices, too. Indeed, we may believe they will buy more of any good at lower prices. Thus, we generalize from our single case to all goods (induction). Further experiments will be necessary to test each generality (deduction).

The use of the words *hypothesis, theory,* and *law* is to a degree arbitrary. Theories usually contain several interrelated hypotheses only some of which have been tested. One could think of a hypothesis as a more tentative statement than a theory. A theory may be thought of as intermediate between a hypothesis and a law. Acceptance of a theory is not as strong as for a law. Our belief in a law is stronger because it has had greater substantiation than a theory. There is no hard separation among a hypothesis, a theory, and a law for general agreement.

Notice that the beginning squares in Figure 1-1 allow for an accidental discovery or for a measurement that conflicts with the existing theory, or a new observation that fits no existing theory. In some situations better data may lead to rejection of what formerly was accepted as a credible theory.

IS SOCIAL SCIENCE POSSIBLE?

Some people do not believe human behavior can be studied scientifically, or even that it should be—for its study poses some troublesome ethical questions. Since a social science is the study of human behavior, it can run into problems when it uses words that have ordinary conversational meaning about human behavior. Words can have emotional content, and can trigger symbolic associations. Still, it is difficult to convert controversial words into impersonal mathematical language. Economics is the most mathematical of the social sciences. This is not surprising because it relies on measures of prices and quantities of goods. Yet there are two major criticisms leveled at economics, and at social science in general.

First, *human beings are complex*. There are too many variables that influence human behavior. It is difficult to run reliable controlled experiments on human beings as is done in the physical sciences. If a physicist wants to measure the effect of temperature change on the pressure of a gas, he may control the volume of the gas, and observe the relationship between the temperature and the pressure of the gas. Economists must take the environment as it is and cannot run controlled experiments. Thus, if taxes are cut, and an economist wants to observe the exact effect of the tax cut on consumer spending over the year, it is not possible to hold fixed such factors as the money supply, interest rates, costs of production, wages, and the many other variables that affect the decisions that people make.

It is easy to overlook some significant variable in attempting to explain behavior. Even where controlled experiments are tried in psychology and sociology, it is difficult to be certain that the tester is not affecting those tested, or that the contrived situation does not overlook something significant that might arouse the suspicion of those tested about the naturalness of the event.

In studying economics—as is the case in all sciences—the student must proceed in small steps, examining bits and pieces at a time and carefully limiting the scope of study. For this reason modern economics avoids ambitious designs that try to describe *all* sociopolitical influences in one sweep. This is both a virtue and a fault. Economic questions are narrowed so as to make measurement more precise.

Economics studies the implications of individual choice. But theories are tested on observations of groups, and what is true for the group need not apply under the stated conditions for everyone in the group. Therefore, economics employs probability concepts and statistical techniques. If it is predicted that more people will use umbrellas during a heavy rain than during a light rain, one cannot say definitely that Wally Wethead will use an umbrella. One can only calculate a probability that more people will use an umbrella.

The second major criticism is that because in social sciences humans observe and measure the behavior of other humans, the studies will always contain some *inherently subjective elements.* The tester is also the tested. But objectivity is still possible. There are, after all, rules of logic that apply to the human thinking process. Medical scientists can understand many things about the human body, chemists about body chemistry. In a similar manner, economists can observe whether people buy more when prices fall, given the stated conditions.

LIMITATIONS OF SCIENCE

Science and the scientific method are not infallible, nor can science answer all questions. But science is superior to any other game in town for sorting the facts. Scientific conclusions are always tentative, always at the mercy of new evidence and new theories that may spring from the new evidence. Science has always operated to throw away the old and put on the new. Of course, at times the old appears to be subsumed in the new. Science is cumulative, building step by step. While it has been successful and beneficial, there is also the danger that science may become the new folklore, the arbiter of all values or no values.

The economist who casually proposes that unemployment would solve our inflation problem might not be taking into full account the immediate human costs on some individuals, even though in the longer run the economist's theories may confer benefits on citizens at large. Thus positive economics can, in turn, have normative consequences. On many issues economic science can, indeed, be valuable as a source of advice on how to get where you want to go. It is less a source of advice, however, on whether you should try to get there. Normative issues are always very much with us, and presumably always will be.

THE ECONOMIC PROBLEM

It is the goal of this chapter to introduce the constraints that humans must confront when solving the problem of physical survival. Economic theory is a very useful tool in helping us at least to ask the right questions, if not always to come up with the right answers. How do people go about solving the problem of physical survival, given the finite size of the earth and its resources? How should they go about it if they desire to get the maximum from their efforts and the earth's limited bounty? What lies behind the process of choosing to solve the problem this way or that way? In answering these tough questions economics can be useful in sorting out ideas that are fertile from those that are barren. A few well-chosen concepts and tools can cut quickly through the maze and assist us in avoiding the myriad paths of confusion and frustration. Therefore, we begin by examining the fundamental nature of what we call the economic problem.

BASIC ASSUMPTIONS

In economic theory we make frequent use of a few basic assumptions about human behavior.

People Act in Their Own Self-Interest This assumption states that individuals want to make themselves as well off as possible. For example, if I find I can have milk delivered to my doorstep more cheaply by a different dairy than the one I now buy from, and I act in my own self-interest, I will shift dairies. With this reasoning, an economist will predict that if one dairy offers lower prices it will take business from the other dairy. This is a testable proposition. Empirically, it is refutable. We can observe the response of people in the community to a change in price.

People Prefer More to Less No matter what your current situation is, you would like just a little more, or maybe a lot more, of something else—some object, some experience, or some goal that has eluded you in the past. We all know of instances where it has not been true that people prefer more to less—that is, when it was refuted by observation. Nevertheless, as a *general* proposition it seems to hold. If you give things away, most of the time people will take them. As an economic proposition, therefore, we will often assume that people will be willing to accept any goods added to their disposal.

People Are Rational Rational behavior simply means that people use the most efficient means they know of to attain their goals. Given the hard way and the easy way, the rational economic person chooses the easier way. It implies choosing the path of least resistance to reach a goal. Of course, what is the best way for one person may not be the way that suits another person. But the individual will act according to what he perceives is the shortest path to his objective.

These assumptions of self-interest, more being preferred to less, and rationality in human behavior are often violated in real life. But from them we can derive descriptions of human behavior that enable us to predict the economic results of various occurrences. If the price charged by a competing supplier falls, self-interest will lead us to shift to that supplier. If we have a chance to have more, we'll take it. If we see a better way, our rational behavior will lead us to choose it. Of course, rational behavior is in our own self-interest. Thus, our assumptions are not always mutually exclusive. They imply each other in many cases.

SCARCITY

We opened this chapter by making the observation that humanity must provide for its survival by extracting the necessary provisions from nature. For most individuals this requires a process of exchanges with others who also extract essential goods from nature. In most cases no effort is required of children, but the time does come when nearly everyone must put aside childlike activities and face the economic condition—they must provide for their well-being.

What is the economic condition? Imagine for a moment a world where, at the age of ten, everyone automatically receives a super credit card. Anytime you want something you simply insert it into a slot at the Perpetual Warehouse Incorporated and order whatever you want in any amount you desire. You might put in for more steak, more records, medicine, a jacket, more space, or even more time. When your request has been processed, the card is coughed back out. There was no effort or sacrifice required from you except the formality of using your super credit card. Goods and services are limitless and free.

From childhood this kind of abundance has not been part of your experience. As a child typically you did not get all you wanted at Christmas. Playtime was limited; you had to stop playing when you did not want to. If your mother gave you some spending money for the local candy store, you never had enough money for all the things you liked.

In similar fashion, the authorities do not seem to be able to satisfy all the demands of competing groups in society for the funds in the government coffers. The schools want more funds, as do the handicapped, scientists, the military, consumer groups, truckers, farmers, the poor, the middle income people, the maritime industry.

The clamor for more never ceases. More may be preferred to less but it is not possible for everyone to have as much as each wants. There is a resistant force out there. And it is not your government, your union, or your employer who is the real culprit; everyone and every institution lives under constraints. The fact is that the world is finite. Space, time, knowledge, minerals, water, timber are finite; they are limited. This is the fact of scarcity. When combined with the behavioral assumptions with which we started, we are faced with the economic condition of scarcity. *Resources are limited, humans wants are unlimited.*

As you are aware by now, in economics many commonly used words are adapted to be used in a rather special way. They are defined more narrowly in economics than in common usage. To begin with, goods not desired are not economic goods. Only desired goods qualify as scarce goods. These goods are called **economic goods**. Garbage is available in limited supplies but not wanted; it is not desired and therefore is not an economic good. To obtain economic goods also requires a *sacrifice* of some kind; something must be given up. The ocean and the air are not economic goods. While desired, they are freely abundant.

Economic goods are desired goods that are scarce.

Given the condition of scarcity, one is forced to choose among alternatives. For if one cannot have everything he or she wants, then the choice of one thing means giving up something else. The economic condition of scarcity means that choices must be made. This fact of life introduces another element into the study of economics; namely, the hard knocks of decision making. Choices made under the constraint of scarcity necessarily involve costs. There is no way out of it. We conclude that an *economic good is something that is desired and scarce. In order to acquire it, something else has to be sacrificed.*

OPPORTUNITY COST

Opportunity cost is the value of the sacrifice you make in choosing to consume or produce one economic good or service instead of another.

The value of the sacrifice you make in choosing to consume or produce one economic good or service, instead of some other good or service, is known as **opportunity cost** or simply *cost* for short. The economic cost of anything is measured by the highest valued alternative currently foregone.

So long as scarcity is a fact of life, making choices involves costs. Time is a scarce resource. The time spent doing one thing means not doing something else. Do you study for tomorrow's exam tonight or watch the football game on television? The cost to you of watching the game might be twenty points lost on the exam by not studying as hard as you could have. The cost of studying for the exam is not viewing the game. The cost of doing the same thing can vary under different circumstances. If you take a walk while the Super Bowl is on, and you are an avid football fan, the cost of your walk is higher than it would be if the game were not on television at that time. Cost in economics is measured not by the value of what was done, but by the value of what was thereby not done.

Opportunity cost in economics is a deeper and more fundamental concept than is normally found in everyday conversation when we tell a friend how much something cost us. It is, perhaps, the major principle upon which economic theory is constructed. Unfortunately, the basic concepts of a discipline are sometimes among the most difficult ones to get straight.

Cost in economics means something more than the daily money outlays you make when buying things. To be more exact, *opportunity cost is the value of the highest-valued, sacrificed alternative coincident with a choice or decision.* Cost represents the value of something you decide to do without, because of a choice you make. The appearance of the word *highest* in the definition of cost is deliberate and crucial. Opportunity cost is not the sum of all the other things we could have bought or could have produced. It is measured by the highest-valued alternative, not by *all* of the alternatives. Because scarcity exists, the cost of having one thing is the loss experienced from not having something else. If there were no scarcity, we could have as much of anything we wanted without having to do without anything else. Without scarcity, there would be no allocation problem; everything would be free. Nor would we have to concern ourselves with getting the most out of what resources are available. Economics would be unnecessary in the Garden of Eden.

Consider the choice of going off to college. Hypothetical annual expenditures are as follows:

Tuition and fees	$2,000
Books and supplies	230
Dormitory fees	2,500
Recreation	380
Transportation, laundry, etc	120
Total outlays	$5,230

Is $5,230 the full cost of going to college? Let us examine the entries one by one. Tuition fees, books, and supplies are costs totaling $2,230. This money could have been spent on a tour of Europe, or on meditating with your favorite guru in the Himalayas. What about the $2,500 for dormitory fees, including meals? Is this a cost of going to college for a year? Ask yourself if you would have needed food and shelter had you not enrolled in college. Of course you would! You still need food and housing regardless of where you are and what you do. This is the cost of staying alive. (For the sake of argument we are assuming that food and shelter fees are the same in the college dormitory as they would be wherever you would choose to live.) It is unlikely that you would forsake housing, food, recreation, and clothing if you did not attend college. These expenses are incurred under any circumstances. They are not costs uniquely associated with going to college.

You realize that going to college while living at home instead of living in a dormitory might have reduced out-of-pocket costs. Any *difference* between dormitory expenses and at-home expenses should be added to the cost of going *away* to college.

Assume you do not live at home. Have all the opportunity costs of attending college been covered? Namely, the $2,230 for tuition, books, and supplies? Were there any other sacrifices beside the $2,230 you saved to go to college?

You are right. There is something else you sacrificed when you went to college. It was the money you *could have* earned from a job. Assume you graduated from high school last June. And suppose you had a job offer and could have made $6,000 for the year. But you gave up this job in order to attend college. Now you can calculate the full opportunity cost of the decision to attend college. It is $2,230 + $6,000 = $8,230. However, if you are unskilled and unemployed, and did not have a job opportunity where you could earn $6,000, then this is not an opportunity cost. The $6,000 is not sacrificed if it could not have been earned. No resources were lost to society, because according to the market you had none to give. In this case, going to college only costs you the $2,230 you spend on tuition, books, and other supplies.

Because costs are measured not only by what is done but also by what is not done or foregone, the full meaning and measure of costs is often misunderstood and understated. Members of Congress, state and local officials, and many agencies often underestimate the costs of projects because they do not fully understand opportunity costs. Some costs are left out. The result is often the misallocation of scarce resources that we call inefficiency: not getting the most from the finite resources available. More precisely, *increasing* **efficiency**

Increasing *efficiency* occurs when we rearrange the use of resources so as to benefit some person without reducing benefits to any others.

occurs when we rearrange the use of resources so as to benefit some person without reducing benefits to any others.

In nontechnical language, opportunity cost can be expressed by the slogan, "There is no such thing as a free lunch." If someone might dispute that catchy phrase using the example of free lunches provided to school children, he would be right—so far as school children go. But he would be wrong for society as a whole. Somehow, somewhere in the society, resources had to be used to produce this food. Behind those free lunches are farm costs, capital, labor, and transportation costs. These resources could have been used to produce goods and services for others. Tax money to provide "free" school lunches could have been used for many other purposes.

Thus far we have been making the strong implicit assumption that money outlays are accurate measures of opportunity costs. Often this is not true. Actually, costs reflect alternatives that are sacrificed—services rendered and physical goods that could be produced and exchanged. Money is principally a measuring device, a medium of exchange that we use in order to make the trading of goods and resources easy to carry out. When we imply that price equals opportunity cost, we are assuming that the very special conditions of a competitive market are in effect. We will be saying more about this topic in later chapters. For now, it is sufficient to treat money price as if it were equal to opportunity cost; this simplifies the explanation of some concepts we want to talk about first.

Let us turn to an example where full costs are underestimated: Congress in its yearly anguish over the military budget.

THE VOLUNTEER ARMY

An excellent way to illustrate the concept of opportunity costs as the true measure of costs is to compare the military draft to the volunteer army. You have, no doubt, heard complaints about the cost of the volunteer system. But is it any higher than that of the draft mechanism?

In 1974 the military draft was abolished and replaced with a volunteer army. The new system has brought about significant changes from the traditional lives of GIs. Enlistees now have the option of being served hamburgers and soft drinks for lunch. And who is serving these meals? Other GIs? No, not anymore. There is no KP (kitchen police) from dawn to dusk, from 3:30 A.M. to 9:00 P.M. or later depending on the whim of a mess sergeant who has allowed you only a few minutes to sit during the whole day for brief meals. Civilians are hired to do the grub work. No longer must you try to sleep among the commotion and stacked beds in old barracks. Now there are four- and eight-man apartments that can be, within limits, decorated to individual tastes. When basic training is completed, an apartment can be rented off base and no pass is needed to leave the post. There is hazard pay for volunteering for combat duty. Married personnel receive tax-free allowances for housing. Does all this represent a more costly and inefficient use of resources than the old universal draft method?

Consider Private Hargrove who, as a civilian, had been making \$8,000 a year two years after having graduated from high school. When he is involuntarily drafted he is paid \$1,200 a year plus his room and board worth approximately \$2,500 over the year, for a total of \$3,700. The \$8,000 measures the market value of his services as a civilian, say as a stock clerk. This is his opportunity cost, the value of what he sacrifices in his control over resources when he becomes a soldier. At \$3,700 for his services as a soldier, the government is paying him less than his opportunity cost. In essence he is being *taxed* \$4,300 a year for the privilege of losing some of his freedom. Also, when \$3,700 is allocated in the federal budget for Hargrove's services, the \$3,700 outlay understates the opportunity costs by measuring only budget costs. These are only *part* of true economic costs to the society.

Under the volunteer system, the budget costs more accurately reflect true costs, because to induce Hargrove to volunteer requires paying him at least his opportunity cost as determined by the market value of his civilian services. No longer are the true costs of the draft disguised. If Hargrove had been unemployable as a civilian, the opportunity costs of his labor services would have been zero, and in the economic sense he would receive more than his worth in the market by being paid the army wage and receiving benefits in kind (food, lodging, clothes).

By being forced to compete for human resources in the market under a volunteer system, the government must pay the full opportunity costs to acquire personnel. Furthermore, under the draft the engineer who is used as a cook is being used inefficiently because such mismatching reduces the total output of society. Even if the army uses the engineer as an engineer, he may not be performing those particular engineering tasks for which he is best suited and therefore most efficient.

Since it was instituted, many people have voiced disaffection with the volunteer army. It is costing too much; it is hard to attract quality personnel; army manuals are now written at the sixth-grade reading level; and there are too few doctors and dentists and too many minorities in proportion to the numbers in the total population. All these criticisms give evidence of the full cost of the draft system. Just think of the even larger expenditures that would be required for the military to obtain the quality people it really wants.

Of course, one could argue for the draft by taking the normative position that U.S. citizens *should* be required to make a sacrifice. They should be expected to devote their resources to the defense of the country for a time. And those who are drafted should be chosen randomly in order to prevent anyone from avoiding it through real or contrived exemptions. However, this does not alter the full cost of having a military draft. It merely enforces the opportunity cost concept and brings the point home with a vengeance.

The true economic cost to society of a conscripted army is at least as large as, and probably much larger than, the cost of a volunteer army. If you have to draft people to get them to take a job in the army, they go against their will. This means that the value of the highest alternative employment—their job at the gasoline station, say—is greater than the value of their army job. Opportunity costs are greater than those measured by their army pay check. If all who join the service have done so voluntarily, however, then the dollar pay check does come close to measuring the cost of the army to the public. Thus, to society, it is clear that the real economic cost of a volunteer force is considerably less than the cost of a conscripted force. This means that a volunteer force is economically more efficient because in fact it is less costly to society.[1]

Allocation

One can see why efficiency is important once the notion of scarcity is clearly understood. Scarcity exists if there is not enough to give everyone all that he or she wants. Therefore, we are better off if we can at least obtain the *most* output from what is available—stretch the dollar, so to speak. To be efficient means that at least we do not waste what we have available. The study of economics is vitally concerned with efficient allocation. We do not have efficient allocation if it remains possible for us to make at least one person better off without making anyone else worse off by rearranging the way our resources are used.

To be efficient, we must decide *how* best to use scarce resources to produce as much as possible of *what* we want. Having decided these questions, we turn to the problem of *for whom* goods and services should be provided. Who gets them? These questions *how, what,* and *for whom* are concerned with the allocation problem. Economic theory has made substantial progress in developing the tools to analyze and solve the conditions for efficiency, if not the achievement of it. Our intention in the first few chapters is to develop and describe those principles that lead to the maximization of output and consumption and minimization of costs and expenditures, given the condition of scarcity and the unavoidable reality of costs.

The free movement of *relative prices* is the guiding principle in achieving efficiency.

The guiding principle in achieving efficiency is the free movement of relative prices. Prices are like beacons in the economic sea directing the traffic of resource movements and providing information to guide these resources to their most productive ports of use. As long as goods are desired and scarce, prices will be attached to them. Note that we refer to **relative prices** and not just dollar prices. What directs resources is not just how high or low prices are—not just their level—but how high they are relative to one another.

Distribution of Output (Income)

A far more difficult problem is uncovered when we open the question of the *distribution* of the output. As output is received by people, they call it their income. The question is *how much* should each individual receive of the economic pie? Allocation is concerned with who gets it. But *distribution* deals with how much those who get it, get. The approach of positive economics cannot lead to an answer to this question; that is, it cannot help us make the decision about who ought to get how much. This is a normative question. The efficiency criterion itself can be satisfied for a whole range and variety of different income distributions. Which one is fair, or the fairest?

As economic theory now stands, this normative question cannot be an-

[1]If a draftee were allowed to hire a replacement, the money expenditures made to the replacement would be a measure of the tax imposed on the draftee by conscription.

swered with purely analytical techniques. What economics can do is shed some light on many of the likely positive consequences of different normative programs that the society may choose. These programs are often introduced through political action. The citizens express their preferences by voting for different arrangements of taxation, subsidization, welfare payment, property use, and so on. It may be that different judgments made by society as to how the pie is to be sliced will also have the effect of changing the size of the entire pie. Taking from workers and giving to nonworkers may reduce the incentive to work and leave a smaller pie to be divided. Here differences among socialists, capitalists, Marxists, and all the other "ists" you can think of make their appearance and have their followers and their fanatics. Economic theory should be of help in comparing the allocation effects of the programs established by different political systems. It may be possible for economics to make reasonable connections between the *way* a society solves its allocation problem and the resultant income and wealth distribution the society realizes. If economic theory is scientifically based and has an internal logic of its own, it should help people of all economic systems to solve their common problem of scarcity. People of each system may thereby decide for themselves how they want to redistribute total output, to satisfy their beliefs about the just society while adhering to the guidelines for efficiency suggested by economic principles.

Economics is the study of how people allocate and distribute scarce resources among competing ends over time.

Given that the problems of distribution should be explicitly included in our definition of economics, we might define **economics** as the study of how people behave to allocate and distribute scarce resources among competing ends over time.

Microeconomics and Macroeconomics

Typically, in the study of economics, the subject is divided into two major sections. One section covers what is called microeconomics and the other is called macroeconomics.

Microeconomics is the study of small economic units: the firm, the industry, the consumer, and markets for individual goods or services.

A _market_ is made up of a group of buyers and sellers who trade or exchange a definable commodity.

Microeconomics is the study of small economic units (*micro* meaning *small*). In micro (short for microeconomics) we study the firm, the industry, the consumer, and markets for individual goods or services. A **market** is made up of a group of buyers and sellers who trade or exchange a definable commodity. In most of the first part of the book we shall be discussing the details of markets in a market economy—how prices are determined, profits maximized, and efficiency attained. The guiding principle of a market economy is the free movement of relative prices of commodities and of productive resources.

As long as there is scarcity, goods and services are not free. Prices will be attached to them. But meaningful economic prices are relative prices, not just absolute dollar prices. To explain why this is so, let us suppose that you paid 1,000 cruzeiros for your watch (the cruzeiro is the currency used in Brazil, like the dollar in the U.S.). If you happen to be familiar with Brazil, then just pretend it is the Greek drachma, or any other unfamiliar currency. Did you get a good deal by paying this price? Is it an expensive watch or a cheap watch? If you are unfamiliar with what a cruzeiro will buy, the information that you paid 1,000 cruzeiros does not enable you to place a value on the watch. But while touring Brazil, you had to pay 50 cruzeiros for a sandwich for lunch, 250 for a shirt, 750 for a hotel room, and 1,000 for a pair of shoes. With this information you would come to relate the price of the watch to other prices, and only then would you get a feeling for the watch's value. The watch cost the same as a pair of shoes. You could have bought 20 sandwiches for the value of the watch. If, furthermore, you recognize that in the U.S. you could pay $2 for a sandwich, $10 for a shirt, $30 for a hotel room, then the watch is worth about $40 and a cruzeiro is worth about 4 cents.

Microeconomics is often called price theory; *relative prices,* rather than nominal prices, are economically meaningful.

Only because we have had past experiences with a *variety* of prices expressed in dollars and/or cruzeiros can we interpret the value expressed by the citation of a single price expressed in terms of a monetary unit. Thus, **relative prices**, rather than nominal prices, are the economically meaningful prices. Microeconomics is often called price theory.

***Macroeconomics* is the study of the *aggregate* economy: the combined action of all firms, households, and industries.**

While microeconomics is the study of how relative prices are determined within the submarkets that comprise the total economy, **macroeconomics** refers to the study of the *aggregate* economy, the all-inclusive picture (*macro* meaning *big*). Macro (short for macroeconomics) is not concerned with just one firm, household, or industry as micro is, but with the combined action of all firms, households, and industries. It develops and studies concepts like gross national product (GNP), national income, investments, and consumption, and focuses on national issues of employment, inflation, total output, the balance of trade, income distribution, taxes, and the supply of money.

Macroeconomists divide the aggregate economy into four sectors—the *household sector,* the *business sector,* the *government sector,* and the *foreign trade sector.*

Macroeconomists divide the economy into four aggregate sectors: aggregate spending and saving of the **household sector**; aggregate investment spending of the **business sector**; government spending and taxation of the **government sector**; and imports and exports in the **foreign trade sector** at the national level. The sum of the spending of the sectors is called aggregate demand. The tools and theories of macroeconomics can be viewed as an extension of the basic concepts and tools developed in microeconomics. One can easily study either macroeconomics or microeconomics first.

Over the history of the development of economic theory, economists have sometimes been more interested in the macro aspects of our economy and sometimes more in the micro aspects. Before Adam Smith (1723–1790), most economists were concerned with mercantilist ideas. Mercantilists were international traders who developed trading from Europe to Asia and described the effects of such trading on the property of the countries involved. Economic property and depression were perceived to be related to the nature and volume of foreign trade. Adam Smith, on the other hand, pointed to the importance of individual businesses and the effect of the search for profit on consumer welfare. For Smith the emphasis was on micro aspects of the economy.

As economies grew and developed, they became subject to wide swings in business activity—periods of prosperity followed by periods of depression. After the Great Depression of the 1930s, which left few countries of the world untouched, economists became more interested in how the macro economy worked. It is important to realize that the macro economy is different from, and more than, the sum of the individual parts that make it up, just as the parts of a watch laid out on the table do not make a watch—they do not tell the time. For timepieces and for economies the whole is different from the sum of the parts.

FACTORS OF PRODUCTION

Inputs that are used in the production process to create output are called *factors of production.*

Inputs that are used in the production process in order to create output are called **factors of production**. They include land, labor, capital, and management.

Land

***Land* includes minerals, water, and other natural resources.**

Land includes minerals, water, and other natural resources. Of themselves, such resources do not produce output. Human effort must be applied. Fish do not jump out of the water into nets and boats. Trees must be cut, transported, and milled. Coal and iron ore must be dug and oil must be drilled and refined. Only the sun, air, and the water come free, and even these are not always freely available in modern cities.

Labor

***Labor* consists of wage-earning workers.**

Nothing gets done without the use of **labor** somewhere in the process. Can labor be increased? Yes, in the sense that individuals through training, experience, and education can become more productive. Despite unemployment, labor is a scarce resource; that is, skilled labor. What society would not want higher quality scientists, teachers, and managers than it has? In our strict terminology, workers who are unemployed are not scarce. They are not wanted for their labor services. But skilled workers are scarce.

Capital

***Capital* refers to man-made units of production: buildings, factories, and tools.**

We do not mean capital in the sense of finances or money. **Capital** as used here refers to man-made units of production. These are the buildings, factories, machines, and tools that produce goods and services. Capital without labor cannot possibly provide any output. And labor without capital is greatly impaired in its ability to provision society. Combined with capital, labor is much more productive. Hence, capital and labor both contribute to output.

Management

***Management* is comprised of decision makers who coordinate the use of capital and labor to produce output.**

Management is a special kind of labor. Managers are decisionmakers who coordinate the use of capital and labor to produce output. The importance of the managerial function, especially in a highly industrialized economy such as the U.S., should not be underestimated. Managerial efficiency is one of the main reasons for the vitality of the U.S. economy. Managers have perhaps the hardest job of all—decision making. The constant stress of this chore can sometimes cause greater physical discomfort than digging a ditch with a shovel. A wrong decision can be very costly to the individual concerned and to the production workers.

PRODUCTION POSSIBILITY CURVE

Figure 1-2 and Table 1-1 show the various combinations of outputs that can be produced with given resources and technology in a two-good world. Suppose the goods are cattle and corn, with cattle expressed in thousands of units along the vertical axis and corn in millions of bushels along the horizontal axis. The *assumptions* of the model are as follows:

1. A two-good economy.
2. The level of technology and technique is held fixed.
3. Factors of production—land, labor, and capital quantities are held fixed.

Figure 1-2

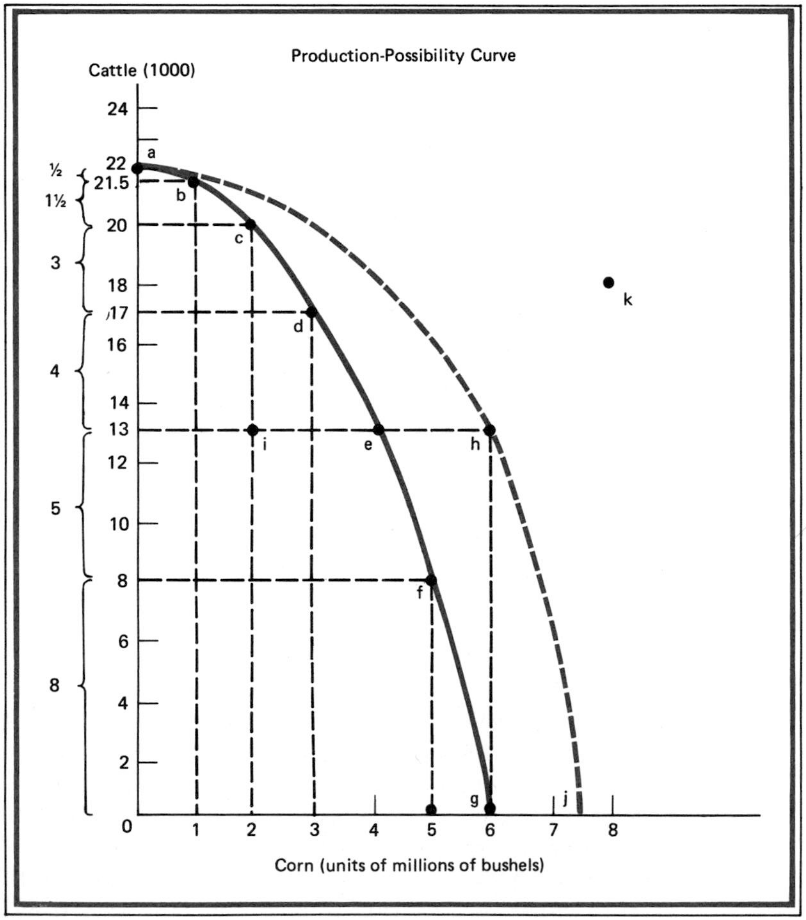

TABLE 1-1
Production Possibility Curve

Points	Cattle	Corn (millions of bushels)
a	22,000	0
b	21,500	1
c	20,000	2
d	17,000	3
e	13,000	4
f	8,000	5
g	0	6

4. Points on the solid curve (*a* to *f*) represent full employment output and maximum efficiency in the use of the factors of production.

Scarcity is evident in this graph. Suppose the people would like to have 8 million bushels of corn and 18 units of cattle as represented by point *k* that lies to the right of the curve. These might be the amounts the people would consume if they could have all they wanted of both goods. The curve itself represents the constraint on consumption. Constraint is implied when we speak of production possibility. We are constrained to consume only what is technologically possible to produce.

If people chose to produce only cattle, and no corn, they could produce 22,000 head, as at point *a*. Or if they chose to produce only corn they could produce 6 million bushels, indicated at point g. The economy's possible output of various combinations of cattle and corn are depicted by the solid curve going from *a* to g.

Assume that people devoted all their resources to production of cattle and produced the full component of 22,000 head. Then they decided they wanted some corn too, so they diverted resources toward producing corn and grew 1 million bushels. They would find that their output of cattle would fall by 500 head. Output would consist of 21,500 cattle and 1 million bushels of corn, as illustrated at point *b*. What is the opportunity cost of acquiring 1,000 bushels of corn? It is the 500 cattle given up. In order to acquire 1 million more bushels of corn (for a total of 2 million bushels), the economy would have to give up another 1,500 cattle. Therefore, the opportunity cost of the additional 1 million bushels of corn is 1,500 cattle. And so it goes. The opportunity cost of producing another million bushels of corn (the 3 millionth bushel) is 3,000 cattle. The combination then produced is 17,000 cattle and 3 million bushels of corn (point *d*). At point e, 13,000 cattle and 4 million bushels of corn are grown, with the opportunity cost of going from the 3 millionth to the 4 millionth bushel of corn being the 4,000 cattle sacrificed. At point *f* the combination produced is 8,000 cattle and 5 million bushels of corn. Finally, the opportunity cost of getting the remaining one million bushels of corn is 8,000 cattle. You have noticed that as the economy proceeds along its production-possibility combinations from *a* to g, the *additional* cost of obtaining *additional* bushels of corn progressively increased. It becomes more and more expensive to get the additional bushels of corn, in the sense that larger amounts of cattle must be given up as corn output increases.

This example of increasing opportunity costs seems to be the real-world situation for most goods. For now, let us explain it by saying that it arises because as the economy substitutes more of its resources from cattle to corn production, more resources of labor and capital that are specialized in the production of cattle must be used in the production of corn, where they are less suitable.

We have expressed costs in terms of cattle for corn. If we reverse the situation the analysis is precisely the same. That is, assume the people produced only corn, and no cattle at all as depicted by point g. Then, let them decide they did not like the meatless diet and wanted 8,000 head of cattle. Moving from point g to point *f*—moving from right to left up the curve—they would have to accept a 1-million-bushel decline in the amount of corn. Increasing the production of cattle by moving up the curve would show that more and more corn would have to be given up to get additional head of cattle. The opportunity cost of cattle would increase.

Both cattle and corn are produced under conditions of increasing opportunity costs. A curve that bulges outward, as in Figure 1-2, illustrates this increasing cost situation. If the curve were a straight line from one axis to another, the opportunity cost of acquiring cattle would not increase as more cattle were produced. Neither would the opportunity cost of corn increase as more corn was produced. This would reflect a constant-cost tradeoff between corn and cattle.

Point *i*, with relatively small levels of output of both corn and cattle, represents an economy performing *below* its capacity. In this case, either resources are not fully employed or the resources are not being used at maximum efficiency.

At point *h* the coordinates are 13,000 cattle and 6 million bushels of corn. This combination of outputs is unattainable. Our hypothetical economy does not have the capacity to reach point *h* under current specified conditions.

Allow one of the assumptions to be changed. Suppose improved technology—a new fertilizer—is introduced in the growing of corn. The effect is to shift the production possibility curve to its new, dashed, contour running from *a* to *j*. Now, we find that point *h* is attainable. Given the same resources, two states of the economy could provide different results. The one without fertilizer could operate at e and the economy with fertilizer could operate at *h*.

We have shown costs in terms of commodities: corn for cattle and cattle for corn. If money were introduced, then opportunity costs could be expressed in dollar values.

MARKET AND NONMARKET ALLOCATION

Scarce goods, by hook or by crook, are allocated to various uses. Societies organize the allocation process in a variety of ways. These organized processes can be classified into three broad categories. They are *traditional economies, market economies,* and *command economies.* Mixed variations of these three types of economies typically exist in every society, but some are strongly traditional, some principally market, and some largely command. Let us briefly note some of the principal characteristics of these three types of allocation systems.

Scarcity and the Dismal Science

In 1798 Thomas Robert Malthus, an English economist, published a provocative work, An Essay in Population, in which he argued that natural laws of biology and economics would doom mankind to inevitable misery. From biology it was the law of exponential growth (he called it geometrical growth) of population where each generation (25 to 30 years) the population would double, progressing as 2, 4, 8, 16, 32, . . . 2^n, where n equals the number of generations. Unfortunately, said Malthus, the production of food to provide subsistence would only grow arithmetically, as 1, 2, 3, 4, . . . n. His pessimistic conclusion was that "overpopulation" would only cease through "positive checks," namely, famine, disease, war, and pestilence – the four horsemen of the Apocalypse. He modified his pessimism in the second edition in 1803, introducing the concept of "preventive check" to population growth. This took the shape of moral restraint on the sexual appetite and use of birth control practices because he believed that man, as a reasoning being, would see the error of his ways and by correct behavior avoid inevitable and disastrous consequences. In the interim he also realized that the point of crisis could be delayed through improved efficiency in the production of food, by employing better techniques, and by introducing innovative technology. This would give mankind more time for the "preventive checks" on population growth to take hold before the "positive checks" would be activated. The figure shows that for 1970 levels of food productivity, the crossover point of declining arable land that could support the population would occur around the year 2000 (point a). Should food productivity be doubled, the crossover point would occur around the year 2025 (point b), and if quadrupled sometime before the year 2050 (point c). Economists have observed that as per capita income rises significantly, the birth rate falls. This forecast offers hope of stabilizing the world population. The question remains, will it occur before Malthus's positive checks take over? Any serious crop failure in the 1980s in major food-producing countries like Canada and the U.S. would no doubt result in many deaths in poor countries of the world.

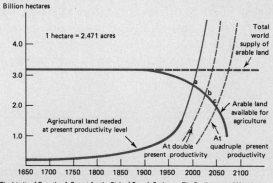

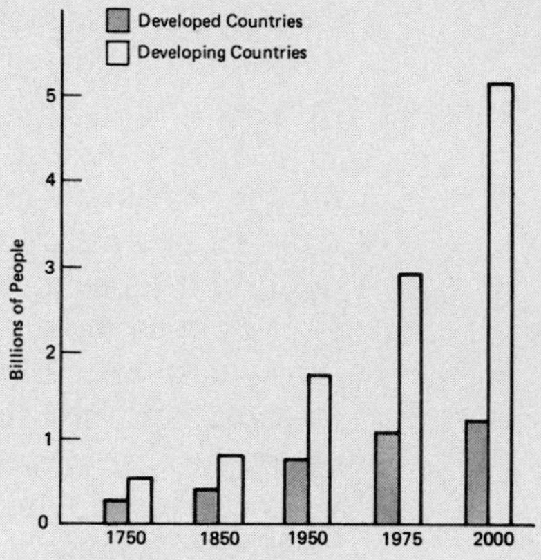

Data: Rockefeller Foundation
Source: Business Week, June 16, 1975

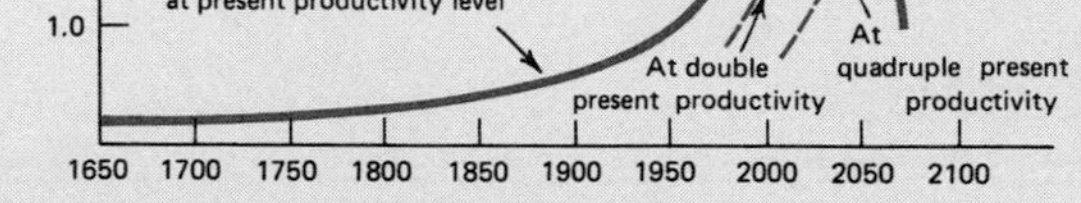

The Limits of Growth: A Report for the Club of Rome's Project on The Predicament of Mankind, by Donella H. Meadows, Dennis L. Meadows, Jorgen Randers, and William W. Behrens III. A Potomac Associates Book. Published by Universe Books, New York, 1972.

Traditional Economies

Traditional economies are based upon social customs to produce and allocate commodities. These customs are passed on from generation to generation.

Many tribal societies rely principally upon customs and traditions to guide scarce resources to their ultimate uses. If the hunters bring in bounty, it is divided among the society's members according to tradition, often accompanied by ritualistic celebrations. Such rituals serve to preserve traditions and ensure that they are passed on from one generation to the next.

Labor services in **traditional economies** are also bound by customs. A son will enter his father's trade, and family names become associated with the trade. John the (Black) Smith will find his son Henry is called Henry Smith. Individuals rarely if ever challenge their places in a traditional economy, principally because cultural traditions wield strong powers over all individual activities.

Obscure remnants of traditional economies may still be found in even the most modern and economically advanced societies. Usually they are found in family tradition. In an American family, for example, the eldest son is still likely to receive first claim to funds for a college education.

Market Economies

Market economies are based on the private ownership of capital and the free exchange of property rights in a decentralized market place at market-determined prices.

Markets exist whenever people come together to exchange things. In well-developed markets, the prices at which things are bought and sold are not set by individuals but rather by the broad and impersonal forces of the market itself. If markets function effectively and efficiently, then market prices will serve to guide the allocation of scarce resources. The market system is also often called the pricing system. This is the system that sets the foundation for what is known as capitalism.

Fundamental to the operation of a market is the ownership of property. An individual must be capable of owning something if he is to offer it for sale in a market. Ownership is transferred to the buyer when an exchange takes place. Thus, a prerequisite for a **market economy** is the right of ownership of property, and property rights must be enforced by the state if a market economy is to operate.

It is imperative that producers, consumers, and laborers be free to enter and exit from markets if markets are to work. When government either restricts free entry to markets or fails to prevent others who may, by threat or force, restrict entry to markets, the market system cannot work effectively. Freedom of market participation is essential to the capitalistic economy, and it is always the case that in countries where individuals have political freedom through democratic processes, one will find considerable market freedom as well. Whether political and economic freedom tend to go hand in hand is an unsettled issue.

Command Economies

In a **command economy** the means of production are collectively owned and centrally controlled. Allocation is organized around a long-range plan developed by central bureaus, rather than following the daily cues communicated by

Command economies **are based upon social ownership of capital with production decisions made and prices set by a centralized authority.**

market prices. The production apparatus is run by the state, presumably for the best interests of the individual. The intent of the plan is to avoid the uncertainties and whimsical movements of the market economy and to provide needed public goods. Production by command is for the common welfare and not a source of individual profits.

Government units operate in a descending hierarchy starting from the national level, to the regional level, to the district level, on to the local level. The national government may regulate railroads, shipping, and the banks, while mining, textiles, and wheat farming may be managed at the regional and district levels. Music halls, health care, and fresh produce may be managed at the local level. Though property rights are substantially redefined under socialism, some individual ownership and entrepreneurship exists. There is usually room for the small private farm, private appliance, and shoe repair shops.

The central authority defines the boundaries over which consumer preferences can range by the imposition of physical quotas on production and the rationing of consumer goods. Scarcity prices as determined by supply and demand do not direct resources; administered prices are used for accounting purposes and to check on allocative efficiency. That is, markets and prices exist but do not respond to day-to-day supply and demand movements.

In an authoritarian command economy, labor is assigned by the central authority to specific activities. Pay scales are centrally administered. Even in an authoritarian socialistic system, however, there is typically some freedom of job choice. Wage differentials are designated to direct choices toward those jobs that are considered as most socially beneficial. Engineers are paid more than writers.

The idea is to create a sense of community and an adequate income for all. All citizens are motivated to do their best for the system and for social purposes, and to disavow selfish individualism and narrow ambitions that do not advance the larger society.

Mixed Systems

In reality, there exists no economy that is either a pure traditional economy, or a pure market economy, or a pure command economy. Even tribal societies have some external market trade. To varying degrees capitalistic market economies often employ nonmarket government allocation and regulatory policies. Command economies often move away from total reliance on a central authority by reducing target production goals and employing greater use of market pricing. For example, communist Yugoslavia has come near to using competitive market prices within its socialist framework of planning and collective ownership of capital.

In principle, a system does not have to be capitalistic to have some free markets, nor does it have to be socialist to have some national planning. A country can have a degree of capitalism under a dictator or a degree of socialism under a democracy.

The U.S. has a mixed economy, with many governmental programs and regulation in many markets. Britain has experienced substantial nationalization of major industries under its Labour Party. Sweden, though democratic and mostly capitalistic (over 90 percent of capital is privately owned), has substantial welfare programs under socialist political parties. Taiwan, though capitalistic, is not democratic politically, tending to monarchy. Russia has softened its once austere application of Marxian economic principles and moved to include more market prices to make allocation decisions. China is more controlled in its communism. Much of its economy is a barter economy.

Economic Theory in Practice

Institutional arrangements—political, social, legal—affect human behavior; they constrain and direct the choices that are made, given the available options. Whatever the institutional setting, economic theory provides the universal conceptual underpinnings of how people make economic choices subject to the institutional constraints.

In this text we focus our principal attention toward the market system. This is because the theoretical principles of demand and supply are applicable to *every* type of economy. For example, if the price of a good is set too low by central authorities in a command economy, the theory of the market will explain why queues of people will appear for the right to buy it. This queuing phenomenon will be predicted by demand and supply. Or, if there is a religious prohibition on using an input in production, for example if pigs or cows cannot be slaughtered or some kind of seasoning is not allowed, then these traditions can be translated into formal economic theory by stating that the cost (social) of consuming them is high, hence the quantity demanded of them is low or zero. Economic theory applies everywhere that goods are allocated just as it applies in a market-oriented economy.

CHAPTER SUMMARY

Scarcity exists whenever human wants are greater than the goods available to satisfy them. Economics is the study of how individuals and society choose to allocate scarce goods to alternative uses.

Economics is a science that deals with positive statements about how economic forces are related to each other. Positive or scientific statements differ from normative statements, which are about how things ought to be.

The scientific method is a rigorous method of posing and answering questions objectively. A hypothesis must be operationally meaningful, that is it must be *possible* to run experiments to test the hypothesis for its predictive content. Science does not prove anything. It only seeks predictable relations.

It is more difficult to develop science when science deals with human behavior than when it deals with physical objects or plants, primarily because societal experiments present more problems to the scientist. But although social sciences are less exact than the physical sciences in many ways, they remain sciences in their own right.

A fundamental concept in economic reasoning is the concept of opportunity cost. The true economic cost of anything is measured by the value of the highest valued alternative foregone. This concept was applied to the question of having a volunteer army or a conscripted army. The real economic cost for the conscripted army is as much as or more than the volunteer army, because most draftees must forego better-paying employment opportunities.

Resources used to produce goods and services are comprised of land and materials, labor and management, and capital. These factors of production are scarce, just as commodities are scarce. They can be used to produce alternative goods, and in our example of a production possibility curve we noted that the farms of the country could produce either corn or cattle or some combination of these two goods. In production, farmers face a trade-off because resources are scarce. If more corn is to be produced there must be fewer cattle produced, and vice versa.

Different societies around the world have constructed different systems for dealing with the economic problem of allocation. In tribal societies tradition plays a great role. In command societies the state intervenes to guide resource allocation. In Western capitalist societies the state is less involved and the impersonal pricing system is allowed more range to guide production as consumers exercise individual freedom of choice in the marketplace. Whatever the system, economic theory provides the common tools to analyze the system.

QUESTIONS

1. Designate which of the following statements are positive and which ones are normative.
   a. Some corporations are too large for the good of the country.
   b. The rich get richer and the poor get poorer.
   c. "Profits are obscene."
   d. There are physiological differences between men and women.
   e. There are mental differences between men and women.
   f. Movie stars who make a million dollars a picture are overpaid.
   g. National health insurance is inflationary.
   h. The majority of U.S. citizens believe that nuclear arsenals are immoral.
2. Physicist Luiz Alvarez said, "To prove a theory you have to get everyone (experts) to agree with you." Does he mean this literally? What is it about the scientific method that he is ironically commenting on?
3. Is fortune telling a science? If not, why not?
4. Why is astronomy a science but not astrology? They both use precisely calculated charts of the motions of the planets, do they not?
5. The heliocentric theory of Copernicus (the sun is the center of the solar system) replaced the theory of Ptolemy (the earth is the center). Both describe the motions of the planets. Why did one theory replace the other?
6. A friend of yours says, "One way to determine income strata (low, middle, or upper) is to observe how married couples seat themselves in an automobile. Low-income people tend to sit with man and wife together in the back and front seats; middle-income married people sit with the men in front and the women in back; while upper-income married people tend to sit with the man and wife as mixed couples in the front and back seats."
   a. Is this a hypothesis? Why or why not?
   b. Is it testable?
   c. Are definitions required?
   d. Does the seating arrangement (the observation) have to conform to the statement every time to establish the essential correctness of the statement?

7. In 1972, Dr. Kenneth Woodrow concluded a year-long experiment conducted with 41,000 Californians testing their ability to stand pain. The test consisted of subjecting the heel of each person to the pressure of a vise-like machine until they signaled they could no longer stand it. Contrary to some popular myths, women on the average were able to bear only half as much pain as men. In fact, some men tolerated as much pressure as the machine could produce. Both sexes were able to tolerate less pain as age levels increased. Men over sixty could stand less than three quarters of the pressure borne by men in their twenties. (*Newsweek*, May 15, 1972).
   a. Can you state the hypothesis?
   b. Why is the fact that women bear children not a useful datum in determining the pain tolerance of women?
   c. If some women performed better than some men, does this invalidate the conclusions?
   d. The sensation of pain is an individual experience. Does this invalidate the experiment's results?
   e. Some might argue that cultural factors are the reason for the difference in pain tolerance between the sexes. Does this mean that when any test indicates different results between the sexes, it is only due to cultural factors? Therefore any tests that show a different result between the sexes are incorrect? Is there a flaw in this argument? Explain.
8. Is garbage an economic good? If a pig farmer were allowed to collect garbage, would it be an economic good?
9. If goods have a price because they are scarce, why are rotten eggs not high priced?
10. Suppose someone says that the scarcity concept does not always apply. Take as an example the case of a renewable resource, timber, where the concept of "sustainable yield" on government lands is applied. The idea is to cut the trees at such a rate as to insure a constant supply of lumber forever. Does this contradict the concept of scarcity? Explain.
11. What might the opportunity cost be to you of studying to get a grade of B as opposed to a D in this course?
12. A miser prefers to keep cash at home rather than in a savings account at a bank. Is there an opportunity cost to him for this choice?
13. You take some old books you have no use for to a secondhand book store to acquire some cash for them. What is the cost to you of not selling them?
14. "The government should not charge a fee for people to camp in national parks. After all it does not cost the government anything for the land." Do you agree? Comment.
15. What would be the opportunity cost—and to whom—if environmentalists were successful in permanently getting 100 million acres in Alaska declared as wilderness area?
16. Does the concept of opportunity cost help explain why so few people choose to earn their living at handcrafts?
17. What is the cost of smoking 2 packs of cigarettes a day at 70 cents a pack for 30 years?
18. A Greyhound bus ad goes, "Take a bus and leave the driving to us." Explain why it might be "cheaper" to take a plane rather than a bus to see your aunt in another city.
19. Around the year 1800 the earth supported about 900 million people. Malthus believed this to be near the earth's limit. Today world population is approximately 4.5 billion. Has the world population now expanded, as Malthus contended, to where it is using up the earth's means of subsistence? Discuss.
20. Suppose you take 3 hours off one evening and take your car and go to a movie with a friend. Assume the ticket costs $5, gasoline for the trip costs $1, and you passed up tutoring a student that night at $5 an hour. You could also have used the 3 hours to do $20 worth of typing. What were your opportunity costs of going to the movie?
21. "Nothing is too good when it comes to education." Comment.

22. As the demand for skiing in Colorado grows, what is the cost to a rancher of using this land for raising cattle? Is he greedy if he sells out to developers? Are tree lovers less greedy if they do not want to pay the market price to keep the land in its natural state?
23. Roughly draw a production possibility curve showing an increasing cost trade-off between oil and all other production, with oil on the vertical axis and all other goods on the horizontal axis.
    a. Indicate the change in the output mix as more oil and less of other goods are produced.
    b. Suppose more and more capital in the U.S. is diverted to oil drilling in order to get at the deeper, harder to drill, residual oil remaining in many old wells, and to provide more offshore drilling so as to maintain oil production at its current level. Show the effect on the production possibility curve.
    c. Suppose a way is found to produce solar equipment and energy more cheaply. Illustrate the effect on a P-P curve for oil versus solar energy.
24. Suppose you own your house "free and clear." This means that you have paid off the mortgage. Does this mean you live in it free after taxes?

Chapter 2

Exchange, Transactions Costs, and Property Rights

PROGRESS REPORT

A. In Chapter 1 we discussed the scientific method as a technique to be used in asking, evaluating, and answering questions objectively and carefully. We examined the fundamental economic problem of scarcity. Other basic economic concepts such as opportunity cost, relative prices, allocation, distribution, factors of production, and increasing costs were also introduced.

B. In this chapter we concentrate on the nature of exchange, and examine why people find it advantageous to specialize their efforts and offer to trade what they have produced with others who have also specialized. We shall find that the ability to trade and to benefit from trade requires an ability to own what one produces, and that there are certain transactions costs incurred by society and by individuals when trading occurs. That is, the act of trading in and of itself is not costless. We shall then discuss whether agreements (so-called contracts) among traders can take place without or prior to institutions or governments looking over the shoulders of the traders to make sure legal and social rules are followed; and whether trade can take place between two traders outside or prior to established institutional rules whenever traders realize they are both better off following through with their private agreements and promises to one another.

C. In Chapter 3 we shall take a formal look at trade as we know it in a market or exchange economy. To do this we shall show the reader how to construct and apply the tools of supply and demand.

EXCHANGE

There are over 225 million people in the U.S. Over 100 million of them have jobs producing the thousands of goods we take for granted every day. An automobile consists of over 10,000 assembled parts, an airplane many more. You, as a consumer, use or buy the final assembled good. When you negotiate for these finished goods you are engaging in voluntary exchange. A paper asset—money—is traded for the physical object at some agreed-upon ratio. Trade also takes place when you buy a ticket for a movie, go to a restaurant, get your hair done, buy a bond, hassle at a swap shop, or sign up for class. When you take a job you agree to trade your labor services for money income over some time period.

Trade involves voluntary exchange. But trade is only one kind of exchange. Gift giving is a voluntary act of exchange on the part of the giver. Another kind of exchange, theft, needless to say, is not voluntary on the part of the giver.

Contrary to what you might believe, people do *not* trade or exchange things that are equal in value to them. If one party gives up something, he expects to receive something of *greater* value to him. Otherwise the bother of negotiating the trade would not make it worthwhile. The parties to the exchange would be worse off than they were before trade took place. Trade is motivated by the intention of being better off then before. The expectation of increased wealth or satisfaction of **both parties** must exist to motivate trading.

Trade increases the welfare of *both parties.*

Take a make-believe example. Suppose Mary and Jerry both have 10 pieces of bubble gum and 6 licorice sticks. These combinations represent the initial wealth position of each child. Let us say that Jerry likes licorice better than gum, and if he could trade 3 bubble gums for 1 licorice he would be no more or less happy than before the trade. In this case we say that Jerry's personal rate of substitution, that is, his willingness to substitute bubble gum for licorice without loss of satisfaction, is 3 bubble gums to 1 licorice (in shorthand notation this substitution preference is written 3B:1L). Let us assume that Mary has a different willingness to trade bubble gum for licorice sticks. Let her personal rate of substitution be 1 bubble gum to 1 licorice stick (1B:1L).

Now suppose that Jerry and Mary meet on the corner and decide to trade with each other at an exchange ratio of 2 bubble gums for 1 licorice stick; that is, Jerry needs to give up only 2 bubble gums to get 1 licorice. He is better off, because he would have been willing to trade up to 3 bubble gums to get 1 licorice. What about Mary? She was willing to give up 1 licorice to get a bubble gum. So Jerry gives her 2 sticks of bubble gum for a licorice. By trading at an exchange of 2B:1L they *both* increase their levels of satisfaction. Even though the total number of bubble gums and licorice in the economy is the same, exchange has made *both* better off.

Jerry might like both treats very much and Mary may not like candy very much. But to make trade worthwhile it does not matter how *much* they like gum and licorice. All that matters is that before they make their trade they have

Before trading takes place, the parties involved must have *different substitution rates*.

different substitution rates. For if Mary's tradeoff was also 3B: 1L, they could not gain from trade.

Jerry and Mary might consider a second round of trading, and in this case the terms of trade might change. Remember that Jerry, after one round of trading, now has 8 bubble gums and 7 licorice sticks whereas Mary has 12 bubble gums and 5 licorices. Assume that Mary would like to trade again at the ratio 2B:1L, that is, she would like to give Jerry another licorice and get from him another 2 bubble gums. But Jerry now has less bubble gum than before and he values his seventh and eighth pieces of gum more than the ninth and tenth ones he traded for the licorice stick. Also, acquiring an eighth licorice stick has less value to Jerry than obtaining the seventh one did. The upshot is that after his first trade Jerry has less bubble gum and now the gum has increased in value *relative* to licorice. He will only negotiate a second trade with Mary at an exchange of 1 bubble gum for 1 licorice stick (1B:1L). But after trade, Mary's substitution rate changes too. She now wants 1 1/2 gums for 1 licorice stick. Hence, there is no further trade since she cannot increase her level of satisfaction by trading bubble gum for licorice at the new relative prices that Jerry wants.

	Mary	Jerry
Before trade	10 gum 6 licorice	10 gum 6 licorice
After trade	12 gum 5 licorice	8 gum 7 licorice
Satisfaction	greater	greater

A final important point is that the exchange of 2B:1L expresses the current market value for gum and licorice, a market created by Mary and Jerry. Were another person to enter the picture and offer 2.5B:1L, that is, offer more than 2 bubble gums for 1 licorice, this *last trader* will determine the market value for all traders. Why is this? As long as all traders clearly know and understand what the exchange rate is, then all traders will be trading at the same market rate of substitution. All traders are then said to possess **perfect information** in the market. If another trader enters the market and offers more (2.5) bubble gums to Mary for 1 licorice, she will buy exclusively from the last trader. In order to meet the competition, Jerry will have to exchange at 2.5B:1L or find no taker for his bubble gum. He will not be able to acquire more licorice. In this manner the **last trader** sets the exchange ratio for all traders when there is perfect information in the market. In a later chapter we shall study perfect information in the context of an idealized model which economists have created and have labeled perfect competition. Of course, traders in the real world seldom operate with perfect information.

Traders possess *perfect information* in the market when all clearly know and understand what the exchange rate is so all trade at the same rate of substitution.

The *last trader* sets the exchange ratio for all traders when there is perfect information in the market.

GAINS FROM SPECIALIZATION

What applies in the realm of consumer tastes also applies to the production process. In the trading off of job chores, efficiency can be improved and output increased.

When labor performs *specialized* tasks, productivity can be greatly improved using the same number of workers.

This fundamental point was emphasized by Adam Smith in *The Wealth of Nations,* published in 1776. When labor is divided into performing **specialized** tasks, productivity can be improved immmensely using the same number of workers. Smith gave an example of a pin factory where 1 man working alone could produce 10 pins a day. But if 10 men worked together, each performing a different part of the operation, as many as 48,000 pins a day could be made, an average of 4,800 pins per worker.

Another astonishing example is found in the activities of Henry Ford, the tycoon who introduced specialization in the manufacture of Model T automobiles. Before 1908, cars were hand built and cost around $7,000 each. Obviously they were produced in small quantities at those prices. In 1905, 24,000 cars were sold—2,000 of them were Fords. By introducing job specialization in the production of the very simple Model T car in 1908, Ford sold his cars at the unbelievable price of $629 each. He soon had over 25 percent of the market. In the first year after specialization was introduced in the production process, 6,000 cars were sold at a profit of $1 million. By 1913 the car's selling price fell to $500, with the cost of building it at $364. Around 183,000 of them were sold at a total profit of $25 million. In 1914 Ford introduced the moving assembly line. By 1916 Ford cars comprised 60 percent of the market; 2,000 a day were being produced. The average working time spent on the assembly for each car dropped from 728 minutes to 93, and along with the drop in time there occurred a drop in the price of the car. As the prices fell, the quantity demanded by the public increased. The Model T was retained until 1927, when the Model A was introduced.

In the 1920s Henry Ford doubled wages from $2.50 a day to an unheard of $5 a day. Through specialization of labor, productivity increased, prices fell, wages rose, and the nation's total output increased. The rising demand for cars created greater demand for workers at higher wages. Streamlining automobile production led consumers to reduce their opportunity costs of transportation, leaving more of their income to be spent on nontransportation goods. The public's increased demand for cars created more jobs and higher income, which rippled through the system and stimulated economic growth.

Calculating Gains from Specialization

Barney and Herb work at the Ford Motor Company factory. During a 10-hour shift, Barney and Herb install both horns and fuel pumps in cars moving on the assembly line according to the following schedule:

Before Specialization

	Horns per shift		Fuel pumps per shift
Barney	30	+	20
Herb	20	+	20
Total	50		40

In 10 hours Barney and Herb have installed both horns and pumps in 40 cars. The additional 10 cars have only the horns installed.

Henry Ford comes along and tells the foreman, "We can do better." "How?" asks the foreman. "Specialization," says Mr. Ford. He shows the foreman the following table:

After Specialization

	Horns per shift		Fuel pumps per shift
Barney	60	or	40
Herb	40	or	40

Thus, if Barney only installed horns, he could do 60 of them in one shift. If, on the other hand, Barney only installed fuel pumps, he could install 40 of them in one shift. Similarly for Herb. He could either install 40 horns in 10 hours if he only worked on horns, or 40 fuel pumps in 10 hours if he only worked on fuel pumps. To Mr. Ford, it is obvious that Barney is more efficient at installing horns, and that Herb is *comparatively* more efficient at putting in fuel pumps. This surprises the foreman, since Herb does not seem to be any better than Barney at either task, though he does realize that Herb is as good as Barney installing fuel pumps. But Mr. Ford understands opportunity costs. He reasons thus: if Barney specializes in installing only horns, he can do 60 of them in one shift, during which period he forgoes installing 40 fuel pumps. Therefore, the opportunity cost for Barney to install horns is 60H:40F (where H stands for horns and F for fuel pumps and the expression is read, 60 horns to 40 fuel pumps). The numbers can be reduced by dividing both sides by 60 to obtain

1H:2/3F Cost of Barney installing a horn is 0.67 of a fuel pump.

This ratio says that for each horn installed, Barney sacrifices installing 0.67 of a fuel pump. Thus, the opportunity cost of a horn is 0.67 of a fuel pump.

(Obviously, one does not install 0.67 of a fuel pump, instead, one can think of being 0.67 along the way to getting one fuel pump in place). Conversely, we can look at the ratio the other way around and find the opportunity cost of Barney installing a fuel pump instead of a horn. It is obtained by dividing both sides of 60H:40F by 40 instead of 60.

1F:3/2H Cost of Barney installing a fuel pump is 1.5 horns.

This is simply the inverse expression of the first result. Therefore, for each fuel pump installed by Barney, the opportunity cost is 1.5 horn installations that are sacrificed. In a similar manner, the tradeoff for Herb in a shift is 40 fuel pumps or 40 horns, i.e., 40H:40F. Dividing by 40 gives

1H:1F Cost of Herb installing horn is 1 fuel pump.

The opportunity cost to Herb of installing 1 horn is 1 fuel pump foregone. Conversely, the opportunity cost to Herb of installing one fuel pump is one horn foregone or

1F:1H Cost of Herb installing fuel pump is 1 horn.

To see the difference specialization brings, compare the figures with the results when the workers were not specializing. The numbers in parentheses show the *change* in output after specialization occurs, as compared to output before specialization.

After Specialization

	Horns	Fuel pumps
Barney	60 (+30)	0 (−20)
Herb	0 (−20)	40 (+20)
Total	60 (+10)	40 (0)

Again, 40 cars have both horns and pumps installed. But there is a net gain since now some 20 additional cars have horns installed whereas before specialization only 10 additional cars had horns installed. The reason for the improved result is that while Barney is 1.5 as fast (60/40) as Herb in installing horns, he is only equally as fast (40/40) as Herb in installing fuel pumps. Hence, more output is achieved if Barney only does the horns while Herb is confined to fuel pumps.

Note, however, there would be no advantage to specializing the tasks if the opportunity costs were the same for the two workers at both tasks. Only when the opportunity costs for each worker as between the two jobs is *different* does Herb have what we call a **comparative advantage** installing fuel pumps.

A *comparative advantage* occurs when the opportunity costs for each worker as between two jobs is different.

Though Barney has an *absolute advantage* over Herb in installing horns (he can install them more rapidly), and Barney is just as good as Herb installing fuel pumps, Herb has a *comparative advantage* installing pumps. It is *relatively* cheaper to have Herb work on fuel pumps than to have Barney do it, because the same number of pumps can be installed yet there is no corresponding reduction in the number of horn installations. Moreover, Herb would still have a comparative advantage even if Barney had an absolute advantage in both tasks, as long as their opportunity costs differed. Thus, specialization leads to increased efficiency in the use of scarce resources.

TRANSACTIONS COSTS

Transaction costs are unavoidable costs incurred that do not always show up in the price at which the exchange is made.

Up to now we have more or less assumed that when trade occurred, the parties involved carried out their transactions smoothly, conveniently, quickly, and with certainty. The traders were in direct contact with one another and each one was certain about the price, the amount, the time, as well as any other characteristics and alternatives related to trading. But prices at which trade is negotiated often do not measure all the (opportunity) costs of that transaction. There are unavoidable costs incurred by the transactors voluntarily participating in the trade that do not show up in the price at which the exchange is made. These are **transactions costs**, of which there are three kinds: information costs, contractual costs, and policing costs.

Information Costs

Information costs are incurred before an exchange is made when individuals gather information about the good or service they intend to purchase.

Many times, before an exchange is made individuals proceed to gather information about the commodity or service they are intending to purchase. For example, if you want to move you will get in touch with moving companies and compare their prices. Or you may want to consult self-service operators who rent trucks in order to assess their prices, inter-area connections, and drop-off points. In this way the potential consumer gets some idea about quality and the distribution of prices. The rational searcher will always include the **information costs** attached to the search. He or she will not spend a dollar's worth of gasoline driving around town to avoid spending a quarter for a conveniently placed parking meter.

If in your search you take too much time to get the best price and service, you may be late getting to work at a new job. This might mean a loss of income and getting off to a bad start with the new boss. Also, while extending your search you may have less time to devote to packing and getting in a few more hours of pay from the current job. Hence, the lower the opportunity costs involved in gathering information, the higher the net gain that can be realized from the exchange or transaction. The additional gain should at the least cover the additional cost of searching. This *additional* cost is called a **marginal cost**; the *additional* gain is a **marginal benefit**.

The additional cost of searching (the *marginal cost*) should be covered by the additional gain (the *marginal benefit*).

There are also situations in which the opportunity cost of search is relatively low, and a greater amount of time is then devoted to information gathering. If you are looking for an $8 pen, you may devote some time to looking for it, but not a great deal. You will certainly not take a day off from work to look for it. Yet, if you are looking for a new car, or more significantly, a new house or apartment, the cost of search will be higher. But the gain from search is here significantly greater. Therefore, you will spend more time looking. You might even take time off from work. In this situation, the additional or marginal opportunity cost of looking for a new residence is relatively low as compared to the additional marginal gain of better housing.

Contractual Costs

These are opportunity costs not reflected in the sale price that arise from actually processing the exchange. When a house is bought, legal papers must be read and signed, mortgage companies contacted, and sundry minor details sorted out. Perhaps other negotiated clarifications are needed concerning property lines and property rights. Such additional opportunity costs involved in trade are called **contractual costs**. Waiting in line at the post office to buy stamps is an example of a contractual cost.

Contractual costs **are opportunity costs not always reflected in the sale price and arise from actually processing the exchange.**

A supermarket may have to acquire a new stock boy to stamp unit pricing labels to satisfy the requirements of a new consumer protection law. Garages have to itemize and cost out suggested repairs before they can touch your car, and call you for permission if the repair costs look like they are going to be higher than first estimated.

Perhaps a firm has to hire a part-time accountant because of a new tax law, or hire some lawyers because it decides to incorporate or to merge with another company, or to get a zoning variance because it is going to modify or expand existing facilities. These all involve negotiation or contractual costs.

Policing Costs

Policing costs **involve the expenses sometimes necessary to protect your property or convince the other party to uphold his end of an agreement (contract).**

Policing costs are related to contractual costs. These may involve the legal expenses sometimes necessary to convince the other person or party to uphold his end of an agreement (contract). More dramatically, suppose the laws against theft were dropped. This would require individual citizens to assume direct participation in the protection of themselves and their property. To become your own policeman would mean high opportunity costs to you. You would have to ride shotgun over your property or you would have to find and hire someone trustworthy to be your hired gun. You might have to end up volunteering some of your valuable time and sleep joining with neighbors to patrol the neighborhood day and night. As it is now, you pay taxes to support a police force. Protection is a public service and not a privately supplied service except in special cases—for example, among famous people who hire bodyguards.

If lumber companies could have no guarantee that their lumber would not be stolen, either they would not produce it or they would greatly reduce the amount they produce. The cost of housing would rise as the supply of materials and houses decreased. If there were no laws against car theft, General Motors

Those Transactions Costs

A present study by the U.S. Department of Commerce found that losses from theft and dishonesty, and other costs imposed on firms to meet safety programs and environmental protection laws, have caused a decline in business productivity (output per man hour). Theft requires policing. Safety regulations relate to contracts between employers and workers. Environmental laws concern social contracts. These transactions costs are significant in the modern exchange economy.

would produce fewer cars or maybe none. People would also have less desire to buy them if there were a high probability they would be stolen. The costs of producing and owning cars would be substantially increased to both seller and buyer because of the disincentive effects of the higher policing costs of ownership. The result would be that the total wealth of society would be substantially reduced.

MIDDLEMEN

In a highly industrialized economy, middlemen play a very large and active role in the complex process of allocation. Most of what we purchase is certainly not directly obtained from primary producers. The retailers through the intermediation of middlemen, like truckers and packers, themselves purchase through wholesalers, jobbers and other specialized distributors. For not only is production highly specialized but so is distribution of what is produced. It is the much maligned middleman who provides these specialized services.

We have discussed how specialization increases efficiency and reduces costs by increasing output. How, you might ask, do middlemen reduce costs when everybody knows they raise costs? In fact, in 1977 for the first time the labor costs required to transport food products to retail outlets was greater than the cost of the food at farm prices. So, what good are middlemen to us?

Middlemen specialize in providing information and _reducing_ transaction costs.

Middlemen specialize in **reducing** transactions costs. In particular, they specialize in information. They know the ins and outs of the markets. The fact that they continue to thrive is testimony to their usefulness. Consider the costs to each individual if he or she had to negotiate each intermediate step taken from the time the crop leaves the farm to the time it ends up in the store.

One of the persistent, romantic myths is that costs can be reduced and savings realized by living on communes—do-it-yourself communities that attempt to eliminate somewhat the need for services of middlemen. The quality of such communes still depends crucially on the middlemen in our society. If members of a commune use electricity do they have their own generator? If so, did they build it themselves? If so, did they machine every part that goes into the generator down to mining the iron ore that must be fired into steel? If they did machine the parts, they surely needed a lathe and other supplemental tools, and did they make these too? If their commune is in California and coal is mined in West Virginia and steel forged in Ohio, how did these resources get to California?

Suppose they do not use electricity and have no need for a generator. They will surely want candles or kerosene lamps. Any materials they want and do not have will have to be bought from people in the outside society, perhaps by finding out with whom to trade through an ad in the newspaper—a middleman. If it is a kerosene lamp they want, they might go to a nearby salvage yard or secondhand shop—a middleman. By the way, how did they find out about the availability and the price of the land they are using? Through a real estate agent? Another middleman. Did one of them write a check on a local bank to pay for the land? Was the check sent through the mail? While people in communes may be enjoying themselves, they are nevertheless incurring costs in order to live in that style.

Middlemen help bring producer and buyer together. They coordinate market activities. In doing so, they reduce transactions costs. Suppose there were no newspaper ads for housing and no real estate agents. Would the costs to you of selling your house or purchasing one be easier or less costly to you? Would you not have to assume your own printing costs for an advertisement and transportation costs to distribute ads? Or perhaps you would pay a youngster with a bicycle to deliver them. That's right—if you do, you have just hired a middleman!

CALCULATING GAINS AGAIN

Let us return to Jerry and Mary. Suppose Mary lived on one end of the block and Jerry on the other end so they never knew about one another. One day Sammy Survivor moves into the neighborhood. He is poor so he hustles around the territory looking for some action. In time he gets to know both Jerry and Mary. Remember that they each started out with 10 bubble gums and 6 licorice sticks. Jerry's substitution preference was 1 licorice stick to 3 bubble gums. His level of satisfaction would not be altered if he gave up 3 bubble gums to get a licorice stick. But he would still like an extra licorice stick. Recall, also, that Mary would be indifferent if she gave up 1 licorice stick to get 1 bubble gum. But she would still like an extra piece of bubble gum. Sammy has learned all this. He goes to Jerry and tells him he will get a licorice stick for him if he gives Sammy 2.5 bubble gums. Otherwise Jerry will have to do the searching for himself. And Jerry does not want to do this because he wants to spend his daylight hours practicing as much soccer as he can so he can make the school soccer team. Mary cannot search around either because she goes to special music classes after school. Jerry and Mary simply do not move in the same circles. Sammy takes Jerry's 2.5 sticks of bubble gum and finds out where Mary's music tutor holes up and catches Mary after class. He offers Mary 1.5

sticks of bubble gum for 1 of her licorice sticks. She agrees, since this offer is even a better deal than what she would have originally traded for a licorice.

As a result, Jerry is better off because he only had to give up 2.5 bubble gums instead of 3 for a licorice stick, and Mary is better off because she got 1.5 bubble gums instead of just 1 for selling her licorice stick. Sammy is better off because he has earned a much desired bubble gum, which is rather good since he was flat broke.

Notice that Sammy is taking advantage of the difference between the bid and asking price for licorice. He buys the licorice from Mary for 1.5 bubble gums (asking price) and sells it to Jerry for 2.5 bubble gums (bid price). The tally is:

	Mary	Jerry	Sammy
Before trade	10 gums	10 gums	0
	6 licorice	6 licorice	0
After trade	11.5 gums	7.5 gums	1 gum
	5 licorice	7 licorice	0
Satisfaction	greater	greater	greater

In principle, Sammy is the prototype of all middlemen. We all use them and need them. Did you have all the information you would have liked about buying a used car or in choosing a college or taking a particular course and about the instructor for the course? How much would you have been willing to pay for the information? Twenty dollars to pay a mechanic to check over a used car you are thinking of buying? If you attend a large university, did you purchase the lecture notes and the old tests from the Lecture Notes Service Center?

Middlemen, of course, compete with one another by offering a better service at the least cost possible. This reduced cost reduces your opportunity costs by lowering your search and contractual costs—if the market for middlemen services is competitive.

SPECULATORS

***Speculators* are specialists who buy and sell currencies or commodities hoping to gain by correctly predicting their future prices.**

Another economic decision maker who is often misunderstood is the speculator. **Speculators** are specialists operating in a particular market. We are all speculators to some degree. Any time a decision is made, risk exists. That is, there is a chance of a loss. When is the best time to buy or sell a house or a car? And at what prices? Should I get a car, a house, or life insurance? Should I take the statistics course now or in the spring quarter when there is a better chance Professor Snap, who is an easy A, will teach it? But there is also a chance Professor Tough will teach it then, and he is an easy D. As the manager of a steel mill, should I stock up with excess coal now, even though there is a a good chance the price will come down later? But contract negotiations are coming up for the miners and there is a chance of a strike with little possibility of getting enough coal if they strike for long. Should I take the new job offer now, or stay here because there is a good chance for a promotion?

Do you take advantage of department store and supermarket special sales? Do you try to get there on the first day or wait until the end when the stock may have disappeared? Yes, you are a speculator even if you do not act. As a home buyer you face a loss if the market price rises and you have already sold your house or other assets.

The professional speculator is a specialized trader. A speculator assumes risks with the intention of making profits when he or she correctly anticipates price movements. The speculator nevertheless plays an important role in helping to allocate scarce resources over time. For example,commodity speculators who are involved in hedging help to smooth price fluctuations in industries like farming. Assume that the June wheat crop is quite large, causing the price of a bushel of wheat to be lower than usual when it is harvested. Some speculators believe, however, that at such a low price the quantity bought will be substantially increased, with the consequence that eight months after June (in February) the supply will be low to the point of a shortage. A speculator purchases a future contract for 20,000 bushels of wheat to be delivered in February at a price of $3 a bushel. The seller of the contract agrees to deliver the wheat at $3 a bushel to the speculator (buyer) in February. The speculator, of course, is betting that the market price in February will be higher than $3, maybe $3.25 a bushel. If he is right, he will sell it and make a substantial profit. If he is wrong and the price is $2.85, he will lose.

The speculators, acting together, will cause the price of wheat to be less volatile. How? If they had not entered the market in June and not caused the owner to hold back the delivery of wheat to the market then by buying a contract for it, there would have been more wheat delivered and its price would have been less than $3.00. This would have meant that less wheat would have been available in February, with the price going above $3.25 a bushel at that time. Of course, there may be occasions where speculative activity could push prices up or down beyond the range dictated by fundamental economic forces. It is often said that foreign exchange markets are subject to excessive speculation. But for the overwhelming majority of the cases, speculation serves to bring prices into line with basic economic forces through the process of arbitrage. **Arbitrage** is the buying of either currency or commodity in one market and selling it simultaneously in another market at a higher price. Eventually the differential is competed away, resulting in a single market price. Only in rare cases does it appear that speculation can destabilize prices. In 1979 speculators, believing the U.S. dollar would continue to weaken, sold dollars to buy gold. This very act forced the value of the dollar down against other currencies and gold. At one point gold reached over $800 an ounce, when earlier it was below $200 an ounce. Chapter 8 will give further details about speculation in the commodity market and what are called hedging activities.

***Arbitrage* is buying a currency or commodity in one market and selling it simultaneously in another market at a higher price.**

RISK AND UNCERTAINTY

Risk can be measured when possible outcomes of an event are known and probabilities can be calculated.

Because of uncertainty, decision making necessarily involves **risk**—a chance of loss. Since future events are unknown, and the implications of events that are known now have effects in the future that are unknown, the world is an *uncertain* world. But there is a more specific meaning to the words *risk* and *uncertainty*—a technical distinction separates the two terms. Risk is said to exist when we know what the chances are that one or the other outcome will occur, that is, when we know the probability of an event. For example, if a coin is tossed, the possible outcome is either a head or a tail. That much is quite certain. What is not certain is whether it will be a head or a tail on any given throw. Because the possible outcomes are known, the probability that it will turn up heads can be calculated. It is one half. Or, we say you have a 50–50 chance of getting a head. Similarly, you have a 50–50 chance of getting a tail. When we bet on heads we know we have a 50–50 chance of losing. That is, we know what our risk of losing is. When probabilities are known, risks of loss in trading decisions can be taken into account.

By studying population data and death rates among the population at different age levels, insurance companies can estimate the risk involved in insuring a client, depending on the client's age. Using large population groups they can calculate the expected lifetime of each client after a medical examination. Because women on the average live longer than men, women may pay smaller premiums than men of corresponding ages. Since death is a certain event, then a reliable estimate of the ages at which death will likely occur can be calculated. Insurance companies then appropriately price their life insurance fees to ensure a profit after paying death benefits.

Uncertainty exists when possible outcomes of an event are not known and no probabilities can be calculated.

With **uncertainty**, however, the probability of possible outcomes is not known. For example, ocean currents can shift off the coast of Peru, causing most of the anchovies to disappear from that ocean area; *when* this happens is not an outcome whose probability could be computed, like that of a coin toss or the throw of a die. Nor can we compute the probability that cold weather in Brazil will destroy many coffee trees.

Insurance companies share risk and uncertainty when they take the precaution of pooling their coverage with other companies in the same geographical area. Events like earthquakes are not precisely predictable; heavy winter snows with spring floods to follow cannot be accurately predicted; a freak train wreck that releases lethal gas that wipes out a whole town is an uncertain event; so is a fatal illness like the 1919 influenza epidemic that killed millions of people in the Western world. These are uncertain events, for which no probability calculation can be meaningfully made.

Business also faces other kinds of uncertainties like wildcat strikes, changing legal definitions of liabilities made by the courts, unanticipated rates of inflation, unexpected decisions by the Environmental Protection Agency (EPA), and changes in safety regulations by the Occupational, Safety, and Health Administration (OSHA). Information theory is an outgrowth of uncertainty and is an attempt to reduce uncertainty by the active gathering of evidence and knowledge.

Speculators can experience losses as well as profits when an expected event does not occur. The author of a best seller who once managed the investments for a Swiss bank lost $60 million for them speculating in cocoa futures. Prices fell when he bet they would rise. Decisions are made in an environment that includes both risk and uncertainty.

PROPERTY RIGHTS

In this chapter so far we have been taking something for granted: We made an implicit assumption that trade and bargaining takes place among people who own private property and have rights associated with that property. Property rights, some claim, are natural rights. Legally they are institutions of society, and are defined by government and the courts. Property rights help people to form expectations that they can reasonably hold when negotiating trade with others. The conditions of property ownership and the rights of property are expressed in the laws, customs, and ethics of the society. The rules on property are enforced by the courts, the police, and the military.

What exactly is meant by property and property rights? In the hands of lawyers this becomes a very complicated question. Property as defined by government takes many forms, being constantly redefined. For our purposes, property means either objective, physical things—your shirt, your car, your house, and it can also mean intangible things like ownership of an idea implemented in a copyright privilege. With property rights you may do what you want with what you own so long as you do not infringe on someone else's right to do what he wants with his property.

Let us pursue this a little further. Property rights are not unlimited; they do not confer a *carte blanche*. Property rights, while subject to constraints, do allow harm or benefit to be imposed on another person or persons. You can inflict damage on a competitor by marketing a better product than he does—putting him out of business. But you cannot remove competition by shooting your rival or bombing his store, without fear of punishment by society.

Property rights **involve the right to 1. alienate your property, 2. legally exclude others from use of your resources, and 3. have the government protect your property from others.**

More specifically, the basic concepts connected with **property rights** are

1. *The right to alienate* your property. You can abandon, sell, or give away what you own. Rights to use property can also be transferred by renting it without yielding ownership.
2. *The exclusion principle.* Nonpayers and nonowners can be legally excluded from using resources you own.
3. *Protection.* The government has the obligation to protect your property from nonowners, and in some cases from owners. For example, an act of arson on your own property for the purpose of collecting insurance is prohibited. It is also prohibited if it endangers your neighbor's property.

Property ownership and the rights to property are distinct things. Property usually refers to a physical thing. Consider the renter: he or she does not own the apartment but he or she has certain rights to the apartment. A stockholder owns a piece of paper that entitles him to receive dividends, and it may confer a voting privilege. Yet, unless he owns all the stock he does not have exclusive say about decisions regarding the operation of the property owned by the corporation. If one holds a patent one does not possess ownership of some physical thing, but does own the rights to the design of the physical object. A can opener sold at a store is not owned by the inventor, but the design implemented in the can opener is. This distinction also holds true for copyrights. An idea can be converted into legally recognized property. Thus, the writer does not own the book sold to a buyer, but he does own the printed rights to the content of the book. Without property rights, the ideas of writers and inventors would be unprotected. There would probably be underinvestment in new ideas, since the originator could not be certain of reaping any benefits from them. Undiscovered ideas are subject to capture for individual benefit, and because of this the community benefits from the individual's contribution. When property rights are permitted, the first one to throw the intellectual net over a new idea is able to receive the maximum benefits and has an incentive to create.

Private property rights and the relative market prices at which property rights are transferred give an important social measure of the value of the use of property in different activities. That is, what the market price is on a piece of private property depends on what the property is being used for. What the property is being used for in turn depends upon the preferences of society. If housing is very strongly desired by the public, then land for use as development will bring a higher price than will its use for a family farm. The developers will outbid the potential farmers for the use of the land, thus indicating the measure of social value of the property. Thus, prices help to allocate scarce resources in an economically efficient way.

Laissez-faire and Institutionalism

Economists inclined to favor the pure free-market approach to the allocation of scarce resources often find themselves in vigorous conflict with a group called institutionalists. The pure institutionalists contend that the historical development and the current structure of society's institutions have more influence on the allocation and distribution of resources and the determination of relative prices in the immediate period, and over the long stretch of time, than do market forces. They argue that the agreements individuals make when they engage in economic trading are fundamentally conditioned by the social values they have historically inherited. The institutionalists claim that economic exchange is embedded in both past and existing cultural arrangements, and that these arrangements and social dispositions toward exchange must have existed before economic bargaining could have taken place. They believe that these social rules and customs are, in fact, what makes economic bargaining and exchange both possible and rewarding. Their explanation lies in the belief that social rules, sustained and enforced by government, encourage those individuals who agree to trade with each other to play by certain rules of behavior and see to it that each trader follows through on his or her promise. If the agreement is broken by one of the traders, society sees to it that the violator either accommodates the injured party or is punished. Society must also ensure that economic exchange takes place without force by one individual or the other, or by some other form of antisocial intimidation. Therefore, the institutionalists argue, economic exchange and an economic system cannot be sustained without legally enforced rights and liabilities for the trading parties. Society must reduce the transactions costs to traders primarily through its policing action if economic exchange is to be possible and beneficial.

Laissez-faire **means little or no government interference into private economic matters.**

Pure market economists, those who support the system of **laissez-faire** (let do [as they please]), loosely meaning "little or no government interference into private economic matters," contend that bargaining and economic exchange can take place without the need to impose culturally and socially defined relations and regulations on economic agreements. These pure market economists argue that individual trading that is rational can and will lead to improved social welfare without, and prior to, society's (that is, government's) influence, particularly when the transactions costs in reaching agreement between the traders are near zero, or very small. In fact, they claim government interference often or usually leads to raising the private transactions costs between bargainers, thereby causing a reduction in social welfare below what it could have been without outside interference. The higher transactions cost imposed by government interference either reduces the output in the markets by making the agreement more expensive, creates inefficiency, or thwarts the output completely by discouraging the agreement because interference makes it too costly to carry out.

Two Approaches to Exchange

Over 2300 years ago the Greek philosopher Plato, in Book II of the *Republic*, described two basic approaches in an agreement to bargain and trade:

1. Even though it costs something to trade, *both* participants in an exchange *gain more than they lose* by agreeing to the exchange. They can produce more by cooperating and by working together than they can produce by their individual efforts. Understanding this, individuals are led to create social contracts not on the basis of minimizing transactions costs alone but by establishing social rules that are applied to everyone. These rules are the social relations that are agreed upon *before* any bargaining takes place. When the rules are violated, action is to be taken against the violator who bargained outside the rules.

2. In contrast, two people may freely bargain with each other in order to reduce their losses. They have more to lose than to gain if they fail to agree. For example, if a single log spans a body of water and two men are coming opposite ways, say, Robin Hood and Friar Tuck, they can battle it out to see who crosses over first. But each could be seriously hurt or killed. Realizing this, the rational solution is to allow the other to pass first. No social laws or governmental ground rules are required. The transactions costs are essentially zero in negoti-

ating the exchange. All that is required is that the two behave rationally, that is, attempt to achieve their goals with the minimum of cost. This is the pure market economist's position. It is cheaper to agree than to fight because the transactions costs are so much lower and the net benefits greater. In this example, no social structure is necessary for a rational and beneficial bargain to be reached.

Thus, some markets will develop out of a sheer recognition of self-interest, and social contracts may not always be necessary. However, institutionalists argue self-interest is not enough. And they opt for the first approach. Trust is essential, and to obtain it a social structure is necessary. If one of the participants violates the *contract*, there are social actions that may be taken against the violator by society for so doing. **Contracts** are based on the social agreement created by members of the society, who agree to cooperate in a certain way. You might ask, "Was not the agreement to set up social rules for transacting itself a transaction prior to the social contract?" "Yes," say the institutionalists, "but that agreement was based on trust." Trust derives from cooperation learned not only from parents but also from the extended family—a social unit which sets up the basis for cooperation and for rules that are applied within and between families and then to other communities of families. Transacting must involve social values. To an institutionalist, cooperation is based on the principle that if people adhere to socially determined rules regulating how bargaining is to occur, more can be gained than lost. Should the government actively interfere in free markets by imposing value-laden political rules that differ from free-market values?[1] Can government intervention improve efficiency and social welfare by taking an active economic role, or will it distort the market and reduce social welfare? Does government unintentionally create inefficiency and reduce social justice by infringing on the freedom of privately negotiated agreements consented to in the marketplace? There are many strong opinions about the role of government and its relation to a free and economically viable economy. History is a stingy laboratory. The long spans of time over which social and economic dynamics can be observed change so many of the parameters that most predictions, wrong or right, no longer apply. This, of course, does not mean we cannot learn from history.

Social contracts are based on trust and the agreement of members of the society to cooperate in a certain way.

The rationale for government involvement into free markets arises for two reasons in addition to that of social justice and order embedded in social rules. One is the existence of **public goods**. These are goods that can be used simultaneously by more than one person, without reducing anyone's consumption of it; for example, police and fire protection. People who do not pay taxes cannot be prevented from benefitting. The private market would not provide them, since nonpayers could not be excluded except at great cost. We shall discuss this topic in a later chapter.

Public goods are goods that can be used simultaneously by more than one person without diminishing the use of them to anyone.

The other reason is the problem of **externalities**. We shall cover this topic in a later chapter also. In passing, we shall only say that an externality is either a cost or a benefit conferred on others who are not a party to the contract. For instance, you buy a gasoline-powered lawn mower. Its use wakes up your neighbor on Sunday morning. Market economists believe that in many cases the market can deal with an externality by providing for a market arrangement

Externalities are either costs or benefits conferred on others who are not a party to the contract.

[1]For more details see S. Todd Lowery, "Bargains and Contract Theory in Law and Economics," *Journal of Economic Issues* March 1976.

with the affected third party. Your neighbor offers to compensate you if you will wait until noon. At this time a majority of economists do not believe that externalities can so readily be internalized into a market arrangement. Government intervention therefore is necessary: a law is passed limiting the use of noisy lawn mowers on Sunday morning. The degree of government involve-

The Economic Organization of a POW Camp

R. A. Radford lived through the experience of being a British prisoner of war of the Germans during World War II. While imprisoned, he was able to observe with fascination the emergence of a very competitive, complex market system from what started out as a simple barter economy. It is also an example of one of those rare situations in economics where a real world event closely approximated a controlled experiment. The films King Rat and Stalag 17 may have been inspired by Radford's article.

The camps usually contained 1,200 to 2,500 people housed in separate but intercommunicating bungalows consisting of about 200 to a building. Between individuals there was active trading in all consumer goods and some services. Supplies consisted of rations provided by the Germans and mostly Red Cross food parcels.

Soon after incarceration, people realized that it was both undesirable and unnecessary, given limited size and equality of supplies, to give away or accept gifts of cigarettes or food. Hence "good will" developed into trading as a more equitable means of maximizing individual satisfaction.

Once, when a new Red Cross package arrived, exchanges already set up multiplied in volume. Starting with simple direct barter such as a nonsmoker giving a smoker friend his cigarette issue (25 to 50 per man per week) in exchange for a chocolate ration, such trade expanded. Stories circulated of a padre who started off the round with a tin of cheese and five cigarettes and returned with a complete parcel in addition to his original cheese and cigarettes: the market was hardly perfect. Within a week or two, as the volume of trade grew, rough scales of exchange value came into existence. A tin of jam became worth a half pound of margarine plus something else. The Sikhs insisted on having jam and margarine, and eagerly traded their tins of beef. A cigarette issue became worth several chocolate issues, and a tin of diced carrots worth nearly nothing. The cigarette became the unit of account and the store of value. People began wandering through the bungalows calling their offers—"cheese for seven" (cigarettes). The hours soon after parcel issue led to bedlam. The inconvenience of this system shortly led to its being replaced by an exchange and mart notice board in every bungalow where under the headlines "Name," "Room Number," "Wanted," and "Offered" sales and wants were advertised. When a deal went through, it was crossed off the board. This led to cigarette prices being well known, lending to equality throughout the camp. There were, however, always opportunities for an astute trader to make a profit from arbitrage. Now even nonsmokers were willing to sell for cigarettes. Only sales in cigarettes were accepted; shirts would average say 80, ranging from 60 to 120 according to quality and age. Loans could be made of food from a shop that was set up as a public utility from surpluses of food, toiletries and clothing and sold at fixed prices of cigarettes, on a nonprofit basis. Loans could be made and repaid by a small comission taken on the first transaction.

There was an emerging labor market. Even when cigarettes were not scarce, there was usually some person willing to perform services for them. Laundry men advertised at two cigarettes per garment. A good pastel portrait cost 30 or a tin of "Kam." Other odd jobs had similar prices.

There were also entrepreneurial services. There was a coffee stall owner who sold tea, coffee, or cocoa at two cigarettes a cup, buying his raw materials at market prices and hiring labor to gather fuel and to stoke the fire. He actually enjoyed the services of an accountant at one stage. Such large scale enterprises were rare, but several middlemen or professional traders existed. The more subdivided the market, the less perfect the advertisement into the private decision process, particularly in the economic marketplace, is a lively issue these days and will remain so in this century. It is an issue that will appear throughout the chapters ahead. It comes down to the question, Is economic freedom a necessary precondition in maintaining political and individual freedom?

ment of prices; and the less stable the prices, the greater was the scope for these operators. One man capitalized on his knowledge of the Urdu language by buying meat from the Sikhs and selling butter and jam in return. As his operation became better known, more and more people entered this trade, prices in the Indian bungalow began to approximate more nearly those elsewhere, although to the end a contact among the Indians was valuable as linguistic difficulties prevented the trade from being perfectly free. Middlemen traded on their own account or on commission. Price rings and agreements were suspected and the traders certainly cooperated.

One trader in food and cigarettes, operating in a period of shortage, enjoyed a high reputation. His capital, carefully saved, was originally about 50 cigarettes, with which he bought rations on issue days and held them until the price rose just before the next issue. Also, several times a day he visited every Exchange Notice board and took advantage of every discrepancy between prices of goods offered and wanted. His knowledge of prices, markets, and names was phenomenal. By these means he kept himself smoking — his profits — while his capital remained intact.

Credit entered into many transactions. Some paid in advance for their own purchases of future deliveries of sugar.

A tiny minority held that all trading was undesirable as it engendered an unsavory atmosphere; occasional frauds and sharp practices were cited as proof.

More interesting was opinion on middlemen and prices taken as a whole; opinion was hostile to the middleman. His function and his hard work in bringing buyer and seller together were ignored; profit was not regarded as a reward for labor, but as a result of sharp practices. Despite the fact that his very existence was proof to the contrary, the middleman was held to be unnecessary in view of the existence of the Exchange and Mart as well as the shop mentioned earlier. Appreciation only came his way when he was willing to advance the price of a sugar ration or buy goods at spot (current price) and carry them against future sale prices. In these cases the element of risk was obvious to all since prices could be very unstable and therefore uncertain because prices were affected by air raids, the nonmonetary demand for cigarettes, good and bad war news, and the interruption of the flow of Red Cross parcels.

Middlemen as a group were blamed for reducing prices or because of special knowledge (for example, knowing Urdu) of cornering certain markets. Nonetheless, most people dealt with a middleman, consciously or unconsciously, at one time or another.

There was a strong feeling that everything had its fair price in cigarettes. This price varied between camps. As soon as prices began to fall with a cigarette shortage a clamor rose, particularly against those who held reserves and who bought at reduced prices. Also, the question arose, "Should nonsmokers get a cigarette ration?" When inflation occurred, curious arguments were advanced to justify price fixing. One argument ran as follows: Not everyone has private cigarette parcels. Thus, when prices were high and trade good in the summer of 1944, only the lucky rich could buy. This was unfair to the man with a few cigarettes. When prices fell in the following winter, then prices should be pegged high so the rich, who had enjoyed life in the previous good times, should put many cigarettes into circulation. The fact that those who sold to the rich in the summer had also enjoyed life then, and the fact that in the winter there was always someone willing to sell at low prices were ignored. Such arguments were hotly debated. But prices moved with the supply of cigarettes, and refused to stay fixed in accordance with a theory of ethics.

Condensed from R. A. Radford, "The Economic Organization of a POW Camp," *Economica*, Vol. 12 (1945).

THE CONTRACT

Contracts **are both explicit and implicit agreements between two parties or groups.**

In our discussion about two approaches to exchange, we have been talking about what in legal jargon is called a *contract.* We have used the concept more loosely here. Agreeing to meet your friend after your ten o'clock class is a contract. Paying for a loaf of bread at the grocery store is a contract. Agreeing to stop at a red light is a contract. Thus, **contracts** are both explicit and implicit understandings; they are promises. In the legal, technical sense contracts take diverse forms. They all amount to a legal expression of the rules regarding a promise and of carrying out that promise, which in any case applies to an economic bargain or transaction between individuals or groups. More precisely, "A contract is a promise or a set of promises for the breach of which the law gives a remedy, or the performance of which the law in some way recognizes as a duty."[2] A contract brings the future into the present. It commits the parties to an agreement made today that binds them to that agreement over a designated time into the future. The contract therefore provides for the stability and continuity of social and business relations. For instance, property rights on a house remove any uncertainty about ownership of the house in the future.

The institutionalists argue that contracts are a *necessary* condition for exchange to occur. The pure market economists do not deny the importance of contracts in negotiating trade. They ardently agree that the government should diligently enforce legal contracts between trading parties, but that the government should not meddle with a consensus reached by the parties to the contract if it is a victimless agreement, or if an agreement can be made with a victim without government intervention. They say that the government's only function should be to ensure that the contract is enforced.

Most economists fall between the extreme positions of the pure institutional and the pure market approaches. They believe that "appropriate government intrusion" can often reduce transactions costs, raise efficiency, provide more justice, and increase the economy's output and the people's standard of living by modifying the conditions of contracts and social relations, and by redefining property rights in some situations. The question remains, What is appropriate? To answer this, defenders of intrusion might cite new laws applying to civil rights, union rights, and government-supported or government-assisted construction projects.

Discrimination imposed a high transaction cost on many people in acquiring education and job experience. Because of social attitudes it has been more difficult for minorities to *contract* for higher education or for a better paying job. For this reason the government instituted provisions under which minorities would find it easier than before to contract for education and work, for instance, for entrance to medical school and for jobs on construction sites. It is anticipated that people who would otherwise have been prevented from doing these things will make a fuller contribution to the economy, benefiting

[2]Victor P. Goldberg, "Toward an Expanded Economic Theory of Contract," *Journal of Economic Issues,* March 1976: 46.

others as well as themselves because of the reduced contractual costs to minorities.

The right of workers to unionize, to contract with employers about the conditions of property rights to jobs, was legally granted in 1935. Through reducing violence and by avoiding severe disruptions at job sites, a stable environment was made possible, enabling the economic system to increase efficiency and output by lowering the transactions costs associated with labor and employer disagreements. Policing costs were greatly reduced. This was made possible by changing the social relations attendant to contracts between workers and employers motivated by government action.

However, intrusion by government into private contractual arrangements may also make them more costly. As we indicated above, price controls and other regulations in product and labor markets will often distort economic activity. Thus, the continuous problem facing government and its economic advisors is just where the lines of regulation should be drawn.

CHAPTER SUMMARY

It is presumed that exchange makes all parties better off. Otherwise, they would not freely engage in trade.

People also gain from specialization. If they specialize they can produce more. To gain from specialization it is important for individuals to do those tasks in which they have a comparative advantage over others.

Trading activities involve costs. These are called transactions costs. In some types of transactions the associated costs are very large. In buying a house, for example, there are large information costs, costs of making a contract, and policing costs associated with enforcing a contract. In some trades, of course, transactions costs are quite small.

The essence of the activities of middlemen is to reduce transactions costs of specializing in the business of distributing goods. Retailers and wholesalers bring goods to shops in the neighborhood, where consumers have easy access to them. This reduces the transactions costs that consumers would otherwise have to pay.

Speculators make forecasts about the way prices are going to move, and speculative activities help to smooth out price movements over time.

When people engage in production and exchange they inevitably face risk and uncertainty. A farmer plants wheat but may or may not have wheat to sell the next year. He faces the risk that bad weather will destroy the crop. If the probability of bad weather is known, he can calculate the risk of crop failure. If the probability of risk cannot be calculated, we say the farmer faces uncertainty.

In order for exchange to take place, and for markets to work, the individuals in the society must have rights to their property. These involve the right to sell it or give it away, the right to keep others from using it, and the right to expect government to protect one's property for one's use. These rights may be called the right to alienate, the right to exclude, and the right to protect.

In the pure laissez-faire market economy the major activity of government is to protect property rights and enforce contracts. But sometimes government is led to play an additional role. Government is asked to provide public goods. These are goods that can be used by more than one person simultaneously. Lighthouses over the rocky shore can protect many ships at the same time. All shipowners, through government, should contribute to their maintenance. Government may also wish to mediate when costs and benefits occur outside of or external to the market—when there are externalities such as air and water pollution created by some to the detriment of others, and where the transactions costs for individuals to contract for compensation are too high.

There is a fundamental conflict between pure market economists and so-called institutionalists about the bases for exchange. Institutionalists believe that social rules play a major role in carrying out trade and are a precondition of trade. The market economists contend that trade is initially motivated by the economic benefits to be gained, with social rules following once the potential benefits are understood, and provided the transactions costs of carrying out trade are small.

Most economic science has developed around understanding the workings of a modern exchange economy. It is this kind of economy that our attention is focused on in this book.

QUESTIONS

1. Buckminster Fuller has 26 patents to his name. The one for the geodesic dome has made him rich. He is also a poet. He was quoted as saying, "Too much is being left to specialists. A highly educated doctor will spend money to have a plumber fix his sink; why can't that doctor do the job himself?" Comment.
2. Mr. Pro hustles contracts for his consulting firm. He is also the best computer programmer in the firm. Should he do his own programming for the firm? Comment.
3. Mr. Volt, president of the Spark Electrical Company, was the best engineer the company ever had. Why did they make him president of the company? It seems such a waste. Comment.
4. Would you be willing to pay for a specialist to trace your genealogy back 500 years? Could you not do it instead? Why might you choose not to?
5. Suppose the retail cost of over 10,000 unassembled parts of a Ford Maverick is $13,000 whereas the assembled car is retailed at $6,000. Suppose you could spend $3,000 at a salvage yard and obtain all the parts to assemble the car yourself. Would you save some costs?
6. During the protests of the late 1960s, did the well-known rock singers who toured the country with their multiwatt amplifiers—over which they blasted protest songs about pollution, materialism, the evils of technology, and hypocrisy—ever have to deal with middlemen? Did they do so willingly? Why?
7. When authors contract with publishers for publication of their books, they arrange to receive a royalty income of from 10 to 15 percent on sales revenues instead of selling the rights to publication for a lump sum. What burden is being shared? Can the author be sure of selling a given number of copies of his book? Why does the firm take the larger burden instead of the author? Can speculation be said to be involved here? Explain.
8. Suppose a person went into business finding *reliable* secondhand cars for people who desire to buy them. Does this make any sense? What concept(s) discussed in the chapter would be involved here? Can you think of any other market where people actually seek out others for certain services?
9. The opportunity cost (price) of shirts was around 80 cigarettes in the POW camp, while a portrait cost 30 cigarettes and cheese 7 cigarettes. Why do you think the relative prices (opportunity costs) of the goods differed?

10. Liverpool Larry and Sangupta the Sikh live in different parts of the POW camp. Each has 10 cigarettes and 10 tins of jam. They have a different substitution preference between the two goods. The Sikh is willing to trade off more cigarettes to get jam than is Larry. Hence, Sangupta trades 4 cigarettes for 2 tins of jam. This leaves him with 6 cigarettes and 12 tins while Larry ends up with 14 cigarettes and 8 tins.
    a. What is the cost to Larry of acquiring 4 cigarettes?
    b. What is the cost to Sikh of acquiring 2 jams?
    c. Does Larry value his tenth jam as much as his first jam?
    d. Did Larry and the Sikh reach a preferred position after the trade?
    e. Now assume that Larry and Sangupta are unknown to one another. Enter the padre who by diligently asking around learns of Larry and Sangupta's preferences. In fact, he knows that the Sikh would be willing to give up 5 cigarettes for 2 tins and that Larry would willingly part with 3 tins to get 4 cigarettes. Thus, the padre trades Larry 4 cigarettes for 3 tins and then trades 2 tins for 5 of the Sikh's cigarettes. The padre ends up with one more cigarette and one more tin than he started with.
        1. What is the padre's function here?
        2. Did he perform a service?
        3. Did he cheat anyone?
11. Suppose a rule was passed against the padre's activities described in problem 10e. Would this prevent the Sikh from getting extra jam? Does passing laws against certain economic activities prevent these activities from occurring? Why not? Can you think of any examples in the U.S. today?
12. Prisoners who built up reserves of goods when prices were low, and sold them later at higher prices when incoming parcels were slow in arriving, were severely criticized. Were they cheating? Or did they serve a useful allocative purpose? Do such activities occur in our economy today? Give an example.
13. In the POW camps loans were made and repaid with a commission in units of cigarettes. By what other term can this commission be called. Does it have a function? What is it?
14. Cigarettes were described in the camps as a medium of exchange, a unit of account, and a store of value. Actually, what was the function of cigarettes in the camps?
15. At first the prisoners bartered directly for goods without using cigarettes. Later scales of exchange evolved based on cigarettes, and an exchange board was set up listing prices. Did this trend reduce the costs of exchange and trade? If so, what costs?
16. Was the exchange board a form of advertising? Did it have a positive or negative effect? Why?
17. In reference to the padre's caper in the camps, the author said, "The market was not yet perfect." What do you think he meant?
18. At the end of the article on the POW camps there is a description about arguments over "price fixing" when prices did not stay fixed in accordance with a theory of ethics. A "just price" was considered by some to be the price that prevailed when times were good, i.e., abundant parcels and lower prices. Are high prices immoral when parcels are more scarce? Would a "just price" be a good allocator? Would price controls work?
19. Suppose each prisoner were given the identical initial quantity of goods and cigarettes—a rule passed by a governing prisoners committee. Would the distribution of goods end up unequal over time? Will some prisoners end up with more than others? Why, or why not? Suppose another rule were passed that said that every two months all goods and cigarettes would have to be redistributed equally. What would the effect be? Would it be fair? Would the prisoners be better off?
20. Two prisoners, Jeb and Josh, are digging a tunnel hoping to escape from the camp. An injured third prisoner acts as a lookout. Jeb can dig 1.5 tons of dirt or lug 25

one-hundred-pound sacks every hour. Josh, in one hour, can dig 1 ton of dirt or he can lug 20 one-hundred-pound sacks. Should Jeb and Josh both dig and lug? Or should Jeb only dig and Josh only lug, or vice versa?

21. Consider two countries, Germany and the U.S. Using the same capital facilities and the same level of skilled labor, the production of coal and steel for the two countries if they produced only all coal or all steel is as follows:

	U.S.	Germany
Coal (tons)	100	50
Steel (tons)	60	50

Suppose the U.S. is currently producing 50 tons of coal and 30 tons of steel and Germany is currently producing 30 tons of coal and 20 tons of steel.

a. What are the opportunity costs for the U.S. and Germany to produce coal and steel?
b. Which country has a comparative advantage in producing coal? In producing steel? Why?
c. Assume that the U.S. and Germany agree to trade at the exchange ratio of 1.33 coal to 1 steel. Which commodity will the U.S. export? Which one will Germany? Suppose the U.S. exports 40 tons of what it specialized in. What would be the final consumption levels of coal and steel for the U.S. and Germany?
d. Suppose the Germans wanted to trade at the ratio of 2 of what it produces to 1 unit of what the U.S. produces. What will happen?

22. Suppose information costs were zero. What would this imply about the real world?
23. Which of the following involves transactions costs, and which kind?
    a. Looking for a house.
    b. You bribe the bartender to lower the sound of the jukebox.
    c. You and your friend have blind dates. Who pairs with whom?
    d. There are three economics sections, each with a different instructor. Which section do you take?
    e. Extra store detectives are hired during the Christmas season.
    f. You have to file the long income tax form this year. You go to H. & R. Block for help.
24. In 1978, a poll showed that 91 percent of freshman college students thought high school grading was too easy. For the first time more students had A averages than C averages. In 1961 about half of Harvard University seniors graduated with honors. By 1974, cum laude or better went to 82 percent of the seniors. The average grade at the University of Wisconsin soared from C plus to B plus in just 9 years. Some people would like to do away with grades.
    a. What purpose do grades serve to potential employers?
    b. If grades are artificially inflated, how might employers sort out the real As from inflated As?
    c. Do you think employers would be "right" in devising means to discriminate between real As and inflated As?
25. There are 10 multiple choice questions left and only one minute remaining in an exam you are taking. You guess at the answers, of which there are four possibilities for each question. Is this an example of risk or of uncertainty? Why?
26. Is the cost of search relatively higher for a tasty pizza or for a large appliance? For which one would you spend more time looking? Why?
27. Did Henry Thoreau depend on middlemen in his forest retreat next to Walden Pond? Explain.
28. At times people receive mail containing an advertisement that includes sample cloth for trousers. The trousers are offered at a discount. Why would you, even at the cut-rate price, be less inclined to order the trousers, preferring instead to pay more at the local clothing stores?

Chapter 3

Demand and Supply

PROGRESS REPORT

A. In Chapter 1 we discussed the scientific method, scarcity, and the concept of opportunity cost. If you covered Chapter 2 you learned why people trade, and how individual preferences determine at what ratio individuals will trade one thing for another without explicitly introducing money prices. We saw that the middleman serves to reduce transactions costs. These are costs associated with the act of trading independent of the exchange price of the product being traded.

B. In this chapter we examine the mechanisms of supply and demand, which are fundamentally based on the opportunity cost concept: how supply, demand, and cost are translated in market prices and how the interaction of supply and demand in a free, competitive market serves to allocate scarce resources through the establishment of a market equilibrium. We then discuss how interference in a free market can prevent a competitive equilibrium from being reached, resulting in a misallocation of resources reflected in either the creation of shortages or surpluses.

C. In Chapter 4 we shall examine a property of demand curves called price elasticity, namely the sensitivity of quantity demanded to changes in price. Then a distinction is made between what individuals pay for something and the satisfaction from using the thing they buy, called utility. The chapter ends with a discussion of utility maximization.

We mentioned earlier that in a market economy allocation of scarce resources is achieved by the system of relative prices. The mechanism of supply and demand determines relative prices in the marketplace. We are now ready for a more formal and rigorous discussion of supply and demand. They are concepts deceptively simple in appearance and extraordinarily useful in application. When fully understood, supply and demand bring coherence to what would appear to be diverse and unrelated events.

DEMAND

We know that scarcity means that choices must be made. These choices necessarily involve opportunity costs, since alternatives must be sacrificed once a choice is made. If there were no scarcity, opportunity costs would be zero; there would be no allocation problem. Desired goods would be free goods.

Consider the demand for more automobile safety. How much more would you be willing to pay for a safer car? It is conceivable that cars and roadways could be designed to greatly reduce the incidence of death and the number of severe injuries from accidents. Cars could be built with heavier gauge metal, shoulder and hip seat belts, air bags, specially designed shock-absorbing bumpers encircling the whole car, and roll bars. Roads could be equipped with computerized conveyor belt systems on which your vehicle could hitch a ride to its destination, thus removing any possibility of human driving errors.

But safety is not the only thing you are consuming when you drive a car. Many individuals would not want to consume that much safety if the car would thereby be too expensive. Hooking onto a conveyor belt is inconvenient and greatly reduces the flexibility and choices of destinations. Furthermore, the safer but heavier vehicle burns more gasoline, making it more expensive to drive.

Convenience and economy of transportation are some of the goods that drivers consume. The higher the safety factors built into a car, the higher the opportunity cost or sacrifice involved in owning a car. Evidence indicates that many drivers are not willing to give up their current degree of convenience and economy for greater safety. The opportunity cost of absolute safety is too high. It is also true that as the opportunity cost (price) of owning or driving a car rises, fewer cars will be bought. Other forms of transportation would be substituted.

The *law of demand* states that the quantity people are willing and able to buy is inversely related to the price (opportunity cost) of the good, *ceteris paribus*.

There are also substitutes for gasoline. How can that be? Gasoline, and in some cases diesel fuel, is the only thing that can be used as fuel in automobiles. But you are thinking in all-or-nothing terms. Substituting for gasoline as its price rises does not imply doing without, but doing with less. You can buy a smaller, lighter car that uses less gasoline per mile. You may learn the simple procedure of keeping it tuned up, thereby keeping the car at peak running efficiency and causing it to burn less gasoline. You may reduce recreational driving as well as use the car less often for short shopping trips. To substitute is not necessarily to replace totally, but to reduce usage. The tradeoff can be expressed in a general statement in economics that portrays the quantity consumed of something as inversely related to the opportunity cost (sacrifice) of consuming it. The more of other things that have to be given up to consume something, the less of it we tend to consume. This, in essence, is the **Law of Demand**. *The quantity people are willing and able to buy is inversely related to the price (opportunity cost) of the good, ceteris paribus.* **Ceteris paribus** means other things remaining equal, and signifies that all other parameters are held constant when quantity and price of the good in question vary. Thus, if the price falls the quantity bought will increase.

***Ceteris paribus* means "other things remaining equal," and signifies that all other parameters are held constant when quantity and price of the good vary.**

It really should be called the law of *effective* demand. Notice the words *willing* and *able*. People are free to buy or not to buy, but if they want to buy they must also be *able* to buy what they desire. They must be able to afford it. The law of demand does not state what consumers ought to or should buy, nor for that matter what they should be able to buy. The law of demand is a positive statement, not a normative one. It deals only with those wants that can be converted into effective purchases.

While we assume that other things are held constant, we realize that price is not the only variable affecting the quantity demanded of a commodity or service. Income, tastes, expectations, season, population size, transaction costs, and the prices of related goods also play a role in determining the quantity that people will buy. To observe the relation between the two variables, quantity demanded and price of a single good, we want to remove the influence of changes in these other variables, because if we did not they would obscure the relation between quantity and changes in the price. Therefore, these other variables are treated as parameters for the particular discussion involving the relation of quantity changes to price changes.

Thus, to discover the relation of the quantity of automobiles demanded to the price of automobiles by observing changes in quantity that follow changes in price, an economist might observe these variables in suburban communities where the typical income is in the range of $20,000–$30,000 per year. Keeping the income class of the consumers constant is making income a parameter—a constant while looking at price and quantity. This is called **partial equilibrium analysis**

***Partial equilibrium analysis* examines the effect of one variable on quantity demanded while holding other variables constant.**

In the shorthand of symbolic notation, the law of demand can be written as

$$Q_d = f(P_o)$$

$Q_d = f(P_o)$ states that the quantity demanded is a function of the price of the good.

The symbol Q_d stands for quantity demanded per unit of time and f is the symbol for "is a function of." The letter P_o is the symbol for the price of the particular good being studied, as distinct from all other related goods. P_o refers to *this* or our good, and not *that* good. The price P_o is the independent variable, and the quantity Q_d is the dependent variable. The *ceteris paribus* condition is *always implied*. That is, we do not explicitly state all the parameters that are being held constant each time we write the equation.

Needs: a Comment

Hardly a day goes by that you do not hear the cry about needs. Everyone has needs or wants. Unfortunately, it is not a useful concept to economists. Need is a normative term that cannot be objectively measured. One person's need may be another person's luxury. Need cannot be the basis for allocating scarce resources, since there is no objective method to determine whose needs take priority. Moreover, the word *need* seems to impart implicit blame. It tends to imply that society or someone is responsible for not satisfying another's wants—as if a moral imperative is being violated. Economists prefer the concept of *demand* for two reasons. One, it is a positive concept, not a normative one. It expresses a preference or want that is carried out in the marketplace and is an observable economic act, therefore measurable. Two, very importantly, demand takes into explicit account that satisfying wants is not costless; alternative resources must be sacrificed.

Market Demand

The *market demand curve* is obtained by adding the quantity demanded horizontally at each price of each segment of the market.

Table 3-1 illustrates a demand schedule in tabular form; it explicitly itemizes the individual coordinates of price and quantity. Figure 3-1 portrays the corresponding graphic form of the demand schedule. Figure 3-1 illustrates two demand schedules, one for Joe and one for Alice. Assuming these two individuals compose the total market, the **market demand curve** is obtained from the graphs by *horizontally* adding the quantities from Joe's graph and Alice's graph for each price. At the price of $7, Joe would intend to buy 4 records and Alice 1 record. The market quantity demanded at $7 is the sum of 4 + 1 or 5 records as listed in the table and also indicated in the graph. By adding the individual quantities that Alice and Joe intend to buy at each price, the demand curve for this entire two-person market can be derived.

A demand curve should always be expressed for some time period. The horizontal axis is therefore labeled Q/t or the quantity per unit of time, be it a day, a week, or a month. In our example, our two consumers may buy 5 records each month when the price is $7 per record.

TABLE 3-1

Joe		+	Alice		=	Market Demand	
Price	Quantity/ time		Price	Quantity/ time		Price	Quantity/ time
11	0		11	0		11	0
10	1		10	0		10	1
9	2		9	0		9	2
8	3		8	0		8	3
7	4		7	1		7	5
6	5		6	2		6	7
5	6		5	3		5	9
4	7		4	4		4	11
3	8		3	5		3	13
2	9		2	6		2	15

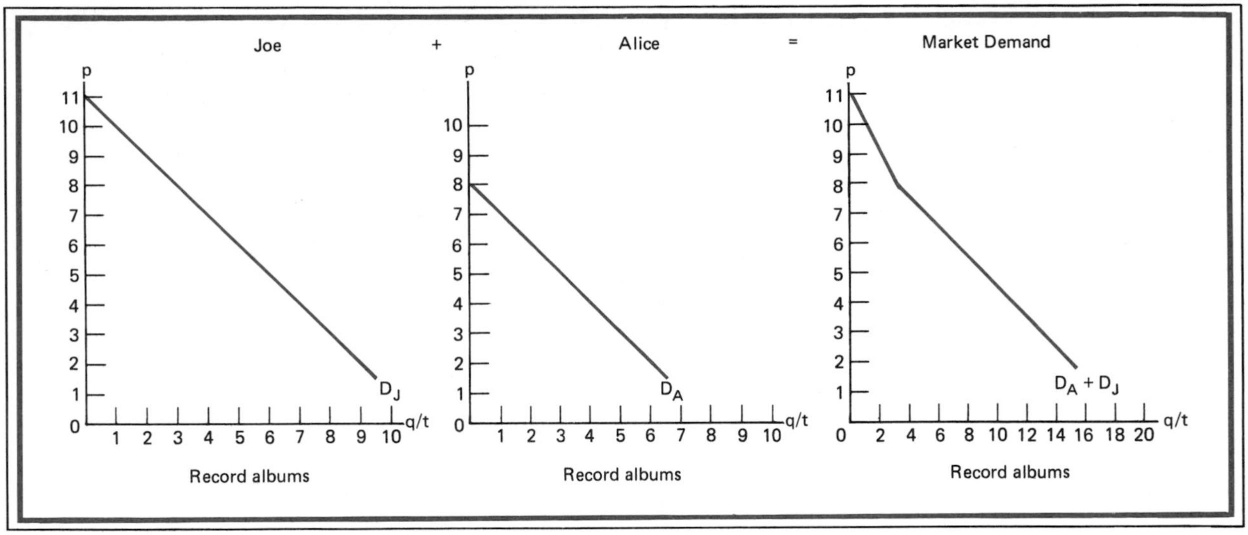

Figure 3-1

Supply and Marginal Cost

The *marginal cost* is the extra or incremental cost of producing an additional unit.

The concept of opportunity cost underlies not only the demand curve but also the supply curve. To see why this is so, let us reproduce the production possibility curve from Chapter 1 in panel *A* of Figure 3-2. From it, it is possible to construct the supply curve for corn in panel *B*. Start out with 22,000 head being produced by this potentially two-good economy. According to the figure, the cost of producing 1 million bushels of corn is the reduction in the size of the cattle herd by 500 head. This puts us at point *b* in panel *A* and also at point *b* in panel *B*. In panel *B*, this tells us that 1 million bushels of corn will be supplied at a cost of 0.5 thousand head of cattle. This cost, or opportunity cost, is also known as the **marginal cost** *(MC)* of 1 million bushels of corn. *The marginal cost is the extra or incremental cost of producing an additional unit* of corn. The unit can be one bushel or a specified amount of corn bushels. In this case the corn unit is millions of bushels. To produce 2 million bushels of corn, that is, an additional 1 million bushels, the marginal sacrifice, hence cost, is 1.5 thousand head (1.5 units) of cattle that cannot be raised. This moves us to point *c* in panel *A* and to point *c* in panel *B*. The supply curve generated in panel *B* is observed to result from the *change* in total costs shown by moving along the curve in panel *A*. Thus, the marginal cost of producing corn can also be derived by calculating the change in the total cost (sacrificed cattle) and dividing it by the change in the total number of corn units. Therefore, the marginal cost of producing another million bushels of corn for a total of 3 million bushels is as follows:

$$\text{marginal cost of corn} = \frac{\text{change in cattle units sacrificed}}{\text{change in corn units produced}} = \frac{20 - 17}{3 - 2}$$
$$= 3 \text{ cattle units}$$

or 3,000 head of cattle. This puts us at point *d* in each panel of Figure 3-2. What we are deriving in panel *B* is, actually, the supply curve for corn. *The supply*

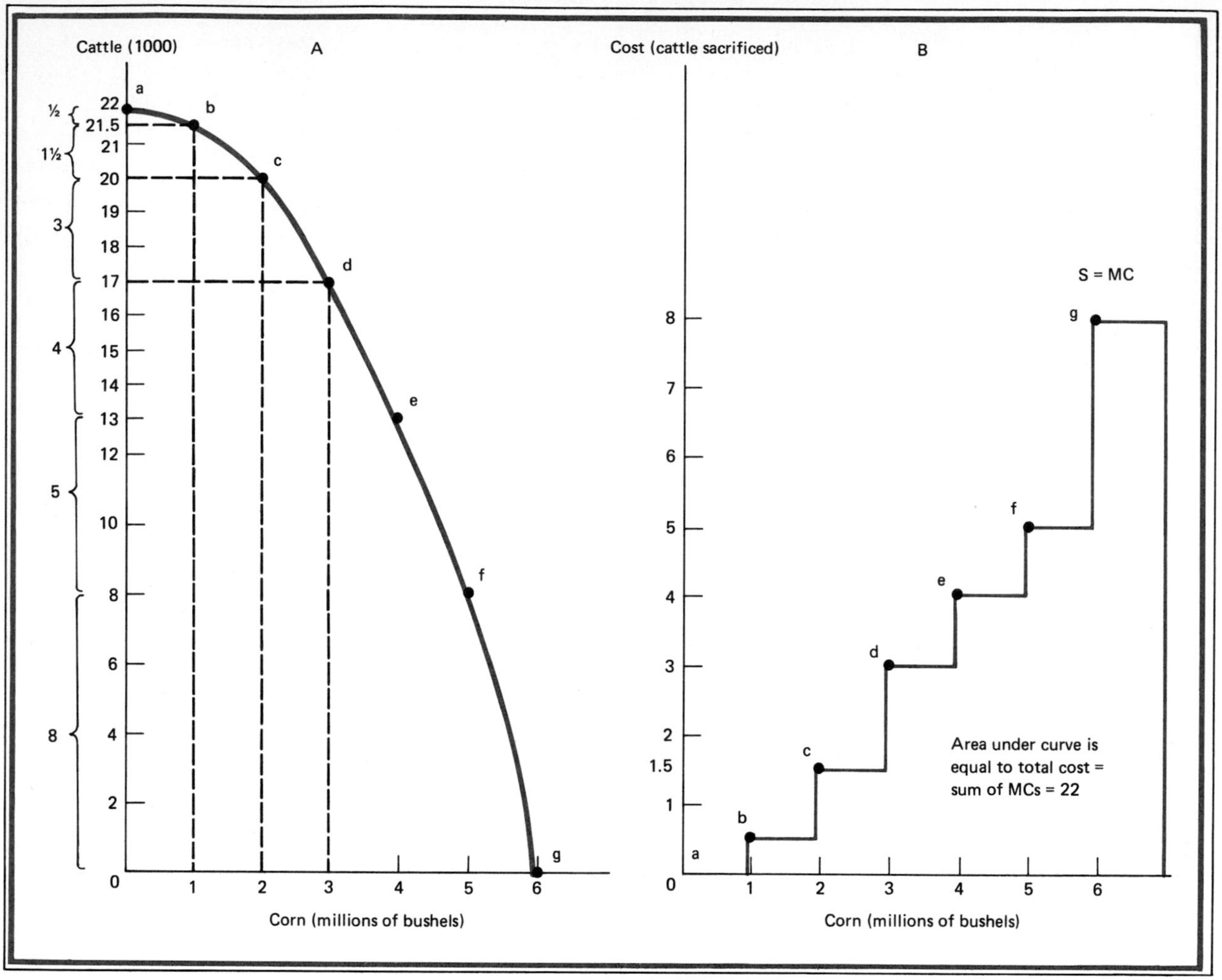

Figure 3-2

The *marginal cost curve* is also called the *supply curve.*

curve for corn is the curve showing the marginal cost of corn. It is also called the **marginal cost curve**.

The decision to produce more and more corn requires that less and less cattle be produced. Resources devoted to the raising of cattle must, of necessity, be bid away from the growing of cattle and applied to the growing of corn. Thus, the supply price of corn, in terms of cattle foregone, is based upon the concept of opportunity cost. In order for cattle growers to switch to corn production they must pay a higher and higher price in terms of foregone cattle production. To willingly release more resources to corn production, the producer must have greater incentive. Society, to get more corn, must bid resources away from being used to raise cattle. That is, it must pay a higher price for corn. Therefore, the supply schedule of corn represents what society must bid in order to draw these resources away from another use and bring forth the amount of corn it wants. The marginal cost or supply price is that price that is just enough to outbid the next highest bidder in an assumed environment of competition and perfect information. The supply price is a price that is just barely higher than the price the resources could command in all other uses. As more corn is produced, the cost of producing the additional corn rises disproportionately, as shown by points *e*, *f*, and g in both panels. Therefore, as the supply curve rises it becomes steeper. Notice that the area under the supply or *MC* curve for corn is equal to total cost. For example, 22,000 cattle were given up in order to produce 6 million bushels of corn, and this represents the total cost of the corn.

The *law of supply* states that the quantity producers are willing and able to provide varies directly with the price (opportunity cost), other things being equal.

The **Law of Supply** *states that the quantity producers are willing and able to provide varies directly with the price (opportunity cost) per unit of time, other things being equal.*

Again, the key words *willing, able,* and *ceteris paribus,* appear. Symbolically, the law of supply is written in equation form as

$$Q_s = f(P_o)$$

with the *ceteris paribus* conditions implied.

Market Supply

Deriving the market supply schedule involves the same mechanical process as deriving market demand. At each price, individual quantities are summed to determine total market quantity. Refer to Table 3-2 and Figure 3-3. At a price of $4, firm *A* would supply 4,000 units and firm *B* 5,000 units. Assuming these producing firms constitute the industry, the total quantity supplied is 9,000 units when the price is $4 per unit. All the points on the total supply curve can be found by adding the separate firm supply curves, horizontally. The table provides all the numbers designated in the figures. Thus, we can describe the supply curve in the same four ways that we described the demand curve: in writing, in equation form, in a table, and in a graph.

TABLE 3-2

Firm A		+	Firm B		=	Industry	
Price	Quantity/ time		Price	Quantity/ time		Price	Quantity/ time
8	9,000		8	11,000		8	20,000
7	8,000		7	9,000		7	17,000
6	7,000		6	7,000		6	14,000
5	6,000		5	6,000		5	12,000
4	4,000		4	5,000		4	9,000
3	2,000		3	4,000		3	6,000
2	0		2	1,000		2	1,000

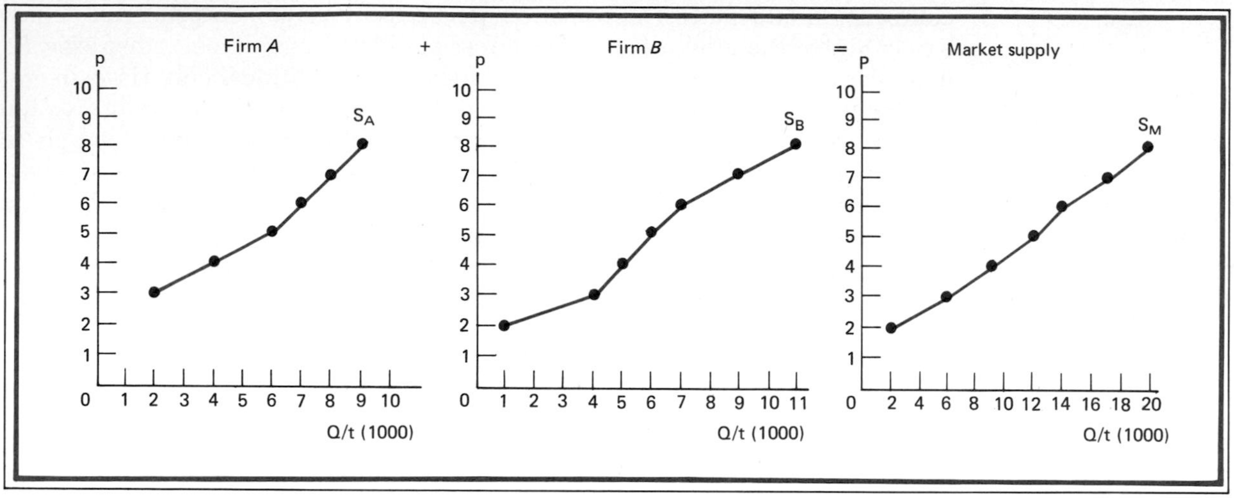

Figure 3-3

Equilibrium

Perfect competition exists when there are many buyers and many sellers trading in a given product, and when no one buyer or seller is large enough to affect the market price.

In this discussion and the relations described in it we have assumed the existence of **perfect competition**—a state of affairs in which there are many buyers and many sellers trading in a given product, and in which no one buyer or seller is large enough to affect the market price. Each seller and buyer trades in volumes that are too small for each to have any market power. They are said to be **price-takers** as contrasted with *price-setters.*

We are now ready to explain, given our assumptions of perfect competition, how a market price is determined. The demand and supply equations are, respectively,

Figure 3-4

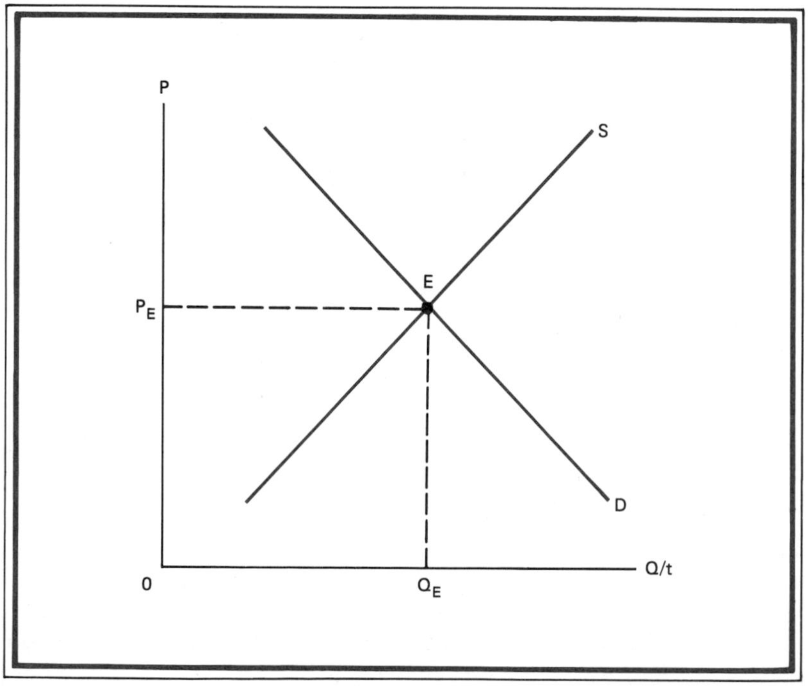

Figure 3-5

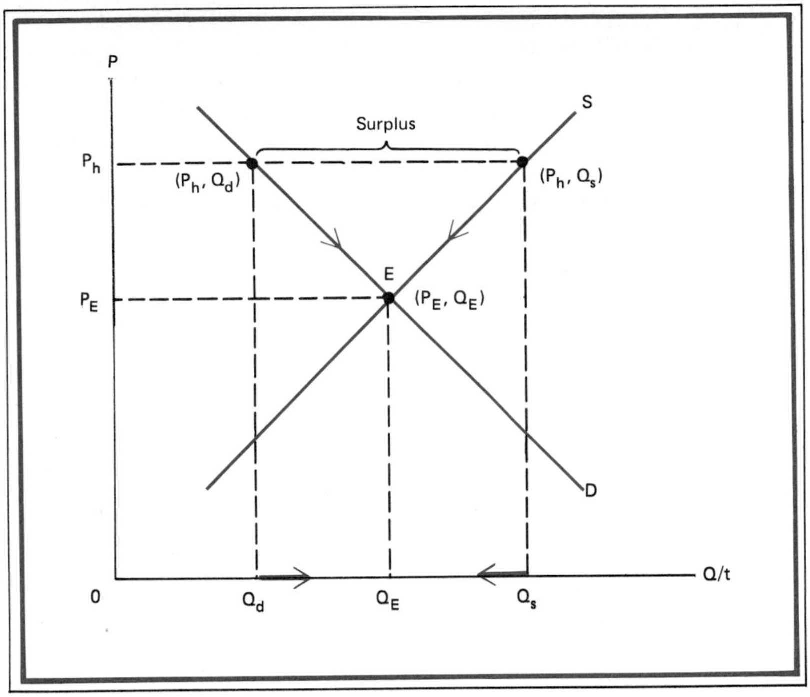

Price-takers are each too small to affect market prices.

$Q_d = f(P_o)$ and $Q_s = f(P_o)$

These equations have two variables in common, the quantity and price. These two variables can therefore be expressed on the two-dimensional diagram shown in Figure 3-4, and related in the demand and supply curves. Remember, the demand curve is a schedule of prices and of the respective quantities that people intend to buy at those prices. The supply curve is also a schedule of intentions, showing the quantities producers or sellers would offer at various prices. There is only one point at which the intentions of buyers and sellers coincide. That occurs where the curves share an identical coordinate point. They share coordinates (P_E, Q_E) designated by E. Point E is called the **equilibrium point** since the quantity supplied equals the quantity demanded at only one price. This price is the equilibrium price, P_E. The market is said to be cleared so that $Q_s = Q_d = Q_E$. The symbol Q_E refers to the equilibrium quantity. When the market is in equilibrium there is no tendency for the system to move off point E unless there is a change in one of the parameters.

The *equilibrium point* is at the price where the quantity supplied is equal to the quantity demanded.

SURPLUS OR EXCESS SUPPLY

Consider the situation depicted in Figure 3-5. Suppose the price in the market is temporarily at P_h, a higher price than the equilibrium price P_E. The market is not cleared. For at the higher price P_h the quantity supplied Q_s is greater than the quantity demanded and is symbolized as $Q_s > Q_d$ where $>$ means greater than. This can be alternately written as $Q_d < Q_s$ where $<$ means less than. Competitive forces act to restore equilibrium. Since the $Q_s > Q_d$, inventories of unsold goods rise. Sellers compete with one another by lowering their prices. As prices fall, some of the sellers will not or cannot lower their prices. In the former case they hold onto inventories longer, hoping prices will rise again. In the latter case they drop out because at the lower prices they cannot earn a profit. They are driven out of business. Surviving firms proceed to reduce production. The total effect on the market is a reduction in the quantity supplied. As the price falls toward P_E, the law of demand operates. Consumers increase the quantity purchased with P_h approaching P_E. The quantities Q_d and Q_s approach one another until they are equal, with $Q_s = Q_d$. The market is said to be **cleared** and in equilibrium. Once again, there is no inclination for the system to move from point E unless some outside force acts on it.

The market is *cleared* when it is in equilibrium, that is, when quantity supplied equals quantity demanded.

SHORTAGE OR EXCESS DEMAND

Consider the situation where the market price is dislodged from equilibrium, as illustrated in Figure 3-6, such that the temporary market P_l is below the equilibrium price P_E. At price P_l the corresponding quantity demanded read off the demand curve is Q_d. But the corresponding quantity supplied obtained from the supply curve is Q_s. We see that the quantity demanded at price P_l is greater than the quantity supplied ($Q_d > Q_s$). In reaction to the lower price of P_l, con-

Figure 3-6

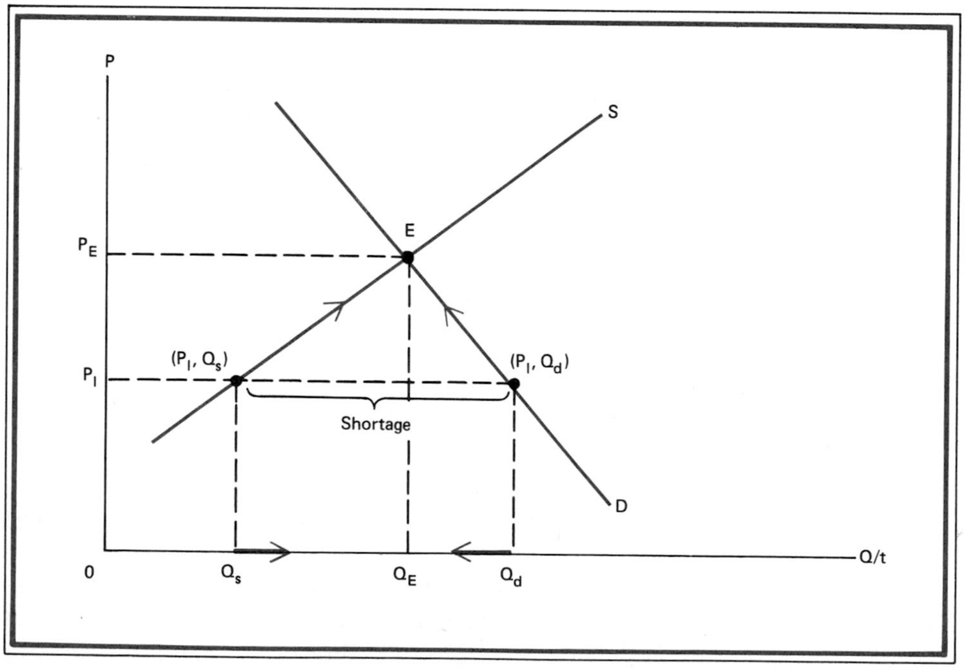

sumers move down along the demand curve and increase their quantity demanded as the law of demand predicts they should. But the law of supply predicts that at the lower price P_l, suppliers are less willing or able to provide goods to the market, hence the quantity supplied declines from Q_E to Q_s. The quantity supplied is now less than the quantity demanded at the price P_l. There exists a shortage of the commodity at the price P_l. But this is an unstable situation. The price cannot remain at P_l. Consider an available apartment that five people want. In a free, unregulated market, the highest bidder will get the lease. Price is the rationing mechanism. The consumers compete for the scarce resource and drive up its price until a price is reached at which, finally, only one bidder is willing and able to pay the equilibrium price P_E.

You might ask how can the apartment units be increased when the price rises? In a short period with market pressure very strong, a building can be partitioned or converted for housing as the opportunity cost of *not* renting it becomes too high. The result is that as the equilibrium quantity Q_E is being attained, the prices will move until the equilibrium price P_E is reached. Effective demand is matched by supply. Equilibrium prevails and $Q_d = Q_s$.

SHORTAGE VS. SCARCITY

Scarcity is the condition of our world; there is only a given amount of resources at a given time with a given technology.

Shortage signifies a price below the equilibrium price, with the result that people want more than producers will provide.

Quantity supplied refers to the quantity provided at a price.

Scarcity is a condition of our world. There is only a given amount of resources at a given time with a given technology. In economic terms, shortage is not the same as scarcity. Shortage signifies a price below the equilibrium price, with the result that people want more than producers will provide. It does not mean that more is not available. A **shortage** signals that at the lower price, it is not economically feasible for many suppliers to provide the good. The quantity supplied of goods will generally rise if their prices rise. Crude oil is an example. As oil becomes harder to get, because wells have to be drilled deeper or offshore, the costs of drilling for it rise. Producers will only be willing to drill for that oil if they can cover the higher costs. This implies higher prices. **Quantity supplied** *refers to the quantity provided at a price.* To talk about quantity supplied without referring to price has no economic meaning. It might mean something to geologists, but it has no operational meaning to economists. There may be plenty of oil in the ground, but if the producers cannot drill for it and receive an incentive price, there will be no supply of oil. A shortage? Yes. Scarcity? Yes. If the price is an equilibrium price, is there shortage? No. Scarcity? Yes.

Disequilibrium

It is understood that equilibrium exists when the intentions of buyers coincide with those of sellers regarding price and quantity. How then can a market once in equilibrium get out of equilibrium? How could excess supply or demand occur, if equilibrium implies a tendency to stay in equilibrium and not to move from it? There are two reasons why disequilibrium can result. These are outside interference into the market by the government, and a change in one of the parameters violating the *ceteris paribus* condition which disturbs the initial or existing equilibrium and causes a shift in the supply curve or demand curve or both.

Government Price Controls

When prices are not legally allowed to fall below a minimum level, it is called a *floor price.*

When prices are not legally allowed to rise above a maximum level, it is called a *ceiling price.*

A permanent disequilibrium may exist in the market when the government sets a price ceiling or a price floor preventing the market from reaching a price that clears it. When prices are not legally allowed to fall below a minimum level, it is called a **floor price**. It is usually a price set above the equilibrium price. When prices are not legally allowed to rise above a maximum level, it is called a **ceiling price**. It is usually a price set below the equilibrium price. Floor prices are in effect on sugar and milk, and usury laws are examples of ceiling prices. Legislated prices exist on or have existed on natural gas, crude oil, and housing among many other things. Wage and price guidelines or controls broadly applied across all markets in the economy have been in effect at times in the past. These controls are often misguided, causing an emerging disequilibrium in the market to become more severe. They cause people to use more resources trying to get around the controls, thus withdrawing resources away from the production of other goods and services. The controls may be motivated by a desire of politicans to help some economically affected group who, more than other groups, is feeling the impact of a certain price movement—up or down—in some market. Sometimes the price controls are motivated by groups with political influence who succeed in getting regulations passed to gain economic benefits for themselves—often making appealing arguments directed at explaining how these controls really benefit you, the consumer. Price controls distort allocation of resources by choking off or suppressing price signals, and usually serve one private interest group at the expense of another, or give rise to illegal activities requiring the government to spend money watching over firms, industries, and individuals. Price controls actually prevent the market from correcting a disequilibrium by getting at the source of it. Hence, over time the problem usually gets worse.

Shifts in Demand

In our analysis so far we have described the formation of an equilibrium price and quantity by forces of supply and demand. We have also described the distortions that follow on the heels of artificially imposed price controls whether they are ceilings or floors. But we have not yet analyzed the movement of price from one equilibrium to another in response to shifts in demand or supply. Our analysis, so far, is called *static* analysis. It is static in the sense that, once equilibrium values of price and quantity are reached, the situation remains unchanged over time.

In this section we shall describe how shifts in the position of the demand curve bring about changes in price and quantity. We shall simply observe the changes in price and quantity that occur as we move from one equilibrium point to another. We shall treat these changes as if the price and quantity jump

Consumer Protection?

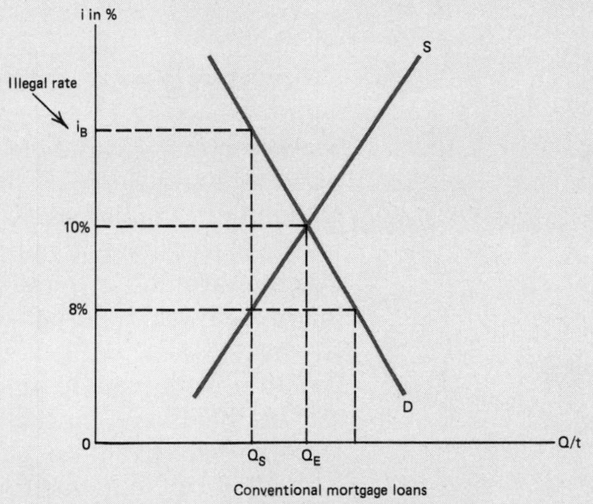

Before May 1976, the state of Minnesota had a usury law setting a ceiling interest rate of 8 percent on instate mortgage loans, loans to individuals, incorporated businesses, and farmers. However, the Federal Housing Administration (FHA) and the Veterans' Administration (VA) mortgage markets were unregulated, being administered by the federal government. The intent of the law was to prevent the unwary consumer from paying excessive interest rates. In the periods from June 1969 to January 1971 and from October 1973 to April 1976, the market rate of interest rose above 8 percent, reaching a high of 10.4 percent in September 1974. The situation is illustrated in the graph. At 8 percent, the quantity demanded is greater than quantity willingly supplied by lenders. The effects were that higher-risk (usually lower-income) borrowers ended up paying more than 8 percent or went without loans. It seems that lenders found means to, in effect, charge illegal higher rates of interest approaching the unregulated market rate prevailing on FHA and VA mortgages. This was achieved by lenders requiring higher down payments and shortening the maturity length of the loan. Also, they raised their "handling charges." In essence, they charged a blackmarket price of i_B shown in the figure.

Many who could not get loans at 8 percent resorted to the government market, willingly paying the 10 percent rather than doing without the loan. Though housing construction was not seriously impaired by the usury law (it can be seriously affected by higher interest rates), the lenders raised their fees to builders. The builders passed on their higher costs by raising the base price of their houses to consumers. Thus, the law did not achieve its purpose of protecting house buyers.

In May 1976 the law was modified, with the ceiling allowed to float 2 percentage points above the interest rate on long-term U.S. government bonds. Housing construction remained unaffected. Financing increased in the conventional mortgage market and decreased in the federal market. But down payment requirements did not decline, nor did maturity lengthen for months after the modification in the law. In effect, the market rate remained above the regulated rate of interest.

Primary source: D. Dahl, S. Graham, A. Rolnick, Federal Reserve Bank of Minnesota Quarterly Review, April 1975 and Spring 1977.

to their new equilibrium positions. Observing such changes is called *comparative statics*—one equilibrium can be compared with another.

Analyzing such jumps is a limited form of *dynamic* analysis. It does not directly trace each movement of price over time. That is, in dynamic price analysis the *time path* of a price movement is noted. Since we are only concerned with jumps to a new price in comparative statics and not with time paths, it is not dynamic in the full sense of the term. Of course, we know markets cannot instantly adjust to new information or to some changing force. There are time lags and gradual adjustments. So we must keep in mind in what follows that while there is an awareness of the existence of adjustments over time, we shall avoid describing exactly how the system travels from one equilibrium to another. We shall only observe the system essentially at its stopping points—comparing one static position to another static equilibrium position.

Demand Parameters

There are many variables held fixed when *ceteris paribus* conditions are applied to a given demand curve, such as shown in Figure 3-7 for men's pipes. One of the variables stated as a parameter is income Y, assumed held fixed at a level of $\overline{Y}_1$ for demand curve D_1. As income rises, a modest prediction would be that men would buy more pipes at the same prices over the next time period. If many men were to lose their jobs, presumably men would buy fewer pipes over the next period. Earlier in the chapter we expressed quantity demanded as a function of the single variable, price. We now explicitly introduce variables that are held fixed for the discussion and refer to them as parameters. To indicate they are fixed we place a bar over them and now indicate the relation embodied in the demand curve D_1 in Figure 3-7 as

$$Q_d = f(P_o, \overline{Y}_1)$$

where income is fixed at the level of $\overline{Y}_1$. The price P_o is the independent variable; the quantity demanded Q_d is the dependent variable. For further details see the Appendix, The Tools of Economics. Assume that average income doubles over the next period, rising to $\overline{Y}_2$. Buyers can now afford to purchase more smoking pipes at the same prices the pipes sold for in the prior period. How can we show that smokers will buy more pipes when the prices of pipes themselves are unchanged? The answer is shown in Figure 3-7 by demand curve D_2.

Figure 3-7

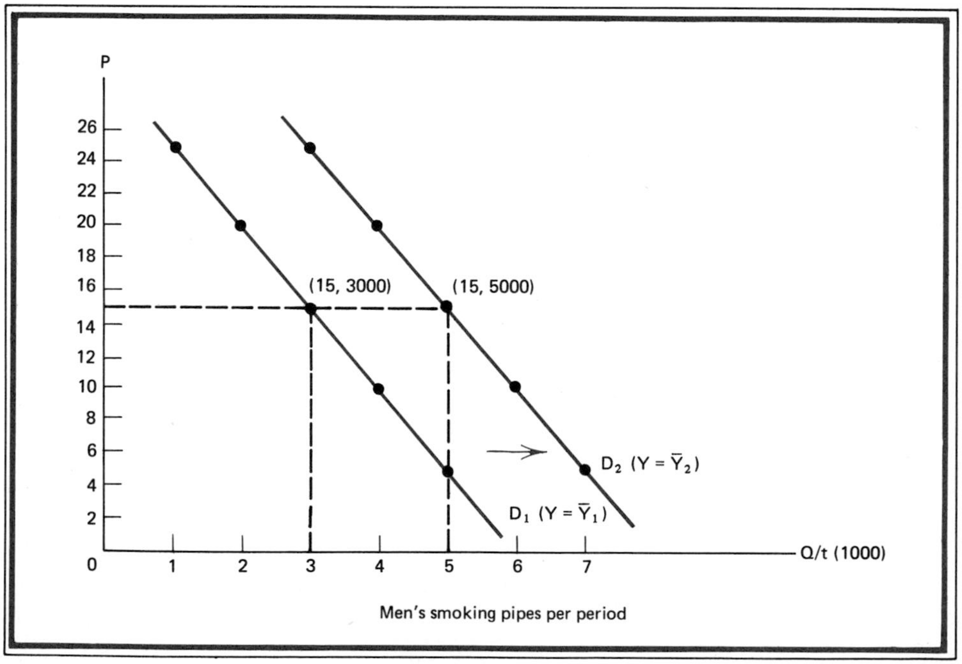

TABLE 3-3

Price	From D_1 Quantity/time	From D_2 Quantity/time
25	1,000	3,000
20	2,000	4,000
15	3,000	5,000
10	4,000	6,000
5	5,000	7,000

The demand curve D_1 has shifted to D_2 because the condition that income is fixed at a level of Y_1 under which D_1 was drawn no longer applies. The curve D_2 shows the demand curve under the new *ceteris paribus* condition when income is at a new higher level of $\overline{Y}_2$. When a barred variable (i.e., a parameter such as income Y) changes, always anticipate a shift in the curve. When demand increases (shifts right) to D_2, the interpretation is that a greater quantity would be demanded at *each* price. This is illustrated in Table 3-3. The price is unchanged, but the quantity demanded at each price is larger. Hence, the coordinate points for D_1 differ for those from D_2, though they share the identical prices. Thus, when the price of men's pipes is $15 each, men buy 3,000 pipes per period given that the barred income parameter is $\overline{Y}_1$. But when the barred income parameter rises to $\overline{Y}_2$, the same buyers purchase 5,000 pipes at the same price of $15 per pipe. Thus, in general,

Old demand curve D_1: $Q_d = f(P_o, \overline{Y}_1)$

New demand curve D_2: $Q'_d = f(P_o, \overline{Y}_2)$

Observe that $\overline{Y}_2$ is the new parametric demand condition applying to the current period.

Seven major variables specified as *demand parameters* are (1) income *(Y)*, (2) prices of related goods *(P_R)*, (3) tastes *(t)*, (4) expectations *(E)*, (5) seasons *(S)*, (6) population growth *(G)*, and (7) transaction costs *(T_R)*.

Income is not the only parameter impounded under the *ceteris paribus* demand condition. The seven major variables specified as **demand parameters** that we shall use are

1. *Income (Y).* If income rises, the original demand curve shifts to the right. If income drops, demand shifts to the left.
2. *Prices of related goods (P_R).* Many pipe smokers like cigarettes and cigars too. If the price of cigars falls significantly, men may do less pipe smoking and more cigar smoking. They substitute toward the now cheaper good. Should the cost of pipe tobacco fall, they may smoke pipes more often. Pipe tobacco is a complementary good to a pipe. The cheaper the tobacco, the more income they have to spend on pipes and the demand for pipes shifts to the right.
3. *Tastes (t).* People have preferences for some things over others even if at the same price and quality. Fads develop. Some things are in while others are out. Changing tastes signifies the adoption of a new con-

sumption schedule. A former fad begins to fizzle, so demand shifts to the left and fewer are now purchased at each price.

4. *Expectations (E)*. If consumers expected the government to increase taxes by 40 percent on tobacco on the first of next month, they would likely stock up on tins of tobacco. Their demand over the current month would increase sharply as they act on their expectations. Conversely, if they expect that two months from now the tax on tobacco will fall substantially, they might temporarily reduce buying as much tobacco until the price goes down. Therefore, there would be a shift of the demand curve to the left.
5. *Seasons (S)*. Not surprisingly, the consumption of soda and ice cream is higher in the summer than during the winter. Households consume more fuel in winter than in summer. Air conditioners are in higher demand in summer than in winter. These effects could also be included under tastes, for example, a taste for warmth or coolness as illustrated in Figure 3-8.
6. *Population growth (G)*. Clearly, as the population grows the demand for most things grows with it, and the demand curve shifts right. Were the population to fall, the demand curve would shift left.
7. *Transactions costs* (T_R). As we noted in the previous chapter, transactions costs can be of three kinds, information, contractual, and policing.

    Information is often costly. Are you more apt to buy a watch from a jeweler or someone who wants to sell you one on the street at a lower price? You pay the jeweler more because you want a reliable watch and a guarantee he will honor because he wants your business in the fu-

Figure 3-8

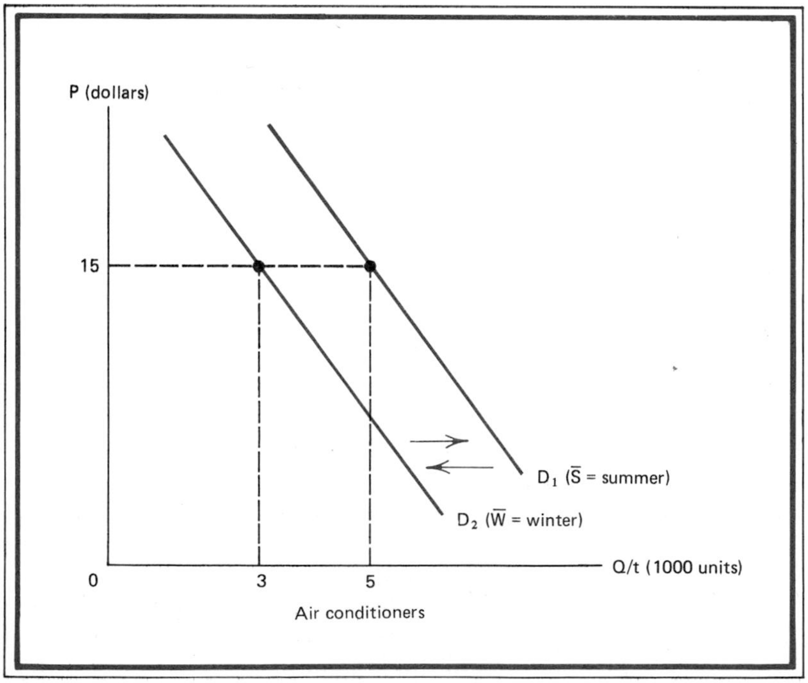

An Exception to the Law of Demand?

A letter writer in Seattle, Washington once wrote to a local newspaper asking why Washington – the leading apple-growing state – exported its best apples to other states while leaving the inferior apples for the local markets. Since the good apples are more expensive, one would expect people in New York to buy fewer apples at the higher price. This would fit the law of demand, which says people buy more when the price is lower and fewer when the price is higher. Therefore, are not Washington apple exporters losing revenues by exporting their best apples?

Careful attention to relative prices tells us that if exporters send both types of apples to the East, the people in New York demand more of the quality apples even though the quality apples are more expensive. This may seem to violate the law of demand. But it does not. For relative prices allocate resources. Consider the following hypothetical numbers:

	Washington		Transportation		New York
Inferior apples	15¢	+	5¢	+	20¢
Good apples	20¢	+	5¢	+	25¢

Both types of apples are higher priced in New York than they are in Seattle because of transportation costs. However, the relative price of quality apples to inferior apples is in the ratio of 20/15 = 1.33 in Washington state while in New York the ratio is 25/20 = 1.25. Therefore, in New York the relative price of good apples is lower than it is in Seattle. At lower relative prices, New Yorkers buy more good apples as the law of demand predicts. It may be easier to understand the point if you imagine that a Washingtonian goes to New York. When in Washington, buying the good apple meant the sacrifice of 1.33 inferior apples. But in New York buying the good apple means sacrificing only 1.25 of the inferior apples. Hence, good apples are relatively cheaper in New York than they were in Washington.

Alternatively, one could say that as far as New Yorkers are concerned the opportunity cost of buying good apples is lower than the opportunity cost for Washingtonians. Hence, quality apples sell relatively better in New York than in Washington and Washington apple exporters are better off. The law of demand holds. The lower the (relative) price the greater the quantity demanded. The general proposition holds for all exported or transported products. This is why one often sees "export quality" on a label. People have come to know that export quality is good quality and commands a premium price.

ture. You pay him more because of the better information he provides about the quality of the watch and the guarantee on the watch.

Contractual costs involve the cost of carrying out the transaction itself, like waiting in line to buy a ticket for a concert. You could avoid the waiting by paying someone else to wait for you. You still pay the cost of waiting while avoiding the act of waiting. Thus, there is a cost aside from the box office price of the ticket. This is the contractual cost of negotiating the exchange of money for a ticket.

Policing costs are costs which affect demand, too. Your demand for owning a car would likely be reduced if it were no crime to steal cars. If you are honest you would have to take extra precaution, hence more expense, to reduce the chance of your car being stolen. The overall effect would be to reduce the demand for cars, thus shifting the demand curve to the left. If an individual's policing costs were reduced by rigorously enforcing laws against theft, then demand would shift to the right.

Because it would be cumbersome to write out the parametric conditions in longhand every time, we resort to stating them in the shorthand notation of equations. The above parameters would be expressed as follows:

$$Q_d = f(P_o, \overline{Y}, \overline{P}_R, \overline{t}, \overline{E}, \overline{T}_R, \overline{S}, \overline{G})$$

QUANTITY DEMANDED VS. DEMAND

The important distinction between quantity demanded and demand must be kept firmly in mind. It embraces the difference between moving along an existing demand schedule when the price P_o changes, and a change in the whole schedule—a shift—when a barred parameter changes.

A demand curve or schedule is just that, a schedule. It is a list of prices, and the quantities corresponding to those prices, under certain parametric conditions. But if one or more of those conditions change, this leads to a different quantity being associated with each change in the price. There is a new list of coordinates (p, q) locating the new demand curve.

But on the new demand curve D_2 the law of demand still applies. According to Table 3-3, if the price of pipes falls from \$15 to \$10 apiece, consumers who would have bought 4,000 pipes on an income of $\overline{Y}_1$ a year, represented by demand curve D_1, would now purchase 6,000 pipes on an income of $\overline{Y}_2$ a year.

1. When the price changes, the *quantity demanded* changes as the buyer moves along his existing demand curve with no change in any of the demand parameters.
2. If one of the barred parameters changes without any change in the independent variable P_o, there is a *shift in the demand* curve. When P_o changes thereafter, the buyer moves up or down along the new demand curve according to the law of demand.
3. When a barred variable changes, there is a shift to a new demand curve. When the price changes, there is no shift, only a movement along the existing demand curve. The demand curve is composed of many price-quantity coordinate points. Which particular quantity on the demand curve is purchased depends on the price. That *quantity* is then read off the horizontal axis. Thus, *demand* refers to the whole schedule of paired prices and quantities, whereas *quantity demanded* refers to a particular quantity from that schedule associated with a particular price from that schedule. When the demand curve shifts, each price is then paired with a new quantity. There is a different schedule of paired prices and quantities, hence a new demand curve.

Shifts in Supply

As with demand, the law of supply is stated under *ceteris paribus* conditions. Figure 3-9 shows a supply schedule or curve for men's smoking pipes labelled S_1, and Table 3-4 provides the corresponding data from which the supply curve S_1 is constructed.

Figure 3-9

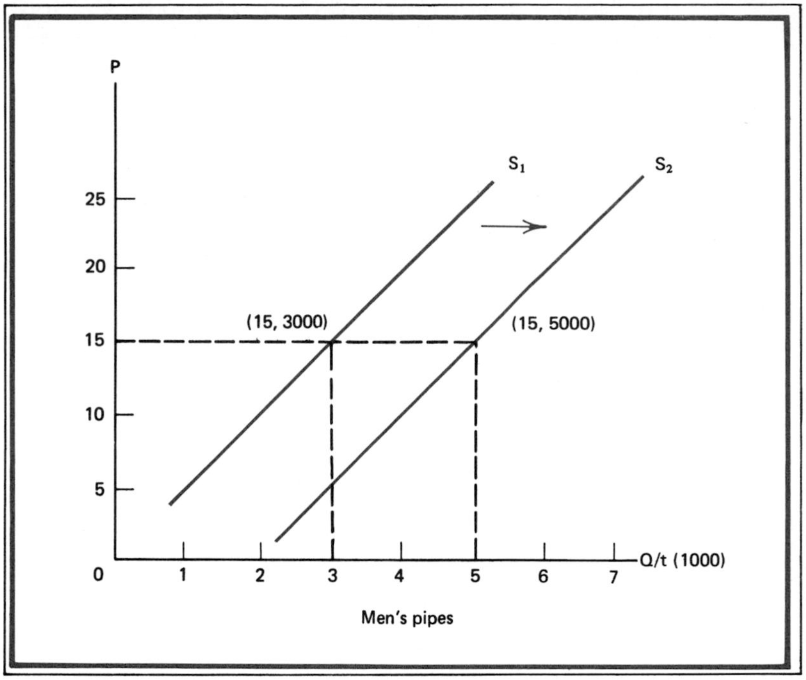

An obviously important variable on the supply side of things is the cost of factors of production. As the price of an input rises or falls the supply curve shifts, since cost is a parameter that is held fixed for a given supply curve. Suppose the cost of an important input were to fall from $C = \overline{C}_1$ to $C = \overline{C}_2$. Then because the firm would earn a higher net return per pipe it would have an incentive to increase its production. This is represented in Figure 3-9 by a shift of supply S_1 to S_2. There is an increase in supply and at *each price* the quantity supplied is greater. In shorthand notation,

Old supply curve S_1: $Q_s = f(P_o, \overline{C}_1)$

New supply curve S_2: $Q'_s = f(P_o, \overline{C}_2)$

TABLE 3-4

Price	From S_1 Quantity/time	From S_2 Quantity/time
25	5,000	7,000
20	4,000	6,000
15	3,000	5,000
10	2,000	4,000
5	1,000	3,000

Consequently, at a price of $15 a pipe, producers would be willing to manufacture 3,000 pipes per period when the given parametric cost was $\overline{C}_1$ for the supply schedule S_1. But when the cost fell to $\overline{C}_2$, producers would be willing to provide 5,000 pipes per period at $15 a pipe, as indicated on curve S_2. For each price the quantity supplied is greater for supply curve S_2 than for S_1. The coordinates of curve S_2 share the same price variable with S_1, but the quantity variable that is read along the horizontal axis is different.

Cost is only one kind of parameter subject to the *ceteris paribus* supply condition imposed on curve S_1. The six **supply parameters** of interest to us are as follows:

The six *supply parameters* are: 1. factor costs *(C_f)*, 2. technology *(T)*, 3. expectations *(E)*, 4. transaction costs *(T_R)*, 5. the number of suppliers *(N_S)*, and 6. season *(S)*.

1. *Factor costs (C_f).* Factor costs are costs of land, labor, and capital inputs in the production process. If any or all of these costs increase, the supply curve shifts to the left. At each price the quantity willingly supplied by producers declines. When input costs fall, the supply curve shifts to the right and the quantity supplied at each price increases.
2. *Technology (T).* Technology refers to the state of the art. When new, more efficient techniques and equipment increase productivity (increase output per unit of input), using the same size labor force, output can be increased at each price. The supply curve shifts to the right.
3. *Expectations (E).* If price controls exist on a commodity and the price controls are to be lifted a month from now, firms will build up inventories and not release them on the market until the price does in fact rise. This will cause shortages in the period prior to decontrol because of the temporary leftward shift in the supply curve. On the other hand, if rising prices are anticipated, and as a consequence rising profits as well, then firms would be encouraged to expand supplies. This would certainly apply if any price controls that were once in effect were lifted. Supply would increase and the supply curve would shift to the right in the period following a lifting of price controls, because of the expectation that higher prices would yield more profits.
4. *Transactions costs (T_R).* There exist information, contractual, and policing costs on the supply side too. Information costs rise, for example, when firms pursue a marketing analysis to determine whether a potential product will strongly appeal to consumer tastes. Contractual costs would be incurred by businesses when they are required to file an environmental impact statement before they can expand an existing plant or build a new one. The necessity of beefing up security and paying higher insurance costs raises policing costs. All of these examples can shift the supply curve to the left, resulting in less quantity being supplied at each price. Of course, transactions costs can also fall, causing the supply curve to shift to the right.
5. *The number of suppliers (N_S).* An industry can increase quantity supplied as firms within the industry raise output. But industry supply can also rise because new firms enter the industry, attracted by the potential of high profits. Conversely, if some existing firms in an industry leave because of losses and little prospect of recovery, the industry supply curve will shift leftward. It should be mentioned, however, that the N_S parameter is only significant in what is called the long run; new firms cannot enter an industry overnight. We shall have more

to say about the distinction between the short run, when entry into an industry by a firm is not possible, and the long run, when entry can occur. The same warning applies to the technology parameter also.

6. *Season (S)*. For farming the effect of this parameter is obvious. It also brings into focus the importance of the time period. The strawberry crop cannot be increased during the winter, but can be increased from one season to the next by more intensively planting as the next season approaches. Unseasonal weather is also important. In Figure 3-10, if a freeze destroys much of the Brazilian coffee trees, the supply curve S_1 shifts left to S_2, and the quantity supplied at each price declines. For price P_1 quantity falls from Q_1 to Q_2 in the next period. A dry spell will reduce the supply of crops while favorable rainfall will increase it.

Specific variables will be required in the examination of the supply forces affecting specific goods. These might often be subsumed under "technology." In shorthand notation, the variables and parameters in the supply equation can be written

$$Q_S = f(P_o, \overline{C}, \overline{T}, \overline{E}, \overline{T}_R, \overline{N}_S, \overline{S}).$$

The letter C stands for production costs, T for technology, E for expectations, T_R for transaction costs, N_S the number of suppliers, and S for seasons. When any one of the parameters changes, look for a shift in the supply curve. If more than one changes, the direction of the shift will be determined by which effect is dominant. You will not be confronted here with that possibility, since that takes us beyond the goals of this course.

Figure 3-10

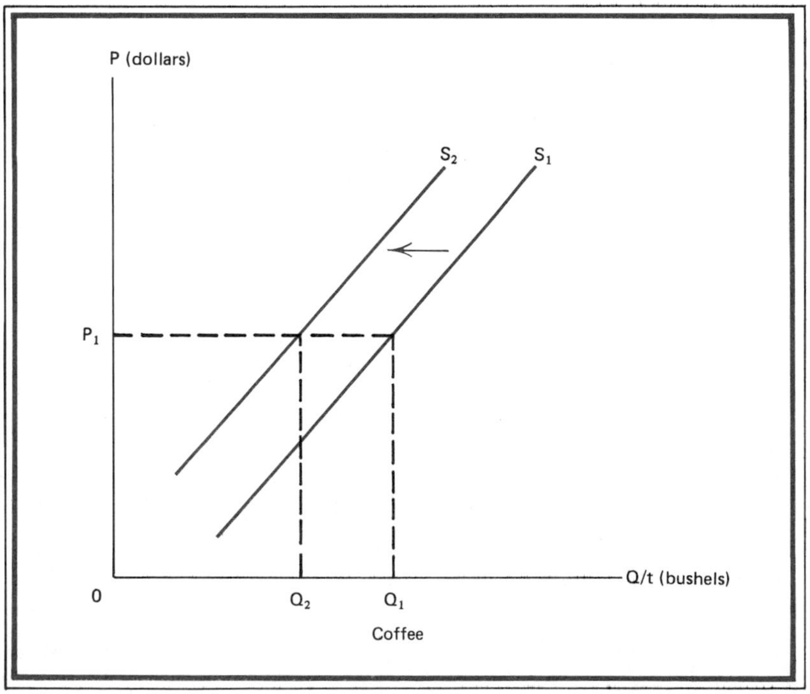

Related Goods

We have seen that by putting supply and demand together, a market equilibrium emerges with an equilibrium price and an equilibrium quantity. When the market equilibrium price changes, one must always ask, What caused it to change? Was it because of a shift in supply or demand, or both? Figure 3-11 depicts an equilibrium in both the corn and soybean markets, designated in each graph by E_1 with initial prices P_1 and Q_1. These prices and quantities are numerically different in each market. We shall assume that corn and soybeans are related on the demand side and act as substitutes. These two crops can be grown on the same land. Farmers on a seasonal basis can easily shift from growing corn to growing soybeans and vice versa.

Assume that because soybeans are discovered to have superior health benefits consumers increase their demand for soybeans, causing soybean demand to shift from D_1 to D_2. The equilibrium position in the soybean market changes from E_1 to E_2 with the new equilibrium prices and quantities P_2 and Q_2 respectively. As a result there is a decrease in demand for corn, represented by the shift in demand for corn from D_1 to D_2. At the original corn price of P_1, however, the quantity demanded of corn declines to Q_3 from Q_1. There is now an excess supply of corn amounting to $Q_1 - Q_3$ with the corn market momentarily at point T. Consequently, the producers of corn lower their prices in order to remove the surpluses. As the corn price falls, according to the law of supply, so does the quantity supplied, because for some farmers the price falls too low and they choose to bury their corn. Others continue to lower their prices. As the price declines, consumers increase the quantity of corn demanded by moving down along the new demand curve D_2. Eventually the new equilibrium price P_2 is reached, where $Q_s = Q_d = Q_2$. Again, there has been no decrease in supply

Figure 3-11

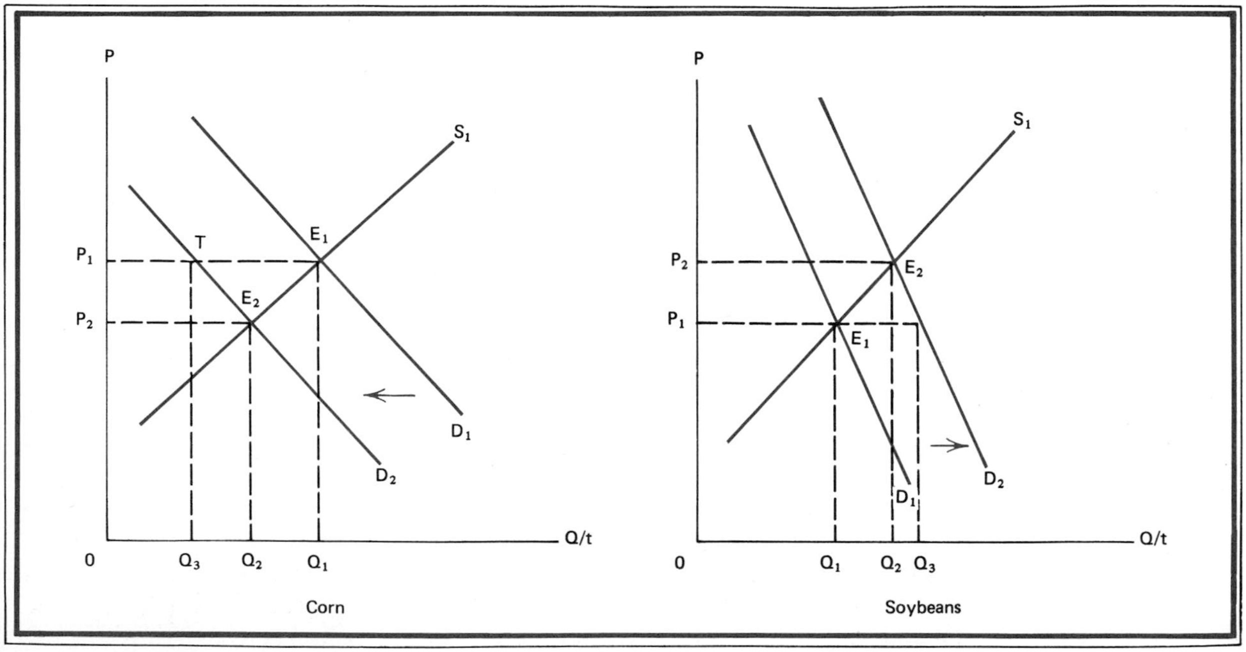

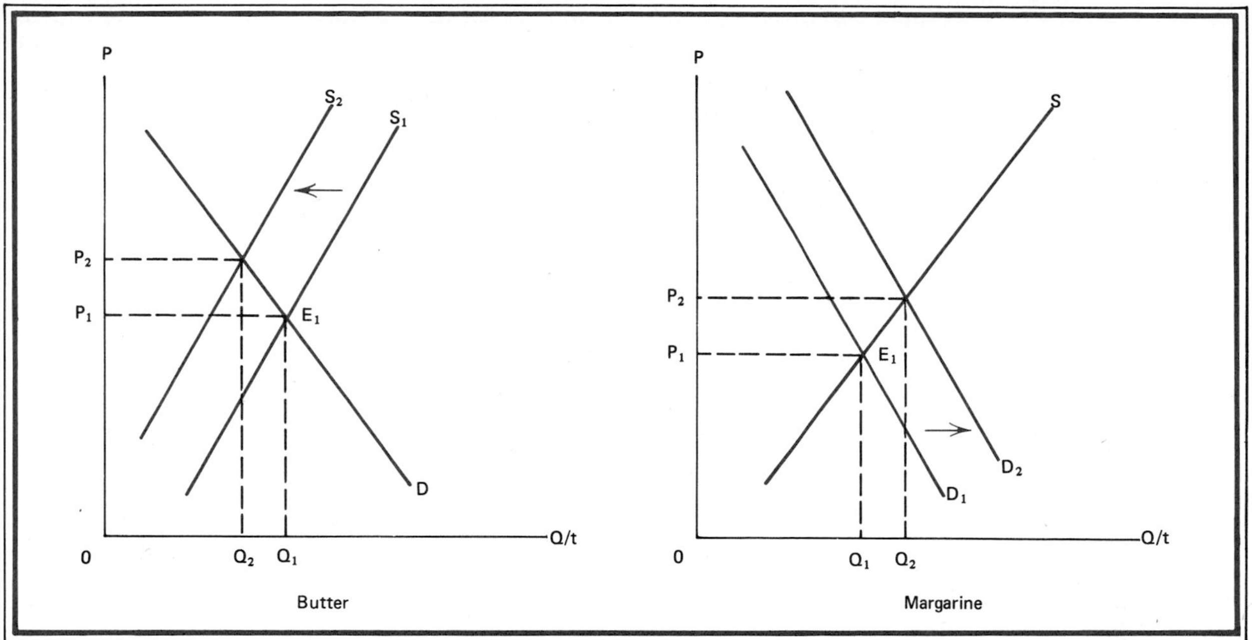

Figure 3-12

because the supply schedule has remained unchanged. No *parameter* changed to make it shift. But quantity supplied fell because the price P_0, a variable, decreased. Thus, suppliers moved down along the existing supply curve S_1 to the new equilibrium E_2.

Let us take another example, using margarine and butter. We shall not be as explicit with the details this time. Figure 3-12 portrays the two markets in initial equilibrium at E_1 for each market. Suppose hoof-and-mouth disease destroys a large share of the dairy cattle stock. As a result, the supply curve of butter, which is a dairy product, shifts left to S_2. The price of butter is substantially higher at P_2, so consumers move up along their demand curve and reduce their quantity demanded to Q_2 at the new equilibrium in the butter market. Margarine is a substitute for butter. And one of the parameters in the demand for margarine is the price of a related good P_R, which in this case is the butter. So look for a shift, in this case to the right, representing an increase in the *demand* for margarine as people substitute toward the *relatively* (not necessarily absolutely) cheaper margarine and away from the relatively more expensive butter. As a result, the price of margarine also rises and so does its quantity demanded. As the price of margarine rises, the suppliers of margarine move up along their supply curve and increase the quantity supplied. Thus the quantity supplied rises but supply is unchanged, that is, the supply curve has not shifted. The price of margarine at P_2 is lower than the new P_2 price of butter. Note carefully, however, that the decrease in supply precipitated the rise in the price of butter, and the increase in demand caused the price of margarine to rise. But the quantity demanded of butter fell because of the higher price of butter—a movement up *along* the demand curve. The rise in quantity demanded of margarine, however, went up because demand went up and this caused the price to rise, a movement up along the supply curve by suppliers in response to the increased demand. These distinctions are important if you are to understand the difference between a *shift* in demand and the subsequent movement *along* the supply curve, and a similar shift in supply and the subsequent movement along the demand curve.

The Opportunity Cost Connection

Supply and demand are connected through opportunity cost. The static construct of the production-possibility curve at the outset of the chapter illustrated all the potential tradeoff combinations between corn and cattle. What determines, among all these possible combinations, the actual quantities of corn and cattle that will be produced? It depends on the relative demands for corn and beef. The choice between whether the system will produce another cob of corn or another pound of beef is determined at the margin. More of both cannot be produced at full employment. Suppose Mr. Jaws wants another corn on the cob while Mr. Chew wants another ounce of beef. Whose preference will be satisfied? It depends on the relative values Mr. Jaws and Mr. Chew place on that extra corn and that extra beef, respectively. How badly does each one of them want his preference realized? If Jaws places greater value on the additional amount of corn than Chew places on the additional amount of beef, then Jaws outbids Chew for the additional resources that will provide corn instead of beef. If we introduce money prices, think of Mr. Jaws bidding 19.5 cents for the corn resources while Mr. Chew's best bid is 19 cents for the beef resources. Jaws places greater value on his preference than Chew does on his. What then is the cost of the corn? It is the value of the resources in their highest valued alternative use, namely, the beef that Chew gave up because he was outbid; it is 19 cents as determined by Chew's demand for the beef. The 19.5-cent supply price of corn is a price just marginally above the value of those resources in their use in providing the beef, a value measured by what Chew was willing to pay for the beef. Thus, the equilibrium price is essentially a price equal to the opportunity cost, where in essence Chew's demand price at the margin sets the supply price facing Jaws for his extra unit of corn. The higher that Chew values beef, the more is Jaws faced with an increasing supply price for corn, and we say Jaws is faced with a rising marginal cost for more corn.

As long as the value of resources in their use to provide beef is lower than the value of those resources in producing corn, then more resources will be allocated in the production of corn. But as more corn is produced, the value of an additional corn on the cob to Mr. Jaws will decline until a point is reached where the value of more corn will be no greater than the value of those resources in producing another increment of beef is to Mr. Chew. When that point is reached, the transfer of resources from one use to another ends, and no more corn will be produced. The system is in equilibrium.

Perhaps another example will be helpful. A firm pays $10 for a unit of steel. It thereby sacrifices its claim on whatever else the $10 would buy, perhaps a unit of tungsten. Moreover, the $10 measures, in money prices, what it took to win the steel away from another use. The $10 represents the cost barely above what the *last* unsuccessful bidder offered and beyond which he would not go. Suppose it was a toaster manufacturer who had outbid a hammer manufacturer. Does this description imply that the tool-producing firm can obtain no steel to make hammers? Certainly not. The price of the steel is determined at the margin where price essentially equals opportunity cost for this marginal or additional unit of steel. The toaster firm, once in business, is not deciding whether to build no toasters or 100,000 of them, and the tool firm is not deciding whether to manufacture no hammers or 150,000 of them. The toaster firm is deciding, in principle, on whether or not to produce the 100,001th toaster and the tool firm whether or not to build the 150,001th hammer. The value each places on that additional steel and the competition it creates will determine the price of that steel and all other similar units of steel. The competitive market equilibrium price of $10 represents the opportunity cost to the steel-producing firm of providing the additional steel determined by the value, as reflected in the demand for its steel, placed on it by the highest bidder. Actually, the *cost* is measured by the next highest bidder who lost out—since that represents the alternative use of the steel. If the toaster firm won out, then the marginal cost of the steel is the value placed on it and is expressed by the price offered by the tool firm. Since this is just a shade below $10, we accept the $10 price as being equal to opportunity cost.

Thus demand has much to do with determining the supply price, and the supply price reflects the cost of the commodity. Costs provide signals about the value of a resource to potential buyers who submit bids by offering dollars for resources. It is the bidder's value, his offered price, that helps clear the market resulting in $Q_s = Q_d$. One might say that a market is cleared by demand forces, in the first instance, and by the supply response that follows. Thus, price and quantity are determined by the interaction of supply and demand.

CHAPTER SUMMARY

Market prices are determined by demand and supply forces. The demand for goods stems from consumer desires. The supply of goods depends on the decisions of producers to make them available.

The law of demand states that the quantity of a good that people are willing and able to buy will increase if the price of the good is lowered. Price and quantity are inversely related.

Supply depends upon costs, and supply curves may be thought of as marginal cost curves. Marginal cost is the addition to cost that occurs when output each period is increased by a unit. Usually, the quantity supplied varies directly with the price.

Individuals have demand curves, and when individual demand curves are added together they make up the market demand curve for a good. Market supply curves, too, are made of the sums that all those producers who are willing and able to supply the good decide to bring to market.

Equilibrium exists in a market whenever the price is such that the quantity that people demand is the same as the quantity that producers supply. There may be excess demand if the price is too low, and excess supply if the price is too high.

Sometimes government introduces price controls. These can be either ceiling prices or floor prices, although usually they are ceiling prices. When a ceiling price is set below what the market would otherwise set, then the quantity demanded exceeds the quantity supplied and there is excess demand and disequilibrium in the market.

Demand curves often shift positions. For normal goods, if consumer income increases, consumer demand for a good will also increase. That is, the demand curve shifts to the right and shows that the consumer will buy more at each price than he did before. Other forces can also shift the demand curves—prices of related goods, tastes, expectations, and so forth.

The distinction between an increase in demand and an increase in the quantity demanded is very important. If price falls, then the quantity demanded increases. This describes a movement down along a demand curve. If the quantity demanded at a given price increases, this means the demand curve has shifted rightward. To avoid confusion, one must always be careful to distinguish between a shift in a curve and a movement along it.

Supply curves can shift, too. Again a clear distinction should be made between a change in the quantity supplied as the price changes, and a change in the position of the supply curve itself. Supply curves will usually shift positions when factor costs change, technology changes, the number of suppliers changes, and so forth.

QUESTIONS

1. In 1976 a hospital in Burien, Washington, had to change its billing system for expectant mothers when it discovered that near-term women were waiting in the hospital parking lot until after midnight had passed because that was the end of billing day. As a result of this discovery, the hospital switched to charging an hourly rate of $5.25 an hour instead of by the day. This change, it was hoped, would stop near-term women from playing baby roulette in the parking lot and enter the hospital earlier.
   a. Why were women waiting in the parking lot?
   b. Does the above description indicate a distinction between need and demand? Comment.
2. Several years ago in a small town outside Seattle, a price war on bread developed among three retail chains. Bread prices fell below 10 cents a loaf at one time. Customers were carting loaves of bread to their home freezers. Someone wrote to a local newspaper on "the unbelievable greed of the American shopper . . . typifying the selfishness so prevalent in the human race . . . it is this unthinkable greed and selfishness that leads to most of the woes of the world today." Was this behavior an example of greed or was it an example of something else?
3. In the 1960s General Electric and Westinghouse were convicted of fixing prices on electrical equipment. For our purposes, assume the prices of light bulbs were fixed by the two companies. The radicals claimed that such white-collar crime is as bad as or worse than injurious street crime, given those involved. On the other hand, they argued that looters in riots should not be shot, since it is only property, not human life, that is threatened to be lost. Using supply and demand analysis, can you evaluate their attitude toward white-collar crime versus street crime? Are they consistent? Is there a fallacy in their argument?
4. At the equilibrium price in the market $Q_s = Q_d$, the market is said to be cleared. In a free market, why is equilibrium at the price and quantity it is, and not anything else? Also, does scarcity exist at equilibrium? Does a shortage? Explain.
5. Meat prices are known to fluctuate over time. When hamburger is $2.00 a pound is there more exploitation than when it is a $1.50 a pound? Who is exploited at the higher price? At the lower price? What price would not be an exploitative price? Is there another reason for a higher price? For a lower price?
6. Given the following data:

P($)	9	8	7	6	5	4	3	2	1
Q_s	50	47	44	42	41	39	35	30	25
Q_d	31	33	35	36	37	39	41	46	50

a. What is the equilibrium price and quantity?
b. Is there an excess demand (shortage) or excess supply (surplus) at a price of $8? How much, if any?
c. Is there an excess supply or demand at a price of $2? How much, if any?

7. It is common to see long lines of people waiting—sometimes overnight—to get tickets for rock concerts.
   a. What does this tell you about the costs to people waiting in line for long hours? What evidence do you have for your opinion?
   b. What does it tell you about the price of the tickets?
   c. What reason might rock groups have for setting the price of the tickets as they do? Are live concerts the only source of revenue to rock groups? Explain.
8. A newspaper columnist said, "Television used to be in the business of producing entertainment, and along the way made money. But increasingly television is in the business of making money, with entertainment little more than a by-product." Is this statement consistent with demand theory? Why, or why not?
9. Suppose a $6 tax is imposed on all shoes sold. What would likely happen to the sales of expensive shoes *relative* to the sales of cheaper shoes? Is the law of demand not applicable here? Comment.
10. A newspaper quote: "Airline passengers are more affluent than other travelers. The farther they come, the longer they stay and the more they tend to spend." Can you use demand theory to explain this spending behavior of airplane traveling vacationers?
11. During the oil and gas shortage of 1974, when cars were lined around the block to get gasoline, a motorist was quoted as saying, "If gas goes up to a dollar a gallon, motorists won't put up with it. The American motorist will blow up the storage tanks." Graph the result of such an action. Would the United States motorist be better off? Comment.
12. There was an astronomical jump in shrimp prices from $2.39 a pound in 1973 to over $4 a pound in 1975. A newspaper writer wondered why, if people refused to buy shrimp at those outrageous prices, the price wouldn't come down. The president of the National Fisheries Institute replied, "Under basic economics the price should drop as people like you and me eat less shrimp because we can't afford it. But the laws of economics don't stand up in the market place where the product is becoming increasingly scarce." Do you agree with the president's analysis? Discuss.
13. It has been difficult for nursing homes in Washington state to get enough attendants. They do not stay for very long. The future looks bleak for getting the personnel needed. Since nursing homes cannot draft attendants, what alternative would you suggest? Why?
14. The unemployment rate among black teenagers has risen from 16.5 percent in 1954 to 36.3 percent in 1978. One partial cause, it is believed, is the rise in the minimum wage set by law. Graph and explain the effect of the minimum wage on black employment. Does your analysis explain why the average age of people working in fast-food chains has risen from 17 to 20?
15. Over the past three decades there has been a steady increase in the price of automobiles. Yet the number of autos sold has also increased. Does this refute the law of demand? Why, or why not?
16. Suppose a state has a usury law limiting the ceiling on mortgage lending by banks and savings and loan associations to 10 percent. Thereafter the market rate of interest reaches 11.5 percent. Graph the housing market and the market for government treasury bills (bonds), whose interest payment fluctuates with the market.
17. Federal environmental rulings have forced sharp limits on street parking in down-

town New York City. As a result, parking rates have risen in parking garages. The New York Consumer Affairs Commissioner announced a crackdown on parking garage "gougers." How would you explain the situation? Suppose price controls are imposed on parking garage fees? What would be likely to happen?

18. Apply supply-and-demand analysis using graphs to the following situations, showing initial and final prices and quantities. Indicate which variables or parameters are significant.
    a. A technological breakthrough introduces open-end spinning equipment in the textile industry.
    b. Cattle herds are struck by disease. What happens to the *relative* price of chicken? Why is relative emphasized here?
    c. Long hair for men goes out of fashion. What happens to the relative price of hair sprays?
    d. There is evidence that four aspirins a day reduce cerebral strokes in men but have no effect on women. What happens to aspirin prices?
    e. It is expected that gasoline prices will jump next month. What happens to the supply, demand, and price of gasoline?
    f. Dormitory expansion has stopped in a college town as enrollment continues to rise. What happens to the rental price of apartments in the private market in town?
    g. It becomes easier and less risky for users to find drug pushers. What happens to the relative price of drugs?
19. The law of supply suggests that, typically, more will be offered when prices are higher. The petroleum shortage seems to indicate less is available at higher prices. Does this violate the law of supply? If not, what government actions might account for the observed behavior of the market?
20. Suppose you are hired as an economic consultant by a private swimming club. You convince them of the importance of knowing the demand curve for their product if they are to maximize profits. They consent, and you are assigned the task. Mrs. Fudge says she will patronize the pool more frequently if the price is lowered. Mrs. Scoff says she will attend the pool more often if prices are raised. Does this conflict with what you learned about demand in this chapter? Water is water, isn't it, more or less?
21. A two-good economy produces board erasers and flashlights, as shown in the graph.
    a. What is the opportunity cost of producing 3 flashlights? The third flashlight?
    b. What is the total cost of producing 3 flashlights? The marginal cost of producing the third flashlight?
    c. Derive the supply curve for flashlights.

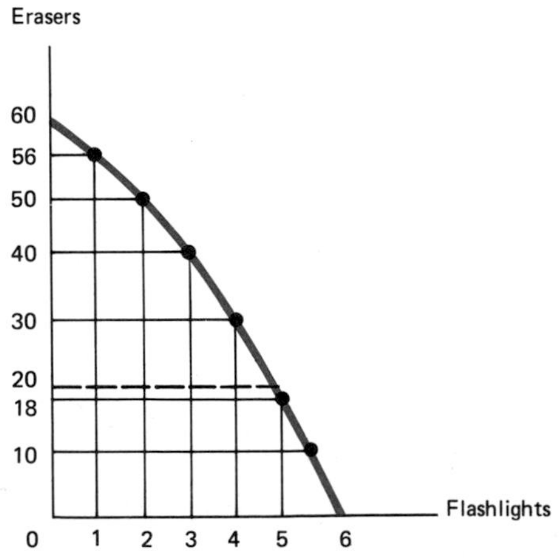

Appendix

Tools of Economics

"That's a great deal to make one word mean," Alice said in a thoughtful tone. "When I make a word do a lot like that," said Humpty Dumpty, "I always pay it extra."

—Through the Looking Glass

Mathematics is the language of science. Of all the social sciences economics is the most mathematical. Many top mathematical economists and theorists hold masters' degrees or their equivalent in mathematics. Economists like Paul Samuelson, Michael Kalecki, and Gerald Debreu have made original contributions to mathematics. Our sights will be set much lower and confined mainly to a few graphs. Our primary purpose is to describe several economic concepts, and to do this graphs will be very helpful in many places. Therefore, we need just that amount of understanding of equations and graphs that is necessary to describe simple relationships such as the relation between the price of something and the amount of it that people wish to buy, or the relation between the cost of producing a good and the volume of production. Such relations as these have certain uniformities that will help us describe the real world with our theories, and help us to be able to predict the effects of many economic events such as a drought that leads to a crop failure, a discovery of a new resource to provide energy to industry and consumers, or a new tax policy introduced by government. Therefore, in this appendix we shall describe what variables are, and the way they are used to construct functions and equations. "Pictures" of these equations can be shown in graphs and we shall discover how simple graphs are drawn from an equation. Finally, we shall describe how curves in graphs are subject to shifts.

Variables, Functions and Equations

You met the term *variable* in Chapter 1. A *variable* is a symbol for a quantity or a quality the symbol represents. It is a symbol of a thing but not the thing itself. It quantifies some characteristic or quality of a thing—its amount, velocity, weight, price, color, motivation, beauty.

Some variables are *discrete,* and some are *continuous.* An example of a discrete variable would be the number of students in a classroom. If there are 5 classrooms the number of students in each might be 18, 22, 34, 38 and 43. This number varies by classroom, but only by specific or discrete amounts. This can be contrasted with a continuous variable such as the length in inches of a sample of sticks, say 2.35, 6.48778, or 18.1. In these cases the lengths may vary in small amounts, and variation is limited only by the precision of your measuring instrument. Continuous variables, such as length, type, weight, and volume, can take on *any* value—measures can differ by infinitesimally small amounts. Discrete variables are "lumpy" and can assume only specific values—number of days, number of people, number of apples. Of course, as a practical matter, if there are lots of discrete values that a discrete variable may take it is possible to treat it as a continuous variable with minor loss of accuracy. And continuous variables can be broken into classes and treated as "discrete." Thus, as a practical matter we shall usually assume that our variables are continuous for analytical purposes, but all the while we shall remember that actual measurement of economic quantities will often involve discrete variables.

In economics, if we want to observe the relation between the price and quantity demanded of something, we can speak of the price variable, p, and the quantity variable, q, as changing during our experiment. We might be interested in understanding just how p and q are related under certain given conditions. We might desire to know, for instance, when p changes how q changes in response to the change in p. When we establish that a relation exists between p and q, we say that the two variables are functionally related. In symbolic or shorthand notation it is written as

$$\text{(A.1)} \qquad q = f(p).$$

The f stands for *is a function of*. Verbally translated, the expression says that the quantity q of a commodity *depends* in some way on its price p. The letter q is thus referred to as the *dependent* variable and p as the *independent* variable, because changes in the independent variable p lead to changes in the dependent variable q and we say q depends upon p.

In economics the problem of establishing functional relations among variables becomes complicated rather quickly. The reason lies in the perplexing fact that, in economics, variables can be independent in some cases, and then as if by a whimsy of nature, operate as dependent variables in other situations. Thus, the one-way directional relation from p to q expressed in equation A.1 is a simplification devoutly wished but rarely granted to students of economics. We find that p and q are *interdependent*, that each depends on the other—q depends on p *and* p depends on q. Recognizing the interdependent nature of economic variables is an essential part of the process of forming economic models that we shall discuss below.

Let us be more specific about the function $q = f(p)$ by assuming that the relation between price and quantity for a certain good, say, apples, is

$$\text{(A.2)} \qquad q = 50 - 5p.$$

An equation is said to be satisfied by particular values of its variables only when the left side of the equation equals the right side, that is, after numerical quantities are substituted for the variables. Thus, in equation A.1 if $p = \$4$, then $q = 50 - 5(4) = 50 - 20 = 30$ units. Therefore, the paired values $q = 30$ and $p = \$4$ are said to satisfy the equation. Thus, equation A.2 describes how people will *behave*. It predicts that if apples sell for $4 per carton, people will buy 30 cartons each period, assuming everything else is held fixed.

If the price falls to, say, $3, the equation that describes our hypothesis about people's desire for apples tells us people will buy $q = 50 - 5(3) = 35$ units each period. With this equation we can "predict" the response of people to changes in the price of apples.

It is very important to realize that an equation is only true for *certain* paired values of p and q, and not for all or any paired values of p and q. To see this, arbitrarily select $p = 6$ and $q = 15$. Then substitute 6 for p and calculate q using equation A.2. You should get $q = 20$ and not 15. Therefore, the pair of values for p and q, $p = 6$ and $q = 15$, does not satisfy equation A.2. These values do not make the left side of equation A.2 equal to its right side. This result tells us that people behave in a manner such that when a given item is $6, they do *not* buy 15 units of it—they buy 20 units.

Thus, what we are saying when we write $q = 50 - 5p$ is that the quantity of apples people will buy depends upon the price of apples, and that if we know what the price is we can predict how many they will buy. Furthermore, if the price changes we can predict how consumers will change the quantity of their purchases. The equation describes consumer behavior when it describes the response that consumers make when price changes.

Stocks and Flows

Mention should be made of a common source of error in economics. A pitfall that has beset many a practitioner is confusing a stock with a flow variable. A *stock* variable is the quantity representing that variable at a given time. Consider a gasoline tank that has 15 gallons in it on Tuesday morning at 9 a.m. The stock of gasoline is 15 gallons at that time. A *flow* variable is the measure of the *change* in the stock variable over some period of time. If by Thursday at 9 a.m. the stock of gasoline is 3 gallons, then the *flow* of gasoline has been 12 gallons *per 48 hours* or 6 gallons per day. The factory that has 10 machines in place on January 1 and 12 machines by December 30 of the same year, has a stock of 10 machines in January and 12 machines in December. The flow (investment) of machines is 2 per year. The *change* in the capital stock over the year represents the *investment* (flow) in machines over the year.

In the case of price and quantity variables, the quantity is nearly always quantity per period of time. On many occasions we write "quantity per period" to remind the reader that we have a flow variable in mind. Sometimes to shorten our sentences we leave off the "per period" but the reader should infer what is meant. On those infrequent occasions when a quantity refers to a stock of something, we nearly always indicate this by explicit use of the term "stock." Most variables in economics are flow variables.

GRAPHS

Finding the Gold Life: Or the Search for the Mother Lode

A graph is nothing more than a map. It helps one locate things and find the relation between two different things. In economics, graphs describe the relation between variables. A graph is a pictorial representation of the relation. Suppose we start out with two prospectors, Walt and Mitty, who hope to discover gold in the territory of El Dorado.

They set up base camp at the point designated by 0 in Figure A-1, the origin of their search. Through 0 are drawn two perpendicular lines (lines which form a 90-degree angle between them) which divide the space into four quadrants reading counterclockwise *I, II, III,* and *IV.* The letters *N, E, W,* and *S* (the origin of the word news, by the way) indicate the geographical direction as on a map. In Figure A-2 quadrant I is reproduced by itself with grid lines included. Grid lines are guide lines drawn parallel to the northern line and the eastern line passing through the origin at 0. The northern and eastern lines that pass through the point 0 are special grid lines called the *axes.* The grid lines, being parallel, are drawn at equal intervals. In this case they are drawn to scale of 100-yard intervals along their lengths. These distances are shown on the northern and eastern axes on Figure A-2. Our two prospectors set out in differ-

Figure A-1

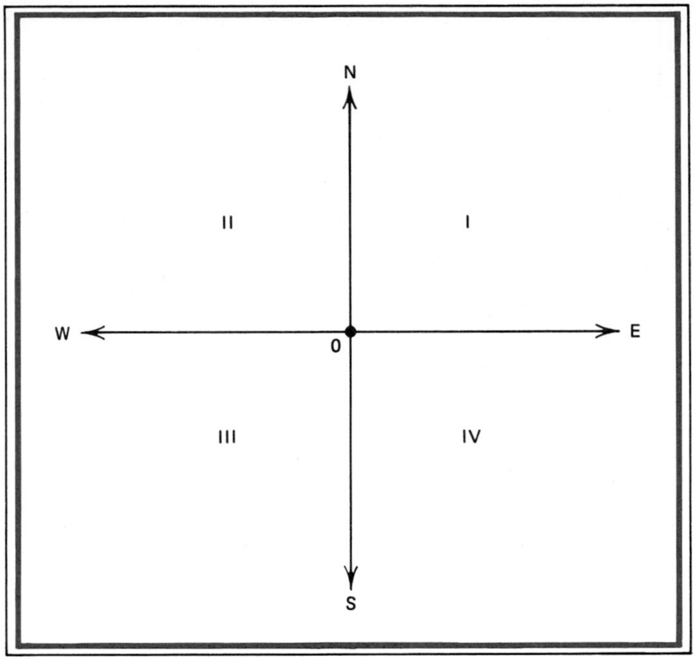

ent directions from the base camp at 0. Walt heads north and Mitty heads east. Walt discovers the beginning of a gold mine. To make sure he can find it again, he designates his position with the letter *A* and next to it inscribes 0, 600. He has recorded a coordinate point with the coordinates 0 yards in the easterly direction and 600 yards in the northerly direction from the base camp at 0. Mitty, meanwhile, has discovered gold while heading straight east at point *F*.

Figure A-2

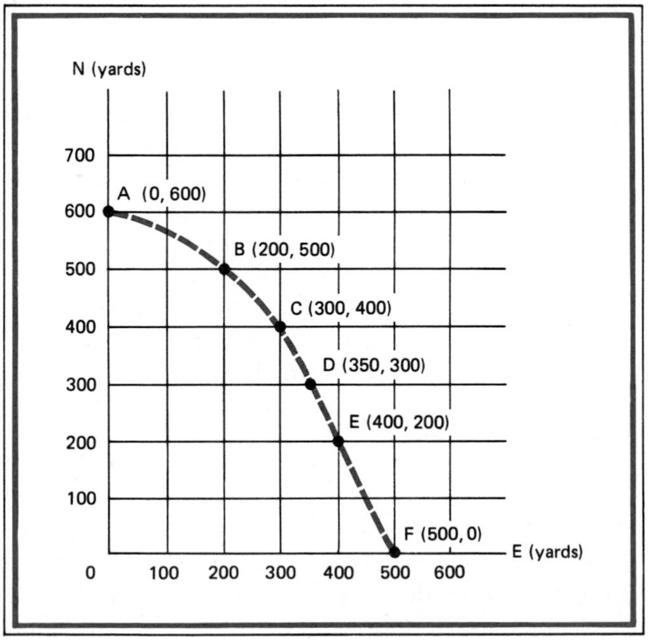

Figure A-3

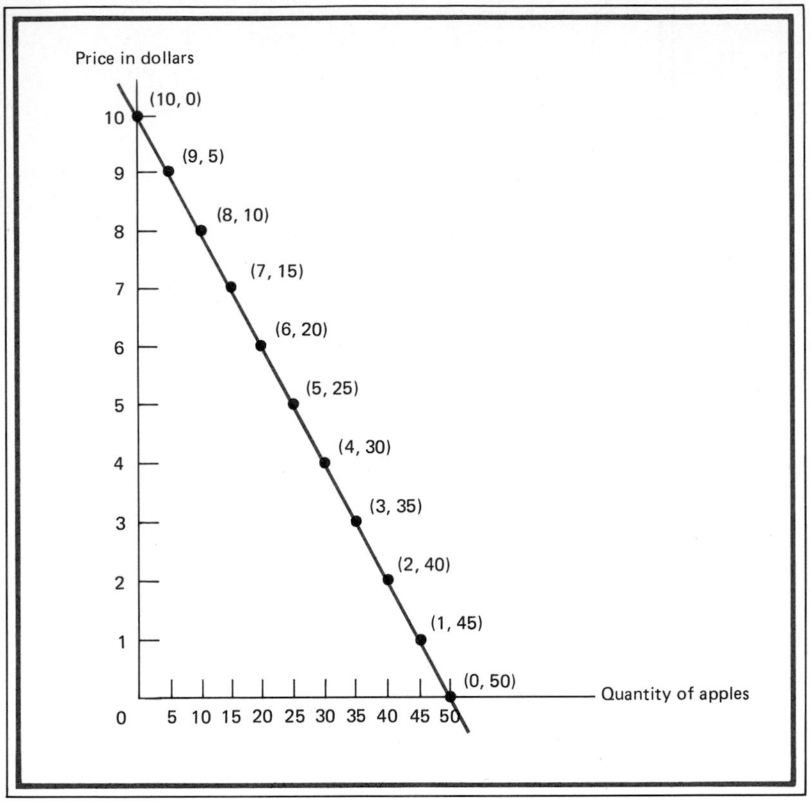

He records 500, 0 indicating that the gold is located 500 yards straight east and 0 yards north relative to the base camp. Walt and Mitty proceed to trace the path of the gold vein. Walt proceeds feverishly along to point *B* where he records his position as 200, 500 while Mitty casually moves along to point *E*. He apparently has done this kind of thing before and it proved to be fool's gold. So he will not commit himself yet. Walt picks up the pace and reaches point C and records 300 yards east and 400 yards north as 300, 400 on the map next to C. Mitty rests a while and wanders up to point *D*, recording his location there as 350, 300. He is tired so he sits down to rest his bones and enjoy the scenery. Walt tracks the vein to point *D* and finds a sleeping Mitty. He wakes him and they put all their information on one graph and draw in a dotted line connecting all the points representing the location of the gold. Walt knows the real thing when he sees it. All of the intermediate points between the recorded points can also be located with their own coordinate points as to their north and east position relative to the base camp.

In this way, the relation between economic variables can be plotted or graphed. Consider again the equation

$$\text{(A.2)} \qquad q = 50 - 5p.$$

Designate the vertical axis as the price axis as in Figure A-3 and the horizontal axis as the quantity axis for apples. Those who recall their high school algebra will notice that the dependent variable q is measured along the horizontal axis whereas the independent variable p is measured along the vertical axis, just the

TABLE A-1

p	q
10	0
9	5
8	10
7	15
6	20
5	25
4	30
3	35
2	40
1	45
0	50

reverse of the way mathematicians do it. This custom dates back to 1890 and the writings of Alfred Marshall. The price-quantity relation is one of several equations in economics that are graphed in this way.

Assume the functional relation between price and quantity demanded for apples is that shown in Table A-1. The quantities are obtained by substituting the different prices into equation A.2 and solving it for q. Thus, for $p = \$10$, the equation—our hypothesis—predicts that $q = 50 - 5(10) = 0$. Each p and its corresponding q determine a coordinate point in the quadrant of Figure A-3, with all the points calculated from equation A.2. The solid line is drawn in connecting them. This line, as we shall see later, is a demand curve. It does not actually curve. Straight lines are a special case of a class of mathematical entities called curves.

The reader may notice that the scales on the axes are different from one another—going from 0 to 10 on the vertical axis and from 0 to 50 on the horizontal axis. The line we have drawn seems steep. But if we were to measure the axes differently the curve would change its level. For example, if we measured from 0 to 10 on the vertical axis by the *same* distance as we measured 0 to 10 on the horizontal axis, the curve would be very flat, and would intersect the vertical axis where the number 1 is now. Thus one's choice of measurement scale will affect the appearance of the graph.

You might be wondering why the other three quadrants have been ignored. In beginning economics there is not much use for them, since prices and quantities are always positive. In advanced economic theory and in disciplines like mathematics and electrical engineering, the other quadrants are often useful. The arrows in Figure A-4 illustrate that coordinates in quadrant *I* increase positively in both directions away from the origin whose coordinates are of course zero, i.e., 0, 0. Point *A* has coordinates 3, 4 in quadrant *I*.

Figure A-4

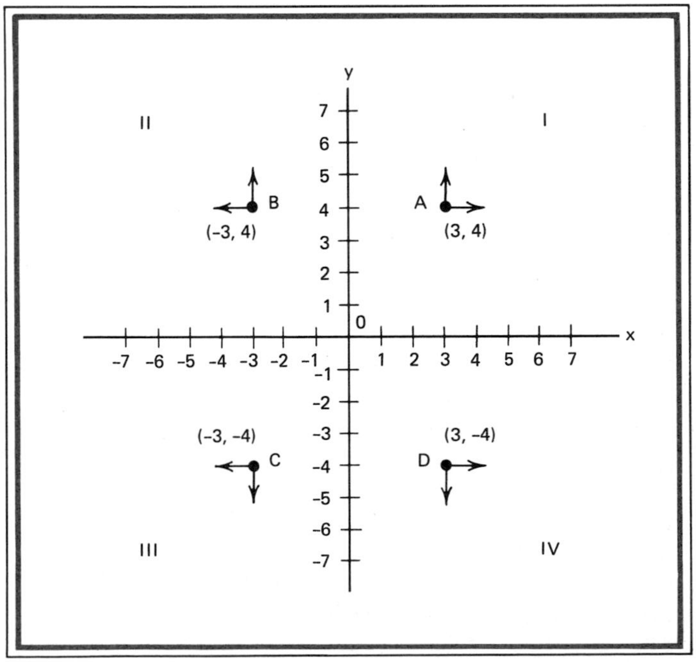

The coordinates for the points *B*, *C*, and *D* are so indicated. For point *B* they are −3 in the negative x direction and +4 in the positive *y* direction or −3, 4. For point *C* they are −3 in the negative x direction and −4 in the negative *y* direction relative to zero at the origin designated by 0. Point *D* has the coordinates +3 in the positive x direction and −4 in the negative *y* direction, or 3, −4.

THE SLOPE

There will be a number of occasions in the text when you will need to be familiar with the *slope* of a curve at a point. If the curve is a straight line the slope is the same at every point. Figure A-5 depicts the graph of the equation of the straight line

$$(A.3) \qquad y = 50 - 5x.$$

The independent variable x is plotted along the horizontal and the dependent variable y along the vertical axis. The slope is defined as the ratio of the length of the vertical side of the triangle to the length of the horizontal side. Thus, the

Figure A-5

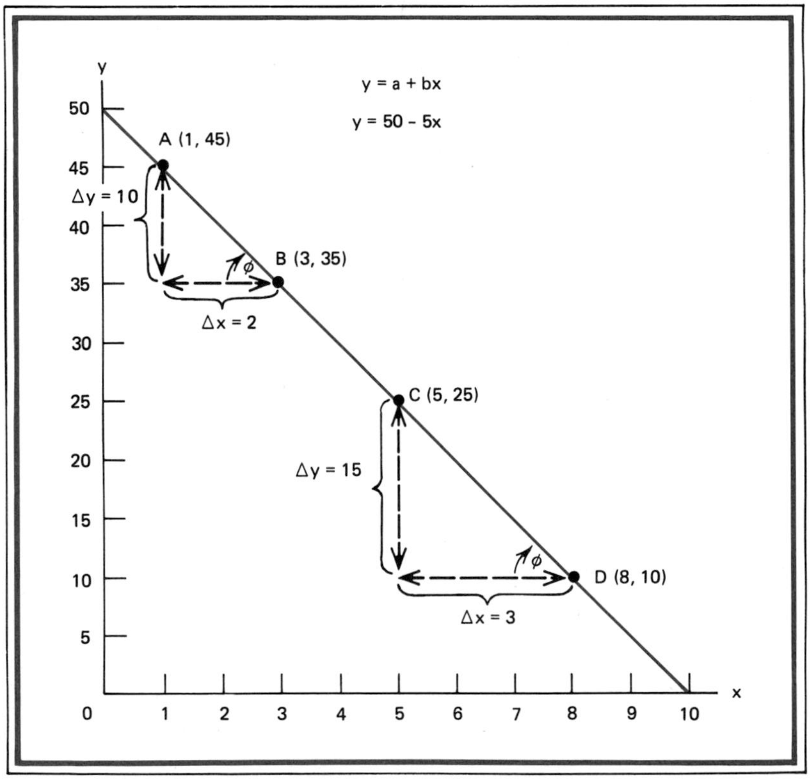

$$\text{slope} = \frac{\text{vertical side}}{\text{horizontal side}}.$$

The length of the vertical side is determined by subtracting the y coordinate of point B, the 35 in 3, 35 from the y coordinate in point A, the 45 in 1, 45 to get $45 - 35 = 10$. This length is labeled Δy in Figure A-5 on the upper triangle and represents the difference between two values of y, i.e., $\Delta y = y_2 - y_1$, with $y_2 = 45$ and $y_1 = 35$. The symbol Δ is the Greek letter, delta. It signifies a difference between two values in context.

Moving from B to A along the horizontal side of the triangle, Δx is calculated. The length of the side is 2, but the difference is -2 since x moves from right to left. Going from A to B instead of from B to A, the value of Δy would be -10 instead of $+10$. But Δx would then be $+2$ instead of -2. So, Δy and Δx take either plus or minus signs depending on the direction moved. But when it comes to calculating the slope, it makes no difference if we go from point B to point A or from point A to point B so long as we pair off the x and y coordinates of points A and B properly. Thus,

$$\text{slope} = \frac{\Delta y}{\Delta x} = \frac{45 - 35}{1 - 3} = \frac{10}{-2} = -5$$

or

$$\text{slope} = \frac{\Delta y}{\Delta x} = \frac{35 - 45}{3 - 1} = \frac{-10}{2} = -5.$$

The slope simply tells us that for every 5 units we move down in the negative y direction, we move to the right one positive unit in the x direction. Or, alternatively, for every 5 units up we move in the positive y direction, we move one unit left in the negative x direction. The line is said to have a negative slope, i.e., it is slanted downward going left to right (or upward going right to left). In general, the equation of a line has the form $y = a + bx$. The b parameter is the slope of the equation. In our particular discussion $b = -5$. The a term is called the *intercept* of the line. It is simply the point where the line intercepts or meets the y axis. This point is easy to find using the equation for the line shown in Figure A-5, namely

$$y = a - 5x.$$

The graph tells us that when $x = 0$, $y = 50$. The equation confirms this result. Substitute $x = 0$ and $y = 50$. We obtain

$$50 = a.$$

Therefore, the intercept occurs at the coordinate point 0, 50 and agrees with the graph. The fully explicit equation is now

$$y = 50 - 5x.$$

In similar manner, the x intercept can be determined from the equation by setting $y = 0$. Thus

$$0 = 50 - 5x$$
$$5x = 50$$
$$x = 10$$

which confirms what we see in Figure A-5. In the same manner you should be able to calculate the slope of the line using the coordinates of the two points *C* and *D* on the line. Thus

$$\text{slope} = \frac{\Delta y}{\Delta x} = \frac{y_2 - y_1}{x_2 - x_1} = \frac{25 - 10}{5 - 8} = \frac{15}{-3} = -5.$$

While the triangle formed using points *C* and *D* is larger than the triangle using points *A* and *B*, you should get the same value for the slope of the line. The reason is that the angle formed by the ratio of the two sides of the triangle is the same for both triangles. The ratio of the sides is the same although the sides themselves are bigger for the lower triangle than for the upper triangle. Such triangles are not equal triangles; they are called *similar* triangles.

Nonlinear Curves

Figure A-6 illustrates a curve that is not a straight line (as gratuitous as that statement might sound). It is referred to as a nonlinear curve. Unlike the straight line or linear curve, each point on a nonlinear curve is associated with

Figure A-6

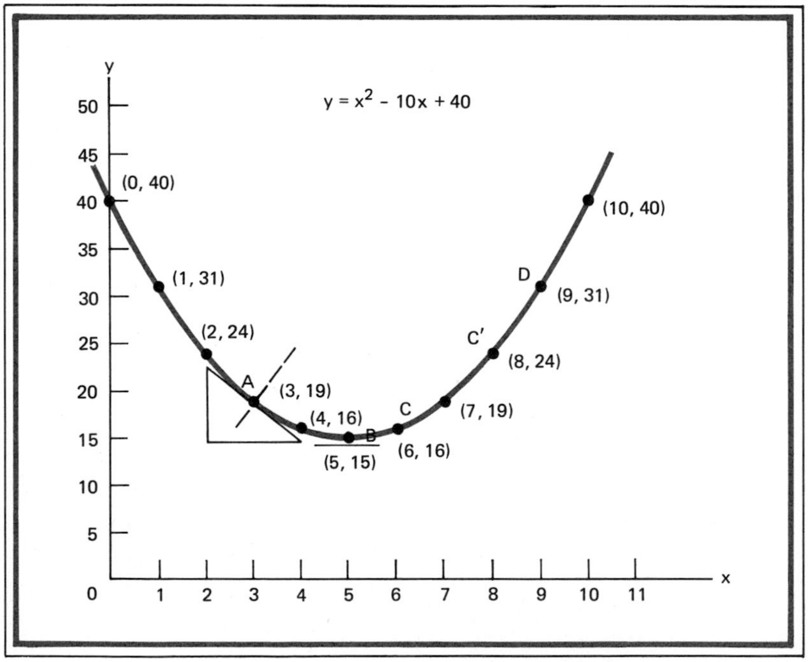

a different value for the slope. The value of the slope at point A is different than the value of the slope at point C, and point C from point D, and so on. At the minimum point, B, the slope is zero. If you are careful enough, you can geometrically calculate the slope at each point on the curve by drawing the hypotenuse of the triangle tangent to that point as shown at point A. The tangent touches point A only, and must be drawn perpendicular to the dashed line passing through point A, which is itself perpendicular to the curve at A.

The next step is to measure the ratio of the sides of the triangle constructed and then calculate the slope = $\Delta Y/\Delta X$. As you can imagine, the geometrical approach would be difficult to perform accurately. Purely mathematical techniques are superior. However, we shall not describe these mathematical techniques here since we shall be using simple linear curves when we want to do measurements.

Parameters

In the examples above we have referred to variables x and y that we use for general notation, and economic variables p and q that we use when we wish to refer to price and quantity. Given a relation between p and q that we write as $q = f(p)$ we recognize that as p varies q will also vary. When we wrote $q = 50 - 5p$ we specified the relation between the variables p and q. The numbers 50 and -5 are constants in the equation. These constants are given when we observe a *particular* relation—say, when we want to discuss a particular commodity such as apples. These numbers would surely be different if we were discussing oranges. For oranges the equation might be $q = 60 - 4p$. Since the constants have changed from what they were when we were talking about apples, would it be correct to say they are variables?

There exists a concept that stands between a constant and a variable that we call a parameter. A parameter simply is a constant that is subject to change. It is a constant for a particular problem, but may take on a different value for a different problem. Hence, when we spoke of apples the constants were 50 and -5, but when we spoke of oranges they were 60 and -4. In general form we can write

$$\text{(A.3)} \qquad q = a + bp.$$

In this equation, a and b are parameters. In the case of apples they were 50 and -5, respectively. And, in the case of oranges they become 60 and -4. Thus, parameters a and b assume particular values when addressing a particular relation, but will be different when looking at a different problem. In a general sense, then, parameters are constants that are subject to change.

Besides assuming different values when treating different subjects, parameters in an equation can also change in value in another important but quite different respect. A change in a parameter may reflect a change in circumstances surrounding a particular problem. To explain, let us return to the apple equation, $q = 50 - 5$ and its graphical form shown in Figure A-3 and redrawn in simpler form as the solid line in Figure A-7. (The reader may observe that the scales of the axes differ in the two graphs.) This equation and the graphs may describe the relation between the price and the quantity of apples bought in a

Figure A-7

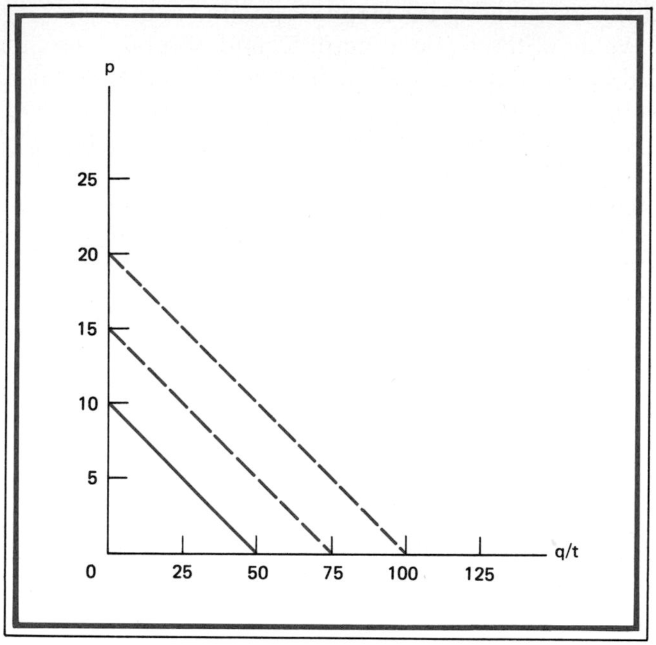

poor community. In a wealthier community (either a different community or the same community after the buying power of the people has risen) the people might decide to buy more apples at each possible price. If this were the case, what would the graph look like? It would shift to the right, and the dashed lines would represent the relation between *p* and *q* under higher and higher income.

Using the equation to read the graph, we note that when the original relation was $q = 50 - 5p$, the intercept with the horizontal axis was 50. At a higher level of income the intercept is 75, and at an even higher level it becomes 100. Thus, in the equation $q = a + bp$ the value of *a* changes from 50 to 75 and then to 100 as a result of rising income that lets people buy more apples. When the intercept changes, the curve shifts and we can call *a* a *shift parameter*. Because we have measured *q* on the horizontal axis, *a* is the value of the intercept of the curve with the horizontal axis. That is, *a* is the value of *q* when *p* takes a value of zero.

The slope of the line, as indicated by the value of *b* in the equation, does not change as the curve shifts from one position to another. In some circumstances, however, the slope can also be affected by changes in buying ability. Thus, it is quite possible for *both* parameters *a* and *b*, that is, both the slope and the intercept, to be affected by changes in buying power.

Again, because we measure *q* on the horizontal axis, the slope of the line in the graph is $-1/5$, not -5. It would be -5 if the axes were reversed. If we redraw the same line putting *q* on the vertical axis and *p* on the horizontal axis, then the parameter *a* in the equation $q = a + bp$ would be the intercept on the vertical axis at $q = 50$, and the parameter $b = -5$ would represent the slope of the line. But since our axes are reversed, we have $a = 50$ on the horizontal axis instead, and the *reciprocal* of *b* as the slope. (Slope is $-1/5$ instead of -5.)

Equations and Identities

We have examined the meaning of the terms function and equation. There exists another kind of relation that is different from the equation that one uses to describe a function or a relation. It is called an identity. Identities, because they often appear in the form of an equation, are often and easily mistaken for functional relations. Actually they are *disguised definitions*. Recall that a definition is an expression of the meaning of a word. It is one of the agreed-upon ground rules that make communication possible. It is the same with identities, most of which result from the process of classification. For example, assume we take all the apples in a barrel and divide them all into two piles, one pile for the rotten apples and one for the good apples. Since all apples are accounted for and there are precisely two classes of apples, and since no apple can be placed in both piles at the same time, we say that we have two mutually exclusive classes. It follows that the total number of apples will equal the total number of rotten ones plus the total number of good ones. But this equality holds *by definition*. We have simply defined which apples are good and which are rotten.

If we write the equation

Total apples = good apples + rotten apples

we have an identity, not a functional relation.

In accounting we sometimes say net receipts = gross sales less expenses. This is an identity expressed as an equation. In national income accounting we will say that national income = consumption plus investment. This is also an identity. In economic analysis we sometimes say that money expenditure will equal money receipts—two sides of the same coin.

Identities such as these are very useful in economic analysis. When economists and others write the equations for these identities, proper notation suggests we should really not write them with an equal sign (=), but instead we should use the identity sign (≡), but the equal sign is commonly used and is acceptable so long as we understand what we are doing.

Statistics

Economists make constant use of statistical methods, a branch of mathematics. Those economists who specialize in the use and development of statistical techniques to analyze economic problems are econometricians. What they study is called *econometrics*.

Statistical techniques are used in science when precise measurement cannot be made, where certainty in measurement does not exist. Thus statistical methods make use of probability statements, and are based on the laws of probability.

We shall briefly discuss a few statistical concepts. A population consists of all members of a group. There can be an infinite number of members in the group or a finite number. The population of all even integers is infinite (2, 4, 6, . . .). In the real world of economics, populations are finite but they can be quite large.

Suppose the Bureau of the Census wishes to ascertain the average age of citizens of the U.S. over the next year. Though large, the number of people in the U.S. is finite. There is a limited number in the total population, some 226 million. For practical reasons of time and cost the Bureau of the Census will not request the age of every person. Instead, it takes a statistical sample that is representative of the population as a whole. How does it know the sample is representative of the whole U.S. population? The sample has to be scientifically picked. Such a sample is called a *random sample.* This means that each person in the total population has an equal chance to be chosen to be in the sample. The idea of providing an equal chance is to eliminate any *bias* in the sample. A bias is a prejudice or influence introduced into the sampling process that causes the sample to have a certain tendency. For instance, if people in the sample were drawn mainly from retirement homes, this would cause an upward bias in estimating the average age of the U.S. population. On the other hand if the sample were drawn disproportionately from people in prisons, the bias would be in a downward direction, below the true average age of the U.S. population, because the average age of prisoners is below the average for the U.S. population. Since we are concerned only with determining the age of the U.S. population and nothing else, we only want to calculate the age of the sample. This will be our estimate of the age of the population.

After obtaining the estimate, we want to determine its reliability. How well have we guessed? Suppose we want to be 99 percent sure that the estimate is within a narrow range of the true average age. This means we are willing to accept some margin of error. The larger the number in the sample, the smaller will be the margin of error. This introduces the concept of the *law of large numbers.* If we toss a coin 100 times we can predict that approximately 50 times it will come up heads. For 100 tosses we can expect as much as a 15 percent error as a routine matter. If the coin is tossed a thousand times, we can expect a maximum error of 5 percent, and if tossed 10,000 times, an error of 1-1/2 percent.

Another example: Were 5 people asked to measure the distance a javelin is thrown, there would be a good chance of some large differences among them. But if 500 people were to make the measurement, there would be a greater likelihood that there would be many small errors among them, both shorter and longer than the true distance such that they would cancel one another out. And the number of these smaller errors would tend to overshadow the much smaller occurrence of large errors.

Statistical techniques are used to predict election results when only a small percentage of the returns are in. Insurance companies also survive on the basis of the probability calculations of average life spans of their policy holders. Although a policy holder may die at 25 and the company lose out in this one situation, it is predicted that enough people will live to 70 or more and that their premiums will more than cover the loss.

Models

We are all familiar with model airplanes—toys made of balsa wood or plastic. There are also aircraft prototypes that airplane companies examine in wind tunnels for airfoil characteristics. These are models, too. Artists sometimes build models and then paint them. Sculptors will draw models and then build them. Economists construct models, too.

Economic models, like other models, are descriptive idealizations or abstractions about relations connecting events in the real world. A *model* is really an approximation that summarizes the interdependencies of the variables used to describe some aspect of an economic system. It is used for purposes of understanding the nature of economic relations, and for deriving predictions. Economic models are usually stated in mathematical form using equations and/or graphs. They employ parameters that are usually estimated by using statistical techniques.

QUESTIONS

1. Let s = savings, y = income. What does $s = f(y)$ mean? What is the expression called? What is the independent variable? The dependent variable? Now, explicitly, suppose $s = c + dy$. What are the variables? The parameters? What is the slope of the expression? Is this an equation, an identity, both, or neither? Is it a model?
2. Let I = investment, i = the rate of interest and T the level of technology. What does $I = f(i,T)$ tell you? What are the variables? Is there a parameter? Suppose $I = a - bi$. What designation can be applied to the expression? What are the parameters if any? What are the variables? Suppose $I = 22$, $a = 16$ and $i = 8$. What is the numerical value of the slope?
3. Consider

   $$\text{(A)}\quad (y - x)^2 = (2x + 3)^2$$

   and

   $$\text{(B)}\quad (y - x)2 = 2x - 2y.$$

   Pick any two numbers for x and y and substitute them into equations A and B. Compare the left hand sides of each with their right hand sides. Pick two new numbers for x and y and compare the respective sides again. Then, let $x = 5$ and solve A and B for y. Again, let $x = 7$ and solve A and B for y. Can you conclude whether A and B are identities or equations? Explain.
4. Which of the following refer to flows or stocks?
   - **a.** There are 60 albums in my record collection.
   - **b.** I add 10 albums a year to the stock of my record collection.
   - **c.** There is currently $900 in my savings account.
   - **d.** The U.S. imports about 9-1/2 million barrels of petroleum products a day.
   - **e.** I deposit $400 a month into my checking account.
   - **f.** Jack earns $900 a month.
   - **g.** The U.S. labor force consists of 96 million people.
   - **h.** Over the year an average of 20 million people had colds in the U.S.
   - **i.** Interest payments are due on the national debt.
5. It has been noted from data starting in the nineteenth century that babies are not born at the same rate through the 24-hour day. The peak in births occurs toward the end of the night and the first hours of the day. The lowest number occurs during the

early hours of the afternoon, the next lowest number is late in the afternoon. Labor pains begin twice as often at midnight as at noon. At midnight the mother's body is most relaxed and deliveries then are the easiest and fastest. This phenomenon is explained by the circadian theory—the body has a natural, daily rhythm, a timer, that controls the woman's nervous and hormonic activities. (See Michel Gauguelin. *The Cosmic Clocks: from astrology to a modern science,* published by H. Regnery, Chicago, 1967.)

a. What are the basic variables?
b. What is the functional relation? Can you indicate it symbolically?
c. What are the independent and dependent variables in your function?
d. Suppose you have the following data for hospitals in a city. Are the data discrete or continuous? Sketch a rough graph of the functional relation.

Births	**Period of day**
14	10 p.m.–2 a.m.
10	2 a.m.–6 a.m.
5	6 a.m.–10 a.m.
3	10 a.m.–2 p.m.
6	2 p.m.–6 p.m.
11	6 p.m.–10 p.m.

6. Given the graph of two curves *I* and *II*, for each curve designate the coordinates at the points indicated.

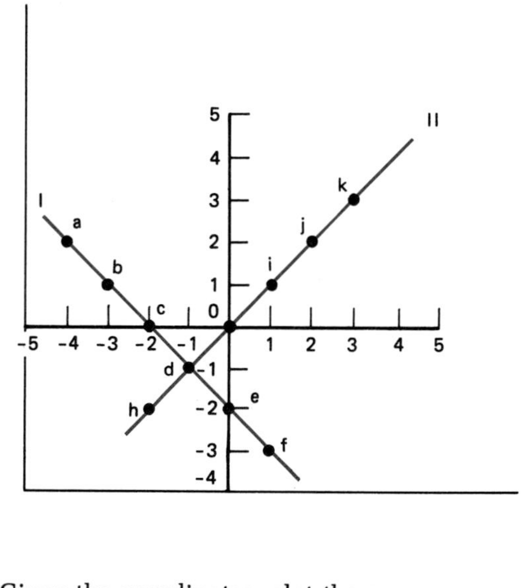

7. Given the coordinates, plot the curve.

x	−20	−10	0	10	20	30	40	50	60
y	50	40	30	20	10	0	−10	−20	−30

8. Given a vertical price axis and a horizontal quantity axis, what are the coordinates of this line at the designated points on the graph?

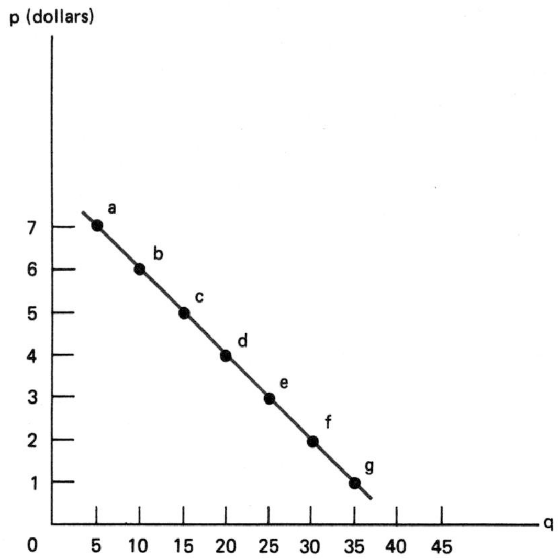

9. What are the coordinates of the curve at the designated points for the quantities of goods *A* and *B* shown on each axis?

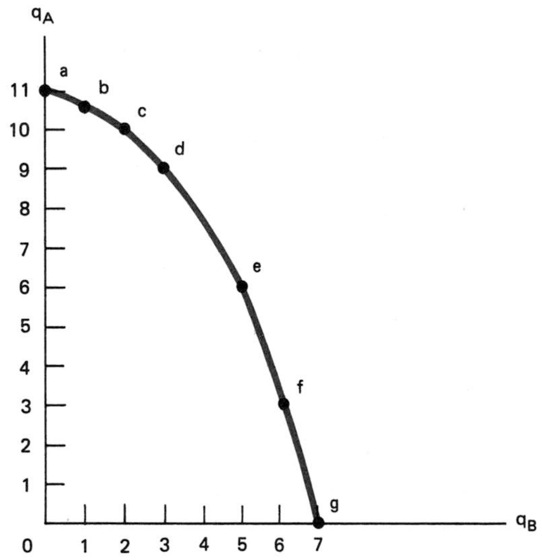

10. What are the coordinates of this curve at the designated points? Fill in table also.

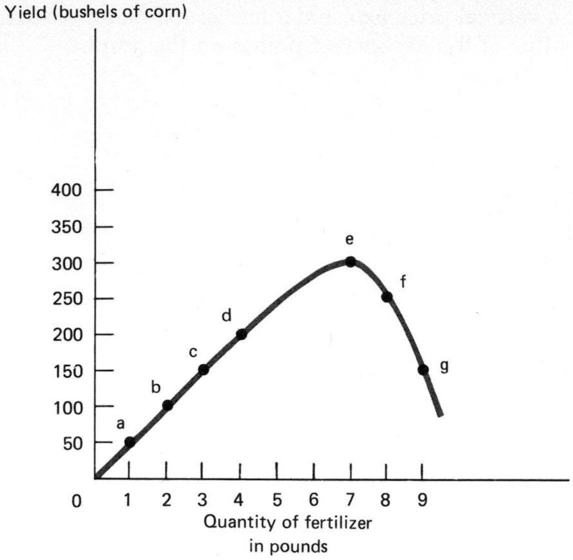

Yield	Fertilizer

11. Given the following data in the table, plot the curve, with price measured on the vertical axis.

p	q
20	15
30	30
40	45
50	60

a. What is the explicit equation of the line and the value of the slope when $q = f(p)$? When $p = f(q)$?

b. What are the quantity and price intercept values?

12. In problem 6, what are the slopes of lines *I* and *II*? What is the slope of the line in problem 8? In problem 9 is the slope more negative at point *b* or point *e*?

13. Given $C = 200 + .8Y$, where C is annual consumption and Y is annual income. What is consumption when income is zero? What is C if income is \$10,000? What is value of the slope? What does the slope tell you here? At what level are consumption and income equal? Can you plot the equation?

MICRO-ECONOMICS

Chapter 4

Elasticity, Utility, and Consumer Surplus

PROGRESS REPORT

A. In Chapter 3 we learned how supply and demand combine to determine a market price, and that there is an important difference between demand and quantity demanded as well as supply and quantity supplied.

B. In this chapter we learn that supply and demand curves have a useful property called price elasticity, and that as price changes the elasticity, i.e., the sensitivity of quantity to price changes, differs over the price range of the demand curve. We shall learn that the demand curve is intuitively based on the concept of utility. The notion of marginal utility then gives rise to the concept of consumer surplus and a reservation price.

C. In Chapter 5 we shall delve deeper into the concept of opportunity cost, expanding on points initially introduced in Chapter 1.

The Agriculture Department believes that if farmers grow less corn or wheat, the farm industry will collect more money from the public when it sells these products. (Amounts of money collected from sales of a certain good are called sales or revenues, or *sales revenues* to be precise). Governments sometimes believe they can increase their tax revenues by raising the tax on alcohol. But transit authorities may believe that if they raise their fares beyond a certain level, revenues might not increase; rather they are likely to fall. Why do revenues rise when prices increase in some instances, but fall in other situations when prices are raised?

PRICE ELASTICITY OF DEMAND

Whether or not sales revenues increase or decrease in response to a change in price depends on how much more or less of the good people buy when price changes. That is, from the law of demand we know that people buy less when the price rises—but the question is, do they buy a lot less, or just a little bit less? If they buy a lot less at the higher price, then sales revenues will decline. But if they only buy a little bit less, sales revenues will increase. This degree of responsiveness of the quantity bought to changes in price is measured by a coefficient called the *price elasticity of demand*.

The *price elasticity of demand* is a measure of the sensitivity of quantity bought to a change in price.

Mathematically, the **price elasticity of demand**, hereafter referred to as the *elasticity of demand*, is defined as the ratio of the *percentage* change in quantity demanded to the *percentage* change in price. Price elasticity is a measure of the sensitivity of quantity bought to a change in price, or

$$E_d = -\frac{\text{percentage change in quantity demanded}}{\text{percentage change in price}}$$

Make note of the minus sign. It is arbitrarily included in front of the expression on the right side of the equality sign, in order to guarantee that the elasticity will always come out positive. If the minus sign were left out, demand elasticity would be expressed as a negative. The sign makes no difference in meaning, and it is more convenient to deal with a positive coefficient. What is important is the numerical value of the coefficient.

A percentage is mathematically defined as

$$\text{percentage} = \frac{\text{final value} - \text{initial value}}{\text{initial value}} \times 100$$

or as

$$\text{percentage} = \frac{\text{change in the value}}{\text{initial value}} \times 100.$$

Consequently, if the initial price is 100 and it rises to 110, then the percentage change in the price is

$$\frac{110 - 100}{100} \times 100 = 10\%.$$

The symbol Δ (the Greek letter delta) indicates a change in a variable from one (initial) value to another (final) value, or $\Delta Q = Q_f - Q_i$. Thus, the percentage change in quantity may be written as $\frac{\Delta Q}{Q} \times 100$.

The *elasticity measurement* applies over a designated price range of a demand curve.

The **elasticity measurement** applies over a designated price range of a demand curve (also for a supply curve).

The formula is:

$$E_d = -\frac{\Delta Q/Q_1}{\Delta P/P_1} = -\frac{\Delta Q}{\Delta P} \times \frac{P_1}{Q_1}.$$

A problem that arises when this formula is used concerns the discrete change in the price variable from one value to another. A 50 percent increase in price occurs when price goes from $1 to $1.50. But then, a 33 percent reduction in price will move the price back from $1.50 to $1, because a different initial price is being used when going back from $1.50 to $1. Because of this, percentages are not reversible. This can cause a problem in measuring elasticity. Suppose the price rises from $100 to $110 and the quantity demanded changes from 50 units to 45 units. Substituting these values into the elasticity formula gives $\Delta Q = -5$ and $\Delta P = 10$, where $Q_i = 50$; $Q_f = 45$, $P_i = 100$ and $P_f = 110$. We obtain

$$E_d = -\frac{-5/50}{10/100} = -\frac{-1/10}{1/10} = -\frac{-10}{10} = 1.$$

Now reverse the direction and let the price decline from $110 to $100 while the quantity demanded now increases from 45 to 50 units. Then,

$$E_d = -\frac{5/45}{-10/110} = (-)\,(-)\frac{5}{45} \cdot \frac{110}{10} = \frac{2.4}{2} = 1.2.$$

For the same numerical values of P and Q, we obtain a different answer for the elasticity of demand depending upon which set of prices and quantities are used for the initial and final values. To avoid this ambiguity, a slightly modified formula for calculating elasticity is used.

The *modified elasticity* averages the price and quantity numbers and thereby removes any bias resulting from where one arbitrarily begins and ends.

The **modified elasticity** averages the price and quantity numbers and thereby removes any bias resulting from where one arbitrarily begins and ends.

$$E_d = -\frac{\Delta Q \Big/ \frac{Q_f + Q_i}{2}}{\Delta P \Big/ \frac{P_f + P_i}{2}} = -\frac{\Delta Q/AQ}{\Delta P/AP}.$$

AQ and *AP* stand for average quantity and average price, respectively. Now, using the same values for *P* and *Q*, irrespective of which *P* and *Q* you start or end up with, either $P_i = 100$, $Q_i = 50$, $P_f = 110$, and $Q_f = 45$ or $P_i = 110$, $Q_i = 45$, $P_f = 100$, and $Q_f = 50$. Using the second set of values we obtain

$$E_d = -\frac{-5\Big/\dfrac{50+45}{2}}{10\Big/\dfrac{10+100}{2}} = \frac{-5/47.5}{10/105} = \frac{105}{95} = 1.1$$

If the first set of values were used instead, $E_d = 1.1$ must result again. Try it.

In general, for commodities and services, the elasticity coefficient E_d can assume values between zero and infinity. But we choose to break this range of elasticity values into parts. When the coefficient E_d is less than 1 say .33 or .5, we say that the demand is *inelastic*. When the coefficient is greater than 1, say 2 or 7, then we say the coefficient is *elastic*. In the special case when the coefficient happens to be 1, we say demand is of *unit elasticity* or is *unitary elastic*. Formulas with inequality signs indicate these ranges of coefficients. Thus, when

$E_d < 1$ demand is inelastic

$E_d = 1$ demand is unitary elastic

$E_d > 1$ demand is elastic.

It is important to keep in mind that price elasticities are ratios of percentages; they are therefore pure numbers. You cannot always tell if a designated range over a curve is elastic or inelastic simply by looking at it.

Figure 4-1

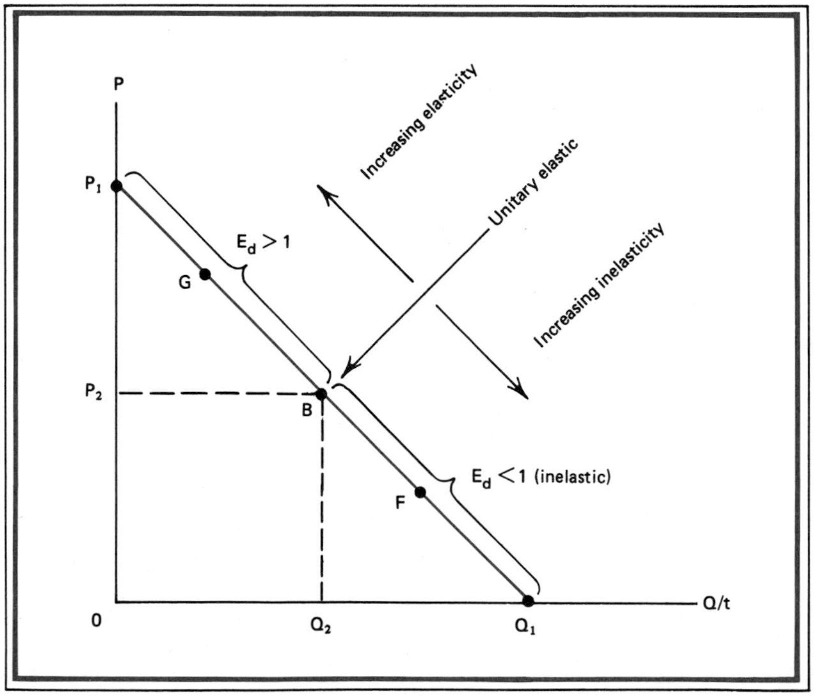

For convenience, some economists suggest that a steeper demand curve is usually more inelastic than a flatter one. But steepness and flatness can be deceptive. You must carefully observe the numerical scaling of the graph designated on the axes. Moreover, elasticity also varies at each point on the demand curve.[1] In Figure 4-1, the demand curve is the line segment $P_1 Q_1$. The line segment must have a midpoint, say it is at point B. It follows that the midpoint of OP_1 is at P_2 and the midpoint of OQ_1 is at Q_2. While we shall not show it here, it is easy to prove mathematically that the ratio of the distance from point Q_1 to a specific point on the line *divided* by the distance from that point on to point P_1 will yield the value of the elasticity coefficient. It is clear that at the midpoint, point B, the segments are the same, and the coefficient is 1. Also,

at point G: $E_d = \dfrac{Q_1G}{GP_1} > 1$, and demand is elastic at all points on the line between B and P_1

at point B: $E_d = \dfrac{Q_1B}{BP_1} = 1$, and demand is unitary elastic only at this point

at point F: $E_d = \dfrac{Q_1F}{FP_1} < 1$, and demand is inelastic at all points between B and Q_1.

Moving toward P_1, elasticity becomes greater, and moving toward Q_1 elasticity become smaller.

As a mechanical way of remembering the elasticity formula in terms of line segments, just think of starting out at point Q_1 and moving to the relevant point on the line at which you wish to evaluate the coefficient. Call this distance Q_1G, and put it in the numerator, then go from point G to point P_1, call this GP_1, and put it in the denominator. Thus $E_d = \dfrac{Q_1G}{GP_2}$, and let G represent any point you choose. If you choose point B, put B in where G is; if you choose F, then replace G with F.

REVENUE AND ELASTICITY

There is a strict relation between price elasticity and the effect on sales revenues when price changes. Total revenue is defined as

[1]Elasticity is different from the slope. To see this, break out the elasticity formula into $-\dfrac{\Delta Q}{\Delta P} \cdot \dfrac{P}{Q}$. The $\dfrac{\Delta P}{\Delta Q}$ = slope. Hence, $\dfrac{\Delta Q}{\Delta P} = \dfrac{1}{\text{slope}}$. Thus, $E_d = -\dfrac{1}{\text{slope}} \cdot \dfrac{P}{Q}$. Since the slope of a straight line is constant, so is $\dfrac{1}{\text{slope}}$ a constant. It follows that E_d only varies with change in P and Q while moving along from point to point on the demand curve. For example, at point G in Figure 4-1, the price is above the halfway mark at P_2, and the quantity is below the halfway mark at Q_2. Thus, $P/Q > 1$. And at point F, the price is below P_2 and the quantity is greater than Q_2 so that $P/Q < 1$.

***TR* = *P* × *Q* tells us that total revenue is the product of price times quantity.**

$$TR = P \times Q = \frac{\textbf{price in dollars}}{\textbf{unit}} \times \textbf{no. of units} = \textbf{dollars of revenue.}$$

Total revenues are described by rectangular areas in a graph. Since the area of a rectangle is obtained by multiplying the length of one side by the other, if price is one side and quantity the other, then their product is total revenue *TR*.

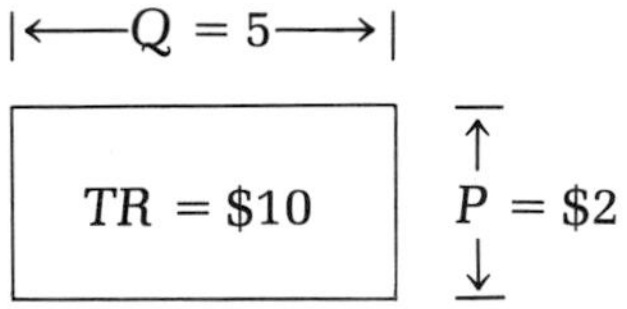

It will be useful to examine the three cases of elasticity and the relation to total revenue.

Price Inelastic ($E_d < 1$)

For our purposes, assume that in Figure 4-2 the price rises from P_1 to P_2 and stays within the inelastic range of the demand curve. In response to the rise in price, quantity demanded falls from Q_1 to Q_2. Because the range of the price change lies along the inelastic segment of the demand curve, the percentage change in the quantity demanded is less than the percentage change of the rise

Figure 4-2

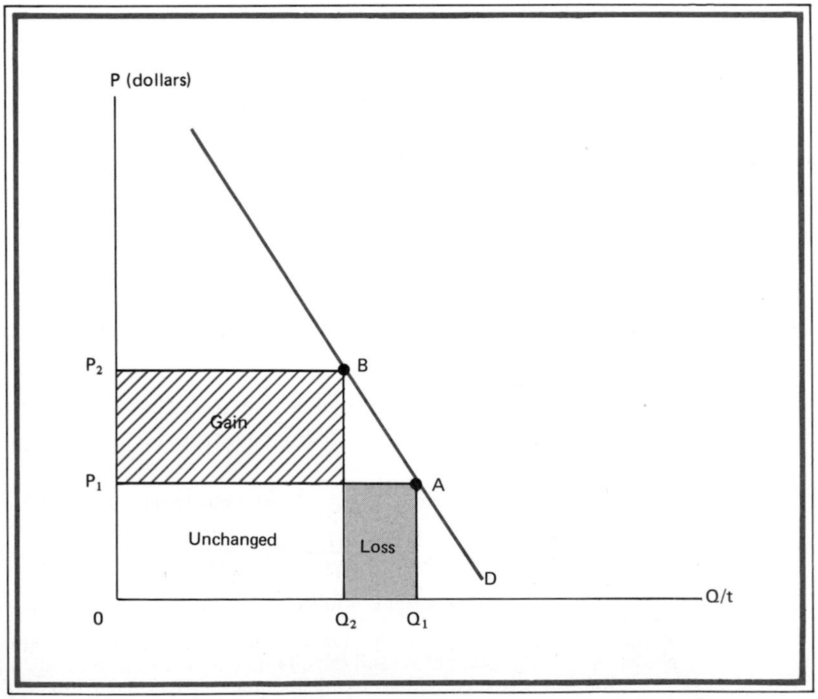

Figure 4-3

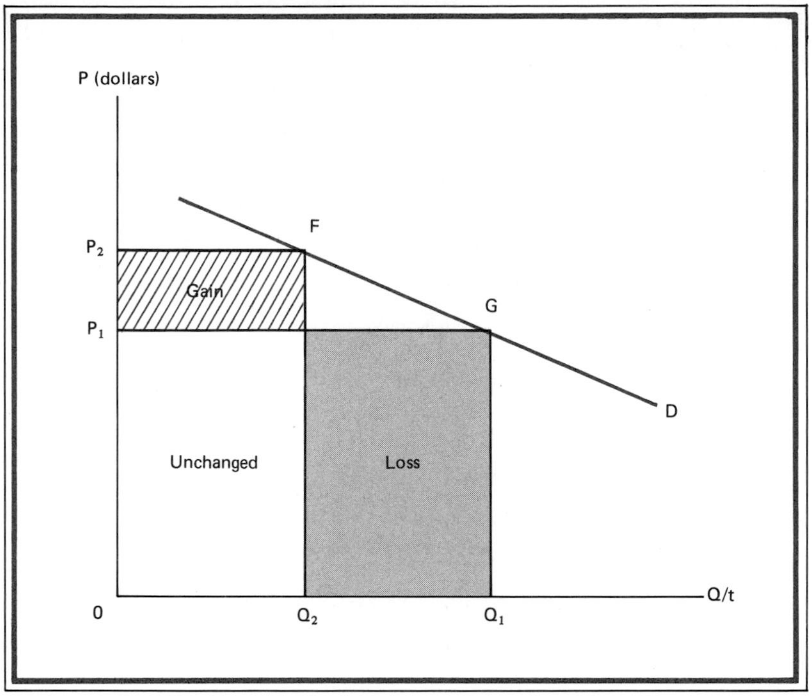

When $E_d < 1$, the quantity demanded is relatively insensitive to a change in price, and demand is price inelastic.

in price. The interpretation is that the quantity demanded is relatively insensitive to the change in the price, and total revenue rises. Geometrically, rectangle P_1AQ_10 is smaller than rectangle P_2BQ_20. The unshaded area is shared by both rectangles. The rectangle P_1AQ_10 experiences a loss, indicated by the shaded area when the price rises. The gain incorporated in rectangle P_2BQ_20 is shown by the striped area. Since the gain is greater than the loss, total revenue increases when the price rises from P_1 to P_2. Conversely, when the price falls from P_2 to P_1, total revenue declines, the loss (striped area) being greater than the gain (shaded area) when demand is inelastic.

Price Elastic ($E_d > 1$)

When the price rises from P_1 to P_2 in the elastic range of the demand curve, total revenue falls. By the geometry of Figure 4-3, the revenue rectangle P_1GQ_10 is larger than rectangle P_2FQ_20 if we assume we are moving in the elastic range of this demand curve. Again, the blank rectangle is shared by both rectangles. When the price rises, rectangle P_1GQ_10 loses the revenue shown by the shaded area, and rectangle P_2FQ_20 gains the revenue shown by the striped area. Clearly, the loss is greater than the gain, so that total revenue declines when the price rises from P_1 to P_2. When demand is price elastic, quantity demanded declines proportionately more than the price rises. The percentage change downward in quantity demanded is greater than the percentage change upward in the price, and the net effect is that total revenue falls. Conversely, when demand is elastic and the price falls from P_2 to P_1, total revenue rises. When demand is elastic buyers spend more when the price is lower.

When $E_d > 1$, the quantity demanded is more sensitive to a price change, and demand is price elastic.

Figure 4-4

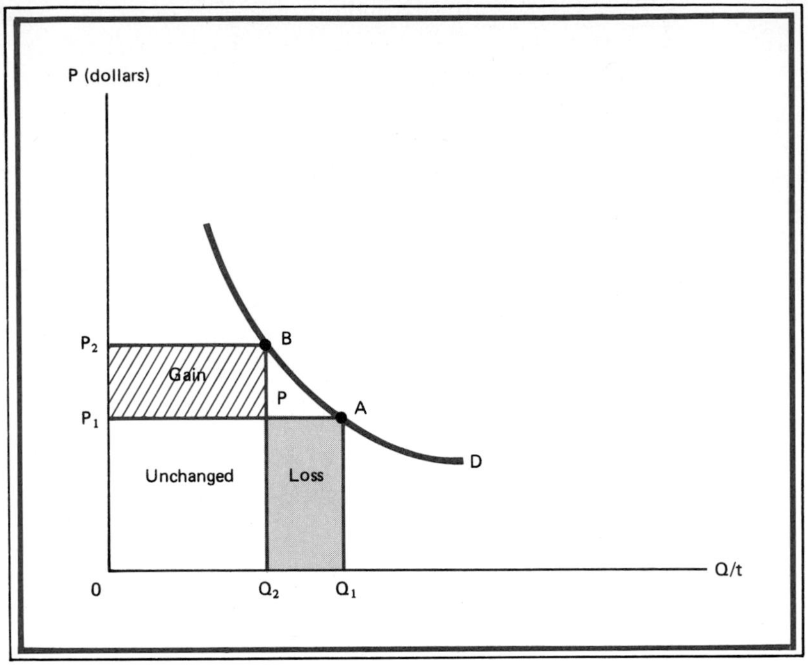

Unitary Elastic ($E_d = 1$)

When $E_d = 1$, the quantity demanded changes in exact proportion to the price changes.

Figure 4-4 provides an example of a unitary price elastic demand curve. Notice it is not a straight line. For our purposes all we have to know is that total revenue remains unchanged when the price rises or falls. At every point on this demand curve elasticity is equal to 1. Thus, when price rises from P_1 to P_2, the shaded area representing the loss area of the lower price rectangle exactly equals the striped area representing the gain area included in the higher price rectangle. The areas P_1PQ_20 and P_2BQ_20 are equal because of the property of this particular demand curve. Total revenue remains unchanged whether the price goes up or down. The quantity demanded changes in exact proportion to the price changes.

WHY ELASTIC OR INELASTIC?

There are four major reasons that the demand for some goods is elastic whereas for others it is inelastic over different price ranges.

In what follows, elasticity should be understood in the context of comparable price ranges.

Availability of Substitutes. When there are other choices, a rise in the price of one commodity finds consumers switching to the purchase of close substitutes.

The degree of elasticity of demand for goods is determined by (1) availability of substitutes, (2) degree of necessity, (3) share of the budget and (4) time.

Food as a group is inelastic in demand over a large price range (we have to eat something). However, the demand for individual food items is often elastic; for example, many vegetables and fruits are substituted for one another by season. There are many highly substitutable pairs of goods such as margarine and butter, orange and grapefruit juice, beef and pork and chicken, and corn flakes and Wheaties. While the demand for these items is not necessarily elastic, it is relatively more elastic in light of the options they provide to the consumer. If you find it too expensive to leap over buildings in a single bound by eating breakfast brand A, you can eat brand B or C. The demand for a good may be inelastic if there are few available substitutes. Consumers tend not to reduce their consumption of tobacco, alcohol, and gasoline much as prices rise; this observation is not lost on government officials who often raise the tax on these commodities to increase government revenues. If the price rises high enough on very inelastic items, the price elastic range of the demand curve will be reached eventually, leading to the often painful decision of reducing the consumption of much desired goods.

Degree of Necessity. The less necessary items are the more demand elastic they are. One is more apt to give them up or, short of that, reduce one's consumption of them. You use the money on more necessary things. Goods one finds hard to do without tend to be price inelastic. Items such as coffee, cigarettes, and automobile transportation come to mind.

Large Budget Item. Items that are a relatively large part of one's budget tend to be more elastic in demand, for example, color television sets and stereo equipment. But we must be careful here because automobiles are a large budget item,

The Price of Losing

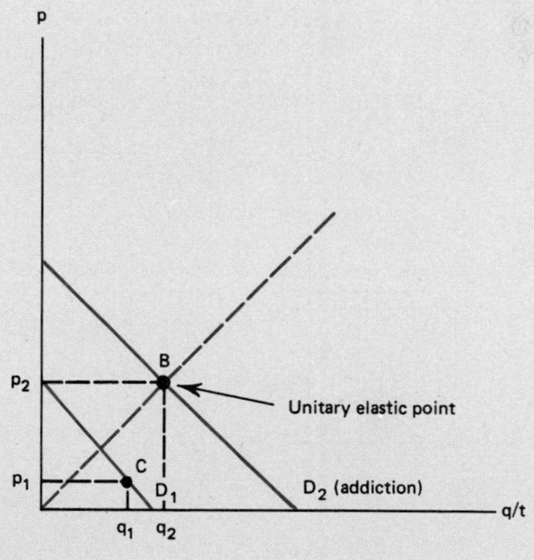

The pusher on the street understands price elasticity of demand. The D_1 curve represents the demand curve for heroin by the nonaddict. At first the pusher may charge nothing or a very low price for a small amount at C, where the price is p_1, the quantity q_1. After the buyer is hooked, his demand curve shifts to D_2 (a change in tastes) and the pusher owns him. The pusher by now has raised the amount to q_2 and now raises the price to p_2 at the unitary elastic point B. Revenue is increased and also maximized. At a price above p_2 demand is elastic and total revenue is lower. At a price below p_2 demand is inelastic and total revenue is also lower. (The dashed line divides the demand curves into two equal segments.) Beyond the price p_2 in the elastic range there are substitutes—Methadone treatment, gradually coming down under medical supervision, or cold turkey.

yet demand for them appears to be inelastic. The reason lies in the degree of necessity for transportation for a public that has long considered public transit a poor substitute for the private automobile. Degree of necessity must be simultaneously considered with other factors that affect demand elasticity. The same reasoning applies to food as a group; it is a large budget item but it is demand inelastic because it is a necessity. In most cases, however, items which are a large part of the budget are also demand elastic. Conversely, it follows that commodities which take up a small part of one's budget, necessities or not, tend to be more demand inelastic. Potatoes, salt, and newspapers appear to qualify. In Table 4-1, note that the elasticity coefficient for potatoes is 0.3.

Time The longer the time period, the more likely is the demand for a commodity to become more elastic over a price range, as shown by the rotation of the demand curve counterclockwise about point *R* in Figure 4-5. Over time, consumers can gather more information and discover alternatives, thereby expanding the range of substitutes. Information costs are therefore a factor not only affecting the level of demand but the elasticity of demand as well. People do not usually adjust instantaneously to large price changes; often they cannot. Most of them, for example, cannot sell the big car and buy a small car tomorrow because crude oil prices rose today, or insulate their homes tomorrow, or convert to natural gas or solar energy overnight. Hence demand is more inelastic in the short period. But as people learn of substitutes and can undertake the transactions costs of converting to other items, the demand curve for big cars, for

TABLE 4-1
Elasticities of Some Goods and Services in Short Run (SR) and Long Run (LR)

Food Items[1]		Nonfood Items[2]	Services
White potatoes	0.3	Stationery SR .4693 LR .5638	Foreign travel by U.S. residents SR .3151 LR 1.7707
Green peas, fresh	2.8	Rental value of owner-occupied housing SR .0351 LR 1.2150	Medical care and hospitalization SR .3136 LR .9162
Green peas, canned	1.6	Toilet articles SR .1993 LR 3.0391	Legal services .3707
Tomatoes, fresh	4.6	Tobacco products SR .4556 LR 1.8919	Household gas (utility) SR .1458 LR 10.7386
Tomatoes, canned	2.5		
Cabbage	0.4		

[1] D. Milton Shuffet, "The Demand and Price Structure for Selected Vegetables." *Technical Bulletin No. 1105*, U.S. Department of Agriculture, 1954.
[2] H. S. Houthakker and L. D. Taylor, *Consumer Demand in the United States: Analysis and Projections* (Cambridge: Harvard University Press, 1970).

Figure 4-5

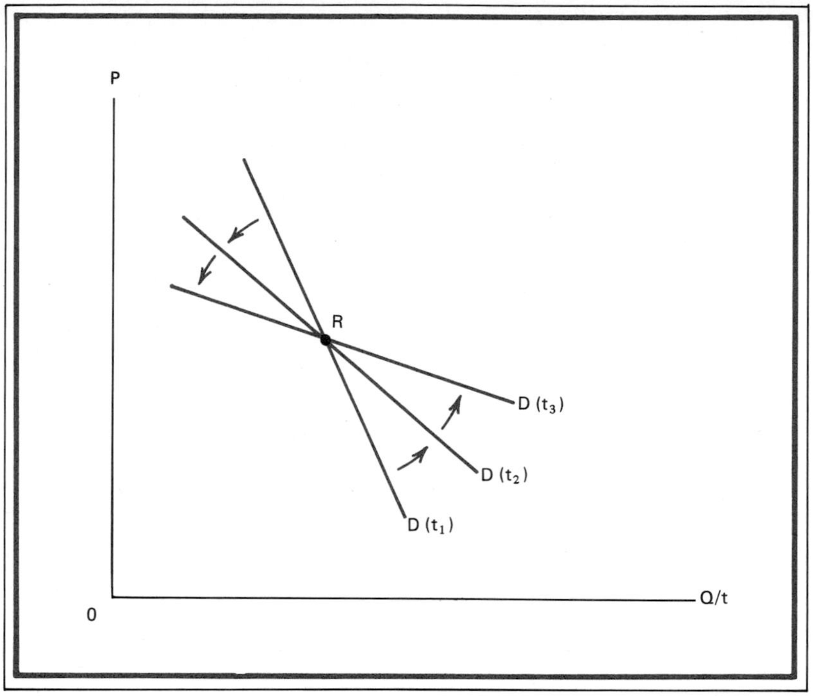

gasoline, and for crude oil will become more elastic as prices become high enough to motivate them to seek alternatives. Table 4-1 compares elasticity changes between the short and long runs for a few goods.

Special Cases

There are two extreme examples of demand elasticity illustrated in Figure 4-6. The flat demand curve is an example of a perfectly elastic demand curve with $E_d = \infty$ (infinity). At a price of P_1, the quantity demanded can be q_1, q_2, or q_n on to infinity in principle. But for a price above P_1, the quantity demanded collapses to zero. There is simply no demand curve above the P_1 price. Mathematically the percentage change in quantity demanded is undefined, being infinitely large. The absolutely vertical demand curve is an example of perfectly inelastic demand. Here, the quantity Q_1 is fixed. A price rise from P_1 to P_2 causes no change in the quantity whatsoever. The elasticity of demand $E_d = 0$.

The logical implication is that the demand curve is zero inelastic over its whole range and that the same amount would therefore be bought no matter the price. This, of course, is not believable. Any demand curve, even if perfectly inelastic over some price range, is bound to have an elastic range if the price gets high enough. Even for items where there appear to be no substitutes, a rising price means people have to sacrifice more of all other goods—substitutes or not—and they will reach a point where they will not do it. Therefore, as prices rise high enough reaching into the elastic range, which *every* demand curve must have as shown by the broken line in Figure 4-6, people will consume less whether it is tobacco, alcohol, house heat as fuel prices rise, large cars as gasoline prices soar, or coffee.

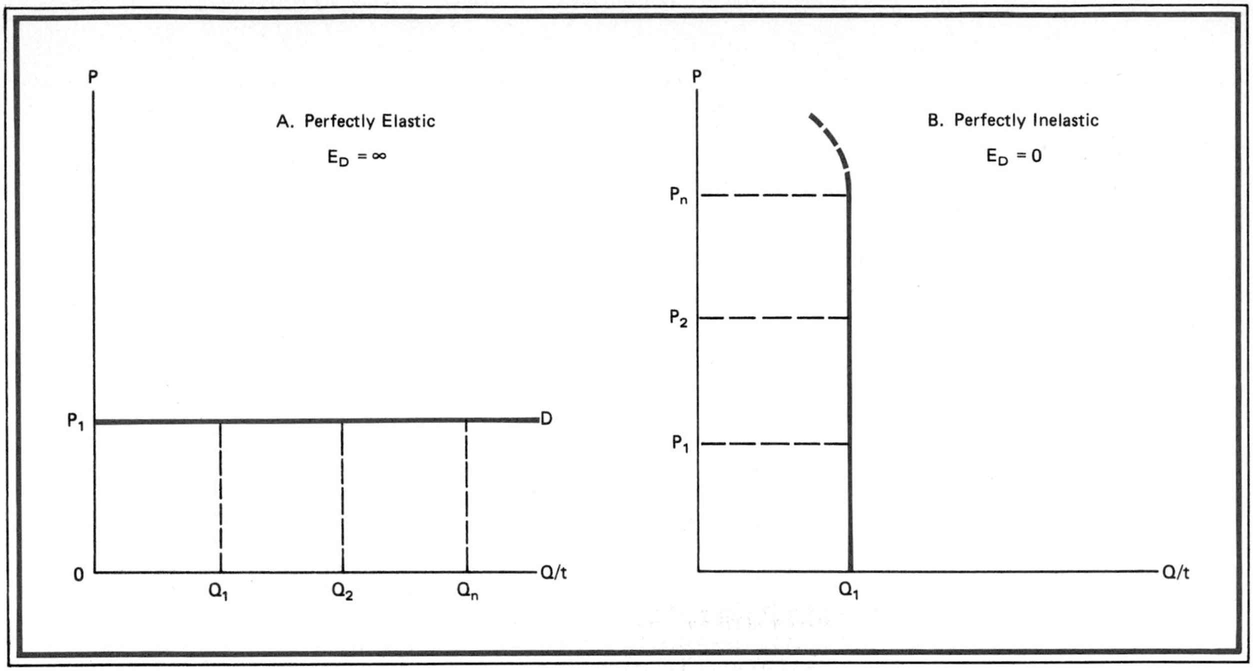

Figure 4-6

ELASTICITY OF SUPPLY

The *supply curve* is progressively more price elastic as the period of production passes from the momentary period, to the short run, to the long run.

The formula for elasticity is general. Any equation and any line in a graph showing the relation between two variables will yield a coefficient of elasticity. Thus, when we are looking at a supply curve, we look at quantity as a function of price, and after choosing a particular price we can compute the value of a coefficient of elasticity of supply E_s as

$$E_s = \frac{\text{percentage change in quantity supplied}}{\text{percentage change in price}} = \frac{\Delta Q/Q}{\Delta P/P}$$

with $\Delta Q_s = Q_f - Q_i$ and $\Delta P = P_f - P_i$ where f stands for the final value and i for the initial value. Elasticity of supply can also be calculated using the modified elasticity formulation.

In this formula there is no need to introduce a minus sign before the fraction on the right side. Because both price and quantity move in the same direction, the coefficient will always be positive so long as the supply curve rises upward from left to right, that is, so long as it has a positive slope.

Elasticity of supply is affected by several factors.

Time The longer the time period, the more elastic is the supply curve. Over time, product modification can be made. Learning by doing increases efficiency and output at each price as workers find ways to reduce the number of steps or movements, thus reducing the time in performing their tasks. Managers discover better ways to organize operations that remove production kinks. Better communication and arrangements are made with suppliers of inputs, transportation schedules are improved, information within and among different sectors of the company are improved, causing a reduction in transactions costs. Actually three kinds of time periods can be defined that explain the different elasticities of supply, shown in Figure 4-7 as time progresses from time 1 to time 3.

The *momentary period* is so short that output cannot be increased no matter what the market price; all inputs in production are fixed.

Momentary Period The curve S_1 is perfectly inelastic ($E_{s_1} = 0$). The period is so short that output cannot be increased above Q_1 no matter what the market price. All inputs in production are fixed and committed. For the farmer, all the corn that can be grown has been grown. The season is over and supply cannot be increased until the next season. For the firm in manufacturing, the time is too short to hire more workers or to receive a new order of materials.

The *short run* represents a time period in which some inputs are variable and can be changed but others cannot.

Short Run The S_2 curve represents a time period in which some inputs are variable and can be changed but others cannot. The farmer can apply more labor and fertilizer to the cornfield during planting or while the stalks are young, resulting in an increased yield. The manufacturer can order more materials and run the plant overtime. But the period is not long enough for the farmer to acquire more acreage or the manufacturer to enlarge the factory, or for the purchase of another tractor or a new machine. At the price of P_1 output expands to Q_2.

Long Run The S_3 curve signifies the long run, a period in which all inputs are variable. New tractors can be rented or purchased and more land acquired. The

Figure 4-7

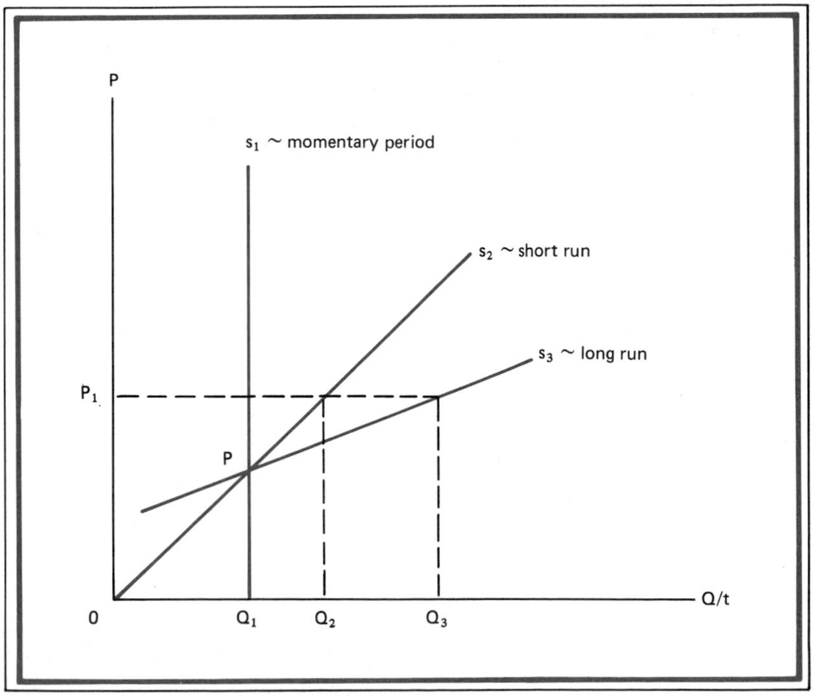

The *long run* represents time sufficient to vary all inputs.

manufacturer can modify or expand the factory, or build another factory. Old firms can leave the industry and new ones enter. Output at price P_1 rises to Q_3. In the long run it is possible for the supply curve to be horizontal—showing perfectly elastic supply at every point.

Table 4-2 provides some estimates of supply elasticities for a few selected goods. Cabbage has a short-run supply elasticity coefficient of .36. Thus a 10 percent increase in the price of cabbage leads to a 3.6 percent increase in the quantity supplied. If the price of cabbage rises by 10 percent from 50 cents, to 55 cents, and the Q_s at 50 cents was 1,000 head, then at the price of 55 cents $Q_s = 1{,}036$. To see this we substitute into the elasticity formula as follows:

$$E_s = .36 = \frac{\dfrac{Q_f - 1000}{1000}}{\dfrac{55 - 50}{50}} = \frac{Q_f - 1000}{1000} \cdot \frac{50}{5}$$

or

$$\frac{Q_f - 1000}{100} = .36. \quad \text{Thus } Q_f = (.36)100 + 1000 = 1036.$$

Suppose that the rise in prices stimulates cabbage growers to plant more cabbage for the next season. The result is that the coefficient of the long-run elasticity of supply rises to 1.20. Thus, a 10 percent rise in price causes the Q_s of cabbage to increase by 12 percent to 1,120.

Special Cases

Figure 4-8 portrays a perfectly inelastic supply curve ($E_s = 0$) and a perfectly elastic supply curve ($E_s = \infty$). We recently learned that for the momentary period $E_s = 0$. But $E_s = 0$ can also occur for the short and long runs when a resource is highly specialized or its quantity is absolutely fixed. A star quarterback or the services of a famous movie actor are essentially unique. There is no one exactly like them. As a result of some unique feature, the quantity is fixed. No price rise can increase the quantity supplied of a famous star—on the field or in the cinema. What can increase is the number of their performances as the price rises.

The other extreme exists when the supply curve is perfectly horizontal. No matter what quantity is supplied there occurs no change in the price. An industry produces any amount of a commodity or service at the identical price per unit. A special example is the post office. When it comes to producing postage stamps, it *is* the industry. No matter what quantity of postage stamps it produces, it sells every one of a denomination at the same price.

Who Pays the Tax?

Does the consumer really pay the full amount of the tax on any item? You might immediately respond, "Of course he does." However, the answer depends on

TABLE 4-2
Selected Supply Elasticities

Item	Short Run	Long Run
Cabbage[1]	0.36	1.20
Lettuce	0.03	0.16
Onions	0.34	1.00
Tomatoes	0.16	0.90
Watermelons	0.23	0.48
Spinach	0.20	4.70
Cucumbers	0.29	2.20
Fertilizer and lime[2]	0.03	0.14
Machinery expense	0.06	0.28
Machinery inventory	0.02	0.26
Labor	0.03	0.25
Real estate	0.03	0.08

[1]M. Nerlove and W. Addison, "Statistical Estimation of Long-run Elasticities of Supply and Demand," *Journal of Farm Economics* (Nov. 1958) for food items.
[2]L. G. Tweeten and C. L. Quance, "Positive Measures of Aggregate Supply Elasticities: Some New Approaches, *American Economic Review,* Papers and Proceedings, 59 (May 1969): 175–183 for nonfood items.

what are the elasticities of supply and demand for the product. Whom the tax is levied on is the *incidence* of the tax. But who actually ends up bearing the brunt of the tax is called the *burden* of the tax. The following analysis applies whether the tax imposed is a percentage of the sale price (10 percent of sales

Figure 4-8

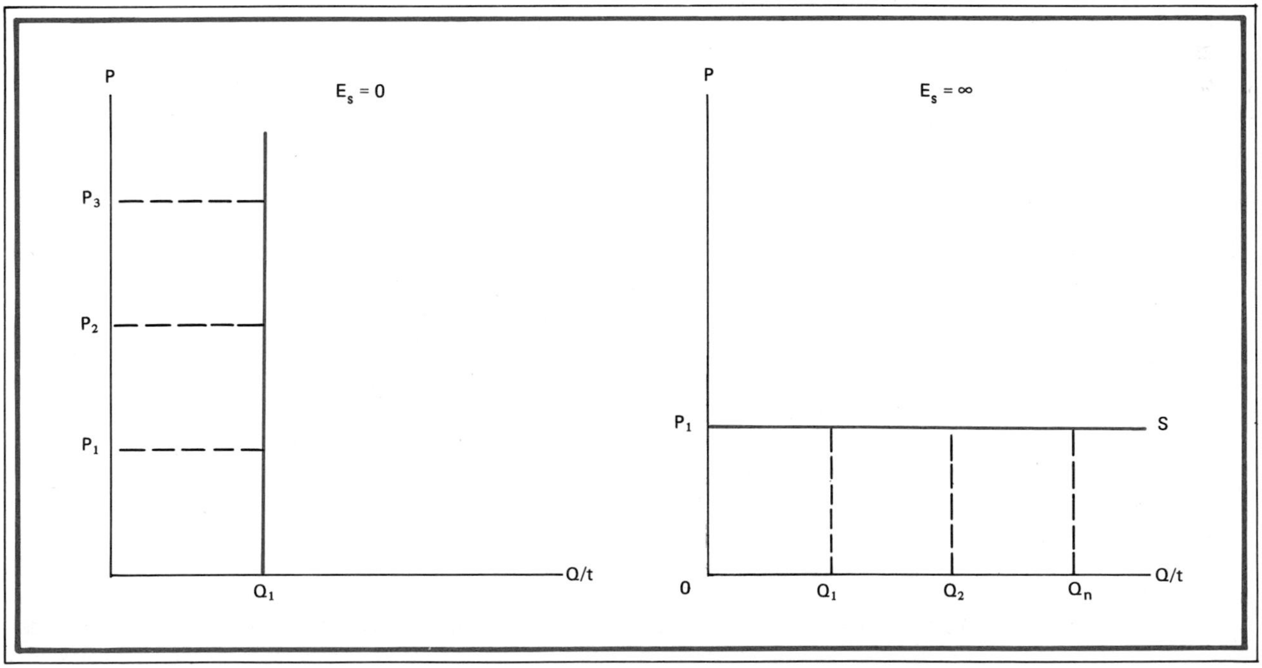

Bombing is Faster

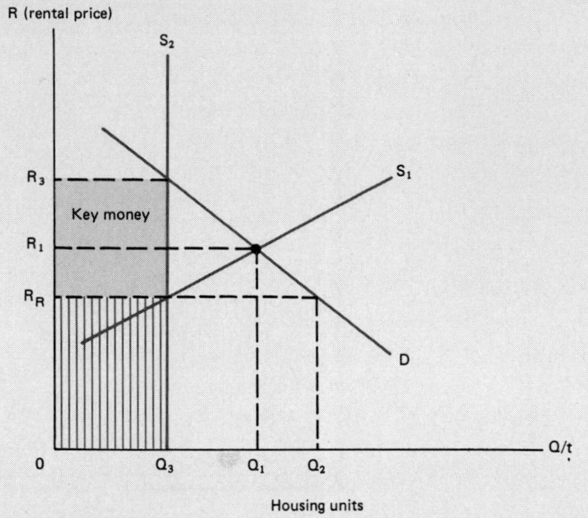

Rent control acts like a delayed time bomb. It destroys housing. In recent years more than 230 communities have operated or instituted rent controls. Politicians who vote in rent control honestly believe they are protecting the poor, the weak, and the old from "legal extortion and exploitation." For a while it does protect them from higher rents. Rent control is, in effect, a tax upon landlords and a subsidy to tenants. But rent controls create an excess demand for shelter by pricing it below its market value and distorting the housing market, all the more as time goes on. New York City is often used as a classic example. Most rent controls were removed after World War II ended, but New York City retained wartime rent controls imposed in 1943 on approximately one million housing and apartment units. The purpose was to allow low-income residents to be able to spend more of their income for nonhousing goods. Unfortunately, the costs of maintenance, mortgage interest, and taxes rose faster to landlords than rental prices were permitted to rise. This caused the return on property investment of owners to fall substantially. The rental rate R_1 is the rate applying in a free market (on a statistically standardized unit). The government regulated rental rate is R_R. At this rate, quantity demanded is Q_2 per period and quantity supplied is Q_3. Over time, the free market rate R_1 rose above the regulated R_R rate even though they were initially the same when the law was passed. As a result of the low investment return, there was little new construction of apartment buildings that might become regulated if built. Therefore, in the long run the supply of low-income units became essentially perfectly inelastic as shown by S_2. At the regulated price R_R, there is a shortage of $Q_2 - Q_3$. In fact, the low level of R_R actually increased the quantity demanded to Q_2. Pinched by rising costs and falling profits, an alarming percentage of private landlords defaulted on property taxes, resulting in city ownership of the properties. Other owners abandoned buildings and banks foreclosed on the mortgages; since the banks cannot sell the building they refuse to pay the taxes and again the

price), or is fixed at some amount levied on a unit of sales (8 cents per gallon of gasoline) no matter what the sales price of the commodity is.

Suppose a new \$1 tax is levied on quart bottles of wine that were previously selling for \$5 a bottle. Figure 4-9 illustrates the analysis. Before the tax, equilibrium existed at point E. The price was \$5 and the quantity demanded was Q_1. The \$1 tax on the seller (assuming that the seller must forward the money to the government) raises the cost to him, causing the supply curve S_1 to shift left to S_2. This creates a new market equilibrium at E'.

Let us assume that the supply and demand elasticities are such that the seller absorbs a fourth of the tax or 25 cents, and the consumer absorbs three fourths of the tax or 75 cents. As a consequence, the seller passes on only three

city ends up owning the abandoned buildings. The city will likely own 75,000 dilapidated apartment buildings by 1985.

Numerous other effects followed from the law over the long run. The striped rectangle in the figure represents landlord revenues under price controls. But the shaded area labeled "Key money" represents illegal income transfers from new renters to subletters. For example, if the legal rate on an apartment was $300 a month, you might have to pay the current renter $200 to get the key if you wanted to sublet the unit. The black market price is P_3 on the very inelastic stock of regulated units Q_3. Another variation required buying the subletter's furniture. Aside from the substantial costs to the taxpayer of the city administering the program, the city receives no taxes on the illegal income transfers.

Other effects were the much higher transactions costs of search to those looking for apartments. Also, the rents on unregulated units were higher than otherwise because owners feared changes in the law that might include them in the future. And they would be stuck with charging the lower rates. Owners on regulated units, as a result, performed less maintenance. The low rents attracted more lower income people into the city (combined with higher welfare rates), which further eroded the city's tax base. While rent controls did help poorer people buy more nonhousing goods, the total gain to them was far less than the costs to the landlords, the city, and to higher bracket taxpayers. Also, though the average renter was poorer than the average landlord, there were also renters who were richer than landlords, so there were random income distribution effects. Rent control is a typical example of trying to solve a market problem by altering the demand side while overlooking or underestimating the supply side effects. An unregulated rental market, but with rent subsidies provided to poor people, would have been a superior approach.

In 1969, the city imposed the rent stabilization program over all post-1947 rental construction previously free of controls. It is less rigid than rent controls and allows for some increases in rents based on lease renewals. Thus some units remained under rent controls while others came under rent stabilization. In 1971 the state passed The Vacancy Decontrol Law which allowed vacated units, stabilized or controlled, to be rented at free market rates. Some 900,000 units are rent stabilized while only 400,000 remain rent controlled. The state replaced the 1971 law with The Emergency Tenant Protection Act which allowed for vacated rent controlled units to come under the rent stabilization act and extended coverage to Nassau, Westchester, and Rockland counties. Nonetheless, New York City spends nearly two-thirds of its Federal Block Grant monies on maintaining properties taken for nonpayment of real estate taxes.

Sources: Edgar Olsen, "An Econometric Study of Rent Control," Journal of Political Economy, Nov./Dec. 1972. And Monte I. Radack, Memo: Rent Regulation in New York City, Savings Bank Association of New York, June 12, 1979.

fourths of the tax to the consumer. The shaded area shows the amount of the tax absorbed by the seller, and the other area indicated shows how much the consumer pays. The market price of the quart wine bottle does not rise from $5 to $6 but only to $5.75. The producer absorbs 25 cents of the $1 tax. At the higher price of $5 + .75 = $5.75 consumers, by the law of demand, move back along the demand curve to purchase only Q_2 bottles. The producer therefore nets $5.75 − 1 = $4.75 per bottle.

While the producer absorbs less of the tax than the consumer, the fraction of the tax that each pays depends on the relative elasticities of supply and demand. If demand is perfectly inelastic, as when the demand curve is vertical, the consumer will absorb all of the tax. If demand is perfectly elastic, on the

Figure 4-9

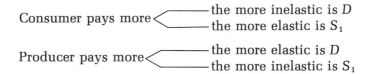

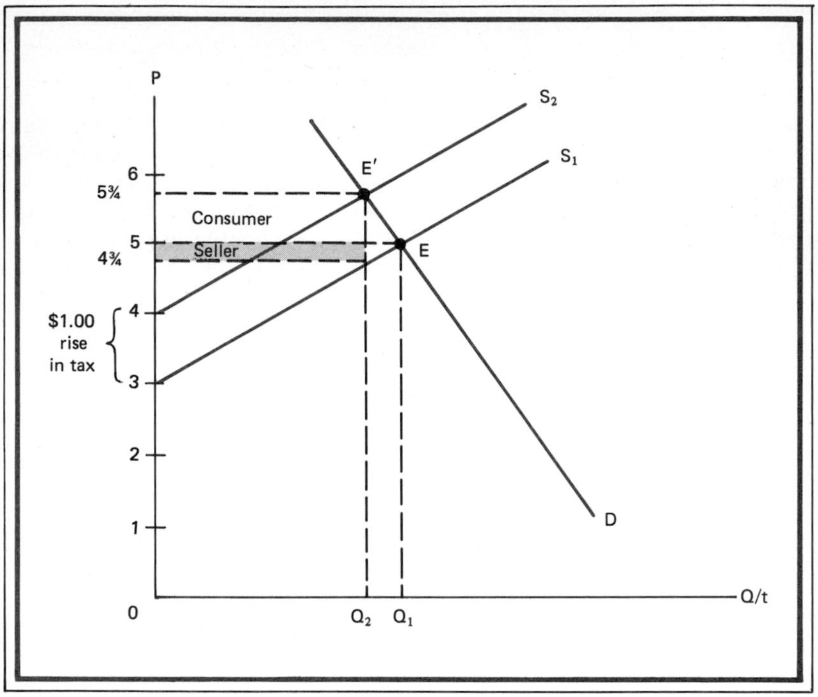

other hand, the producer will absorb all of the tax while the consumer pays none. Can you verify the following by rotating the S_1 and D curves through point E?

Consumer pays more — the more inelastic is D; the more elastic is S_1

Producer pays more — the more elastic is D; the more inelastic is S_1

In reality, the analysis of the incidence of a tax and its burden is not so simple. Depending on whom the tax is initially levied, the chain between the initial producer and the final buyer is connected by the many links of middlemen. Firms do not usually produce one product, nor do middlemen deal in only one commodity. The *ceteris paribus* condition only exists in the idealized world of theory. In reality, there are very complex interdependencies among the economic actors. For example, suppose a new, very heavy tax is levied on gasoline. People react by trying to sell their big cars and replace them with cheaper, smaller cars. This switch leads to a drop in the demand for steel, and the total revenues of steel producers fall. Thus they are "paying" for part of the tax increase. Because of a decline in steel revenues, the government collects less tax from steel producers and also collects less tax from steel workers. The government is forced to change what it spends the tax money for, and on whom to spend it, or on whom else to levy additional taxes to make up for the loss in steel taxes. Ultimately the consuming public, or certain members of the consuming public, are able to buy fewer resources to use while the government might end up with more to use for different members of the consuming public. Furthermore, when the steel firms cut back production, what effect is there on stockholders' investment earnings? How many junior executives are fired? How many production-line workers are laid off? Thus, when a new tax is levied, who ultimately benefits and who ultimately bears the burden is very hard to sort out.

MARGINAL UTILITY: ANOTHER VIEW OF DEMAND

In the previous chapter we talked about the highest price one would be willing to pay. The reason that someone is willing to buy something has to do with the satisfaction, or what we call the *utility,* one expects to experience by consuming the good or the services that the good provides. By some complicated mental process we translate the satisfaction we expect to experience into a price we are willing to pay in order to obtain that satisfaction—what we have dubbed utility. Obviously, the price we are willing to pay is not the desire itself but the price of satisfying it. Price is one way to measure what something is apparently worth to someone.

Since, "more is preferred to less" is a behavioral assumption, the logical conclusion is that we must experience or anticipate more utility from having more than less. You might say, "Okay, I'll buy that. But the more I consume of something isn't it likely I'll reach a point I'll become bored or saturated with it?" Very likely, and we describe your insight by means of the principle of diminishing marginal utility.

The principle of *diminishing marginal utility* states that a point is reached where consuming additional units would increase total utility but at a decreasing rate as marginal utility begins to decline.

The Principle of Diminishing Marginal Utility While initially marginal utility might increase as more of a good is consumed, a point is reached where consuming additional units would increase total utility but at a decreasing rate as marginal utility begins to decline. Additional units of consumption could result in smaller and smaller additional units of satisfaction, assuming the amounts consumed of other commodities remained unchanged.

This law is really the law of demand masquerading under a new identity. Diminishing marginal utility operates under *ceteris paribus* conditions. If on a very hot day after a vigorous schoolyard basketball game you drink a cold bottle of soda pop, you will experience a high level of satisfaction. If you follow with a second soda, then a third, then a fourth, you will increase the total amount of pleasure. However, it is unlikely that the second bottle of soda pop, though satisfying, was quite as good as that first drink. And that the third bottle was not nearly as good as the second. That is, the additional utility that you got from each successive bottle declined. Though total utility was increased with each bottle, it increased at a decreasing rate. It is like a runner who is beginning to slow down. He is increasing the total distance he is covering, but at a reduced rate.

This additional utility obtained from consuming another bottle of soda is

TABLE 4-3

Q Soda	TU Total Utility	$\frac{\Delta TU}{\Delta Q}$ Marginal Utility
0	0	
		12
1	12	
		10
2	22	
		8
3	30	
		4
4	34	
		0
5	34	
		−6
6	28	

called *marginal utility* (MU). It measures the change in total utility from consuming an additional bottle. In shorthand notation,

$$MU = \frac{\Delta TU}{\Delta Q}.$$

Table 4-3 provides hypothetical data. Utility is measured in utils—a unit of pleasure—and is arbitrarily assigned numerical values. We have let the change in Q be 1 in all cases, so that the denominator in the fraction $\Delta TU/\Delta Q$ is also 1. Thus, total utility *(TU)* measures the sum of the discrete changes in utility resulting from each unit increase in quantity consumed. The first unit of consumption provides 12 units of satisfaction. The second unit provides an additional 10 utils; the third an additional 8. Thus, if 3 units are consumed, the total utility is made up of 12 plus 10 plus 8, or a total of 30 utils of satisfaction. Notice that when the fifth bottle is consumed, total utility falls, and the marginal utility of consuming the sixth bottle is actually negative. The individual has drunk to the point of physical discomfort.

Figure 4-10 also illustrates the relationship between total and marginal utility. We can observe that total utility increases up to a maximum level of 34 as the number of sodas increased. In the lower graph we note the added utility obtained from added units of consumption. This marginal utility declines until it becomes negative when the sixth unit is consumed.

Price is *proportional*—not equal—to the marginal utility.

Diminishing marginal utility can explain the demand curve. As one obtains less and less satisfaction from consuming additional amounts of an item, then one can only be induced to consume those additional units at correspondingly lower and lower prices. The quantity demanded increases as the opportunity cost (price) falls. The less the utility, the less the good is worth to you; the smaller is the sacrifice you are therefore apt to make for the diminished plea-

Figure 4-10

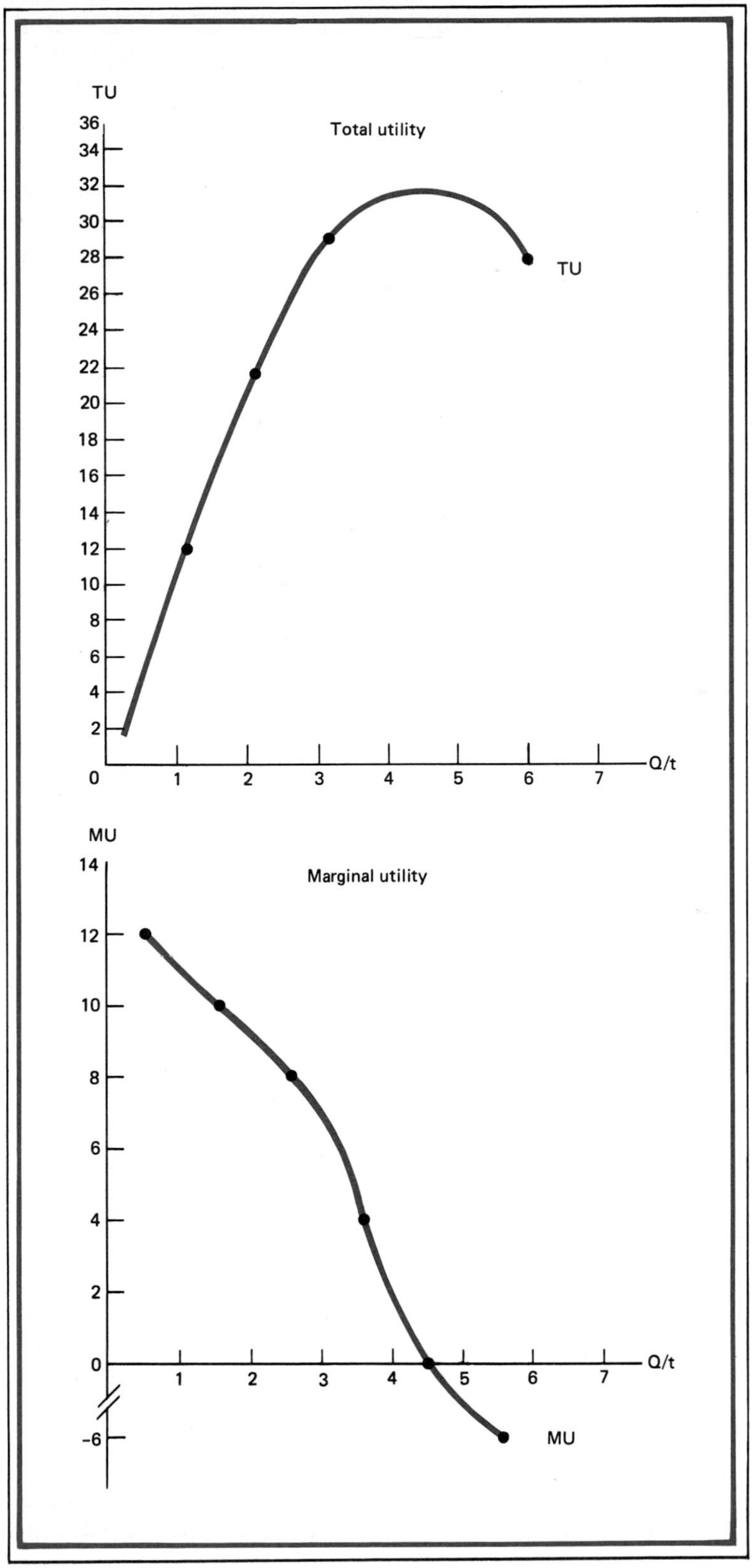
TU
Total utility
36
34
32
30
28
26
24
22
20
18
16
14
12
10
8
6
4
2
0
1
2
3
4
5
6
7
Q/t
TU
MU
Marginal utility
14
12
10
8
6
4
2
0
-6
1
2
3
4
5
6
7
Q/t
MU

sure of consuming it. But price is **proportional**—not equal—to the marginal utility of the last unit consumed. The marginal utility curve, the lower curve in Figure 4-10, corresponds to an individual's demand curve for soda pop.

MARGINAL UTILITY AND EXCHANGE

In Chapter 2 we discussed how two people can increase their welfare through trading. Each person possessed some of both items, licorice sticks and bubble gum. However, each person's preferences differed and these differences provided a basis for trade. Instead of assuming both persons had some of both items, let us simplify the example and let Jerry begin by holding only licorice and Mary only gum—four sticks in each case. Assume their utility schedules are as shown in Table 4-4.

If marginal utility to Jerry of obtaining a bubble gum is 9 utils and the marginal utility to Mary of acquiring one licorice stick is 8 utils, then Mary and Jerry can benefit from a trade. Should Mary trade her 4th bubble gum worth 5 utils to her, she will acquire 1 licorice stick worth 8 utils to her. In similar fashion, Jerry sacrifices his 4th licorice stick worth 5 utils to him for 1 bubble gum worth 9 utils to him. Therefore, Jerry ends up with a net gain of 4 utils for a total of 35 and Mary ends up with a net gain of 3 utils for a total of 34.

MAXIMIZING UTILITY

The principle of *equimarginal utility* states that if the marginal utility experienced from spending the last dollar on one commodity equals the marginal utility experienced from spending the last dollar on another commodity, total utility is maximized.

The marginal utility principle, if properly applied, leads to maximization of individual utility. Though no one actually has an explicit mental table of util values, one nevertheless does operate as if the marginal utility concept were in operation. In describing this behavior we introduce the notion of **equimarginal utility**: the marginal satisfaction you get from spending your last dollar (or penny) on one good just equals the marginal satisfaction you receive spending the last dollar or penny on another good so that total utility is maximized.

Let us give an example. Have you ever seen a child in a candy or grocery store deciding how to allocate his or her candy budget? Assume our friend Mary enters a candy store with 15 cents. She has 14 cents to spend on candy plus 1 cent for the governor.

She finally narrows her choice down to Tootsie Rolls and gumdrops. Tootsie Rolls are priced at 2 cents apiece and gumdrops at 1 cent apiece. Table 4-5 shows her utility schedule.

To maximize utility, the equimarginal principle states that Mary should equate the marginal utility per penny spent on gumdrops to the marginal utility per penny spent on Tootsie Rolls, while staying within her budget. The

TABLE 4-4

Licorice	Jerry's Total Utility	Jerry's Marginal Utility	Bubble Gum	Mary's Total Utility	Mary's Marginal Utility
0	0		0	0	
		10			10
1	10		1	10	
		9			9
2	19		2	19	
		7			7
3	26		3	26	
		5			5
4	31		4	31	

marginal utility from a 2-cent Tootsie Roll equals the marginal utility from a 1-cent gumdrop. In shorthand,

$$\frac{MU_T}{P_T} = \frac{MU_G}{P_G}.$$

TABLE 4-5

Number of units	Total utility: tootsie rolls	Marginal utility: tootsie rolls	Total utility: gum drops	Marginal utility: gum drops
0	0		0	
		9		4
1	9		4	
		8		3
2	17		7	
		6		3
3	23		10	
		5		2
4	28		12	
		4		2
5	32		14	
		3		1
6	35		15	
		2		1
7	37		16	
		2		1
8	39		17	

For five Tootsie Rolls the expenditure is 10 cents. For four gumdrops it is 4 cents. Referring to Table 4-5, we see that

$$\frac{MU_T}{P_T} = \frac{4}{2} \text{ and } \frac{MU_G}{P_G} = \frac{2}{1}.$$

Therefore,

$$\frac{MU_T}{P_T} = \frac{MU_G}{P_G} = \frac{2}{1}.$$

Mary's total utility is 44 utils equal to 32 from consuming 5 Tootsie Rolls plus 12 from consuming 4 gumdrops.

Let us check the other combinations that are within her budget. They yield a smaller total utility and they violate the equimarginal principle. For example, 4 Tootsie Rolls costing 8 cents and 6 gumdrops costing 6 cents yield a total utility of 28 + 15 = 43 utils.

$$\frac{MU_T}{P_T} = \frac{5}{2} \text{ and } \frac{MU_G}{P_G} = \frac{1}{1}.$$

The ratios are not equal. With $MU_T/P_T > MU_G/P_G$ the way to establish equality of the ratios is for Mary to increase her consumption of Tootsie Rolls from 4 to 5 and reduce her consumption of gumdrops from 6 to 4. An important point is that the maximizing rule does not state that the *MU* of both items must be identical. Rather, it says that the *ratio* of the marginal utility per dollar spent on one good must equal the *ratio* of the marginal utility per dollar spent on the other good.

Suppose finals begin next Monday. You must decide how much time to spend on French, math, and economics. To get the highest possible grade average, you should ration your time such that the extra benefit you get from spending the last hour on each of the three subjects is equal. If you are much better at French than math, you will spend less time on French than math, but to the point that the benefit you get per hour on French equals the benefit you get per hour studying math, which in turn both equal the benefit that you will receive per hour studying economics. Doing this maximizes your grade point average.

THE WATER-DIAMOND PARADOX

In the time of Adam Smith (1723-1790), a controversy brewed on the continent. Why was water, which is so useful, so cheap, whereas diamonds, then much less useful, so expensive? Around 1750 Fernando Galiani got close to but did not quite reach the answer, for he stopped just short of the marginal utility concept. Galiani argued that the price was proportional ($\propto$) to the ratio of use to scarcity, that is,

$$\text{Price} \propto \frac{\text{use (utility)}}{\text{scarcity}}.$$

Water was very useful but it was very abundant, hence its price was low. But diamonds, though less useful, were very scarce; hence the relative price of diamonds was higher than that of water.

It was another 120 years before the marginal concept was discovered. The point to remember is that consumers are not choosing to consume a whole reservoir of water or none at all. They are deciding whether to consume only a small quantity of water at a given time. Time is important to understanding the analysis. The individual is not normally negotiating for a certain amount of water for a whole year, but for an amount for a shorter period of time. He is not estimating the total utility of the water in the reservoir, but the marginal (additional) utility of a much smaller amount, maybe a gallon or so, at the moment. It is the value to him of this incremental quantity that helps decide the price he will pay. The exchange price is based on the marginal unit traded. If you have been stranded in the desert and come upon a town of wells owned by a number of Arab businessmen, you are not paying for all the water in the wells. You are negotiating the value of a mere canteenful. You willingly pay a lot for the first canteen. Thereafter, the value of additional canteens of water have declining marginal utility to you, and you will offer to pay less and less for them.

Refer to Figure 4-11. It shows the marginal utility curves for water and diamonds. Recall that the total utility is measured by the area under each marginal utility curve. With all due account taken of the fact that diamonds are in units of carats and water in gallons, we can make a reasonable comparison. Price is proportional to (not equal to) marginal utility, and the marginal utility

Figure 4-11

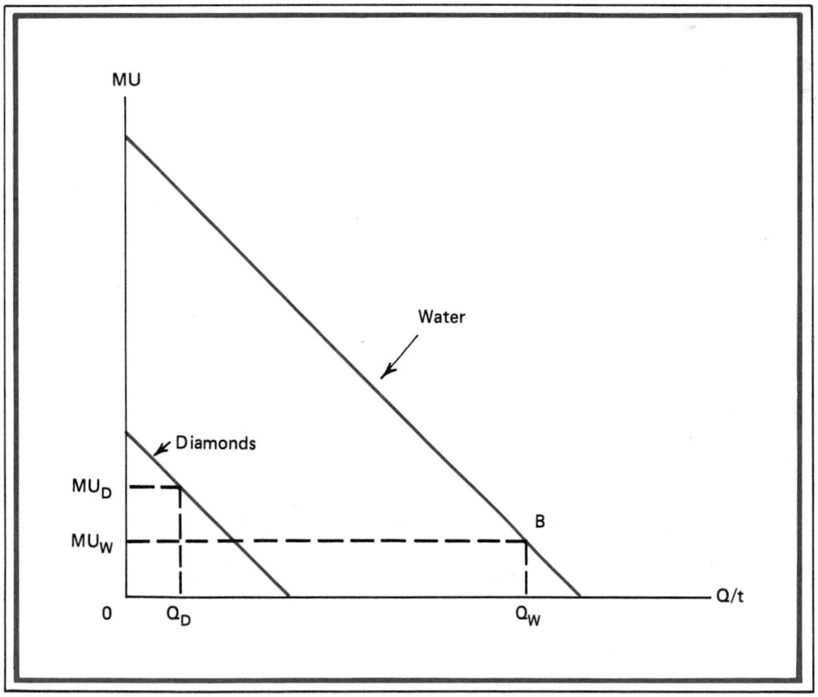

of water at B is low because people consume so much of it that they are not willing to pay much for an additional amount. But diamonds are scarce and expensive. People stop buying them at the amount Q_D where the marginal utility is high, higher than that of the marginal utility of the $Q_W{}^{th}$ unit of water.

ISSUES OF CONCERN

Since utility is the quality a good has by which it satisfies a desire, it is a subjective thing. The question arises, can utility be measured? Would it be possible, for example, for an individual to say that a milkshake has exactly twice the utility of a glass of soda pop? To answer this question, it would be necessary to construct a set of cardinal numbers (1,2,3,. . .) so that a person can say that a glass of soda pop gives him or her 5 utils of satisfaction while a milkshake provides 10 utils. Economists have argued this issue for years. They now believe that, in theory, but under rigid assumptions, one might be able to construct such a set of numbers. But the subject is complex and still unresolved. However, we are lucky. We can derive diminishing marginal utility curves and downward sloping demand curves by ranking individual preferences. That is, we can say that a milkshake is preferred to a glass of soda pop which is in turn preferred to a glass of water. We rank the milkshake first, soda pop second, and water third in an order of preferences. Measuring utility in this fashion, ordinally instead of cardinally, serves us just as well. Therefore, while an absolute measure of a subjective thing like utility is still of concern to theoretical economists, we can proceed with our analysis of demand based on the utility concept.

Besides the measurability question, there is another concern that economists have worried over. It is the question of the indivisibility of a good. In many cases goods that people buy come in discrete units. You cannot always increase your rate of consumption of goods by small increments. The consumption of an additional bag of peanuts is simple enough. But while the buying of a first typewriter costs much more than the first bag of peanuts, its marginal utility is much higher. The ratio of the marginal utility to the price of the second typewriter is lower, and may be lower than the ratio for the second bag of peanuts. The point is that it is not always possible to reach the exact equimarginal point because some goods are not as divisible as others.

Stock is quantity at a given time.

But this may not be a big problem. Unlike a bag of peanuts, an appliance such as a typewriter provides a stream of services into the future. To put it figuratively, the typewriter is not consumed immediately as a bag of peanuts usually is. Therefore, what must be compared are the much smaller packages of consumption spread out over time that the typewriter provides. The typewriter is a **stock**, but it provides a **flow** of services. What should be compared is the marginal utility of the flow, that is, what is the rate of service flow of the typewriter and the corresponding marginal utility of those flows. In this way, the typewriter is divisible and those divisibilities are what is compared to the many bags of peanuts one could have bought over time with the money spent on the purchase of the typewriter.

Flow measures the _change_ in quantity over time.

Figure 4-12

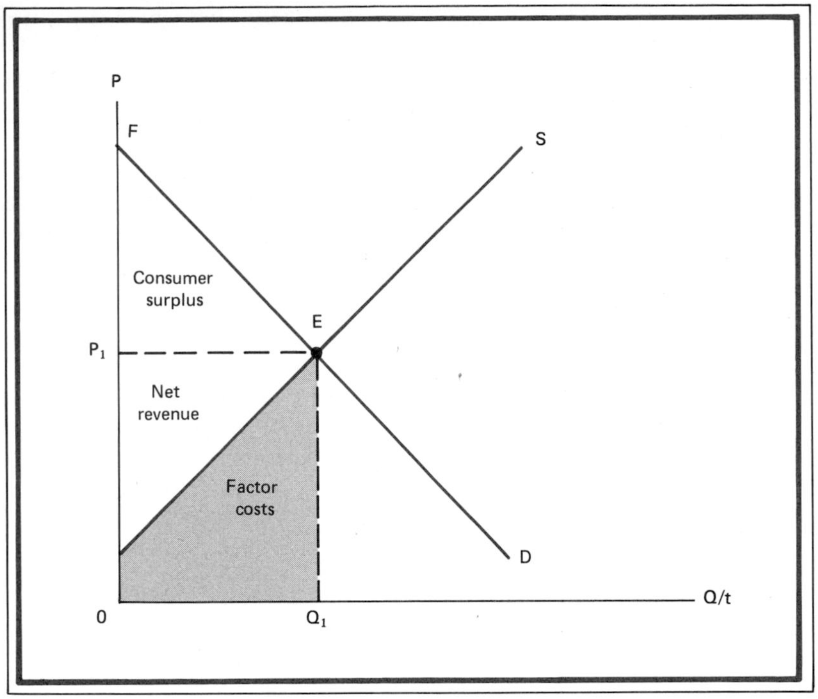

Consumer Surplus

Examine the graph in Figure 4-12. Keep in mind that the supply and demand curves are market curves comprised of many individual suppliers and many buyers. They are aggregate curves. Equilibrium occurs at a market clearing price of P_1, where $Q_s = Q_d = Q_1$. What does the segment of the demand curve above E to F mean? It signifies that there are many consumers who would have been willing to pay a higher price than P_1 to obtain the commodity. For example, suppose $20 is the tuition price per hour to take dancing classes. There are people who would have been willing to pay more than $20 per hour, but because they only have to pay $20, they actually receive a gain, a surplus. This is referred to as a *consumer surplus*. Those people who would have only been willing to pay $20 and end up paying $20 are right at the margin of the benefit they receive from taking the dancing class and what it costs them. Their consumer surplus is zero. For people who are not willing to pay $20 an hour, they fall at a point below E on the market demand curve. Hence, they consume no dancing lessons.

People who would have been willing to pay more than $20, but do not, can spend the money they saved by consuming goods and services they would not otherwise have bought. This represents a real benefit to them. Some receive greater gains than others. The person who would have paid $30 an hour, receives more gain than one whose *reservation* price was only $25 an hour. The *reservation* price is the maximum amount a consumer would pay and beyond which he will not go. The total market value of the consumer surplus is measured by the shaded area confined by FEP_1.

REVENUES AND EXPENSES

Factor costs are the cost of bidding away resources from alternative uses.

Figure 4-12 contains additional information. If $Q_1 = 1000$ and lessons are sold per month at $P_1 = \$20$ per lesson, then the total revenue to the industry is $P_1 \times Q_1 = 20 \times 1000 = \$20{,}000$ a month. The gross revenue is represented by the rectangular area P_1EQ_10. But to get net revenue or producer surplus P_1EG, the shaded area $0GEQ_1$ indicating factor costs must be subtracted from total revenue. **Factor costs** are payments to inputs like dancing instructors, heating fuel, electricity, as well as payments that have to be made even when no lessons are given at all, called fixed or overhead costs, like rent, license fees, and equipment that depreciates whether it is used or not. Factor costs are part of the costs of being in business; they are the cost of bidding away resources from alternative uses. More details about these topics will be developed in later chapters.

CHAPTER SUMMARY

Price elasticity of demand is another term for *stretch* or *responsiveness*. A cord has elasticity if when it is pulled it stretches, and when it is released it returns to its original length. If price is changed, how much does the quantity bought change? The elasticity coefficient answers this question for us. The coefficient is the percentage change in quantity divided by the percentage change in price (with a minus sign added).

If the coefficient of elasticity is less than 1, demand is said to be inelastic. If it equals 1, demand is unitary elastic. And if it is greater than 1, demand is elastic.

Revenues flowing to sellers of a good may either increase or decrease as prices change. If demand is price elastic, the quantity bought will increase when the price falls, and total revenue will go up. When the price rises, less is bought and total revenue will decline. If demand is price inelastic, the quantity bought will increase when the price falls but total revenue will decline. And when the price rises, less will be bought but total revenue will increase. If revenues do not change with a change in price, the demand is unitary elastic.

The concept of elasticity is applicable to the supply curve as well. The elasticity of supply measures the responsiveness of the quantity supplied to changes in the price of the good.

Marginal utility means that as a consumer increases the consumption of a good, the addition to his satisfaction will diminish. That is, marginal utility is the increment in utility that accompanies an increment in the consumption of the good. The increments in utility become smaller and smaller as more of a good is consumed. This is the principle of diminishing marginal utility.

Because marginal utility diminishes as consumption increases, there comes a point where the consumer is unwilling to spend any more money on that particular good.

According to the equimarginal principle, in order to maximize a utility a consumer will have to allocate the money from a budget in such a fashion that the ratios of the marginal utilities of the various goods to their respective prices are all equal to each other.

Consumer surplus is a measure of the difference between the amount consumers would be willing to pay, as a reflection of the utility they receive, and the amount they actually pay for a commodity.

QUESTIONS

1. The elasticity of demand for color television sets is less than the elasticity for RCA color television sets, which is less than the elasticity of demand for small, portable RCA color television sets. Do you agree? Why, or why not?
2. "Medical care is a necessity, right? Therefore the price elasticity of demand for it is perfectly inelastic. After all, there is no substitute for medical care." Comment. After you answer the questions, refer to problem 1 of Chapter 3.
3. Subway prices in Washington, D.C. are raised from 40 cents to 55 cents during rush hour, and revenues during rush hour increase. What does this tell you about the demand for subway rides during rush hours?
4. Some people argue that even if lawyers advertise prices and no-fault insurance becomes the law, lawyers will simply raise their fees to make up for the lost revenue resulting from fewer accident cases going to court. What is being assumed about the demand for lawyers' services here?
5. What arguments can you make against someone who says that there is only so much land and the use of it is perfectly inelastic in demand?
6. Why are such commodities as tobacco and liquor heavily taxed? Does this mean that taxes on them can keep going up, *ceteris paribus*? Why not?
7. "It appears to us that higher taxes on gasoline at this time for highway building is not a wise move, because people are being encouraged to use less gasoline. How can you plan to raise more money on a product that is declining in demand?" Comment.
8. A local sports writer is quoted as saying, "Our team charges higher prices for baseball tickets than any other team in the majors. One reason it's necessary is that we have more outdoor recreational opportunities available to us than do baseball fans of many other cities. Thus, we have to charge higher prices." Some facts: The team never sold out the stadium for any game during the past season. All of the expensive box seats were sold out before the season started.
   a. Would you accept the sports writer's reason for the higher price of the tickets? Comment.
   b. Would the above facts suggest the price of box seats was too high? Explain.
   c. Was the team not maximizing revenues by charging prices for general admission seats that did not fill the stadium? Explain.
9. Mary could just as easily go to an opera, a jazz, symphonic, or rock concert. Jane only likes rock concerts. Who has the greater elasticity of demand for rock concerts? Why?
10. You are given the following data (*Forbes*, July 15, 1975, p. 13):

1969 price	1976 price (est.)	
$ 2,500	64,800	1925 Rolls Royce roadster
650	3,650	1953 Studebaker hardtop
2,500	7,909	1958 Ford Thunderbird
19,500	98,496	1931 Cadillac V–16 convertible

   a. Why has the price gone up?
   b. What can you say about the elasticity or supply of these cars? Why?

11. "The elasticity of demand for food is perfectly inelastic. After all, you need to eat." Do you agree? Why, or why not?
12. How do brown lawns during a water shortage indicate that the demand for water is not perfectly price inelastic during a dry spell when households are charged proportionately much higher prices per gallon as more water is used?
13. No matter how much water you use out of your tap, the price per gallon the public utility charges you is the same. What does this tell you about the elasticity of supply of water as you see it? Why?
14. Suppose a grocery store sold 200 packs of cigarettes a day when the price was 50 cents a pack and sold 195 packs a day when the price rose to 60 cents a pack. Calculate the price elasticity of demand for cigarettes sold by that store? (Use modified elasticity.) Is it elastic or inelastic? Would revenues from selling cigarettes have risen or fallen?
15. In 1941, when the U.S. entered World War II, it took Kaiser Shipyards 245 days to build the first liberty ship. At the end of a year it took them 4 days to build a liberty ship. What can you say happened to the elasticity of supply of liberty ships? Why?
16. Which of the following are examples of increasing marginal utility or decreasing marginal utility?
    a. "Smoking more but enjoying it less."
    b. "The more the merrier."
    c. "Two's company, three's a crowd."
    d. "His eyes were bigger than his stomach."
17. Newspapers run daily ads for people wanting to give away pets for free. What does this tell you about:
    a. The marginal utility of the buyer of the ad for keeping an additional pet?
    b. The marginal utility of pet destruction to the buyer of the ad?
    c. The marginal utility of a pet to the average reader?
    d. Are your answers to a and c consistent with the datum that the pets are offered at a zero price?
18. In equilibrium the price of a commodity equals the marginal utility of consuming that good. Do you agree?
19. A presidential candidate intends to campaign for election in the last four states remaining along the campaign trail. He or she has $480,000 left in the budget. How should the candidate allocate these campaign funds in order to maximize the num-

	State A (6 million voters)	**State B (1.5 million voters)**	**State C (5 million voters)**	**State D (2 million voters)**
Expenditures (thousand $)	**Voters (millions)**	**Voters (millions)**	**Voters (millions)**	**Voters (millions)**
$ 0	.35	.17	1.10	.250
40	1.00	.47	1.60	.450
80	1.50	.67	2.00	.550
120	1.90	.77	2.30	.630
160	2.20	.85	2.50	.700
200	2.40	.92	2.60	.760
240	2.55	.98	2.68	.810
280	2.65	1.03	2.75	.850
320	2.78	1.07	2.81	.880
360	2.84	1.10	2.86	.900
400	2.93	1.12	2.90	.910
440	2.97	1.13	2.93	.915
480	3.00	1.135	2.95	.918

ber of popular votes? The table at the bottom of p. 132 relates the dollar expenditures to the expected number of votes in each state.

20. George likes the outdoors and lives in a cabin in the forest during the summer. Jerry also likes the outdoors and goes hiking every weekend during the summer.
    a. Who most likely has the higher total utility for the outdoors? Why?
    b. Which one most likely has the higher ratio of marginal utility to total utility for the outdoors? Why?
21. Assume the market price of a paperback is $1. If Sandra buys 4 books, she then values the 5th book at $1. Suppose Sandra's ratio of utility to price is 4 to 1. What is Sandra's total utility from buying 5 books? What is the marginal utility to her of the 5th book? Her consumer surplus in utils? In dollars?

Utils	8	7	6	5	4	3
P	$2.00	1.75	1.50	1.25	1.00	.75
Q_d	1	2	3	4	5	6

22. "I'll get whatever brand they have since I don't have time to shop around." What can you say about elasticity of demand here? Explain.
23. Children can be very fussy about what they eat. As people grow older they often like the very same foods they did not like as a child. In what way does this reflect a change in elasticity for particular foods?
24. You can be sure the elasticity of demand for sugar is less than for bicycles. Do you agree?

Chapter 5

Cost

PROGRESS REPORT

A. In Chapter 2, we discussed at length the concept of opportunity cost because it is fundamental to the understanding of economic efficiency. We extended our discussion of cost in Chapter 3, and it gave us the supply function we used in analyzing demand and supply. In Chapter 4 we applied elasticity not only to demand but also to supply.

B. This chapter carries the concept of cost a little farther, particularly where a long-lived asset is concerned. We shall find that the time period over which an asset is consumed is an important factor in determining costs. We shall also find that money expenditures do not necessarily equal real costs in many instances. Various classifications of costs are explained. The concepts of fixed and variable costs that are associated with production are discussed, and the difference between relevant and irrelevant production costs is examined.

C. In Chapter 6 the classification of costs, their calculation, and their curves specifically associated with production will be discussed.

Economist J. M. Clark stated two commonly used definitions of cost.[1] The first, "Cost in the alternative sense records the unfavorable side of any given decision which may be made, and always involves a comparison between the policy that was chosen and the policy that was rejected." The second, "Cost in the absolute sense records all diminution of assets." These may seem like quite different definitions, one about choice and one about assets. But it turns out that there is no incompatibility between them once it is understood what an asset is, and once explicit consideration of time is introduced.

DEFINITIONS OF COST

Definition 1

***Cost* is the value of the highest-valued currently-sacrificed alternative associated with a decision.**

As previously defined, **Cost** *is the value of the highest valued currently sacrificed alternative associated with a decision.*

When a choice is made from a set of possible opportunities, a cost is incurred. Time, human resources, and physical resources are scarce. Doing or using one thing means there is less time that can be devoted to something else, or means doing without *that* other thing now or later on because we decide to do *this* thing now. Choice always involves a cost. Cost is determined by the highest-valued option foreclosed on by enacting a decision. Recall the example about deciding whether to watch television or study for tomorrow's exam. Add in the additional option of playing touch football in the nearby playground. If you opt for the playfield you do not sacrifice *both* studying for the exam and watching the game on television. The cost you incur by acting on the decision to frolic on the playfield is the value of whichever alternative was most valuable to you. The cost is either the points lost on the exam because of insufficient studying or the satisfaction of watching the game on television. However, if there were no televised game or no exam the next day, the cost of working up a sweat on the playfield is not the same. Furthermore, if a friend joined you at the playground, the cost to him might be different than the cost to you. Maybe he was supposed to meet his girl friend at the library. Therefore, when evaluating the cost of a decision you must ask yourself, "The cost of doing what, when, and from whose viewpoint."

Terms in common use such as *cost* often carry many meanings. In economics, commonly used terms are defined more narrowly to mean something quite specific. This is done so that the logic of analysis can be more precise. If you go to Nevada and lose a lot of money on gambling you are inclined to say "that trip really cost me a lot of bread." Your partner in conversation understands perfectly well that the statement means that you lost at gambling—not that the expenses of your trip were high. Suppose your friend went sailing yesterday, and from failure to secure a backstay properly, the boat's wooden mast was broken when a gust of wind blew up—a "costly" sail, he might say.

[1]John M. Clark: Studies in the Economics of Social Overhead Costs (Chicago: University of Chicago Press, 1923), p. 39.

A *windfall loss* is an unexpected cost.

In cases like these the economist would prefer to say that you and your friend suffered windfall losses. A **windfall loss** is an unanticipated cost. The expected cost of sailing the boat might have been the screen door that could have been put in at home. But when the mast broke, the cost of going sailing turned out to result in a cost greater than expected, hence a windfall loss was incurred. The difference between the actual cost and the anticipated cost is an additional cost and a windfall loss. The actual cost is higher because replacing the mast means sacrificing consuming other goods in addition to not putting in the screen door.

These examples for the most part were situations where the full costs were essentially incurred when the decisions were made since the decisions were acted upon shortly thereafter. They were analyzed in the context of definition 1.

Definition 2

Cost in the absolute sense records all diminution of assets.

The government employs many accountants in the Department of Commerce whose job it is to classify all transactions that take place in the economy over the year. They measure the value of all consumer and capital goods that are produced as well as the value of all services provided, like haircuts and television repairs, down to the last possible dollar. Every item in the economy is put into its precisely defined slot. They distinguish between consumer nondurable and durable goods, and capital goods. **Consumer nondurable goods** are those lasting for less than a year, for example perishable goods like food, and nonfood items such as socks, nylons, or pencils. **Commodities** lasting a year or more are called either **consumer durables** or **capital goods**. Consumer durables are items like cars, washing machines, and home furniture. Capital goods are most things that firms use as inputs in production such as buildings and equipment. However, a car owned by a firm is classified as a capital good, not as a consumer good. These are arbitrary classifications. For this discussion we shall treat all commodities as assets.

Consumer nondurable goods are those commodities that last for less than a year; *commodities* that last for a year or more are either *consumer durables* or *capital goods.*

Assets *are property rights of ownership that embody claims on future streams of services or of income* the asset yields. An asset is a *stock* and the services or income streams it provides is a **flow**, as described in the Appendix. Thus, a car provides a chain of services (rides) over many years. A bond provides a flow of annual income until it matures. This time dimension of an asset requires us to be much more careful when talking about the concept of *opportunity cost,* or simply *cost,* especially when we speak of the cost of a capital good as contrasted with the cost of a consumption good.

An asset represents property rights to a stock which yields a chain of services or of incomes called *flows.*

Outlays versus Costs

Money outlays or money expenditures do not necessarily equal full cost. At any time you may own a stock of assets. You may lay legal claim to a car, a house, clothes, books, the food in your refrigerator. Some of these assets will last a very long time. When you buy a car, a boat, a fur coat, or a bond with some of that cash you have, your wealth or your asset level has not changed. What has changed is your asset portfolio, namely the form in which you have chosen to hold that level of wealth. If Sal the salesman buys a boat for $20,000 his wealth position is unchanged; he has merely substituted a financial asset, cash, with a physical asset, the boat. His wealth position is the same because he has not diminished the level of his asset position, that is, his wealth, but only the form in which he is holding it. In business terms, he has adjusted or diversified his portfolio. The number of eggs you own is not altered by keeping them in one basket or putting them in several baskets. Therefore, the expenditure of $20,000 need not immediately involve any cost so long as Sal could turn around and resell the boat for $20,000. The $20,000 apparently foregone can be retrieved. There is every possibility he could decide to keep the boat for a year and then sell it for $19,000. Even if the boat had never moved from its moorage, the cost of possessing the boat for one year is $1,000, and only that amount, because that is how much Sal reduced the level of his wealth, other things remaining constant. So long as the boat can be resold at a later date and is still useful, he continues to have options at each moment in the future; that is, he can continue to sacrifice the remaining chain of alternatives so long as he keeps the boat. Unlike the apple that was eaten upon purchase, the full benefits of the boat are not fully consumed at purchase; they are spread out over the depreciated life of the boat.[2] Money outlays are not necessarily costs, because there may still be residual alternatives ahead. In the case of the apple, its services are immediately consumed. The time element between the buying and the eating of the apple is so short that expenditures on it are nearly simultaneous with costs.

Suppose Sal works on the West Coast for a large national firm. Because he expects to remain on the Coast, he bought the boat with the intention of keeping it over at least its depreciated life. But Sal is transferred to the dry flatlands of Kansas where there is little opportunity to sail a boat. Ignoring inflation effects, assume the market value of the boat a year later is $19,000, having depreciated by $1,000. The highest valued forgone alternative of owning the boat from that time forward would be the alternative stream of income or services he could now purchase with the $19,000. On the other hand, had he *intended* to sell the boat after one year, the cost of purchasing and using the boat is the value of other things he might have acquired and held for one year. For example, he could have spent his $20,000 on a bond yielding 10 percent annually. In this case he would have sacrificed $2,000 (.10 × 20,000) by owning the boat for one year. Thus, on the occasion of buying the boat, the projected full opportunity cost of holding the boat over the next year would include $2,000 sacrificed in interest plus $1,000 in depreciation for a total of $3,000. Of course, a year later this $3,000 is no longer an opportunity cost of owning the boat. It lies in the past. It has been incurred. The opportunity cost of owning the boat a year later is, once again, the value of the alternative streams of services or of money income that the $19,000 boat, if sold, could bring in the future. Since the salesman chose to hold the boat for one year and it cost him $3,000 in forgone alternatives over that year, he must have planned to obtain at *least* $3,000 worth of utility from owning it.

[2]Depreciation is the decrease in value (price) of an asset because of physical deterioration, destruction, or obsolescence. An allowance is made for it in bookkeeping and accounting. Obsolescence results when new, technologically superior assets make the old asset worth less.

Reconciling Definitions 1 and 2

Given what has been said, the two definitions of cost quoted from J. M. Clark are not two conflicting definitions at all, but really one definition once we realize that many assets are not completely consumed immediately. The time period is crucial. Cost is measured by the price of the highest-valued alternative currently forsaken as in definition 1. But as time goes by, if only part of the asset is consumed it still retains some value, though it is a diminished value, as in definition 2. Consequently, the choice to continue to use the asset's services in the future means you intend currently to sacrifice what is perceived to be the value of those future sacrificed alternatives as you estimate their value today.[3] With long-lived assets, the opportunity costs—the highest valued sacrifices—still lie in the future. But as you hold the asset over time and consume its flows (services), the value of the asset declines as you use up more alternatives associated with the asset's lifetime flows. Thus are Clark's two definitions of cost reconciled.

Utility and Cost

If you were to compare consuming $4 worth of entertainment at the movies with banking $4 and earning interest over the period of a year, you would be comparing apples to oranges. A common measure is lacking. If you choose to go to the movie, the dollar value you place on the satisfaction you get from attending the movie must be worth more to you than the interest earned from saving the money. You do choose to go to the movie; to give a logical answer to the problem posed, we assume that the marginal utility of going to the movie was no less than, say, 4.04 cents. Otherwise you would not have gone to the movie. Thus, it is again emphasized, in discussing costs there are different kinds of problems and purposes that must be sorted out for which we need different kinds of information about the forgone alternatives, that is, the costs. For this reason cost is measured by the value of the *highest* valued currently forsaken opportunity of a decision that is acted upon.

When Outlays Are Costs

It is a hot day and you spend 30 cents for an ice cream cone instead of a bottle of soda you were also considering. What was the cost of the ice cream cone? That depends on whether you have eaten the cone or not. But you rise up in protest. How long is an ice cream cone going to last in the hot sun? Once you put down your 30 cents, there's no turning back. You immediately assumed a 30-cent cost represented by avoiding the consumption of a 30-cent soda! In practical terms you are right. But we insist on being perfectly consistent and logical with our definitions of cost. A cost is only experienced when you actually eat the cone. Suppose you could have put it in the home freezer and sold it to your sister

[3]The method of determining the cost or value today of a chain of events that will incur costs or confer benefits in the future is called the method of *present value*. It will be discussed in Chapter 14.

later. There was no cost in the *purchasing* of the cone (assuming transactions costs are zero). There are still options open to you so long as it has not been eaten; there is still a possibility of resale, so the value of your asset position is unchanged. You can still avoid the loss of subsequent choices by not eating the frozen cone, and reselling it. Of course, there certainly are circumstances where a direct expenditure is a cost even when applying our definition of cost with merciless and humorless rigor. Have you ever deposited a coin in a machine to weigh yourself or to have your aching feet vibrated? The time period between the decision to drop the coin in the machine and the desired event itself is for all practical purposes zero. The cost is thereby incurred immediately.

SUNK COSTS

A *sunk cost* is an expenditure made in the past and is not an opportunity cost because it represents no current alternative.

When discussing the boat example, we argued that the opportunity cost of owning a $20,000 boat for one year is the sacrificed interest of $2,000 if buying a bond were the highest-valued alternative. But when the market value of the boat a year later is $19,000, what does the $1,000 represent? A cost? No. Not a year later. Costs are only currently sacrificed alternatives. A year later the $1,000 represents no cost at all, for it represents no current option. It is a thing of the past, history, a bygone. It is called a **sunk cost**. The fact that you paid $20,000 for the boat and its market value is only $19,000 a year later only tells you that $1,000 no longer represents an opportunity cost. The $1,000 is history and should have no effect on your current decision to sell or retain the boat. The opportunity cost is what you sacrifice now by not selling the boat for $19,000. At the moment you bought the boat, you estimated the opportunity cost as being $3,000 for the coming year when you included the forgone interest, because this represented the total value of your future sacrifices. If you made the right decision, you received at least $3,000 worth of value during the year. As far as you were concerned you put the $20,000 to its best use, at least for a year. As we said, when dealing with long-lived assets, direct expenditures do not immediately involve costs identical to those expenditures for two reasons. First, costs are measured by the alternatives passed up only over the period of time you *intend* to possess the asset. Second, you can change your mind later and sell the asset at its secondhand market value. What you cannot recover is sunk and is no longer an opportunity cost.

You bought the boat for $20,000 and a year later you can sell it for $19,000. The $1,000 you cannot recover is a sunk cost and not an opportunity cost since it represents no alternative that you can avoid losing in the future through a choice made today. Yesterday's opportunity cost is today's sunk cost. All past costs are sunk costs. A sunk boat implies $20,000 in sunk costs.

When Cost Equals Sunk Cost

To drive home the cost definitions to their logical conclusions, take the example of putting a 5-cent piece in a machine to weigh yourself. The interval between the outlay of 5 cents and the act of consuming the services of the machine is essentially zero. With time so collapsed, the division between sunk cost and opportunity cost disappears. Once the nickel is deposited it is sunk. Simultaneously you also sacrifice the highest-valued alternative that was available to you, because you cannot resell or renegotiate the weighing of yourself. Hence, in this instance the cost and the sunk cost are both 5 cents and occur simultaneously and instantaneously.

There are no costs when there is no scarcity, for if there is no scarcity then nothing is sacrificed when one thing is chosen over another. Nor would there be a cost if a machine, for instance, had no other function than it has in its current use. Nothing is sacrificed by using a machine that is so specialized in its use that it cannot be used to do anything else. Yet again, even in this special case, the original decision to build the machine does have a cost. It is another situation where opportunity cost and sunk cost are immediately equal to one another. However, this statement is not quite true if the metal composing the totally obsolete machine has scrap value. Then the machine's opportunity cost is not quite zero: it is the scrap value. The effective sunk cost is the original price minus the scrap price. An opportunity cost always exists when an alternative is still available to you, for then any decision you make means forfeiting one of the alternatives. In this sense, opportunity costs reflect current options as they are now perceived. But a decision made in the past is irreversible, hence sunk costs should have no bearing on the cost of the decision now facing you. Only opportunity costs are the relevant costs.

The Boat Case Revisited

It might occur to you that it was not necessary to pass up the use of $20,000 by using it to buy the boat. Sal can borrow $20,000, purchase the boat, and at the same time spend his own $20,000 on a summer cottage. Nothing was currently sacrificed to get the boat because he got the cottage too. But there is still a cost. The loan must be repaid in the future. At such time he will have to reduce his consumption below what it would have been had he not received the loan. But, you might respond, can he not refinance the cottage, that is, borrow against the cottage using it as collateral to, say, buy a new car? Why can he not simply continue to use assets, for the acquisition of which he has already borrowed money, as collateral against making loans to acquire even more assets? Where is the opportunity cost? Where are the sacrificed alternatives? The sunk costs? He is getting it all now, isn't he?

This reasoning denies something quite important—transactions costs. The banks will charge high rates of interest to refinance a car or house. Sal might even be denied a loan when the lender sees how thin he is spread. Also, a point is reached when the future consumption that has to be sacrificed to live high now may become too great for Sal to want to do it.

An Implicit Cost, not a Profit

Sometimes what a businessman calls a profit is really a cost.

***Explicit business costs* are direct outlays that do not include implicit opportunity costs.**

Take the situation of a person who owns and runs a small gasoline station or garage. His costs per year represent what are required to bid these resources from other uses. These direct outlays are often referred to as **explicit business costs**. They could be the following:

Rental of property	$ 3,600
Utilities and taxes	300
Hired help	10,000
Equipment depreciation	2,000
Miscellaneous	1,000
	$16,900

As seen by an accountant, the owner's total annual costs are $16,900. But to an economist some costs are being left out, namely, some opportunity costs that are not explicitly included in the list. First of all, his own salary may be largely a cost and not a profit. Should he be able to earn $20,000 a year managing a station for someone else or working for another garage as a mechanic, this would represent his opportunity cost—an implicit cost—of running his own business instead. Thus, his forgone salary is a measure of the cost of choosing to run his own station and should be added to the $16,900.

In addition, if he had invested $30,000 of his own money in the business, and the local credit union is paying 6 percent on a savings deposit, there is $1,800 (.06 × 30,000) in forgone interest. This, too, is an implicit cost that should be added in order to estimate the full opportunity costs. Thus, to the explicit money outlays of $16,900 we add $20,000 in implicit wage costs and another $1,800 in implicit interest costs, for a total of $38,700. If the business takes in less than this amount it is losing, and if it takes in more it is making a profit.

As another example, take a couple who own their house free and clear. What is the cost to them of living in their home for another year? The cost would be what the highest valued alternative is, namely, what would they collect in rent if they did not live in their house. Or, it might be what they could earn by selling the house and earning interest on the income from the sale. The highest-valued of these possibilities is the opportunity cost, because the choice remains open to them of changing their current situation. So long as a course of action remains as an available option, an alternative can be sacrificed, hence there is an opportunity cost involved. If someone says to you, "I own my home, so it doesn't cost me anything to live there," he has neglected to recognize the opportunity cost of living in his home.

Production Costs

Up to now we have taken a very broad but fundamental approach to costs. All real economic costs are opportunity costs, but many subclassifications can be made. We have discussed sunk costs, explicit costs, and implicit costs. These several common classifications of cost are narrowly defined for certain purposes.

Some costs are directly associated with production activities. Consider the man or woman who owns a factory that manufactures aluminum pots and

Fixed costs (overhead costs) are the contractual commitments to make payments over a designated time period whether there is production or not.

pans. The owner is said to face **fixed costs** after the plant with its machines and inventories are purchased. These costs continue to flow even though the plant is idle, that is, there are fixed costs of production even when no production occurs.

Other examples of fixed costs are interest on borrowed funds, property taxes, rental payments if the property is leased, and any other commitments to make payments embodied in fixed contractual agreements applying over some designated period of time. In common business language, fixed costs are often called **overhead costs.**

Variable costs are the *operating costs* of producing output.

Variable costs are costs associated only with the production of output. Fundamentally, these are opportunity costs just like any real cost. When the decision to produce is acted upon, workers must be hired, materials and utilities purchased. The greater the output, the greater the variable costs. Variable costs include what businessmen call **operating costs**. In the case of a boat, the more it is used the greater the variable costs for fuel, oil, and wear and tear.

In reality it is not always easy to separate fixed from variable costs. Some salaried executives and some production workers are guaranteed an annual wage whether the company produces anything or not. Yet the firm would not usually hire these workers if it were not in production. Therefore, when it does go into production, how much of the wage bill is a fixed cost and how much is not? It is hard to say. Some wage costs that seem to be variable are, in fact, more or less fixed.

It is also the case that some costs that seem to be fixed can be variable to an extent. When a farmer buys a tractor for $15,000 and sells it two years later for $12,000, the $3,000 fixed cost is unavoidable to a great degree. But if the tractor had been used less and had only 20,000 miles on the odometer instead of 30,000, then it might have been resold for $13,000 and the fixed cost would have been $2,000. As a practical matter, what a business accountant considers fixed and what he considers to be variable depends on the particular situation.

Marginal Cost

Marginal costs involve changes in total variable costs related to changes in output.

An especially common and important cost concept is **marginal cost**. When production decisions are being made, they do not normally involve all-or-nothing decisions. Instead, they are made at the margin: more or less of this, more or less of that. As we saw in Chapters 3 and 4, the supply curve is really a marginal cost curve. It can measure the additional cost of producing an additional unit or an additional batch. Thus marginal cost involves a decision about additional production and is therefore a variable cost; is also an opportunity cost since current sacrifice is involved. Marginal costs are actually changes in variable costs. In the sailboat example, marginal costs are the change in the level of total variable costs to Sal in deciding, say, to deliver some goods to destination A. But suppose Sal decides to go on to deliver other goods to destination B. Then there is a marginal cost which is made up of the additional costs that Sal incurs when he goes from A to B. However, if before leaving for destination A Sal knew he would also be stopping at destination B, the marginal cost of stopping at A and B calculated as a single trip might be quite different from that of planning to go to port A, then only later deciding to go to port B.

KINDS OF COSTS

There are many different kinds of costs, because different practitioners use different terminologies for different situations. When discussing production *per se* the traditional concepts of fixed and variable costs are useful. Economists, accountants, and businessmen often disagree on cost terminology and government often mixes in its own jargon. Our list of types of costs is suggestive but not definitive. In interpreting cost information it is important to keep in mind the costs for what purpose, from what viewpoint, at what point in time, and over what time period. To avoid confusion, you and others with whom you are talking must first make clear the meanings of the terms and associated concepts that are to apply. Suggestive pairings are as follows:

Sunk costs	Fixed, overhead, and depreciation—costs incurred in the past that are not recoverable.
Opportunity costs	Variable, operating, explicit, and implicit—costs you can decide to incur or not to incur as you make choices.

Short Run and Long Run

There was mention of momentary, short, and long periods above and in Chapter 4. The momentary period is so short that the supply curve is vertical; output is fixed. The short and long run, though associated with clock time, do not truly refer to clock time. They are operational definitions. The short run signifies that some factor or factors are fixed. What that translates into in actual clock time depends on the industry under review. There is no single absolute measure of time that separates the short from the long run. What is the short run for the steel industry may be much longer in chronological time than the short run for the hamburger stand business. Factors that are fixed in the short run would be things like the size and number of buildings and the type of equipment installed. Demand might increase, but existing space and capacity cannot be quickly expanded. Of course, output can be stepped up by using the existing facilities more intensively. The long run is defined as that period over which all factors become variable. There are no fixed factors. It is possible in the longer period for the factory to be expanded or a new one built. New, more efficient machinery can replace the older, obsolete machinery, and so on. However, in the long run all costs are viewed as opportunity costs.

Fish or Cut Bait

A large oil company recently purchased a $10 million oil tanker. It is deciding whether to use it to ship a cargo of oil worth $250,000 from Saudi Arabia to the U.S. Given that the cost of the oil, the ship's fuel, the merchant seamen salaries, docking fees, and cargo insurance is $100,000 for the trip, should the tanker

Tina McToaster

A college student, Tina McToaster, rents a room in a large house where other renters share the kitchen facilities. Needing a little extra income, she decides to go into business on the side by purchasing an $8.00 electric but nonautomatic toaster and charging 5 cents to toast a slice of bread for the other renters. She intends to use it for four years, until she graduates. The opportunity cost could be the interest she could have earned in four years on the $8 if she had put it in a bank or, if the alternative were better, the returns from a second-hand mixer had she sold milkshakes instead. She decides the toaster is the best use of the $8. She should also include the depreciation she expects on the value of the toaster over the four years.

Were she to change her mind one year later and sell the toaster for $3, the sunk cost would be $5 plus the interest foregone on $8 for one year. Were she not to sell it, the opportunity cost would be the $3 that could have been recovered by selling the toaster; to be more specific, it would be what she sacrifices by not selling the toaster for $3 at this time.

Now examine the four-year situation using the more narrow classification of costs as it applies to production. In the short run the fixed cost is $8. What are her variable costs? They are whatever she buys in bread plus the electrical costs on the toaster, assuming it is metered.

The total cost equals the fixed costs plus the variable cost. She charges 5 cents a slice, with her variable costs being 3 cents a slice. She is covering her variable costs. If she were not covering her variable costs of 3 cents a slice, she should shut down and minimize her losses. As it is she is making a net of 2 cents a slice. In the long run she has to sell at least 400 slices to cover her total costs (the toaster, bread, and electricity). Actually, since the toaster is nonautomatic she will probably burn some bread, so she will have to sell over 400 slices. But there is another item. If she had put the $8 in the bank for four years at 6 percent she should have earned about $1.56 in interest. So she has to sell additional slices to cover the return on investment, for that is an opportunity cost of running the business.

But that is not all. There is the possibility that she could have chosen to live in another household where she could have been hired as a toastmaker using someone else's toaster. Her wages doing that should be added to total costs (toaster, bread, electricity, salary, and return on the investment). We have now included the full long-run opportunity costs of her going into business.

Suppose Tina covers her total costs in two years plus a small profit. She sells the toaster for $1. With two years to go before graduating she purchases an automatic toaster for $14. She can lower the price on the toast because she no longer has to cover any losses from burning toast, and can use her time for other things since there is no need to keep an eye out for smoke. Because of the technological superiority of the automatic toaster, her short-run supply curve for toast has shifted to the right. The price of toast falls as the marginal and average cost of toasting bread has fallen in the long run, when the old toaster is no longer considered as a fixed factor. The new toaster is, however, a fixed factor over the next two years.

make the trip? That depends on the costs and the revenues involved. If you think the costs are $10 million and the revenue $250,000, then you are arguing the company is running this operation at a loss. But you would be including costs that are not relevant to this particular trip. The $10 million paid for the ship should not affect the decision to transport the cargo; the relevant costs are the $100,000 in variable or marginal costs. The revenue from delivering the oil is $250,000. Hence, the company makes a profit of $150,000. This net revenue goes toward defraying other costs the company has incurred, such as the fixed cost of the ship. If the ship makes enough of these profitable runs, it will pay for all of its costs and then some.

Revenue from delivery	$250,000
Cost of transportation and cargo	100,000
Net revenue used to pay off part of fixed cost	$150,000

In the short run, so long as variable costs or marginal costs are being covered, a firm or operation should stay in business since it is defraying some of its fixed costs. In the long run all costs are variable, and to stay in business a firm must cover both fixed and variable costs. The decision to enter a business requires consideration of the full opportunity costs of that decision at that time. In the short run the fixed costs do not have to be covered. But in the short run if even variable costs are not being covered by current revenues, the firm should shut down altogether; by doing so it minimizes its losses.

CHAPTER SUMMARY

Cost is the value of the highest-valued alternative currently forgone from an action taken.

Historical or past expenditures (sunk costs) are not opportunity costs since they do not represent current alternatives. Such costs are not relevant to current production decisions.

If there are no alternatives there are no opportunity costs.

Expenditures or money outlays do not necessarily indicate the full amount of the opportunity cost at the time the expenditure is made, since assets yield a flow of services (or of income) in the future all of which cannot be instantaneously consumed.

Costs can be deferred by borrowing if transactions costs can be neglected. Even then there are costs (sacrifices) to be faced in the future.

In the short run, some costs are fixed costs because some factors of production are fixed in supply to the producing firm. In the long run, all costs are variable costs because all factors of production can be varied in their use by the firm.

If a firm earns enough revenues to cover its short run variable costs, it remains in production even though it may not cover all of its fixed costs, too. In the long run, of course, it must cover all costs, fixed and variable, or it will cease production.

QUESTIONS

1. If you sign up for 10 skiing lessons for $100 and you miss 1 lesson, what is the cost to you of missing the lesson?
2. The price of canned peaches rises. The store owner does not raise prices on his existing inventory of canned peaches. Is there any cost to him, since he has already paid for his older stock of canned peaches?
3. If the economy is suffering heavy unemployment, is there a cost to society for government programs that employ otherwise unemployable people? Explain.

4. Is the monthly fee you pay for your local telephone calls a fixed or variable cost? What about long distance calls? What about your original choice of having a telephone installed?
5. Amtrak is deciding whether or not to add another passenger car on its Chicago to New York line for one run. Suppose the fixed costs associated with the extra car is $7,000 and it is anticipated that 100 people would use it if tickets are $50. Adding the car would cost the railroad $3,000 in extra fuel, maintenance, yard fees, and cleanup. Should the railroad add the car?
6. A car salesman on television says the bank is breathing down his neck. He has to move his cars fast, so he will give you a "real good deal" on the price. What costs are meaningful here?
7. You see an ad in the newspaper: "1971 Datsun, R/H, AM/FM, rebuilt engine, $300 into it, papers, bluebook is $800. Willing to sell at a loss for $950." Assume the price of the car new was $2,500,
   a. What is the owner's sunk cost if he sells it for $800?
   b. Suppose he sells it for $900, has he incurred a loss?
   c. Suppose he can only sell it to a car lot for $500; has he sold the car at a loss? Why, or why not?
8. It is common for arrested marijuana smugglers caught on ships or planes coming into Florida from South America to jump bail set as high as $200,000. They are usually not caught again. What kind of cost does the bail represent to the smugglers?
9. A tramp ship determines it earns $3 a cubic foot to transport washing machines, which take up 20 cubic feet each. What was the cost of shipping 1,000 of them?
10. When are direct money expenditures considered as costs, and when are they not costs?
11. After several months of going along with other downtown retailers in being open on Sundays, a downtown manager of one of the stores said retailers' sales had not increased. "It only shifted buying patterns from midweek to Sunday. Our costs have gone up but we will continue to stay open on Sunday despite that." Why is the retailer going to keep his store open on Sundays despite no significant increase in sales revenues? Is this problem similar to why taverns have "happy hours"—a period of a few hours one day a week when prices of pitchers of beer are temporarily lowered?
12. On national television March 17, 1976, an anchorman reported on an urban homesteading policy by a city. The city government had ended up owning houses when former owners had abandoned them because the houses were unprofitable and unsalable. Now empty, vandalized, and deteriorating, the houses were offered at $1 on the condition that the buyer repair the house within a year and a half, using a $6,000 city loan to be paid back in 3 years. The homesteader would then become the legal owner. It was costing the city $7 a day to keep the houses. Determine the costs and sunk costs to
    a. The former private owners
    b. The city
    c. Society.
13. You are enrolled in a 5-credit course for a 15-week semester at $18 a credit. If you drop the course before 5 weeks of the semester have passed, you can get a 40 percent refund. Beyond that no refund. Halfway through the semester, you drop the course.
    a. Is the $90 you paid for tuition a sunk or marginal cost?
    b. Suppose you drop out after 3 weeks, what are the costs?
    c. Suppose you do not drop the course, and with 5 weeks left in the semester you pass up a morning job for 3 hours at $4 an hour 5 days a week. What are your sunk costs? Your opportunity costs?
    d. Suppose you did take the job? What are the different costs?

14. A woman owns a small Xerox reproduction service shop. She replaces one of the fully depreciated machines with a newer model and sells the old machine for 30 percent of its original price. What are the sunk, opportunity, fixed and variable costs? Also, distinguish between the short and long run as it applies to costs.
15. American Motors sought a $100 million loan. An AMC executive said, "The loan proceeds would be used to help develop new car models over the next several years. It wouldn't be used for operating expenses. We don't need to meet the payroll." What is meant by operating expenses? Should the $100 million loan enter into the retail price of AMC cars? Why, or why not? Under what conditions is the $100 million an opportunity cost?
16. Suppose you paid $5,000 for your car and it depreciates at the rate of $500 a year whether or not it ever leaves the garage. Gasoline, oil, lubrication, and other operating costs amount to 10 cents a mile for every mile it is driven.
    a. What would be the sunk cost of owning the car for 2 years if it were never driven?
    b. After 2 years of never driving the car you sell it for $4,000. What is the opportunity cost? What is the sunk cost if the rate of interest is 10 percent and your highest-valued alternative?
    c. What is the total cost per year and the average cost per mile if you drive the car 8,000 miles the first year and 11,000 miles the second year?
    d. Suppose you drive 1,000 miles on business. Since you end up near where an old friend lives, you decide to detour 100 more miles to see him, chalking it up to a little relaxation. What was the marginal cost of stopping off to see your friend?
    e. Can you calculate the difference between the fixed costs associated with business traveling and the fixed costs in traveling to see your friend?
    f. Suppose you had planned from the start of the trip to include seeing your friend. Could it have made a difference in the marginal cost of the total trip, as compared to the marginal cost of the total trip when visiting your friend was an afterthought? Why?
17. Dentists charge a lot because their education is costly to them. Does this mean that educational costs should determine their fees? In what way do dentists' training costs affect the fees they charge? Before answering the question, consider the person who has just opened his first dental office as compared to the dentist who has been in business 25 years.
18. Wrigley Field in Chicago is one of the two privately owned baseball stadiums in the major leagues. There are no lights for night games and no advertisements on the outfield walls. The playing field is still grass and natural dirt, bucking the trend of most teams toward substituting an artificial turf.
    a. What is the cost to the owner of choosing to grow ivy vines on the outfield walls?
    b. What is the cost of playing daylight afternoon games?
    c. Should construction costs enter into the determination of ticket prices?
    d. When would construction costs be a factor in estimating the costs of that decision to the owner?
19. Assume education is only a consumption good. Tuition at State University is $2,000 a year where the student enrollment is 32,000.
    a. Would the $2,000 be a cost for attending State U for a football player who is not on a scholarship?
    b. Under what circumstances would a prospective football player not consider the $2,000 expenditure as not being a cost? What would it be?
    c. Is the $2,000 necessarily the full cost to the university of educating him? Why not? (Hint: What is the marginal cost of his registering and taking a seat in three classes of 100 students each?)
    d. Is an alumnus who donates $2,000 to the athletic program also donating to non-athletic students' academic programs without realizing it? Why?
20. Why would a firm that is losing money hire another worker?

Chapter 6

The Firm, Productivity, and Production Costs

PROGRESS REPORT

A. In Chapter 5 we examined the concept of opportunity cost in detail. There we saw how the economist evaluates the cost incurred by the act of consumption and the cost incurred when using the services of an asset.

B. This chapter examines the legal definitions of business enterprises and investigates what is meant by a firm. A few fundamental relations between productivity, costs, and output are examined. The concept of a production function is introduced and graphs of cost curves are illustrated and explained, using the law of diminishing marginal returns. The short run and long run are defined, and this leads us to the distinction between diminishing marginal returns applicable to the short run and internal economies of scale applicable to the long run.

C. Chapter 7 will contain a description of the perfectly competitive model, and how the firm and industry adjust to market disturbances in the short run and the long run. Profit maximization and external economies of scale will also be discussed.

BUSINESS ORGANIZATIONS

Firms in a market economy combine scarce inputs to *produce* output for profit.

It is the function of **firms** in a market economy to combine scarce inputs to **produce** outputs of goods or services for the purpose of making a profit. An efficiently run firm that satisfies consumer preferences will likely earn a profit. If it does not it will not survive for long. There are three legal kinds of business enterprises.

A *sole proprietorship* is an individually-owned small business; the owner has unlimited liability.

Sole Proprietorship. A sole proprietorship is individually owned and the jack-of-all-trades to the business. There are permits to be obtained from the various local governments at a fee, but there is no necessity to draw up legal papers establishing the structure of the firm. All one needs is a license to hang up a shingle once it passes the scrutiny of the local building inspectors. The advantages that accrue to the sole owner are usually low setup costs—since these are usually small businesses—independence, pride, and total possession of the profits. A disadvantage is that it may be quite difficult to raise enough money to see the owner through the early periods before the business begins to pay its way. Another disadvantage is that there is unlimited liability. The owner assumes all the risks. A business that goes bankrupt might also involve the loss of the owner's personal possessions such as his or her house and car as collateral against the debts incurred. If the business is successful, the sole owner finds it difficult to finance a much larger operation. Good prospects combined with little collateral do not make banks enthusiastic about making large loans to underwrite growth.

A *partnership* consists of two or more partners in a business venture; legal papers establish the structure and ownership shares.

Partnership. A partnership consists of two or more partners in a business venture. Legal papers establishing the structure and ownership share of the business are necessary, though reasonably simple. Profits are shared as provided in the contract. One advantage is that it too has relatively low startup costs, shared as they are among the partners. Also, the partners can specialize in different tasks in the business, thereby increasing the efficiency of running it. A disadvantage is that liability is unlimited. Furthermore, disagreements among partners can appear, turning a potentially successful operation into a distasteful failure. It is also plagued by difficulty in obtaining financing if there is a desire to substantially expand the business. A partnership is automatically dissolved when a partner dies. But it can easily be legally reestablished.

A *corporation* is a legal entity charted by the state; it has the advantage of limited liability.

Corporation. A corporation is a legal entity charted by the state. Legal papers describing its structure are necessary and are considerably more complicated than for solely owned businesses and partnerships. One important virtue of a corporation is the advantage of limited liability. An owner—a stockholder—can only lose the amount he or she has invested. Also, the successful corporation can generate more funds by selling more issues of stock. Thus, its possibilities for financing growth are much better than for other business structures. And larger size can mean greater efficiencies and greater net revenues. A disadvantage is that stockholders as owners have no daily direct input into the decision-making process of the business. That function is performed by managers who might or might not also own stock. Of course, stockholders can be involved in electing members of the board. Also, corporate stockholders are

TABLE 6-1
Business Enterprises, 1976

	Number (thousands)	Percentage of all firms	Percentage of all receipts
Proprietorships	11,358	78.0	9.0
Partnerships	1,096	7.5	3.9
Corporations	2,105	14.5	87.1
	14,559	100.0	100.0

Source: *Statistical Abstract of the United States, 1979,* p. 553, Table 913. Percentages were calculated from the table.

doubly taxed. Corporate profits are taxed and then taxed again when dividend payments become stockholders' personal income. Table 6-1 provides some information for 1976. Sole ownership is the most numerous business enterprize while corporations by far account for most of the business receipts. Partnerships continue to decline in number and in percentage of receipts.

THE FIRM

We have described the legal kinds of business structures in existence, but we have not yet stated what exactly is a firm. What are firms? Why do firms exist? Surprising as it may seem, the answer to the second question is relatively easy—to make a profit—but the answer to the first is much more complicated. For a simple answer we can say that a firm is any producing unit.

In Chapter 2 we saw how a middleman can reduce costs by specializing in information, and we pointed out that the essence of specialization is producing more with the same number of inputs. Managers of firms use specialization to make their operations more efficient, to reduce costs, to maximize revenues, and to compete with other firms in the market place. Many firms act as middlemen between the consumer and the primary producer. But why does the firm have to be a team of middlemen? Why do not individuals acting as sole proprietors individually contract in the market with other sole proprietors for each input, with each owner acting as an independent owner-middleman?[1] Instead of a single huge oil company managing the production and distribution of large amounts of oil products, why not many thousands of independent individuals drilling a well or two, contracting at some market price with individual truck owners who in turn negotiate a contract with individuals who refine the crude oil? They in turn would contract with individuals at some exchange price, who

[1]This section draws on Ronald Coase, "The Nature of a Firm," *Economica* (Nov. 1937); and Armen Alchian and Harold Demsetz, "Production, Information Costs, and Economic Organization," *American Economic Review*, Dec. 1972.

then would sell gasoline to the public. There is, indeed, a considerable amount of individual contracting of this kind, particularly in long-haul trucking and wildcat wells. But typically we observe organizations composed of groups of people working under some kind of authority where operations are combined within a unit called the firm. Why does this unit called the firm emerge—the larger organization devoted to the coordination and management of productive activity?

When one firm deals with other firms to acquire inputs, it negotiates its exchange via the market mechanism by paying market prices that are determined *outside* the firm. Yet many allocations of resources *within* the firm are not explicitly coordinated by using prices, because there is no market within the firm. One has to be careful here, however, for many larger, modern firms have people employed as specialists who are assigned the job of calculating what are called shadow prices. These are estimates of what prices would be if each intrafirm department behaved *as if* it bought and sold resources (paper clips, paper, bolts, and other inputs) from other departments within the company, just as the firm itself buys inputs from other firms outside the company. Nevertheless, in most firms, large and small, there are intradepartmental allocations of resources not subject to any form of internal pricing, including personnel, that are instead coordinated by decisions of supervisors or managers.

If we are to accept the assumption of rationality, firms exist because they have advantages. Economic agents, in coordinating their activities by establishing a business firm, are taking the most appropriate means to reach a desired goal. The principal advantage of creating a firm is that it is cheaper to form a team than it is to use the market to make individual transactions for each input. Individual contracting is much more costly than the transactions involved in supervising a team. The individual workers agree to perform certain chores under the direction of supervisors, who exercise flexibility in the organization of the inputs, workers included, without having to enter into an explicit, written, long-term contract with each worker on each specific activity. The supervisor can then give orders, within reasonable limits, to direct resource use.

A firm will grow as long as the additional *benefits* of hiring another worker are greater than the transactions costs of hiring and retaining the worker.

Thus, the organization we call a firm will emerge and grow so long as the **benefits** from hiring another input are greater than the transactions costs of hiring it and paying it a wage to retain it if it is labor, or buying or renting it if it is land or capital. Moreover, as we shall soon see, there must be a residual income, that is, a net revenue or profit, to the entrepreneur who organizes the firm, otherwise he would not go to the trouble of forming a team of workers.

As the firm expands, a point may be reached where the additional cost to organize one more transaction within the firm is just equal to the cost of contracting for it outside the firm at market prices with another firm or entrepreneur. Beyond this point, it will not pay to bring an additional exchange transaction under the organizing internal authority. Simply put, the additional input is not worth the additional cost in the form of its price and the added bother (transactions costs) attached to its employment.

Measuring Productivity

The above still does not fully explain why it is cheaper, up to a point, to organize into a team, or what is meant by a firm. Certainly it is obvious that someone who works for himself is motivated to be more productive than if he worked for someone else. But how is working for the firm more beneficial to the individual, since working in a team means one must share the rewards with others?

One explanation is that the team effort is more productive than the sum of the individual efforts. Depending on the sizes, having twenty percent of a larger pie is often better than having all of a smaller pie. This will be the case if the output of the team effort is greater than the output of the sum of the individual efforts. In a sense, one could say the whole is greater than the sum of its parts. Cooperation leads to increasing returns. Two movers can carry a couch upstairs, where either one of the two, individually, cannot.

Measuring the contribution of each input in *joint production* is difficult; it is easier to measure the total output of the team as a unit.

The problem of determining reward based on individual productivity still remains. One man may have lifted more of the couch than the other—maybe the one on the bottom end. There is a problem in measuring the contribution of inputs in **joint production**. Measuring individual productivity for purposes of rewarding the movers for what they produce can be difficult in the real world, where *ceteris paribus* is not always a reasonable assumption to make. What can be measured more accurately is the total output of the team as a unit.

The Manager

A *centralized authority* is a manager or owner who allocates and directs the completion of tasks.

The boss, supervisor, or manager can organize the team to make it more productive by policing and observing individual behavior. He or she keeps on the lookout for shirkers who attempt to go undetected under the cloak of team activity. The manager functions as a **centralized authority** who directs (contracts with) inputs to perform certain chores. He can redirect (recontract) with individual inputs by transferring, demoting, firing, or promoting them without at the same time changing the conditions of employment that have been contracted with the other inputs. But who watches the manager? If it is a corporation or a large nonincorporated business, then competition among the lower echelon middle managers competing for room at the top provides the incentive for them to make the team (firm) more productive. This involves adding icing to the cake by making the manager a residual claimant and paying him or her a larger share proportionate to the increase in the team's productivity resulting from his or her decisions.

The Entrepreneur

The owner of a business is an *entrepreneur.* Risk-taking is the essence of the entrepreneur; the reward for risk-taking is profit.

The entrepreneur differs from the manager because he is an owner, hence a risk taker. Entrepreneurs can also be managers but managers are not necessarily entrepreneurs. While managers earn rewards, in the administrative hierarchy it is the entrepreneur who is the ultimate residual claimant and decision maker. It is the entrepreneur who launches into risky business adventures, who innovates, who introduces new commodities and services. His role is unique because of its responsibility and breadth. But risk taking is the essence of the entrepreneur, and the reward for risk taking is profit.

It now becomes apparent there is always a fixed factor of production in the firm even in the long run—namely, the entrepreneur. The larger the firm becomes, the larger will be the number of transactions that must be organized by the entrepreneur. The harder it then becomes for the entrepreneur to combine inputs efficiently and to oversee a growing number of middle managers and operations. There will eventually be diminishing returns to his skills as they are spread over more diverse kinds of transactions. Also, there are diminishing returns to his energy and to his time, since the day is limited to twenty-four hours and the growing firm might become dispersed over a larger geographical area. Given these constraints, there are diminishing returns to the negotiation of each additional transaction. Thus, in the long run the entrepreneur might be the ultimate reason for declining efficiency to set in. His productivity falls and the firm's marginal costs rise as he becomes more vulnerable to mistakes. The larger the firm the more costly the mistake can be. With the greater risk the more conservative are the decisions likely to be. The desire for additional profit is moderated by the greater uncertainty of a large loss.

Firms exist to make profits. They are efficient at doing this because by combining into a team they can alter the use of inputs with more flexibility, and reduce the transactions costs by contracting with inputs within the firm rather than negotiating individually with those inputs in the outside market. Because of the greater efficiency of firms, society increases its wealth and gains beyond what it could produce if inputs did not agree to contract according to prescribed rules of the team, under the direction of a centralized authority.

We conclude that *a firm is a team of inputs hired under an unwritten or written contractual arrangement organized to produce output under the direction of a centralized authority who is a residual claimant to the profits.*

EFFICIENCY AND LEAST-COST

A firm can combine inputs in a variety of ways and still produce the same amount of output. In order to maximize its profits and minimize its costs in a competitive environment, it is forced to be as efficient as possible with its resources if it is to survive. Exactly what is meant by resource efficiency? As you might expect by now, economists view efficiency in a different way than do specialists in other disciplines. An economist is interested in the opportunity cost involved. In a competitive market prices reflect opportunity costs; hence, costs can be measured in dollar terms. Therefore, the economist is interested in **economic efficiency**, defined as follows, where value signifies dollars:

***Economic efficiency* is achieved when costs are minimized.**

$$\text{Economic efficiency} = \frac{\text{value of output}}{\text{value of input}}.$$

The higher the ratio the greater the efficiency. Even where the same amount of output is being produced, the firm can alter the combinations of inputs—broadly speaking, capital and labor—to attain the **least-cost** combination. As the relative price of inputs change, firms will tend to substitute away from the input rising in price and substitute toward that input whose relative price is falling. You have no doubt seen films about China where it appears that 500 people with brooms are sweeping a street. In the U.S., this chore is done by one person running a large, mechanized sweeper. Why the difference between the

The *least-cost* combination of inputs varies with whether a society is labor intensive or capital intensive.

two countries? It is because China's economy is relatively labor intensive while that of the U.S. is relatively capital intensive. In China, the supply of labor is higher relative to the supply of capital. Relatively speaking, therefore, in China the price of capital is much higher than the price of labor. The productivity of the individual worker using a broom is relatively low; hence wages are lower. Labor is abundant and cheap; capital is scarce and therefore expensive. By comparison, labor in the U.S. is relatively scarce, hence more expensive, whereas capital is more abundant and relatively cheap, that is relative to labor. Therefore, when input prices differ, firms and the economy will use different production technologies and differing capital-labor combinations in production.[2]

A firm is interested in maximizing profits. In order to do this it also has to be minimizing costs. What guides a firm in making those decisions that will maximize its profits? The answer has already been suggested.

PRODUCTION FUNCTION

All firms must hire inputs, or what economists like to call "factors of production." The technical or engineering relation between the amount of inputs per period to the amount of output per period that they produce is embodied in the production function symbolized by

$$Q = f(K, L, \bar{T})$$

where Q is a rate of output—the amount of the product the firm produces each period—*K* is the amount of services from capital used each period, *L* is the amount of labor per period, and *T* is a parameter representing the current state of technology or the current wisdom. The equation states that output depends upon inputs for a given technology. Thus, *a production function reveals the different combinations of capital and labor in minimum amounts required to produce various amounts of output using existing technical knowledge.*

Table 6-2 illustrates the different combinations for labor and capital per period to produce widgets whose amounts are shown by the numbers in the blocks. Thus, reading across the row for 3 machines, the initial entry is zero since there is no output without labor, nor in today's economy is there output without capital. When 1 labor unit is combined with three widget-producing machines, 260 widgets are produced. As you proceed along the row adding additional labor units, it leads to an increasing number of widgets. Thus, for 2 labor units, 360 widgets are created; with 3 labor units and 3 machines, 450 widgets are manufactured, and so on. Alternately, moving down the column holding labor inputs fixed at, say, 2 workers, no output of widgets is forthcoming without a widget-producing machine to collaborate with labor. However, with 1 machine 210 widgets are produced, with 2 machines and 2 workers 300

[2]Economist Joseph Schumpeter (1883–1950) introduced the expression "creative destruction." It makes sense to, say, replace a perfectly operating steam engine with a diesel engine. That is, to destroy something working well with something new because it is more economically efficient.

TABLE 6-2
Production Function for Widgets per Period

Quantity of Capital per Period (K)	Quantity of Labor per Period (L)						
	0	1	2	3	4	5	6
0	*0*	0	0	0	0	0	0
1	0	*150*	210	260	300	330	340
2	0	210	*300*	360	410	450	480
3	0	260	360	*450*	510	560	600
4	0	300	410	510	*600*	660	710
5	0	330	450	560	660	*750*	810
6	0	340	480	600	710	810	*900*

widgets are produced, with 3 machines, 360 widgets are manufactured, on down to 480 widgets produced when 2 units of labor combine in production with 6 machines.

Diminishing Marginal Productivity

In the short run, combining increasing amounts of a factor which is allowed to vary with another factor that is being held constant results at some point in proportionately less output being produced. We define this situation as the *Law of Diminishing Marginal Productivity. When successively equal increments of a variable factor are combined with a fixed factor, at first the addition of incremental amounts of the variable factor leads to correspondingly increasing increments of output. Eventually a point is reached where adding extra equal amounts of the variable factor will yield smaller and smaller increases in total output.*

Except for the initial effect of increasing returns, diminishing marginal returns are demonstrated in Table 6-2. Move to the right along any row or down along any column (except zero) and observe what happens to the number of widgets produced. Assume that all workers have equal ability. Table 6-2 reveals that 1 worker with 1 machine produces 150 widgets. Adding the second worker results in 210 widgets for an increase of 60 widgets. Now include a third labor input which increases total output to 260 widgets for a change in total output of $260 - 210 = 50$ widgets. The fourth worker adds an additional $300 - 260 = 40$ units. And the fifth and sixth labor units respectively increase total output by 30 and 10 widgets per period when capital is held fixed at one machine. While the number of widgets is increasing, it is increasing at a *slower* rate in accordance with the law of diminishing returns. It is an example of the old expression, "too many cooks in the kitchen." Moving down the column while holding the labor input fixed is exemplified by altering the aphorism to read "too much kitchen for the cook."

Lift Row 1 from Table 6-2, representing the output from combining one machine with zero workers, then with one worker, and progressively on up to six workers:

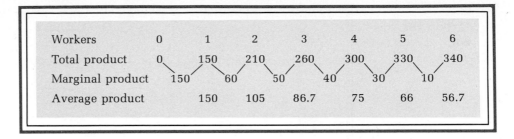

Workers	0	1	2	3	4	5	6
Total product	0	150	210	260	300	330	340
Marginal product		150	60	50	40	30	10
Average product		150	105	86.7	75	66	56.7

The law of diminishing marginal returns is evidenced by the decreasing marginal productivity from 150 to 10 units of output from successively adding one on up to the sixth additional worker. The marginal productivity of labor is defined as the change in total output by adding an extra labor input.

$$MP_L = \frac{\Delta Q}{\Delta L}.$$

Adding 1 worker to 1 machine increases output Q from zero to 150, hence $\Delta Q = 150$, $\Delta L = 1$, and the $MP_1 = 150$. Adding the second worker in combination with 1 machine increases output Q from 150 to 210, or $\Delta Q = 60$, $\Delta L = 1$, hence

$$MP_2 = \frac{\Delta Q}{\Delta L} = \frac{210 - 160}{2 - 1} = 60$$

is the marginal productivity of the second labor input. Figure 6-1 graphs the relation between total product *(TP)* and marginal product *(MP)*, using data from the row for 1 machine in Table 6-2. As the marginal product declines, the total product rises but by smaller and smaller amounts.

A Clarifying Point

In the tables and graphs we have measured labor input by number of workers. This is a convenient measure and easy to understand because people generally are hired as individuals. However, to be more precise we should be measuring not workers but, say, days of labor service. Strictly speaking, a labor input to the production process is not a worker as such, but the worker's services.

This is a minor point, but by clarifying it we can also clarify our understanding of the concept of marginal productivity. At the beginning of the chapter we assumed that all workers are equally productive. If we now think in terms of labor service, then a day's worth of labor service is the same no matter which worker performs it. So we no longer need to worry about potential differences in productivity of different individuals. What we mean is that by hiring another worker the firm has increased the variable factor—the amount of days of labor service applied to a fixed factor in the production process. We shall continue to refer to number of workers instead of days of labor service because it is easier to talk about number of workers. The reader should be aware that we are using number of workers only as a proxy measure.

Figure 6-1

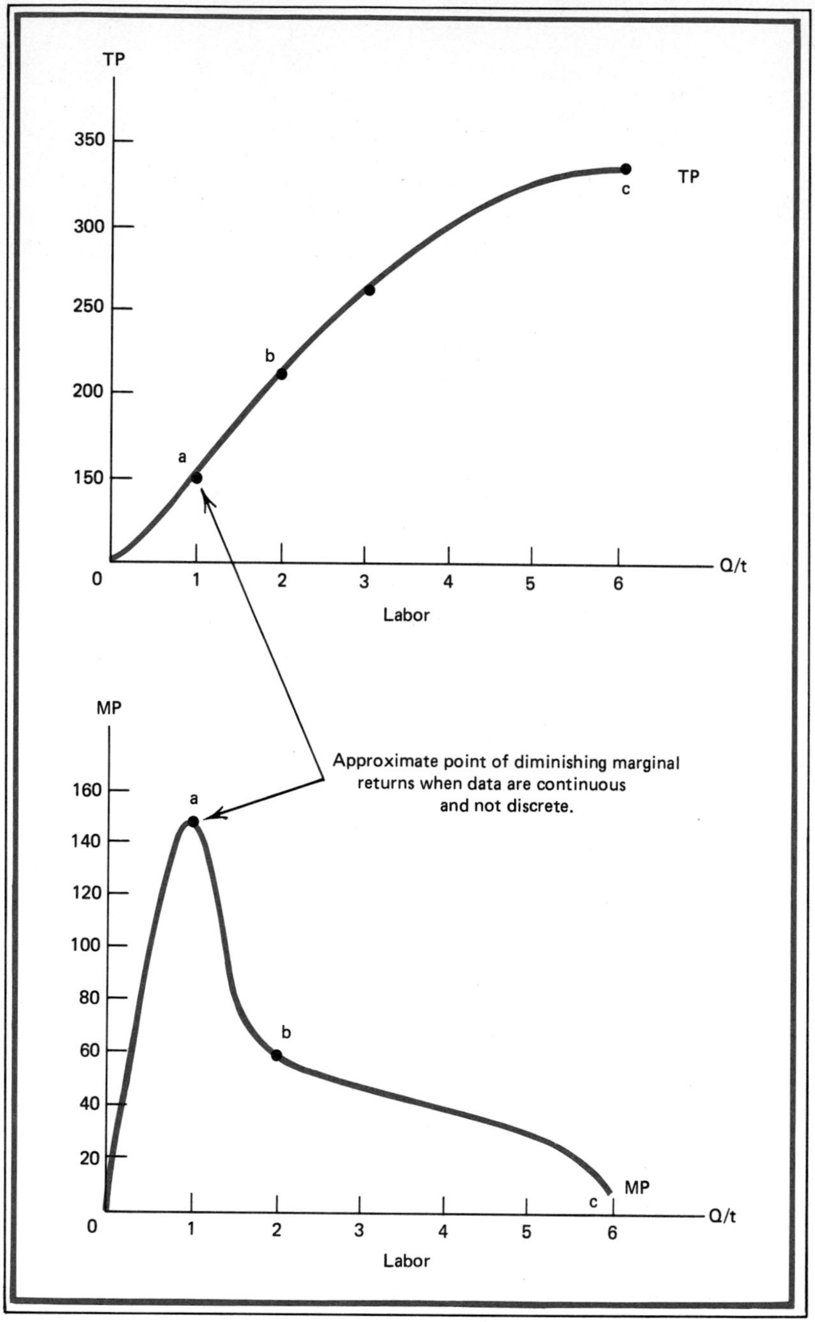

Marginal and Average Productivity

Refer to the row for one machine Table 6-2. If the fourth worker is added, the marginal productivity of labor when 4 are working is

$$MP = \frac{\Delta Q}{\Delta L} = \frac{300 - 260}{4 - 3} = 40 \text{ units.}$$

Similarly, the average productivity when 4 are working together is

$$AP = \frac{Q}{L} = \frac{300}{4} = 75 \text{ units.}$$

As one proceeds along the row to the right, the marginal productivity of labor declines. Also notice that the average productivity declines too. Consistent with the lower graph of Figure 6-1, if the marginal product were to increase as one proceeded along the row, the average product would also increase. However, the marginal product precedes the average product. Thus when the marginal product is above the average product the average product is rising. And when the marginal product is below the average product, the average product must be falling.

Variable Proportions and Scale Effects

Diminishing marginal productivity applies when there is a fixed factor such as the number of workers or machines. However, when all factors can be varied, diminishing marginal productivity does not strictly apply and we approach the concept of *economies of scale*, sometimes referred to as *returns to scale*. When both capital K and labor L are allowed to vary simultaneously, there then being no fixed or unchanged factor, there can result a proportionate or more than proportionate increase in output. For example, if increasing both K and L by 5% results in a directly proportional increase in output by 5%, then *constant economies of scale* or *constant returns* are said to exist. If increasing K and L by 5 percent, however, leads to an increase in output of more than 5 percent, then *increasing scale economies* or *increasing returns* are said to exist. And if a less than 5% increase in output results, then *decreasing economies of scale* or *decreasing returns* are said to exist. The constant return situation is aptly illustrated in Table 6-2 when the input combination of 1K and 1L is increased to 2K and 2L and output rises from 150 to 300. Thus, increasing both inputs by 100 percent will also increase output by 100 percent. When 4K is combined with 4L for another increase of factors by 100 percent, total output rises to 600 units for an increase of 100 percent over the previous 300 units. This is an example of constant economies of scale. We have throughout the discussion assumed technology is unchanged as well as the price of inputs.

Short Run and Long Run

When one factor is held fixed and the amount of another factor is allowed to vary, it is said to be a *short-run* situation. There is neither time nor the opportunity to, for instance, acquire more land, change the crop once it is planted, or acquire another machine. Having defined the short run as a period when some factor is fixed, we see that the law of diminishing returns is a short-run phenomenon. It is demonstrated in Table 6-2 when one moves either across a capital row or down a labor input column. But the long run is also indicated in Table 6-2. The *long run* is said to occur when all factors are variable (though the entrepreneur may be the one exception). New acreage can be planted, additional machines acquired as well as more workers hired. Thus, when we speak of economies of scale we are implicitly considering the long run period. Scale economies are expressed in Table 6-2 when changing both K and L while moving along the diagonal when inputs are increased proportionately, or changing K proportionately more than L while moving down the table faster than moving across the table, or changing L proportionately more than K while moving across the table faster than going down the table.

Costs and Curves

The *law of increasing marginal costs* is a corollary to the law of diminishing marginal productivity, and states that in the short run, marginal cost (*MC*) varies inversely with the marginal product (*MP*).

Productivity and costs are two sides of the same coin. Or they can be looked upon as mirror images of one another. The corollary to the law of diminishing marginal productivity is the **law of increasing marginal costs.** In the short run, marginal cost (*MC*) varies inversely with the marginal product (*MP*).

$$\text{MC varies as } \frac{1}{\text{MP}}.$$

Thus, when the marginal product increases, the marginal cost decreases. And when the marginal product decreases the marginal cost increases. For the interested student the relation is derived in the footnote.[3]

The relations between cost and productivity curves are shown in Figure 6-2. Note carefully where the curves appear at the outputs q_1, q_2 and q_3 in all four graphs. At q_1 the marginal product curve is at a maximum (*e*) and must line up with the marginal cost curve at its minimum (*e′*). For output q_2 the marginal product curve intersects the average product curve from above at the

[3]Assume the amount of capital *K* is fixed. Let *L* = amount of labor, *Q* = the change in total output, P_L = the price of labor (wage), and *L* = change in workers hired. Then neglecting raw material costs, marginal cost is defined and redefined:

$$\underset{(1)}{\text{MC}} = \underset{(2)}{\frac{\Delta \text{TC}}{\Delta \text{Q}}} = \underset{(3)}{\text{P}_L\frac{\Delta \text{L}}{\Delta \text{Q}}} = \underset{(4)}{\frac{\text{P}_L}{\Delta \text{Q}/\Delta \text{L}}}.$$

Expressions 1 and 2 make up the original definition of marginal cost defined as the change in total cost (*TC*) associated with an increase in production of Q. Expression 3 follows from expression 2 because the change in total cost results from hiring one more worker at the current price P_L equal to the wage; that is, the change in total cost is equal to the wage per worker times the change in the number of workers hired, or $\Delta TC = P_L \times \Delta L$. It is possible to get from expression 3 to 4 by realizing that $\Delta L/\Delta Q$ can also be written as $\frac{1}{\Delta Q/\Delta L}$. This step is exactly the same as writing 4/1 as $\frac{1}{1/4}$. For when dividing by a fraction, simply bring the fraction from the denominator to the numerator and turn the fraction upside down. In step 4, the direction is reversed, going from the numerator to the denominator and flipping the fraction $\frac{\Delta L}{\Delta Q}$ to $\frac{1}{\Delta Q/\Delta L}$. But since $\Delta Q/\Delta L$ by definition is the marginal product of labor or MP_L, then we can rewrite the relation between expressions 1 and 4 as

$$\text{MC} = \frac{\text{P}_L}{\text{MP}_L}.$$

Thus, the marginal cost and marginal product are inversely related.

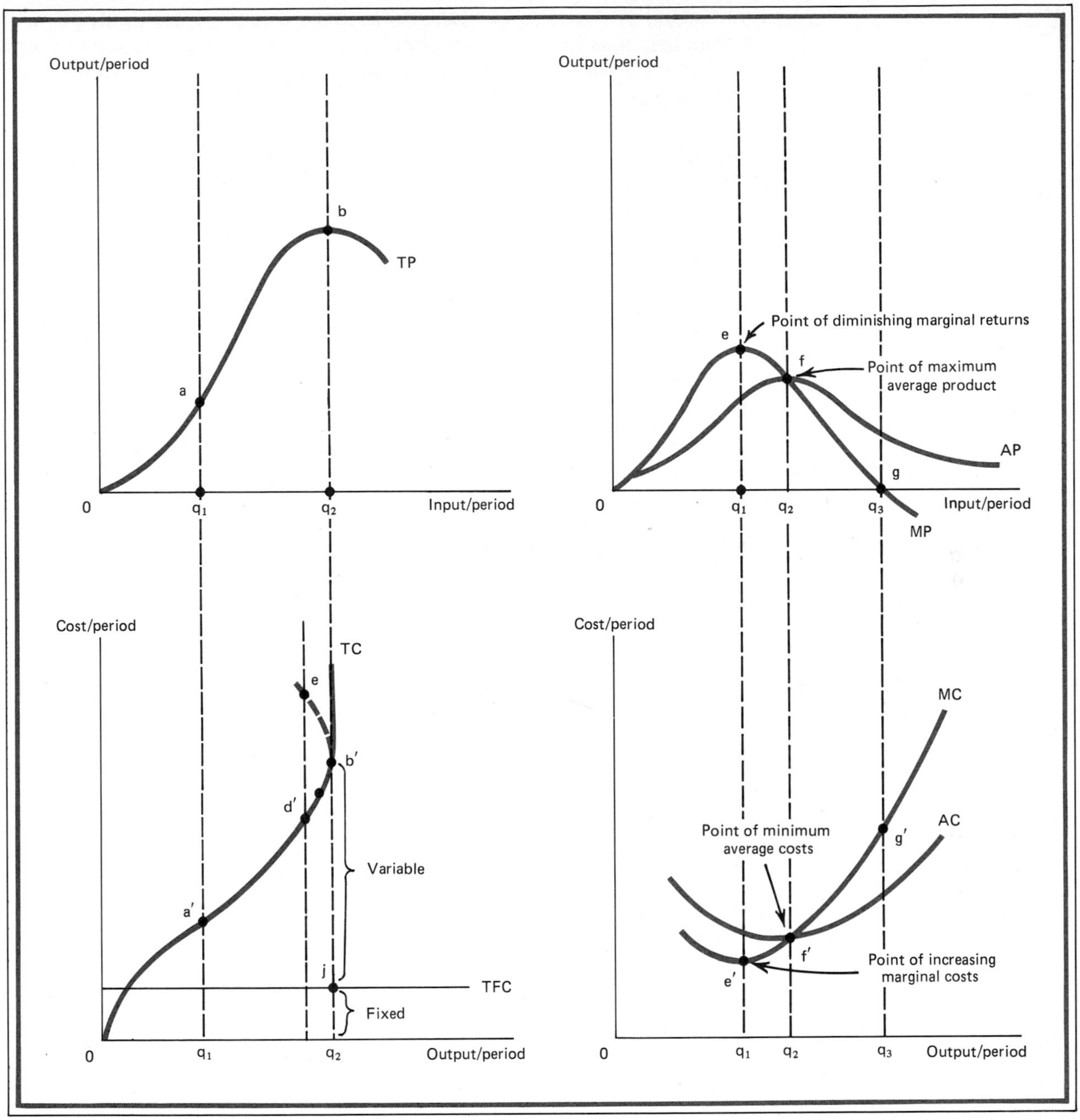

Figure 6-2

average product curve's maximum point *(f)*. Therefore, it logically follows that the marginal cost curve intersects the average cost curve at its minimum from below *(f′)*. At q_3 the marginal product curve is at zero and continues its decline. Hence, the marginal cost curve continues its rise. Beyond output q_3 the marginal product curve is negative whereas the marginal cost curve rises rapidly. When the average product curve is rising, not surprisingly, the average cost curve is falling. The reverse pattern between total product and total cost is no exception. Initially, the total product curve rises steeply before output q_1 is reached, then becomes less steep, and finally levels off to its maximum at point b. Alternatively, the total cost curve rises slowly near q_1, then picks up the pace once output is greater than q_1. It continues to rise even more rapidly when it becomes vertical at output q_2. Actually, if we pursue the logic of the inverse relation between total product and total cost, the total cost curve would bend back on itself as more inputs were hired, indicated by the dashed line. But in reality the output represented by point e would have already been produced at a total cost represented by point d′ on the total cost curve.

Cost Relations

Total cost (TC) Total cost is composed of total fixed cost (*TFC*) and total variable cost (*TVC*) with $TC = TFC + TVC$. The relation is illustrated in Figure 6-3. Total costs begin at *f* because there are still total fixed costs when output is nonexistent and $TVC = 0$. By vertically adding at each level of output the total fixed cost to the total variable cost, the total cost curve can be derived. At output *q* total fixed cost is equal to the vertical segment *qa* which in turn must be equal to the segment *bc*. *TVC* is the total variable cost and is equal to the segment *qb*. When *qb* is added to *bc*, it sums to total cost *TC* equal to *qc*. When $q = 0$, then $TC = TFC$ since at zero output $TVC = 0$. In Table 6-3, total cost in column 4 is obtained by adding Columns 2 and 3.

Average total costs (ATC) To obtain average costs merely divide total costs by the quantity of output. Hence, divide each term in $TC = TFC + TVC$ by *q* to get

Figure 6-3

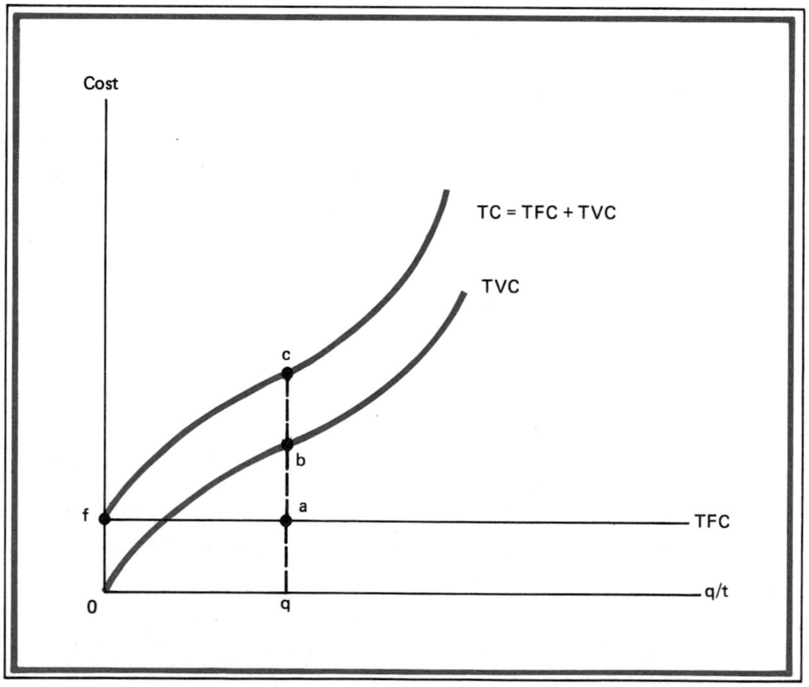

(1) Output	(2) Total fixed cost TFC	(3) Total variable cost TVC	(4) = (3) + (2) Total cost TC	(5) Marginal cost $= \frac{\Delta TC}{\Delta q}$ MC	(6) $= \frac{(4)}{(1)}$ Average total cost ATC	(7) $= \frac{(2)}{(1)}$ Average fixed cost AFC	(8) $= \frac{(3)}{(1)}$ Average variable cost AVC
0	$1000	$ 0	$1000	—	∞	∞	—
1	1000	50	1050	50	1050.0	1000.0	50.0
2	1000	90	1090	40	545.0	500.0	45.0
3	1000	120	1120	30	373.3	333.3	40.0
4	1000	140	1140	20	285.0	250.0	35.0
5	1000	180	1180	40	236.0	200.0	36.0
6	1000	240	1240	60	206.7	166.7	40.0
7	1000	320	1320	80	188.6	142.9	45.7
8	1000	420	1420	100	177.5	125.0	52.5
9	1000	570	1570	150	174.4	111.1	63.3
10	1000	800	1800	230	180.0	100.0	80.0
11	1000	1100	2100	300	190.9	90.9	100.0

TABLE 6-3

$ATC = AFC + AVC$. In Table 6-3, average cost in column 6 is obtained by dividing column 4 by column 1; average fixed cost in column 7 is derived by dividing column 2 by column 1; and average variable cost in column 8 is derived by dividing column 3 by column 1. For output $q = 0$, average total cost (*ATC*), average fixed cost (*AFC*), and average variable cost (*AVC*) are not defined since dividing by zero has no meaning.

Marginal cost (MC) To obtain marginal cost merely take the change in total costs and divide each term by the change in output. Thus divide each term of $\Delta TC = \Delta TFC + \Delta TVC$ by Δq. But since total fixed costs are constant, the change in total fixed costs is zero ($\Delta TFC = 0$) leaving $\Delta TC/\Delta q = \Delta TVC/\Delta q = MC$. For example, marginal cost equal to 40 in column 5 of Table 6-3 is obtained when output q is increased from 1 unit to 2 units. Thus $\Delta q = 1$ and the change in total costs (ΔTC) is $1090 - 1050 = 40$, or marginal cost can be determined by observing that the change in total variable cost (ΔTVC) is $90 - 50 = 40$. Hence, marginal cost (*MC*) is equal to both the change in total costs and the change in total variable costs. The lower graph of Figure 6-4 illustrates the various cost curves. It requires some explanation.

When the marginal cost curve lies *below* the average cost curve, the average cost curve is falling. When the *MC* curve lies *above* the *ATC* curve, the average cost curve is rising. The marginal cost curve passes through the minimum points of both the average variable cost and average cost curves from below. Notice there also exists a range of output from q_0 to q_2 where the marginal cost curve is rising but the average variable cost curve is falling. But the marginal cost curve still lies *below* the average cost curve, so that the average cost and average variable cost curves are declining.

Figure 6-4

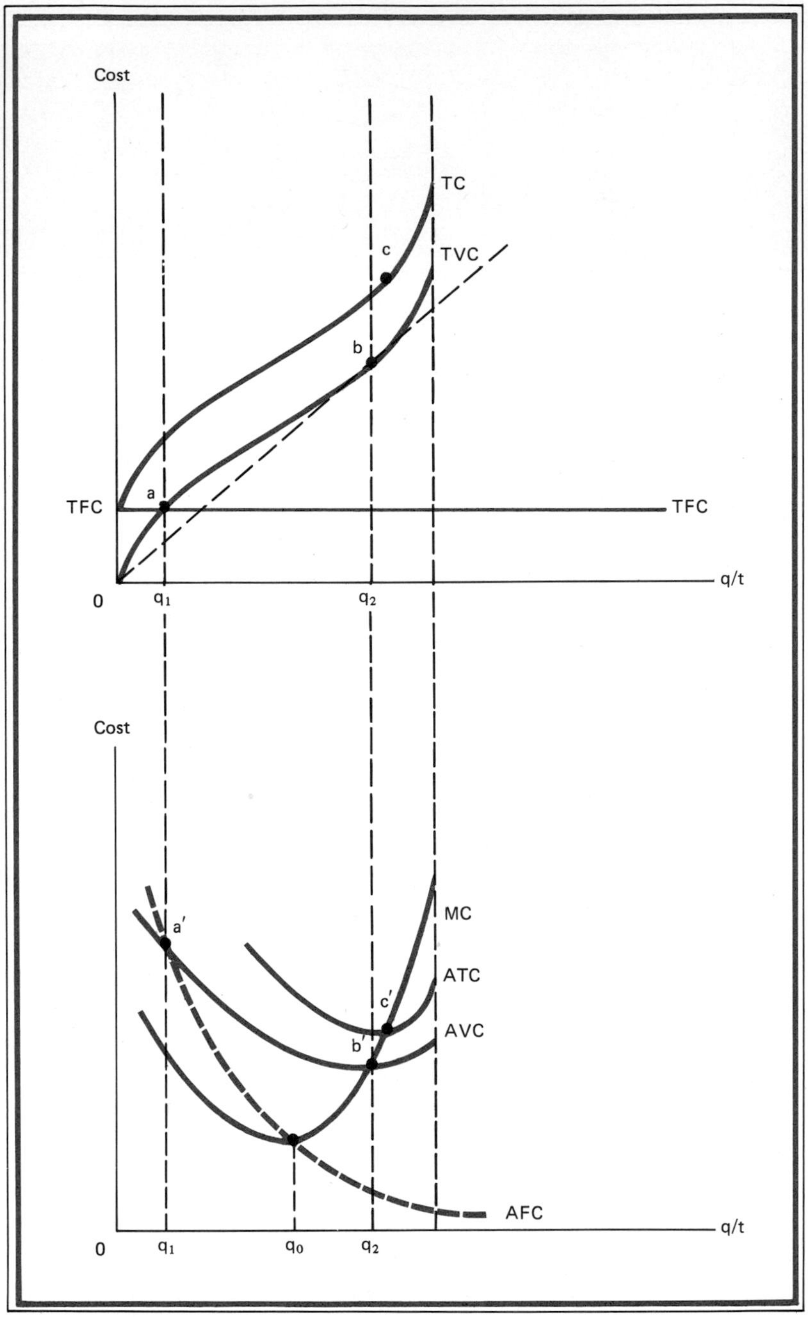

Average fixed cost (AFC) The average fixed cost declines and approaches zero as output q rises. As total fixed costs are spread over more units of production, the average cost per unit falls. This is easy to show. Suppose the outlay for a machine is \$1,000, its total fixed cost. When 1 unit of output is produced $AFC = TFC/q$ = 1000/1 = \$1,000. For 2 units AFC = 1000/2 = \$500; for 3 units AFC = \$333.3, and so on down column 7 of Table 6-3.

Average variable cost (AVC) Average variable cost is not defined for zero output. When production is begun, average variable cost falls since initially there are decreasing marginal costs (increasing returns). However, as production continues it reaches a minimum and thereafter increasing marginal costs (decreasing marginal returns) set in, pulling up the average variable cost curve. For low output the vertical distance between the average total cost (*ATC*) and average variable cost (AVC) curves is greater than for larger outputs where the average total cost (*ATC*) and average variable cost (AVC) curves begin to come together. The reason is that at low levels of output, average fixed costs (*AFC*) are high, but at higher output the average fixed costs (*AFC*) becomes much smaller as indicated by the dashed curve.

Observe that the minimum point c' of the average total cost (*ATC*) curve is slightly to the right of the minimum point of the average variable cost (*AVC*) curve at b'. This is because the average fixed cost curve *AFC* is both falling and is below the average variable cost curve *AVC* beyond output q_1. When the average variable cost curve begins to rise after passing through its minimum point at b', it is not yet rising fast enough to outweigh the effect of the declining average fixed cost curve AFC. Eventually the rising average variable cost (*AVC*) curve begins to dominate the declining average fixed cost (*AFC*) curve so that the average total cost (*ATC*) reaches its minimum after the *AVC* does. Observe that in the upper graph of Figure 6-4, the total fixed cost (*TFC*) intersects and equals the total variable cost (*TVC*) at point *a*. Therefore, the average variable cost (*AVC*) curve must intersect the average fixed cost (*AFC*) at a' corresponding to output q_1. Exactly where the intersection of the average variable cost (*AVC*) and average fixed cost (*AFC*) curves occurs depends on a firm's ratio of capital costs (fixed costs) to total costs. Firms with a low fixed cost to total cost ratio would find the average fixed cost curve intersecting the average variable cost curve to the left of the minimum point of the average variable cost curve at b', or the total fixed cost (*TFC*) must intersect the total variable cost (*TVC*) curve to the left of the point *b* in the upper graph. For firms with a high fixed-total cost ratio, the total fixed cost curve could intersect the total variable cost curve to the right of point *b*. This also implies that the average fixed cost curve would have to intersect the average variable cost curve to the right of the minimum point of the average variable cost curve at b'.[4]

Long-run Costs

Capacity **is the maximum quantity of output that can be produced in a fixed period of time, given the existing stock of capital.**

At a moment in time the managers or owners of a firm can envision building a plant of varying size. Blueprints can be drawn up in which the size and costs of operating different facilities can be projected. Therefore, during the planning stages managers can treat *all* factors of production as if they are variable—even the amount of plant and equipment. When all factors are variable we call it the long run, and from the long overview all costs are variable. Yet at any given time, a firm that is operating and producing a product will have a limited capacity. **Capacity** refers to the maximum quantity of output that can be pro-

[4]See William D. Gunther, "Inconsistencies and Omissions in the Treatment of Fixed Costs: A Note," *The American Economist*, Spring 1977: 67.

duced in a fixed period of time, given the existing stock of capital. Some people prefer to define capacity output as the level of output related to the minimum point of the average cost curve *ATC*. But it is possible for a firm to produce more than this, so that its "maximum" output would be its capacity output. There is no uniform agreement among economists on the definition of capacity, and whenever the term is used to refer to a measurement that says, for example, "the steel industry was operating at 82% of capacity last month," one must see how the measurement was made in order to know how capacity was defined. We shall not pursue it further here.

The point is, no matter what size plant is finally constructed its productive capability will be limited, and as such it exists in the real context of the short run. As far as actual production goes, therefore, the long-run average cost curve *LAC* is a planning curve only, a projected long-run schedule. It is not an empirical curve from which a manager will determine the costs of productive decisions for the week, the month, or the year. Those decisions can only be made on the basis of the current existing facilities. At any time the manager can envision a larger plant that would reduce the average costs of producing for the week, the month, and the next year. But he cannot currently use it.

A comment about the use of the word plant: Plant does not necessarily imply one building or factory. It may refer to the whole complex that may consist of several factories with interrelated operations. In the long run existing factories can be enlarged, or new ones built to replace the older ones, or additional factories and buildings could be added to existing ones. In each case the size of the plant has been expanded. The stock of capital has been enlarged. Figure 6-5 illustrates three different sizes of plant, each with its corresponding short-run cost curves. At output q_1, plant number one is producing where MC = minimum ATC and is operating at optimum capacity. If the bosses

Figure 6-5

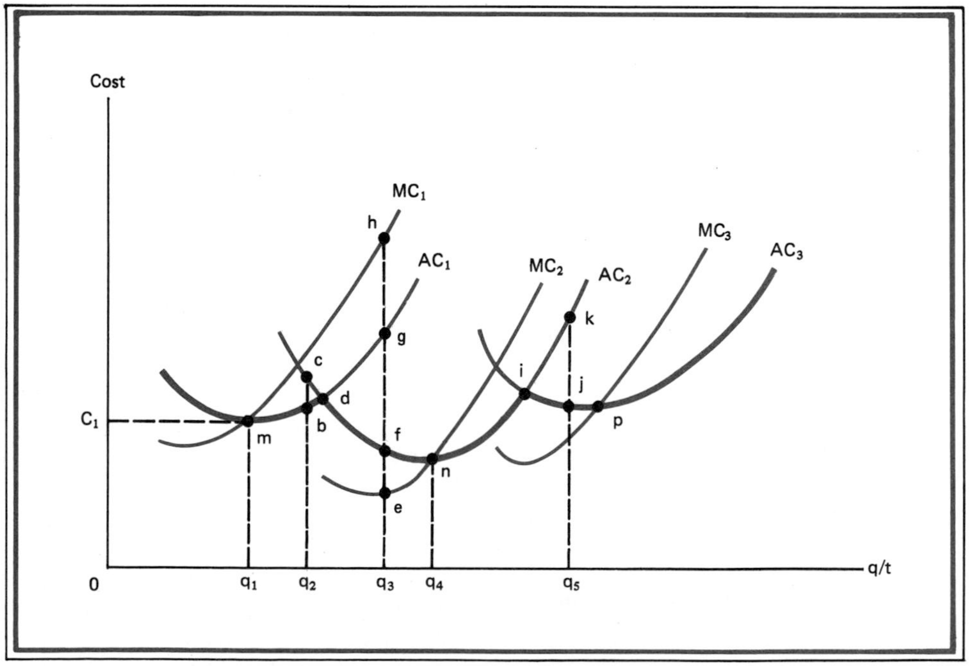

decided to increase output to q_2, what size plant would be more efficient to achieve that level of output? Point *c* of the ATC_2 curve is above point *b* of the ATC_1 curve. Thus, it is more costly per unit of output to produce a total level of output q_2 with plant size two than it is with a plant size one. Therefore it is cheaper to overuse plant one than to underuse plant two. If the managers, however, projected that it would be desirable to produce output at the level of q_3, since market conditions for the future appeared quite good, a plant of size two would be preferable. At output q_3, point *f* on the ATC_2 curve is much lower than point g on the ATC_1 curve. Therefore, the average cost per unit to produce output q_3 is much lower with a plant of size two. It would even be lower should production rise to q_4. But beyond output q_4, additional output would lead to rising costs per unit using plant size two.

From the evidence of curves ATC_1 and ATC_2 one concludes that for output q_3, it is cheaper to underuse plant two rather than to overuse plant size one. Also, observe that for output q_3, the marginal cost of producing the q_3 unit is at point *h* on the MC_1 curve and only at point *e* on the MC_2 curve.

Moving on to the production of output q_5, would you say it is cheaper to use a plant of size three or of size two? We observe that plant three has lower average costs for output q_5 since point *j* on curve ATC_3 is lower than point *k* on curve ATC_2. We conclude that it is better to underuse plant three rather than overuse plant two if output q_5 is the production target.

The points *d* and *i* depict the crossover points of the *AC* curves of adjacent short-run plants, where it becomes cheaper per unit of output produced to move from the smaller to larger plant. The heavy line indicates the long-run average cost (LAC) curve. It shows the cost per unit of producing various levels of output by varying the size of plant. It is important to keep in mind that at any actual level of output the firm will be combining inputs on one or another of the short-run average cost curves. The parts of these short-run curves, taken together, constitute the *LAC* curve.

Imagine an abstract blueprint in which the short-run average cost *(SAC)* curves are drawn infinitesimally close to one another. Drawing a very large number of these short run curves will create a new curve, each with one point of the short-run curve also being on the long-run curve. Seen in this way, the most general *LAC* curve would become a smooth line as portrayed in Figure 6-6. The minimum point of the *LAC* curve occurs at output q_m. This is the optimal long-run size of plant. At this output $p = SMC = \min SAC = \min LAC$, where *SMC* is the short-run marginal cost curve.

For output levels below q_m, the *SAC* curves touch (are tangent to) the *LAC* curve to the left (e.g., point *a*) of their minimum levels (e.g., point *b*). At levels of output beyond q_m, the *SAC* curves are tangent to the *LAC* curve to the right (e.g., point *d*) of the minimum point of the *SAC* curves (e.g., point *c*). Only at point *m* does the minimum point of the *SAC* curve coincide with the minimum point of the *LAC* curve. This is the point of long-run optimum capacity using a given production function where the level of technology is fixed.

Why LAC Can Fall

The question that remains to be answered is why the *LAC* curve can decline over a large range of output. The answers lie in internal economies of scale that derive from several sources.

Figure 6-6

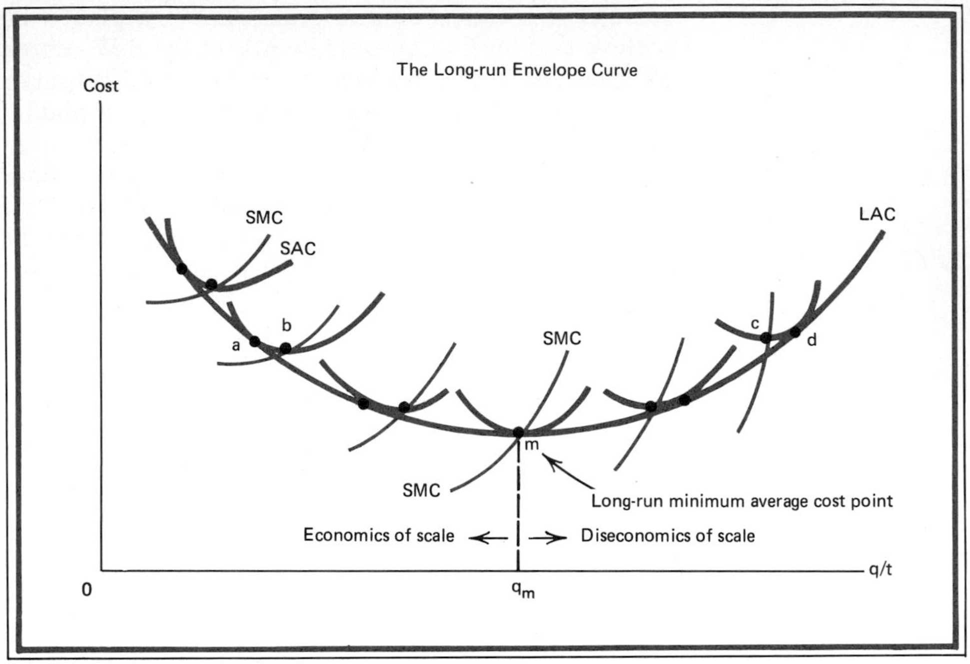

Internal Economies of Scale In the long run all factors are variable and can be increased or decreased. As stated earlier in the chapter, when both inputs are increased output can increase proportionately or disproportionately. Increasing K and L by 5 percent might result in a 5 percent increase in output. This is the situation of constant returns to scale. If output increases by over 5 percent, there exist increasing economies of scale which give rise to declining long-run average costs as firms grow larger. If output increases by less than 5 percent, there are decreasing economies of scale.

The sources of scale effects are often classified by whether they are *external* to the firm or *internal* to it. Internal scale economies result from changes within the firm and will be treated here. We shall defer a discussion of external economies until we reach Chapter 7. Internal economies affect the shape of the planning curve, but not its position, that is, internal economies do not cause the *LAC* curve to shift. In Figure 6-6 we would say there are internal economies to the left of the q_m and internal diseconomies to the right. Why is the curve shaped the way it is? Why does average cost fall as output rises from lower levels up to q_m, and then increase beyond q_m? To answer these questions we must look to the factors that give rise to scale economies.

Causes of internal economies include *efficiencies of size, divisibility and specialization, by-products,* and price *discounts* on volume purchases of inputs.

Efficiencies of Size There are several aspects of size that lead to efficiency. A slightly larger machine may be more productive than a smaller one. One big machine that produces as much as three smaller ones may take up less space than three smaller ones. The number of machine operators is reduced from three to one. One building is easier to maintain and increases the amount of work space without proportionately increasing the materials to build them. For example, a 2-foot cube has a volume of 8 cubic feet and a surface area of 24 square feet. A 4-foot cube has a volume of 64 cubic feet and a surface area of 96 square feet. By doubling the length, width, and height of the cube the area is increased by 4-fold and the volume by 8-fold. By building another 2-foot cube the volume is only increased to 16 cubic feet and the area to a 48 square feet total for the two smaller cubes combined. This relation between area and volume is even more dramatic if we deal with cylinders and spheres instead of cubes. This is why storage containers on oil-tank farms are usually cylinders and some gas storage tanks are spheres—the volume created is greater for the given amount of construction materials used to build the surface of the container.

Moreover, it is cheaper per unit of output to light and heat one large building than to stoke up the furnaces and run the generators for each of three smaller buildings.

Divisibility and Specialization Adam Smith examined specialization in his description of the pin factory. In a small operation one worker may perform several tasks. In a larger one he would specialize, performing the one task more efficiently than any of the other multiple tasks. He learns shortcuts to perform his job. Machinery and other forms of capital do not always conveniently come in the exact sizes that are most appropriate to a particular task. Thus, perhaps a larger machine can be utilized and one may avoid using one smaller machine to full capacity and the other small one at one-half capacity. With bigger machines and plants and a larger work force, more flexible arrangements of capital and labor are possible. And greater flexibility allows for inputs to be combined more efficiently.

By-products Large firms can take advantage of marketing of by-products, whereas small firms cannot. Examples are large lumber firms which manufacture presto logs and chipboards from scraps. The large chemical companies can also afford to market numerous chemical by-products from the residues of chemical processes. Wool is a by-product of raising sheep—or is lamb the by-product? Actually they are *joint products.* We shall say more about this later.

Volume Discounts Another example of the declining long-run average cost curve results from inputs which can be purchased in volume as well as output that can be sold in volume, leading to lower unit delivery costs. The distributor can offer lower prices to the volume buyer because it then becomes cheaper for a distributor to transport larger shipments of materials less frequently to the retail outlet. As a case in point, it is becoming more difficult for the small, local grocer to order from wholesale distributors unless the order at least reaches a specified minimum amount. Transportation costs to the distributor are too high per unit of goods delivered by truck to justify what are considered small orders. The loading and unloading time for both buying and selling firms is reduced by large-volume orders. Another consideration is that the larger the order and the greater geographical area over which a distributor sells its products, the more efficient the operation, because a driver is able to make many deliveries at points far from the plant.

Why LAC Can Rise

Internal Diseconomies of Scale In the long run when all inputs are variable the LAC curve can rise. Why is this?

Of all factors of production, even in the long run, it may be necessary to consider the decision maker as a fixed factor. The larger the plant becomes, the longer are the lines of communication from the lower levels to the top of the pyramid. Hence, transactions costs rise. As the specialization intensifies, it is harder for the ultimate decision maker to be knowledgeable in all pertinent areas, to be able to keep in touch with the daily refinements in each department and subdepartment. The subheads may find some conflict between maximizing the welfare of the company and that of maximizing their own welfare. The bigger the plant, the less able is the top manager to sort out the intrigues of subordinates which could decrease workers' morale and efficiency. In addition, management is constrained by time. There is only so much a manager can get done in even a twelve-hour day. Therefore, in the long run, treating management as a fixed factor leads to diminishing marginal returns.

Some companies, like General Motors and Ford, have found it more efficient to subdivide into smaller divisions, each with its chief, an example of diversification. Just where diversification of plant and economies of individual plant size cross is not known. But General Motors evidently has not reached it, since there is no indication it is experiencing internal diseconomies of scale over its total operations as yet. Figure 6-7 illustrates three different situations. In the first figure, firms elicit economies of scale for a large range of output before the turning point is reached. In the second figure, firms reach internal diseconomies of scale after relatively smaller levels of output. And in the bottom figure, such firms demonstrate constant returns to scale over a large middle range of output. The last case seems to be quite common. But measurements are difficult and results can vary.

JOINT PRODUCTS AND BY-PRODUCTS

Most firms produce more than one product. These jointly produced goods are called joint products or by-products. If the Indian Hunter kills a buffalo, the meat may be the principal product, but after some further processing the hide is used to provide a cover for the tepee. Similarly, a modern slaughterhouse produces many joint products from beef and hog carcasses.

Modern sawmills also produce by-products. In the Northwest, sawmillers discovered that the mounds of chips and sawdust that once were discarded could be profitably processed into salable commodities. The sawdust is rolled into a compact cylinder, creating what is generally known as a presto log that people use as firewood in their living room fireplaces. The chips are made into chipboard, a sheeting material widely used in construction. Bark is used both for chemicals and as a decorative mulch for landscaping. The principal product of a typical sawmill, of course, is lumber for building purposes. We call all these other goods by-products.

We are interested here, of course, in how one can measure or observe the

Figure 6-7

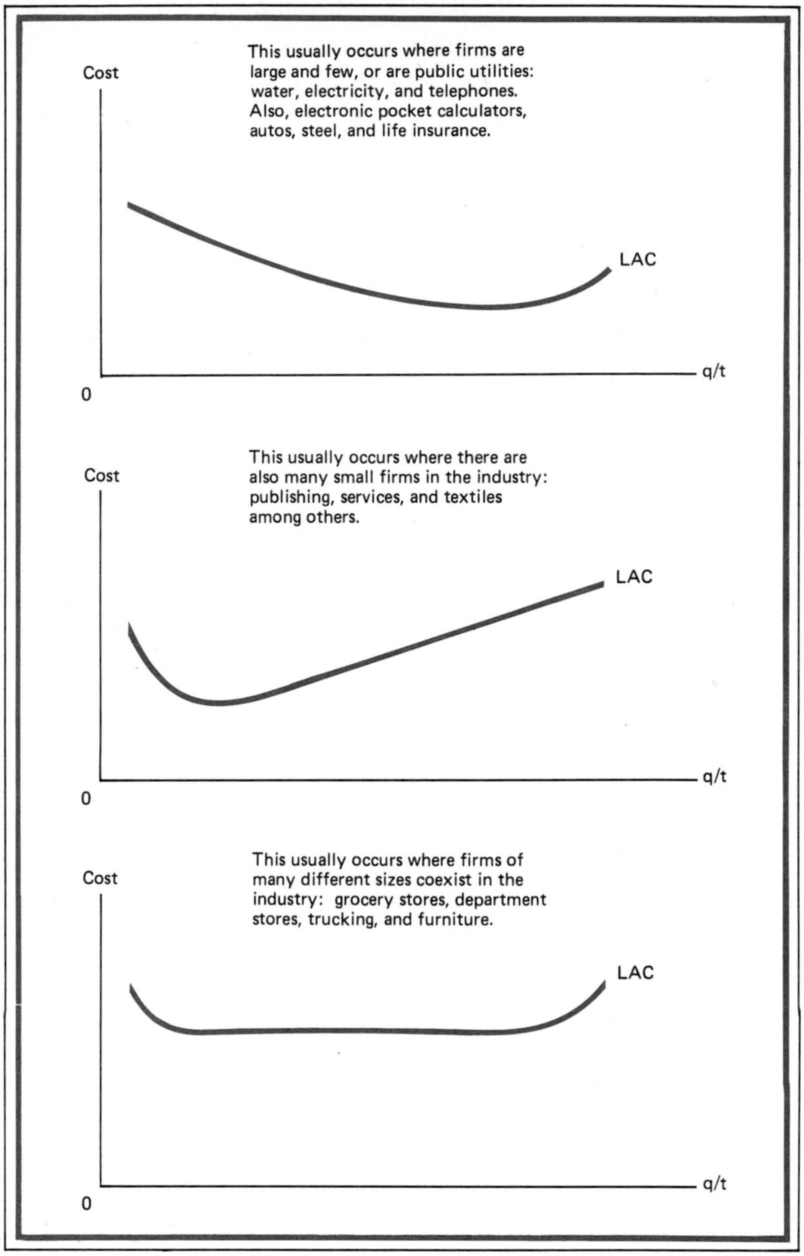

cost of production of a by-product, because at first it would appear that the concept of cost becomes cloudy when we are dealing with by-products. We shall find that careful attention to economic cost as opportunity cost helps clear up some problems that arise in accounting for the cost of providing a joint product.

Take the case of the presto log. We know, of course, that the cost of labor and machinery that is used to process the sawdust left over from the mill's operations is directly related to the cost of production. But what of the sawmill itself—the originator of the sawdust? Should not part of the costs of the mill be absorbed by the presto log division? Or, say a single manager is paid a salary to run both the sawmill and the presto log operations. If we allocate costs, should we not divide up that part of his salary that applies to one operation and that part that applies to the other, in order to know what it costs to produce Presto logs? But, how do we make such a division when the manager's decision-making activities often affect both operations simultaneously?

When accountants make decisions like this—allocating overhead costs among the various product lines—the rules they use are arbitrary and are recognized to be arbitrary. And, in many cases involving such things as tax liabilities, some arbitrary procedures must be followed as a practical matter. Thus, the accountants do the best they can with the information they have. But, the business manager can recognize that output decisions should be made on the basis of opportunity cost by treating the joint products as a package. Imagine, for example, that for some reason the price of lumber falls to very low levels while the price of presto logs stays high. The manager might then decide to take perfectly good timber and grind it up into sawdust as an input to the presto log production. He would do this because the opportunity cost of lumber has fallen.

Alternatively, imagine that the price of Presto logs falls to very low levels while lumber prices remain high. In this case, the manager will take care to produce as little sawdust as possible, because its value in the form of presto logs is nil. Furthermore, if it is costly to dispose of the sawdust by burning or dumping, it might even pay to produce the Presto logs at a loss if the loss is less than the cost of otherwise disposing of this unwanted by-product of the sawmill's operations. In this case the opportunity cost of the sawdust in Presto logs is negative because the alternative is itself costly. If costs are negative, this means that there is a net benefit to the firm from having its Presto log alternative handy. It loses less by selling Presto logs than it would if it disposed of the sawdust byproduct in some other way.

Hence, in the case of joint products, the production process will usually involve processing both products simultaneously—beef and hides, for example. To allocate part of the production costs to one product and part to another simply does not make sense. It is impossible to do except in a subjective way. Accountants must do it for certain record-keeping purposes. But from an economic point of view, if you can achieve small increases in the output of one product at the expense of the other, the opportunity cost is clear. Once you have decided on a volume of output, whether or not you expand or contract that volume depends on the benefits you expect to derive from the two products produced jointly, and the opportunity costs of the resources that you must devote to this joint expansion of output.

CHAPTER SUMMARY

Three legal kinds of business enterprises are sole proprietorships, partnerships, and corporations. Liability is unlimited for the first two, whereas owners of corporate stock can only lose the amount of their stock investment. But stockholders, individually, have much less influence in running the business than single owners and partners.

Conceptually, a firm is a team of workers who contract to specialize in performing certain tasks under the centralized authority of a boss, manager, or owner. Those in authority, and the ultimate owner, are motivated by being residual claimants to the profits. The reward is greater the greater their efficiency in organizing the activities of the team.

The firm will grow as long as the benefits from contracting to hire another worker is greater than the transactions cost of hiring him plus the wage cost, or of purchasing or renting another piece of equipment.

Economic efficiency is not measured in physical units, only in monetary units. As the relative prices of inputs change, firms alter the combination of physical inputs in the production process in order to minimize costs.

The production function is the relation of the amount of inputs of capital in combination with labor, to the amount of output per period, assuming a given technology.

Diminishing marginal productivity occurs in the short run when a point is reached where further additions of a variable factor in combination with a fixed factor result in smaller incremental increases in output.

Since all factors of production can vary in the long run, then diminishing marginal productivity does not apply. The concept of economies of scale takes over. There can be increasing, decreasing, and constant returns to scale.

Marginal costs are the mirror image of marginal productivity. Thus, the law of diminishing marginal productivity has its alternative expression in the law of increasing marginal costs. Marginal cost is the change in total cost or in total variable cost resulting from producing additional output. In the short run, marginal costs vary inversely with marginal productivity.

The various cost constructs are related. Total cost equals total fixed cost plus total variable cost. Totals are converted to averages by dividing by quantity. Thus, average cost equals total cost divided by quantity, average fixed cost equals total fixed cost divided by quantity, and so on. The marginal cost curve intersects both the average cost and average variable cost curves at their minimum points.

A firm's planning curve is its long-run average cost curve composed of one point from each of a theoretically infinite number of short run average cost curves.

The shape of a firm's long run average cost curve is affected by internal economies of scale. These are changes originating from within the firm and resulting from efficiencies of production associated with size, specialization of tasks, and marketing by-products. Diseconomies of scale occur because the specialized resources of the entrepreneur may be the one fixed factor in the long run. As operations grow, he becomes less efficient in coordinating activities.

Most firms produce more than one product or joint products. In costing out such products, the opportunity cost of the joint package is the relevant cost.

QUESTIONS

1. Is it a firm when a weekend mechanic fixes cars in his backyard? Suppose he is also the sole owner and employee of a corner auto repair business. Is this shop a firm? What about if he employs three mechanics and a bookkeeper-secretary?
2. There is occasionally a basketball team in the NBA that does not possess any superstars, or any player picked by the voting fans to play in the annual all-star game. Yet the team wins a divisional championship (and revenues) against teams whose players are better (individually more productive) in individual matchups position by position. Much of the team's success, it is believed, is due to the coach's ability to

select and integrate the complementary skills of certain players and mold them into a winning unit. Does this description fit the description of a firm? Is the whole greater than the sum of its parts? Is there a residual claimant? Aside from the seasonal contracts that players and coaches sign with the owner, how does the coach "contract" with each player during the game?

3. According to the chapter's description, is a government agency a firm? Does it have residual claimants? What standard of efficiency is lacking that distinguishes it from a private firm? Is it therefore likely to be more inefficient than a private firm? Why, or why not? Does the fact that in 1976 only 226 Washington, D.C., civilian government employees out of 2.8 million lost their jobs due to inefficiency affect your answer? Explain.
4. Would profit-sharing schemes likely work better for small firms than for large ones? Does your answer depend on in which situation the greater percentage of the loss from shirking is absorbed by the shirker? Explain.
5. In 1980 the British talked about substituting blimps for jet cargo planes. Is this an example of the often discussed inefficiency of the British economy? Comment.
6. Why do milk companies use gas-guzzling trucks instead of horse-pulled wagons to make store deliveries? They used to do it, didn't they? Comment.
7. Recycling bottles and aluminum cans, it is said, uses less energy, thus it is more efficient than producing throwaways. Does this conclusion necessarily follow? Discuss.
8. In automobiles the combustion engine is more efficient than steam-powered engines. How do you know this is true without knowing anything about automobile engines? Which concept of efficiency is being discussed here? Suppose electric automobiles begin to appear everywhere, what would you conclude?
9. The prevailing philosophy for success in economic development in the 1950s and 1960s was founded on the notion that growth was an automatic and direct function of the amount of capital investment. Why might large capital investment for India be an example of gross waste and incompetence?
10. The Interstate Commerce Commission began to deny rate increases that enabled railroads to earn more than 180 percent of variable, or average, costs. An executive of the Association of American Railroads said, "We need 165 percent of variable costs to cover full costs, so 180 percent isn't even 10 percent above average costs." Assume the executive means average variable costs when he speaks of 180 percent of variable and average costs:
    a. Does he really also mean average cost at the end of his statement? Explain.
    b. Suppose *AVC* is $100. What revenue rate must be set to earn 180 percent of *AVC*?
    c. If *AVC* are $100 and 165 percent above *AVC* is the necessary rate per unit of cargo shipped, what is the *AFC*? What is the *ATC*?
    d. What does 10 percent above "average costs" represent here?
11. Mr. Clutter says he needs more space in his small shop. "I'm stepping over everything and can't find half the things I'm looking for. It sure reduces the time I can spend with my customers." What cost curve is significant here and what is happening to it? Is there a related concept and curve that can also describe Clutter's situation? Can you indicate and graph the costs curves that would suggest a solution for him?
12. Mrs. Potter runs a plant shop and has been setting her retail prices at twice the cost per plant charged her by the supplier. Hence, her markup is 100 percent. "So if a plant is $1, I charge $2: one for us and one for them. But lately our costs have been rising and our prices haven't because of competition. Our profits are falling." Was her profit really 100 percent? Explain.
13. Book publishers are feeling the pressure of higher costs, among them the rising costs of paper. Pulp Printing Inc. plans to publish fewer new titles this year. The

company expects to come out ahead by publishing 1 book that attracts, say, 30,000 buyers, rather than 6 books that sell 5,000 copies each (*Newsweek*, October 28, 1974, p. 88). Why will this action reduce costs? What costs?

14. Can you draw an analogy between a student cramming the night before studying for a big exam the next morning and the *TP*, *AP*, and *MP* curves?
15. The ships that carry the oil and other bulk freight across the oceans of the world have gotten bigger over the last several decades—some reaching 500,000 tons. "The bigger they are the cheaper they are." Does this quote mean total costs of larger ships are actually less than for smaller ships? Explain the relevant concepts.
16. Several years ago K-Mart stores began opening up smaller stores of about 40,000 to 50,000 square feet, down from their earlier stores of 84,000 to 95,000 square feet. The policy was to build many more smaller units and few large units. Would you conclude that K-Mart has reduced the economy of scale of its operations? Explain. A spokesman said, "We are far from the saturation point in the Northeast." (*Forbes*, October 15, 1975, p. 52). What does this imply?
17. Is the average expenditure to you of buying a car greater or less than the average expenditure to you of a public bus paid in part by your taxes? Therefore, is the marginal cost to you of driving your car to work greater compared to the *MC* to you of taking a bus? Why in the past have a majority of people preferred to take their cars?
18. A firm that is experiencing increasing returns to scale cannot therefore be subject to diminishing returns as well. Do you agree?
19. Why does the *SAC* curve descend faster than the *LAC* curve?
20. You collaborate with a friend on a homework assignment for an economics class. He provides you with the following data as an example of increasing returns to scale:

Output (units)	ATC
30	20
40	16
50	12
60	10

Should you continue to collaborate with him?

21. Given the following information, calculate the marginal costs of producing the output of each additional worker and his marginal productivity. Is there evidence of diminishing returns, assuming the number of machines is constant and the daily wage is $40 per worker?

Workers	Wages	Total costs
0	$ 0	$ 800
1	40	1,000
2	80	1,140
3	120	1,260
4	160	1,360
5	200	1,480
6	240	1,630
7	280	1,810
8	320	2,020

22. "It costs the same to send a bus down the road with one passenger as it does full." What costs was this Greyhound executive talking about?

23. This problem covers most of the concepts in the chapter. Can you fill in the blanks using the clues provided? Use fractions instead of decimals when answers are not whole numbers.

Output	TC	MC	AC	AFC	TVC	AVC	TFC
0		—	—	—		—	
1							
2							
3							
4							
5							
6							

a. *AFC* for 6 units of output is 6-2/3.
b. *AVC* for 4 units of output is 21.
c. *TVC* is increased by 10 when the 5th unit of output is added.
d. *AC* of 6 units of output is 4-4/5 less than AC of 5 units of output.
e. *AFC* + *AVC* for 2 units of output is 45.
f. *MC* is 18 for a change in output from 2 to 3 units.
g. It costs 30 more to produce 1 unit of output than to remain shut down.

Chapter 7

The Competitive Model

Competition may be the life of trade, but it's the death of profit.

—Anonymous

PROGRESS REPORT

A. In Chapter 6 we discussed the firm and the economic rationale for the existence of firms in an exchange economy. Fundamental relations between productivity and costs were also examined, illustrating the law of diminishing marginal returns in the short run. The chapter ended with a discussion of internal economies of scale.

B. The purpose of this chapter is to integrate the firm and the industry into the competitive model. The condition required for profit maximization is discussed. In addition, external economies of scale are introduced and distinguished from internal economies of scale in order to explain why industries experience either increasing, decreasing, or constant long-run costs. Finally, the economic concept of Pareto efficiency is detailed.

C. In Chapter 8 we shall examine farming as an example of a potentially perfectly competitive industry.

PERFECT COMPETITION

The *perfectly competitive model* assumes that: firms are small and many, the product is the same among sellers, mobility is unimpeded, perfect information exists in the market, and no advertising is necessary.

We now have enough tools to describe what economists refer to as the **perfectly competitive model**. It is a very useful abstraction and a helpful reference in describing resource allocation in the real world.

There are five major assumptions that apply to the perfectly competitive model.

Firms are small and plentiful There are many buyers and sellers. The word "many" cannot be given a precise numerical value; it simply means there is a large enough number of potential buyers and sellers that no single buyer or seller can buy or produce enough output to affect the market price. Participants in the market are *price-takers*. In this case the demand curve faced by a competitive producer for his product is perfectly elastic ($E_d = \infty$). No matter how much he brings to the market he receives the same price per unit. The firm or individual has no price policy.

Homogeneous product The product that is exchanged is identical in all respects among all the sellers. Thus, it makes no difference to the buyer from which seller he makes the purchase. Since the product is completely undifferentiated across all sellers, there is no possibility for any one seller to alter the demand curve he faces by introducing a different attribute unique to his product. Corn is corn is corn.

Mobility of resources There exists no impediment to resources—human and nonhuman—moving either in or out of the industry. There is perfect mobility for inputs to seek their best use. There is no discrimination of any kind that sets up arbitrary conditions for entry; initiation fees, licenses, patents and/or copyrights are not required. That is, we are assuming that transactions costs of resources switching from one use to another are trivial.

Perfect information All buyers and sellers are assumed to know the prices at which all transactions are taking place, and what the possible alternatives are. That is, the consequences of actions taken are known with certainty. Information costs are zero. In this environment no one consumer is able to buy at a lower price than his competitors because he is privy to some special information. He is not able to sell his product at a higher price because other sellers or the buyers are ignorant of some market conditions. Therefore, no one is able in the long run to earn windfall gains while others absorb windfall losses.

No advertising Since the product is identical no producer has anything to gain by advertising a product indistinguishable from what competitors produce. Thus, the only competition among them comes down to price competition.

Perfect competition does not exist in the real world, although several major industries approximate it surprisingly well. Among them are farming, cotton textiles, tanker rates on shipments of crude oil, bituminous coal, and some raw materials bought and sold in the highly organized commodity markets like tin, zinc, and copper. Yet, upon careful examination, even these industries do not reflect *perfect* competition. There are different grades of corn, potatoes, and other crops. There are government subsidies in farming. It is not costless to shift resources among different applications. Uncertainty is the rule, not the exception. And some economic agents do have inside or prior information. Some of these agents are quite small, others quite large, as for example the family farm compared to the corporate farm. Nevertheless, the competitive model is a sufficiently close approximation to the real world in a few industries that it is extremely useful as an analytical tool for predicting price and output changes as supply and demand change, and on which to build more realistic models.

PROFIT MAXIMIZATION

A basic assumption of economics is that firms desire to *maximize profits.*

One of the assumptions of economics is that the firm desires to **maximize** its **profits**. The normal meaning of profits to most people is the excess of total revenues above total costs, sometimes called net revenue. We shall stick with the word profit (π), where $\pi = TR - TC$. Recall from Chapter 5 that a distinction between accounting and economic profits was made. Accounting profits do not include the opportunity costs of the sole owner (his implicit wage) or of the corporate owners—the investors (stockholders)—dividends as a part of total costs. Hence, profits, equal to the difference between total revenue and total costs, are greater than zero. But when the rate of return earned by investors on their investment in the business is also correctly recognized as an opportunity cost, then we shall see that in competitive equilibrium pure profits are zero. The investor is considered as having earned a normal return. This return, however, includes no element of pure profits above and beyond opportunity costs, that is, what the resources could earn in their next best use. More particularly, if the investor earned an 8 percent dividend in the skateboard industry and the economy as a whole was in a long-run general equilibrium situation so that no industry was yielding either more or less than an 8 percent rate of return, then the opportunity cost of the investor is 8 percent. That is his next best alternative. The solution to the competitive model determines that the investor's or owner's opportunity cost (sacrifice) is 8 percent, because no more than 8 percent could have been earned by him had the money been invested in another industry. Thus, zero or normal profit includes the opportunity cost of the investor or the sole owner. They earn no pure profits. Zero profit signifies that only a normal return has been earned. However, temporary pure profits—sometimes called quasi-profits—can be earned in the short run until they are competed away in the long run under perfect competition.

Price-taker

Panel *A* of Figure 7-1 depicts the individual firm as a price-taker. The price is determined by supply and demand in the industry as shown in panel *B*. The combination of all the buyers and all the sellers (producers) creates a market.

The supply and demand schedules express the intentions of these buyers and sellers under various prices. When those intentions are in agreement, a market price emerges and it is the price at which all transactors trade for the commodity or service. It is an equilibrium price because the quantity bought equals the quantity that suppliers offer to sell, and the market is said to be cleared.

The individual firm of panel *A*, however, has no control over the market price. The firm is a price-taker; it produces such a small share of total industry output that its negligible contribution does not shift the industry supply curve to the right far enough significantly to alter the market price. Therefore, the demand curve it faces is perfectly elastic. Whether the firm produces output q_1, q_2, or any output within a feasible range, it still receives the same price per unit of output. If it attempts to charge a higher price than the market determined price of P_1, its customers will go to competitors to make their purchases and it will sell nothing. If the firm attempts to charge a price below P_1, its price will be below opportunity costs and it will incur losses and eventually may go broke. This situation closely approximates the situation faced by the individual American farmer.

Notice that the firm's demand curve is also its price line, and price also equals average revenue. Furthermore, the price is also equal to marginal revenue, since total revenue always changes by the amount each additional unit is sold for, namely P_1. Thus, if $P_1 = \$10$ then the change in total revenue from selling 1 unit is \$10, from selling a second unit is \$10, from a third unit is \$10; so marginal revenue = \$10 and is constant. Also, since each unit sells for \$10, it is obvious that the average price each unit is sold for is \$10, thus the average revenue from selling 5, 10, or 15 units is \$10, Therefore, price equals both marginal revenue and average revenue and all coincide with horizontal demand curve *d*. We can also express the relation as $P_1 = MR = AR$.

Figure 7-1

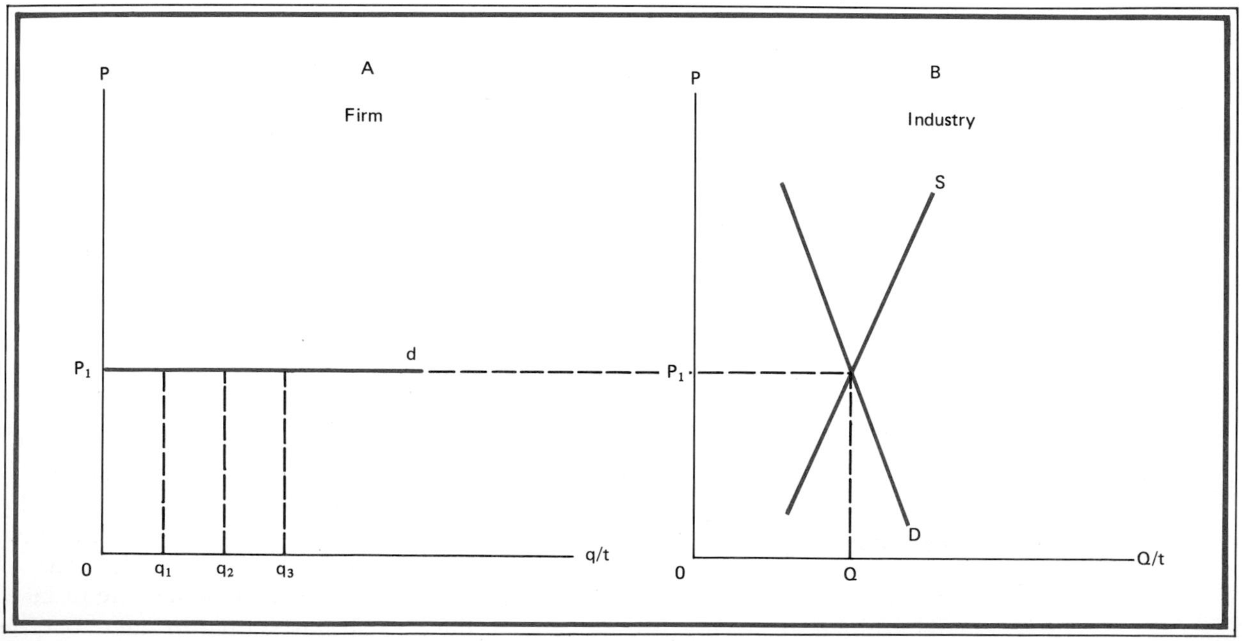

Figure 7-2

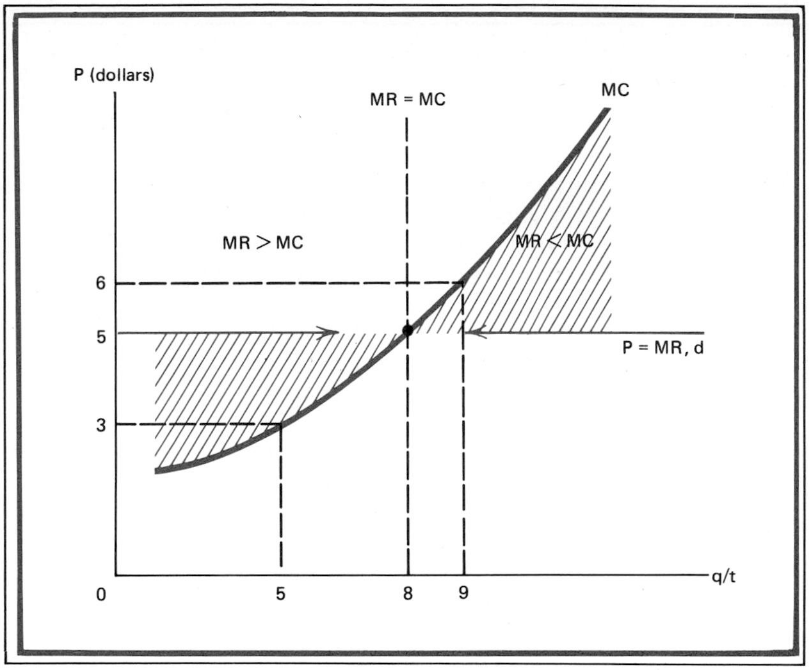

Marginal Revenue Equals Marginal Cost *(MR = MC)*

If a firm desires to maximize its profits, then it makes sense for it to increase production so long as the additional (marginal) revenues from selling the increased output are greater than the additional (marginal) costs. Figure 7-2 shows a marginal cost curve for a firm. Assume the price of the output it produces is $5. The marginal cost curve rises, signifying that the firm experiences increasing costs as it sells more output. Recall that the marginal cost curve is another name for the short-run supply curve of the firm, and also represents the opportunity costs of acquiring the additional inputs as well as the cost of producing the additional output. As long as output (q) is less than 8 units, the marginal revenue of producing each additional unit is greater than the marginal cost. For example, suppose the cost of providing the fifth unit is $3. This is its marginal cost. Since the additional or fifth unit sells for $5, marginal revenue is greater than marginal cost *(MR > MC)* and it is profitable for the firm to provide the fifth unit. The marginal cost of the sixth unit is greater but still less than $5. This is true until the eighth unit is produced. At that point marginal revenue equals marginal cost and the eighth unit earns an extra revenue of $5 just equal to what it cost the company to provide it. There is no profit made on the eighth unit, nor is a loss experienced. Suppose the firm produced a ninth unit at a cost of $6. Since the market price of the good that the firm produces is $5, the firm's marginal revenue from selling the ninth unit is $5. For all units sold, price equals marginal revenue. Hence the firm earns less ($5) than it costs ($6) to provide the ninth unit. That is, marginal revenue is less

Taxicabs of the Sea

They move day and night, over 20,000 of them a year, along the eight major ocean trade routes of the world. Ships of all nations hauling cargo along gateways that range over the North Atlantic route, the Mediterranean-Asiatic-Australasian route to the South African and Pacific routes. There are two major types of service provided for cargo, liner service and tramp service. Ocean freight rates on liners are not based on competitive supply and demand pricing. Liners tend to belong to conferences that are organizations of steamship lines operating in different countries who set rates in order to avoid competitive price wars. Liner rates are individually determined for each type of cargo. Also, liners run on fixed schedules of repeated sailings whether full or not. Tramp ships are a different breed. They are free to negotiate rates and accept cargo anywhere in the world. They're the gypsy cabs of the sea. They cling to no fixed schedule and make runs only when and where they figure they can make a profit. Indeed, they fit surprisingly well into the competitive model. They provide an identical product: cargo hauling in an open competitive market where a difference in bids of a few cents a ton will determine which ship is chartered.* At any given time the same rates approximately prevail for hauling the same commodity of nonperishable bulk cargo like coal, ore, oats, grain, cotton, cement, fertilizer, and sugar.

No single country dominates tramp shipping and no permanent group of operators is subsidized by a national government. Should a tramp owner set his price above those of competitors, he'll lose charters from shippers who will seek out other carriers. If set too low, he cannot earn a survival profit. How can such a world-wide market be so highly competitive? The answer is by means of modern communications and the functioning of middlemen. Through use of radio, teletypewriter, and telephone via ocean cables, a ship owner of any nation can bid on cargo in most any port of the world. The ship broker often performs this task for the carrier since he can be in constant touch with ports and shippers. He finds cargoes for ships and ships for cargoes and negotiates prices and conditions. But the ship owner makes the final decisions.

* Lane C. Kendall, The Business of Shipping (Cambridge, Md.: Cornell Maritime Press, Inc., 1973), p. 41.

Profits can be increased if marginal revenues are greater than marginal costs *(MR > MC)*; profits are *maximized* when marginal revenues are equal to marginal costs *(MR = MC)*.

than marginal cost. In fact, for all output beyond the eighth unit, marginal revenue is less than marginal cost and the difference grows as more units are produced. Hence, profits rise when marginal revenue is greater than marginal cost and fall when marginal revenue is less than marginal cost when another unit is produced. Thus, the firm increases profits when it produces more as long as marginal revenue is greater than marginal cost, but does not go beyond the point where marginal revenue equals marginal cost. At marginal revenue equals marginal cost, profits are maximized.

By the Numbers

Assume that Figure 7-3 represents the costs and revenue chart for Blast Inc, a producer of rock-and-roll records. The upper graph displays a relation between total revenue *(TR)* and total cost *(TC)*. The lower graph illustrates the demand *(d)*, the average total cost (ATC), and the marginal cost *(MC)* curves. The numbers in Table 7-1 go with Figure 7-3. In our example we assume that the first three columns of Table 7-1 are given. These show the price of the product, the output rate, and the total cost of producing that rate of output each period. The remaining columns can all be derived from these three. In Table 7-1, it is assumed that total fixed costs are $15 before any records are produced, as you can see from column 3 where total cost is $15. As production begins, additional

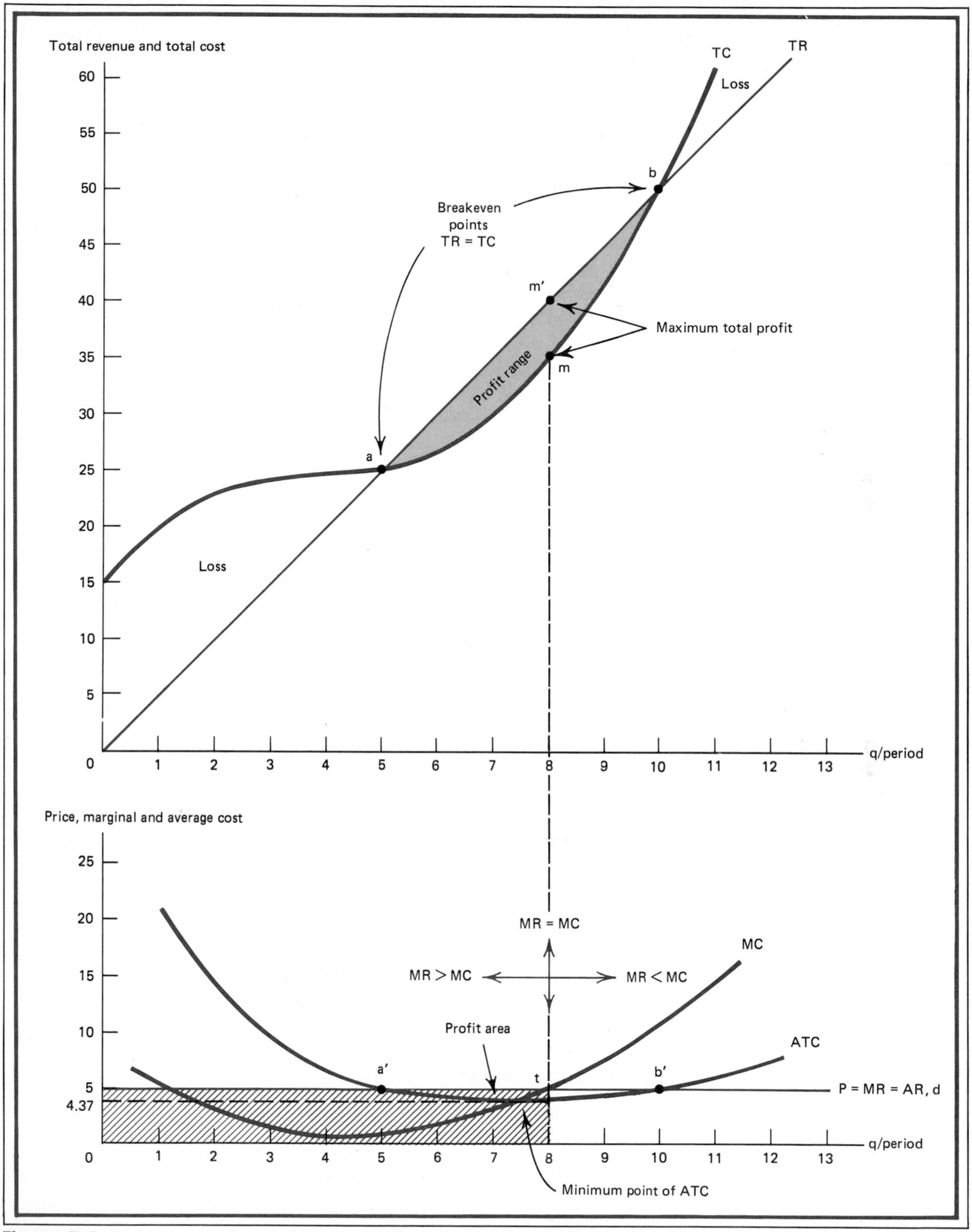
Total revenue and total cost
60
55
50
45
40
35
30
25
20
15
10
5
0
TC
TR
Loss
b
Breakeven
points
TR = TC
m'
Maximum total profit
m
Profit range
a
Loss
1 2 3 4 5 6 7 8 9 10 11 12 13
q/period
Price, marginal and average cost
25
20
15
10
5
4.37
MR = MC
MC
MR > MC
MR < MC
Profit area
ATC
a'
t
b'
P = MR = AR, d
Minimum point of ATC

Figure 7-3

costs are incurred with each record produced. These are the variable costs discussed earlier. Column 3 contains some hypothetical numbers to illustrate a possible cost situation facing Blast Inc. In particular, column 3 provides the numbers for the total cost curve labeled *TC* in Figure 7-3.

As we draw the curves from the number in the tables, we shall present smooth and continuous curves and not just jump from one number to the next. That is, we are using discrete numbers in our table, but we wish to ignore this discreteness by drawing smooth curves. This leads to minor inaccuracies and on occasion to use of approximate numbers.

The total revenue (*TR*) is calculated by multiplying the price per unit by the total number of units sold. Glancing back at Figure 7-1, panel A, we see a horizontal demand curve facing the firm. Assume Blast Inc. sells its records to the retail stores for $5 each, and that the price remains at $5 no matter how much this firm produces and sells. This is shown in column 1 of Table 7-1. Since total revenue is price times quantity, we have multiplied $P \times Q$ shown in columns 1 and 2 and presented the results in column 4 as *TR*. Transferring the numbers from column 4 to Figure 7-3, we plot the straight line labeled *TR*.

Points *a* and *b* indicate the breakeven points where total revenue equals total cost for outputs of 5 and 10 records respectively. The shaded area in the upper graph indicates the profit range between outputs of 5 and 10 over which total revenue is greater than total cost. Total profits (not profit per unit) is a maximum when output is 8 records, and at that output the vertical distance between total revenue (*TR*) and total costs (*TC*) is the greatest ($5) indicated by the distance *m′* to *m*. The point of maximum profit should also occur for an output of 8 records where marginal revenue (*MR*) equals marginal costs (*MC*) in the lower graph, which it does at point *t*. Also, notice that in the lower graph

TABLE 7-1 Hypothetical Numbers for Blast Inc.

	(1) P	(2) Q (Records)	(3) TC (FC + VC)	(4) TR (4) = (1) × (2)	(5) MR $(5) = \frac{\Delta(4)}{\Delta(2)}$	(6) MC $(6) = \frac{\Delta(3)}{\Delta(2)}$	(7) ATC $(7) = \frac{(3)}{(2)}$	(8) π (8) = (4) − (3)
	5	0	15.0	0	—	—	—	−15
	5	1	20.0	5	5	5.0	20.00	−15
	5	2	23.0	10	5	3.0	11.33	−13
	5	3	24.0	15	5	1.0	8.00	−9
	5	4	24.4	20	5	0.4	6.10	−5
	5	5	25.0	25	5	0.6	5.00	0
	5	6	27.0	30	5	2.0	4.50	3
	5	7	30.0	35	5	3.0	4.29	5
MC = MR →	5	8	35.0	40	5	5.0	4.37	5
	5	9	41.0	45	5	6.0	4.55	4
	5	10	50.0	50	5	9.0	5.00	0
	5	11	61.0	55	5	11.0	5.55	−6

when output is either 5 records or 10 records, average revenue (AR) equals average total cost (ATC). Both can be multiplied by output again to get total revenue equal to total cost. To the left of output $q = 8$ marginal revenue is greater than marginal cost ($MR > MC$), hence total profit is lower than it is at its maximum when 8 records are sold. To the right of $q = 8$ marginal revenue is less than marginal cost ($MR < MC$), and again total profit is smaller than when $q = 8$.

Since price is equal to marginal revenue and average renveue when the demand curve is horizontal, then $P = MR = AR$, and column 1 entries are identical to column 5 entries. The marginal and average cost curves are plotted from columns 6 and 7. Total revenue is equal to price times quantity ($TR = Pq$). At an output of 8 records each selling at \$5, Blast Inc. earns total revenues of \$40, as represented by the striped rectangle in the bottom graph of Figure 7-3. Because total cost equals average cost times quantity ($TC = ATC \times q$), then for $q = 8, ATC = 4.37$, so that total cost (TC) is \$35 with profit being \$40 − \$35 = \$5.

A final point: Profit is also \$5 when output is 7 records as well as when output is 8 records. This occurs because records cannot be subdivided into smaller units or fractions of records. If they could, the curves would really be continuous as we have indeed drawn them, and the maximum profit output would occur somewhere between 7 and 8 records where the marginal cost curve intersects the minimum point of the average total cost curve. At that point, maximum total profit would be slightly higher than \$5.

THE SHUTDOWN POINT

In Chapter 5 we mentioned that the firm should shut down when it cannot cover its variable costs. Managers of the firm will decide whether to produce, by comparing marginal cost with marginal revenue or price since price equals marginal revenue for the price-taker firm. When $P < MC$ the firm should increase output. As output rises, marginal cost becomes greater and the firm moves up along the marginal cost curve until the point is reached where price just equals marginal cost. Thus, the firm's supply curve in the short run is its marginal cost curve. Marginal cost is an opportunity cost associated with a decision to produce more output. Since marginal cost is an incremental cost it is associated, of course, with variable costs. And, if price is so low that revenues are not sufficient to cover all variable costs, the firm should close up shop. If it does this it will suffer losses equal to fixed costs. Moreover, if revenues do not cover variable costs, losses will be even greater than fixed costs if it continues to produce, because then the firm will lose *both* the amount equal to its fixed costs *and* that part of its variable costs that it does not recover. Thus, it will minimize losses by shutting down.

For example, assume Blast Inc. has cost charts looking like Figure 7-4, where we now use a different set of numbers than appears in Table 7-1. If the company produced and sold 45 records and the market price were \$11, it would be operating at point *a* with total revenues equal to total cost of \$345. Total revenue equals $P \times q = \$11.50 \times 30 = \$345$, and the total cost equals

Figure 7-4

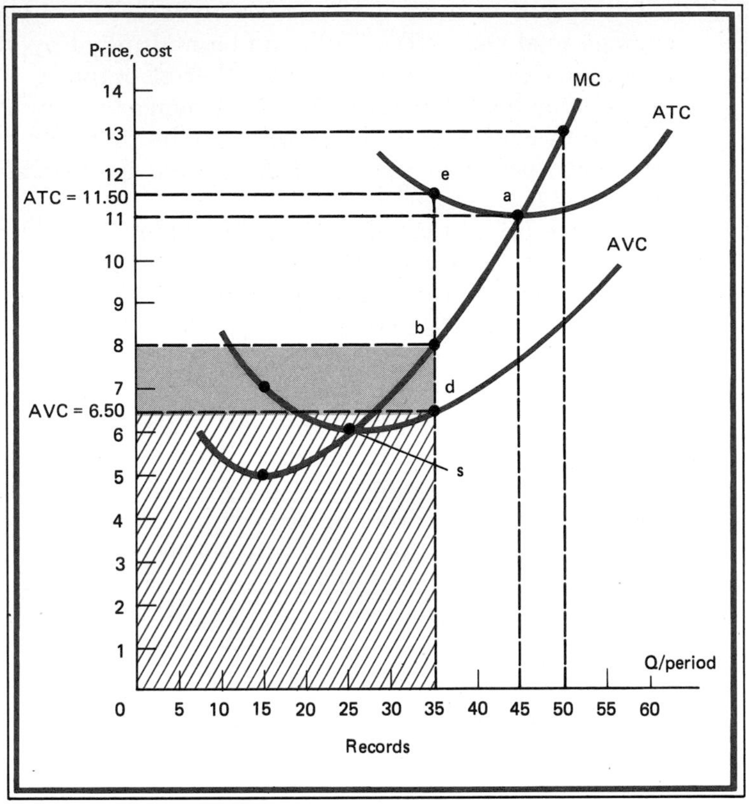

ATC × q = \$11.50 × 30 = \$345. If Blast Inc. were to sell the records for \$8 each, it would move down along its marginal cost (supply) curve to point *b* and produce 35 records. Its total revenues are now \$280 (\$8 × 35). Its total costs are now \$402.50 (\$11.50 × 35). Its total variable costs are \$227.50 (\$6.50 × 35). Therefore, Blast Inc. is not covering its total costs, but it is more than covering its variable costs by \$52.50 (\$280 − \$227.50). This \$52.50 is indicated by the shaded rectangle. The difference between total costs and total variable costs is the total fixed cost \$175 (\$402.50 − \$227.50). Thus, the average fixed cost (AFC) is \$5 (\$175/35) indicated by the distance *d* to *e* on the graph, and the average variable cost is \$6.50 (\$227.50/35) for an output of 35 records. As it stands at point *b*, the firm has accounted for \$52.50 worth of its total fixed costs of \$175. But it still has \$122.50 (\$175 − \$52.50) to go in order to cover all of its fixed costs. This residual of \$122.50 is represented by the unshaded rectangle (\$3.50 × 35). If the firm could have charged a price of \$11 per unit, it could have covered all of its total costs—fixed plus variable. But at a price of \$8, the firm only managed to cover its variable costs plus some of its fixed costs. It is therefore more than covering its short-run opportunity costs or variable costs. However, in the long run, unless something changes so it can charge a price of \$11 a record, or unless something happens that lowers its costs somehow, Blast Inc. will suffer *long-term* losses and should eventually exit the industry, as there will be no incentive to replace worn-out equipment.

If the firm were selling at price of \$6, it would just be covering its variable costs (point *s*) but not offsetting any of its fixed costs in the short run. The firm is operating at the shutdown point *s*. If the market price of the records were below $6, the firm would not even be covering its variable costs in the short run. It is operating below point *s* and should close down operations immediately. There is no supply curve below *s*. Thus if Blast Inc. were receiving $5 a record, and if it produced 15 records, its total revenue would be $75 ($5 × 15) but its total variable costs would be $105 ($7 × 15). It will increase its losses for each time period it remains open by $30 ($105 − $75) plus the $175 in fixed cost it is carrying along. By shutting down it only absorbs the fixed costs plus whatever net operating losses it incurred to that point. If it remains open the operating losses will further accumulate. Therefore, this firm would not produce at an output below 25 records if it intends to minimize losses.

Should the firm be in the fortunate position of being at a point above *a* in Figure 7-4 charging, say, $13 and producing 50 records, the $13 it receives per unit is above cost per unit, total revenue is greater than total costs, and the firm would be earning a pure profit.

Shutdown Point and Shutdown Period

Firms may cease production temporarily but not permanently. For example, the lumber mills of the Northwest will start up and shut down in response to seasonal demand, and in response to cyclical swings in prices for lumber. If the current price received for the output is below variable cost, the firm will stop production but owners of the firm may expect the price to rise again soon, and they will not sell their plant and equipment for its scrap value. Instead, they will continue to spend money for necessary maintenance so production can be resumed on short notice. They anticipate that the shutdown *period* will be a short one.

If the firm's plant remains shut for a long period of time, the machinery and equipment may become obsolete. If it does, then its only value is what it will bring as scrap. In this case, reentry to the industry would *not* mean starting up the old machinery, but rather it would mean building a new production unit. This would be a new investment decision on the part of the firm's owners.

Thomas Edison Selling Below Cost?

I was the first manufacturer in the U.S. to adopt the idea of dumping surplus goods upon the foreign market. Thirty years ago my balance sheet showed me that I was not making much money. My manufacturing plant was not running to its full capacity. I could not find a market for my products. Then I suggested that we undertake to run our plant on full capacity and sell the surplus products in foreign markets at less than the costs of production. Every one of my associates opposed me. I had my experts figure out how much it would add to the cost of operating the plant if we increased this production 25 percent. The figures showed we could increase the production 25 percent at an increased cost of only 2 percent. On this basis I sent a man to Europe who sold lamps there at less than the price of production in Europe. By doing this I was able to employ more labor to run my plant at full capacity.

Source: Wall Street Journal, Dec. 20, 1911.

***Entering and exiting* an industry is more or less difficult depending on the amount of capital involved.**

We wish to point out that **entering and exiting** an industry is more or less difficult depending upon the amount of capital required. The larger the capital requirements, the more difficult it is to enter, and the more difficult it is to exit. By difficult, of course, we mean costly in the sense of opportunity cost. In the case of starting a firm there are large opportunity costs if the amount of capital investment required is large.

Similarly, the larger the amount of capital that is idle when the firm is temporarily shutdown, the larger will be the fixed loss to the firm. This is because there may exist a large number of highly valued opportunities given up if the firm's plant and machinery are kept idle and not put into alternative uses. In other words, to scrap the firm's capital is not necessarily the only alternative. The larger the number of higher valued alternatives, the more imperative it is that the firm's owners examine and engage in *any* alternative uses of the plant and equipment that will help reduce the extent of the period-to-period losses. What we wish to emphasize here is that those fixed costs that represent losses to the firm's owners should be viewed as opportunity costs. This in contrast to the examples often given in terms of historical accounting costs. In other words, just because you spent a lot of money on equipment in getting into the business does not mean you necessarily have to suffer large losses in getting out. It depends on whether or not there are alternative uses to which your plant and equipment can be put. Indeed, alternative uses of your plant should become highly desirable. When, for example, a broken-down warehouse could become a successful restaurant in a refurbished area of town, then the opportunity cost of *not* converting it would be high. Even though the warehouse appeared to be making a profit as a warehouse, as its alternative-use value grew its opportunity costs rose until it no longer paid to keep it as a warehouse. Thus, the decision to scrap equipment and sell the property will be made more rapidly the larger the opportunity cost of capital.

Shutting down temporarily is one kind of decision; selling the machinery and property to be used in some other trade is another. Shutting down temporarily is an operating decision; shutting down permanently is an investment decision—but that investment decision is one that must be reassessed period by period, for opportunity costs are always changing.

SHORT-RUN EQUILIBRIUM OF THE FIRM

In the short run the firm can adjust to demand and price changes by using existing facilities either more or less intensively as the situation demands. Workers can be laid off, new ones hired, or regulars worked overtime. Machines can be used for part of the day or for two shifts. Figure 7-5 illustrates three situations of short-run equilibria. In each situation the price P_1 equals marginal cost when output is q_n.

Panel A The firm is in short-run equilibrium. It has no incentive either to contract or expand output away from q_n which is its optimum output. The firm is operating at the minimum point of its average total cost *(ATC)* curve, so it is

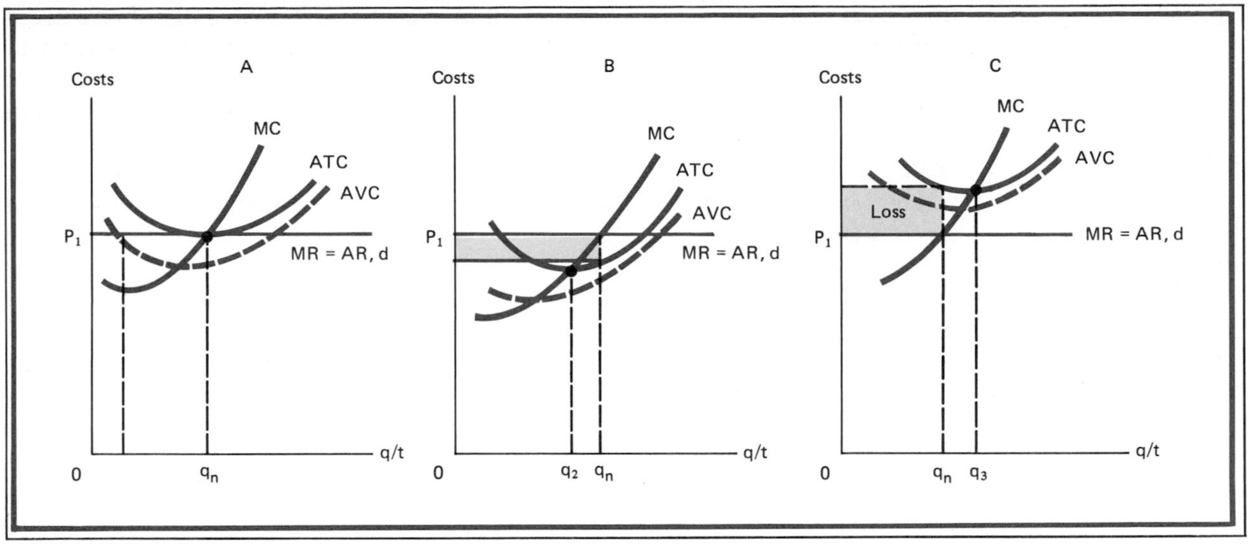

Figure 7-5

producing at its capacity. Total revenue $TR = P_1 \times q_n = \text{ATC} \times q_n = TC$. The firm is earning a normal return. There are no pure profits.

$P_1 = MC = MR$: Marginal cost represents the value of resources required to produce the q_n unit. It is an opportunity cost and signifies what amount of dollars it took to bid these resources away from another use. Since $P_1 = MC$, the value of the resources required to produce the q_n unit just equals, at the margin, the benefit to consumers—for P_1 is what the consumer is willing to pay for that last unit of good. And this price is the same for all consumers. Thus, the resources earn their keep and provide utility to consumers that is no more than these resources could provide in alternative uses. The statement $P_1 = MC$ indicates maximum efficiency in the use of resources. Taken together, $P_1 = MC = MR$ suggests that society—the group of buyers and producers—is achieving both maximum efficiency and satisfaction in the current allocation of resources in this use.

The $MC = MR$ relationship says that output q_n is the profit maximizing output. There is, therefore, no desire to expand or contract output. Thus, $P = MC = MR$ is the short-run equilibrium condition.

Panel B In panel B the marginal conditions $P_1 = MC = MR$ still apply except that now the market price is greater than the minimum average total cost (min *ATC*). Since $P_1 = MC$ there exists no inefficiency in resource allocation. Firms are paying to produce the q_n unit exactly what consumers are willing to pay. However, the firm is producing at an output level beyond its normal output of q_2 because the higher price has motivated it to produce at the higher level q_n. Since $MC = MR$ the firm is maximizing its total profits and it is also earning a pure profit. Pure profits are shown by the shaded area. In the short run, resources applied to produce this product are earning more in their current use than they could earn in any highest valued alternative use. Thus, their earnings are greater than their opportunity cost. You might wonder whether this implies misallocation and waste. No. We said that $P_1 = MC = MR$. In this condition we know there is efficiency even though $TR > TC$ and pure profits exist. There is no resource misallocation; there is simply an extra transfer of income from consumers to the owners of the resource. These profits are sometimes called an economic rent—a topic more fully discussed in Chapter 13. The consumers buying the product are paying a price equal to the marginal revenue which corresponds proportionately to their marginal utility. They are willing to buy the amount they do at price P_1 because they gain utility. They are not paying more than they are willing to, and they are buying as much as they want to at the P_1 price.

Panel C The market price P_1 is below the minimum average total cost. Again the firm produces where $P_1 = MC = MR$ but at an output q_n, below normal capacity output q_3. However, average revenue is now less than ATC per unit, and $TR < TC$. Profits, indicated by the shaded area, are negative in this case. The firm is operating at a loss. Resources are earning less than their opportunity costs. They could earn more in an alternative use. Moreover, P_1 is also less than minimum average variable costs. The firm is not even covering its variable costs under these conditions. It should shut down completely and perhaps sell off its fixed factors to minimize its losses. If the firm responded by producing more at the P_1 price, it simply would increase its losses. The shaded area would become larger. We could, of course, have indicated a situation where the firm had a loss but remained in business because its losses were less than they would be if it chose to shut down, as we described in the previous section.

What we have shown in the three panels is the short-run equilibrium position of a firm when it makes zero profit, positive profit, and negative profit. Now we wish to consider long run-equilibrium of the firm and the industry.

LONG-RUN EQUILIBRIUM OF THE INDUSTRY

The assumptions of the competitive model logically lead to the conclusion that, for any firm, price will equal opportunity cost in competitive equilibrium. This viewpoint has interesting implications for allocation of resources by the market and for how firms and the industry adjust to short-run and long-run changes in market conditions. We shall consider the industry details first.

Constant-Cost Industry

When the cost of production per item remains the same no matter how many items are produced, it is called a *constant-cost industry*.

Let us examine the skateboard industry. Assume it is a highly competitive industry. Note that the supply curve for the industry is horizontal in Figure 7-6. This signifies that no matter how many skateboards the industry produces, the costs of production per skateboard are the same. When industry costs remain unchanged as more output is produced, we call it a **constant-cost industry**. This result occurs for an industry that uses no specialized resources. Resources in the economy at large can be bid away from other uses and substituted for use in the skateboard industry without driving up the price of those unspecialized

Figure 7-6

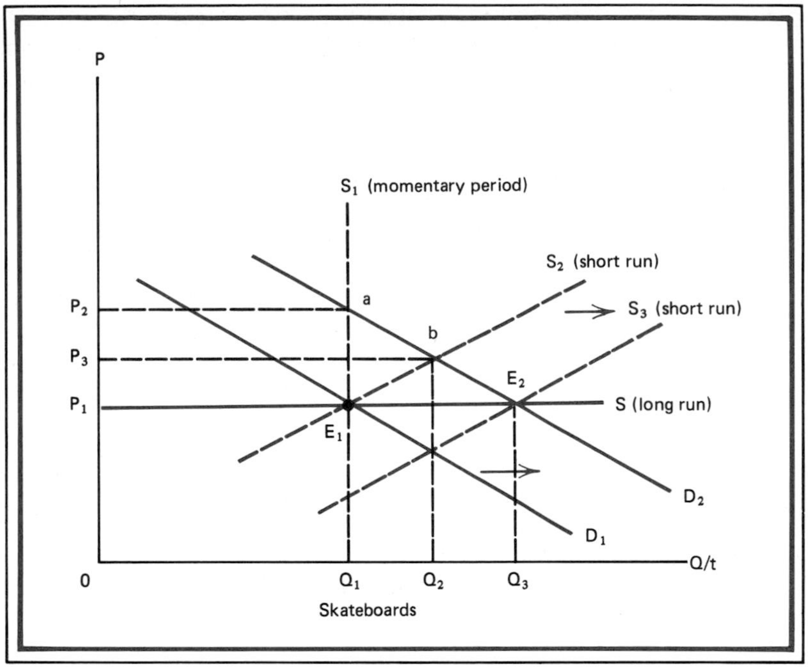

inputs. Also, it is assumed that the skateboard industry makes such a small claim on the total resources of the whole economy that it does not affect the market price of inputs it purchases.

The skateboard industry starts out at equilibrium at E_1, where supply S and demand D_1 determine the market price to be P_1 and the quantity to be Q_1. A new craze for skateboards causes the demand curve for skateboards to shift to D_2. In the momentary period, the immediate effect is to drive the market price up to P_2, where the quantity remains at Q_1 since there is not time for suppliers to respond. Hence, the momentary period supply curve S_1 is perfectly inelastic ($E_s = 0$). Soon the inventories of retailers and wholesalers dwindle, and the factories are hit with a sudden increase in demand from wholesalers and retailers. The supply curves represent the long-run opportunity costs of production. The price P_2 is now above opportunity costs associated with the supply curve S, resulting in pure profits being earned by existing firms in the industry. Momentary equilibrium exists at point *a*.

In the short run, existing firms cannot increase plant capacity but they can, nevertheless, step up production by using current facilities more intensively. They can go into overtime and hire more workers. As this happens, the quantity supplied increases to Q_2 as the industry moves up along the short run supply curve S_2.

The short-run supply curve S_2 is more elastic than the momentary period supply curve S_1 illustrated as rotating clockwise through point E_1. The industry can only sell the additional skateboards $Q_2 - Q_1$ by individual firms competing the price down to P_3 in the short run. Therefore, short run equilibrium exists at point *b*. But P_3 is still greater than opportunity costs represented by price P_1 per unit of output. The glitter of profits remains though slightly dimmed. By the assumptions of the perfectly competitive model, resources are mobile and potential producers also have all the information they want about prices, costs, and those alluring pure profits. The market signals beam loud and clear. Entry by new producers takes place. As we learned in Chapter 3, when the parameter N_S (the number of suppliers) is increased the supply curve shifts to the right. Hence S_2 now shifts to S_3 as the industry is compelled toward long-run equilibrium at point E_2. Once again the price is P_1 and equal to opportunity costs, but industry output has risen to Q_3. Under perfectly competitive conditions prices cannot remain above opportunity costs in the long run, because pure profits attract more resources into the industry and the pure profits are competed away.

Figure 7-6 needs some clarifying explanations. Notice that the long-run supply curve S is obtained by connecting the two short-run equilibria points E_1 and E_2. But you may puzzle over why the short-run supply curve S_3 also passes through point E_2. It sounds like a contradiction, but it is not. The reason lies in the nature of the long-run supply curve. The long-run supply curve S is actually made up of points from all short-run supply curves such as S_2 and S_3; one point from each short-run supply curve. At any given point in time firms in the industry are operating from their short-run supply curves, that is, their marginal costs curves, where the industry supply curve is the sum of the firms' supply curves. For if the price were again to rise above P_1, the industry would not move along S right away. In the momentary period the industry would only produce Q_3 and the momentary supply curve would be perfectly inelastic through Q_3. But in the short run the industry, having some time to adjust, would move along a more elastic supply curve S_3 because individual firms are increasing output along their short-run marginal cost curves (not along their long-run average cost curves *LAC*) because plant capacity cannot be expanded in the short run.

Increasing-Cost Industry

It is worth while to apply the competitive model to the situation of an increasing-cost industry. As shown in Figure 7-7, the coal and oil industries display rising long-run supply curves rather than flat ones, where the short-run supply curves have been left out. This situation can occur if the industry under study is so important to the whole economy that its output represents a significant share of the total output. It cannot purchase more inputs without having repercussions on the prices of inputs also needed by other industries.

The other explanation for increasing costs is that the industry uses highly specialized equipment as well as highly skilled, more scarce, labor inputs. Resources bid away from competing uses cannot be so easily substituted and adopted to other uses without a decline in efficiency, that is, a fall in their marginal productivity. The less efficient, the less productive is the input and consequently more costly to employ. In some cases resources cannot be transferred from one use to the other at all. For instance, land under which depleted oil fields lie cannot be converted to coal production. Thus, as more variable factors are applied to the fixed coal resources, diminishing marginal returns set in and the variable costs of producing coal rise.

The energy bill passed by Congress in October 1978 was designed to dis-

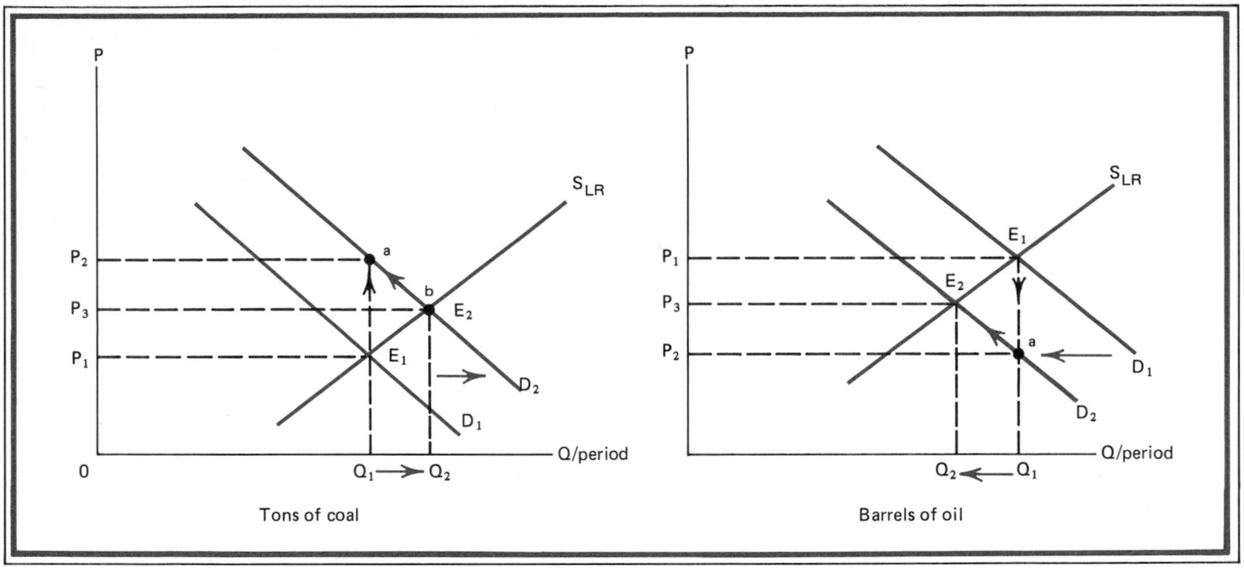

Figure 7-7

courage use of oil and increase the use of coal. The effect is a *relative* decrease in the price of oil. This, however, does not mean that the *absolute* price of coal will end up higher than the *absolute* price of oil. It is relative prices that allocate and ration scarce resources. The purpose of the energy policy was to stimulate the demand for coal so that D_1 would shift to D_2. In the momentary period, the existing amount of coal Q_1 increases from its former equilibrium price of P_1 at E_1 and rises to the temporary disequilibrium price of P_2 at *a*. The process shown in Figure 7-7 is identical to that of skateboards, with the one exception that the long-run supply curve S is upward sloping. At the price P_2 pure profits exist. There is now an added incentive to dig for the harder-to-mine coal and also to mine more of the readily available coal. Extra workers are hired, or overtime is implemented, or another shift is added. Perhaps all of these options are adopted by the current companies in the industry. In the short run existing firms step up production and in the long run new firms enter. Eventually the price falls to P_3, but does not return to the old equilibrium price of P_1, though output is higher at Q_2 along the long run supply curve S_{LR}.

The reverse process occurs in the oil industry. If costs rise when industry output expands in an increasing-cost industry, then costs should fall when industry output contracts under perfect competition. Initially, equilibrium in the oil industry is at point E_1 where the price is P_1 and output is Q_1. If the energy policy discourages use of oil, then demand shifts left to D_2. In the momentary period, temporary equilibirum exists at point *a* and the price falls to P_2 as firms compete to sell off the less desired oil. However, the price P_2 is below opportunity costs that exist at point E_1. The industry is experiencing pure losses—a windfall loss. In the short run, firms, hence the industry, respond by cutting back production through either introducing shorter work days or directly laying off workers. As firms cut back production the price rises above P_2 and consumers move up along the new demand schedule D_2 and reduce quantity demanded below Q_1. But the price is still below opportunity costs. Thus, in the long run some firms leave the industry. A new equilibrium is established at point E_2 representing a price P_3 below the initial equilibrium price of P_1, and a quantity Q_2 below the initial equilibrium quantity of Q_1.

Some firms that were covering all their opportunity costs at the P_1 price can no longer do so at the new P_2 price. As a result, some labor and capital resources leave the oil industry seeking higher rewards elsewhere—in this case, coal mining. In fact, several oil companies do own coal mines.

The market is a vast communications system sending information signals to all of the economic agents. Any disparities in supply, demand, and price are soon known to all the decision makers, and the market begins to adjust until the shortages, surpluses, and pure profits—or losses—in the temporary short-run equilibrium have been eliminated. When the new long-run equilibrium is reached, prices are once again equal to opportunity costs, and maximum efficiency in the use of resources has been attained since resources can earn neither more nor less in alternative uses.

LONG-RUN INDUSTRY SUPPLY AND EXTERNAL ECONOMIES OF SCALE

Internal economies **affect the shape of a firm's planning or *long-run average cost curve (LAC)* as the *firm* projects cost reductions due to expansion and reorganization.**

External economies **affect the position of the cost curves of member firms when the *industry* increases output in response to increased demand.**

Industries experience either increasing or decreasing long-run costs because of *external* scale economies. These differ from the **internal economies** of scale outlined in Chapter 6. Internal economies deal with the shape of a firm's planning or long-run average cost curve *(LAC)* as the *firm* realizes cost reductions from increasing plant size and reorganizing inputs into more flexible and efficient combinations. But they cause no shift in the firm's *LAC* curve up or down, because the technical and price relations of inputs expressed in the production function remain unaffected, though the number of inputs can change. However, **external economies** of scale are associated with the effect on the cost curves of member firms as the *industry* increases output in response to an increase in demand by moving *along* the industry's long-run supply curve. The individual firm has no control over outside economic forces affecting it. External economies cause individuals firms' long-run and short-run average cost curves *LAC* and *SAC* to shift downward while external diseconomies cause them to shift upward. Until now we have more or less implicitly assumed three things:

1. As the industry changes size, input prices remain fixed.
2. The level of technology is fixed.
3. The number of complementary firms or industries had no effect on the individual firm's production function.

When any one of these assumptions is relaxed, external economies or diseconomies of production enter, to fundamentally alter the economic or technical relations in the production functions of firms.

There are two classifications of external economies and diseconomies—price and nonprice.

External Price Economies and Diseconomies[1]

Where *external price diseconomies* exist, input prices rise when product demand and production are increased.

When the industry expands production in response to an increase in demand by moving along its long-run supply curve, it also increases its demand for inputs and drives up input prices. The single firm cannot affect input prices, but the industry as a whole can as new firms enter the industry. Rising input prices shift the cost curves of member firms upward in the case of an increasing-cost industry when **external price diseconomies** exist. Conversely, as an industry expands, it may cause firms who supply inputs to the industry to expand as well, increasing their efficiency (internal economies of scale) and permitting them to supply inputs to the purchasing industry at lower prices. The cost curves of the purchasing firms would shift downward as they realize external economies of scale. The purchasing industry would undergo decreasing long run-costs and exhibit a downward sloping long-run industry supply curve.

External Nonprice Economies and Diseconomies[2]

Where *external nonprice economies or diseconomies* exist, production costs are incurred because of the impact of complementary firms or industries.

In this situation input prices do not change when there is an increase in demand for the industry's product and a responding increase in output. However, production costs to member firms change because of the impact of new firms entering an industry or the impact of one industry on another industry. There are two cases, complementary firms and complementary industries.

Complementary Firms External nonprice diseconomies can arise when, for example, new firms set up in a logging area and congest a common road so that deliveries take longer, raising transportation costs to the original firms. Input prices are fixed, yet costs go up. The firms imposing the additional costs do not pay the external costs they have imposed on the other firms in the industry. The new firms could impose external economies if when they enter the area they improve and widen the road, actually reducing the congestion and lowering transportation costs to all firms in the industry, leading to a downward sloping long-run industry supply curve.

Complementary Industries The growth or appearance of one industry can either enhance or disrupt the efficiency of another and confer economies or diseconomies on it. Steel firms are usually located near the source of the iron and coal fields, automobile plants near steel mills, textile mills near seaport towns where cotton enters, and aluminum plants near dams providing abundant sources of water and cheaper electrical power. Railroads and shipbuilding initially merged and grew where primary producing raw material firms could more readily supply manufacturing firms and enlarge the size of the market.

The opposite effect can also occur. A growing industry can impose higher costs on other industries, shifting their cost curves upward. Oil spills by large tankers pollute shrimp beds; nuclear waste raises river temperatures, killing

[1]More formally known as external pecuniary effects.
[2]More formally known as external nonpecuniary effects.

fish; airports expand operations and raise noise levels, upsetting farmers' chickens and causing them to lay fewer eggs. In these situations, external nonprice diseconomies of scale reduce the productivity of affected firms in an industry.

SHIFTS IN LONG-RUN INDUSTRY SUPPLY

The foregoing examples of price and nonprice effects involved increases in production motivated by increases in demand for the industry's products, that result in either increasing or decreasing long-run industry costs. Technological innovation is another example of an external effect. When more efficient technology is introduced in an industry supplying inputs to another industry, input prices can fall allowing the purchasing industry to realize external economies of scale even though—and this is the difference from the prior examples—there has been no change in demand for its product. This causes its member firm cost curves to fall and for the industries' long-run supply curve to shift downward. The same decline in costs and product prices can also result from a technological change occurring within the industry. Figure 7-8 illustrates a shift in the industry supply curve in the situation where the industry is an increasing-cost industry. Remember that the phrase *increasing cost* refers to a movement *along* a given supply curve. However, that curve can shift downward because of new technology. The introduction of a new, cheap process for making chips for electronic pocket calculators was the major cause for the

Figure 7-8

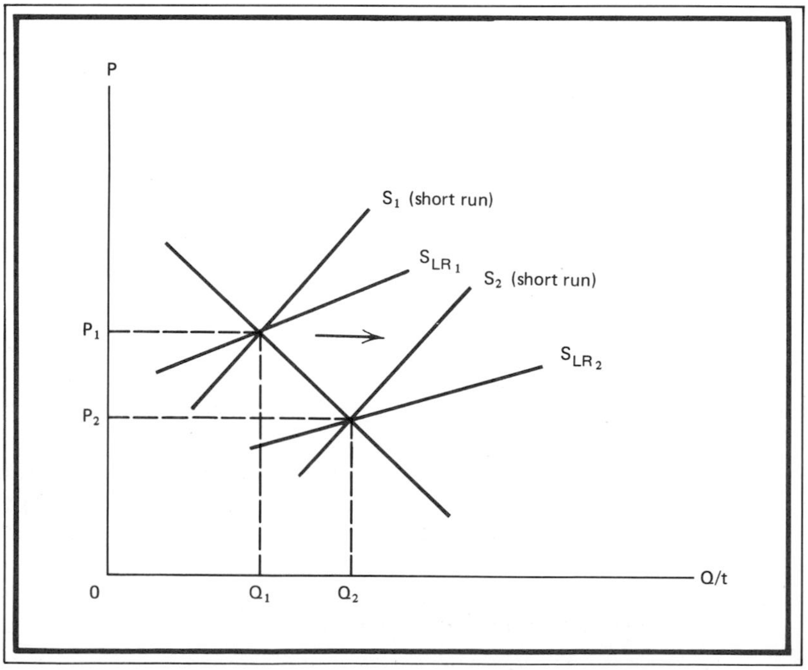

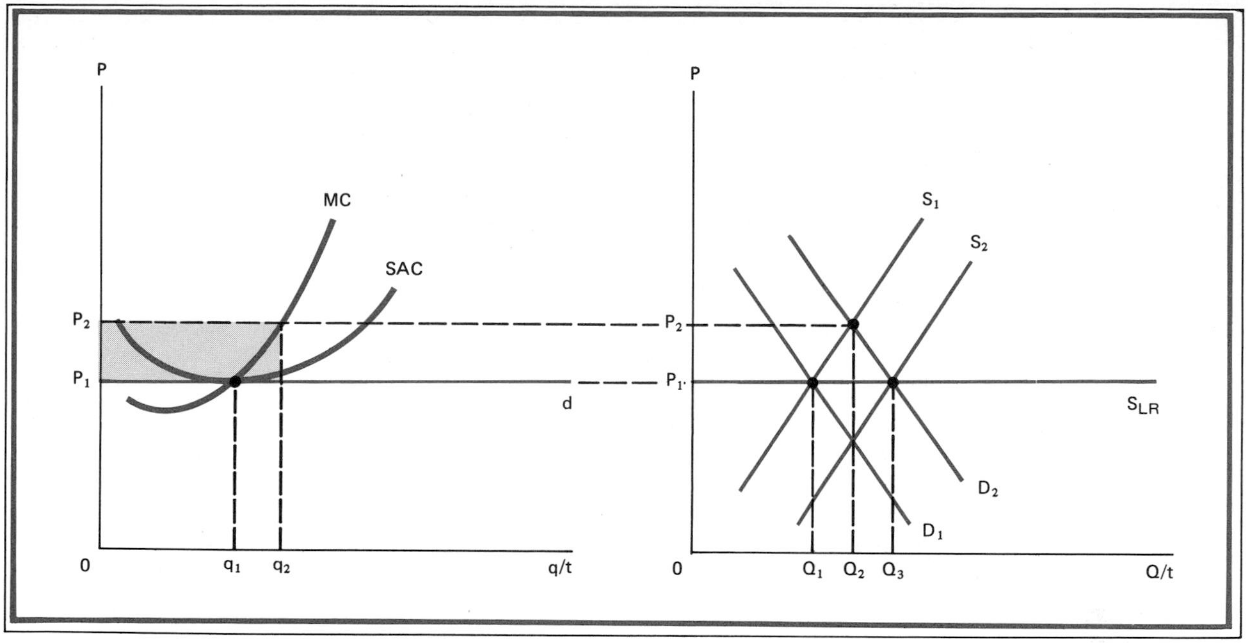

Figure 7-9

declining prices and the resulting increase in the quantity demanded for calculators in the 1970s.

The various externality effects, internal and external, operate simultaneously. The net effect of them will determine whether an industry will experience rising, decreasing, or constant long-run costs.

SYNTHESIS: FIRM AND INDUSTRY

We now take up the analysis of the firm and industry as they adjust to long-run competitive equilibrium for the three situations of long-run industry costs.

Constant-Cost Industries When external economies and diseconomies balance, the long-run supply curve is horizontal. Assume, initially, that the firm and industry are both in equilibrium when the market price is P_1 with the firm producing q_1 and the industry Q_1, as illustrated in Figure 7-9. There is an unanticipated increase in demand from D_1 to D_2 that drives up the market price to P_2 in the short run (we bypass the momentary industry supply curve here). In response, firms move up their short-run supply curve and increase output to q_2, with industry output rising to Q_2. As a result pure profits are being earned by existing firms shown by the shaded area. Lured by the pure profits, new firms enter the industry in the long run. With more firms now in production, the supply curve of the industry shifts to the right to S_2, raising industry production to Q_3 and lowering the price back to P_1. As a result of the lower price, firms move back down along their *MC* curves until at a price of P_1, they are supplying

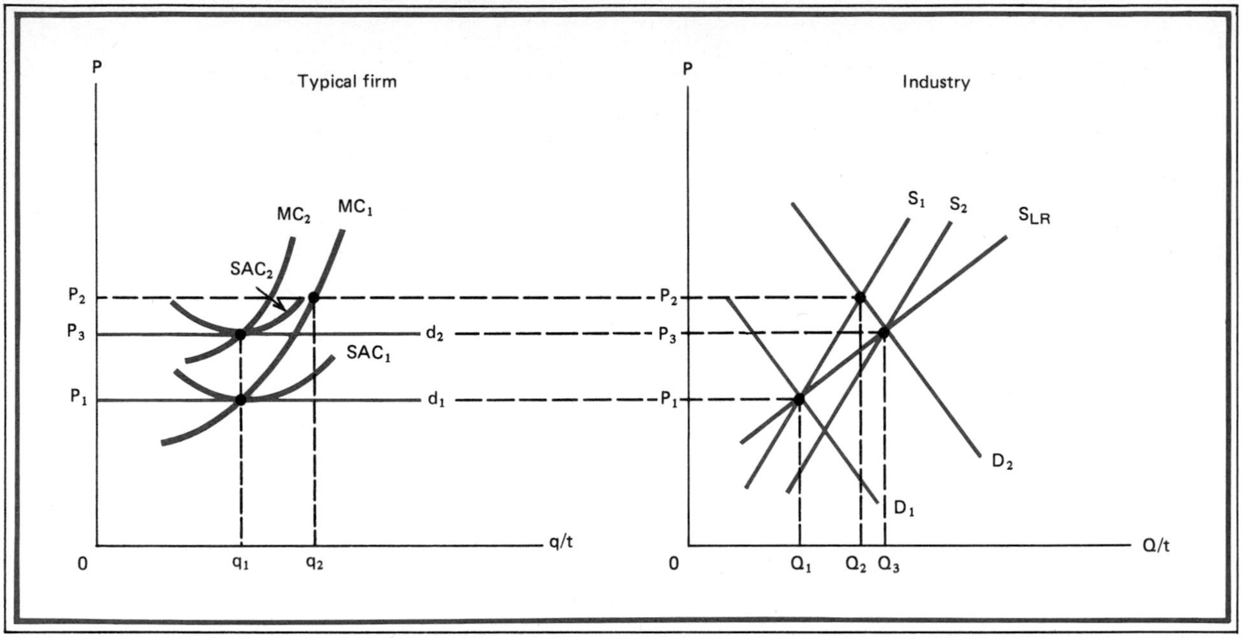

Figure 7-10

output q_1 once again. Although each of the original firms has now reduced its output back to its previous level, the output of the industry has increased because more firms are now in production. The long-run supply curve for the industry, S_{LR} is derived by connecting the two short-run equilibrium positions.

In long-run equilibrium all firms are earning only a normal profit, and for the firms $P = MC = MR = \min SAC = \min LAC$. In the long run, pure profits cannot be sustained. They are competed away as new firms appear, attracted by the higher profits.

Increasing-Cost Industries When industry output expands, all firms' costs curves may shift upward as the external *dis*economies of increased input prices take effect. Initially, in Figure 7-10 the industry is in long-run equilibrium at price P_1, producing output Q_1. The typical competitive firm as a price taker is facing the market price P_1 and earning zero profits while producing output q_1. Assume there is an increase in demand causing a shift to D_2; a new short-run equilibrium price P_2 results with output rising to Q_2 in the industry. As a consequence, the existing firms increase output by more intensive use of current facilities. The typical firm motivated by the higher price P_2 increases its short-run output to q_2. Firms are now earning pure profits. The pure profits attract new firms into the industry and the industry supply curve shifts to S_2, establishing a long-run equilibrium price of P_3. Industry output expands to Q_3. The industry long-run supply curve S_{LR} is obtained by connecting the two equilibrium positions.

The effect of industry expansion causes, at the same time, input prices to be bid up above the old prices that prevailed under the initial equilibrium. This simultaneously causes the cost curves of the firm to shift upward. The combination of falling prices as new firms enter, and rising costs as the demand for factors of production increases, tend to shrink profits to the zero level for all remaining firms in long-run equilibrium.

Decreasing-Cost Industries In this case there are external economies that cause firms' productivity to rise, resulting in their cost curve shifting downward. The long-run industry supply curve slopes downward, with prices falling as output rises. A young and growing industry may initially experience declining long-run costs, but increasing costs eventually result. If not, competition cannot survive. This special situation is discussed in the chapter on monopoly.

FIRM SIZE

It is interesting to ask how many firms will be in the industry for any given demand and cost situation. This will depend on the optimal size of the firm. How big is it when it is producing at both its minimum short-run and long-run average cost (*SAC* and *LAC*)? One measure of a firm's size is the output it produces each period. This implies that a certain amount of fixed capital input is working along with other variable inputs and producing at minimum long-run average cost. Thus, in the long run all firms will tend toward production with this optimal amount of fixed capital input—we might say the optimal-sized plant. That is, if there is an optimal-sized plant, firms will tend to be the same size.

If the total quantity demanded at price P_1 is known, then we can also determine how many firms it takes to produce this output level. Since output is the same for all firms and industry output is the sum of all firms' outputs, the number of firms in the industry will equal industry output divided by a firm's output.

Of course, if the firm's long-run cost curve as developed in Chapter 6 is horizontal for a stretch, then firms can vary in size and be equally efficient, in the sense of producing at minimum average total cost (min *ATC*). In this case there would be no single minimum average cost rate of output common to all firms. Hence, the number of firms in the industry may be indeterminant. And their optimum sizes can differ.

At any time we will observe different sized firms in production because historical decisions were made to build certain sized plants, and therefore different cost situations were faced by different firms. Furthermore, demand changes over time, and while firms adjust their outputs, they again will not be expected to have identical output. The importance of our analysis is, therefore, to point out that in many industries pressure exerted by cost realities exist that incline firms to become **look-alikes** in terms of size and choice of plant capacity.

In many industries, the pressure of cost realities inclines firms to *look alike* in terms of size and choice of plant capacity.

EFFICIENCY

We have seen how under perfectly competitive conditions the long-run characteristics are different from those prevailing in the short run, in that

1. For each firm in the long run, all factors are variable.
2. Entry and exit of firms is possible in the long run, whereas they are fixed in number in the short-run.
3. In long-run equilibrium all firms are making a normal or what we have called a *zero* profit.
4. In the long run the system as a whole is maximizing both consumer utility and output.

This last characteristic needs additional explanation.

Pareto optimality

Pareto optimality **(efficiency) exists in the system when the allocation of resources is such that no change in allocation can be made without reducing the satisfaction of at least one party.**

Pareto optimality (or efficiency) exists in the system when the allocation of resources is such that no change in allocation can be made without reducing the satisfaction of at least one person. It is not possible to make one person any better off than he now is without making someone else worse off. Thus in this restricted sense of the term, public satisfaction is said to be maximized when Pareto optimality prevails (named after Vilfredo Pareto, an Italian economist and sociologist, 1848-1923).

To express precisely what Pareto optimality is, we can use our marginal utility and marginal cost concepts. Let the analysis be confined to two goods and one consumer, for purposes of exposition. The goods are goods *a* and *b* and they are produced under cost conditions such that MC_a is 5 and the MC_b is 1. Also, assume that a consumer's marginal utilities from consuming these goods are $MU_a = 3$ and $MU_b = 1$. In this example we are looking at an initial and temporary *disequilibrium* situation in order to describe how a movement to equilibrium will improve things. In equation form we write

$$MU_a/MU_b = 3/1, \text{ and } MC_a/MC_b = 5/1.$$

Thus, for this consumer and for the two goods in question,

$$3 = MU_a/MU_b < MC_a/MC_b = 5. \tag{1}$$

The ratio of the marginal utility the consumer receives from goods *a* and *b* is less than the ratio of the marginal cost of producing these two goods. Since the two ratios are not equalized at the margin, society's efficiency and satisfaction can be increased by altering the production of goods *a* and *b* and changing the relative consumption of the two goods. The law of diminishing marginal utility suggests that the ratio of the MU_a and MU_b can be raised if the consumer reduces consumption of *a* and increases consumption of *b*. To do this requires producing less of *a* and more of *b*. Under conditions of rising marginal cost, producing less of *a* means moving down the rising MC_a curve and reducing MC_a (and price), and increasing the production of *b* raises the marginal cost (and price) of *b*. As a result, the ratio MU_a/MU_b can be raised and the ratio of MC_a/MC_b can be lowered until the ratios are equal to one another, say both ratios equal 4/1. At that point consumers are maximizing their utility. The inequality is removed and the ratios brought into balance by producing and consuming less of *a* and more *b*. When 1 less unit of *a* is consumed, the MU_a rises.

From our theory of the firm we know that $P = MC$ in competitive long-run equilibrium. Thus, the marginal conditions facing the consumers and the producers can be expressed as

$$MU_a/MU_b = P_a/P_b = MC_a/MC_b = 4/1. \quad (2)$$

The ratios indicate that relative product prices reflect not only relative consumer preferences but also relative marginal costs of production. The consumers are receiving a marginal benefit (utility) from consuming their last unit of *a* that is proportional to the price paid for *a*, and a price that is equal to the marginal cost of producing that last unit of *a*. The same holds for good *b*. The prices, marginal costs, and marginal utilities of *a* and *b* are not equal in some absolute sense, but in equilibrium their *ratios* are equal. Pareto optimality holds. Satisfaction is maximized and costs are minimized.

The General Case

In our example we have assumed two goods and one consumer, but of course there are many goods and many consumers in an exchange economy. Thus, the conditions expressed in the equality of ratios should hold for *all* consumers and *all* pairs of commodities in order for maximum efficiency to hold everywhere in the economy at one time.

It should be obvious that no economy is static and unchanging. Indeed, we have spent most of this chapter describing the adjustment processes by which firms respond to changing conditions over the short and long run. We suggest that these adjustment processes are working in a competitive exchange economy to push the economy toward the Pareto optimum—toward maximum efficiency in production and maximum satisfaction in consumption.

Several notes of caution are in order. First, recall that we are restricting the meaning of the word *maximum* here. It is used in the limited sense that no one can be made better off by either consuming different proportions as a consumer or producing different proportions as a producer. Second, we have assumed competition so that there is no monopoly. Third, there are no unaccounted-for social costs such as pollution that distort efficiency, because market prices do not reflect full marginal costs of production to society. Fourth, the Pareto optimum deals with allocative efficiency and maximization of utility under the existing distribution of society's income. In theory, there are an infinite number of possible income distributions, each of which can meet the conditions for Pareto efficiency. Therefore the Pareto optimum deals with maximizing utility only in the efficiency sense, not in the equity sense. Pareto optimality has nothing to say about whether or not the distribution of society's income is fair. It could be that total utility of society might be increased by a redistribution of income that makes incomes more equal. But since it is not possible to compare everyone's utility level with everyone else's utility level, we may never be able to find out just what distribution is best from an equity standpoint. Interpersonal comparisons of utility lie outside the analytical reach of a Pareto optimum. All that can be said is that the optimum exists when at least one person is made worse off whenever someone else is made better off, irrespective of the distribution of income.

CHAPTER SUMMARY

The perfectly competitive model is an idealized but useful description of markets on which a more realistic analysis is based. It assumes many buyers and sellers are trading a homogeneous product with none of them individually able to alter the market price. They are price-takers. Decision makers possess all the available information about prices and alternative market possibilities. The transactions costs of converting resources to alternative uses is small and not prohibitive. Finally, there is nothing to be gained by advertising a product that is undifferentiated.

Firms are motivated by the quest for profit maximization. Accounting profits calculations do not include opportunity costs, whereas economic profit calculations do. Thus, profits equal total revenue minus total opportunity costs. When all opportunity costs are included, a competitive firm in long-run equilibrium earns zero economic profits; but total opportunity costs include a normal return.

Firms maximize profits by following the rule that production should proceed so long as marginal revenue is less than marginal cost.

A firm will stay open in the short run so long as revenues are covering variable costs. If it is not covering variable costs it should shut down and minimize its losses. In the long run, since all costs are variable, the firm's revenues must cover all costs.

Firms may shut down temporarily because they are not covering variable costs, but they may not shut down permanently because they expect variable costs can be covered in the future when market conditions are likely to be more favorable.

Thus, shutting down for a while is an operating decision. However, shutting down permanently and exiting the industry and then entering another industry is an investment decision. Whether a firm decides to permanently exit one industry and enter another depends on the opportunity cost of its idle capital.

The short run is defined as a period during which the firm cannot alter its fixed factor(s). Sudden changes in demand require using existing facilities either more or less intensively. Pure profits may exist in short-run equilibrium. Price = marginal revenue = marginal cost is the short-run equilibrium condition. Price equal to marginal cost indicates maximum efficiency, since the value society places on the marginal unit just equals the additional cost of bidding the necessary resources away from an alternative use.

Long-run equilibrium for the typical competitive firm exists when price = marginal cost = marginal revenue = minimum short-run average cost = minimum long-run average cost. Pure profits cannot exist in the long run, since they are competed away by the entry of new firms.

Industries are either constant-cost, decreasing-cost, or increasing-cost industries. The long-run industry supply curve is either horizontal, falling, or rising, respectively.

External economies of scale determine the behavior of industry long run supply. They are costs imposed on member firms from outside the industry that alter their production functions, causing their short-run and long-run average cost curves to shift.

External scale economies are of two kinds, external price economies or external nonprice economies of scale. The former arise when input prices are driven up as an industry responds to increased demand by stepping up output. The latter arise, not because of increased demand for the industry product, but because new firms or new industries make their appearance and shift firms' cost curves.

Also, the industry's long run supply curve itself can shift because of technological innovation.

Theoretically, competition forces firms to operate at their optimum size in the long run, where min SAC = min LAC, so that firms will be of the same size. But at any given moment we observe that firms in an industry exist in a variety of sizes. However, planning decisions were made at different, earlier periods for different firms so that firms are observed at different phases of their planning curves (*LACs*). In the short run, nonetheless, firms in an industry are in the process of converging to similar sizes, technologies, and output levels.

For a given level of income distribution in the society, maximum efficiency is achieved when it is no longer possible to make one person better off without at the same time causing at least one other person to be worse off. Maximized consumer welfare and allocative efficiency coexist when $MU_a/MU_b = P_a/P_b = MC_a/MC_b$ for all consumers and all goods.

There is theoretically an infinite number of different income distributions for which the Pareto optimum can exist. Therefore, it is incorrect to conclude that *total social* well-being is necessarily maximized when there is a Pareto optimum. All that can be said is that society's efficiency for a given income distribution, however viewed by all its members, is maximized when the Pareto optimum conditions are met.

QUESTIONS

1. "The greater my sales the greater my profits." Do you agree?
2. Given the following data for a firm, what output should it produce to maximize total profits?

Q	TR	TC
100	$440	$400
101	480	420
102	515	445
103	545	475
104	565	515
105	575	575
106	580	635

3. Some people claim that on days when welfare checks are paid out in ghetto areas, small store owners raise prices temporarily, and that store owners in these areas generally charge higher prices and make "excessive" profits.
   a. If "excessive" profits are earned by small store owners in these areas, what does economic theory predict should happen?
   b. Suppose the accusations are true that higher prices are charged by small ghetto stores. Does it necessarily follow that profits are proportionately higher than for small stores outside these areas? Explain.
   c. What services do neighborhood stores provide that supermarkets do not? What name might you give to the price of that service?
4. In these days of the large retail chains like Sears, Penney, Montgomery Ward, the small businessman is often heard to lament that it is increasingly difficult to make a go of it. In 1978 Congress changed the tax laws and reduced some taxes to businesses. For small businesses in a highly competitive retail market, will a cut in taxes increase their profit rate? Discuss.
5. The chapter discusses the principle that firms in competitive equilibrium earn normal profits or zero pure profits, since the industry equilibrium price exactly

equals opportunity costs. Suppose demand falls causing the price the product sells for to decline. Do firms cease to earn a normal return because the price has fallen below opportunity costs? How do firms therefore survive? Or don't they, with the industry ceasing to exist?

6. Structurally, the paper and paperboard industry is considered to be one of the most competitive among the primary industries in the U.S. It is composed of some 350 corporations operating approximately 750 plants. The top 4 firms only have a market share of about 35 percent and the top 18 of 50 percent, and there is no price leader. There are over 3,000 converter plants which turn paper into cardboard, bags, and so on. Assume the industry is an increasing-cost industry. Suppose there is an increase in demand for paper products. Describe the change from one equilibrium to another for the typical firm and for the industry through the momentary, short-run and long-run periods. (Note: From 1975 to 1978 36 companies pleaded guilty to charges of price-fixing on coffee bags and folding cartons, claiming the industry is so competitive that some people take risks).
7. The crab-fishing industry can be considered as a perfectly competitive industry. The product is homogeneous, there already exist many fishermen, and entry and exit is easy since it is relatively simple for the existing boats to equip their vessels with the necessary crab gear when the crab beds are full. After the catch, when the beds are reduced, fishermen return to catching other sea creatures, while the crab beds are replenished by natural processes. Suppose there is a decrease in the demand for crab because they are found to be suspected of containing cancer-causing chemical pollutants. Describe the adjustment of the industry and of a typical firm, assuming the industry is a constant-cost one.
8. It can be said that marginal cost is an operating decision (deciding how much to produce). But average cost is an investment decision (deciding whether to set up shop at all). True or false? Why?
9. Reread the box by Thomas Edison and draw a graph for the cost curves of the firm.
   a. What might Edison mean by "full capacity" here?
   b. When Edison chose to sell surplus products at less than "costs of production," was he selling at a loss and therefore earning negative net revenues?
   c. When output rose by 25 percent and "costs" increased by only 2 percent, what costs was he talking about? On a diagram of the firm, show in what section of this cost curve the plant was operating initially. Then show where it was operating after Edison's new policy?
   d. Were economies of scale indicated in the box?. Comment.
   e. What grade would you give Edison for the economic analysis contained in the box?
10. According to the 1972 U.S. *Census of Manufactures* there were 7,539 cotton textile mills, employing 20 or more people, which take raw cotton and weave or knit it into a standardized cloth and sell it to the apparel and textile industry where it is cut and sewed into a variety of fabrics. No firm (composed of one or more mills) produces enough of the cloth to significantly affect total industry output and the market price. Exit from and entry into the industry is easy. Assume that cheap synthetic fiber as a substitute for cotton cloth is introduced and that the cotton textile is a constant-cost industry. Describe and graph the step-by-step adjustment of a typical firm and the industry.
11. a. What is the difference between internal and external economies?
    b. What effect does an internal economy have on a firm's *LAC* curve?
    c. What effect does an external diseconomy have on a firm's *LAC* curve?
12. Designate whether the following are either internal or external economies or diseconomies of scale, and why:
    a. "Work schedules were reorganized to remove padding, since labor accounts for

70 percent of the company's operating costs. About 15 percent of the packing jobs were eliminated, saving $6.5 million a year."

b. "Continental Can shut down or reduced in scale 15 plants; others were moved closer to customers and new equipment was installed over a three-year period."

c. A corrugated board mill official said, "Energy costs today are 10 percent to 15 percent of finished product costs, versus 5 percent six years ago.

d. "We don't want a plant to get over 350 people. That's all the division manager can handle effectively. When our divisions get too big for close personal relationships, we split into two divisions."

e. American Motors Corporation and Renault merge and agree to allow each other to use their car dealerships in the U.S. and Europe to retail each company's cars.

f. As the demand for television sets exploded after 1950, the real price of television sets declined in the years that followed.

g. The Bessemer process was a great improvement over the open-hearth process for making steel.

h. The steel industry developed along with the growth of the automobile industry.

i. The real cost of ocean transport fell per ton as the shipping industry went from sail to coal to oil fuel propulsion.

13. Farming is a highly competitive industry. Suppose a new farming technique for growing soybeans is discovered that drastically changes when and how soybeans are planted and nurtured respectively. The technique can increase yields by 35 percent per acre.

a. Diagram and explain what effect the new technique would have on those farmers who immediately convert to its implementation.

b. Diagram and explain the long-run adjustment of the industry.

c. Diagram and explain the effects on those farmers who do not convert to the new technique.

14. The 1972 U.S. *Census of Manufactures* recorded a total of 8,071 sawmills which sawed rough lumber and timber from logs and bolts into specialized patterns and dimensions for a variety of purposes. No single company controls more than 3 percent of the market. Entry is easy. New mills can be on line in less than two years. But the industry in the Northwest has been having its troubles. The lumber companies have been exporting more and more logs to Japan, which bids top prices for them, causing a number of sawmills in the U.S. to shut down. Lumber companies have been building more mills in the southern U.S. Sawmills are relatively labor-intensive operations.

a. Based on the above description, would you conclude that the Northwest sawmill industry is likely to be a constant-cost, increasing-cost, or decreasing-cost industry?

b. What kind of economies of scale, if any, are suggested by the above paragraph? Why?

c. Describe and graph the adjustment of a typical mill and the industry from one equilibrium point to the next in the short and long runs.

15. Prices are determined by the costs of production in the long run. When is this statement true and when is it false?

16. Suppose all markets are in competitive equilibrium and then the price of a commodity is set by the government below the equilibrium price. Some consumers cannot buy as much as they want, lines form, and some shortages occur in other markets:

a. Is there a Pareto optimum? Explain.

b. If price were permitted to rise to the equilibrium level, what would happen to aggregate welfare? How did you reason to your answer?

Chapter 8

Perfect Competition; Farming

PROGRESS REPORT

A. In Chapter 7 we learned how price and output respond to changes in demand as firms adjust their individual output levels to bring marginal costs into line with prices. We discovered that this competitive system leads to an efficient use of scarce resources.

B. Our explanation in the previous chapters was quite technical with a lot of graphs and detail. In this chapter, therefore, we wish to use the farming industry as an example of the competitive model that we have described. In the real world the farming industry comes closest to behaving like the theoretical model we constructed. Interestingly enough, it is also an industry that has been highly regulated and often subsidized. Therefore, in farming we not only have an example of how the competitive system works, but also an example of how the system responds to disturbances from outside.

C. In Chapter 9 we shall depart from our analysis of the competitive firm in a perfectly competitive industry and begin our examination of imperfect competition. We shall start there with analysis of a monopoly.

The typical consumer in the U.S. takes the abundance of food for granted. In the 1970s U.S. residents spent an average of about 16 percent of their real disposable income on food—less than that of any other country in the world in history. Yet in recent years angry farmers have blocked food shipments coming in from Mexico, held rallies in Kansas, picketed the White House, and driven tractors over city parks in Washington, D.C., causing over a million dollars in damage. They threatened to strike—that is, refuse to plant crops. At other times in the past farmers have destroyed potatoes and slaughtered chicks rather than bring them to the market. Dairy farmers have deliberately spilled milk on the ground. What is going on?

Economists have typically used the farming industry as an example of a perfectly competitive industry. While no industry, not even farming, fits the perfectly competitive model totally, farming probably comes the closest. In a perfectly competitive industry the individual sellers of a product are price takers. Each farmer sells his product at the going market price, and the price does not change if he sells more or less of it. No individual farmer's volume of sales will affect the price. There are so many sellers of a product that no one farmer feels that he is in competition with any other farmer for the consumer's dollar. The industry is perfectly competitive for all practical purposes.

But farming has been influenced by government in many ways. Farmers have some special tax privileges, farm prices are sometimes supported, farm technology is enhanced by research, and so forth. The actions by government tend to interfere with the free movement of farm prices that we would expect to see in a perfectly competitive market. In one sense, then, even farming departs far from the model of perfect competition because of widespread government intervention. On the other hand, the responses by farming to government actions are precisely the kinds of responses the competitive model would predict. Such predictable responses tend to verify that farming is, indeed, close to being a perfectly competitive industry.

BRIEF HISTORY

According to the USDA, a *farm* is any establishment which during the census year had, or normally would have had, sales of agricultural products of $1,000 or more.

Before going further let us first give the government's official definition of a **farm** as offered in the *Census of Agriculture* published by the U.S. Department of Agriculture (USDA). A *farm* is any establishment which during the census year had, or normally would have had, sales of agricultural products of $1,000 or more.

In the colonial period Congress passed the Ordinance of 1785. It provided for the rectangular survey and sale of small parcels of public land at auctions. In 1885 it was modified to permit credit on land sales. Thomas Jefferson had argued for easy access to land by the people. He wanted farms to be of small-family size and privately owned. In contrast, Alexander Hamilton preferred that land sales be limited in number and offered on the market in large blocks to the highest bidders, who would most likely be speculators. In this way he believed that the market price of the land would reflect its best use. Jefferson won out and small farmers picked up land very cheaply from the government.

In 1862 the Homestead Act offered free government land to those who would clear, live on, and develop it.

On May 15, 1862 the USDA was signed into law by President Lincoln. The USDA obtained cabinet status in 1889. The government thereafter turned its activities away from handling problems of land distribution toward support of agricultural research and development. Under the Morrill Act of 1862, land-grant colleges were set up to perform much of the research. By 1900, as a direct result of extensive research effort and programs designed to improve farming technology, farm productivity had increased significantly. But this caused supply to increase more rapidly than demand and prices of farm products fell. Then there was a surge in the population and, in the period 1910-1914, demand grew and prices rose again. Farmers were prosperous and the 1910-1914 years came to be known as the golden years for farmers. By the early 1920s the rate of population growth subsided and prices fell again. Excess supply became a problem. By 1926 the farm problem had emerged and was here to stay. Prices fell sharply. By 1933 the purchasing power of the typical farm family was only about half of what it had been in the 1910-1914 period. For 1933 was the worst year of the Great Depression, which extended from 1930 to 1941.

To serve the public interest, the Agricultural Adjustment Act of 1933 was passed. Its objective was to reduce the excess production of crops by assigning acreage allotments to farmers in the hope of lowering supply and thereby raising prices and farmers' incomes. Adhering to government programs, farmers ploughed under some ten million acres of cotton and over six million pigs were slaughtered and never brought to market. The prevailing view was that government intervention was necessary because of the erratic and unpredictable nature of the free market. Solemn bureaucrats would enter where nature played freely. It was felt that action was necessary to remove market instability. The farm problem was one of overproduction combined with fluctuating swings in prices and incomes. What are the causes of the erratic behavior of farm income?

The Fluctuations

The obvious problems affecting farm output are weather, insects, and disease.

Weather, Insects, Disease The obvious causes of variations in farm output have to do with the weather, insects, and disease. While research brought about chemical pesticides that solved many insect and disease problems, human knowledge and influence does not yet extend to the control of weather. Too much water or water too late and unseasonal freezes have played havoc with supplies of wheat, coffee, lettuce, and oranges, among other crops. A bad season is often followed by a season of good weather—it is feast or famine.

Industry supply and demand for farm products are highly *price-inelastic* and highly *income-inelastic.*

Price and Income Elasticity Empirical evidence confirms that the industry supply and demand for farm products are highly **price-inelastic** as well as **income-inelastic**. When prices rise total expenditure on farm products rises, and when prices fall expenditure falls. Assume the price in year 1 is P_1, shown in Figure 8-1. In year 2, the weather is poor and supply declines to S_2, price rises to P_2. Total expenditure on farm products—revenues—is now P_2bQ_20 and has increased from P_1aQ_10. In the following year, year 3, the yield is abundant; supply shifts to S_3 and price falls to P_3. But so does total revenue, which is now the area P_3cQ_30. There results an abrupt change in farm income and prices from year 1 to year 3.

Figure 8-1

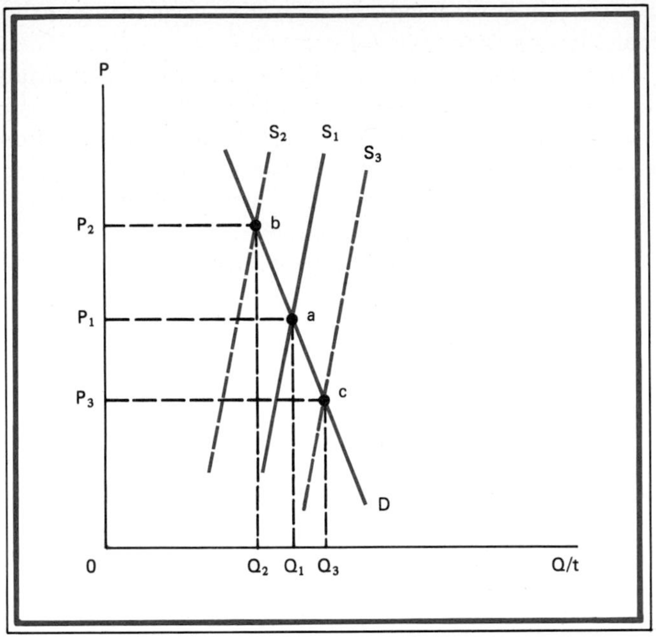

Since incomes rise when production falls, you might wonder why farmers do not choose to grow less. The reason is that there are millions of farmers. If the individual farmer grew less it would only mean that his revenues would fall. Not only that; should he grow less, there is no certainty that other farmers would not simply grow more. Thus he would sell less crop and earn a lower income. At a national level, there are simply too many farmers for any one or any group to control output. Transactions costs of coordinating and negotiating what each should produce are so high as to make a volunteer program impractical. But the government can reduce transactions costs to the farmers by acting as the central coordinator. We shall have more to say about government's income stabilization programs farther along in the chapter.

The income elasticity of demand for farm commodities is also low.[1] As consumer real income rises (i.e., income adjusted for inflation), consumers spend proportionately less of their income on food and more on nonfood items. Food is basic. Rich people do not eat that much more than poor people, i.e., $0 < E_Y < 1$. The rich may spend more for food than the poor but not *proportionately* more. Once this basic need is satisfied the rich, middle-income, and the poor do not spend very much of any additional income on food. For example, a 20 percent rise in income may mean that consumers only spend 5 percent more on farm products, giving an income elasticity of .25, and while total expenditure on food products may rise, it will rise by only a small amount in comparison to expenditures on other things.

[1]Income elasticity is defined as

$$E_y = \frac{\text{\% change in quantity demanded}}{\text{\% change in income}}$$

where $0 < E_y < 1$. The value of this coefficient is less than 1 for farm products and greater than zero.

Farmers' reaction to current costs and prices and their anticipation of future prices and costs give rise to widely *fluctuating* agricultural prices and incomes.

Inherent Cycles Market forces affect prices. How farms react to prices, and what farmers anticipate prices and costs will be in the future, give rise to two problems confronting the farming industry. Prices tend to **fluctuate** widely, and farmers face large swings in income. Some of the swings in price and income are caused by seasonal shifts in supply in combination with the highly inelastic nature of both the supply and demand for farm products. Weather irregularities also shock supply. In addition, shifts in supply arise because farmers guess (speculate) on what they believe future product prices and input costs will be next season. Such guessing gives rise to a well-known cycle peculiar to farming.

Corn-Hog Cycle

Hog prices seem to rise and fall in two year-periods. The price variation appears to have two sources: the price of corn, and the response by farmers to changes in hog prices which causes more instability in prices as they change the size of breeding herds.

To understand the chain of events in the corn-hog cycle, assume at time t the supply and demand for hogs (pork) is represented by S_1 and D in Figure 8-1. The price and quantity in equilibrium are P_1 and Q_1 respectively. Suppose good weather yields an abundant corn crop, causing corn prices to fall. Feeding costs to hog farmers fall, so they plan to increase the size of their stock. But to do so they must increase the size of the breeding herd by selling off fewer hogs for slaughter in the short run. Therefore the supply curve for hogs shifts to S_2 in the short run and prices rise to P_2. Since demand is inelastic, total revenue rises. But increasing the breeding herd increases the demand for feed corn and drives up corn prices. The result is that farmers liquidate much of their breeding stock to cut what they anticipate might be even higher feed costs. Also, in the long run, as a result of the expanded herds, there are many more hogs. Thus the supply curve shifts to S_3 as more hogs are slaughtered for the market. Since demand is inelastic, total revenue now falls when the market price drops to P_3. But then the cycle begins anew. With the breeding herd substantially reduced, the demand for corn feed falls and corn prices drop. The farmers expand the breeding herd by slaughtering fewer hogs, which drives up hog prices. And so on. Corn is used to feed hogs, and other grain is used to feed cattle. The analyses for both hogs and cattle is the same, except that the cattle cycle is longer since the lapse of time between breeding and marketing is about 24 months for cattle but only 9 months for hogs.

LONG-TERM TRENDS

As we mentioned earlier, the demand for farm products tends to be income inelastic. For this reason rising real incomes earned by consumers do not lead to proportionate increases in food purchases and consumption. Hence, as the economy grows there is a tendency for farm supply to exceed consumer

Hedging: Not a Crap Shoot

Everyone has heard of the stock market. But what is this business about the commodity market, where someone can buy five trainloads of pork bellies for a week through a commodity exchange?

There are about twenty licensed exchanges in the U.S. The six major ones are the Chicago Board of Trade, the Chicago Mercantile Exchange, and the New York, Kansas City, Minneapolis, and London exchanges. Trading in commodity futures began in the U.S. in Chicago in 1848. It is an organized market, that is, what buyers are willing to bid and sellers to ask is easily determined and quickly transmitted, so that a known single market price emerges. The commodity market is based on expected future prices of over forty commodities, some of which are wheat, potatoes, soybeans, frozen orange juice, pork bellies, silver, tin, cocoa, cotton, propane gas, plywood, live cattle, and hogs. Some items like tea, coal, steel, oil, uncanned fruit and vegetables, and others are not traded on the commodity or futures market. To qualify, the good must be homogenous or identical and must be easily identifiable by established grades and standards. The supply and demand of the commodity must be large–worldwide–to prevent one speculator from cornering the market. Supply must flow freely, unhampered by government quotas and price regulations. The good must not be perishable but storable or maintainable (for example, livestock).

Futures are purchased contracts that promise to sell a commodity at a specified date in the future at a price agreed upon now. Goods not traded on a commodity exchange by using futures are traded in the physical sense in the spot market, with delivery at the current local price on the spot. This is also called the cash market. In the futures market the physical good is not actually bought. What is purchased is a contract for a future delivery of a certain quantity and grade (5,000 bushels of #2 yellow corn), at a specified time (July 1980), at a particular location (Chicago), at a designated price ($1.70 a bushel). Delivery months vary for commodities. For corn they are July, September, December, March, and May. A trader can contract with another participant either to take a short position (agree to deliver the commodity) or a long position (agree to accept the commodity, paying on delivery). Futures are bought on very low down payments, called margins, of 5 to 10 percent. Thus a small price change in the commodity future can turn into large gains or losses. Buyers such as grain-elevator operators, bakeries, and export firms often contract to buy wheat at a certain price at some time in the future. This protects them against the risk of price changes. They are hedging. It is like covering a bet by making an offsetting bet. It is a form of insurance.

There are basically two types in the futures markets – hedgers and speculators. Hedgers use

demand, causing *relative* prices to trend downward over time. Essentially farm production in the U.S. has outpaced the increasing food demands of a growing population. As a result, the *relative* prices of commodities sold off the farm has fallen compared to the prices charged by the manufacturing sector of the economy. This is shown in Figure 8-2. The vertical axis depicts the price of farm goods relative to nonfarm goods. The short-run supply curve has been shifting rightward over time. The demand curve also shifts rightward, but not as much. The result is a downward sloping long-run supply curve obtained by connecting the short-run equilibrium points. Relative prices are falling while the quantity supplied increases. The farmer pays more for his inputs but gets relatively less for his output—a profit squeeze. In recent years receipts averaged about 40 percent of the consumer dollar spent on a typical market basket of farm products, the other 60 percent going to processors and retailers. On bakery and

futures to eliminate risk. Speculators are really crapshooters; they hope to earn windfall profits by taking the risk of future price changes. Thus, a speculator might figure that the current price of wheat at $4 a bushel is too high and must come down. He buys a futures contract promising to sell wheat four months from now at $4 a bushel. He wins if the price goes to $3.50. He sold a contract at $4 and now buys it back at $3.50. Rarely does actual delivery and payment for the physical commodity take place. The contracts are bought back or covered before the delivery date arrives.

When delivery does occur (to a public warehouse), the difference between the futures price and the spot price is the basis. It varies among locations and for the most part reflects transportation and storage costs as they change from month to month.

Large farmers tend to hedge their growing crop in order to set a price for it, rather than speculate on what the price will be at harvest time. For example, suppose that in July the futures price of soybeans is $4.20 per bushel. If, typically, the November basis price in his area is 15 cents per bushel, the farmer knows the futures price of $4.20 translates into a net local price of $4.05 Suppose he decides to sell his expected output of 5,000 bushels (the minimum contract) at $4.05 for November delivery. But by November he finds the local price of soybean bushels to be $3.85. Adding the basis, the futures price on the Chicago Exchange is $4. He sells his beans locally for cash at $3.85 and at the same time buys back his futures contract at $4. He makes 20 cents a bushel on the futures contract, since it was agreed on in July that he would sell for $4.20 in November. He loses 20 cents a bushel on the crop itself. The cash price of $3.85 plus the 20 cents per bushel on the futures transaction yields the farmer $4.05 a bushel. The net gain (or net loss) is zero despite the price change from July to November.

Cash market	**Futures market**
July: Anticipated crop 5,000 bu. (expected price $4.05 a bu.)	July: Sells 5,000 bu. still growing at $4.20.
November: Actually sells 5,000 bu. at $3.85 a bu.	November: Buys 5,000 bu. at $4. a bu. ($3.85 × $.15 for basis).
On net: The loss is 20 cents a bu.	On net: The profit on futures contract is 20 cents a bu.

Suppose, instead, that the spot price in November had turned out to be $4.16 and not $3.85. With the 15-cent basis included the farmer buys back the futures contract for $4.31. He then loses 11 cents ($4.20 − $4.31) on the futures contract. The cash price including the loss he receives on his crop is still $4.05 ($4.16 − $.11). Hence, he is protected against price level changes.

cereal items the farmer's share of the dollar is closer to 17 percent, on processed fruits and vegetables about 20 percent, and on milk about 50 percent.

Table 8-1 illustrates several trends in agriculture. From it we see that in the 1920s, for the first time, more than half the U.S. population became city dwellers. Around 1910 the number of farm workers peaked at approximately 13.6 million when unpaid family members are included. Thereafter the numbers declined slowly, then more rapidly after 1950. The number of farms fell to below 2.8 million in the 1970s. In the 1980s the number of farms will fall below 2.3 million. From 1870 to 1970 output increased over 600 percent. However, USDA data reveal that average income per farm only increased by approximately 200 percent from 1910 to 1975, from $1,126 to $3,456, adjusted for 1967 dollars. This is consistent with falling relative farm prices and the declining long-run supply curve we described in Chapter 7 and in Figure 8-2.

Figure 8-2

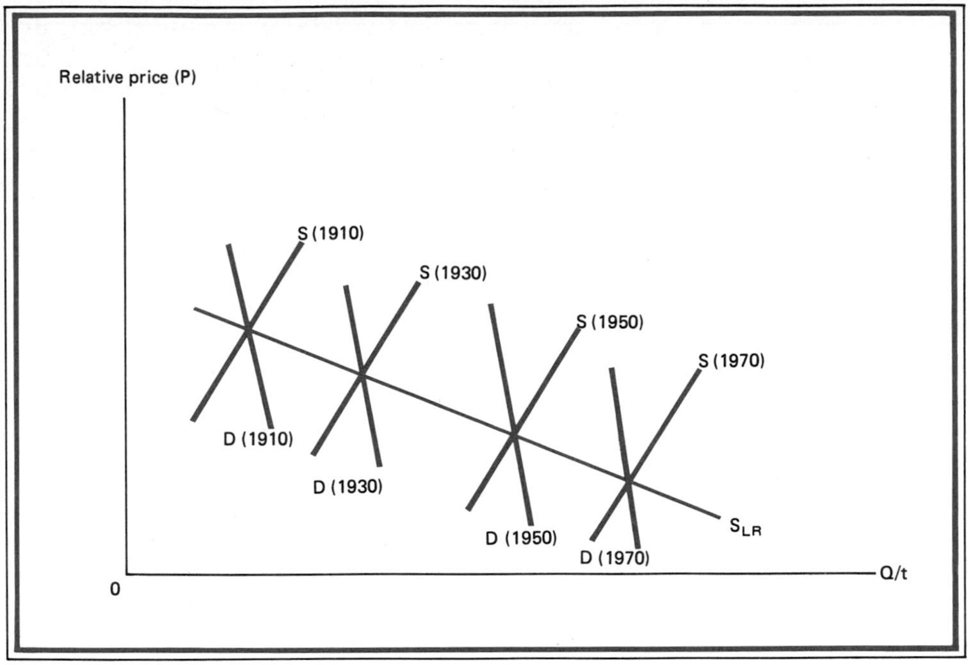

TABLE 8-1
Some Long-Term Trends in Agriculture

Year	Total population (1000)	Percent of population: Urban	Percent of population: Rural	Farm employment (1000)	Percent of total employment	Index of Farm Output per Man-hour (1958-100)	Number of farms (1000)
1870	38,558	25.7	74.3	—	—	20.1	2,660
1880	50,156	27.9	72.1	—	—	23.9	4,009
1890	62,947	35.1	64.9	—	—	25.1	4,565
1900	75,995	39.7	60.3	11,050	41.0	29.8	5,740
1910	91,972	45.6	54.4	11,260	32.5	31.0	6,366
1920	105,711	51.2	48.8	10,440	26.6	31.3	6,454
1930	122,775	56.1	43.9	10,340	23.4	35.6	6,295
1940	131,670	56.5	43.5	9,540	15.4	42.7	6,102
1950	150,698	64.0	36.0	7,160	12.2	61.9	5,388
1960	179,323	69.8	30.2	5,458	8.3	106.5	3,962
1970	203,202	73.5	26.5	3,462	4.4	191.5 (est)	2,954

Sources: Population statistics calculated from *Historical Statistics of The United States, Colonial Times to 1970,* Bicentennial Edition, Part 1, series A57–72, pp. 11, 12. Farm Employment, Part 1, series D6 and D16, pp. 126–127. Index of output, Part 1, series D686, p. 162. The number of farms, Part 1, series K1, p. 457.

Table 8-1 also shows that by arbitrarily setting the output index to 100 for 1958 in the column showing the index of farm output per man hour, the rapid growth of output can be compared over the years. Notice the accelerated rise in the output index for farms as a whole and per man hour after the 1930s.

Despite this impressive growth in output and productivity, small family farming continued to earn a much lower average income than farming generally. Costs of inputs have risen faster than the prices farmers receive for their crops and animals. As a result, many small farmers receive at least half of their income from nonfarm sources. Normally, people would exit businesses that experience ongoing losses. The result would be fewer producers—in this case farms—but bigger more efficient ones producing at lower per unit costs.

But the farming community is represented by politically powerful organizations and lobbying groups such as the American Farm Bureau Federation and the National Farm Organization. Personnel numbers in the USDA have not fallen, although the number of farms continues to decline. Many marginal and less than marginally efficient farms remain operating, and the successful ones get richer through government-sponsored farm subsidy and loan programs.

Cause of Long-run Trends

Improved productivity accounts for *declining long-run relative prices*, fewer farms, and the great increase in U.S. farm output.

The major reason for **declining long-run relative prices**, fewer farms, and the fantastic increase in U.S. farm output is explained by improved productivity. Between 1910 and 1929 farm output ascended slowly; thereafter it rose rapidly. The causes of this rapid rise lie in government policies and economies of scale. The government research and development programs expanded agricultural knowledge. As the technology improved, generous government credit and loan programs enabled individual farmers to purchase expensive capital equipment that made possible greatly increased economies of scale.

The irony here is that government policy designed to increase the farmers' welfare helped them to be more productive, which resulted in overproduction and falling relative prices and even more severe problems for them as their income dropped. No doubt the farmers, without government help, would have increased crop yields, but the availability of government financial assistance greatly encouraged them, particularly since 1933 when the government set up the Commodity Credit Corporation (CCC). The government policy of subsidy payments perversely affected the small farms while unintentionally bestowing large benefits to the larger farms. This can be ascertained by studying Table 8-2.

The data in Table 8-2 indicate that the number of farms under 500 acres has declined significantly, particularly those of 180 acres or less. In contrast, the number of farms over 500 acres has substantially increased. There is no conclusive evidence, however, of a takeover by big family farms or by nonfamily corporate agribusiness.

Because of the large decline in the number of very small family farms, the average farm size has risen to about 450 acres. Still, the *relative* distribution of farm size has remained rather consistent. In 1970, some two fifths of the farms produced approximately 80 percent of total farm output. The bottom two fifths of farms produced about 10 percent of total farm output. The middle one fifth produced the residual 10 percent of output. Moreover, over 60 percent of those

TABLE 8-2 Number and Size of U.S. Farms, 1959–1974

No. of Farms (by acres harvested)	1959 3,710,503	1964 3,157,857	1969 2,730,250	1974 2,314,013
1–49 acres	1,675,125	1,375,258	1,078,252	872,024
50–99	563,699	462,698	372,178	315,586
100–199	536,667	454,885	364,295	315,601
200–499	351,983	329,726	311,035	318,226
500–599	60,176	64,010	73,770	100,511
1000 and over	13,655	15,117	20,101	32,752
1000–1999	NA	NA	NA	26,890
2000 and over	NA	NA	NA	5,862
Average size in acres	303	352	389	440

NA = Not available.
Source: 1974 *U.S. Census of Agriculture.*

farms that are also corporate farms are nevertheless family owned, while over 12 percent are individually owned. The remaining 20+ percent are owned by groups larger than a family. The family farm is defined as one that hires less than 1.5 workers per year. Figure 8-3 shows the trend in farm size and number.

Source: Federal Reserve Bank of Kansas City, *Economic Review,* November 1980.

Figure 8-3

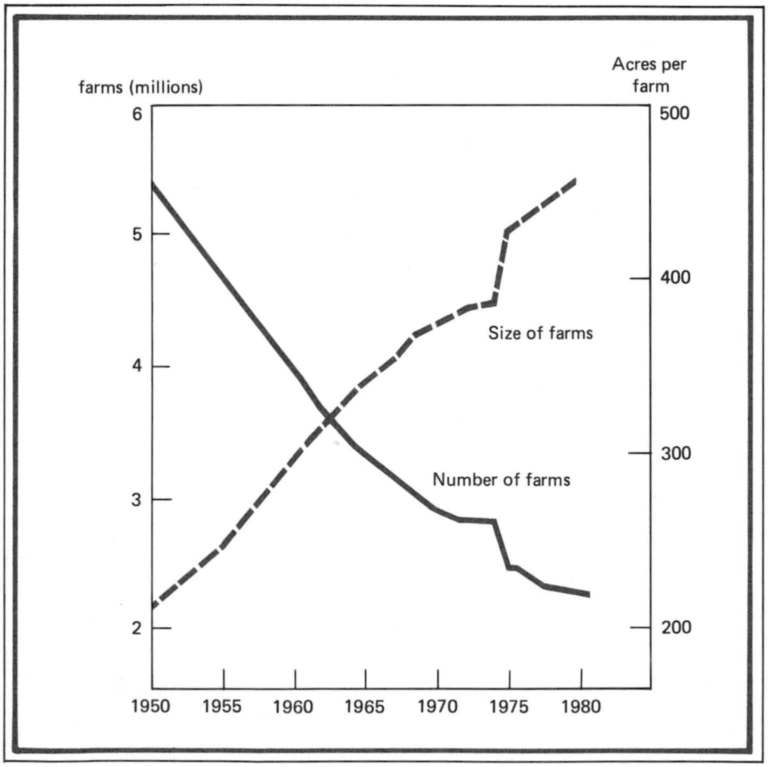

Figure 8-4

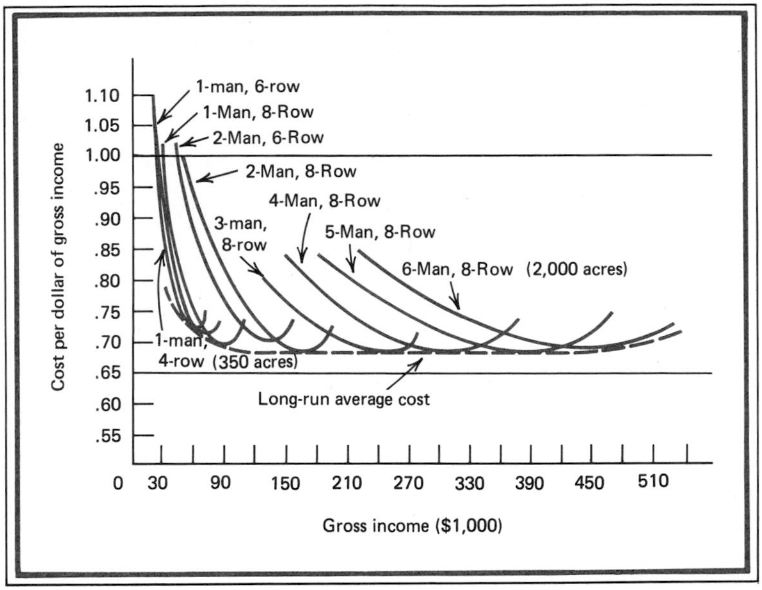

As farms became larger, they became more efficient. And the larger they became the more they could borrow from banks by offering the land as collateral, and the more economical it became for them to buy more expensive capital equipment. Farm productivity leaped.

In 1820 one farm worker fed 4.1 people; in 1870, 5.1; in 1920, 8.3; in 1930, 9.8; in 1940, 10.7. By 1950 one farm worker fed 15.5 people, nearly doubling in 30 years, and by 1964 the figure more than doubled, to 33.0. In 1970 one farm worker fed 47.1 people, and by 1977 the number approached 60.0.[2] Malthus, where is thy sting?

New knowledge about cropping methods, irrigation, and new crop varieties combined with new forms of fertilizer have caused yields to leapfrog. In 1928 the average hen produced about 128 eggs and the average cow 4,516 pounds of milk in one year; in 1970 the average hen produced 220 eggs and the average cow over 9,000 pounds of milk a year. In 1950 it took 22,000,000 dairy cattle to meet the demand for milk. The demand for milk was about the same in 1980, but it only took 11,000,000 cattle to meet it. New technology embodied in tractors, milking machines, and other machinery, particularly after 1933 when government capital became available, increased efficiency greatly. The number of farms peaked in 1935 to about 6.7 million and has been declining ever since because of the dramatic improvements in input technology.

Figure 8-4 illustrates the point. A 1969 study of nine types of cash-grain farms in Illinois revealed that for farms ranging from 350 to 2,000 acres internal economies of scale were in effect. Fixed costs were spread over more output and average total costs fell until the minimum average total cost was reached. In the figure we can see from the curve that it was reached when 2 regular workers used 8-row machinery. To realize scale economies, therefore, the grain farm must employ at least 2 men per year but fewer than 6. The capital require-

[2]U.S. Department of Agriculture, *Agricultural Statistics.*

ments necessary to achieve these economies rise in cost faster than small farms can generate the income and collateral backing on loans to acquire such equipment. Overextended, they face a cash flow problem: land rich and penny poor. In the 1980s grain farms smaller than 200 acres are likely to find it very difficult to remain self-sufficient. Currently the most efficient farm size runs from 800 acres for corn and soybeans to 2,000 acres for wheat and barley. Fruit and vegetable farms do not have to be as large in order to be self-sufficient.

PARITY

Parity is the concept of comparing the prices received by farmers for their products with the input costs they incur to produce in order to calculate yearly changes in farmers' purchasing power.

How has the government responded to (a) the short-run instability in farm prices and income, (b) the long-term trend in declining relative prices of farm goods, and (c) the cash flow problem of the small farms? It has introduced a variety of price support programs based on the concept of parity. This is a concept that first appeared during the 1920s and was incorporated into the Agricultural Adjustment Act of 1933. **Parity** embodies the calculation of prices for farm products sold by farmers which will provide the farmer with the same purchasing power in the current year as he had with the income he earned on the average in the 1910-1914 period. The idea is to compare the prices received by farmers for the commodities they sell to the prices that farmers must pay for inputs to their production.

If prices paid by farmers for inputs rise, an adjustment is made to lift the prices of farm products so as to raise the income of farmers to the same relative level they earned in the 1910-1914 base period. The idea is to keep the prices farmers receive for their products in line with the farmers' production costs. It does *not* mean incomes are made equal. Rather it aims to make real purchasing power of the farmer equal in the two periods.

For example, if the price of fertilizer, taxes, farm wage rates, and consumer goods all rise an average of 10 percent, then so should the average price of the crops the farmer sells. This ideally helps him to buy not only the same amount of inputs but also the same amount of consumer goods. The index of input prices is called the parity index.

Parity indexes are averages of prices, and are calculated from a statistically selected representative sample. The construction of price indexes is more thoroughly covered in Chapter 20. All we need to know for now is that the price indexes of inputs and outputs are derived by using the years 1910-1914 as the base period, because 1910-1914 were good years for farmers' purchasing power.

Parity Calculations

The ratio of prices received for outputs to the prices paid for inputs is called the **parity ratio** When the parity ratio is divided into the current price per bushel of a crop, we obtain the **parity price**

The ratio of prices received for outputs to the price paid for inputs is called the *parity ratio;* when this is divided into the current price per bushel of a crop we obtain the *parity price.*

In computing the parity price, the calculation of the parity ratio must be made first. Assume that the farmer's crop is wheat, and with the income from selling the wheat the farmer buys various inputs as well as consumption goods. It is to be understood that the farmer will be considered as *buying* a basket of typical goods. For the period 1910-1914 the basket will be assigned an arbitrary index of 100. In addition, the index of commodities the farmer *sells* in the 1910-1914 period is assigned an arbitrary value of 100. The input and the output indexes for subsequent years will then both be referenced to the base period 1910-1914. Thus, for the year 1940 the parity ratio equals

$$\frac{\dfrac{\text{Price received by the farmer for outputs in 1940}}{\text{Price received by the farmer for outputs in 1910-14 } (=100)}}{\dfrac{\text{Prices paid by farmers in 1940 for inputs}}{\text{Prices paid by farmer in 1910-14 for inputs } (=100)}}$$

$$= \frac{\text{Price index of outputs in 1940}}{\text{Price index of inputs in 1940}}.$$

If we use the numbers from Table 8-3, the parity ratio equals

$$\frac{97}{120} \times 100 = 81.$$

The parity price per bushel of wheat in 1940 is therefore,

$$\frac{\text{price farmer received in 1940}}{\text{parity ratio}} = \frac{\$.85}{81} \times 100 = \$1.05.$$

This can be rewritten by substituting for the parity ratio and bringing the ratio up into the numerator and inverting it yielding the parity price:

$$\begin{array}{c}\text{1940 price}\\ \text{for wheat}\end{array} \times \frac{\text{price index of inputs}}{\text{price index of output}}.$$

TABLE 8-3
Parity ratio and parity price

Year	Price of wheat per bushel (1)	Price index of prices received for outputs (2)	Price index of prices paid for inputs (3)	Parity ratio = (2)/(3) × 100 (4)	Parity price = (1)/(4) × 100 (5)
1910–14	\$.88	100	100	100/100 × 100 = 100	.88/100 × 100 = \$.88
1940	\$.85	97	120	97/120 × 100 = 81	.85/.81 × 100 = \$1.05

In this form we can see that if input prices to the farmer rise faster than output prices, the parity price would increase. But if input prices did not rise as much as output prices then the parity price would fall. In essence, it is the change in the parity ratio that pretty much determines the direction of the parity price when the wheat price changes very little. When the wheat price also changes, that too is taken into account. If, as we have assumed, the actual market price of a bushel of wheat in 1940 was 85 cents, then according to the parity calculation the 85 cents received in 1940 signifies that it amounted to 81 percent of the parity price, i.e., .85/1.05 = .81 or 81 percent. Not since 1952 have farmers received a 100 percent parity price for commodities.

In 1948 the old parity formula was modified. The new formula is more complex, and we shall not describe it here.[3]

Deficiencies of Parity

Parity has several deficiencies.

1. Parity does not adequately provide for increased farm productivity. For example, in the 1910-1914 period a $1 bushel of wheat could buy one pair of shoes. With wheat, say, currently at $3 a bushel, it would take

[3]*Parity Handbook*, U.S. Department of Agriculture, 1952. Also, W. Wilcox, W. Cochrane, and R. Herdt, *Economics of American Agriculture*, 3d ed. (Englewood Cliffs, N.J.: Prentice-Hall, Inc, 1974), p. 442.

TABLE 8-4
Size and Distribution of Federal Farm Program Payments (Dollars per Farm)

Farm size class	1970	1973	1975	1977	1978
$100,000 sales and over	$9,263	$4,985	$1,179	$2,204	$3,476
Percent of payments	14.2	26.2	20.4	19.6	21.5
Percent of farms	1.9	4.8	5.1	6.0	7.0
$40,000 to $100,000 sales	$4,056	2,135	739	1,770	2,800
Percent of payments	19.4	25.5	28.7	33.9	36.0
Percent of farms	6.1	11.0	11.3	12.9	14.6
$20,000 to $40,000 sales	$2,583	1,410	539	1,280	2,012
Percent of payments	22.7	17.8	21.6	22.6	21.5
Percent of farms	11.1	11.7	11.7	11.9	12.9
$2,500 to $20,000 sales	$1,111	638	202	407	647
Percent of payments	36.3	24.8	24.7	20.2	18.2
Percent of farms	41.1	35.9	35.5	33.9	32.0
Less than $2,500 sales	$ 235	145	37	71	92
Percent of payments	7.4	5.7	4.6	3.7	2.8
Percent of farms	39.8	36.6	36.4	35.3	34.3
Total government payments					
Billions of dollars	3.7	2.6	0.8	1.8	3.0
Millions of farms	2.9	2.8	2.8	2.7	2.7

Sources: U.S. Dept. of Agriculture, Farm Income Statistics, July 1979. Federal Reserve Bank of Kansas City.

Parity deficiencies are: (1) it does not adequately provide for increased productivity, (2) it does not provide farmers with incomes equal to nonfarming incomes, and (3) it does not include government payments.

10 bushels to buy a $30 pair of shoes. This sounds awful for the farmer. But with modern equipment, a farmer can produce a lot more bushels per acre, and at significantly lower cost per unit.

2. Parity does not provide farmers on the average with incomes equal to incomes in nonfarm occupations. The technological race requires that farmers buy more sophisticated and expensive equipment that is vastly more productive, with the inverted result that higher production has caused average farm income to rise more slowly than the national average. As a fraction of total national income, farm income has fallen from 10.2 percent in the 1935-1939 period to less than 3 percent in the 1970s.
3. Parity does not include the payments that government provides to farm households as part of the farm subsidy program. Parity prices therefore can be higher than they need to be. (See Table 8-4)

Government Programs

The farm problem did not begin in the 1920s or 1930s. Fluctuating prices caused by overproduction in the U.S. goes back over 340 years to Virginia tobacco farms when growers deliberately destroyed their crop. But not until 1933, after farm prices dropped 57 percent between 1929 and 1932, did the government engage in a massive system of quotas and acreage allotments to limit the production of corn, tobacco, wheat, peanuts, cotton, and rice. In 1956 the soil bank program permitted compensation to be paid to farmers either in the form of direct payments or in crops from government storehouses, in exchange for retiring land from production. This works differently from acreage allotments, where a maximum acreage is set for harvesting and if the acreage is exceeded the farmer is not eligible for price supports. Let us sketch an analysis of three programs to aid farmers.

Price Support

The *price support program* is a method of guaranteeing a certain target price to the farmer for his crop and is linked to parity.

The price support program is a method of guaranteeing a certain target price to the farmer for his crop. The level of the price support is linked to parity. You will often hear the expression "prices on corn set at x percent of parity." In Figure 8-5, P_E is the free market price without government intervention. The supply curve is shown as perfectly inelastic, since output cannot be changed until next season once the crop is harvested. The price P_S is the government's support price. For instance if the market price of wheat is estimated to be $2 a bushel, the government sets the price P_S at, say, $3 a bushel. At the higher price P_S, farmers produce a quantity Q_1, but at that price consumers choose to buy an amount Q_0. The surplus $Q_1 - Q_0$ is purchased by the CCC at the support price and stored. The shaded area represents the tax burden to society and a transfer of income to the farmers. The government cannot sell the stored commodities because it would drop the price below the level the government agreed to support. Incidently, there are no price supports on beef, pork, fruits, vegetables, poultry, and eggs. But since these farmers use grain to feed cattle, chicken, and hogs they suffer from price supports on feed grain.

Figure 8-5

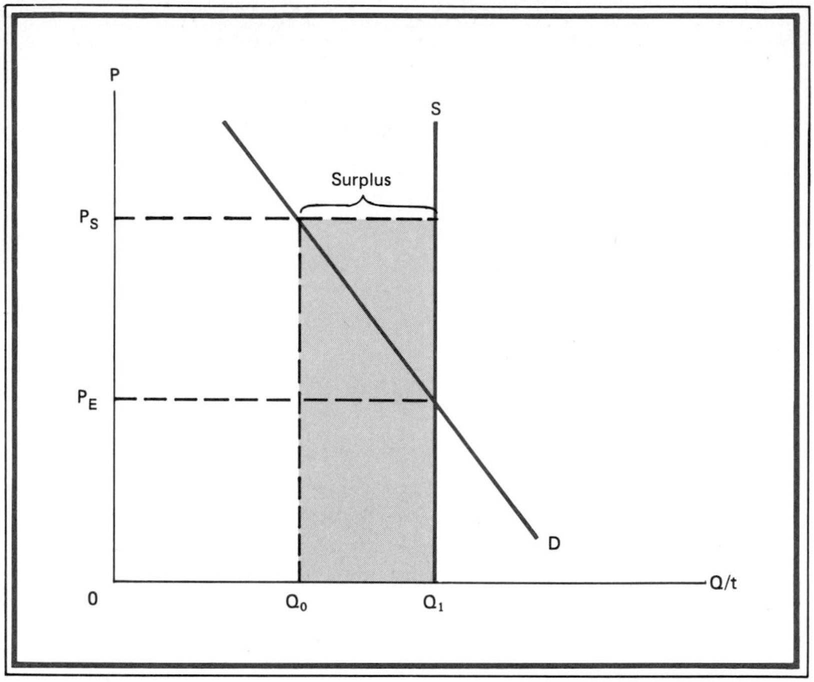

Crop Restriction

***Crop restriction* requires famers to reduce acreage to qualify for support payments; this reduction of supply raises prices and should raise total farm revenue.**

The idea here is to require farmers to reduce acreage if they are to qualify for support payments. Also, because demand is inelastic, reducing supply raises prices and consequently should raise total farm revenue. This is illustrated in Figure 8-6. Planting is reduced, shifting supply leftward from S_1 to S_2 and the price up to P_2. The gain in revenue to the farmer shown by the shaded rectangle is greater than the loss in revenue to the farmer shown by the crossed rectangle, so that the net change in total revenue that the farmer receives is positive. The farmer has gained at the expense of the consumer.

The consumer's loss, on the other hand, is the area of both the crossed and striped spaces. The striped triangular area represents the loss in consumer surplus that is not, in turn, gained by the farmers. It is therefore a deadweight loss—or waste—to society as a whole.

In addition to price support, farmers often receive government payments on land they voluntarily retire from production. These are transfer payments from taxpayers to farmers. The program is sometimes called the soil bank program, as if land left idle was somehow being saved for future use.

Unfortunately, the success of supply management depends on the ability of the Agriculture Department's economists to predict both demand and supply. They need to estimate how large the crop should be in the coming season—a tricky business. If they are wrong, or if they change their estimates too often, farmers get upset and uncooperative. The program is, after all, voluntary.

Moreover, supply management does not work well. Farmers tend to retire their lowest yield land and intensively cultivate the better land. Thus, between 1940 to 1960, while harvested acreage declined 15 percent, crop yields

Figure 8-6

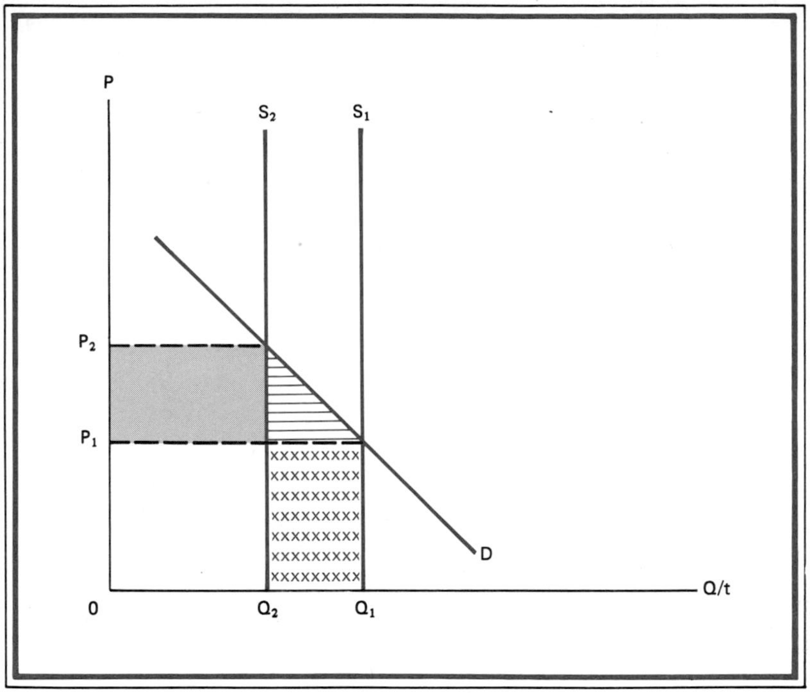

increased nearly 70 percent. And the government still had to pay off on the surplus. This policy encouraged smaller, less efficient farms to hang on.

Lest one get the impression that America is the only country with agricultural subsidy programs that usually make little sense economically, let us hasten to provide an example from Europe. In late 1979 the European Economic Community (EEC) sold 7 million pounds of butter to the Soviet Union for 58 cents per pound. At the same time the British were paying $1.75 per pound at the grocery. What was happening? The British under the auspices of the EEC was buying unsold butter at support prices. Then, the EEC negotiated with the Russians to get whatever they could for it, outside the EEC. The ultimate result was that the relatively poor British housewife ended up subsidizing the Russian consumption of butter in order to keep the British dairyman in business. There is a certain irony about it all. The people in England and the EEC would have been somewhat better off to implement a resale plan.

Resale Plan

In a *resale plan* the purpose is to support incomes instead of prices.

In a resale plan the purpose is to support incomes instead of prices. It involves playing musical crops with the CCC. There is no crop restriction or soil bank policy or any storage of crops. In Figure 8-7, P_S is the parity support price and P_E the free market equilibrium price. Assuming the crop is wheat, $P_S - P_E$ represents the price differential per bushel of wheat. The tax burden to the public under the resale plan becomes the shaded area in the form of direct payments to farmers.

To see how this burden comes about, consider an example. Suppose the

Figure 8-7

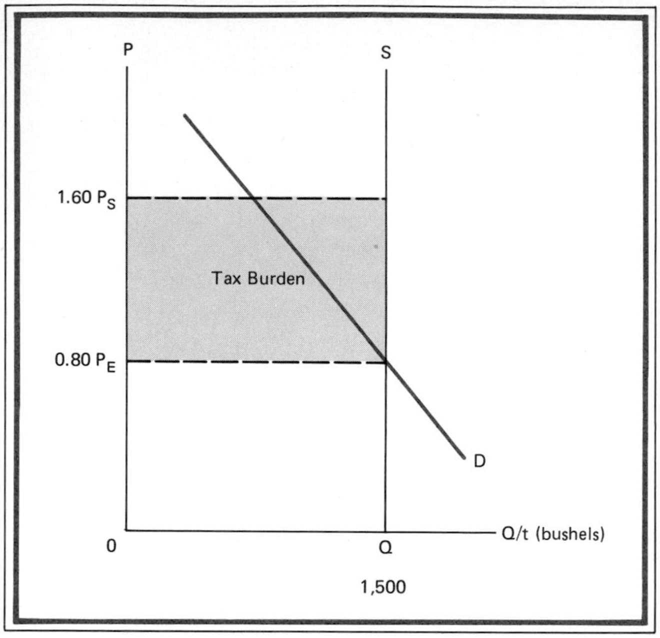

parity price of wheat is $2 a bushel and the CCC sets the support price at 80 percent of parity. The support price is therefore (.80) ($2) = $1.60/bu. The farmer is guaranteed this price per bushel. Suppose the farmer grows 1,500 bushels. The farmer receives a loan in the form of a government payment (a check) for (1,500) ($1.60) = $2,400, and the farmer stores his crop (we ignore storage costs here). Should the market price of wheat be above $1.60 a bushel, say $2, the farmer will sell his 1,500 bushel crop that is in storage for $3,000, and with the receipts of this sale he pays back the $2,400 government loan and keeps the extra $600. But should the market price fall below $1.60 a bushel, the farmer makes less than $2,400 from selling his crop. Say it falls to P_E = 80 cents shown in the figure. He keeps the government check and turns the crop over to the government. Essentially, the government has now bought his crop at the support price of $1.60 and paid $2,400 for it. The government then sells the wheat at its current market price of 80 cents and receives $1,200. Taxpayers pick up the difference.

In terms of allocation of resources this program is in some ways more efficient than the other programs, for there is no lost consumers' surplus, no government storage costs, and the consumer pays the low free-market price. However, the public is taxed to pay for the income transfers to the farmer.

Marketing Orders For many fruits and vegetables each year the USDA sets minimum sizes and grades for what may be sold through normal wholesale outlets. The orders keep the quality of produce in stores high. By raising size and grade requirements when crops are large, and lowering them when crops are small, the USDA reduces the supply to keep prices higher. Milk-market orders keep the price of fresh milk above the price of milk used in powdered milk and cheese. There is also a floor price set by the USDA on milk, a price below which milk cannot be sold. Import quotas and rules restrict foreign produce. During the U.S. tomato crop harvest, the USDA keeps out small sun-ripened tastier Mexican tomatoes in favor of the larger Florida tomatoes, which are picked green, are hard, reddened with gas, and have little flavor. The USDA also sells at low price surplus food items to schools for their lunch programs.

Effects

The income redistribution effects on government farm aid programs have unfortunately fallen very unequally on farmers. Since the larger farms can retire more acreage, grow more crops, and obtain better credit for expansion, it is they who have mostly benefited from government generosity. For instance, in 1972 there were some 2.9 million farms. The 600,000 largest, about 20 percent of all farms, received about 60 percent of all federal subsidies. The average was about $3,000 per farm. The other 80 percent received 40 percent of the total and averaged less than $600 per farm. This is an average only; many did better than $600 but others survived partly or totally from nonfarm income. Nevertheless, some small farms survived because they did receive government aid. The total of subsidies was in the neighborhood of $5 billion in 1972.

Some select farms really benefited. In 1971, two California farm firms were paid more than $4 million each and four of them more than $1 million each. One Florida and two Hawaiian firms received over $1 million each.

In 1973 another act was passed limiting any person under the wheat grain and upland cotton programs to $20,000 ($50,000 on rice). The limit did not cover loans or purchases. Crop restrictions were removed. The farmers had a good year because of a world food shortage caused by droughts in Africa and a poor harvest in Russia. Domestic surpluses found a strong export market. In 1979 the payments ceilings were raised to $45,000. In 1978 many small farms were again in a cost-price squeeze. Farmers talked of strikes, threatened to plant no crops, and wanted 100 percent parity. The government responded by introducing a set-aside program in the Agricultural Act of 1978. If farmers volunteered to set aside 20 percent of their wheat acreage and 10 percent of their corn acreage, they would receive $100 per acre. In this we have, essentially, a return to the soil bank program. It is, no doubt, not the end of a continuing stream of agricultural acts.

Despite nearly forty years of government policies strongly influenced by powerful farm lobbies representing the large operations, the farm problem remains.

CHAPTER SUMMARY

Farming is an industry that potentially approximates the perfectly competitive model. But government programs have tended to interfere with the free movement of farm prices and production.

The depression of the 1930s initiated the introduction of new major farm policies, after years of government-sponsored research going back to the late nineteenth century had vastly improved agricultural productivity.

Farm income undergoes wide fluctuations because of natural conditions like the weather, and because the price elasticity of demand for farm products is inelastic, reinforced by a low income elasticity of demand.

Because of vast improvements in productivity, the long-run prices of farm products declined relative to prices in other sectors of the economy. Prices farmers receive have fallen relative to the costs of inputs they buy.

To rectify this problem, the government introduced the parity concept and other price support programs. Parity, in principal, is designed to adjust prices farmers receive in such a way as to maintain the purchasing power that existed in the best farm purchasing power years, 1910-1914. The parity calculation was modified in 1948.

Other government programs have been price supports in which farmers are guaranteed a price for their crop, crop restriction where the farmer is paid to retire acreage, and the resale plan—all of which involve transfers of income from taxpayers to farmers.

The effects of these farm aid programs have tended to benefit the large farms much more than small ones. Thus small farms still suffer from a cost-price squeeze. Despite government programs, the number of farms continues to decline in a profit-squeezed industry, though not nearly as fast as they would have without the programs.

Speculators and hedgers in the commodities markets help to smooth farm prices and protect large farms, grain operators, and other large buyers and sellers of farm products from fluctuations in market prices.

QUESTIONS

1. "We (U.S. citizens) eat more food and spend less of our income for food than people in any other country." If true, does this violate the law of demand? Explain.
2. If the income elasticity of the demand for shrimp is +1.1, an increase in consumers' spendable income will not increase the consumption of shrimp. Do you agree?
3. Farmer Plow says, "If there are no subsidies, only 1,000 large farms will be left and instead of spending 20 percent of your income on food you will be spending 100 percent. Give the farmers 100 percent parity." Assume that food prices would rise if subsidies were eliminated and only 1,000 large farms would be left. Does this mean food "costs" would rise? What is the difference between price and cost here? Would food prices necessarily rise?
4. There continues to be a conflict between the inefficient, small farms on the periphery of surburban areas whose owners desire to keep their land for farming, and some of their farm neighbors who have chosen to sell their farmland for top prices to housing developers. Millions of acres are lost to developers every year.
   a. What fundamental economic principle is displayed once again about resources?
   b. Is farmland therefore perfectly inelastic in supply?
   c. Are housing developers benefiting at the expense of the rest of us? At the expense of the farmers? Are farmers benefiting at the expense of the rest of us?
   d. Can you say with confidence that U.S. farmland will not completely disappear? Comment.
5. In the late 1970s the Japanese discovered a process for converting corn syrup into sugar that is as sweet as beet sugar. Corn syrup sugar sold at one third the price of beet sugar even after transportation of the corn from the U.S. to Japan for processing and returning it to the U.S. as sugar.
   a. For the industry only, graph the effect in the foreign and domestic sugar industries of the new sugar process.

b. The U.S. sugar industry is guaranteed a minimum price for sugar at about 14 cents a pound. Can you show the effect of a sugar price-support program if Japanese sugar drives the price below the support price for U.S. sugar farmers?
c. What do you anticipate that U.S. candy, ice cream, and other food manufacturers will do? Are they being unpatriotic? To whom?

6. It is not uncommon for a typical farmer to write into a magazine or newspaper, "If every business went to Washington, D.C., to get a government payment everyone would laugh, because as costs go up to the small businessman so do his prices to cover the extra costs. But the farmer can't raise the price of his wheat. A tractor that cost $10,000 in 1950 costs $150,000 in 1980. Bread was under 20 cents a loaf in 1950 and the farmer got $3 a bushel for his wheat. Today bread is over 70 cents a loaf and the farmer still gets $3 a bushel."
   a. Why does the farmer still get $3 a bushel for his wheat?
   b. Suppose all government subsidy programs to farmers were stopped. What would happen in the industry? Would it automatically follow that U.S. residents would have less food to eat, and at much higher prices? Does Table 8-2 help you to answer this question?
7. Many farmers argue that crop restriction programs do not really help them, because the subsidy they receive per retired acre does not make up for the loss of profit from growing less. What are they implicitly assuming about the price they will receive for their crop in the situations of crop restriction versus no crop restriction? Does it make a difference if the farm is small or very large?
8. Suppose today farmers are receiving a 70 percent parity price for wheat? Is this a clear indication that farmers' purchasing power today is less than what it was in the 1910-1914 period? Explain.
9. Suppose the average price of wheat in 1978 was $3 a bushel. Given that the price index for farm products was 320, calculate the parity price for corn for the year 1978 if the 1978 price index of inputs was 480. What percent of parity are the farmers currently earning per bushel? If the support price were set at 80 percent of parity, how much would they earn per bushel?
10. A farmer sells an amount in futures contracts based on the size of his expected crop at a price he considers acceptable. He then agrees to buy back the same number of futures contracts from a local dealer. If the cash price of the crop falls below what the farmer expected, does the farmer gain or lose when his crop and futures market dealings are combined? What is this activity of the farmer called? Did the dealer gain or lose? What is his activity called? Why one name for the dealer's activity and another for the farmer's?

Chapter 9

Monopoly and Price Discrimination

PROGRESS REPORT

A. In Chapter 8 we studied the farming industry. We chose to study it principally because it is a very important industry and because most farm products are sold in nearly perfectly competitive markets. Farmers are considered to be price-takers. However, this industry is also strongly affected by government programs designed to support farmers.

B. In this chapter we examine the monopoly model, industry regulation, and price discrimination. Instead of a large number of firms existing in an industry, monopoly is a single firm which is the industry, and is the sole producer and/or seller of a commodity. We explain why monopolies exist in some industries. A monopolist as an imperfect competitor is a price-searcher rather than a price-taker. Price discrimination is discussed, and then a distinction is made between a simple monopolist who does not price discriminate and a discriminating monopolist.

C. In Chapter 10 other models of imperfect competition will be introduced. These are intermediate between the pure monopoly of this chapter and perfect competition discussed in Chapter 7.

FALLING AVERAGE COSTS: THE "NATURAL" MONOPOLY

Try to imagine a town in which two telephone companies competed for the customers' dollars. Half of your friends might be hooked up to company A and the other half to company B. You would have to sign up with both companies if you wanted to get in touch with all your friends by phone. Then there would be two sets of wires to each person's house. The same is true of gas lines, water pipes, electricity service, and railroads.

Two telephone companies would never exist side by side in a given town because it would always be cheaper for one to sell out to the other, which would then maintain only one set of poles and wires. Costs would be lower if the two firms merged. When costs are lower with a single firm producing the entire output of an industry than they are with two or more firms, then we say the industry faces declining average costs.

What happens when a competitive firm expands and long-run costs continue to decline in the region of industry demand, as shown in Figure 9-1? Eventually the long-run average cost curve may turn upward. But by that time a single firm's output may be so large that there are no rivals or potential rivals left. Only a single seller—the pure monopolist—remains. This single producer is not only the firm, but also the industry.

It is possible that when the *LAC* curve of a dominant, but not exclusively dominant, firm does finally begin to turn up only a few firms will have sur-

Figure 9-1

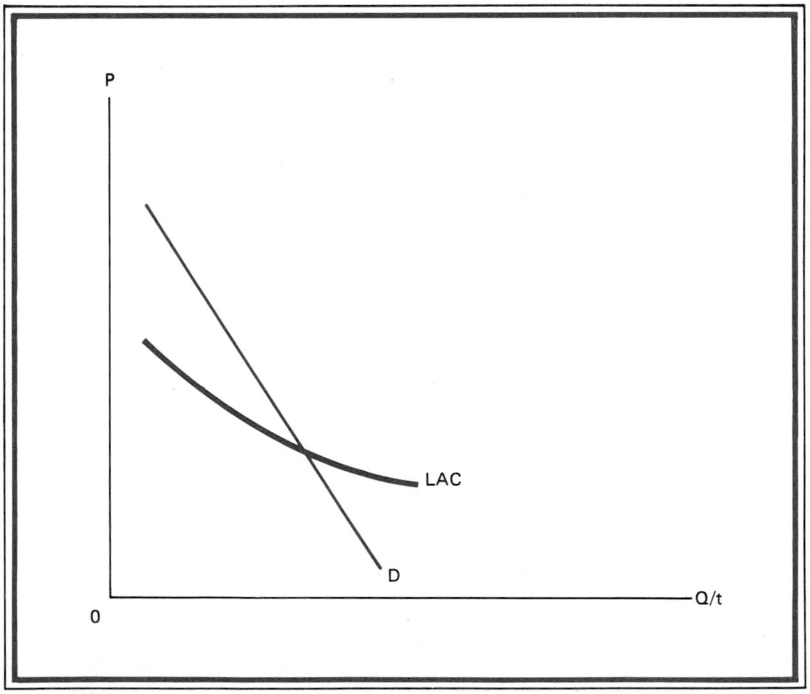

vived. The industry becomes a concentrated industry with only a few sellers sharing most or all of the market. Such an industry is called an oligopoly, meaning few sellers. Most of the time this is the actual situation when people refer to monopoly.

Business firms sell their wares in a market. Economists classify markets according to their structure. If a seller has no control over the price of the good he sells, he is called a price-taker and the market he sells in is called perfectly competitive. Most farm products are sold in markets like this. Many other products are sold in fairly competitive markets, that is, while the seller has some discretion over the price he or she charges, the range of prices is quite small. A new corner restaurant may open up and the owner can set any price on a hamburger. But the price had better be within a "competitive" range if the owner expects to stay in business. Firms operating in slightly imperfect markets like this behave almost exactly the same as those in perfectly competitive markets, and the theoretical models of cost and demand that have been developed in previous chapters can be readily applied to these industries as a reasonable approximation. There are, however, a few industries that by their nature tend to have only a single producer. When there is only one producer, and no other potential producers, we say this industry is a **monopoly**. In this case, the price set by the owner can be set without concern over the reaction of competitors because there simply are no competitors. Thus, we can characterize market structure as a continuum from the price takers of perfect competition to the price-setters of monopoly. Because nonperfect competitors may exercise a little, moderate, or a great deal of control over the price, they are sometimes called price-searchers.

An industry is a *monopoly* when there is only one producer with no other potential producers.

Thus, we classify market structures as **perfectly competitive**, **imperfectly competitive**, **or monopolistic**. Under the heading of imperfectly competitive we have various other subcategories. If there are two producers we call it a duopoly. If there are only a few producers, we call it an oligopoly. We also refer to monopolistic competition in which the industry is highly competitive but each firm holds a slight monopoly position because of trademarks or other property rights.

Market structures can be *perfectly competitive, imperfectly competitive, or monopolistic.*

In this chapter we wish to describe monopoly. Like the theory of perfect competition, the theory of monopoly is quite well developed. The monopoly model applies to a very few industries, but some of these industries are also very important to the consumer—public utilities, for example.

The Single Seller

If as a competitive firm expands it realizes declining costs, known as economies of scale, it encroaches on the market share of its rivals. Because rival firms now sell less, they must cut back production and begin to shut down plants. They are forced to move to higher short-run average cost curves and are compelled to charge higher prices. Unable to compete with price, they continue to lose sales until they depart the industry. A single seller of a homogeneous product remains, the monopolist.

In practice, the case of a single seller of a product is exceedingly rare. When such sellers exist, they seldom sustain their predominate position for long. Studies seem to indicate that long-run average cost curves tend to turn upward before a single firm's output approaches the industry output in nearly every industry. In fact, many large manufacturing firms for the most part appear to display constant returns of scale, that is, they operate where long-run average cost is constant. The necessary conditions for **pure monopoly** to be sustained are that no close substitutes for the product are produced and no entry by other producers is possible. We shall say more on these natural monopolies later in the chapter. Pure monopoly, like perfect competition, is a textbook idealization. The only situation where it can persist for any significant period is where it is the result of government regulation and permission, as in the case of regulated public utilities.

The necessary conditions for *pure monopoly* to be sustained are that no close substitutes for the product are produced and that no entry by other producers is possible.

The two conditions mentioned are hard to maintain in the long run. Alcoa was a monopoly in the production of tin until 1945. Dow Chemical, until 1969, produced 90 percent of the magnesium metal in the U.S. But these firms could not keep their privileged positions. In 1881 Standard Oil controlled over 90 percent of U.S. refining capacity. By 1911, when the Supreme Court decreed the breakup of the company, there were already at least eight other U.S. oil companies competing with it.

It is difficult to think of a commodity produced by one company today for which no substitutes exist. Coca-Cola sells throughout the world. Its recipe is unique and a jealously guarded secret by the company. But it is not a monopoly because many close substitutes exist. The definition of a monopoly critically depends on the definition of the product. Plastic pipes, concrete, beams, and nylon cord can substitute for metal in a variety of uses. The Volkswagen Rabbit has a single producer but other compacts act as close substitutes for it. Nor is size a reliable indicator of monopoly. The only shop in town that silvers glass or machines automobile brake discs may be more of a monopoly than Boeing Airplane Company in Seattle, since Boeing competes in a worldwide market consisting of national and international rivals.

Check the yellow pages of the phone book to see whether you can find a single seller of any commodity or service. If you do it is likely to be a small local business and not a company listed in Fortune Magazine's yearly compilation of the 500 largest U.S. firms. If there happens to be only one Peugot dealer in town, you can no doubt discover alternatives for car repairs and parts.

Moreover, should a firm be a monopolist in a particular market, it is highly unlikely to remain so. In a changing world fortunes change, protective walls erode, and eager rivals manage to trickle in. Given that entry is difficult to prevent in the long run, what makes entry difficult in the short run?

Size and Capital Costs

Where a monopoly has emerged, why might the firm be large? The reason is to be found in high setup costs, that is, the high costs of fixed capital (plant and equipment). For a new firm to enter the industry it would have to start big. A large, established producer would already possess an extensive network of affiliated or franchised retail outlets. This would often represent a prohibitive barrier to a potential entrant. The chance of breaking into the industry with significant impact entails risk. Newcomers would only be willing to take such a large risk if they firmly believed a substantial share of the market could be captured in a relatively short time—of which there is certainly no guarantee.

The Postal Service

Empowered by the Constitution, the U.S. Postal Service has had a monopoly on the delivery of first class mail since 1792. In 1970 Congress established the Postal Service as an independent establishment of the executive branch. The Post Office delivers first class mail—letters, bills, Christmas cards, and most common business documents. Second class mail is comprised of magazines and newspapers, third class deals with advertising circulars, and fourth class with bulk packages. Competition for fourth class delivery comes from Greyhound package, REA Express, local and short haul truckers, and United Parcel Service. The Post Office monopoly on first class mail allows it to protect its revenues. But it has been running huge deficits for many years and deliveries are less frequent.

Whenever it is threatened by a private competitor in a local area the Post Office forces it out of business through arguments based on the legal definition of what is a letter. Any firm can deliver its own letters legally but may not deliver for others. In March 1976 in Pittsburgh, a local firm was shut down that was delivering first class mail locally for 3 cents a letter as compared to 13 cents by the Post Office. It guaranteed delivery on the same day if the letter was mailed before noon. Independent Postal System of America, Inc. in Oklahoma sold private postage stamps for 5 cents in 1971 to deliver Christmas cards to local and surrounding areas when the Post Office was charging 6 cents. The postal union brought suit against the company, saying the potential jobs of 200,000 Post Office employees it represented were in danger. The court ruled the company was a nuisance and declared Christmas cards were letters and shut down the private operation.

The Post Office is a legal, not a natural, monopoly, for if it were a natural monopoly it would not need the benefit of the law to make it a monopoly.

The Postal Service makes money on first class mail, but loses on third and fourth class mail where private firms do it more cheaply with better service. Prices on first class letters have changed as follows:

Year	Price of First-Class Stamp	Deficit (millions)
1932	3	$ 205.5
1958	4	$ 890.6
1963	5	819.4
1968	6	1,020.9
1974	10	2,188.0
1976	13	1,175.8
1979	15	469.8
1981	18	306.9

It can raise rates no more than 33 percent at a time by law, yet it still loses money.

Empirical studies do not show that the Post Office evidences economies of scale for large operations. Nor does it have high fixed capital costs. The Post Office is labor intensive, with about 85 percent of its costs due to labor. It has over 40,000 branch offices in the U.S. and employs over 650,000 people. Whether you send a letter across town or across the country the price has been the same ever since Congress established the uniform rate in 1863. Small branch offices around the country incur costs much greater than revenues. An example is Colbert, Washington. With a population of 25 in 1976, revenues were $9,624 and expenses $61,269, or $2,450 per person. Major cost saving innovations have come mostly when private operators have been then taken over by the Post Office and the private deliveries declared illegal. The old Pony Express was one example. In the 46 states where United Parcel Post is permitted to do business it outperforms the Post Office in reliability.

Heading into the 1980s, private firms will step up the use of private electronic mail techniques, avoiding the Postal Service altogether. Many firms, like the Wall Street Journal, use their own delivery systems. This trend will probably eventually reach into homes as the volume of mail the Post Office handles continues to decline while its subsidies rise.

An incumbent company that produces goods like large appliances or automobiles usually carries a network of dealerships and specially trained personnel to service the equipment and honor warranties. The manufacturer is backed by warehouses and distributors with a ready inventory of replacement parts. The convenience of service that these supportive activities provide make consumers reluctant to take a chance on a new product whose reputation has yet to be established and whose services are apt to be spotty, possibly unavailable, and in any case untested.

The upshot is that in situations where the lowest average cost of production is achieved at very large output rates, the amount of capital employed by the firm will be large, and entry to the industry will be difficult.

Capital Market Imperfections

For an activity that requires high volumes of fixed capital such as that found in the steel, oil, shipping, and automobile industries, the costs of borrowing investment funds are high and obtaining credit is difficult. A potential entrant will often find it hard to convince lenders to provide the large amounts of venture capital needed for risky operations. Lack of adequate knowledge on the part of the lenders on the future behavior of the market, or about the new entrepreneur's business acumen, discourages lending institutions and wealthy individuals from making direct loans to the new firm or from purchasing its stock. If information were costless, investment funds could be freely allocated and all frictions removed with the lubricant of certainty. In reality, information is not free.

The potential lender in a high stakes business venture faces a very imperfect capital market, that is, lenders simply do not know enough about the borrower. Lenders no doubt at times lose out by not lending when they should and lending when they should not. But the larger the amount requested, the higher is the rate of loan rejections, given the same amount of information. For this reason it is unlikely another U.S. car manufacturer will be able to generate enough financial backing to break into the U.S. automobile manufacturing industry. A notable attempt was made after World War II with the introduction of the radically designed Tucker automobile. The designer could not obtain the capital backing or the credit on steel purchases he needed to start up mass production. Today there are only eleven or twelve Tucker cars in existence.

Sole Owner of an Input

Monopoly can come about because a firm has managed to corner the market on an essential resource. Alcoa, as mentioned, was the only owner of the only known high-grade bauxite mine. Bauxite is necessary for the production of aluminum. But Kaiser and Reynolds both managed to discover new sources of bauxite ore and broke Alcoa's monopoly even before the government took effective antitrust action against the company.

Alcoa's monopoly on the bauxite input did not allow it to have a monopoly on a consumer good. While for a period it was the only seller of aluminum pots and pans, it did not have a monopoly on all pots and pans because of close substitutes, mainly steel and cast iron pots and pans.

The Organization of Petroleum Exporting Countries (OPEC) has formed an international monopoly called a cartel. They set prices of crude oil and then produce only what buyers will ask for at those prices. They produce a majority of the world's crude oil.

Legal Barriers

Government can grant *temporary monopoly* rights to individuals and firms through the issuance of patents and copyrights.

Through the issuance of patents and copyrights the government can grant **temporary monopoly** rights to individuals and firms. Patent rights last for seventeen years; copyrights are for twenty-eight years and are renewable for another twenty-eight years. Exclusive property rights are granted on plays, television events, songs, poetry, novels, and textbooks. Clearly novels, songs, and so on have close substitutes. Nonetheless, popular music has borrowed many melodies from classical music because the copyrights have expired on the works of Chopin, Rossini, Bach, and others. However, the degree of exploitation of a temporary monopoly that exists under a copyright involves much less money than the amounts derived from patents on manufactured products and production processes, since the market is potentially much larger. The purpose of patents and copyrights is to stimulate the search for and to reward new ideas and technologies.

Patents granted on drugs have led to enormous price markups above costs of production. Drug companies claim this is necessary to cover research and development costs. In the 1960s the drug tetracycline, used for urinary infections, was sold by drug companies to wholesalers for $30.60 per bottle of 100 capsules. The cost of producing a bottle varied from $1.60 to $3.80 in that period. Later when the patent right expired and renewal was doubtful, other unlicensed firms began to produce it at about $2.50 a bottle.

A large, established company which feels threatened by a technological innovation that is related but different from a process or device the company already has patented can delay implementation by tying up the small competitor in long court battles that deplete the smaller capital resources of the upstart entrepreneur. The large, incumbent company often settles out of court by buying up the patent right for its own use.

Regulation and Licensing

Many industries though not monopolistic are significantly insulated from the full force of price competition. Industries like taxicabs, airlines, banks, utilities, and interstate commerce that encompasses transportation by truck, barge, ships on internal waterways, and railroad are monitored by government regulatory agencies with the intention of ensuring competition, avoiding chaos, and preventing monopoly.

In the case of individuals, the industry requires a license by the practitioner be he doctor, dentist, optometrist, or lawyer, or requires certification as in the case of primary and secondary school teachers, barbers, dog trainers, accountants, plumbers, and so forth. Licensing such as this tends to restrict entry into the industry and hold up the prices received for services provided by those individuals who are licensed. Insofar as licenses indicate that the person providing the services is competent, the licenses help provide information to the public and help protect the public from quacks and con artists. Often, however, members of licensed groups will press for restrictions on entry far beyond what is necessary to protect the public interest. When this happens, consumers are ill-served because suppliers are held back and prices are higher than economics would dictate.

The American Medical Association

The status of physicians in U.S. society has much to do with the influence and policies of the American Medical Association (AMA). The AMA was founded in 1847. Today a minority of doctors are members. Ordinarily, to gain membership a physician must be accepted into the county medical society. The AMA is structured in an ascending order starting at the county level, then to the state and federal levels.

The AMA has diligently pursued policies to enhance the quality, prestige, and income of doctors. This was accomplished by the licensure of doctors and control of accreditation of medical schools. It achieved these goals around 1906 as a result of the Flexner study, which claimed there were too many doctors and too many schools, many of them below standard. Of 160 medical schools only 82 were allowed to remain open, and some merged. There were only 88 medical schools by 1966 and 116 in 1978. In 1904 the ratio of doctors to population was 157 per 100,000. It fell to 132 per 100,000 in 1957. Because of public pressure it increased to 162 per 100,000 in 1976, up since 1970.

The Flexner study was genuinely concerned about standards, but in 1932 as the Depression hit, the AMA became restrictive about entry and has remained so. The result has been to stifle fee competition, to control doctor supply, and to increase dramatically the income of doctors.

While AMA spokesmen often berate government interference, it is state governments that have granted the AMA the power and wherewithal to control medical training and practice. To get a license a potential doctor must pass standards set by one of the 55 medical examining boards—one in each state and the 5 U.S. territories. These standards require that the doctor graduate from an accredited medical school. The AMA decides which schools qualify. Also the state examiners tend to agree with the AMA standards. Since "only professionals can police their ranks competently," the state boards are mostly peopled by members associated with the medical profession. By threatening schools with removal of accreditation, the AMA can ensure the proper ratio of doctors to the population, reached through setting quotas on interns at hospitals and students entering medical schools. Loss of accreditation would make it unlikely that a hospital could get interns.

There are other sanctions available to the AMA to discipline nonconformists to obey their policies. "Unethical" conduct includes things such as advertising prices, competitive price cutting, and participation in prepaid health organizations not approved by the AMA. When their good standing is lost in the county medical association, doctors can be denied graduate medical training, admission to specialty exams, and the use of hospital facilities. To surgeons this last sanction would be a disaster. But not to psychiatrists; hence they are more rebellious than other equipment-dependent doctors.

The AMA has attacked group health clinics. They are still illegal in some states, for these organizations charge a fixed membership fee to all patients no matter what their income. Thus, price discrimination as such is not practiced among group health clinics.

The place of medicine in any social setting is complex. The decisions that doctors must make, and the responsibility they must assume, fosters a need for professional credibility on the part of the public. It is beyond our purpose here to analyze the sociology of medicine. But from the strictly economic point of view we observe that restriction of entry into the profession under AMA supervision tends to make medical services more expensive. When any industry becomes monopolized, the services provided by that industry become more expensive. Not only do prices tend to be monopoly prices, but also price discrimination is widely practiced.

Whether this is good or bad for society we cannot judge. What the AMA does is little different from what other trade and professional organizations do or would like to do. The influence of the AMA is weakening. In 1970 over half of the MDs were full time dues paying members, about 168,000. In 1980 the 150,000 dues-paying members were only about one-third of the nation's MDs.

There are ten major federal *economic* regulatory agencies and seventeen major *social* regulatory agencies at the federal level. At the state level there are over 1,500 agencies across the nation. Federal agencies account for over 72,000 pages in the Code of Federal Regulations. The cost to consumers of regulations runs over $125 billion a year.

MONOPOLY OUTPUT AND PRICING

Monopolists have some latitude in setting prices but face a *demand curve;* they cannot force people to buy a product.

Do not be misled into accepting the falsehood that a monopolist can charge any price his whimsy dictates. Though he is a single seller, the monopolist does face a market **demand curve**. He cannot force people to buy his product if they are either unwilling or unable. But the monopolist does have latitude in setting price that is unavailable to the price-taking perfect competitor.

The demand curve confronting the monopolist is less than infinitely elastic. Therefore, the quantity he decides to sell depends on the price he sets. In this regard he is a price searcher. He can choose the price. But he chooses the price with cunning because he wishes to maximize his total profits. The highest price he can charge will not maximize profits, and neither will the lowest price he can charge. How then does he find the optimum price?

Recall that under perfect competition the price that the producer receives per unit equals both average revenue and marginal revenue per unit ($P = AR = MR$), since the demand curve is perfectly elastic. But when demand is less than perfectly elastic, it is no longer true that price (average revenue) is equal to marginal revenue per unit.

Consider Figure 9-2 and the hypothetical data in Table 9-1 on which the figure is based. The upper panel portrays demand and marginal revenue and the lower panel total revenue.

If the monopolist charges $60, consumers buy nothing. They will buy one unit at $55, given the demand schedule. The change in total revenue from selling one unit is also $55, since marginal revenue is the change in total revenue from selling one more unit of output.

$$MR = \frac{\Delta TR}{\Delta Q} = \frac{\$55 - \$0}{1 - 0} = \$55.$$

When the monopolist lowers the price to $50, he is able to sell two units. Because the monopolist cannot sell one unit for $55 and the other for $50 when he offers two identical units for sale, he charges $50 for each unit and sells two units each period. The total revenue from selling two items is $100. The marginal revenue (MR) from selling the second unit is the addition to total revenue, or

$$MR = \frac{\Delta TR}{\Delta Q} = \frac{\$100 - \$55}{2 - 1} = \$45.$$

Observe that on the second unit sold, the price is $50 but the marginal revenue is only $45. Therefore, for a monopoly seller price is not equal to marginal revenue ($P \neq MR$). In fact, it is greater than marginal revenue ($P > MR$).

Figure 9-2

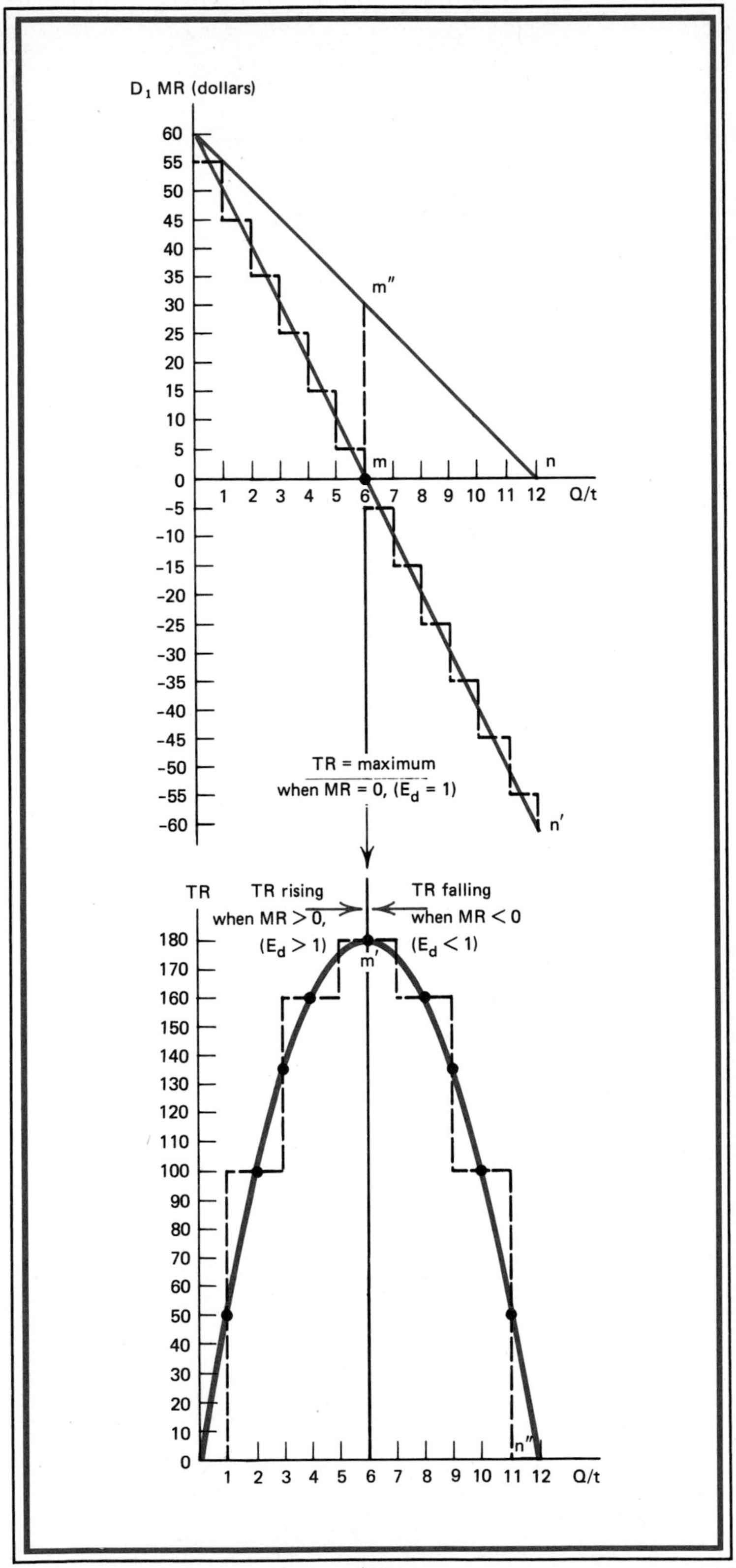
D$_1$ MR (dollars)
60
55
50
45
40
35
30
25
20
15
10
5
0
-5
-10
-15
-20
-25
-30
-35
-40
-45
-50
-55
-60
m″
m
n
n′
1 2 3 4 5 6 7 8 9 10 11 12 Q/t
TR = maximum
when MR = 0, (E$_d$ = 1)
TR
TR rising
when MR > 0,
(E$_d$ > 1)
TR falling
when MR < 0
(E$_d$ < 1)
m′
n″
180
170
160
150
140
130
120
110
100
90
80
70
60
50
40
30
20
10
0
1 2 3 4 5 6 7 8 9 10 11 12 Q/t

TABLE 9-1

Price	Quantity	Total revenue	Marginal revenue
60	0	0	
55	1	55	55
50	2	100	45
45	3	135	35
40	4	160	25
35	5	175	15
30	6	180	5
25	7	175	−5
20	8	160	−15
15	9	135	−25
10	10	100	−35
5	11	55	−45
0	12	0	−55

To sell three units the monopolist would have to price them at $45 each. Total revenue rises to $135, and the marginal revenue earned on the third unit is $35. On this occasion the price is $10 above the marginal revenue.

In general, the price is greater than the marginal revenue by the amount of income lost on the *previous* units. Hence, $5 each was lost on the first and second units for a total of $10 ($P(\$45) > MR(\$35)$). Go to 4 units. The price is $40 per unit. By our reckoning $5 should be lost on the first, second, and third units, so that marginal revenue should be $15 less than the price of $40. Indeed the marginal revenue from selling the fourth unit is $25, or $15 less than price. As more units are sold the price read off the demand curve continues to diverge farther away from marginal revenue and is always above the marginal revenue. Furthermore, for linear demand curves the marginal revenue curve will intersect the horizontal axis halfway between the origin and the point where the demand curve intersects the horizontal axis. In Figure 9-2 the marginal revenue is zero at 6 units and quantity demanded is zero at 12 units.

The dashed lines for marginal revenue and total revenue are included to make the point that when discrete or lumped data are used, the curves really look like steps. They are not smooth. If the data were continuous, then there would be many points to connect into a smooth line. For purposes of explanation we use the solid, continuous curves for marginal revenue and total revenue. Notice that we have drawn the solid marginal revenue curve through the midpoints between units zero and one, one and two, two and three, and so on. Thus, the marginal revenue equals 55 for 0.5 unit and 45 for 1.5 units.

Relation Between MR and TR

Marginal revenue is greater than zero for output less than 6 units. So long as marginal revenue is positive the total revenue will rise. Also, as the price is lowered the total revenue rises so that from 1 to 6 units the range of the demand curve is price elastic. At exactly 6 units total revenue is a maximum at point m' in the lower figure and marginal revenue is zero at point m in the upper figure. At point m'' only, demand is unitary elastic. When the price is zero, demand is a maximum at point n and marginal revenue is at its maximum negative value at n'. Not surprisingly, when the price is zero, total revenue is zero at point n''. Observe that total revenue increases but at a decreasing rate between one and six units.

Because marginal revenue is negative beyond 6 units and total revenue begins to decline, the monopolist would only produce on the elastic range of his demand curve where $MR > 0$. Being a price searcher, he would ideally look for the unitary elastic point on the demand curve he faces in order to maximize his total revenue. However, once costs are introduced, the output which maximizes total revenue does not necessarily maximize total profits. Thus, while the monopolist might not produce exactly where $E_d = 1$, he will certainly produce where $E_d > 1$ since $MR > 0$ in that range of output.

Maximizing Total Profits

To maximize profit the monopolist will expand production so long as the $MC < MR$ and stop expanding when $MC = MR$. The graph for the monopoly situation is shown in Figure 9-3. The maximizing profit output is Q_1. That is the rate of output for which $MC = MR$. The price P_1 is obtained from the demand curve. The shaded area indicates the pure profit area P_1adT. Total revenue is equal to the rectangular area P_1aQ_10 and total costs are equal to the rectangular area TdQ_10.

Were the monopolist to charge prices higher than P_1 and produce outputs below Q_1, total profits would not be maximized and the shaded area would be smaller. Alternatively, should the monopolist produce outputs greater than Q_1 the price would have to be lower than P_1 and again profits would not be maximized. For outputs below Q_1, $MC < MR$. That is, the additional cost of producing another unit is less than the revenues obtained from selling it. For outputs beyond Q_1, $MC > MR$. That is, in this range it costs more to produce another unit than is obtained for it when it is sold.

Changing Scale

Even though not threatened with entry, the monopolist could decide to change the size of plant in the long run in anticipation of a growth in demand. He may or may not build an optimum scale of plant. It depends on anticipated market

Figure 9-3

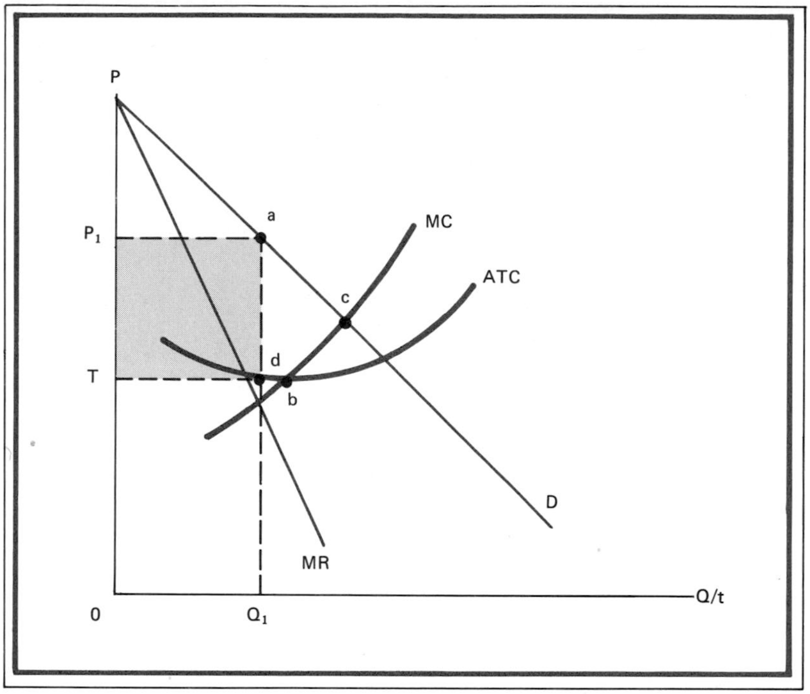

conditions. Thus the short-run market equilibrium can stay where it is into the long run. The monopolist can utilize the existing plant to accommodate shifts in demand or a greater elasticity of demand facing him over the longer run.

A monopolist may also face a decline in demand for his product because of the introduction of some new substitute. The decline could shift the demand curve so far left that it would lay entirely below the average total cost curve. In this case no profits would be earned. However, so long as marginal cost equals marginal revenue, at least short run losses would be minimized. Over the longer run, the monopolist would abandon production just as the perfect competitor would.

Monopolist Supply Curve

We have learned that the supply function relates the quantity supplied to the price of the product, other things being equal. When the price rises, suppliers are willing and able to produce more. We observed that in perfect competition when the price rises, individual firms and the industry they comprise increase output by moving up along their supply schedules. Conversely, when the price falls, firms and the industry reduce output, this time moving down along their supply curves in the short run.

But the monopolist has no supply schedule or curve in the sense we have just described. When demand decreases, causing the price to fall, we can predict what competitive firms will do—they will reduce output. However, when it comes to the monopolist, we cannot be sure how he will react when demand decreases. Figure 9-4 provides an example. Suppose demand declines, shifting

Figure 9-4

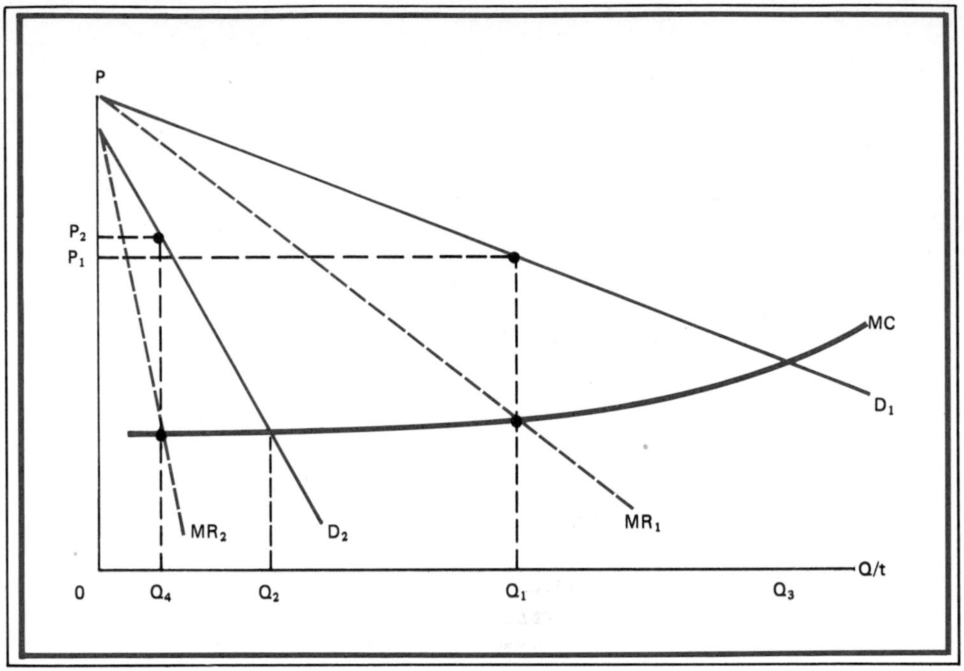

from D_1 to D_2. If the marginal cost curve were for the moment considered as the supply curve for a competitive industry, the price would drop and quantity demanded would decline from Q_3 to Q_2.

However, the monopolist's MR_1 curve would shift to MR_2 as demand shifted to D_2. Output, being determined by where $MR_2 = MC$, would fall to Q_4. The price would not fall but would rise from P_1 to P_2. In each case, the monopolist sets the price depending on the point where marginal revenue equals marginal cost.

The monopolist has no consistent schedule of intended quantities that he would supply at different prices, that is, a greater quantity supplied at higher prices and a lower quantity supplied at lower prices. Instead, the monopolist searches for and sets that price that will maximize profits. An example applicable to Figure 9-4 is when the demand for automobiles temporarily declines, as it often does, yet prices are not cut. If dampened demand persists, the work force will be reduced before prices are. Though auto manufacturers are oligopolists and not monopolists, Figure 9-4 is still relevant to the auto industry.

Effects of Monopoly on Efficiency

A quick check of the monopoly graphs shows that price is greater than the marginal cost ($P > MC$). As a result, the monopolist is not producing at the most efficient level of output. For instance, in Figure 9-3 for a level of output Q_1, P_1 at point *a* is greater than *MC* at point *b*. When output is at Q_1 consumers are willingly paying a price P_1 for the Q_1 unit, while the additional cost of producing that Q_1 unit is only 0*T*. But along the segment of the demand curve from *a* to *c*, the price is greater than marginal cost and output is greater than Q_1. It is the quantity consumers are willing to buy and which the monopolist could produce and still earn a profit. Granted it would not be the maximum total profit possible, since $MC > MR$ beyond output Q_1. But is it not produced, nor do consumers derive the additional benefit. There is a welfare (utility) loss to society.

The graphical formulation of the welfare loss is illustrated in Figure 9-5. For purposes of exposition, assume that marginal cost is constant. Thus $MC = ATC = S$ where S is the supply curve of the perfectly competitive firm. Thus $P_c = MC$ and $TR = TC$ satisfies the perfectly competitive conditions. The industry demand curve is D and MR is the marginal revenue curve facing the monopolist. The perfect competitor produces at point C where supply equals demand and where the price is P_c and output is Q_c. On the other hand, the monopolist sets $MC = MR$ and produces output Q_m at a price of P_m with $P_m > MC$. When the price is P_c the consumer surplus is the triangular area acP_c. The monopolist, by setting the price at P_m, reduces the consumer surplus to abP_m and takes away from the consumer the surplus shown by the striped area P_mbdP_c. The consumer surplus bcd, the shaded area, is lost by the consumer but not recaptured by the monopolist. Who gets it? No one. It is output the consumer does not get and income the monopolist does not receive. Since $P_m > MC$ there is inefficiency in allocation of resources. The price paid for the last or mth unit by the consumer is greater than the opportunity cost to society of the resources used to produce the last unit. The area bcd represents a deadweight loss to society. Neither buyer, producer, nor seller gets it.

Under a monopoly, prices are higher and output is lower than in perfect competition; $MC = MR$ is necessary to maximize profits.

Under a monopoly, prices are higher and output is lower compared to perfect competition. It is not ill will, incompetence, or callousness that compels a monopolist to produce less than he would under perfect competition. As a rational economic decision maker the monopolist uses the $MC = MR$ rule to maximize total profits, just as a perfect competitor would.

Figure 9-5

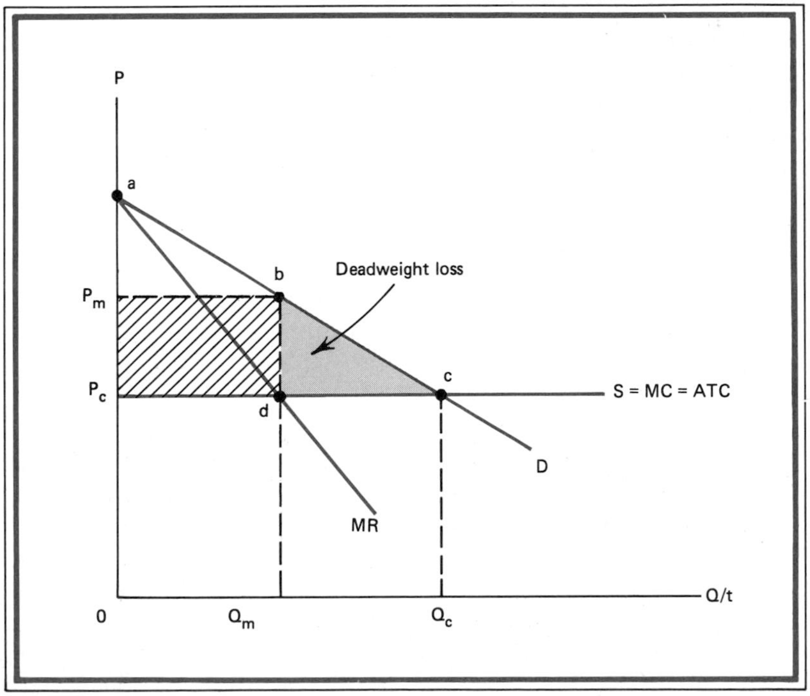

Taxing Monopoly Profit

The pure profits of a monopoly can be reduced by taxation. There are two approaches.

A *lump-sum tax* is one way to reduce pure profits of a monopoly and is an additional fixed cost.

Lump-Sum Tax A fixed tax is levied on the city's only golf course. The tax is simply an addition to fixed costs and therefore does not affect variable or marginal costs related to changes in output. The ATC curve shifts right and upward to ATC_2 reducing total profits as shown in Figure 9-6. The price P_1 and the quantity Q_1 remain unchanged since the $MC = MR$ point at a is unchanged and pure profits are reduced to the shaded area.

A *variable tax* is a tax on output and increases as output expands. It raises marginal and variable costs, but not fixed costs.

Variable Tax This is a tax that varies with the amount of output sold. It is often imposed on state liquor stores. Here, variable and marginal costs are affected as well as average total costs, since variable costs are part of total costs. In Figure 9-7, both the ATC_1 and MC_1 curves shift upward to ATC_2 and MC_2 and a new $MC = MR$ point at b (instead of at point a) exists, determined by $MC_2 = MR_1$, thus resulting in the price rising to P_2 and output falling to Q_2. Total profits are maximized, given the tax, but the total profits are now lower than they were before the tax existed.

PRICE DISCRIMINATION

Price discrimination exists when a seller offers the same good or service to different buyers at different prices, even though the price of producing and selling the commodity to each buyer is the same.

Any seller who is confronted with a downward sloping demand curve might have either a little, a moderate, or a great deal of control over the market price. Provided certain conditions are met, such a seller can practice price discrimination. **Price discrimination** *exists when a seller offers to different buyers the same good or service at different prices, even though the cost of producing and selling the commodity to each buyer is the same.*

For a monopolist to price-discriminate successfully, two conditions must be met.

For a monopolist to price-discriminate successfully, the market must be *separable* by sex, income, age, volume, time, or geography.

1. The market must be **separable**; that is, resale of the good is either impossible or too costly to make it worthwhile. For example, if you have brain surgery it is not likely you will ever be able to sell off a little bit of the surgery service you received to someone else. If you go to the store to buy a single washer to fix your faucet and you find they only come in a package containing an assortment, it is possible you could sell off the ones you did not really want by waiting around outside the store for someone to come along who wanted just what you had to offer. But it is unlikely you would do this because it is not worth the time; the transactions costs are too high compared to any gains. Thus, what separation means is that if one individual or subgroup is required to pay a higher price than another individual or subgroup of buyers, the group paying the lower price cannot or does not find it profitable to resell to the other group by acting as a middleman. The market can be separated in several ways: by sex (ladies' day at the baseball game), by income (first-class passengers re-

Figure 9-6

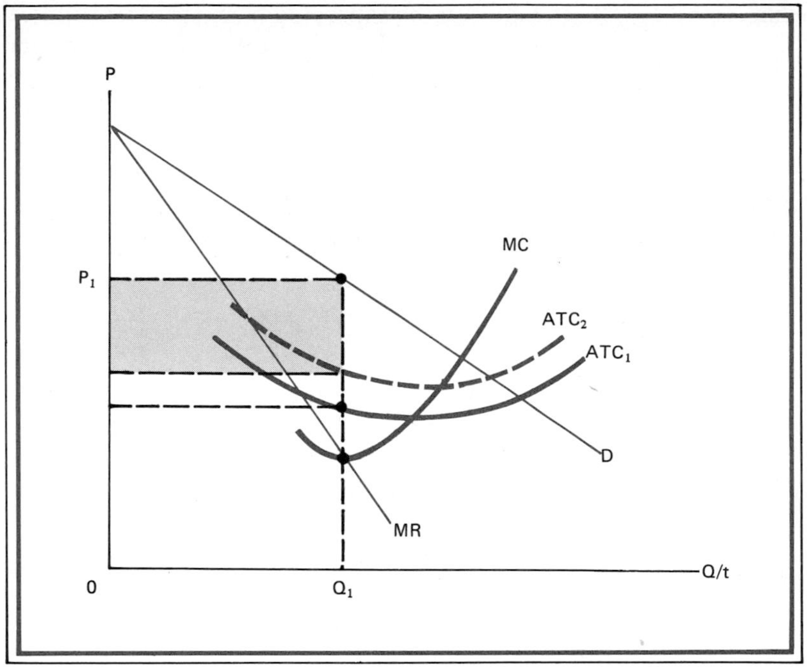

ceive free drinks on airplanes), age (children pay less than adults for movies), volume (large-volume buyers pay less per unit, for example in electricity fees), time (matinees are cheaper than evening shows), geography (out-of-staters in Oregon pay a camping fee, Oregonians do not).

Figure 9-7

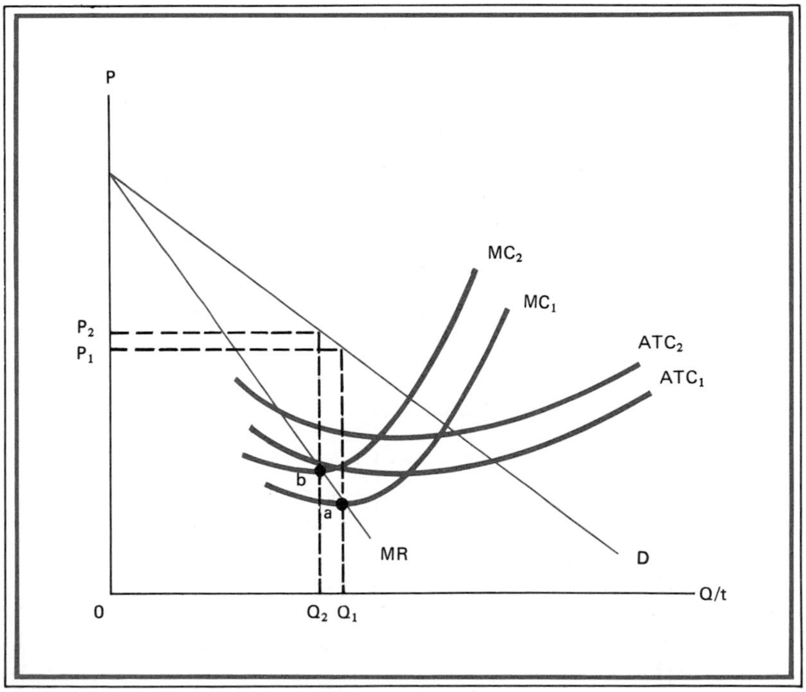

The second condition for successful price discrimination is that *demand* in the separated markets *must differ.*

2. **Demand** in the separated markets **must differ**. Once the submarkets are separated, the demand must also differ. Otherwise there is no point in separating the market because the prices charged will be the same anyway. Thus, the demand by students for movie tickets is understood to be lower than for adults because students, on the average, earn lower incomes. Therefore, the quantity demanded by adults and students differs over the range of the tickets' prices.

There are three degrees or types of price discrimination, varying in descending order of control, in achieving income maximization by the seller.

First-degree Price Discrimination

A *reservation price* is the absolute price you would be willing to pay for something.

Understanding first-degree discrimination requires the reader's familiarity with the concept of ***reservation* price**. It is the absolute limit you would pay for something as compared to what you would ordinarily be willing to pay. Reservation price is a price beyond which you will not go. Suppose you have to pull off the road into an isolated garage because your rear tire is coming apart and you have no spare. The garage owner offers to sell you a very expensive replacement tire. He is offering to sell you more tire than you want. You are stuck in the boondocks and have no other option except to drive slowly on a bad tire until you reach the next garage. But that could ruin the wheel on which the tire fits. Nonetheless you balk at the price. The owner searches for your price. He may offer another tire at a slightly lower price He is trying to find your reservation price. You finally buy a tire but it is still much more than you would have been willing to pay under more normal circumstances. The garage offers you an amount of tire q_2 at a price of p_2 illustrated by point a in Figure 9-8. It is more

Figure 9-8

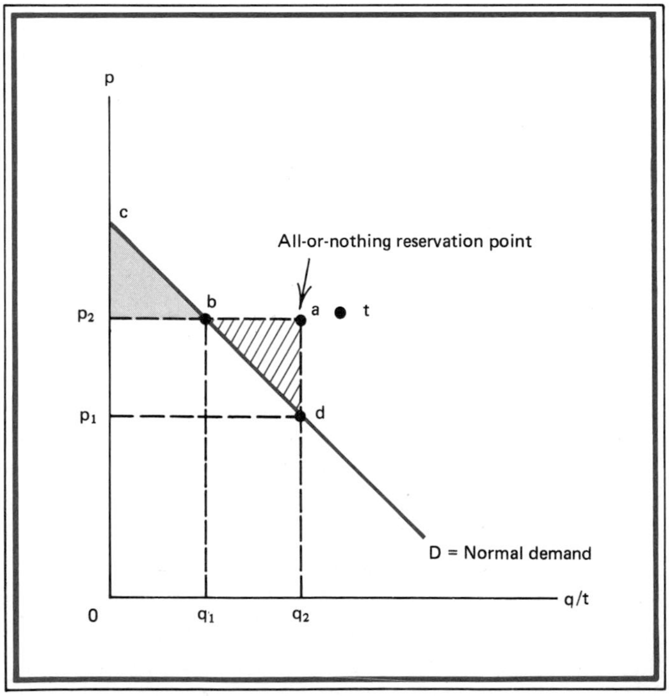

tire than you need or want. You normally would only be willing to buy the amount q_2 if the price were p_1. But the seller makes an all-or-nothing offer, take it or leave it. Point *a* or nothing. At the price of p_2 you would normally buy the amount q_1. Now you are being asked to take q_2 and pay your reservation price of p_2. It might appear that you are getting more for the same price, but you are really not better off.

When the price is p_2 consumer surplus is shown by the shaded triangle p_2cb under the normal demand curve *D*. However, the seller recaptures that surplus from you, indicated by the striped area and appropriately labeled *bad*. Thus, the net consumer surplus is zero. There is no net gain to the buyer, since you either buy the more expensive tire or no tire at all. The flat tire prevents you from driving to other garages where you might obtain the lower quality and cheaper tire that you really prefer. Hence, any consumer surplus you would normally receive is haggled away by the seller who finds and charges you your reservation price.

You might ask why the seller does not force you to point *t* and capture a larger consumer surplus than *bad*? The reason is that the striped area would now be larger than p_2cb, and consumer surplus would be negative. You would prefer to walk to the next station or call a tow truck rather than pay one penny more than p_2.

The *tie-in sale* is a kind of first-degree price discrimination whereby you must buy the accompaniments of an item to obtain the item itself.

Tie-ins A first-degree price discrimination of sorts is the **tie-in sale**. Examples abound. You cannot buy the table without buying the chairs, the book without buying the whole set; you must buy two shock absorbers, not just one; you cannot buy only one minipackage of Corn Flakes, you must also buy the minipackages of the other cereals included with it. At one time, until the restriction was declared illegal, IBM refused to sell IBM cards to users of non-IBM keypunch machines. You had to buy the off-line equipment from IBM when you bought its computer if you wanted to get the cards, since no one else produced them for IBM's machines.

Second-degree Price Discrimination

How often have you seen ads for magazine subscriptions offering price discounts the longer the period of time covered by the subscription? The longer the time period, the cheaper is the per-copy price. You are, no doubt, familiar with the difference in price per ounce between buying the small-, medium-, or economy-sized box of soap, jug of apple cider, package of dry dog food, or sack of sugar.

We have mentioned the benefits realized from internal economies, and how unit costs can be lowered to retailers who buy in volume from distributors. **Volume discount buying** is an example of second-degree price discrimination. A specific example is when you go to the local tavern for beer and pizza. The price of the 8-inch pizza is \$3, the 12-inch pizza \$4.50 and the 16-inch one is \$6. Consequently, the price per square inch for the 8-inch pizza is 5.96¢.[1] For the 12-inch pizza it is 3.98¢, and for the 16-inch pizza it is 2.98¢. The graphical

***Volume discount buying* is an example of second-degree price discrimination; some consumer surplus remains for the benefit of the buyer.**

[1]The area of a circle is πr^2. The 8-inch pizza has an area of $A = \pi r^2 = (3\text{-}1/7)(4)^2 = 50.3$ square inches. The price per square inch is \$3/50.3 = 5.96 cents.

Figure 9-9

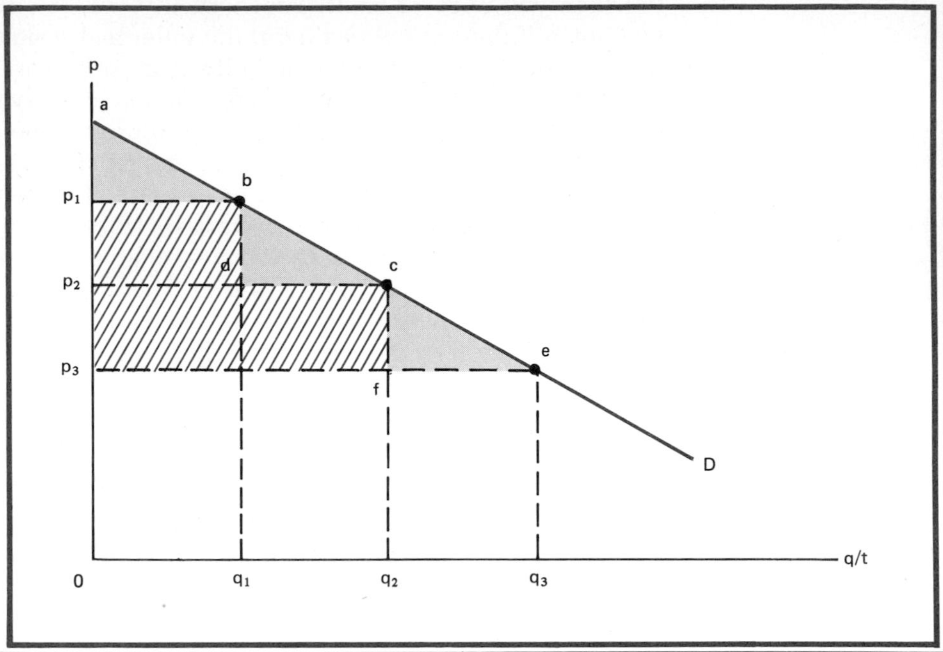

analysis is illustrated in Figure 9-9 for the general case. The horizontal axis can be denominated in weight such as ounces, kilowatts, or some other measure as it applies. When an amount between 0 and q_1 is purchased, the buyer pays a price p_1 per unit. The consumer surplus is the shaded triangle abp_1. When the amount between q_1 and q_2 is bought, the consumer is charged a price p_2 per unit. The consumer surplus includes the additional shaded triangle *bcd* . Were the consumer to buy an amount between q_2 and q_3, the price would be p_3 per unit, and the buyer picks up an additional consumer surplus indicated by the shaded triangle *cef*. By selling $q_1 + q_2 + q_3$ units, total consumer surplus would be the sum of the three shaded triangles. The striped triangles constitute the consumer surplus captured by the seller, since he does not sell all the units at the same price. If p_3 were the only price charged for output from 0 to q_3, the consumer surplus would be the large triangle aep_3. *With second-degree price discrimination some consumer surplus remains for the benefit of the buyer.* The seller is not able to capture it all, as he is able to do in the case of first-degree discrimination.

An important example of second-degree discrimination occurs when public utilities charge lower prices per kilowatt hour the more electricity large industrial users consume. Costs differ in supplying industrial and household users, but an element of second-degree discrimination remains. If the local electric utility company went to each household and priced the service directly so that each paid different fees, then it would be possible for the company to practice first-degree price discrimination. But since it usually must set rates so that all households and all industries in an area pay the same rates, it can capture part of the consumer's surplus but not all of it.

The Cover Charge A cover charge consists of a fee charged to enter night clubs, amusement parks, racetracks, tennis clubs, as well as the fixed fee charged to have a telephone installed and the electricity turned on. You pay to have the pilot light for gas turned on and kept on whether you use the range or not. It is levied, supposedly, to cover the large fixed capital costs of these ventures. After paying the cover charge, you are thereafter charged according to use. It would seem to be a variation of second-degree price discrimination. With more use, the average fixed cost represented by the fee declines.

If consumers had identical demand curves for the services of, say, an amusement park—which they do not—the cover charge could be set at a level that captures all of the consumer surplus. But there is no way an owner could determine each entrant's reservation price. The owner levies the same fixed charge to all, and increases his revenue. He does not capture all of the consumer surplus, but has to be careful the cover charge does not drive away any customers since that would be less efficient than charging no cover at all. The cover charge is efficient to the seller if the price of the rides is set at marginal cost and the cover price deters no potential customers from buying a ticket. In Figure 9-10, the shaded rectangular area indicates the income from setting the price of each ride at marginal cost ($p_1 = MC$). The striped area is the income derived from the cover charge of $p_2 - p_1$ and illustrates the consumer surplus captured by the seller.

Third-degree Price Discrimination

Under first-degree price discrimination all of the consumer surplus is captured by the seller. In second-degree discrimination some of the consumer surplus

Figure 9-10

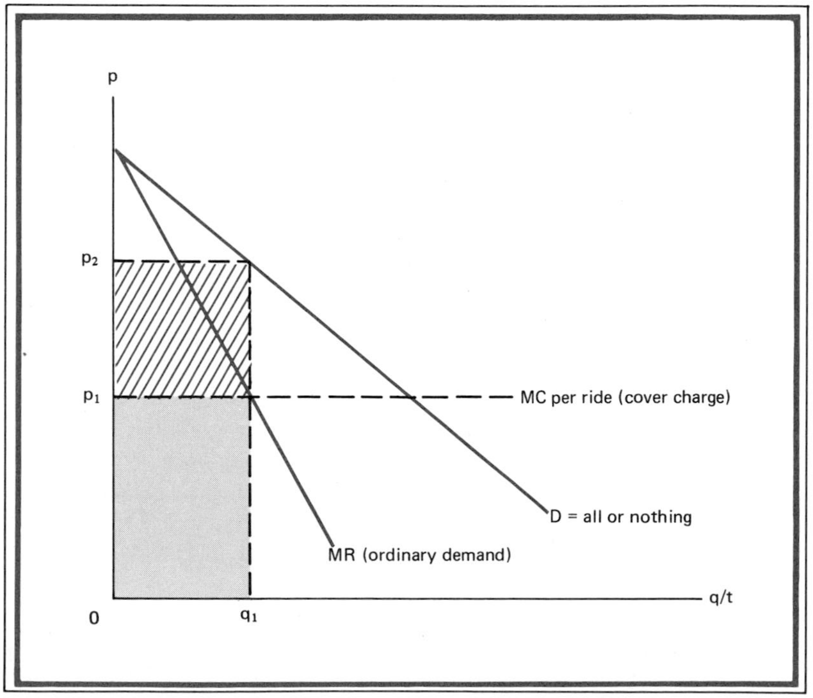

In third-degree price discrimination, some of the consumer surplus that is captured is *transferred* from one subgroup of buyers to the other subgroup.

accrues to the seller. In third-degree price discrimination some of the consumer surplus that is captured from one subgroup of buyers is **transferred** to the other subgroup. Indeed, we shall find that some subgroups may get more consumer surplus than they could have if no discrimination occurred. Again, third-degree price discrimination relies on the seller's being able to partition the market between buyers who have different demands. Also, a necessary condition is that the buyers cannot enter into arbitrage or cannot benefit from arbitrage, since the marginal revenue from bargaining as a secondary seller is less than the marginal cost.

Circus Tickets In this example of third-degree price discrimination we assume that the monopolist can discriminate among customers by age—we shall assume that customers are either adults or students under twenty-two. Therefore, in going to a circus, you find that admission tickets are sold for two different prices. How can we explain this, using economic theory?

First, we know it is a traveling show, and for any given week it is the only circus show in town. Thus, the circus is to a small degree a short-lived monopoly.

Second, we recognize that while both adults and students like circuses we also know that in general working adults have more spending money than students. Thus, the effective demand for a seat in the tent is greater for adults than it is for students so that their price elasticities also differ. Drawing demand curves for adults and students in Figure 9-11, we see that the demand curve on the left for adults is greater than that shown in the middle for students. For example, at a ticket price of $6 the adults will buy 2 tickets, but students will not buy any. At a price of $2, however, the adults would buy 4 tickets and the students would buy 2 tickets. Thus, adults buy more tickets than students do at any given price, and this is what we mean when we say that adult demand is greater than student demand.

When we add the two demand curves together, as shown on the panel on the far right, we see the total number of tickets bought by both groups at various

Figure 9-11

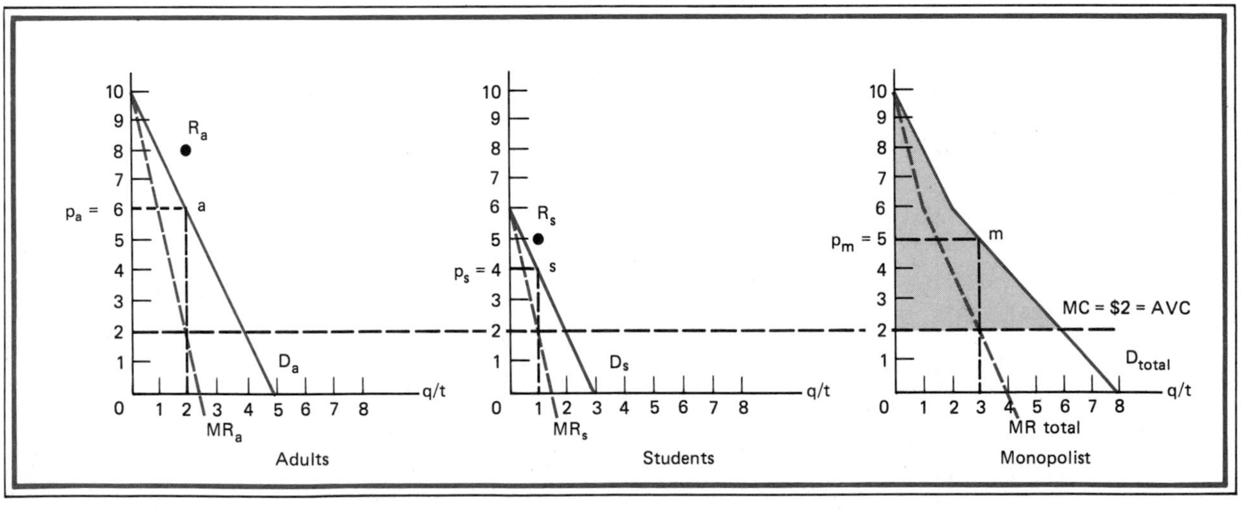

prices. Thus, at a price of \$4, there will be 4 tickets bought altogether, 3 of which will be bought by adults and 1 by a student. The reader might want to check these numbers. By adding the student demand curve to the adult demand curve we have formed the market demand curve faced by circus owners.

Let us make the simplifying assumption that the average variable cost to the owner of providing seats for the show is \$2, and that it is constant in the range of our analysis. We have drawn in a dashed horizontal line across all three graphs to represent this constant average variable cost. Since average variable cost is constant the marginal cost is also constant.

Now let us examine the right-hand panel showing the market for the circus in town. It the market were perfectly competitive we would have price equal to marginal cost. Thus, price would be \$2, and adults would buy 4 tickets and students would buy 2 tickets for total sales of 6 tickets. This represents what we can presume would be the price and the number of tickets sold under perfect competition.

Now let us assume the circus owner is a simple monopolist rather than a discriminating monopolist. A simple monopolist charges the same price to everyone. He would maximize his profits by setting the price at \$5. Here, the adult would buy 2.5 tickets and the student would buy only 0.5 tickets. (Please excuse the idea of a half of a ticket—it happens because we are trying to keep the numbers small and simple.) The monopolist sells 3 tickets at \$5 and collects \$15. His costs are \$2 per ticket for 3 tickets, for a total cost of \$6. These values are seen in the right-hand panel in the form of areas. Thus, 5 times 3 is 15 and equals the shaded area below the line where $p_m = 5$ and point m on the demand curve representing sales of 3 tickets. This is his total revenue. His total cost of \$6 is observed in the area below the dashed AVC line. His profits, $TR - TC$, will be \$9, or the area between the p_m to m line and the AVC line. Thus, we observe in the figure both the competitive solution and the solution arrived at by a simple monopolist who maximizes profits.

Now let us assume that this monopolist has the ability to segregate adults from students. "Show your ID or you'll have to pay the adult price." In this case the two graphs for the subgroups of customers become the relevant graphs for the discriminating monopolist. To maximize profits now, the circus owner will set the price at \$6 for the adult and sell 2 tickets, and at \$4 for the student, selling 1 ticket. Selling 3 tickets means that total costs are again \$6. But now, he takes in \$12 from adults and the profit he makes from the adults is \$8 because his costs are only \$4. Essentially he makes a profit of \$4 on *each* of the 2 tickets. By selling 1 ticket to the student for \$4 the monopolist makes \$2 profit. Thus, total profits for the discriminating monopolist practicing third-degree price discrimination are \$10. We see that this is \$1 more than he would collect by acting as a simple monopolist.

Notice that $MC = MR$ in all cases. What happens is that if the markets can be separated the monopolist simply sets prices where $MC = MR$ in *each* of the separated markets. The monopolist can make more profit doing this than by allowing the markets to be merged into one.

Another thing to observe in these panels is the consumer surplus realized by the ticket buyers. For the adult it is represented by the area under the demand curve in the triangle above the dashed line from $p_a = 6$ to point a. This area represents \$4. The same area above the dashed line p_s to s for the student represents $1. Thus, the total amount of consumer surplus under price discrimination is $5. For the simple monopolist of the right-hand panel, the area representing consumer surplus is $6.50. Thus, under discrimination, consumers *as a group* lose $1.50 in consumer surplus. Notice that *individually* the *student* is *better off* under price discrimination. He pays the lower price of $4 instead of the monopoly price of $5, and gains consumer surplus of $.75. When the price goes up from $5 to $6 to the adult, the adult *loses* $2.25 in consumer surplus. Thus, the monopolist in getting his extra dollar of profit from discrimination leaves the student better off to the tune of $.75 of consumer surplus, and leaves the adult worse off to the tune of $2.25 of surplus.

In the right-hand panel of Fig. 9-11, the shaded area under the demand curve above the marginal cost curve is 20 units. This would all be consumer surplus under perfect competition. If the price were $5, the area would be 6.5. Thus, consumers lose surplus of 13.5 under a simple monopoly. If there is third-degree discrimination, consumers receive only $5 of surplus—that is they have lost another $1.50 in consumer surplus.

We have represented adults and students as if there were submarkets consisting of these two groups. But what if the market could be subdivided by individual consumer so that the circus manager could negotiate separate contracts with each? In this case he could practice perfect price discrimination—discrimination of the first degree. In the graph for the adult, notice the price labeled R_a—representing the individual adult's reservation price. The circus manager says to the adult, "I'll sell you 2 tickets for $8 each—take it or leave it." The adult is indifferent at this point, for if he takes it he will *lose* all his consumer surplus. Then, as the smallest inducement to act, the manager offers a free box of popcorn. The popcorn gives the adult just enough consumer surplus to induce him to buy the tickets. The monopolist gets all but a neglibile amount of the adult's consumer surplus by presenting him with an all-or-nothing offer. Similarly, the monopolist can set reservation price $R_s = \$5$ to the student.

Thus, in these diagrams we can observe what a competitive solution would be, what the simple monopoly solution would be, what a third-degree discrimination would be, and what a first-degree discrimination would be.

Whatever happened to second-degree price discrimination? It seems as though we have lost it, but we really have not because it is not a different form of discrimination, it is an in-between form. It is part first-degree and part third-degree. It is like third-degree because the markets are divided into submarkets and groups of individuals make up the submarkets. It is also like first-degree because a quantity discount is like the all-or-nothing offer. For example, suppose the adult was faced with the following offer: "I'll give you one ticket for $12 and throw in the second ticket for $4." This is $16, or $8 per ticket for the two tickets. Adding in the popcorn to tilt the balance means that this quantity discount is really no different from the first-degree price discrimination. In general, though, quantity discounts apply not to single individuals but to groups like the group of householders who buy electricity. All householders face the same quantity discount. Thus, the monopolist picks up a lot of consumer surplus from some individuals and less from others, so that we do not have perfect price discrimination in this case, only second-degree. Thus, second-degree discrimination is a combined version of first- and third-degrees.

Is It Really Price Discrimination?

The case for price discrimination does not hold up if you can successfully argue, in the example of discount pricing under second-degree price discrimination, that you can buy the bigger box of soap and use it for a longer period of time. That is, in effect you are really buying a different product than when you purchase the smaller box. Also, if it costs the seller more per box to produce 2 smaller boxes than 1 larger box, then price discrimination is not taking place according to the definition. If it is more costly for the breakfast cereal manufacturer—and the retailer—to sell the minipackages separately than it does to sell the total package, than a lower price for a larger quantity does *not* imply price discrimination; it is merely a reflection of cost differences.

Justifiable Price Discrimination

It is possible that without practicing price discrimination a good or service might not be provided at all because the nature of the activity is not profitable. An example is illustrated in Figure 9-12. For a level of output q_1 total cost ($0bdq_1$) is greater than total revenue ($0feq_1$) because the ATC curve is higher than demand and holds for all levels of output. Some private utilities have been in such a predicament. However, if the seller can negotiate separate contracts with buyers, arriving at a different selling price to each in a first-degree price discrimination arrangement by charging on the average, price *b*, then the added revenue portrayed by the shaded areas *will* cover total costs by capturing the

Figure 9-12

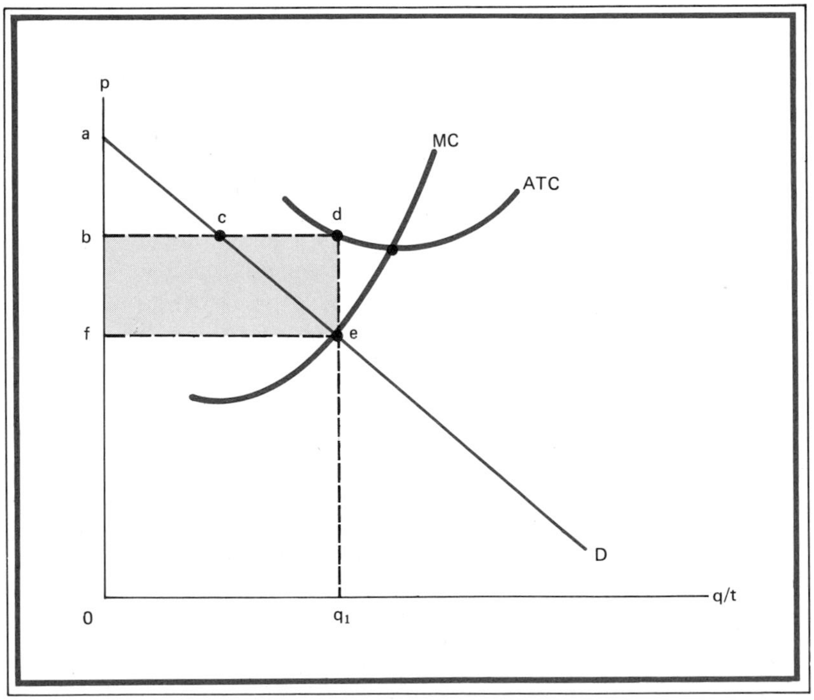

consumer surplus *aef* when output is q_1. In other words, when *acb* is equal to triangular area *cde*, total revenue will just equal total costs. If *acb* be greater than *cde*, some pure profit would be earned. If price discrimination is disallowed by the government, as happens with utilities, and if there are net benefits to society for the firm to continue to exist, a subsidy would have to be provided to bring total revenue up to par with total cost. If the subsidy is not provided, there will be zero benefits to society. Other real-world examples are government subsidized transportation systems such as intracity bus service and some railroads.

Public Utility Pricing

Left to itself, the company would maximize profits by setting $MC = MR$ and charging a price p_1 per unit of output, and produce a level of output q_1 as illustrated in Figure 9-13. But output is too low and price too high. In addition, because $p_1 > MC$ there is underuse of the resource and waste. The commission could opt for *average-cost* pricing by setting the price $p_2 = ATC$ per unit. The company would increase output to q_2. At this output level $TR = TC$ and pure profits are wiped out. But still a price $p_2 > MC$ occurs. Resources are earning more in their current use than in an alternative use. The marginal utility of consumers is greater than the marginal cost to provide the q_2 unit. The system is shy of equality at the margin. More can be produced and greater efficiency achieved by pricing at marginal cost. When *marginal cost pricing* is employed $p_3 = MC$ and output rises to q_3.

Resource efficiency is now attained but $TR < TC$; the utility is losing

Figure 9-13

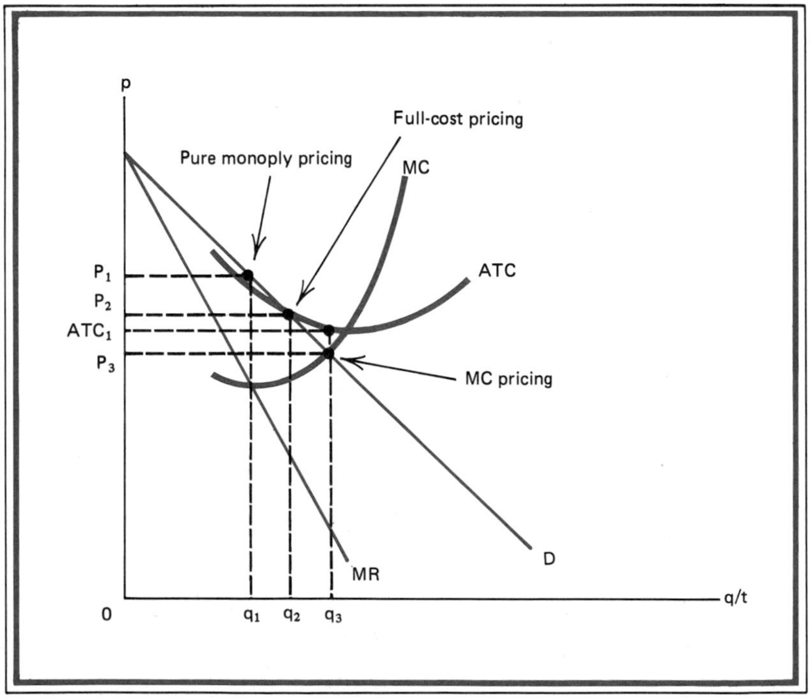

money. At output q_3 total revenue is $p_3 \times q_3$ but total cost equals $ATC_1 \times q_3$ and is greater. The deficit could be subsidized through taxes. But regulatory commissions usually have no power to collect taxes and provide subsidies. Taxes and subsidies involve political maneuvering for benefits to certain regions of the state over others and cannot be handled by a commission. Subsidies may mean taxing some who do not use the utility and who derive no benefits; hence, it is possible for inequitable income redistribution to occur. What regulatory agencies have tended to do, therefore, is permit second-degree price discrimination, where large-volume buyers get a discount and thus have an incentive to use more than they otherwise would.

Rate of Return

Utilities like electricity, gas, and telephone service are privately owned but monitored by public agencies on matters of rate setting. Price changes by utilities must be reviewed and given approval by state regulatory commissions, who have the authority to audit company finances in order to make an informed decision. This raises the question of where prices should be set and what is a fair rate of return on investment to owners (stockholders).

When regulatory commissions set prices they are often called fares or tariffs or rates. If they involve price discrimination they are, in many respects, like taxes. In any case, the amount of revenue collected by a utility, say, must be sufficient to cover all the utility's costs, including a full return to the investors who bought stock in the enterprise. This is the cost of capital, and it must be covered if all costs are to be covered.

The next question is to determine the rates, or tariffs, necessary to provide a fair rate of return on invested capital. If most shares of stock are earning 8 percent, then the fair market rate of return is also 8 percent, for 8 percent is the opportunity cost of capital. Utility commissioners would allow tariffs high enough to cover all operating costs plus an 8 percent return to invested capital.

Providing for a fair return is, of course, a normative act and economic theory is of limited help here. But our theory can help determine what is reasonable. The return to capital allowed will have significant impact on how the utility chooses its mix of inputs and how it runs the whole operation.

CHAPTER SUMMARY

A pure monopolist is the sole seller of a homogeneous product for which there are no close substitutes, and no entry is possible.

In reality pure monopoly will break down. Permanent monopoly, however, can exist with government permission, as in the situation of natural monopolies like public utilities.

Monopoly can arise because of high fixed-capital costs, the difficulty of borrowing a large amount of funds, legal, licensing, and regulation barriers, and because of sole ownership of an important input that prevents entry by new firms.

The monopolist is a price-searcher and faces a less than perfectly elastic demand curve for his product, so that price is greater than marginal revenue. However, the monopolist follows the marginal revenue-equal-marginal-cost rule in order to maximize profits.

The monopolist has no supply schedule in the ordinary sense. Given demand, the monopolist searches for the price that will maximize profit. The supply curve is a point, not a schedule. The monopolist does not produce on the inelastic portion of the demand curve he faces, since marginal revenue is negative.

Because the price the monopolist charges is greater than marginal cost, he is not producing the most efficient level of output. It is too low. And because total revenue is greater than total cost, the monopolist earns a pure economic profit and captures some consumer surplus while also creating a deadweight loss to society.

Price discrimination occurs when a seller charges different prices to different borrowers for the same good or service when the cost of providing same to both does not differ.

To price-discriminate, two conditions are necessary. The different buyers must be separated so that one buyer cannot renegotiate with another buyer, and buyers' demand schedules for the product must differ.

There are three cases of price discrimination, first, second, and third degree. Under first-degree discrimination all consumer surplus is captured, with second degree some is captured, and in third degree some is captured from one group and increased to another, for a net capture by the seller of consumer surplus. The cover charge is a variation of second-degree price discrimination. Some economists contend there is only third-degree price discrimination, since costs to different buyers do differ in the other two cases.

Price discrimination can be justified where without it the good or service would not be provided; that is, where production is not otherwise possible because the average cost curve lies above the demand curve. Exercising price discrimination can bring total revenue up to total cost.

The question of how regulated monopolies like public utilities should price their product, and what rate of return they should earn, is a continuing one. Marginal cost pricing is efficient but may impose losses on the firm. Average cost pricing covers costs but is not efficient since price is greater than marginal cost. Left to itself the monopoly would set $MR = MC$, charge too high a price, and provide too little service.

State regulatory commissions target what is a fair rate of return to capital investment in order to encourage purchases of the utilities' stocks and bonds by the public. They also determine the price that is charged in order to provide that target rate of return.

QUESTIONS

1. In January of 1979 the Federal Communications Commission (FCC) voted to end Western Union's monopoly over domestic telegraph service that it had granted in 1943. The FCC statement said that "decades of regulation of this service haven't succeeded in making it either profitable to Western Union or affordable to the public generally" (*Wall Street Journal*, Jan. 26, 1979).
   a. Did Western Union have a monopoly on message transmission?
   b. Despite having a telegram monopoly Western Union was losing money on this phase of its business. Why could it not simply raise its prices to cover its rising costs?

2. Howard Johnson's received a 38-year lease in 1940 to operate the only restaurants on the 470-mile Pennsylvania Turnpike from the state. Contracts on 11 of the 26 facilities expired in January 1979. The Turnpike Commission had to decide whether to renew the contracts with Howard Johnson's or consider competitive bids from three other food services as well. Maine sought $3 million in excess profits it said Howard Johnson earned on its lease in that state since 1971. A Howard Johnson executive said there is no merit to the charge since "food prices are close and that's the same for everybody" (*Wall Street Journal,* Oct. 18, 1978).
   a. Is Howard Johnson's Turnpike food service a monopoly? What market structure is implied by the executive? Comment.
   b. Might it make a difference in Turnpike food prices that would be charged if Pennsylvania accepted competing bids on the 11 facilities as a unit rather than on each facility individually?
3. A specific style of stereo set is sold at Sears Roebuck to both the informed buyers, say, electronics engineers, and uninformed buyers, say, recent graduates of the school of education.
   a. Is Sears a monopolist? Explain.
   b. Would the price be the same to the uninformed buyer and the informed buyer? (Hint: See Chapter 2 on exchange describing the setting of the exchange ratio by a middleman.)
   c. If each sale were based on bargaining between the salesman and the customer, would you expect the *average price* of the stereo models to be higher or lower than the price at which they were sold in *b*? Explain.
   d. Is there price discrimination in *c*? If so, to which type is it most similar?
4. You read in your local newspaper that "when times are good people flock to get their real estate sales and brokers' licenses. Too many enter the field, causing chaos. There must be new laws raising the passing grade on state exams and requiring that applicants earn more certified credits in real estate education. The business can certainly be carried out by far fewer licensed people. Many of the newcomers are old, only interested in part-time work, many grossing $6,000 or so on two or three sales a year. The business is not suited to people desiring a regular income. There's a need for more stringent entrance requirements to protect the public from incompetents."
   a. What appears to be the problem? What is the proposed solution?
   b. What is meant by the term chaos?
   c. Who is likely to support the proposed solution in *a*?
   d. Do you think the public would benefit from fewer, more professional real estate brokers? Discuss.
5. In 1975, the chairman of the AMA's Board of Trustees stated, "It's ironic that the FTC should attack a code devised and operated as a standard of conduct in the best interests of the patient . . . (price) advertising by a professional is the very antithesis of professionalism . . . we think there is enough hucksterism without huckstering medicine. . . ." Some facts: There are documented cases of punitive action taken by the AMA against doctors who announced or advertised their fees. The AMA has argued that it is a scientific and educational organization which benefits the general public. The medical industry should be exempt from antitrust action. A further note: In 1976, because of employee layoffs many workers lost health benefits. There was a drop of 0.4 percent in patients entering hospitals, and paid visits dropped 3.8 percent by outpatients.
   a. Do you think the public's need for Dr. A's services would be greater than for Dr. B's if it knew A's prices were 40 percent higher than B's?
   b. When college and universities make their tuition prices available, is this hucksterism? Are faculty members not considered as professionals?
   c. Do the grocer, the shoemaker, and the television repairman benefit the general public? Is information on their prices readily obtainable?

6. A doctor who raised his fees said, "Unfortunately there was simply no way we could avoid charging more and expect to make what any doctor considers a fair return on his time and knowledge. Doctors should be able to make a 50 percent profit or it just isn't worthwhile." Can the farmer or the local grocer just as easily raise prices so as to earn profits of 50%? In order to mark up profits to a designated target above costs, you have to be rather certain about the level of income forthcoming. What does this indicate about the market for medical care?
7. Many economists prefer "performance standards" over rigid regulations. Can there be standards without regulation? What regulates standards according to these economists?
8. Several years ago in New York City, a group of doctors and acupuncturists opened up a clinic offering both traditional Western treatment to patients and acupuncture techniques. Pressure forced the clinic to shut down. The courts agreed, arguing that doctors were not qualified as acupuncturists and acupuncturists were not qualified as doctors.
   a. Who likely brought the pressure on the clinic?
   b. Was the reason for the shutdown of the clinic really because of lack of qualification of its personnel?
9. There is an active illegal market for white babies in the U.S. In the eastern states only the state adoption agencies can place babies in foster homes. However, in California lawyers can legally act as middlemen in arranging for couples to adopt the forthcoming babies of pregnant women so long as a state social worker interviews the donor prior to her using a lawyer's services. In California official adoptions run 26 to 100,000 while in the eastern states it is about 7 to 100,000. In the eastern states babies can go for as high as $20,000 on the black market while in California lawyers handle roughly 80 percent of the adoptions.
   a. Would you expect the lawyer's fees in California to be less than $20,000 per adoption?
   b. Why the disparity between the eastern U.S. and California in the number of adoptions and the prices, assuming the pregnancy rate is about the same?
10. Theaters charge higher prices to adults than they do to students. Car dealers charge the same price to both. Is it because car dealers do not like students? Discuss.
11. At one time the prostitutes in the red-light district of Amsterdam, Holland, opposed a citywide tolerance policy toward prostitution. They wanted hookers outside the district arrested.
   a. Why did the prostitutes want to see other prostitutes harassed by the police? Was it because the other prostitutes were offering an inferior product?
   b. Does the complaint of the red-light district prostitutes differ in principle from the policies of the trucking industry, the AMA, and the plumbers union? Explain.
12. Fleet car operators and automobile insurance companies pay less per car for auto repairs than do individual drivers. Why? Is there price discrimination going on? If so, what kind?
13. The Van Gogh art exhibit comes to Metropolis Museum in your town. It charges different prices to students and adults. Assume the marginal cost of admitting a viewer is $2. The demand schedules are shown at the top of p. 259.
   a. What prices would maximize profits? What is the amount of the profits?
   b. Calculate the consumer surplus for adults and students.
   c. What conditions are necessary for your policy? Is this price discrimination? Comment.
   d. If the conditions cannot be met, what pricing policy would maximize profits? What is the amount of profit?
14. What is a cover charge? What is its purpose?
   a. Why would Disneyland have a cover charge but not Sears Roebuck?

Students		Adults	
Price	Quantity	Price	Quantity
11	0	15	0
10	1	14	1
9	2	13	2
8	3	12	3
7	4	11	4
6	5	10	5
5	6	9	6
4	7	8	7
3	8	7	8
2	9	6	9
1	10	5	10
		4	11
		3	12
		2	13
		1	14

b. Why is the price of a football ticket or the entrance fee to a zoo not a cover charge?

c. Often nightclubs require a cover charge and restaurants do not. Why the difference in policy? The food is not necessarily better in nightclubs, is it?

15. You go to a foreign car dealer to get a new rear brake light lens for your car, since yours is broken. You are told you cannot just buy the lens; instead you must purchase the whole rear lighting unit.
    a. Is this price discrimination? What sort?
    b. Are special sizes without available substitutes that are sold only by the manufacturer—so-called captive items—an indication of poor engineering, or something else? Comment.
16. A common complaint made by the Post Office when it is suggested that private firms also be allowed to deliver first class mail, is that private firms would "skim off the cream." What is meant by "cream"? Why does it exist? Would it disappear if private firms were allowed to deliver first class mail? Comment.
17. A public utility publishes the following schedule for natural gas rates:

Usage in therms	Rate
0	$ 4.32
1	$ 4.71
2	5.11
3	5.51
4	5.91
5	6.31
10	8.31
15	10.31
20	12.31
25	14.31
30	15.76

a. Is there price discrimination? How do you know?

b. Does the rate column indicate anything similar to a cover charge? Comment.

18. You are selling electricity to 10 houses and you are a monopoly seller. Two households have identical demand curves for electrical power and the remaining 8 have differing demand curves, also different from one another. The cost of serving each household is the same.
    a. If you charge the same prices to all 10 households, is this price discrimination? If so, what kind?
    b. Suppose the two households with identical demand curves are charged the same price for volume discounts? Is there therefore no price discrimination involving these two households?
19. Which of the following are examples of price discrimination?
    a. A car manufactured in the Ford plant in Detroit, Michigan, sells for $5,000 in Lansing, Michigan, and for $5,200 in Oakland, California.
    b. U.S. Steel sells 15,000 tons of steel to Company A for $20 a ton and 32,000 tons of steel to Company B for $19 a ton.
    c. People on standby pay less for a ticket than do regular ticket buyers.
    d. The corner mechanic will replace the water pump of Mary's Pinto for $20 an hour, but charge $30 an hour to replace the water pump in Jane's Pinto.
    e. The dental association requires that only dentists sell dentures to clients, and that the denturists cannot sell directly to the public but only directly to dentists because only dentists are qualified to fit dentures.

Chapter 10

Imperfect Competition

PROGRESS REPORT

A. In Chapter 9 the pricing behavior of pure monopoly was discussed. The monopolist was viewed as both a price setter and a price searcher.

B. In this chapter we bring the models of the firm and industry closer to reality. We observe that both pure monopoly and perfect competition are rare and that prices on apparently the same products do vary to some degree, that there is advertising, and that firms in the same industry exhibit great disparities in their size. In other words, firms actually appear to function in differing degrees somewhere between the two extremes of price setting and price taking. We now undertake to explain the alternative industry structures of oligopoly and monopolistic competition.

C. The oligopoly of this chapter is extended in Chapter 11 to the study of concentration in the industry, whereby few firms account for most of industry output and what might constitute what is sometimes called a shared monopoly. It is subject to potential antitrust action by the government.

THE COMPETITIVE CONTINUUM

Pure monopoly is on one end of a continuum of forms of competition. There is only one seller of a commodity, and this seller can set prices—even discriminatory prices when markets can be separated. Perfect competition is on the other end of the competitive continuum. There are so many real and potential competitors that no producer has any control over price and each producer ends up as a price taker. Thus, on the two extremes of the continuum we have price setters and price takers.

As we look around us we see that most producers are somewhere in between these two extremes. Most have some price-setting power, but few are sole producers of a commodity with absolute price-setting power. Thus, the theoretical models of perfect competition on the one hand and monopoly on the other are, for the most part, abstractions. In good theory, one always abstracts from reality. The chemist uses pure (distilled) water in experiments, but in the real world there is no pure water. Even rainwater picks up dust particles as it falls through the air. The engineer assumes a frictionless world in calculating the mechanical advantage to be gained from a set of pulleys, but there is always friction. Both the chemist and engineer can, in practical application of their theories, make useful and accurate predictions in preparing solutions and building bridges, recognizing that their theories are based on abstract assumptions.

So it is with the economist. Pure competition rarely, if ever, exists. But in a multitude of cases there is sufficient competition so that prediction is effective. Pure monopoly rarely exists. But some degree of monopoly power can often be found and the proposition that the producer is acting *as if* he were a monopolist turns out to be useful.

When the engineer makes calculations about mechanics, he makes an extra allowance for friction, and when a chemist prepares a tonic, he also allows for variation away from purity in the water. But the basic principles still hold. The economist knows that every hot dog stand operator can set his own price. But for ostensibly the same product the economist also predicts that a stand with a high price will lose customers to the one with a lower price around the corner. Thus, the price set by the competitor must be within a narrow range of the price that would be predicted by the model of perfect competition. But when the concessionaire at the ball park is given a monopoly over hot dog sales by the stadium owners, then you will find the monopoly model works—hot dog prices will be higher than they are outside the park. Thus, both models are extremely useful despite their abstraction.

In this chapter we shall examine some attempts to find theoretical consistencies in the midrange of the competitive continuum.

The competitive continuum ranges from *pure monopoly* to *duopoly* (two sellers) to *oligopoly* (a few sellers) to *monopolistic competition* (high competition with differentiation) to *perfect competition.*

Pure monopoly	Duopoly	Oligopoly	Monopolistic competition	Perfect competition

On the line we observe *duopoly,* meaning *two sellers* of a product. Next is *oligopoly,* meaning *a few sellers* of a product (for simplicity we shall often use the term oligopoly to include duopoly, meaning either two or a handful of sellers). Then comes *monopolistic competition,* the term economists use to describe a market that is highly competitive but in which each producer differentiates his product from that of others by packaging, attaching brand names or labels, and so forth.

COMPETITOR REACTION

The essential ingredient of a duopoly or oligopoly is that each competitor must worry about how his competitor will respond to changes in price or output. A monopolist has great latitude in setting the price, but when a second producer enters the ring then the former monopolist will have to watch how the new producer will respond to any change in price the former monopolist might wish to make.

Kinked Demand

The concept of kinked demand is a useful device to explain the problem of competitor reaction that duopolists and oligopolists face. As we shall see, this is a theory of "sticky" prices, and is incomplete as a theory of duopoly or oligopoly prices and output. The kinked-demand model was suggested among others by Paul Sweezy in 1939 to explain why prices tend to be relatively more rigid or sticky when oligopoly exists. To explain it we refer to Figure 10-1.

Starting at point k, p_1 represents the price that the oligopolists are charging. The demand curve that one firm faces is the curve dd' with a kink in it at k. If it raises its price above the existing industry price of p_1, the firm would move up along the demand curve segment dk, but other firms would not raise their prices too. Their reaction is to keep their prices fixed at p_1. By not changing their price they will capture the loss in sales experienced by the price-raising firm while sales of the price-raising firm will fall off. The dk segment of the demand curve is relatively more elastic.

Alternately, by starting at p_1 and then lowering prices, rival producers will react by lowering their prices too. Thus, when the price-lowering firm drops its price, it is not able to increase its sales because of the way other producers respond. Its sales revenues will decline. Therefore the kd' segment is relatively more inelastic than the dk segment. Hence, in considering price changes an oligopolist perceives a kinked demand curve. At point k there occurs an abrupt switch in the price elasticity in the curve. Associated with the dk segment of demand is the curve labeled MR, and associated with the kd' segment is the MR' curve. The kink in demand at k translates into a discontinuity or break in the MR–MR' curve. You might prefer to think of the dashed segment connecting MR to MR' as a vertical line between b and a. Leaving out the ATC curve for now and looking at the MC curve, it can intersect the

Figure 10-1

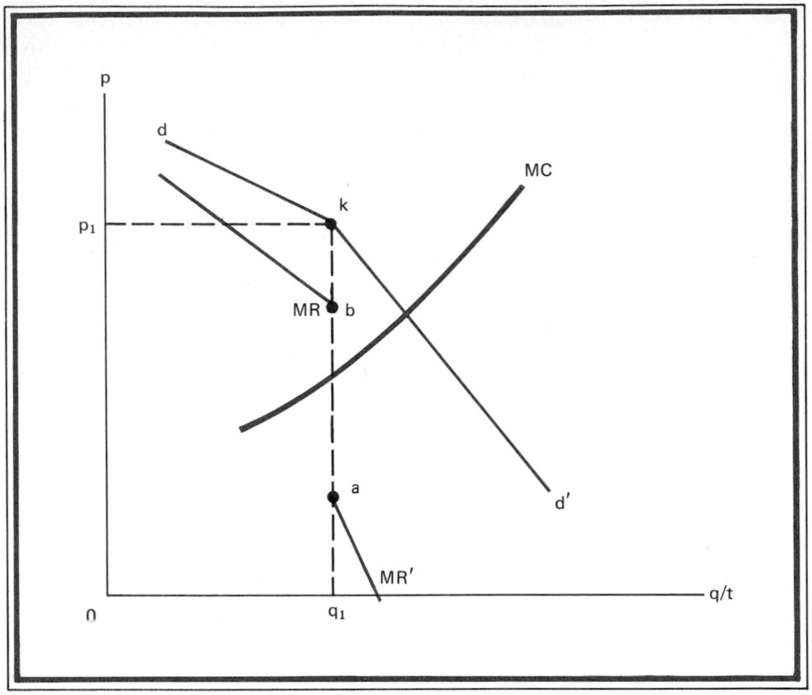

vertical section of the MR–MR' curve at any point between b and a. Thus, the maximizing point $MC = MR$ can occur at many points, all of them yielding the same equilibrium price p_1 and quantity q_1. A rationale for price rigidity has been provided. Costs can change and the MC curve can shift up or down to a considerable extent while still intersecting MR between b and a, and without having the price change.

You must be warned that the kinked demand model is not a general theory of oligopoly behavior. It is only a single model among several. It has deficiencies:

1. It fits only a few actual industry situations that have been examined. There have been many occasions in which price increases were matched by rivals, the opposite of what the theory predicts. Similarly, in other cases price decreases were not matched by rivals, again going against the theory.

2. It is a static model. It does not explain how or why the kink occurs at price p_1 and not at some other prices. Nor can it explain how a new price would be reached once it was dislodged from its current equilibrium. While it might provide for a short-run equilibrium, it cannot explain a stable long-run equilibrium.[1] Thus, it is not a theory of oligopoly price-setting behavior.

Despite these deficiencies, the kinked demand theory is helpful as an explanation of short-run stickiness of price and output, and is interesting because of the focus it places on the necessity for duopolists to consider each other's potential reaction to any changes in price and output.

[1]For fuller details see Kalmen Cohen and Richard Cyert, *Theory of the Firm*, 2d ed. (Englewood Cliffs, N.J.: Prentice-Hall, Inc., 1975), pp. 255–257.

OLIGOPOLY

When we think of oligopoly we usually have in mind a situation in which a few large corporations dominate an industry. However, in some oligopolistic industries there could exist dozens of firms but with only two or three producing the major share of the industry's output. Oligopoly is often mistakenly referred to as monopoly by the public. It is estimated that as much as fifty percent of all manufacturing in the U.S. is produced by industries that we would probably call oligopolies.

Examples of oligopolistic industries abound: automobile and truck manufacturing, turbine engines, airplanes, lawn mowers, television picture tubes, writing pens, cereals, razor blades, rubber tires, computers, and shoe machinery to mention a few. Because individual firms in these industries possess substantial market power, they can set their prices over a wide range.

Sources of Market Power: Barriers to Entry

How do oligopolies come into existence, and once established how do they behave in order to maintain their position? Answers to this question include reference not only to natural causes, but also to artificially created man-made causes.

Natural barriers to entry arise from economies of scale. Early in the century industries that would have been classified as competitors are now considered oligopolistic. For example, around 1900, there were 97 domestic car manufacturers in the U.S. Today there are only 4. The smallest, American Motors, merged with Renault of France. Chrysler Corporation is in financial trouble. Only a 1980 government loan saved it from bankruptcy—for now. A major reason for this apparently relentless process to reduce the number of automobile manufacturing firms is economies of scale, which we studied about in Chapters 6 and 7. The efficiencies of large-scale production, sales outlets, and parts distribution permit a few automobile firms to end up serving the entire market. Since smaller operations must necessarily operate at higher per-unit costs, they become noncompetitive. They are forced to charge higher prices to cover higher per-unit costs of production and distribution.

The natural barriers accompanying economies of scale are:

Absolute Cost The high fixed costs required to set up shop are too large for the potential entrants to finance and overcome. The capital costs required to start up an automobile plant or steel mill are formidable.

Barriers to market entry include *absolute cost, high risk, technology,* and *government restriction.*

High Risk Given the risk of failure and the perceived difficulty in capturing a large enough share of the market in order to overcome the high absolute fixed costs in the long run, entry is discouraged.

Technology In some industries the level of technology required for efficient, large-scale production is quite sophisticated and expensive. Also, people with high levels of technical talent are scarce. The incumbent companies can afford to pay top price for this capital and talent.

Government Restriction In addition to these natural barriers there are government-created barriers. Deterrence to entry is achieved by licensing requirements, patent rights, personnel certification, and other laws administered by state and national regulatory agencies as well as the restrictive legislation sought by unions and other special interests.

Oligopoly Pricing

While profit maximization provides the motivating behavior of producers, the day-to-day price and output policies of oligopolies can be extremely complex in reality. Because of the interdependence among them, price competition is often avoided. They struggle to maintain or increase their market shares by adopting nonprice competitive strategies. What forms might these take? The number appears to be limited only by human imagination and the circumstances of the market.

The Prisoners' Dilemma

To understand why oligopolists use nonprice competition we can examine the problem known as the *prisoners' dilemma.* Two people are arrested as suspected burglars. The police interrogate them in separate rooms. Neither suspect can know what the other will say in answer to questions. Neither one of the suspects knows what concessions the police have offered to the other in exchange for information about the crime. If neither is bribed by police, they will probably receive equal treatment. But if one confesses and the other does not, the one who refuses to confess might receive a stiff sentence while the other might receive a light one or even be released. What strategy should the prisoners use? Choice of a strategy means that each suspect must estimate the combination of possible responses, and make the best choice under the circumstances. The Rand Corporation has simulated this situation with games for the military concerning strategy about the possibility of a nuclear war. If the U.S. does one thing, what can it expect the Russians to do in response? The Russians, knowing we are thinking how they might react, will react to how they think we will react to how they react—and so it goes. Under some conditions an optimum outcome can be determined.

This kind of "payoff" strategy was initially worked out by J. Von Neuman and O. Morgenstern in *The Theory of Games and Economic Behavior* (Princeton University Press, Princeton, N.J., 1944, 1947). Unfortunately their work turned out to be of limited value in analyzing oligopolistic pricing behavior because of the complexity of economic activities. If we take the prisoners' dilemma example and extend it to 7 or 8 firms and add a multiplicity of variables they can each manipulate, anticipating the price and strategy moves of one another leads to a staggering array of combinations and possible outcomes.

As a result there is, today, no generally accepted theory of oligopoly behavior. Each particular situation must be analyzed on the basis of its individual characteristics. Some strategy situations can be shown to be unstable. That is, they possess no stable equilibrium toward which they tend to converge. Once dislodged from any assumed initial point of equilibrium, it is never regained. Most other models of strategies are simply too complicated to arrive at any equilibrium solution.

Of course, oligopolistic firms can reach agreements either tacitly or by direct and illegal collusion to fix prices, set quotas, or make other arrangements about setting prices and establishing market shares.

Pure Oligopoly: Pricing Strategies

Under pure oligopoly, it is assumed that the few firms in the industry are producing an identical product. Possible examples are the aluminum, steel, and cement (wholesale) industries. Four different pricing strategies might be followed: independent pricing, tacit price agreements, markup or target pricing, and explicit price-fixing (direct collusion).

Under *independent pricing* firms do not collude to fix prices. They set their own prices with the implicit understanding not to start price-cutting wars.

Independent Pricing While mutual dependence is recognized by the oligopolists, there is no direct collusion. Yet because no individual firm wants to rock the boat and splash into the hostile waters of price-cutting wars, there exists a mutual understanding that cooperative behavior is best for the group. Enough sales are left for everyone.

Suppose two firms constitute the industry. They have identical costs and an equal share of the market. Hence they have the same demand schedule. The situation is illustrated in Figure 10-2. The *D* demand curve is total market demand facing the industry. The *d* demand curve represents the demand faced by both firms and represents 50 percent or half of total demand. There is of course the usual *MR* curve to the downward sloping *d*-demand curve. Output

Figure 10-2

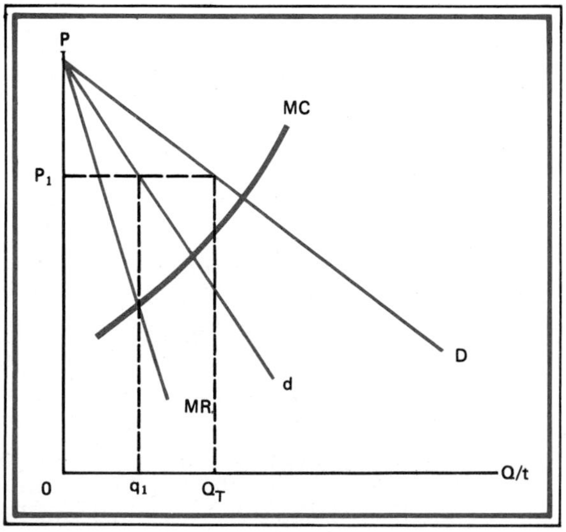

Figure 10-3

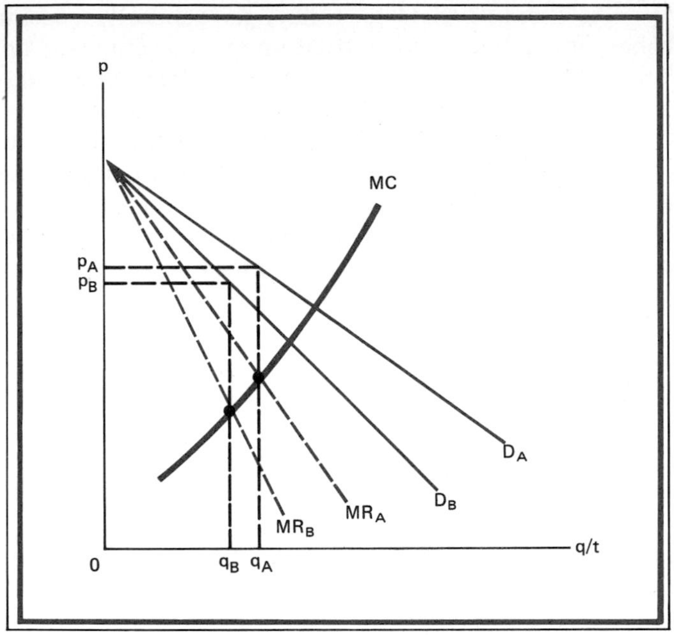

q_1 is equal to half of Q_T for each firm. It is determined by setting $MR = MC$, which establishes the price of P_1 from the d demand curve.

Figure 10-3 portrays the alternative situation of identical costs but different market shares for firms A and B. Assume the sales of firm A are 55 percent of the market and the sales of firm B are 45 percent. In this situation, the smaller firm B sells less than A does and charges a lower price P_B. Unfortunately, this is not likely to be a stable price situation in the long run. But just how a mutually acceptable price could be arrived at without some kind of an agreement could be difficult. There is a greater likelihood that rival firms would have slightly different cost and similar demand schedules. One company, being smaller than another, would experience lower fixed costs, but its marginal cost is apt to rise much faster by comparison. In this situation, firms pricing independently will end up producing different quantities and charging different prices. The analysis is shown in Figure 10-4 where A refers to the bigger company and B to the smaller one. Being unstable, this relationship can lead to price competition. The policy adopted is for firm A to set the price at p_A with B given little choice but to follow this lead. Otherwise B is in peril of losing its market share by setting its price at p_B.

Tacit price strategies **involves price leadership, whereby the dominant firm signals the price to be followed by the industry simply by announcing its price and without secretly colluding with other firms.**

Tacit Price Strategies–Price Leadership How is it decided at what level to set the price? Since independent pricing could still lead to unstable and intolerable conditions, it is compelling and advantageous for rivals to reach an unspoken understanding about when prices should be adjusted and by how much. Outright negotiation—collusion—is illegal in the U.S. One solution is for a dominant firm, if one exists, to sniff the market atmosphere and adjust the price barometer. Alternatively, price leadership may rotate among the firms. In some understandings it may be left to the oldest or most prestigious firm with the most experience to make the decision that the industry as a whole will follow. This approach lies between independent pricing and direct price-fixing.

But even tacit agreements do not follow a general overall theory providing reliable predictions. Even within the same industries market variables change over time, calling for different arrangements, for instance rotation of the price leadership role. In the past, companies like International Harvester, Standard Oil of New Jersey, U.S. Steel, and The Great Atlantic and Pacific Tea Company performed in leadership roles. On occasions there is a dominant firm selling a major share of the market, rivaled by a number of smaller satellite firms; then, where the dominant firms sets its price will determine the size of the share for them all.

Under *markup pricing* the firm sets the price by a percentage above average cost.

Markup or Target Pricing Industry discipline among the corporate oligopolists is often introduced by means of a rule-of-thumb markup above average cost. A targeted rate of return is added onto average cost per unit to determine a market price that yields a fair return on capital investment. Only firms with some market power can target price. Such pricing is rationalized in several ways. For example, next year's demand for television sets is uncertain. Given that a manufacturer has been earning about 15 percent on investment after taxes, he would like to maintain it. If he expects to produce at 85 percent of capacity, he can calculate approximately what the average cost per unit will likely be. He then adds on a 15 percent markup. The final price with this built-in adjustment, understood by all rivals, helps establish a reference retail price.[2]

Some economists claim that full-cost pricing violates the maximization hypothesis so fundamental to economic theory, since it essentially ignores

[2]F. M. Scherer, *Industrial Market Structure and Economic Performance* (New York: Rand McNally and Co., 1973), pp. 173–175.

Figure 10-4

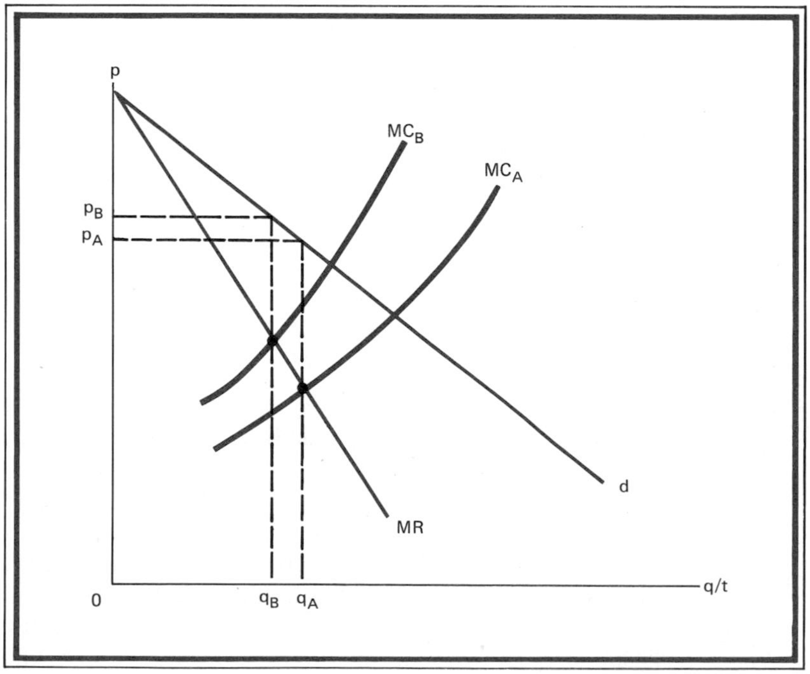

demand considerations and focus exclusively on costs. What is being maximized instead is sales, not profits. Higher profits are sacrificed in order to gain a larger market share. In essence, they claim the $MC = MR$ rule is ignored when calculating sales maximization. Others reply that full-cost pricing is profit-maximizing behavior for it incorporates into business decisions the wider effects of the uncertain and complex real world. Some executives have in fact stated they do not believe they could increase net profits by adopting other than full-cost techniques.[3] Full-cost pricing is also used because in reality it is very difficult, if not impossible, to measure MR and MC so as to set $MR = MC$.

***Collusion, covert* and *overt,* is an illegal pricing strategy whereby firms agree to set higher prices.**

Collusion, Covert and Overt Outright agreement to fix prices is illegal in the U.S., but human nature being what it is, gain is measured against risk and illegality is indulged in when the odds are acceptable. Cartels are the name given to formal price-fixing agreements among colluding firms. They unite and reap the gains of monopoly by setting higher prices. Arrangements other than price alone are also made. Quotas are set. In some cases, areas of operation are specified. At one time or another industries like milk distribution, erasers, plumbing supplies, cardboard, electrical equipment, typewriters, cigarettes, oil, and steel have been charged with collusive activity. Nonetheless, even with an explicit agreement, maintaining discipline among the members is difficult and the cartel eventually breaks down. There is a temptation to cheat, particularly for some firms experiencing lower profits than the other culprit firms. A profit pinch can arise because of changing demand and cost factors introduced by a downturn in the business cycle. If one of the companies increases sales by lowering prices, thereby breaking the agreement, it invites retaliation. A price war results, destabilizing the markets. This cannot occur under perfect competition, because individual firms are price takers, not price searchers.

Differentiated Oligopoly

In the case of pure oligopoly it is assumed that the product is homogeneous and therefore that both sellers will sell for the same price. However, under differentiated oligopoly sellers usually differentiate their products by packaging or brand names. The characteristics of differentiated oligopoly are that there exist:

The characteristics of *differentiated oligopoly* are that there exist a few large firms, difficulty of entry, strong mutual dependence, differentiated products, and heavy advertising.

1. A few large firms (numbers of small ones possible).
2. Difficulty of entry.
3. Strong mutual dependence.
4. Differentiated products with property rights to some characteristic.
5. Heavy advertising, usually at the national level.

Thus, differentiated oligopoly includes the first three items relating to pure oligopoly plus the fourth and fifth, and is the dominant market structure in manufacturing in the U.S.

Once product differentiation is introduced, the complications magnify. When the product is identical, the oligopolists must find some way to determine a single price in order to prevent the wounds inflicted by price wars and other varieties of retaliatory bloodletting by rivals.

[3]Ibid., p. 175.

Differentiated oligopoly therefore introduces additional aspects absent from pure oligopoly. There is of course some difference in prices because of variations in the product (including patents). For reasons already stated, when the gap in prices becomes too large, expect trouble. But the differentiated oligopolists can resort to nonprice competition to protect themselves from devastating price wars.

Furthermore, differentiated oligopoly can add additional barriers to entry besides the natural and created barriers that already exist. Because the product is differentiated, creations of new artificial barriers are possible.

There are three overlapping approaches to survival. The first two are examples of nonprice competition while the third is an example of an artificially price-created deterrent to entry confronting new rivals.

Promotional gimmicks **are an example of nonprice competition whereby one firm encroaches on a rival's market share by subtly enticing consumers.**

Promotional Gimmicks Encroaching on a rival's market share involves gimmicks like contests with prizes awarded in goods or trips, and better warranties. It might be a technological innovation that improves quality, packaging or safety features, or labeling and design which serves as subtle lures for the customer.

Advertising **is another form of nonprice competition, and promotes a firm's image.**

Advertising The above information must be brought to the public's attention whether the differences are real or not. Thus differentiated oligopolies tend to advertise heavily. A newcomer to an industry would have difficulty because of the large costs related to such heavy advertising.

Under *limit pricing* a low price is set by established firms to discourage the entrance of potential rivals.

Limit Pricing Suppose a new firm attempts to obtain a share of the market (see Figure 10-5). The demand for its product has to be at least d_2 and the price it sells at p_1 in order to cover total costs. Because the firm is just setting up, it is higher up on the long-run average cost curve (*LAC*) at b, assuming in the long

Figure 10-5

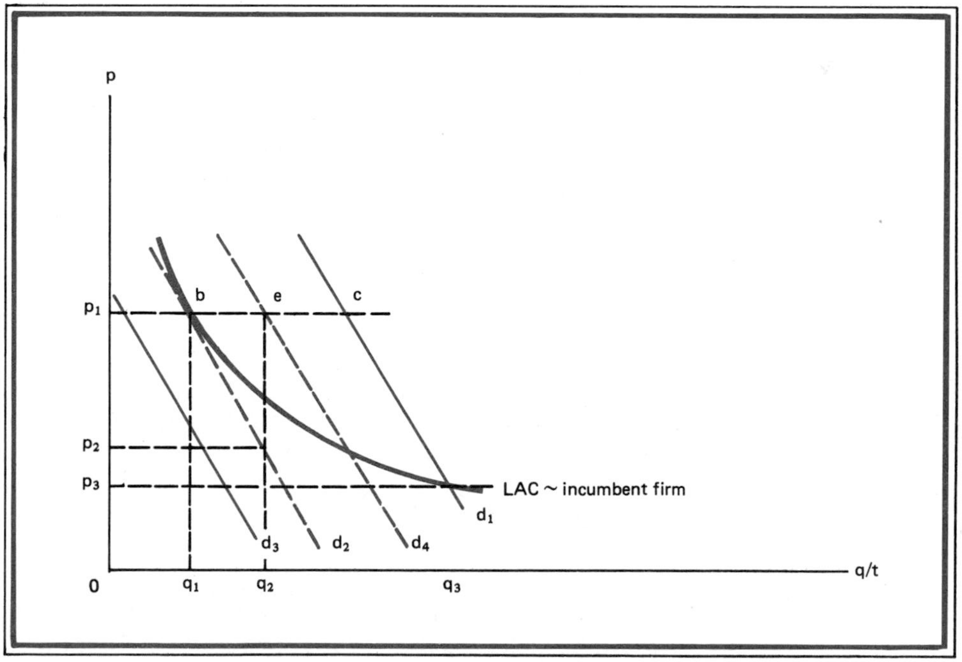

Taps for Taps

In 1933, when Prohibition was ended and the taps were opened, there were approximately 740 breweries in the U.S. By 1978, over 660 local breweries had been shut down or absorbed in mergers. In 1990, it is expected by some industry experts that only 4 or 5 national breweries will remain. Their regional outlets will have replaced all the local breweries. Chicago, the host to 32 breweries in 1934, had only one in 1978.

Over 45 breweries closed down or sold out in 1978. Since 1960, some 125 breweries have perished. In 1960 the top 5 produced 33 percent of all U.S. beer shipments. In 1968 they accounted for 47 percent, in 1978 they shipped 70 percent. Some observers believe that by 1990 only Anheuser-Busch and Miller will remain. By 1980 these two will account for 60 percent of the market share.

The top 5 brewers were, in descending order in 1979, Anheuser-Busch, Miller, Schlitz, Pabst, and Coors. Of these only Coors of Colorado is family owned, and it sells in roughly 15 Western states. The small local breweries have charged the nationals with predatory price-cutting. But on their premium beers the national breweries charge, and get away with, prices on six-packs 10 to 20 cents above the local brands. Part of the explanation may lie in the large expenditures the nationals put into advertising—television commercials that employ well-known sports figures. The local breweries can only fight back by lowering prices, since these days there does not appear to be significant quality differences, though there probably was in the pre-chemical past. The nationals can and do, however, launch aggressive promotional schemes. They temporarily drop prices, hit the quality pitch hard, and drive out the local breweries. Interestingly enough, many buyers who switch to the national brand during the price-cutting caper do not switch back to the local brand when the nationals raise their prices again. Some of the smaller regional companies have lobbied states for price-posting regulations. They want laws requiring that brewers announce price changes in advance and that they be maintained for fixed time periods—up to as much as a year. Others want anti–price-cutting laws passed.

The national breweries use the extra income earned on the higher prices they charge for their premium beers to build more efficient, automated plants and to underwrite advertising costs. Beer—being price inelastic in demand—is heavily taxed, distribution is expensive, and the average hourly wage of labor is surpassed only by wages in the construction industry. Some regional breweries have been very successful after automating. Most cannot afford to. Moreover, the Justice Department has often prevented smaller locals from merging, which they must do in order to stay competitive. There is to be no foam in their future.

run its scale of production would eventually be identical with the established company. This, of course, includes large advertising expenditures. At the price of p_1 the incumbent firm would be making pure profits at point c, which is the reason for the new entrant's appearance in the first place. If the entrant's market share was such that its demand was d_3, it could not survive since revenues would be less than costs. If it faced demand of d_2, it would reduce the demand facing the incumbent to d_4 from d_1. But by practicing *limit pricing* the incumbent firm can cut its price to p_2. At that price the new entrant would only sell q_2, not enough to cover its costs. In fact, with some foresight, the established firm or firms can discourage any attempts at entry altogether by setting its price initially at p_3.

There is yet another facet to oligopoly strategy. Even if the entrant were faced with a d_2 demand curve and it set its price at p_1, the incumbent firm would be making a pure profit at point e. Investors who own the existing firm's outstanding (already issued) stock will receive higher retained earnings and dividends than those holding the entrant's stock. Therefore, the new entrant will have difficulty selling new stock issues needed to generate funds for capital expansion, and never really become competitive with the senior company. All the incumbent company has to do is lower its price some and drive the upstart out.

MONOPOLISTIC COMPETITION

In 1927 Edward H. Chamberlain submitted a doctoral thesis at Harvard University in which he offered alternative models of the firm and its markets. It was a new breed of model, neither pure monopoly nor perfect competition. Still it contained elements of both—a hybrid model he labeled as monopolistic competition.[4] Chamberlain referred to it as competition among monopolists. Obviously this is not the monopoly described in Chapter 9. Rather it is an example of competition among monopolists producing highly substitutable but not identical commodities. Thus, a monopoly in producing Camel cigarettes does not constitute a monopoly in all cigarettes. It is a monopoly on a *brand* of cigarettes, a product that is differentiated slightly by taste and slightly by packaging. There are, however, many rival producers of cigarettes who, as a group, constitute what we could call the cigarette industry. Clearly, industry as used here is more loosely defined than that for perfect competition, for in the perfectly competitive market we assumed an identical or homogeneous product.

The characteristics of *monopolistic competition* are that there exist many buyers and sellers, easy exit and entry, slightly differentiated products, some possible mutual dependence, and some advertising.

The characteristics of monopolistic competition are that there exist:

1. Many buyers and sellers.
2. Easy exit and entry.
3. Slightly differentiated products with property rights to some characteristic.
4. Some mutual dependence is possible.
5. Some advertising, usually local.

The first two characteristics—many buyers and sellers, and easy entry and exit of firms—are also the familiar characteristics of the perfectly competitive model. The third characteristic mentioned is the crucial one—the one that sets the theory of monopolistic competition apart. Because the good produced by the individual firm is somehow differentiated from that produced by other firms, each firm is a seller of a quasi-unique product. To the extent that it is unique one could say the producer is a single seller and has a monopoly over the production of goods with that unique quality. The good does not differ greatly from what rivals produce. One brand of toothpaste, laundry soap, or gasoline might have slightly different characteristics from another, and often you are led to believe in the importance of the difference through advertising.

[4]Joan Robinson, in England, independently published somewhat similar results a year later. She stopped short of Chamberlain's monopolistic competition and did not introduce the element of advertising. See her *Economics of Imperfect Competition* (London: Macmillan & Co., Ltd., 1933).

Examples of monopolistic competition are found in television and appliance repair, most services including travel agencies, most retail outlets like grocery stores, gasoline stations, laundromats, restaurants, fast food restaurants, flower shops, real estate agencies, and auto repair shops.

One often sees clusters of these *retail* businesses in a given area: two or more gasoline stations at an intersection; several grocery outlets, flower shops, and clothing stores congregated on the same road stretch, neighborhood, or shopping center. For instance, there were approximately 106,500 gasoline stations in the U.S. in 1979 (down from 204,500 in 1972) with about 60,000 changing hands or shutting down each year.

Downward Sloping Demand

Product variation may be based not only on the properties of the product itself but also upon the conditions that surround the sale.[5] Conditions surrounding the sale may be intangible. They might include convenience of location, hours of business, availability of credit, delivery service, and whether checks and food stamps are acceptable. Other intangibles are reputation for honesty, courtesy, quickness of service, honoring of warranties, exchange policy—in short, the general atmosphere of the establishment. These intangibles can be viewed as tie-in sales for a product sold at the same price by all the sellers, and amounts to a subtle form of price discrimination.

It follows that the market of each seller is not completely merged with that of rivals. Buyers and sellers, unlike perfect competitors, are not paired in a purely random manner. Some buyers seek certain sellers and vice versa. As a result there is a basis for price variation, meaning the seller does not face a perfectly elastic demand curve but a slightly downward sloping one instead. Therefore, the seller can exercise some small control over the price. There is a price range within which he can operate. Unlike the situation under perfect competition, he does not sell an unlimited amount at an inflexible price. He can lower the price should he wish to sell more. Were the seller to raise prices too much, buyers can resort to purchasing close substitutes from rivals. Although the seller has a monopoly of sorts, monopolistic-competition is still highly competitive.

Mutual Dependence

The fourth characteristic of monopolistic competition mentioned above is that some mutual dependence exists among firms. We shall explain precisely what we mean by using a graph.

Because the seller's demand curve is downward sloping, the marginal revenue curve lies below the demand curve as in monopoly. The graph for the monopolistic competitor is essentially the same as that for pure monopoly, except as a matter of degree. Generally, the demand curve for a monopolistic competitor is believed to be more elastic than for a monopolist and less elastic

[5]Edward H. Chamberlain, *The Theory of Monopolistic Competition* 8th ed. (Cambridge: Harvard University Press, 1965, p. 56.

Figure 10-6

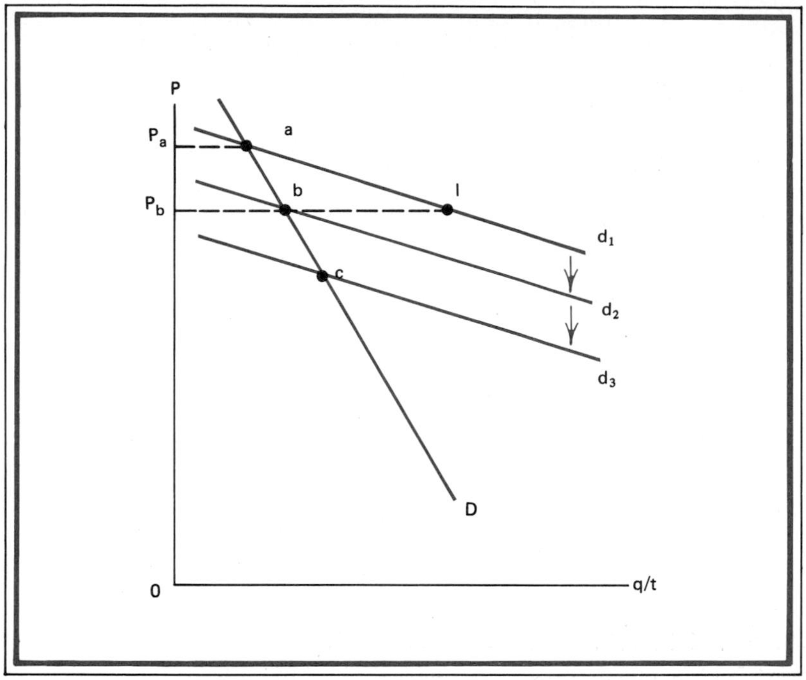

than that of a perfect competitor. Let us examine Figure 10-6. In it we have drawn two types of demand curves, D and d, and we must explain what each represents. The d demand curve, say d_1, is what a firm faces when the amount of *all other competing products and their prices are given.* It represents what a firm will sell at various prices, assuming that other rivals do not change their prices too. The firm in question can, for instance, lower its price while the other firms do not lower their prices. It is presumed that rivals do not notice that the first firm has changed its price. But if all firms take note of one another's behavior and respond alike, causing all of the rivals to lower their prices when the first firm does, then the d curve of the typical firm will shift down. The typical firm, by intending to move along its d curve unnoticed, finds because it is noticed that its d curves will shift.

The shifting d curve will generate for the firm a demand curve that we have labeled the D curve. As the individual firm lowers its price in order to sell more, it attempts to move along its d_1 curve from say, a to l. But other firms in the industry respond by lowering their prices too. As all firms lower their prices the quantity demanded by consumers increases to all firms, hence to the whole industry.

Thus, the initiating firm does sell more, indicated at point b, but not as much as that indicated at point l. The shifts in d_1 to d_2, d_3 generate the D demand curve for the initiating firm made up of points a, b, c. As a result the D demand curve is more inelastic than the d curve because as the individual firm drops its price, the quantity demanded of the initiating firm's output does not respond as much because other firms react by lowering their prices.

In Lynnwood, Washington, in 1976 several grocery chains found themselves in a price war on bread. As prices were cut by one grocer to attract more customers, rivals cut their prices too. It ended up with 60-cent bread selling for less than 10 cents a loaf. Before 1974, gasoline price wars were frequent in some cities, and they may return again since prices are deregulated. Thus, mutual dependence of prices can be observed in the marketplace.

The position of *D* demand curve of the firm depends upon the number of rivals in the loosely defined industry (loose since the products are not homogeneous). The more sellers there are the further to the left lies *D*. The reason is that the given firm must share the total market demand with more firms, hence its own share of the market is reduced at each price. Conversely, the fewer rivals there are the flatter the *D* demand curve will be since each firm shares a larger part of total sales. The firm's *d* demand curve is more elastic than its *D* demand curve because of the assumption of retaliation by rivals in the industry to price cuts.

We should mention here that Chamberlain made the heroic assumption in developing the monopolistic competitive model that both demand and cost curves within each product group are the same, with consumer preferences more or less evenly distributed among the different brands. That is, although the products are different, they are not so different that significant variations in costs of production exist among them.

SHORT-RUN EQUILIBRIUM

Assume the typical firm is in short-run equilibrium with $MC = MR$ at point *b* in Figure 10-7. Thus, it charges a product price of p_1 and sells q_1 units at point *c*.

Figure 10-7

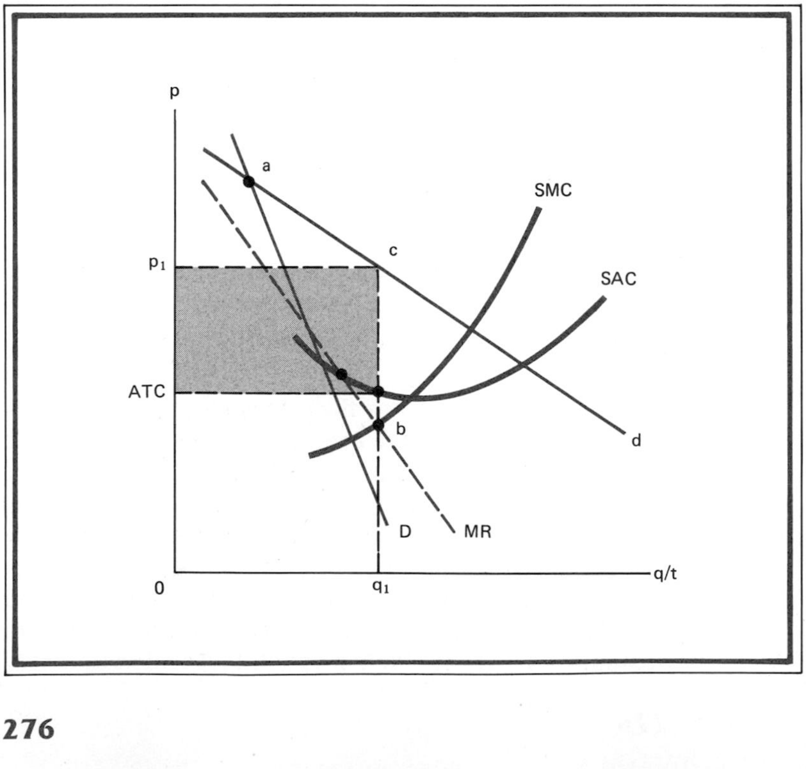

Figure 10-8

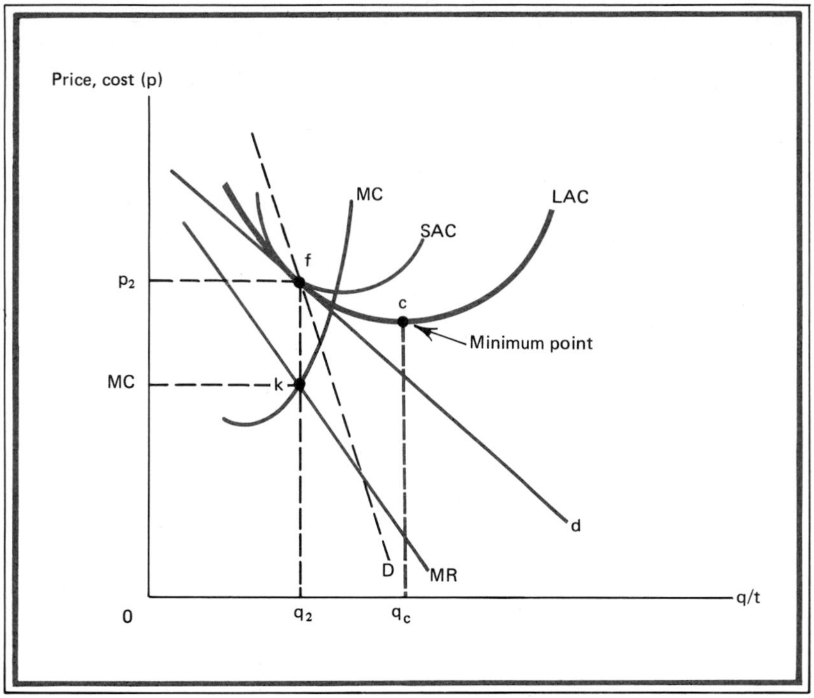

Point *a* shows the intersection between the *d* and *D* demand curves. In the short run the graph is identical in appearance to pure monopoly, except for inclusion of the *D* demand curve. The firm is earning pure profits, indicated by the shaded rectangle. Pure profits can happen in perfect competition too. In perfect competition new firms will enter production and short-run profits will disappear from the industry. In monopolistic competition entry is also easy, and new firms will also enter the market just as soon as they notice that existing producers are skimming off some pure gravy. And just as in the case of perfect competition, profits are competed away in monopolistic competition in the long run.

LONG-RUN EQUILIBRIUM

In Figure 10-6 we described how the market demand curve for an individual firm's product was subject to shifts in response to changes in price that the firm put forward. These shifts occur because rival firms respond to price policies of the initiating firm. As pure profits attract entrants into the industry, larger quantities can only be sold by reducing the price. As new firms enter and the price falls, the typical firm is forced down along the *D* demand curve as the *d* demand shifts. As *d* shifts downward the typical firm is experiencing a decline in its market share as well as a decline in the price it gets for its product. Eventually the long-run equilibrium situation illustrated in Figure 10-8 results. The firm ends up producing q_2 which is less than q_1 in Figure 10-7, and at price p_2 which is less than p_1 in Figure 10-7.

At point *f* the firm's *d* demand curve is just tangent to the *SAC* curve, thus $TR = TC$ in the short run and profits are zero. However, there is no incentive to change the price and move along the *d* demand curve because this would only lead to losses. Also, there is no incentive for new firms to enter the market, therefore point *f* is on both the *d* demand curve and the *D* demand curve. Furthermore, at point *f* the *d* demand curve is also tangent to the *LAC* curve, so that long-run profits are zero too, and there is no incentive for the firm to change its size over the long run. Entry has stopped and long-run equilibrium is established at point *f*, with marginal cost equal to marginal revenue at point *k*.

There are several aspects of this long-run equilibrium solution toward which the forces of monopolistic competition drive the industry.

1. Long-run profits are zero, as in perfect competition.
2. At point *c* long-run average costs are a minimum, therefore the firm has in a sense "excess capacity," indicated by the difference between q_c and q_2. This is a different result from the long run solution in perfect competition.[6]
3. At output q_2 in Figure 10-8 we find that price is greater than marginal cost, $p_2 > MC$. Thus, in this system there is a departure from the Pareto efficiency condition that p_2 should equal *MC* if optimum use of resources is to be attained. The failure to achieve Pareto efficiency is reminiscent of monopoly.

Thus, in monopolistic competition prices are higher and output lower than would prevail under perfect competition, even though profits are zero. There are too many firms producing with too much slack. Firms also indulge in wasteful use of resources by adopting advertising and promotion programs that stress nonprice competition such as gifts of sliverware, drinking glasses, and at one time coupons issued by gasoline stations when purchases were made. Also, some advertising is used to promote product or service differentiation.

One should distinguish between the monopolistic competitor who operates at the retail level from those found among distributors and manufacturers. Car manufacturing companies are more likely to be classed as oligopolists and not monopolistic competitors, but car dealerships on the other hand are more likely to be classified under monopolistic competition. Ford will undertake much more advertising than Joe's local car lot. It turns out that defining the product is a basic problem in discussing oligopoly and monopolistic competition. Are plastic containers and tin cans in the same industry?

CRITICISMS OF THE THEORY OF MONOPOLISTIC COMPETITION

While rich in theoretical content, many economists remain quite skeptical of the concepts of monopolistic-competition and its practical relevance.

[6]One of the authors had the privilege of being a student of Professor Chamberlain and recalls that, in a private conversation, Chamberlain attributed at least part of the tremendous ability of the U.S. economy to expand its production of war material during WW-II to the widespread existence of monopolistic competition and the general slack below-capacity levels of production that most firms maintained, as the theory suggests.

1. Since the product is differentiated, what constitutes close substitutes? They could include only a few other commodities or a good chunk of the economy, depending how you choose to define an "industry." And since the products are differentiated, what is meant by industry? In perfect competition an industry supply curve is the sum of supply curves for individual firms producing identical products. Also, how much less than perfectly elastic can the demand curve facing a monopolistic competitor be before it is not considered a perfect competitor or becomes an oligopolist?

2. What kind of diversity in products is required so that producers act as monopolists on one hand, and as competitors on the other? Where there are no barriers to entry such as farming and retail clothing, the product is so slightly differentiated that the perfectly competitive model is a reasonable approximation of reality.

3. Where product differentiation is clear enough and a few individual firms are producing a handful of different brands, there tend to be relatively few rival firms. Such a situation is classed as oligopoly, and not monopolistic competition. Thus there may, in fact, be only rare instances in which one or the other theory would not be better.

4. Where there are supposedly a large number of small firms such as grocery stores, a price change by one retailer will only affect those rivals who are within the same marketing area. There is interdependence in the immediate geographical area but not over a larger area. The interdependence can again be better analyzed using oligopoly theory, whereas monopolistic-competition theory does not pertain over the larger area because the interdependence does

Threads of Collusion?

The women's garment industry embodies more than 4,000 manufacturers who sell to around 200,000 retailers across the U.S. A major wholesale supplier may have from 4,000 to 10,000 retail accounts. Yet it is not uncommon for one seller to have over 50 percent of his volume being sold to only 250 of the larger retailers. Still the industry is without any single, dominant firm. It is unlikely that any wholesaler or retailer can claim more than 10 percent of each one's respective markets. Of course product differentiation exists, but there are close substitutes. Despite the imagination of fashion designers, as nature knows, there is a limited number of ways a garment can be styled.

Small companies whose sales extend from $5 million to $30 million a year constitute most of the estimated 4,000 producers who offer specialized lines of coats, dresses, sportswear, and other garments. Nonetheless it seems that even in such a highly fragmented industry there is evidence of price setting among some of the large wholesalers and retailers. In 1975 the Justice Department obtained guilty pleas from three internationally known retailing firms in New York City – Saks Fifth Avenue, Bergdorf Goodman, and Genesco Inc., the parent company of Bonwit Teller. They were each fined $50,000. If price fixing did occur, say some insiders, it does not exist now. Given the multiplicity of firms and the fierce competition, companies cannot afford the transactions costs to seek out only those retailers who will agree to keep their prices up. There is too much risk involved for a collusive-minded group to stake out the market from among so many. Others disagree, claiming that price fixing still goes on. The markup is a necessity because no store, no matter what its size, could cover rising costs without it. Unlike elastic waistbands, there is little stretch in the profit margin.

Reference: New York Times, Feb. 1, 1976

not exist. If it did, oligopoly theory would again be a more appropriate tool of analysis.

5. Some economists argue monopolistic competition is an unstable market structure. If there are no diseconomies of scale from operating more than one plant, then firms with plants operating at excess capacity could beneficially merge into one firm. Demand would be the same but the merged plant would operate with lower per-unit costs derived from increased scale. Some smaller plants could even be closed down. Perhaps the reason this does not happen is that the transactions cost, or costs of negotiating the merger, are too high. Nevertheless, as firms did merge in this fashion, the structure of industry would move toward oligopoly.

6. Firms are shortsighted. If it is known ahead of time that pure profits will be competed away by entry, why do not the incumbent firms price initially at the minimum point of their average total cost curves, prevent entry, *and* end up with a larger share of the market?

Appraisal

Monopolistic competition is not necessarily wasteful if the market, through differentiation of products, can satisfy a greater range of consumer preferences. A perfectly competitive world offering only homogeneous products to the public would be a boring one. It appears that consumers have a positive preference for differentiated products, and if firms offer these, then they are responding to consumer demand and satisfying consumer desires. Henry Ford in the 1930s began to experience loss of his market share to Sloan's Chevrolet Company when Sloan introduced car colors other than black, as well as different styles and sizes. Chevrolet eventually grew to become General Motors. Thus variety is a luxury item, but as standards of living rise, there is more demand for luxury items.[7] Hence, for competitive firms to move toward monopolistic competition may be a natural accompaniment to a maturing economy in line with the goal of accommodating consumer preferences.

CHAPTER SUMMARY

Unregulated pure monopoly and perfect competition are abstractions. In reality, firms exist in a world of imperfect competition between the extremes of price-searchers and price-takers—a world of varying degrees of oligopoly and monopolistic competition.

An oligopoly is a concentrated industry consisting of a few firms having market power in setting prices. Duopoly is an industry consisting of only two sellers and is a special subset of oligopoly.

Oligopoly, like monopoly, arises because of natural barriers to entry; namely, economies of scale. To compete, a new entrant must enter big with the latest technology.

[7]A luxury item is defined to have an income elasticity of greater than 1 ($E_Y > 1$), signifying that as income increases, there is more than a proportionate increase in its consumption—for example, diamonds.

Hence, setup costs and risk are high. There are the additional artificial barriers created by government regulations such as licensing, patent rights, and other permits.

Oligopoly pricing tends to avoid price competition because it can destabilize the industry, creating large losses. It is a manifestation of the pricing interdependence of oligopolistic firms. To avoid price competition firms engage in forms of nonprice competition like advertising, better warranties, and contests.

The kinked demand hypothesis describes how interdependence among firms creates sticky, that is somewhat inflexible, prices in oligopolistic industries. However, the hypothesis does not show how the price got to be what it is, only why it does not easily change. And contrary to the model's predictions, at times rivals have often matched price increases initiated by other firms.

Pure oligopoly consists of a few firms in the industry who are assumed to sell an identical product. Four pricing strategies among potentially many are independent pricing, tacit price agreements led by the dominant firm, markup or target pricing, and outright price-fixing agreements.

Under differentiated oligopoly there is product differentiation, hence a heavy reliance on advertising, usually at the national level, thus introducing further complexities into its analysis.

Limit pricing is another artificially created barrier to entry created by the firms themselves. Incumbent firms can lower the price to the point where new firms starting out with smaller sized plants would have higher average costs, preventing them from earning survival profits at the lower price at which they are forced to compete.

Monopolistic competition is characterized by the existence of many buyers and sellers, easing exit and entry, some advertising which is usually local, perhaps some interdependence, and with small differentiations in the product from those of competitors. Differentiation may also involve conditions surrounding the sale such as hours, buy-back policies, courtesy, location, and so forth.

The monopolistic competitor faces a less than perfectly elastic demand curve for his product and therefore a small range over which he can vary the price.

In the short run, equilibrium for the firm occurs at that price where marginal revenue equals marginal cost—the profit maximizing rule. However, because price is greater than average cost, some pure profit is earned.

In the long run, because of easy entry, pure profits are competed away. However, long-run equilibrium occurs to the left of the minimum point of the long-run average cost curve, so that some excess capacity exists. The inefficiency is reflected by the price being greater than the marginal cost. Thus, prices are a little higher and output a little lower than would exist under perfect competition.

There are several criticisms of imperfect competition. The dividing line between firms considered as being monopolistic competitors or oligopolists can be a fuzzy one. Since each firm produces a slightly different product, how can there be an industry demand curve? And where competition is rigorous, the competitive model serves just as well in analyzing market adjustments.

QUESTIONS

1. The Canadian auto rental business experienced a rental rate-slashing war between Budget Rent-a-Car and Tilden Rent-a-Car. Prices fell from $22.95 a day to as low as 1 cent a day for the first 2 days, and $6.95 a day thereafter. The price war was confined to Canada's 9 international airports covering about 50 percent of the

short-term rental market. The American companies, Avis and Hertz, tried to stay out of it (*Wall Street Journal*, Feb. 15, 1979).

a. Is the rent-a-car business an example of monopolistic competition or oligopoly? Why, or why not?
b. Is the kinked demand curve model useful in explaining why Avis and Hertz avoided the price war? Why, or why not?

2. When Morris the TV cat died in the summer of 1978, there was a debate within the Heinz Corporation, producer of 9-Lives pet food, whether or not it should announce Morris's death or just switch to a stand-in cat. Does it matter? Does the fact that 6 companies produce 71 percent of the pet food in the U.S. help you to determine an answer?
3. There continues to be an expansion of market share by a handful of major beer brewing companies. Small beer makers continue to be absorbed by the larger companies or quit the business. It seems that the higher priced premium beers of the larger national companies sell better in the local markets than many of the locally brewed beers which are priced lower. Does this violate the law of demand? Why, or why not? What information activity occurs in concentrated markets that does not occur in perfectly competitive markets? Why?
4. Many of the supermarket chains sell in-house brands of tuna fish at lower prices than the name brands. Yet you observe people buying the higher priced Chicken of the Sea or Starkist tunafish. Are they not identical products? Can you offer an explanation?
5. Sometimes you may observe that a regionally or nationally franchised department store charges $10 to $20 more for the same dress or coat than a small one-owner shop charges. Why, if the wholesale cost of the coat is presumably the same to both? Are the coats really identical? Or are there factors that make them not identical? Discuss.
6. No pure profits will be earned in a pure oligopolistic industry in the long run if there is free entry. Do you agree? Does your answer depend on whether there is collusion or noncollusion in the industry? Explain.
7. The price elasticity of demand for the product of a firm will be more elastic the greater the degree of production differentiation. True or false? Why?
8. Suppose the local supermarket lowers the price of its oatmeal cereal from 80 cents a box when it sold 2,500 boxes a day, to 76 cents a box and sells 3,000 boxes a day. If the store is a profit maximizer, then it can be assumed that $MC = MR = 76$ cents a box. True or false? Discuss.
9. Suppose the demand for RCA television sets increases (an oligopolistic industry). Use the kinked demand curve to show how quantity is affected but the price is not.
10. During Prohibition days of the 1920s, various gangs in Chicago fought for turf in which to be the sole distributor of illegally produced alcohol. From time to time the gangs met to settle their disputes about rights to territory and to stop the bloodletting. What industry structure is suggested here? In that vein, why was the "industry" so unstable?
11. From time to time the large supermarket chains in Chicago have indulged in price wars. One approach was to run specials on certain items by offering discounted prices on them (lead items). One of the supermarket executives said, "Specials take 4 percent off gross margins. But everyone is afraid to be the first to chicken out."
    a. What economic theory is consistent with the executive's theory, if any? Explain.
    b. Is there any conceptual difficulty in deciding whether supermarket chains fit the oligopoly model or the monopolistically competitive model? Comment.
12. There are 12 major airplane manufacturers in the U.S. Right after WW-II there were many more. Today, defense budget analysts argue that the U.S. has too many airplane companies, resulting in idle factories and depots. Some half million dollars could be saved by cutting 19,000 nonproduction employees. In fact, if 2 or 3 of the

companies went out of business, the industry would still experience excess capacity. The government keeps some of these companies afloat. It bailed out Lockheed in 1978 with a guaranteed loan. "The whole thing is inflationary."

a. Graph the excess capacity situation.
b. Suppose the government stops picking up the tab on unneeded idle capacity, graph the effect in the long run.
c. Does the inefficiency of the airplane industry hurt national defense in the long run by artificially stretching out production over too many firms? How? Keep in mind who pays for defense.
d. Should company survival depend upon political decisions?
e. Boeing Co. is in Senator Jackson's Washington, General Dynamics in Senator Tower's Texas, Mc Donnell-Douglas in Senator Eagleton's Missouri, and Rockwell in Senator John Glenn's Illinois. Does this information affect your answer to *d*?

13. A corporate executive is quoted as saying, "You've got to have some impact in the marketplace or you're always dancing to someone else's tune. He's making the dough and you're always playing catch-up."
    a. What kind of market structure is typified here?
    b. While increasing market share at the expense of some profit seems to violate the rule of profit maximization, might there be no inconsistency if a distinction is made between the short and long run? That is, what would likely happen to a company's stock prices in the long run even though it accepted lower profits in the short run by lowering its prices in order to increase its market share?
14. In 1973, before OPEC's effective emergence, a mayoral candidate of a large city proposed that limitations be imposed on gasoline service stations. "We have enough service stations on every corner. We need legislation that puts tight controls so that we have only enough stations to service people—enough to meet public demand and give existing operators a chance to make a living and a profit without too much competition."
    a. Who "needs" this legislation? Who gains? Who doesn't?
    b. What number of service stations is required to meet public demand? Is demand fixed?
    c. What is enough to "make a living"?
    d. How much competition is too much competition?
    e. Does the fact that from 1970 to 1980 the number of service stations in the U.S. fell from about 225,000 to 106,000 affect your answers to the above?

Chapter 11

Business Structure

PROGRESS REPORT

A. In Chapters 7 to 10 several types of industry structures were analyzed. They ranged from farming in Chapter 8 treated from the viewpoint of the competitive model, to the natural monopolies of public utilities in Chapter 9, the oligopolies that exist in much of manufacturing, and the monopolistic-competitive model of many small and several large businesses such as gasoline stations and the retail grocery business in Chapter 10.

B. In this chapter we are interested in the market power of companies in an industry and in the economy, how different concentration ratios are defined and used to measure market power, the history and the application of antitrust policy, what multinational companies are and whether they are good or bad, and finally a brief look at the oil industry.

C. In the Chapter 12 we leave the study of industry models, industry structure, and outputs to look at the markets for inputs to the production process.

Chapter 6 identified three legal ways to set up business in the U.S., namely sole ownership, the partnership, and the corporation. When students talk about business in the U.S. they usually mean *big* business, the mega corporation, and the effects of the concentration of economic power in a few hands. Thus, according to the 1972 Census of Manufactures approximately 2,500 manufacturing companies controlled over 86 percent of the manufacturing industry assets and earned around 88 percent of industry profits. The top 100 manufacturing firms accounted for over 53 percent of all manufacturing assets. The 10 largest banks held 25 percent of all bank assets in the U.S. and the largest 100 were responsible for over 50 percent of all banking industry assets in 1972. The fear is of the discretionary power large firms may wield.

But businesses fail, both large and small ones. It has been estimated that in the U.S. about 10,000 businesses fail on the average in any given year. Only about 8 or 9 of every 100 new businesses stay in operation for as long as 5 years. Put the other way around, 91 to 92 percent of new businesses do not last for as long as 5 years.[1] So, while our emphasis here is on growth and size and structure of existing businesses, we should always keep in mind that we are looking at the ones that survived.

MARKET POWER

Market power can be measured by the value of a company's assets, the total value of sales, the net profit on sales, the value of shipments, or the percentage of physical output contributed to total industry output.

Economists have several ways of measuring market power. Conceptually, some are more meaningful than others. But theory is severely constrained by the limits of useful available data. Market power can be measured by the value of a company's assets, that is its land, factories, equipment, and inventories; the total value of sales; the net profit on sales; the value of shipments; the percentage of physical output that it contributes to total industry output; or some combination of these measures.

For instance, in 1975 Chrysler Corporation ranked tenth in sales of all industrial corporations; it was seventeenth in assets, and 492nd in net income on sales. In 1980 it required a $1.5 billion government loan guarantee to survive. Greyhound Bus Lines was 41st in sales, 114th in assets and 115th in net income. Each year *Fortune* magazine ranks the leading 500 corporations in the U.S. by assets and by sales in its May issue. Table 11-1 shows the asset ranking for the top nonfinancial corporations for selected years.

Aggregate concentration is a method of measuring market power whereby the largest firms in the whole economy are measured for the percentage they contribute to total production.

Aggregate Concentration

There are two basic approaches that economists and government statisticians use to measure market power. The first to be discussed, *aggregate concentration,* makes no distinction between firms and industries. It lumps the largest firms in the economy, regardless of the industry these firms are in, and meas-

[1]Cecil Scaglione, "Thinking of Starting Your Own Business? Think Again," *News Extra,* Aug. 1979: 27.

ures their gross production as a percentage of the total production of the economy.

Since manufacturing is one of the most important sectors of the economy, comparisons of aggregate economic concentration are usually centered on this industrial sector of the economy. Aggregate concentration measures economic power by calculating the value added of 50, 100, 150, and 200 largest industrial firms. Value added is approximately equal to the difference between a firm's sales in dollars and its purchases of intermediate output, that is, the materials it buys from other firms. At each stage of production, value is added by each producer. The total value of the product is the sum of the individual values added at each stage. For example, the mining company uses $1 of diesel fuel to operate equipment to dig a ton of iron ore which it sells for $5 to Intermediate Steel Company, thereby adding $4 of value to the iron ore. The steel company converts the ore into flat steel and sells it to Equipment Inc. for $15, which

TABLE 11-1
Top Ten Nonfinancial Corporations by Assets

1909[1]	1917[2]	1929[2]
1. U.S. Steel	1. U.S. Steel	1. U.S. Steel
2. Standard Oil	2. Standard Oil (N.J.)	2. Standard Oil (N.J.)
3. American Tobacco	3. Bethlehem Steel	3. General Motors
4. International Mercantile Marine	4. Armour	4. Standard Oil (Ind.)
5. International Harvester	5. Swift	5. Bethlehem Steel
6. Anaconda Copper	6. International Harvester	6. Ford Motor
7. U.S. Leather	7. Du Pont	7. Standard Oil (N.Y.)
8. Armour	8. Midvale Steel & Ordinance	8. Anaconda Copper
9. American Sugar Refining	9. U.S. Rubber	9. Texas Co.
10. Pullman	10. General Electric	10. Standard Oil (Cal.)
1945[2]	**1966[2]**	**1977[2]**
1. Standard Oil (N.J.)	1. Standard Oil (N.J.)	1. Exxon (was Standard Oil)
2. U.S. Steel	2. General Motors	2. General Motors
3. General Motors	3. Ford Motor	3. Mobil
4. Socony-Vacuum Oil	4. Texaco	4. Texaco
5. Du Pont	5. Gulf Oil	5. IBM
6. Standard Oil (Ind.)	6. U.S. Steel	6. Ford Motor
7. Bethlehem Steel	7. Sears, Roebuck	7. Standard Oil (Cal.)
8. General Electric	8. Mobil Oil	8. Gen. Telephone & Electric
9. Texas Co.	9. General Electric	9. Gulf Oil
10. Ford Motor	10. IBM	10. Sears, Roebuck

[1]From N. Collins and L. Preston, "Turnover and Growth of Largest Industrial Firms, 1906–1950," *Review of Economics & Statistics* (Feb. 1957): 79–83.
[2]*Forbes Magazine* (Sept. 15, 1977): 127.

converts the steel into a shovel for a bulldozer, creating $10 of additional value. Equipment Inc. sells it to Construction Retail Supply Company for $40. Thus $25 is added at this stage of production. Finally, the retailer sells the shovel for $60, creating an additional $20 in value added.

	Sales price	Value added
Diesel fuel	$ 1	$ 1
Mining company	5	4
Steel company	15	10
Equipment Inc.	40	25
Supply company	60	20
Total sales	$121	$60

Notice that the final retail price of $60 for the shovel is identical to the sum of the value added created at each stage. The total of sales prices is $121 and is higher than total value added of $60. The reason is that the sales total double-adds the value added figures. It counts them more than once. The $1 is counted five times, the $5 four times, the $10 three times, and so on.

Table 11-2 illustrates the changes in aggregate concentration for selected years from 1947 to 1972 in manufacturing. As you can see there has been a steady, gentle upward trend since 1954. Keep in mind that these figures do not necessarily include the same firms throughout this period. A company is defined as the total of its industrial establishments including its warehouses and central administrative offices. Value-added data are used here since availability of the data is relatively good. It also sidesteps the double-counting problem that plagues other approaches. For example, if value of shipments from plants is used, double accounting results for plants that ship to other plants within their own company. Yet value of shipments still has an important use in the measurement of concentration.

The table reveals that between 1947 and 1972 the value-added market share of the 200 largest firms increased 13 percentage points from 30 to 43 percent, that is, from less than 1/3 to more than 2/5 of the total manufacturing share. From 1954 to 1972 the increase was only 6 percentage points.

The aggregate concentration approach as a broad overview cloaks behavior in individual industries. Furthermore, it is confined to manufacturing. Other important industries are found in the services, financing, food, construction, and transportation sectors. These sectors tend to have a more competitive structure than the manufacturing sector. Also, within manufacturing itself, industry structure varies greatly between companies that provide producer goods and those that provide consumer goods. Producer goods are goods sold from one firm to another whereas consumer goods are sold to households by firms at the retail level. Producer goods are things like tractors, drill presses, railroad cars, and all other inputs that firms need to produce goods for consumers such as washing machines, stereos, and T-shirts.

Concentration Ratios

Concentration ratios **measure the market share produced by the largest 4, 8, 20, or 50 firms in an industry.**

A concentration ratio might measure the market share produced by the largest 4, 8, 20, or 50 firms in an industry. The most common ratio quoted is the four-firm concentration ratio (FFCR). As an example, if the total number of widgets produced in the whole widget industry is 10,000 per month and 4 firms produce 2,000 of them, then the FFCR is 20 percent. When it comes to industry concentration ratios the Census Bureau primarily uses value of shipments as a criterion in manufacturing. Only for a few manufacturing industries does it use value-added data.

SIC Code

The *Standard Industrial Classification (SIC) Code* separates and classifies industries numerically.

Every five years the Census Bureau publishes the Census of Manufactures. The Bureau uses the Standard Industrial Classification (SIC) to separate and classify industries and to determine what products belong under what classification. A number code is used. The first two digits distinguish the major group. Thus, 31 indicates that the commodity is produced in the leather and leather products industry within the manufacturing sector where the manufacturing code ranges from 20 to 39. The more digits, the further the classification refinement. Going to 3111 confines the commodity grouping to leather tanning and finishing. Breaking it down to 5 digits of 31111 subdivides the grouping to finished cattle hide and kip (untanned hide of calf or lamb) side leathers, and 31112 indicates finished calf and whole kip leathers. There is no 6-digit coding. The

TABLE 11-2
Share of Total Value Added by Manufacture Accounted for by the 50, 100, 150, and 200 Largest Manufacturing Companies: 1972 and Earlier Years

	Percent of value added by manufacture								
Company rank group	1972	1970	1967	1966	1963	1962	1958	1954	1947
Largest 50 companies	25	24	25	25	25	24	23	23	17
Largest 100 companies ...	33	33	33	33	33	32	30	30	23
Largest 150 companies ...	39	38	38	38	37	36	35	34	27
Largest 200 companies ...	43	43	42	42	41	40	38	37	30

Note: 1962, 1966, and 1970 data are based on the Annual Survey of Manufactures: "Largest companies" are those which were the largest in each of the specified years.
Source: U.S. Bureau of the Census; *Census of Manufactures, 1972*. Special Report Series, Concentration Ratios, Table 1, p. SR2-4.

narrowest classification is to 7 digits, thus 3111115 is sole leather and 3111133 is bag, case, and strap leather. There are no concentration ratios at the 7-digit level. Industry concentration ratios find their greatest use at the 4-digit industry level. Other examples of code numbers are product code 2023212, referring to canned evaporated milk; 20232, referring to the "product class" canned milk; and 2023, which includes the meat and kindred dairy product sectors in which coding consistency requires that canned evaporated milk be included.

Complications arise in abundance by forcing things into standard industrial codes (SIC). Some codes are defined in terms of equipment or processes used while others are defined in terms of the actual product made. An example is womens' sweaters produced in knitting mills (2253) and also made in cut-

TABLE 11-3
Share of Value of Shipments in Manufacturing 1947–1972 (Percent)

SIC Code	Industry	1972		1967		1963		1958		1954		1947	
		4-firm	8-firm	4-firm	8-firm	4-firm	8-firm	4-firm	8-firm	4-firm	8-firm	4-firm	8-firm
2011	Meat packing plants	22	37	26	38	31	42	34	46	39	51	41	54
2051	Bread, cake and related products	29	39	26	38	23	35	22	33	20	31	16	26
2086	Bottled and canned soft drinks	14	21	13	20	12	17	11	15	10	14	10	14
2083	Malt beverages	52	70	40	59	34	52	28	44	27	41	21	30
2043	Cereal breakfast food	90	98	88	97	86	96	83	95	88	95	79	91
2095	Roasted coffee	65	79	53	71	52	68	—	—	—	—	—	—
2111	Cigarettes	84	NA	81	100	80	100	79	99+	82	99+	90	99+
2371	Book publishing	19	31	20	32	20	33	16	29	21	32	18	29
2514	Metal household furniture	13	24	14	24	13	20	13	22	16	26	26	37
2371	Fur goods	7	12	5	8	5	8	5	8	4	6	3	5
2771	Greeting cards	70	78	67	79	57	71	45	62	42	57	39	55
2822	Synthetic rubber	62	81	61	82	57	80	60	86	53	81	100	100
2911	Petroleum refining	31	56	33	57	34	56	32	55	33	56	37	59
3773	Ready mixed concrete	6	10	6	9	4	7	4	7	—	—	—	—
3334	Primary aluminum	79	92	—	—	NA	100	6	NA	100	100	100	100
3494	Valves and pipe fittings	11	21	14	23	13	23	17	27	17	27	24	32
3672	Television picture tubes	49	71	49	69	41	62	—	—	—	—	—	—
3312	Blast furnaces and steel mills	45	65	48	66	48	67	53	70	55	71	50	66
3111	Leather tanning and finishing	17	28	20	31	18	30	18	30	27	39	22	34
3171	Women's handbags and purses	14	23	10	17	11	18	10	15	8	14	7	13
3861	Photographic equip. and supplies	74	85	69	81	63	76	65	74	—	—	61	70

Source: U.S. Bureau of the Census, *Census of Manufactures, 1972.*

and-sew shops (2339). To retain the industry of origin concept, it is necessary to assign different code numbers to women's sweaters depending where they are made.

In 1972 the Census Bureau defined 20 broad 2-digit groups, 143 3-digit groups, 451 4-digit groups, 1,293 5-digit groups, and around 10,500 7-digit groups. Table 11-3 provides 4-digit concentration ratios for some selected industries. In this table the ratios are based on value of shipments by companies in the U.S. Where "NA" appears the numbers may have been deliberately left out because market shares of individual companies could be inferred. This might violate the privacy of the company agreed to by the Bureau.

Problems with Concentration Ratios

The Census Bureau collects and prepares concentration ratio data from confidential questionnaires sent to firms. The data are not in the form most advantageous to economic analysts who are trying to ascertain important facets of industry structure and behavior. There can arise serious understatement and overstatement of industry concentration. Not only that, the state of the art is such that it is difficult to determine exactly what the truth is on particular questions.

Overstatement of concentration occurs for industries that import a significant amount of goods. Foreign competition is ignored and the ratios are higher than they should be for U.S. domestic firms.

Also, the concentration calculations are critically dependent upon what is to be included and not included in the industry product group at the 4-digit level. Basic materials are increasingly substitutable for one another. Yet many are classified under completely different product groups and therefore industry groups as well.

On construction sites, plastic, wood, metal, and concrete materials are interchangeable for many functions. Metal cans, glass bottles, and for some purposes paper containers are close substitutes, but these all come under different SIC codes. Thus, some industries are too narrowly prescribed and this causes higher concentration ratios to appear.

Understatement of ratios is the other possibility. Many companies are multiproduct companies. They produce small amounts in many categories or they may be involved at only one stage of production of some items. General Electric in 1972 was found to be involved in 74 of the 430 4-digit SIC categories. In almost all of these categories its share of the market is small, yet it is one of the large corporations, ranking ninth in sales and eleventh in assets in 1975 according to *Fortune's* 500 list.

Another source of understatement of the industry concentration ratio arises because the distinction between national and regional markets is obscured. What might appear to be a relatively unconcentrated industry at the national level could be quite concentrated at the regional or local level. Examples are milk, bread, and cement, where in each local area only a few companies share the market. Since A & P has shut down most of its stores west of the Mississippi River in recent years, 1972 data overrepresented it in the West and underrepresented it in the East, a datum obscured by the national concentration measure.

A&P on the Rocks

Beginning in 1972 A&P launched a price-cutting drive to recapture market shares it had lost to Kroger, Safeway, Grand Union, and other supermarket grocery chains. However, the other chains often did not respond with their own price cuts. One cause for A&P's loss of customers was that it retained many older, smaller sized stores in the cities while competitors had been building larger units in the suburbs. By 1974 A&P's counterattack seemed to work, profits rose, and they began to raise their prices again to market levels. Indeed, on many items A&P's prices rose above their major competitors.

But in 1975 they again ran into trouble in sustaining their successful recovery. A&P responded by hiring new management, who concluded that the company was not keeping pace with trends in supermarket techniques. Many stores were dirty, poorly stocked, and utilized outdated or poorly conceived merchandising. Managers and checkout clerks were ill-trained. By June 1977, the new management had closed over 1,600 stores with the intention of closing 120 a year until 1981 while planning to construct and open 370 larger sized stores of 30,000 square feet or more. Most stores west of the Mississippi River have been shut down, with less than 2,000 stores remaining open in ten states, plus Washington, D.C., and Canada. By 1978, A&P's market share declined to 3.2 percent, down from 6.1 percent in 1976 and 7.69 percent in 1969. A&P's outlets were down to less than 1,747 by mid 1979 and more of them will be closed. A&P is now third in sales behind Safeway and Kroger.

The innovative trend in the retail grocery business seemed to be toward very large combination stores that sell both food and general merchandise. But now the more significant trend is toward limited-service stores which carry between 450 to 800 items and no fresh fruit, vegetables, or meat. Products are left in their original delivery boxes, so prices are lower. More than 12,000 items were sold in a traditional supermarket. A&P started joining into this competition after 42 percent of its voting shares were acquired by Tenglemann Group, a West German retailer, and A&P will open more than 50 of these limited-assortment stores as it tries to stem its decline going into the 1980s.

For all these reasons, high concentration ratios do not necessarily mean lack of competition, nor do low ratios necessarily imply a high level of competition. Nor does bigness necessarily mean monopoly and smallness mean lack of market power. The economy is dynamic. Over time while the largest 4 firms may account for 50 percent of shipments, they may not be the same 4 firms in any 2 years. However, some of the very large corporations have been in the top 10 for a long time.

TRENDS IN CONCENTRATION

About one third of the value of all goods and services in the economy in a given year is attributed directly to manufacturing. Economists agree that measures of *aggregate concentration* are indicating higher levels of concentration from year to year. However, the results on *industry concentration* ratios are mixed. In some industries the ratios are up, in others down, and often they are irregular.

Table 11-3 shows the concentration ratios are down, for example, in the production of cigarettes and aluminum. For cigarettes (2111) the ratio dropped from 90 to 84 at the four-firm cutoff. In aluminum (3334) it fell from 100 to 79 between 1947 and 1972. Cereal breakfast food (2043) went up from 79 to 90. Photographic equipment and supplies (3861) went from 61 to 74.

In food and kindred products (SIC 20) the concentration has tended to rise while in chemical and allied products it is down.

Trends in concentration are hard to isolate because of changes in the SIC code from time to time. For industries whose shipments are valued at $2.5 billion or more, concentration has apparently risen. The ratio has risen in textiles. Transportation equipment, as it relates to motor vehicles and parts, has also trended upward, but as it applies to aircraft engines, railroad cars, and street cars concentration has fallen some.

While industry concentration ratios have increased in the first half of the twentieth century, it appears that only a slight increase in concentration has occurred since 1947. In some places, increases are balanced by decreases in other places. Still there is good evidence of a definite increase in the very large industries. The fact that the aggregate ratio for industry has risen does not necessarily imply that the industry concentration ratios must have gone up too. Part of the explanation for this apparent paradox is growth of conglomerates. A company can grow in size by acquiring other firms in other industries. It can therefore increase the aggregated concentration figure without increasing its concentration in any one industry.

There seems to be no inherent and inevitable momentum in the U.S. economy that would lead one to conclude that monopolies, or a very few companies, will end up producing almost all the output in the U.S. by the end of this century. There is much effective competition perking in the pot of the economy.

MERGERS

There are essentially four ways for a company to expand and integrate its operations. The first is internal growth that comes about as the firm reaps the associated benefits from internal economies of scale. In earlier chapters we examined the cost structure of the firm and saw how economic efficiency could arise from scale economies. But there are other forms of expansion that are important.

Horizontal Integration

***Horizontal integration* merges two firms which produce the *same* product at the *same* stage of the production process.**

Integration can take several forms: when a company acquires firms which are producing the same product it itself produces, then *horizontal integration* exists. The merging companies both produce at the same stage of production. Examples would be when General Motors absorbed Pontiac, Oldsmobile, Buick, and Cadillac, and Pabst Brewing absorbed Carling Brewery. In fact, horizontal merging in the beer brewing industry continues apace. In 1932 General Electric and Westinghouse were ordered to relinquish control of RCA. Crown-

Zellerbach was prevented from absorbing St. Helen's in the production of unrefined paper, and in the 1950s Bethlehem Steel was prevented from acquiring Youngstown Sheet and Tube. Republic Steel came about from the horizontal merger of 30 small steel companies in 1900.

Horizontal mergers offer a much greater possibility of leading to a monopoly than do vertical mergers, since essentially a single product is involved.

Vertical Integration

Vertical integration merges two firms which produce the *same* commodity at *different* stages of the production process.

When two firms decide to merge and one of them is a supplier of inputs to the other, then *vertical integration* is the result. It entails the combining of firms which produce at separate stages of the production process of the same single product. Examples of vertically integrated industries are the large oil companies, which once owned both their foreign and domestic oil fields and continue to own the pipelines, refineries, and many of the retail gasoline stations. Ford Motor Company produces much of its own steel, has its own railroad and iron ore ships, and franchises dealerships; Pepsi-Cola owns Pizza Hut (they do not serve Coca-Cola); and U.S. Steel owns iron ore deposits, coal mines, and many railroad cars to haul ore and coal. In June of 1978, the Supreme Court ruled in a Maryland case that states may pass laws preventing oil companies from owning gasoline station outlets. Its effect is likely to spread to some other states. Vertical integration does not tend to lead to monopoly, since the takeover of other companies does not involve capturing a greater market share of the same final product.

Diversification and Pure Conglomerate Mergers.

Diversification merges two firms which may produce the same product but in different locations, produce inputs for each other, or produce unrelated products.

There is another kind of merger that has some of the characteristics of either horizontal or vertical integration, but might also possess little or none of their properties. These mergers are often referred to as **diversification**. One example of such a merger is where the integrating firms produce and sell the same products but continue to operate independently in different geographical regions. This is similar to horizontal integration in that the same product is being produced, but it differs because they do not directly merge their production activities. Instead, they "diversify" into different locations and different marketing areas. They do not necessarily take advantage of economies of scale in the sense of bringing the whole operation into one plant. You might say that it is as much an acquisition of one firm by another. Yet by doing so they do extend their market by diversifying geographically, thus increasing their market share.

Vertical integration can also be classified under diversification; for example, Ford Motor Company could produce its own steel. However, with vertical integration Ford only sells the steel to its own car manufacturing plants. But if Ford also sold the steel to outside firms, this would be diversification that goes beyond vertical integration. Ford is said to be extending its product line.

There is a form of diversification which involves a combination of two companies producing, for all intents and purposes, unrelated commodities. Thus, RCA owns Hertz, Anheuser-Busch owns amusement parks, Philip Morris owns Lowenbrau Beer, International Telephone and Telegaph (IT&T) has corralled Avis Rent-a-Car and Continental Baking among others, and Teledyne has acquired insurance companies. This kind of diversification is referred to as **pure conglomerate merger**. One purpose of a conglomerate merger is to stabilize the company's income over the ups and downs of the business cycle. Thus, if during the summer when people travel more RCA sells less television sets, it may rent more of its Hertz cars. But during the winter when people travel less and stay home more, sales of television sets rise while car rentals fall. Pure conglomerate mergers therefore do not tend to lead to monopoly power, because the product lines are unrelated.

The *pure conglomerate merger* combines two companies which produce *unrelated* products.

Department of Justice Merger Guidelines

Horizontal Mergers

1. Where the four-firm concentration ratio is 75 or more, a merger will ordinarily be challenged if the firms involved possess the following market shares:

Acquiring firm		Acquired firm
4% or more	and	4% or more
10% or more	and	2% or more
15% or more	and	1% or more

2. Where the four-firm concentration ratio is less than 75, a merger will ordinarily be challenged if the firms involved possess the following market shares:

Acquiring firm		Acquired firm
5% or more	and	5% or more
10% or more	and	4% or more
15% or more	and	3% or more
20% or more	and	2% or more
25% or more	and	1% or more

3. Other mergers may be challenged, especially those where the acquired firm has at least 2 percent of the market, if either the acquiring firm or the acquired firm is among the 8 largest firms in that market and the market share of the 8 largest firms has increased 7 percent or more in the 10 years preceding the merger.

Vertical Mergers

1. Mergers will be ordinarily challenged where the firm supplying inputs accounts for 15 percent or more of sales in its market and the purchasing firm accounts for 6 percent or more of the purchases in the same market.
2. Mergers will ordinarily be challenged where the firm which is purchasing inputs accounts for 6 percent or more of purchases in the market and the supplying firm accounts for 10 percent or more of the sales in the same market.
3. Other mergers may be chállenged outside of the above limits.

Conglomerate Mergers

1. Mergers will ordinarily be challenged where (a) the acquired firm has 25 percent of the market; (b) the acquired firm is one of the 2 largest firms in the market and the top 2 firms have at least 50 percent of the market; (c) the acquired firm is one of the 4 largest firms in the market and the top 8 firms in the market have at least 75 percent of the market and the acquired firm at least 10 percent of the market; (d) the acquired firm is among the largest 8 firms in a market where the largest 8 firms have at least 75 percent of the market.
2. Mergers will ordinarily be challenged where a danger of reciprocal buying might result.
3. Mergers will ordinarily be challenged where the acquisition might increase the acquiring firm's market power or raise barriers to entry.

Source: U.S. Department of Justice, Merger Guidelines, May 30, 1978, Commerce Clearing House, Trade Regulation Reporter, 1, Paragraph 4430.

In most cases in recent decades, America's largest firms have been created by merger and not through internal growth. Economists seem to agree that there were three major periods of merger in U.S. *history*. These were 1895–1905, 1920–1930, and 1950 through the 1970s. The first wave of mergers was rather massive, and the second wave was less significant, but mergers acquired some new zest in the third period. The first wave of mergers created many of the well-known corporations thriving today: Among them DuPont, U.S. Rubber, Diamond Match, National Biscuit, International Harvester, and Standard Oil of New Jersey.

The 1895–1905 period of mergers consisted of both the horizontal and vertical variety, most scholars conceding that horizontal dominated (steel and oil). It resulted in significant increases in concentration ratios in the U.S. The second wave of mergers was both horizontal and vertical, with a substantial rise in vertical integration above that of the first merger wave. The third wave of mergers led to over 25,000 mergers through 1970, and it is still going on. Initially they tended to be more the horizontal type, but in the 1970s pure conglomerate mergers have dominated. There is no question of the speedup in conglomerate mergers since the end of World War II.

CONCENTRATION: PROFITS AND PRICES

You might expect the profits of firms to be higher in industries with higher concentration ratios. There is some evidence for this in industries where barriers to entry are strong and where firms are fewer and larger. Still there remains the question, Are profits high because firms are big and few in an industry, or are firms big and few because profits are high as a direct result not of bigness but of being a superior competitor arising from better cost efficiency, that is, from lower unit costs derived from economies of scale? To show a correlation between bigness and higher profits is one thing; to explain the reason for the correlation between profits, bigness, and concentration is quite another and more difficult thing. The measurement of profit rates is therefore not clearcut or straightforward. High profits can occur whether industries are competitive or concentrated.[2] The theory is difficult to check out or refute, but strong feelings about it abound and presumptions of what the results should be keep politicians in office. There is a confusing maze of complexities connected with accounting conventions and the intricacies of tax laws. Also, profit rates reflect risk. The higher the risk the higher the profit rates must be in order to attract capital. Return on capital of a steady 10 percent on a low-risk venture may be more profitable over time than an average of 20 percent on a high-risk operation where returns swing widely from year to year.

What is the evidence on the relation of profits to mergers? Interestingly enough, when it comes to relating profit rates to merger activity the results

[2]For a brief survey of the issue with a selected bibliography see Harvey Goldschmid, H. Michael Mann, and J. Fred Weston, eds., *Industrial Concentration: The New Learning* (Boston: Little, Brown and Company, 1974).

suggest a weak relationship. One has to seek other reasons for merger activity like a desire to achieve growth, to reduce risk, to utilize existing tax loopholes not otherwise available, to raise the company's price-to-earning ratio on the stock, or a desire for managers to maximize their prestige, hence their saleability and salaries. None of these has provided conclusive evidence as a reason for merger, but the growth hypothesis seems to be the strongest reason.[3]

While profits are tricky to measure, prices are much easier to track. Keep in mind that high prices do not necessarily signify higher profits, nor lower prices signify lower profits. It is the price-to-cost relation that is important, as we have already described. But we can digress from profits per se to observe how prices behave in concentrated industries compared to unconcentrated industries.

In business cycle upswings prices tend to rise more slowly in concentrated industries. Conversely, in periods of business downswings prices in concentrated industries tend to fall by less or not at all, while the amplitude of prices fluctuates more widely in nonconcentrated industries. This observation is consistent with the price stickiness associated with oligopolistic industries. Because of scale economies, concentrated industries could have lower prices than if the industries were fragmented. The computer, refrigerator, and stove industries have undergone declines in their real prices (prices adjusted for inflation).

ANTITRUST

The *Federal Trade Commission* (FTC) and *Justice Department* enforce antitrust laws by regulating mergers and stopping price-fixing.

The monitoring and controlling of "unfair practices" and stopping those mergers that might destroy competition are activities that fall to those who enforce the antitrust laws in the U.S. There are both national and state antitrust laws. Our principal concern, however, is with the national regulation of potential monopoly. The watchdog function and enforcement of antitrust violations is the responsibility of the **Federal Trade Commission** (FTC) and the **Justice Department**. These agencies can deny or allow mergers and rule on some pricing policies and other transactions of business activity. On rare occasion they have ruled that a certain large firm must divest or break up into several smaller, independently owned units. Their intention is to preserve a competitive environment in which public welfare is increased by means of competition and lower prices.

History

Prior to the Civil War of 1860, the notion of market competition in the U.S. sprang from English common law that pursued policies to remove restraints on trade. These were, for the most part, developed case by case on a small scale in

[3]For details see Peter Steiner, *Mergers: Motives, Effects, Policies* (Ann Arbor: University of Michigan Press, 1975), p. 31.

response to private grievances. But after the Civil War, given the great immigration flows and the huge land, water, and mineral resources, economic patterns grew quickly and far beyond the small, individual, and local markets. New advances in communication such as the railroads, the telegraph, the postal system and the linking of canals expanded the size of the market to the extreme boundaries of the nation. Economies of scale became important requiring vast capital expenditures and government land privileges for right-of-way for the railroads. The corporation for the first time emerged as an economic threat to small, independent producers. Mergers and discriminatory pricing practices were rampant, so that by 1880 the oil and railroad industries were showing signs of concentrating as the business tycoons wheeled and dealed and did battle on the expanding economic frontiers.

In the post-Civil War period farmers began to complain of high and discriminatory freight rates as the financiers and tycoons maneuvered for position and advantage. The possibilities of pure monopoly were seen as real. As a result of pressure by angry farm organizations, the Sherman Antitrust Act was passed in 1890 after the Interstate Commerce Commission (ICC) was set up in 1887. The word *antitrust* derives from stockholders who received a trust certificate on transferring title to their stock over to trustees. These trustees came to represent stockholders for many different companies. This put them in the position of being able to control company elections and to run the combination of companies as one big business called a trust. The stockholders got the profits but the trustees acquired the power. Standard Oil, owned by Rockefeller, first implemented this controlling scheme in 1879.

Sherman Act (1890)

The Sherman Act added little that was new to antitrust legislation that did not already exist under the restraint of trade and tendency to monopolization provisions that had previously evolved under common law, and which were being ineffectively applied in some 18 states. The Sherman Act reaffirmed the prohibition of such practices as restricting output, partitioning sales territories, profit pooling, price fixing, and in general conspiracies that were aimed at keeping competitors out of foreign and domestic markets. What was important and new in the Sherman Act was that antitrust practices came under federal law as misdemeanors, with the federal government given powers of enforcement and authority to level fines and jail sentences. It was stated in broad language, and did not clearly spell out what constituted trade restraint and monopolization tendencies. Its purpose was to combat monopoly once it had become a fact as determined by the courts.

Clayton Act (1914)

The Clayton Act was passed in response to criticism that vagueness made the Sherman Act ineffective. The Clayton Act was intended to prevent monopolization before the fact, and specifically forbade price discrimination on identical products unrelated to transportation costs; exclusive contracts, where a seller could not sell to a buyer's competitors; tying contracts, where a buyer had to buy another product tied to the purchase of a given product; interlocking directorates, where the same person would be a member of the boards of competing firms; and interlocking stockholdings, where a firm would buy into the stock of a competing firm. However, the Clayton Act did not prohibit asset acquisitions; that is, stop a firm from purchasing the physical assets of a competitor. Exempted from the law were agriculture, some regulated industries, and unions.

Robinson-Patman Act (1936)

Sometimes known as the chain-store law, the Robinson-Patman Act essentially revised Section 2 of the Clayton Act relating to price discrimination. Small, independent wholesalers and retailers after World War I were confronted with survival by the emergence of large chain stores that charged prices that were "too low." The small stores argued that there was predatory pricing by the chains aimed at driving them out of business. The chains were able to charge lower prices because they were able to buy from suppliers at lower prices. The chains were volume buyers, which gave them bargaining leverage with distributors who desired their accounts. Suppliers gave chains price discounts on large purchases and for letting suppliers advertise their products in the chain stores. They also reduced costs to the chains by delivering to them instead of having the chains picking up their own supplies. The independents asked Congress for help. Congress responded, limiting the cost concessions provided by the suppliers—and the public paid higher prices.

Cellar-Kefauver Act (1950)

The Cellar-Kefauver Act closed the asset acquisition loophole in Section 7 of the Clayton Act and also prohibited one corporation from purchasing or using as proxies the stock of two or more competing corporations within an industry where this might significantly reduce competition and tend toward a monopoly. The stock restriction was necessary because subsequent court decisions had weakened a somewhat similar provision in the Clayton Act.

Shared Monopoly

Today, antitrust continues to be a lively football in the halls of the FTC and in Congress. In the 1970s the FTC began pushing the concept of a shared monopoly. The idea is that when only a few producers share a market they can act as a monopoly even without conspiring or colluding. If in a concentrated industry dominated by four big rivals a single product price is attained, then these firms may be setting anticompetitive prices even though their executives do not meet on golf courses or in secret. The pricing policies the FTC is concerned about are those of companies fixing prices by published price lists, price signaling through announcements in the press and in trade journals, uniform prices to consumers even where transportation and production costs of the rival firms differ, and price-protection clauses in contracts that prevent one producer from deviating from the agreed price by requiring that a discount offered to one customer must be offered to all customers. Some economists have taken the FTC to task, arguing that intense rivalry does exist in concentrated industries, and that a uniform industry price reflects that competition. Moreover, if large companies do collude, then small price-taking companies in the industry should earn above-normal profits, protected as they are by the price umbrella of the large price-setting firms. But research indicates that large firms earn higher rates of return than smaller ones, suggesting again that scale efficiency is the source of big firms' higher rate of profits. Of course, this need not rule out price collusion by the large firms. However, studies reveal that the more profitable companies grow faster than the industry as a whole does. Therefore, they must either be charging lower prices and selling more, or selling more aggressively, or innovating at a faster pace than their more sluggish competitors.

As for the closely related issue of corporate mergers which increase a company's size, this sometimes involves the acquisition of failing firms as witnessed when the prices of their stocks have fallen below the replacement value of their physical assets. Thus, conglomerates at times buy badly managed companies and run them more efficiently. In this situation, shared-monopoly attacks by the FTC can actually be twisted by critics into an example of the government protecting inefficient firms while penalizing the efficient ones, as well as penalizing the consumer indirectly, by causing prices to rise. Most often, acquired companies actually perform better after their acquisition. The ultimate cost of small-is-beautiful regulation may well be loss of efficiency, of price competitiveness in the international markets, slower growth, and greater unemployment. There are more companies today both large and small than there have ever been.

MULTINATIONALS

A *multinational corporation* is a corporation that owns at least 25% of an overseas corporation's stock or has at least 25% of its total sales overseas.

What exactly is a **multinational corporation**? The very name suggests global operations, a business organization that operates across the political boundaries of nation states. But not every company that has an overseas plant qualifies as a multinational corporation. Broadly speaking, multinational corporations are mostly private, not public, corporations. They operate in many countries; carry out research, development, and manufacturing in these countries; have parent and subsidiary administrative management; and have multinational ownership of all or at least an operating share of the stock. More specifically, a company is designated as multinational if it owns at least 25 percent of the stock of an overseas operation or if the sales of its overseas affiliates amount to at least 25 percent of total sales. In addition, there is the requirement that it operate in 6 or more countries and have sales of over $100 million abroad. An example is Caterpillar Tractor with 11 plants in 9 foreign countries in 1975. It is not one of the bigger U.S. based multinationals. A majority of the multinationals are U.S. based. General Motors is the largest but Royal Dutch/Shell is in the top 10, British Petroleum is not far behind, while Hitachi of Japan and Volkswagen of Germany hover around the twentieth largest.

History

Strictly speaking, multinationals are not a twentieth-century phenomenon. The British East India Company dates back to the seventeenth century. In 1850 there were about 50 U.S. corporations with about 25 overseas operations.[4] At that time the U.S. was an underdeveloped country.

Foreign funds helped finance the development of American railroads. The post-World War II period brought an explosion in the growth of U.S. multinationals, for it fell to the U.S. to launch the rebuilding of the war-torn economies of Western Europe and Japan, which sought out U.S. technology and capital. In the 1950s the growth of multinationals was particularly rapid, increasing an average of 10 percent a year until 1974, when they grew 25 percent. Thereafter growth slowed considerably, declining to 5 or 6 percent. This downward trend is expected to continue.

The Multinational Controversy

The existence of multinational corporations has been a source of heated debate. The pros and cons of some of the points of issue follow.

Economic and Political Power. Critics Multinationals make selfish economic decisions without regard for the welfare of the host countries, particularly if the host country is underdeveloped. Because of the multinationals' size and power they threaten the autonomy of foreign host governments. Motivated solely by growth and profit, they operate without regard for the development of poor nations striving for industrialization and a place in the sun of the modern world. "More is taken out in profits by the multinationals than they put in," is the rallying cry. Because investments by multinationals are capital intensive as compared to labor intensive, they do not create many new jobs. Also, being dependent, these poor nations end up with political debts owed to the global corporations, debts that might not be in the poor country's best political interests.

Defenders Multinationals do not bully the governments of any nation because they cannot. In the 1970s an average of 93 companies a year were nationalized by foreign governments. By exporting technology, resources, and know-how efficiently around the world, multinationals have been a major factor in blurring political boundaries of nation states. They have overcome many cultural barriers and through the universal language of business have made political and economic stability a greater possibility. The multinationals will prove to be the most creative institutions of the twentieth century in providing a common means to bring people of the world together in beneficial cooperation. Consider the developing trade between the U.S. and China. Certainly there are cases where multinationals have been harmful, where they have not utilized host country resources in the best way. But this was not done through malicious-

[4]N. Fatemi, G. Williams and T. DeSaint Phalle, *Multinational Corporations: The Problem and Prospects* (Cranbury, N.J.: A. S. Barnes and Co., 1975), p. 19.

ness, rather by misjudgment. As for excess profits, the local governments can increase taxes on profits, as many already have done.

The higher the risk the higher the profit rate in order to attract investment funds. As for taking out more than they put into a country, the multinationals often build schools, roads, and power plants where they set up business. This social overhead capital becomes part of the assets of the host country and is considerably larger than the profits multinationals received. Peru has, for example, nationalized foreign companies from time to time without any noticeable change in the income distribution of the country.

Multinationals also invest overwhelmingly in other developed countries. In 1973 around 34.7 percent of direct investment by U.S. multinationals was in Western Europe, up from 21 percent in 1960; in Canada it was 26.2 percent, down from 35.0 percent in 1960; in Latin America it was 17.2 percent, down from 26.0 percent in 1960. Investment in the remaining countries was 21.9 percent, up from 18.0 percent in 1960. Of this, U.S. investment in Japan accounted for 2.5 and 1.0 percent respectively in 1973 and 1960.[5] There is also reverse investment. In the 1970s Volkswagen and Volvo opened plants in the U.S. The oil-exporting countries have been investing in Western Europe and the U.S. Foreign investment in the U.S. is expected to continue to grow in the 1980s.

Loss of domestic jobs. Critics Labor unions vehemently contend that the multinationals export jobs and technology, sending overseas the new capital necessary to improve productivity at home that keeps prices of U.S. goods competitive in world markets. Furthermore, the multinationals contract work out to foreign sweatshops which pay the cheapest wages in the world. As a result Taiwan, Japan, Korea, and Hong Kong have taken over much of the radio, television, and electric components production from the U.S. The AFL-CIO estimates that since 1966 over 800,000 jobs have been lost because U.S. consumers prefer to buy cheaper foreign-made items. The result is a loss in labor's share of national income and weakening of unions' collective bargaining. Finally, the exportation of U.S. technology lessens U.S. technological superiority since foreigners can adapt it without paying the research and development costs.

Defenders U.S. multinational corporations have created more jobs at home than they have destroyed. It is true that in some domestic industries jobs have been lost because of overseas investment, but the overall effect has been to increase jobs in other more efficient sectors of the economy and to stimulate domestic growth. Moreover, a major share of the output of U.S. foreign subsidiaries is consumed in host countries. A 1972 Department of Commerce study concluded that host countries bought 72 percent of their own output, 27 percent was sold to others with 7 percent of that sold to the U.S. Of course that 7 percent has impacted strongly on the television, radio, electronics parts, and automobile manufacturing sectors of the U.S. economy. But U.S. overseas investment creates jobs at home because U.S. foreign affiliates often purchase materials and parts from the U.S. based parent company. Also, the incomes earned by foreigners working in multinationals and by domestic firms which

[5]Ibid., p. 49.

grow up to serve them create a demand for U.S. goods. Thus, the export sector of the U.S. economy grows and creates a host of jobs there. It is a simple fact that foreigners will not or cannot buy U.S. goods if we do not buy their goods. Exporting is one way they accumulate dollars to buy U.S. goods. In many cases the U.S. could not have exported these goods because foreign countries threatened to set up trade barriers if U.S. firms did not build plants overseas.

While it is true that wages are lower in Asia, this is no longer true for Western Europe and Canada, which account for a majority of U.S. direct investment abroad. Loss of jobs to competitors has more to do with both U.S. government and union policies themselves.

A study by the U.S. Chamber of Commerce revealed that for the decade of the 1960s 121 multinationals experienced a rate of job growth in their U.S. based companies greater than the national average. Only 9 multinational firms in the U.S. experienced declines in the period from 1960-1970.[6]

Tax loopholes. Critics As of this writing U.S. corporations do not pay taxes on foreign earned income until it actually enters the coffers of the U.S. based parent company. This keeps potential investment funds out of the U.S. Furthermore, any taxes that are paid by subsidiaries to foreign governments are deducted dollar-per-dollar as a tax credit on U.S. taxes. Suppose a subsidiary earns $100,000 in France and at 30 percent pays the French government $30,000 in taxes. The U.S. then taxes the remaining $70,000 at the corporate rate of 46 percent or $32,200. The U.S. government than subtracts from the $32,200 the taxes already paid to France. Thus the U.S. parent company only pays $32,200 – $30,000 = $2,200 in U.S. taxes, thereby receiving a $30,000 tax credit from the U.S. government. The multinationals should pay both taxes yielding a total of $62,200 or roughly a 62.2 percent tax. An acceptable modification is the tax deferral bill. Here the multinationals in our example would pay the $2,200 in U.S. taxes as soon as the income is earned overseas and not deferred until it is imported by the home company. This, say the unions, would supply more funds for direct capital investment at home.

Defenders Eliminating the tax deferral on income earned abroad but not as yet imported to the home company would certainly reduce U.S. investment abroad, but also reduce imports to the U.S. of goods desired by U.S. consumers. It would also reduce the taxes paid into the U.S. government. Nor would these foreclosed overseas investments be replaced by investing in the U.S., because there would be no market for these goods abroad as a result of the retaliatory trade barriers that would no doubt be instituted by foreign countries. Besides, there are over 25 double taxation agreements the U.S. has signed with foreign countries. If the U.S. repealed the tax credits for its multinationals abroad, so would other cosigning countries. World trade would suffer greatly and worldwide inflation would become even more severe.

Balance of Payments. Critics Already a serious U.S. problem, the balance of payments situation is worsened by U.S. multinationals exporting investment funds to be used abroad instead of invested at home for domestic capital proj-

[6]Ibid., p. 85; and the U.S. Chamber of Commerce, *United States Multinational Enterprise Survey* (1960–1970), pp. 25–30.

ects. As the foreign countries accumulate the dollars multinationals spend, these dollars do not get converted into a demand for U.S. goods, so the U.S. trade deficit grows larger. A weakened dollar caused by increasing trade deficits tempts multinationals to convert their dollars abroad into stronger foreign currencies such as the German mark and Swiss franc. This speculative activity by the multinationals guarantees further declines in the dollar against other currencies.

Defenders In the long term, profits return to the U.S. from multinationals' foreign investments as foreigners spend to buy the multinationals' products. The branch companies often buy inputs from the parent company in the U.S., thus causing dollars to flow into the U.S. The more dollars foreigners have, the more buying they will do from the branch company. A 1973 report by the U.S. Tariff Commission indicated that multinationals do not use their potential to speculate in currency changes and cause possible disruptions, though the temptation is there.

OIL

The U.S. oil industry looms as an example of both a concentrated industry and an industry with multinational corporations. While there are several hundred companies, the seven sisters (five American, one Dutch-British, and one British) dominate production outside communist countries. In 1900 coal accounted for about 71 percent of all energy consumed in the U.S., oil for about 2 percent. By 1950 the proportions were 36 percent for oil and 37 percent for coal. In the late 1970s the proportions were over 47 percent for oil and 19 percent for coal. Natural gas composed a substantial part of the remainder. The U.S. imports nearly half of its oil, most of it from the Middle East. Some is also imported from Africa, Venezuela, and Mexico.

Background

The emergence of the Middle East as the world's leading oil producing area occurred after World War II, though abundant oil reserves were found in Iran in 1908. After World War II there was an immense increase in demand for crude oil. Production in the Middle East fields was rapidly expanded. At this time so much crude oil had been discovered and produced in the U.S. that the oil industry persuaded Congress to enforce import quotas on foreign oil to protect domestic oil producers from falling prices that increased supplies from abroad would cause to drop further. Also, the Texas Railroad Commission was given regulatory authority over oil in the State of Texas and it placed restrictions on the amount of oil that could be pumped daily at the wellheads in Texas. These kinds of regulations spread to other states and helped U.S. oil companies gain significant control over the world price of oil. At first, in the Middle East, U.S. oil companies paid the host countries a yearly rental fee until oil was discovered, then a royalty on each barrel produced. Not long after, oil companies added a 50/50 profit arrangement with the oil producing countries. Had import restrictions not been allowed by the U.S. government, prices would have been lower, we would have imported more, and U.S. oil reserves in the 1970s would have consequently been higher.

Until the end of the 1950s the Middle East countries were satisfied with the arrangement—selling oil resources for which they had very little use. The Middle East accounts for about 80 percent of the noncommunist world's known oil reserves. But 1960 was a pivotal year. Market forces had forced world prices down, and unsettling price fluctuations occurred from time to time as instigated by the policies of the oil companies. The major oil companies, arguing diminished profits, told oil-exporting countries that they would be paid less for their oil. Revenue to the host countries in 1960 was 80 cents on a typical barrel going for $1.80. The revenue per barrel had been 86 cents in 1957. Unhappy with the oil companies' pricing policies, 13 countries created the Organization of Petroleum Exporting Countries (OPEC) in 1960. Later others would join, raising the membership to 24. They did not expressly have cartel (international monopoly) in mind. They were seeking to prevent price fluctuations that destabilized their revenues.

In the 1960s, to satisfy an ever increasing demand for petroleum at home and because conditions were favorable (the marginal cost of pumping up an additional barrel of crude oil from Middle East fields amounted to a few pennies, and U.S. reserves were beginning to dwindle) the U.S. oil companies got the import quotas raised, thus stepping up production abroad. OPEC members could not obtain further price increases above $1.80 a barrel because they could not agree to limit output. As demand increased, OPEC's position became stronger, aided by the U.S. inflation starting in 1967 resulting from monetary and fiscal policies during the Vietnam War. The OPEC members held their reserves in U.S. dollars. The U.S. inflation was eroding the value of their dollar holdings. There was also the matter of the leverage the OPEC members wanted to exert on the U.S. concerning U.S. policy toward Israel about the Palestinian issue. Contrary to antitrust policy, the major oil companies were allowed by the State Department to negotiate as a group with OPEC. In 1971 the OPEC members demanded and got a greater ownership share in the oil companies' production operations. They were still unhappy with the price agreements. Prior to October, 1973, as Table 11-4 shows, prices were around $2.30 a barrel. By the end of 1973 the price reached above $10 a barrel. OPEC was calling the shots. By September of 1975 the price reached $11.50 a barrel. In 1978 it was over $12 or roughly five times the 1959 level of $1.80 a barrel. By the end of 1980 it averaged about $35 a barrel.

You might wonder why OPEC members do not take over completely from the U.S. oil companies in their own countries. There is a mutual dependence between the oil companies and the host countries. OPEC members are dependent on the oil companies for technical know-how, for their high degree of marketing and distribution skills, and refining facilities not possessed by the OPEC members.

U.S. Reaction

In mid 1979 long gasoline lines began to appear, as they had in 1973, at the pumps across the U.S. because of a decline in oil exports by Iran. Saudi Arabia increased production to take up some of the slack. Gasoline prices reached a dollar, more in some places in the U.S., and the lines subsided significantly. President Carter in July of 1979 asked Congress for a standby rationing plan to be used if necessary, and decided to retain price controls on gasoline and fuel oil until October 1981. President Carter also asked Congress that a windfall profits tax be imposed on the oil companies in order to finance a public corporation to create synthetic fuel substitutes for oil. This was done in early 1980 but price controls remained. President Reagan removed the price controls in January 1981, but the profits tax remained, although weakened.

Entitlements

Government policy has paradoxically led to actually subsidizing imports of oil through its program of entitlements. Oil refiners who are more dependent on higher priced crude oil imports are entitled to payments or rebatable tickets from those refiners who on the average use greater amounts of cheaper old oil.

TABLE 11-4
Cost and Profitability of Middle East Oil Historical Data Illustrating Trends

	Year-end						
	1948	1951	1960	1970	1973[1]	1974	1975
Participation, Royalty, Taxes							
Host government share of production	0%	0%	0%	0%	25%	60%	60%
Host government royalty rates	[2]	[2]	12 1/2%	12 1/2%	12 1/2%	20%	20%
Host government tax rates	0%	50%	50%	50%	55%	85%	85%
Prices—*Dollars per barrel*							
Posted price (i.e., list price)	2.05	1.75	1.80	1.80	2.90	11.25	12.40
Typical sales price	2.05	1.75	1.80	1.40	2.30	10.45	11.50
Costs—*Dollars per barrel*							
Operating cost (Explor. & Prod.)	(.60)	(.20)	(.20)	(.10)	(.15)	(.15)	(.25)
Host government take[3]	(.25)	(.75)	(.80)	(.95)	(1.80)	(10.10)	(11.00)
Profits—*Dollars per barrel*							
Oil company producing profit margin	1.20	.80	.80	.35	.35	.20	.25

[1]June—prior to large price increases in October.
[2]Many original concession agreements called for a fixed payment in gold for each ton of oil exported. A ton of oil contains about 7 1/2 barrels or 315 gallons.
[3]Includes royalties, taxes and other payments, but excludes receipts from sales of government-owned oil to non-concession holders (third parties).
Source: Middle East Oil, Public Affairs Department, Exxon Corporation, New York, N.Y.

Under past policy there were two prices on domestically produced oil. Known oil reserves that are readily available and were discovered before 1972 were priced at $5.25 a barrel (42 gallons), while oil produced after 1972 was set at the OPEC price, say $30. At one time the large refiners had to pay an entitlement of about $3 a barrel (now 96 cents) to the smaller refiners who have to buy imported OPEC oil. Thus a small refiner who pays $30 a barrel, sells for $30 a barrel and receives $3 a barrel in entitlement fees and thereby earns a profit. This subsidizes imported oil to the tune of $3 a barrel. The biggest payments go to refineries with a capacity of 10,000 barrels a day or less. Refiners producing up to 175,000 barrels also receive a small payment. The aim of the rules is to protect the small 170 or so refiners by equalizing crude oil costs to all refiners. This encourages growth in the number of small refiners (refining less than 175,000 barrels a day) who the large refiners say are inefficient because economies of scale begin with plants refining more than 175,000 barrels a day.

Furthermore, because the large oil companies are vertically integrated, both producing and refining domestic and foreign oil, they end up paying entitlements to themselves. Those profits lost in production because of price controls are gained back in refining because of the entitlement rule. But for companies that are not vertically integrated, the rules shift profits from domestic crude oil production to domestic refining of imported OPEC oil. In other words, entitlements encourage greater U.S. dependency on imported oil. Domestic refiners, according to May 1979 data, used about 375 million extra barrels of imported oil per year as a result.[7]

Prices and Profits

Table 11-4 reveals that OPEC has acquired a majority 60 percent ownership of its oil wells over time. Notice, too, the change in the proportion of what the companies earn per barrel and how much OPEC receives out of the posted price of a barrel. Pure profits to OPEC have soared and those to oil companies on a per barrel basis have fallen. However, a more significant measure of profit rates is the rate of return on capital, also referred to as the rate of return on net worth or equity. Table 11-4 does not go beyond 1975 because the oil companies now own too small a share of the Middle East oil wells.

Table 11-5 indicates that the oil industry realized a higher rate of return than all manufacturing in 1950–1957. From 1958 to 1972, on the average it fell below the average for U.S. manufacturing. In 1974, as a result of the OPEC oil embargo, prices jumped and profits did increase sharply, going above that for manufacturing. The recession slowed profits down and oil profits have run at about 3 percent higher on the average than for manufacturing. Of course some individual oil companies may earn 20 percent and others 6 percent. In a period of shortage profits will rise, directing that more resources be devoted to increasing supply or finding substitutes. Current regulation and environmental policy hampers this adjustment.

In 1980, the windfall profits tax on U.S. oil companies was passed by Congress with the understanding that price controls would be phased out by

[7]Kenneth Arrow and Joseph Kalt, "Why Oil Prices Should be Decontrolled," *Regulation*, Sept./Oct. 1979; based on a forthcoming American Enterprise Institute monograph.

TABLE 11-5

	1950–1957	1958–1969	1974	1969–1978
Petroleum	14.7%	11.4%	19.9%	12.8%
All manufacturing	13.8	11.9	15.4	12.4
Difference	0.9	−0.5	4.5	0.4

Source: First National City Bank, *Monthly Economic Newsletter,* April Issues. Studies by The Treasury Department and The Federal Trade Commission are consistent with these figures, though not identical with them. See Sherman Clark, *Oil Industry Earnings 1950–1975,* Rose Institute of State and Local Government, Claremont Men's College, 1976.
*The source of the 1969–1978 column is The Federal Trade Commission, and includes coal companies because of industry SIC reclassification in 1974.

October 1981. Because of the rise in OPEC prices, much of which was passed on to consumers, and lagging supplies, Congress concluded oil companies were earning windfall profits—or what is called economic rent, a concept to be discussed in Chapter 13. The tax revenues are to be used to discover new, synthetic fuels and to pay fuel subsidies to the poor. It remains to be seen whether Congress will continue with decontrol in 1981. Uncertainty arises from Congress's perception of equity versus economic efficiency, that is, whether gains in efficiency from decontrol outweigh spending power losses to consumers from decontrolled prices.

Arrow and Kalt calculated that even without a windfall profits tax—which is directed toward equity—comparing the unfavorable income effects on the poor with the gain in efficiency to producers of decontrolled oil prices would create benefits to society that exceeded costs. This would result even when it is assumed that all the benefits go to producers, although they would not since decontrol would stimulate income generating investment and employment of benefit to both producers and consumers. The additional taxes generated could be used to compensate the poor, who are disproportionately hurt by the higher prices. The real issue, they argue, is not the political pot boiler between consumers and oil companies. Rather, it is the conflict of interest between the companies that are primarily refiners and those that are primarily crude oil producers, since controls subsidize refiners and punish producers.

Decontrol should stimulate supply because there are approximately 600 prospective petroleum basins in the world. Of these, 160 are commercially productive, another 240 only partially explored, and the remaining 200 mostly untouched. In 1979, discoverable world oil reserves amounted to about 1,142 billion barrels, of which the U.S. claimed 163.8 billion barrels, with 122.1 billion assigned to the Soviet Union. The Middle East recoverable reserves total about 562.1 billion barrels. There is still large, untapped oil in the world's basins economically feasible to drill for at higher prices. There are enough known natural gas reserves for at least two centuries and enough coal in the U.S. to last for at least 300 years at current use. The U.S. coal deposits amount to about 40 percent of the world's total. U.S. and Mideast government policies, not nature, will determine if there will be an energy crisis in this century.

Gasoline Prices: A Perspective

Compared to the price of other goods, the real price of gasoline fell by nearly 20 percent between 1950 and 1973. That is to say, gasoline prices increased but by 20 percent less on the average than for other goods taken together. This meant consumers had more of their money left after buying gasoline to spend on other goods in 1973 than they did in 1950. Even after the huge jump in prices in 1976, the real price of gasoline was 2 percent lower than it was in 1956. While crude oil prices had leaped 500 percent by 1977 over 1960 prices, the price of a gallon of gasoline had only doubled. However, by 1980 gas prices had tripled and led the price index.

CHAPTER SUMMARY

Production in some industries tends to be highly concentrated among just a few large firms. In other industries there are a few large firms and many small firms. And in most industries there are many small firms. When economists discuss the number of firms in an industry they speak of industry or business structure.

The aggregate concentration ratio is simply a measure of the proportion of the production that the largest firms produce in some sector of the economy. For example, in 1972 the 200 largest firms in the economy produced 43 percent of the total output of the manufacturing sector of the U.S. economy.

Industries can be broken down into smaller classifications according to the Standard Industrial Classification (SIC) code. And concentration can be measured by observing what part of the share of a market belongs to the largest 4 firms.

While it is easy to understate and to overstate concentration ratios because of the problems that arise with data, it is less of a problem to observe the trend in concentration. Over the years in some industries concentration is down. This has been the case with cigarettes and aluminum. But in the food industries it has tended to rise.

Concentration can increase as mergers take place if there is horizontal merging that is, merging of two firms in the same industry. Mergers involving vertical integration do not necessarily involve greater concentration. Vertical integration takes place when a firm mergers with its supplier (or its customers). Conglomerate mergers take place when one company acquires another company in a different product line.

Whereas there may be a tendency for firms in the more concentrated industries to earn higher profits on the average than firms in more competitive industries, the evidence is not conclusive. However, the prices changed by concentrated firms seem to fluctuate less over the business cycle than for firms in less concentrated industries. In some concentrated industries real prices have shown some declines.

Antitrust laws are designed in the hope that undue concentration of economic power will be prevented. Most large businesses will clear their mergers with the justice department to ensure that antitrust criterion are satisfied before the merger takes place. In the world of financial institutions any mergers must be approved in advance.

Multinational corporations operate in many nations, as their name implies. Whether or not they exploit the people of less developed countries is questionable. It is likely that they have helped the economic development of poorer countries in most cases.

The oil industry is highly concentrated in many respects and its concentration along with its regulation has created an extremely complex situation.

QUESTIONS

1. Between 1937 and 1972, the share of *value of shipments* in manufacturing of the 200 largest manufacturing firms increased from 41 percent to approximately 43 percent, whereas the share of *value added* increased from 30 percent to 43 percent during that same period. Furthermore, the share of manufacturing *assets* of the 200 largest firms increased from 46 percent to 61 percent.
   a. Suppose from 1930 to 1965 the large companies did less fabricating work on products they shipped than did the average-sized manufacturer and did more fabrication after that period. Which of the three measures of industry concentration would be changed, and in what direction?
   b. The fact that by 1972 the value of shipments and value added were both 43 percent tells you what about the structure of the large versus the average manufacturer?
   c. Suppose asset concentration was calculated by dividing domestic U.S. manufacturing assets into the total assets of the top 200 manufacturing companies. How could this yield a higher concentration ratio than either value added or value of shipments?
2. Often large firms specialize in producing only a few products of an industry. Suppose a farmer wants to buy a tractor where the output share of tractors of the 4 largest firms accounted for in the 5-digit code is higher than for the 4 largest firms in the 4-digit SIC industry, farm machinery and equipment. Does this understate or overstate the concentration ratio as calculated by the Census Bureau? Can you say in this case that the production of tractors is more highly concentrated than the industry as a whole?
3. a. Since sales in domestic markets also include imported goods, would this tend to overstate or understate the concentration ratio?
   b. Suppose the good is produced overseas in a factory owned by a domestic U.S. company. Would your answer change compared to *a*? How?
4. The national beer breweries have their own malt houses, where barley is soaked, sprouted and dried prior to brewing. Small brewers do not. What kind of integration by the large brewers is this?
   If Jack buys out Jill's lemonade stand, what kind of integration, if any, is this?
   Suppose Coca-Cola purchases Continental Can. What would this maneuver be called?
5. A local television repair shop owner is upset about the electronics shop down the street which sells radio and nonpicture television tubes at 60 percent of the retail price. It is able to do this because it buys the tubes from its own factory.
   a. Why is the television repair operator angry?
   b. What kind of market integration is the electronics shop engaged in?
   c. Who loses and who gains?
   d. Is this situation any different from the doctor who owns a prescription-selling drug store? Should it be allowed? Why, or why not?
6. How might transactions costs be a deterrent to conglomerate mergers?
7. The Robinson-Patman Act (1936) made it difficult for chain stores to underprice the local grocers without being called for predatory pricing. Aside from desiring a larger market share, what other reason does economic theory give for chains being able to underprice small grocery stores? Is this unfair competition? Define unfair. Who loses and who gains?
8. Many (but not all) studies indicate that price increases in concentrated industries

have been smaller than in the less concentrated industries. For example, aluminum prices have risen less than have auto repair prices in the last decade. What does this suggest about the comparative size of profit rates for smaller, less concentrated firms? Does it make any difference whether it is in the long or short run? Comment.

9. It is common to see many graphs showing the oil (and energy) "crisis" drawn something like the following:

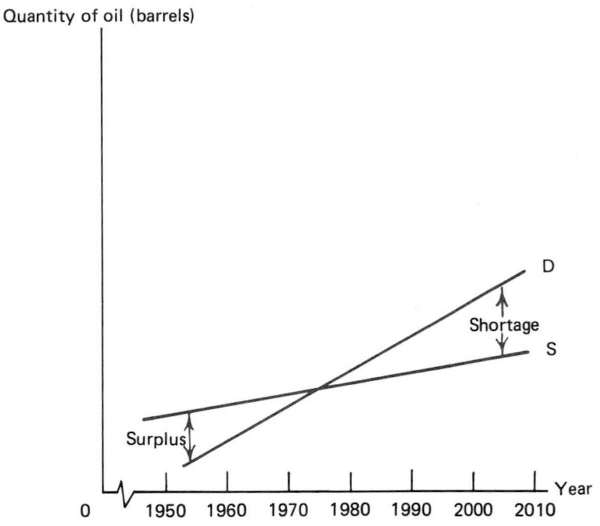

   a. As an economist, what do you see as wrong and misleading about this graph? What essential factor is missing?
   b. What government policies would ensure that what the graph is describing could occur in 1990?
   c. What is being implicitly implied about the inventory of oil (and other energy) resources in the year 2000, 2010, and 2020? Does a supply curve for oil depend on how much projected oil is in the ground or will be in the ground at some period?

10. Suppose the government issues gasoline coupons to consumers which they would have to turn in plus paying money at the regulated price of gasoline. Assume the regulated price is 90 cents a gallon while the free market price is $1.50 a gallon. The coupons are allowed to be bought and sold in a secondary market.
   a. At what price would the coupons sell? And what would the consumer actually be paying for a gallon of gasoline?
   b. What would the price of gasoline be if the government issued cash instead of coupons?
   c. Suppose the coupons were issued on the basis of every registered car a person owned. What would be likely to happen? Would you want to be an auto-salvage yard owner? Comment.
   d. Suppose 50 coupons worth $1 each were issued each month per registered car, and rationing of gasoline was expected to last for 3 years. What would the minimum value of a junked car in your salvage yard be? Would the actual price of gasoline be 90 cents a gallon to a customer who purchased two junks from you? Explain.
   e. Would the poor benefit from the regulation?

11. The cost of pumping a barrel of oil in Saudi Arabia is about 40 cents. But we know that oil rigs that pump oil are very expensive—into the thousands of dollars. How

can these prices be so divergent? What costs are significant here, and why is there no inconsistency in these prices?

12. Professor Adelman of MIT believes the OPEC oil cartel can be broken. He proposes the U.S. remove domestic price controls and set a quota on the amount of oil it wants to import; then auction off oil tickets in a secret ballot with the oil exporting countries bidding on them. This would force the oil price down as countries bid for a share of the U.S. quota. Critics claim it would not work because (a) oil is a nonrenewable resource, hence OPEC is not like other cartels, and (b) nobody would come to the auction because the U.S. is too dependent on OPEC for oil and OPEC certainly knows that. What do you think? Before answering ask yourself:
    a. In addition to OPEC regulating its oil supply, what else makes the oil expensive?
    b. If the U.S. stood firm, would there be a temptation for one or more of the 13 OPEC members to reduce their price?
    c. Are countries like people? That is, do they prefer to live off income or live off savings?

Chapter 12

The Labor Market

We're paying him too much, but he's worth it.

— Sam Goldwyn

PROGRESS REPORT

A. In earlier chapters we focused attention on production functions, cost curves, and the firm's operations under different forms of market structure. In Chapter 11 we looked at the extent of concentration in the manufacturing industries and examined antitrust policy and OPEC.

B. At this point we turn from the study of the markets for outputs to the study of inputs: labor, land, and capital. We focus on the labor market in this chapter and on the marginal productivity of labor. The equimarginal principle is then applied to all inputs in order to arrive at the least-cost combination concept and at the understanding that firms must produce at least cost if they are to maximize profit. Finally, marginal productivity and criticisms of it as a theory of income distribution are discussed.

C. In Chapter 13 the concept of marginal productivity is extended to the demand for land as a factor of production. The supply of land and the concept of economic rent is clarified.

A production function describes the relation between output and various inputs we call factors of production. We often classify factors in three broad categories: land, labor, and capital.

The price one pays for the use of labor is the wage rate. The price one pays for land has a special name, rent. And the price charged for the use of capital also has a special name, interest. There is one good reason these particular prices have special names. It is because these prices not only allocate inputs to alternate uses, but they also determine the incomes to the owners of the factor; wages are the income to laborers, rents are income to landowners, and interest is the income to owners of capital equipment.

The *marginal productivity theory* of the distribution of income to factors of production describes how wage rates, rents, and interest rates are determined in the markets.

We need a theory to describe how wage rates, rents, and interest rates are determined in the markets for factors of production, and therefore how factor incomes are determined. In line with earlier procedure we shall first assume that markets for factors of production are perfectly competitive. The theory is called the **marginal productivity theory** *of the distribution of income to factors of production.* Assumptions under which the marginal productivity theory of income distribution is offered are very restrictive. Our theory is not meant to provide an ethical basis for income distribution. However, it does offer some insights into why some factors earn the return they do. The theory emphasizes only broad economic relations and takes as given the institutional, sociological, and political structure. In this chapter we concentrate primarily on labor inputs, and we leave our discussion of land and capital inputs for following chapters.

DEMAND FOR LABOR

Just as consumers have a demand for a commodity, and will buy more of it at lower prices according to the law of demand, so too do producers have a demand for a factor of production, like labor, and will employ more of it the lower its price, other things being equal. In constructing a demand schedule for labor we are describing what determines the number of workers an employer will hire at different wage rates. True to the tradition followed in this book, it should come as no surprise to you that the employer will make a decision at the margin. The entrepreneur will not hire another worker if that worker has to be paid more than the revenues that his or her production brings into the business. That is, the worker's marginal revenues are compared with his marginal costs. In making this comparison, the entrepreneur makes an objective economic decision about hiring the worker. We are not concerned with whether the worker ought to be hired based on some noneconomic or moral grounds, say, to better distribute income and perform acts of social justice as individuals and/or groups perceive it. Such considerations are normative issues, so we shall focus on purely economic relations.

Marginal Productivity of Labor

As we learned in Chapter 4, diminishing marginal utility can be used as a concept to explain why the demand curve for a product is downward sloping.

The demand for labor by a firm depends on its *marginal productivity*. The marginal productivity is the change in total product per period from hiring an additional worker. It decreases as more labor is added, holding other factors fixed.

In a similar manner, the concept of **diminishing marginal productivity** initially discussed in Chapter 6 provides the rationale for the downward sloped demand curve for workers.

Recall from Chapter 6 that for a given input the marginal product (MP) is defined as the addition to total output each period from hiring another unit of input. Assume the input is labor, then

$$MP_L = \frac{\Delta TP}{\Delta L} = \frac{TP_f - TP_i}{L_f - L_i}$$

where f and i designate the final and initial values under consideration. When labor inputs L change by one unit, then $\Delta L = 1$ and the formula becomes simply:

$$MP_L = \Delta TP$$

The marginal product is expressed in physical units of output. For a simple example assume that total output is 100 units a day and this is produced by 10 workers. On the average these workers are producing 10 units each. Now hire another worker, the 11th. Output may go to 106 units a day. Thus, the additional output that accompanies the hiring of an additional worker is 6 units a day. This is the marginal productivity at the 11th worker. The total product has risen, but the marginal product is falling. Total product increases but at a decreasing rate. Falling marginal product as additional workers are hired is an expression of the law of diminishing marginal productivity.

The reader should not think of the marginal worker as less productive than any other worker just because marginal product falls. Any of the 11 workers in the example could be thought of as the 11th. Of course, we know that in real life different workers have different abilities and these are reflected in their individual productivities. But here we are abstracting from these individual characteristics and assuming that every worker is of the same skill as every other worker.

To convert from physical units of output to dollar revenues, the MP is multiplied by the market price P_o of the product being produced to obtain the **marginal revenue product *MRP*.**[1]

The *marginal revenue product* is obtained by multiplying marginal product by the price of the product.

$$MRP = MP \times P_o$$

In the example assume that the 100 units of output sell in the market for \$2 each. Thus, the total revenue would be \$200 per day before the 11th worker is added. When the 11th is added output rises to 106 units and revenues go up to \$212 since the additional 6 units of output are also sold for \$2 each. Thus, marginal revenue product is \$12 and is found by multiplying the marginal product of 6 units by the price of that product, \$2. With P_o fixed, when marginal product declines as more workers are hired, it naturally follows that the marginal revenue product will also decline. This schedule of declining marginal revenue product is the demand curve for labor, an example of which is

[1]The marginal revenue product is sometimes called the value of the marginal product if the product market is perfectly competitive.

Figure 12-1

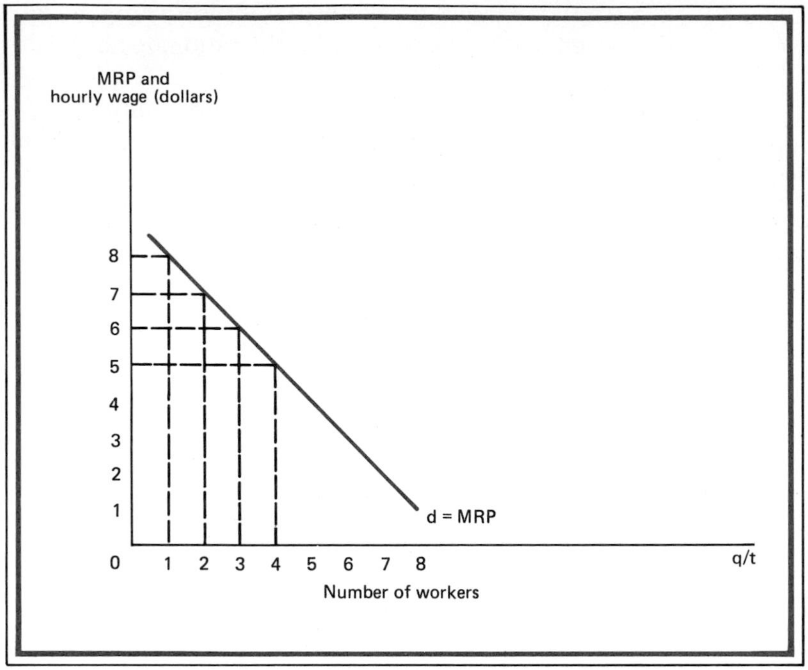

The *quantity of labor hired* by a firm depends not only on the marginal productivity of labor but also upon the price of the product.

portrayed in Figure 12-1. It tells us how many workers will be hired by the entrepreneur at different wage rates. As the figure indicates, the first worker hired produces revenues of $8 an hour. This is his or her *MRP*. The second in combination with the first has an *MRP* of $7 an hour. When working with the other two the *MRP* of the third worker is $6 an hour and the *MRP* of the fourth worker is $5 and so on. Thus, the quantity demanded of labor is a function of the *MRP*, or in shorthand notation, $Q_L = f(MRP)$.

The firm will hire another worker as long as the marginal revenue product of that worker is greater than the marginal factor cost, the worker's wage.

How Many Hired? The market wage is determined as illustrated in panel B of Figure 12-2. We are assuming that a perfectly competitive labor market is in operation. Since the employer is a perfectly competitive buyer of inputs, he is a price-taker, and therefore faces a perfectly elastic supply curve of workers for hire. Assuming the competitive wage to be $6 an hour, how does the employer decide how many workers to employ? According to our assumptions about economic behavior the entrepreneur wants to operate at maximum efficiency and at a maximum rate of profit. As we know, viewed from the product side, profits are maximized when marginal revenue equals marginal cost. But profit maximization also results when marginal revenue product equals marginal factor cost—which is derivable from the marginal revenue equals marginal cost condition. When the firm is in equilibrium, as illustrated in panel A of Figure 12-2, the price of the labor input P_L = wage = MRP = MFC. It occurs when the wage is $6 and here 3 workers are employed.

Why are all of the workers paid $6 an hour when the first and second workers have *MRPs* of $8 and $7 respectively? Remember that any of the homogeneous workers, working in conjunction with the other 2 workers, could be considered the marginal worker. Thus, each worker's *MRP* would be $6. Hence, this is the wage that applies to all of them in the group. There is no exploitation here; each worker is equally skilled and receives the same hourly pay.

The firm would not hire the fourth worker because marginal revenue product is less than marginal factor cost. That is, the fourth worker when combined with the other three has an *MRP* of $5 an hour, while he must be paid the going wage rate of $6 an hour. If he were hired his cost would be greater than the value of his production, and profits, while they may be positive, would not be maximized.

Figure 12-2 panel A also shows the total wage bill of $18 (6 × $3) to the firm per hour; what remains is the net income earned by the firm per period. What labor does not get is the income going to owners of other factors of production with which labor works, like payments to capital, interest costs on borrowing, rents on land, and the opportunity cost of the entrepreneur's own efforts.

Thus, the marginal revenue product curve is important because along with the going wage rate it tells the business manager how many employees to hire. It also indicates how the income is distributed among the various factors of production.

Shifts in Demand for Labor

If we take all of the marginal revenue product curves for all of the firms in the economy and add them together, we have constructed the aggregate demand curve for labor services. This demand curve is illustrated in panel B of Figure 12-2. Also in the figure is a market supply curve for labor. It is made up by a combination of population characteristics and the willingness of the people to work.

Figure 12-2

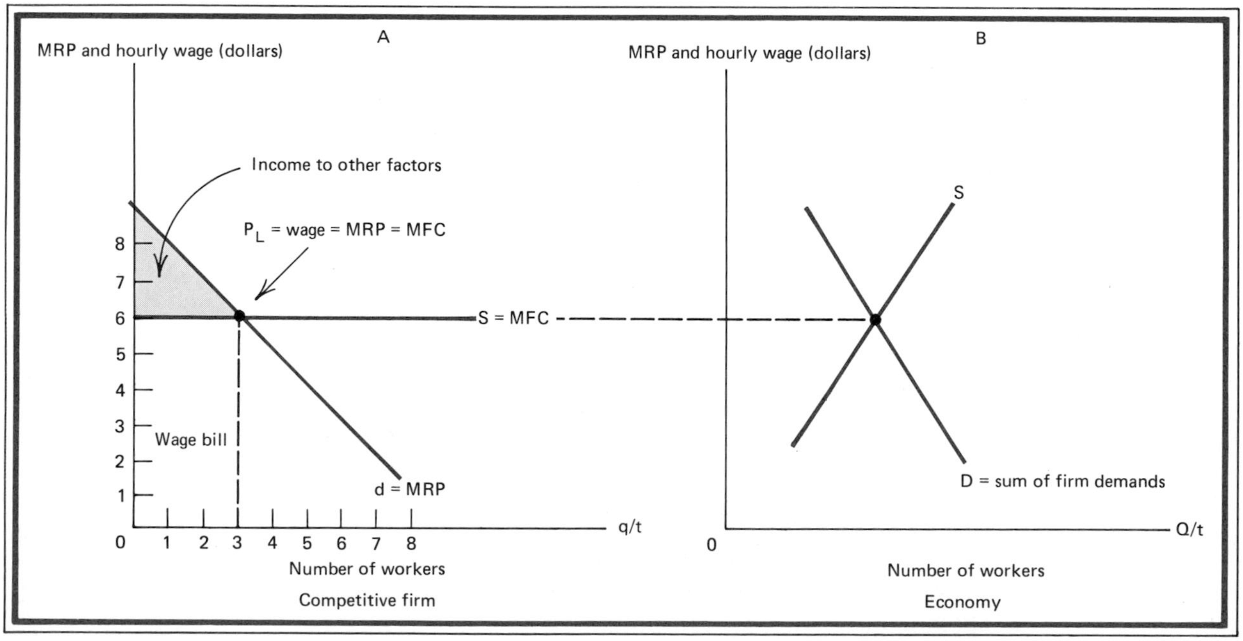

Thus, in Figure 12-2 the two panels both show demand and supply curves for labor. Panel A shows the demand for labor on the part of an individual firm. It is the marginal revenue product curve. The supply curve the firm faces is horizontal because the amount of labor it employs is so small it can buy all the labor service it wants at the going wage rate. Panel B, on the other hand, is the economy's demand and supply of labor and shows the result of all firms' demands and all the labor that is offered in the job market.

In panel A of Figure 12-3 the individual firm's demand curve for labor is shown shifting to the right from d_1 to d_2. This will occur if the price of the product sold by the firm rises. Since the marginal revenue product is the marginal product multiplied by the price of the product any increase in price will also increase marginal revenue product and the curve shifts. At each wage rate the workers earn greater marginal revenues for the firm.

In panel B the demand curve for labor is depicted as shifting left. This could occur because the price of a labor-saving machine falls. The machine is substituted for some of the work force so that at each wage rate the quantity demanded of workers declines.

Many other factors may affect the position and shape of the firm's demand curve for labor. It is generally believed that improvements in technology lead to a reduction in demand for labor. This is because a great deal of technological improvement involves the discovery of labor-saving machinery. It is also possible for technological development to be such that the firm's demand for labor will increase because labor's marginal product goes up.

The economy's demand for labor will, however, more than likely shift to the right because of technological discoveries. New labor-saving machinery may reduce one firm's demand for labor, but the new machinery must be produced and there will be an increase in the demand for labor by the firms that produce the new machine.

DERIVED DEMAND CURVES AND THEIR SHAPES

Demand curves for labor are called *derived demand curves* because they are *derived* from the consumer demand for labor's products.

Since the ultimate goal of all economic activity is to satisfy consumer demand, it is often useful to recognize that producers exercise their demand for various factor inputs principally because they are in the business of providing consumer goods to consumers. Therefore, we can think of the demand for a factor of production as, in a sense, derived from the consumer demand for the good that the factor is used to produce. Factor demand curves arise because factors are used to produce consumer goods. Thus, we say that the demand for a factor of production is a *derived* demand.

If factors are classified into broad categories, such as labor and land, then we do not have much insight into the shape of the demand curve. Millions of firms hire labor of one sort or another, and if wage rates rise by 5 percent, say, we really cannot say whether or not firms would hire 5 percent or 10 percent less labor service. That is we cannot say whether the aggregate demand for labor service in general is elastic or inelastic—highly sensitive to wage rate changes or insensitive to them.

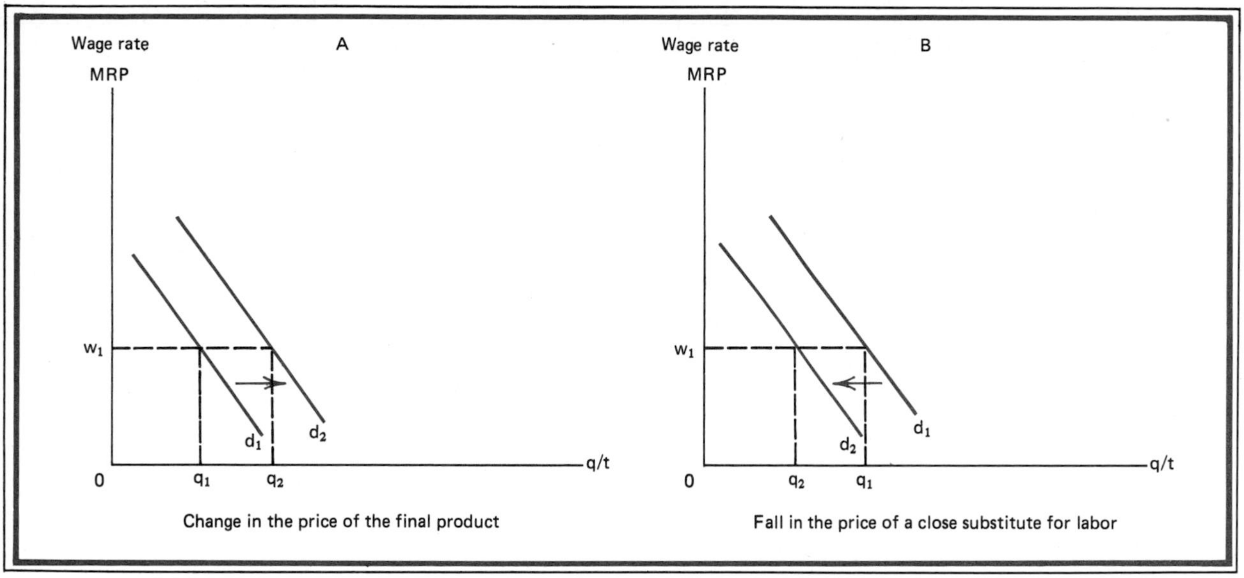

Figure 12-3

On the other hand, if we construct narrow classifications of skilled or specialized forms of labor service, then we can begin to infer something about the shape of the demand curve for that particular factor. For example, in France there is a handful of people who are called *noses* because they sniff perfume in the making in order to ensure quality. Famous exotic French perfumes could probably be duplicated elsewhere if it did not require the input of these highly skilled individuals. The demand for the services of these noses is probably quite inelastic—if their wage rate were to rise, it is likely they would still be hired to work nearly as many hours as they worked before the wage went up.

To say that factors of production are highly specialized is to say that they have few good substitutes. And, in general, few substitutes means that the demand will be relatively inelastic. Thus, just as we analyzed the shapes of demand curves for consumer goods, we can also generalize about the shapes of the derived demand for factors. Let us make a list beginning with the point we have just made about specialized factors.

1. The more specialized the factor, the fewer substitutes it will have, and in general the less elastic will be the demand for the factor. There is no substitute for bauxite, the raw material used in producing aluminum. Thus, the demand for bauxite by aluminum producers is surely less elastic than the demand for other factors also used in producing aluminum because other factors have substitutes and bauxite does not.

2. In the short run the demand for a factor is likely to be inelastic. But if a factor price rises, over the longer run the business manager will be encouraged to seek out substitutes. If machinists' wages rise, the firm will continue to employ the workers until such time that a new piece of equipment can be put into production that replaces the worker. Generally, the longer the time frame, the more elastic will be the demand for factors.

3. If the factor is a small item in a producer's budget, it is likely that producers' demand for it will be inelastic. Salt is such a small part of a consumer's food budget that its price could double or be cut in half and the con-

sumer would not change the amount purchased. Similarly, a small and standard bolt used in the production of an expensive consumer appliance costs such a small amount, and represents such a small part of the overall expense of production of the appliance, that the demand for that bolt will be relatively inelastic. The amount of bolts used will be relatively insensitive to changes in the price of bolts.

4. Because the demand for a factor is a derived demand, there is, in some cases, good reason to believe that the shape of the demand for a consumer's good *may* relate to the shape of the demand for that specialized factor used to produce the consumer's good. We used the example of bauxite above. Since bauxite must be used to produce aluminum, the demand for aluminum will be related to the demand for bauxite. If the price of aluminum rises and if the demand for aluminum is quite elastic, then the amount of aluminum bought will drop off sharply. And the quantity of bauxite bought by producers will also drop sharply. Thus, both the demand for aluminum and the demand for bauxite used in producing it are elastic. In general, we can conclude that in the case of specialized factors of production the price elasticity of demand for the factor will be a reflection of the price elasticity of demand for the good that that factor is used to produce.

The more elastic (inelastic) the demand for the final product, the more elastic (inelastic) is the demand for the factors producing it likely to be.

LEAST-COST PRINCIPLE

The most efficient input combination in the production function occurs when a dollar expended for any input adds as much to total physical product as a dollar expended for any other input adds to total product. Consider three inputs A, B, and C. The **least-cost** combination to produce the given output is reached when

$$\frac{MP_A}{P_A} = \frac{MP_B}{P_B} = \frac{MP_C}{P_C}. \qquad (1)$$

Using some numbers, let us say that the prices and marginal products of these three inputs are such that

$$\frac{4}{\$1} = \frac{12}{\$3} = \frac{32}{\$8}.$$

Since these three ratios equal each other we know that a necessary condition for profit maximization exists. These ratios say that an optimal combination of factors is being used. If the firm spent \$4 on factor A, it would produce 16 more units of output, and if it spent \$4 on factor C it would also produce 16 more units of output. No matter which input was expanded in use the dollars spent would yield the same increment in output. The least-cost principle turns out to be the equimarginal principle applied to factors of production.

Firms are producing output at *least-cost* when the ratio of the marginal productivity of each input to the price of the input equals that ratio for all other inputs. This is the equimarginal principle applied to factors of production.

But producing at least cost does not necessarily mean that the firm is maximizing profits. The equimarginal principle does not tell a firm at what level of total output to produce or what price to charge. Therefore equation 1 does not spell out the absolute amounts of output to be produced or the absolute amounts of inputs to hire. It simply says that no matter what those amounts are, this is the way to determine what combination of inputs to use in order to produce the given output level most efficiently.

But the firm also desires to maximize its profits. The maximum profit position was shown in Figure 12-2. There we saw that when P_A was \$6 then marginal revenue product equaled marginal factor cost and both were also \$6. In equation form this is $MRP = MFC = P_A$. By dividing both sides of the equation $MRP_A = P_A$ by P_A we can write

$$MRP_A/P_A = 1.$$

Profit maximization **occurs when the ratios of the marginal revenue product to the price of the input equals one for all inputs.**

If there are 3 inputs, A, B, and C, then **profit maximization** requires the satisfaction of the equimarginal condition.

$$\frac{MRP_A}{P_A} = \frac{MRP_B}{P_B} = \frac{MRP_C}{P_C} = 1. \tag{2}$$

This may also be stated in the form of a list of equations.

$$MRP_A = P_A$$
$$MRP_B = P_B$$
$$MRP_C = P_C.$$

To go from equation 1 to equation 2 we have simply multiplied marginal product times the price of the product. For example, if the firm hires an additional unit of factor A it may produce 4 more units of output, its marginal product. If these 4 units of product are then sold for \$6 each there is \$24 in additional revenue taken in by the firm each time period. Thus, the marginal revenue product is \$24. And \$24 is also the price of factor A. If factor A is labor then the daily wage rate might be \$24. The marginal revenue products of each factor input must equal the prices the firm pays for those inputs if the firm is to maximize its profits.

We wish to point out that there are a number of rates of output for which equation 1 holds, that is for which marginal products are proportional to factor prices. But given the usual conditions there is only one rate of output where marginal *revenue* products all equal their respective factor prices. That rate of output is given when the product's price is given. At the going market price of the product the firm will set the total output such that equation 2 holds.

To maximize profits, a firm must be producing at a *least-cost* combination of inputs, but it can be producing at least-cost but not be maximizing profits.

Thus, equation 1 sets the **least-cost** combination of factors and this is *necessary* for profit maximization. But introducing the product's price gives us equation 2, which determines the amount of product produced and hence the amounts of the factors of production used to produce that rate of output. That is, in order for condition 2 to hold, condition 1 must be satisfied. But it is possible for 1 to be satisfied but not 2 because the firm is producing too little output. If the firm is meeting condition 1, it is producing this output with the least-cost combination of inputs. However, it can maximize profits by hiring more of both inputs and producing more output until condition 2 as well as condition 1 is met.

COMMENTS ON MARGINAL PRODUCTIVITY THEORY

The criticisms of the analytical limitations of marginal productivity theory are numerous, but none has been strong enough to dislodge the theory from a position of preeminence. First of all the factor markets are assumed to be perfectly competitive; given the difficulty of acquiring information about people's abilities and potentials, discrimination, union quasi-monopoly powers and restrictive policies, perfect competition is a gross simplification of reality.

As a result of the existence of strong price-setting firms and restrictions imposed by unions and the government on working conditions relating to hiring, firing, seniority, and fringe benefits, employment rates do not always correlate well with wage rates in a manner conforming to a highly abstract factor demand curve concept. Nor is there a perfectly lubricated, unhindered flow of labor resources being allocated to their best uses and being rewarded accordingly with a wage equal to their marginal revenue product.

There is, claim opponents, no stability to the demand curve for labor because noneconomic influences dominate economic forces and cause shifts in the demand curve for labor. Consequently, firms and industries do not possess well-defined demand curves where the quantity demanded by the firm is associated with a specific wage rate. Wage rates can rise and the quantity demanded by the firm may not fall at all, or large increases in output and product prices can result without substantial change in the number of workers employed. Some economists believe that the firm's demand for labor is not nearly so much affected by wage rates as it is affected by projected sales volume. These observations indicate that the employer operates in very imperfect factor markets where marginal product theory is not applicable.

Another claim, and a strong one, is that employers cannot pay a worker his or her marginal revenue product because they simply do not know what it is. Employers find it difficult to calculate individual marginal revenues and marginal costs. They usually stick with the average revenue product for the group. When interest, advertising, pension, social security, and fringe benefit costs are included along with the joint costs associated with a multiproduct firm, precise calculation at the margin where $MR = MC$ is virtually impossible, and may be in and of itself too costly to try to calculate. The critics say that marginal productivity theory is thus not a good predictor of wage rates in the short run.

In response to the criticism that employers do not know what a worker's marginal productivity is, let us reflect on why the filling station closes at 7:00 p.m. instead of at 10:00. The manager of the filling station knows that the amount of income taken in by sales after 7:00 do not warrant the cost of keeping an extra hand for 3 more hours. This means that the manager is, in fact, estimating the marginal productivity of an extra 3 hours of labor service, even though he would not understand the term as economists use it.[2]

[2]For a thorough discussion of the validity of marginal productivity theory see Lester Thurow, *Generating Inequality* (New York: Basic Books, Inc., 1975), pp. 211–230.

In conclusion, while marginal productivity theory is not a good predictor of wage rates in the short run, it is a good predictor in the long run when enough time has elapsed for the labor markets fully to adjust to changes in supply and demand, which also incorporate the effects of union agreements and government rules and regulations.

Supply of Labor

The *supply of labor* is the quantity of work per time period that will be offered at a given wage rate; in general, the higher the wage rate the greater the quantity of labor supplied.

The supply of labor is a schedule of the quantity of work per time period that will be offered at different wage rates. What the actual wage will be in the market depends on both supply and demand for labor. Panel *A* of Figure 12-4 depicts an upward sloping supply curve of labor for a single individual. The wage per hour is on the vertical axis and hours worked per day on the horizontal axis. Notice that the curve bends backwards. This means that if wages rise to very high levels, people may choose leisure over work and actually work fewer hours than they would at a lower wage. Point *a* of Panel *A* indicates that q_1 hours of labor would be offered at a wage rate of w_1. As the wage rate rises to w_2, then q_2 hours would be offered. Work would be substituted for leisure as the opportunity cost of leisure increased. To point *c* the supply curve is upward sloping as the opportunity cost of leisure continues to rise. By not working, higher wage income is sacrificed and leisure becomes more expensive to consume in terms of opportunity cost. Beyond point *c* the supply curve bends backwards. As the wage rate rises to w_4, quantity of work in hours offered declines from a maximum of q_3 to q_4. Beyond *c* the additional income from working another hour each week provides less utility than the satisfaction received by consuming more leisure. More leisure is substituted for work.

Figure 12-4

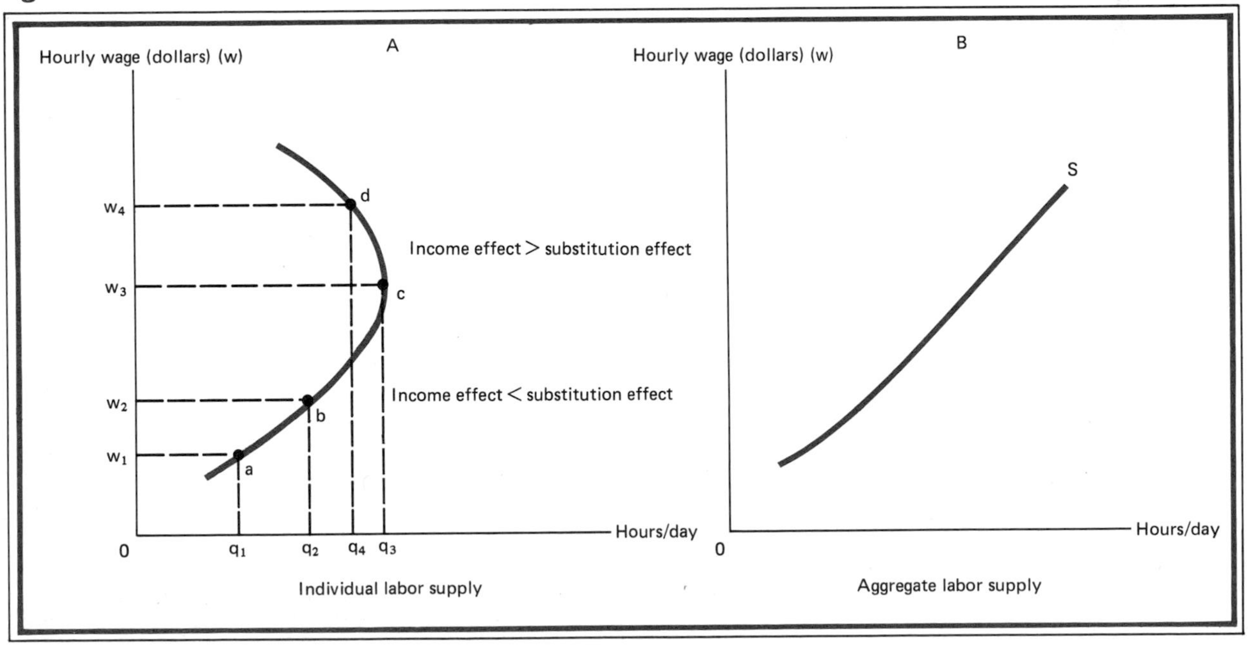

In panel *B* the supply curve for the economy—the aggregate supply curve—is not backward bending. The horizontal axis here represents the participation by the workforce. As wages rise more people are induced to work. The higher the wages the greater the participation rate. Although some individuals may be operating on the backward bending part of their own supply curve, for the economy as a whole higher wages attract workers. At higher wage rates more housewives and other part-time workers would take jobs. Some students might pass up time in school as the wage situation improves. Therefore, in the aggregate the supply curve of labor is not likely to be backward bending.

EQUALIZING WAGE DIFFERENCES

We observe that some people prefer to take lower paying jobs because of other nonmonetary rewards associated with the present job. Some jobs offer a more pleasant physical environment in which to live. Thus, many people prefer the coast areas of the U.S. over the midlands. Or, you may like your boss and the people you work with so you turn down a higher paying position. You can be more of your own boss with more flexible hours in another job. A scientist or scholar may prefer working in an academic environment on a research project rather than in a higher paying business setting. This suggests that there are nonmonetary rewards or satisfactions that could be called psychic income. When added together monetary and psychic income equal the total compensation earned on a job. The psychic income reflects an *equalizing difference.* Psychic income makes the difference in total benefits equal between two different paying jobs.

Nonequalizing differences are cases where even with psychic income taken into account, there are real differences in total compensation among jobs. Some jobs are not only better paying but more enjoyable than others. This concern fits better in Chapter 16 on income distribution, and we shall return to the subject there.

MARGINAL PRODUCTIVITY AND INCOME DISTRIBUTION

The worker's wage will tend to equal his marginal revenue productivity if firms are free to hire as much labor service as they wish to hire. This means that if a worker contributes $50 worth of output to the firm's total output then the workers wage will also be $50. Since his wage is his income from labor, we can say that under a free enterprise system workers tend to be paid according to the value of what they produce. This is a different criterion than that suggested by Marx and Engels. In the Communist Manifesto they wrote "From each according to his ability, to each according to his needs." This has very different ethical connotations from the statement "From each according to what he produces, to each according to what he produces."

Everyone knows that in capitalist societies there are many departures from the marginal productivity criterion. Also, we know that rewards in communist societies depart from the criterion of need. After all, if a communist society produces income in excess of what individuals need then what criterion is to guide the distribution of the excess production among citizens?

More will be said about this in Chapter 16 on income distribution. In this chapter on the labor market we merely wish to point out that the theory of wage determination, with the demand for labor based on marginal productivity, is also a theory of the distribution to workers of the society's output.

MONOPSONY

Monopsony **means that there is a single buyer in a market.**

Up to now we have assumed perfect competition. We now abandon the assumption that perfect competition holds in the factor market. Instead we shall assume that buyers or labor service have some power over the setting of wage rates. The corollary to monopoly in a market for a good is *monopsony* in the market for a factor. Monopoly means there is a single seller while monopsony means there is a single buyer.

Figure 12-5 portrays the situation of a monopsony buyer of labor. The S

Figure 12-5

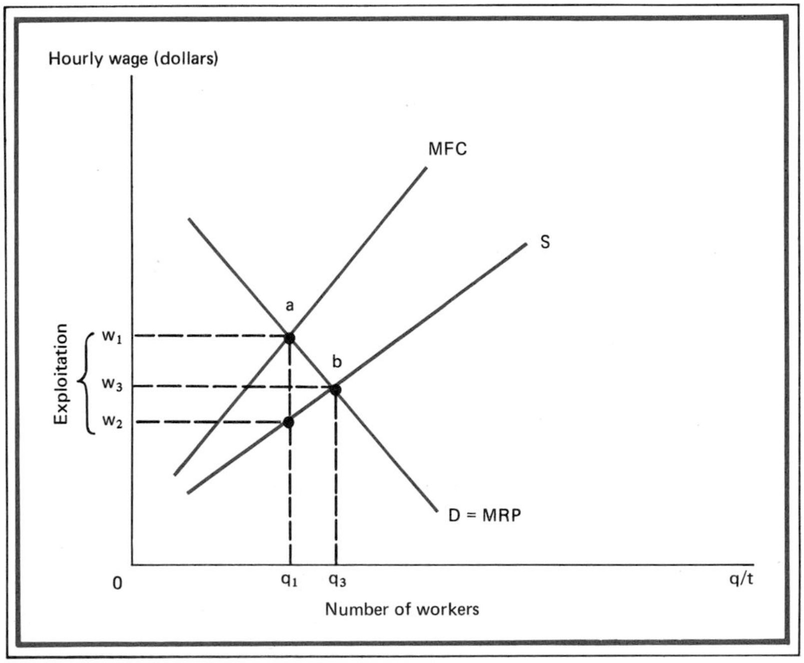

curve is the normal supply curve for labor, and *D* is the demand curve for labor by the monopsonistic firm. The perfectly competitive buyer of labor depicted back in panel *A* of Figure 12-2 sees a perfectly elastic supply curve confronting him. This means that no matter how much labor he hires he will not affect the market wage rate. But the monopsonist, the single buyer, faces an upward sloping supply curve of labor. Since the supply curve he faces is upward sloping, to hire more workers he must pay a higher wage rate, and this higher rate must be paid to all workers. Otherwise the previously hired workers could quit and be rehired at the new wage. This means that the marginal cost of hiring another worker is much greater than the wage that he himself receives. Not only does he get his pay but every other worker gets a raise too. So, to add a worker the firm suffers a high marginal cost that is greater than the average wage rate.

Referring to Figure 12-5, let us assume that the wage rate is w_2 and the quantity of labor hired is q_1. Each worker receives a wage equal to w_2. If w_2 were $10 per day and there were 10 workers, then the daily wage bill would be $100. Now assume the firm hired another worker, but had to pay a wage of $11 per day. But it will also have to pay $11 to the other 10 original workers. Thus, to hire the additional worker would require a wage of $11 for him and, in addition, another $1 for each of the other 10 workers. This makes the marginal factor cost of hiring the 11th worker to be $21, and not just $11. This high marginal factor cost would be represented by wage w_1 and point *a* where q_1 workers are hired. Thus marginal factor cost lies above the labor supply curve.

If the monopsonist firm wishes to maximize profit it will hire workers up to the level at which marginal cost equals marginal revenue. In this case it is where marginal factor cost *(MFC)* equals marginal revenue product *(MRP)* and is represented in the diagram by the intersection of the respective cost and revenue curves at point *a*.

The employee's marginal revenue product in this case is equal to w_1. But, the employer only pays a money wage of w_2 in order to induce q_1 workers to be on the job. Thus, the value of what the typical employee produces is greater than his paycheck by the difference between w_1 and w_2. It could be said that, in this case, the worker is exploited. If w_1 were $21 and w_2 were $10 as in our example, we could say the worker produces $21 worth of output but gets only $10 in wages. The extent of his exploitation is $11.

However, this exploitation by the employer can be removed. To see how, let us assume that government becomes aware of this exploitation and requires that the firm raise the employees' wages. Assume it is like a minimum wage law imposed on this particular firm. As wages were pushed up by law, the firm would hire more workers because the firm will hire to the point where $MRP = MFC$, which now occurs at q_3. When the wage equals w_3 the firm would hire q_3 workers. At this wage, the firm's marginal factor cost imposed by government of w_3 is exactly equal to the marginal revenue productivity of the workers. The workers receive in wages the value of what they produce. There is no longer any exploitation of labor and no longer any profits being earned by the firm. Thus, perhaps it would be better to view the extent of exploitation as the smaller difference between w_3 and w_2 than the larger difference between w_1 and w_2.

How realistic is the monopsonist model? These days it is not very signifi-

Rational Discrimination in Action

Can a case for discrimination be made on purely economic grounds? Many companies prefer not to hire handicapped people because they argue their marginal productivity is too low where a union wage rate is in effect. But some firms do specialize in hiring handicapped people in nonunion shops. Assume they are equally as productive as normal workers. For example, some firms in New York City hire blind people to do piecework. As a result many of these workers receive less than the minimum wage if their wages are calculated on an hourly basis. Consider the situation illustrated in the figure below. The S_N curve is the supply curve faced by a firm which is a competitive employer of normal labor. The competitive wage of $4 is determined where $D = S_N$ at c. Assume the firm is the only employer in town of handicapped workers. It is therefore a monopsonist regarding the employment of handicapped workers. It faces an upward sloping supply curve for handicapped people S_H and a MFC_H curve marginal to it. Will it hire only handicapped people? If not, how many relative to other workers? The handicapped fit the requirement for a monopsonist to exist because they lack mobility and other job options. We assume the firm starts out hiring handicapped workers at below the competitive wage that exists for other workers. It continues to hire handicapped workers until the point is reached at a where the $MFC_H = MFC_N = MRP$. Thus q_H are hired, but they are not paid their marginal revenue product of $4 an hour; instead, according to the supply curve S_H, they are paid $3 an hour indicated by point d. Beyond q_H only normal workers are hired, $q_N - q_H$ of them, and handicapped applicants are discriminated against in hiring thereafter. In this way the employer maximizes his profits.

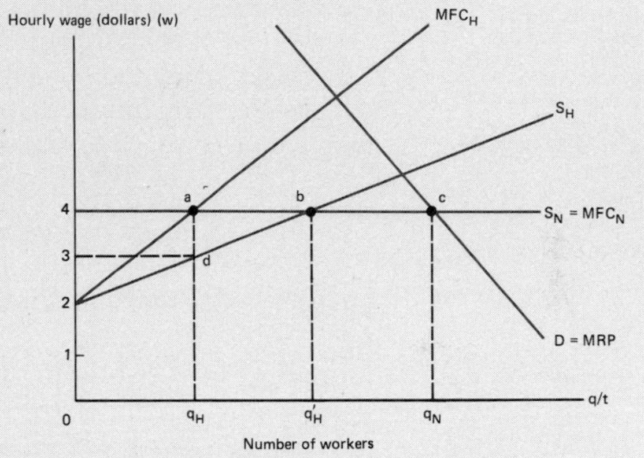

If another competitor entered the market and paid handicapped workers the competitive rate of $4 an hour, the discriminating firm would be forced to pay $4 to get handicapped workers. He would then move to point b along S_H and hire more of them to q'_H, at which point he is indifferent toward the hiring of normal and handicapped workers.

If a firm is the single buyer of a service, it can pay lower wages than those in a competitive market; today's labor mobility makes this situation less common today.

cant. In the past when transportation facilities were minimal and incomes were low, poor people did not find it as easy to move to other areas and find new jobs. They were more likely to be stuck in small rural towns where one company hired most of the locals. There are some special cases where at first glance monopsony might seem to be applicable. For instance, the Hanford Nuclear Works employs most of the engineering and technical labor force in Richland, Washington. Yet companies there do not have monopsony leverage. Workers are highly skilled and cannot make the same wages taking other jobs in town, but neither can the company draw upon the local labor to replace them. For such skilled people the job market is often national in scope, and information about openings elsewhere is good. Moreover, these employees have sufficient income to make the cost of traveling to other jobs not prohibitive. Indeed, such costs are often paid by the new employer. We conclude, therefore, that monopsony power in labor markets was more important in earlier days than it is now.

CHAPTER SUMMARY

The demand for labor by a firm depends on the marginal productivity of labor service, that is, it depends on the added output following from an increase in the amount of labor service hired. As more labor is hired its marginal productivity declines.

The quantity of labor hired by a business firm will depend not only on the marginal productivity of labor but also upon the wage rate labor receives and the price of the product that labor produces. The formula is $MP_L \times P_O = P_L$. The left hand side of this formula is called the marginal revenue productivity of labor (*MRP*).

Demand curves for labor are called derived demand curves because they are derived from the consumer demand for those goods that labor effort produces.

Maximizing output and the firm's profit requires that the equimarginal principle is met. The principle is that the ratio of the marginal revenue product of a factor of production to its price is the same for all factors of production that the firm hires.

$$\frac{MP_A}{P_A} = \frac{MP_B}{P_B} = \ldots \text{ for all factors, in order to minimize costs.}$$

In order to maximize profits

$$\frac{MRP_A}{P_A} = \frac{MRP_B}{P_B} \ldots = 1, \text{ for all factors.}$$

To understand the determination of wage rates it is necessary to understand not only how the demand curve is derived, but also where the supply curve comes from. In terms of work and leisure, economists believe that the labor supply curve for an individual is backward bending. Usually, if wages rise, people work more, but if wage rates rise to very high levels, workers will start to work fewer hours rather than more. But when all the individual supply curves of all the workers in the community are added together, economists believe that the supply curve of labor for the economy is positively sloped. Higher wage rates will, in general, induce people to work longer hours.

Monopsony is the case of the single buyer of a service. If one company owned a town, it could make itself the only buyer of labor in that town. Monopsonists will offer a lower wage than would exist if the labor market were competitive, in the same way that a monopolist will charge a higher price for a good than would be set under competition. But in today's world with modern communications, there is little reason to suppose that any one buyer of labor has a significant degree of monopsony power.

QUESTIONS

1. Why is the short-run demand curve for a factor of production downward sloping? What is meant by the short run?
2. Why is the supply curve faced by a perfectly competitive buyer of a factor perfectly elastic? Suppose it is not; what would that imply?
3. Why would a firm that is losing money hire another worker in the short run?
4. Does marginal productivity theory have more predictive power in the short or the long run? Why?

5. Using marginal productivity theory, what do you make of the oft repeated proposal of spreading the work by having people work shorter hours and share the same job?
6. Does marginal productivity theory suggest that there is a limit to the share of national income that can go to labor? What would occur if unions tried to push labor's share beyond that limit?
7. Can you apply marginal productivity theory to the grade you get in this course? Can you also apply the backward bending supply concept to your effort in this course if the instructor says nobody will get less than a B if he or she comes to all the classes?
8. Smith prefers the day shift even though the night shift pays more. Is Smith's income less for this reason? About what income are you talking?
9. Dr. Dip made $100,000 more than the average doctor did last year. He decided to reduce his working hours and play more golf even after the passage of the Medicare law, even though the number of hours practiced by the average doctor rose at that time. What is the cost to Dr. Dip of playing more golf? Is Dr. Dip violating the law of supply whereas the average doctor is not? Can you reconcile this apparent inconsistency?
10. If two factors X and Y are purchased at prices P_X and P_Y respectively such that $MRP_X/MRP_Y < P_X/P_Y$, then total output can be increased by using more of X and less of Y. True or false? Explain.
11. If two inputs X and Y both sell for the same price, then the least-cost principle is satisfied if each factor X and Y is used in equal amounts in the production process. Do you agree? Explain.
12. Before 1974 Burlington Textile Company was the major employer in Fayetteville, North Carolina. Now it competes for workers with DuPont, Rohm & Haas, and Black & Decker. Burlington used to pay an average $3 an hour compared to $4 for all manufacturing. To ease its employment problem Burlington raised its wage rates by 13.3 percent in one year. A spokesman for the company said, "We'll solve our labor problem by modernizing our plant and minimizing the need for less skilled jobs."
    a. Analyze the situation assuming Burlington was a monopsonist. Then illustrate what happens when new firms sprang up in the city?
    b. Is your analysis consistent with Burlington's desire to modernize and employ fewer but more highly skilled workers?
13. One student studies 20 hours a week on his physics course and receives a C grade. Another student studies 8 hours a week and misses a few classes but receives an A grade. The C student complains to the professor saying he worked hard and deserves an A too. Is this situation any different from the roofer who sweats in 90-degree heat at $8 an hour while a corporate consultant sits in an air-conditioned office for $300 a day? Is the roofer paid less than he is worth since he worked so hard and the consultant paid more than he is worth since he "didn't lift a finger"? You might first ask yourself (a) what is the roofer worth? The consultant? (b) What is fair? Is fairness implied in the marginal productivity theory in that one is paid in proportion to what one produces? Does the consultant really produce? If not, then what is the consultant being paid for?
14. Assume all workers are homogeneous. A small producer and shipper of one-gallon metal cans works up data for his plant and equipment as shown at the top of page 330.
    a. What is the marginal productivity at the 3rd worker? At the 6th worker?
    b. What is the average productivity at the 3rd worker? At the 6th worker? Why does the question say *at* rather than *of* the 3rd or 6th worker?
    c. At which worker hired does diminishing marginal productivity first occur? For which worker does average productivity first begin to decline?
    d. Suppose each worker is paid $80 a day and that each can sells for $1.10. How many workers should the owner hire in order to maximize profits?

Number of workers	Cans per day
0	0
1	50
2	120
3	220
4	300
5	360
6	400
7	430
8	450

e. Suppose the union gets wages raised to $90 a day, what number of workers would maximize profits?

f. Suppose, instead, the price of cans goes to $1.40. How many hired workers would maximize profits?

g. Assume the owner is confronted with the following options, where wages are $80 a day and containers are selling for $1.10 each as in part *d*. Which option should the owner choose?
   1. Hire another worker who will produce *100* more cans a day.
   2. Buy a machine that depreciates $4 a day and would increase product by 6 cans a day.
   3. Rent space from the adjacent warehouse for $70 a day with production increased by 50 boxes a day.

h. After the changes in g are calculated, what further changes would the owner have to make in order to realize the least-cost combination of inputs? That is, indicate whether he would have to increase or decrease in each case the amount of machines, workers, or space. What criterion should be used to make his judgment?

15. In a competitive market the product price is 50 cents and input prices are $P_A = \$5$ and $P_B = \$8$.

(1) Inputs of A	(2) MPP_A	(3) Inputs of B	(4) MPP_B	(5) MRP_A	(6) MRP_B
1	35	1	52	17.5	26
2	30	2	48	15	24
3	25	3	44	12.5	22
4	20	4	40	10	20
5	15	5	34	7.5	17
6	10	6	28	5	14
7	5	7	20	2.5	10
8	1	8	16	.5	8

What is the least-cost combination of factors needed to produce 274 units of output? What combination of factors will maximize profits? What is output then? Are factors still being combined efficiently at that output?

16. The supply curve of labor for an industry will ordinarily be more elastic than the supply curve of labor for the whole economy, and the supply curve of labor for a given industry will ordinarily be more elastic than the supply curve of labor for a given locality. Do you agree? Comment.

Chapter 13

Land, Rent, and Profit

The spirit of property doubles man's strength.

— Voltaire (1769)

He that hath nothing is frightened of nothing.

— T. Fuller (1732)

PROGRESS REPORT

A. In Chapter 12 we discussed various aspects of the factor input, labor. The wage of labor was shown to be equal to its marginal revenue product in a competitive factor market.

B. In this chapter we find that the marginal revenue product of land is equal to rental payments. We examine the notion of pure economic rent where owners of both the factor, land, and of labor services receive income beyond these factors' opportunity costs even when the factor market is perfectly competitive. We then investigate the different definitions of profit and the important function of profit in allocating resources efficiently.

C. In Chapter 14 we shall examine the marginal revenue product of capital — the rate of interest — and see how the value of long-lived capital assets is determined.

In a competitive market, rent paid for land equals its *marginal revenue product.*

Rent payments for the use of land are made to owners of land. The greater the demand for the use of the land, the greater the rent, that is, the greater the price charged for the use of land. In equilibrium where the supply and demand for the land are equal the rental payments equal the **marginal revenue product**.

How is land priced? It is not man-made and therefore involves no cost of production to bring it into existence. Thus, the amount of land in the economy is essentially fixed (as we shall see, this is not quite true). For the whole economy the supply of land, therefore, is perfectly inelastic, as illustrated by the solid line in panel A of Figure 13-1. But it is important to realize that the supply of land *in a particular* use is not perfectly inelastic, as shown in panel B. How much land is actually made available for a particular use depends on the price that would be paid to use that land for a specific purpose.

You might wonder at this point about the relation between the price of a plot of land and its rental price. One must keep in mind the distinction between a stock (the land unit) and a flow (the services the land provides over time). Land is a physical asset that yields a flow of services over time, for which a rental payment is required of the user by the owner. With this in mind it is important to explain what the graphs for land really mean. The graphs can be constructed showing the supply and demand curves for a stock—a piece of land at a given time, for example, now. The supply and demand determine the price of the stock or asset as a whole entity. The graphs can also express the supply and demand of flows of service yielded by the land that determine a rental price per period for the use of the land—not its selling price. Rental payments for the services of the land yield an income stream over time. We choose the flow approach so that the vertical axis is expressed in terms of the rental payment per period for the use of the "acreage flows," that is, acreage used for the year. And the horizontal axis indicates the quantity of acreage demanded over the period. In the case of the demand for the quantity of serv-

Figure 13-1

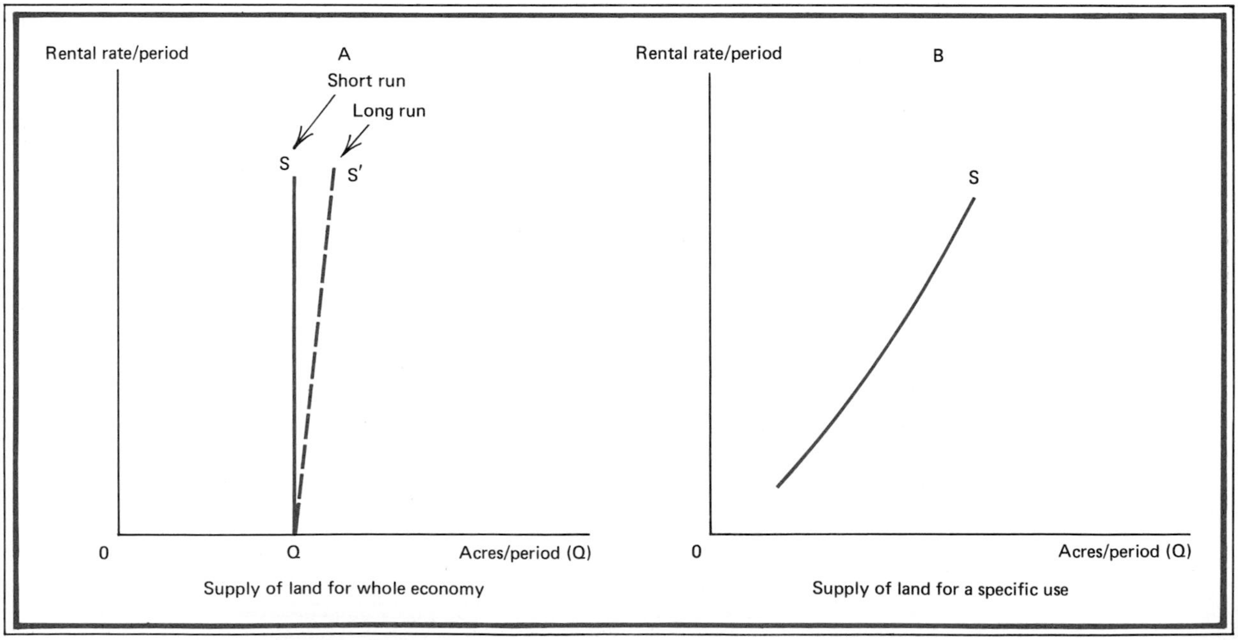

ices of the land we should note that this demand derives from the demand for the products produced on it. For this reason the graphs used here can be labeled to indicate the demand for land to be used to produce certain products. The demand for acreage flows provided by the land is a derived demand, stemming from the demand for the flow of the commodity produced on the land.

In Chapter 14 we shall explain how to determine the price of the stock (the land) based on the flows of income (rental of acreage) the stock earns over time.

In panel A of Figure 13-1, the supply of land in the U.S. is shown to be perfectly inelastic. However, in the long run this is not necessarily true. The dashed long-run supply curve S′ is not perfectly inelastic. In the long run it is possible for some lands to be reclaimed: water can be pumped, the swamps can be filled with garbage and packed with dirt. The Dutch are famous for building dikes to hold back the North Sea, thereby creating more land mass in their densely populated country. They even have small vegetable gardens interspersed between airplane landing and takeoff paths at some airports.

But the fixed land mass can be used for many purposes. It can be used for recreation, military training, weapons testing, housing, farming, mineral sources, historic landmarks, and wilderness areas. Where there is private ownership if the demand for housing increases because of population growth and the demand for farmland decreases because fewer farms are needed to grow even more food, prices of land for housing will rise and farmland prices will fall. More land becomes available in the market for housing and less for farming. Thus, as the price rises the quantity of land supplied for housing development increases according to the principle of supply. Hence, the supply of land for housing is not vertical, as shown by panel B of Figure 13-1; nor is it perfectly inelastic in supply for purposes of farming either. In some parts of the country land is desired for ski resorts. If the market looks strong enough, buyers will bid land away from housing developers to supply recreational services. The higher the demand for skiing facilities, the higher the price developers will be willing to bid for that land for that purpose. Thus, the quantity supplied of skiing resort acreage will increase with a rising price in accordance with the law of supply. People in the real estate business refer to land being put to its highest-valued use.

Defining Economic Rent

The meaning of the word *rent,* as used here, is nearly the same as its meaning in common usage, where it signifies payment for the use of an asset, like renting a car or the monthly payments for shelter services made to landlords. But for an economist the phrase "economic rent" has a unique connotation. In a world of perfect competition price will equal marginal costs, and these costs are, of course, opportunity costs. *Economic rents are incomes received that are greater than necessary to bring forth the services of the factor of production.* Rent tends to arise when the factor in question is fixed in supply or highly specialized or unique in some sense. Let us examine a few examples to impart the meaning of economic rent more intuitively.

Example 1 Panel A in Figure 13-2 depicts an individual farmer with a fixed acreage of land. The supply curve of his land is perfectly inelastic in a perfectly

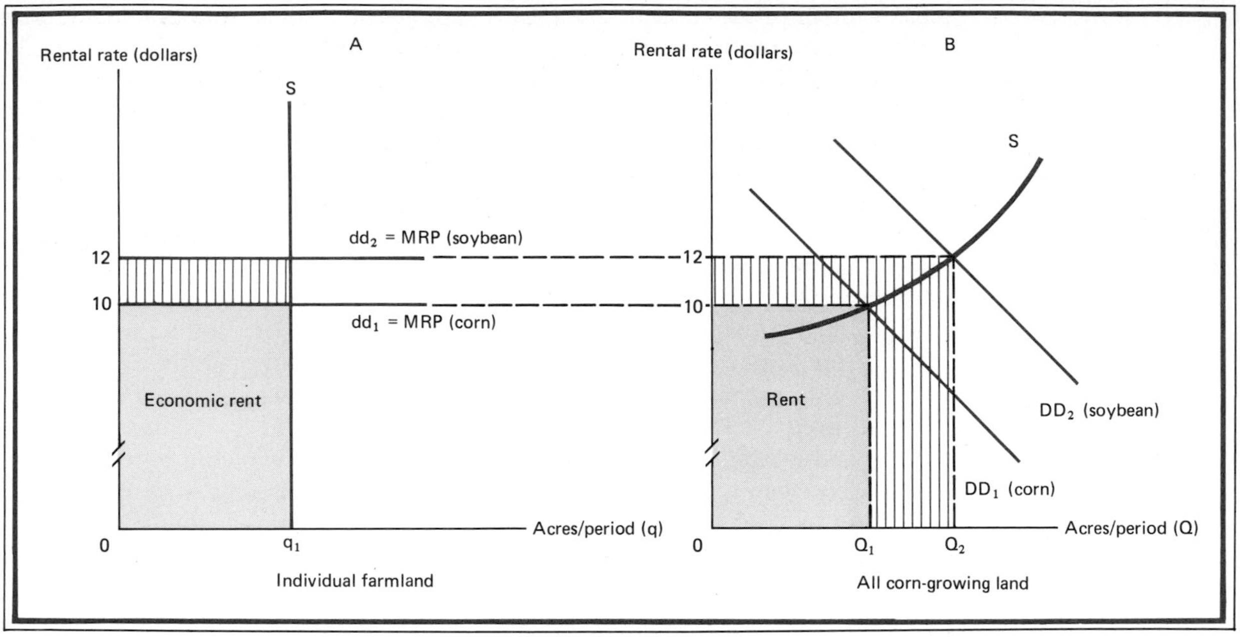

Figure 13-2

competitive industry where the individual farmer is a price-taker. The industry demand curve for corn DD_1 in panel B indicates the marginal revenue product of the land when it is used to grow corn. The curve is labeled with a double D in order to bring out the point that the demand for land to be used in the growing of corn is a *derived demand* for land. Acreage is demanded because consumers want to buy corn. Assume for now that the land has absolutely no other use than for the growing of corn. Since the land has no other use, nothing else is sacrificed by growing corn, hence the opportunity cost of growing corn is zero. Of course there are fertilizer, equipment, taxes, and labor costs, but for purposes of making a point we set these costs aside.

Suppose the industry demand for corn is DD_1, which translates into a demand for corn land, and given the supply of corn land, determines that the rental rate of an acre of land is \$10 per period. The competitive farmer faces a perfectly elastic derived demand for his land of dd_1 when it is used to grow corn. Curve dd_1 represents the marginal revenue product of the land, shown in panel A. Ignoring operating costs, the rent earned by the individual farmer is represented by the shaded area in panel A and the rent earned by the farm industry in the growing of corn is indicated by the shaded area in panel B.

Economic rent **earned by a factor is income earned above the factor's opportunity cost.**

The rent that the individual farmer in panel A earns is also called an **economic rent**. It represents income the farmer earns above and beyond his opportunity cost. We define economic rent as

economic rent = owner's income − opportunity cost.

Therefore, it is rent as residual income to the owner above his costs—his opportunity cost. It represents a transfer of income from buyer to seller that has no effect on how many acres of land the owner will devote to growing corn. For example, suppose the price of corn which had been selling for \$3 a bushel falls to $2 a bushel the following season because consumers for whatever reason decide to eat less corn and corn-based products. The farmer still has q_1 acres of land on which to grow corn and he does not reduce his acreage. Remember, we assumed the land can only be used to grow corn. Thus, so long as the price of corn is above zero (and revenues are greater than operating costs), he will make use of the q_1 acres and grow the usual corn crop and receive an income above opportunity cost, even though this economic rent is lower than that earned in the prior season. Observe, therefore, that economic rent, whether higher or lower from period to period, does *not* affect resource allocation. The supply of acreage to grow corn q_1 does not fall although the rental value of the land does change as corn prices change.

Opportunity Cost Not Zero

Assume the land does have another use. The farmer could easily substitute a soybean crop for the corn. Now the amount of acreage that can be devoted to the growing of soybean and of corn is variable, though the total acreage is still fixed. Suppose the market price of soybean is $3 a bushel while that for corn drops to $2 a bushel. Assume that the industry demand curve DD_2 suggests that the marginal revenue productivity (*MRP*) or the rental rate of land in its use for growing soybeans is $12 an acre as compared to $10 an acre in its use in the growing of corn. Thus, the individual farmer faces a derived demand for his land of dd_2 in panel A of Figure 13-2, since soybean demand is greater than corn demand. What then is the cost to the individual farmer of the land?

The answer is its value as soybean land. The soybean brings a higher income, hence the value of the land in its use in the growing of soybean is greater than its value in its use in the growing of corn.

If we concentrate on the annual income earned by the farmer instead of the price of the land, then in any given period the opportunity cost of growing soybeans is the annual income sacrificed by *not* growing corn. Assume there are 100 acres and each yields 50 bushels of soybean or 50 bushels of corn. At $3 a bushel for soybean and $2 a bushel for corn the economic rent from the growing of soybean in a period is

$$\text{Economic Rent} = (3)(50)(100) - (2)(50)(100) = \$5{,}000.$$

The $5,000 represents an income per period beyond what the farmer could earn growing corn. The shaded areas in Figure 13-2 now represent a cost, since each is the sacrificed alternative. The vertically striped area is the rent earned by the farmer in panel A and by the industry in panel B from growing soybeans.

Example 2 Unfortunately, in the land example the terminology causes confusion. Users make rental payments to owners, but economic rent is not the same thing as rental payments although economic rent, where land or property is involved, is calculated using rental payments. Therefore in this example we will talk about economic rent without making any reference to rental payments.

Garbage collectors earn over $20,000 a year in many cities. Figure 13-3 portrays a supply curve for garbage collectors, indicating that more people would be willing to collect garbage the higher the union negotiated wage rate.

Figure 13-3

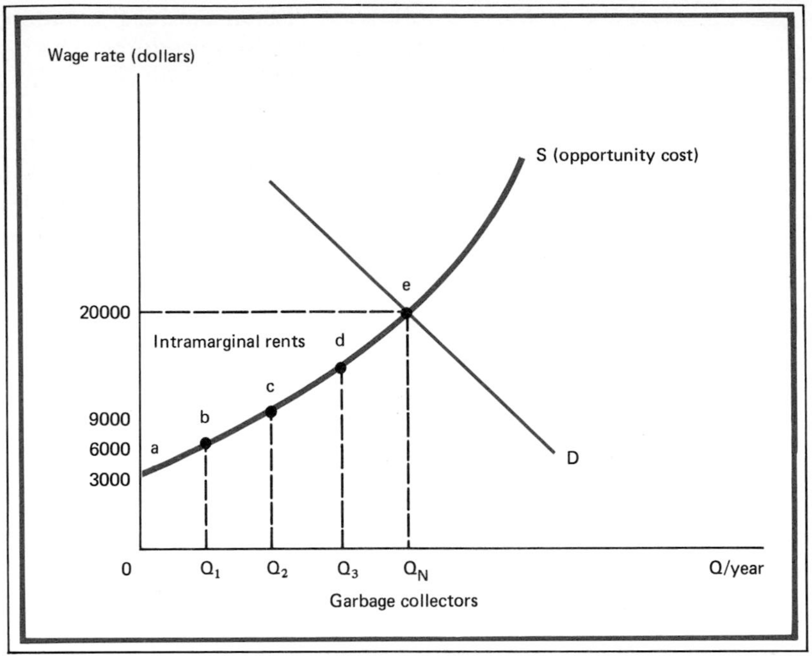

At $20,000 a year, there is often a waiting list. For our purposes we shall assume that $20,000 is an equilibrium wage where $Q_s = Q_d$. The number of men hired is Q_N. At point *a* on the supply curve no one would be willing to haul dirty, 60-pound cans over his shoulders 6 to 8 hours a day at a wage of $3,000 a year.

The supply curve represents what workers could earn at other jobs. It relates their opportunity costs in alternative activities. Thus, some workers must be paid more than $3,000 a year to lure them away from other activities or out of retirement. Point *b* shows that Q_1 people would work for $6,000 a year. It is better than anything else they can get and beats unemployment compensation even after taxes. At point *c*, the wage is $9,000 and induces Q_2 workers to haul garbage. And so it goes up to point *e*. The last man hired, the Q_N one, is paid a wage of $20,000 a year, which would equal his marginal revenue product (if it were a competitive labor market). Yet all workers are paid the same wage. Hence, all previous workers, the intramarginal haulers, earn more than would have been necessary to induce them to collect garbage. They are earning rents since the $20,000 is greater than their opportunity costs. For example, the Q_2 workers who would have taken the job for $9,000 a year are earning economic rents or a surplus of $11,000 a year. That is, $11,000 more than would have been required to employ them in this particular activity.

Thus, economic rent though it is a surplus is still a rationing device. Like other prices, rent serves to allocate resources to their most productive use. Factors will move into activities where demand is the strongest or where price is the highest.

Example 3 Several years ago there was an unexpected shortage of canning lids, and every home-canner and jar-using company was scrambling for them

Figure 13-4

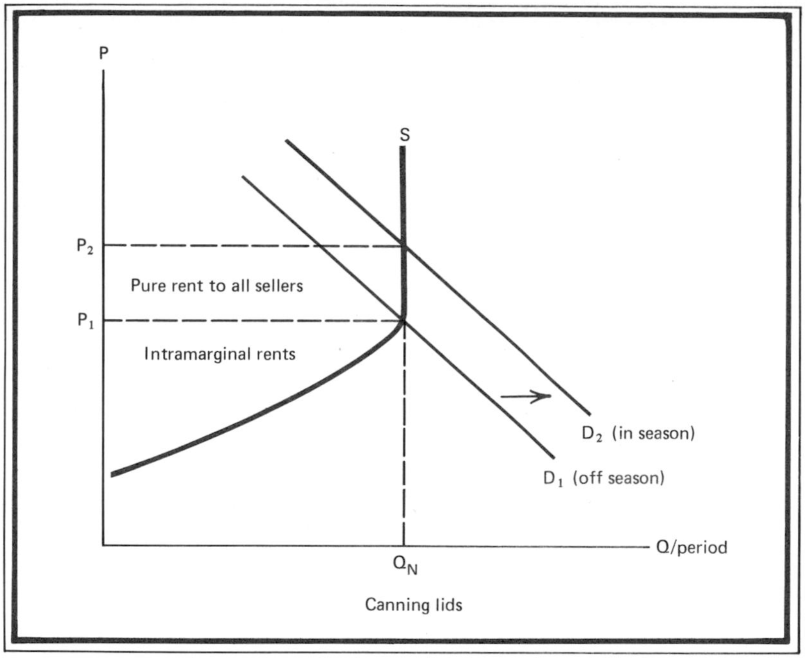

during canning season. Prior to the crisis, assume that the demand for canning lids was D_1 and the price was P_1. At the market price of P_1 some intramarginal producers of canning lids were earning economic rents. The marginal producer was not. On the arrival of canning season, demand shifts to D_2 in Figure 13-4. However, during the market period there is no increase in supply of lids because those being made are already committed to those companies which had signed contracts for them earlier in the year. The magnitude of the surge in demand was unanticipated.

Therefore, those buyers without contracts face suddenly higher prices. Hence, above price P_1 supply is temporarily perfectly inelastic. The same amount of lids, Q_N, are available as before, there being no increase in quantity when prices increased. Thus, the same amount of resources are being devoted to the production of canning lids. When the price rises, there is a transfer of income from lid buyers to suppliers. Now all producers earn a pure economic rent, even the producer of the last or marginal lid.

When canning season has passed, demand falls back to D_1. But there is no reduction in the resources devoted to producing lids or in the amount of lids produced. The extra economic rents to all producers disappear and once again only intramarginal rents are earned.

It would appear that at price P_2 the pure economic rents were unearned, the price P_2 being above opportunity costs for society. It is important to state, however, that pure rents do perform an allocative function. In the longer run, with higher demand anticipated, more of the economy's resources will be devoted to producing lids. This would shift the supply curve to the right, lowering price and reducing, if not removing, the pure rents. These short-run rents are sometimes called quasi-rents because they are perceived as temporary and in the long run competition from new producers will remove them.

Implications

Rent allocates the use of land toward its *most efficient use.*

Economic rent does serve a useful allocative function—driving resources to be applied to their best and therefore **most efficient use**. That is, land in its different uses varies in its productivity. In neighborhoods where the college student population grows, the rental on business property rises. In order to survive paying the higher lease costs, owners must sell products that students are more apt to buy. It is not surprising to see, for example, hardware stores and television repair shops move out of these immediate areas to be replaced by small clothing stores, fast-food restaurants, record and book shops, and other stores offering copy services. Those rental payments owners of land receive earn them an economic rent or a surplus greater than their opportunity costs.

In these circumstances it is demand that determines both the rental price and the economic rent, and ultimately for what purpose the land will be used. *The price of soybeans is not high because the price of land is high. Rather, the price of land is high because the price of soybeans grown on the land is high.*

In the case of college shopping areas, the demand for land to lease is competitive. When the demand for blue jeans is higher, the store owners earn more income selling jeans than they do selling hardware to college students. It is the demand for clothing that drives up the lease cost to the hardware store operators. If he does not sell enough hardware because consumer preference in the area is not strong enough, he does not renew the lease. The landlord derives a surplus income from renting the property to a clothing store operator rather than to the hardware store operator, because the clothing store operator is willing to make higher payments to the landowner than the hardware store operator is willing to make. Therefore, the owner offers the same amount of land resources on the market but earns a residual income by renting to the jeans seller. This residual is above what the owner could earn from leasing to the tool seller. The discussion is summarized in Figure 13-5, illustrating the market for property in the area located nearby a university or college.

Economic Rent — A Matter of Your Point of View

High economic rent is often earned because a factor is highly specialized in its function. What rent is charged will vary depending on what the alternatives are. Garbage collectors are not specialized, but professional athletes are. Let us consider another example. Joe Throw is a superstar quarterback for the National Football League (NFL). He possesses a unique talent as a quarterback; he is one of a kind. What is his economic rent? That depends on his opportunity cost; only then can a residual income be determined. For, again,

$$\text{Rent} = \text{owner's income} - \text{opportunity cost.}$$

Suppose Joe Throw makes $100,000 a season. Given that his next best alternative outside of football is $30,000 a year he could make as a salesman, then his economic rent is $70,000 while avoiding 280-pound tackles pursuing his body. As long as he can make over $30,000 a year playing football he would stay with

Figure 13-5

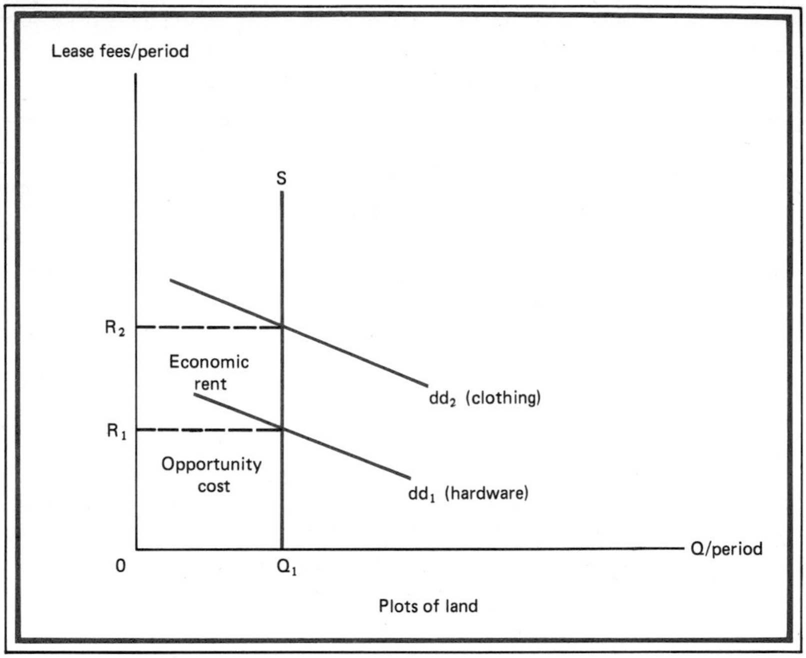

the NFL. Whether he made $100,000 a year or any amount above $30,000, does not in theory reduce his quarterbacking resources devoted to football. In terms of opportunity cost any amount above $30,000 is pure gravy earned by playing football.

Suppose now that Joe Throw plays for New York. What then is his economic rent within football; that is, could he earn more if he played for Dallas than for New York? Suppose he were not a free agent; only New York could trade him to Dallas. Then New York would sell his contract to Dallas, in which case Joe Throw would also earn $100,000 by signing with Dallas. Thus *among teams in the NFL* Joe Throw's economic rent is zero since his opportunity cost playing for another team is $100,000.

Finally, what is Joe Throw's economic rent relative to the economy as a whole? To determine this one would have to know what minimum wage he would accept working at any other kind of job in the economy, and below which he would choose not to work at all, but prefer unemployment compensation or beach bumming. Suppose that is $5,000 a year. In this case, his economic rent is $95,000 a year. Rather than waste away in a low-paying job, he'd offer to play football as long as the income was over $5,000 a year. In summary, Joe Throw's pure rent or surplus is as follows:

As a quarterback versus a salesman	= $100,000 − $30,000 = $70,000.
As a New York player versus playing for another team in the league	= $100,000 − $100,000 = 0.
As a football player versus a salary below which he would not work at anything	= $100,000 − $5,000 = $95,000.

THE SINGLE TAX

Henry George (1839–1897) was a sailor, gold prospector, jack-of-all-trades, unsuccessful candidate for mayor of New York City, and an economic writer. He preached the doctrine that all taxes should be removed except for the tax on land. This tax was to be set at 100 percent. His reasons were twofold: economic rent on land is immoral, and the economy would be better off.

Because land is a gift of nature, owners of land earn a pure economic rent—a surplus they surely do not deserve. Also, since pure economic rent has no effect on the allocation of resources, and only represents a redistribution of income from users to owners, a 100 percent tax on economic rent would remove this undeserved surplus income. He argued that those who made the land productive should earn the income on the goods and services they provide. If all other taxes were removed, users would have more incentive to make the factories on the land and the land itself more productive. Thus, he argued that the economic rent on land derived solely from land ownership. These rents should be returned to the public and not be kept by the individual owner. The public at large is responsible for the increased value of the land, and therefore the public at large should share in its return. When a railroad is built, a bridge, or a sewer system, it is the effort of others that increases the land's value. Nearby landowners have done nothing. George believed it was purely luck or circumstances that in an expanding western frontier, the people who got there first received monopoly income claims on land they were allowed to own.

Land ownership also motivates speculators to withhold land from productive use while they wait for new migrants or a new railroad to cause the land values to jump. By taxing away all the rent on the land, the government would remove the motive of speculators. And the land taxes would be all that would be required to finance government services. Henry George's argument for the single tax was a compelling one and caused quite a stir in the 1880s.

Criticisms

First, it is doubtful (though maybe desirable) that the single land tax would bring in enough revenues to finance all government functions.

Second, George overlooked the fact that buying of land to be used for housing, recreational areas, or farming involved substantial risk. While land prices have tended to rise, there is no certainty they will rise in a specific area and be profitable for the particular use the speculator may have in mind. Speculators can also experience capital losses. Thus, it is incorrect to argue that speculators as a group gain from land development. There are as many who lose as there are who gain.

Third, land is not the only factor of production to receive a pure economic rent. Some capital and some labor also earn rents. On grounds of fairness and morality, should owners of land resources be the only ones to have their rents taxed away? Why not movie stars, sports figures, plumbers, doctors, and even garbage collectors? Are not the skills in sports, music, mathematics to a large degree arbitrary gifts of nature?

Fourth, while the total amount of land is fixed, land in a prescribed use is not. In fact, it might be naturally more productive in one use than another and is therefore never perfectly inelastic in supply to any particular use. If the owner of land had all the income he earns from renting it taxed away, why would he bother to own it? He could supposedly make some use of it for his own recreational purposes. Under the tax the effect would be that economic rent would be prevented from performing its allocative function, that is, the determination of what is the best use of the land. (However, if the tax on economic rent were set at 90 or 95 percent, it might not frustrate the allocation function of economic rent.)

Fifth, what land, capital, and labor each contributes to the value of output cannot be neatly separated. Therefore the economic rent of land alone cannot be precisely determined.

PROFITS

In a poll conducted by Opinion Research Corporation of New Jersey in 1976, a majority of the respondents expressed the belief that companies averaged 33 cents profit on a dollar of sales. A Standard and Poor's survey revealed that college students believed the return on a dollar to be 45 cents. Actually the profit on sales has averaged about 5 cents on the dollar.

Without profits there is no growth. Without profits capital is not replaced and income not generated. A portion of profits earned by businesses is plowed back into the company to replace worn-out or obsolete capital and to generate research and development that creates new products and increases productivity, thereby raising wages which when spent create new markets and jobs.

Another portion of profits is not kept by firms but paid out as dividends to stockholders—the owners. While it is claimed only the rich can afford to own stock, and that individuals are becoming a declining share of stockholders, this overlooks a significant institutional change that has been going on in the U.S. Nearly half of all stocks are owned by company and union pension funds which they invest to earn income for retired workers. Insurance companies and colleges also invest in stocks, insurance companies to pay off on policies and colleges to provide endowment funds for scholarships and other programs.

The healthier the profits, the higher the dividend payments going to individuals via the pension programs where workers' funds are invested by financial managers for purposes of making a profit.

Some researchers believe that corporate profits have been on a downward trend since 1965. Whether it is merely a temporary decline or will continue as a permanent change is hard to say at this time. But if true, it portends a lower standard of living in the future because it will seriously impair future productivity, since profits are the major source of spending for capital expansion and improvement.

One reason that there seems to be much disagreement about the amount of

Which Accounting Profit?

Businesses calculate accounting profits in several ways, including the rate of return on net sales and the rate of return on capital which ignores opportunity costs. Other measures of profitability are net earnings per share of stock, gross profit on sales (operating profit), rate of profit on stockholders' equity both before and after taxes, and the ratio of stockholders' equity to total debt. Two common calculations are:

1. Rate of profit on net sales

$$= \frac{\text{net income (profit) per period}}{\text{net sales per period}}.$$

Notice the difference between profit (net income) and the rate of profit. Profit is an absolute dollar figure, whereas rate of profit is a ratio of dollars to dollars and is a pure number, that is, a percentage. If a firm has sales of $1,000,000 and a net income of $80,000, then the rate of profit is 8 percent.

2. Rate of return on capital

$$= \frac{\text{net income (profit) per period}}{\text{total capital employed per period}}.$$

The rate of return on capital can also be viewed as consisting of two components, (a) the rate of profit on net sales already described, and (b) the turnover of capital equal to

$$\frac{\text{net sales per period}}{\text{total capital per period}}.$$

For example, suppose a grocery store sells its inventory (current capital) once every month. In a period of a year it turns over its stock of inventory capital 12 times. Of course, the store has fixed capital or assets too, namely plant, equipment, tools, and so on. Thus, multiplying components a and b yields:

Rate of return on capital

$$= \frac{\text{net income}}{\text{net sales}} \times \frac{\text{net sales}}{\text{total capital}}$$

$$= \frac{\text{net income}}{\text{total capital}}.$$

Economists prefer this approach over that of the profit on sales because it is a much better measure of the return to real resources.

Assume the following hypothetical numbers

profits and the rate of profit is that businessmen and economists have several different measures of profit, because they are really trying to measure different things and different phases or aspects of business operations.

Net Income

In everyday usage profit is the difference between total revenues and total costs when revenues and costs are measured by accepted accounting rules. They are sometimes called accounting profits. In the discussion of profits immediately above we have been referring to accounting profits.

Pure economic *profit* is a return above total costs; included in total costs are the implicit or opportunity costs of owners. Accounting profits are higher because they omit these implicit costs from total costs.

But economists often prefer to use the word **profit** in a more limited way. The reason is that in accounting there are some costs that accounting rules do not treat as costs. It is not that accountants do not like to include some items. There is no difference of opinion among accountants and economists. Rather it is a matter of being able to measure certain costs. The costs in question are mostly certain implicit opportunity costs. For example, an accountant may tell the operator of the local gas station that he made $30,000 profit last year. This amount is what the operator took home for himself after paying all other costs.

apply to a company for the year in its assets and income statements.

Assets

Current (cash, inventories, etc.)	=	$110,000
Fixed (plant, equipment minus depreciation)	=	70,000
Total assets		$180,000

Liabilities and equity

Short-term debt	=	$65,000
Long-term debt	=	45,000
Equity (stock and net earnings)	=	70,000
Total liabilities		$180,000

Income account

Net sales from previous period	=	$450,000
Less costs of goods sold	=	380,000
Gross profit on sales	=	$70,000
Taxes and other costs	=	44,000
Net income	=	$26,000

The rate of accounting profit on net sales is

$$\frac{\$26{,}000}{\$450{,}000} = 5.77\%.$$

The rate of return on capital is

$$\frac{26{,}000}{450{,}000} \times \frac{450{,}000}{180{,}000} = (2.5)(5.77) = 14.4\%.$$

Depending on the industry the firm is in, a firm can have low profit on sales and a high turnover on capital or vice versa. Some industries have a high sales volume and relatively low capital intensity; others a low sales volume and a relatively high capital intensity. Therefore, some writers suggest combining the two measures of profitability to even out differences and to provide a better comparison. Consider some actual data:*

	Rate of return on sales	Turnover of capital	Return on capital
Weyerhaeuser Timber Co.	12.10%	0.763	9.23%
Penn Fruit Co.	1.40	4.600	6.44

The third column provides useful information for investors to draw conclusions about a company's comparative performance.

*Reuben E. Slesinger, "Measuring Investment Returns, Journal of Economics and Business, Winter 1974.

This is income to the operator, but it is not profit if the owner could have earned $30,000 working as a mechanic with another firm. The opportunity cost of the labor put in by the operator himself was $30,000. Had this cost been accounted for by the accountants, the operator would have been told that the firm's economic profit was zero. Thus, to economists, total costs include *all* opportunity costs.

In the situation when a corporation pays dividends to stockholders, these payments may be called a distribution of profits by accountants, but are really costs to the firm of acquiring capital from the point of view of the economist. As for the stockholder, if he or she were to receive, say, 8 percent on an investment but could have earned 8 percent by purchasing a government bond or a savings and loan certificate, the 8 percent is not a profit even though it is income to the stockholder.

The same analysis applies for a self-employed doctor, farmer, or the local owner of an auto repair shop. Payments made to themselves—wages or salaries—are a return for supplying themselves as inputs to production. These payments may not represent economic profits. Instead they represent opportunity costs or implicit costs.

Risk and Uncertainty

In the perfectly competitive model we assume perfect information. Since supply and demand conditions in the future are known, any discrepancies in prices and efficient resource use will be shortly corrected. There is assumed a certainty about the future. In reality, of course, the future is uncertain. The past is not prologue; we do not have tomorrow's paper today. Thus, what has happened in the past provides no guarantee that the same outcomes will be repeated in the future. The entrepreneur can only make calculated guesses and take a chance. Changes in technology, unforseen strikes, bad weather, a political coup, and new rivals are only a few of the things that can affect the supply and price of a commodity. A change in tastes and new products might affect the demand side. Some economists have argued that economic profit is best viewed as a return to the entrepreneur for assuming risk and facing uncertainty.[1]

Let us elaborate this point with an example. If you deposit $1,000 in a bank at 5 percent interest you expect $1,050 at the end of the year. Suppose, on the other hand, you buy stock for $1,000. After a year you sell the stock for $1,150. Is your profit (a capital gain) the entire $150? Economists would say no, since you could have had a sure $50 from the bank. The extra $100 you got from the stock could be viewed as profit. By investing in the stock you gave up the opportunity of earning $50 from the bank. Thus, $50 represents the value of an opportunity forgone and is an opportunity cost.

Now suppose the stock had sold for only $1,050 instead of $1,150. In this case your economic profit would be zero. Although your income is $50, this is interest income and not profit as such. If the stock had sold for only the amount you paid for it, $1,000, what then is the profit? It is minus $50 because you could have earned $50 from the bank. Thus profit is revenue earned above expected opportunity cost, and in the real world of constant change and uncertainty, profits are often negative (losses).

Risk is a Cost

Individuals can insure against risk for certain things like fire and theft. But the companies insuring the insured are not themselves insured in the same way. Risk differs from uncertainty in one important aspect: The probability of possible outcomes can be calculated; the odds are known. The chances for your number to come out on a roulette wheel is 1 in 36. This is **risk**. The odds of picking an ace from a straight deck is 1 in 13. That too is risk. By examining data carefully, insurance companies can calculate the probability of x number of fires in a city of 100,000 and adjust their rates to more than cover the payout costs—this is an example of calculating risk.

The probability that a 45-year-old white female will live to be 72 is known to insurance companies. Of course, Hardluck Holly might have a brick fall on her tomorrow. That's uncertainty. But enough 45-year-old white females will live to 72 to make insuring Holly a profitable venture. Thus, the distinction between risk and uncertainty is that risk probabilities can be calculated while uncertainty remains when you cannot calculate the probability of an outcome.

[1] Frank Knight, *Risk, Uncertainty, and Profit* (New York: Sentry Press, 1921).

Thus, risk is insurable, uncertainty is not. Entrepreneurs cannot buy insurance on their pricing, output, and investment decisions.

In a world of *risk* and uncertainty, profit is a return above total costs; but included in total costs must be an allowance for risk.

Because of risk and uncertainty, investors want a higher rate of return when they invest in a speculative venture than what they could earn on passbook savings with a bank at 5 percent. They would only give up the certainty of 5 percent return if the risky venture paid 10 or 11 percent. To be induced to invest they need a return that includes a premium over the nonrisky or pure interest rate. The premium paid to the investor for assuming risk is, therefore, very much a part of the costs of doing business. Where the risks are high, expected accounting profits must be high in order to motivate investors to take chances. Economic profits may be low, however, because the high accounting profits are necessary to bring in investors.

If one decides to innovate by trying to build a better mousetrap and spends $50 on each of five failures, then when the sixth one is a success it must be priced to cover the cost of the five failures—and then some. The "and then some" is the extra profit to motivate an individual or a company to earn enough to cover the losses incurred with the five failures plus a favorable profit on the capital investment. Hence in a competitive market the selling price is the sum of wages, interest, rental payments, other opportunity costs, and a return to cover risk called the risk premium. Only those returns greater than the amount necessary to cover all these costs would be called economic profit.

Profits and Economic Rent

At this point you might be pondering what difference there is between pure economic rents and profits. In many situations there is for practical purposes no difference; in others there is a difference, depending on from what vantage point a situation is observed. Firms may earn economic profit but resources or inputs earn economic rents. To the firm a profit is a return in excess of the amount required to ensure that the firm will stay in business over the long run. In other words, profits could fall to zero but the firm would keep producing. To a factor of production a rent is a return greater than the amount necessary to attract that factor into the particular activity in which it is engaged. In other words, the factor would stay employed where it is even if the pay it received were to be reduced so that it no longer earned rent.

Economic rents earned by resources are costs to the firms that hire those resources. The firm pays the direct costs to factors such as rental payments for land, wages to labor including the salary to the entrepreneur, the interest on borrowed funds, and the implicit costs of dividends to stockholders. As far as the firm is concerned, opportunity costs such as interest on capital and economic rent earned by managers or executives are part of total costs. Any income it might earn above all these costs is a profit.

CHAPTER SUMMARY

In a competitive market, rental payments made for the use of land and property will equal the marginal revenue productivity of the property.

Economic rent is a term with a special meaning for economists. It means the payment made for a resource in excess of that necessary to bring forth the services of the factor of production. If certain land is useful to grow corn, and for little else, an increase in the demand for corn will drive up the price of the land and land rents. But if the demand and price were to fall, the land would still be used to grow corn. Thus, economic rent arises when the price is pushed above that required to bring forth its use. It is the price above the land's opportunity cost.

Rent is a rationing device. Like other prices, it serves to guide the use of land toward its most productive use.

Because of the economic nature of rent a man named Henry George put forward a unique idea. It was that since economic rent is not necessary to bring forth the use of the factor, the government could tax away the rent on land without distorting or reducing economic production. There are several problems with this idea, but it refuses to die.

There are several different measures of profits, and the term is often used with emotion when people fail to distinguish among them. Accounting profits arise when gross sales revenues of the firm exceed costs. These are the profits on which firms pay taxes. But economists argue that accounting costs do not include many implicit opportunity costs. Thus, accounting profits often exceed real economic profits. Furthermore, some profits are required in order to give owners of firms some payment for accepting the risk and uncertainty necessary to bring forth entrepreneurial activities. The assumption of risk is costly and this cost must be covered too.

Pure economic profit, to an economist, is the same kind of thing as pure economic rent. It is a payment in excess of that needed in order to induce the entrepreneur to produce the product. In the case of rent it is the factor of production that comes forward and in the case of profit it is the firm's output that comes forward. Profit accrues to a firm, rent accrues to a factor of production. Otherwise, they are the same.

QUESTIONS

1. Suppose you owned a large amount of farmland which had equally fertile soil, but varied in distance to product markets. Would you expect to use equal amounts of labor, fertilizer, and so on, on each plot of land? Why, or why not? Is the concept of economic rent helpful in order to answer the question? How?
2. A local newspaper investigating a tight housing market in the city conducted a short survey of apartment house dwellers. Of the 20 queried, all but two believed they were paying too much for what they were getting. "Rents in this city are dictated by what the landlord can get, not what the apartment is worth," said one tenant. "There's a shortage of good apartments, so renters pay through the nose."
   a. Is the landlord a monopolist?
   b. Why are *all* landlords charging higher prices? Is there collusion?
   c. What is an apartment worth? From whose viewpoint?
   d. Is the landlord earning windfall profits? What else is this called? Is this wrong?
   e. What would you expect to occur in the housing market of this city if rent controls are not imposed? With what effect?
   f. Is this problem in any way similar to the controversy surrounding oil companies' earning windfall profits when price regulations were removed?
3. Is the theory of economic rent in conflict with the concepts of market supply and demand? Discuss.
4. A highly skilled pipe welder who makes $20,000 a year in Texas takes a job in Alaska at $35,000 a year welding a new natural gas pipeline that is being built to

transport gas to the Midwest United States. What does the $15,000 difference represent to the welder? To the pipeline company?

5. Michel de Montaigne, sixteenth century French writer, entitled one of his essays, "The profit of one man is the damage of another." Do you agree? What if all gain from exchange were outlawed, what do you think would happen?
6. In April of 1977, Red Adair received $6.6 million for capping a North Sea oilwell blowout which took him about 10 days. Was Adair overpaid? Of what did most of his payment consist? Was this a misallocation of resources? Explain.
7. "Some people have better managerial instincts than others: the stiffer the competition the better they perform. Arnold's the best in the business. Our company could make more profits than any in this rat-race industry if he were at the helm." Why might you conclude that a perfectly competitive company would not earn extra profits even if hiring Arnold would eventually result in lowering the firm's average variable costs?
8. In 1927 Babe Ruth was the first baseball player to be paid $100,000 a year. When it was mentioned that the President of the U.S. (Hoover) did not make that much, Ruth replied, "I had a better year than he did." Does this facetious remark contain an element of sense? Explain.
   a. Was Ruth earning an economic rent? Comment.
   b. In what sense may he have not been earning an economic rent?
9. If a single tax on land was set at, say, 50 percent of the economic rent, would it misallocate land use? Discuss.
10. A businessman corners the market on the currently available supply of saccharin by paying higher than the current price because he expects the FTC to ban any further production of it in the near future because it is reputed to cause cancer.
    a. If he is right, he can raise prices and earn a pure profit. This extra profit includes a return to what? Is he immoral? Would your answer depend on whether you are a diabetic or not? What return on his or her expenditure for saccharin, if any, does the diabetic earn?
    b. Suppose he is wrong, and he has to lower the price to reduce the less valuable inventory, thus taking a loss. Is this unfair or immoral? To whom?
    c. What do you think would occur if the FTC banned saccharin?
11. Suppose an investor anticipates a 10 percent return on his investment. Suppose the best rate of interest is 8 percent and the investor only earns 6 percent on his investment. Is this a negative profit (loss)? Explain.
12. "Sellers will charge what the market will bear." Is this necessarily bad? Can profits be too high? How do you know when they are?
13. Do profits have a function in planned or socialist economies? If it is believed that profits do not exist in planned economies, what is being implied? That is, do production goals always turn out as expected?
14. Are those citizens who are frightened by the uncertainty of inflation protecting themselves from uncertainty by buying gold and silver? Comment.
15. More than half the corporate stocks these days are owned by union pension funds, insurance companies, college endowments, and even churches. Do high corporate profits threaten the existence of these institutions? Do corporate profits go into padding the pockets of corporate fat cats? Are their salaries pure profits? If not, what are they?

Chapter 14

Capital, Investment, and Present Value

PROGRESS REPORT

A. In Chapters 12 and 13 the return to the factors labor and land was reviewed. The marginal revenue products of land and labor were discussed and the allocative function of economic rent was examined.

B. In this chapter, capital and investment are examined. Just as one pays a rent for the use of the services of land and a wage for labor, interest payments are made for the use of the services of a machine. The concept of saving and the rate of interest are discussed, as well as the relation between saving and investment and the connection to capital growth. We observe that a capital asset yields a chain of income or services over time. The method of calculating the value today of those future income streams leads to the concept of present value.

C. In Chapter 15 we bring a few of the tools developed thus far to an analysis and discussion of one of the institutions of our society—labor unions.

CAPITAL AS A FACTOR OF PRODUCTION

We have classified factors of production into three broad categories: land (including raw materials), labor, and capital. These are inputs in the production process. Land is a gift of nature. In the aggregate, the amount of land is more or less fixed. However, in any particular use a buyer of the service of land must compete with other buyers. Hence buyers must make rental payments—the price of the use of land—in an amount equal to the land's opportunity cost in order to ensure that the services of land continue to flow to a given use. Thus, the pricing of land by charging rents serves to allocate the limited amount of land to its alternative uses. In a free society, individuals may offer their services in the market as factors of production. They receive a wage for their services. This wage represents the price of their services and it must be paid to ensure the continued flow of labor service to that activity. The wage represents the opportunity cost of labor and it serves to allocate the limited amount of labor service that is available to its alternative uses. There are many different kinds of land, and many different kinds of labor, each of which can be treated as a unique factor of production.

Capital is not endowed by nature but produced by man.

Capital, too, comes in many sizes and shapes, but in the aggregate we separate capital from both labor and land as a class of productive input simply because capital is man-made. That is, part of society's production activity is devoted to production of capital goods. We sometimes say that capital is a produced means of production. Land, labor, and capital are used by businesses to produce capital goods just as they are used to produce consumer goods. We often speak of capital goods industries in the same way we speak of consumer goods in domestic production.

In general, real capital goods are tools of production. These tools consist of equipment and machinery. Broadly constructed, this includes everything from hammers and saws to the factory building in which production takes place. It also includes inventories of nuts and bolts and nails—for these have been produced by man, but not yet put to use. However, they will be used in the future in the process of producing either more capital goods or consumer goods, and hence inventories are in most pertinent respects a produced means of production just like tools and machinery.

At any given time, the aggregate amount of capital in the system is fixed, just like land. But, also like land, any particular piece of capital can be used in many ways. A piece of land can be used to produce corn, wheat, or barley. A welding set can be used to repair cars, boats, or trailers. Thus, to ensure continued use in a particular activity, a piece of capital must receive a payment called **interest**. Interest is the return to capital and represents its opportunity cost.

To ensure continued use in a particular activity, a piece of capital must receive a payment called _interest._ Interest is the return to capital and represents its opportunity cost.

Just as in the case of land and labor, the payment made to capital is a payment for a flow of services from capital. One pays a rent for the use of land, a wage for the services of labor, and interest for the services of a machine. Sometimes we even speak of renting a machine as when your mother rents the carpet cleaning equipment from the local grocery store. Economists call this kind of payment a quasi-rent. Since, at any given time, the aggregate amount of capital is fixed, like the aggregate amount of land is fixed, it may be appropriate to call the return to capital a kind of rent, for the only difference is that land was a gift of nature to the people, while the existing capital was produced by the people. Thus, existing capital can earn rent just as existing land does.

Demand for capital is derived from the demand for the goods that the capital is used to produce.

The **demand** for capital is a derived demand—derived from the demand for the goods that the capital is used to produce. Since people want and are willing to buy clothing, there is a demand for textile equipment and machinery by businesses that produce clothing. As an individual textile company buys or hires the use of additional machines, the marginal productivity of machines declines. If we add together all the declining marginal productivity curves for all the textile producers, we have a declining market demand curve for services of textile machinery. Therefore, existing capital, as a factor input, can be treated using marginal productivity theory in the same way we treated other factors of production.

The Special Complexion of Capital Theory

Since we can treat existing capital like land and other factors of production, why do we sort it out for special treatment? The reason is that it is a *round-about method* of increasing production at lower cost. By choosing to defer current consumption and pursue capital formation, there exists the possibility of greater consumption later and a subsequent rise in the standard of living.

Investment is a flow and an addition to the stock of capital.

Investment is the addition to the stock of capital. We can write

$$I = \Delta K \text{ or } I = K_2 - K_1$$

where I represents investment and K represents the stock of capital, subscripts representing time. Thus, if the stock of capital grows from date 1 to date 2, the difference in the stock between the two dates represents investment or capital formation that occurred between the two dates.

The wisdom of a capital investment can be determined through *benefit-cost* analysis.

Capital creation requires that we compare the **costs** (time and resources) of producing it, with the **benefits** (returns over many periods in the future) of having it to use in the production of other goods. Since we invest now in order to get the fruits of capital from its use over a period of many years, time, saving, and the rate of interest play important, interrelated roles.

SAVING AND INTEREST

Most people are concerned not only about their current economic well-being but their future economic well-being too. For this reason they often save, that is, they are willing to trade off some current consumption for more future consumption. **Saving** involves the substitution of future goods for current goods. The more future goods are preferred, the greater is saving and the lower is the current consumption of goods. However, given the choice of consuming

Saving is deferred consumption.

something now and the same amount of it later, people will usually choose now because it it more convenient to consume what is currently available. Therefore, for people to give up the convenience of early consumption for the inconvenience of later consumption requires a positive return.

The *rate of exchange* between future versus current consumption of goods is measured by the interest rate covering the accounting period.

Suppose your neighbor says her tree will not yield peaches until next summer. She proposes that if you lend her 20 jars of canned peaches this summer she will repay you with 25 jars of canned peaches next summer. The **rate of exchange** or substitutability between future versus current consumption of goods is measured by the rate of interest i covering the accounting period (normally a year). Its value when multiplied by 100 is

$$i = \frac{25 \text{ repaid} - 20 \text{ lent}}{20 \text{ lent}} = \frac{5}{20} = .25 \text{ or } 25 \text{ percent.}$$

Notice that the higher the rate of interest, the lower is the current or present value to you of consuming future goods, hence future consumption is substituted for current consumption. That is, more is saved when interest is higher. Thus, if you could obtain 30 jars of peaches next summer by doing with the inconvenience of not consuming 20 jars prior to next summer, then the rate of interest is 50 percent. The present value of future peaches falls. You would, therefore, more likely be willing to substitute future peaches for current peaches. Saving goes up and consumption goes down.

Each consumer has some rate of substitution between the inconvenience (marginal disutility) of delaying consumption and the increased satisfaction (marginal utility) of consuming more later. Thus, the rate of interest is positive because there must be a reward for waiting if saving is to take place. A second reason that the rate of interest is positive is that capital formation is risky. In a world of uncertainty, there is no guarantee that the new project or machine will be more productive at a lower cost. The increase in future consumption is therefore not guaranteed. To call forth the necessary saving required to free resources for capital formation, a guarantee of an interest payment is necessary—and the higher that payment, the more willing are people to risk sacrificing current consumption and to save more.

Let us examine two hypothetical examples that will illustrate the concepts of the marginal productivity of capital, saving, interest, and profits associated with the process of capital formation.

An Example: Stranded on a Desert Island

Suppose you are stranded on an isolated island where it takes you a full day to catch 2 fish by spearing them with a pointed stick you found near a stream on the island. You decide to build a fishing pole because the wooden spear has low productivity. You estimate that it will take 2 days of your time to build the fishing pole and line—the process of capital formation, or investment. This means that you must go 2 days without fishing and therefore without catching your normal quota of 2 fish per day, or 4 fish altogether. Your hope is that the fishing pole will improve your ability to catch fish. You hope to be able to catch as many as 12 fish in a single day with your pole, cook them and eat 2 of them a day for the next 6 days. In this way you can free up your labor time and build a shelter, hunt, and perhaps farm some land or provide other necessities during the 6 out of every 7 days that you have free from fishing.

Assume that on the third day the fishing gear is completed and you do succeed in catching 11 fish. This is 1 short of the number you planned to catch but nevertheless your fishing pole turned out to be a good investment.

The *marginal productivity* of capital is defined as the change in total product divided by the change in the capital stock.

Let us do a few simple calculations. The **marginal productivity** of capital MP_K is defined as the change in total productivity divided by the change in the capital stock, or

$$MP_K = \frac{\Delta TP}{\Delta K}.$$

The MP_K is expressed in physical units, the fishing pole as an input and the fish as output. If money prices were being used, then the price of the fish would be P_0 and when it is multiplied by the MP_K we would obtain the marginal revenue product *MRP*, which is equal to the change in total revenue divided by the change in the capital stock.

$$MRP_K = MP_K \times P_0 = \frac{\Delta TR}{\Delta K}.$$

However, for the next several pages we shall ignore money prices and measure input and output in units of fish. We therefore set P_0 equal to 1. The price of a fish in terms of fish is 1.

The MP_K of the fishing pole is therefore

$$MP_K = \frac{11 - 2}{1 - 0} = 9$$

or 900 percent when multiplied by 100. The 2 appears in the numerator because it is the total product without the use of a fishing pole. Observe that while total productivity is 11 fish, the marginal productivity is 9 fish. As soon as it is recognized that time is a cost—a cost in fish sacrificed in order to build the fishing pole—then you would be concerned not only with how productive the pole is, but how long it took to construct it. Explicitly introducing time leads to the more important calculation—the rate of return r to new capital formation.

You were willing to sacrifice 4 fish over 2 days in order to build a fishing pole with which you could catch 11 fish. During the third day you use the pole to catch 11 fish. Let R equal the total return on the first fishing pole. Then R − C equals the net return and C is the initial cost. The ratio of net return to cost per time period yields the rate of return.

$$r = \frac{R - C}{C} = \frac{11 - 4}{4} = \frac{7}{4} = 1.75 \text{ or } 175\%.$$

The 4 is a cost because it includes the 4 fish sacrificed when building the pole, the opportunity cost of building the pole. The rate of net gain is therefore 175 percent over and above what you would have caught using the wooden spear.

Real Interest Rates

The rate of return r goes by several names, including the real rate of interest, the internal rate of return to investment, and the marginal efficiency of investment. We shall use these three terms interchangeably.

What if you constructed 2 poles instead of only 1? Having 2 poles to tend while fishing at the stream might allow you to catch 7 more fish for a total of 18 for the day—11 from the first plus 7 from the second pole, assuming you put in the same amount of labor and effort in fishing as before. But producing the additional pole takes another 2 days and implies a loss of another 4 fish. Thus, the internal rate of return *to the second pole* is

$$r = \frac{7 - 4}{4} = \frac{3}{4} = .75, \text{ or } 75\%.$$

What about adding a third pole that adds another 5 fish? For this

$$r = \frac{5 - 4}{4} = \frac{1}{4} = .25 \text{ or } 25\%.$$

Figure 14-1 shows the relation between the return *R* in the form of fish on the vertical axis and the number of poles on the horizontal axis. Cost C in fish is also measured on the vertical axis. The figure shows a schedule of *R*'s plotted against the number of fishing poles. Except for the problem with the first fishing pole, the *R*'s are the MP_K of each additional pole. For the first pole R = total product but $TP_K > MP_K$. This happens because we started at zero amounts of capital and because of the problems encountered when using discrete data—lump changes in the amount of capital and fish instead of continuous changes. (It is like measuring changes in the amount of water when it is a fluid compared to when it exists as discrete cubes of ice.) Thus, the marginal product of the

Figure 14-1

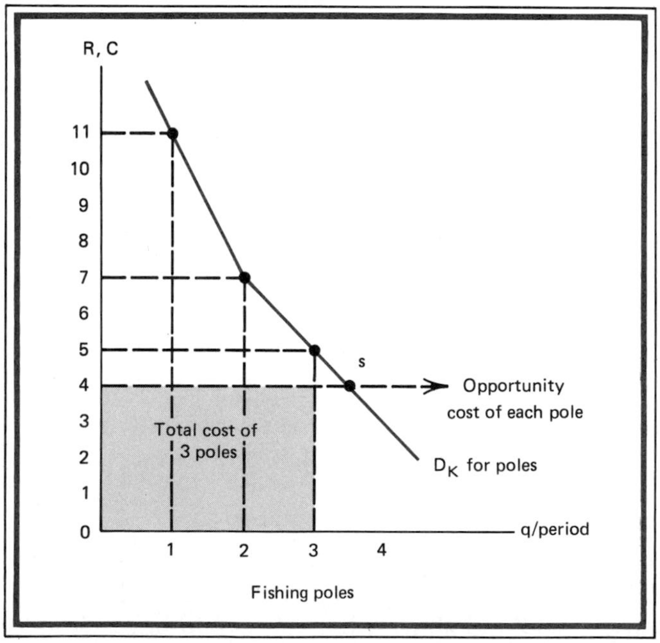

second pole is $(18 - 11)/(2 - 1) = 7$; of the third pole it is $(23 - 18)/(3 - 2) = 5$. The demand curve D_K for fishing poles is downward sloping, reflecting diminishing marginal returns to capital. The total number of fish you can catch *each* day with 3 poles is 23 $(11 + 7 + 5)$. The opportunity cost of building the 3 poles is 12, equal to 4 fish per pole and is illustrated by the shaded area. In general to maximize net product $(TP - TC)$, you should continue to invest in poles until the demand curve and cost curve cross at $R = C$ $(MP_K = MC)$. This happens where $r = 0$ at point s for 3.5 fishing poles (the discreteness problem again).

The same information as that shown in Figure 14-1 can be shown in Figure 14-2 where the vertical axis represents r instead of R and C, and r is expressed in percentages. There, the curve shows the marginal efficiency of investment for various amounts of investment, and is often called the MEI schedule, or simply the investment demand schedule. Figure 14-1 illustrates the demand for capital (poles) and the increase in product each pole adds to the total stock. Figure 14-2 tells us the rate r that is earned from each new investment. But r is also affected by how fast the capital stock is being increased. Since time is a cost, the speed at which investment is occurring is intimately related to cost measured here in terms of sacrificed fish. This time-cost critically affects the rate of return to investment, and together with the marginal product of capital MP_K determines the **rate of return** r. It is important to know in making investment decisions how quickly the project will be completed before it begins to yield its marginal product.[1]

The *rate of return* is the ratio of net return to cost per time period.

INCONVENIENCE AND THE REWARD FOR WAITING

From our illustration so far, it appears that you will take a full 6 days off from fishing and construct 3 fishing poles to get the total of 23 fish per day of fishing that the poles will provide. But this is probably not the way things will work

[1]The rate of return r does not equal the marginal product of capital $(MP_K \neq r)$ unless cost C is zero, meaning the pole was created instantaneously. Or, when the additional output from the new capital is realized within the same time period in which the capital is produced. Consider the first fishing pole. If the production period were 11/20 of a day during which 1 1/10 fish could be caught (using the ratio of 2 fish per day caught with the stick), then

$$r = \frac{R - C}{C} = \frac{11 - 1.1}{1.1} = 9, \text{ or } 900\%,$$

which equals

$$MP_K = \frac{\Delta TP}{\Delta K} = \frac{11 - 2}{1 - 0} = 9, \text{ or } 900\ \%.$$

However, when the production period of the capital (fishing pole) extends beyond 1 period, r is less than MP_K. Thus, the relevant decision variable is the rate of return r. Though the first pole yields 11 fish a day, if it were to take such a long time to build that you would starve to death first, then you would conclude that the rate of return r is too low. Actually, you would try to construct it a little bit at a time. This would guarantee that $r < MP_K$ would result. But $r < MP_K$ is not important. It is r relative to the opportunity cost of new investment that is important. And that opportunity cost critically depends on the time period of production.

Figure 14-2

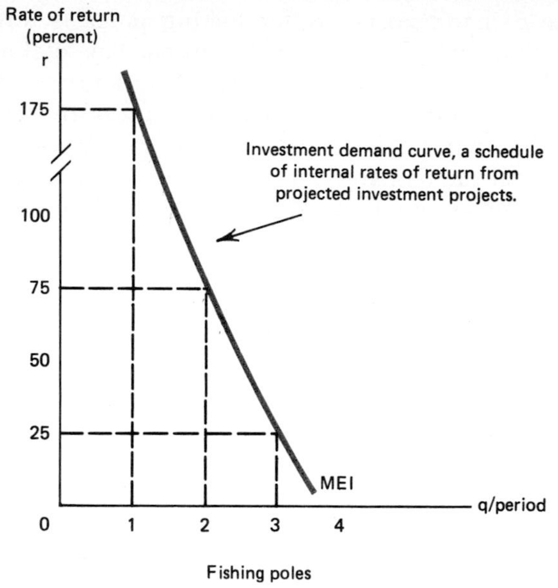

out. The reason is that you are sure to get quite hungry if you have to go for 2 days without eating in order to have a single pole. It is more likely that you find your hunger awfully inconvenient, and quit work on the first pole when it is only half finished. That is, you work on the pole 1 day, then fish 1 day to eat, then work on the pole another day. Assume that you finish building a pole at the end of a second day's work that allows you to catch 9 fish. You fish the third day and get 9 fish. At this point you begin to reap your rewards for waiting.

These 9 fish will sustain you for 3 days if you now increase your consumption to 3 fish per day. You now must fish only 1 day out of every 3 in order to sustain your new higher level of consumption, and building the second pole will mean giving up 3 fish per day. That is, the opportunity cost of the second pole is now higher, because more consumption must be given up to acquire the second pole.

Now, assume that you decide to fish 2 days in a row, catch 18 fish, but keep your consumption level at 3 per day, and spend the next 4 days building the additional poles. You took 2 days to catch the fish and 4 days to build the poles for a total of 6 days. Eating 3 fish per day for 4 days depletes your inventory of 12 fish. But you now have 3 poles to put to work. That is, you produced 18 fish over 2 days but only consumed 6 fish while fishing and saved a total of 12 fish that sustained you while building the additional poles.

Saving Equals Investment

It turns out that saving and investment will equal each other, by definition. What you produce is your income. Savings are what you have left over after

For the aggregate of all consumers and all investors, *saving equals investment.*

you have consumed that part of your income you desire to consume. But when you have produced something and not consumed it, you have added to the stock of capital—invested. Thus, investment too is what has been produced but not consumed, the same thing as saving. On the island you added to your inventory of fish—saved and invested simultaneously, then you depleted (consumed) the inventory of fish while you built the fishing poles—replaced one form of investment with another. Finally, the new poles were functional and the reward of greater production began to be felt.

In the isolated economy you invested and saved simultaneously, but in a market economy, different people do the saving and investment. Some people do some of each. Nevertheless, the equation that saving equals investment holds for the aggregate of all consumers and all investors.

THE OPPORTUNITY COST OF CAPITAL

The *opportunity cost of capital* is determined by the return on the next best investment alternative.

We have not pursued the possibility that other kinds of capital besides a fishing pole—a shelter for example—can also provide benefit to you if you are abandoned on a deserted island. In our case, the only opportunity cost we considered was the loss of fish. But having 1 pole you might fish for 2 days and use your savings to sustain you for 4 days, then build a shelter during those days rather than construct additional poles. In other words, the value of the shelter to you may be greater than the value of the added poles. By constructing the shelter you forgo either the added fish you could have caught and stored up in your inventory of fish, or the added poles you could have built. Thus, the various returns on various investment alternatives that you perceive will determine the opportunity cost of capital. These returns are generally expressed as percentages.

THE DEMAND FOR INVESTMENT AND THE SUPPLY OF SAVING

By graphical analysis we can now use demand and supply to show how the equilibrium rate of interest is determined. In Figure 14-3 the demand for investment funds is expressed by a marginal efficiency of investment (MEI) schedule as it was in Figure 14-2, and a positively sloped supply of saving schedule is added to it. In a market economy this demand curve is the result of the adding up of all the marginal efficiency of investment schedules for all the firms in the economy. Also, the supply of saving schedule is the result of adding all the supplies available from all consumers.

As in the case of the firm in perfect competition, the amount of the single firm's demand for new capital is sufficiently small that it has no effect on the

Figure 14-3

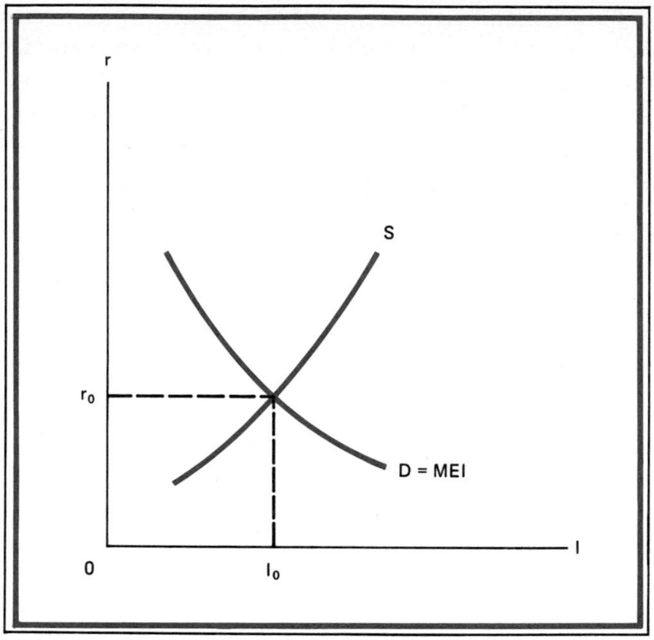

r—now an expression of both the cost of capital and the return on capital. Thus, to the individual firm the r is given by the market. In equilibrium, the rate of return r_0 is just high enough to induce the aggregate of savers to save the required amount, and this rate is also equal to the return from the investments undertaken by all the business firms in the society.

Three Man Island

Assume there are 3 people on the island each catching 2 fish a day with spears. Two of them offer to provide Mr. Innovator, the third man, with 1 fish a day each for 2 days while Mr. Innovator builds a net with a long pole that will catch 14 fish in a day.

The 2 men earn an income of 2 fish a day. They are each willing to save (not consume) 1 fish a day for 2 days for use by Mr. Innovator provided he will pay them 4 fish each in return. The interest payment to the men includes the inconvenience to them for deferring consumption plus a risk premium. That is, part of the interest also includes a markup because there is no certainty that Innovator will succeed. Therefore the rate of interest for borrowing 2 fish is 100 percent, since he must pay back 4 fish on the third day. Let us use *i* to designate the interest rate that the borrower must pay the lender.

$$i = \frac{8 - 4}{4} = 1 \text{ or } 100 \text{ percent.}$$

Mr. Innovator still gets his 2 fish a day to eat.

The rate of return to Innovator is

$$r = \frac{14 - 8}{4} = \frac{6}{4} = 1.5$$

or 150 percent over the two-day accounting period. The cost, 8 fish, is composed of 4 fish that Innovator borrowed (financial capital) representing the saving by the other 2 men plus the opportunity cost, namely the interest rate payments of 4 fish. Notice that if Innovator had not borrowed but starved for 2 days his opportunity cost would still be the 4 fish he could have speared had he not been building the net. You can readily see that interest is a cost, an opportunity cost, not profit. Profit is the return above opportunity cost and risk. As it is, r is greater than opportunity cost, that is, so long as $r > i$ the project is profitable and beneficial to everyone.

Suppose it is anticipated that the fishing net would only yield 11 fish: $r = (11 - 8)/4 = .75$ or 75 percent, which is less than the $i = 100$ percent above. In this case $r < i$, and Innovator would not undertake the project. The fishing net is still productive, but not productive enough to invest in because the return is too low to overcome the opportunity cost.

When there is a free exchange and competition in the marketplace, the owner of capital can invest in one of two ways. He can invest by sacrificing current income and use it to create capital that will yield more income later; or he can loan a part of his capital stock to another person and charge interest. Where risk is nonexistent the investor is at a point of indifference between either approach. No pure profits would occur and $r = i$ would be the fact. Where any discrepancy exists between r and i, assuming $r > i$ of course, a pure profit or economic rent would occur. But in a competitive market further investments would be encouraged which would eliminate the difference. The rate of return is driven down by new investments until it is equal to the interest rate. When $r = i$, no *new* investment occurs.

INVESTMENT, CAPITAL, AND ECONOMIC GROWTH

The standard of living of a group of individuals in an economy is the measure of the community's well-being. When this standard rises over time we say that the economy is growing. To a considerable extent, economic growth occurs because people save, invest, create capital, and are able, therefore, to realize greater production from their limited labor and land resource base. It is true, of course, that training and education make labor more productive, a form of investment in human capital, that fertilizer makes land more productive, and that new technology makes all factors of production more productive. Thus economic growth is related to science, technology, and workforce training. But another considerable portion of growth derives from investment in plant and equipment and the expanded supply of capital that it implies.

Machinery has both figuratively and literally taken the burden off the shoulders of mankind. While working conditions during the Industrial Revolution (1750-1850) seem dismal by most standards today, the industrial environment then was quite an improvement over the poverty on many farms at that time.

So long as the productivity of capital is large enough so that the return on investment is high enough to persuade people to save, the country's economy will grow and net investment will take place continuously over time. In theory, there could come a day when investment opportunities seem to offer only a small return—a return insufficient to induce any net saving in the economy. In such a case, the economy could stop growing and could fall into what economists refer to as a stationary state equilibrium—an equilibrium without growth. Only worn-out capital is replaced.

Stability of the Real Rate of Interest

The *equilibrium rate of interest* is determined by the demand for investment and the supply of saving.

The real rate of interest has been surprisingly constant over this century. When a more productive technology is introduced into a new piece of capital, the demand curve for investment shifts to the right and causes the rate of interest to rise. The more productive the capital, the higher the rate of interest because the prospects of good returns to investment are present. The higher interest rate increases the quantity supplied of savings as well. As the capital stock expands, diminishing returns to capital occur. With diminishing returns to capital as the capital stock increases, it becomes less desirable to add to the capital stock. Thus the rate of return will tend to fall from r_0 to r_1 as shown by the movement from point *a* to point *b* in Figure 14-4. Initially, this makes it appear that real rates of interest will remain at the lower level. But if diminishing returns to investment are offset by improved technology, the MEI_1 curve

Figure 14-4

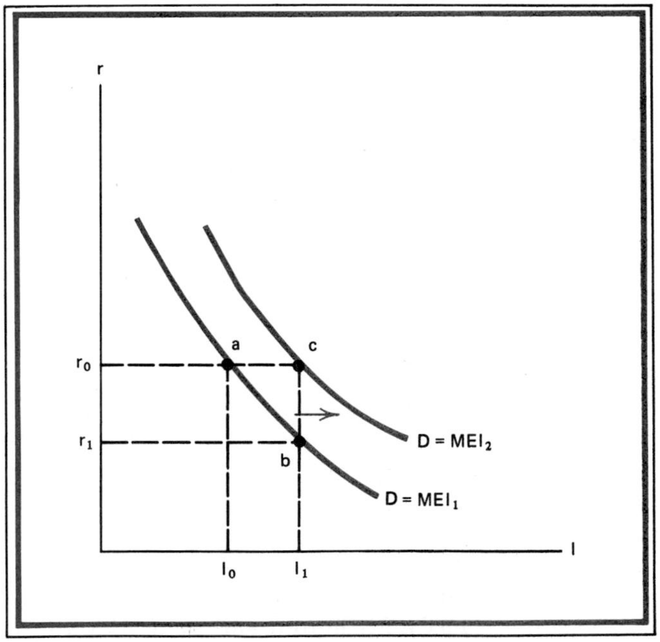

shifts to MEI_2 which more or less maintains the real rate of interest at r_0 at point c. It is not surprising, therefore, to find the real rate of interest remaining quite stable over time. The interest rate i is always positive. It is not likely ever to reach zero. As long as some investor believes something can be improved or done a little better, yielding a worthwhile return r, interest will be positive since the expectation exists that borrowed funds can be turned into a profit.

TIME AND PRESENT VALUE

Not only does it take time to produce capital, it also takes time to consume it or use it up. Capital has a durable life. Different kinds of equipment have different life spans. Some land improvements may last forever. The fishing pole may last 6 months, 1 year, 2 years or more. During these time periods, capital yields a stream of services or income. Therefore, when money prices are introduced, the value or worth of new capital can be estimated by taking into account not just the income it produces next year, but the entire chain of income streams expected in future periods. Let us now digress to explain how to estimate the value today of income to be received in the future. Finishing that, we can connect the results of this discussion to the value of a long-lived asset.

Since income received in the future has less value to you today because of its later availability, future income is discounted, in a sense it is marked down, by using the interest rate to calculate the amount of the deduction. Because the interest rate reflects the rate of substitution between current and deferred income (or consumption), the interest rate is needed to calculate the value of that future income to you today, namely its present value. As the interest rate rises, the present value of future income falls, and as the interest rate falls, the present value of future income rises.

For instance, how much money would you give me for \$1 if I offered you \$1 right now? Obviously only \$1. One dollar now is worth \$1. Suppose you are asked what you would pay for \$1 today if it were to be given to you 1 year from today? That's a different question. Having one dollar to use now is worth more to you than having that dollar to use one year hence.

The present value of \$1 to be paid to you 1 year from now has to be discounted for 1 year. Thus, the present value is

$$PV = \frac{1}{1 + i}$$

where the interest rate i is the discount rate. If the rate of interest equals 6 percent, the present value of \$1 paid a year from now is

$$PV = \frac{R_1}{1 + .06} = \$.943 \text{ or } 94.3 \text{ cents.}$$

The 94.3 cents is the value today of \$1 received a year from today. And 94.3

cents lent today at 6 percent would yield \$1 in a year. The present value of R_1 dollars payable a year from now is shown in this equation.[2]

$$PV = \frac{R_1}{(1+i)}.$$

Farther Ahead

Suppose you were asked, instead, how much you would pay today for \$1 that would be paid to you 2 years from now? Since 2 years is farther into the future, the dollar would even be worth less to you. The present value formulation is

$$PV = \frac{1}{(1+i)^2}$$

If the rate of interest equals 6 percent, then the value of a dollar today payable 2 years from now is

$$PV = \frac{1}{(1+.06)^2} = \$.890 \text{ or } 89 \text{ cents}$$

The longer the wait, the less is the dollar worth today. If R_2 dollars were to be paid 2 years from now, and the rate of interest were i, then this equation would hold.[3]

$$PV = \frac{R_2}{(1+i)^2}.$$

Again, let $R_t = \$1$ and $i = 6\%$, and let $t = 7$ years. The present value of one dollar payable 7 years from today at 6 percent is

$$PV = \frac{1}{(1+.06)^7} = \$.665 \text{ or } 66\ 1/2 \text{ cents}$$

[2]Discounting is the reverse of accumulating interest. If present value PV is the principle, then in 1 year the principle will earn R_1 dollars, equal to the principle PV plus the interest on the principle $PV \times i$, or

$$PV + PV(i) = R.$$

Therefore, factoring PV gives

$$PV(1+i) = R_1.$$

Dividing both sides by $1 + i$ gives

$$PV = \frac{R_1}{1+i}$$

[3]With R_1 as the return after the first year, it becomes the principle for the second year yielding a return of R_2 after a year or $R_1 + R_1 \times i = R_1(1+i) = R_2$. For a one year wait $PV = R_1/(1+i)$. Thus, substitute $R_1 = PV(1+i)$ in the expression for R_2 to get $PV(1+i)^2 = R_2$. Solving for PV by dividing both sides by $(1+i)^2$ yields $PV = R_2/(1+i)^2$.

The Real and Money Rates of Interest

When paper money is explicitly excluded, the rate of interest is expressed in goods and is a real rate of interest. Thus, if a machine can be built at home that is able to can 40 jars of peaches a year forever once it is built, but requires the sacrifice of canning 400 jars while devoting time to create it, then the cost of the machine is 400 jars of canned peaches. The formula for the real rate of interest, when a machine lasts forever, is modified to

$$r = \frac{R}{C} = \frac{\text{40 jars a year forever}}{\text{400 jars sacrificed this year}}$$
$$= .10 \text{ or } 10\%.$$

This is the real rate of interest in a moneyless economy. However, when money is introduced, money as a measure of value does not always retain its value over time. Money can be cheapened by inflation and this gives rise to the money rate of interest diverging from the real rate of interest. The real rate reflects the productivity of the canning machine. The money rate of interest is defined as

$$i = r + P^e$$

where r is the real rate of interest and P^e is the expected rate of increase in the price level. If the anticipated rate of inflation is zero, then $P^e = 0$, and the money rate of interest would equal the real rate.* But if the expected inflation rate is 5 percent, then the medium of exchange—paper money—that is being used to buy and sell real goods is declining in value because the same amount of money will purchase fewer jars of peaches, making the money rate of interest greater than the real rate. Adding the real rate of 10 percent to the inflation rate of 5 percent yields a money rate of interest of $i = 10 + 5 = 15\%$. Therefore, the money rate of interest must rise by the inflation rate to make up for the expected decline in the value of money relative to future goods (peaches). The rational lender will mark up the real rate of interest by the expected inflation rate in order to be paid back with more dollars so as not to realize a loss from saving. The lender will charge this money rate of interest, composed of 10 percent due to expected inflation plus another 5 percent to ensure a positive rate of return to his saving.

* Actually the money rate of interest does not reflect the full amount of the inflation rate. See S. C. Tsiang, "Keynes's 'Finance' Demand for Liquidity, Robertson's Loanable Funds Theory, and Friedman's Monetarism," The Quarterly Journal of Economics, May 1980: 467–491.

In general, the present value of R_t dollars payable t years from now is

$$PV = \frac{R_t}{(1 + i)^t}.$$

As t gets large the calculations become complicated. However, tables are conveniently provided so that repetitive and tedious calculations can be avoided. Also, many hand calculators are programmed to do them. Table 14-1 shows the present value of a dollar for various years and various interest rates. As an example, calculate the present value of $5 payable 6 years from now when the interest rate is 4 percent. Setting up the problem,

$$PV = \frac{5}{(1 + .04)^6}.$$

Refer to Table 14-1. Since the number of years is 6, move down the column headed "Years hence" until you reach 6. Then proceed across that row until

TABLE 14-1 Present Value of $1.00 $\left(PV = \frac{1}{(1 \quad i)^t}\right)$

Years hence (*t*)	1%	2%	4%	6%	8%	10%	12%	14%	15%	16%	18%	20%	22%	24%	25%	26%	28%	30%	35%	40%	45%	50%
1	0.990	0.980	0.962	0.943	0.926	0.909	0.893	0.877	0.870	0.862	0.847	0.833	0.820	0.806	0.800	0.794	0.781	0.769	0.741	0.714	0.690	0.667
2	0.980	0.961	0.925	0.890	0.857	0.826	0.797	0.769	0.756	0.743	0.718	0.694	0.672	0.650	0.640	0.630	0.610	0.592	0.549	0.510	0.476	0.444
3	0.971	0.942	0.889	0.840	0.794	0.751	0.712	0.675	0.658	0.641	0.609	0.579	0.551	0.524	0.512	0.500	0.477	0.455	0.406	0.364	0.328	0.296
4	0.961	0.924	0.855	0.792	0.735	0.683	0.636	0.592	0.572	0.552	0.516	0.482	0.451	0.423	0.410	0.397	0.373	0.350	0.301	0.260	0.226	0.198
5	0.951	0.906	0.822	0.747	0.681	0.621	0.567	0.519	0.497	0.476	0.437	0.402	0.370	0.341	0.328	0.315	0.291	0.269	0.223	0.186	0.156	0.132
6	0.942	0.888	0.790	0.705	0.630	0.564	0.507	0.456	0.432	0.410	0.370	0.335	0.303	0.275	0.262	0.250	0.227	0.207	0.165	0.133	0.108	0.088
7	0.933	0.871	0.760	0.665	0.583	0.513	0.452	0.400	0.376	0.354	0.314	0.279	0.249	0.222	0.210	0.198	0.178	0.159	0.122	0.095	0.074	0.059
8	0.923	0.853	0.731	0.627	0.540	0.467	0.404	0.351	0.327	0.305	0.266	0.233	0.204	0.179	0.168	0.157	0.139	0.123	0.091	0.068	0.051	0.039
9	0.914	0.837	0.703	0.592	0.500	0.424	0.361	0.308	0.284	0.263	0.225	0.194	0.167	0.144	0.134	0.125	0.108	0.094	0.067	0.048	0.035	0.026
10	0.905	0.820	0.676	0.558	0.463	0.386	0.322	0.270	0.247	0.227	0.191	0.162	0.137	0.116	0.107	0.099	0.085	0.073	0.050	0.035	0.024	0.017
11	0.896	0.804	0.650	0.527	0.429	0.350	0.287	0.237	0.215	0.195	0.162	0.135	0.112	0.094	0.086	0.079	0.066	0.056	0.037	0.025	0.017	0.012
12	0.887	0.788	0.625	0.497	0.397	0.319	0.257	0.208	0.187	0.168	0.137	0.112	0.092	0.076	0.069	0.062	0.052	0.043	0.027	0.018	0.012	0.008
13	0.879	0.773	0.601	0.469	0.368	0.290	0.229	0.182	0.163	0.145	0.116	0.093	0.075	0.061	0.055	0.050	0.040	0.033	0.020	0.013	0.008	0.005
14	0.870	0.758	0.577	0.442	0.340	0.263	0.205	0.160	0.141	0.125	0.099	0.078	0.062	0.049	0.044	0.039	0.032	0.025	0.015	0.009	0.006	0.003
15	0.861	0.743	0.555	0.417	0.315	0.239	0.183	0.140	0.123	0.108	0.084	0.065	0.051	0.040	0.035	0.031	0.025	0.020	0.011	0.006	0.004	0.002
16	0.853	0.728	0.534	0.394	0.292	0.218	0.163	0.123	0.107	0.093	0.071	0.054	0.042	0.032	0.028	0.025	0.019	0.015	0.008	0.005	0.003	0.002
17	0.844	0.714	0.513	0.371	0.270	0.198	0.146	0.108	0.093	0.080	0.060	0.045	0.034	0.026	0.023	0.020	0.015	0.012	0.006	0.003	0.002	0.001
18	0.836	0.700	0.494	0.350	0.250	0.180	0.130	0.095	0.081	0.069	0.051	0.038	0.028	0.021	0.018	0.016	0.012	0.009	0.005	0.002	0.001	0.001
19	0.828	0.686	0.475	0.331	0.232	0.164	0.116	0.083	0.070	0.060	0.043	0.031	0.023	0.017	0.014	0.012	0.009	0.007	0.003	0.002	0.001	
20	0.820	0.673	0.456	0.312	0.215	0.149	0.104	0.073	0.061	0.051	0.037	0.026	0.019	0.014	0.012	0.010	0.007	0.005	0.002	0.001	0.001	
21	0.811	0.660	0.439	0.294	0.199	0.135	0.093	0.064	0.053	0.044	0.031	0.022	0.015	0.011	0.009	0.008	0.006	0.004	0.002	0.001		
22	0.803	0.647	0.422	0.278	0.184	0.123	0.083	0.056	0.046	0.038	0.026	0.018	0.013	0.009	0.007	0.006	0.004	0.003	0.001	0.001		
23	0.795	0.634	0.406	0.262	0.170	0.112	0.074	0.049	0.040	0.033	0.022	0.015	0.010	0.007	0.006	0.005	0.003	0.002	0.001			
24	0.788	0.622	0.390	0.247	0.158	0.102	0.066	0.043	0.035	0.028	0.019	0.013	0.008	0.006	0.005	0.004	0.003	0.002	0.001			
25	0.780	0.610	0.375	0.233	0.146	0.092	0.059	0.038	0.030	0.024	0.016	0.010	0.007	0.005	0.004	0.003	0.002	0.001	0.001			
26	0.772	0.598	0.361	0.220	0.135	0.084	0.053	0.033	0.026	0.021	0.014	0.009	0.006	0.004	0.003	0.002	0.002	0.001				
27	0.764	0.586	0.347	0.207	0.125	0.076	0.047	0.029	0.023	0.018	0.011	0.007	0.005	0.003	0.002	0.002	0.001	0.001				
28	0.757	0.574	0.333	0.196	0.116	0.069	0.042	0.026	0.020	0.016	0.010	0.006	0.004	0.002	0.002	0.002	0.001	0.001				
29	0.749	0.563	0.321	0.185	0.107	0.063	0.037	0.022	0.017	0.014	0.008	0.005	0.003	0.002	0.002	0.001	0.001	0.001				
30	0.742	0.552	0.308	0.174	0.099	0.057	0.033	0.020	0.015	0.012	0.007	0.004	0.003	0.002	0.001	0.001	0.001					
40	0.672	0.453	0.208	0.097	0.046	0.022	0.011	0.005	0.004	0.003	0.001	0.001										
50	0.608	0.372	0.141	0.054	0.021	0.009	0.003	0.001	0.001	0.001												

you come under the column headed 4%. The number is .790. This signifies that \$.790 or 79 cents is the present value of \$1. Then \$5 × .79 = \$3.95 is the present value of \$5 under the stated conditions.

Valuing Capital

The value of new investment capital will vary according to the length of its useful life, and by what the interest rate is. An investment good such as a fishing net or a computer is a real asset. A real asset is a legal claim on a stream of services that have exchange value. A money or financial asset is a legal claim to future fixed streams of income, for example, a bond.

The *present value* of an asset is the sum of the discounted values of its expected yearly net income flows.

Capital is an asset embodying claims to a sequence of yearly earnings, or services with a market value, over t years. The yearly incomes are expected net incomes (*NR*) derived by subtracting expected operating costs from expected revenues for each year. The **present value** of an asset, therefore, is the discounted sum of its expected net income receipts. It is called *capitalizing* the value of the asset.

$$PV = \frac{NR_1}{(1+i)} + \frac{NR_2}{(1+i)^2} + \ldots + \frac{NR_t}{(1+i)^t} \qquad (NR = TR - TC).$$

The Decision Rule

In making an investment decision, the profit-maximizing firm will undergo the investment so long as the present value of the project is greater than the cost. That is,

If $PV > C$, invest in the machine
If $PV < C$, do not invest.[4]

Assume a piece of machinery costs \$2,500 and the net revenues expected over the 3 years of the machine's life are \$500, \$1,000, and \$1,500. The market rate of interest is 5 percent. The table does not list figures for 5 percent. By taking the entries for years 1, 2, and 3 and averaging the values for 4 percent and 6 percent, the 5 percent figure can be calculated close enough. For the first year $i = \frac{.962 + .943}{2} = .952$ with rounding. Hence,

$$\begin{aligned} PV &= 500(.952) + 1{,}000(.908) + 1{,}500(.865) \\ &= 476.0 + 908.0 + 1{,}297.50 \\ &= \$2{,}618.50. \end{aligned}$$

[4]The alternative form of the same decision rule compares the rate of return r (or the marginal inefficiency of investment) to the market rate of interest; hence,

If $r > i$, invest because this usually implies $PV > C$.
If $r < i$, do not invest because this usually implies $PV < C$.

However, in some cases $r > i$ would not yield $PV > C$. Then go with present value.

The present value of the machine is greater than its cost on the basis of what the decision maker believes will be the expected net revenues over the next 3 years. The machine is a profitable venture by all appearances. Of course, unpredictable events could change that once the machine is purchased and losses could result instead.

Sometimes the decision to invest is a difficult one. The entrepreneur may have to decide between a machine lasting 7 years as compared with one lasting 10 years; or whether to replace the old machine or purchase a more expensive new one utilizing improvements. The higher cost of the new machine must be justified by its higher rate of return.

If it is assumed that the estimated net earnings each year are the same, that is, $NR_1 = NR_2 = \ldots NR_t$, then the formula becomes

$$PV = NR\left[\frac{1}{(1+i)} + \frac{1}{(1+i)^2} + \ldots + \frac{1}{(1+i)^t}\right].$$

The common NR term is factored out. We observe that the longer the capital equipment is in use, the greater is the present value since more terms are being added. But each successive term adds less than the prior term since they lie farther into the future and their individual present value contribution is therefore smaller.

We can now see how the price of a piece of land used for the growing of corn is related to the stream of rental payments from the land. We can also see that the stronger is the demand for corn, the higher the rental payments are for renting the land, hence the greater the yearly net revenues earned by leasing the land to corn growers. From this it follows that the present value of the land is also larger the greater is the demand for whatever the land is being used for.

Moreover, since present value depends on what expected revenues and expected costs are, the profit is determined by the excess of revenues over those expected costs. That is, if net revenues end up being even greater than anticipated they confer a capital gain.

In brief, the rate of interest is determined by the supply and demand for investment funds. The supply is provided by savers including businesses themselves. At the point of short-run equilibrium the rate of interest will be equal to the rate of return of new capital and to the marginal rate of substitution between the present and future consumption by savers, also equal to the rate of interest.

If the long-run competitive equilibrium of the economy occurs at a lower rate of interest than currently exists, then in a dynamic system prospects will emerge for new investments whose return r is greater than that long-run interest rate. The stock of capital will be increased, diminishing returns set in, and the interest rate falls until another short-run equilibrium position is temporarily attained where $r = i$.

Capitalizing Profits

It can be shown that when capital is assumed to last forever, known as perpetuity, then as t approaches infinity, the formula becomes

$$PV = \frac{NR}{r}.$$

In this form it is easy to show why pure profits garnered by a monopoly seller do not transfer to the buyer of the capital earning such monopoly profits. Suppose a business has a market price of $80,000. Maybe it is the only local tavern and yields an annual net return of $16,000 a year. The tavern yields a net return

$$r = \frac{NR}{PV} = \frac{\$16{,}000}{80{,}000} = .20 \text{ or } 20 \text{ percent.}$$

Had the owner borrowed the $80,000 at 8 percent, then at what price would he sell the tavern? The owner is making a pure profit of 20 − 8 = 12 percent. The buyer is assured of $16,000 a year. The owner would sell it at a *capitalized value* of

$$PV = \frac{16{,}000}{.08} = \$200{,}000.$$

The owner capitalizes his profits into the selling price and captures the pure profits that he could have earned had he retained ownership. Does the buyer get anything? Yes, a normal return. He gets a rate of return

$$r = \frac{NR}{PV} = \frac{\$16{,}000}{200{,}000} = .08 \text{ or } 8 \text{ percent}$$

This is a normal return equal to the market rate of interest, the opportunity cost.

Profit is the return above opportunity cost and risk.

But no pure **profit** is earned above opportunity cost. Present value is wealth. Even if the owner had not sold the tavern, his wealth increases when the tavern's value increases.

CHAPTER SUMMARY

Capital is a man-made tool of production. Just as labor earns wages for the flow of services it provides and land earns a rent for the flow of services it provides, capital earns interest for the flow of services it yields. This interest is sometimes called a quasi-rent since the return to a machine is a kind of rent similar to what land earns.

Like labor, capital is a derived demand—being derived from the demand for the goods that capital produces. Marginal productivity theory also applies to capital.

Capital, however, is a special input because it is a roundabout method of increasing future production by sacrificing current consumption. Therefore, capital formation requires that there be saving. Furthermore, capital is a stock variable and the change in the capital stock per period is a flow variable, namely investment. Thus saving equals investment. Since investment requires both sacrifice and time, there are opportunity costs to creating capital. When benefits are greater than costs, capital yields a positive rate of return, or a profit.

Saving will only occur if the interest rate is positive. The higher the interest rate the higher the amount of saving. In a moneyless economy, the interest rate is a real rate of interest and measures at what rate goods are sacrificed today in order to consume more goods in the future. The higher the rate of interest, the lower is the value today of consuming future goods or the higher is the value of waiting to consume future goods. Each consumer has a rate of substitution between current consumption and the greater satisfaction of consuming more later.

The interest rate is also positive, not only because of the future reward it promises, but because capital formation is risky. Therefore, the interest rate also includes a risk cost in order to induce people to take chances and forgo current consumption.

The marginal productivity of capital equals the change in total product divided by the change in capital input. Thus it is expressed in physical units independent of time. Time imposes a cost. Therefore, the length of the period required to produce a piece of capital must enter into the calculation of its rate of return—also known as the real rate of interest or the marginal efficiency of investment. The important decision variable is not the marginal productivity of capital but the rate of return on investment, since the latter explicitly incorporates both the marginal productivity of capital and the costs of constructing capital. The rate of return on an investment equals net revenue divided by the cost of capital.

The interest rate is a cost, hence for a project to be profitable the rate of return must be greater than the rate of interest. In a perfectly competitive market the rate of return would be driven to where it equaled the rate of interest. The quantity of investment is inversely related to the rate of interest, *ceteris paribus*.

Although capital takes time to produce, it also takes time to consume since it may last for many years. When goods are denominated in paper money, the present value of a piece of capital can be calculated by discounting the future streams of net income the capital is expected to yield. Since income to be received in the future has less value today, the value of future income must be marked down. The discounting factor used is the interest rate. The higher the rate of interest the lower the present value of an asset. And the lower the rate of interest the higher the asset's present value. If the present value is greater than the original cost of the machine, the machine is a profitable investment. If present value is lower than cost, the investment is not profitable.

When capital is assumed to last forever, the present value formula simplifies and allows for an easy demonstration of why monopoly profits are earned only by the original monopolists, since they are capitalized when the monopoly is sold.

The real rate of interest only equals the money rate of interest in an economy without inflation or deflation. Thus, when there is inflation, the money rate of interest must equal the real rate plus an adjustment for the expected rate of inflation.

QUESTIONS

1. "If the owner (of forest land) has actually borrowed money to acquire the property and if he is paying interest on the borrowed capital, this interest is a real cost, and the owner in all likelihood will reduce his growing stock somewhat, in order to pay back borrowed capital. He may do this even though he intends to cut the same amount of lumber each year (sustained yield). For a wealthy landowner, on the other hand, who owns property outright, interest is not a real cost." (Quote, slightly edited, from Meyer et al., *Forest Management,* 2d ed. New York: Ronald, 1961, p. 70.)

a. Would the owner necessarily reduce his growing stock if he had to pay interest on borrowed funds? What item is being overlooked in the present-value calculation? What affects present value despite the owner's selling the same amount of lumber each year?
b. For the owner who owns the land free and clear, is it true that the interest rate is not a cost to him since he does not have to borrow money? Yes or no? Explain.
c. What significance does the interest rate serve in the economy?

2. Does adding much more of the same type of capital raise or lower the rate of return? Explain. Does adding much more of capital embodying new technology raise or lower the rate of return?
3. Why is it unlikely the interest rate will ever be zero? Discuss.
4. Is pure profit being earned if the rate of return is greater than the interest rate? Why would it ever be less than the rate of interest? (Do investors have perfect information about the future?)
5. When is, and when is not, the *MRP* of capital equal to the rate of interest? Explain.
6. You buy an auto tune-up kit from Sears during a sale for $60. It includes a dwell-tachometer meter, a timing light, a compression and fuel-pump checker, and a remote starter switch:
   a. How would you estimate the cost of owning the kit for 1 year? For 2 years?
   b. Describe how you would estimate the marginal revenue product of the tune-up kit if you intend to use it for one year. For two years.
   c. How would you determine the current value of the kit if you intend to use it for the next 10 years? Calculate whether or not you would purchase it.
7. A woman who owns the neighborhood copymart shop purchases a new Xerox machine for $20,000. Its market value after the first year is $17,000. Assume the rate of interest is 8 percent.
   a. What is the cost of purchasing and owning the machine for 1 year?
   b. Suppose its resale value after 3 years is $11,000. What is the cost of owning it for 3 years? (Note, compare the answers here with those in question 14 of chapter 5)
8. Big Log Timber Co. estimates that the profits from each Douglas fir it sells depends on the tree's age when sold. You are given the following information:

Age of Tree	Profit per Tree	Interest Rate
50	$1,000	10%
51	1,100	"
52	1,200	"
53	1,300	"
54	1,200	"

   a. Calculate the year that yields the highest present value for cutting and selling the tree.
   b. What is the best age to cut the tree if the rate of interest is zero?
9. Suppose you have the opportunity to purchase a vacant lot for $10,000. You estimate that in 5 years you will be able to sell the lot for double its purchase price. You now own $10,000 worth of corporate bonds which are yielding a 10 percent annual rate of return. Should you sell the bonds and buy the lot? Assume no inflation.
10. A college superstar signs with a National Basketball Association team for over $5 million. He gets $100,000 now for signing plus $1.25 million at the end of each of the next 4 years. Is the cost to the owner of signing him $5.1 million, assuming the rate of interest is 8 percent? Set up the calculation.
11. You sign up for a 2-semester course covering a period of 8 months with every intention of completing it. The hardback textbook required for the course is priced

at $17. But the price of the two paperbacks, each one covering only one semester, sell for $9 apiece. Suppose the rate of interest is 9 percent. To reduce your book expenses, should you buy the hardback or one paperback now and the other paperback 4 months from now at the beginning of the second semester? (Note: Interest is based on a year. Thus 6 months would mean interest of 1/2 of the yearly rate.) Show your calculations.

12. Is it always inefficient to keep the old machine and not adopt the new machine that incorporates the newest technology? Discuss.
13. Does the softhearted parent who cannot say "no" to his or her child, but suffers when the child grows up because it has not learned self discipline, have a higher or lower discount rate for facing up to unpleasant parental obligations than the parent who consistently but fairly disciplines the child? Does it therefore follow that the indulgent parent has a present-value benefit greater than the present-value benefit of the more firm parent? What assumption is necessary here to answer the question? Comment.
14. George Goodguy sees himself as fair-minded and always eager to be contemporary with the latest sociological fashions. He knows that in a competitive market the worker is paid his marginal revenue product. His company on the average pays women less than men and therefore assumes women are less productive than men. He then observes workers on the assembly line and is shocked to discover the women are performing as productively as the men while they are—and have been—paid less. Racked with guilt and self-doubt, George has a breakdown and is replaced by a former economist, Harvey Humbug. He studies the operation of the plant and discovers the following:
    a. A plant employee produces $10,000 worth of output a year.
    b. It costs $1,000 in administrative costs to hire a worker.
    c. It costs $1,000 to train a worker.
    d. All women work 3 years and quit and other women replace them.
    e. All men move to better jobs in the company after 6 years.
    f. The interest rate is 6 percent.

    He wants to know
    1. What is the present value of a woman worker?
    2. What is the present value of a male worker?
    3. What happens to the difference in the present value of the salaries between men and women (if there is a difference) if
        a. The interest rate falls?
        b. The cost of hiring doubles?
        c. The cost of training is cut in half?

    Assume all workers are already hired and trained to begin with. (Note: It is not necessary to make detailed calculations. You can ascertain the answers by simply setting up the problem correctly.)
15. Simon Legree owns an apartment building. In its current form he expects to earn $25,000 annually from the property above maintenance and operating costs. He decides to remodel. The contractor will do the job for $45,000 down plus $85,000 on completion—two years from the start. Simon believes that the remodeled apartments will *net* $35,000 a year from increased rents he will be able to charge. Assume the apartment will have to be shut down during remodeling.
    a. Explain how Simon would decide whether to remodel or not.
    b. Now set up how Simon would calculate whether to remodel or not.
    c. Assume the rate of interest is zero. Then answer *b* again.
    d. If $i > 0$, would the time for remodeling to pay for itself be greater or less than the time in *c*?
16. In Chapter 13 on economic rent we read how an athlete would provide his services so long as his salary was greater than his supply price, i.e., his opportunity cost. Yet

we see holdouts who lose half a season's pay. Is this irrational on their part, since much of their pay is economic rent anyhow? Explain.

17. Suppose the owner of a timber stand withholds his timber from the market even though it has reached biological maturity. He believes it can be sold for a higher price later. Is this decision, based on a desire to make more profit, socially irresponsible? Why, or why not? Suppose the price falls instead?

18. a. Assume the inflation rate is zero, so when interest rates (and mortgage rates) go up, the demand for future housing services goes down and people switch their preferences to consuming more nonhousing services.
    1. What happens to the present value of houses? Why?
    2. What happens to the price of houses?

    b. Now suppose the demand for future housing services rises, increasing the present value of housing and causing the mortgage rate to rise. However, to be consistent with a above, when the demand for future housing services increases, this implies that people switch from wanting nonhousing resources to desiring more future housing services. Thus they substitute future goods for current goods and save more, which should lower the interest rate. But we just said interest rates went up. How can the present value fall when interest rates rise, as it does in *a*, yet rise when interest rates rise as in *b*? Can you reconcile the apparent contradiction?

Chapter 15

Unions

PROGRESS REPORT

A. Earlier chapters covered the pure theory of factor allocation and incomes, for the most part outside of the influences of the institutional environment.

B. In this chapter the union role in the determination of the wage rate is described. Some background, current trends, the structure of labor unions, the impact unions have had on labor's share of the economy's total income, and union effects on income distribution are all examined. Legislation regarding labor unions is covered and the role of the National Right to Work Committee in combating compulsory unionism is mentioned.

C. In Chapter 16 the full issue of income distribution is examined going beyond the material of this chapter.

Unions **are organizations of workers who collectively bargain for wages, working conditions, and assorted benefits.**

Unions are organizations of workers that bargain with employers for economic and job benefits. They exist to create and wield political and economic power against private management and the government to achieve their goals. These goals are primarily higher wages, better working conditions, and job security. The arrangements made to achieve these goals are usually complex in their social and psychological detail.

The union movement has its origin in the old guilds of medieval times, when a skilled craft was looked upon as a property right handed down in the family from generation to generation. With industrialization, the single craftsmen working alone underwent displacement by larger shops and factories owned by noncraftsmen.

Union movements occurred in the latter years of the 1700s in the U.S. Carpenters, printers, and shoemakers formed organizations as early as 1791 in Philadelphia, Boston, and New York. These arose largely over economic conflicts between workers and employers when rapid changes in a young developing country began to break down the familiar methods of production and the close ties between worker and employer.

A long, hard drive for legalization of unions ensued. Unions fought with companies and unsympathetic courts for legitimacy and status. Unions were seen as a threat to free enterprise and private property, and therefore to political and economic stability. Arguments against unions usually took the form of "conspiracies in the restraint of trade." The courts often agreed. They were also considered radical, and companies resisted them vigorously. Violence was frequent on both sides. The government at times moved in state police and the National Guard to suppress the more fierce conflicts. It was not uncommon for companies to hire goon squads (hoodlums) to beat up strikers. Union workers themselves often punished other workers who did not support their policies.

Unions in the U.S. have always maintained a practical orientation, in contrast with the strong ideological bent of their European forebears. They have not adopted radical ideologies or unrealistic utopian goals. The world is full of scarcity, particularly jobs as union labor sees it. A major force in union organizing in the early part of the century, Samuel Gompers, took a pragmatic approach. He disdained the intellectuals in the labor movement as well as radical and utopian socialist theories. He was for "bread and butter unionism" or "pure and simple unionism." He was interested in immediate, practical gains—higher wages and shorter hours. He sided with no political party, only with politicians who could help whether Republican or Democrats. As for socialists, he felt them to be "economically unsound, socially wrong, and an industrial impossibility." They bored him. From 1949 to 1950 eleven local unions were expelled from membership in the Congress of Industrial Organizations (CIO) because of communist domination. In 1978 the AFL-CIO pulled out of the International Labor Organization (ILO) because of its communist domination. Until the Roosevelt era unions sided with no political party. Friends were those who helped; enemies those who did not. Since the 1930s, however, labor unions have typically supported more Democratic party candidates than Republican ones. But no Democratic presidential candidate can be assured that the union vote is in his pocket.

The Wagner Act

Unions actively existed long before the *Wagner Act* (1935) legitimized the right of workers to organize and to bargain with employers.

In July 1935 the Wagner Act was passed by Congress. It was the most important legislation in the history of the labor movement in the U.S. In one stroke labor obtained what it had struggled for for so long. It guaranteed employees the right to organize unions and to bargain with employers. It outlawed company unions and yellow-dog contracts, which required as a condition of employment that the worker must pledge not to join a union. To assist its implementation, the National Labor Relations Board (NLRB) was simultaneously created. The NLRB consists of five members appointed by the President for five-year terms. It was given powers to rule on unfair labor practices that interfere improperly with union organization and bargaining, to determine the bargaining unit in cases of union disputes on jurisdiction, and to call for plant elections when requested by workers. The NLRB does not interfere in wages and working conditions negotiated between unions and management, nor is it an enforcer of contracts. Antagonists must petition the courts for enforcement.

The NLRB proceeds in three steps. It receives the complaint, has a hearing on it, and then issues an order based on its findings. Some feel that its rulings have tended to favor labor more than management. Many disputes on which it made decisions have reached the Supreme Court for final resolution.

Things changed rapidly after 1935. Today unions that were once considered aberrations in society are looked upon as a conservative element, part of the status quo.

When World War II ended, both unions and management called for the immediate removal of wage and price controls that had been imposed during the war. There were numerous strikes and industrial disturbances. Often union discipline was nonexistent as wartime grievances and frustration pent up during the 1941–1945 period were unleashed.

Congress concluded that the balance between labor and management had tipped too far in favor of the unions.

Taft-Hartley Act 1947

Prompted by union abuses the *Taft-Hartley Act* (1947) restricted some union activities, including secondary boycotts and closed shops.

***Secondary boycotts* are those against the suppliers of a company being struck.**

This act, essentially an amendment to the Wagner Act, was passed over presidential veto. Some of its provisions were as follows:

1. It prohibited coercion of members by members.

2. It outlawed **secondary boycotts**. These are picket lines set up against companies who are suppliers of a company being struck. They are illegal although they still occur, but less frequently now than before 1947. *Boycotts* are attempts to get consumers not to buy a company's product. By punishing them economically the unions hope to make the company agree to the union's terms.

3. It prohibited jurisdictional strikes against a company because two unions are in conflict over which union will do which type of work, for example, whether the longshoremen or the teamsters load up trucks at the docks after the ships have been unloaded.

Closed shops require union membership; *open shops*, membership after 14 to 30 days employment.

4. It outlawed the **closed shop** and allowed for the *open shop*. The *closed shop* exists when a worker must join a union as a condition of employment. The *open shop* requires that the worker join the union after a time period, usually from 14 to 30 days after being hired. The *agency shop* is one where the worker does not have to join the union but must either pay union dues and initiation fees or designate a charity which would receive them if the union does not. The agency shop is a device for unions to circumvent the provisions of right-to-work laws that exist in twenty states. In a *check off* system union dues are deducted from the pay check by the company for the union.

5. Employers and the unions can petition the NLRB for elections. This requires that when 30 percent of the workers in a shop sign union representation cards, then an election is required to be held to determine if a union local is to be certified by the workers to negotiate for that shop. Also, when 30 percent of the workers want to decertify the union representing them, the NLRB must conduct an election. Firms often call for union decertification elections when they know the union is weak.

6. The certification and decertification elections must be conducted under a secret ballot.

7. A decertified union has to wait one year before it can petition the NLRB for a new election.

8. Unions may also be guilty of unfair labor practices.

9. Government employees are forbidden to strike. This is often ignored (railroad workers are exempt and come under the provisions of the Railway Labor Act).

10. The President can order an 80-day cooling off period to delay a strike, with court approval only, if there is demonstrable danger to national health and safety. This order has been rarely used.

11. All states are permitted to pass state right-to-work laws if they choose.

Despite the setbacks and restrictions imposed by the Taft-Hartley Act, complaints of union bullying and corruption continued. While not that numerous, some allegations were well documented and scandalizing. Particularly damaging was evidence of some of the unions' connections with syndicate mobsters, for example, the New York Longshoreman's Union. The film *On the Waterfront* was inspired by it. The Teamsters, led by Jimmy Hoffa, were investigated. In 1957 the Teamsters and the Bakery and Laundry Workers Unions were expelled by the AFL-CIO.

Landrum-Griffin Act (1959)

The *Landrum-Griffin Act* (1959) required government audits of unions and secret ballots in union elections.

When Congressional hearings on union activities revealed that racketeering and other undemocratic procedures were common in union ranks, this led to more intervention by the government, and another modification of the original Wagner Act. The Landrum-Griffin Act signaled entry by the government into labor-management relations and tighter control of internal union operations. Major provisions of this act were as follows:

1. Secret ballots were required in union elections.
2. Members had the right to remove leaders, and to be protected from charges against them without due process.

3. Secondary boycotts and picketing were more stringently regulated.
4. The union's constitution, by-laws, fees, fines, officers, membership qualifications, and election procedures were to be detailed in regular reports.
5. Union officials were required to file reports on their own finances and audits on union finances were required. All data were to be made available to the public.

Since 1955

Between 1936 and 1944 union membership jumped. From 1944 to 1955 membership rose but at a much slower pace. However, since 1955 labor union growth has stagnated, and as a share of the total labor force it has declined. This is shown in Figure 15-1. As a precentage of the total labor force union membership has dropped from around 24.0 percent in 1950 to 20.1 percent in 1978. When only nonagricultural establishments are considered, the percentages are 31.5 percent in 1950 to about 24 percent in 1980.

To seek some answers for this phenomenon it is helpful to look at the changing structure of the U.S. labor force. In the mid 1950s the number of white collar workers passed the number of blue collar workers. The white collar workers have offered greater resistance to unionization in the past, though that may be changing now. Also, because of technological change and large-scale movement of manufacturing from the Northeast to the less unionized South, the absolute number of unionized manufacturing jobs declined. Since 1963 this decline has been more than made up by inroads in white collar and

Figure 15-1

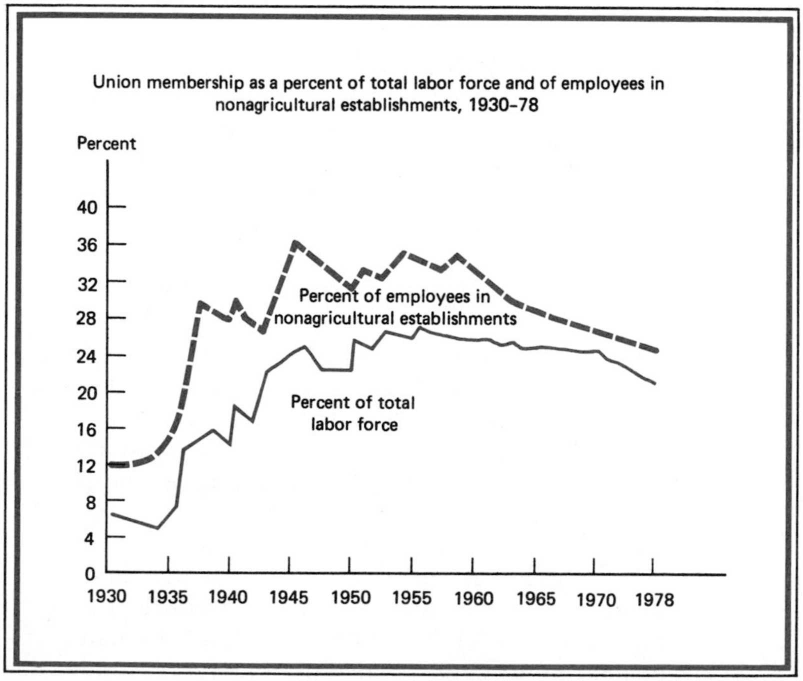

public sector unionization. Growth in membership, however, has not been great enough to increase the unions' share among the total labor force.

In the first ten years after the Wagner Act was passed, the basic manufacturing industries were unionized, leaving exempt only the white collar workers who ply in the service and retail trade sectors.

Over half of the nation's union members are found in six states: New York, Pennsylvania, California, Illinois, Ohio, and Michigan. The Northern states have lost many manufacturing jobs to right-to-work states in the South, and continue to lose plants and jobs to the rapidly growing Southern industrialization.

In part, some union decline is explained by the legislation of 1947 and 1959, the amendments to the Wagner Act. These amendments left the unions with less control over nonstrikers and nonunion employees.

In addition, the union's public image suffered in the 1970s, and public unions in particular will probably become a source of greater exasperation to the public. Unions are no longer viewed as the underdogs they were in the 1930s.

The leadership of unions, as seen by the public, and by some union members, is sometimes self-serving. Evidence of association with racketeers has created public skepticism of the leadership. In 1977, labor unions lost 54 percent of their secret ballot elections and over 75 percent of decertification elections, whose frequency tripled from 1968 to 1978. In 1979 unions won only 46 percent of the over 8000 representation elections, the smallest in 45 years.

THE PROSPECTS

Do not be misled into believing that unions are less powerful than they were, or that the future looks bleak for them. Unions are strong in the fundamentally important manufacturing sector. Even as the South continues its rapid industrial expansion, unions have a good chance of making further inroads there. Manufacturing industries in many cases are composed of large companies with nationwide plants. Their northern branches are unionized. As time passes, this should make it easier to gather in the flock among the southern branches of the companies. The United Automobile Workers (UAW) was certified in an Oklahoma General Motors plant in 1979. One of Stevens' Textile plants was unionized in 1980. Also, unions will diligently pursue legislation compelling more public employees to join open or agency shops as a condition of maintaining their jobs. No doubt pressure will be put on the new Department of Education to seek agency shop arrangements in all public schools. Enlarged revenues from this source are spent in mounting powerful lobbies in Congress and state legislatures to gain union goals.

Though the law says revenues collected from agency shop dues cannot be used for political contributions, as it stands there is no practical way to prevent it. In this manner unions can wield political power in greater proportion to their numbers. They can use these funds to mount volunteer doorbelling campaigns, phone banks, registration drives, free rides to elderly voters, and baby-sitting services to parents of young children, without violating the political expenditure laws. Such public relation operations can gain them votes for the candidates they support. In the future they might reverse the disappointments they experienced in Congress in 1977 and 1978 on both the Common Situs Picketing and Labor Law Reform Bills that came very close to becoming law.[1]

Unions can look to gains in the wholesale and retail trades, the large chain grocery and department stores that should become more vulnerable to unionization, more so than the small and diversified retail outlets that are hard to organize. Bank clerks and even the professional occupations employing engineers, college faculty, even some doctors may fall in line. Of course, given a world abounding in uncertainty, one cannot be sure of anything. What direction the union growth will take will depend greatly on the competitiveness of the U.S. economy and the moderation of public unions. Should the U.S. become less competitive in the world economy, unions will fight hard to keep what they already have. Whether they gain protective legislation will depend on what the public understands is beneficial to it. If protection of domestic industries can gain public sympathy, the unions will become stronger. But if the public believes protectionist policies will lower the U.S. standard of living, union persuasion will decline further.

KINDS OF UNIONS

There are three kinds of unions: *craft, industrial,* and *public.*

There are three general categories under which unions can be classified.

Craft Unions Craft unions are comprised of workers in the same craft or in a group of related crafts such as plumbers, carpenters, or plasterers, those in the construction trades, and others like ferry boat pilots, printers, and shoemakers.

Industrial Unions Industrial unions include all workers in an industry or related industries irrespective of the type of work performed. These unions are most often found in mass production industries like automobiles, steel, coal, rubber, and transportation. In other situations the separation between craft and industrial does not apply. Consider teachers, barbers, and newspaper and television reporters. In many plants skilled and unskilled assembly line workers are often represented by different unions.

Public Unions Public unions are neither craft nor industrial, and are composed primarily of white collar workers. However, they do include mechanics and machinists who work in the motor pools of cities and towns and policemen, firemen, and animal control workers.

[1]The Common Situs Picketing Bill if passed would have allowed unions to shut down the whole job site in disputes with nonunion contractors who are working alongside union contractors. Taft-Hartley's secondary boycott provision now prevents this. Now, when plumbers, for example, are striking, carpenters may go through their picket lines. The Labor Law Reform Bill would have made it easier to organize resistant companies faster. It would also increase the size of the NLRB to speed up hearings and, some claim, weight the Board more heavily in the union's favor.

Sources of Union Power

What is power? One definition is the ability to get what you want against the will of others. Goals can be achieved by the compelling logic of an argument, by education, by political influence, by intimidation, and by force.

Union ambitions can be realized by the use of work slowdowns, consumer boycotts, informational picketing, keeping nonunion products from the market, controlling the supply of labor, illegal strikes, strikes sanctioned by the rank-and-file, and government intervention into strikes.

Strikes The purpose of the strike is to impose financial hardship on companies because of the loss of sales and profits. This is particularly true with companies that are highly capital intensive with high fixed capital costs. In some companies supervisory personnel are able to handle the equipment. However, as the strike lengthens, maintenance becomes a serious problem. Companies in the same industry can retaliate by locking out all workers even in nonstruck plants. They can also hire nonunion replacements. This is often the cause of violence.

When it appears that a union will likely be the loser in a labor-management conflict, it is to its advantage to request government intervention. Since the unions wield considerable political influence through donations to candidates out of their reserves, the government is inclined to seek a solution less harmful to the union than if the union fought it out alone.

Strikes in the private sector have some different characteristics from those in the public sector. In the private sector, in manufacturing industries, loss of output and wages can to some extent be recovered with overtime once the strike is settled. But there is some loss to the workers and to the company which is permanent. Also, there is some loss to the public from reduced output. The firm and the union each calculates the present value of what they can gain by holding out. Is the current sacrifice worth the future gain? If it is, the present value of benefits won in the future is greater than the cost—the sacrificed wages for unions and the sacrificed sales and revenues for the companies.

Strikes of public employees, however, can impose large permanent costs on everyone, including those not involved in the dispute. There is a larger loss to the public of monopolized public services from a strike. Public workers provide government services such as transportation, fire and police protection. Loss of them can lead to pubic disorder. A building burned down, protection lost, and a bus ride missed are services that are sunk; they are gone forever. Also, higher wage increases without commensurate improvements in quality or efficiency cause taxes to rise, but the benefits received do not rise proportionately.

Collective Bargaining What do unions want? What are unions trying to maximize? And how do unions convey what they want? Collective bargaining as defined in the Taft-Hartley Act is "the performance of mutual obligation of the employer and the representative of the employees to meet at reasonable times and confer in good faith with respect to wages, hours, and other terms and conditions of employment, or the negotiation of an agreement, or any question arising thereunder, and the execution of a written contract. . . ."

While the statement of purpose is simple enough, the legal implications

Unions negotiate for a package of items at contract time with priority given to wages and job security, and then to benefits.

and practical applications are complicated. Today, **negotiations** require each side to have seated around them at the bargaining table lawyers, accountants, and business agents. There is a constant need to have the NLRB monitor what comes out of these agreements as laws and situations change, and make the necessary interpretations as they apply to changing institutional arrangements. The contracts not only cover wages but a host of other items like safety rules, seniority, job classifications, promotion grievances, and job security. Some contracts are over 300 pages in length.

Deadlocked employers and unions, especially in the public sector, may resort to the *binding arbitration* of an independent third party.

When agreement cannot be reached, **binding arbitration** is entered into. This involves each side giving up freedom of decision and calling in a third party to make a decision that is binding on both sides whether they like the decision or not. This is not done often, and when done it usually happens in the public sector since by law public unions are not allowed to strike. Of course they engage in sick-outs and other charades which are, in effect, strikes.

Collective bargaining introduces an institutional approach to wage determination as a substitute for determination of individual wage rates by the supply and demand of labor. The unions believe this is necessary because the individual worker is at a gross disadvantage relative to the large firm. In a market situation workers are not competing with the firm, they are competing with one another for jobs. With collective bargaining workers in principle join as one; they agree not to compete with one another, but to compete against the leverage of the firm with their own unified power. For this reason unions bargain for all workers—union and nonunion—at a plant. The unions want to prevent any form of competition among workers, and resist raises based on merit that would cause disparities in wages within the same plant. What evolves instead is a stratified system of job classifications.

It is quite possible that institutional bargaining does not end up with results that are significantly different from a market solution, because negotiations are constrained by market conditions, like it or not. To negotiate wages that are too high results in a trade off—some unemployment. Highly skilled, ambitious workers held back by union policies can quit the unions, or go into supervisory jobs as management members if there is an open shop requirement. Some go into business for themselves.

Aside from wages, unions are passionately concerned about protecting their members' jobs. They see their jobs as rights on property, a tradition going back to the old guilds. Thus seniority is a very important factor and is jealously guarded. Working conditions, pensions, and health plans are also important. It is hard therefore to say that unions maximize any one thing, though wages are important and various fringe benefits are really indirect wages. But it is the package that is important, and particular trade-offs within the package are often necessary.

The Leadership

In bargaining there are not two parties but more than two. The union leaders who represent the members at negotiations are not necessarily maximizing the identical variables that the rank-and-file is. The union leader must come up with an acceptable contract. If he caters too strongly to the members' desires, which may be unrealistic under the existing conditions, the union itself may be in jeopardy. It could lose, disintegrate, and go broke. If he acts too independently of their desires he will lose touch with the members and be disobeyed or replaced. Maintaining discipline is extremely important if a leader is to be effective. While he must recognize his democratic obligations to the members, there are times when he must be autocratic and throw some weight around. If he overdoes it his arrogance will be resented, but if he is weak and cannot deliver then he will be accused of selling out.

There is a tendency for unions to bargain for high wages that cause some loss of jobs. There may be a good reason for this result. If the leader negotiates for a wage increase lower than what the membership expected but involves no loss of jobs, no one will be happy. However, if he bargains for a generous wage increase that results in the workers with lowest seniority being laid off, then most workers are pleased and only a few are not. Thus it is better for the leader to please the majority and displease a small minority than to please no one. Also, the minority eventually laid off may not see the connection between the new contract and their eventual release, because of other intervening circumstances.

IS MARGINAL PRODUCTIVITY APPLICABLE?

There is controversy over the ability of *marginal productivity* theory to predict wage rates and labor allocation.

Does collective bargaining seem to leave marginal productivity theory in the position of being a useless textbook construct? Some would say it does, because it does not appear to determine wages in an institutional setting. To others, however, marginal productivity theory retains its validity.

Critics Some of the arguments against the use of marginal productivity theory are as follows. Businessmen do not have good enough data to calculate marginal values like marginal revenue product and marginal costs. The data are skimpy and often in unusable form. Nor is it possible to ascertain just how much capital and how much labor each contributes to the final product. Moreover, plants are usually designed to accommodate a fixed target of workers so that management is thinking in terms of total units and total costs. They merely rely on estimates of average and total revenues and average and total costs.

Also, marginal productivity is calculated under *ceteris paribus* assumptions, whereas contract talks involve a host of factors dealing with work rules and worker rights and other intangible, nonmonetary decisions that impact on costs and affect marginal productivity in ways that cannot be determined. The theory assumes workers are homogeneous and equally productive, which they are not.

Unions and firms most likely negotiate wages using some notion of an average productivity of the whole unit, not elusive marginal productivity figures.

Defenders On the other hand, there are arguments favoring the view that marginal productivity theory is consistent with collective bargaining theory.

First of all, if the union hammers out a wage agreement that makes wages higher than the competitive wage because of its monopoly power in its factor market, there is room for the company to manipulate the number of workers employed and readjust the level of output so as to force the negotiated wage closer to a more efficient marginal productivity figure. Thus, the employer will attempt to combine inputs as efficiently as possible, given costs and the constraints imposed by union contracts. As a result, it may be true in the long run that the bargaining power of labor is still constrained by labor's productivity. If the firm is not competitively productive it loses its competitive edge, some workers will lose jobs, and the firm might not survive. Hence, unions must temper wage demands with some awareness of long-run productivity and the trade-off in the amount of unemployment a membership can live with. Cases exist where unions have reduced wage demands because of declining business. This has happened on the New York docks and in construction. The struggling Chrysler Corporation requested and received wage restraints from the UAW in its 1979 contract negotiations. Therefore, the notion of marginal productivity remains intact, being implicit in the calculated hunches and guesses of company decision makers.

The Union-Nonunion Wage Difference

Although unions have raised money wage rates, evidence of whether they have raised real wage rates overall is inconclusive.

Are the relative wages of union workers higher than those for nonunion workers? And if so, are unions responsible for the difference? Do skilled craftsmen earn higher wages because they are unionized or because they are more skilled? Or is it some unknown combination of the two? Do many workers earn less than union workers because they are nonunion or because they are less skilled, with lower marginal productivities?

The labor economist, Albert Rees, while recognizing the inherent statistical difficulties and allowing for them as best he could, concluded that about one third of the trade unions have raised wages of their members somewhere between 15 and 20 percent above what they would have been without the union, another one third of the trade unions have raised members wages from 5 to 10 percent above what they would have been without the unions, and one third had no influence at all.[2]

In 1963, Gregg Lewis reviewed earlier studies of union-nonunion earning differences, and estimated that in the late 1950s unions increased union workers' earnings by 10 to 15 percent. A study in 1966 by Leonard Weiss also measured an 8 to 15 percent differential. A study by Adrian Throop covering the 1950s estimated an average hourly wage differential of 26 percent between union and nonunion production and nonsupervisory workers in the private nonfarm sector. Later investigations by Frank Stafford measured differences of about 25 percent for union craft workers versus nonunion workers, adjusted for differences in sex, education, region, and occupation. Research by Michael Boskin fixed the differential at 15 percent for craft and kindred workers and 25 percent for laborers. These estimates are incorporated in an article by Paul Ryscavage, who estimates the union-nonunion differential at 20 to 25 percent per hour, and as high as 44 percent in transportation equipment operative

[2]Albert Rees, *Wage Inflation* (New York: The Conference Board, 1957), pp. 27–28.

occupations (e.g., trucking).[3] Others believe that the evidence that unions have made a difference is tentative because of the complexity of the measurement problem.[4]

The more fundamental issue is whether unions raise real wages. Real wages reflect actual buying power and are defined as

$$\text{Real wage} = \frac{\text{money wage}}{\text{general price level}}.$$

Unions say they do raise real wages. Others are not so sure. While wages may rise in the short run, they may not rise in the long run if increases in real wages are greater than increases in worker productivity. For then inflation will cancel the gain in money wages. Firms will substitute capital for labor and will lay off some workers. The overall effect is that the real wage bill may not rise. Those laid off often find lower paying jobs in the nonunionized sector. Also, those seeking jobs may be forced into low paying nonunion jobs because union wages slow down the growth of jobs in the unionized sector. There is an income distribution effect. Labor economist Clark Kerr calls it the Jesse James effect, where union workers gain by taking from nonunion workers, as distinct from the Robin Hood effect where unions gain by taking from employers.

There are other clear-cut effects. Unions have continued to close the gap between the wages of the lowest skilled workers and the highest skilled blue collar workers on the average. They have also shortened the wage difference between all blue collar workers and white collar workers on the average. In the crafts, some members are paid considerably higher wages than many white collar workers. Plumbers can earn more than bank clerks, garbage collectors can earn more than public school teachers.

Unions have closed the wage gap among workers doing the same jobs; this is the *wage contour* concept.

Unions have certainly closed the gap between workers in one company and those in other companies doing the same job. This is the **wage contour** concept and has to do with the unions' insistence on equity. Dock workers in Seattle should make what dock workers in Oakland do. Firemen should get what policemen do, and so it goes.

How Unions Raise Wages

Craft unions attempt to raise wages by limiting the supply of workers; *industrial unions* do so by unionizing all workers in an industry.

Craft unions and industrial unions do not necessarily pursue the same methods in their goal of raising members' wages. **Craft unions** rely more on restricting the supply of members into their organizations. A straightforward supply and demand analysis results in higher wages for working members, as shown in Figure 15-2. There, the supply curve has shifted to the left and the wage rate is higher for fewer workers.

The **industrial unions** aim to unionize the whole industry. As illustrated in Figure 15-3, by making all workers members they can then bargain for higher wages for q_2 workers, who retain their jobs. ($q_1 - q_2$ do not.) If some firms remained nonunionized in an industry, these firms would pay lower

[3]Paul M. Ryscavage, "Measuring Union-Nonunion Earning Differences," *Monthly Labor Review*, Dec. 1974: 3–9.
[4]C. J. Parsley, "Labor Unions and Wages: a Survey," *The Journal of Economic Literature*, Vol. xviii, No. 1 (March 1980): 1–31.

Figure 15-2

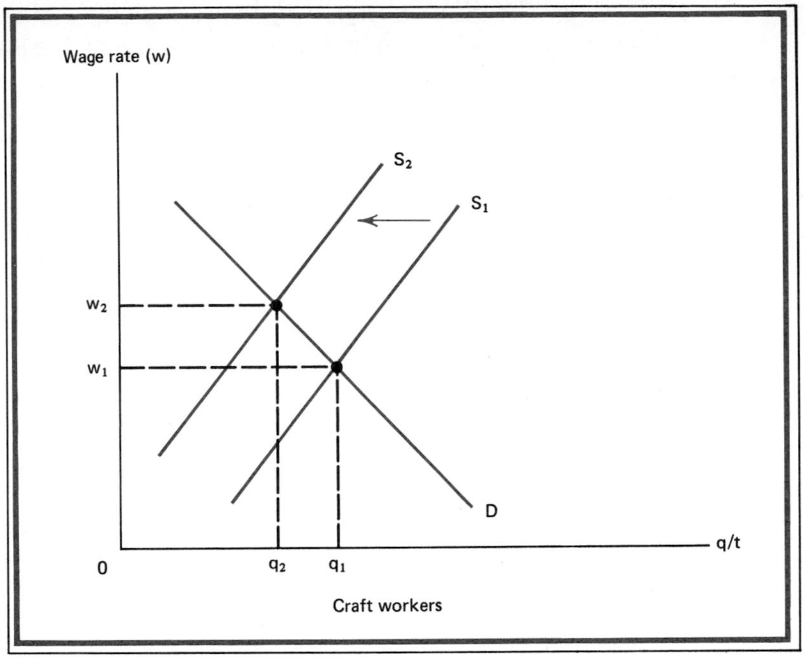

wages and consequently charge lower prices for their products. The law of demand implies that the quantity demanded for their lower priced products would increase, reducing the quantity demanded for union produced goods, thereby causing unemployment among union workers, which harms the union. When all workers are members, then setting the wage w_2 means that only q_2 of workers will be hired, because that is all the labor that management will buy at

Figure 15-3

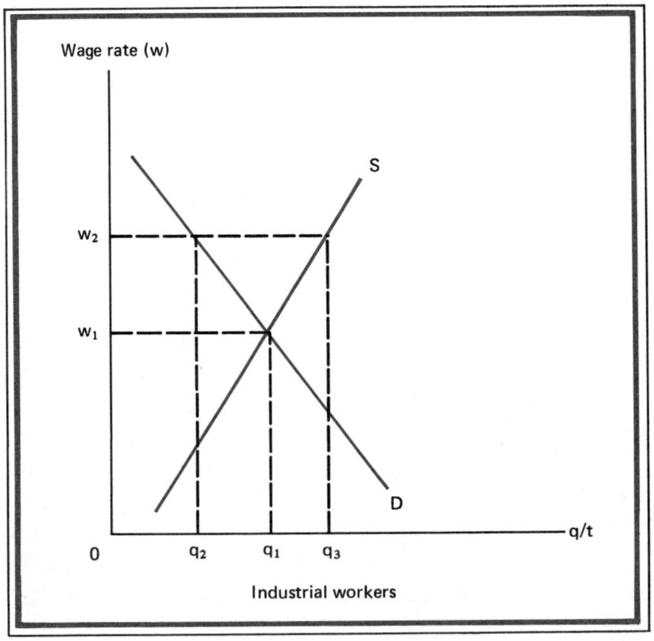

that wage. The difference ($q_3 - q_2$) represents the labor that would like to work at wage w_2, but who cannot find jobs. In this way, the amount of labor supplied to the industry is restricted.

Thus craft unions tend to moderate increases in membership, and industrial unions to encourage it. In both cases the effect is to achieve higher wages for members.

Limiting Supply

Unions can *control the supply* of workers through high initiation fees, lengthy apprenticeship programs, union certification, and other means.

1. Some unions pressure Congress for immigration barriers. The AFL-CIO is not happy about the large entry of illegal aliens from Mexico, who, they claim, are taking jobs from U.S. workers. A reply would be that the immigrants are taking jobs that U.S. citizens will not take, such as stoop labor in farm fields and low-paying jobs in textile plants.

2. Many of the craft unions require high initiation fees, some running in the hundreds of dollars. Poor minorities are discouraged by this device.

3. Undue length of apprenticeship training discourages many from finishing their qualifying training periods. Many trades can be learned in a much shorter period of time. Even when classroom work is completed, one or two years of apprentice work are required on the job.

4. Licensing and certification mean control of entry into the industry, pure and simple. We went over this ground in Chapter 9.

5. Discrimination has been a deterrent in the past. Minorities threaten the control over entry which craft unions so carefully want to limit in order to keep wages higher by keeping the competition for jobs down.

Increasing Demand

1. Wages can be raised by causing an increase in demand for union workers and for union-made products. One way to do this is to agitate in Congress for import restrictions or for higher import taxes (tariffs) in industries where foreign competition is keen. The idea is to increase the demand for domestic products, and since labor is a derived demand, increase the demand for domestic labor by making the prices of imported goods less competitive. Examples are the steel, textile, and shoe industries.

2. Members can be encouraged to buy union made products, often identified by a union label.

3. Bargaining for better working conditions and fringe benefits can increase worker morale and because of that can raise productivity in unionized firms.

4. Collusion with the employer can result in a higher monopoly-like price for the product. This shifts the demand curve to the right for labor. The firm earns some pure profits and the workers some pure economic rent. This was supposed to have occurred in the coal industry in John L. Lewis's days. Unfortunately, firms and consumers substituted coal and natural gas for coal, and unemployment soared in the coal mines over the years since the late 1940s. The Teamsters Union is against deregulation of the trucking industry, a cause it shares with trucking firms.

Monopsony and Union Power

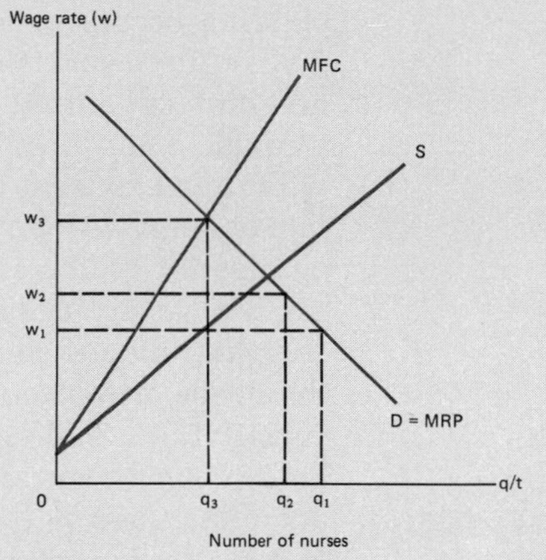

According to C. Link and J. Landon, the market for registered nurses is well suited to the study of monopsony and a union's ability to improve the starting salaries of nurses.* The job demands considerable training and skill, which limits supply. There are few occupations that are close substitutes for nursing. Also, nurses tend to function as secondary wage earners relative to their husbands. This often limits their mobility and confines them within geographical regions.

On the other hand, the buyers' side of the labor market for hospital nurses approximates the monopsony model in several characteristic ways. For instance, over 70 percent of the 7,000 hospitals in the U.S. in 1973 were located in one-hospital communities, while only a few hospitals serve in each of a large number of other communities. In 1969 unions represented only 3 percent of registered nurses. At this time there was constant talk of a nursing shortage. This, too, is consistent with a monopsony-like structure in the market. As single buyers, hospitals face a rising supply curve and will hire nurses so long as the marginal factor cost is less than the marginal revenue productivity ($MFC < MRP$). Thus they hire q_3. They would pay them a wage w_1; at this wage they could move to hire $q_1 - q_3$ more to fill these "vacancies." But with unions in place, the workers would not accept w_1. Those who wish to maximize wages would raise them to w_3. But if employment is also a goal, they might seek wages of w_2 and q_2 nurses would be hired instead of only q_3.

Link and Landon sent questionnaires to 520 hospitals in 65 cities that included the 50 largest. Of these, 317 usable questionnaires were returned. Union membership on nurses was requested. Data were collected on the percentage of all nonagricultural workers who were unionized within the state. This was done to account for any free-rider effect a strongly unionized state would have on nonunionized nurses salaries. Location was also considered to net out any differences in real wages due to differences in the regional cost of living. In addition, the monopsony criterion used was that of a four-firm concentration ratio obtained by taking the total number of hospital beds and calculating the percentage of beds accounted for by the four largest hospitals in the area. Five different models were tested.

One monopsony effect, as measured by a 100 percent increase in measured hospital concentration, was associated with a reduction in the yearly salary for beginning nurses from $619 to $383 depending on the model tested. When there was unionization of at least 75 percent of the nursing staff at a hospital, the union effect was associated with increases in annual salaries ranging from $500 to about $800 for beginning nurses depending on the model. Also, the union, as expected, was much more effective in raising wages of the relatively unskilled nurses than for the skilled nurses.

* Charles Link and John Landon, "Monopsony and Union Power in the Market for Nurses," Southern Economic Journal: April 1975, 649–659.

Unions can *increase demand* for workers by encouraging a buy-the-union-brand policy, featherbedding, and lobbying for import quotas.

5. Featherbedding takes many forms but all involve using more manpower than is really necessary. Examples have been three pilots in an airplane cabin; a fireman on a Diesel train; stagehands idle backstage during talk shows because of minimum quotas. Construction materials that could be assembled at the factory site must be done instead on the job site. Thus, prefabricated metal forms into which concrete can be poured to form columns cannot be used.

Carpenters must build them of wood each time on the job site.[5] Plumbers must thread pipe on the job, pipe cannot be threaded beforehand. A form of featherbedding occurs when output is limited within a time period. Thus, unions dislike piecework since it introduces competition among workers and places no limit on output per worker. Employees on piecework have been fired through union pressure when they worked too fast, and fired by companies with union consent when they worked too slow. There was an agreed average rate of output—for everybody. Related to featherbedding is union resistance to automation which is the substitution of capital for labor. As a policy, unions are not strictly against automation; they are, however, concerned about the short-run displacement of workers it brings. When they are not satisfied that the needs of workers will be taken into consideration, they will resist capital substitution. So long as automation is translated into higher wages, fringe benefits, and shorter hours, with affected workers slotted to other jobs in the company, they will cooperate. In the long run featherbedding is eventually eliminated, although with the railroads it has persisted for a long time. Firms find ways around it or the economics of the industry make its continuation impractical, unless the industry is regulated as are the railroads.

6. Unions have kept the pressure on to have the minimum wage raised. The effect is to increase the demand for union workers relative to nonunion workers, even though it is primarily the unskilled nonunion worker who will be paid the minimum wage. In fact, some of these unskilled people will end up without jobs. Thus, the minimum wage can have an income redistribution effect toward greater inequality.

7. In certain situations unions can increase the number of workers hired and their wages by eliminating the monopsony leverage of the employer.

Allocation and Distribution

The drive to raise wages and protect jobs leads many economists to argue that unions are a significant element in misallocating resources (*where* resources are to be used) and in redistributing income (*who* gets it). The arguments surrounding the income inequality issue frequently overlook the income distribution patterns set in motion by union policies already described. Some workers gain at the expense of others. And, as we shall see in the upcoming discussion on labor's share, labor has gained very little at the expense of corporate profits.

It can be argued that unions cause misallocation because they introduce higher costs per unit of output. These higher costs result from higher union wages and often from inflexibilities unions introduce in the use of labor inputs. Larger companies have compensated for these costs by bringing new technology on line that increases productivity. But only the larger firms can do this. Small businesses do not have the market size or capital to counteract higher costs imposed by union policies. Without significant expansion they cannot readily absorb or compensate for higher per-unit costs, and are not able to survive because they cannot sustain price competitiveness. Thus, the unions help create the large business units that are often the object of their disdain. The unions have no doubt speeded up structural changes in the U.S. economy.

[5]For more details see Lloyd Reynolds, *Labor Economics and Labor Relations*, 6th ed. (Englewood Cliffs, N.J.: Prentice-Hall, Inc., 1974), pp. 530–535.

By changing the relative rewards to factors they force changes in resource allocation.

Adding to these changes are union jurisdictional disputes that result in resource inflexibilities, provide economic rents to some workers, and drive up costs. Thus, union plumbers cannot use ripsaws, nor union carpenters pipe wrenches, on construction sites. Pipe carrying laborers get paid wages closer to plumbers than to those of other manual laborers. Five men are required where three might do, or, more likely, five inflexible inputs produce less than five workers whose activities are not rigidly specified and jealously guarded. When wages are bargained too high some workers are laid off, increasing the supply of them for nonunion jobs. Their wages and marginal revenue product is lower in these other occupations. Thus, the nonunion sector becomes relatively more

The Open Shop War

In the 1970s vandalism, beatings, and even murder in one incident occurred at construction job sites in at least 22 states across the nation. A study by Opinion Research Corporation revealed that 570 open-shop contractors encountered violence on job sites over a two-year period. Some 2,170 received threats of violence and 4,000 sites were subjected to vandalism.* Leon Altemose, a nonunion Philadelphia contractor, was beaten on the streets of Philadelphia in August 1972.† The suspects were acquitted despite testimony from policemen at the scene. On June 5, 1972 some 800 men stormed Altemose's construction site at Valley Forge and did $300,000 worth of damage. Twenty men from Roofers Local 30 were convicted and sentenced to from 1 to 5 years in prison. Altemose reportedly starts his car with a remote control device.

The cause of these passions is the growth of the nonunion shop in the construction industry from less than 30 percent to over 50 percent of all construction. The AFL-CIO does not condone the violence of a few "but it results from the total frustration our guys feel." The nonunion contractors say votes taken indicate their men do not want a union, for good reason. While their pay may average $2 or more an hour less than that of union workers, unlike the average union worker they can work all year around because of the absence of strikes and because the nonunion operators can underbid union contractors by 10 to 15 percent or more on jobs. The underbidding is due primarily to being able to avoid costly work rules which unions impose. Nor do manual laborers get paid at close to the wage rates skilled workers do.

In most cases, the AFL-CIO has reacted to the competition by junking work rules and introducing selective pay cuts. But the trend to nonunion shops has not ended. There are still embedded restrictive practices that hurt the unions. Plumbers have experienced the competition. The unions no longer control the licensing boards in Pittsburgh. Plumbers Local 27 in Pittsburgh, as a case in point, runs its own apprentice school requiring 864 hours of night school over a 4-year period, as against 576 hours required by the local nonunion program.‡ The union also requires 1,700 hours a year of on-the-job experience. It charges no tuition, being funded by the employers. The nonunion school charges fees of $280 for residents and $470 for nonresidents.

Home repair demand has fallen off, and the unions have cut the sizes of their classes. Yet they charge as much as $10 an hour more than the nonunion plumbers do. As a result, substitutes have arisen. Home remodeling centers and large retailers have provided new apparatus and information for do-it-yourself home plumbing. The introduction of copper (it bends easily) and plastic piping has made formerly difficult plumbing jobs easy for budget-conscious homeowners.

* Associated Press, April 1976.
† Business Week, June 9, 1975.
‡ Wall Street Journal, July 24, 1978.

labor intensive and the unionized sector more capital intensive, and factor rewards are altered.

Others reply that there may be some misallocation but that it is not that large. The social benefit is greater than the loss. Job security and decent wages for the majority more than balance the loss of a few jobs to some and lower earnings to others. Over all, unions have assisted goals of economic and political stability. Yet high unemployment levels among minority youths must in part be due to union job restriction policies, the willingness to trade off some lost jobs for higher wages, and union influence behind minimum wage legislation. Yet it would be grossly unfair to attribute all minority unemployment to unions. The problem is not that simple. Perhaps one union street cleaner earning $20,000 a year, creating an excess supply of applicants for an unskilled job, could be replaced by two idle teenagers or young adults paid $10,000 apiece per year. If so, the streets would be cleaned more often and fewer of the young would be unemployed.

Labor's Share

In the long run, the rise in real wages for labor has been caused not by union policies but by rising productivity derived primarily from better technology.

We have established that some unions have probably had significant influence on increasing money wages. But what about increasing labor's overall share of national income? Given the redistribution and allocative forces set into motion by unions, we can study aggregate data to answer a few related questions. What is the share of national income per year going to labor? What is the share of labor income to property income? And what is labor's share of income compared to corporate profits as a percentage of national income? Not surprisingly, the data problem is a difficult one and results vary with the definitions adopted. Government accounting of the historical data shown in Table 15-1

TABLE 15-1 Relative Shares of National Income, 1900–1980, in Period Averages of Individual Years

Decade	Employee Income	Proprietors' Income	Corporate Profits	Net Interest	Rent	Total
1900–1909	55.0%	23.7%	6.8%	5.5%	9.0%	100%
1910–1919	53.6	23.8	9.1	5.4	8.1	100
1920–1929	60.0	17.5	7.8	6.2	7.7	100
1930–1939	67.5	14.8	4.0	8.7	5.0	100
1939–1948	64.6	17.2	11.9	3.1	3.3	100
1949–1958	67.3	13.9	12.5	2.9	3.4	100
1959–1969	71.5	10.2	12.1	3.1	3.1	100
1970–1980	75.5	7.3	9.2	6.1	1.9	100

Source: Irving Kravis, "Income Distribution: Functional Share, *International Encyclopedia of Social Sciences*, vol. 7 (New York: Macmillan and Free Press, 1968), p. 134, for data up to 1958. Data for 1959–1980 are calculated from *The Economic Report of the President*, 1979: Tables B-18, B-19; pp. 204–205; and same report, 1981 issue: Table 22, p. 155.

indicates a steady increase in labor's share of national income. Prior to 1972, however, the numbers do not suggest that it has come at the expense of the corporate share. Since 1972 there does appear to be a shift, with labor's share rising and the corporate profit share falling. Whether this is a permanent shift is not yet clear. Some believe it is. Other studies show a decline in corporate profit shares beginning in 1965. We stated this earlier in Chapter 13 when discussing profits. But the glaring shift in shares from 1900 to 1978 toward labor has been gained at the expense of small shopowners and property owners—not from corporate profits and professionals. Since unions grew in strength beginning with their legalization in 1935, it appears unlikely unions were primarily responsible. Rather the shift has likely arisen because of a shift out of self-employment into wage and salary employment and from the structural change from an agricultural to an industrial economy. In the change from sole ownership to corporate run business, unions may have speeded up the change, as we mentioned earlier in the chapter, as firms introduced labor-saving technology to avoid higher labor costs. This change entailed the growth of plant size and larger investment in fixed capital to realize economies of scale and lower per-unit costs. Therefore, technological change must be the major factor behind the rise of real wages and of profits from 1900 to 1948 and roughly constant profits from 1948 to 1968.

Study of the data casts further doubt on the unions' responsibility for increasing the workers' income share. The largest jump in worker compensation occurred in the 1920s, the decade of prosperity and before unions were either legal, large, or powerful. Conversely, the fastest growth in union membership was from 1935 to 1945, yet labor's share only rose by 2.5 percent. Apparently the Great Depression and World War II price controls distorted the signals. There was stagnation in union growth from 1955 to 1981, but the percentage rise in labor's income share was over 7 percent from 1955 to 1972. Of course, labor's power is real. Nonetheless, there seems to be little or no correlation between union growth and the rise in labor's share of national income. But, as it is, Table 15-1 is misleading. The government definitions of income embodied in this table do not fit neatly into economists' requirements for analysis; rather they express institutional and legal arrangements of society. After adapting for these conceptual differences, will labor's share show the trend as indicated in Table 15-1?

First, proprietors income in the table is composed mostly of wages and salaries. Yet most small businesses provide their own capital and entrepreneurship. Therefore part of small owners' income is a payment to interest, rent, and profits. Furthermore, part of employee income includes not only wages and salaries but transfer payments from government to people being paid for things like education and manpower training. Corporate profits also include the interest received by firms. Therefore, separating labor income from property income (rent, interest, and profits) and taking the aforementioned refinements into account, national income shares show a remarkable constancy over time of about 80 percent to labor and 20 percent to property. Thus, labor's total share has remained relatively constant according to this breakout of the data. With real wages having risen, yet total labor share more or less constant, then technological change must be the most significant factor in explaining the constancy of the labor/property ratio. Also, since the labor share consists of union and nonunion components, and given the gradually creeping rise in the unem-

TABLE 15-2
Manufacturing Jobs: Net Gain/Loss, 1969–1979

Right to Work States	Year of Adoption	Employment Gain
1. Texas	1947	269,500
2. Florida	1944	109,400
3. North Carolina	1947	104,700
4. Tennesse	1947	59,400
5. South Carolina	1954	57,000
6. Mississippi	1954	53,100
7. Georgia	1947	50,800
8. Kansas	1958	50,400
9. Alabama	1953	50,000
10. Arkansas	1947	48,800
11. Arizona	1947	48,200
12. Virginia	1947	42,100
13. Iowa	1947	33,300
14. Utah	1954	33,100
15. Louisiana	1976	32,400
16. Nebraska	1947	12,400
17. Nevada	1952	11,500
18. South Dakota	1947	11,000
19. North Dakota	1947	7,600
20. Wyoming	1963	2,900
Total gain 1,087,600 jobs		

Source: Bureau of Labor Statistics, U.S. Department of Labor.

ployment ratio, there would appear to be a shift in income distribution from nonunion toward unionized workers.

Finally, while unions might succeed acquiring a larger real share, over the short run, many believe that in the long run, when all factors are adjustable, unions cannot raise their real income share. If substitutability of capital formation slows, hence productivity too, rising money wages gained by unions can only raise prices that wipe out any real gains. In the long-run only rising productivity can raise real earnings.

Right-To-Work Laws

Whether compulsory unionism should be the law of the land or not is an emotional issue that continues to ferment on the American scene. The union shop requires that a newly hired employee join the union after a specified probationary period. Section 14b of the Taft-Hartley Act permits states to pass right-to-work laws, in other words to ban the union shop and make the condition of joining a union a voluntary decision of the individual. Section 14b is the most hated and frustrating piece of legislation to the AFL-CIO and they have rallied their efforts unsuccessfully against it since 1947. The most organized resistance to the union shop, or as dissenters say, compulsory unionism, is the National Right to Work Committee (NRTWC), bitterly despised by the union. As of 1978 20 states have outlawed the union shop. At one time as many as 24 states had passed right-to-work laws, but subsequently the laws were repealed in 5 of them—by legislatures, not by a state referendum. Following that the latest right-to-work state was Louisiana in 1976. Table 15-2 lists the states which have banned the union shop. In these states public employees cannot be required to join a union. In 18 other states some public employees must join a union shop, ranging from California where it only applies to public school teachers to Alaska where only public school teachers are exempt. In Kentucky, for example, only public employees in cities with populations greater than 300,000 must join the union. There are 5 states where all public employees must join the union and 5 states where the law is silent about voluntary or compulsory unionism for public employees.

A study by economist Alan Reynolds reported in the *New Haven Register* July 13, 1977 that real income after deducting taxes is lower in New York and

TABLE 15-3
Manufacturing Jobs: Net Gain/Loss, 1969–1979

Non Right to Work States	Employment Gains or Losses
1. California	+339,300
2. Wisconsin	+ 71,600
3. Colorado	+ 65,600
4. Oklahoma	+ 53,400
5. Minnesota	+ 50,600
6. Kentucky	+ 47,100
7. Oregon	+ 46,900
8. Washington	+ 27,100
9. Idaho	+ 18,700
10. New Hampshire	+ 18,100
11. New Mexico	+ 14,400
12. Vermont	+ 7,400
13. Alaska	+ 5,300
14. Rhode Island	+ 4,400
15. Montana	+ 2,800
16. Hawaii	− 1,600
17. Maine	− 1,700
18. Missouri	− 2,500
19. Delaware	− 3,400
20. West Virginia	− 5,000
21. Indiana	− 11,400
22. Massachusetts	− 12,300
23. Connecticut	− 37,300
24. Maryland–D.C.	− 40,000
25. Michigan	− 42,000
26. Ohio	− 88,200
27. New Jersey	− 93,800
28. Illinois	−138,600
29. Pennsylvania	−193,400
30. New York	−371,900

Total loss 271,000 jobs.

Source: Bureau of Labor Statistics, U.S. Department of Labor.

Massachusetts than in right-to-work states like Alabama and Arkansas. In fact, real earnings on the average are higher in right-to-work states than non-right-to-work states.

Table 15-3 details changes in employment for the 30 non-right-to-work states from 1969 to 1979. There has been a decline in number of jobs on the average for states without right-to-work laws.

Be warned that raw data like those shown in the table do not prove that right-to-work laws have been solely responsible for the growth in non-right-to-work states. The South was much less industrialized than the North and its labor force less skilled and more agricultural. Thus, its wages were lower to begin with. An added attraction for companies to move South are the generous tax benefits promised to firms that move operations there. This may be a stronger reason than the lack of union strength in these regions, although weaknesses of unions in the South probably plays some part.

CHAPTER SUMMARY

Unions are organizations of workers who collectively bargain for wages, working conditions, and assorted benefits. Union activity existed long before the Wagner Act in 1935 legitimized the right of workers to organize and to bargain with employers.

Over the following ten years unions experienced a rapid growth, thus power grew, and with it some abuses of that power emerged. In response to pubic complaints, Congress passed the Taft-Hartley Act in 1947 that imposed some restrictions on unions and on employers as well. States were also permitted, if they chose, to pass right-to-work laws requiring that workers need not join a union as a condition of employment.

The Act also outlawed the *closed shop* and permitted the *open shop*. Under the closed shop a worker had to join a union to get a job with a unionized company. Under the open shop the worker must join after a period of 14 to 30 days' employment. An *agency* shop requires payment of dues even if membership is not required.

The Landrum-Griffin Act was passed in 1959 in response to union corruption and links to organized crime. It made changes in certain internal union affairs such as government audits and provision for secret union election ballots.

Since 1955 labor union membership has slowed from 31.5 percent of the nonagricultural labor force to about 24 percent in 1980. In part this has occurred because of the changing structure of the work force, with harder to unionize white collar workers increasing greatly in numbers relative to the more easily unionized workers in the slower growing manufacturing sector. Another reason is the relocation of more manufacturing firms from the North to the South, where union influence is weaker and a majority of the right-to-work states exist. Unions, however, are vigorously unionizing workers in the public sector and have gained in some areas of the Southern textile industry.

Unions are of three kinds—craft, industrial, and public. Craft unions are composed of workers in the specialized skill crafts and tend to exercise tight control over entry. Industrial unions are made up of the less skilled and specialized workers and desire to make all industry workers union members.

Unions negotiate for a package of items at contract time, with priority given to wages and job security, and then to benefits. When negotiations are deadlocked employers and unions sometimes resort to binding arbitration by an independent third party who will make the final, binding, decision. This device is more typical of the public sector. When negotiations fail, the union can resort to its most powerful weapon, the strike, to impose economic costs on the employer.

Because wages are determined in an institutional setting, some critics contend that marginal productivity theory is not a good predictor of wage rates and labor allocation. Others disagree, arguing that in the long run it is a good predictor, for if negotiated union wages are higher than marginal productivity, companies will reduce the number employed to where the wage rate does equal marginal productivity.

Although unions have succeeded in raising money wage rates, evidence of whether they have raised real wage rates overall is inconclusive. In certain occupations they have been successful, but on average throughout the economy the evidence is tentative because measurement is extremely difficult.

Craft unions can raise wages by controlling the supply of workers through high initiation fees, lengthy apprenticeship programs, union certification, and other means. They can increase demand for workers, encouraging a buy-the-union brand policy, featherbedding, and agitating for import quotas.

It is believed, however, that union policies have caused a change in the distribution of income in favor of unionized workers at the expense of unskilled, nonunionized workers. Studies indicate that the share of national income going to labor has remained at about 80 percent during this century, and that the rise in real wages is the result of increased productivity derived primarily from better technology.

Many economists believe, however, that unions have had a negative effect in some sectors on resource efficiency and allocation. Higher wage demands and union work rules forced firms to speed up technological change and to build larger plants to gain scale economies that lower unit labor costs. Small businesses serving smaller markets cannot expand in order to reduce unit labor costs. Hence, they become less competitive, account for a smaller share of the nation's total output, and find it more difficult to survive.

QUESTIONS

1. Economist Thomas Sowell angered Bayard Rustin of the NAACP when he wrote, "Somebody among the black leadership has to say out loud, that their young people are idling away on the street corners for the greater glory of the AFL-CIO—regardless of how much that offends liberal allies and regardless of how much the NAACP or the Black Caucus in Congress are in hock to George Meany and Company." (*Wall Street Journal,* July 28, 1978)

   Bayard Rustin responded ". . . if organized labor had to rely on the current inadequate minimum wage to prop up the union scale, organized workers would be in serious trouble. . . . The labor and civil rights movements have a basic commitment to social justice which includes a guarantee of a fair wage. To sacrifice this fundamental guarantee with the unsubstantiated hope of creating millions of low-paid, undignified jobs strikes me as unrealistic." (*Wall Street Journal,* Aug. 8, 1978)

   a. To what causes of unemployment among young blacks is Sowell referring?
   b. Why do the unions come under attack here by Sowell? Are unions not for higher employment? How is the Black Caucus, supposedly, in hock to the AFL-CIO?
   c. Is Rustin implying that Sowell is not concerned about social justice? What is social justice?
   d. Is Sowell supporting an "inadequate" wage? What is an adequate wage? Can you avoid using normative terms in defining it?
   e. What are the "undignified jobs" Rustin refers to? Is the garbage collector who

makes $20,000 a year in San Francisco holding an undignified job? Do you think he would exchange it for a school teacher's dignified job that pays $14,000 a year?

f. Rustin refers to the "unsubstantiated hope of creating millions . . . of jobs." Of what is Rustin so skeptical?

g. Would you prefer to live in a society where it was against the law to be unemployed? Comment.

2. Labor union trade journals often claim that the growth and prosperity of the country has been and is a result of labor unions. Does it follow that for Third World countries to be assured of economic prosperity, they should unionize their labor force? What about unionization of migrant workers? Would employment of migrant workers be increased by unionization?
3. While being interviewed by Tom Snyder in February 1979 on the "Tomorrow" show, Leonard Woodcock, former president of the UAW, said the UAW does not really rotate among the four U.S. automobile companies it will strike when contract negotiation time for the UAW arrives. He said Ford Motor Company was struck more than the other three companies over a 15-year period. The largest company, General Motors was struck the least among the big three and American Motors not at all. Why did the UAW tend to strike neither GM nor AMC, choosing Ford and then Chrysler the most often? Because they did not like Ford and cherished AMC? Explain.
4. Suppose you are the president of the Retail Clerks' and Amalgamated Meatcutters' Union. In which one of the following is the union's ability to raise wages the greatest? The least? Explain your choices.
   a. Unionized checkers and meatcutters in Safeway stores.
   b. Unionized checkers and meatcutters in all large chain stores in the area.
   c. Unionized checkers and meatcutters in all stores—chains and small neighborhood groceries.
5. Why do you think that unions would prefer an hourly wage rate paid to workers instead of a piecework arrangement? Against whom do workers compete?
6. Why would a craft union prefer to limit its membership whereas an industrial union would prefer to enlarge membership throughout the industry?
7. Is labor service a commodity? If not, what is it?
8. If low wages are "unfair" or "inhumane," how might low prices be unfair and inhumane?
9. Does featherbedding in a trade necessarily create jobs? Might your answer differ for the short run and long run?
10. Labor gets paid according to its marginal productivity whether or not unions are instrumental in setting the wage rate. Do you agree? What if there is featherbedding?
11. Are nonunion workers "free riders"? If required to join a union are they "forced riders"? Comment.
12. In the box on unions and the nurses, is it implied that the wage elasticity of supply of nurses is relatively elastic or relatively inelastic in a given region or area as described in the box? Explain.
13. If a union negotiates a fixed wage rate for a particular type of labor for a given time period, regardless of the number of those workers a company hires, what elasticity of supply does the union create?
14. Would labor racketeering—i.e., extortion payments extracted by corrupt union leaders—more likely occur in industries where there is a high turnover of workers, indicating that union leadership is hard to organize against by members, as for instance in the building, entertainment, and longshore industries? Why would extortion also be more frequently practiced against firms which have high fixed capital costs? To answer this, recall what is the difference between fixed and variable costs and what serves as the major bargaining weapon of a union.

Chapter 16

Income Distribution

PROGRESS REPORT

A. In Chapter 15 we discussed labor unions as social institutions, each with varying degrees of power in determining wages and redistributing income.

B. In this chapter we study several influences on marginal productivity, and we examine income distribution data in much more detail and offer some interpretations and implications of the data.

C. In Chapter 17 we shall examine why market prices do not rise and therefore cannot operate to allocate resources efficiently – what is called market failure. The assignment of property rights is crucial when market failure and externalities occur.

Income is a flow of goods, services, or money received per time period; *wealth* is a measure of the dollar value of all assets at a moment in time, and is the source of income streams.

A good deal of discussion in the U.S. concentrates on wealth and income distribution. The desire to be as well off as the next person, to be equal, to have expectations of upward mobility are part of the U.S. tradition. A distinction between wealth and income should be made. Income data are much easier to obtain than data on wealth. **Income** is a flow of goods, services, or money, or some combination thereof, received per period. Income is normally measured by recording the flow of payments received over a time period, such as $500 a month or $20,000 a year. **Wealth** is a stock of assets. Your wealth is the dollar value of your assets at a moment in time. Assets are physical goods like land, buildings, and automobiles, or claims on such goods. They include financial items such as stocks, bonds, insurance equity, and cash. Assets yield a stream of income or services over time. They are sources of income. One's wealth may be a source of income to others, for example, the salary you pay someone to manage apartment property you own. Some of the income received from the property is diverted to others who are not owners of the property. Also, inher-

TABLE 16-1A Money Income of Families – Percent of Aggregate Income and Income at Selected Positions Received by Each Fifth and Highest 5 Percent: 1929 to 1977

Item and income rank	1929*	1950	1955	1960	1965	1970	1975[1]	1977[1]
Percent of Aggregate Income								
All families	100.0	100.0	100.0	100.0	100.0	100.0	100.0	100.0
Lowest fifth	3.5	4.5	4.8	4.8	5.2	5.4	5.4	5.2
Second fifth	9.0	12.0	12.3	12.2	12.2	12.2	11.8	11.6
Middle fifth	13.8	17.4	17.8	17.8	17.8	17.6	17.6	17.5
Fourth fifth	19.3	23.4	23.7	24.0	23.9	23.8	24.1	24.2
Highest fifth	54.4	42.7	41.3	41.3	40.9	40.9	41.1	41.5
Highest 5 percent	30.0	17.3	16.4	15.9	15.5	15.6	15.5	15.7
White	NA	100.0	100.0	100.0	100.0	100.0	100.0	100.0
Lowest fifth		4.8	5.2	5.2	5.6	5.8	5.7	5.6
Second fifth		12.4	12.7	12.7	12.6	12.5	12.1	12.0
Middle fifth		17.4	17.8	17.8	17.8	17.7	17.6	17.6
Fourth fifth		23.2	23.5	23.7	23.7	23.6	23.9	23.9
Highest fifth		42.2	40.8	40.7	40.3	40.5	40.7	40.9
Highest 5 percent		17.2	16.2	15.7	15.4	15.5	15.4	15.5
Black and other races	NA	100.0	100.0	100.0	100.0	100.0	100.0	100.0
Lowest fifth		3.5	4.0	3.7	4.7	4.5	4.7	4.4
Second fifth		10.3	10.4	9.7	10.8	10.6	10.1	9.6
Middle fifth		17.6	17.8	16.5	16.6	16.8	16.7	15.9
Fourth fifth		25.2	25.6	25.2	24.7	24.8	25.1	25.2
Highest fifth		43.4	42.2	44.9	43.2	43.4	43.3	44.9
Highest 5 percent		16.5	14.3	16.2	15.1	15.4	15.4	16.1

[1]Beginning 1975, not strictly comparable with earlier years due to revised procedures.
Source: U.S. Bureau of The Census, Current Population Reports, series P–60, No. 118, p. 452.
*Historical Statistics of the United States, Colonial Times to 1970, part 1, series G 319–336, p. 301.

ited wealth, like property, creates income and additional income makes it possible to add to existing wealth.

MEASURING THE DISTRIBUTION OF WEALTH AND INCOME

The distribution of wealth in our country is more unequal than the distribution of income.

The distribution of wealth in our country is more unequal than is the distribution of income. Tables 16-1A and 16-1B illustrate the standard method of presenting income data. The population is divided into fifths or quintiles, where each fifth of the population's share of money income earned by families is shown. The poorest 20 percent of the population received 5.4 percent of the total U.S. income in 1976. The highest 20 percent of the population received a disproportionate 41.1 percent of national income in 1976.

There is evidence of significant changes toward more equality in the distribution of family income between 1929 and 1947. Thereafter income shares seemed to have stabilized.

Table 16-2 provides some data on the distribution of family wealth in the U.S. in 1962 and 1970. To interpret the data accurately, the official definition of the income unit is important. Furthermore, income figures are affected by

TABLE 16-1B Money Income of Families – Income at Selected Positions, by Each Fifth and Highest 5%, in Current and Constant (1977) Dollars: 1950 to 1977

Income at selected positions	1950	1955	1960	1965	1970	1975[1]	1977[1]
Current dollars:							
Mean, all families	3,815	4,962	6,227	7,704	11,106	15,546	18,264
Upper limit of each fifth:							
Lowest fifth	1,661	2,221	2,784	3,500	5,100	6,914	7,903
Second fifth	2,856	3,780	4,800	5,863	8,320	11,465	13,273
Middle fifth	3,801	5,082	6,364	7,910	11,299	16,000	18,800
Fourth fifth	5,283	6,883	8,800	10,800	15,531	22,037	26,000
Highest 5 percent	8,615	10,605	13,536	16,695	24,250	34,144	40,493
Constant (1977) dollars:							
Mean, all families	9,604	11,229	12,742	14,797	17,332	17,504	18,264
Upper limit of each fifth:							
Lowest fifth	4,181	5,026	5,697	6,722	7,959	7,785	7,903
Second fifth	7,190	8,554	9,822	11,261	12,984	12,909	13,273
Middle fifth	9,568	11,501	13,022	15,192	17,633	18,015	18,800
Fourth fifth	13,299	15,577	18,007	20,743	24,238	24,812	26,000
Highest 5 percent	21,687	24,000	27,698	32,065	37,845	38,444	40,493

[1]Beginning 1975, not strictly comparable with earlier years due to revised procedures.
Source: U.S. Bureau of The Census, Current Population Reports, series P–60, No. 118, p. 452.

TABLE 16-2
Distribution of Family Wealth 1962 and 1970

1962*		1970†	
Wealth rank	Percent	Wealth rank	Percent
Lowest 25.4	0.0	Lowest fifth	Less than 0.5
Next 31.5	6.6	Second fifth	1
Next 24.4	17.2	Third fifth	5
Top 18.7	76.2	Fourth fifth	18
(Top 7.5)	(59.1)	Highest fifth	76
(Top 2.4)	(44.4)	(Top 5 percent)	(40)
(Top 0.5)	(25.8)	(Top 1 percent)	(25)

*Dorothy Proctor "Survey of Financial Characteristics of Consumers," *Federal Reserve Bulletin* 50 (March 1964); 285.
†Survey Research Center, University of Michigan.

population patterns and employment structure as well as by changes in life styles. Each factor should be examined separately. When such things are neglected, raw data will broadcast misleading and erroneous signals.

The government defines income as salaries and wages (money earnings).

Definition of Income The Census Bureau includes as income payments in wages and salaries, or **money earnings**. Since 1960, the government has stepped up transfer payments to households through Social Security, Aid to Dependent Children, and in other ways. There are over 100 federal government programs conferring benefits to the people. Many of these benefits are called noncash or in-kind transfers that are not direct cash payments but things like public housing, food stamps, school lunches, and Medicaid, all of which, in effect, increase incomes to recipients since they are left with more money to spend on other things. As an example, Table 16-3 compares income shares for three periods with and without the inclusion of in-kind transfers.

For 1972, apparently, adjustment for in-kind transfers resulted in a doubling for the lowest fifth from 5.4 percent to 11.7 percent and a decline for the highest fifth from 41.4 to 32.8 percent, with only slight changes among the in-between groups. When noncash transfers are included, the distribution of income has definitely become less unequal, although it still remains significantly unequal. By 1972 the government had become the largest source of income for families in the lowest quintile.

Income Unit and Undoubling

Since 1950, living patterns have undergone a definite change brought about by increased prosperity, some changes in sexual standards, and the higher percentage of high school graduates who go on to college. The data of Table 16-1 apply to families. Therefore, the number of single person and legally unattached person households has increased sharply since 1950. Many young adults can now afford their own apartments; many more unmarried couples

Government income statistics do not reflect in-kind government transfers, or distortion caused by living arrangements within families, the different financial pictures shown by varying accounting periods, or after-tax income distribution.

live openly together; more old people live alone or separately from children. The process of moving out of the family unit and setting up another household is called *undoubling*. It changes the measurement of income distribution because it increases the number of households without proportionately increasing total income. As a simple example, when a young working person moves out of the home to an apartment his or her income is now counted separately instead of as part of total household income. Now two households earn the same amount of income as one formerly did. This lowers the average income per household. Also, people living away at college may receive intra-family transfers (allowances) that go unreported. And retired people may be drawing on savings as a source of income aside from pensions and Social Security payments. These savings are not included in income data. Table 16-4 indicates that when broken out by individual income, the distribution has not changed much since 1950.

Accounting Period

The accounting period over which income statistics are compiled affects the distribution. Assume person A earns $2,000 one year and $30,000 the next, while person B earns $30,000 the first year and $2,000 the next year. If the accounting period is taken as 1 year, income distribution would be very unequal and unstable. But if the accounting period is 2 years, measured income

TABLE 16-3
Money Income Shares by Percent

	1952	1962	1972
Lowest fifth	4.9	5.0	5.4
Second fifth	12.2	12.1	11.9
Third fifth	17.1	17.6	17.5
Fourth fifth	23.5	24.0	23.9
Highest fifth	42.2	41.3	41.4

Money Income Shares by Percent Adjusted for In-kind Transfers

	1952	1962	1972
Lowest fifth	8.1	8.8	11.7
Second fifth	14.2	14.4	15.0
Third fifth	17.8	18.2	18.2
Fourth fifth	23.2	23.1	22.3
Highest fifth	36.7	35.4	32.8

Sources: U.S. Bureau of The Census; and Edgar Browning, "The Trend toward Inequality in the Distribution of Net Income," *Southern Economic Journal*, July 1976.

TABLE 16-4 Money Income of Unrelated Individuals – Percent of Aggregate Income and Income at Selected Positions Received by Each Fifth and Highest 5%: 1950 to 1977

Income rank	1950	1955	1960	1965	1970	1975[1]	1976[1]	1977[1]
All unrelated individuals	100.0	100.0	100.0	100.0	100.0	100.0	100.0	100.0
Lowest fifth	2.3	2.5	1.7	2.9	3.3	4.0	4.0	4.1
Second fifth	7.1	7.2	7.3	7.6	7.9	9.0	8.8	9.0
Middle fifth	13.8	13.3	13.7	13.6	13.8	14.7	14.8	14.7
Fourth fifth	26.5	24.7	26.0	25.0	24.4	24.3	24.1	24.0
Highest fifth	50.3	52.4	51.4	50.9	50.7	47.9	48.3	48.2
Highest 5 percent	19.3	22.5	20.2	20.0	20.8	18.7	19.3	19.6

[1]Beginning in 1975, not strictly comparable with earlier years due to revised procedures.
Source: U.S. Bureau of The Census, *Current Population Reports, series* P–60, No. 118, p. 452.

distribution would average to equality and be quite stable. Over a person's lifetime yearly income can vary dramatically and distort the picture. Extending the accounting period to 5-year intervals may show it to be relatively stable.

Taxes

The Current Population Surveys (CPS) of the Census Bureau reflect only before-tax income. Some families, while making the same income and owning the same value of assets, may well pay different taxes because of the different structure of each one's assets. Their property tax and capital gains tax may differ. Thus, their net income after taxes will also differ.

What about the effect of taxes on income classes expressed in the quintile groupings? The impact of taxes on various income levels was described in the *Economic Report of the President for 1969,* for the year 1965. Its major conclusions were that the federal income tax system since the mid 1930s has, in effect, been proportional for lower and middle income classes, but progressive in structure for the highest fifth. A progressive tax on income is a tax whose percentage rises as income rises. Thus it may be 15 percent on the first $10,000 income but 20 percent on income from $10,000 to $15,000 and 25 percent from $15,000 to $25,000. A proportional tax on income is a tax whose percentage stays constant as income rises, for example, 15 percent on any amount. A regressive tax on income is a tax whose percentage declines as income rises. It might be 15 percent on the first $1,000, 10 percent on income from $1,000 to $10,000, and 8 percent on income from $10,000 to $20,000.

A *progressive tax* on income is a tax whose percentage rises as income rises.

In a study by Joseph Pechman and Ben Okner[1] on the total effect of federal, state, and local income and payroll taxes in 1966, they found that families

[1]Joseph Pechman and Benjamin Okner, *Who Bears The Tax Burden?* (Washington, D.C.: Brookings Institution, 1974).

TABLE 16-5 Average Tax Rates by Quintiles of Households in 1976 (percentages)

Quintile	Sales and excises	Payroll	Income	Corporate and property	Total
First	2.1	4.2	1.6	2.7	10.7
Second	3.7	6.5	4.2	3.4	17.8
Third	4.8	8.5	7.5	3.3	24.0
Fourth	5.2	8.2	10.4	3.6	27.3
Fifth	5.4	5.0	13.2	12.5	36.1
All quintiles	4.9	6.4	10.3	7.7	29.3

Source: Edgar K. Browning and William R. Johnson, "Taxes, Transfers, and Income Inequality," paper presented at a conference on Regulatory Change in an Atmosphere of Crisis: The Current Day Implications of the Roosevelt Years. Washington State University, April 1978.

in the lowest fifth paid an effective income tax of about 8 percent while those earning between $500,000 and $1 million paid an effective rate of 23 percent. For families below an average age of 65 and earning between $5,000 and $50,000 the effective rate was proportional, not progressive, and about 15 to 16 percent on the average.

The President's report also concluded that state and local taxes tend to be regressive throughout the income scale, but when federal taxes are included along with state and local taxes the tax burden is heaviest on the bottom and top quintiles, and lowest in the middle brackets. However, the transfer payments received by the poor outweigh the tax burden to them. This would make Okner's results consistent in direction with the government's study.

Income and payroll tax changes since the mid 1960s indicate a slightly more progressive structure, and would suggest a movement toward more income equality.[2] See Table 16-5 for a 1976 measure of tax progressivity. In addition, there seems to be some, but not conclusive, evidence that the corporate income tax is borne by stockholders primarily. Therefore the trend toward more equality is even stronger.

The tax impacts on income redistribution are not nearly as large as the impact that follow from in-kind transfers. Nonetheless, even after allowing for all these adjustments there is consensus that the distribution of income has not changed much since 1950.

New Adjustments

Beginning in 1975 Morton Paglin[3] attacked the conventional wisdom enshrined in the Census studies and stirred a controversy. Paglin concentrated on in-kind transfers, the accounting period, and on the fact there is no consist-

[2]Edgar K. Browning and Jacquelene M. Browning, *Public Finance and the Price System* (New York: The Macmillan Co., 1979), pp. 400–404.
[3]Morton Paglin, "The Measurement and Trend of Inequality: A Basic Revision," *American Economic Review*, 65 (Sept. 1975): 598–609.

ent methodology to apply to the analysis of poverty statistics. New methodology would include in-kind transfers. But Paglin believes the conversion of in-kind transfers into their cash equivalent is not done very well and is therefore inaccurate. For example, housing is undervalued by the Congressional Budget Office since it uses budget figures and not market values. But it is Paglin's adjustment in the accounting period that has drawn the real fire. It is generally understood that, over a lifetime, earnings are low when young, peak in the middle years, and low again at retirement age. Therefore, the Census comparison of income shares over time as shown in Table 16-1A does not account for the fact that families who were young and poor in 1950 are not the same families in the lowest quintile in 1976.

Inequality of income is strongly linked to age among other things. Paglin believes more accuracy in income distribution measurement is possible by calculating family income by age grouping and comparing the degree of income inequality over time for the same age group. That is, compare those who were 30 in 1950 with those who were 30 in 1976, adjusting, of course, for inflation. We should not look at families at different stages in their lifetime but at the same stage of their life cycle. The age difference over time should be used to adjust the inequality figure. When this was done, Paglin found a marked trend in income equality since World War II. Criticism of Paglin's study centers primarily on technical arguments. Some say he is not measuring what he thinks he is. Others that his use of CPS data distorts his measure of long-run inequality.[4]

POVERTY

Exactly what is poverty? How many poor are there in the U.S. and who are they? While one may have an intuitive notion of poverty, arriving at an objective measure of poverty is futile. How many poor there are depends on the definition chosen. For poverty is to some degree a subjective evaluation.

Poverty counts are tallied in the March edition of the CPS and consist of a scientifically selected random sample of 55,000 households totaling over 150,000 persons. The survey is conducted on a monthly basis by the U.S. Census Bureau. A household (not always a family) is considered to be in a condition of poverty if its total money income for the prior calendar year falls below a set standard that is dependent on family size, age of members, and whether the family is living in a farm or nonfarm situation. The poverty standards were originally developed in 1963 and have been adjusted for inflation since.

A household is below the *poverty level* if its total money income for the prior calendar year falls below a standard depending on family size, age of members, and whether or not the family lives on a farm.

The 1963 poverty line for a nonfarm family of 2 parents and 2 children was $3,100. In 1978, the poverty line for the standardized family was set at $5,850. In 1973, there were 23 million people classified as poor, according to the official definition, compared to 33 million in 1965. Table 16-6 provides figures for other years.

It should be mentioned that farm families are excluded from this defini-

[4]The debate is recorded in the June 1977 issue of the *American Economic Review*.

TABLE 16-6
Persons Below Poverty Level: 1959 to 1978

Year	Number (millions)	Percent of total population
1959	39.5	22.4
1960	39.9	22.2
1966	28.5	14.7
1967	27.8	14.2
1968	25.4	12.8
1969	24.1	12.1
1970	25.4	12.6
1971	25.6	12.5
1972	24.5	11.9
1973	23.0	11.1
1974	23.4	11.2
1975	25.9	12.3
1976	25.0	11.8
1977	24.7	11.6
1978	24.5	11.4

Source: U.S. Bureau of the Census Statistical Abstract, 1980.

tion and the standards are set lower for them since they consume some of their own output, and an imputed income is calculated to account for the value of what farm families consume out of their own production.

The Congressional Budget Office (CBO) contends that poverty figures are overestimated because of underreporting by respondents of their income and supplementary welfare payments. When income is adjusted for taxes, underreporting, and conferred benefits from food and housing programs, the 25 million poverty number for 1976 falls to 18.2 million. Table 16-2 showed the change in the share of income received by the lowest quintile when adjusted for in-kind transfers and education benefits, and after subtracting income and Social Security taxes.

Paglin's studies show that for 1975 the percentage of people in poverty falls from the CPS figure of 12.3 percent to only 3.0 percent. This converts into 6.4 million people living below the poverty level.[5]

The poverty standard is a subjective measure, and relative to societal norms. Two people making the same annual income might classify themselves differently. One might consider himself as poor, the other as "not too bad off." Those living below the official poverty level in the U.S. would be considered rich by the poor in Bolivia or the destitute in the slums of Calcutta.

Data show that real earnings, that is, money income adjusted for inflation, have continued their overall upward trend. The total income of the poor buys more real goods and services than it did 20 and 30 years ago. Table 16-7 uses 1967 as the base year. In it income is arbitrarily set at 100 and the index change in real purchasing power from 1947 to 1976 is shown. Thus, in 1968 real pur-

[5]Morton Paglin, "Poverty and Transfers in Kind: A Reevaluation of Poverty in the United States (Stanford, Calif.: Hoover Institution Press, 1979).

TABLE 16-7
Index of Real Wages, 1947–1980

Year	Adjusted average hourly earnings	Year	Adjusted average hourly earnings
1947	63.7	1964	95.1
1948	63.8	1965	96.9
1949	67.5	1966	98.1
1950	69.3	1967	100.0
1951	69.0	1968	102.0
1952	70.9	1969	103.2
1953	74.4	1970	103.9
1954	76.6	1971	106.7
1955	79.4	1972	110.0
1956	82.3	1973	110.1
1957	83.4	1974	107.4
1958	84.5	1975	107.1
1959	86.8	1976	108.3
1960	88.4	1977	109.2
1961	90.2	1978	109.6
1962	92.2	1979	105.8
1963	93.7	1980	101.8

Average annual rate of increase: 1947–62, 2.5%; 1962–76, 1.2%
Source: U.S. Dept. of Labor, *Monthly Labor Review*, August 1977, p. 8; and 1977 to 1980 from subsequent monthly issues.

chasing power was 2 percent higher than in 1967. The trend is upward, though there are occasional dips such as in 1974 and 1975 when oil prices suddenly impacted on the U.S. economy. Wage adjustments take time to catch up to sudden and large price changes because of contract rigidities and other institutional lags. In 1976, the average wage earner could buy 56.3 percent more goods and services than the average wage earner could in 1950:

$$\frac{(108.3 - 69.3)}{69.3} \times 100 = 56.3$$

Therefore, the poor in absolute terms are better off without necessarily having increased their relative share, exclusive of government cash and noncash transfer payments.

Who Are the Poor?

A study of 5,000 families by the University of Michigan's Institute for Social Research showed that there is a pool of the poor whose level is slowly declining because more are leaving the pool than entering. Between 1967 and 1973, using the Census Bureau's definition of poverty, they counted an average yearly poverty population of 19.6 million people. Over the seven-year period covered by the study only about 20 percent were poor during the whole period.

But some 75 percent were poor at least half of this time, that is, four or more years. Correcting for this fluctuation, the researchers concluded there were still 13.7 million permanent poor during this period, or one out of approximately every 15 people in the U.S.[6] People who divorce often qualify for the poverty definition, as do those who leave home. Others move out of poverty at the same time by marrying, changing jobs, or getting more education. Who are the poor? They are more likely to be children and the elderly, to live in the inner city and in rural areas rather than in the suburbs; nearly half live in the South, they have on average less schooling, and two-thirds of them are white. This last statistic may surprise you. In absolute numbers there are more poor whites than nonwhites but the percentage of nonwhites who are poor is over three times that of whites. The poor would also include many of the blind, chronically ill, or otherwise disabled. Table 16-8 summarizes the data prior to 1978 based on official government definitions of poverty.

A majority of the poor tend to be the elderly, dependent children of single-parent households, and the disabled.

Unmarried women with dependent children are twice as likely to be poor as married couples without children. Women who are widowed, separated, or divorced are more inclined to fall into poverty, particularly if they retain custody of the children. This is further compounded among black women, who have higher divorce rates and more children on the average. Women who alone support children are apt to remain on welfare for long periods until the children leave home or they remarry. A surprising conclusion arrived at by researchers in the University of Michigan's Institute for Social Research was that unemployment was not the most significant cause of the poverty problem, although it compounds it. Family breakups, increasing poverty through undoubling, seemed to be a bigger factor. Consistent with this conclusion was the startling discovery of a five-year experimental income-maintenance program covering 4,800 two-parent families in the Seattle-Denver area conducted in the early 1970s. When intact families were given government cash welfare grants, the chances the family would break up was found to be slightly greater than for intact families not given these cash payments. Why this caused breakups is open to conjecture. The experiment also showed, as predicted, that when the government cut welfare payments after the family head took a job, the family head worked slightly fewer hours per week.

SOURCES OF INCOME INEQUALITY

Inherited Wealth

Income inequality stems from differences in inherited wealth, choice, environment, health, labor market information, institutional restrictions, and, above all, human capital.

Some people start out with more wealth than others, just as others start out life with more musical, athletic, or mathematical ability. The latter characteristics economists refer to as *human wealth* as distinct from financial and physical wealth. The expression "it takes money to make money" has more than a ring of truth to it. Wealth is a source of income, the more income the wealth produces, the more wealth that can be obtained with which to produce more

[6] *Wall Street Journal,* March 3, 1978.

TABLE 16-8 Demographic Correlations with Poverty, 1978

	Number	Percentage of all poor
Age		
Under 18	9,931,000	40.5
18–64	11,333,000	46.2
Over 64	3,323,000	13.3
Residence		
Inside central cities	9,285,000	37.9
Outside central cities	5,805,000	23.5
Outside metropolitan areas	9,407,000	38.4
Region		
South	10,255,000	42.0
North and west	14,242,000	58.0
Race		
Whites	16,259,000	66.3
Blacks	7,625,000	31.1
Spanish origin[1]	2,607,000	10.6

		Percent of families below poverty level	Percent of families above poverty level
Education of heads of households over age 22			
Elementary:	Less than 8 years	22.2	7.8
	8 years	11.9	8.0
High school:	1 to 3 years	25.0	13.2
	4 years	27.5	35.6
College:	1 year or more	13.4	35.4
		100.0	100.0

[1]persons of Spanish origin may be of any race.
Source: U.S. Bureau of the Census, Current Population Reports, July 1980 series, P–60, No. 124, pp. 2, 11, 45.

income. The greater the income, the greater the source of savings. It is from savings that investment is made. The wealthy can save more and accumulate a pool from which further income can be generated. The process is cumulative and it is not surprising that the distribution of wealth is more unequal than the distribution of income. However, except for the very rich, most income classes inherit insignificant amounts of nonhuman wealth. Of these maybe 5 percent of the nonrich inherit a significant amount of wealth. Among males whose parents are in the highest income groups, less than half earn income placing them in the highest quintile. A few end up in the lowest quintile. For the very rich,

Lorenz and Gini

A well-known graph that economists use to depict income distribution is the Lorenz curve. It is the solid curve in the figure below. The horizontal axis gives the percentage of families and the vertical axis the percentage share of family income. The 45° line dividing the graph in half represents absolute equality of income distribution among families. At point *1* on the 45° line, 20 percent of families earn 20 percent of total income. At point *2*, 40 percent of the families earn 40 percent of total family income, and on to point 3 where 100 percent of the families, not surprisingly, earn 100 percent of total family income. The other extreme, absolute inequality, where nearly all families earn no income but one family earns all of it would be shown by a horizontal line along the horizontal axis to the right hand corner of the box then shooting up the vertical axis to show the last family with 100 percent of the income at point *3*.

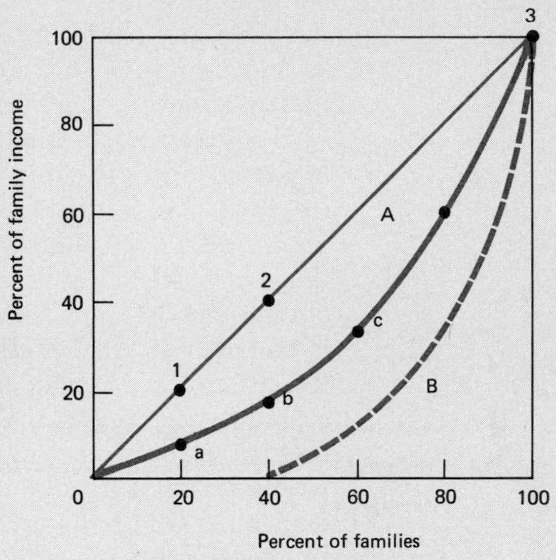

The Lorenz curve for 1976 data from Table 16-1A is the solid curved line with points *a*, *b* and *c* on it. At point *a* 20 percent of the lowest income families earned 5.4 percent of total family income. The next 20 percent of families earned 11.8 percent of total income. But the Lorenz curve is cumulative. Thus 40 percent of families earned what the lowest fifth and the second fifth together earned. Therefore, point *b* represents 40 percent of families earning 5.4 + 11.8 or a total of 17.2 percent of total family income. At point *c*, the graph illustrates that 60 percent of families earned 34.8 percent of total income. The dotted curve represents wealth distribution and, as stated, its distribution is much more unequal than income distribution.

The farther away from the 45° line is a Lorenz curve, the greater the degree of inequality. Corrado Gini early in the century was able to quantify the degree of income inequality by comparing the area of inequality lying between the 45° line and the Lorenz curve labeled A, to the total area $A + B$ under the 45° line (ignore the wealth curve). Thus, the Gini coefficient = area A/area $(A + B)$ = degree of inequality. The coefficient must range between zero and one. If the Gini coefficient equals zero, then area A would be zero, which can only be true if the Lorenz curve was identical with the 45° line illustrating perfect income equality. When the Gini coefficient is equal to one, then area A equals the whole area under the 45° line, or $A + B$, and absolute inequality would exist. In most industrialized countries the Gini coefficient ranges between .35 and .50 and it becomes higher in most poorer, less industrialized countries. It indicates more equality in wealthier countries. It is below .40 for the U.S., Britain and Canada, between .40 and .50 for West Germany, and over .50 for France and Sweden. If the measures for Sweden included appropriate allowance for housing subsidies, its coefficient would be lower.

Since only five income classes are used, the Lorenz curve would not be a curve, but a series of 5 points that could be linked together—straight line segments going from 0 to *a*, *a* to *b*, *b* to *c*, and so on. This would divide the five segments under the 45° line into subareas of A made up of triangles and areas under the Lorenz "curve" consisting of trapezoids. The Gini coefficient can then be estimated, since areas A and B can be determined by piecemeal calculations for each quintile.

those with an average wealth of $1.5 million, using 1962 data, inheritance is a dominant factor as an income source. About 57 percent inherit a major portion of their assets and 66 percent report inheritance was substantial but not dominant as an income source.[7]

Fortune magazine listed 39 people in 1973 who made from 50 to 700 million dollars within the previous 5 years without either inheriting wealth or being represented in *Fortune's* list among the wealthiest. These large fortunes were not and could not have been earned through a long process of patiently saving and investing and then reinvesting. Lester Thurow discussed this instant-wealth phenomenon. These rapidly acquired huge fortunes are earned by risk takers operating in imperfect capital markets that present opportunities for large, multiple gains for the financial pioneer. While the amount that can be lost is only what the investor went in with, he is motivated by a small probability of a very large return which is a multiple of the initial outlay. Thurow reasons that there exists a very wide range in the rate of return on such ventures that could not exist in perfectly competitive markets where information is assumed to be complete, that is all economic agents know about all the possible alternatives. Thus, if everyone had information that light bulbs were going to be very scarce six months from now, then those who are holding light bulbs would sell them at what they anticipate would be the future scarcity price. No pure profits would be made later by today's buyers when the shortage occurs. Today's buyers would bid up the price of light bulbs in anticipation of making profits later. But because buyers bid up the price to what they believe will prevail when the scarcity occurs, when they sell the bulbs six months from now they will not earn a pure profit because the original holder of bulbs capitalized those profits in the original sale. Competition drives pure profits to zero six months later, and the speculative seller will only earn a normal return.

However, suppose that Mr. Bright is the only one who has information about the future scarcity of light bulbs—at least he thinks he is right. He takes a chance and corners the light bulb supply by buying them at the current lower price. Mr. Bright has a good business reputation, and is able to borrow heavily to do this. Ms. Glow also believes the light bulb prices will soar, but she is an unknown and cannot get a loan to finance the purchase of a huge inventory of light bulbs. The capital market is imperfect. Bright gets the loan but Glow does not. Lenders do not know as yet how capable she is, so they will not bet on her. If Bright is wrong, he essentially loses only an amount based on his initial outlay. The potential profits are much greater than the potential losses on his investment; hence, the imperfect information in the market holds out a promise of a very high return with a low probability of success. But if he is right, instant riches are possible. Once they are achieved, Mr. Bright will tend not to speculate; instead he will spread his risks to minimize the chances of losing his new wealth. He will do his best to remain rich and be able to some day pass his wealth on to his children.

Choice

Take the example of twin brothers Jules and Jim who start out with the same tastes, backgrounds, abilities, and level of assets. But they do have different

[7]Lester Thurow, *Generating Inequality* (New York: Basic Books, Inc., 1975), p. 130.

time preferences about saving and consumption. Jules as a teenager prefers to play stickball in the street and run with the boys while Jim hits the books, intending to enroll in college. They both work at part-time jobs. Jules spends his money on girls and other leisure activities while Jim does so occasionally but saves as much as he can toward tuition. Over the long haul Jules ends up working at temporary low-paying jobs while Jim ends up in a permanent high-paying job. Because they have different attitudes about the future and different time preferences about consumption and saving, they discount the future differently. In this regard Jules has chosen to be poor and Jim to not be poor.

Environment

Environment is very important. The chances of being more productive and earning a higher income are affected by an environment where the traits necessary to acquire skills, habits, discipline, and motivation are present.

Health

The impact of health on income is obvious. An unhealthy person simply cannot sustain the momentum needed to accumulate skills and experience that gradually yield financial long-run payoffs.

These considerations aside, economists try to look at things easier to measure and analyze. For instance, some 75 percent or more of earned income comes by way of wages and salaries. Why are there steep differences in wages earned among individuals and groups? There are several separate yet somewhat overlapping concepts involved.

Nonequalizing Differences

Some wage differences are compensated for by psychic income. The professor's salary may be low, but he is able to pursue his own interests rather than work for others. Some people not only have more interesting and pleasant jobs but they also earn higher wages and salaries. There are several explanations for real wage differences not compensated by psychic income.

Imperfect Labor Markets Individuals do not have full information about job openings and the most promising future careers. A person who entered the teaching profession in the 1970s did not realize the boom in birth rate coming after World War II would bottom out about the time he or she entered the market. By the end of the 1970s there was an excessive supply of teachers at the prevailing wage rates. It is difficult to know what skills will be required for a new technology to be discovered five or ten years hence and what other skills will become obsolete or in much less demand. In other cases, individuals lack the resources to travel long distances to where the new jobs are.

The Modification of Property Rights Institutional practices bestow benefits on some while excluding others, e.g., unions and professional restrictive prac-

For Better and for Worse

According to 1979 Bureau of Labor statistics data, the percentage growth in the number of jobs expected through the mid 1980s for occupations is as shown in the partial list below.

Up		Down	
1. Dental hygienists	118.9%	1. Telegraph messengers	−50.0%
2. Medical secretaries	80.3	2. Farm wage laborers	−43.3
3. Flight attendants	79.3	3. Farmers and farm managers	−33.1
4. Architects	52.2	4. Keypunch operators	−26.8
5. Paperhangers	50.0	5. Elevator operators	−25.6
6. Bulldozer operators	49.6	6. Research workers	−22.3
7. Dental assistants	47.8	7. Stenographers	−22.0
8. Geologists	42.5	8. Newspaper carriers and vendors	−19.4
9. Office managers	39.6	9. Secondary school teachers	−18.9
10. Doctors	36.6	10. Postal clerks	−11.0
11. Guards	36.0	11. Compositors and typesetters	−7.9
12. Buyers, sales managers	35.2	12. Porters and bellhops	−6.2
13. Mathematicians	34.0	13. Bus drivers	−5.7
14. Psychologists	33.2	14. Shoe repairers	−4.0
15. Veterinarians	29.2	15. Authors	−3.3
16. Economists	26.9	16. Bakers	−1.6

tices such as licensing confer monopoly earnings on selected individuals. Doctors' incomes are higher than, say, physicists not because it is intellectually more difficult to become a doctor than to earn a Ph.D. in physics but because entry into medicine is much more tightly controlled. One can learn and practice physics without a degree if one is good enough but one cannot legally practice medicine. The government confers large amounts of subsidies to the farm and maritime industries. Taxis require licenses, called medallions, in New York City where they sell for $50,000. However, in Washington, D.C., where taxi licenses are not restricted, the cost is less than $500. Affirmative action programs, fairly or unfairly, have attempted to redistribute income. Arbitrary zoning ordinances can substantially rearrange individual income rewards.

***Human capital* embodies education, training, and job experiences that enhance an individual's productivity.**

Human Capital This is an extension of the concept of capital to human characteristics, both acquired and innate. It encompasses the skills, training, experience, and education a worker possesses. The more human capital one has the higher the individual's productivity, implying a higher wage-earning capacity. Many economists now believe human capital is the single most important element explaining the differences in wages and salaries. It complements the marginal productivity theory approach of factor rewards. Education is a prime consideration in the enhancement of human capital, particularly an academic education. Various studies have confirmed that the lifetime earnings of individuals are strongly related, on the average, to years of schooling.

By referring to Table 16-8, we see that inadequate education correlates highly with poverty. In the late 1970s the rate of return to education began to fall and its advantage over nonacademic training declined. But education is not the only determinant of income; sheer innate ability is a factor. But what relative weight to give to natural ability on the one hand and to environmental influences on the other may be impossible to discover. There is a complex interaction between the two.

Human capital is also created by on-the-job training as well as vocational training. Yet there are people with identical training on jobs who do not make the same income. White college graduates on the average earn more than black college graduates. Men earn more than women on the average for what is ostensibly the same occupation. But how much of the difference is due to discrimination and how much to other variables? Measurements are imprecise, but some partial answers are possible.

Lester Thurow is not convinced of the general power of human capital theory to explain income differentials.[8] He argues that human capital theory, based as it is on the vaguely applicable marginal productivity theory, predicts inconsistently. One would expect that the productivity analysis would see equality of education matched by equality of earnings. Thus, an educational program that transforms a person with little or no skills into one with higher skills should raise that person's earnings. It should reduce the total supply of low-skilled workers, thereby raising the wages of the low-skilled workers. It should increase the supply of higher-skilled workers and result in a lowering of their relative wages. The end result should be that wages would be close together for all workers, combined with a higher average income.

Thurow feels that by now education in the U.S. should have begun to reach its equalizing impact. Empirically it has not.[9] He believes that there are other systematic factors going on in the labor market undetected by the marginal productivity theory. While the theory may not be wrong, it may be too simple to explain fully the various deviations in income that are observed. There might be another explanation, a better theory. But then no other economist believes marginal productivity theory fully explains income distribution either, given its assumptions. It remains, however, the best predictive model around. It is still useful even though we observe exceptions to it. People do tend to behave as if marginal productivity theory operates. People expect to be rewarded for being productive.

Discrimination

In order to acquire human capital that makes for more productive workers who appeal to employers, you must have the opportunity to receive the education and the job experience that enhances human capital. Minorities have often been cut off from these opportunities or received inferior ones. The more prevalent that discrimination is against a group, the less likely its members are to believe that effort will be rewarded and should be undertaken. One performs

[8]Ibid., Chapter 3.
[9]In the 1970s, claims Richard Freeman of Harvard, returns to college education declined and have come closer to earnings of noncollege graduates.

at a lower level of achievement because that is expected. The biases of discrimination then become self-fulfilling.

The *statistical discrimination hypothesis* is that employers stereotype a group's productivity, and therefore discriminate against qualified individuals of that group.

Statistical Discrimination Hypothesis This has given rise to the statistical discrimination hypothesis.[10] If in the past employers have decided that certain groups, ethnics, and women, have on the average had higher turnover rates, tardiness rates, and absentee rates, all factors reducing long-run productivity, then even individuals with acceptable personal characteristics are discriminated against because they are stereotyped as having the average characteristics that have come to be associated with other members of the group, rightly or wrongly.

The *Family Specialization Hypothesis* is that the motherhood role has limited women's job mobility and the kinds of jobs they can take, resulting in lower pay.

Family Specialization Hypothesis As regards women in particular, a more cogent theory is the family specialization hypothesis that points to wage differentials that arise from role differentiation and its implication for the choice of occupation women enter.[11] Women tend to have reduced job mobility, being confined to areas where their husbands work; jobs must be close enough to home in order to be available when children return from school. For this reason, mothers often require flexible hours that affect hourly earnings and the kinds of jobs women take.

Thus, women tend to enter occupations that pay less than occupations that men enter. Women are directed into teaching and office work that pays less than, say, construction jobs where physical obstacles make it difficult for women to participate as efficiently as men.

Discrimination against women may result in lower pay to women for the same work and less mobility into higher positions. However, not all income differentials between men and women doing ostensibly the same work can be attributed completely to sex discrimination. Studies indicate that sex discrimination may account for about 35 percent of the income differentials between the sexes. The remaining 65 percent can be explained by other factors, particularly human capital investment.

Role specialization would predict that job experience would lead to wage differences. Women of child-bearing age who take time out to raise children disrupt the process of development of human capital through job experience—they tend to drop in and out of the job market. Their skills rust and productivity falls below that of men, hence so do their wages. In general, except perhaps for professional women, the female job turnover rate is considerably higher than for men. It is more costly for employers when they have to hire and train personnel more frequently. Hence, their productivity is lower and with it wages. Even when men and women display equal productivity, there is still about a 35 percent earning difference due to discrimination. But what of the remainder? With productivity equalized, income differentials still exist because women work less hours than men on the average.

Yet differences in real productivity do arise. For example, women perform significantly lower than white males in mathematics, which is an important

[10]Lester Thurow, op. cit., Chapter 7.
[11]Victor Fuchs, "Differences in Hourly Earnings Between Men and Women," *Monthly Labor Review* (May 1971): 9–15; Cynthia Lloyd, ed., *Sex Discrimination and the Division of Labor* (New York: Columbia University Press, 1975).

subject for entering many of the higher-paying fields such as science and engineering. Special efforts have been made in recent years to improve the mathematical skills for women. And some jobs do require greater strength as in fire-fighting, police patrol, and heavy construction. Women are more productive in textile work. Most of the production force in textiles are women. Tests indicate women on the average have better finger dexterity than men. Hence, they *are* better typists than men and faster grocery clerks.

However, let it be noted that pay scales for single women are much closer to those for single men because, no doubt, of greater career orientation by single women that yields strong work histories and more on-the-job training than for married women. Another interesting statistic is that women who operate their own businesses average less income than men who run their own businesses. But even more startling is that on the average, single middle-aged men make less than single middle-aged women who work full time.

As the barriers fall, more women will no doubt enter into jobs traditionally reserved for males. In the 1970s many more women have enrolled in law, medical, and dental schools. Enrollment by women in business courses is up sharply. Given the lower birth rates, longer life spans, and the women's movement, more married women will enter the workforce and the trend toward life-long careers by women will continue to rise. While black female participation rates have remained constant, more or less, the participation rates of white females have climbed dramatically. The biggest pay gap is between married men and married women, and it increases with age.

Age It has already been hinted that age is a factor in the distribution of income. Most men reach their maximum earning power in their early forties and sustain it until retirement. At middle age they reach the cumulative peak of the many years of adding to their stock of human capital. On the basis of age alone income will be distributed unequally, the very young and the very old earning much less on the average than those in between. Age is a contributing factor in income differentials among ethnic groups, for age is not randomly distributed among different groups. The median ages of blacks, Puerto Ricans, Mexican Americans, and Indians is at least 10 years lower than the median age of the Irish or Japanese Americans. The median age of Jews in the 1970s is over 40 years, some 20 years greater than for the poorer minorities.[12] The explanation lies in the disparity of the birth rates of various groups. Thus, aside from discrimination, blacks are also poorer because more of them are younger. The poor tend to have higher birth rates.

Black-White Income Title VIII of the 1964 Civil Rights Act outlawed discrimination on the basis of race, color, religion, sex, or national origin in hiring, pay, and promotion. The notion was equal opportunity and equal pay for equal work. It was intended that black, Chicano, and Indian pay scales and income be raised to the level of whites. Concentrating on black-white comparisons, we find from Table 16-9 that the black-white income ratio did rise in the 1960s, reaching a peak of 0.64 in 1970. But, the ratio then declined for three years beginning in 1971. Black unemployment, as shown in Table 16-10 remains high despite the various government programs such as manpower training and

[12]Thomas Sowell, *Race and Economics* (New York: David McKay Co., 1975).

TABLE 16-9
Median Income of Families: 1964 to 1976 (In current dollars)

	Race of head				
Year	Black and other races	Black	White	Ratio: black and other races to white	Ratio: black to white
1964	$3,839	$3,724	$6,858	0.56	0.54
1965	3,994	3,886	7,251	0.55	0.54
1966	4,674	4,507	7,792	0.60	0.58
1967	5,094	4,875	8,234	0.62	0.59
1968	5,590	5,360	8,937	0.63	0.60
1969	6,191	5,999	9,794	0.63	0.61
1970	6,516	6,279	10,236	0.64	0.61
1971	6,714	6,440	10,672	0.63	0.60
1972	7,106	6,864	11,549	0.62	0.59
1973	7,596	7,269	12,595	0.60	0.58
1974	8,265	7,808	13,356	0.62	0.58
1975[1]	—	8,779	13,408	—	0.62
1976[1]	—	9,242	15,537	—	0.59

[1]Current Population Reports, Special Series Studies P–23, No. 80. Table 139, p. 194.
Source: U.S., Bureau of the Census, Current Population Reports, Special Studies, Series P–23 No. 54, *The Social and Economic Status of the Black Population in the United States,* 1974, Table 9, p. 25.

affirmative action. Data for 1964 to 1974 indicate that 1) the earnings of blacks who were fully employed year-around increased relative to whites, 2) changes in family composition have been a factor in the decline of black family income relative to white family income, and 3) black employment has fallen relative to white employment.[13] These employment and income trends should be examined carefully, and an explanation offered of why the antidiscrimination laws and policies did not produce greater employment and wage benefits for blacks, as would be predicted if a perfectly competitive labor market existed after discrimination practices had been removed from the labor market. In 1976 the typical black family earned about 60 percent as much as a typical white family—about what it was in 1969. Yet between 1964 and 1969, by contrast, the income gap narrowed from 54 percent to 61 percent, as shown in Table 16-10A. From 1970 to 1975, earnings of black males increased from 66 to 73 percent of that for white males. Black females increased earnings from 85% to 97% of that for white females. Some of this was due to affirmative action programs. However, while median[14] family income for blacks increased from 54 to 61 percent of white median family income by 1969, the gain disappeared in the 1970s and

[13]For fuller details see Alicia Munnell, "The Economic Experience of Blacks: 1964–1974," *New England Economic Review,* Federal Reserve Bank of Boston, Jan./Feb. 1978.
[14]The median is the middle value of a set of numbers arranged in order of magnitude. There are as many numbers above median as below it. When there are an odd number of observations, the median is the middle value. When there is an even number the median is the average of the two middle values. For 1, 4, 5, 6, 9, 12, 19 the median is 6. Note that the average or mean is 56/7 = 8.

fell back to a black-white income ratio of 0.58. In 1978 the gap widened again. (When the black-white income ratio equals 1 it signifies equality between the median income of the two groups.)

The progress that was made in earnings was confined mostly to blacks with specialized skills and higher education, not across the board to blacks generally. The erosion of median black family income relative to white family income after the increase in the 1960s appears to be due to the changing composition of the black family. The rising divorce rate and the easier access to welfare has increased the proportion of black households headed by a woman. Such households earned about 40 percent of what intact black families earned, who often have more than one breadwinner. While the percentage of both black

TABLE 16-10
Unemployment Rates for Persons 16 Years Old and Over: 1948 to 1975

Year	Unemployment rate: Black and other races	Unemployment rate: White	Ratio: black and other races to white
1948	5.9	3.5	1.7
1949	8.9	5.6	1.6
1950	9.0	4.9	1.8
1951	5.3	3.1	1.7
1952	5.4	2.8	1.9
1953	4.5	2.7	1.7
1954	9.9	5.0	2.0
1955	8.7	3.9	2.2
1956	8.3	3.6	2.3
1957	7.9	3.8	2.1
1958	12.6	6.1	2.1
1959	10.7	4.8	2.2
1960	10.2	4.9	2.1
1961	12.4	6.0	2.1
1962	10.9	4.9	2.2
1963	10.8	5.0	2.2
1964	9.6	4.6	2.1
1965	8.1	4.1	2.0
1966	7.3	3.3	2.2
1967	7.4	3.4	2.2
1968	6.7	3.2	2.1
1969	6.4	3.1	2.1
1970	8.2	4.5	1.8
1971	9.9	5.4	1.8
1972	10.0	5.0	2.0
1973	8.9	4.3	2.1
1974	9.9	5.0	2.0
1975	13.9	7.8	1.8

The unemployment rate is the percent of the civilian labor force that is unemployed.
Source: U.S. Department of Labor, Bureau of Labor Statistics and Bureau of Census Current Population Reports, Special Studies Series P–23, No. 80, p. 69

and white male heads of households declined between 1967 and 1976, the loss has been much greater for black heads of households.

The upgrading in earnings for fully employed blacks has increased. But as Table 16-10 shows, there has been a decline in minority employment relative to white employment beginning around 1970. Part of the reason is the sharp increase in young blacks attending college. On the negative side it is believed that the rising minimum wage has caused substantial increases in black teenage unemployment. Also, the large influx of young, inexperienced white females into the labor market has taken jobs from young blacks. Employers filling unskilled jobs prefer females, both black and white, but the largest gain has been among white females. For teenage black males 16 and 17 years of age only 21 percent were employed, whereas 45 percent of the whites in that age group were employed.

While affirmative action appears to have been of some help in raising black earnings, there has occurred the offsetting phenomenon of an increase in black unemployment relative to white unemployment, particularly as between black males and white females. Possibly the gains in the 1960s were derived from an expanding economy. When the economy declined in the early 1970s government minority policies were ineffective, particularly as they affected black family income contrasted to skilled and educated black individuals. The primary reason for the ineffectiveness of affirmative action on median income for black families seems to be seniority clauses and wage rigidity. Seniority translates into last hired and first fired for the unskilled. As such, this institutional arrangement keeps the labor market separated because of past discrimination that made it difficult for blacks to acquire seniority. The Supreme Court has upheld union seniority clauses. As for wage rigidity, employers will not hire more workers unless the wage is lowered for all workers so that the total wage bill is not increased to the firm. But because of contract agreements and minimum wages, employment cannot be expanded to include blacks who on average possess less human capital.

Affirmative action and antidiscrimination laws have had less impact on the income gap between whites and blacks than population trends and the health of the economy.

Thus, unless the economy is expanding, **affirmative action** will not increase the total number of jobs, and evidently only had a small effect on the redistribution of jobs in the 1970 to 1975 period, in an imperfectly competitive job market exhibiting seniority clauses and wage rigidity.

This is not to say blacks have not made gains. More blacks than ever own their own homes, some 44 percent of black families. Blacks have doubled their enrollment to 10 percent of all college students. Over 200 hold elected political offices. Several are mayors of large cities. They hold 15 percent of all full-time federal government jobs, and hold more white collar and union jobs than they did in earlier years. Among intact black families living outside the South, and in the under-35 age bracket—in this one category—blacks achieved economic equality with whites as of 1975. The gains are very fragile and any serious economic slump may hit blacks the hardest.

Ultimately, long-term gains for blacks cannot be achieved by government programs. Thomas Sowell emphasizes this point. "The economic progress of blacks has come largely through the front door [meeting the standards]. Frantic efforts to keep the back door [quotas] have much more to do with the vested interests of affirmative action officials and civil rights activists than with any demonstrated benefits to minorities. Those with a vested interest in victimhood

and its rewards."[15] A study by Richard Freeman of Harvard found that young black and white adults with similar cultural exposure in their childhood and similar adult educational experience earn the same incomes. The goal, argues Sowell, is to equalize backgrounds that pay off in ways that make personal effort matter. There are many vehement dissenters to Sowell's views.

PROGRAMS TO HELP THE POOR

Among the numerous programs to help the poor and underprivileged have been the growth in Social Security, unemployment insurance, veterans' programs, workmen's compensation to injured workers, Aid to Dependent Children, food stamps, Medicare, Medicaid, nutrition for the elderly, housing subsidies, day care, student aid, Head Start, Upward Bound, school lunch and breakfast programs, vocational education, Job Corps, Neighborhood Youth Corps, work study, talent search, migrant workers, Manpower Training Act, Job Opportunities in the Business Sector (JOBS), and public employment policy—over a hundred in all.

Have inroads been made on the war on poverty and income redistribution? Yes. But hard-core poverty remains and the public is beginning to rebel at the costs for the small benefits gained. In particular, the causes of poverty have not been remedied, so the high expenditures must continue to sustain the improvements in income levels already reached. In particular, the various education and training programs have not significantly increased the skills and productivity, hence the earnings, of inexperienced, low-skilled workers. Why this is so is not known. As is too often the case, most welfare programs concentrate on the demand side without giving due consideration to productivity on the supply side that can increase earning power.

Negative Income Tax (NIT)

A *negative income tax* is cash transferred directly from the government to the poor in proportion to the income earned by the individual; thus, it should not destroy the work incentive.

A direct approach to income redistribution that might avoid the vast, overlapping bureaucratic structure is the negative income tax. It has the appeal that the giver, the government, does not make subjective determinations of what is best for the recipients. It should require a much smaller bureaucratic structure because the administrators needed would for the most part come from the existing Internal Revenue Services (IRS) facilities. Since the existing programs have raised income levels without curing the causes, the NIT would achieve the same goals by making direct cash payments to the poor without large expenditures being diverted to pay for administrative overhead costs to dispense checks to the poor. Variations of NIT go under the name of guaranteed income and income maintenance. The idea that making direct payments to the poor is the most efficient way to help them is an old one. Milton Friedman proposed and promoted the idea of a comprehensive NIT in the mid 1950s.

[15]*Wall Street Journal*, July 28, 1978.

TABLE 16-11

Personal Earnings	The tax + or −	After-tax income
$ 0	−3,000	$3,000
1,000	−2,500	3,500
2,000	−2,000	4,000
3,000	−1,500	4,500
4,000	−1,000	5,000
5,000	− 500	5,500
6,000	0	6,000
7,000	+ 500	6,500

The NIT works in the following way. When a person earns *below* a prescribed income, instead of paying an income tax to the government the government pays the individual. The figures in Table 16-11 illustrate one way in which the proportion of those payments might be related to earnings. The numbers are suggestive for purposes of explanation. If a person earns nothing over the year, then he is paid a negative income tax—a subsidy—of $3,000. Thereafter, up to a total of $6,000, for every marginal dollar the person earns he receives a 50 cent reduction in the subsidy. Note how the person who works and earns some income still gets some welfare. Welfare payments are reduced, but not taken completely away if a person has a job. Therefore, there is still an incentive to work. There is no abrupt cutoff point where a person would be better off not working because the reduction in the subsidy is greater than any additional income he could earn by working, as is the case under many welfare programs. The individual is not told what he should do with the money if he qualifies for it.

Friedman is of the opinion that the many unfair and excessively costly welfare programs, including the Social Security system, could be abolished if the NIT were introduced. Undoubtedly there would be significant administrative problems in operating such a system but they could hardly be greater than the present ones.

Critics of NIT counter with several arguments. They contend that it would not be cheaper than the current grab bag of programs and would grow in cost. What is established as a minimum poverty level nationally would be too low for New York but too high for Mississippi, and in any case, it can only supplement and not replace current welfare programs. For example, it is not sufficient to cover medical expenses. The biggest obstacle to NIT appears to be political. Many voting citizens might rankle at the thought of people being paid cash directly for doing nothing. Experimental income maintenance programs already conducted revealed that cash payments to poor families did not have a large disincentive effect on working. However, heads of households did work about two hours less per week on average when welfare benefits were added from earnings. The NIT would not interfere extensively with the efficiency of private markets as current programs often do. For example, the public housing program, it is claimed, has destroyed more housing than it has created.

IS EQUALITY DESIRABLE?

In 1972, 122 million Americans were income recipients. They earned an average income of $6,375 and a median income of $4,713. The average wealth in the U.S. obtained by dividing total wealth by the total population was roughly $21,700 per person.

Suppose the wealth and income of the country could be equally divided among all citizens by fiat. Would this make everyone better off? Most everyone better off? It is not likely in the long run. Assuming the tax structure remained the same, the more enterprising, the healthier, the more skilled, the luckier, and the more clever would still end up with more than the others through trading and risk taking. If the tax structure were changed to prevent this random lottery from existing by force of law, the fiat would destroy any incentive for the most productive people to produce. Investment and growth would be stifled and there would necessarily be more coercion to keep people from scheming to get more. By preventing large amounts of income and wealth from accumulating in individual hands and dividing wealth into small units, saving would decline; economies of size would be more difficult to achieve, and productivity for this reason alone would suffer. As productivity fell, so too would income, hence there would be less in tax receipts to redistribute to everyone. As the size of the public sector increased at the expense of the private sector, where most wealth is produced, it would further dampen the private sector. As income fell, so would demand fall, markets would shrink, and efficiency would decline. As productivity declined in the private sector and taxes were raised to maintain public expenditures, the system would wind down—it would become like a lizard eating its own tail. There is presumably some unknown optimum, although unequal, distribution of income that is required to keep the economy healthy. If income is too unequal, social and political instability will result, but if it is forced too far toward equality by government interference, it may kill the golden goose. Somewhere in between the extremes lies an optimum range of inequality in the distribution of income.

CHAPTER SUMMARY

The distribution of wealth is more skewed than the distribution of income. Wealth is a measure of the value of the stock of all assets. Wealth yields a stream of money payments over time called income, and income in turn can be reinvested to create additional wealth. The Lorenz curve depicts the income distribution of the population by dividing the population into fifths or quintiles, illustrating the share of total national income each quintile receives. Between 1929 to 1947 there was a noticeable improvement in income distribution, with, however, little significant change since.

For 1972, adjustments for in-kind (noncash) government transfers resulted in a doubling of the share of total income of the lowest quintile from 5.4 percent to 11.7 percent.

The manner in which calculations are performed affects the distribution outcome. The percentages for families are different for persons than for family units. For instance, because of "undoubling," when some family members move out to live alone, average household income declines because the same amount of income is now divided between two households. Also, the accounting period over which the statistics are compiled alter income distribution figures, since fluctuations may average out over longer periods.

Moreover, government income statistics count income before taxes. Because of different wealth structures across families, they may pay different taxes while earning the same incomes so that after-tax incomes vary.

Morton Paglin challenged the conventional method of calculating income distribution. He argued that the cash equivalent of government in-kind transfers has been underestimated. Also, comparisons of income earnings should be compared between the same age groups at different time periods, since age is an important determinant of income.

A majority of the poor tend to be the elderly, dependent children of single-parent households, and the disabled. In general, sources of income inequality arise from differences in inherited wealth, environment, health, information about the labor market, and most importantly human capital. The last embodies education, training, and job experience that enhance individuals' productivity. Access to improving human capital have hindered minorities and women in the past. As regards women, the motherhood role limits the mobility and kinds of jobs many women can take, which tend to be lower paying than the kinds of jobs men take.

Affirmative action and antidiscrimination laws have not led to any significant closing of the income gap between blacks and whites in the 1970s. These laws seemed to have mostly helped minorities already possessing highly marketable skills and those already fully employed. For the young unskilled minorities the influx of white females in the labor market, union seniority rules, to some extent the minimum wage, and the higher black birth rate, have increased the ratio of black-white unemployment among the young. These ratios become worse during economic slowdowns. More and better education for blacks that raises their human capital seems to be the way out. One study indicated that young blacks and whites with similar education and cultural exposure earn about the same incomes. By and large the vast government programs begun in the latter 1960s do not appear to have helped the employment situation for blacks so necessary to bring long-term improvements in income distribution.

One approach to improve the plight of the poor is the negative income tax: a program that qualifies the poor for receiving direct cash transfers. These payments decrease in proportion to any income the person receives from working, but in such a way that the incentive to work is not destroyed.

The question remains of how far a society can use the tax system to redistribute income more equally without destroying the incentives of those whose incomes are more heavily taxed in order to help provide for income transfers to the poor.

QUESTIONS

1. Beginning male fashion models in New York (1978) start out at $60 an hour. They rarely achieve the average of $100 an hour that many female fashion models do. Is this discrimination? Is it equitable (fair)? What else might account for the difference?

2. You may have heard the expressions, "The cream always rises to the top" or "talent will out." What is being implicitly assumed about the workings of the human capital market in these statements? Would you agree? Explain.
3. Suppose the average age of the population falls. How would this change likely affect the Lorenz curve? Discuss.
4. Black males in the 25–44 age bracket have lower unemployment rates and higher income than whites in the 16–20 age group who are not attending school. Is this fact easily explained?
5. This century has seen a steady migration of farmers to the cities. What effect would this have on the Lorenz curve? Explain.
6. Some researchers claim there has been little improvement in income distribution in the U.S. since 1950. Others say this is not true, for adjusted income which shows an improvement in income equality. What do these "adjustments" entail?
7. Insofar as the marginal utility of income declines as income rises, would a change resulting in a more equal income distribution in the economy understate or overstate the improvement in the aggregate utility of society? Explain.
8. "You cannot make the poor rich by making the rich poor." Should there then be no income redistribution policy? Comment.
9. What do changing life styles have to do with undoubling? What about the divorce rate?
10. Several studies have concluded that the middle income class is the main benefactor of state subsidized universities and colleges because they represent the highest percentage in attendance at these schools and pay tuition amounting to only a fourth to a third of full cost. If this fact is included in the Census data, how would the Lorenz curve be affected? Explain.
11. Virtually every instructor has listened to a touching story from a student about why he or she is not performing well on exams and papers. Some of them plead for consideration based on a variety of excuses, real and otherwise. Suppose at the end of the term, instead of basing grades on exam scores, each student is allocated three minutes during finals week to explain vocally to the instructor the various hardships during the term that caused their performance to be poor or less than what they "know they can really do." The more heartrending the tale, the higher the grade one receives.
    a. Is this criterion more or less fair than evaluation based on test grades, given that people have different schooling backgrounds, life experiences, native skills, income, and so on?
    b. Suppose everyone had a B.A. degree conferred on them when they turned 16, with attendance at college classes optional thereafter. Would job allocation and income distribution be much different than it is now? Explain.
12. Eleanor Maccoby and Carol Jacklin, psychologists at Stanford University, rigorously researched differences between males and females (What We Know and Don't Know About Sex Differences, *Psychology Today,* December 1974). They claimed to have definitely dispelled eight popular myths about sex differences. They were uncertain about differences in eight others. Four differences, however, were clearly established. They were that (1) boys are more aggressive (combative), (2) girls have greater verbal ability, (3) boys distinctly excel in visual-spatial ability, and (4) boys excel in mathematical ability. Moreover, the Johnson O'Conner Human Engineering Laboratories believe their studies show a high correlation between visual-spatial ability and excellence in engineering, physics, mathematics, and mechanical skills.
    a. What would the above predict about the sex distribution in English and language classes as compared to engineering and physics classes? As between sociology and economics classes?
    b. What other hypothesis might also explain the sex distribution in college classes?
    c. Some biologists attribute mental differences in the sexes to the higher testoster-

one levels in males. The sociobiologists attribute it to genetic imprinting rather than cultural bias. Do you think cultural reconditioning can overcome innate differences if they do exist? Suppose there are really innate differences. What might result from imposing social engineering programs to get people to have the "right behavior?" Do you see these things happening now?

13. Jews comprise about 3 percent of the U.S. population. They, however, account for about 27 percent of Nobel prizes won by Americans. Their representation on the faculties of colleges and universities is far greater than 3 percent.
    a. Does the above suggest that the Jews in Western societies have traditionally received preferential treatment?
    b. Would Jews tend to support racial or ethnic quotas for entering medical schools? Explain.
14. A 1964 study done at Johns Hopkins University measured how much time families allocated to do-it-yourself projects around the house. Using opportunity cost, they estimated the value of these projects if they spent the equivalent time outside at them, e.g., carpentry. They discovered that a family whose money income was between $5,000 and $6,000 typically increased its income about $4,100 through unpaid household work. For a family whose money income was between $10,000 and $15,000, increased but unpaid household income was raised by $4,400. Would these results, if included in the Census data, increase or decrease income inequality?
15. If a city spends $1,000 a year in taxes to educate a child in a public school, this outlay by the city can be interpreted as an increase in the nonmoney income of the child's family (i.e., consider the cost of sending the child to a private school). Is there a name for this sort of income transfer? How would income distribution data be affected if the $1,000 of public education were included in household income?
16. Would it make sense to say that natural ability is more evenly distributed among the population than are incomes? Why?
17. Use the graphs to answer questions *a* through *c*.

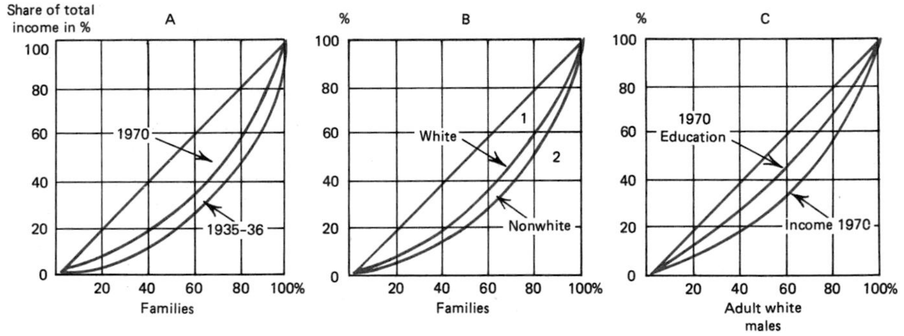

    a. What does Figure A indicate about income inequality as between 1935—1936 period and 1970?
    b. What does Figure B indicate about the distribution of income among whites and nonwhites and between the two groups? For which group is the Gini coefficient higher?
    c. What does Figure C indicate about the distribution of education and income among adult white males in 1970?
18. If it is true that women get paid less for the same work as men do, what does the perfectly competitive model predict would occur in industries that discriminate against hiring women? Is your answer consistent with the fact that most production workers in the highly competitive U.S. textile industry are women? Is there any other hypothesis consistent with women being employed in lower-paying jobs?

Chapter 17

Dealing with Externalities; Pollution

PROGRESS REPORT

A. Property rights have been mentioned intermittently throughout the text. When discussing supply, demand, and exchange, private property rights were implicitly assumed. In Chapter 16 we discussed income distribution. In order to earn income an individual must own rights to the gains from his property, encompassing his labor, capital, and land.

B. In this chapter we discuss how poorly defined property rights do not permit markets to exist. When markets cannot exist there arises a problem that economists call the externality problem. We shall examine the nature of this problem in some detail and discuss the attributes of what are called common property resources. These are resources that are not owned by any individual, corporation, or government. Having examined the problem of externalities, we shall then consider some suggestions that economists have proposed to deal with them. Finally we shall see that income distribution questions are entwined with solutions to the problems of externalities.

C. In Chapter 18 the difference between private goods and public goods is examined and shown to be a concept distinct from the notion of private and public ownership. Thereafter, problems associated with arriving at group decisions on economic issues in a democracy are discussed.

THE ECONOMY AND THE ENVIRONMENT

One of the major dilemmas of the modern industrial world is the conflict between the industrialism associated with economic growth and the quality of the environment. While technological development in such fields as medicine, agriculture, and transportation has greatly improved the quality of life, this same technology also endangers it in many instances. Concern over pollution has reached the point in the U.S. where dam construction to provide electrical energy has been interrupted in order to prevent extinction of endangered species such as the furbish louse wart, a lowly wildflower, and the simple snail darter, a small guppy-like fish. But the issues go deeper than concern over endangered species of plants and animals when humankind is the species being threatened.

Large deposits of toxic man-made organic chemicals have been found in the Great Lakes of the U.S., in the ice of Antarctica, and in the snows of Greenland and Alaska. Oil spills have destroyed shrimp beds in the Mexican Gulf, ruined oyster beds off the coast of France, and killed fish and birds off the coast of California. The Colosseum is being eroded by the acid in the Roman air; there is similar concern in Athens over the Parthenon. Pollution plays no ideological favorites. It destroys the fish in the rivers and streams of America as well as in Lake Baikal or the Volga River in Russia. It exists where there is industrialization. Nor is pollution a modern phenomenon. The drinking waters of ancient Rome were polluted. In 1775 an English doctor, Percivil Pott, noticed the relationship between chimney sweeps exposed to soot and tar and the incidence of scrotal cancer among them. Smog snuggled over the mining and steel towns of nineteenth century England. Edinburgh, Scotland is still affectionately called "Old Reeky" because it used to reek of coal smoke from home fires.

Externalities

Externalities **are uncompensated costs or benefits inflicted on people by others' decisions.**

Industrial pollution is a subset of a larger set of phenomena that economists have labeled externalities. To economists, air pollution, water pollution, and noise pollution are perceived as externality problems. When a factory pours smoke into the neighborhood, or a neighbor plays his stereo too loud, externalities occur. There are adverse affects, or costs, imposed on others who were not in any way involved in the decisions resulting in factory smoke or stereo noise. In the case of the factory smoke, neighborhood houses must be painted more often, one's clothes need cleaning more frequently, and a person's hair needs washing much more often. Thus, an *externality arises when the costs borne by the decision maker do not include all of the costs of his decision. Some are inflicted on people who were not involved in the decision. There are social costs of production that are not accounted for in private cost calculations.* Externalities also go under other names, such as third party effects, spillover effects, side effects, and neighborhood effects. An externality can be positive or negative. When it is positive it confers a benefit, when it is negative it imposes a cost.

Externalities were first studied formally by economists beginning in the 1920s (A. Pigou, 1877–1959). Marginal costs are at the center of any analysis of externalities. Earlier we saw how, in expanding output, producers compare the cost of the additional output—the marginal cost—to the marginal revenue. It is the familiar $MR = MC$ rule. In these cases the MR and MC refer to *private* additional benefits to consumers, and *private* additional costs to producers. The costs to the producer are the costs to society as well, since they measure what these resources would have cost society in an alternative use, signified by the factor costs paid by the producer. In the situation where externalities exist, the producer, while absorbing the factor costs, does not absorb the full social cost of production because his business decisions impose costs on others who are not party to the operation. Thus social cost equals private costs plus external costs. Since we are interested in relations at the margin, instead of writing $SC = PC + EC$ we write

$$MSC = MPC + MEC$$

The *marginal social cost* of production equals marginal private costs plus marginal external costs.

where MSC stands for **marginal social costs**, MPC stands for marginal private costs, and MEC stands for marginal external costs. When externalities are zero, then marginal external costs are zero and marginal social costs equal marginal private costs, or $MSC = MPC$.

Take the case of a polluting factory and list some of the private and social costs involved.

Private costs	External costs
Rent	Dirty houses
License	Offensive odors
Business taxes	Eye sting
Property taxes	Dirty clothes
Fuel	Respiratory afflictions
Electricity	Lower property values
Equipment	
Materials	
Wages and salaries	

Private costs are paid by the producer as the decision maker. The external costs follow from side effects on local residents. Start with the industry in equilibrium at E_1 in Figure 17-1, with quantity at Q_1 and the price P_1. The typical price-taking firm in the industry faces a perfectly elastic demand curve $d_1 = MR_1$. The marginal private cost to the firm of producing q_1 is indicated at point a. But to produce q_1 the firm imposes an additional marginal external cost of ab, which when added to marginal private costs places marginal social costs

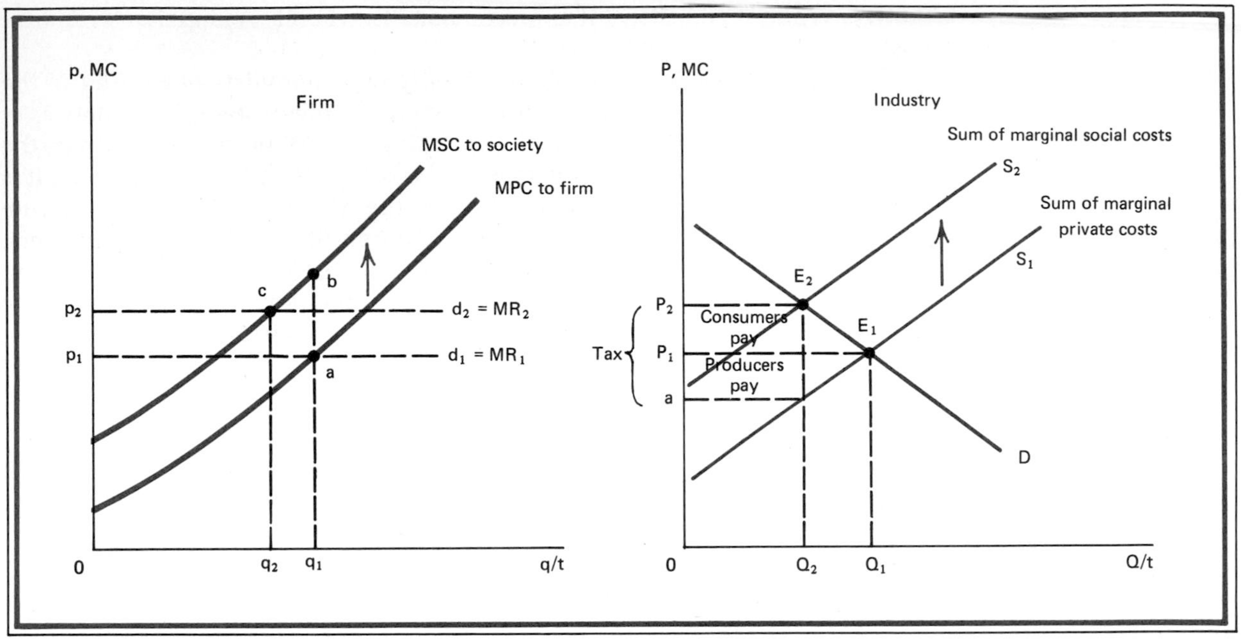

Figure 17-1

at the level indicated at point *b*. As far as the individual firm sees it, it is maximizing because $MPC = MR_1$. However, because $MSC > MR_1$, the full costs to society are greater than the benefits indicated by MR_1 at point *a*.

Let us assume that society intends that producers will pay the full social costs of production. It attempts to do so by having the government impose a tax on the output of the industry in the amount $P_2 - a$. It shifts the industry supply curve from S_1 to S_2 and raises the market price to P_2. By the law of demand, industry quantity demanded would decline from Q_1 to Q_2. Since the typical firm is assumed to be a price-taker, the firm now faces a price P_2 at which it sells its output. Because the firm now pays a tax, it incorporates this tax into its *MPC* curve. If the tax is just the right amount, the *MPC* curve shifts up until it is superimposed on the *MSC* curve. A new equilibrium is established at point *c* where $MSC = MR_2$, output is q_2, and resource allocation is efficient because marginal social costs now equal marginal revenue. However, as we learned in Chapter 4, part of the tax is absorbed by the producer and part by the consumer, depending on the elasticities of industry supply and demand. The price of the commodity shown in Figure 17-1 does not rise by the full amount of the tax. Producers absorb $P_1 - a$ of the tax per unit and consumers pay an additional $P_2 - P_1$ of the tax per unit. Thus, an efficient solution can follow as the tax leads to a rise in price and a subsequent reduction in production shown by point *c*.

There is an array of examples where externalities occur; some can be easily quantified, others not so easily. In Alaska, lumber companies often leave too much slash and stumpage after cutting because it is not economical to remove it. Not economical means that the marginal cost of removing it is less than the marginal revenue from selling it. Nevertheless there are social costs. The act of leveling the trees may remove protection from wind for nearby houses. In some areas this causes fuel bills to rise in the winter. There are other consequences.

By leaving the slash, reforestation may be delayed. What would take about 70 years by natural means may take up to 100 years on slash-covered land. The present value of the extra 30 years of lumber is lost to consumers. There is no inefficiency to the firm if the present value of the trees, delayed by 30 years from achieving full growth, is less than the present cost of removing the slash. But there may be an additional marginal external cost if the area remains an eyesore for an extra 30 years.

Let us consider a quantitative example involving two towns, Upstream and Downstream. Upstream city does not treat its sewage and dumps it into the river that flows through Downstream, where it has to be purified. If Upstream were to install a sewage treatment plant, Downstream would require a much less expensive purification system.

Downstream city water costs per year:

Without Upstream's sewage treatment	—	\$3,000,000
With Upstream's sewage treatment	—	\$500,000

Upstream city sewage treatment costs per year:

Without sewage treatment	—	zero
With sewage plant	—	\$1,500,000

Upstream city benefits:

Without sewage treatment	—	zero
With sewage treatment	—	\$2,000

Keep firmly in mind in what lies ahead that private costs are associated with Upstream's decision to build or not build the sewage plant. The social costs enter when considering the effect of that decision on Downstream's water purification costs. As far as Upstream is concerned it would receive marginal benefits of \$2,000 from, for example, the estimated value of recreation to people in Upstream who would use the beaches and clean water. The \$2,000 is what they collectively and willingly would pay to have a clean recreational water facility. The marginal cost to Upstream is the cost of the sewage treatment plant, namely \$1.5 million. From their perspective the sewage plant would not be an efficient allocation of their resources, since marginal costs are greater than marginal benefits—the benefits being translated into dollars as an objective measure of public preference. Without a sewage treatment plant the cost to Downstream to purify the water is \$3 million. Downstream is absorbing the external costs imposed by Upstream's pollution. Suppose the two towns are in the same county and county officials decide that Upstream should have a sewage treatment plant. Upstream builds the plant. Now, the tally is

Marginal costs for sewage treatment:

(Private)	Upstream city	\$1,500,000
(External)	Downstream city	zero
(Social)	Total	\$1,500,000

Marginal benefits from sewage treatment:

(Private)	Upstream city	\$2,000	
(External)	Downstream city	\$2,500,000	(reduction in purification costs)
(Social)	Total	\$2,502,000	

Perspective

Environmentalists like to get back to nature. But how is it done without help from many nature-polluting industries? Consider the following quote: "Spring is the time of the year many of us get the urge to go back to nature, to strip ourselves of the last vestiges of civilization, and join the Neanderthal, the Natty Bumppos,* and the foraging societies. We get a lump in our throats when we hear phrases such as tuning-in to nature, accepting nature on her own terms, and stripping our lives to essentials.

It is that last one that appeals to me, and I'm always grumbling about "things." Things and gadgets own us. Own only what you can carry on your back, I say.

So what do I carry on my back when I hike back to nature? A backpack made of aircraft aluminum alloy, a coated nylon sack, and a padded hip-belt filled with a petrochemical foam, nylon-coated raingear, silicone waterproofing for my vegetable-oil tanned boots. Aluminum pots and pans. A stainless steel cup, polarized sunglasses, reprocessed wool-and-nylon shirt, freeze-dried and dehydrated food in plastic containers, nylon-taffeta tent with coated nylon rainfly, nylon guy lines, aluminum stakes, and fiberglass poles.

Add to this the cameras and lenses, sophisticated brass stove, white gas, plastic bottles, crystals for soft drinks, and a dozen or so other "necessities" that would have made Meriwether Lewis† blink and scratch his fleas – I'll bet he would have loved a bottle of Off."

* A frontiersman in James F. Cooper's novels.

† Of the Lewis and Clark expedition.

Source: Archie Satterfield, Adventures in Washington, The Writing Works Inc., Mercer Island, Wash., p. 52, By Permission.

The external benefit to Downstream is $2,500,000, since that is the reduction in purification costs experienced by Downstream city. Thus, marginal social benefits include the $2,000 realized by Upstream plus the $2.5 million Downstream citizens can now spend on other things, for total benefits of $2,502,000. This is greater than the combined costs to both cities. Thus marginal social benefits are greater than marginal social costs *(MSB > MSC)*. That is, net social benefits equal $2,502,000 − $1,500,000 = $1,002,000.

To repeat, in this example private costs and private benefits accrue to Upstream city, whereas external costs and external benefits accrue to Downstream city. But social costs and benefits are experienced by both Upstream and Downstream cities as members of the county viewed as a single unit. The externality is internalized.

Guidelines for Policy

The determining factor in such decisions is not whether social costs are less than or greater than private costs or whether social benefits are greater or less than private benefits. Given scarcity and the desire for efficient, nonwasteful resource use, the issue concerns the relation between social benefits and social costs and who should pay the external costs. In the example of Upstream and Downstream cities, social benefits were greater than social costs and the project was feasible.

Society receives a net benefit when *marginal social benefit is greater than marginal social cost.*

We emphasize that it is not a matter of total benefit exceeding total cost. We must know whether **marginal benefit exceeds marginal cost**. For instance, assume the cost of getting a lake 95 percent clean is $2 million. However to get it 99 percent clean would cost $5 million. The marginal cost of getting the extra 4 percent of purification is $3 million. Should the additional purification be undertaken? Perhaps an environmentalist would immediately say yes. An economist would first ask several questions.

What would be the measurable benefits and costs from having the lake 95 percent clean? And, what are the marginal benefits and marginal costs from the additional 4 percent increase in purification? At the 95 percent level, if the marginal benefits equal the marginal costs of purification, then the system is optimal, and no further expenditures should be made. It would therefore be grossly wasteful to spend an additional $3 million to obtain only $500,000 worth of additional benefits. Put it this way: What is the benefit from tolerating some pollution, or what products are sacrificed by removing pollution?

The calculation not only of total benefits and total costs but also the calculation of marginal benefits and marginal costs associated with a given clean-up project allows us to *optimize*. Our approach is to find the marginal *trade-off* between additional water purity on the one hand and the additional cost of achieving it on the other. We call this an attempt to optimize.

A necessary condition for optimization is that $MSC = MSB$. It is our old friend $MR = MC$ with external benefits and costs thrown in. Figure 17-2 illustrates the principle. Prior to reaching point *m*, the *MSB* curve lies above the *MSC* curve, indicating that $MSB > MSC$ and that further gains in purity would also increase efficiency in resource use. At point *m* the optimal point is reached where the additional gains to society from purity are equal to the additional costs of obtaining it. At *m* the water is 95 percent clean. Beyond point *m*, the *MSC* curve lies above the *MSB*; hence, the additional costs to society for further cleansing of the water are not justified by the additional gains to society.

It is not easy to measure the dollar value of benefits. Suppose at the 95

Figure 17-2

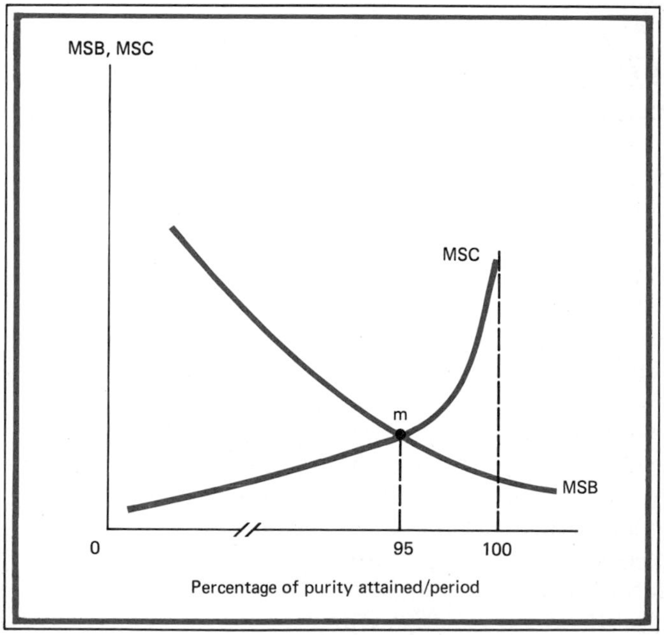

percent level, 1 percent of the stock of fish are killed by the residual 5 percent pollution. Assume the fish sell on the market for $10 each, and the additional cost to clean the lake in order to prevent 1 percent of the fish from dying comes to $100 per fish. Society values the additional fish at $10 as revealed by what people pay for fish at the market for fish—not at $100. Thus, if the purpose of cleaning the lake is to save fish it would not be worth it to spend more on cleanup efforts. To an environmentalist, however, the clean lake may be worth more than just the value of the fish it produces. Take another example. Cattle ranchers in Colorado were severely criticized by environmentalists for selling their land at good prices to ski resort developers. The price was high because developers estimated that the demand for skiing was going to be high and they were prepared to bid high prices for the land. The issue was between the preference of 30,000 potential skiers and the preference of fewer people who wanted to look at the trees. In a purely market sense, the tree lovers, if they want the land conserved for their purposes, should better the market bid offered by the developers. In this way the market helps signal the value of consumer preferences so that national decisions can be made about environmental cleanup projects.

This approach reduces everything to dollars and cents. What the analysis is trying to do is to incorporate human considerations and translate them into comparable dollar values that measure, however imperfectly, consumer preferences in terms of an observable common denominator. Since market prices cannot be directly observed to measure such things as quiet and beauty, proxy calculations using prices are the best that can be done. Thus, it can be determined how much people would willingly pay for a clean beach by taking the property values in the neighborhood where the beach is located and subtracting the property values of physically equivalent houses where a beach does not exist. The difference would reflect the value to the neighborhood of the beach.

EXTERNALITIES AND THE ABSENCE OF PROPERTY RIGHTS

Private property rights **are exclusive rights to deciding how property will be used and exchanged. The holder of these rights is the owner.**

Suppose a windstorm blows debris onto your property. You would probably clean it up. Suppose that same storm scatters debris in the park down the street. Would you pick it up? Probably not because the park is not all yours. Private property rights are exclusive rights to deciding how property will be used and exchanged. The holder of these rights is the owner. People have private property rights to the yard but only shared rights to the streets and parks. Externalities occur when property rights are not clearly defined, are shared, difficult to define, or not defined at all, hence unenforceable. Where well-defined private property rights exist, these rights can be exchanged in the market at some exchange price. The use of these resources is thereby allocated by actions of private owners according to the preferences of buyers and sellers in the market. Where private property rights exist, exchange of ownership can take place and prices will operate to allocate resources by the system we have described in earlier chapters.

Externalities arise when:

Externalities arise when private property rights are undefined because they are hard to define, hard to enforce, or the government chooses not to price the use of publicly provided goods.

1. Private property rights are hard for government to *establish* for technical reasons, and without property rights it is impossible for a market to develop. We can survey the land and pound in stakes to designate ownership. It is not so easy to mark a portion of a lake.
2. Property rights are hard for government to *enforce*. For example, it is difficult enough to establish rights to the air and the ocean as compared to the ease of setting up property rights to land. But this is a small problem compared to tracking the ownership of fish swimming back and forth across legal but intangible ocean boundaries.
3. Society may choose not to price certain "publicly provided goods" because of a desire for fairness—that they be available free to the poor as well as to those who can pay. Only small fees, if any, are charged for access to national parks such as Yellowstone.

Pollution is allowed to impose its external costs because waterways and fresh air are not privately owned and property rights to them are hard to establish and enforce. If city *A* pollutes the air for city *B* in the next state, or industrial fumes from Britain kill trees in Southern Norway, nothing can be done unilaterally. The areas lie under different political jurisdictions. City *A* and city *B* could, of course, be brought under a national policy. Britain and Norway can form a treaty. This means that a national government, or a world body in the case of nations, must redefine or modify property rights to correct the problem when it can. With no clear property rights established, no one feels responsible for cleaning up pollution. Since nobody owns the air space, firms do not feel responsible for it. Drivers do not feel individually responsible for the exhaust pollution they cause. Nor is there an incentive to install voluntarily antipollution devices even if others do not, because the marginal cost is much greater than the marginal benefit, which is essentially zero. But the government can modify property rights for all car owners and producers by requiring purification devices. When everyone is forced to cooperate, the social benefits (clean air) can justify the private costs to all manifested in the higher price of the car because of the antipollution devices installed in them.

MARKET FAILURE, GOVERNMENT FAILURE, OR NEITHER?

It is often said that the existence of externalities indicates that the market has failed to do its job of allocating benefits and costs. Upon reflection however, one could more appropriately say that government, not the market, has failed. A market does not exist because without property rights transfer of ownership or rights cannot take place at market prices. It can hardly fail to work in areas where it does not exist. On the other hand it is government's job to establish and enforce property rights. And if government has not done its job then government, not the market, has failed.

Of course, government may have failed for good reason—it may be technologically impossible or extremely costly to establish rights. In such cases government may undertake various methods of dealing with externalities. We must conclude that when externalities exist there will be a role for government to play in economic affairs. But neither the government nor the market should be viewed as having failed. In the case of the market it is prevented from playing a role because of the absence of property rights and in the case of government it is usually prevented from establishing property rights because it is either impossible to do so, or prohibitively costly to do so.

COMMON PROPERTY RESOURCES

Common property resources are those that no one owns.

Resources on which no property rights exist can be said to be owned by no one. However, it is a resource to which everyone has access. Examples are air, the ocean, and oil in underground beds. In some instances, the government permits publicly owned goods to be treated as if they were common property resources, for example beaches and parks where no fee is charged for their use. Not surprisingly, a common property resource is not treated with the consideration that attends to one's private property. Since there is no exchange price for its use by one person or another, no one can be excluded. Instead, "first come, first served" is the unwritten rule.

When it Rains it Pours, or the External Effects of a Causeway

The Morton Salt Company of Salt Lake City, Utah, has gotten a bad shake. It seems that in 1959 the Southern Pacific Company constructed a 13-mile railroad causeway across the Great Salt Lake, completely dividing it into two lakes that have become quite different in depth, color, and mineral content—particularly salt. The southern section is fed by fresh water tributaries. As a result the salt content has dropped from 16 percent to less than 11 percent. The northern section, cut off from its former tributaries, has increased in salt content from 16 percent to 26 percent. Unfortunately, the Morton Salt Company is located on the shores of the southern section, causing a drop in its salt collection from 300,000 to 100,000 tons a year. Also, NL Industries Incorporated, magnesium miners, reports a drop in magnesium concentration from 0.74 percent in 1964 to 0.45 percent in 1975.

Morton Salt and other companies on the southern shore filed suit to force Southern Pacific to drill holes in the causeway to make the lake a single body of water again. Drilling would be too expensive, said the railroad. The court found in their favor, arguing that the companies had no guarantee of a specific salt level when they set up. Morton's loss on the southern shore has been a gain to companies on the northern shore. They have offered to sell to the Morton Company the salt they unavoidably harvest while gathering sodium and potassium phosphate instead of dumping it back into the lake. But it is too expensive for Morton Co. to haul to its own plant. Also, the state of Utah is now able to attract more companies to the northern shore because of the now higher concentration of other minerals the causeway caused. Furthermore, boaters are now attracted to the southern shore of the lake since the water is fresher and the reduced amount of salt concentration will not corrode their boat hulls and deck equipment. This translates into more tourists and higher tax revenues for the state.

Source: Business Week, June 9, 1975.

Therefore, with common property resources you can expect pollution, overuse, and potential depletion. The air is poisoned, beaches littered, and the ocean becomes an overfished, industrial dump. One company drilling for oil is unknowingly tapping a common well below ground, thereby taking oil from another company which has exclusive property rights above the ground where its oil rig is legally located, so that one oil company imposes an externality on another.

Many countries have extended their offshore boundaries to 200 miles out to sea. By establishing property rights that far out, countries can then regulate the use of the resource allowing it to yield net benefits. A public lake will be overfished if no restrictions on catch are enforced. But where private property rights are introduced, an owner can price the use of a lake in accordance with the supply and demand for fish. The owner will find the appropriate price to guarantee that the lake will not become depleted and be a useful resource well into the future if he intends to maximize his profits not for one year but for many years. The same holds for tree management by privately owned lumber companies. In precisely this way firms ensure that Christmas trees will always be available. The owner wants to maximize his return and protect the quality of the resource not for one year, with nothing coming in thereafter, but over many years. He will operate to maximize the return from his own property. However, overused, common property resources are not used efficiently or put to their highest-valued use.

SOLUTIONS TO POLLUTION

As we have seen, the source of pollution in one area affects the environment in other geographical areas. In many situations only the larger jurisdiction of government can deal with the externality problem. Since pollution results from the common-property nature of some resources, a price-allocating mechanism cannot systematically function. When no private market can be operated because property rights are vague or nonexistent, externalities arise. It falls to the government, which defines all property rights, to define them especially when external costs exist as a wedge between private and social costs. How can the government redefine property rights to account for externalities and achieve maximum efficiency? It may need a great deal of information to determine the level of pollution, the source of it, and the most efficient means to control it.

Government can redefine property rights to take into account the full social costs of production by (1) taxing the public and companies, (2) regulating through threats of fines and shut downs, and (3) bringing the external costs into the pricing system.

There are several ways a government can deal with the external costs of pollution. One is simply to undertake spending to remove it directly. A second is to regulate those who pollute. A third is to force firms to internalize an externality by a system of taxes or subsidies. Let us glance briefly at each of these possible approaches by government to the problem of pollution when property rights cannot be established.

Public Spending for Cleanup Facilities Local governments usually construct and maintain sewage treatment plants. Taxpayers are required to pay for these facilities. A local manufacturer can usually pour his or her waste into the sewer without incurring any but the usual tax burden that everyone pays. The cost and selling price of the manufactured product is unaffected. There is no incentive for the firm to reduce its waste or divert it from the sewage system.

Regulation If pollution by a particular firm becomes excessive, however, government can pass pollution regulations. Gasoline stations, for example, are simply not allowed to pour used motor oil into the city's sewage system. If they do they will be subject to fines. They may also be shut down if violations continue.

Regulations can often be arbitrary and capricious. For example, assume that an anti-air-pollution device that cleans up the cigarette smoke in a local tavern costs $1,000. If it is required in all taverns then a little place with a handful of patrons is burdened with the same expense as a larger place. A very heavy expense might unintentionally run the small tavern out of business.

Instead of fining a polluter, or barring his activity by law, it is possible for a government to tax the firm that pollutes. We have shown in Figure 17-1 how a tax can raise a firm's marginal private cost of production until it equals the marginal social cost of production. A government can also achieve this goal not by taxing the product produced by the firms, but by taxing the waste produced by the firm instead. A tax based on the volume of waste the firm produces will encourage the firm to cut back on pollution and install a pollution prevention device whenever they are low-cost enough that the firm can save on its taxes to warrant installing them.

If exhaust emission regulations are national, then car buyers in Montana may be helping pay to reduce smog in California. If automobile use is price inelastic in demand, this means that most of the costs of regulation are passed on to the consumer. But, of course, the consumers who demand these products are part of the problem too.

Internalize the Externality One way to remove external costs is to internalize them. Internalizing means finding a way to redefine property rights so as to incorporate the external costs the firm imposes into the firm's pricing policy. There are several possible ways to do this. Two are mentioned here.

1. Pollution Rights The government may determine a socially acceptable level of pollution and then open up bids for licenses to pollute by certain amounts. The government must limit the number of licenses in order to restrict the cumulative, external effects and confine them to a socially optimum level. Each firm determines what the license is worth to it and it buys permission to pollute to the point where it is cheaper than cleaning up. Licenses can also be transferable and can be sold in secondary markets. The government does not coerce companies or threaten them or tell them the best equipment to use, although firms have an incentive to seek better equipment. A tanning factory might pay more for a license than a firm that produces much less pollution. Since it is necessary for a firm to buy pollution rights, firms will make the optimal decisions for themselves. In this way, the polluter is paying the full social cost of his action if the government has accurately chosen the amount it allows. We say firms internalize the social cost of pollution when there is a market for pollution rights.

2. ***Compensation*** Private agreements can be arranged to internalize an externality. You might arrange with your neighbor to compensate him for topping his tree so you can have a view of the lake. Or you bribe the bartender to shut off the jukebox for ten minutes or have him lower its noise volume. If he does not because, say, three other customers in the bar want the noise, you can negotiate with each of them and find the price at which they would be compensated for removing the external cost to you. In these examples the transactions costs of negotiating a contract are low. Thus, property rights can be exchanged relatively cheaply and the divergence between social and private costs removed.

However, this cannot be done by people who live near airports, or near a smelter that spreads a stench over the whole town. The transactions costs to an individual citizen to change property rights is prohibitive, and much greater than the gain. They would be better off moving. In the example of the loud jukebox in a crowded bar, it is too expensive relative to the gain to transact with and compensate each patron. Either you do not attend or, if you really want to concentrate on a game of pool, you buy construction-worker type ear caps and wear them and absorb the external cost with the price of the ear caps. The compensation principle is impractical in most situations because of the high transactions costs involved.

In theory, government can go a long way toward solving many of the economy's more serious pollution problems. Nevertheless it faces many difficult practical questions. In the auto exhaust question, do you tax the automobile producer or the driver of the car? Who pays? Who benefits? How are incentives affected? Creating a market mechanism using prices would often be better than direct regulation and control, since it allows for the expression of producer and consumer preferences, and may be more efficient than direct regulation by government.[1]

DISTRIBUTION OF SOCIAL COSTS

When marginal social costs exist, someone must be paying them. The previous pages describing a few possible solutions to the external cost problem necessarily involve income distribution effects because these schemes attempt to transfer some or all of the payment of the external costs to others. Aside from efficiency considerations, solving the externality problem is also intimately related to the equity problem of who gains and who pays when government redefines property rights.

[1]Larry Ruff, "The Economic Common Sense of Pollution," *The Public Interest,* Spring 1970.

CHAPTER SUMMARY

There is a twofold effect to economic growth; the benefits of a higher material standard of living and the costs of environmental destruction and dangers from pollution. Pollution is but one aspect of externalities. Externalities are uncompensated costs inflicted on those who are not party to a decision made by others. Uncompensated costs are imposed on others in society not party to a decision so that the costs to others and the decision maker—social costs—become greater than the private costs incurred by the decision maker alone. When externalities exist, social costs equal private costs plus external costs. Externalities are sometimes called neighborhood, third-party, spillover, or side effects. When external costs are nonexistent, then social costs and private costs are identical. And when there is an external cost imposed on one, another is benefitting by not paying. Thus, external costs are the mirror image of external benefits. It follows that external costs can be treated as negative external benefits. Consequently, social benefits equal private benefits plus external benefits. The analysis of externalities can then be done using this alternative relation.

In order to use resources efficiently, the rule for evaluating benefits and costs requires comparing the additional benefits to the additional costs of an additional action taken. In this way total net benefits to society will be maximized. The rule therefore is to proceed—with cleanup, for example—as long as marginal social benefits are greater than marginal social costs.

Externalities arise because property rights are imprecisely defined or not defined at all. When clear rights are absent, there is no exclusive ownership, hence a market does not exist whereby the property is efficiently allocated by means of market-determined exchange prices. Absence of clearly defined property rights can occur when such rights are either difficult to establish, hard to enforce, or because of deliberate government policy about certain kinds of resources, for example, free access to public beaches. In all cases there is an absence of a market allocating system.

The typical point of view is that externalities are an example of market failure. However, in a sense a government failure to define property rights adequately allows externalities to persist. The government can create markets where they did not previously exist by delineating property rights. This can be done in several ways. In the case of common-property rights for which there is no ownership by anyone—like the oceans—nations can meet and negotiate property rights among them. Otherwise the danger is that common-property resources will be overused, polluted, and depleted. At the national and local levels government can redefine property rights to take into account full social costs of production by (1) taxing the public and companies to pay for cleanup facilities, (2) regulation with threats of fines and shutdowns for violators, and (3) internalizing the externality, that is, setting up a mechanism to bring external costs into the private pricing system. One way to do this is for the government to sell pollution rights to polluters after it is determined what the safe pollution level is. Another method is to arrange for private individuals to negotiate a price to either remove an externality imposed by another or to tolerate it by compensating the transgressor or the transgressed. However, except for the simplest situations, the transactions cost for individuals in negotiating compensation are so high as to be impractical.

When social costs exist, someone must be paying them. When property rights are redefined so that costs are redistributed, it must also follow that income is redistributed.

QUESTIONS

1. "Give a man secure possession of a bleak rock, and he will turn it into a garden; give him a nine-year lease of a garden and he will convert it into a desert." (From Arthur Young, *Travels in France and Italy During the Years 1787, 1788 and 1789*. New York: E. P. Dutton and Co., 1915.) Can you relate this quote to concepts in this chapter?
2. What do zoning laws have to do with property rights?
3. "Who is going to use his land downtown for a park when he or she can put an office building on it?" Why do owners not use the land for a park instead, for the benefit of all? Comment.
4. Is 15,000 tons of filth dumped into the air of Los Angeles County every day a lot or a little? How do you know?
5. A Chicago journalist commenting on the educational radio station said, "If we don't open up the wilderness, then it won't be swamped the way Disneyland is—and that's fine. Who wants a lot of people spilling over the wilderness with companies going in there opening up mine and lumber operations for their own benefit."
   a. Is it only the companies who benefit from mining and lumber operations? Explain.
   b. Who are "we" in the statement?
   c. Would it have been better not to build Disneyland and not have it swamped with people, keeping the area as a park or forest instead? Discuss.
6. "Children are our greatest natural resource. We should spend whatever it takes to give them good education." Is there then no logical stopping point in the funding of education? Explain.
7. Suppose a methane producing plant is relocated in the middle of cattle land. And suppose the by-products it burns create a "dust" which settles on the ranch grass, causing the cows to grow much bigger so the farmers end up getting better prices for their cows. (Assume that any extra costs to ranchers of repainting their barns because of the dust is worth the extra cow prices they receive. Also, assume the ranchers and the chemical company are price-takers in their respective markets.)
   a. Will the chemical plant and the ranchers produce too little, too much, or exactly the socially efficient amount of methane and cows respectively? Answer in terms of the marginal private and social costs for the rancher and the chemical plant.
   b. Suppose both the chemical plant and the ranchers are owned by the same individual. Would resources be better allocated than in *a*? Explain.
   c. Suppose the chemical plant allows the cows to roam on its land, depositing their dung, which is greater than usual because of the larger sized cows. Now the plant benefits from the free dung since it is used to produce methane fuel, just as the farmers benefit from the plant's dust. Does this change the answers to *a* and *b*?
   d. Going back to *a*: If government intervention is requested by the chemical plant, what kind of tax or subsidy scheme could be used to achieve the socially efficient level of methane fuel output, if social efficiency is not maximized in *a*?
8. While visiting a park in Kansas, you observe that it is littered with beer cans. However, there are no Coors cans among them. But Coors happens to be the biggest seller in Kansas. Can you therefore conclude that Coors drinkers are more ecology-minded than those who drink other brands? If not, using economic reasoning, what can you conclude?

9. Suppose a dress shop opens up across the street from yours and in six months puts you out of business. According to economic theory, is this an externality? Why or why not?
10. Many marine biologists believe the ocean is being overfished and there is danger of some species becoming depleted. Is it not in each fisherman's interest to let the fish grow to a bigger size? What are the private and social costs of doing this? Would an educational program explaining to fishermen how many and what size fish they should catch remedy the problem? Explain.
11. "George Perkins Marsh pointed out a century ago that greed and shortsightedness were the natural enemies of prudent resource policy. Each generation must deal anew with the "raiders," with the scramble to use public resources for private profit, and with the tendency to prefer short-run profits to long-run necessities. The nation's battle to preserve the common estate is far from won." (John F. Kennedy—quoted from the introduction to *The Quiet Crisis,* by Stuart Udall, New York: Holt Rhinehart & Winston, 1963, p. xii.) Critically evaluate.
12. Benefits and costs are mirror images of one another. An external cost is a negative external benefit, so that $MSB = MPB + MEB$ is the alter expression to $MSC = MPC + MEC$. Using Upstream and Downstream city figures can you (a) show that $MSC > MPC$ and that MSC equals $3 million when Upstream operates without a sewage treatment system? (b) Can you also show that under these circumstances $MSB = -\$2.5$ million? (c) Now assume Upstream puts in a sewage treatment plant. Can you show by how much MSC is less than MPC?

Chapter 18

Public Goods and Publicly Provided Goods

PROGRESS REPORT

A. In Chapter 17 we looked into the concept of an externality, and we briefly discussed how government has a role to play in the abatement of pollution.

B. In this chapter, decision making in the public or government sector is discussed further. The important distinction between a public good and that of a publicly provided good is emphasized. Different techniques for evaluating the costs and benefits of government programs are examined and compared. The importance of the interest rate that the government uses in evaluating different production projects is discussed.

C. Chapter 19 continues with the application of economic theory to public choice, with an examination of the democratic system through the lens of economic theory. The emergence of property rights and government are covered and an examination of voting and political parties. The importance of information costs is emphasized.

Many goods and services are provided by local, state, and national governments. We now must make a distinction between *public goods* and goods that are *publicly provided,* that is, provided by government. They are not necessarily the same thing. In the next few pages we shall distinguish between *ownership* of a good and certain *attributes* of a good that make it a public good.

Private and Public Goods

Most goods have an attribute of *exclusiveness.* When one person is using a good it cannot be simultaneously used by another person. For example, a book you are reading cannot (at least, not easily) be simultaneously read by another. Two people cannot eat the same milkshake unless they are nose to nose, each one sucking on a straw. But then they are only dividing it, and neither one is consuming the whole milkshake. Each one is consuming, exclusively, a different portion of the milkshake.

A bicycle you are pedaling cannot be pedaled at the same time by another; a car you are driving cannot be simultaneously driven by another—back seat drivers notwithstanding (actually an automobile is a *shared* good, since other riders receive transportation services). In Chapter 2 we mentioned the characteristics of private property rights, which were the right to transfer ownership, the right to exclude nonpayers, that is, to prevent nonpayers from using one's property, and the right to government protection of one's property. We are now concerned not with ownership but with certain properties of the good itself that determine the number of people who can use it at the same time. Thus, a **pure private good** *is a good that cannot be used by more than one person at a time.* The very nature of the good excludes others from using it at the same time. However, there are other goods for which concurrent use is possible. These are **pure public goods**. They have different attributes than pure private goods. A *pure public good* is a good that can satisfy the desires of as many people as wish to consume it simultaneously. Examples are the light house on the shore that simultaneously guides any number of ships that pass in the night. One ship's use of the shore light does not diminish the use of the light by another ship. Your own fireworks display is a public good since you cannot prevent others from seeing it. By definition, an idea or a concept or information in general has the potential of concurrent use and qualifies as a pure public good. Everyone can think of the idea at the same time without reducing the ability of anyone else to think about it. National defense and public health are examples of public goods. To protect one is to protect all. And anyone can turn on the television set and receive the picture that everyone else is receiving.

A *pure private good* cannot be used by more than one person at a time. The user has exclusive use of it.

A *pure public good* can be used concurrently by many people without diminishing its use to any of them.

Since more than one person can use a public good, the opportunity cost of someone else using it is zero. In the case of a private good, a key element of the opportunity cost of my use of it is that its use is denied to you. It could have been allocated to you, and you would have willingly paid for it. But a public good does not have this problem. If you use it, I get to use it too and there is no opportunity or alternative use forgone to you because I use it.

In reality most goods are neither *pure* private nor *pure* public goods. Most goods have a little of both characteristics of nonsimultaneous and simultaneous use and are called **mixed goods**. Examples occur where the Federal Communication Commission (FCC) assigns a frequency to radio station X in a cer-

***Mixed goods* have properties of both public and private goods.**

tain region. No other radio station in the area is allowed to use that frequency. Thus, the frequency itself is a private good. But if station X were to increase its power, it might reduce the reception of the signal from station Y; hence, the radio space cannot be used concurrently. But what about the program received in the home? Many houses can receive the program concurrently without reducing its availability to other houses. Programs are public goods. But programs have properties of both a public and a private good if one radio program interferes with another because power was increased. Such mixed goods are sometimes also called crowded or impure public goods.

A free concert in the park would, at first thought, be considered as a pure public good. If the park becomes *too* crowded, and the presence of others diminishes your enjoyment of the concert, then it is a public good only to an extent. You may be far from the stage where the sound may be distorted. Hence, the concert takes on aspects of a mixed good. If you end up in a bad spot because of the congestion, the concert at that point becomes a private good. You cannot concurrently share it with others because their use of it denies your use of it.

GOODS AND OWNERSHIP

Having established the concepts of private, public, and mixed goods, we now introduce the condition of ownership. Ownership exists over both private and public goods. A private good, such as a chair, can be either privately owned or publicly owned. A chair in a city-owned office is a private good because only one person at a time can sit in it. It is publicly owned—owned by *the government*—but it is not a public good. A reverse situation may also exist. That is, a privately owned good may become a public good. For example, you may own another piece of land in the desert. It is privately owned but others can trespass on it simply because the transactions (policing) costs to you of preventing their trespass are so high. Thus, in effect, anyone can use your property and it becomes somewhat like a public good.

Consider the Post Office. Its courier services are government owned (except in special cases where firms employ their own messengers to deliver directly to customers). But first class mail *delivery* is a private good. There is a sacrifice of real resources, a marginal cost, whenever an additional letter is delivered whether the government delivers the letter or a private firm delivers it.

Although an idea is a public good, a copyright on a book that expresses the idea is owned by the author. If the government prints a book, the book is still a private good but it is publicly owned and provided. A theatre is a mixed good. It is a public good until all the seats are sold. When the last seat is sold it becomes a private good no matter whether it is privately or publicly owned. The reason, again, is that the presence of others taking all the seats prevents you from obtaining a seat.

A good may have private, government, or mixed ownership.

Just as there can be mixed goods there can be mixed ownership. For instance, the government maintains some patent rights on inventions it shares with a private patent holder, and fishing grounds that are publicly provided and owned can often be used by private citizens if they buy a license.

The Free Rider

When people cannot be excluded from consuming a public good, they can do so without paying; this is the *free rider effect.*

In the case of privately owned goods, it is legal for an owner to exclude nonpayers. Thus, you can be legally prohibited from entering a theater if you do not pay the price of the ticket. This is called the *exclusion principle.* In the situation of a good where nonpayers *cannot* be excluded the **free rider effect** exists. It can occur for both privately and publicly produced goods. If the city uses taxpayers' money to provide fireworks on July 4, there is no way to prevent nontaxpayers, out-of-towners, from being free riders. They get to consume the spectacle, but they do not have to pay.

In many instances, the free rider problem gives rise to a clamor by citizens for government provision of a public good. If I pay taxes and you do not, then I pay for the national defense. But you are protected by the nation's missiles and you do not help pay for them. One argument in favor of military conscription is that *everyone* should help provide for national defense. If you get it, you

Prime Time Network Players

Television in the U.S. is a good example of a public good and of the free rider effect. The marginal cost of another viewer tuning in to a television station and its network is zero. However, as a public good television does not adequately reflect the full range of consumer preferences. The networks and the local stations compete with one another to attract the greatest number of viewers, for this means larger advertising revenues. As a result most programming is pitched to the tastes and level that appeal to the average viewer, so there is little diversity across networks in the same time slots. One sees variations of sitcoms, celebrity talk shows, soaps, and quiz shows that are considered safe by the networks. Those who do not buy the advertised products but watch the shows are free riders. Because the price of viewing a show on television in your home is zero, there is no direct pricing mechanism for all potential viewers to reveal their preferences. But there is a potential market.

In recent years 200 public television stations (PBS) offering programs such as "Nova," "Masterpiece Theater," and National Geographic specials, have received total pledges of over $15 million annually from an estimated 500,000 donors. During one of their 6-1/2 hour television pledge festivals featuring a variety of performers and sample shows, PBS estimated it reached 35.6 percent of all television viewing audiences.

This suggests that PBS can overcome its own free rider problems by receiving enough viewer subscription donations to sustain programming for which a significant segment of the population is willing to pay. Thus, there would appear to be some justification, as is done in England, for a government tax-subsidized public channel, making all television set owners forced riders. Still, there remains the problem of government indoctrination and also on deciding how to allocate the time across various interests. Even artistic material is a subtle transmitter of values, just as editing on news shows is.

Another way to tap this substantial submarket is through pay television. Subscribers are charged an installation and deposit fee on a decoding unit that corrects a scrambled signal, carrying programs that viewers wish to see. This would get rid of the free rider problem. But the program offered is still a public good and, for economic efficiency, no fee should be charged because the real opportunity cost of viewing is zero. The fee is like a tax, not like a price for a service required to ration a good.

should help pay for it—clearly a normative position. Because of the free rider issue, most public goods are government provisioned and are paid for by taxes levied generally on the public, so that no citizen is given a completely free ride.

Allocation and Efficiency

A privately owned zoo would generally charge a price greater than marginal cost if it were a monopoly and operated where marginal revenue equals marginal cost. But how does the government price a park or a zoo? The government, unlike a private firm, is not trying to maximize profits; it is attempting to maximize public satisfaction through the services it offers, frequently without due regard for efficiency. The remainder of this chapter is concerned with how governments decide what goods and services to provide from among alternatives.

Spillover effects may occur when government supplies goods and services that the private sector will not, cannot, or is not allowed to provide. In the situation where there are spillover or side effects, the government may modify property rights when the transactions cost of internalizing the externality are too high for private parties to negotiate. The redefining of property rights, through the evolutionary process of government, often leads to a *mix* of private property rights with government property rights. Publicly provided or government owned goods also emerge when, for whatever reason, government fails to establish clearly determined property rights, or when markets are not allowed to operate to create a system of exchange so that prices can act to ration scarce resources. The economy, then, is prevented from attaining maximum efficiency as manifested in the Pareto optimum conditions (Chapter 7) where the ratios of marginal productivity, marginal costs, and marginal utility per dollar are equated at the margin. Whenever transactions costs are too high for private parties to redefine property rights by internalization, it is likely that costs for the government to clarify rights may also be very high. Political processes connected with public decision making are often costly.

Publicly provided goods may have side effects. They may bestow external benefits on some and external costs on others. They most certainly have distributional consequences for individual incomes. Where transactions costs are very high and the gains to the contracting parties low by comparison, who gains and who loses in the redefinition of property rights by the government will depend most significantly on the political influence and power of vested interests—corporations, small businesses, unions, property owners, farmers, the poor, the middle income, the rich, teachers, churches. An example is pollution control; the government is likely to be the best source of efficiency in redesignating property rights where widespread pollution occurs. Or, rather, it could be the best potential source of efficiency if it acted wisely. There is no guarantee it will. It could make inefficiency and income distribution worse. A factory located in a poor neighborhood may close and jobs may be lost in the local community if pollution standards are too costly for the factory to survive. The income lost from the jobs can be greater than the gain to residents of having a cleaner neighborhood. Their personal utility preferences are not reflected in the control levels required of the firm by the government regulations.

Where a vital resource is threatened, the government may convert what was once a privately owned good into a publicly owned good. For instance, most public transportation in cities was once privately run. Some colleges, once purely private, now receive additional revenues from states, turning the college programs into publicly provided goods. Let us examine public goods in a little more detail.

Public Goods and Prices

Once government has provided a public good, the *marginal cost* to the state of an additional user is zero; hence, for maximum efficiency the price for its use should equal zero.

As we saw earlier, when a pure private good is consumed by one person its consumption by others is not possible. Pure public goods are collective goods concurrently consumed by many people. Once provided, the **marginal cost** of one more person consuming a public good is zero; hence, its efficient price should be zero. The marginal cost to a television station of someone turning on a television set to watch the station's program is zero. The cost of one more person driving over a bridge or down a freeway, is essentially zero if there is no traffic jam. For social efficiency the price should also be zero since marginal cost is zero. The cost to the state of your driving over a bridge is zero since no other resources are sacrificed by the state. For this reason a private entrepreneur would not build a bridge if he were required to operate it at maximum efficiency, because the price he would have to charge in order to maximize efficiency is zero. An owner of a private bridge, however, would likely be a monopolist and would charge a price higher than marginal cost. The state does sometimes charge a toll; it does so mostly to pay off the interest and principal on the bonds the state sold in order to raise funds to build the bridge. Once the mortgage is paid off, the toll is usually lifted. On rare occasions tolls are charged for the explicit purpose of preventing congestion.

Estimating the Demand for a Public Good

Because nonpayers cannot be excluded, the private market would not provide a public good. Suppose the government decides to build a lighthouse that will provide services for many years. The higher the lighthouse the greater the cost, hence the marginal cost curve rises as the height is increased. For simplicity, assume there are only 5 fishermen who will use the lighthouse for navigational purposes. If it were possible to have a private market for the services of a lighthouse, the amount each fisherman consumed would be a function of the price of the service. The higher the lighthouse, the greater the distance it can be observed. Fishermen would only want a higher lighthouse, hence a greater observable distance, if the price per foot of lighthouse were lowered in accord with the law of demand. Each fisherman given his own demand curve, would consume differing amounts at any given price, as indicated in Figure 18-1 by the demand curves d_A to d_E. The total quantity demanded at each price would equal the horizontal summation of the individual quantities demanded, as is the normal situation for a private good. But the private market will not provide the services of a public good like a lighthouse. Assume it is decided that the government will build an 80-foot-high lighthouse. Now the height of the lighthouse is fixed and the amount of it consumed is the same to all fishermen, as is characteristic of a public good. Suppose fisherman A would willingly pay nothing, indicated by the demand curve d_A going through the origin at 80 feet,

Figure 18-1

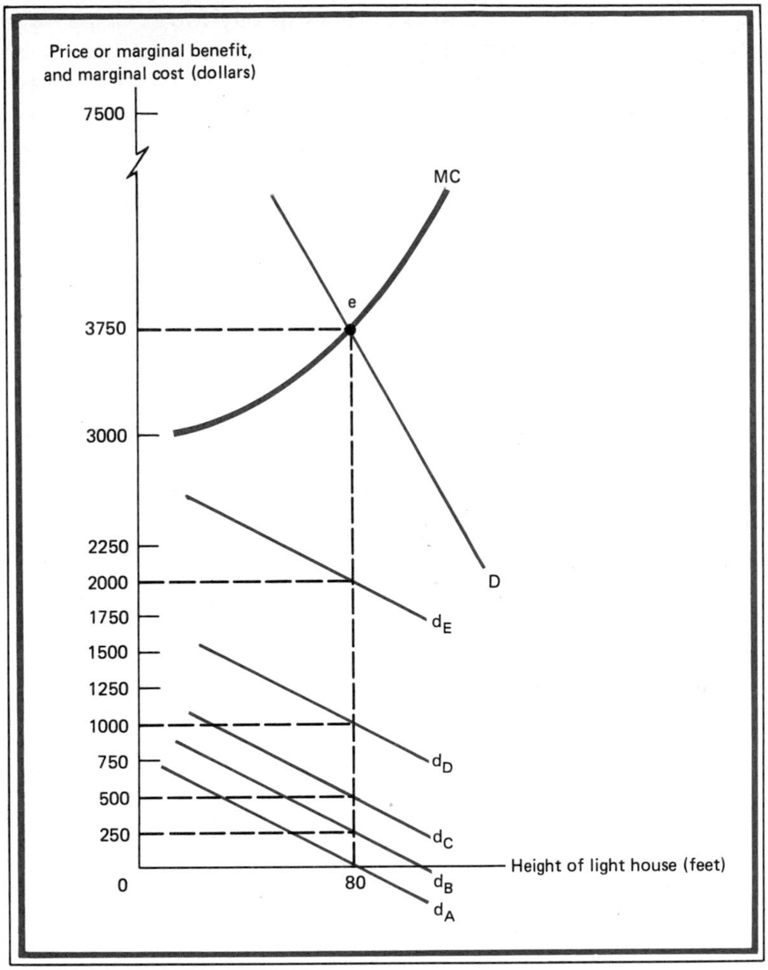

Theoretically, the total *demand* for a public good is the vertical summation of the individual demand curves at a given quantity all users consume.

fisherman B would pay $250, fisherman C $500, fisherman D $1,000, and fisherman E $2,000 to have it built. Each price reflects the marginal benefit to each fisherman respectively. Notice that since the quantity is fixed, the total marginal benefits are the *vertical* summation of the individual benefits equal to $3,750. In this case, equilibrium exists at point e where the sum of the marginal benefits equals marginal cost. Society's preferences are satisfied and the solution is economically efficient.[1]

Unrevealed Preference

In the example above, we implicitly assumed that people revealed their true preferences. Actually, people would likely not reveal their true preferences for a public good because of the free rider effect. An individual would be tempted to understate his true preferences, that is, announce a willingness to pay out-of-pocket costs below what the real benefit to him would be. The reason is that

[1]In earlier centuries lighthouses were sometimes privately funded and earned revenues from fishermen.

he might be able to get others to pay for it, or pay a larger share than he and reduce his own outlay. Given the nonexcludability characteristic of a public good, he nevertheless still consumes as much of it as others do. On the other hand, a citizen would overstate his or her preference by offering to pay a higher tax when it is understood others will be taxed that amount also, because the citizen receives services that his or her individual taxes alone could not provide. Therefore, economic theory predicts that when it comes to the government provision of a public good, individuals will not reveal their true desires.

Who Should Pay?

Two criteria for deciding who will pay for a public good are *benefits received* and *ability to pay.*

When government decides whether to provide a good or not, it must also determine who is to pay for it. In the case of the toll-free bridge, some will use it more than others, and some will use it not at all. Even where a toll is imposed, who will eventually pay the construction costs of the bridge? How should the burden of financing public goods be distributed among the taxpaying citizens? There are two commonly applied principles: benefits received and ability to pay.

Benefits Received Benefits received places a tax on the user or citizen who receives the good. It applies where excludability of nonpayers is possible. Thus, a gasoline tax is directly imposed on drivers only. In this manner the tax money used for expenditures for the construction, operation, and maintenance of roads is linked to the users of roads. In other situations the marginal benefits received principle may not work well because relatively few would use it, so that revenues obtained would be woefully inadequate. This can occur because the proposed expenditures would likely be greater than the tax revenues received, since potential users would hide their true preferences. Taxing on the basis of benefits received is an attempt to realize both equity and efficiency. But, it is usually difficult if not impossible to obtain information on what individual marginal benefits are, and therefore to determine the appropriate amount of tax. For example, those who do not use a bridge and do not pay gasoline taxes may still receive benefits. The woman who eats watermelons the truck brings across the bridge into her community receives a benefit—she gets watermelon and other goods at lower prices because of the reduced transportation cost the bridge provides.

As a practical matter, therefore, government can only approximate in very rough ways the goal of taxing those who receive benefits. Furthermore, when taxes take the form of excise taxes, such as 10 cents per gallon of gasoline, the tax itself distorts the allocation of resources away from the Pareto optimum, since price no longer equals marginal cost. Thus, taxing on the basis of benefit received is a controversial matter.

Ability to Pay Ability to pay emphasizes equity considerations. Payment depends on one's income or wealth—those who can afford to do so pay more than others. It is becoming more common public policy to give fare discounts to elderly bus riders, who are presumably living on low and often fixed incomes. In some areas the elderly pay lower utility rates. Some who fall below a certain level of earned income receive welfare payments while others above it, though still not well off, do not. Consequently, there are unavoidable redistribution effects that derive from decisions about publicly provided goods.

The ability to pay approach is not a means of employing the price mechanism to allocate scarce resources efficiently. It is used instead as a differential tax which redistributes income. Because some pay more tax than others, income is redistributed. In the case of bus rides, those who are under 65 subsidize bus rides for those 65 and over. These external effects and their fairness are necessarily subjective. To describe in detail the way these decisions affect each individual is impossible, since individual utility functions are unknown to the government. Yet without this information social welfare cannot be maximized, hence the tradeoff between efficiency and equity is only vaguely understood. Nevertheless, it is believed that action taken is at least in a useful direction, and in rough fashion ability to pay policies are therefore adopted.

PROGRAM EVALUATION

Public agencies are often confronted with a choice to be made among alternative programs. Government expenditures on dams, bridges, roads, and so on are really investments in what is known as social overhead capital. Other government programs amount to investments in human capital, for example, manpower programs, loans to students, Job Corps, and the like. The various policies and programs must be evaluated in order to make comparisons of their benefits and costs, as well as their efficiency and equity, given budget constraints and objectives.

Planning Program Budgeting System (PPBS)

The *Planned Programming Budgeting System (PPBS)* first determines which programs are in greatest demand and which programs will yield the most benefits, then adopts the least costly procedure to implement the chosen programs. It emphasizes services.

One technique instituted by the federal government in 1965 is called PPBS for short. The government agency determines what the demands are for public goods and services. It directs its activities toward estimating the demand for programs, the output those programs should provide, and the benefits they yield. While it must work within limits of a budget, it emphasizes programs. It does not give priority to what can be spent on different programs, but rather it emphasizes what programs are needed and directs expenditures to different programs according to the demand for each. It focuses on the goal or the mission and relates ends to means. It therefore devises a plan to achieve its outputs given a budget, then measures how the program performs. Nonetheless, two elements must be considered in government programs—effectiveness, where costs are given and then benefits are maximized within the cost constraint, and efficiency, where benefits or goals are given and costs of attaining those targets are minimized. The main purpose of PPBS is to look at different programs that have different structures but the same objectives and compare them for potential outputs, that is, benefits. This is the effectiveness approach. It is less concerned with inputs, that is, costs. That is to say, once it is decided which of several programs will yield maximum benefits, one is chosen that can be carried out at minimum cost. PPBS differs from conventional budgeting in that the program is not confined to one fiscal period. Its program plans are evaluated on benefits that may only be fully realized in future periods.

PPBS is a rather subtle concept of planning and budgeting, and full details cannot be provided here. By 1971, however, PPBS was, in effect, dead in Washington, D.C. For one thing, just measuring the output of most government services is a tricky business. For example, how is the output of the Health and Human Services Department (HHS) measured when its output is comprised of welfare payments, health care, and consumer protection? One cannot use physical units of output as the producer of nuts and bolts can do. Outputs by government tend to be benefits to the community at large, such as vaccination programs. These are hard to convert into measurable dollar benefits. Thus, PPBS was unpopular in Congress because members had to justify programs they supported for political reasons—pork barrel[2] programs that got them reelected at home but were an inefficient use of monies when viewed from the perspective of the total economy. While there may have been definite benefits from some of these programs, measurement difficulties made such benefits hard to confirm. Most importantly, PPBS threatened to place more budget power in the hands of presidential administrators and less into pet agencies created by congressmen.

Zero Based Budgeting (ZBB)

Zero based budgeting (ZBB) **assumes a starting budget of zero, then sets descending priorities; it emphasizes the costs of providing services.**

Zero based budgeting was introduced by the Carter administration in 1976 in an attempt to reduce government spending. The idea is that in setting its budget each agency should start at a budget of zero with no programs and then set its priorities. Each program is to be considered one at a time in descending priority. Zero based budgeting emphasizes the input side. What has to be supplied and at what cost? In this manner each program is compared to all other alternative programs within each agency and to programs in other agencies. The hope is to reduce duplication and overlapping among agencies. It nevertheless has the same difficulties in measuring output as does the PPBS method, and also requires expensive, detailed calculations. Moreover, it conflicts with the desires of agency chiefs, who jealously protect their programs and the budgets needed to supervise them. ZBB is a real threat to empire builders.

BENEFIT-COST ANALYSIS

Whether PPBS, ZBB, or any other scheme is used to allocate budgets and implement program benefits, a technique of evaluating alternative programs is necessary. Systems analysis is the general name given to the package of tools and techniques used to measure the efficiency of a complex system, be it an office or an operation comprised of many suboperations. One of the most used

[2] A pork barrel is the term for legislation pushed by congressmen who get money appropriated to gain votes, as for example local improvements to please constituents.

and useful tools is the technique of benefit-cost calculations, especially where programs will have effects extending well into the future.

The most consistently accurate way to calculate the *benefit-cost ratio* of a public program is present value: discounting expected benefits net of costs.

A bridge may last for 70 years or more, a dam for 100 years. Benefit-cost analysis is a practical way to compare alternative projects. It requires that benefits and costs be identified, enumerated, and evaluated. Benefit-cost studies must draw on information provided by engineers, agriculturists, marine biologists, and experts from many disciplines. A proposed project is then quantified by estimating all future annual anticipated benefits and costs to determine net benefits per period. These projected benefits are then discounted to the present, using an interest rate.

To choose a simple example, assume that the Army Corps of Engineers plans to put in a breakwater that is expected to last indefinitely if maintained. Benefits to ships are assumed to be valued at $150 per year, and maintenance cost each year is estimated at $50 per year. Net benefits are the benefits less costs, or $100 per year, $NB = B - C$ or $\$100 = \$150 - \$50$. Because the flow of benefits and costs are expected to last more or less forever it is appropriate to estimate the discounted present value of the future stream of net benefits with the formula

$$PV = \frac{NB}{i}$$

Where i is a rate of interest that is called a discount rate in this context. In our example, if $i = 5$ percent or .05 then $PV = \$100/.05 = \$2{,}000$. The project of putting in the breakwater is economically appropriate in this case if construction costs are less than $2,000. If costs are more than $2,000 then the project is not expected to provide sufficient benefits to make it worth what it costs to install. The reader can see that this is the same kind of analysis that is used when private investors make investment decisions. The difference, when government invests, is in the calculation of benefits. Benefits are not simply money profits, but are dollar estimates of the services of public goods for which no price may be charged.

In the early days of benefit-cost analysis, instead of using straight present value figures it was often the case that government officials would calculate a benefit-cost ratio, where

$$B/C = \frac{\text{Present value of annual future benefits}}{\text{Present value of annual future costs + construction costs}}.$$

If $B/C > 1$, then the project was justified. If $B/C < 1$ it was not. Most of the time using the present value and comparing it with construction cost will lead to the same decision as the B/C ratio. However, in some unique situations the answers may differ. In these cases use present value.

Measuring Benefits

Because a project is long-term, estimating future social benefits is subject to uncertainty. There are future events over which no one has control and that no one can predict with confidence. There is also the difficult question of quantification. What value does one place on clean air, scenic beauty, the drownings prevented by flood control projects, and manpower programs? Furthermore, there is the element of externalities. Should they be included? If an irrigation project actually increases the production of food on farms, the value of the increased output is a benefit to be included. But if a new bridge brings more business to a gasoline station and raises the value of the property, this is not a benefit that should be included. For gasoline stations operating under the same fiscal authority (a city) higher profits and increases in property values (which are capitalized in the selling price of the station) are merely transfers of income and are only income distribution effects and not output changes. More gas sold at this station simply means less sold on routes that some cars previously took, or represents the increase in trips made because of the convenience. There is no increase in production as a direct consequence of the bridge being built. The gasoline station operator is merely earning some economic rent; his opportunity cost is unchanged.

Measuring Costs

When calculating social costs, it is opportunity cost that is involved—all forgone costs. While the direct opportunity costs of material and labor are obvious and immediate, other future forgone costs are less conspicuous. When a dam is built, there are the direct resource costs of cement, steel, hydraulic equipment, and labor. In competitive markets their prices reflect their opportunity costs—what it takes to bid them away from other uses.

There may also be external costs that must be included in order to arrive at the full social costs of a public project. If a pesticide program is being subsidized by the government, the market price—the private cost—of the chemical would be misleading if it did not include all negative effects of toxins that enter into mothers' milk and into babies' systems because of the toxin being absorbed by grazing cows. Or if a dam to provide electricity kills fish, what is the cost to the state fisheries program to replenish the stock of fish? Both full social costs and full social benefits are difficult to measure precisely in practice.

In practice, it is difficult to *measure full social costs* and *full social benefits,* and to choose the correct interest (discount) rate.

What Interest Rate to Use?

Besides the difficulty of measuring costs and benefits, there remains the difficult choice of the appropriate interest rate to use with which to discount the anticipated net benefits of a project. There are many financial markets each with different interest rates reflecting things like differences in time periods, risks, taxes, and inflation rates. There are bond markets, certificates of deposit markets, the market for treasury bills, and the rate of return on investment in physical capital in the private sector. Thus, at any time interest rates may range from 5 percent on a savings account to a rate of return on capital of 20 percent or more. Obviously, different interest rates will yield different net benefits. In fact, the same project may be economically justified at one rate of interest and unjustified if a higher rate of interest is chosen for the discount rate. This lesson was learned in Chapter 14. The lower the interest rate used, the higher the present value of net benefits. Lower interest rates tend to favor projects that yield anticipated benefits farther into the future. This can easily be seen by noting that the interest rate appears in the denominator of the formula. The larger the interest rate the lower the present value, and vice versa.

The "right" interest rate is of importance, since achieving optimum social welfare is the goal of the project. The best rate to use would be the one that accurately reflects the willingness of the community as a whole to sacrifice current consumption, that is, to save in the expectation of future benefits. Such an interest rate is referred to as the marginal social rate of time preference. This single rate of interest could then serve to compare benefits and costs of public projects that displace capital that could have been used in the private sector if the public projects had not been undertaken.

The point of the tale is that the government is often criticized on the ground that it uses an interest rate that is too low. This charge has given rise to a lively debate. Critics argue that part of the reason is the political pressure put on the federal budget that is processed through Congress. Pork barreling may dominate economic prudence. The lower the interest rate chosen, the higher the net benefit calculation, hence more projects are ruled as economically and socially beneficial and government grows. Choosing a discount rate remains a controversial subject.

COLLECTIVE CHOICE

In a democratic society individual citizens have the right to vote. The transactions cost of voting for most people is quite low. If elections were held on Sundays it would be even lower. A vote for a program of public expenditures or some sort of institutional change is required where competing programs exist. In most situations the choice is dependent on a majority rule, that is, over 50 percent of those voting. At times at the local level a 60 percent rule might apply on a school levy issue, and two thirds is required on a constitutional amendment or for overriding a presidential veto. Political solutions are sought to decide what action is to be taken to maximize the common good. Decisions about pollution, education, transportation, national defense, taxes, and school busing are cases in point. Unless the vote is unanimous (100 percent), the majority decision will impose externalities on the minority. In fact, the decision to utilize a majority rule is also a collective decision, imposing externalities. As far as is possible, one goal of the public decision is to internalize the externality that brought about a need for the vote, and thereby produce a gain in efficiency and social welfare (however that may be defined, if at all). Of course, when the voting population is large, each citizen does not directly vote on every issue. Citizens vote for representatives who compare the social and economic worth of alternative programs.

Arrow's Impossibility Theorem

Nobel prize winner Kenneth Arrow demonstrated that there are problems with majority rule that may make it impossible to arrive at a consistent solution

Arrow's impossibility theorem **suggests that majority rule may make consistent public decisions impossible.**

when three or more alternatives exist, and three or more decision makers or groups are involved. Most public decisions are multidimensional and involve more than three decision makers. What follows is a very simplified version of Arrow's theory.

Consider the following problem. A 3-member school board has to make a decision about busing. One member is a conservative, the second a moderate, and the third a liberal. The alternatives are no busing, voluntary busing, and forced busing. The numbers in the table 1, 2, and 3 stand for order of preference. The rankings by the board members are arranged in the table. Can a clear, consistent decision for the community be ascertained by examining the preferences of the three public officials? Not necessarily. Assume each board member has a consistent ordering of preferences. The word *consistent* implies that, if *A* is preferred to *B* and *B* is preferred to *C*, then *A* is preferred to *C*.

Program

	A No busing	B Voluntary busing	C Forced busing
Conservative	1	2	3
Moderate	3	1	2
Liberal	2	3	1

The numbers refer to the order of ranking of each policy *A*, *B*, and *C* by each member. But consistent individual preferences do not ensure a consistent outcome of voting. Let us start by matching the members two at a time. Pairing the conservative and the liberal reveals that both would opt for no busing over voluntary busing, since for the conservative *A p B* (read as *A* is preferred to *B*) and for the liberal *A p B*. However, if the conservative and moderate were paired they would rank voluntary busing over forced busing (*B p C* and *B p C* respectively). Assuming that preferences are consistent, then because the members on a pairwise basis prefer no busing to volunteer busing and volunteer busing to forced busing, it logically follows that no busing is preferred by the board to forced busing. That is, *A p B* and *B p C* implies *A p C*. But that is not what happens. Pairing the moderate and the liberal reveals that they would prefer forced busing to no busing, since *C p A* and *C p A* respectively. Thus, the decision, if any, will depend on the sequence of the pairings, that is, on the order in which the alternatives are considered when voting on them pairwise.

The real world is full of examples of this dilemma posed by unrevealed preferences and strategic voting. It exists in U.S. primary elections for President when there are five or six candidates at the start and numerous issues. Strategy and funds will determine which candidates will be paired in which state primaries, since it is not likely all of them will enter every primary. Strategic voting also occurs where the primaries are open at the state and local levels.

Voters can switch their vote, crossing party lines. For example, a Democratic voter could vote for a weak Republican candidate against a strong Republican one to prevent the strong candidate from competing against the Democratic incumbent who is likely to win his party's candidacy easily.

A senator from an oil and natural gas producing state like Oklahoma might agree to vote for national health insurance provided a Northern liberal senator promises to vote for removal of price controls on all natural gas. Such vote trading is called *logrolling*. Compromise is often the only way to get legislation passed in a majority rule system that could otherwise not reach a collective decision. Thus, in a democratic society operating under majority rule the wide range of issues and the diversity of vested interests makes consistent social choices very difficult.

CHAPTER SUMMARY

There is a distinction between public goods and publicly provided goods. A public good is a good that possesses certain qualities or attributes, whereas a publicly provided good refers to ownership by government. A public good may or may not be owned by the government. A pure public good is one that can be concurrently used by many people without diminishing the use of it to any one of them. This is in contrast to a pure private good that possesses the property of exclusivity. One person's use of a private good excludes or diminishes its use by another. Therefore, for one person to use a private good requires bidding away its use by another—hence a marginal cost is incurred. But with a pure public good there is no additional sacrifice from another person using it, so the marginal cost of another person consuming a pure public good is zero. The government, of course, also owns many private goods.

In reality most goods are neither pure private nor pure public goods: they are mixed goods. Thus, a movie theatre has the attribute of a public good—until all the seats are sold, whereupon the person who takes the last seat imposes a sacrifice on the person who did not get a seat. The film at that point becomes a private good, not in the ownership sense, but in the attribute sense.

Also, aside from goods having mixed private and public good characteristics, there can be mixed ownership. An individual can share patent rights with the government.

Because public goods can be simultaneously consumed by more than one person at a time, the free-rider effect arises. People can enjoy consuming the good without paying because there is no way to exclude them from doing so. A Christmas display outside a house is privately owned but is a public good where passersby are free-riders. A large Christmas tree display funded with local taxes cannot be collected from out-of-towners who see it free of taxes. The nature of a public good presents problems in pricing the use of it in order to efficiently allocate resources. If the state provides a public good, the marginal cost to the state of an additional user is zero. Hence for maximum efficiency the price should equal zero. How then is it determined whether the good is economically justifiable? This is done by estimating the demand for it. For a private good the quantity demanded is the sum of individual quantities demanded at a given price. The individual demand schedules are horizontally summed at this price to determine total demand. With public goods everyone consumes the same amount of the good. That amount is fixed, and the different prices individuals would willingly pay according to each one's demand curve for this same amount is summed to determine total revenue. Thus, total demand for a public good is arrived at by the vertical summation of individual demand curves, but at the same quantity for everyone. If these marginal revenues (prices) sum to marginal cost, the production of the good is economically efficient.

However, because of unrevealed preference, individuals when queried would understate the out-of-pocket costs they would pay, hoping as free-riders to receive use of the good by having someone else pay for it. In other situations they would overstate their preferences.

The question of who should pay for a publicly provided good is viewed in two lights. One is the benefits-received principle. Those pay who use it. The other is the ability-to-pay concept. Those pay more who can afford to do so.

The government can resort to different methods for evaluating and choosing among programs. A PPBS or Planned Programming Budgeting System first determines what programs are in greatest demand and which programs will yield the most benefits, and only then adopts the procedure that is least costly. ZZB or zero-based budgeting assumes a starting budget of zero, then sets its priorities in descending ordering. It therefore emphasizes the cost side. Benefit-cost analysis is the tool that is used no matter what budgeting scheme is adopted. When the benefit-cost ratio is greater than 1 the project is feasible. However, the most consistent calculation is present value, discounting expected benefits net of costs. If present value is greater than costs, the project is feasible. However, measuring benefits and costs is inexact. Also, a major problem is determining with what interest rate to discount. If the government uses too low an interest rate, projects will yield higher present values and be deemed feasible when indeed they are not.

Finally, in a democratic society, Arrow's impossibility theorem suggests that majority rule may make it impossible to arrive at consistent public decisions.

QUESTIONS

1. Determine if each of the following best fit the definition of a pure public good, a pure private good, or a mixed good. Can any of them be privately provided?
   a. A swimming pool.
   b. A parade.
   c. A seat in economics class at the college.
   d. The lecture in economics class at the college.
   e. An idea for a new mousetrap.
2. Explain under what conditions a public good becomes a private good.
3. Explain how one of the goods in question 1 can involve mixed ownership.
4. Is a vaccination against measles for which you paid the doctor a public good, a private good, or a mixed good? Explain.
5. A classic example of scarcity and opportunity cost is the trade-off between guns and butter. Suppose someone says, "It isn't a choice between getting fat on butter or skinny on guns. It's a matter of buying guns to save our butter."
   a. What is the good in question here?
   b. Why is it a publicly provided good and not a private good?
   c. Is there an implied benefit-cost ratio? What is the benefit? What is the cost?
6. Why is the marginal cost to the city of the marginal consumer using a city-provided public good zero?

7. Economists believe that high income people may be more willing to pay proportionately more for government services than low income people.
   a. What does this statement imply about income elasticity for government services?
   b. Can you explain the relative preferences of high versus low income groups for government services in terms of who pays and who receives the major benefits?
8. The city council proposes that a convention center be built downtown to accommodate business and other assorted conventions. A city spokesman said that "over a 20-year period, the revenues would cover 5 times the original cost of the site."
   a. Is this statement economically correct? That is, do you agree that the cost is only the original outlays for the site and the building?

   Also, it was suggested that a tax be levied on hotels and restaurants to pay off the bonds sold by the city to raise the funds for the project. However, the hotel managers and restaurant owners preferred that a sales tax be levied instead.

   b. Which type of tax do you think should be levied? Why?
9. The Port of Plenty, a public institution, is expected to approve $500,000 in its budget to provide baggage and ticket facilities on currently unused land it owns for use by the airlines that want to expand their services at Flyby Airport. A port administrator is quoted as saying, "There is enough unused space to accommodate expansion. But if too many airlines expand, gate sharing will become necessary."
   a. Should the original purchase price of the land by the port authorities enter into the port's cost calculations on whether to spend $500,000 for extra airline facilities?
   b. What is the cost to the Port of creating new facilities for the airlines? Should the $500,000 affect the rental fee that is to be charged the airlines? Explain.
   c. Does your answer to *a* change if the airlines choose to use only half the space made available to them by the port?
   d. What is the cost to the airlines of using the additional space exclusively for office and lounge facilities for its employees?
   e. Are land costs relevant if the Port had to expand facilities because gate-sharing led to congestion and confusion? Or is your answer the same as in *a*?
   f. Who gains and who loses from the Port expanding airline facilities?
10. Why is the government the major provider of intracity mass transit rather than private firms? Frame your answer in terms of average and marginal costs to the individual of taking a bus or buying and driving a car to work.
11. Suppose the Army Corps of Engineers intends to construct a waterway that it says will save shippers $500,000 a year in lower shipping costs since it would provide them with a straight shot by barge to the iron ore fields. Assume it takes one year to build at a cost of $4 million, and thereafter it will require $200,000 per year to maintain. The waterway is expected to be in use for at least 50 years. The federal rate of interest used by the Corps is 4 percent because the tax money it uses is treated as if it were funds borrowed in the federal market.
   a. What is the benefit-cost ratio?
   b. What is the present value of net benefits?
   c. Would you recommend construction of the waterway?
   d. Suppose the Corps used the market rate of interest instead of the federal rate, and it was 8 percent, would you recommend building the canal?
   e. Suppose the waterway cut through a national park destroying the natural habitat of much wildlife. How would you account for this in your calculations?
12. The Tennessee-Tombigbee (Tenn-Tom) 232-mile waterway running from Northeastern Mississippi to Demopolis, Alabama has been called nothing but a huge earth-moving project. There it connects to the Tombigbee River to Mobile and the Gulf of Mexico. It will cost at least $1.6 billion to finish by 1987. The Army Corps of Engineers avers that every dollar spent will earn $1.20. But an economist disagrees,

saying it is only 64 cents if the Corps used the market rate of 6 5/8 percent instead of the government rate of 3 1/4 percent.

a. What benefit-cost ratio did the Army Corps of Engineers calculate as compared to the economist's?

b. Despite much protesting from the railroads and the Environmental Defense Fund Inc. the project was continued. Who do you think wanted it continued? Why?

c. Which of the following should be included in the estimation of benefits in the benefit-cost calculation:

1. The 100,000 new jobs it is supposed to create by the year 2000.
2. The taxpayers, since the project was discounted at a rate lower than the market rate of interest, so taxes were lower in paying the interest on borrowed funds.
3. Wages and fringes received by skilled workers in constructing the canal.
4. The reduced shipping costs to the coal industry from having direct access to the Gulf of Mexico if they use ships, or if they do not use ships, by not using the more expensive railroads.
5. Additional profits earned by local businessmen due to the economic growth stimulated by the canal.
6. Current landowners who will end up owning waterfront property.

d. Which of the following should be included as costs in the benefit-cost calculation:

1. Economic rents earned by construction workers.
2. The loss in revenues to the now less competitive railroads.
3. Wildlife destroyed by upsetting their environment.
4. Former landowners who must move, since the canal will pass through where the houses formerly stood.
5. The higher property taxes businessmen will have to pay because of the increased value of their property as the area develops because of the canal construction.
6. The 400 formerly unemployable workers who would be put to work on the construction.
7. The value of the cotton crop the former farmland produced.
8. Future flood control prevention.

13. A mother asks her three children if they prefer to go to the zoo, on a picnic, or watch television. Two of them choose the zoo and one the picnic. The majority rules and they all go to the zoo.

a. Is this a Pareto optimal solution? Explain.

b. If the situation is not Pareto optimal, how can the children reach a Pareto optimal solution? Or can they not?

c. Suppose the children, Linda, Marge, and George, have the following preferences:

	TV	Picnic	Zoo
Linda	3	2	1
Marge	1	3	2
George	2	1	3

1. If Linda and Marge are paired, what would be their choice?
2. If George and Linda are paired what would be their choice?
3. Is a unanimous choice among the three therefore possible? Explain.
4. Suppose George and Marge were paired first. Would the outcome differ? Explain.

14. Indicate which of the following are examples of the benefits-received versus the ability-to-pay principle?
    a. Food stamps.
    b. Revenue bonds to be paid by bridge tolls.
    c. Tax on diesel fuel used by pleasure boats.
    d. Property tax.
15. Assume the state government has just built a bridge for $60 million, financed by revenues from taxes. If there is no congestion on the bridge after it is built, what price should be charged if the government intends to maximize consumer surplus? Why?
16. "If oil companies are given permission to construct the Northern Tier oil pipeline from Alaska to Minnesota, the act of building it will create jobs. These jobs are a pure social benefit." Do you agree? Discuss.

Chapter 19

Economic Theory of Democratic Government

A fanatical belief in democracy makes democratic institutions impossible.
– Bertrand Russell

PROGRESS REPORT

A. Chapter 18 contained a discussion of the difference between characteristics of a public versus a private good, as well as the difference between the public and private provision of a good whether that good is a public or private good in its characteristics.

B. This chapter develops a positivistic economic analysis of a democratic political system. It builds an analysis based on the concepts of property rights, information costs, and choices or tradeoffs founded in marginal analysis. The analysis of collective choice includes discussions on voting and political parties, ending with an examination of the behavior of bureaucracy.

C. Chapter 20 introduces the student to macroeconomic analysis beginning with national income accounting. Macroeconomics is the study of the aggregate economy, not of individual markets and industries, but of all markets and industries taken as a whole. The focus of macroeconomics is on employment, inflation, and economic stability.

ECONOMICS OF COLLECTIVE CHOICE

Collective choice and government representation in a democratic society lead to the study of political parties, elections, information, voting, special interest lobbying, and bureaucracies.

Government decisions do not make everyone better off, but they must make enough citizens believe they are better off if they are to gain approval. Therefore, to understand the nature of democratic government we shall analyze the actions of political parties and the voter from a perspective that is different from that used in the past by political scientists and sociologists. We shall develop an economic approach based on the kinds of fundamental assumptions introduced in Chapter 1. That is, we want to develop a model employing economic tools and use it to predict the likely consequences of majority voting in a democratic political system.[1]

The Model

Economic tools, to some extent, can be used to analyze the political decisions of *producers, consumers, voters, politicians, and bureaucrats* in a democracy.

Our model of a democratic political system contains five major decision-making groups—**producers, consumers, voters, politicians, and bureaucrats** They are, of course, overlapping. However, our interest in this chapter is concentrated on the government sector and voters engaging in a political process of collective choice. Therefore there is little mention of the producer and consumer in the private sector. We only refer to the private sector to make comparisons to it in order to explain decision making in the government.

Behavioral Assumptions

Economic theory assumes that an individual or group will promote its self-interest, maximize its utility, and act rationally. To be *rational* is to seek a goal in the easiest or most efficient way.

Self-interest is assumed in the behavior of all agents. When describing the private sector, economic theory operates on the maximization hypothesis. Choices are made by producers who, preferring more to less, want to maximize profits. The **rational** producer is one who will endeavor to reach this goal with the minimum of effort and in the most efficient way. The producer will therefore direct resources into those activities that yield the highest returns and move them out of activities yielding the lowest return. In order to satisfy efficiency requirements, the producer will pursue a course of action so long as the additional revenues are greater than the additional costs. In a similar manner the consumer prefers more to less, and will maximize satisfaction within a budget constraint.

The Political Process

The voter is acting under self-interest and is assumed to be rational in that he or she will pursue the easiest way to select the representatives and political party and the anticipated programs they offer that will maximize his or her utility.

[1]The economic theory of how various political forces interact is relatively recent and nothing said here should be taken as fixed in the security of certainty. Much of this chapter is based on a pioneering book by Anthony Downs, *An Economic Theory of Democracy* (New York: Harper & Row, 1957). Copyright © 1957 by Harper & Row, Publishers, Inc.

Thus, if one is an irrational voter, it simply implies he or she is inefficient in obtaining the political goals being sought. That is to say, the additional gains derived from a decision are less than the additional costs. Hence, if the voter or politician discovers his method is mistaken, while he believes his goals are not, he will not repeat the mistake once he realizes it; he will also not repeat the mistake if the mistake is costlier to him than any benefits forthcoming even if the goal is finally achieved. So long as the chain of anticipated benefits is perceived to be greater than the chain of future expected costs, he will pursue the given course of action consistent with the maximizing principle.

Political parties are assumed to be trying to receive enough votes to win the election subject to financial constraints. They will try to offer a slate of candidates who offer a package they believe will yield net benefits to a majority of the voters, and a package the voters believe will yield them net benefits. We use the word *package* because it is rare for voters to have all their preferences satisfied, or for voters to have a chance to express their preference on only a single issue. Thus, parties try to maximize political power by offering the package that will gain them the necessary amount of votes.

Bureaucrats are assumed to be acting in their self-interest by maximizing security, by increasing the certainty of keeping their jobs, and by establishing seniority through climbing the civil service ladder in order to administer larger programs and earn larger salaries.

In all situations all economic agents, producer, consumer, politician, and bureaucrat, are operating in an environment of uncertainty and incomplete information. The choices they make are constrained by the limitation in the information they have. Such choices are therefore subject to the influence of, and dependent upon, those people and institutions who provide them with information about economic policies and about political strategy.

The Political Party and Politicians

Political parties **try to create the best vote-gathering image by supplying a political package the consumers want or are led to believe is in their individual interest and in the public interest.**

Just as a business in the private market supplies a product to the market, so too does the political party supply a product engineered by its politicians and party image makers. In a two-party democratic system the party wants to win election after election. Similar to the firm as a team with its managers directing inputs of labor and capital, the party is a team organized to delegate different functions to its various members. The aim of the party is to attract a majority of the voters.

Rational ignorance **occurs when voters choose to be ignorant about issues and politicians because the cost in terms of marginal effort of obtaining more information exceeds the marginal gain to them. Ignorance is viewed as being more efficient.**

Individual politicians and party members are maximizers too, driven by personal ambition. Thus do the social political functions mesh with personal goals. In order to be successful the politician must make the voter believe he is acting in the voter's interest and, by corollary, in the public interest. Unfortunately, there is no guarantee that what the politician or the public believes is in the public interest is really in the public interest. Thus the total costs of running a government program may turn out to be greater than total benefits to society. A decline in total benefits may result because the voter may be **rationally ignorant**. The voter may choose to not be better informed because the additional cost is greater than the additional benefit he or she may realize, particularly if the voter believes that the more informed vote will have no effect on the outcome of an election. As a result voters may be efficient at obtaining the wrong policies with the wrong representatives.

Uncertainty, Information, and the Voter

In an ideal world where the voter experiences zero costs of obtaining information, the voter can easily acquire information to compare the additional benefits to the additional cost to him of programs advertised by the competing political parties. He would be perfectly efficient. The voter then operates with certainty in making decisions, since information on which to base the decision is complete. All options are known, and who bears the tax burden with each option is also known. However, the reality is that the voter lives in a world of uncertainty. Once the illusory veil of certainty is dropped, less is revealed rather than more. Uncertainty is the lack of knowledge about all the options and of future events, as well as the lack of knowledge concerning the implications of currently known events. The voter, in order to make an intelligent decision about a candidate, must have information about the candidate and about the implications for the voter as well as the implications for the programs the candidate supports. The cost to the individual voter of being informed may exceed any benefits to him or her. Thus, for many voters it is logical to be to some extent rationally ignorant. Being ignorant however, they may make the wrong choice—make a rational mistake.

Certainly voters are aware that at times the country does not seem to be working very well. But they are not sure why. And the cost is too high for them to try to find out. Is it the government, the oil companies, or OPEC that is causing inflation, oil shortages, and unemployment? The cost to the voter of finding out how the inner decisions of the government energy bureaucracy are made, and how oil company policies are determined, is formidable. The explanations offered by competing politicians are often unclear, even contradictory as they subtly shift position on issues and clarify their previous comments in response to feedback from the public, political colleagues, and enemies. Thus, the voters are unsure why things are a mess. In light of these information difficulties, it is hard for the voter to estimate the stream of future benefits and costs to him of choices from among alternative issues. If they vote for the politician and party who intends to, say, support legislation providing for national health insurance, decontrol of oil prices, windfall profits tax on oil companies, or nationalization of the oil companies, will the voters be better or worse off? Will the country? Nor do voters have reliable information on the party machinery, or the tactics being discussed in party caucus meetings by the professionals in the backrooms. Voters are therefore uncertain of what the options are or could have been.

Voters have different backgrounds stretching over the full range of educational, regional, and work experience. For some their focus is wide and their interests many; for others their focus is narrow and interests very few. Still others have more leisure with which to seek out more information on the issues and on party officials.

Even those institutions whose business it is to provide information, the watchdogs of society (newspapers, television, the popular magazines) usually pitch the content at a low level to maximize their audiences. Hence most offer human interest stories and shallow analyses of events. All too often sensationalism takes priority over accuracy and integrity of reporting. Thus, even in such a communication-obsessed society as the U.S., thorough acquisition of the facts by the voter requires a costly effort, in terms of diligence and concentration in seeking and sorting out information from books, from quality periodicals, and from televised discussion and analyses of current events. Most voters do not make this effort.

There is lack of information and uncertainty from the party's viewpoint, too. What are the voters thinking? What information should be imparted to the voter and what should be withheld? Given a package of issues being discussed nationally, how much will be gained and how much lost by emphasizing some of the issues and downplaying others? What is the net gain in capturing votes supporting one policy but the loss to individual politicians in personal financing by supporting it? The net increase or decrease in votes through affecting consumer utility (benefits) must be balanced against the net decrease or increase in campaign finances, and the likelihood of staying in office once there. How does the politician package his image of fairness, competence, and honesty while at the same time designing his policies so that it is clear to those who will benefit that they will indeed benefit, while keeping the issues unclear or ambiguous to those who will incur the costs—usually in the form of deliberately hidden taxes? For example, taxes imposed on business often end up being paid by consumers.

Uncertainty and the Party

Parties employ selective propaganda to reduce a voter's information costs; special-interest lobbies reduce the information costs to political parties.

The uncertainty of the voter and politician is passed on to create uncertainty for the party. Some voters from habit and tradition always vote unconsciously for the same party. But the independents must be persuaded by party propaganda to believe that their future stream of benefits will be maximized by voting for "this" party. The party is trying to maximize votes and to remove uncertainty in the voter's mind. Therefore it will provide only the "right" information because it knows how voters are, not what idealists would like them to be. The party will resort to catchy slogans in which complex issues are grossly simplified. Though outright falsehoods might be avoided, only the partial truth is imparted. For instance, one presidential candidate claims that employment is rising, while the opposing party candidate claims unemployment is rising. Who's right? They both are. As new workers enter the labor force, total employment rises. But if all of them do not get jobs, unemployment goes up too. If the doughnut represents employment, and the hole represents unemployment, then as the population grows both the doughnut and the hole grow. Most voters lack enough information to evaluate many statements made by politicians and industry spokesmen. Even those voters who possess a great deal of information often have no outlets to communicate it to many other voters.

The party will maximize votes subject to a budget constraint by making additional expenditures so long as the net votes gained are worth it. If an extra $5 million from the campaign fund will swing the state of California and win the national election, then the expenditure is made. However if the extra $5 million were to be spent to swing the state of Rhode Island, with no effect on the national outcome, then it would be irrational and nonmaximizing to spend it there.

The party does not attempt to maximize the utility or well-being of the country as a whole. It only needs to persuade a majority of the electorate to vote for it. It must persuade a majority that it is to its benefit to vote for the party by pleasing its members with the package, without having to satisfy them on each separate issue. Because voters are uncertain, to get out the message the party presents voters with leaders with presence and image, considered as honest and liked, to solve the problems and influence the uncertain voters. Because the leaders are supposed to be more certain about what the country needs and how to get the job done than is the average voter, leaders can direct the voter to choose "what is best for the country." Thus the uncertainty about attitudes among independent voters forces the party to rely on local party leaders to persuade and to gather the necessary information at the local levels, which leads to decentralized power.

Special Interests and Lobbies

There are many small minorities who form organizations with a common purpose. The National Rifle Association, the Sierra Club, the American Farm Federation, the AFL-CIO, and many others are well known and have well-financed lobbies. By forming into teams they substantially reduce the costs associated with trying to influence the party or the government decision makers in their favor, as compared to the huge personal costs that would accrue to each individual acting alone to influence legislators.[2]

As we said, the common existence of voter rational ignorance means that voters often do not know, for example, which politician is on which Senate or House committee that would be the originating source of a law favoring the voters' interests. Nor do politicians always know what the voters' interest is. But a lobby can breach the information gap and reduce the transactions costs of informing both the politician and the voter. Lobbies can help focus citizen attention to pressure the appropriate committee. Consequently, large gains may accrue to supporters of a lobby while only reflecting a small addition to total cost. A few can substantially benefit, with total costs dispersed over the larger population so that each individual absorbs only a very small part of the cost, though the total cost may be substantial. Consider, for example, the Interstate Commerce Commission (ICC) before it significantly deregulated the trucking industry. Its entry and price regulations bestowed higher profits on trucking companies and, as a direct result of that, higher wages on teamster drivers and higher prices spread over all consumers of trucked items because of the higher transportation costs that industry protection from free entry and price competition had caused.

Because some voter groups carry more influence than others under the electoral system, a benefit-cost analysis reveals that one-man-one-vote is not the best strategy for a party.

Special interests which do not often support lobbies, such as the poor, have nevertheless gained favorable legislation transferring income to them because they represent a large voting bloc. However, "one man, one vote" is in name only. In reality parties do not normally follow it in making decisions.

Aside from lobbies and special-interest influences, the existence of the electoral college means that parties may pursue a different strategy than they would if the popular vote determined the outcome of national elections. Party strategists direct more money and time to voters in cities with their large blue-

[2]See E. Browning and J. Browning, *Public Finance and the Price System* (New York: The Macmillan Co., 1979), pp. 262, 267.

collar and ethnic blocs, since a victory in a large urban center can carry the whole state. Thus, some voters are considered as more important than others. Party emphasis on the cities can change, of course, if a coalition of middle class voters emerges in the future leaving the suburbs as the largest voting bloc.

Ideologies

The party's aim is to get a majority of the votes, not all of them. That would not be efficient. Because of both the party's and the voter's uncertainty and lack of information, the party will try to reduce its costs of getting its message to the people. The shortcut takes the form of the party identifying with an ideology which is perceived by the voters as differentiated in one or more ways from that of its competitor. The voter cannot expect the party to satisfy him on each decision. Nor, as we have said, does the voter frequently know enough about each issue to have an informed opinion on it. Yet if the voter can identify his major desires—usually economic—with the ideological image manufactured by the party's public image, the information costs to the voter of connecting his preferences with the party ideology are significantly reduced. "If Senator X said it, and he's a good Democrat, then it's okay by me. If the union newspaper says vote for it or against it, then its interest is in my interest too. It's their job to keep track of these things for the membership."

The opposition party also provides information to voters about the incumbent party that would otherwise be difficult and costly for the average voter to obtain. The opposition acts as a watchdog, ready to blow the whistle on any hanky-panky like kickbacks or conflicts of interest.

Is Voting Rational?

We suggested earlier that it makes sense for the rational voter to be rationally ignorant. It is more efficient for a voter to devote most of his time to decisions about his private life and to goods and services in the private sector, because he perceives a direct relation between the decision and net benefits. Time devoted to making informed choices in the public sector has much less, if any, influence on the final outcome. Even if he becomes well informed on an issue and votes for the outcome that is best for him and the country, it has little or no effect on the outcome, and he sees his efforts conferring no immediate benefit to the country and to other voters who opt to remain uninformed. The effect of one voter's vote is essentially nil; hence benefits are lower than costs and it is not rational to vote. If the voter is at the point of indifference between the benefit and the cost, he abstains. Many citizens still vote, however, because they believe it is necessary if democracy is to survive. Thus, in the long run, voting is seen as rational (efficient) by many citizens.

For the individual, voting is usually seen as efficient even though his marginal gain is less than the transactions costs of acquiring information and voting.

There is also a *free rider* effect. That is, where public goods are concerned (goods that can be simultaneously consumed by many people without diminishing their use by the other users, for example, national defense) you can benefit by letting others provide them. By letting others absorb the transactions costs of voting, you obtain the benefits of the democratic system. Of course, a better informed public would be more aware of the long-term outcome of its decisions. However, the public usually does not connect the short-term benefits to it of winning on a specific issue with the long-term costs to it that winning may impose. For example, the short-term effects of rent control seem like a good thing. Thus short-sightedness prevents the public from seeing the long-term bad effects. And the longer the effect is delayed, the less likely is the public to make the connection between their choice and the ultimate effect.

Logrolling

***Logrolling* is trading votes to get a bill passed that could otherwise not receive a majority vote.**

Logrolling occurs when voters are forced to consider several bills at the same time. For instance, when a major bill on military expenditures has a rider attached to it that includes passage of the President's latest Strategic Arms Limitation Talks (SALT) peace agreements with the Russians, this is called logrolling. It results when politicians are resigned to trading votes in order to get a majority on another bill they want. Less than a majority of the Senate may want the military budget provided for in the bill and sponsors can only get a majority by agreeing to the SALT rider attached to it. By the same token, the senators who want the SALT bill can only get a majority by also agreeing to the part of the bill on the size of the military budget. It is therefore possible that a bill will be passed that the majority of the voters do not want—neither the increased military expenditures nor the President's SALT agreement with the Russians.

There is disagreement as to whether logrolling results in too much or too little government expenditure and expansion. In the sense that bills get passed that otherwise would not without vote trading, there could be overexpenditure. But if logrolling prevents passage of bills, it reduces government expenditures. Logrolling provides one explanation why minority voters can negotiate legislation favorable to them by agreeing to support other bills favored by a majority or by a coalition of other minorities. When one minority bill that is logrolled also ignores the interest of other minority groups and organizations, the successful minority's preference is satisfied out of proportion to its representation in society. As a result, some observers believe logrolling leads to inefficiency in government spending allocations, because small groups can receive large benefits while large costs are hidden since they are spread out over the rest of the population with each individual absorbing only a small part of the total cost.

But when such spending programs are multiplied, there is overproduction of publicly provided goods and services. The total cost is greater and the individual burden of the taxes to support the expenditures is neither hidden nor small. However, others claim that this effect is outweighed because of rational ignorance. The typical voter does not realize all the benefits he is getting and is much more sensitive to the cost. Hence, there is on net an underproduction of government-provided goods, and because of advertising an overproduction of unnecessary private goods. As yet, tools of analysis are not adequate to test these hypotheses. But our experience is that government has continued to grow.

Government Size

In 1929 federal government expenditures accounted for about 8 percent of gross national product. Today it is over 21 percent. The growth in expenditures by state and local government has proceeded faster than the growth in federal expenditures in recent years. But one must remember that states and cities are encouraged to spend more by the federal government with the frequent promises of matching funds to states and cities for various projects initiated by local governments. Also, federal monies come to local governments by way of intragovernmental transfers from the federal government for roads, hospitals, social services, schooling and a host of pork barrels.

So long as the majority of voters believes that government programs will increase its net utility, government will continue to grow.

If the majority of the voting population has something to gain and little to lose through redistributing income by creating certain government programs, then government will grow and continue to grow. Given that there are more people who are relatively poor than are relatively rich, then in a universal system of voting the implication is that there will be a tendency to elect politicians who will act to tax higher income recipients and redistribute the taxes to the lower income groups. The government would grow as long as the majority gained from the growth.

Then what is there to stop government growth? Why did not the majority achieve better redistribution long ago, at a much faster pace? Might there occur undesirable effects on society from a massive redistribution in the longer run? If the higher income recipients by and large are also the more productive, excessive taxes might destroy their incentives to continue to produce at the same level or even higher. This makes leisure more attractive to them and also tends to make them consume more now instead of sacrificing some current consumption now (for example investing in their education) to be able to consume more later. If taxes become too high, the doctor might work fewer hours. Those thinking about going into medicine might conclude that it is not all that worth while to invest in medical education today and end up not being able to consume that much more tomorrow because of the high income taxes. So they spend the money today instead of using it for medical tuition. The result is a decline in future medical services to society. The cost is borne by everyone since total medical services produced and consumed will decline. But the below-average income voter operating under rational ignorance sees net benefits to him now and does not connect the possibility of the future absolute decline in benefits to him and others that could result much later.

When the slowdown in overall productivity finally begins to become serious and recognizable as information spreads, society may slow down the redistribution process by agreeing to lower taxes for both business and high income earners. As the economy picks up again, and the income inequality reemerges as an issue, those who are less successful in the private market will resort to political pressure to up their share. Because there are more voters below the average income figure they represent the largest voting bloc, a fact which the politician cannot ignore. As a result, government will expand as long as these policies do not destroy the expected net gains to the individual voter as he perceives them. Only at that point will expansion in government size stop. Until then, the government sector will continue to grow faster than the private sector, as it has done in the last 50 years.[3]

All this is not to say government growth is wrong or right. Positive economics merely tries to describe what is and predict what will happen, given certain initial conditions. If larger and larger government increases net total

[3]See Allen Metzler and Scott Richard, "Why Government Grows (and Grows) in a Democracy," *Public Interest*, Summer 1978.

utility, it is considered to be efficient. If it threatens seriously to decrease net total utility to society in the form of, say, less individual freedom, it will be seen as inefficient.

BUREAUCRACY

The government provides collective services. To do this it must also collect information and decide what services to provide and how much of them. It therefore depends on its bureaucracy to provide the government with costly information, since the government lacks full information and is therefore often uncertain about what services to provide to the citizenry. Bureaus operate with considerable independence in the decision-making process by the kind of information they pass up to the government leadership and the kind of services they provide. Thus, to a certain extent a bureau can increase its funding by always making sure its existence is necessary. A bureau is thought to be necessary if it makes some headway in solving a problem and establishing credibility.

A *bureaucracy* is a large public or private organization with layers of authority.

The word bureaucracy originated in the eighteenth-century French government. The desks of French government officials were covered with cloths *(bureaux)*, and *bureau* came to identify government by certain kinds of officials. Today *bureaucracy* refers to a large organization that tends to be identified in the public's mind with a large public or private organization of faceless officials.

Government *bureaus* are nonprofit operations whose services are not priced in markets.

Unlike private firms, government **bureaus** are nonprofit organizations and do not sell their product services directly to the public but to Congress, which budgets them on an annual basis. A bureau's output is not priced in markets external to the organization as, for example, is General Electric's output. Thus, government agencies will not provide Congress with information on waste and inefficiency which would be sooner apparent to the heads of a private organization whose profits are falling. Bureaus provide information that is favorable to their future funding and growth. In this way bureaucrats can convince Congress that they are raising the public's utility, hence increasing the chances of incumbent members of Congress being reelected. Information is costly for Congress to obtain for itself because there are hundreds of programs in existence. Therefore Congress depends on government agencies and their research departments. In turn, the citizens who vote congressmen into office depend on their having appropriate information, because the voter chooses to be rationally ignorant. If true, agency budgets tend to be too large. The Congressional Budget Office (CBO) was created in the 1970s by Congress to double-check for Congress the budget requests of bureaus.

Bureaus strive to maximize their budgets, and hence their security.

Bureaus, being motivated by security, will try to maximize their salaries, reputation, power, patronage, and output (services). They can maximize these goals by maximizing the size of the yearly budget allotment from Congress. Niskanen[4] argues that the budget they use to carry out their functions must be

[4]William Niskanen, Jr., *Bureaucracy and Representative Government* (Chicago: Aldine-Atherton, Inc., 1971).

at least as large as the minimum costs of supplying the services that their congressional sponsors expect them to provide. Bureaucracies are created because the services they provide are considered necessary. What is considered necessary comes about by the head bureaucrat convincing others that his or her organization is rendering useful services. To sustain itself the bureaucracy must be big enough to be effective to enough people and old enough to establish credibility with the group or groups it is servicing. The size and age requirements are called the bureau's "initial threshold of survival."[5]

An established bureau reaches this threshold usually with rapid growth after the high degree of its social need is demonstrated to Congress. The Department of Health, Education and Welfare (HEW) was an example of an agency with a steady clientele, rapid growth, and importance of function. A bureau can also decline in size if it loses its credibility or does its job too well. A bureau in trouble, in danger of losing its credibility, and concerned about negative outside evaluation of its performance, will suppress unfavorable information. Many school boards and principals do this. So did the Government Accounting Office (GAO). In fact, the first line of defense for a bureaucracy is to withhold information, and to only moderately extol its successes in order not to attract too much attention.

Bureaucracy is sometimes efficient; overall, however, bureaucracies are inefficient because they are more conscious of votes and budgets than costs.

However, even when bureaus appear that they are going to sink they can manage to take on new responsibilities. Because bureaus devote their energies to selected identifiable groups who benefit from their existence, the bureaus' clients can insure their survival by pressuring politicians to keep the bureaus afloat. Thus, bureaus tend to survive. There is one still in existence in Italy, set up after World War II, to provide services to World War II orphans.

By the Book

Why are bureaus inflexible? One reason is efficiency. When everybody knows how something is to be done, it is much less costly to just do it and not try to bend the procedure to fit the details of individual cases. Individual cases may be complex and costly to administer if new rules have to be created every time.

Moreover, since bureaus are nonprofit organizations they do not have to worry about a market price that is related to economic survival. They need not be as cost effective as they are vote effective for the politicians who sponsored them. Without a market price to guide the efficiency of the bureau's decisions, it is hard for them to price their activities when there is no market demand curve by which consumers can signal prices to express the dollar values they place on their preferences.

Therefore, the next best procedure is to construct formal rules to act as behavioral guidelines. These rules must apply to everyone both inside and outside the bureau. Going by the book and acting only on written approval enables bureaucrats to pass the buck if a decision could be a blunder. Formal rules also enable workers to know exactly what their chores are. In the absence of rules, different customers would be treated differently and the bureau could be charged with discrimination. No government unit wants to have such charges placed on it, since politicians taking credit for the programs the bureau administers could lose votes.

[5]Anthony Downs, *Inside Bureaucracy* (Boston: Little, Brown and Co., 1967).

Without written rules governing procedures, the bureau chiefs would be left to make their own judgments about the amount of spending and for what purposes, operating on the principle that more spending means better programs. Thus, formal rules are designed to prevent self-indulgence as well as prevent fighting with other heads over the funds.

Inertia

The common lament is that bureaucrats take too much time to get anything done. One reason might be that setting up a bureau and getting operations to go smoothly involves a substantial investment cost. A building must be built or rented, equipment ordered, personnel selected, and rules written. Once done,

HEW (Now HHS)

The Health, Education and Welfare Department (HEW) touched the lives and pockets of more Americans than any other federal agency. HEW was an example of a bureaucracy growing from within and also absorbing bureaus outside of it. HEW accounted for over 33 percent of federal outlays. Its budget was virtually shrinkproof. More than half its revenues came from Social Security payroll taxes.

HEW was created on April 11, 1953 as the tenth cabinet level department of the executive branch. As it existed up to 1980, its subdepartments were the offices of Consumer Affairs, of External Affairs, of Civil Rights, of Human Development, the Public Health Services, Social and Rehabilitation Services, the Education Division, and the Society Security Administration, which became part of HEW in 1963. Its budget was the largest of any agency including the military, and it employed over 156,000 workers. It manned about 306 advisory committees. Its agencies, bureaucrats, and lobbying groups competed for checks form the U.S. Treasury as they scrambled to fund entitlement programs with costs rising in proportion to new appeals from citizens for beneifits. A few of the programs among the 300 major ones it funded included preschool Head Start, medical assistance for the elderly and the down-and-out, counseling for troubled and pregnant teenagers, hospitals for merchant seamen, a printing house for the blind, and services for Eskimos.

It controlled or monitored to some degree things like physical education peformance standards in gym classes that could "arbitrarily" discriminate against females, funding of female athletic programs by schools and universities, inflammability of children's clothes, what people eat, drink, and smoke, statistical information on the sex distribution in classes in high schools and colleges, busing, whether junk food should be available in high schools. It even prohibited the formation of choral groups restricted to either girls or boys, and wanted selections to be made according to the octave range of the voice. Universities came under significant pressure from HEW to make them conform to its notions about hiring, and promotion, with threats of cutoff of federal funds if they did not meet HEW standards.

The largest expenditures of HEW were made for Social Security payments, then health, public assistance, education, and manpower programs in that order. About 95 percent of HEW's budget fell under "uncontrollable" outlays. These are funds that must be spent as mandated by law. The funding and spending can only be stopped by passing another law.

In 1980 much of the education division of HEW was transferred into a separate Department of Education, and HEW became the Department of Health and Human Services (HHS).

Bureaus do not like to change because of high fixed set-up costs and the ease of acquiring budget allocations for previously successful programs. However, bureaucracies do change and grow, due primarily to the growth of new agencies threatening their domain.

the outlay in dollars is large. These large setup costs are *fixed costs*. Moreover, a bureau once it gets going does not like to change the way things are done, particularly when it is hard to measure the net benefits without market prices to guide them. It will only make the change if it is clear that the additional benefits are greater than the additional costs. Thus, the larger the fixed costs the greater is the resistence to change. Furthermore, bureaucrats, being risk-averse, would risk the sacrifice of security only if the personal value of the change is much greater than the possible loss the change could cause. The more entrenched and the greater the power of the bureaucrat, the greater is the opportunity cost of a change, hence the greater the resistance to it and the greater the conformity of behavior. Another explanation is that for an established bureau to branch out requires that it recalculate its budget needs. The previous year's budget has already been worked out and shown to be satisfactory in meeting its expenditures. The future benefits to the bureau of maintaining the status quo are therefore known with greater certainty than are uncertain, untried programs or massive procedural reorganizations.

Yet change can occur. A new bureau may rise up, threatening the domain, power, and size of an incumbent bureau. Thus, the Department of Education was torn from the grasp of HEW. Such threats to the incumbent's security give it an impetus for change as it regroups for self-defense. It could discover new problems that need looking into, it can arouse its clients to make greater demands on it, hence a need for more funds to implement new programs. The Army Corps of Engineers can usually flush out a new water project by illustrating the benefits it promises to clients and politicians.

Our experience is that bureaucracy continues to grow. The monster often outdoes its creator, the servant threatens to dominate the master. Bureaus have more information, more experts, than do the politicians responsible for funding them. Bureaus are often required by law to spend budgeted money. They are often not allowed to not spend it.

The politician who created a bureau passes on, but the bureau continues and knows better than the political replacement what is going on. The bureau can justify funds for a program more persuasively than politicians can offer reasons for refusing them. And because of this rational ignorance of politicians, bureaus operate with surprising independence—they have become entities of power and decision making unto themselves.

Postscript

Lest the student lose perspective, he or she must realize that much of what has been said also applies to large, bureaucratic organizations in the private sector, and that the business sector is also a lobbyist in Congress seeking tariff protection, subsidies, fewer restrictions, and bailout loans from government agencies. Furthermore, the nature of an industrial society can create insecurities for individuals because of rapidly changing technology, the dangers of pollution, industrial accidents, natural disasters, unemployment, and family fragmentation. Ideally, government agencies are set up to provide services to alleviate the effects of these adversities. Many people today, though, perceive that it too often provides less than a dollar in services for a dollar paid in taxes.

CHAPTER SUMMARY

Economic tools, to some extent, can be used to analyze the democratic political process and make predictions about political decision making as it applies to voters, parties, party heads, and party ideologies.

The economic model includes five decision making groups: producers, consumers, voters, politicians, and bureaucrats, with emphasis on the last three here. Behavioral assumptions are self-interest, maximization of utility, and rationality. The last refers to the decision maker pursuing the most efficient course to achieve political ends. Namely, as long as the marginal gains are greater than the marginal costs of a given course of action, then continue with it.

Political parties try to receive enough votes to be elected and reelected, subject to their budget limits. To do this they must supply a political package the consumers want or are led to believe is in their individual interest and in the public interest. However, because information is imperfect and costly to acquire, voters may choose to be rationally ignorant. That is, the marginal effort of obtaining more information about issues and politicians is greater than the marginal gains, so the voter chooses to be ignorant since it is more efficient. It reduces transactions costs. However, as a result voters may make wrong choices for the public interest. Ignorance creates voter uncertainty, which creates uncertainty for the party. To convince a voter to support its candidates, a party must convince the voter through party propaganda that his or her future stream of economic benefits will be maximized by supporting the party. The party, therefore, is selective about the information it promulgates. The party leaders must create the best vote-gathering image to keep the party's traditional voters attracted by its traditional ideology, and must be knowledgeable about how to attract sufficient numbers of the independent vote. Many special-interest groups form lobbies. This greatly reduces the transactions costs of influencing Congress. And because of rational ignorance, lobbies can reduce the information costs to politicians about what constituents think. Large voting blocs, because of their numbers, can also influence Congress even without special-interest lobbies.

Parties have not operated under the one-man-one-vote principle because it is not maximizing strategy. Some voter groups carry more influence than others under the electoral system.

Since one person's vote rarely affects an election outcome, and the transactions costs of acquiring information and of voting is higher than the marginal gain from the economic efficiency perspective, it may be irrational (inefficient) to vote, whether one is well-informed or not. The free-rider effect is a factor. In the case of public goods, a nonvoter can benefit from others doing the voting.

Logrolling is the trading of votes—compromises—that allows a minority-supported rider bill in Congress to be passed because the minority promises to help achieve a majority vote on another bill to which the minority bill is tacked. It is not clear whether logrolling results in too much or too little government expenditures.

It is proposed that the government has continued to grow because there are relatively more poor voters than rich voters. Poor voters tend to support government income redistribution programs and politicians who sponsor them. Moreover, voters are shortsighted. They more easily perceive the short-term gains and lose sight of long-term costs. Growth of government will stop or slow down when people become aware that long-term costs are greater than the benefits. However, so long as the majority of voters believe government programs will increase their net total utility, government will continue to grow.

Bureaucracy is a large organization with layers of authority that exist in both the private and public sectors. Government bureaus are nonprofit operations whose services are not priced in markets outside the bureau. Government bureaus act to maximize their security by portraying themselves as providing necessary services and by creating dependency among politicians on the information and voter patronage that bureaus offer to them. A measure of their survival ability is the size of their yearly budget allotments from Congress. They must maintain credibility, hence they defend themselves by not attracting too much attention and by not being overly generous with information. Bureaus are inflexible because it is more efficient to apply the same rules for everyone than to accommodate each unique situation; nor do they wish to be accused of discrimination. They tend, however, not to be efficient because they are more vote and budget conscious than cost conscious. Because of the high fixed costs of setting up operations and establishing formal rules, bureaucracies do not change easily. For budget reasons they do not like to break up a winning combination once they find it. Yet bureaus can and do change, primarily from growth of new agencies threatening their domain. Thus bureaucracy grows, and because of politicians' rational ignorance, they operate independently of the control of individual congressional members.

QUESTIONS

1. What is meant by rationality in this chapter?
2. What is rational ignorance? Under what special circumstances would rational ignorance not exist?
3. Can we conclude from the discussion in the text that the average citizen is lazy, and that is why election turnouts are not larger than they are?
4. Can you give a positivistic economic answer why governments continue to grow in a democratic system?
5. In the 1970s there was a tremendous influx of new and independent members of Congress with much less commitment to party loyalty and discipline who did not believe in the old rule, "to get along, go along." Is this fragmentation something that would work for or against the advantage of narrow interest groups in society? Why? Does your answer contradict the notion discussed in the chapter that a decentralized decision process is the best way for the party to acquire a voting majority?
6. Aside from lobbying, what are other nonvoting methods of political participation?
7. Why might politicians prefer to supply selective information on issues instead of full information?
8. What is it about the structure of Congress that makes elected officials likely to lean toward serving vested interests than the general interest?
9. According to the text, what is the economic argument offered for not voting?
10. In a democratic political system, what creates the demand for and the supply of ideologies expressed by competing parties?
11. If each citizen has perfect knowledge, could any one citizen influence another's vote?
12. Why is lobbying a rational act?
13. Why might the first line of defense for a government bureaucracy be to withhold information yet spend large funds on public relations advertising?
14. The Occupational Safety and Health Administration (OSHA) spends large sums of money on publicity urging workers to file complaints against their employers about hazards on the job. Is this effort solely due to OSHA's concern about workers? What else might be involved?

15. How might fixed costs be a reason for the slowness of bureaucracies to change?
16. Though there is increasing dissatisfaction with public schools, why is it that so few parents are involved in changing the public school system?

MACRO-ECONOMICS

Chapter 20

Measuring the Nation's Economy: Income and Prices

"It is fortune, not wisdom, that rules man's life."

– Cicero

PROGRESS REPORT

A. This chapter begins the study of macroeconomics. It is useful to know the official definitions that government accountants use to measure the aggregate activity of the economy, and to gain some understanding of the major sectors of the economy that will appear throughout the later developments in the book on macroeconomic theory and policy.

B. Chapter 21 focuses on the analysis of one of the sectors mentioned in this chapter, namely the government sector and its expenditure and taxing functions.

It is rare these days to watch the network news on television without seeing some newscaster speaking of the health of the economy by using terms such as gross national product, the consumer price index, the producer price index, and so forth. We now investigate the meaning of several of these mysterious measures compiled by government agencies, and attempt to make clear why such indices are useful.

NATIONAL INCOME ACCOUNTING

The national income accounts record the nation's economic activity over time.

The national income accounts published by an arm of the Department of Commerce, the Bureau of Economic Analysis (BEA), are records of the economic activity of the economy. The accounts are used to reach a better understanding of the pattern of economic activity, and also to provide economists and other researchers with the empirical base upon which abstract but revealing and useful models of the economic system can be built. These accounts are used by those in government to formulate appropriate short-run stabilization policy, by business to anticipate market trends and subsequent investment expenditures, and by those who prepare forecasts of the economy such as large banks interested in predicting where future credit demand will be the greatest. Compiling the accounts is an extremely complex and detailed task, becoming more sophisticated with each new publication of the *Survey of Current Business*.

The primary purpose of the national accounts is to measure the value of the nation's output of goods and services over the year. There are three approaches to measuring the nation's yearly output called the *gross national product* or GNP for short.

Product-Expenditure Flow

Figure 20-1 is a simplified description of the economy consisting of households and business, with the government and foreign sectors left out. The upper half of the figure indicates the flow of goods and services produced by business and is shown flowing in the counterclockwise direction, while money expenditures made by households to business are shown flowing in the clockwise direction. A dollar spent by a household for a *final* product is a dollar in sales received by the retail firm. When the retail price of each final product is multiplied by the quantity sold of each product produced during the year, the yearly receipts of the firm are determined for each product.

The gross national product (GNP) is the measure of the market value of all final goods and services produced in an accounting period of one year.

However, some goods produced by firms in the period may not get sold in the period, resulting in an increase in unsold goods known as business inventories. For accounting purposes these additions to inventory are treated as if firms buy their own unsold goods. Then, the total expenditures for final products (products sold to final users) must by definition be equal to total revenues. Thus *GNP is the measure of the market value of all final goods and services produced in an accounting period of one year.*

Figure 20-1

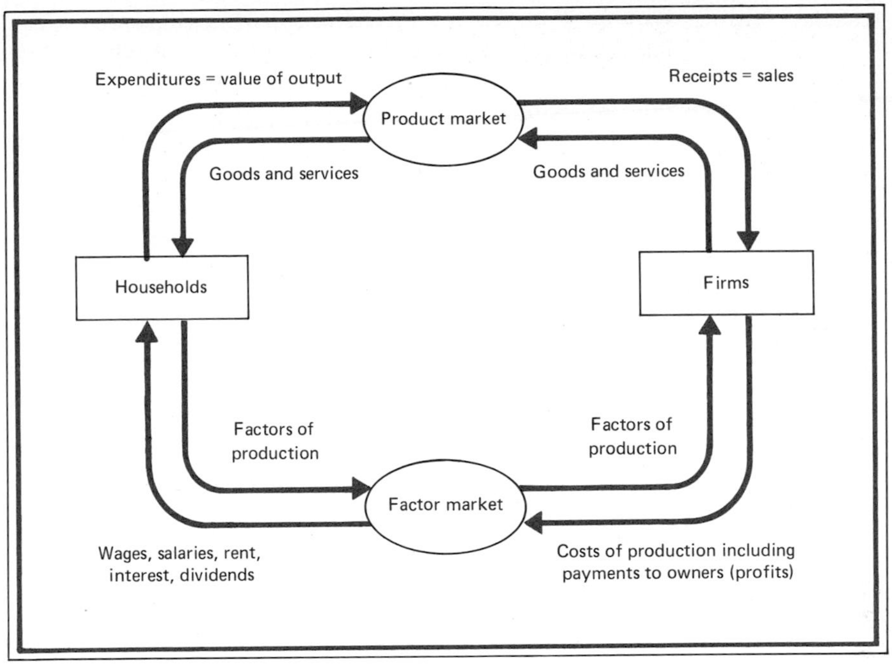

Take the simple example of an economy that only produces two goods: 5 lemons and 4 limes with lemons 15 cents apiece and limes 20 cents apiece. Let p = price and q = quantity, then

Lemons: $p_1 \times q_1 = 15 \times 5 = 75$ cents

Limes: $p_2 \times q_2 = 20 \times 4 = 80$ cents

then

GNP = dollar value of lemons + dollar value of limes

or

$$\text{GNP} = p_1 \times q_1 + p_2 \times q_2$$

hence

GNP = 75 cents + 80 cents = \$1.55.

Factor Cost-Income Flow

The *factor cost-income flow* approach to calculating GNP is based on the fact that costs to one must be incomes to another.

The lower half of the circular flow depicting the factor market also provides a measure of the GNP. All payments made by firms for inputs—factors of production—are costs of production to the firm. At the same time these costs represent income to factors for productive work. Earned income and costs are reflections of one another—two images of the same calculation. What firms pay out to hire inputs (land, labor, and capital) must equal what those factor inputs receive as earned income. Therefore, all costs of production represent income to someone. In our example, assume that out of the 15-cent retail price of the lemons 1 cent goes to the landowner, 2 cents to the farmer, 3 cents to the wholesaler, 5 cents to the trucking firm (of which 2 cents goes toward paying for the truck and 1 cent to payment of interest on a loan), and 4 cents to the retailer in these processes that lead from the farm to the grocery store shelf. Profit is a term that is used in many different ways. Here it is being used simply to mean a payment to owners. Thus, profit is a payment to those who provide capital and other entrepreneurial services and, as such, is a cost that must be included in order to establish the accounting identity of total cost being equal to total earned income. Hence, from the product market at the top of the figure we see that, leaving out the government and foreign sectors,

Gross national product = gross national expenditures

and from the factor market at the bottom we see that

National factor cost = gross national income.

To illustrate the equivalence more fully, let us look at another example. Suppose a bottle of beer costs 70 cents at a grocery store, as indicated in Table 20-1. We start from the bottom at the farm level and trace the figures up through the retail level.

The farmer receives 6 cents in revenue from selling the barley and hops that is included in the bottle of beer ultimately sold by the grocer. On the production side the 6 cents is accounted for by costs for inputs or payments to factors of production. The fertilizer, rental payments for the land, wages (including the farmer's), and interest total to 5 cents. To bring total cost into equality with total revenues, the 1 cent profit is included as part of total cost. With what has been said in Chapter 1, the return to owners of capital is an opportunity cost. In this case it is the farmer who receives a return beyond the opportunity cost of his own wages, and earns a return on his investment which under assumed competitive conditions equals the return he could earn investing in a nonfarming endeavor. A less complicated way of looking at it is that, from a strict accounting approach, in order to insure that total revenue equals total cost, profit is the residual that forces this equality.

Income of 6 cents to the farmer is correspondingly an input cost to the brewer and bottler. The miller's function of crushing the barley has been combined with the brewer's function here to shorten the example. The brewer malts the barley by crushing and grinding it, and then softens it by soaking it in water until it sprouts and then is kiln-dried. It is fermented and brewed into beer which is flavored with hops. The brewer has to pay factors of production such as wages, equipment, hops, fuel, rent, and interest that are all involved in converting the barley into beer. Again the profit of 4 cents is the difference between total revenue of 35 cents and total cost of 31 cents. Or, if you prefer, it is the opportunity cost equal to the rate of return to those who invested their capital in the brewing business. That is, it is what owners could have earned if they had invested in some other industry.

The brewer sells the bottled beer to the wholesaler for 35 cents. The wholesaler must stock the beer and arrange for delivery to retailers. The wholesaler must pay for its hired factors of production, labor, capital, and borrowed funds and pay 2 cents to stockholders. He sells and delivers the bottle of beer to the retailer who must stock it, display it, pay clerks for negotiating its sale, hire

TABLE 20-1
From Farmer to Consumer

Income from sales (cents)		Costs (cents)	
Grocery			
	70	Bottled beer	50
		Wages	14
		Rent	2
		Interest	1
		Profit	3
Total revenues	70	Total costs	70
Wholesaler			
	50	Bottled beer	35
		Wages	10
		Rent	2
		Interest	1
		Profit	2
Total revenue	50	Total costs	50
Brewer			
	35	Barley & hops	6
		Bottle	2
		Wages	20
		Rent	2
		Interest	1
		Profit	4
Total revenue	35	Total costs	35
Farmer			
	6	Fertilizer	0.5
		Land rent	0.5
		Wages	3
		Interest	1
		Profit	1
Total revenue	6	Total costs	6

TABLE 20-2
Final Product Price and Value Added in Cents

Stage of production	Sale price (cents)	− Price of intermediate product (cents)	= Value added to intermediate product (cents)
Farmer	6	0	6
Brewer	35	6	29
Wholesaler	50	35	15
Retailer	(70)	50	20
	161	91	(70)

a manager to oversee the clerks, pay an accountant, bookkeepers, and property taxes. After that the retailer includes his profit of 3 cents making a total of 70 cents. Only the 70 cents is counted as part of GNP. It is the revenue received on the sale of the final product at the final stage of production.

Value Added Approach

The *value added approach* to the GNP is based on the concept that the total retail value of a final product is equal to the sum of the values added to it at each stage of production.

Table 20-2 suggests a third way of calculating the GNP. Instead of adding the expenditures for the final products produced in the current year, simply add together all of the values that are *added* to the bottle of beer at each stage of production. At each intermediate step the product is an intermediate product—unfinished in some aspect. Only when it is finally sold to the consumer is it no longer an intermediate product.

Table 20-2 is condensed from Table 20-1. The sequence begins at the farm level where the matured barley is sent to the brewery company to be processed into beer for transport to the wholesaler. One must be careful, however, not to count the barley in the bottled beer more than once. It is counted the first time at the farm level. Its crude value should not be included again when it goes through the brewing process. Only what the brewer *added,* that is, the brewing and bottling should be tacked onto the crude value of the barley because the farmer's sale price already has been counted in the first stage. The value of the crude barley is 6 cents. That is what the brewer pays for it. The brewer charges 35 cents for the bottled beer; he has added 29 cents in value to the product. The balance of 29 cents in costs also represents income to the factors of production involved in enhancing the product as it passes through the second stage of production. These are payments made in wages, rent, and interest, and just enough profits to keep the business going. The brewer then ships these out to convenient wholesale centers throughout the country where, of course, part of the brewer's costs are transportation costs and take the form of payments to truckers and the railroads. The wholesaler in turn must pay out to factors wages, rent, and other costs, and he adds a value of 15 cents to the 35 cents it costs him for the beer. So for 50 cents he sells it to the retailer who, after making all his payments to various factors of production, including advertising costs, breakage, and so forth, sells it from his shelf at a price of 70 cents. He has added value of 20 cents to the product. Since we assume the farmer initiates the process his selling price of 6 cents is the total value he adds to the product. He pays for no intermediate products. (Strictly speaking this is not true but we must start somewhere so we simply ignore such things as the farmer's costs for seeds in our simplified example, but these costs are estimated for inclusion in the official data.) The final product price is 70 cents and the sum of the value added is also 70 cents. Both equal the GNP figure. Notice that if you had added the final sales price at each stage you would have gotten a figure of $1.61, which involves counting the crude barley 4 times and the bottled beer 3 times and therefore grossly overstates the value of GNP. The value of the society's output during the period—the value of what was produced—is $.70 and not $1.61. When the government sector is included, wages and salaries of government workers are counted as value added contributed by government.

Injections and Leakages

In the simple circular flow of Figure 20-1, a *leakage* is said to occur when spending leaves the circular flow. Thus, household saving is a leakage. However, savings by households pass through the banks and other financial institutions to be borrowed by firms to make *investment* expenditures. When firms invest, the *savings* reappear as *injections* into the circular flow. Businesses save too and also account for some of the savings leakage.

Adding the Government and Foreign Sectors

When the government and foreign sectors are included in the GNP accounts, money injections into the circular flow and leakages from it arise. Government expenditures on goods and services are *injections* into the circular money flow. In addition, unearned income—transfer payments—paid to households on welfare are *injections*. The government also makes unearned transfer payments to businesses, called subsidies. Among those receiving subsidies are the farming and maritime industries.

To finance its expenditures the government collects taxes from households and businesses. These taxes represent money leakages from the circular flow.

Revenues earned from selling *exported* goods are *injections* as spending enters the circular flow, whereas outlays for *imported* goods are leakages since money spending exits the circular flow. In summary,

Injections	Leakages
Household consumption	Household savings
Business investment	Business savings
Government expenditures	Taxes
Exports	Imports

Table 20-3 illustrates the equality between the product-expenditure calculation of GNP to the factor-cost–income approach of gross national income (GNY), with the government and foreign sectors now included. We shall now describe additional details of GNP accounting, with the government and foreign sectors included.

Product-Expenditure Approach

The product-expenditure side of the accounts equals personal consumption plus government purchases plus gross private investment plus net exports.

The GNP is the total of all expenditures on final goods, or alternatively the market value of all final goods and services produced per period. There are four major components.

Consumption Purchases Household consumption is the largest expenditure element of GNP and is roughly two thirds of GNP. Consumption is divided into three parts, as shown in the left side of Table 20-3. *Consumer* **durables** are defined as commodities lasting a year or more and includes items such as furniture, cars, books, television sets, records, maps, and some toys. *Consumer* **nondurables** are commodities defined as lasting less than a year. They include food, tobacco, clothing, shoes (indeed!), drugs, seeds, and a host of other everyday things. **Services** include expenditures on laundering, transportation, radio and television repairs, haircuts, recreation, and so on.

Consumer commodities are broken down among *durables* (lasting a year or more), *nondurables*, and *services*.

Government Purchases This entry accounts for the second largest expenditure component in GNP. The government spends to provide goods and services. A partial list includes national defense, highways, synthetic fuels, education, health, dams, and bridges. It does not include transfer payments. Total government expenditures account for about one fifth of total GNP. Approxi-

TABLE 20-3
Gross National Product and Gross National Income, 1980 in Current Dollars (Billions)

GNP = C + I + G + (X − M) Product = expenditure approach			GNY = NY + IT + BT + Dep. Factor cost = income approach	
C	Personal consumption	1,671.1	Employee compensation	1,596.7
	Durable goods	211.6	Proprietors' income	133.6
	Nondurable goods	674.3	Rental income	31.9
	Services	785.2	Corporate profits before taxes	182.1
G	Government purchases	534.8	Interest income	180.1
	Federal	199.2	National income	2,124.4
	State and local	335.6	Indirect business taxes	212.2
I	Gross private domestic investment	396.8	Business transfers	10.5
	Fixed investment	399.8	Other transfers	6.2
	Changes in business inventories	−3.0	Depreciation	275.5
(X − M)	Net exports	26.1	Gross national income	2,628.8
GNP	Gross national product	2,628.8		

Preliminary data; may not add due to rounding.
Source: U.S. Dept. of Commerce, *Survey of Current Business*, Jan. 1981, pp. 13, 14.

mately two thirds of these government expenditures have been state and local in the last decade.

Investment purchases **consist of residential construction, nonresidential construction, and changes in business inventories.**

Investment Purchases Investment in capital goods is the third largest component of GNP and accounts for approximately 16 percent of GNP. Fixed investment consists of *residential construction,* namely houses and apartments, and other residential dwellings; and *nonresidential construction,* primarily businesses such as warehouses, stores, factories, farm buildings, machinery, petroleum and gas drilling equipment, and tools among other things. *Changes in business inventories* are included. The word *change* is emphasized. Final products that have not been sold do not appear under consumption. At the end of the period, additions to inventory are counted as investment. If more goods were sold than produced in the accounting period, then those goods that were sold but not produced must have come from inventories carried over from the previous period, in which case the change in inventories is negative. Fluctuations in investment expenditures are considered a major cause of the business cycle.

Net Exports This entry is the smallest component of GNP. Exports are domestically produced goods sold abroad, whereas imports are foreign produced goods purchased domestically. Since GNP is the measure of the value of domestically produced goods and services, the value of imports must be subtracted from the value of exports. If the value of what is imported is greater than that exported, then net exports would be recorded as negative purchases.

Expanded Factor Cost-Income Approach

Factor income consists of employee compensation; proprietor's income plus rental income; corporate profits; interest income; indirect business taxes; business transfer payments; and depreciation.

Recall that GNP can be calculated by measuring the other side of the coin of the market value of produced goods and the expenditures made to acquire them, by adding income earned by factors in the creation of those goods and services. We refer now to the right side of Table 20-3.

Employee Compensation This consists of monetary income of employees, including corporate officers, tips, commissions, bonuses, and receipts in kind that represent income to recipients.

Proprietors' Income This includes monetary income and in-kind income of sole owners and partnerships, including the independent professions (doctors, lawyers) and producers' cooperatives.

Rental Income This is monetary income of persons obtained from rental of real property except the income of persons engaged in the real estate business; the imputed net rental income of owner occupants of nonfarm dwellings; and the royalties received by persons from patents, copyrights, and rights to natural resources.

Corporate Profits Before Taxes Over 45 percent of this goes for taxes. The remainder is either distributed in dividends or retained and reinvested in plant and equipment.

Interest Income This is interest paid to domestic business and persons by government minus interest received by government, plus net interest received from abroad.

Thus far all earned income has been accounted for and is defined as national income. It still is short of being equal to GNP. The next three entries will make up the gap. However, they are not part of income earned by factors of production.

***Indirect business taxes* are taxes not paid by those on whom they were originally levied.**

Indirect Business Taxes Sales, property, excise, and license taxes qualify as indirect business taxes. Such a tax is defined as an indirect tax because it is not paid by those on whom it was initially levied. The grocery store passes the sales tax on to the consumer. These taxes do not represent earned income by factors of production. They are income transfers from the private sector to the government sector. For example, suppose a loaf of bread is priced at 90 cents plus 5 cents sales tax. The 90 cents represents payments to factors in producing the bread. The 5 cents does not. Since the tax is part of the market price of the bread, it appears on the product side. Thus to get the income side equal to the expenditure side the 5 cents must be included.

***Business transfers* include both transactions for which a firm receives only advertised goodwill and losses from unpaid customer debts.**

Business Transfers These are transactions for which the firm receives nothing except advertised goodwill (prize money on television shows, donations, scholarships, contests) or losses from unpaid consumer debts. Business transfers must also be added in order for national income to equal GNP, because they are income paid to recipients from whom there was no corresponding production. If it is a car won in a contest, the car has already been counted on the product side. However, prize recipients cannot be counted as earning factor income, so the business transfer has to be added to national income to bring the income side into equality with the product side.

***Depreciation* is a bookkeeping procedure where part of the total cost of a machine is deducted from a firm's total revenues for each year of the machine's depreciated lifetime.**

Depreciation Over the years capital depreciates, meaning that capital in a bookkeeping sense is used up and must be replaced. For tax purposes depreciation is allowed as an expense of doing business that the entrepreneur legally deducts over the lifetime of the machine equal to the original cost of the machine. For example, if a truck costs $10,000 the business can allow for $2,000 a year as a cost for each of 5 years of the truck's lifetime, until the full cost of $10,000 is covered. Use of the truck is a cost of doing business, and as it is owned over the years its depreciated value is deducted from revenues as an expense. This is strictly a bookkeeping operation that, in effect, reduces the profits earned by the business as expressed in the accounts. It thereby reduces the firm's tax liability on profits. But to include depreciation in national income would be double-counting earned income connected with the truck. This is because payments have already been made to factors employed by the firm that built the truck.

Gross Investment Refer now to Figure 20-2, for a diagrammatic representation of the gross investment–net investment–depreciation relationship. Gross investment is the total amount of new construction and plant and equipment put into place during the year. It is a flow variable. But some existing plant and equipment is used up during the year. It depreciates. Therefore, net investment during the year is simply gross investment less depreciation. We see that net

Figure 20-2

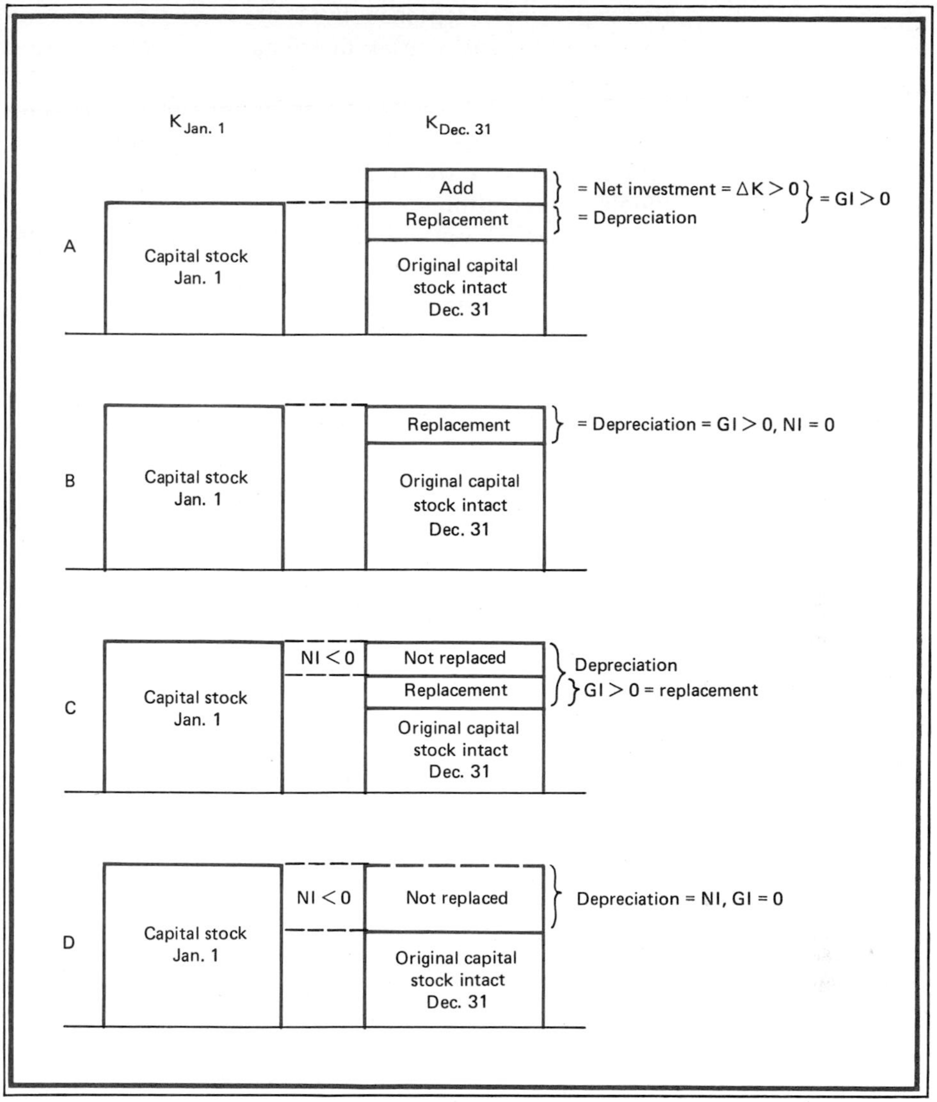

Gross investment is the total value of new construction and new equipment put into place during the year. *Net investment* is gross investment less depreciation of old equipment.

investment is the change in the capital stock that takes place during the year. The letter *K* stands for the amount of capital stock at a given time.

$$\text{Net investment} = K_{\text{Dec. 31}} - K_{\text{Jan. 1}} = \Delta K$$

and

$$\text{Net investment} = \text{gross investment} - \text{depreciation}$$

or

$$\text{Gross investment} = \text{net investment} + \text{depreciation.}$$

In panel A, the stock of capital by the end of the year has increased above the amount that existed at the beginning of the year. Not only has the depreciated capital been replaced, but there is a net positive investment of new capital. Since gross investment = depreciation + net investment, gross investment is also positive.

In panel B, there has been no net addition to the capital stock, hence net investment equals zero. The only investment was in replacing depreciated capital. But since depreciation is positive so is gross investment, which now equals depreciation.

In panel C, not only has there been no new investment, but not all of the depreciated capital has been replaced. Hence net investment is actually negative and the capital stock has actually declined. Gross investment = depreciation. Since depreciation is lower than it is in panel B, gross investment is still positive but smaller than in panel B.

In panel D, the capital stock is reduced more than it is in panel C. Not only is net investment negative but none of the depreciated capital stock has been replaced. The decline in investment identically equals the depreciated capital; thus since gross investment equals net investment (which is negative) and net investment now identically equals depreciation (which is positive), then gross investment equals zero. Note that gross investment can never be less than zero, because depreciation can never be less than zero. What capital there is can only depreciate if it is not replaced.

Other Common GNP Accounting Definitions

Gross national product and national income are not the only measures of the economy's performance. Other accounting concepts related to them are also useful indicators. The relations among them are illustrated in Table 20-4.

TABLE 20-4
Gross National Product in 1980 in Current Dollars (Billions)

Measure		Amount (billions of dollars)
GNP	Gross national product	2,628.8
	Subtract: Depreciation	275.5
NNP	Net national product	2,353.3
	Subtract: Indirect business taxes	212.5
	Business transfers	10.5
	Other transfers	6.2
NY	National income	2,124.4
	Subtract: Corporate profits (before taxes)	182.1
	Social Security taxes	203.7
	Add: Government transfer payments to persons	283.9
	Dividends	54.4
	Net interest paid by government and consumers	256.6
	Business transfers	10.5
PY	Personal income	2,161.0
	Subtract: Personal taxes	399.8 (est.)
DY	Disposable personal income	1,761.2 (est.)

Preliminary data; may not add due to rounding.
Source: U.S. Dept. of Commerce, *Survey of Current Business*, Jan. 1981, Table 1.7.

Net national product is calculated using net instead of gross investment.

Personal income includes households' personal income plus unearned transfer payments from business and government.

Household disposable income is income that can actually be spent after subtracting taxes.

Unspent disposable income is defined as *savings.*

When depreciation is subtracted from the GNP, **net national product** (NNP) results, since only the net additions to the capital stock, namely net investment, is counted. It should be mentioned that GNP is a more reliable measure than NNP because GNP is measured at market prices on the product side where the data are reasonably good. The data on depreciation are rough estimates and it is hard to know what firms' real depreciation costs are. When indirect taxes and business transfers are netted out, we arrive at **national income** (NY), an item we discussed earlier. In going from NNP to NY, we move from valuing products at their market price to valuing output at factor cost. **Personal income** (PY) includes income earned by individuals and nonprofit institutions plus unearned income transfers from business and government. The transition to personal income requires subtracting the share of profits retained by corporations for reinvestment as well as Social Security taxes paid by employees who have earned income but do not currently receive the income. Government transfer payments for things like welfare, veterans' benefits, farm subsidies and so on are unearned income transfers. Dividends paid to stockholders are earned income. These are the corporate profits that people actually get. The interest on the government debt is income to owners of government bonds. It is treated as a transfer payment and not as a payment for current goods or services. To obtain the measure of **disposable income** people actually get to spend, it is necessary to deduct personal income taxes. Unspent disposable income is personal **savings**

PUTTING THINGS IN THEIR PLACE

One should not be misled by the apparent simplicity of the preceding statements. What is actually included and omitted in estimates of GNP by those in charge of creating the numbers is often surprising and arbitrary. Furthermore, what is considered to be an intermediate product, sold from one business to another, is often hard to distinguish from final products that consumers buy. One definition of *a final product is a purchase that is not resold* to another intermediate producer, whereas *an intermediate product can be defined as a purchase that is resold* to another producer. For example, an automobile bought by a consumer from a dealer is a final good if it is bought in the same year in which it is produced. As should now be understood, the steel, rubber, plastic, and cloth sold to the automobile manufacturer are intermediate products and should not be included more than once in GNP. Only the final price of the car should be counted, since the intermediate goods are contained in the price of the final good—which, by the way—includes dealer preparation costs. This is fairly straightforward. But how do the accountants treat such things as the carpenter who must buy work clothes, the mechanic who buys a wrench, or the check-out clerk who buys bus transportation to work—all of which can be considered as input costs—or intermediate costs—of earning a living? The staff of the BEA must, and does, make decisions on such issues. How many times have you seen a film where a character says while leaving the office, "I'll be back at two, I'm taking a client to lunch"? Is the restaurant lunch a consumer expenditure for a final good, or is it a business expenditure and therefore an intermediate product? Without the amenities of the lunch the sale may not go through. Hence, it could be considered as a business expense.

Aside from the problem of deciding what is a business purchase and what is a consumer purchase, there are some purchases that do not enter into GNP at all. Instead of a new car, suppose you bought a secondhand car off a used-car lot. This purchase is not included in GNP for the current year; the car has already been counted for in a previous year. The purchase represents the transfer of ownership, and not production of a good. However, the salesman's commission would be included in GNP, since that is earned income for a service rendered in the current period.

The GNP does not include transactions that do not officially pass through the market, such as illegal activities and some domestic activities.

Then there are those purchases that, in principle, should be included in GNP but for obvious reasons are not recorded, for example prostitution and illegal drug sales. Consider an old painting picked up at a garage sale which turns out to be a lost painting of a master and is consequently sold for a large profit. This capital gain is not included in GNP. Then there is the classic example of the man who marries his maid and GNP falls because the value of household chores performed by housewives are not counted as part of GNP whereas the former maid's chores were. In the same vein, if you fire your gardener and pay your son to mow the lawn, GNP falls. The value produced by those people who contribute their time to work for political organizations, hospitals, and other welfare activities without receiving wages are excluded from GNP calculations. Do-it-yourself projects are not recognized in the GNP accounts. Some economists argue that such activities should be evaluated at opportunity cost or at some imputed market value. In conclusion, an activity or transaction that does not pass through the market is sometimes computed by imputation. There are some exceptions.

TO IMPUTE OR NOT TO IMPUTE

The GNP does include some *imputed* (estimated) domestic activities such as the value of home-grown food on farms.

To impute is to estimate or ascribe. There are several goods and services that contribute to the official calculation of GNP but do not pass through the market. Therefore, the accountants must impute value for this part of the nation's output. Three examples are noted here. First, there is a modest amount of fuel and food produced and consumed directly on the farm although these items count for less than 10 percent of farm income. Second, there are the imputed values of the services of owner-occupied homes. If an owner does not live in the house or apartment, he or she most likely receives rental income from the property. If the owner does live in his or her own home, a typical market rent is used to impute the value of the services received. The BEA bases these imputations, not unreasonably, on rents paid in similar locations for similar types of housing units. Third, there are imputations for goods and lodgings furnished by business firms to their employees.

Partly Finished Goods

Those who measure GNP concentrate on market transactions for final goods and services, but what about a half-finished refrigerator or half-built apartment building or even a play in rehearsal that has not yet opened? These should be counted in GNP. The apartment building is not finished yet plumbers, carpenters, and other workers are still receiving paychecks. The actors are receiving rehearsal pay. Hence, this earned income is certainly part of GNP when it is measured by factor costs. Such goods-in-process are simply treated at cost rather than at final market value. For finished goods held in inventory, their sale price is set at the sales price of goods already sold and is averaged over the year. The estimated value is listed under an item in the accounts called *inventory valuation adjustment.*

Public Goods

Some unfinished goods and most *public goods* are calculated at cost instead of at market prices.

A public good is a special creature because more than one person consumes it at the same time. Many of the goods provided by federal, state, and local governments are public goods. Expenditures on the nation's defense are perhaps the largest among the costs of providing the community with public goods. But these public goods do not sell in a market at a market price, and therefore we have no measure of their value to the consumer. BEA accountants solve this problem of measuring their value by simply recording the *cost* of the inputs devoted to the production of these goods, and using these costs as estimates of the value of the output of services provided by the government sector. Everyone recognizes that the costs of production may differ greatly from the actual value of output at market prices. However since we have no way to estimate this value we simply make do with an arbitrary judgment.

Consumption or Investment

Not the least of the problems is the classification of what is a consumer good and what is an investment good. A truck purchased by a moving company is classified as an investment good, but a pickup truck purchased by a consumer is considered a consumption good. Many consumer durables (goods lasting a year or more) actually provide a flow of services for many years, just as a unit of capital purchased by a firm yields a flow of services over time. Nevertheless, the consumers are counted as purchasing durable consumption goods. One exception is if a consumer builds or buys a newly built house. All homebuilding is considered investment by the BEA accountants. But things like home appliances are placed in the category of consumption. Furthermore, when government is included, all spending by government comes under the label of government spending even though it is clear that many of the things it contracts for would, if built by private business, be categorized as investment, for example, bridges, dams, and highways. One reason for this is that it is hard to differentiate between intermediate and final products of government. If private firms were allowed to buy government resources just as they buy other inputs, their outlays could be considered as payments for intermediate products rendered by government. Instead, the government collects compulsory taxes and does not separate services to the business sector from those to the final consumer. Similarly, if individual consumers were able to pay directly for services of government as they do for those of dentists, their payments could be counted as the market value of a government final product. To meet this problem, accountants for the BEA simply define payments made by business firms to government as intermediate services provided by the government. In like manner, direct payments by private citizens to government are measured as final services provided by government to ultimate consumers. For example, tuition payments to attend a state college.

Transfer Payments

When the government is introduced into the analysis, we shall treat various welfare payments and subsidies to households and business by government as expenditures which are *not* included in the national income accounts because they are treated as income transfers from one group to another. Only *income earned* from current period *production* is counted. If transfers were included too, it would be double counting again. Of course, such payments increase the personal income of the receiving households, so that while all factor costs are income, it does not follow that all incomes are correspondingly factor costs from the national income accounting viewpoint.

Consumer Price Index

The *consumer price index* suggests a national price level by calculating the average price of a "market basket" of many commodities commonly purchased by consumers; however, it does not accurately reflect current living costs for many individuals.

In this section we discuss an abstract invention of statisticians that probably has as much effect on the economic policies and decisions of the country as anything else—the consumer price index (CPI). Government officials, labor leaders, businessmen, and homemakers sometimes react to it with the same intensity that some teenagers respond to the wails of the latest rock singer. *Inflation* looms large among our national concerns, and the CPI is supposed to measure it. The CPI is widely used and sometimes misused. It measures month-to-month changes in the total price of what is called a basket of goods and services. This basket consists of several thousand items typically consumed by the urban and suburban population, representing 80 percent of the total population.

The CPI was first estimated during the years of World War I when, not surprisingly, there were rapid changes in prices, particularly in the shipbuilding areas of the country. An index of prices was felt to be essential for wage negotiations. At that time, in order to allow for variations throughout the different regions of the nation, studies of family expenditures were conducted in industrial centers from 1917 to 1919. The estimations are now prepared by the Bureau of Labor Statistics (BLS) of the Department of Labor, and their publication is called the U.S. Department of Labor Statistical Bulletin.

Over five million workers have labor contracts with cost of living adjustment (COLA) clauses that are based on changes in the CPI. Over 3 million of the government's retired military and civilian retirees, over 35 million Social Security recipients, over 20 million food stamp recipients, and approximately 12 million school children who receive school lunch benefits have these government transfer payments pegged to the CPI. A change of .1 of a percent means millions of dollars to these groups. If the index rises .4 of a percent it translates into 1 to 2 cents an hour under most COLA clauses.

Deficiencies in the CPI stem from sampling errors, unreflected quality changes, and rapidly changing consumer preferences.

The news media and others often mistakenly refer to the CPI as a cost-of-living index, but it does not accurately reflect current living costs to individuals because they do not always buy the same goods, and when relative prices change consumers do not continue to buy the same basket of goods. The CPI is only what it says it is—a price index—a statistical average of prices.

Weighting

In constructing the index the statisticians must decide which items to include in the basket, and after that just how much influence each included item should have. How many eggs are to be in the basket? How many boxes of potato chips? Should steak be included? If so, what kind? And, how much? Should Fords be substituted for Datsuns, or should both items be included? Should the index contain a full range of typical food items, or only items included in a typical breakfast, lunch, and dinner?

The problem of how much of each good to include is what statisticians called weighting. The quantities in the basket of goods are kept constant except when the weighting is to be revised. The new weights are introduced in such a way that they cause no change in the index. Any change that does result in the basket's cost is caused by price changes alone. The bundle deals with prices actually charged to consumers and includes sales and excise taxes as well as such things as real estate taxes on owned homes, since these are part of the cost of home ownership. The CPI ignores Social Security and income taxes.

Data Sources and Collection[1]

At intervals of ten years or more the BLS conducts new surveys and revises the basket of goods, because relative prices and tastes change over time, new goods appear, and some old ones disappear. The revision of the old 1960–1961 basket was started in 1969 and the figures were not released until 1978. Two CPI indexes are now published. A revised old one, CPI-W, is based on those goods bought by urban wage earners and clerks. It covered about 45 percent of the total population. The new index, CPI-U, is based on goods bought by all urban and suburban households and excludes rural households for now. However, it covers about 80 percent of the total U.S. population. The old, unrevised index has been dropped. The reason the old, revised CPI-W index continues to be published, and not the new CPI-U alone, is that the labor unions did not want to abandon the old index because they were afraid the new index would lower the inflation rate used in their wage adjustments, the COLA of their wage contracts. The CPI-W will be dropped eventually.

When it was stated above that the CPI-W index covered 45 percent of the total population, it does not mean that 45 percent of the population was directly surveyed. The sample is much smaller than that, but is scientifically selected in such a way that it is as if 45 percent were surveyed. The old CPI was constructed from a basket of 398 typical goods that people bought in 1960–1961.

The new basket was expanded from the original 398 items to several thou-

[1]For a fuller discussion of price indexes, see William H. Wallace and William E. Cullison, *Measuring Price Changes,* 4th ed., The Federal Reserve Bank of Richmond.

sand items in the *Consumer Expenditure Survey* of 1972–1973. Price movements to determine the CPI-U index are observed in a sample of 85 urban and suburban areas that had more than 2,500 inhabitants in 1970, including areas in Alaska and Hawaii. Rural areas are excluded. The survey includes about 2,300 food store outlets, 18,000 rental units, and about 18,000 housing units to estimate property taxes. Prices on food, fuel, and other goods and services are collected monthly, and the pricing of food is done throughout the month.

The new basket reflects significant changes in spending habits since 1960–1961. Women's stationary hair dryers have been replaced with portable blow dryers, recapped tires are out, while warm-up suits, fast-food restaurants, pool cues, pocket calculators, CB radios, and crockpots are in. The new CPI-U index increases the weights accorded to housing and transportation but reduces it for food, apparel, and medical care.

Calculating the CPI: Market Basket Approach

Consider the three items in Table 20-5, a subset of the bundle the typical urban consumer buys. The weight column shows the quantity, hence the influence, of each good in the bundle. Hypothetical prices for the years 1972 and 1980 are shown, the years for which the percentage change in the price levels is to be compared. The values for each year are obtained by multiplying the weights for each good by the price of each good. Thus, for eggs, 10 dozen times 70 cents per dozen equals 7 dollars. The base year is taken as 1972, so the index for 1972 is set equal to 100. Remember, it is changes we are interested in, not absolute levels. By choosing 100 for the base year, the calculations are made easier and are readily interpreted. The formula is

$$CPI_{1980} = \frac{\text{Value of 1980 basket}}{\text{Value of 1972 basket}} CPI_{1972}.$$

Since 1972 is the base year, let it be 100. We can now calculate the 1980 basket in what is called "1972 constant dollars."

$$CPI_{1980} = \frac{698}{527} \times 100 = 132.44.$$

TABLE 20-5
CPI Example for Three Goods

Item	Weight (Q)	Price in 1972 in Dollars	Price in 1980 in Dollars	Value in 1972	Value in 1980
eggs	10 dozen	.70	.80	7	8
gasoline	400 gallons	.30	.60	120	240
color television	1 set	400	450	400	450
				527	698

This says that the price of the consumer basket rose 32.44 percent from 1972 to 1980. Notice that the price of

eggs increased 14.3%
gasoline increased 100%
color television increased 12.5%.

Because of the influence of the television set, the total index rose only 32 percent even though gasoline increased by 100 percent in price.

WEAKNESSES OF THE CPI

The CPI is *not* an exact measure of price changes. It is an average, and it is subject to sampling errors and reporting errors that may cause it to deviate from the results which would otherwise be obtained. If actual records of *all* retail purchases could be used to compile the index, the accuracy might be improved. Larger samples, however, are costly.

But sampling and reporting errors are not the only types of errors that plague the index. For example, a serious deficiency in calculating the index is in accounting adequately for quality improvements in products and the introduction of new products. These are often understated by the CPI. In earlier years television sets were black and white only, now many people own color television sets. The change that introduces color television as part of the package of goods is, again, arbitrarily decided upon, just as black and white television was in the original sample. But the quality improvement represented by color may not be accounted for by the higher price attributed to color television, so that the CPI is biased upward. The consumer is paying more but getting more too.

To adjust for quality changes—and it is only a partial adjustment—the BLS compares the prices of the old and new item when both are available in the market at the same time. The difference in their prices is assumed to be a measure of the quality difference and is adjusted out of the price of the new item. However, when the items are not available at the same time, differences in the manufacturing costs are estimated and taken as a measure of the quality change, and then factored out of the new price. Thus the higher cost color set is compensated for by the improvement in quality and consumer satisfaction. This example also reflects a change in consumer tastes. Although the price index rises by introducing more expensive changes in consumption, this does not mean that consumers are less well off. The index does not quickly adapt to changes in consumer buying habits. For example, the movement by consumers out of high priced coffee to lower priced substitutes is not immediately picked up by an adjustment in the index. The index assumes that people continue to buy goods the way they did before prices shot up. They frequently do not. The index does not catch up to the shifts in tastes until much later. Other imperfections are that the CPI does not include income taxes, and that new housing is overweighted in the basket. Table 20-6 lists data for the CPI for the years 1909–1980 in 1967 constant dollars.

TABLE 20-6
Indexes of Wholesale (Producer) Prices and Consumer Prices

Year	Wholesale prices 1967 = 100	Consumer prices 1967 = 100
1909	34.9	26.1
1910	36.4	27.6
1911	33.5	28.5
1912	35.6	28.9
1913	36.0	29.7
1914	35.2	30.1
1915	35.8	30.4
1916	44.1	32.7
1917	60.6	38.4
1918	67.6	45.1
1919	71.4	51.8
1920	79.6	60.0
1921	50.3	53.6
1922	49.9	50.2
1923	51.9	51.1
1924	50.5	51.2
1925	53.3	52.5
1926	51.6	53.0
1927	49.3	52.0
1928	50.0	51.3
1929	49.1	51.3
1930	44.6	50.0
1931	37.6	45.6
1932	33.6	40.9
1933	34.0	38.8
1934	38.6	40.1
1935	41.3	41.1
1936	41.7	41.5
1937	44.5	43.0
1938	40.5	42.2
1939	39.8	41.6
1940	40.5	42.0
1941	45.1	44.1
1942	50.9	48.8
1943	53.3	51.8
1944	53.6	52.7
1945	54.6	53.9
1946	62.3	58.5
1947	76.5	66.9
1948	82.8	72.1
1949	78.7	71.4
1950	81.8	72.1
1951	91.1	77.8
1952	88.6	79.5
1953	87.4	80.1
1954	87.6	80.5
1955	87.8	80.2
1956	90.7	81.4
1957	93.3	84.3
1958	94.6	86.6
1959	94.8	87.3
1960	94.9	88.7
1961	94.5	89.6
1962	94.8	90.6
1963	94.5	91.7
1964	94.7	92.9
1965	96.6	94.5
1966	99.8	97.2
1967	100.0	100.0
1968	102.5	104.2
1969	106.5	109.8
1970	110.4	116.3
1971	113.9	121.3
1972	119.1	125.3
1973	134.7	133.1
1974	160.1	147.7
1975	174.9	161.2
1976	183.0	170.5
1977	194.2	181.5
1978	209.3	195.3
1979	235.6	217.4
1980	268.7	246.8

Source: U.S. Dept. of Labor, Bureau of Labor Statistics, as compiled in *Facts and Figures on Government Finances*, Tax Foundation, Inc., 1979. Also, Economic Report of the President.

WHOLESALE PRICE INDEX (NOW PRODUCER PRICE INDEX)

The granddaddy of all the price indexes is the wholesale price index (WPI), being the oldest continuous statistical series published by the BLS. It was first published in 1902 covering the years 1890 to 1901. It started with a resolution of the U.S. Senate in 1891, which authorized the Senate Committee on Finance to investigate the effects of tariff laws "upon the imports and exports, the growth, development, production, and prices of agricultural and manufactured articles at home and abroad." The 1890–1901 index published in 1902 was an unweighted average of prices including 250 to 261 commodities. By 1979 the number of commodities had reached 2,800. Separate indexes are constructed for all 2,800 commodities. These are then combined into averages and weighted by the quantity of goods shipped. The WPI is a measure of price changes for goods sold in primary markets. Despite what it says, it does *not* refer to prices received by wholesalers. Primary markets refer to prices received by firms that produce and ship large quantities to wholesalers, jobbers, or distributors. So far as possible these prices are f.o.b. (free on board), which means prices before transportation costs. The WPI is intended to measure "pure" price changes, changes in prices that are not influenced by changes in quality and shipping terms. It consists of many items that are also included in the CPI but at primary market prices instead of retail prices. In particular, the WPI consists of all commodities sold in commercial transactions, including not only those produced in the U.S. but also those imported for sale. It covers manufactured and processed goods as well as goods produced by industries classified as manufacturing, agriculture, fishing, mining, gas and electricity, public utilities, and waste and scrap materials. Not included are construction, transport, communications, government purchases and financing, and industrial services. Price data for the WPI are collected by mail questionnaire on a monthly basis. Reporting is voluntary and confidential, but the sample is not scientifically selected as it is with the CPI.

Generally, the commodities chosen are the largest shipment values. The WPI is used by the government and private research agencies for purposes of market analyses, escalation adjustments of long-term purchases and sales contracts, for formulation of monetary policy by the Federal Reserve, as an indicator of economic trends, and by the Justice Department looking for evidence of monopoly practices of the 550 industries in the sample. Table 20-6 lists the PPI for the years 1909–1980.

Weaknesses of WPI

The WPI is beset by more methodological errors than the CPI. It bases the 2,800 price indexes on only 10,000 items surveyed monthly covering 9,000 firms in a nonscientific sample. And, as we said, it is not really a wholesale price index. Nor does it include quality adjustments. In 1952 office equipment could perform 100,000 computations at a cost of $1.26. With improved computer technology it can be done now for about a penny. But computers are not included in the WPI as part of office equipment. List prices are often not the prices at which actual transactions take place, particularly when demand is weaker during a slowdown in the economy. In these circumstances producers sometimes offer price discounts in various ways, for example in free shipping. Thus, industrial prices actually fall but the WPI is counting list prices, so that prices fluctuate more than the WPI indicates. On the other hand, the WPI contains a hodgepodge of raw materials, intermediate goods and finished or final goods. It can involve double and triple counting, causing it at times to deviate sharply from the CPI. The BLS has initiated some corrections by upgrading the three indexes for shipments of finished goods, intermediate goods, and raw goods, and calling the new three-way calculation the **Producer Price Index (PPI)** as distinct from the old "all commodities" WPI. An extensive overhaul is expected to be completed by the mid-1980s.

The *producer price index* measures price changes on approximately 2,800 goods sold in large quantities by primary producers to wholesalers and distributors.

THE GNP DEFLATOR AND REAL GNP

***GNP deflator* is money GNP converted to constant or real dollars.**

The GNP deflator, also known as the Implicit Price Deflator, is the favorite price index of economists. Unlike the CPI, which includes commodities both old (resold houses and cars) and new (newly built houses and cars), the GNP deflator covers only currently produced goods and services, and unlike the WPI it avoids double and triple counting. Calculation of the GNP deflator is complicated. It is not derived from direct price measurements as are the CPI and WPI; however, it depends on various components in the CPI and WPI.

The purpose of the GNP deflator is to net out the pure price change effects in the measurement of GNP. Recall the lemon-lime example where five lemons each sold at 15 cents and 4 limes each sold for 20 cents, so that GNP of this two-good economy was \$1.55. Assume that in the next year the same number of lemons and limes are produced by the economy but that the price of each has risen by 5 cents so that lemons are now selling for 20 cents and limes for 25 cents. We have

$$\text{Year 1: GNP} = \$1.55$$

$$\text{Year 2: GNP} = \$2.00.$$

However, the increase in GNP in year two is solely the result of inflation. The real output of the economy—the lemons and limes—has not changed. Therefore, in order to determine real GNP from one period to another, money GNP must be deflated by the amount of inflation. The GNP deflator does this. Thus, real GNP in year two in constant year-one dollars is

$$\text{Real GNP in Year 2} = \frac{\text{Money GNP in year 2}}{\text{GNP deflator}}.$$

A History

National Income Accounting evolved from its early beginning in 1921 when the National Bureau of Economic Research (NBER) published its first document entitled Income in the United States: Its Amount and Distribution, 1909–1919. During the 1920s the Bureau published additional volumes on national income. As a result of the Depression of the 1930s Congress pressured for more information on the national economy. From 1919–1938 Simon Kuznets* was most instrumental in shaping the major concepts and methods in the area of National Income and Product Accounts (NIP), for which he received the Nobel Prize in Economics in 1971. The accounts are published in The Survey of Current Business† first published in July 1, 1921 and issued at that time free to subscribers as a supplement to Commerce Reports. It was not numbered. The August 1 edition was numbered and also issued free to all subscribers of the Commerce Reports. At that time the journal was compiled by the Bureau of the Census, the Bureau of Foreign and Domestic Commerce, and the Bureau of Standards, with the major load carried by the Bureau of the Census. It remained a Census publication until June 1930, when it was transferred to the Division of Statistical Research in the Bureau of Foreign and Domestic Commerce (BFDC). The Department of Commerce was reorganized in December 1945 and the Survey of Current Business was lodged in the Office of Business Economics (OBE) of the Department of Commerce. On January 1, 1972 the OBE was changed to the Bureau of Economic Analysis (BEA). The core of BEA's work is the construction of the national accounts from raw data supplied mostly by other agencies (Census Bureau, Office of Manpower, Management and Data Systems, IRS, OMB, and the Treasury are among them). Since these sources do not always meet standards of form and accuracy economists need, the work requires the development of both concepts and estimation methods. The BEA also collects some data of its own – about 15 percent of its budget is devoted to this acitivity.

* NBER, National Income: A Summary of Findings, by Simon Kuznets, 1946.
† U.S. Dept. of Commerce, Survey of Current Business, Vol. 51, No. 7, Part II, (July 1971), The Anniversary Issue.

The GNP deflator is calculated with reference to a base year. Currently the base year is 1972 with the base year index set equal to 100. Thus, real GNP in year two when deflated by inflation should yield $1.55 in year-one constant dollars. In Table 20-7 observe that the deflator rose from 100 for the base year 1972 to 177.2 in 1980. GNP was $1,171.1 billion in 1972 and $2,106.6 billion in 1978; hence, real GNP in 1978, in 1972 constant dollars using 1972 = 100 as the base and 1.521 as the 1978 GNP deflator, was

$$\text{Real GNP 1978 (in 1972 dollars)} = \frac{\$2{,}106.6 \text{ bil.}}{1.521} = \$1{,}365.2 \text{ billion.}$$

Most of the increase in GNP from 1972 to 1978 was the result of inflation. Real growth in GNP was equal to only

$$\frac{\$1{,}365.2 - \$1{,}171.1}{\$1{,}171.1} \times 100 = 16.5\%$$

as compared to a nearly 80 percent growth in money GNP over that time period.

TABLE 20-7
Implicit Price Deflators for Gross National Product

Year	Gross national product deflator (1972 = 100)
1929	32.9
1930	31.8
1931	28.9
1932	25.7
1933	25.1
1934	27.3
1935	27.8
1936	27.9
1937	29.3
1938	28.6
1939	28.4
1940	29.1
1941	31.5
1942	34.8
1943	36.4
1944	37.1
1945	38.0
1946	43.9
1947	49.7
1948	53.1
1949	52.6
1950	53.6
1951	57.3
1952	58.0
1953	58.9
1954	59.7
1955	61.0
1956	62.9
1957	65.0
1958	66.1
1959	67.5
1960	68.7
1961	69.3
1962	70.6
1963	71.6
1964	72.7
1965	74.3
1966	76.8
1967	79.0
1968	82.6
1969	86.7
1970	91.4
1971	96.0
1972	100.0
1973	105.8
1974	116.0
1975	127.2
1976	133.8
1977	141.6
1978	152.1
1979	162.8
1980	177.4

Source: U.S. Dept. of Commerce, Bureau of Economic Analysis as compiled in Economic Report of the President.

CHAPTER SUMMARY

The national income accounts record the nation's economic activity over the year. The dollar value of what the nation produces in final goods over the years is called the gross national product, or GNP for short. There are three ways to measure GNP, namely (1) the product-expenditure approach, where the total dollar value of goods produced must equal the total value of spending to acquire them, so that total spending equals total receipts; (2) the factor cost-income flow, where what are costs to one must be income to another, so payments made by firms for inputs represent earned income to those inputs for productive work; and (3) the value-added approach, where only the value added to a product at each intermediate stage of production is summed to arrive at the total retail value of the final product sold to the consumer. When the government sector is included, government wages and salaries are counted as value added contributed by government workers. The circular flow suggests the movement of goods and services in one direction and the corresponding opposite movement of money income in the other. A leakage occurs when money spending leaves the circular flow; injections occur when it enters the circular flow. Thus, government expenditures, business investment spending, household consumption, and exports are injections, whereas taxes, business and household saving, and imports are leakages.

The product-expenditure side of the accounts equals household spending + government spending + investment spending by firms + net exports. Factor income consists of employee compensation + owners' income + rental income + interest income. In addition, to get the income side of GNP equal to the product side of GNP, indirect business taxes and business transfer payments must be added to national income.

Inventories, unsold goods, are treated as capital investment. Inventories are likened to firms buying their own output—and when firms spend it is investment.

National income is earned income for productive activity. But part of households personal income also consists of transfer payments from government. Household disposable income is income that can actually be spent after subtracting taxes. Unspent disposable income is defined as savings.

Secondhand sales are not included. Illegal activities are not counted, since they are not and cannot be officially recorded as passing through the market. Domestic chores are also left out. For some domestic activities, however, a price is imputed, for example, food grown and consumed on the farm, and the rental value of owner-occupied houses. Unfinished goods in progress are calculated at cost and not at their retail price. The same is true for government-provided goods. The consumer price index is a statistical method for calculating the average price of many of the standard commodities consumers buy in order to determine a national price level. It is not really a cost of living index, because all people do not buy the identical goods. The cost of living does not go up to a nondrinker if the price of coffee doubles, but it does rise to the coffee drinker. Two CPI indexes are now published. The CPI-W is based on goods bought by urban wage earners, and a new more inclusive CPI-U covers urban and suburban households.

Deficiencies in the CPI range from sampling errors to adjusting for quality changes. Moreover, consumers change their tastes faster than the basket of goods from which the index is calculated can be changed. The wholesale price index, now renamed the producer price index (PPI), measures price changes for some 2,800 goods shipped in large quantities and sold by primary producers to wholesalers and distributors. The potential for sampling errors are greater than for the CPI, and double and triple counting can occur. Hence, the PPI can fluctuate more widely and erratically than the CPI.

The GNP price deflator, or the implicit price deflator, covers only currently produced goods and services and avoids double counting. It is used to deflate money GNP in order to determine real GNP, thus netting out the effect on current GNP of price changes so that changes in the real output of the economy can be determined. Deflated GNP is expressed in constant or real dollars.

QUESTIONS

1. What are the three ways of measuring GNP? Explain why each approach will conceptually yield the same magnitude.
2. According to the GNP accounts, which contributes more to economic welfare—a switchblade knife sold to a street kid for $7.95 or a record of Beethoven's Seventh Symphony sold for $7.95 to the Ladies' Musical Guild?
3. The primary objective of economic activity is to provide goods to satisfy the nation's wants. Is national income accounting a measure of how much effort, toil, and trouble economic activity represents? Why, or why not?
4. What are the justifications for including profits as part of costs in the accounts?
5. If auto workers become less efficient at doing their job, will this raise or lower GNP? Why?
6. Does the purchase of a chess set raise productivity as measured on the product side? Does playing a game of chess with it raise GNP? Explain. Suppose the set is unsold in the current period. Does this mean GNP is lower than if it had been sold? Explain.
7. Mary is paid $11,000 a year for a job she finds dull, tedious, and nerve-wracking. Helen also does the same work for $11,000 a year and finds it challenging and fun. Is their combined contribution to GNP $22,000, less than $22,000, more than $22,000, or is it hard to say?
8. Harry pays $50 to a pusher on the street for the same drug that George obtains for $30 through a prescription written by his doctor, who is George's pusher. Is GNP increased by $30, $50, $80 or zero dollars by these transactions? Why?
9. Because a day care center is not available for Sissy to place her child, she remains unemployed. She then gets a job in a day care center and brings her child with her. Does GNP go up? Should it? Why were her services not included in GNP before she obtained the day care job? Should they have been?
10. Suppose an author receives a $5,000 royalty advance on an as yet unfinished novel. Is GNP measured from the income side then greater than GNP from the product side? How is this treated in the accounts, since the income and product price approaches must balance?
11. If your economics professor has a research article published in a professional journal for which he receives no fee, does this mean output is greater than income as measured by the GNP accounts? Explain. Is it possible for output to be greater than income?
12. Which GNP classifications do the following come under—consumption, investment, government expenditures—or none of these if the item is not included in GNP?
    a. Twenty dollars you pay a gypsy fortune teller.
    b. Monthly rent for an apartment.
    c. A new house which you buy.
    d. A 20-year-old apartment building you buy.
    e. A student's monthly allowance from home.

f. A $1,000 purchase of AT&T stock.
g. A new nuclear naval submarine.
h. Social Security payments.
i. A home you live in with the mortgage paid off.
j. $10,000 won on a television quiz show.
k. A $200,000 decrease in Penney's inventories.
l. Purchase of new golf clubs by a golf instructor.
m. A $100 purchase of cocaine.

13. A 1977 all-time movie list had *Star Wars* at the top with earnings of $127 million in 1977 alone. The 1939 film *Gone With the Wind,* in seventh place, had accumulated earnings of $76.7 million. Since "money talks," one presumes that *Star Wars* was the biggest all-time revenue earner. Is this presumption open to serious question? Why? What might be an alternative way of comparing the popularity of films over time?
14. Suppose the price index rises by 30 percent over a 3-year period. Since the CPI measures the cost of living for everyone, it is not possible for Jane to be any worse off than Tom when the price index rises. Do you agree? Comment.
15. Assume that your income rises by 100 percent from 1967 to 1978. Were you therefore financially better off? Make a calculation using the CPI. Why might your calculation understate the inflation?
16. Why might the CPI not rise when the WPI rises?
17. a. Suppose GNP was $1,000 billion in 1977 and $700 billion in 1972, what was real GNP in 1977 using the GNP deflator in Table 20-7, p. 502?
    b. Suppose the population increased by 5 percent over the 4 years between 1972 to 1976. Then real GNP per capita increased by approximately what percentage if the population in 1972 was 200 million?
18. Construct a consumer price index for 1980 using the following:

Item	1971 price	1980 price	Quantity
Apartment	$1,100	$2,000	1
Daily meals	6	12	700
Books	13	20	10

19. A BLS official said, "The CPI does not attempt to delineate changes in the style of living of Americans." Why doesn't it?
20. A principles of economics text in 1974 retailed for $11.95. In 1978 this text sold for $15.95. Did the 1978 edition cost you more or less? By how much?
21. There is a technological breakthrough in the production of electrical automobiles and they completely replace gasoline driven cars. They are also relatively cheaper. Pollution drops drastically when antipollution devices are no longer necessary for automobiles. Houses can be more cheaply heated without using fuel oil. The prices of many products formerly requiring oil in the production process fall slightly. What happens to GNP?
22. Suppose the crude oil supply becomes so low that gasoline and fuel oil are rationed. Half of the driving population ceases to drive cars. Many people lose jobs in the auto industry and take lower paying jobs in other industries. The result is that the neighborhood reappears with a variety of small, local stores springing up to serve local needs. Their prices are higher and their wages are lower. Families end up spending more time at home, sitting down together at meals, and sharing more tasks. The new situation is, however, enjoyable in unexpected ways. Has GNP gone up or down? Are people better or worse off? What is the point of the question?
23. Horses Mouth Company on campus printed and sold $100,000 worth of faculty lecture notes to students last year. It paid $50,000 to a manager and student employ-

ees, and also paid out $35,000 for paper, ink, electricity, and other inputs. Its machines depreciated $4,000 over the year.

a. What was its contribution to GNP?
b. How much were its costs, including opportunity costs?
c. How much was value added?
d. What were its profits before taxes, excluding opportunity costs?

24. You are given the following:

a. Consumption.
b. Wages.
c. Depreciation.
d. Gross investment.
e. Corporate profits (before taxes).
f. Business transfer payments.
g. Government expenditures.
h. Indirect business tax.
i. Government transfer payments.
j. Personal savings.
k. Corporate income tax.
l. Interest paid by government.
m. Net corporate savings.
n. Dividends.
o. Social Security taxes paid by employers.

Using the above,

1. Calculate GNP on the product side using the lettered items (e.g., a + b + c) in the list above.
2. Calculate NNP.
3. Calculate NY in two ways.
4. Calculate net investment.
5. Calculate GNP from the income side.

Chapter 21

Government

"It seems very pretty," she said when she had finished it, "but it's rather hard to understand" (You see she didn't like to confess, even to herself, that she couldn't make it all out).

—Alice in "Through the Looking-Glass."

PROGRESS REPORT

A. In Chapter 20 we discussed the measurement of the nation's economic activity as expressed in the national income accounts. Also, three major price indexes were introduced and some of their weaknesses were mentioned.

B. This chapter first examines how government evolved, based on several assumptions about resources and individual behavior. That done, the discussion turns to the modern U.S. government, its functions, and its goals. Then some of the nuts and bolts of the budget, expenditures, and revenues are scrutinized. The chapter ends with a discussion of government regulatory agencies.

C. Chapter 22 examines one of the component parts of aggregate demand, that of household consumption and its relation to the level of income and other economic parameters.

THE EMERGENCE OF GOVERNMENT

Suppose Ted the Troglodyte becomes dissatisfied with hunting wildlife and nomadic cave-hopping. Being an innovator, Ted realizes that he can supplement his meat diet by planting crops. He heads out over the hill looking for a better life, something more reliable and stable. He desires the permanent possession of land, shelter, and food for his own use to do with as he sees fit. He wants the exclusive use of a piece of land. He intends to increase his well-being by maximizing the amount of shelter and food he can consume by the most appropriate means or in the most efficient way he knows. We say that Ted is being *rational*. Rational means pursuing goals with the least resource waste where the gain is expected to be larger than the cost. One's labor and time are scarce, therefore efficiency is of the essence.

Ted comes upon an area with fresh water and lush green trees and grass and settles down. He marks off a plot of ground, builds a cabin, and grows a crop, doing some hunting on the side. When a few of his restless, unorganized friends see that Ted is eating better, is warm in the winter, and has a stockpile of grain to get him through the cold months, they too leave the nomadic life and create farming plots nearby. At this time there is no such thing called government. After several years more of Ted's old, nomadic friends wander wearily into Ted's territory after a particularly severe winter. They camp in Ted's corn field. Ted alone cannot chuck them off the land he now considers his but which the old gang does not because they have no conception of land as private property. They understand only their spears and animal skins as their property. Nor can he alone prevent them from munching on his crop and tearing out his wooden fence in order to make a fire. Thus, the intruders impose *external* costs on Ted. They are costs Ted incurs because of decisions made by others.

The purpose of Ted's establishing permanent residence, to have exclusive use of property, was motivated by the fact that his labor is a scarce resource; therefore he desired property because he did not want to have to repeat the effort of putting the land into the form he wanted. His purpose was to avoid repetitious labor endeavors by being able to exclude others from using the land. In other words, the risk of loss from others transgressing has to be reduced in order for him to chance the efforts of his labor being put into farming. Without guarantees or property rights there is no incentive for him to build or repair. A person has *property rights* to goods if he or she can make decisions that others may not on how the goods may be used. The person who decides how goods may be used is called the owner.

It so happens that the nomads have trampled on the fields of Ted's neighbors too and they are rather upset about it. Ted and the other tillers of the land have a meeting. They decide to form a community with rules binding them all. They also agree to apply force to throw the interlopers out of the area, which they do. They specify that each member of the community has exclusive possession of his land. Nonowners can be thrown off the land with members of the community as the rule makers and enforcers of the exclusivity right of each owner. A government has been formed. *Government is the exercise of authority*

Government exercises final authority for its citizens in order to control their actions, decide their disputes, and promote their common welfare.

in controlling actions of its members and in the promotion of the common welfare, and acts as the final power in settling disputes.

In Ted's case government has done two things. It has defined private property rights, and backed up those contracted rights with the use of force. In effect, the government has reduced the potential loss to Ted of farming the land. It has reduced his costs of ownership. As a result the quantity of land he will farm is increased beyond what it would be without government assurance.

We know that a corporation is also a collective decision body with certain powers of enforcement. It too was formed by a contract freely agreed to by a group of individuals in order to achieve a common goal more effectively. How does it differ from a government? According to Tullock[1] the government has a broader consensus from among the population and it has more authority. To put it bluntly, it has more power. The organization with the most widespread and final exercise of power is called the government. The biggest fist wins in the end and becomes the government. Thus, institutions like the corporation have continuity because the government sanctions it, protects it, and allows it the privilege of limited liability. (Many economists would contend that it would thrive without government if it were satisfying consumer demands and would not survive even with government if it were not.)

EXTERNALITIES AND CONTRACTS

A *contract* is a promise or a set of promises, the violation of which by one of the parties will be punished by law because the government recognizes the performances of the promise(s) as a duty.

The government enforces contracts. *A* **contract** *is a promise or a package of promises, the violation of which by one of the parties will be punished by the law because the government recognizes the performance of the promise(s) as a duty.* The contract provides for the protection, use, and transfer of private property now and into the future because the government will enforce agreements contained in the contract that are freely entered into. In this way the government allows for the orderly continuity of social and business relationships.

Suppose one of Ted's former Troglodyte friends, Hondo, decides to end the nomadic life and become a member of the community. He, instead, chooses to raise cattle instead of crops. When it rains, however, the runoff from Hondo's ranch carries the cattle waste onto Ted's land and damages some of Ted's crop. Hondo's decision to use his private property to raise cattle bestows an external cost on Ted, who had nothing to do with Hondo's decision to raise cattle. This side effect could easily be handled by Ted and Hondo making a contract whereby Hondo compensates Ted for the crop damage. In this manner the external cost is said to be internalized. A private market price transaction is entered to account for the social cost caused by Hondo. Hondo pays the private cost he incurs raising cattle plus the external cost he imposes on Ted, hence he pays for the full social cost of growing cattle. Thus social cost equals private cost plus external cost.

In this situation the transactions cost, that is, the cost of processing the contract, is low enough to make the agreement economically feasible. But if Hondo is polluting many nearby farms, the transactions costs of negotiating an

[1]Gordon Tullock, *Private Wants and Public Means* New York, Basic Books, Inc., 1970.

agreement among so many people may be too high. If the farmers appeal to the government, the government can resolve the issue by redefining Hondo's property rights, requiring him to desist from polluting the adjacent farms by constructing a series of canals for the waste to run off, or requiring that Hondo make payments for the value of the damaged crop. If not, wasteful social conflict is likely to occur.

Thus, as the *population* grew after the agricultural period had emerged long ago, scarce land resources became a problem. Without a government and the recognition and changing definition of property rights, wealth that was created by scarce labor would have been wastefully destroyed. From this it was realized that respect for individual property rights was of benefit to all and that the creation of government was a logical and rational act. However, once the government became a permanent institution of society, individual preferences became subordinate to the collective decisions of the democratic government. In this sense, since individual wishes can be denied, the collective democratic decision imposes externalities on individuals, on minority and majority groups, and can affect income distribution. By making decisions about externalities caused by a growing population and technology, the government reduces the transactions costs of reaching these decisions. And the government is also saying what is best for the individual by determining what is required of everyone. Implicit here is the presumption that the government has itself nothing to gain by the rules it makes.

Government evolved from the need to ensure the efficient use of scarce labor and resources; it does so through the enforcing and, if necessary, rearranging and redefining of property rights.

As the population grew even larger, it became apparent that the greater the unequal distribution of income—intimately related to property, property rights, and voting privileges—the greater the possibility for antagonisms to arise between the have and have-nots. Hence, numerical strength implies potential power. Controversy could erupt and in the process destroy the wealth of society as the existing property rights are violated. Thus, a democratic government could act as a pressure valve to release social pressures by the members of the society acting through expanded representative government to redefine property rights in order to realize a more equal distribution of income and to ensure political stability through a process of collective choices. As government and its power grows, then the trade-offs in loss of freedom and efficiency versus gains in equity could reach a point where the additional benefits of government authority may be less than the losses imposed on individual citizens and on the whole society. This is the problem confronting contemporary and future societies—the fundamental conflict of interest between the rights of the individual and the rights of the collective state.

In summary, five points were discussed.

1. Individuals are assumed to be rational. They pursue goals efficiently, that is, where the additional gain is greater than the additional cost.
2. Resources are scarce, including labor. There is no desire to have to repeat work that has already been done because others might destroy or confiscate what was created.
3. To ensure that labor efforts need not be repeated, the concept of private property is developed as is the notion of contracts.
4. To enforce property rights and contracts a government is formed that has the final authority in the use of force.
5. The government can redistribute income among the populace by rearranging or redefining property rights.

THE U.S. GOVERNMENT

As the second largest spending sector of the U.S. economy, the government has several roles to play, roles that have grown dramatically since the Great Depression of the 1930s that initiated a decade of massive government efforts to stimulate the economy when it appeared that the free private market all but collapsed. Whether a free market system would have recovered without government assistance is still debatable. Nevertheless, government intervention speeded up what would likely have been a longer period of recovery.

One major role of government is *allocation:* deciding on which goods and services it will spend its budget.

One major role of government is the **allocation** function. The government is a provider of many goods and services. It determines in some circumstances what is to be produced and who is to receive what is produced, for example, a contract award to Boeing to build a long-range missile, which protects every citizen, or funds for the Post Office, whose services are available to everyone. In other circumstances allocation is directed at specific groups. Witness agricultural and other research funds directed to universities by the government or housing for the poor provided by the Department of Housing and Urban Development (HUD). Closely related to the allocation function is the **distribution** function. Here the primary goal is to determine how much of what is allocated each recipient is to get. It introduces considerations of economic justice or equity. Some citizens do not earn what the government considers a minimum income to lead a decent life. Therefore, some of society's income is redistributed through a variety of programs that transfer income through a system of differential taxation.

Government's *distribution* function determines the amount of allocated goods and services each recipient will receive.

Government provides *public goods* that the private sector cannot or will not provide.

Two other activities of government are the provisioning of **public goods** that the private sector does not supply, and the problem of *externalities* discussed earlier.

Government employs fiscal policy (taxes and spending) to carry out its *stabilization* function of encouraging stable prices, full employment, and steady economic growth.

No less important than its other roles, is the government's **stabilization** function. This is the deliberate tuning of the nation's economy by use of government expenditures and taxation—fiscal policy—and by the manipulation of the nation's money supply and interest rates—monetary policy—in order to seek goals of full employment, stable prices, and responsible economic growth. By implementation of these policies, government tries to avoid substantial fluctuations in the economy known as the *business cycle.* While the business cycle cannot always be prevented, proper policy can shorten its duration and reduce its intensity.

As we shall eventually see, stabilization policy is difficult, for modern industrialized economies have been doubly indicted for the rising prices and rising unemployment called stagflation. (Before analyzing the modern edifice of stagflation, some foundations will be constructed in the upcoming chapters.)

Another role of government already mentioned is to enforce *contracts.* Contracts assure that promises made today between buyers and sellers will be binding in the future. By backing contracts the government assists in its goals of providing economic and social stability. In addition, the government functions to *protect the public welfare* with regard to safety, public health, and business competition. Thus, police and fire protection are services it provides, and access to the protection and due process of the courts.

The government is vigilant in seeking out monopoly practices that prevent business competition. It assists farmers and small businesses; it endeavors to protect consumers from defective products and business fraud and workers from unsafe working conditions and in some cases from discrimination and unfair treatment. It also seeks to ensure that new medical drugs are properly tested and safe. Government inspectors check places where food is being processed, as well as stores which sell it and restaurants which serve it. These sundry overlapping roles and functions of government have given rise to a vast, regulatory complex so that the **regulatory function** of the government is a story in itself. We delay some of the further details until the end of the chapter.

The *regulatory function* of government is to protect the public welfare.

Like the weather, people complain about government. Just how big is the government? (It is understood that government refers to federal, state, and local governments unless otherwise specified). Prior to 1789 the U.S. was a confederation of states and not a nation with a centralized government. The federal government is based on the Constitution drawn up in 1787 and ratified in 1789; it has been amended 26 times since then. If the Equal Rights Amendment passes it will be the 27th. Thomas Jefferson spoke idealistically of "a wise and frugal government which shall restrain men from injuring one another and leave them free to regulate their own pursuits."

The founding fathers did not say much about the functions of the executive branch. The Constitution is virtually silent on the subject of executive functions and says even less about its administrative apparatus. When the U.S. operated under the Continental Congress and the Articles of Confederation prior to the Constitutional Convention of 1787, the founding fathers expressed their unhappiness with the confusion and inefficiency of federal government up to that time. It was their intention not to return to this chaotic system. They argued heatedly about what the departments of government should be and how their heads should be selected. They finally agreed the President alone had the right to hire and fire the department heads. The State Department was the first to be established and began operation with 10 employees. There were 3,000 federal employees in the Federalist period, 95,000 by the time of Grover Cleveland in 1881, 500,000 by 1925, 2.4 million by 1946, finally growing to about 2.9 million in 1980.

In 1881 the population of the U.S. according to the U.S. Bureau of the Census was approximately 51 million; in 1925 it was approximately 115.8 million, in 1946 about 141.6 million, and in 1980 it was 226 million. Thus, per capita federal employment was roughly 1 person for every 537 in 1881, 1 for every 232 in 1925, 1 for every 59 in 1946 and one for every 75 in 1980. Though the relative size of the federal government has declined since 1946, government size goes up when local government employment is included. Local, state, and federal governments employed one jobholder out of 7 in 1946, or about 14 percent. In 1975 it was one in 5, about 20 percent. The federal government employs approximately one fifth of all the scientists and engineers in the U.S. The numbers since 1946, however, may underemphasize the growth in government power created by new legislation over the last four decades.

In the face of a continuously growing population and the greater expectations engendered by past policies and promises of politicians, greater demands for services have been placed upon the government, resulting in an increasing growth in the size of government and its influence.

As we shall see, since World War II the federal government has not, in fact, grown as rapidly as state and local government. Therefore, recent disillusion with the federal government—the lack of public trust—is presumably due as much to its performance as its size.

STRUCTURE OF THE FEDERAL GOVERNMENT

The federal government is composed of the executive, legislative, and judicial branches. The executive branch is headed by the President, who is elected for a

Figure 21-1

Outline of branches of the U.S. Federal Government
and civilians employed in rounded numbers, 1980

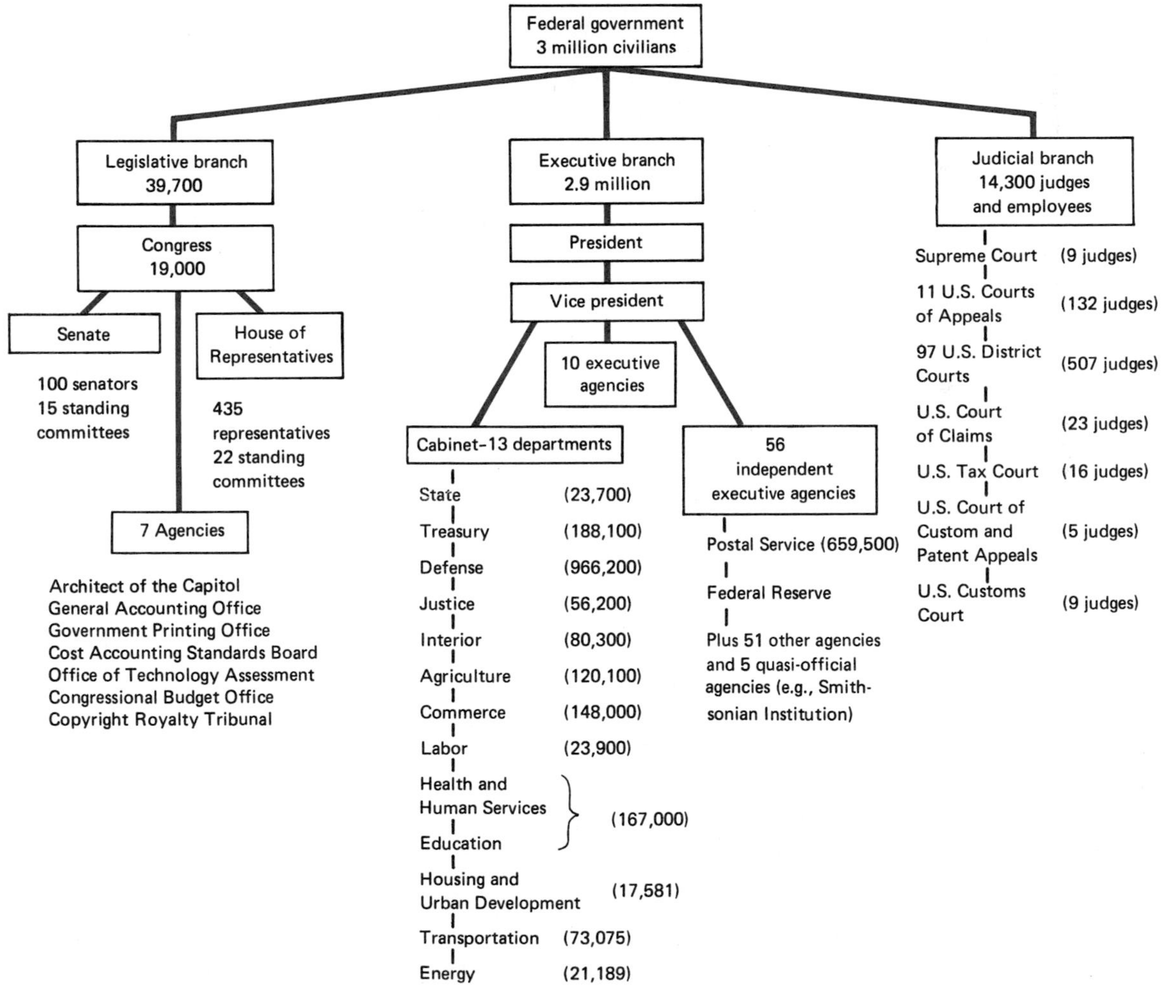

Source: U.S. Government Manual, 1980–1981 and various U.S. government agency and department publications.

four-year term and who cannot hold this office for more than two consecutive terms. Figure 21-1 outlines the structure of the executive branch.

There are 13 Cabinet level departments, 59 agency subsidiaries, and over 1,200 bureaus and commissions. These bureaus and commissions are listed in the annual edition of the *United States Government Manual*. They are responsible for some 1,040 domestic programs and 1,256 advisory boards. There are over 45 million entitlement checks mailed each month either directly or indirectly by the federal government. These entitlement outlays account for over 44 percent of the federal budget.

Some 99 percent of federal jobs are either protected by law under the Civil Service Act or represent employment for specific terms because of specialized skill that is required. This makes federal employees hard to fire or replace. The Hatch Act (1939) also protects them from political coercion and loss of jobs by the party in power.

Not only does the federal government impose its departments, its rules, and its programs on the people, but it is the direct owner of a huge part of the land of the U.S. Some 760 million acres, or 33.5 percent, of the total land of the U.S. is owned by the federal government! As Table 21-1 and Figure 21-2 show, the western states have more of their land owned by government than is the case in the Eastern half of the U.S. The percentage of all land owned by government increases substantially if that owned by state and local government is included.

TABLE 21-1
Portion of States Owned by the Government

Alabama	3.4%	Missouri	4.9%
Alaska	96.4%	Montana	29.7%
Arizona	42.8%	Nebraska	1.4%
Arkansas	9.7%	Nevada	86.6%
California	45.2%	New Hampshire	12.3%
Colorado	36.1%	New Jersey	2.7%
Connecticut	0.3%	New Mexico	33.6%
Delaware	3.2%	New York	0.8%
District		North Carolina	6.3%
of Columbia	26.2%	North Dakota	5.2%
Florida	10.1%	Ohio	1.3%
Georgia	6.0%	Oklahoma	3.5%
Hawaii	9.9%	Oregon	52.6%
Idaho	63.7%	Pennsylvania	2.3%
Illinois	1.6%	Rhode Island	1.1%
Indiana	2.1%	South Carolina	5.9%
Iowa	0.6%	South Dakota	6.7%
Kansas	1.4%	Tennessee	6.7%
Kentucky	5.3%	Texas	1.9%
Louisiana	3.7%	Utah	66.1%
Maine	0.7%	Vermont	4.7%
Maryland	3.2%	Virginia	9.4%
Massachusetts	1.7%	Washington	29.5%
Michigan	9.4%	West Virginia	6.9%
Minnesota	6.7%	Wisconsin	5.2%
Mississippi	5.5%	Wyoming	47.8%

Source: General Services Administration

Figure 21-2

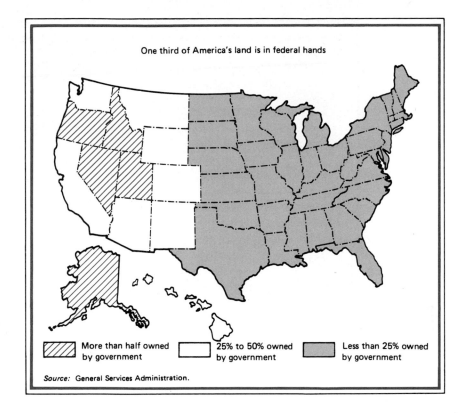

Source: General Services Administration.

GOVERNMENT EXPENDITURES AND THE SIZE OF GOVERNMENT

The data presented above make it quite clear that our economy is significantly affected by government. While many Americans tend to pride themselves on their free enterprise system, they overlook the fact that government itself is big business even if government is less intrusive in the U.S. then in nearly any other country of the world.

How do we measure the size of government in a meaningful way? First, as we know, relative size is often more easily interpreted than absolute size. Thus, one index or measure of government would be that proportion of national income that is comprised of government expenditures. Such proportions appear in Table 21-2. From the table we can see that in 1929 all government expenditure was only 8.5 percent of GNP—1.4 percent from federal expenditures and 7.2 from state and local. Thus, in the 1920s government was small and the federal government was tiny.

A dramatic reversal in these percentages occurred during World War II, and the numbers for 1945 substantiate this. Government accounted for 39.0 percent of GNP; and of this amount 35.1 percent was federal expenditure and only 3.9 percent was state and local. After the war, the federal government's proportion sank to much lower levels, but in the 1970s it remained in the

TABLE 21-2
Government Expenditures and Gross National Product

Calendar years 1929–1980: Dollar amounts in billions.

Year	Gross national product	Government expenditures: Amount — Total	Federal	State and local[1]	As a percentage of GNP — Total	Federal	State and local
1929	103.4	8.8	1.4	7.4	8.6	1.4	7.2
1940	100.0	14.2	6.1	8.1	14.2	6.1	8.1
1945	212.4	82.8	74.6	8.2	39.0	35.1	3.9
1950	286.5	38.5	18.7	19.8	13.4	6.5	6.9
1955	400.0	75.0	44.5	30.5	18.4	11.1	7.3
1960	506.5	100.3	53.7	46.6	19.8	10.6	9.2
1965	691.1	138.4	67.3	71.1	20.0	9.7	10.3
1970	992.1	220.1	95.7	124.4	22.2	9.6	12.6
1975	1549.2	339.9	122.7	217.2	21.9	7.9	14.0
1980	2626.1	534.7	198.9	335.8	20.4	7.6	12.8

[1]State and local expenditures include expenditures for grants-in-aid from the federal government and are not included in the federal data, to avoid duplication.
Sources: *Survey of Current Business* (U.S. Department of Commerce), as compiled in The Economic Report of the President, annually.

neighborhood of 8 percent. In contrast, since the end of World War II state and local government expenditures have risen slowly but steadily from 3.9 percent to around 13 percent. Thus, while the federal government remains large at around 8 percent of GNP, the growth of government in the postwar period has been mostly a growth on the state and local level. In 1980 for *all* government, it was about 20.4 percent of GNP.

THE BUDGET PROCESS

The Budget and Accounting Act of 1921 created the Bureau of the Budget, which required that the executive office plan a federal budget for each fiscal year. After reorganization in July 1, 1970 the Office of Management and Budget (OMB) was established, under whose auspices the federal budget is now initially planned. In 1974 the Congressional Budget and Impoundment Control Act was passed, which introduced some modifications in the budgetary process to be discussed below.

The budget is a spending plan for the government initiated by the execu-

TABLE 21-3
Government Budget Receipts by Source (billions of dollars)

	1977	1978	Estimate 1979	Estimate 1980	Projection 1979 1981	Projection 1979 1982	Projection 1979 1983
Individual income taxes	156.7	178.8	190.1	223.9	262.9	301.7	339.9
Corporation income taxes	54.9	58.9	62.5	69.1	77.7	86.5	94.6
Social insurance taxes and contributions	108.7	124.1	141.9	160.1	186.3	208.4	225.9
Excise taxes	17.5	20.2	25.5	31.1	34.7	36.7	39.5
Other	19.0	18.3	19.7	21.1	22.4	24.3	26.4
Total	356.9	400.4	439.6	505.4	583.9	657.6	726.1

Source: U.S. Office of Management and Budget, annual.

tive office, which sets the national priorities. It is a government blueprint whose size and distribution operates as a crucial instrument of economic policy for the nation. It is a significant, but certainly not exclusive, factor nudging economic variables in expansionary or contractionary directions.

The federal *budget* is a taxing and spending prescription for a fiscal year.

The **budget** is not only a spending plan but a taxing prescription as well for the twelve-month period called the fiscal year. Prior to 1977 the budget covered the fiscal year beginning on July 1 of the current year and on to June 30 of the following year. Since 1977 the fiscal year begins on October 1 and ends on September 30 of the following year. Tables 21-3 and 21-4 and Figures 21-3 and 21-4 provide some data on receipts and outlays.

Figure 21-3

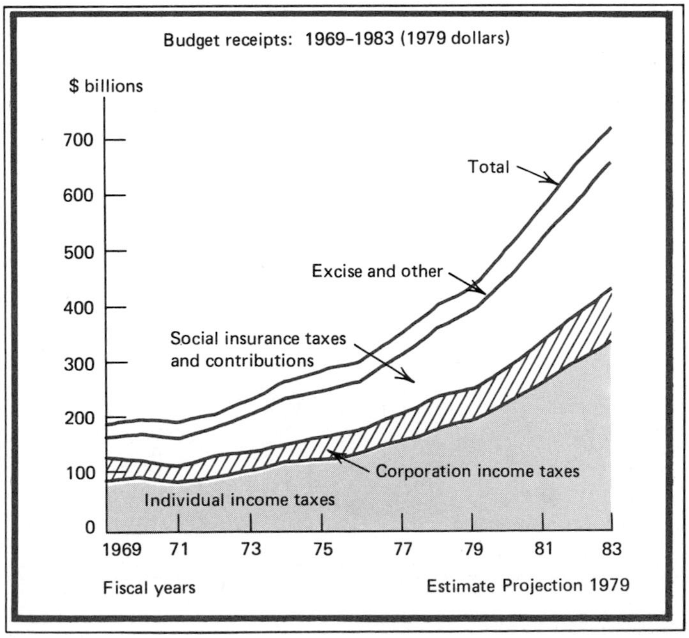

Figure 21-4

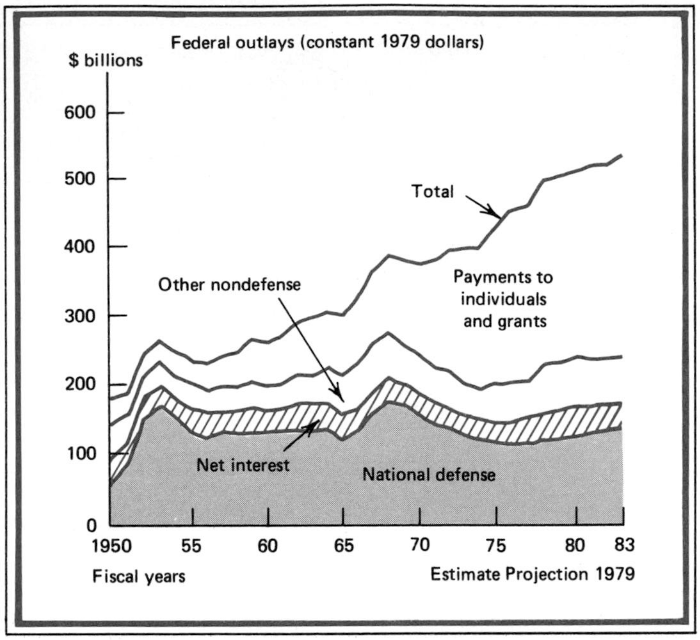

TABLE 21-4
Percentage Composition of Government Budget Outlays

Description	Actual			Estimate		Projection 1979		
	1969	1973	1977	1979	1980	1981	1982	1983
National defense:								
Direct federal payments to individuals	1.3	1.8	2.0	2.0	2.1	2.1	2.1	2.1
Grants to states and localities	*	*	*	*	*	*	*	*
Other	41.7	28.4	22.2	21.5	21.6	22.1	22.5	22.8
Subtotal, national defense	43.0	30.2	24.3	23.5	23.7	24.2	24.6	24.9
Nondefense:								
Direct federal payments to individuals	24.6	33.5	39.5	37.4	37.5	38.6	39.2	39.9
Payments for individuals through states and localities	4.0	5.3	5.7	5.4	5.4	5.5	5.5	5.5
All other grants to states and localities	6.9	11.6	11.3	11.5	11.1	10.8	10.7	10.3
Net interest	6.9	7.0	7.5	8.0	8.0	7.8	7.3	6.7
Other	14.5	12.4	11.8	14.0	14.2	13.1	12.8	12.6
Subtotal, nondefense	57.0	69.8	75.7	76.5	76.3	75.8	75.4	75.1
Total	100.0	100.0	100.0	100.0	100.0	100.0	100.0	100.0

*Less than 0.1%.
Source: U.S. Office of Management and Budget, annual.

Planning the federal budget takes 18 months and has four phases: executive formulation and transmittal, congressional authorization and appropriation, budget execution and control, and review and audit.

There are four main interrelated phases—executive formulation and transmittal, congressional authorization and appropriation, budget execution and control, and review and audit.

The Sequence: Agencies First

Initial steps to building a budget occur some 18 months before the fiscal year in which it is to be implemented. Thus, work on the 1981 budget beginning in October 1, 1981 started around April of 1980.

When preliminary plans are to be devised by the President, he must decide the needs and the behavior of the economy 18 months hence. With the Council of Economic Advisors, the Department of the Treasury, and the OMB, he must predict but without a crystal ball. Will taxes have to be increased or cut? Does the private sector have to be stimulated or cooled down? What of military expenditures and foreign aid? Programs for each agency of the government must be assessed and policy issues identified. After about three months these tentative budget and policy determinations are sent to the various agencies as guidelines from which revisions based on their evaluations are made. After another two months, these agencies such as HHS, HUD, and the BEA submit their budget requests for the coming fiscal year to the OMB. Figure 21-5 illustrates the budget sequence and timing schedule.

OMB Rehash

With 13 months to fiscal countdown, the OMB begins around September to confer with individual agencies over their budget requests, to arrive at a final budget program to submit to the President along with an overall tax policy. After any final appeals by the agencies are considered, the President then makes a final judgment. After these appeals the President's decision is final. Around November 10 the Congressional Budget Committee (CBC) receives an estimate from the OMB on the cost of continuing federal programs at the *current* level. By December 31, the Joint Economic Committee (JEC), composed of members of both the House and Senate, gives the CBC a revision of the OMB figures.

Executive Budget

In January, within 15 days after Congress convenes, the President submits his budget to Congress, in particular to the CBC, in books containing more than 1,000 pages itemizing the details of his proposals. As a consequence of the New Congressional Budget and Impoundment Control Act of 1974, the Congressional Budget Office (CBO) was set up to help the House and Senate committees evaluate the cost and economic impact of the new budget proposals and to look for possible alternatives to deal with various issues. There are also the tax-writing and the appropriations committees in each house that review specific bills. Many programs are authorized for a specific number of years, some indefinitely, referred to as open-ended. Other programs require authorization on an annual basis. The procedure on evaluating appropriations and changing revenue laws begins in the House Ways and Means Committee and in the

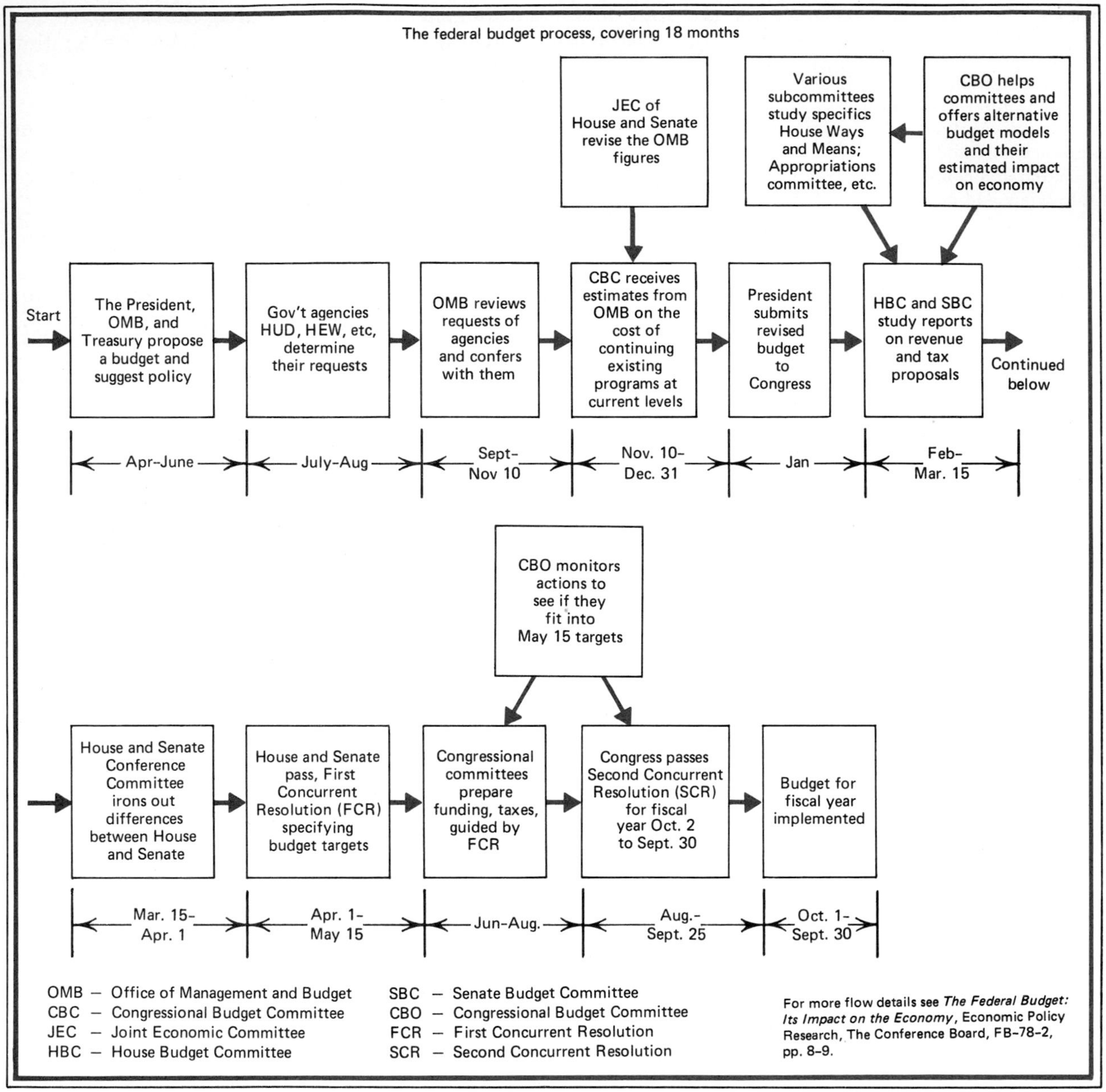

Figure 21-5

Appropriations Committee of the House of Representatives, which make use of a number of subcommittees to study specifics of budget and tax proposals. As parts of the budget are approved by the House after they come out of the House Budget Committee (HBC), they are forwarded to the Senate, where a similar process is followed. Eventually, the CBC receives all of the spending and taxing plans of the various legislative committees by March 15.

Then the CBO provides alternative budgets—high and low, and ongoing—for the committee to consider along with the likely impact of each alternative on employment and other economic variables.

Where disagreement between the House and Senate exists, a conference committee composed of members from both houses resolves the issues and submits a report to the House for approval. This is to be done by April 1.

By May 15, with 6 months remaining to October 1, the House and Senate must vote a concurrent resolution specifying and setting budget targets. These often differ from the President's initial plans. Legislative committees then prepare funding guided by the resolution. During the summer months of June through August, the CBO keeps tabs on funding to determine whether the total will come out above or below the May 15 target. By September 15 at the latest, Congress must pass a second concurrent resolution that sets binding limits on spending and taxes for the fiscal year beginning October 1. If bills passed prior to September 15 do not conform to the second resolution, they must be adjusted so that they do conform. Hence, the appropriations process itself goes from May to September.

The new Congressional Budget and Impoundment Act of 1974 provides authority to the President to regulate the rate—not the level—of spending by delaying the spending of the allocated funds over the fiscal period, but the President's decision may be overturned by either house at any time. He may also cancel funds, subject to the approval of Congress if Congress acts within 45 days of a continuous session. Essentially, this implies that without Congressional approval the President cannot withhold funded money from being spent.

Uncontrolled Outlays

Over half the federal budget consists of *uncontrollable outlays* that the law requires be spent; most are domestic assistance programs.

A major part of the budget now contains payments that must be carried out by law. This biggest single category of expenditures is called uncontrollables, because once Congress provides the legislation and the funding for them, the monies must be spent. The appropriations cannot be changed through the regular budget process. They can only be modified by amendments to the existing law or by repealing the law. Congress is timid about doing this, since they represent transfer payments to large voting blocs—legal entitlements to all eligible recipients. Examples are listed in Table 21-5. Others not shown include veterans benefits, food stamps, unemployment money, and interest on the debt. Social Security taxes continually rise to keep the program solvent. To change this law would be painful to both Congress and consumers, although it is inequitable and actuarially unsound.

The major thrust in federal spending in the last 25 years has come in civil outlays or domestic assistance, most of it handled by HHS. These expenditures are listed in a blue covered catalog, *Federal Domestic Assistance,* often referred to by federal employees as the "goody book." It has over 800 pages and lists nearly 1,200 programs for which federal money is available. There is much feeding at the trough. In 1975, for example there were National Science Foundation (NSF) grants for $260,000 for the study of the origins and nature of passionate love. Most of the spending, however, goes toward expenditures for human services such as Medicare, Medicaid, and Social Security, which constitutes the largest item.

In 1967 these open-ended outlays and fixed costs made up 36 percent of the budget. By 1976 they were $206.8 billion out of a total budget of $394.4 billion, or some 52.4 percent, as can be determined from Table 21-5. By 1980 the ratio is projected to be $275 out of $476.7 billion, or almost 58 percent.

TABLE 21-5
Uncontrollable Outlays in the 1982 Federal Budget

Social Security and railroad retirement benefits	$165.4 bil.
Outlays from previous contracts and obligations	$118.8 bil.
Net interest	$ 75.2 bil.
Medicare, medicaid	$ 65.3 bil.
Federal civilian retirement benefits	$ 30.1 bil.
Unemployment assistance	$ 24.1 bil.
Welfare and assistance programs	$ 21.4 bil.
Food and nutritional aid	$ 17.3 bil.
Military retirement benefits	$ 16.0 bil.
Other obligations	$ 32.8 bil.
Total	$566.4 bil., or 76.6% of all federal spending

Source: U.S. Office of Management and Budget

THE BUDGET: INFLOWS, OUTFLOWS, AND BALANCE

Having discussed the budgetary process at considerable length, we now want to look at a sample of the results of that process. It is important to have an understanding of the budgetary process and its results because of the impact they have on the level of national income. When the government spends, it gives purchasing power to someone. When the government taxes, it takes purchasing power away from someone. If the amount of spending just equals the amount of taxes collected, then the injections of purchasing power just equal the leakages, and the budget is said to be balanced. If spending exceeds tax collections, the budget is in deficit. And if tax receipts exceed spending it is in surplus. Whether or not the budget is projected to be in surplus or in deficit has important implications for the state of business activity. When we develop the theory of income determination this role of government will become explicit. For now, we wish to become acquainted with the kinds of taxes that are used, and the types of expenditures that are made.

Inflows

From Figure 21-6, a pie-chart estimate for 1979, we can observe the ingredients of the federal fiscal pie. Thus, individual income taxes account for 38 percent of the federal government's tax collections. Adding to this the 13 percent in corporate income taxes, we have a total of 51 percent of the pie coming from income taxes of one sort or another. Another 28 percent of the federal government's revenues are collected under Social Security arrangements. Both income taxes and Social Security taxes are collected through withholding from workers' paychecks, leaving take-home pay, or spendable income, equal to gross pay less withholdings. Although the employer pays half of his employees' Social Security, in fact the worker pays it because it includes the wage the employer would be willing to hire him for. Thus, we should add this 28 percent to the category of income or payroll taxes, so the total comes to a full 79 percent that comes out of income.

Taxes such as those on gasoline and long distance telephone calls, and other taxes such as import tariffs and license fees, account for 9 percent of the federal government's revenues. These taxes take spendable income from the pockets of the taxpayer, but in a different way from income or payroll taxes. They raise the price that the seller must charge for the item that is subject to the tax. Thus, excise taxes have price effects in addition to income effects on consumer spending.

One of the ingredients that go into making the pie is borrowing. The existence of borrowing means that the government does not collect enough taxes to pay for all its appropriations, and so it must borrow money to make up the difference. This net borrowing represents the extent of the government's deficit in the year being discussed.

Federal income taxes have risen sharply since 1930. Between 1930 and 1950, federal tax receipts rose from approximately 3.2 percent of GNP to 17.5 percent. Since 1950, the ratio of taxes to GNP has settled at approximately 20 percent.

Outflows

Shifting now to the second pie chart in Figure 21-6, we can see how the pie is divided. The largest category is 37 percent that is paid out to individuals—Social Security, veterans benefits, welfare payments. These are called transfer

Figure 21-6

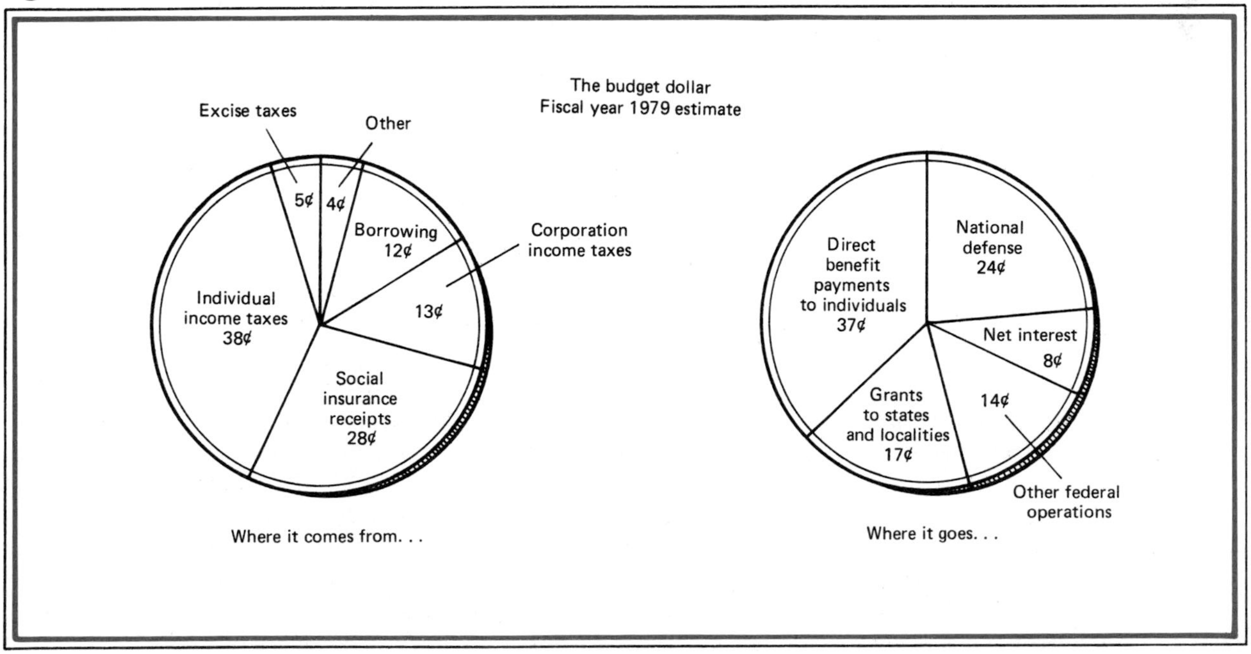

payments because the government's role in this activity is principally to transfer income from those who pay taxes to those who receive benefits. In this manner the government plays the role of reallocating, or redistributing, income among members of society.

The second largest category is 24 percent for national defense. While necessary, it is surely the most dismal of all figures in the budget. One can imagine all the prosperity that could be conferred upon our citizens if $100 billion worth of resources were to be available to produce consumer goods instead of the instruments of war—if we could only feel safe so we could trans-

TABLE 21-6
Federal Budget Receipts and Outlays, 1789–1980 (millions of dollars)

Fiscal Year	Receipts	Outlays	Surplus or deficit (−)	Fiscal Year	Receipts	Outlays	Surplus or deficit (−)
1789–1849	1,160	1,090	+70	1948	41,774	29,773	+12,001
1850–1900	14,462	15,453	−991	1949	39,437	38,834	+603
1901–1905	2,797	2,678	+119	1950	39,485	42,597	−3,112
1906–1910	3,143	3,196	−52				
1911–1915	3,517	3,568	−49	1951	51,646	45,546	+6,100
1916–1920	17,286	40,195	−22,909	1952	66,204	67,721	−1,517
				1953	69,574	76,107	−6,533
1921	5,571	5,062	+509	1954	69,719	70,890	−1,170
1922	4,026	3,289	+736	1955	65,469	68,509	−3,041
1923	3,853	3,140	+713	1956	74,547	70,460	+4,087
1924	3,871	2,908	+963	1957	79,990	76,741	+3,249
1925	3,641	2,924	+717	1958	79,636	82,575	−2,939
1926	3,795	2,930	+865	1959	79,249	92,104	−12,855
1927	4,013	2,857	+1,155	1960	92,492	92,223	+269
1928	3,900	2,961	+939				
1929	3,862	3,127	+734	1961	94,389	97,795	−3,406
1930	4,058	3,320	+738	1962	99,676	106,813	−7,137
				1963	106,560	111,311	−4,751
1931	3,116	3,577	−462	1964	112,662	118,584	−5,922
1932	1,924	4,659	−2,735	1965	116,833	118,430	−1,596
1933	1,997	4,598	−2,602	1966	130,856	134,652	−3,796
1934	3,015	6,645	−3,630	1967	149,552	158,254	−8,702
1935	3,706	6,497	−2,791	1968	153,671	178,833	−25,161
1936	3,997	8,422	−4,425	1969	187,784	184,548	+3,236
1937	4,956	7,733	−2,777	1970	193,743	196,588	−2,845
1938	5,588	6,765	−1,177				
1939	4,979	8,841	−3,862	1971	188,392	211,425	−23,033
1940	6,361	9,456	−3,095	1972	208,649	232,021	−23,373
				1973	232,225	247,074	−14,849
1941	8,621	13,634	−5,013	1974	264,932	269,620	−4,688
1942	14,350	35,114	−20,764	1975	280,997	326,151	−45,154
1943	23,649	78,533	−54,884	1976	300,005	366,418	−66,413
1944	44,276	91,280	−47,004	1977	357,762	402,710	−44,498
1945	45,216	92,690	−47,474	1978	401,997	450,804	−48,807
1946	39,327	55,183	−15,856	1979	465,940	493,635	−27,695
1947	38,394	34,532	+3,862	1980	520,050	579,613	−59,563

Sources: Department of the Treasury and Office of Management and Budget as compiled in The Economic Report of the President, annually.

form swords into plowshares. Grants to states and localities constitute 17 percent of the federal government's expenditure.

Interest payments make up the 8 percent of the total payments. These are payments on the national debt and also represent transfers from taxpayers to bondholders. That is, they do not represent payments for the services of labor, but represent payments necessary to divert financial capital away from other borrowers in favor of the government as a borrower. The final 14 percent of the pie pays for all the remaining federal operations. When you think of it, this is really a small portion of the overall federal budget.

The Budget's Imbalance

A budget *deficit* occurs when outlays are greater than tax receipts; the government borrows to make up the difference.

In Table 21-6 there are listed the actual receipts and outlays for many fiscal years of the federal government's operations. From the string of minus signs since 1970, we can see that the budget has been in **deficit** every year. This means that the national debt has increased in each of those years in which a deficit occurred.

We shall not jump to the conclusion that somehow the government is in danger of declaring bankruptcy, as an individual might if he or she were drifting further and further into debt year after year. The government is not a profit making but a service providing institution. It could pay off all its debt tomorrow simply by printing money if that were in the best interest of the people. But it is not, so it will not.

The reason the government bothers to collect taxes and borrow money is to divert purchasing power from the hands of the citizens to its own hands. If it were to spend by creating money alone, the result would be a disastrous inflation. Responsible government does not print money for its expenditures—it either taxes or borrows.

Extensive borrowing to finance a series of budget deficits by the federal government has brought the national debt to the level of over $900 billion. To the extent that U.S. residents own the debt, then paying interest on this debt simply means that one U.S. resident pays money to another, and the total amount of goods and services produced in the economy is, except in minor ways, unaffected. On the other hand, to the extent that foreigners own the debt, when they collect the interest they may spend it on goods produced in the U.S. and this leaves fewer goods left over for U.S. residents to consume. For years the amount owned by foreigners was very small, but it became significant in the 1970s. Chapter 29 will cover in more detail the controversial issue of who bears the burden of the national debt.

GOVERNMENT REGULATION

The foregoing section emphasized the spending and taxing activities of government. Government agencies also affect households income, spending and saving decisions, as well as business decisions, by the kind of housing, health, ecological, lending, safety, and credit conditions it mandates. Government regulations, expenditures, and transfer payments have an impact on the aggregate economy affecting employment, national income, interest rates, and capital formation, all important ingredients in stabilizing aggregate demand in the macroeconomy.

In order to perform its various roles and objectives, the government has evolved a regulatory network of government agencies. We have catalogued the benefits to be derived from government regulation. There are, however, costs and potential dangers in government efforts to protect the public if agencies should become too zealous.

It may take only a small number of people and expenditure to enforce a vast array of regulations—more so these days, given the tremendous technological explosion in communications systems that we have seen over the past few decades. Direct dialing, computers with vast storage capacities, electronic banking, all make it feasible for regulators to regulate in many areas that they would never have bothered to try to enter a few years back. While we doubt that the paternalistic Big Brother society that George Orwell described in his work *1984* will come about, it is nevertheless the case that his vision of the technological revolution that could make it possible is upon us.

There is concern that the economy's productivity has been impaired by overzealous regulatory agencies.

Finally, the economy can become overburdened with regulations impairing the supply side of the economy, its productivity and vitality. Supply side economics will be taken up in a later chapter.

The Regulatory Maze

Figure 21-7 depicts in a rough way the regulatory maze that anyone dealing with the U.S. today must sort through. The underlying structure of regulation is depicted by the vertical lines. When the federal government, under constitutional authority, established the Interstate Commerce Commission (ICC), its focus was largely on railroad transportation and ultimately on other interstate transport systems. With each of the vertical lines, we have in a broad sense industry-wide regulation—radio (FCC), aircraft (CAB and FAA), utilities, food and drugs (FPC and FDA), banks (FRB and FHLBB).

This pattern of regulation on an industry basis continued to hold up until the 1950s and 1960s with one exception, the Securities and Exchange Commission (SEC). It was formed in the 1930s in the wake of the great crash of the stock market in October 1929. Financial losses were severe and public outcry led to demands for regulation over the market for stocks and bonds for large firms in all industries. It is, therefore, an across-industry regulatory agency. It was 20 years before additional regulatory commissions of significant impact were instituted, but then came a rash of them.

The Consumer Product Safety Commission (CPSC) was established in the wake of the furor raised by Ralph Nader when he testified before Congress that some small automobiles were unsafe at any speed. The idea that producers should ensure the safety of their customers has social merit, but safety requirements may also be costly. Economists have proposed that cost-benefit analysis be used in appraising the regulations that agencies and commissions impose. In general, so long as additional benefits exceed additional costs, a regulation is appropriate. But if the extra costs exceed the extra benefits, it should be

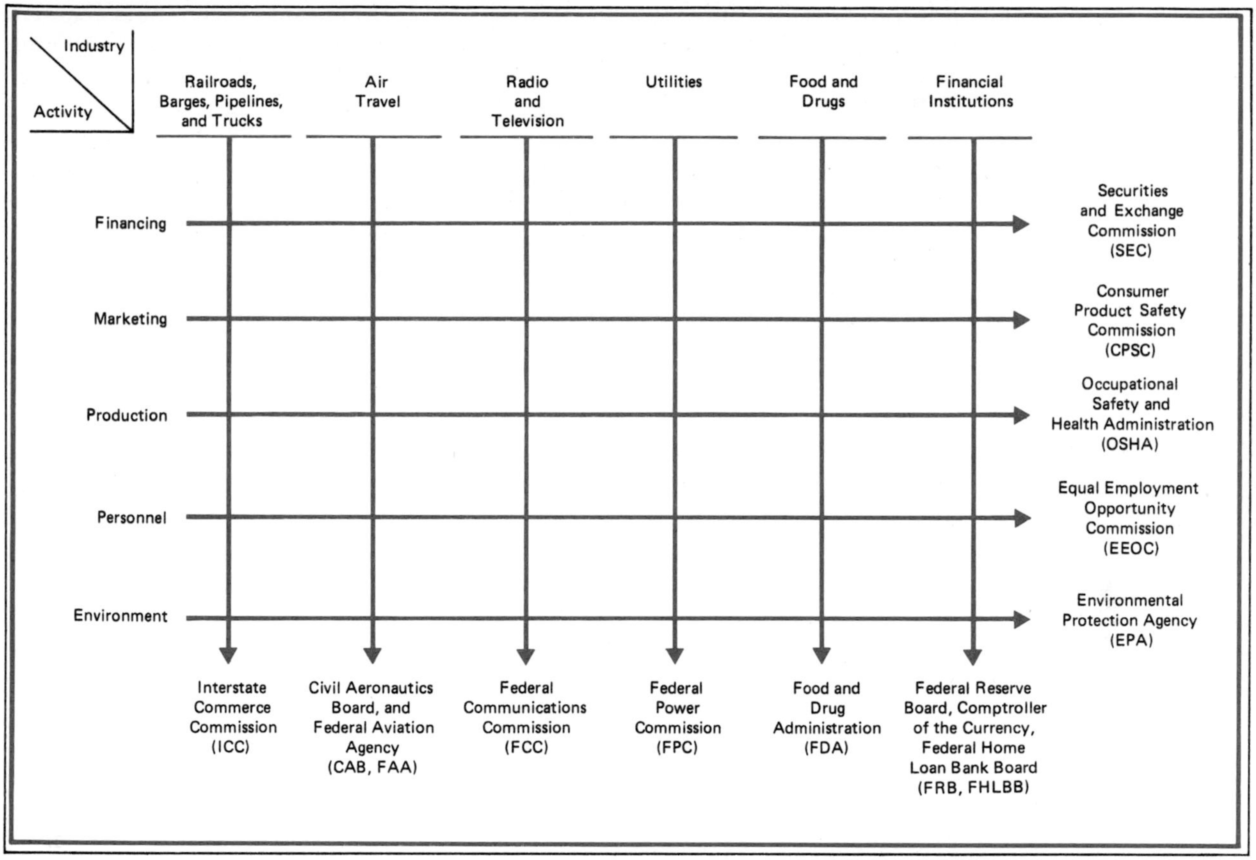

Figure 21-7

dropped. There is little doubt that many benefits have derived from the actions of the regulatory commissions, but there is also little doubt that a tremendous burden has been placed on the society in order to obtain these benefits. The business firm that must file reports will suffer costs. These costs should be added to the administrative costs of the regulatory agency in order to arrive at the total cost of the regulation.

The Equal Employment Opportunity Commission (EEOC) was formed in response to alleged discrimination in employment. Back in the 1940s, job and school application forms had spaces for one to check race, sex, marital status. In the 1950s, in response to pressure to eliminate discrimination, the courts held that people need not fill out such spaces or file pictures that would allow race and sex to be identified. This would, presumably, help prevent discrimination in opportunities. Ironically, in order to do its job of preventing discrimination the EEOC had to know when discrimination occurs, and to find this information it was forced to reinstitute the practice of identifying race, sex, and the like.

There is too much paperwork, nearly everyone agrees. For example, *Newsweek* reported (December 15, 1975, p. 41) that Standard Oil of Indiana yearly sends 250 final reports totaling 24,000 pages (backed by 20,000 subsidiary reports) to 41 government agencies. In the early 1970s the Commission on Federal Paperwork was established. It reported that the various federal agencies produce 10 billion sheets of forms, applications, and reports each year at a cost of around $40 billion. It was estimated that business spent 35.6 million man-hours filling out forms. The new commission itself, with a staff of 36 and a budget of $4.6 million in 1976, has generated a pile of paper. The commission was to be phased out in 1978 after issuing its report.

After adding together all the costs of having and enforcing the regulation, the next step is to place a value on the benefits derived from it. This is not an easy task, and reasonable people may disagree. But the very act of attempting to construct a benefit estimate helps place the decision to regulate or not to regulate in perspective.

CHAPTER SUMMARY

Government is the exercise of authority in controlling the actions of its citizens in promoting the common welfare, and in serving as the final power in settling disputes. Government evolved as people realized that labor and resources are scarce and needed an authority to establish the ownership and define the rights of property so that these scarce resources could be employed and developed efficiently without duplication of labor effort and wasteful destruction of private property. A person has property rights to things if he or she can make exclusive decisions about how the property will be used or transferred to another. Such a person is called the owner.

The government is the final authority in the use of force to settle disagreements and contract violations. Contracts are promises and duties freely and mutually agreed upon, that when broken by one of the participants subjects the violator to punishment. Contracts therefore allow for the continuity and predictability of economic and social relations, hence for social stability.

In situations where costs are imposed on another who is not a participant to the contract, an external cost is said to exist. When the transactions cost to the offended party is too high for him to remove or negotiate with the offending parties, the government can enter and redefine property rights to remove the externality or have the offenders compensate the victim.

As the population grew and with it externalities, it became necessary for government to require individuals to subordinate some of their private preferences to collective decisions. It also began to use taxes to relieve the social pressures caused by large disparities in income among groups in the population, and to otherwise redefine property rights in order to achieve a more equitable and socially stable distribution of income.

The government is the next largest spending sector in the U.S. economy after the household sector. Its size and role has grown greatly since the 1930s, when direct intervention by the government was believed to be imperative in lifting the economy out of its doldrums. One role of the U.S. government is the allocation function—what goods and services to spend its budget on. Another is the distribution function of how much recipients get of what is allocated. Another role is for it to provide goods that the private sector cannot or will not provide, such as highways and roads. The government must use fiscal policy—taxes and spending—as well as monetary policy to carry out its stabilization function of stable prices, full employment, and steady economic growth. The government must protect the health and safety of the public as well as maintain competition in the marketplace. This is carried out through its regulatory apparatus. Although the relative size of the federal government has leveled off in recent years, the local and state governments have continued to grow in response to greater demands for services by the public. The size of government and the kinds of things it does developed into a major political issue in the 1980s.

The federal budget is a taxing and spending prescription for the fiscal period beginning on October 1 and ending on September 30 of the following year. Planning the budget begins some 18 months prior to October 1.

The budget is initially formulated by the President's office and then is sent to Congress, where it goes through the House Ways and Means Committee, the Appropriations Committee, and the Budget Committee. It is then sent to the Senate for similar processing. Disagreements are resolved by joint sessions of committees drawn from both houses, with the budget process under continuous evaluation by the Congressional Budget Office. By September 15 at the latest, Congress must pass a second concurrent resolution setting binding limits on spending and taxes for the upcoming fiscal year.

More than half the budget consists of uncontrollable outlays that the law requires must be spent. Most of it goes toward domestic assistance programs such as Medicare and Social Security. Taxes constitute about 90 percent of the budget inflows and borrowing the remaining 10 percent. The largest budget outflow is for welfare programs, with military spending second. When outlays are greater than tax receipts, the budget is in deficit and the government borrows to make up the difference.

To perform its various functions, a large network of government agencies has evolved. There is concern that the economy's productivity has been impaired in the last decade by overzealous regulators.

QUESTIONS

1. In 1976 government figures showed that $11.4 billion would have raised all the poor out of poverty (as then defined) in the U.S. Yet some $30 billion was spent on programs to raise the poor above the poverty line with 5 million people still ending up below the poverty level. (*Race and Economics*, Thomas Sowell, D. McKay Co., New York, 1975, p. 195) Can you explain these figures? Does it suggest a better way to distribute the $30 billion? Why is it not likely to happen?
2. Some localities have legally changed the name of manhole covers to personhole covers. Does this imply that the government can always change behavior given its legal monopoly in the use of force? Can you give examples where government laws have failed to change behavior of a large segment of the population? Where it has succeeded?
3. Many citizens are disillusioned with the results of the government's economic policies. Many want the government to reduce the size of the deficit while giving more attention to their particular financial problems. Are they being inconsistent and irrational? Shortsighted?
4. Do you believe the government should decide for you what is safe to use or not use? Would your answer change if the government required you to jog at least two miles a day because they claim young people are in poor shape? Is there a way the government could get you to run two miles a day without passing a law forcing you to jog?
5. Do you believe civil servants should be able to be fired more easily for incompetence? What arguments can you give against it?
6. Most localities give anywhere from one hour to the whole day off on election day even though polling places are open after working hours. Private firms in many instances give some time off but without pay. In one study for Austin, Texas, it was

found that overall voter participation was 58.1 percent, whereas for city employees it was 87.6 percent. Why the difference? What relationship, if any, would you predict exists between the income of bureaucrats and the growth of the public sector?

7. A study by Bartell Associates Inc. observed 100 male and 100 female police officers in Philadelphia from mid 1976 to mid 1978. It concluded that women officers on patrol need more assistance, are assaulted more often, sustain more injuries, and have more vehicle accidents than male officers. It tentatively recommended that women be used for nonpatrol duties. A judge later ruled that the city hire women as officers until they make up 40 percent of the police force. He also ordered that the city not use physical tests not approved by the court, of which 97 percent of male applicants passed whereas less than 33 percent of the female applicants did.
   a. Are property rights being redefined here? Whose?
   b. Is there a conflict between equity and efficiency here?
   c. Should equity always take priority over efficiency? Why or why not?
   d. Are any externalities created by the court's decision? If so, on whom?
8. Industrialized countries tend to spend a larger portion of their GNP on government expenditures than the less industrialized countries. Is there a logical, economic explanation for this difference?
9. What is the largest source of government revenues? The largest item under government expenditures?
10. The 96th Congress of the U.S. (1978–1980) had 199 lawyers out of 434 members of The House of Representatives (more than any other group), and 67 lawyers out of 100 in the Senate. State legislatures also have a disproportionate share of lawyers. Might this have any relation to the number of rules and regulations passed through Congress and state legislatures each year?
11. Do you believe a law should be passed that limits government spending to a given percentage of GNP, say 22 percent? Give the pros and cons.

Chapter 22

Consumption

PROGRESS REPORT

A. Chapter 21 discussed government as one of the major components of aggregate spending in the economy.

B. This chapter covers the largest component of aggregate spending in the economy, namely, consumption spending by households. We shall find that consumption levels depend on income. The higher the level of income, the larger the amount of consumption will be. The relation between consumption and income is called the consumption function. Properties of the aggregate consumption function are discussed. Also, a distinction is made between the short-run consumption function and the long-run consumption function.

C. Chapter 23 covers the third largest component of aggregate spending, aggregate investment – the formation of capital goods by firms in the economy.

THE CONSUMPTION FUNCTION

Prior to 1936, economists believed that interest rates determined the level of aggregate consumption: this is the *classical theory.*

Keynes asserted that aggregate *consumer income* determined aggregate *consumption,* and the relation is a stable one.

Prior to 1936 **classical theory** prevailed. Although it was realized that consumption was related to income, it was believed that the particular level of aggregate consumption was primarily determined by the rate of interest. Since the ultimate goal of economic activity is consumption, the classical economists contended that households would only delay consumption—and save—if their savings earned interest. Thus a rise in the interest rate resulted in a decline in consumption with an increase in savings, while lower interest rates implied relatively more consumption and less saving. Keynes rejected the primacy of the interest rate as the major determinant of the level of the consumption-saving shares. Keynes viewed aggregate saving as a residual out of aggregate income, and this income was the major determinant of the level of consumption, hence of savings too. There were reasons other than the interest rate why households would postpone consumption, such as savings for retirement, for a child's college trust fund, for life insurance, and for family inheritance.

In his book *The General Theory of Employment, Money, and Interest* published in 1936, Keynes asserted that there exists a stable, hence predictable relation between consumption and income. The consumption function became one of the building blocks of Keynes's revision of macroeconomic theory. (Classical and Keynesian theories will be analyzed in Chapter 24.)

The consumption function is an example of a functional relation. The relation is expressed in equation form as $C = f(Y)$. The expression $C = f(Y)$ may

Figure 22-1A

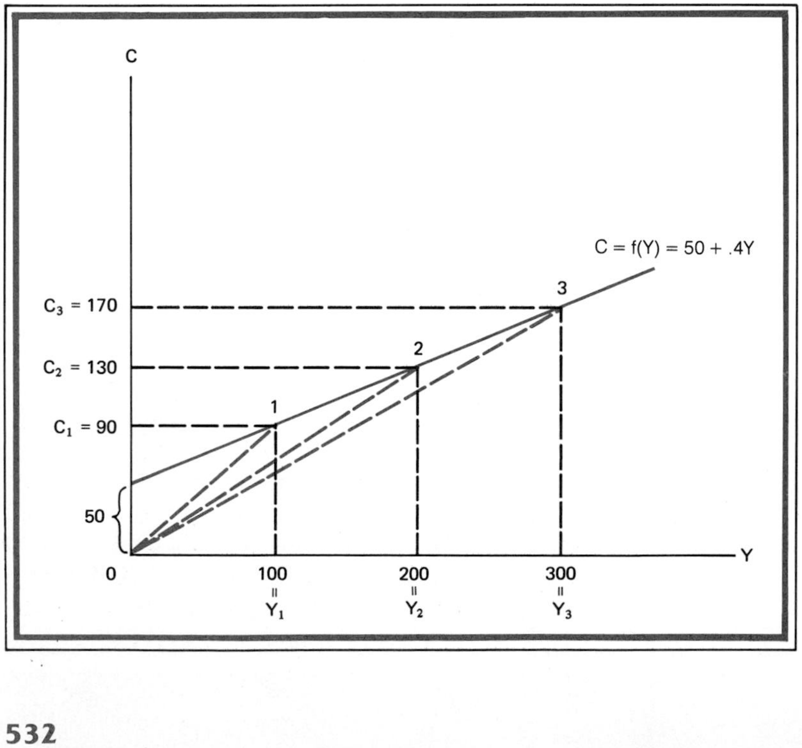

be read "consumption is a function of income," or, "consumption depends on income." In this discussion, income refers to personal income, not to disposable income. In Figure 22-1A, consumption is measured on the vertical axis and income on the horizontal axis.

For purposes of illustration let the specific form of the relation be $C = 50 + .4Y$. By letting income (Y) assume three different values we can show a set of three values for consumption (C).

In table form the numbers are

If Y-	then C-
100	90
200	130
300	170.

The respective pairs of values for Y and C according to the formula are plotted as points *1*, *2*, and *3* in the figure. Since the relation is linear we can draw a straight line through them and this curve is a graphical representation of the relation.

Average Propensity to Consume

The *average propensity to consume* (APC) is the ratio of total consumption to total income.

Point *1* in Figure 22-1A shows the coordinates of consumption equal to 90, measured vertically, and income equal to 100 measured horizontally from zero at the origin. At point *2*, this consumption function indicates that when the level of income is 200, the level of consumption is 130. And at point *3*, consumption is 170 when income reaches 300. In order to see how consumption behaves as income rises, set up a ratio of consumption to income C/Y and compare the ratios at points *1*, *2* and *3*.

Point *1*: $C/Y = 90/100 = .90$
Point *2*: $C/Y = 130/200 = .65$
Point *3*: $C/Y = 170/300 = .57$.

This ratio of C to Y measures the fraction of total consumption out of each level of total income. It is called the average propensity to consume (APC). Hence,

$$APC = \frac{C}{Y} = \frac{\text{total consumption}}{\text{total income}}.$$

The *APC falls as income rises* along a short-run linear consumption function.

Notice how the ratio **declines as income rises** from points *1* to *3*. Both consumption and income are rising in absolute terms, but income is rising faster than consumption. This fact can be seen by noting the declining slant of the dashed guidelines drawn from the origin to each one of the points forming the three triangles. The horizontal side of the triangle formed using point *1* is the income measured by the distance $0Y_1$. The vertical side is the consumption level and is measured by the distance Y_1 to point *1* (or $0C_1$ on the vertical axis). Thus, the APC is the ratio of the vertical side of the triangle to the horizontal side of the triangle with reference to point *1*.

$$APC_1 = \frac{\text{vertical side}}{\text{horizontal side}} = \frac{C_1}{Y_1} = \frac{90}{100} = .9.$$

The triangle formed with point 2 has both a larger vertical and a larger horizontal side than the triangle formed with point 1. However, the *ratio* of the sides is now smaller as shown by the dashed line running from the origin to point 2. It is slanted closer to the horizontal axis, implying that the proportion of consumption relative to income has fallen so that the ratio of *C* to *Y* has decreased (and the ratio of saving (*S*) to income (*Y*) has increased). Therefore, for point 2

$$APC_2 = \frac{C_2}{Y_2} = \frac{130}{200} = .65.$$

Likewise for point 3. The dashed line is even flatter than for point 2, meaning the ratio of the consumption to income has fallen even more, so that

$$APC_3 = \frac{C_3}{Y_3} = \frac{170}{300} = .57.$$

One can see that the average propensity to consume would continue to fall as we moved to points on the function beyond point 3. The figure shows that the average propensity to consume (*APC*) is different at every point, falling as income increases.

Marginal Propensity to Consume

Keynes also hypothesized that there is a fundamental psychological law ". . . that men are disposed as a rule, on the average, to increase their consumption as their income increases, but not by as much as the increase in their income."[1] That is, *changes* in consumption are smaller than changes in income or $0 < \Delta C < \Delta Y$, where delta (Δ) is the symbol for the change in the variable. If each term is divided by the change in income (ΔY), we obtain $0 < \frac{\Delta C}{\Delta Y} < 1$.

The *marginal propensity* *to consume* (MPC) is the ratio of the *change* in total consumption to the *change* in total income. Keynes postulated that MPC is greater than zero and less than one and constitutes a fundamental psychological law: changes in consumption are smaller than changes in income.

The *marginal propensity to consume (MPC)* is defined as the ratio

$$MPC = \frac{\Delta C}{\Delta Y} = \frac{\text{change in consumption}}{\text{change in income}}.$$

Thus, the assertion is that the marginal propensity to consume is greater than zero and less than one, or in shorthand, $0 < MPC < 1$. The *MPC* is something significantly different from the *APC*. Table 22-1 lists the marginal and average propensities to consume.

The marginal propensity to consume (*MPC*) is concerned with *changes* in the level of income, not simply with the absolute level of income. In the table, as income rises from 100 to 200 consumption increases from 90 to 130. The *change* in income is 200 − 100 = 100 and the corresponding change in con-

[1]John Maynard Keynes, *The General Theory of Employment, Money and Interest*, Harcourt, Brace, and World, Inc., 1936, p. 96.

TABLE 22-1
Calculation of the APC and MPC

C	Y	MPC	APC
50	0	—	∞
90	100	.4	.90
130	200	.4	.65
170	300	.4	.57
210	400	.4	.53
250	500	.4	.50

sumption is 130 − 90 = 40. Hence, the ratio of the increase in consumption to the increase in income is .4.

$$MPC = \frac{\text{change in consumption}}{\text{change in income}} = \frac{40}{100} = .40.$$

Figure 22-1B shows the same consumption function as Figure 22-1A. To keep the marginal propensity to consume *(MPC)* from being confused with the average propensity to consume *(APC)*, remember that the average propensity to consume is composed of the ratio of total consumption to total income as measured from the *origin* to points on the consumption line. However, the *MPC* is always measured as the *change* between points *on* the consumption line itself.

Figure 22-1B

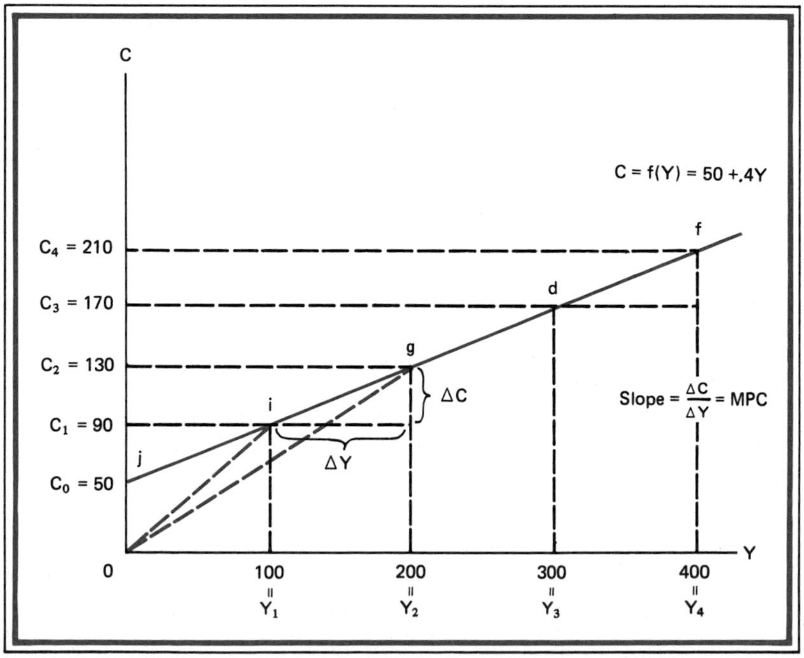

Two points *on* the line are always necessary. For example, the *MPC* can be measured going from point *i* to g on the consumption line. Hence, going from *i* to g the *MPC* is calculated by measuring the ratio of the vertical side to the horizontal side referenced to point *i*, *not* however referenced to the origin. Hence,

$$APC = \frac{\text{consumption level}}{\text{income level}} = \frac{130}{200} = .65, \text{ whereas}$$

$$MPC = \frac{\text{change in consumption level}}{\text{change in income level}} = \frac{130 - 90}{200 - 100} = \frac{40}{100} = .4.$$

The measurement of the *MPC* at point *f* is done with reference to another point *d* (or g, *i*, or *j*) *on* the consumption schedule. The marginal propensity to consume (*MPC*) is also called the *slope* of the line. In this case the slope is constant, for the consumption function shown here is a straight line and the ratio of the change in consumption to the change in income is constant for any two points on the line.

The *average propensity to save* (APS) is the ratio of total saving to total income.

It also follows that the **average propensity to save** is

$$APS = \frac{\text{total saving}}{\text{total income}}$$

and the marginal propensity to save is

$$MPS = \frac{\text{change in saving}}{\text{change in income}}.$$

Income, Consumption, and Saving

People receive income and then usually consume most of it. Whatever is left over out of income is saving. We simply define saving as income less consumption and write

Saving = income − consumption.

By rearranging terms we get

Consumption + saving = income.

If Sarah eats 2/3 of a candy bar, she must not eat 1/3 of it. What she ate and did not eat must add to one candy bar, or 2/3 consumed + 1/3 saved = 1 candy bar.

To get the average propensity to consume and the average propensity to save we divide through by income to form

$$\frac{\text{Consumption}}{\text{Income}} + \frac{\text{saving}}{\text{income}} = \frac{\text{income}}{\text{income}}$$

or by definition

$$APC + APS = 1.$$

Since the marginal propensity to consume represents the fraction of additional consumption out of additional income, and the marginal propensity to save is the fraction of additional saving out of additional income, the *MPC* and *MPS* by definition must also **add to one**. Since,

Since the APC and the APS are the fractions of income either spent or saved, by definition they must *add to one*.

$$\text{Consumption} + \text{saving} = \text{income}$$

then the

$$\text{Change in consumption} + \text{change in saving} = \text{change in income}.$$

When any *additional* income is divided up, part of it goes to consumption and the remainder goes to saving. If we divide through by the change in income

$$\frac{\text{Change in consumption}}{\text{Change in income}} + \frac{\text{change in saving}}{\text{change in income}} = \frac{\text{change in income}}{\text{change in income}}.$$

Or by definition

$$MPC + MPS = 1.$$

The 45° Guideline

Observe the dashed 45° line emanating from the origin in Figure 22-2. It forms a 45° angle with the horizontal axis and is one half of the 90° angle formed by the vertical and horizontal axes. At any point on the 45° line where a consumption schedule passes through, the value of consumption will equal the value of income, $C = Y$. Such a point is called the **break-even point**, and its value here is 83.3.

At the *break-even point*, consumption equals income.

At the break-even point, since consumption equals income, the average propensity to consume ($APC = C/Y$) must be equal to 1. To the left of point *h*, in the shaded area where the consumption function lies above the 45° line, the *APC* is greater than 1. Because consumption is greater than income (symbolized by $C > Y$) the ratio of consumption to income must also be greater than 1 (symbolized by $C/Y > 1$). Consumers are dissaving in this range of the function. Conversely, where the consumption function lies below the 45° line to the right of the break-even point, the *APC* is less than 1 because $C < Y$ so that $C/Y < 1$.

Once parameters *a* and *b* are known, a particular consumption function is specified. Particular levels of consumption can be calculated for different values of income. At point *p* income is 400; consumption is therefore

$$\begin{aligned} C &= a + bY \\ &= 50 + (.4)(400) \\ &= 50 + 160 = 210. \end{aligned}$$

Figure 22-2

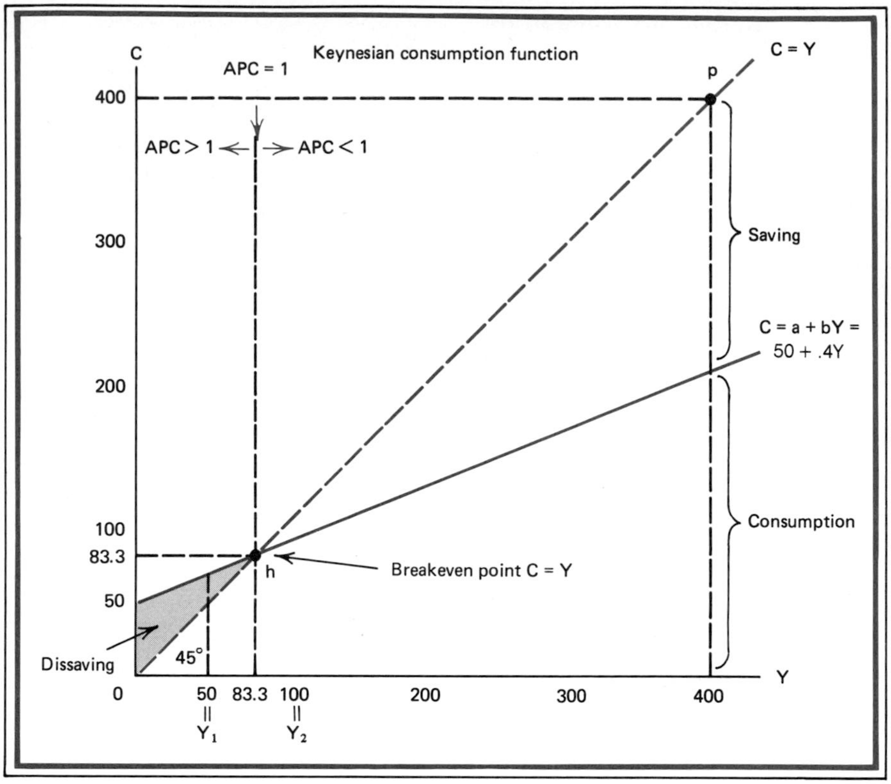

At point p not all of the 400 in income is spent, since $400 - 210 = 190$ is saved. The amount of saving is shown by the distance from point p down to the consumption function. In Figure 22-2 we can see geometrically that consumption + saving = income ($C + S = Y$).

A final point: So long as the consumption function is flatter than the 45° guideline, the marginal propensity to consume is less than one ($MPC < 1$).

SHORT-RUN VS. LONG-RUN CONSUMPTION FUNCTIONS

Cross-section studies analyse the relation of consumption to income at a period in time for different groups and income groupings.

To this point the discussion has been confined to the short-run consumption function. Early empirical studies designed to uncover just what the relation of C to Y was for a given economy usually relied on family budget or cross-section data rather than looking at the changing relation between consumption and income over successive time periods known as time series.[2] **Cross-section studies** are statistical techniques that compare consumption expenditures out of income over *different* groups at the same moment in time; for example, doctors

[2]For details see Gardner Ackley, *Macroeconomic Theory* (New York: The Macmillan Co., 1961) or Edward Shapiro, *Macroeconomic Analysis* 4th ed., (New York: Harcourt, Brace, Jovanovich, Inc., 1977).

can be compared with welders and salesmen. Or cross-section studies can estimate how much of income is consumed across all households by categorizing them by income levels, i.e., from $0 to $2,000, from $2,000 to $4,000, and so on, at a given point in time. With **time series**, consumption and incomes *within* the *same* groups are compared *over* time. Thus, the *same* groups—doctors, welders, and salesmen will be measured for consumption and income *changes* over the years. Or all households can be aggregated and treated as a single unit and analyzed over some time series. A time series is a moving camera recording household behavior over many periods.

Time-series studies analyse the relation of consumption to income for the same groups as income changes over time.

Cross-section studies are like a snapshot freezing the action while we look to see what the relation is at that moment. Remember, we are looking at averages and aggregates and not at an individual's consumption pattern. Although the data show on the average that household expenditures vary consistently with income, there is substantial variation that cannot be explained by income alone. The answer lies in shift parameters that can cause the whole consumption schedule to move up or down. As emphasized in Chapter 3, it is important to distinguish between a *movement along* a schedule and a **shift** in the schedule—in this case the consumption schedule. As we explained, when the level of income changes, consumers in the aggregate move along the consumption schedule, changing the level of consumer expenditures, *ceteris paribus*. However, when important nonincome parameters change, the consumption function can shift up or down. Thus, with aggregate income unchanged, aggregate consumption can still increase or decrease at *each* given level of income because of a shift in the consumption function. For example, as institutional changes occurred in the credit markets, consumer credit (*Cr*) became more available with the introduction of smaller down payments and the creation of installment payments; it allowed people to be able to consume more at *existing* income levels. The result was an upward shift in the aggregate consumption schedule from C to C′ as the parameter $\overline{Cr}$ changed to $\overline{\overline{Cr}}$, illustrated in Figure 22-3.

Over the long term, the short-term consumption schedule can *shift* due to changes in expected income, the expected rate of inflation, the level of debt, the stock of durable goods, the age and size of households, and taxes.

Other changes in other parameters cause the consumption function to shift. If people expect significant changes in their income (y^e), they will consume more now in anticipation of that. If people expect inflation (p^e) to continue to rise, they may choose to spend more because inflation erodes the purchasing power of their savings. Buy more now while money is still worth something. If the level of debt (*d*) is very high, then we expect consumers to slow down spending, so that the consumption will shift down. Another important shift parameter is the stock of durable goods (*g*) households own. Durables last a long time. Thus, once households are stocked up on them, expect the consumption function to shift down. Therefore, when the parameters are included, the shorthand notation for the consumption function is

$$C = f(Y, \overline{p^e}, \overline{y^e}, \overline{Cr}, \overline{d}, \overline{g}, \ldots)$$

Another parameter not listed might include the age composition of households. The younger the family, the more it will consume. Young couples starting out will likely buy all kinds of durable goods to set up house. The size of households is also important. The more children there are on the average, the more consumption there is on perishable goods and the lower is saving. The distribution of income also has a role to play. Lower income groups have a

Figure 22-3

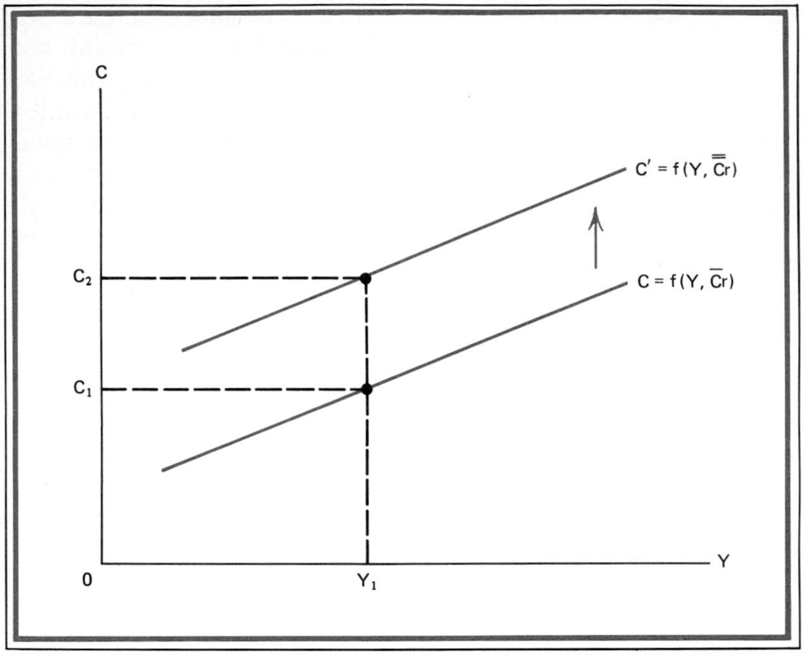

higher average propensity to consume than do better off groups. The greater the number of lower income people there are, the higher is the consumption curve. Keeping up with the Joneses plays a part. U.S. society is characterized by an historical trend of upward mobility. It is the ambition of many U.S. citizens to move to a better neighborhood. Therefore, to give evidence of being a success, of "making it too," implies shifting consumption into higher gear on a par with the Joneses.

When any one of the barred parameters experiences a change in its level, the *C* curve shifts. Of course, one person's expectations are not necessarily another's when dealing in aggregates. When the aggregate consumption function shifts up (or down) it does not necessarily follow that *each* person consumes more (or less). Jack may go out the back door, but the crowd goes out the front door. What is observed is the crowd's movement, not necessarily Jack's individual peculiarities. Another important parameter is taxes. We treat that separately.

The Effect of Taxes

A *lump-sum* tax does not vary with income; therefore, it reduces or increases consumption by the same amount at every income level.

When government is introduced, taxes necessarily follow. There are two broad categories of taxes, those that are independent of income and those that vary with income. A **lump-sum tax** is a tax of a fixed amount that is the same for all levels of income. It is constant. It therefore reduces consumption by the same amount at every income level, resulting in a parallel downward shift of the consumption schedule, as illustrated in Figure 22-3. Obviously, if taxes were already being imposed, then a reduction in the lump-sum tax would result in a parallel upward shift in the consumption schedule.

Figure 22-4

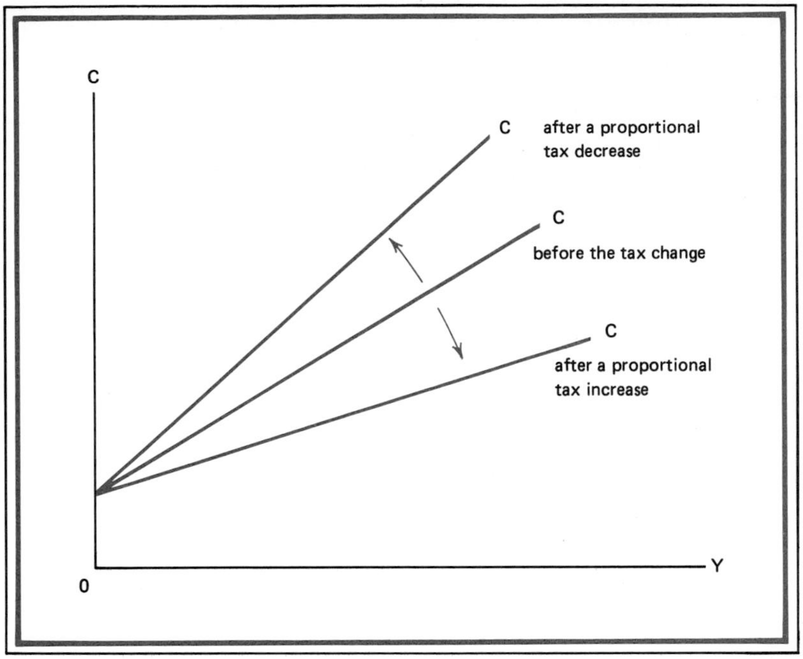

A *proportional tax* varies in proportion to income.

A tax that changes in proportion to changes in income is a **proportional tax**. It could be set, say, at 10 percent of income. As Figure 22-4 portrays, a proportional tax increase rotates the consumption schedule in a clockwise direction since 10 percent of a larger income yields a larger amount of taxes. If a proportional tax were already in existence, and it were lowered, the consumption function would rotate counterclockwise.

The Empirical Surprise

Figure 22-5 illustrates what cross-section data revealed for each of the 5 census years, 1900, 1910, 1920, 1930, and 1940. It is what researchers had come to expect from looking at U.S. data for any given year. Higher income families consume more than lower income families, but their average propensity to consume is lower while their average propensity to save is higher. All this fits well with short-run consumption. Departures from this pattern began to emerge as studies were made near the end of World War II. At that time economists decided to perform time series analysis on consumption and income data. Obviously, over time things change. The camera rolls and the actors move, and the drama is recorded. Income levels are no longer fixed. The results surprised the economists. The character of the consumption function took on a new appearance in the household scene, as illustrated by Figure 22-6. It shows that $0 < MPC < 1$ is still true. However, now the MPC and the APC are essentially numerically identical, since the intercept for all practical purposes occurs at the origin. Therefore, if $a = 0$, then $C = a + bY$ must reduce to $C = bY$. If each term is then divided by Y, then for the long run the slope $b = C/Y$. But it is also true that $b = MPC$ and that $C/Y = APC$. Thus, $MPC = APC$.

Figure 22-5

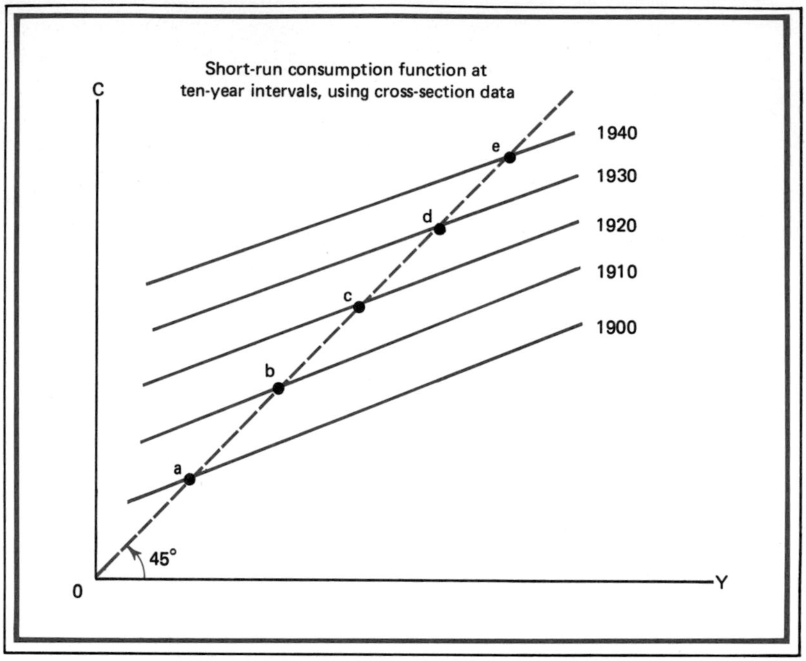

Consumption varies with income, but remains a **constant fraction** of total income, unlike the short-run consumption function where the fraction of consumption out of income falls as income goes up. And because the marginal propensity to consume is still less than 1, the consumption function is flatter than the 45° guideline. How can the long-run historical time-series data be squared with the short-run cross-section data?

Figure 22-6

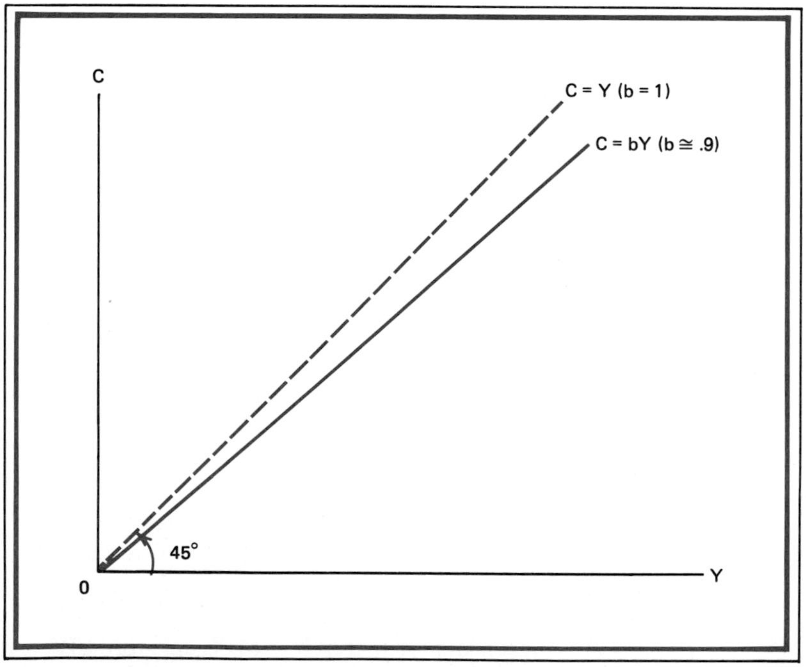

The relation of the short-run consumption function to the long-run consumption function makes some sense when one realizes that level of consumption at any given time depends on all the parameters and not just on income. Yearly cross-section data pick up other influences, both small and large, that tend to average or wash out over longer run time-series data, temporary things like layoffs, illnesses, bonuses, inheritances, and other unexpected losses or gains. During World War II aggregate consumption was down because many consumer goods were not being produced and many goods were rationed. People were pretty much forced to save by circumstances.

Time series studies of aggregate spending and consumption revealed that in the long run, consumption remained a *constant fraction* of income.

Nonetheless, the overall trend is upward and when the data are plotted over time, the short-run consumption function appears to have shifted up, generating the long-run consumption function with points *a*, *b*, *c* illustrated in Figure 22-5. The long-run function is therefore composed of a sequence of adjacent points traced by the shifting short-run function. However, when one looks at consumption at a point in time one does not observe any shift or its intersection through the origin. At moments in time other nonnormal, temporary fluctuations in income are not averaged out, so that short-period incomes do not move smoothly along the long-run function but deviate from it.

PERMANENT INCOME HYPOTHESIS

The *Permanent Income hypothesis* holds that people spend their income based on their longterm expectations of future income.

Several theories have been offered in attempts to harmonize the difference between cross-section (short-run) and time-series (long-run) results. One is the Permanent Income Hypothesis devised by Milton Friedman. Friedman argues that people do not spend on the basis of their current or measured income, but according to the average income stream they anticipate is forthcoming well into the future—their permanent income. An intern bases many of his economic decisions now on what he expects to make as a doctor in the years to come. These expenditures, on the average, would be different for a future high school history teacher who anticipates earning less income in the future than a would-be doctor. Friedman postulates that

Measured income = permanent income + transitory income,

and

Measured consumption = permanent consumption + transitory consumption.

The transitory income component involves chance movements, unexpected short-term effects on income caused by illness, a layoff, overtime, or a small inheritance. Friedman also argues that consumers—households—do not spend, or spend little, out of windfall or transitory income; nor do they reduce their consumption very much when they come onto hard times, because they see their situation as only a temporary setback.

In the long run the unsystematic temporary fluctuations in income average out so that the long-run *MPC* is higher than *MPC* in the short run. The consumption function is therefore very stable. It does not change drastically except in special situations like those after World War II. At that time the influential nonincome shift parameters were primarily the explosion in private capital investment expenditures and pent-up World War II household savings eager to be spent on new postwar goods.

An Example

Refer to Figure 22-7. There is only one long-run consumption function. The other lines represent the short-run deviations of measured consumption and measured income resulting from disturbances which are temporary in nature. These curves are really for aggregates, but for expository purposes let us deal with one individual. Assume Sally allocates her consumption and savings as $C_p = .9Y_p$. Thus, $MPC = APC = .9$. To keep things simpler, assume that transi-

Figure 22-7

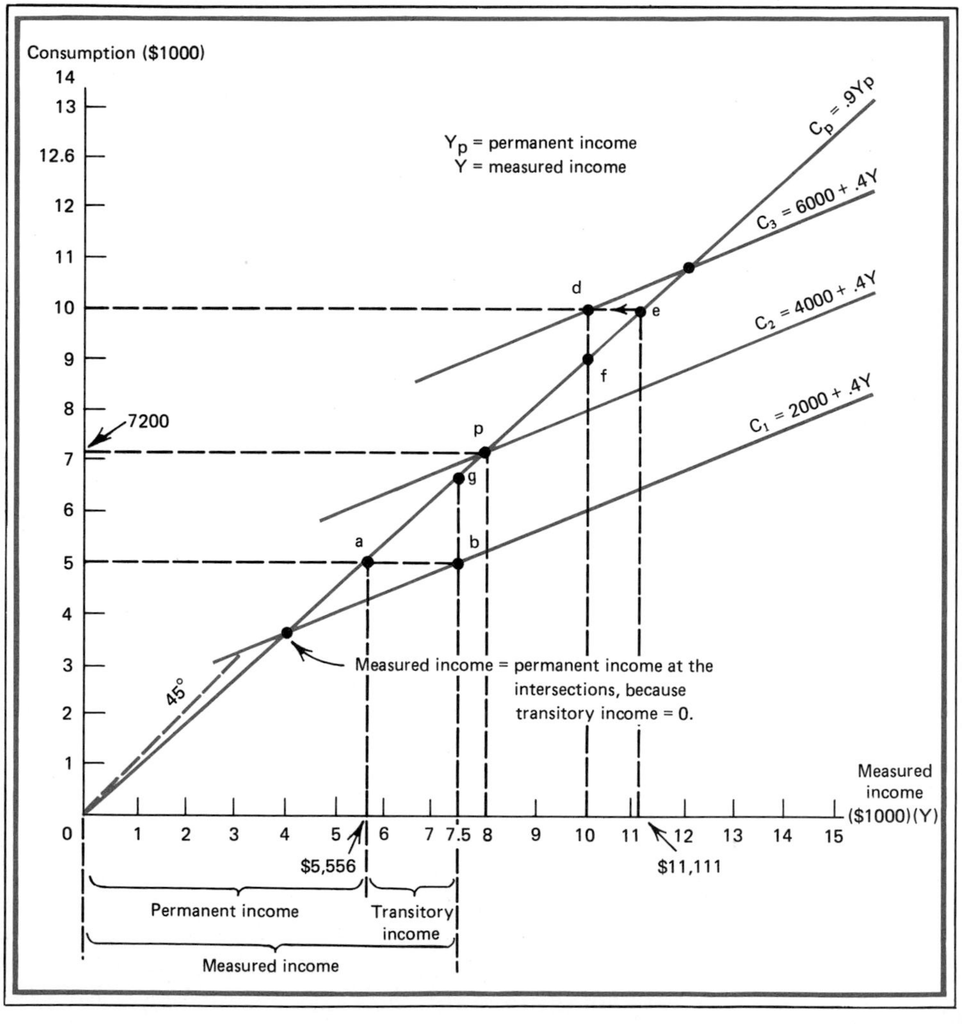

tory consumption in any period is zero, so that measured consumption equals permanent consumption. Assume that the three short-run consumption functions that fit the short-run data are C_1, C_2 and C_3 representing three time periods. (The actual short-run *MPC* is closer to .7. Our choice of .4 is designed to make the graph easier to follow.) We have deliberately chosen some erratic numbers to illustrate the point. Suppose in period one she has some good luck. The company employs Sally for considerable amounts of overtime at the fast-food restaurant and she also wins a small newspaper-sponsored football pool contest. Both are temporary increases in her income and not part of the permanent income stream she expected. Her income for the period (year) is $7,500. Sally spends $5,000 over this period and saves the rest after taxes for tuition because she intends to go to college. This puts her at point *b* in Figure 22-7. It would seem according to $C_p = .9Y$ that she would spend $6,750 designated by point g, but not according to the permanent income hypothesis. The permanent income she expected was $5,556 designated by point *a*; hence she consumed $C = .9(5556) = \$5,000$. Measured income equals permanent income plus transitory income. Hence the segment *ab* represents a transitory income = $7,500 − $5,556 = $1,944. She does not spend out of this transitory income, for transitory spending is zero. She spends according to what she estimates is her permanent income; therefore Sally operates at point *a* in the figure. Thus measured, *APC* is .67, which deviates from the long-run permanent *APC* = .9.

In the second period, Sally is now in college and still working half time at the fast-food restaurant. But she is in a managerial position at night, which is where she expected to be in her career at this time. Sally earns $8,000 in this period and consumes $7,200. Thus she is at point *p*. Transitory income is zero. Measured and permanent income are identical and so are measured and permanent consumption with measured *APC* = *MPC* = .9.

In the third period Sally has graduated from college and anticipates moving up the income ladder. Because of illness she misses some workdays and her income is only $10,000. Sally had hoped to be earning over $11,000, and operating at point *e*. Yet she does not drop her consumption to $9,000 at point *f* because of a temporary setback. She continues to consume according to income she anticipates she will earn and therefore consumes at point *d*, amounting to $10,000 after taxes. Sally can do this by borrowing against future earnings even though transitory income is negative by $11,111 − $10,000 = $1,111. As a result, measured *APC* equals 1 and is larger than permanent *APC* = .9. Again we see that short-run or cross-section data that pick up temporary deviations in measured income from permanent income average out to zero in the long run. And spending is consistent with long-run income that is anticipated and is not significantly affected by temporary slumps or gains in income.

The data are summarized at top of the following page.

Implications

The permanent income hypothesis predicts that consumers do not respond immediately to changes in current income, since unexpected changes are considered a temporary windfall. Instead they base their consumption patterns on what they anticipate will be their stream of future income. Therefore, govern-

	Measured income	Permanent income	Transitory income	$C_m = C_p$ Measured consumption	Permanent APC	Measured APC
Year 1	$7,500	$5,556	+$1,944	$5,000	.9	.67 (5,000/ 7,500)
Year 2	8,000	8,000	0	7,200	.9	.9
Year 3	10,000	11,111	−1,111	10,000	.9	1.0 (10,000/ 10,000)

ment actions intended to alter current consumer spending behavior may have little effect. For instance, a tax cut would be taken by consumers as only a temporary change in their income stream, not a permanent one. It would not affect total public spending significantly if implemented. Only if consumers perceive the tax change to be a permanent one, lasting for say at least three years, would they consider the additional income as a permanent addition to their expected income stream. In this light, because the short-run consumption function has a lower marginal propensity to consume than the long-run consumption function, government spending programs would not have as much influence on stimulating consumer spending and the economy in the shorter period as might be hoped for. The question also revolves around what period of time constitutes the end of the short run and the beginning of the long run. That is, after what period of time do additional income streams come to be considered as permanent income over the longer run? If one could anticipate winning on the horses over the next five years because one has worked out a "system," should these winnings now be considered not as windfall income but as permanent income? Friedman at one time suggested that a time horizon of three years be taken as the cutoff point beyond which windfall income be treated as permanent income.

CHAPTER SUMMARY

In 1936 Keynes advocated that the particular level of aggregate consumer spending depends primarily upon the level of aggregate consumer income. Prior to that time economists believed that the interest rate determined what the particular level of aggregate consumption would be. The higher the interest rate the greater the amount of savings and the lower the level of consumption. When the interest rate fell, the opposite effect occurred.

Keynes asserted that there is a predictable or stable relation between aggregate consumption and aggregate income. Thus, given income, a given level of consumption could be calculated. Income also determined what the level of aggregate saving would be, since saving is defined as unspent income. Thus, the rate of interest was of secondary importance in determining the level of savings, according to Keynes.

The ratio of total consumption to total income is called the average propensity to consume (APC). The APC falls as income rises along a short-run linear consumption function. The ratio of total saving to total income is the average propensity to save (APS). Since the APC and the APS are the fractions of income either spent or saved, they must add to one.

The fraction of additional income that is spent is defined as the marginal propensity to consume (MPC). It is the ratio of the change in total consumption over the change in total income. It is also known as the slope of a linear consumption schedule.

Keynes postulated that the MPC is greater than zero and less than 1 and constituted a fundamental psychological law of aggregate spending behavior. Similarly, the ratio of the change in total saving to the change in total income is called the marginal propensity to save (MPS). Since the MPC and the MPS are the fractions of the additional income that is spent or saved, they must also add to 1.

The 45° line emanating from the origin is a locus of points where consumption is equal to income. Since the short-run consumption function intersects the vertical axis above the origin, there is one point where the consumption schedule must intersect the 45° line. It is called the break-even point, since consumption is equal to income there. To the left of the break-even point, the APC is greater than 1, indicating that consumption is greater than income. For that to occur there must be dissaving. Also, because the MPC is less than 1, the consumption schedule is flatter than the 45° line and must intersect the vertical axis above the origin.

Consumption is a function of income, *ceteris paribus*. When one of the parameters changes, the short-run consumption function can shift up or down. There can be changes in expected income, the expected rate of inflation, the level of debt, the stock of durable goods, the age and size of households, and in taxes, causing the consumption schedule to shift.

A lump sum tax is a tax that does not vary with income. It therefore causes a downward parallel shift in the consumption schedule when imposed, and an upward parallel shift when it is reduced or removed. A proportional tax of say 10 percent would rotate the consumption schedule in a clockwise direction, because 10 percent of a larger income is a larger amount in absolute dollars. Conversely, lowering the proportional tax rotates the consumption schedule in the counterclockwise direction.

The short-run consumption function is derived from cross-section data, where time is held fixed and the consumption levels of the population or of different occupations is compared for different income ranges. Thus, consumption patterns of doctors, machinists, and the like can be compared at a moment in time for different income levels. These studies showed that consumption levels had shifted upward at each given level of income.

Time-series studies apply to the long run, tracing out changes in the relation between aggregate consumption and aggregate income where income varies as time varies. They observe the spending pattern of the same groups or of the overall population through time. They reveal that while the MPC is less than one, the long-run consumption schedule passes through the origin. This means that the intercept term a in $C = a + bY$ is zero, so that the APC and the MPC are identical.

The permanent income hypothesis is only one of several theories reconciling the short-run cross-section data results with the long-run time-series data. It hypothesizes that people spend their income based on a long-run notion of what they anticipate their future income stream will be. At any given point in time there may be temporary deviations in income from their long-run permanent income stream. However, because these deviations are viewed as temporary, people continue to spend more or less on the basis of their anticipated long-run income. These deviations average out in the long run but show up in the short run. Thus short-run shifting consumption schedules are really movements up along the long-run schedule, hence consumption bears out to be a stable function of income.

QUESTIONS

1. Keynes stated that the consumption function was a stable function of income. What did he mean by stable?
2. Keynes said that the consumption function expressed a "fundamental psychological law" of human behavior.
   a. What was the law?
   b. Does it apply in both the short run and the long run? Explain.
3. Suppose the CPI rises by 20 percent, but your money income also rises by 20 percent. Will your APC change? Discuss.
4. Overly Broke consumes all of his income no matter how much he earns.
   a. Draw his consumption function (assume $C = 0$ when $Y = 0$).
   b. Draw his savings function.
   c. What is the value of his MPC?
   d. What is his break-even point? Define it.
   e. What is his APC?
5. Would you expect the MPC out of national income to be higher or lower than the MPC out of disposable income? Why?
6. Since $APC_1 = C_1/Y_1$ and $APC_2 = C_2/Y_2$ and the MPC is defined as $MPC = (C_2-C_1)/(Y_2-Y_1)$, then another way to calculate the marginal propensity to consume is to calculate the change in the APC from one income level to another, or $MPC = APC_2 - APC_1$. Do you agree? Why or why not?
7. A study by New York's Citibank on U.S. family spending yielded the following:

Family Spending by Income in 1973 (before taxes)

Income	\$12,000–\$14,999	\$15,000–\$19,999	\$20,000–\$24,999
Spending	\$10,474	\$12,515	\$15,248

   a. Is this a cross-section or a time-series study? Why?
   b. What is happening to the APC as income rises? Calculate it, using 12,000, 15,000, and 20,000 as the base income for each income group.
8. Consumption is an increasing function of income. How then do you account for the following changes in consumption spending even though money income is unchanged?
   a. An appliance salesman says, "People have jobs but I've lost more than 50 sales because installment debt is now 14 percent of income compared with 12 percent a year ago."
   b. A distributor says "I had a cancellation of 175 microwave ovens from one dealer alone. People are behaving with more caution and want a little extra in the savings account because of the way things are beginning to look."
   c. Inflation is accelerating well into double digits. People are holding less cash and buying things. Saving is down.

d. Most of the neighbors are putting in swimming pools so the Babbitt family does too.

9. With the aid of the 45° guideline, indicate on a graph how
   a. the MPC can remain constant while APC rises or falls as income changes.
   b. The MPC can remain constant while the APC rises or falls when income remains constant.
   c. The APC can be constant at a given level of income while the MPC can rise or fall as the consumption function passes through this income level.
10. If the value of the intercept is $200, and the MPC is 0.8, at what level of income does the break-even point for consumption and income occur?
11. Given a consumption function $C_1 = 20 + .75Y$, what does 20 and .75 represent? Suppose C_1 changes to $C_2 = 10 + .75Y$. What has happened? What could cause this to happen? Suppose C_1 changes to $C_3 = 10 + .80Y$. What has happened, and how?
12. Would your consumption function for 1 year look any different from your consumption function covering 20 years? Why, or why not?
13. You are given the following data:

Family income	Savings
$10,000	−$2,000
14,000	−1,000
16,000	0
19,000	2,000
22,000	4,000

   a. Are the saving and consumption functions linear? What is the evidence for it?
   b. Calculate the APS at income levels of $10,000, $16,000, and $22,000. Then use the APS to calculate the APC at each income level.
   c. Calculate the MPC for each jump in income. Then use it to calculate the MPS.
14. According to the permanent income hypothesis, does a student who skips classes on Friday to play poker put his winnings in the bank or go off and spend all his winnings on pizza and beer? What about the professional gambler Amarillo Slim—assuming he likes pizza and beer?
15. Suppose you know that if you declare one exemption for yourself you will receive an IRS tax refund at the year's end. According to the permanent income hypothesis would this be transitory or permanent disposable income?
16. Would you expect medical interns to spend more on the average than students working on their Ph.D. thesis in political science? If so, can you back it up with a theory?
17. A free-lance typist receives $800 for work she really did not want to do and did not need, but did to keep an earlier promise. However, when she got paid she used it to buy a rug she always wanted. Is this example consistent with the permanent income hypothesis? Explain. Does this mean the permanent income hypothesis has no validity?

Chapter 23

Investment

The business of America is business.

— Calvin Coolidge

PROGRESS REPORT

A. Chapter 22 covered consumption in the household sector, the largest component of aggregate demand. We learned that aggregate consumption spending is stable, behaving predictably with changes in aggregate income.

B. In this chapter we consider the third largest component of aggregate demand — investment. The types of investment spending, the role of investment spending, and the analysis of the main variables that promote or hinder investment spending are explained. The role of investment at the macroeconomic level is emphasized; we then look at investment from the perspective of the firm, since microeconomic investment is the underpinning for aggregate investment. The relation of investment to saving and the importance of investment spending as a major source of upturns and downturns in the economy are touched upon.

C. Chapter 24 will combine the three sectors discussed to that point — government, household, and business, and incorporate them into a model describing aggregate equilibrium, where aggregate supply equals aggregate demand for the whole economy.

MEASUREMENT AND ROLE OF INVESTMENT

The components of investment are *residential construction, nonresidential investment,* and *changes in inventories.*

In the way national income is usually divided into its component parts in the national accounts, consumption is the largest component of GNP; government spending is next; and capital investment is the third largest component. Historically, business investment expenditures have ranged from 9 to 11 percent of GNP. After adding in residential construction, the level of investment normally varies from 14 to 16 percent of GNP. Gross private domestic investment consists of nonresidential construction, residential construction, and change in the level of inventories.

Residential construction includes primarily new houses and apartments. Since most houses are purchased by consumers, why, you might ask, is housing a part of investment instead of being classified as a consumer durable good? Recall that investment is defined as a net addition to the stock of capital, and that capital is a man-made unit of production capable of providing a flow of services over many years. Keeping this definition in mind, we can see why housing is, indeed, an investment good.

A rented house provides not only a current service to a consumer but also promises a future stream of income or services as do other capital goods. If you own the house and rent it out, it offers a stream of income into the future. If you live in it yourself, then you receive directly a stream of services into the future. Consumer durables such as a washing machine which provide a stream of services for a year or more are, however, not classified as investment goods by government accountants.

Nonresidential investment includes what is termed fixed capital investment or simply fixed investment. It refers to plant and equipment such as factories, warehouses, storage bins, barns, tools, equipment, and intangibles like repairs and expenditures for research and development.

Changes in inventories are treated as investment and refer to the adding to or subtracting from the levels of inventories carried over from the previous period. An increase in inventories is not necessarily a good omen. It may be that you ordered a bunch of skis and it did not snow. So, you are stuck with them. But presumably you can sell them next year if the styles do not change. Decreases in inventories are treated as negative investment so that GNP will not be overstated in the year in which the fall in inventory occurs.

Discussions about capital spending on the television news and in the newspapers are primarily about fixed capital expenditures, that is, nonresidential investment spending on plant and equipment. These expenditures are crucial and help determine the health and growth of an economy. They indicate that some new entrants to the labor force will be absorbed into the new jobs created by expansion of facilities.

Many firms receive assistance in making capital or investment expenditures from financial institutions that act as middlemen by borrowing the savings of households and lending to commercial enterprises. As households sacrifice current consumption in order to save, firms acquire the funds with which to improve equipment and facilities, thereby raising productivity. These savings enable households to realize higher levels of consumption later in a growing economy. More explicitly, fixed investment makes it possible for businesses to add to the stock of capital, replace worn out capital (replacement capital), remove obsolete (outdated) capital, and introduce better technologies. It is worth commenting that obsolescence can be brought on by technological change or by changes in input prices such as wages and the price of oil. We shall come back to this point later.

Of the three components of aggregate demand, consumption, government spending, and investment spending, investment is the most volatile. Within investment the item *changes in business inventories* is the most erratic. Changes in investment spending are believed to be one of the major causes of business cycles—those fluctuations in output and employment that often plague market economies. As an example, from 1930 to 1931, the first full year of the Great Depression, aggregate consumption fell by 41 percent while investment declined by 91 percent. Business cycles and the role investment plays in them are the subject of a later chapter.

INDUCED AND AUTONOMOUS INVESTMENT

Induced investment **is a response to increases in consumer demand stimulated by rising income.**

Investment, when it occurs in response to increases in consumer demand stimulated by rising income, is called **induced investment**. An example was the expanding U.S. market that caused Volkswagen to open up a plant in Pennsylvania. Construction of the Alaska pipeline is another case in point. Increased demand for oil and gasoline motivated the oil companies to expand capacity. Induced investment depends on economic growth that pushes the economy up against existing capacity and encourages expansion because profit expectations are strong.

Autonomous investment **is an introduction of new products and technology in the hope of creating new demand and higher profits. It is not initiated by rising aggregate income.**

On the other hand, there is investment that is not instigated by increased demand, but is independently motivated by the introduction of something new and by the expectation that the investment will be profitable. This is named **autonomous investment**. Profits are expected to be made from a new idea or a technological innovation, items such as electronic pocket calculators, video tape decks, skateboards, and the latest fashions, to name a few. It may be hard to separate precisely one type of investment from the other, and they may reinforce one another. A successful corporation that can expand its facilities because demand for its products is strong can also afford to increase expenditures for its research and development division from which the ideas for autonomous investment expenditures may originate. For instance, the Bell System has a large research division. Physicists discovered the transistor in the Bell Telephone laboratories. Modern electronics would be impossible without the transistor.

DETERMINANTS OF INVESTMENT

Investment or capital formation is a flow variable measured by the change in the amount of the capital stock per time period.

The investment process is fundamentally one of adjusting the economy's stock of capital. The adjustment is the result of the accumulated adjustment derived from individual businesses which alter their existing capital stock to attain some desired level. The amount of capital at a given time is a *stock* variable. Changes in the amount of capital over some time period is a *flow* and is what we call investment. Thus, if K_t is the capital stock at time t, and K_{t+1} the amount at time $t+1$, the next period, then investment is the change in capital stock or $I = \Delta K = K_{t+1} - K_t$. The symbol Δ is a capitalized Greek letter delta, and signifies the difference in the capital stock at two different moments of time. If there were 100 machines on January 1 and 110 machines in the plant on December 31 of the same year, the rate of investment was 10 machines per year.

Our concern now is to examine those variables that influence the investment decision. Whatever they may be, they are unquestionably interrelated in a complex and, unfortunately, imperfectly understood way. While it is known that some variables are more important than others, a reasonably exact magnitude of the effect one variable has, as compared to another, is not clear.

The rate of capital formation is affected by the interest rate, changes in national income, the rate of new technology, the price of new capital, the level and kinds of taxes, the cost of inputs, and the degree to which existing plant capacity is being used.

1. The interest rate (i) Although there are different interest rates existing in different markets, we shall talk as if there were one interest rate applying across all markets. Although many large corporations generate enough funds internally, it is necessary for most firms to borrow funds to make capital purchases for purposes of replacing, expanding, or otherwise modifying their operations, such as buying the latest technology. Clearly, the higher the interest costs they must pay to acquire investment funds, the more reluctant businesses are about borrowing money. These funds may be borrowed directly from banks and other financial institutions. Firms also borrow by selling their own bonds on the open market that pay the holder of the bond (the lender) a rate of interest. The higher the market rate of interest, the higher must be the rate of interest (the yield) on the bonds the firm sells; otherwise the firm is not offering a competitive yield and will have great difficulty selling its bonds. Private business must compete with other institutions, such as local, state, and federal governments, for buyers. Thus, a higher rate of interest means a lower level of investment spending as it becomes more costly for the firm to borrow.

2. Changes in national income (Y) When national income increases significantly, business expects that future sales will rise, and with them future revenues. Under a climate of optimism business will increase its inventory levels—a form of investment—and proceed with plans to make new expenditures on plant and equipment to handle a growing market.

3. Technology (T) Technology is a variable associated with autonomous investment. Business is always on the lookout for ways to increase production efficiencies—cut costs—and to increase profits. This often requires adopting new technology. Occasionally a technological breakthrough creates a whole new industry. The invention of printed circuits and then of integrated circuits (chips) and new techniques to speed up their production have had an enormous impact in cutting costs and creating a whole new industry in electronic pocket calculators. Lasers are opening up new possibilities in industry as a cutting tool and possibly for signal transmission. In the past, invention of the Bessemer process to produce steel had a great impact on reducing the costs of building railroads and automobiles, themselves technological innovations that substantially reduced transportation costs and, in turn, provided the motive to find new processes in making rubber and other materials used in production of trains and automobiles. The huge prescription drug industry has exploded on the heels of new developments in chemistry. New technologies create new markets and new jobs. The growth in profits can be plowed back into research and development whereby ever newer technological advances are possible. The technological frontier, and the profits it promises, is an important variable in the investment decision.

4. Acquisition cost of new capital (P_K) When the price of new capital rises, especially when prospects for growth in future sales do not look strong, the incentive to purchase new capital goods diminishes. Also, the greater the number of pollution and safety regulations there are, the higher is the cost to produce capital goods containing these required features. The higher production costs of producing capital equipment are then passed on to the business which buys them for purposes of using them to produce consumer goods. Of course, firms can raise their prices, forcing some consumers to substitute other goods, thereby creating an increased demand for plant and equipment in industries producing the substitutes—and for industries producing the antipollution equipment. Where ready substitutes do not exist, higher priced capital goods act as a deterrent on firms intending to make purchases of new capital equipment. Similarly, higher construction costs may inhibit the expansion of existing facilities and the construction of new facilities. Related to the price of new capital is the cost to the firm of putting the newly acquired capital to actual use. For example, there are costs involved in retraining workers to operate the new equipment and for them to learn the changes in procedures in a revamped operation caused by the introduction of new plant or equipment.

5. Taxes (T_X) The structure of taxes as they bear on business income, depreciation, and the purchase of new equipment is an important consideration in the investment decision of businesses. Significant in varying degrees are depreciation, the investment tax credit, and possibly the Social Security payroll tax among others.

Depreciation is the decrease in the value of an asset through wear and tear, deterioration, or obsolescence. An allowance for it is made in the tax laws. Assume AT&T buys a new power transformer which it will install on a telephone pole at a cost of $30,000. By law it cannot deduct the full $30,000 as a cost of production in the first year and thereby reduce its taxable net income by that amount. It can only deduct from its taxable income the depreciated value of the transformer each year over its depreciated life. That is to say, it does not write off the $30,000 immediately, but only some of it each year until all of the $30,000 is deducted. Suppose the company estimates that the transformer will function for 10 years. Then AT&T has several methods it can legally use to depreciate the transformer. If the law allows for a depreciation period of 8 years, then annual depreciation is $3,750 a year (8 × $3,750 = $30,000). Thus, each year for 8 years it can *straight-line* depreciate the equipment and deduct $3,750 from its total taxable income, leaving only the remaining income to be taxed. Since 1978, the law set the tax rate on corporate profits at 46 percent. Hence, if net income to AT&T is increased each year by the $3,750 it can depreciate the transformer, then it realizes a reduction in its taxes of (.46)($3,750) = $1,725 per year. By choosing to adopt *accelerated* depreciation methods instead, AT&T could depreciate the transformer in 5 years instead of 8 years, despite the fact that useful life of the transformer is 10 years. The yearly depreciation allowance is now $6,000 since 5 × $6,000 = $30,000. The tax reduction is (.46)(6,000) = $2,750 for each of 5 years. But this leaves AT&T with no deduction to claim for the remaining 5 years, so it will pay more taxes in those years. The net effect is to give the investor some money now on which it can earn interest until it has to pay more taxes in 5 years' time. It is as if the government gives AT&T an interest-free loan in the amount of the accelerated depreciation allowance.

The investment tax credit is a tax credit allowed businesses in addition to the depreciation allowance. For example, if the investment tax credit applied to business is 10 percent on equipment lasting over, say, 7 years, then AT&T's tax credit on its $30,000 transformer is $3,000. The company can deduct $3,000 from its income tax in the year of purchase. It is a *credit* directly against taxes and is in addition to any depreciation allowances for which the firm is eligible.

Payroll taxes, applied to labor inputs, also affect investment. Different taxes on the income earned from capital and labor inputs change the relative prices of capital and labor the firm has to pay when it invests or hires. This alters the least-cost combination of capital to labor in the production process, since the firm wants to produce at the lowest possible cost per unit of output that it can. The business Social Security payroll tax is one example. It requires that the employer must pay into the Social Security fund an amount equal to what the employee pays. Suppose the worker earns $10,000 a year and the payroll tax is $100, leaving the worker with $9,900 in income after deducting for Social Security. The employer must also kick in $100 to Social Security. The total tax take by the government is $200. The worker receives $9,900 (before income taxes) and the firm pays out $10,100 to employ the worker. The effect of the payroll tax is to make labor relatively more expensive than capital, and therefore labor relatively less desirable as an input for the firm. The firm substitutes capital and raises its capital to labor ratio (K/L). It is possible that the payroll tax may not have as large a consequence as depreciation and tax credit factors. What can be said is that some parts of the tax system increase investment and some lower it.

6. Costs of inputs (C_I) The demand for capital is related to the price of inputs such as materials, fuel, and labor wages. The ratio of capital to labor may rise because wage increases cause the firm to substitute capital for labor. Capital can become obsolescent, that is, economically inefficient when the price of an input rises. Since 1973 OPEC crude oil prices jumped by over 800 percent, raising the cost of oil-intensive operations. It forced firms to reduce the use of their existing capital stock and adopt more efficient technology using cheaper coal and natural gas. Obsolescence was accelerated and capital expenditures on new technology was speeded up. Many utilities converted to coal generators from oil-powered generators. The transition also provided industries the opportunity to meet new pollution and safety standards.

*7. **Capacity utilization** (C_U)* Capacity refers to the quantity of output that can be produced, given the existing stock of capital, when plants and equipment are operating the average or normal amount of time producing the normal mix of output. Over time the normal period of time has changed as workers gain shorter work weeks and more leisure. Also, what is meant by a normal production mix is subject to variation, and it seems to change with the business cycle. Thus, capacity is subject to a number of interpretations, and this discussion of capacity utilization is only a brief one.

When plant and equipment are not being fully utilized, that is when operations are at less than the theoretical 100 percent of capacity, some equipment may be idle for days or weeks or only for several hours during the working day. Under these circumstances a firm is less likely to invest in new capital facilities. However, when a plant is operating at very high capacity, say 94 or 95 percent, the equipment is being worked to its limit. Under high intensity use there are likely to be more frequent machine breakdowns (down time) during which time more production is lost than would be the case if there were lower capacity utilization. Higher maintenance costs and production losses mean higher operating costs. Moreover, during peak operation, the market looks good and expansion would appear to be a good investment. When capacity utilization of an economy is high, more labor is being hired, and the newer workers are apt to be the less skilled since they are often the last hired, hence unit labor costs rise. Introducing new, more efficient labor-saving capital and other cheaper inputs is therefore an inducement to make new capital expenditures in order to reduce unit costs and raise profits. In periods of slack, the incentive to increase capacity, or even to replace old capital is reduced or nonexistent, particularly if market prospects for the future are pessimistic, meaning expectations about sales growth appear to be dismal.

THE ROLE OF INFLATION

Inflation's effect on investment appears to be linked to expectations of its impact on future sales and future costs.

We have deliberately avoided discussing expectations about future prices—notably rising prices or inflation—in our description of factors affecting investment expenditures. The role of expected inflation is controversial.

In a period of rapid inflation it is possible that some firms will step up their investment expenditures despite the existence of excess capacity. When prices are rising, replacement of older equipment with newer equipment represents a higher replacement cost to businesses. The longer the delay, the more costly it is to replace the older equipment. Yet many businessmen claim they do not respond to inflation by speeding up their investment plans. Instead, they argue, investment spending is increased only to meet expected long-term demand for their products. It has been observed in past periods of strong inflation, however, that when firms were experiencing substantial idle capacity they nevertheless went ahead with new capital expenditures. This would seem to contradict their claim that they did *not* invest in plant and equipment when demand for the products was weak and inflation was strong.

Under some circumstances, there may be no contradiction. Despite low current demand, businesses may be anticipating much higher long-term demand. They view the current downturn as only a temporary thing, so they must take action now if anticipated demand is to be met with higher production in the future, and at as low a unit cost as possible. This objective can only be realized by undertaking the adoption of new, more productive equipment beforehand.

Another possibility is that inflation affects not only the amount of spending on capital, but also the composition of capital. In the 1960s spending on vehicles and machinery was nearly three times as much as spending on plants and structures. Part of the explanation lies in the growth in the complexity and sophistication of equipment compared to structures—the computerization and automation of production. An automated warehouse involves much higher outlays for equipment than an older warehouse that makes more use of manual handling. Furthermore, the huge rise in construction costs leads firms to refrain from building new structures but to install more technically advanced equipment within the existing structures.

UNCERTAINTY AND CYCLES

Fluctuations in investment spending are considered an important source of business cycles in a private enterprise economy.

Because of lack of information, there is uncertainty about the future. Furthermore, decision makers may incorrectly assess the implications of a known current event. With uncertainty as a fact of life, decision makers can only have expectations about future events formulated on what is only partially known about the direction of markets and the economy. Expectations can be either short or long term. Short-term expectations deal with the results anticipated with regard to prices and profits associated with a target output using the existing plant and type of equipment. Short-term or short-run production decisions affect production on a daily, weekly, and monthly basis. Such decisions do not involve changes in plant or equipment, but are confined to decisions that affect inventory levels and how intensively the existing plant and equipment are utilized—the capacity utilization factor. Short-run mistakes, that is, undesirable buildups or depletions of inventory through overproduction or underproduction, can be rectified in a rather short period of time by cutting back or increasing working hours as the situation demands.

Long-term or long-run expectations, however, deal with the expected net rate of return when the existing plant is expanded and possibly new vintages of capital equipment can be employed. The long run is, therefore, concerned with enlarging (or diminishing) the capacity for production. Obviously, the reason this signifies a longer period of time is that it takes longer to alter the capacity of the plant than to change how much the existing plant capacity is being used.

Hence, there is greater risk and uncertainty connected to the long run. Information is also more costly to acquire the longer the time period before the effect of the decision is known. Consequently, long-run mistakes can mean getting stuck with a larger or inappropriate plant operating at inadequate capacity utilization, and it may take years after the initiation of the project to realize the mistake. This was the situation with the American auto industry in 1979 when it did not foresee the sudden shift to small cars by the public. Although production and the variable costs strictly associated with producing output can be reduced, the fixed costs of the expanded facilities remain. This will reduce the demand for investment goods in future periods. If the phenomenon is widespread among several industries, it may cause employment to decline. In the aggregate, the result is a downturn in the level of economic activity. As income falls households have less to spend, so that aggregate demand in the economy declines, reinforcing the downturn. The economy is said to be in the contractionary phase of a business cycle.

In a market economy uncertainty, generated by mistakes and their correction related to investment decisions in the private sector, is thought to be a major contributing factor to fluctuations in aggregate output and employment—the business cycle.

THE MARGINAL EFFICIENCY OF INVESTMENT

Until now we have talked mostly in terms of aggregate investment and discussed those variables that seem to have a major effect on it. But the investment decision is made at the level of the individual firm and aggregate investment is, in a sense, simply the sum of the investment expenditures of individual firms in the economy.

The Pizza Wagon

Unlike the Lone Ranger, Joe the Pizza Wagon rider is not independently wealthy, doing good deeds for the pleasure he gets out of it. Instead, he is probably like each of us—simply trying to make enough to pay next month's dorm bill. How did he get into this business, anyway?

Let us play with some simple numbers to get an idea about the way the decisions to operate pizza wagons are made. First, assume Joe can buy pizza wagons for $1,000 each, and that they last 1 year and then collapse. There is the senior year to finish and he needs to earn some money. Joe has the opportunity of pumping gas for about $5 an hour for a 20-hour week and earning $100 a week or $5,000 for a year (assuming he takes a 2-week vacation). But he decides he would like to investigate the pizza delivery business.

Assume that Joe finds he can buy pizzas for $1 each and sell them for $3. He makes $2. If Joe works 4 hours per evening for 5 evenings a week (a total of

20 hours) delivering pizzas, and if he delivers 20 pizzas per night, or 100 per week, he would make $200. This is twice as much as Joe would make pumping gas. From the $200 Joe should subtract the implicit or opportunity cost of his labor, namely the $100 he could earn as a gas-pump jockey. This would leave him with a net return on his investment of $100. However, Joe would have to pay for his wagon out of the extra $100 per week. Over the year, working 50 weeks, Joe would earn $10,000. The wagon only cost Joe $1,000, which fully depreciates during the year. Operating expenses include gas and oil costs of $1,000, plus the $5,000 in forgone wages. After these operating expenses totalling $6,000 he would earn $4,000 on his original investment of $1,000, for a net return of $3,000 or 300 percent.

This looks like such a good deal that Joe decides to buy a second wagon and hire his roommate at $5 an hour. The trouble is, the dorms he chose to accommodate are located in a cluster. Other dorms are further from campus, so gas expenses go up. Furthermore, there are fewer people in the other dorms, so sales go down. Assume that higher expenses and lower sales mean that the return Joe earns on the second wagon is only 100 percent. This is still good. So, he considers a third wagon. Now Joe discovers he is left with only 15 percent return since the market served by the third wagon is so small. Rather than spending $1,000 for a third wagon Joe could earn about 10 percent on this $1,000 by keeping it in a bank account. So, the 15 percent looks just enough better to him that Joe decides to buy the third wagon. But, no *more* than three, because the return on a fourth would probably be small or negative.

So, what Joe ends up doing if he wants to maximize his income for the year is operate 3 wagons. He keeps hiring or investing in additional wagons until the return on the last one is less than he could make by lending his money to the bank.

For the mathematical student, the formula for the anticipated rate of return is

$$r = \frac{\text{expected revenues} - (\text{expected costs} + \text{depreciation})}{\text{price of capital}}$$

Using data for the first pizza wagon we get

$$r = \frac{10{,}000 - (6000 + 1000)}{1000} = 3, \text{ or } 300 \text{ percent.}$$

Notice that the formula includes the word *expected*. Because of uncertainty Joe cannot be sure that his estimates of future revenues and costs will be realized.[1]

If there is inflation, then the rate of return may not be affected since the variables in both the numerator and denominator may be equally inflated. That is, the costs of inputs rise but so can the product price. Therefore, even as interest rates rise the real rate of return does not necessarily fall. Let us explain.

[1]Actually capital earns a chain of future income since it lasts for more than a year. The student who has already covered chapter 14 (Capital, Investment, and Present Value), will recognize the superiority of the present value approach in estimating the profitability of an investment.

MONEY RATE OF INTEREST VS. THE REAL RATE OF INTEREST

It is possible for savers to consume more later because borrowers can pay them interest. Borrowers can afford to pay interest because they use savers' funds to invest in capital goods that would increase the economy's productivity. Increased productivity means that society is able to produce more, hence consume more later by willingly sacrificing part of current consumption.

The *real rate of interest*, or real rate of return, is measured in goods per period and is the rate at which goods sacrificed today will yield more goods tomorrow.

Ignoring the money rate of interest for the moment, let us see how the productivity of machinery determines the **real rate of interest**. Assume that a machine can produce 3,000 frisbees a year forever once it is built, but this means the sacrifice of 30,000 frisbees that could be produced without the machine during the time that resources were devoted to building the frisbee machine. Thus, the (opportunity) cost of the machine is 30,000 frisbees. The formula for the real rate of interest for a machine that is assumed to last forever simplifies to

$$r = \frac{3{,}000 \text{ frisbees per year forever}}{30{,}000 \text{ frisbees sacrificed this year}} = .10, \text{ or } 10 \text{ percent.}$$

Society, by being willing to trade off 30,000 frisbees this period, can realize 3,000 frisbees per year forever for a real return of 10% per annum. This is the real rate of interest in a moneyless economy.

The *money rate of interest* is equal to the real rate of interest plus the expected rate of inflation.

However, when money is introduced as a medium of exchange the **money rate of interest** can deviate from the real rate. Money, as a measure of value does not always retain its value over time. Money can be cheapened by inflation and this may cause the money rate of interest, what the borrower pays when he goes to the bank, to diverge from the real rate of interest which reflects the productivity in physical units of the frisbee machine. The money rate of interest i is defined as

$$i = r + p^e.$$

where r is the real rate of interest and p^e is the expected rate of increase in the price level. If the anticipated rate of inflation were zero and the prediction is accurate, then $p^e = 0$, and the money rate would be identical with the real rate of interest, $i = r$. And the price of a frisbee today will be the same as its price in the future. But if the rate of inflation is, say, 5% then the medium that is being used to buy and sell real goods—money—is declining in value because the same amount of money will purchase fewer frisbees. The money price of frisbees is higher and the money rate of interest is greater than the real rate. The real rate was 10% and to this is added the inflation rate to get the money rate:

$$i = 10 + 5 = 15\%$$

Therefore the money rate of interest must rise by the rate of inflation to make up for the expected decline in value of money relative to future goods. The rational lender will mark up the real rate of interest by the expected inflation rate so as to be paid back with more money so as not to lose purchasing power. For example, if the rate of inflation is 10% and the real rate is 3% (about its average historical rate), then if I lend you a dollar for one year, I will charge you 13% to account for the inflation. I would charge you this money rate of interest in order to be compensated for the anticipated decline in the value of money by 10%, and I would add another 3% to ensure a positive rate of return to my saving, that is, a reward for being willing to delay consumption.

The Investment Process

A capital investment will be profitable if the expected rate of return is greater than the money rate of interest.

In general, then, the investment process occurs when firms adjust existing capital stock to some desired level, with expectations of earning some acceptable, but not certain, rate of return—a profit. The net return calculation includes the combined effects of many variables. A firm does not have to spend its earnings on a new machine or factory. If the rate of interest it can earn by buying a bond or some other paper asset, or by simply depositing the funds in a saving deposit, is higher than the rate of return that can be earned by investing in the business, the firm is better off by buying the bond. Not only that, but putting the firm's earnings into, say, government bonds or in deposits with a large financial institution is nearly without risk in comparison to purchasing new capital for the firm.

The bench mark that the investor uses to compare the rate of return he expects from investing in capital formation is the rate of interest. The rate of interest is a measure of opportunity cost. What yield does the firm sacrifice by not buying the bond or making a deposit in an account? The sacrificed yield is the interest rate.

The really large corporations usually generate enough earnings from sales and depreciation, after costs are subtracted, to purchase new and expensive capital and expand facilities. Many smaller firms do not. Therefore, they have to borrow and pay back the loan at some market rate of interest. Hence, the rate of return the firm anticipates must also cover the interest cost on the borrowed funds *and* allow enough of a return beyond that amount to justify taking the risk. Why borrow at, say, 8 percent just to earn a return of 8 percent on the investment in capital stock? This applies to internal funds too, for they also have an opportunity cost of 8 percent which they could earn if the firm lent the funds.

A WORLD OF MANY FIRMS AND MANY INVESTMENTS

In Figure 23.1 the vertical axis represents the rate of return, designated as r, expected from a capital expenditure. Suppose some machines or a plant modification costs $2 million. In the graph, the tallest vertical bar beginning at the left indicates that with an expected return of $r = 30$ percent, $2 million in

Figure 23-1

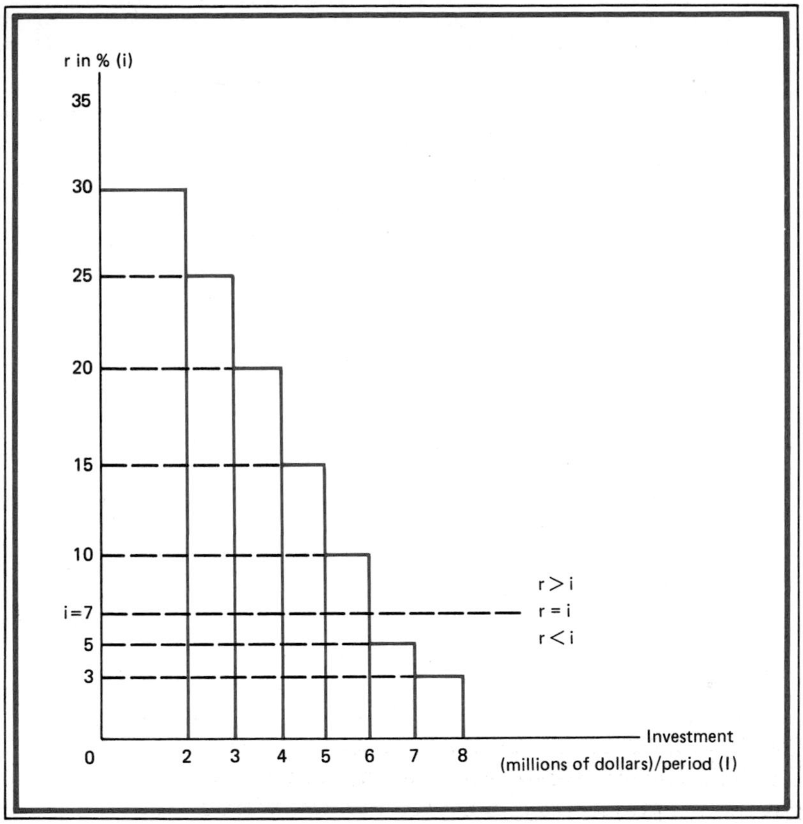

capital investment expenditures will be made as shown on the horizontal axis. Normally a firm is usually considering several investment plans, and it ranks them in descending order on the basis of the rate of return it anticipates from each.

Suppose another investment project in the amount of $1 million is expected to yield a rate of return of 25 percent. Given that the market rate of interest $i = 7$ percent, say from purchasing government bonds, the firm will proceed with the project from among its priorities of projects. This is shown by the second but shorter bar in Figure 23-1. There is now a total of $3 million in potential investment, $2 million from the first project plus $1 million in expenditures from the second project. Yet another project on the boards is expected to yield a rate of return of 20 percent. Since $r = 20$ percent and $i = 7$ percent, then r is greater than i ($r > i$) and the project is anticipated to be a good investment. Hence, the third shorter bar is shown in the future as raising total potential investment projects to $4 million. And so the priorities are itemized. Those projects yielding 15 percent are next, then those yielding 10 percent, and so on.

But for projects yielding a rate of return r *below* i equal to 7 percent, say $r = 5$ percent, it would not be maximizing profit behavior for the firm to make outlays for them. The rate of return on government bonds is greater. In this situation, the opportunity cost of buying the machine or modifying the plant is higher than the return on the machine of plant modification itself. Remember,

Figure 23-2

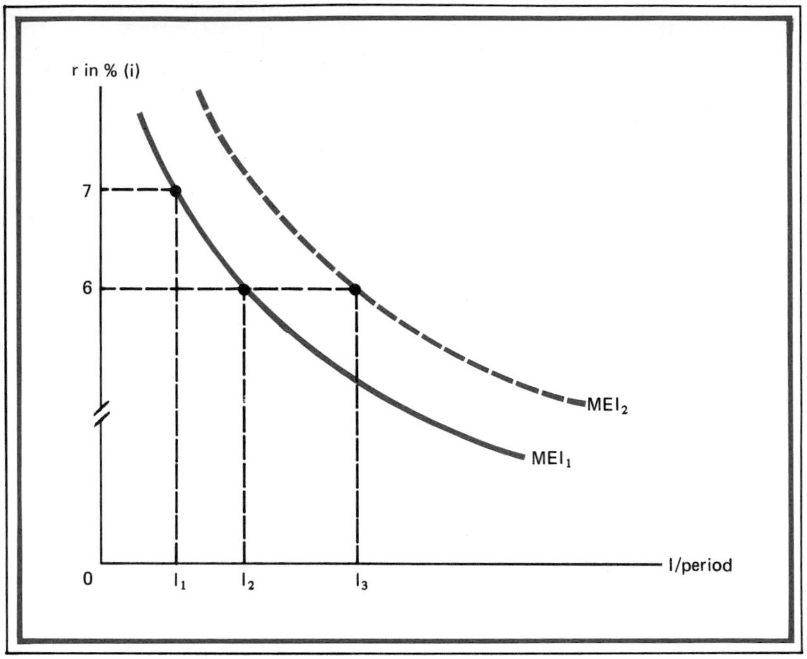

opportunity cost is the value of the next best alternative—in this case the alternative is the return of 7 percent on government bonds, which are essentially riskless. There is little likelihood the government will not pay off the bonds.

Therefore, the bar graph shows the investment priorities as ranked by their expected rates of return. Those above the dashed line are viable and worthwhile; those below are not and should not be undertaken. The graph depicts that the level of investment is greater the lower the opportunity cost (the rate of interest).

To convert the bar graph of Figure 23-1 into a continuous, smooth function shown in Figure 23-2, think of the difference in the amount of spending on each subsequent investment project as being very small. This signifies that the vertical bars would become much thinner and the number of possible projects would be multiplied. As the bars become thinner the upper right hand corners of each bar would come closer to one another. Imagine the additional expenditures on each additional project as being infinitesimally small, so that the corners of each bar would be so close as to form a continuous line as shown in Figure 23-2. This line is a schedule of the rate of return r and is called the **marginal efficiency of investment** *(MEI_1)* schedule—the demand curve for investment. As in the case of all demand curves, the MEI_1 expresses an inverse relationship between the rate of interest in percentage (the price of borrowing) and the dollar quantity of investment (quantity demanded of investment funds). Note that the vertical axis is labeled with the interest rate i as well as r, for the understanding is that in equilibrium $i = r$. Actually r would have to be larger than i because there should be included in the rate of return a reward for assuming risk.

The *marginal efficiency of investment* (MEI) schedule is the demand schedule for investment; it indicates that there is an inverse relation between the quantity of investment and the rate of interest.

As the interest rate falls from 7 to 6 percent in Figure 23-2, the dollar level of expenditures rises from I_1 to I_2. Those projects whose rate of return fall between 6 and 7 percent would or could now be undertaken. Conversely, had the rate of interest risen from 6 to 7 percent, some potential projects would have to be dropped, and investment expenditures would decline from I_2 to I_1 *along* the MEI_1 curve.

Various statistical studies of mortgage rates have indicated that investment expenditures on housing clearly do vary inversely with the rate of interest. Household construction is apparently quite sensitive to changes in the interest rate. The reason is that mortgage payments make up a large part of the total costs of buying a house. For instance, over the life of a 30-year mortgage interest payments can amount to over 50 percent of the total cost. Suppose a mortgage is taken out for 40 years at 9.25 percent on a house selling for $30,000. Annual payments of $2,732.20 over 30 years come to a total of $81,969.13.

Shifts in MEI Curve

As constructed in Figure 23-2, the level of investment (I) is a function of the interest rate *(i)*, *ceteris paribus*. Thus, using shorthand notation,

$$I = f(i, \overline{Y}, \overline{T}_X, \overline{P}_K, \overline{t}, \overline{C}_I, \overline{C}_U)$$

The MEI schedule can shift because of changes in one of the parameters.

where the shift parameters are now barred according to our convention. Shifts in the *MEI* curve occur when one of them changes. For example, if there is a positive change in income *Y*, the MEI_1 curve shifts right to MEI_2. At a rate of return of 6 percent, investment expenditures increase from I_2 to I_3. In fact, there are increased levels of investment at each level of increased income, which is exactly what a rightward shift in the schedule means.

Other factors affecting business decisions might have the effect of shifting the *MEI* curve to the left, indicating a reduction in capital expenditures at each rate of interest.

Returning to the determinants of investment described earlier in the chapter, we can now summarize the effects of each of the six barred variables in the equation.

1. As we have seen, an increase in GNP shifts the *MEI* curve to the right and is represented as an increase in demand for investment goods.
2. If technology, *T*, improves, then to exploit the advantages it offers, businesses will usually expand their expenditures on capital goods. It is possible to have an exception to this rule, because some technological change could be capital-saving and lead to less capital formation. But most technological change seems to stimulate investment. Hence, the *MEI* curve will usually shift to the right with improvements in technology.
3. As the price of capital goods, P_K, rises, less capital will be demanded. Thus, a higher P_K means a shift to the *left* in the *MEI* schedule.
4. A variety of taxes and tax incentives, T_X, affect the investment decision. In general, if T_X is lower, the demand for capital goods rises and the *MEI* schedule shifts to the right; and if T_X is raised, it shifts the *MEI* to the left. However, if T_X is an income tax and if it is raised on the receipts from *all* alternative uses of funds, then the *MEI* curve does not

shift. Thus, to analyze the shift one must specify the tax one has in mind.

5. When the price of an input rises, current capital facilities may become obsolescent. The demand for more efficient technology is speeded up, shifting the *MEI* curve to the right. Conversely, if there is a decline in labor costs relative to capital, the demand for new equipment may decline, shifting the *MEI* curve to the left as firms substitute toward labor relative to capital.
6. The closer that the industry is to full capacity utilization of its plant and equipment, the greater will be its incentive to expand its capacity. Thus, if C_U increases, it implies a rightward shift in the *MEI* schedule.

Thus, the *MEI* schedule showing the relation between *i* and *I* will shift in response to other important variables. It is in this way that economists can analyze the effects of such factors on the aggregate level of investment demand.

Movements versus Shifts

Shift parameters often dominate movements along the MEI curve caused by a change in the interest rate.

Investigators have had difficulty observing the inverse relationship of the level of investment to the rate of interest for plant and equipment. One reason is that *shift* (barred) parameters often dominate any *movements along* the *MEI* curve. For example, changes in national income do appear to have a strong influence on investment. This possibility is demonstrated in Figure 23-4. Suppose the rate of interest rises from i_1 to i_2 because of a decreased supply of credit. There is a corresponding reduction in investment along the MEI_1 schedule from I_1 to I_2. Suppose simultaneously there is an increase in national income (Y) that

Figure 23-3

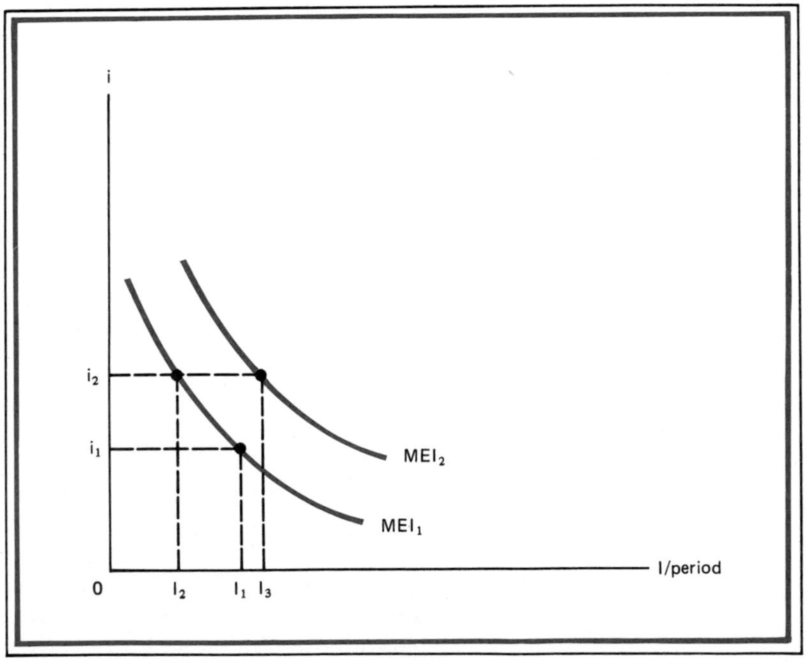

Figure 23-4

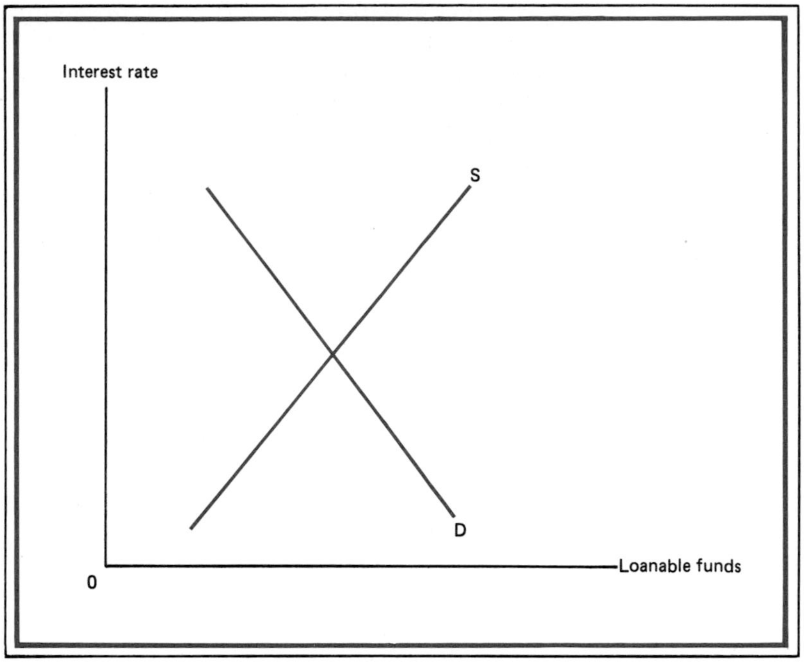

shifts MEI_1 to MEI_2; at i_2 the level of investment is now I_3. Thus, the stimulating effect of the increase in Y dominates the inhibiting effect on investment of the rising interest rate. When observing movements in investment and interest rates over time, therefore, we often observe that investment I and the interest rate i move together. This observation does not, however, signify that the underlying relation is positive. Rather, it means that another force, such as income, causes both I and i to move in the same direction.

Loanable Funds

The interest rate is determined by the supply and demand for *loanable funds*, that is, credit.

The demand for investment funds by firms as described above is a demand for borrowed funds, which falls under the general category of loanable funds. The loanable funds theory holds that the supply and demand for funds in the credit market determine the rate of interest, the price of borrowed funds.

The supply of credit derives mainly from household savings, retained earnings (savings) of business, insurance companies, credit unions, banks, and from the reductions in noninterest-bearing cash holdings of firms and households carried over from the previous period—those idle cash balances that had not been either spent or put to work earning interest as savings.

The demand for loanable funds stems from the desire of households and firms for credit, from banks slowing or recalling loans in order to bolster their reserves, and from households and firms increasing their noninterest-bearing cash balance holdings over those of the prior period. The marginal efficiency of investment *(MEI)* of firms is merely a subset of the demand for loanable funds directly associated with firms' investment borrowing. As Figure 23-3 illustrates, the supply schedule of loanable funds is upward sloping to the right, indicating that the quantity of credit willingly provided is a rising function of the interest rate, whereas the demand for funds is downward sloping to the right, reflecting that the quantity demanded is an inverse function of the interest rate. As the price of credit declines, the quantity of credit demanded rises.

THE STOCK MARKET

The stock market permits a corporation to sell part ownership in order to raise investment funds.

The question of who owns a corporation involves the concept of stocks. A stock certificate is a financial paper indicating that the legal holder owns part of the company. If a person owns 100 shares of stock of 100,000 shares outstanding, then that individual owns 1/1,000 of the company. Stock is issued and sold in order for the company to acquire needed capital for purposes of producing goods and services. When the corporation earns a profit the stockholder receives a dividend—a share of the profit. Someone might have a great idea for a new potato peeler but lacks adequate start-up or venture capital. Thus he or she forms a corporation and sells stock and is said to have "gone public." There are two basic kinds of stocks.

Holders of *common stock* have voting power and unlimited potential dividend payments; owners of *preferred stock* may have no voting power and they receive fixed dividend payments.

Common stock Holders are the actual owners who have voting power. They elect the board of directors. However, common stockholders are the last on the list to receive any payments—taxes, interest on loans, and all other expenses come first. They are also the last group to receive any compensation if the company goes bankrupt and is forced to sell off its assets (liquidate). However, there is no limit on the size of the dividend payment. If profits are high, dividends are also higher in proportion.

Preferred stock Holders are paid dividends before holders of common stock are paid theirs. But the level of the payment is fixed and does not vary with the corporation's profits. Preferred stock may carry no voting power.

When no dividend is declared in a given year, the amount missed may be included in the dividend for the next year, so that dividend rights of preferred stockholders may accumulate over the years.

***Bonds* represent a corporation's indebtedness.**

Bonds To raise financial capital for their investments, corporations also sell bonds. Bonds represent borrowing by the company—the company's indebtedness. The lender (buyer of the bond) expects to receive a fixed rate of return, called interest, on the money spent to buy the bond. When the bond matures, that is, when the period of the loan is up, the bondholder is repaid the principal—the initial amount of the loan or the original price of the bond. A bondholder is not an owner or a dividend receiver.

Those stocks you see listed in the daily newspaper are not newly issued stocks. Stocks outstanding are bought and sold just like secondhand cars. Stockholders are the middlemen who facilitate the transactions by finding buyers for sellers and sellers for buyers. The stock market is similar to a big gambling table where people are speculating not on a throw of the dice but on

Reading the Financial Page

The financial page listing stocks in the typical newspaper looks something like this:

Stock & Div	PE	Sales 100s	Hi	Lo	Close	Net Chg.
Kellogg 1.20e	12	17	21-3/8	21-1/4	21-3/8	+1/4

a. The first column identifies the company and the 1.20 reveals the dividend the company is expected to declare on each share for that year. The letter *e* following the 1.20 signifies that extras are included. If the letter were *b*, it would mean that Kellogg offered a bonus—an additional cash payment as well as the stock dividend. Other letters signify other bits of information. The letters *pf* before the dividend statement signify a preferred stock.

b. The 12 stands for the price-earnings ratio. It is the ratio of a stock's market price to its earnings per share. It is only one of the variables investors observe in making decisions about buying the stock.

c. The 17 signifies that 1,700 shares of Kellogg stock were traded that day. The 17 is multiplied by 100 as the column heading shows.

d. The 21-3/8 under the *Hi* column indicates that the highest price the stock sold for that day was $21.375 a share. The 21-1/4 signifies that the lowest price the stock sold for that day was $21.25 a share.

e. The 21-3/8 under the *Close* column says the last buyer of the day paid $21.375 for each share. Sometimes this column is designated *Last*. Some papers give the time of day—Price 3 pm.

f. The +1/4 signifies that the closing price that day was 25 cents higher than the closing price on the prior day. Thus, the previous day's closing price was 21-1/8. If the net change were −1/8, the closing price was 12-1/2 cents lower than the closing price of 21-1/4 of the prior day.

Dow-Jones

The most widely known and televised stock market index is the Dow-Jones Industrial Average. It consists of an index or average of prices of thirty industrial blue chip stocks. The name derives from the first editor of the *Wall Street Journal*, Charles Dow, who wrote a series of articles on the theory of stock market behavior from 1900 to 1902. Jones was a cofounder of the Dow-Jones Company. W. Hamilton and Robert Rhea interpreted these writings on Dow's theory and came up with the Dow-Jones Index. Actually, there is a Dow-Jones index for utilities and railroads, and a composite index. The Dow-Jones Industrial Index of thirty companies includes: Allied Chemical, Alcoa, American Can, AT&T, American Tobacco, Anaconda, Bethlehem Steel, Chrysler, DuPont, Eastman Kodak, G.E., General Foods, G.M., Goodyear, International Harvester, International Nickel, International Paper, Johns-Manville, Owens-Illinois Glass, Proctor & Gamble, Sears, Standard Oil of California, Standard of New Jersey, Swift, Texaco, Union Carbide, United Aircraft, U.S. Steel, and Woolworth.

Other well-known stock market indexes are the New York Stock Exchange Index, Standard and Poors Index 500, Forbes Magazine, and the New York Times Index.

the price of stocks. The idea is to buy at low prices and sell at higher prices and realize a capital gain. Some investors may purchase stocks in growth companies, where dividend payments are expected to go up, or in blue chip companies, where the dividend payment has been consistent and reliable. The prices of stocks listed by the stock exchanges are determined by the interaction of forces of supply and demand. The stock market serves other purposes, too. It helps to allocate scarce capital. A firm whose stock price is rising will find it much easier to sell new issues when it needs more capital. When people expect stock prices to rise they tend to buy, and this creates a *bull* market. When people expect stock prices to fall, and want to sell, a *bear* market is said to exist.

Most experts believe that stock prices move randomly. By this is meant that there is no consistently predictable pattern or tendency in the behavior of stock prices which can be inferred from stock price movements themselves. Thus, if true, the amateur playing the market has as good a chance as the professional investor of earning capital gains by throwing darts at the stock listings in the daily newspaper. Conversely, if as some believe there is some pattern to stock price movements, the obvious question is, Why aren't they millionaires?

We have been referring to dividend payments as the means by which the stockholder is given a return for the investment he or she made in the company. Actually, the return, or reward, for investment can arise out of an increase in the market price of the stock as well. Let us say a firm has considerable profit in a given year. It keeps the money instead of paying dividends, and buys some additional income-producing property. Now the stockholder's share of the pie is still the same, but the pie (wealth of the company) is now larger than it was before. The market price of the stock should rise. If so, the shareholder can sell his stock for a larger price and his return is *not* in the form of dividends, but is in the form of an appreciation in the value of his or her securities.

DETERMINING AGGREGATE DEMAND

Household and investment sector spending can be combined, to calculate aggregate demand of the two sectors equal to consumption plus investment ($AD = C + I$). The derivation is shown in Figure 23-5. In Chapter 24 the gov-

Figure 23-5

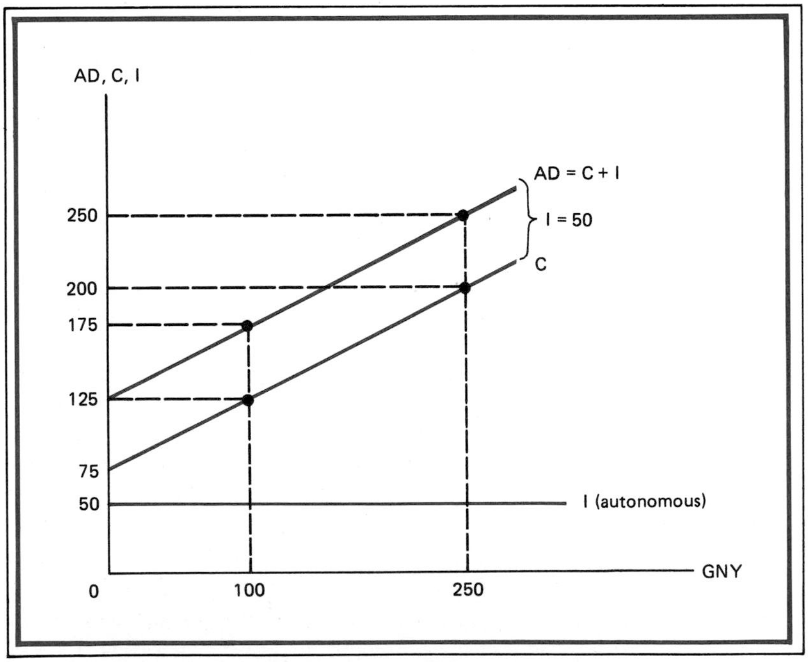

ernment sector will be included. Consumption, measured on the vertical axis, is a rising function of income, measured on the horizontal axis. Autonomous investment, also measured on the vertical axis, is fixed at 50, signifying that it does not change with current period income. We can treat current investment as constant if we assume that investment in the current period is viewed as related to income of the previous period and is therefore independent of current period income.

Gross national income is measured on the horizontal axis. When income is zero, consumption measured on the vertical axis is equal to 75. Aggregate demand, also measured on the vertical axis is the *vertical summation* of consumption and investment for each level of income. Thus, when income is zero, aggregate demand equals 75 + 50 = 125. When income rises to 100, investment remains at 50 while income rises to 125 to yield an aggregate demand of 175. When income increases to 250, investment is constant at 50, consumption rises to 200, so that aggregate demand equals 50 + 200 = 250.

CHAPTER SUMMARY

Investment by the private sector of the economy is the axle on which the wheel of the economy turns. The components of investment are residential construction, nonresidential construction, and changes in inventories. Investment spending is said to be of the induced kind when rising income causes people to demand more goods and services, leading firms to expand facilities and production. Autonomous investment is independent of increases in income and demand. The impetus for autonomous investment derives from the supply side. New products and technology are introduced in the hope of creating new demand and higher profits.

Investment or capital formation is a flow variable measured by the change in the amount of the capital stock per time period. Factors that affect the rate of capital formation are the rate of interest, changes in national income, the rate of new technology, the price of new capital, the level and kinds of taxes, the cost of inputs, and the degree to which existing plant capacity is being used. The change in national income is probably the most important, with interest rates second.

The effect of inflation on capital formation is clouded. Depending on circumstances, it could speed up investment or retard it. It is linked to what impact inflation is expected to have on future sales and on the cost of delaying the replacement of capital. This introduces the notions of uncertainty and the business cycle, and whether current downturns or upturns are temporary, or indicative of long-run trends. The short run is defined to be the period during which the existing capital stock cannot be changed but production levels can. Errors in production are easily corrected and less costly. The long run is defined as the period during which plant size and capacity can be changed. Errors here are more long-lasting and more costly. Fluctuations in investment spending are considered to be an important source of business cycles in a private enterprise economy.

The demand schedule for investment is known as the marginal efficiency of investment (MEI) schedule. It indicates that there is an inverse relation between the quantity of investment and the rate of interest, *ceteris paribus*. The anticipated rate of return from investment is equal to expected net revenues divided by the price of capital $r = \frac{NR}{P_K}$. The real rate of interest, or real rate of return, is measured in goods and is the rate at which goods sacrificed today yield more goods tomorrow. When money is introduced, and money can be exchanged for goods, the price of future goods in terms of money can change because of inflation. This causes the real rate of interest (now expressed in dollars) to diverge from the money rate of interest by the expected rate of inflation p^e so that $i = r + p^e$. Only when the expected rate of inflation is zero will $r = i$, indicating that the value of money in terms of future goods is expected to be unchanged.

So long as the expected rate of return is greater than the money rate of interest, a capital investment is profitable, otherwise it is not.

The rate of interest is determined by the supply and demand for loanable funds, that is, credit. The supply of loanable funds consists of household and business savings, funds in credit unions and banks, and reductions in the holdings of cash not earning interest currently held by firms and households. The demand for loanable funds comes from household and business demand, banks, and households and firms that wish to increase their holdings of cash balances not currently earning interest. The marginal efficiency of investment (MEI) curve is a subset of the demand for loanable funds.

The MEI schedule can shift because of changes in one of the parameters. In some situations, for instance, an increase in national income can shift the aggregate demand curve to the right, increasing the amount of investment spending more than a rising interest rate reduces it while moving up along the MEI schedule.

The stock market permits a corporation to sell part ownership of the company in order to raise investment funds. When it sells bonds, however, it is not selling ownership (equity) but it is borrowing. Stocks are of two general types; common stock where holders have voting power and whose potential dividend payment is unlimited, and preferred stock whose owners may have no voting power and receive only a fixed dividend payment.

Aggregate demand, excluding government spending, is the vertical summation of household and business investment spending at each level of national income. It represents the amount of spending out of each level of income.

QUESTIONS

1. Investment in housing is inversely related to the rate of interest. Why then, with money interest rates rising in a period of serious inflation, would the demand for housing increase as happened in mid 1978. Is this not a contradiction of the downward sloping investment demand curve?
2. A typical builder says, "I'm sitting on land that's already zoned. I'm not going to build a thing until those rates come down." Another builder says, "I don't adjust to interest rates. As long as I can get money, I'll keep building. I can't afford to lose rent and depreciation by not building with my materials costs going up 1 percent a month." Can you reconcile the differing attitudes of these builders? The second builder says he can't afford to lose depreciation by not building. Isn't depreciation a cost? So what does he mean?
3. Do changes in the market rate of interest alter the stock of capital of a firm? The investment process is fundamentally a process of what? Is investment a stock or a flow? Explain.
4. Polonius said to his son Laertes in Shakespeare's Hamlet, "Neither a borrower nor a lender be." Is this good advice for a firm? If not, when should a firm borrow and when should it lend?

5. The economics of expansion is risky business. Why is it more risky for Chrysler Corporation than for the local mom-and-pop grocery? Or is it not?
6. In the 1970s the Northeastern states declared that the South was growing at their expense as hundreds of firms left the North to resettle in new buildings in the South. Northern politicians convinced the House Ways and Means Committee to extend the investment tax credit to the rehabilitation of older buildings. Why did they desire this? Can you frame your answer in terms of the rate of return?
7. In 1980 the average car was 700 pounds lighter than it was in 1975. What effect would you predict this had on capacity utilization in the steel industry, *ceteris paribus?* What situation could change in the auto industry to make you revise your answer?
8. Why would price controls likely have a depressing effect on investment in fixed capital?
9. Which of the following would you classify as either induced or autonomous investment?
   a. Tennis becomes fashionable. So firms buy more tennis racket producing equipment to meet the expected demand.
   b. People can afford more leisure. More outdoor equipment is produced.
   c. Teflon is a byproduct of aerospace research, and Teflon pots and pans hit the market.
   d. The invention of the electric toothbrush.
10. During the 1970s there was a steady decline in the productivity of the U.S. economy. What effect on productivity and on the MEI schedule would you anticipate, and why, from
    a. The average age of the labor force rising by 10 years.
    b. The OPEC oil cartel disintegrating.
    c. More dishonesty and crime.
    d. A decline in expenditures for research and development (R&D).
    e. An easing of government regulations.
    f. An increase in the supply of loanable funds.
11. A long neglected, now resurrected way for raising capital funds is not for firms to borrow money outright from the banks, but for, say, an oil company to sell an interest in the future production from its oil and gas fields with known reserves. The ownership interest is known as a *production payment,* and becomes the collateral for banks supplying the loans. The banks are repaid out of the future revenues yielded by the field. The oil company is not liable for the loans should the yields be a disappointment. Gulf Oil raised $100 million in 1976 in this way for drilling its fields off the Louisiana coast. What obvious advantage is there to oil companies from this type of investment financing?
12. What happens to the interest rate in the loanable funds market, and why, if
    a. Households decrease holdings of cash balances?
    b. Banks begin to recall loans?
    c. Firms step up their borrowing?
    d. Business savings rise?
    e. Firms increase their demand for cash balances?
    f. Insurance companies and pension funds undergo an increase in their retained earnings?
13. Fargo Freddy inherits $800 and decides to buy an old pizza wagon with it that has a year of life left in it. He figures his operating costs for a year would be $1,500 while he anticipates gross revenues of about $4,100. He could earn $1,200 working the same number of hours in the school library. Assume the interest rate is 10 percent.
    a. What is Freddy's rate of return should he buy the pizza wagon? Was it a good investment?

b. Can you express the rate of return in a single formula?
c. Suppose he buys a second wagon for $800 but has to pay another student $1,200 over the period to drive it. The second wagon grosses $3,650 and costs $1,600 to operate. What is the rate of return? Is the second wagon a good investment?

Chapter 24

Aggregate Equilibrium

PROGRESS REPORT

A. We have to this point discussed the three major components of the economy: government, households, and firms.

B. Our purpose in this chapter is to combine the three sectors into an overall model of aggregate equilibrium. Before doing this we back up in history to the classical theory and explain what it was, why Keynes rejected parts of it, and in what ways Keynes's theory differs from the classical theory.

C. Chapter 25 develops the demand for money and then integrates money into the Keynesian model.

The time has come to combine the three major sectors of the economy—government, business, and households—into a macroeconomic model. We want to examine the concept of aggregate equilibrium, a condition of equality between aggregate supply and aggregate demand over the whole economy.

CLASSICAL THEORY

The classical theory's assumptions include perfectly competitive private markets, flexible wages and prices, perfect information, resource mobility, and no longrun money leakages.

Prior to 1936, classical theory and the classical model of Adam Smith, David Ricardo, John Mills, and Jean Baptiste Say, constituted the prevailing wisdom in orthodox economics. With sophisticated modifications, they have experienced a resurgence in the past decade. To understand any model one must first examine its assumptions. (For now we ignore the government sector.)

Competitive markets Classical theory assumes that markets are easy to enter, that there are no monopoly elements, and prices and wages are flexible both upward and downward in response to supply and demand forces. No single seller or buyer of a product has sufficient market power to influence the industry price, nor does any supplier or purchaser of labor services have sufficient market power to influence the market wage rate. Thus, all economic agents are price-takers and not price-setters. Because of the competitive nature of product and labor markets, any disequilibrium can only persist temporarily, in what economists call the short run. The short run is not a chronological measure of time, but an operational definition signifying a period during which the firm cannot change some aspects of its operation. Therefore, some input is fixed. But prices and wages are flexible. Thus, if for some reason the product market were experiencing excess demand in some industry, with quantity demanded greater than quantity supplied, prices would rise until quantity demanded once again equaled quantity supplied. The rise in prices returns the market to equilibrium. On the factor side, if there were an excess supply of workers, wages would decline until equilibrium in the labor market was restored and everyone who wanted to work could find a job. Specifically, suppose there is a decline in aggregate demand because the businesses decide to spend less. At existing prices, aggregate demand is now lower than aggregate supply and prices begin to fall. Temporarily money wages do not fall, so a decline in the price level translates into higher real wages paid by firms. They respond by laying off some workers. In a competitive labor market, unemployed workers compete for jobs by bidding down money wages. As money wages decline, so do real wages. Firms begin rehiring unemployed workers until the economy is again fully employed, with prices and money wages lower but with real wages and output again at their original levels.

Perfect information In classical theory all economic decision makers are assumed to be operating with all the information they needed to make the best decisions. The costs of acquiring information—transactions costs—are negligible. Therefore, consumers, producers, and workers know the prices and wages existing among traders in the markets and are aware of their options. No one would be privy to some special information providing them with an advantage for long. Any information gap would be closed quickly. Because entry is easy, others could enter in a relatively short time and remove any extra advantage being gained by another.

Resource mobility Consistent with the two prior assumptions is the assumption that both human and material resources are perfectly mobile. That is, the transactions costs of directing and redirecting resources to different uses in response to changing supply and demand forces are not inhibitive. Therefore, there is no serious friction in the system preventing resources from moving between slots in response to market forces.

No long-run leakages All this signifies that classical theory rules out any long-term leakages from the circular flow of national income. While leakages can arise, they are only temporary and before long would be reinjected into the economic system. Thus, savings are eventually borrowed and then spent; cash balances are not accumulated and kept unspent. Money is only a medium of exchange to facilitate the acquisition of goods and services desired by consumers. Money is not an end in itself, only the means to an end—spending. Therefore, all income is spent on consumption and investment goods.

The classical theory says that this equilibrium is temporary, since supply and demand adjust wages and prices, eventually returning an economy to *full employment* output and unchanged real wage rates.

Full employment As a result of these assumptions, a prediction of the classical system is that it essentially operates at full employment on a long-run equilibrium path over time. While in the short run unemployment can result, it cannot exist permanently because wage rates would fall when there exists an excess supply of labor. As workers compete for jobs, then by the law of demand wage rates fall and the quantity of labor services hired by firms increases. Alternately, if there were a labor shortage, the wage rate would rise as firms compete for workers. By the law of supply, the quantity of labor hours supplied by households would increase. For short-run periods, the labor market can, of course, be in a temporary state of disequilibrium. The classical economists certainly realized that product and labor resources do not adjust instantaneously and that there are lags in adjustment to market forces. However, the classical model incorporates the notion that the economy is on a long-run moving equilibrium path, and any deviations from long run equilibrium are not permanent because wage and price flexibility can remove excess demands or excess supplies. The conclusion is that if there were indeed any persistent unemployment, it can only be voluntary unemployment or be the result of severe frictions in the economy. But the latter is pretty much ruled out by the assumptions of competition, wage and price flexibility, and readily mobile resources.

SAY'S LAW

***Say's law* holds that supply creates its own demand.**

The classical macromodel is based on Say's law and is often summarized by the catchy phrase, "supply creates its own demand."

From Chapter 20 and the discussion on the national accounts, we learned

Figure 24-1

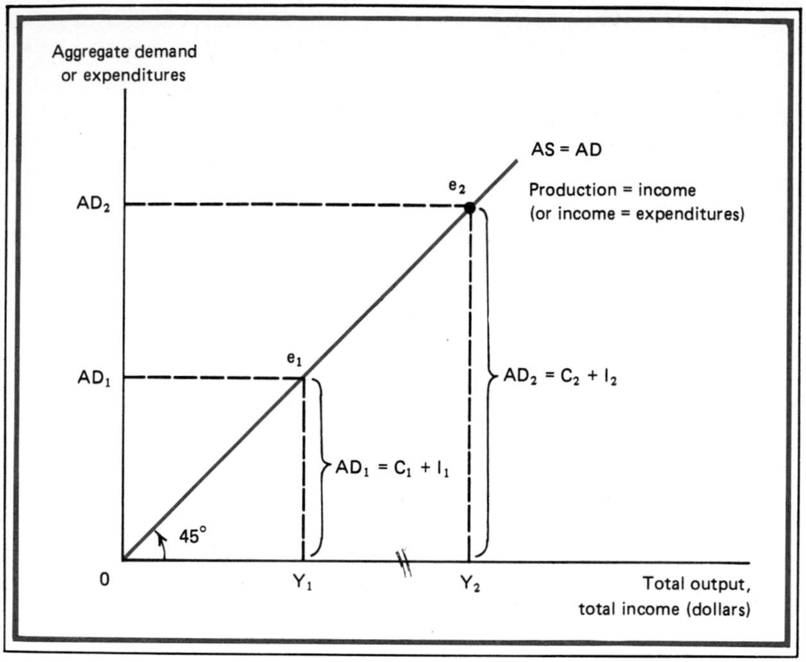

that the value of total output equals the total amount of income to factors of production: land, labor, and capital.

This of course is an accounting identity. It is true by definition. But Say's law says something about plans and intentions, hence about behavior. If producers plan to increase production, they can also create demand. Say's law could be stated, "Planned supply creates its own demand." When production is increased, payments are made to factors of production equal in value to the additional goods and services produced. The logic is that the additional production increases factor incomes by just the amount necessary to assure purchases that will absorb the additional output. That is to say, all the additional income earned by factors of production will be injected into the system because there are no long-term or permanent sources of leakage in the system under the assumptions of the classical model.

Planned Savings and Investment

Under Say's law the income is not only earned, it is also intended to be spent by households on consumer goods, and what is not spent is saved and equals how much producers plan to use to spend on investment goods.[1] Figure 24-1 presents a graphical summary. The 45° line is by construction a locus of points equally distant from the vertical and horizontal axes. Since by definition gross

[1] The following discussion is simplified. You are reminded that both households and business save as well as invest during the time period. Business saves through depreciation and retained earnings and households invest in housing. Business invests by replacing worn out facilities and acquires savings other than through borrowing by selling stock. We shall confine all saving to households and all investment to firms.

national product (GNP) equals gross national income (GNY), the 45° line is a schedule that simply indicates the relation between production and income in dollars. The 45° line can also be thought of as an aggregate supply curve *(AS)* with each point on the *AS* schedule indicating the dollar value of all consumer and investment goods that suppliers would willingly produce at various levels of GNP (or GNY). Since this production generates an equivalent amount of factor income, and we assume there are no permanent leakages from the circular flow according to Say's law, then the *AS* schedule also represents planned aggregate spending of that factor income at various levels of income. This aggregate spending of income can also be thought of as aggregate demand *(AD)* schedule, since each point indicates the level of spending required to absorb all the output produced in the period. Therefore, in the classical world the *AS* and *AD* schedules both coincide with the 45° line.[2] In Figure 24-1, at points e_1 and e_2 on the 45° line, equilibrium exists with aggregate demand equal to aggregate supply. Thus, $AD_1 = Y_1$ and $AD_2 = Y_2$. In the classical scheme, however, aggregate demand can only equal aggregate supply at one of these points, because in any given period there can be only one point at which there is full employment. Say's law is fulfilled as planned supply creates its own full-employment demand.

The Keynesian Cross

When there are no permanent leakages $AD = AS$ at full employment because planned investment expenditures by business equal planned savings by households in our simplified model, and expresses a behavioral assumption of the model. Namely, decision makers spend, and what they do not spend out of income, they put into saving to earn interest. Money income that is neither spent nor saved must therefore be held in the form of cash balances which earn no interest. The holding of cash balances, except for the purpose of making purchases, is rejected in the classical scheme. Now, it is also true that aggregate saving must equal aggregate investment by the imperatives of national income accounting definitions. Letting Y = income, S = saving, and C = consumption, $Y \equiv C + S$. It is an identity expressed with an identity sign ($\equiv$). On the expenditure side, letting C = consumption expenditures and I = investment expenditures, $Y \equiv C + I$ is also an identity. Income equals expenditures. Since the two identities both equal income (Y), they are identical to one another.

$$C + S \equiv C + I$$

Cancelling the C terms common to both sides leaves

$$S \equiv I.$$

Figure 24-2, called the Keynesian cross, illustrates the various income levels where the plans of savers and investors do not necessarily agree. Suppose at the

[2] Some writers prefer to call the 45° line an income-expenditure line, representing the locus of possible equilibria between income and spending. Strictly speaking it is not an aggregate supply curve. However, the aggregate supply-aggregate demand terminology is convenient and seems to be gaining favor over the income-expenditure terminology, so we adopt it here.

Figure 24-2

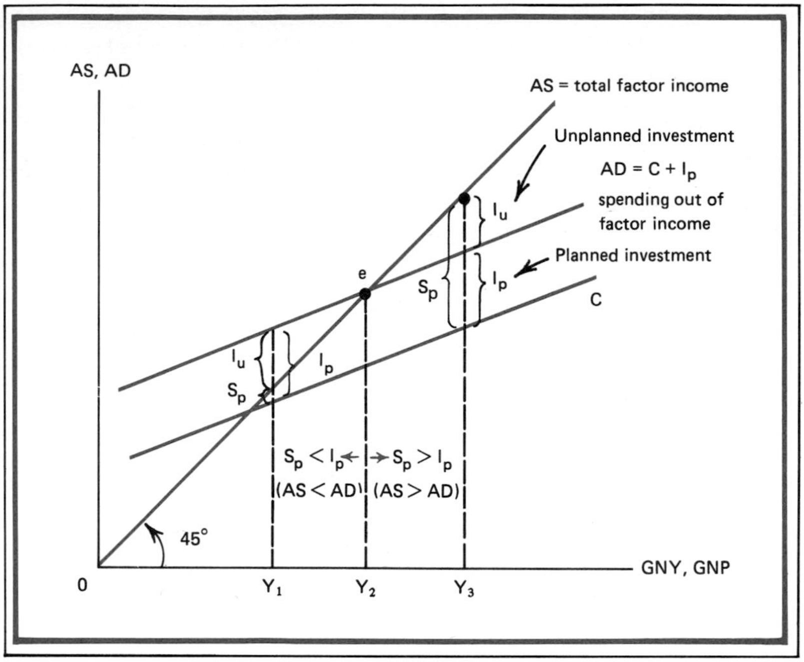

income level of Y_3 there are net leakages. Assume households plan to save more out of their income in the period than firms expect. That is, households plan to spend less than firms expected, implying that planned saving is greater than planned investment, symbolized as $S_p > I_p$. Moreover, it implies that aggregate supply is greater than aggregate demand, $AS > AD$, or that not all income earned is spent in the period. As a result there is overproduction by firms, with producers left with some unsold goods—inventories. Disequilibrium exists, for Y_3 is a nonequilibrium level of income. Recall from Chapter 20 that changes in inventories are treated as investment. The additions to inventory are designated as unplanned investment I_U. By the accounting definitions the actual level of investment must equal the level of saving. The actual level of investment consists of both the planned and unplanned components so that

$$I_{\text{actual}} = I_{\text{planned}} + I_{\text{unplanned}}.$$

Since in the accounting sense this must also be equal to saving, then, picking some arbitrary numbers

$$\underset{(100)}{S_p} = \underset{(80)}{I_p} + \underset{(20)}{I_u} \quad \text{with} \quad \underset{(100)}{S_p} > \underset{(80)}{I_p}.$$

(To avoid unhelpful complications, we always keep actual saving equal to planned saving by assuming that savers realize their saving plans immediately, implying that there are no lags in savers' adjusting their saving plans when income changes.)

When inventories are zero so that $I_u = 0$, then $S_p = I_p$ and there is equilibrium at point e when income is Y_2. Conversely, if income is Y_1, and households save less, that is, they consume more than producers expected, firms will underinvest and underproduce, causing planned saving to be less than

Figure 24-3

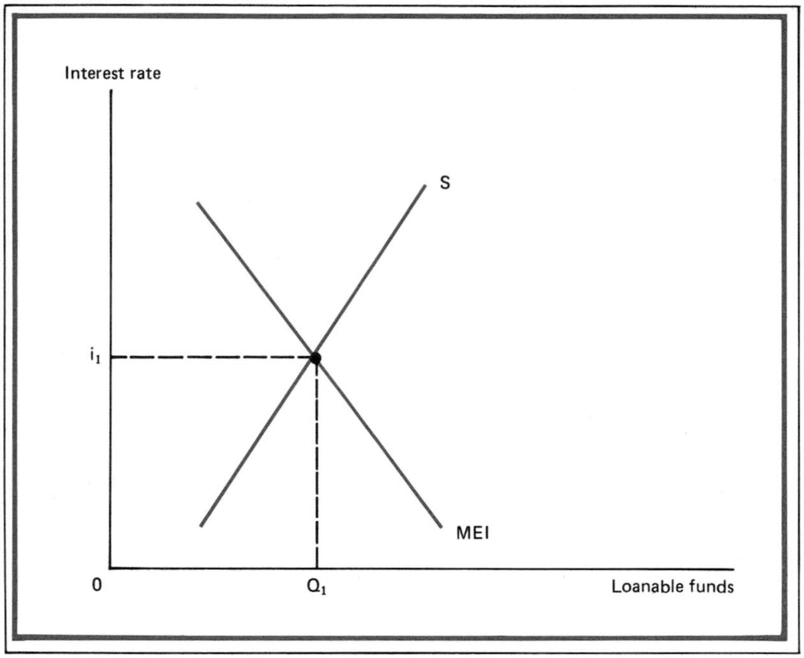

planned investment ($S_p < I_p$). Inventories carried over from the previous period will be drawn down, making unplanned investment negative ($I_u < 0$).

$$\underset{(20)}{S_p} = \underset{(80)}{I_p} + \underset{(-60)}{I_u} \quad \text{with} \quad \underset{(20)}{S_p} < \underset{(80)}{I_p}.$$

This too is a disequilibrium level of income, with aggregate supply less than aggregate demand $A_S < A_D$.

We conclude that $S_p = I_p$ ($A_S = A_D$) only in equilibrium, whereas $S \equiv I_A$ is true by definition in or out of equilibrium. Equilibrium exists when the plans or intentions of savers and investors agree.

The Role of Interest

The natural question to ask is, What brings the planned saving of households into equality with investment by firms? The equilibrating mechanism in the classical model is the interest rate. The classical model predicts that there cannot be any significant deficiency in aggregate demand because there are no long-term leakages from the system. For what is not spent must be saved. Money income does not sit idle under mattresses earning no interest. Cash is not held unless one intends to spend it; and if one does not intend to spend it, money is saved. Saving in the classical system specifically means that money is put to work earning interest. Thus, what is put into savings is borrowed by investors, namely business. How does the interest rate motivate savers and investors to save and invest? If we think of saving and investment in financial terms and as flows of money, then Figure 24-3 reproduces the supply and demand for loanable funds that appeared in Chapter 23. In our simplified analysis, households supply the funds and businesses demand them. Households make savings deposits in banks and businessmen go to banks to borrow this money to buy materials and equipment—to invest. (The role of banking as the intermediary between savers and investors is discussed in Chapters 25 and 26.)

Savers in the classical model are motivated by thrift—a penny saved is a penny earned. The saved penny will earn more the higher is the interest rate. Thus the quantity of funds households would willingly supply rises as the interest rate rises, so the supply curve is upward sloping. The demand for investment funds is negatively sloped because the quantity of funds firms would willingly spend on investment is greater the lower is the rate of interest, *ceteris paribus*, because the cost of borrowing is lower.

Investors are maximizers too. They would like to borrow as cheaply as possible because lower borrowing costs help to create higher profits. Thus investors are motivated by the rate of return r on investments—often called profit—which depends on the net productivity anticipated from the investment. A new machine that will turn out twice as many widgets as the old one means that widgets can also be sold at a lower, more competitive price. Thus, revenues are expected to rise while unit costs of output are expected to fall. As the interest rate falls, former unprofitable projects on the company drawing boards now appear profitable.

Thus, saving and investment are both functions of the interest rate. And because classical theory maintained that wage and price flexibility, and mobility of resources, yielded a condition of full employment of the labor force, the level of national income was at its full employment level no matter what the rate of interest that brought the supply of loanable funds to equality with the demand for loanable funds. Suppose households decide to save more than firms plan to invest, causing a shift in the supply curve of loanable funds to the right. Temporarily, before the new lower equilibrium rate of interest is reached, planned saving is not equal to investment at the old rate of interest. With saving up, total spending is down. The competitive markets of the classical model accommodate the drop in spending by allowing for flexible prices to fall as producers compete to remove the buildup in unsold goods. As employment (or hours worked) declines, so does money income. With prices falling in proportion, real income, or real purchasing power, does not fall. That is, if Y_m is income denominated in money terms and P_l is the price index, real income is $Y_r = Y_m/P_l$. With Y_m and P_l falling in proportion, Y_r remains constant. The same sort of thing happens in the labor market. There is no involuntary unemployment in the classical model. For as unemployment emerges, workers compete for scarce jobs by accepting lower money wages W_m. Firms view this as a decline in the real wage $W_r = W_m/P_l$ so they are willing to rehire laid-off workers. However, as the price level falls in proportion to the decline in money wages, the real wage remains unchanged. Thus, real output, real wages, and employment are the same after a period of adjustment, while money income, money wages, and the interest rate are down. The interest rate must fall too if full employment is to be reached again. It is the real terms that matter in the classical model. Therefore, there was no necessary connection between national income and the amount of savings and investment, since the amount of saving and investment varies only with the rate of interest, given the existing state of technology. In brief, with prices, wages, and interest rates flexible and existing in a system that experiences no severe long-term leakages of unspent or uninvested monies from the circular flow of income, there could be no serious long-term deficiency in aggregate demand in the classical scheme of things.

Supply creates its own demand and all's right with the world.

THE GREAT DEPRESSION

Starting in late 1929 and lasting through the decade of the 1930s, the U.S. economy experienced a disastrous slump. At times officially measured unemployment reached as high as 25 percent of the labor force, so that actual unemployment was no doubt higher. Aggregate demand was down and well below full employment equilibrium. Falling wages and prices apparently did not restore the labor and product markets to market-clearing equilibrium. Why did supply not create demand? Why did deficient aggregate demand persist between 1929 to 1941? asked perplexed economists of the time. Money wages dropped over 20 percent by the worst year of the Depression, 1933, and the price level fell over 25 percent. Unemployment in 1929 was 3.2 percent and peaked at 24.9 percent in 1933. One of every four workers had no job. There was no such thing as unemployment compensation or food stamps. Concerned citizens set up soup kitchens where the out-of-work lined up for a bowl of soup and a slice of bread. Even though hamburgers were a nickle, many people had no money to buy them. People sold their homes and farms or had no money to pay their mortgages and abandoned them to their creditors. Many moved into shantytowns with shelters made of old scrap metal and boxes—Hoovervilles as they were named after the then President, Herbert Hoover. They slept under bridges using newspapers for blankets and begged door to door. All this in a land of the most plentiful resource base—materials, labor, and capital—in the entire world.

KEYNES'S MUTINY

Why did falling wages and prices not restore full employment as classical theory predicted it should? In 1936, the English economist John Maynard Keynes (pronounced Canes) published a controversial, difficult, but pathbreaking book called the *General Theory of Employment, Interest and Money*, to explain this paradox of poverty in the midst of potential plenty. In it he challenged some of the basic tenets of classical theory—a body of theory to which he had already made significant contributions.

Keynes offered three basic causes for the dismal level of aggregate demand in the 1930s.

Keynes held that wages and prices are *sticky downward*.

1. Wages and prices while easily flexible upward tend to be **sticky in the downward direction**. Workers tend to react to the level of their money wage

and not their real wage. Therefore, if aggregate demand falls, firms respond by initiating lower prices in order to stimulate sales. But workers resist a decline in their money wage. To the firm charging lower prices, this resistance by workers amounts to a rise in the real wage that firms are paying the workers.

Consequently, at the higher real wage there was an excess supply of workers. That is, firms laid off workers to reduce their rising real wage bill in view of the declining demand. Once the economy had settled into a situation of high unemployment, a Catch 22 kind of situation emerged. Without money income, unemployed workers could not create sufficient demand. Paradoxically, the firm without anticipated sufficient sales receipts, because of current inadequate demand, could not justify hiring workers to produce goods it could not expect would be sold. Say's law does not always work.

Supply may not create demand, because firms will not increase production if they do not anticipate earning sufficient receipts from sales with which to pay workers. The plans of both firms and workers are thwarted because of the cash flow lag experienced by firms in the wake of a decline in aggregate demand.

Another Keynesian precept is that *saving* is primarily a function of income, not of the interest rate.

2. Keynes emphasized that savers and investors are two different groups with different saving and investment schedules. At the beginning of the period there is no *a priori* (before the event) reason to expect that the intentions and plans of the two groups will be identical. The chance that saving by households and planned investment by firms will be identical is small. Furthermore, the level at which saving would equal planned investment could just as easily exist in an equilibrium below the full-employment level of national income. The reason, said Keynes, is that the dominant influence on saving and investment is the level of income and not the rate of interest.

According to Keynes, consumption is a function of the level of income. The unspent residual, **saving**, is therefore also a function of income. Investment, however, is indirectly related to income because the source of investment funds is saving. As income falls, investment will fall because saving goes down. Since in equilibrium planned saving must equal planned investment ($S_p = I_p$), the *equilibrium* level of both saving and investment depends on the level of income.

Therefore, the primary variable that directs saving and investment, that indeed adjusts saving and investment to equilibrium, must be gross national income. If national income were too low for reasons of unemployment described in 1 above, then aggregate demand would fall short of creating full employment. Aggregate spending is too low to generate enough income for full employment output to be absorbed. What has to be done is to stimulate aggregate demand. In the 1930s the private sector appeared incapable of it. Keynes suggested that the government prime the pump and stimulate aggregate demand by raising government expenditures without raising taxes, and proceed down the avenue of deficit financing where business was unwilling or unable to engage in the necessary level of deficit financing. In Keynes's scheme it is aggregate demand that determines the level of national income. Demand creates supply and not vice versa. If aggregate demand is insufficient, unemployment is the result. Unemployment is involuntary, said Keynes; the jobs just are not there. Jobs must be created, therefore, by stimulating aggregate demand.

3. The classical model did not allow for permanent leakages in its per-

Keynes also held that there are *cash leakages* from the circular flow.

fectly fluid description of the macroeconomy. In an economy that does not trade goods for goods—a barter economy—there can be no leakage. However, in an economy where money is used to buy goods, and goods can be used to buy money, but goods do not directly buy goods, there can be **leakage** in the form of money withheld from the circular flow. The income that consumers do not spend and income they do not save is money they can hold in the form of cash balances. People also have a demand for cash in a money economy. If the nation's money supply has not been increased over the last period, and if the public decides to collect more quarters for coin machines or increase minimum balances kept in cookie jars not yielding interest, cash balances will increase. These are noninterest-bearing leakages from the circular flow. So are excess reserves held by banks, as you will see in Chapters 25 and 26. We shall have more to say about the noninterest-bearing demand for money in Chapter 27. Our purpose in this chapter is to examine thoroughly some causes for inadequate aggregate demand in an economy operating at less than full employment equilibrium. *AD, AS,* and *GNY* are all expressed in money or nominal terms. For now we assume the price index remains constant until full employment is reached.

GAPS AND EQUILIBRIUM

When aggregate demand is greater than aggregate supply, there exists a situation of deficient aggregate supply or a supply gap. When aggregate demand is less than aggregate supply there is deficient aggregate demand or a demand gap. Let us examine how Keynesian theory would restore the economy to equilibrium.

The upper graph in Figure 24-4 shows the system in aggregate *equilibrium* at point e when $AD = AS = \$600$. All goods produced by firms are sold. Therefore total spending equals income.

AS Greater than AD

Suppose that production is stepped up to $1,000 of output. Thus, corresponding factor income is also $1,000. However, at the outset of the chapter we made the point that in the beginning of the new accounting period, the spending by households usually differs from what firms anticipate consumer spending will be. Therefore, planned investment by firms normally differs from planned saving by households. The figure shows that when income is $1,000 consumers spend $700, so that consumers would save $300. Assume firms only planned to spend $100 on capital investment I_p. The result was that firms overestimated how much households would spend (or underestimated how much they would save). Thus, saving is greater than planned investment by $200 ($S - I_p = 300 - 100 = \$200$). What then did the $200 residual represent? It was the unsold inventory accumulated by firms in the period. Firms planned to invest $100 in

Figure 24-4

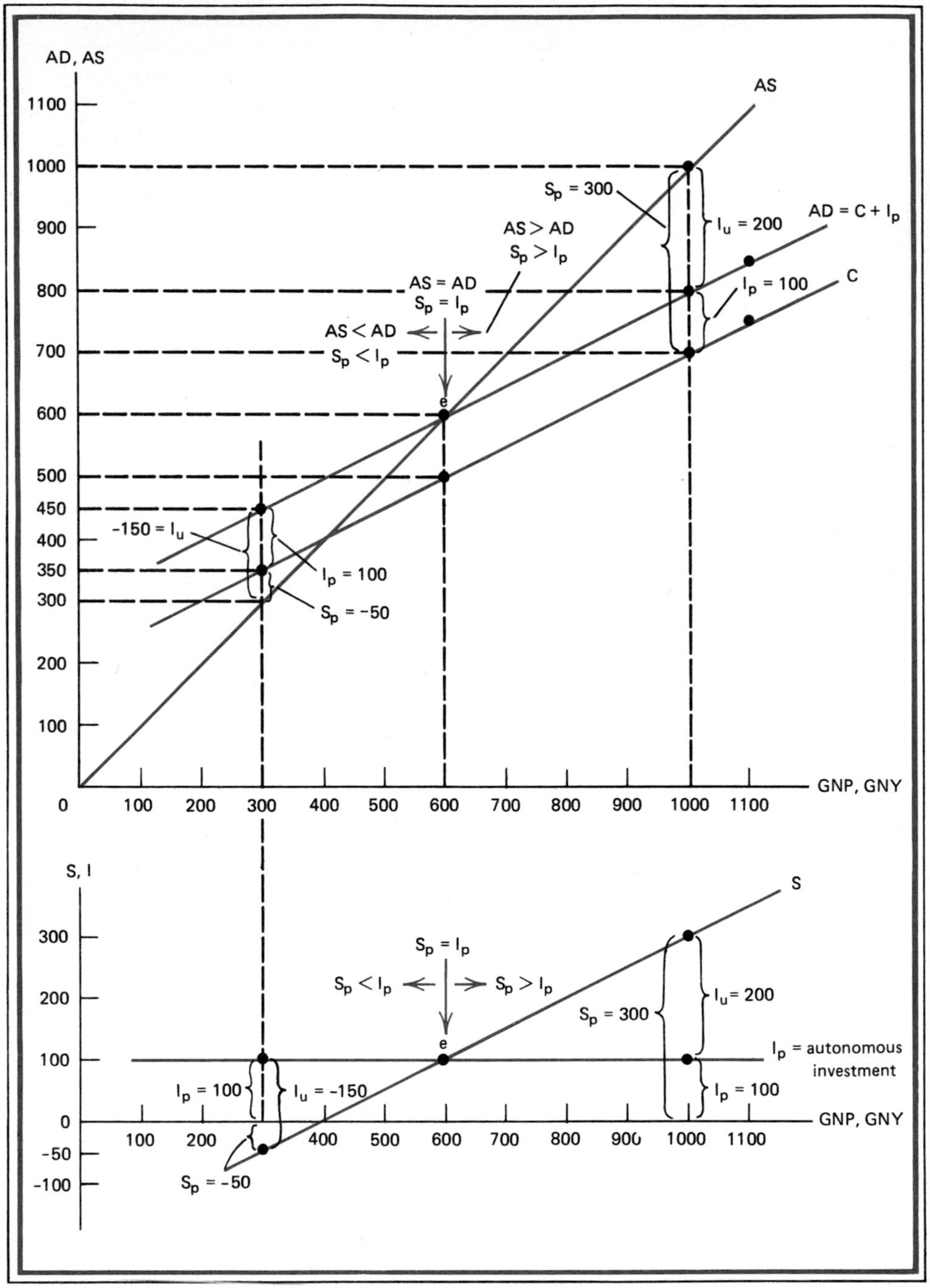

capital goods, in the process creating \$100 of factor income. They also intended to produce \$900 (1000 − 100) worth of consumer goods, thereby creating an additional \$900 in factor income, for a total factor income of \$1,000. However, unpredictably, consumers spent only \$700 out of their total income and saved \$300. Since firms planned to spend \$100 on investment, total aggregate demand was \$700 + 100 = \$800. And since aggregate supply is the value of output produced, and is by definition equal to total factor income of \$1,000, aggregate demand therefore was less than aggregate supply by \$200. There were \$200 worth of unsold goods accumulated by firms over the period. Consumers spent less (saved more) than firms anticipated they would out of a given level of income.

Behavior is one thing and accounting definitions another. At the end of the period, the fact is there were unplanned inventories of goods owned by firms worth \$200. No accountant is going to tolerate bending definitions for very long. The rules of Chapter 20 say saving must equal investment by definition—so be it! So the accountant calls the unanticipated inventories unplanned investment I_u. Think of it as firms buying their own output. Nonetheless, firms do not consume, they invest; hence, the \$200 in unsold goods is an investment expenditure—although an unanticipated one. When this is done saving equals investment. Recall that we should say that *actual* saving equals *actual* investment. Since actual investment I_A is the sum of planned plus unplanned investment, it must equal saving. Thus, in the accounting sense $S = I_A$ (remember, we always keep $S_p = S_A$),

$$
\begin{aligned}
S &= I_p + I_u = I_A \\
\$300 &= 100 + 200 = \$300
\end{aligned}
$$

However, there is a problem because $S_p > I_p$ and $AD < AS$. Demand is deficient and the system is in a state of disequilibrium. Firms have overproduced in the current period. Therefore, in the next period firms plan to reduce the inventory stock by reducing output while selling off the extra stock of goods. They can do this by either reducing the number of working hours or cutting back the work force. In either event, a decline in production over the next period translates into diminished employment and production, leading to a corresponding decline in factor income. Since saving is a function of income, and income begins to fall, saving must fall too, and by association so must consumption. *It is changes in* **national income** *that drive the equilibrating mechanism in the Keynesian model.* But consumption falls more slowly than saving as factor income falls in the short run. We described this in Chapter 22. We learned there that the average propensity to consume (*APC*) falls as income rises and rises as income falls. Thus as income falls, saving falls but by proportionately more than income falls. As income declines the economy moves down along the *AD* curve toward point e. As the inventories represented by I_u decrease, the I_u term approaches zero and equilibrium is reached when income is \$600. The process continues until $I_u = 0$ leaving $S_p = I_p$. However, saving and consumption are both much lower now. The result is $S_p = I_p = \$100$ and consumption is \$500. But since $S_p = I_p$ and $AD = AS$, equilibrium exists. It is the intentions embedded in the aggregate supply and demand schedules that ultimately decide where equilibrium will be, not the definitional imperatives of accountants.

In the Keynesian model, changes in *national income* drive the equilibrating mechanism.

Actual saving equal to actual investment refers to the completed accounting period. At any given time in an economy whose decision makers, firms, and consumers, are constantly adjusting to new signals from the marketplace, saving by households will only equal planned investment by firms through sheer coincidence. This is the crux of the analysis.

AS Less than AD

To be thorough, we should examine the model when income is \$300, below the equilibrium income of \$600 as in the upper graph of Figure 24-4. There is deficient supply. For an income of \$300, aggregate demand equal to \$450 is greater than aggregate supply equal to \$300. Households consume \$150 more than is produced in the current period. To meet the excessive demand, firms reduce inventories carried over from a previous period by \$150. The change in inventories, the unplanned investment I_u, is in the negative direction since inventories are reduced. Saving is also negative by \$50 (\$300 − \$350). To meet expenses, households had to dip into savings built up during prior periods. Summarily, since $S = I_p + I_u$, rearranging terms yields

$$I_u = S - I_p$$

Substituting in the numbers $S = -50$ and $I_p = 100$ gives

$$I_u = -50 - 100 = -\$150.$$

Therefore I_u is both negative and larger in absolute size than I_p. Faced with these circumstances, firms move to increase production in order to meet demand which they have underestimated. More workers are hired or working hours of the existing labor force are increased. Higher employment and output means that higher factor incomes are generated. As income rises, both saving and consumption, being functions of income, also rise. The system simultaneously moves back along the *AD* and *AS* curves, where they converge toward equilibrium at point *e* where $AD = AS = \$600$ and $S = I_p = \$100$ with $I_u = 0$.

You might respond by saying there are no extra inventories available when $AD > AS$, since the system had adjusted to equilibrium in the previous period. In reality, an economy is always in motion, moving through time, now closer to equilibrium, now moving away from it. The simple model here is only meant to explain a basic equilibrium concept and is not to be taken as an analysis that traces the path of a business cycle.[3] However, we realize firms are always in a process of adjusting inventories and carrying over more or less inventories from one period into the next as they try to maintain some target level of inventory to be ready to respond to unexpected changes in supply and demand.

Leakages Equal Injections Approach

Because of the definitional relation between saving, consumption, and income, we can draw a saving function that is a complementary reflection of the consumption function, so that everything we detailed can be analyzed just as well using the lower graph in Figure 24-4. With consumption subtracted from aggregate demand, the analysis can be carried on using saving and investment only. When $S = I_p$ and equilibrium is reached, $AD = AS$ must also hold. There-

[3] Actually, during a downturn in the business cycle inventories would initially build up as sales declined, and only later would inventories be cut back as the downturn persisted.

TABLE 24-1

$$GNY \equiv C + S_p \equiv \underbrace{C + I_p}_{AD} + I_u \equiv GNP$$

	GNY		C		S_p		C		I_p		I_u		GNP	
	300	≡	350	−	50	≡	350	+	100	−	150	≡	300	$S_p < I_p$
equilibrium:	600	≡	500	+	100	≡	500	+	100	+	0	≡	600	$S_p = I_p$
	1,000	≡	700	+	300	≡	700	+	100	+	200	≡	1,000	$S_p > I_p$

fore, saving and planned investment can be analyzed without introducing consumption. The saving schedule appears as a rising function of income. When $Y = 300$, the lower graph directly shows that saving is negative and equal to -50 and $I_u = -150$. Remember, $I_p = \$100$ but it generates factor income of \$100 to those who produce the investment goods. This \$100 is nevertheless factor income with which to buy consumer goods. Hence, it contributes \$100 to consumption and helps reduce inventories. So while I_p is positive, I_u is nevertheless negative in this situation.

Table 24-1 summarizes the relations of Figure 24-4 for the three levels of income.

By definition $GNY = GNP$ equals \$300 in the first row. However, underproduction has occurred because saving (-50) is less than planned investment (100) and a condition of disequilibrium exists with aggregate demand (450) greater than aggregate supply (300). Inventories decrease as producers move to meet the demand, and in the next period they hire more workers and step up production causing *GNP* to rise while moving the system toward equilibrium with $GNP = \$600$ as shown in the second row. In equilibrium $AS = AD = \$600$ and saving equals planned investment at \$100. The third row illustrates

Figure 24-5

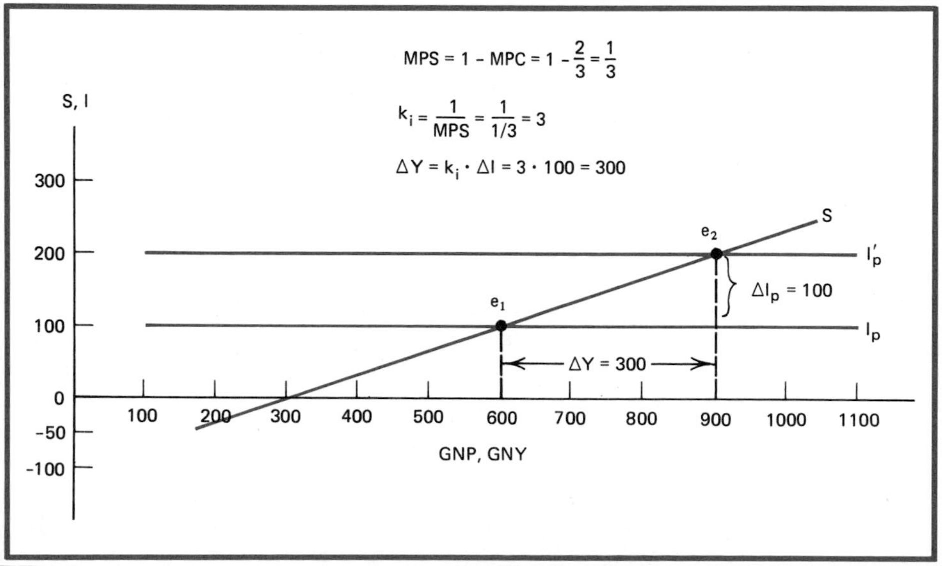

another disequilibrium condition where aggregate demand (800) is less than aggregate supply (1000), a situation of overproduction. Saving (300) is greater than planned investment (100), resulting in some unsold goods. Firms lay off workers and cut back production, causing a decline in gross national income. The economy contracts back to equilibrium at an income of $600.

THE MULTIPLIER

The Keynesian investment *multiplier* equals the inverse of the marginal propensity to save.

Assume that autonomous investment in Figure 24-5 increases from $100 to $200, or $\Delta I_p = 100$. Recall that autonomous investment spending by firms is investment that is not instigated by changes in income, but occurs independently of income because of, say, the introduction of a new technology. Thus I_p is shifted upward to I'_p by $100, causing a rise in aggregate demand by $100. Equilibrium moves from e_1 to e_2 with the equilibrium level of income increasing from $600 to $900 with leakages (S) equal to injections (I_p). Observe that the increase in investment of $100 leads to an increase in income of $300. Investment spending causes the change in income to rise by a multiple of 3 over the initial investment outlay. The figure indicates that the marginal propensity to save $(MPS) = \Delta S/\Delta Y = 100/300 = 1/3$, so the marginal propensity to consume (MPC) must equal 2/3. Let us trace through the process of how an initial expenditure that increases aggregate demand by $100 leads to an increase in aggregate income of $300.

A firm spends $100 for a new machine. The $100, according to the accounting rules, is paid to the owners of the factors of production who created the machine. If $MPC = 2/3$, then in the first round factors of production who earned the income will spend 2/3 of $100 = $66.67 and save 100 − 66.67 = $33.33. The $66.67 that is spent by these consumers who made the machine is spent on other goods which, in turn, represent payments to yet other owners of factors of production who made these other goods. Having received income of $66.67, and given an MPC of 2/3, they in turn spend 2/3 of 66.67 or $44.44 and save $22.23. Now the $44.44 that is spent becomes income to those who produced the $44.44 worth of goods that were sold, and in their turn these factor owners spend 2/3 of 44.44 or $29.62 and save $14.82. So it goes, down to the last dollar. When the last round is reached and income, spending, and saving is tallied, income totals $300. Since the $MPC = 2/3$, then $2/3 \times 300 =$ $200 in additional spending was created, plus additional saving of $100. The table at the top of page 591 summarizes the results.

There is a multiplier effect of 3 on the initial outlay of $100. This Keynesian investment multiplier is designated as k_i and is equal to

$$k_i = \frac{1}{1 - MPC} = \frac{1}{MPS}$$

Using the relation that $MPC + MPS = 1$, yields $1 - MPC = MPS$. Thus, $MPC = 2/3$, so that $MPS = 1/3$ gives

	Investment	Income	Consumption	Saving
Round 1	100	$100.00	66.67	33.33
Round 2	0	66.67	44.44	22.23
Round 3	0	44.44	29.63	14.81
Round 4	0	22.23	13.82	8.41
	.	.	.	.
	.	.	.	.
	.	.	.	.
All other rounds	0	66.96	45.44	21.22
Total	$100	$300.00	$200.00	$100.00

$$k_i = \frac{1}{1/3} = 3.$$

Note that when dividing by a fraction, bring the fraction up into the numerator and invert it.

We can now state, in shorthand, the basic relation between the change in income (ΔY) to the change in investment expenditures (ΔI) as

$$\Delta Y = k\Delta I$$

The multiplier effect is exemplified by a new firm that comes into town. For every job it provides, two others derive from it. The enlarged workforce earnings create a demand for other things such as housing and food. There is more spending on construction materials, on goods sold in local stores, a local restaurant has to hire another waiter, and the local car dealer another salesman, whose spending creates new demands.

Unfortunately, the multiplier cuts two ways. If the local plant were to shut down and lay off 300 workers, it could mean a loss to the community of $3 \times 300 = 900$ jobs. In practice, city planners use a multiplier of 2.

PARADOX OF THRIFT?

Is it possible that because households try to save more they may be ironically forced by the ensuing consequences of that desire to end up saving less? Suppose that the economy is in equilibrium where $S_1 = I_p = \$150$ at $GNY = \$700$, as in Figure 24-6. For whatever reason, households decide to save more at each level of income. This is in effect a shift in S_1 upward to S_2. Households now want to save $200 at the current level of income of $700 instead of $150. But increasing saving out of current income by $50 means that consumption is

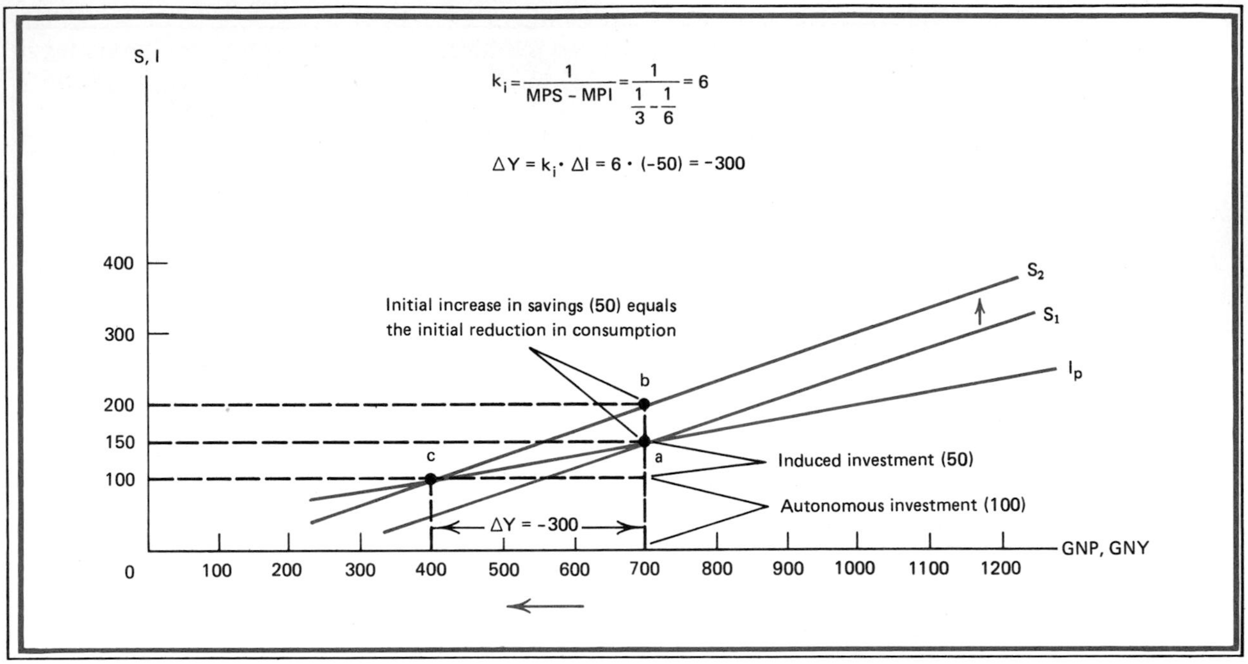

Figure 24-6

reduced by \$50, which shows up as \$50 of unsold goods by firms—unplanned investment. In response, firms reduce production and employment with the result that national income falls to \$400. At \$400 households can only save \$100—and it all started because they wanted to save \$200.[4] Because everyone wanted to save more and spend less, economic activity declined, the economy fell into a slump, and people were forced to save less because they earned less. Evidently, according to the paradox of thrift, an aggregate penny saved is not an aggregate penny earned. What's good for Ben Franklin is not good if everyone behaves as Ben Franklin suggested.

This is apparently explained by invoking the fallacy of composition. What holds for the individual does not hold in the aggregate. It has been proposed that the paradox of thrift could have happened during the Great Depression of the 1930s. As people became very unsure about keeping their jobs, they tried to save more while consuming less—to build up a cushion as security. However, the reduction in aggregate demand this behavior caused guaranteed further job layoffs, declining income, and production. As income fell, so naturally did saving despite the desire to save more.

Some economists reject this paradox. As we already noted, saving is the source of investment funds. Are we to conclude therefore that saving results in a decline in economic growth? If more income is saved creating additional loanable funds, will not the interest rate fall, thereby encouraging further

[4] Notice that the investment function is not constant here but a function of income, so there is an induced disinvestment effect when income falls, associated with the marginal propensity to invest (*MPI*), which is now not zero. Here, the $MPS = \Delta S/\Delta Y = 100/300 = 1/3$ and the $MPI = \Delta I/\Delta Y = 50/300 = 1/6$. The multiplier then takes the form $k_i = \frac{1}{MPS\text{-}MPI} = \frac{1}{1/3\text{-}1/6} = 6$. Hence $\Delta Y = k_i \Delta I = 6(-50) = -300$. We shall take another look at this soon.

investment by firms according to the marginal efficiency of investment schedule analysis? The more capital goods firms buy, the more capital goods other firms must produce. This creates factor income to those factors that produce capital goods just as those factors that produce consumer goods earn income. Thus, the level of income should not fall because people decide to save more. What changes is the ratio of capital goods to consumer goods produced, and not the level of aggregate income and spending. The only way for the paradox of thrift to occur is if the unspent income of households did *not* reenter into the circular flow as investment funds. For that to happen requires that households hold more of their income in noninterest-bearing cash balances by not making deposits in financial institutions such as banks and savings and loans, or even withdrawing funds from them. It would also require that deposits owned by households and held by banks not be reinjected into the circular flow by the banks because they refuse to make loans to businesses. It could be argued, on the other hand, that if the drop in consumption is severe enough and long enough, too much excess capacity would occur, resulting in adverse effects on business expectations, causing the *MEI* schedule to shift left, offsetting the effects of lower interest rates and depressing income and consumption further. All this involves an understanding of the demand for and the supply of money, to be discussed in the upcoming chapters.

AGGREGATE EQUILIBRIUM WITH GOVERNMENT

When the government sector is added to aggregate demand, total output as measured by GNP is

$$GNP \equiv C + I + G.$$

By corollary, gross national income is

$$GNY \equiv C + S + T$$

where G stands for government expenditures and T for taxes collected by government but not including taxes from transfer payments. By definition of the national accounts, GNY≡GNP over the accounting period of one year. Thus

$$C + S + T \equiv C + I + G.$$

Since C can be subtracted from both sides, this leaves the basic national income accounting identity

$$\underset{\text{(leakages)}}{S + T} \equiv \underset{\text{(injections)}}{I + G.}$$

Solving the identity for S by adding $-T$ to both sides, with T disappearing on the left side, we get after rearranging

$$S \equiv I + (G - T).$$

To convert the identity into an equation introducing intentions or plans (using the subscript p for planned expenditures),

$$S = I_p + (G_p - T)$$

where G_p refers to planned government expenditures as proposed in the government budget. The parentheses indicate net revenues in the government sector, as distinguished from the private sector represented by S and I_p. We have three cases.

If $G_p - T > 0$ (or $G_p > T$)	Planned government expenditures exceed tax revenues: a deficit condition with government injections greater than tax leakages.
If $G_p - T = 0$ (or $G_p = T$)	Planned government expenditures equal tax revenues: a balanced budget with government injections equal to tax leakages.
If $G_p - T < 0$ (or $G_p < T$)	Planned government expenditures are less than tax revenues: a surplus with government injections less than tax leakages.

Overall equilibrium with government included occurs when leakages (planned saving plus taxes) equal injections (planned investment plus government expenditures).

Suppose $S > I_p + (G_p - T)$. This implies that the system is out of equilibrium with total leakages greater than total injections. This can occur because private investment is smaller than saving, with net government injections $(G_p - T)$ too small to make up the difference. There are two ways for equilibrium to be reached. Simply let GNP fall until equality between leakages and injections is attained. Or, if government policymakers do not want GNP to fall because it will lead to unacceptable levels of unemployment, the government can expand GNP through increasing net government injections by creating a budget deficit $(G_p > T)$, either by borrowing, then spending, or by reducing taxes, or both.

There is also a disequilibrium when $S_p < I_p + (G_p + T)$, signifying that total leakages are smaller than total injections. It can occur because private investment is larger than saving with net government leakages (negative injections) too small to close the difference. This time a new higher equilibrium can be reached by letting GNP rise. However, if the policy makers are fearful that it would cause inflation, the government can either reduce spending or increase taxes or both, which will increase leakages through creating a budget surplus $(G_p < T)$, thereby lowering the equilibrium level of GNP.

Figure 24-7 presents the graphical analysis of aggregate equilibrium when the government sector is included. Both the government and investment schedules are constant, and have been vertically added to give a constant (flat) $I_p + G_p$ schedule. That is, both are drawn as independent of current period income. We can justify this convenient and simplifying condition by assuming that investment is a lagged function of previous period income, and that current period government expenditures are based upon a budget developed in the prior period.

Aggregate equilibrium is shown by point e in the upper figure, where $AS = AD = C + I_p + G_p$, and where investment I_p has been vertically added to G_p to yield the $I_p + G_p$ line shown in both figures. The bottom figure, as

Figure 24-7

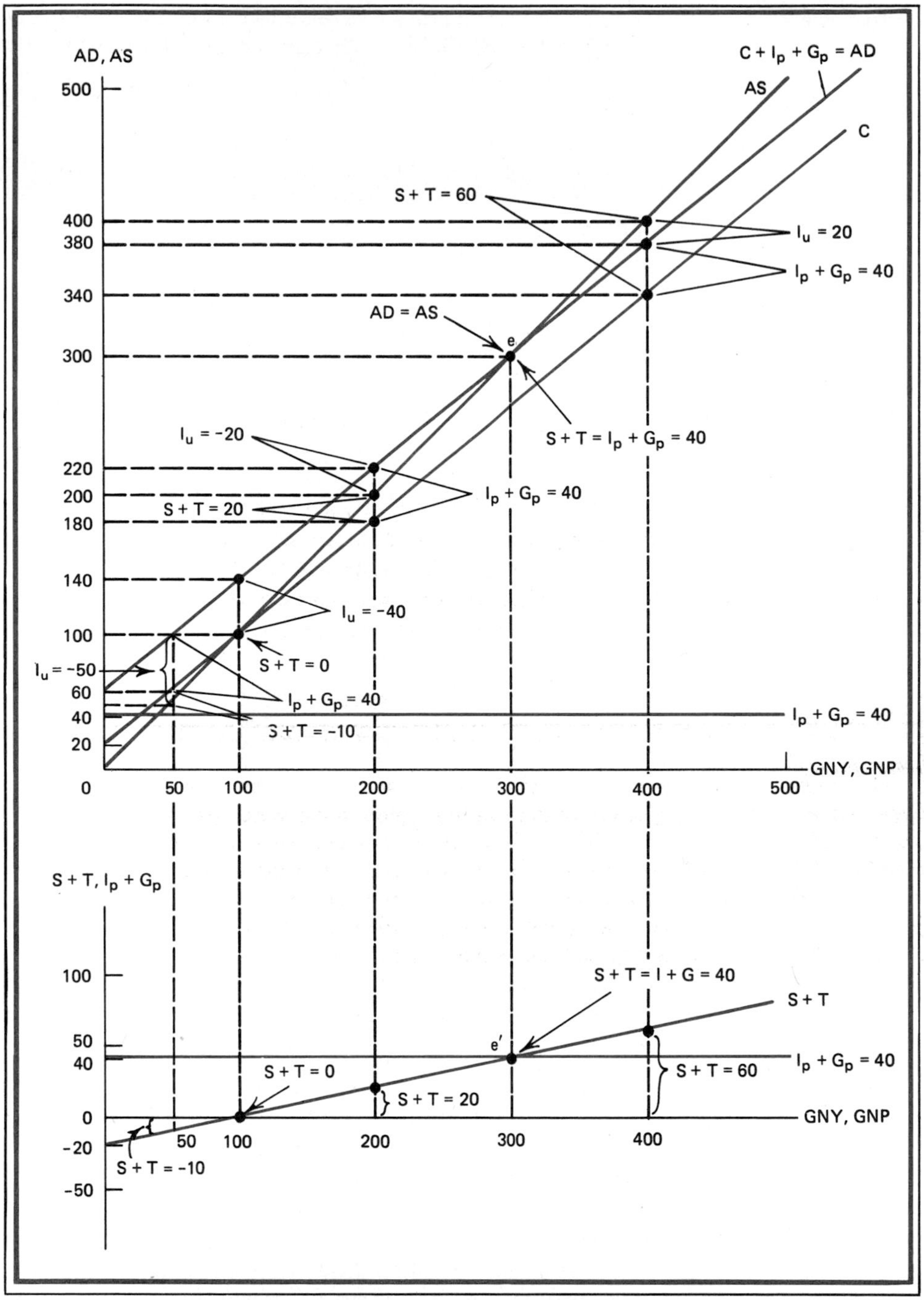

before, has consumption deleted and is the alternative graphical depiction of aggregate equilibrium at point *e′*.

Using Table 24-2 and Figure 24-7, let us trace through aggregate adjustments to equilibrium in the economy. When income is \$50, aggregate demand (\$100) is greater than aggregate supply (\$50) in the current period. Leakages

TABLE 24-2

$MPC = 0.8$

				AD			AS
	$GNY \equiv$	C	$+ (S + T) \equiv$	C	$+ (I_p + G_p)$	$+ I_u \equiv$	GNP
$S + T > I_p + G_p$	50	≡ 60 −	10	≡ 60 +	40	− 50 ≡	50
	100	≡ 100 +	0	≡ 100 +	40	− 40 ≡	100
	200	≡ 180 +	20	≡ 180 +	40	− 20 ≡	200
$S + T = I_p + G_p$	300	≡ 260 +	(40)	≡ 260 +	(40)	+ 0 ≡	300
$S + T < I_p + G_p$	400	≡ 340 +	60	≡ 340 +	40	+ 20 ≡	400
	500	≡ 420 +	80	≡ 420 +	40	+ 40 ≡	500

$S + T$ equal −\$10 and are less than injections $I_p + G_p$ equal to \$40. Since AD is greater than AS by \$50, unplanned disinvestment occurs since inventories carried over from the previous period change by −\$50. Forces operate to restore equilibrium. Production is stepped up to replace inventories and to meet anticipated increases in sales. In the next period production goes up to \$100 with $S + T$ equal to zero. Injections $I_p + G_p$ equal \$40, hence $S + T$ is less than $I_p + G_p$ by \$40. Aggregate supply equal to \$100 is still insufficient to satisfy AD = \$140. The change in inventories I_u is negative and equal to −40, as shown. Suppliers must again draw down inventories in order to meet current period demand. In the next period the level of national income is boosted to \$200, aggregate supply is also \$200 while AD is equal to \$220. Inventories are still being drawn down and change in value by −\$20. Leakages $S + T$ equals \$20, as portrayed on the upper and lower graphs, and are still smaller than injections, which equal \$40. In the next period production is stepped up and the economy moves up along AD and AS, in the upper graph toward point e or along $S + T$ in the lower graph toward point e′. In the process $AD = C + I_p + G_p$ rises in the upper graph, or $S + T$ rises approaching $I_p + G_p$ at e′ in the lower graph as inventories continue to dwindle. When production finally reaches \$300, equilibrium in the upper and lower graphs exists at e and e′ respectively. Aggregate demand equals aggregate supply and $S + T = I_p + G_p = 40$, with inventories equal to zero.

The path of adjustment from disequilibrium to equilibrium is similar when aggregate supply (\$500) is greater than aggregate demand (\$460) when GNP is \$500. As Table 24-2 shows, leakages $S + T$ equal \$80 while injections are only \$40. Thus, there is overproduction and a buildup of unsold goods indicated by I_u equal to \$40. Firms want to reduce the buildup in inventories and reduce production to \$400 in the next period. However, in the next period, disequilibrium remains because AD (\$380) is still less than AS (\$400) and leakages $S + T = 60$ are greater than injections $I_p + G_p$ = \$40. Finally, in the next period production is reduced to \$300, bringing aggregate supply into equality with aggregate demand and leakages equal to injections equal to \$40. The system has been driven to equilibrium by a decline in national income.

INFLATIONARY AND DEFLATIONARY GAPS

When aggregate demand is greater than aggregate supply, there is an inflationary gap. When aggregate demand is less than aggregate supply, there is a deflationary gap.

Assume that full employment income is Y_F in Figure 24-8. When income is Y_F, the aggregate demand schedule AD_2 is in equilibrium with AS at point f' and the system is in full employment equilibrium with neither excess demand nor excess supply. However, if the aggregate demand schedule were AD_3 an inflationary AD gap would exist. Because Y_F is full employment income, $\acute{Y}_H$ is a higher value of income, not because more workers are employed, but because with inflation the full employment levels of goods and services carry higher price tags. Since GNY = GNP and GNP = price level times output, then GNP can rise because the price level rises while output cannot because the economy is already operating at full employment. Thus we say that money GNP rises because prices rise while output is fixed. Thus AD_3 is too high and there is an inflationary aggregate demand gap equal to hf, where point f' indicates full employment aggregate demand without inflation and without unemployment of resources. The corresponding income gap is equal to $Y_H - Y_F$.

Because $AD = C + I_p + G_p$ and AD can rise or fall as C, I or G_p rises or falls, and if we symbolize the change in AD as ΔAD, then via the multiplier the corresponding change in GNY or GNP is $\Delta GNY = k\Delta AD$. Thus, the inflationary AD gap read vertically on the graph can be translated into an inflationary income gap read horizontally. Keep in mind, however, that the size of the aggregate demand gap is not identical to the income gap. They are related through the multiplier.

Figure 24-8

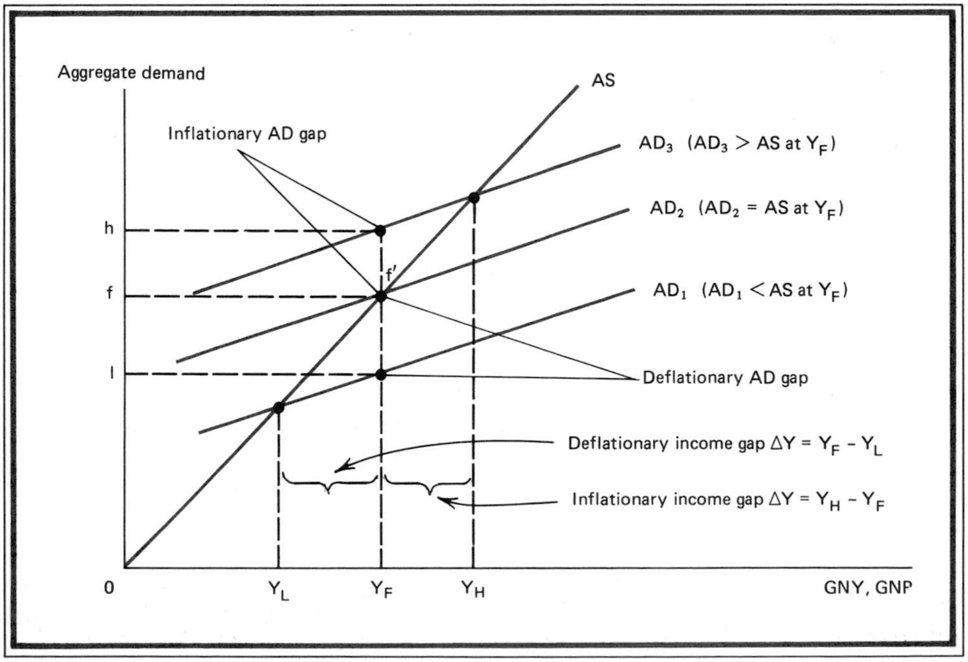

Income Y_L represents an economy operating at less than full employment. It is associated with an aggregate demand AD_1 that is too low. The economy is experiencing a deflationary gap equal to *fl*. Corresponding to the deflationary aggregate demand gap is a deflationary income gap equal to $Y_F - Y_L$. It is for this reason that when private consumption and investment spending are too low in a depressed economy, as they were in the 1930s, that Keynes argued that the government should stimulate aggregate demand with massive doses of government spending. One can foresee a possible dilemma here. Full employment may be incompatible with stable prices. Government expenditures and tax policies undertaken to stimulate aggregate demand in order to reach full employment might start up inflationary forces in the economy. Following that, counterpolicies adopted in order to stop the inflation by reducing aggregate demand may only lead to unemployment without subduing the inflation. Prices go up more easily than they come down. We shall have much to say about this dilemma in later chapters.

FISCAL POLICY AND MULTIPLIERS

Fiscal policy is the manipulation of aggregate demand by altering government expenditures and taxes.

We have already described the investment multiplier. It applies when it is assumed that neither government nor consumption schedules change (shift), signifying that neither the intercepts nor the slopes (the *MPCs*) change. Under these conditions we obtained the *investment multiplier* k_i.

The manipulation of aggregate demand by altering government expenditures and taxes is called **fiscal policy**, and brings into focus the importance of several multipliers.

Government Expenditure Multiplier

Government spending causes a magnified change in national income through the _multiplier_.

Keeping the investment and consumption schedules fixed and letting government expenditures change, the government expenditure multiplier (k_g) takes the same form as the investment multiplier (k_i) so that

$$k_g = 1/MPS$$

With $MPC = 3/4$ and $MPS = 1/4$, the $k_g = 1/\ 1/4 = 4$. Thus, when government expenditures change by $10 billion, the change in national income is equal to the multiplier times the change in government expenditures, or

$$\Delta Y = k_g \Delta G = 4 \times 10 = \$40 \text{ billion.}$$

Of course, when income rises while the consumption schedule is unchanged (i.e., does not shift), the level of consumption nonetheless rises because there is movement along the existing consumption schedule.

Government Spending-Investment Multiplier

When investment is not kept constant but is allowed to vary as income varies, as it does back in Figure 24-7, then a change in government spending leads to a modified multiplier. It takes the form

$$k_{gi} = \frac{1}{MPS - MPI}$$

where the MPI is the marginal propensity to invest out of income. If $MPC = 2/3$ and $MPI = 1/6$, then the $MPS = 1/3$ and

$$k_{gi} = \frac{1}{1/3\text{-}1/6} = \frac{1}{1/6} = 6.$$

A change in government spending, hence of aggregate demand, of $50 million leads to a magnified change in income of $300 because of the multiplier factor.

$$\Delta Y = k_{gi}\Delta G = 6 \times 50 = 300 \text{ million.}$$

Lump-sum Tax Multiplier

Again, assuming the investment and government schedules are constant, what is the effect of taxes on aggregate demand? Consider a tax which is a fixed amount, called a *lump-sum* tax. It is simply a tax of a constant amount that is subtracted from income no matter what the level of income. The lump-sum tax multiplier is[5]

$$k_{tx} = -\frac{MPC}{MPS}$$

Hence, if $MPC = 3/4$, then

$$k_{tx} = -\frac{3/4}{1/4} = -3.$$

Witness that for the same *MPC*, the lump sum tax multiplier is one unit smaller than the simple government expenditure multipliers and also has a negative sign attached to it. The negative sign makes sense because if taxes are increased, it is expected that spendable income, hence, consumption, will be

[5] The derivation of the lump-sum tax multiplier is as follows:

Let $Y = C + I + G$, where T is a lump tax with I and G constant, and $C = a + bY$.

Then: $Y = a+b(Y-T) + I + G$

Thus: $Y(1-b) = a + I + G - bT$

Hence: $Y = \dfrac{a + I + G - bT}{(1-b)}$

Now let T change so that

$$\Delta Y = \frac{-b}{1-b}\Delta T. \quad \text{Therefore, } k_{tx} = \frac{-b}{1-b} = -\frac{MPC}{MPS}$$

lower. The negative sign simply indicates the direction of change. If taxes are cut, then the negative sign will ensure that the calculation yields an increase in income and consumption. Thus, with $MPC = 3/4$ combined with a tax cut of \$10 billion, the change in income equals the tax multiplier times the change in the tax, or

$$\Delta Y = k_{tx}\Delta T = -3(-10) = +\$30 \text{ billion.}$$

Notice, the change (rise) in income is \$10 billion smaller than that obtained when government expenditures were increased by the same amount. The reason is straightforward. When there is a tax cut of \$10 and the *MPC* is 3/4, this tells us that the full \$10 will not be directly injected into the circular flow because according to the *MPC* only \$7.5 will be spent and \$2.5 will be saved. This is unlike the effect of \$10 that the government spends because that is what the government does—spend all \$10 of it. Thus, the effect of a tax cut is smaller because consumers only spend an amount equal to the marginal propensity to consume times the tax cut ($\Delta C = -MPC \times \Delta T = (-3/4)(-10) = 7.5$).

Balanced Budget Multiplier

The balanced budget is a statement citizens hear mentioned frequently in the media. In simple terms it means the government should not spend more than it collects in a given period. Thus if expenditures are increased by \$10 billion, it ought to be covered with increased lump-sum tax collections of 10 billion. What is the multiplier when $\Delta G = \Delta T$ in the fiscal period? The balanced budget multiplier turns out to be equal to one, always.

$$k_{BB} = 1.$$

Figure 24-9

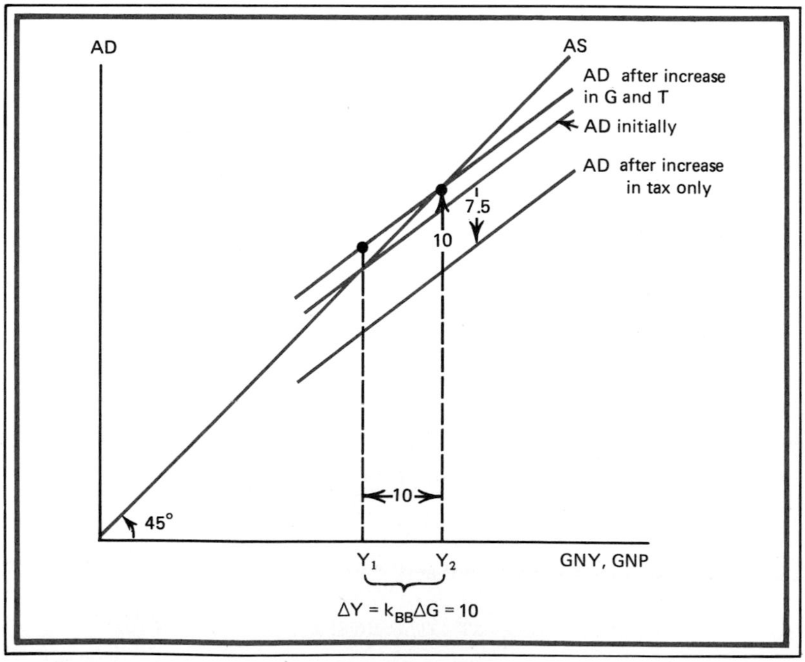

Figure 24-10

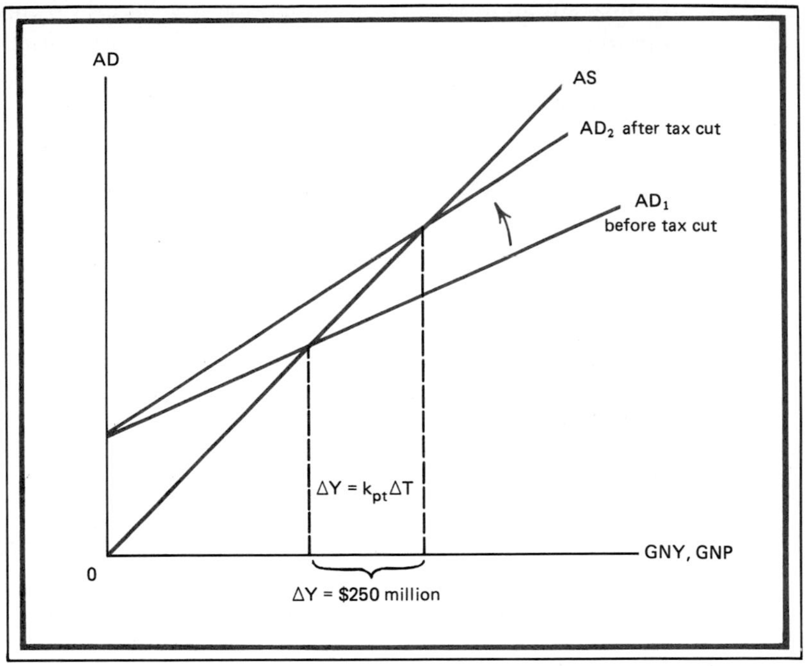

Thus if both G and T are increased by $10 billion, income increases by $10 billion. In this situation the balanced budget is expansionary. Thus

$$\Delta Y = k_{BB} \times \Delta G = 1 \times 10 = \$10 \text{ billion.}$$

If there were a cut in both by $10 billion, then

$$\Delta Y = k_{BB}\Delta G = 1 \times (-10) = -\$10 \text{ billion}$$

and the result is contractionary. The reason for this is that the government expenditure multiplier equals 4 if the MPC = 3/4 and is one unit larger than the lump-sum tax multiplier which equals −3, and hence dominates it. Since an equal change in government expenditures has a stronger but opposite effect of an equal change in taxes, the balanced budget multiplier can be expressed as a combination of the government expenditure multiplier and the tax multiplier.[6] Figure 24-9 compares the effect on aggregate demand of an equal increase in taxes and government expenditures of $10. Observe that the *net* rise in aggregate demand is $2.5 whereas the change in national income is $10.

Proportional Tax Multiplier

When the tax varies in proportion to the change in income, the proportional tax multiplier is

$$k_{pt} = \frac{1}{MPS + MPC \times MPT}.$$

[6] For the interested student the derivation is as follows: Let $k_{BB} = k_g + k_{tx}$
$k_{BB} = \frac{1}{MPS} + \left(-\frac{MPC}{MPS}\right) = \frac{1 - MPC}{MPS}$. Therefore, $k_{BB} = \frac{MPS}{MPS} = 1$

In this situation the aggregate demand schedule rotates: clockwise when the marginal propensity to tax increases, and counterclockwise when it decreases, as shown in Figure 24-10. Thus, when $MPC = 3/4$, the $MPS = 1/4$ and given $MPT = 2/10$, the multiplier is

$$k_{pt} = \frac{1}{1/4 + 3/4 \times 2/10} = \frac{20}{8} = 2.5.$$

Thus, if either government spending or private investment are cut by $100 million, the change in national income via the tax multiplier is

$$\Delta Y = k_{pt}\Delta G = 2.5(-100) = -\$250 \text{ million.}$$

CHAPTER SUMMARY

Aggregate demand is the sum of the spending of households, business, and government in an economy without foreign trade. Aggregate supply is the total value of what the economy produces in a year. Since this must also equal factor income it is also the value of aggregate income. When aggregate demand equals aggregate supply—or if you prefer, when aggregate spending equals aggregate income—the economy is in equilibrium. Classical theory predicted that aggregate equilibrium occurred only at full employment since it was assumed that private markets were perfectly competitive and that prices and money wages were flexible. Producers and workers were price-takers and wage-takers respectively. They lacked price and wage setting power. Thus, if supply or demand temporarily existed, money wages and prices would adjust and eventually return the economy to full-employment output and unchanged real wage rates.

This conclusion also required that economic agents possess perfect information about the markets and that human resources were interchangeable (and hence able to find alternative employment without much delay), and that physical and financial resources were readily adaptable to other uses. There were no permanent or long-run leakages of monies from the circular flow. All cash not directly spent or intended for consumer expenditures was put to work earning an interest or dividend return.

The implications of these assumptions were summarized in Say's law, "supply creates its own demand." By the logic of the circular flow, the total value of output produced must equal total factor income generated where that income is just enough to purchase the output produced, since Say's law implies all income is intended to be spent in one way or another. Thus the 45° line can either be conceived as total income earned or as an aggregate supply schedule showing the value of all goods and services suppliers would provide at different income levels. In the classical scheme, because there are no permanent leakages, total spending, or aggregate demand out of income, coincides at each point with the aggregate supply schedule or the 45° line. However, only one of these points is the actual equilibrium point in the classical model; namely, the one representing full employment income with the equilibrium level of saving and investment out of that income determined by the rate of interest.

Keynes rejected some of the classical tenets because of the experience of the 1930s—at least as an explanation for the short-run before long-run classical kinds of adjustments could occur. He thought adjustment lags would take too long to be practical in solving existing economic conditions. Keynes contended that savers and investors are different groups with different spending plans at the beginning of the period. It is most likely that saving and investing plans of households and firms would differ initially. Thus, if households saved more and spent less than firms anticipated, inventories of unsold goods—unplanned investment—would result, indicating that aggregate demand (intended spending) would fall short of aggregate supply (or total income). Thus, for many income levels it is possible for aggregate spending or aggregate demand to diverge from aggregate income or aggregate supply, leading to the Keynesian cross phenomenon. Keynes held that saving was primarily a function of income, not of the interest rate. When planned saving was greater than planned investment, firms reduced production, hence employment, in order to sell off the extra inventories, and revised their estimates of household spending in the next period. Thus, factor income would fall, and so would saving. Income would continue to fall until planned saving and investment were equal, with the system restored to equilibrium, with aggregate demand equal to aggregate supply. However, unlike the classical model, the equilibrium would not necessarily occur at full employment; that would only happen by chance, since many equilibria states were possible.

Keynes also broke with classical theory by holding that changes in employment, therefore in factor income, restored aggregate equilibrium because money wages and prices were sticky downward. Therefore, when aggregate demand went into decline, money wage rates did not fall. To reduce their wage costs firms laid off workers instead, since workers resisted declines in their money wages. Finally, argued Keynes, the classical system was wrong when it hypothesized households and firms did not hold idle cash balances. As a result there could be long-term withdrawals of monies from the circular flow, permanently reducing spending and causing a longstanding aggregate demand gap. These gaps can be removed by direct government expenditures and tax cuts, causing a magnified change in national income via the multiplier. The simple government multiplier k is equal to 1 divided by the marginal propensity to save. More complicated multipliers can be derived by letting other variables change simultaneously with government expenditures; for example, investment spending and taxes.

When the government sector is included, aggregate demand is augmented so that $AD = C + I_p + G_p$. The overall equilibrium condition then becomes $S_p + T = I_p + G_p$ indicating that total leakages equal total injections. It can be rewritten as $S_p = I_p + (G_p - T_p)$. When the budget is balanced $G = T$ leaving $S_p = I_p$. If there is a budget deficit, G is greater than T so that S_p is greater than I_p. This indicates that in principle aggregate full employment equilibrium can still be attained by government deficit spending making up the spending deficiency of the private sector. Conversely, if S_p is less than I_p, indicating too much spending by the private sector, the government can run a budget surplus ($G < T$) to close the aggregate supply gap. Below full employment, the price index is assumed to be constant in the Keynesian model. This assumption will have to be modified later.

QUESTIONS

1. Under Say's law supply creates its own demand. However, suppose product prices are too high so that people do not have enough income to make the necessary expenditures. How does the classical system assure that they will have enough income to absorb all the output?
2. What could be wrong with the notion that the equilibrium level of national income occurs when saving equals investment from a Keynesian analysis perspective? What do you know about this equilibrium if you are in a classical world?

3. Can you give a reason why reducing wages would not necessarily reduce unemployment or bring the economy back to full employment equilibrium, as the classical model predicts it would?
4. What would be the size of the simple investment multiplier if there were zero leakages? If all income were saved?
5. You are given the following diagram:

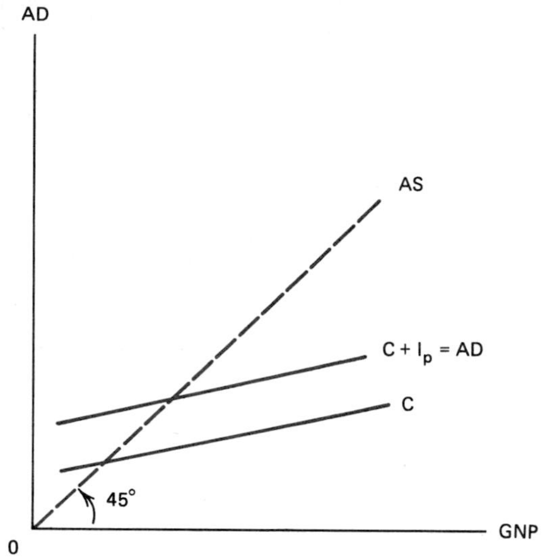

Where is the equilibrium position? Why is equilibrium what it is, and why can it not be anywhere else?
6. If the *MPC* is .9, what is the simple multiplier *k*? If $k = 5$, what is the *MPS*? What is the MPC?
7. If government expenditures increase by $10 million, *ceteris paribus*, and the equilibrium level of income rises as a result by $40 million, what is the *MPC*?
8. The equilibrium level of national income of $100 billion is disturbed by an increase of $8 billion in investment spending, where investment is assumed to be a constant function of income. If the *MPC* is 3/4, what is the new equilibrium level of national income?
9. Suppose the short-run aggregate consumption function is $C = 5 + .80Y$ and $G = 20$ and the equilibrium level of national income is 200, then what is the amount of autonomous investment that firms in the economy are undertaking?
10. Assume no government. If planned investment for plant and equipment is 100, and firms plan to increase their inventories by 10, while consumers spend according to $C = 50 + 3/4Y$, what will be (a) the equilibrium level of income, (b) the equilibrium level of consumption, and (c) the equilibrium level of saving?
11. You are given the data shown in the table at top of page 605 for an economy.
    a. At what level of gross national income do injections into equal leakages from the circular flow? Does planned saving necessarily equal planned investment in equilibrium? Explain.
    b. Does a *GNY* of 580 represent a deflationary or inflationary gap?
    c. What is the value of the *MPC*? The multiplier?
12. If there is a deflationary full employment gap, the economy cannot be in equilibrium since planned saving does not equal planned investment. Do you agree? Explain.

GNY	*C*	I_p	G_p	$S_p + T$
400	420	2	50	−20
430	440	4	50	−10
460	460	6	50	0
490	480	8	50	10
520	500	10	50	20
550	520	12	50	30
580	540	14	50	40
610	560	16	50	50
640	580	18	50	60
670	600	20	50	70
700	620	22	50	80
730	640	24	50	90

13. Is it correct to say that the full employment level of national income *must* occur when actual investment equals planned plus unplanned investment? Why, or why not?
14. If there is a lump sum reduction in taxes by $10 billion, when the MPC is 3/4, will
    a. GNP rise or fall?
    b. By how much?
15. The government expenditure multiplier is 3. Suppose the President planned to cut taxes by $6.4 billion and to cut government spending by $4 billion. What is the effect on GNP? What would the government expenditure multiplier have to be to result in no change in GNP?
16. Assume the economy is confronted with a $10 billion dollar inflationary *aggregate demand* gap. Three bills are proposed on the senate floor by three different senators. *Senator Cutback* proposes that the government reduce its spending by $15 billion to remove the gap and restore the economy to full employment equilibrium income. *Senator Grim* proposes that the government increase lump sum taxes by $10 billion to wipe out the gap and restore the economy to full employment equilibrium. *Senator Balance* suggests that both government expenditures and taxes be reduced by $50 billion in order to remove the gap and reach full employment equilibrium. Assume that the MPC = 4/5. Show why each senator is either right or wrong.
17. What is the size of the multiplier if the MPC = 4/5 and the proportional tax is 10 percent?
18. Assume GNP = 100. With C = 60 + .7Y and I = 20 + .1Y, assume government expenditures increase by 10.
    a. What is the amount of induced and of autonomous investment.
    b. What is the new level of GNP?
    c. What is the amount of new induced investment?
19. Does investment depend upon savings or savings depend upon investment? Does your answer differ if you are in the classical world or the Keynesian world?
20. Suppose the GNP deflator rose by 3 percent last year and GNP was $900 billion with the MPC = .6.
    a. Construct a graph indicating the inflationary aggregate demand gap. Calculate the size of the gap.
    b. By how much and in what direction would government expenditures have to change to remove the gap?
    c. By how much and in what direction would a lump-sum tax have to change to remove the gap?

Chapter 25

Money and Banking

PROGRESS REPORT

A. We have discussed the expenditures of government, of the consuming public, and of the world of business. Within these three broad categories we can represent all the kinds of spending that go on in a society. In Chapter 24 we developed a macroeconomic model that shows the relations among the three spending groups and how national income is determined by them.

B. The macroeconomic model we have put together lacks explicit treatment of an important element – money. We live in an economy that relies on money to facilitate trade and exchange. Money is used for spending and paying off debts. Changes in the amount of money can cause inflation or depression. Therefore, in this chapter we shall examine the characteristics of money and the banking system that helps create it.

C. In Chapter 26 we shall examine how the banks and the money supply are controlled by the government authorities through the Federal Reserve System, the nation's central bank.

MONEY

Money is anything accepted as payment for goods and services and as settlement of debts.

What is money? From where does it come? Who controls the amount of it, and how? The following pages will bring together institutional and theoretical details to enrich the analysis of national income and bring the model a little closer to reality.

We all recognize money. It consists of both coins and paper currency. That, however, is only what some of it looks like. We must therefore distinguish what money is in its most general meaning from specific forms it can take. In general, money is anything that is accepted as payment for goods and services or as settlement of debts. Money can also be a commodity that is generally accepted in exchange for other commodities. In some prisoner of war camps of World War II cigarettes served this function. They also served as money for a time after World War II in some occupied sectors of Germany. In other cultures, money consists of fish hooks, beads, stones, and salt. In the U.S. some of our money is paper and some of it is coin. Taken together they define what is called currency. But these two items compose only a portion of the official money supply in the U.S. There is a much larger third component of the stock of money. What do you think is that other item? Checks. No, but close. It is the bank deposits upon which those checks are drawn.

Functions of Money

Money serves as a *medium of exchange*, a *store of value*, and a *unit of account*.

Before money evolved, exchange between individuals and groups was by barter—the trading of some goods directly for other goods. But as economies developed and more and more trading took place, barter became cumbersome and inefficient. A universally acceptable medium of exchange that reduced the transactions costs associated with barter and facilitated economic growth was money. Money functions as a medium of exchange—something used to purchase goods.

As the **medium of exchange**, money creates greater freedom of choice and increases the specialization and division of labor leading to increased efficiency and productivity of the economic system, for it avoids the severe constraint of the double-coincidence of wants that exists in a barter system. For instance, if Mr. Jones has wood and wants to acquire pears from Farmer Fred, but Fred does not want wood because he needs milk produced by Barnaby who in turn wants wood but not pears, then Jones has to search out Barnaby, trade wood for milk in order to acquire pears from Fred. Direct trade between Jones and Fred could only occur if Jones wanted pears and Fred wanted wood, that is, where there happened to be a double-coincidence of wants. This is extremely inefficient.

Money also serves as an asset or a **store of value**. If put in a bank for some time, it can be used later. Thus, one can hold wealth in the form of money. Assets come in many forms. Besides money there are bonds and stocks and real property. If our bonds and stocks are sold to obtain money we say that we have liquidated our assets. Money is the perfectly liquid asset because one cannot only hold it as an asset but can also buy things with it. Other assets must usually be sold before their owners can buy other things. If an asset is easy to sell for money, it is called a liquid asset. If it is difficult to sell it is called an illiquid asset. Thus, different assets have different degrees of liquidity and we say that some are more liquid than others. The more liquid the asset the lower the transactions costs of negotiating exchange.

Money functions as a **unit of account**. Commodities have relative market values that can be denominated in money prices for purposes of easy comparison and exchange. As a unit of account money is also used in contracts that involve future payments. When used this way money also serves as a standard for deferred payments.

THE NATURE OF MONEY

To have value, money must be *scarce*.

Whatever is used for money must be **scarce**. Because pebbles are not scarce, they would be worthless and therefore useless as money. American Indians used seashells as wampum in certain areas where shells were not free for the collecting. Rare metals such as gold and silver were used as money in antiquity and are still used to this very day. Money must be scarce or it will be worthless.

Another thing to note about money is that, because it is scarce, people will try to find it, or make it, or create it in whatever way they can. Prospectors comb the mountains hoping to find the motherlode. When gold is discovered, the increased supply of this form of money can make prices of goods and services in terms of gold skyrocket, so that a piece of gold will buy much less than before. This is called inflation. On the other hand, when gold becomes more and more scarce and valuable, a small piece of it can buy a lot of goods. Prices fall and this is called deflation.

Money's scarcity can be controlled. Today it is the central government's job to control the supply of money; it alone can legally mint coins and print paper money, and it prosecutes others who infringe on its monopoly by counterfeiting.

In a few pages we shall explain how banks can create money. They profit from creating money because, as part of the process, they can make loans and earn interest. If just anyone were allowed to start a bank or any bank were allowed to create demand deposit money without limit, money would not be scarce any longer. It would become worthless. Therefore, just as we control counterfeiting we must also control the amount of money that banks can print if we are to have a viable medium of exchange. In the U.S. the Federal Reserve System is charged with controlling the money supply and the amount that banks create.

What Is Wrong with Gold for Money?

The problem with using gold as money is basically an economic one. Economists would say that gold is expensive in comparison with paper money and bank money. What do we mean by expensive? Simply that it costs a lot to use gold. The most obvious costs associated with using gold are the costs of mining it, hauling it, and storing it. It is heavy, not easy to move around. If gold is used as jewelry only, then people will mine it so long as the cost of getting it out of the ground is less than its value as jewelry. But when gold is used as money, too, there is even greater demand for it than if it were desired only for its worth as jewelry. Therefore, the opportunity cost of using gold as money is its value as jewelry.

It is clear that paper money and bank money are, in general, much less costly to produce than metallic money. When the Susan B. Anthony dollar was minted in the U.S., it was reported that the coins cost an average of 3 cents each to make, in contrast with a dollar bill which cost about 1 cent each. However, the average useful life of a dollar bill is about 18 months while a coin lasts 15 years or more. So, if coins lasted 4-1/2 years they would be the equivalent in cost to the dollar bill. But these cost estimates only apply to production, and do not include the added costs of handling the bulky coins. The dollar coin will not likely replace the dollar bill not because dollar coins are more expensive to make but because they are more expensive to use.

Prices are not necessarily stable because metallic monies are used. Gold and silver discoveries, happening as they do at more or less random times, mean that an economy can be subjected to periods of inflation by the whims of discovery.

Some countries are rich in gold ores and others are not. Thus, some countries are made rich simply because other countries choose to use gold as money and must pay a lot for gold. These other countries would be well advised to create their own paper and deposit money. It would mean a saving for them.

By having government maintain a monopoly over the money supply, a country can avoid the heavy expenses attendent to the use of gold. It can also insulate itself from the effects on prices of the vagaries of supply and discovery. It makes a lot of sense to use paper money provided the people are law-abiding and will not compromise the plan by counterfeiting, and provided there exists a reasonable degree of political stability to make law respected. It is also necessary for the monetary authorities to exercise prudence and restraint and not allow their control to erode when faced with a call for political expediency. It was in response to this sentiment that Congress, in establishing the Federal Reserve System, made it an agency that was intended to operate, to a considerable extent, independent of the Treasury Department and the Executive Office of the President, in hopes that the Fed would keep a stable money supply while recognizing that it should act as an agency of the government in the interest of the people.

MEASURING MONEY

Without question, that amount of currency in the hands of the public at any time is part of the money supply. Nearly everyone uses some currency to buy something or other nearly every day. But for large ticket items people in the U.S. and many other countries usually pay by check. Thus, if a person has a

TABLE 25-1
New Measures of Money (Billions of dollars, not seasonally adjusted)

	December 1979
M1-A:	
Currency in the hands of the nonbank public	108.1
Demand deposits at commercial banks less those due foreign banks and official institutions	273.0
	381.1
M1-B:	
M1-A	381.1
Other checkable deposits	16.2
(NOW, share drafts, automatic transfers from savings to checking accounts)	**397.3**
M2:	
M1-B	397.3
Savings deposits at all depository institutions	415.0
Small time deposits at all depositary institutions	648.7
Overnight RPs issued by commercial banks	20.6
Money market mutual fund shares	43.6
Overnight Eurodollar deposits of U.S. nonbank residents at Caribbean branches of U.S. banks	3.5
Consolidation component (to avoid double counting of components)	−2.7
	1,526.0
M3:	
M2	1,526.0
Large time deposits at all depositary institutions	222.6
Term RPs issued by commercial banks	22.2
Term RPs issued by savings and loan associations	8.0
	1,778.8
L:	
M3	1,778.8
Other Eurodollar deposits of nonbank U.S. residents	30.9
Bankers acceptances	26.6
Commercial paper	97.2
Savings bonds	80.0
Liquid Treasury obligations (remaining maturities of 18 months and less)	127.2
	2,140.7

Source: *Federal Reserve Bulletin.*

demand deposit in a bank on which a check can be written, and if sellers will, in general, accept a check, this demand deposit is spendable money. Thus, one measure of money consists of currency held by the nonbank public and demand deposits at all commercial banks. It is referred to as **M1-A**. As of December 1979, currency in circulation in the U.S. was $108.1 billion and demand deposits were $273 billion. Table 25-1 shows these numbers.

Checks can be written not only on demand deposits at commercial banks

According to the official U.S. definitions of money, M1-A consists of cash held by the public plus demand deposits at commercial banks and M1-B includes M1-A plus checkable accounts at all financial institutions.

but also against certain savings accounts as well as some deposits in thrift institutions—savings banks, savings and loan associations, and credit unions. These "checkable" or "transactions" accounts are included as part of the money supply under a measure of money referred to as **M1-B**. As the table indicates, it amounted to $397.3 billion in December 1979. Credit cards are money substitutes but not money. The monthly credit card bill is usually paid by writing a check against one's account. Only then is debt discharged.

During the 1980s thrift institutions throughout the country began offering accounts that checks can be written against. It is anticipated that M1-A will eventually be dropped and that M1-B will then become the narrow money supply. It will be called just M1 and will include cash and all checking accounts, not just those at commercial banks, as well as traveler's checks.

A broader measure of money is **M2**. Besides including all the items in M1-B it also includes several items that are treated as "near" money. For example, a student may have a savings account instead of a demand deposit account. If the student were asked how much money he owned, his answer would include the savings item. When he wants to buy something he will take "money" from his savings account. Thus, M2 includes small savings and time deposit accounts as well as a few other items.[1] Over $1,100 billion is added to M1-B to arrive at a figure of $1,526 billion for M2, to make M2 nearly 4 times as large as M1-B.

The Federal Reserve also publishes other measures labeled **M3** and **L**. These broader measures include all items in M2 and several other highly liquid assets that are extremely good substitutes for money even though they cannot be spent directly.

THE ORIGINS OF COMMERCIAL BANKING

Imagine a period when nations, as we know them today, were beginning to be formed, about the year 1400. Traders used gold, and the Spanish ships were about to discover America and other new sources of gold. This gold was held in warehouses for safekeeping. When a trader or merchant would return from a voyage with some bars of gold, he would put them in a warehouse and would be given a receipt for his deposit of gold. The certificate, or receipt, said, "This is to certify that there is on deposit X amount of gold that belongs to Christopher Columbus." Now when Columbus wanted to outfit the Nina, Pinta, and Santa Maria, he may have taken such a certificate to his supplier, and turned it over and written on the back of it, "To Mr. Warehouser, please pay this gold to the order of Mr. Luis Larios." Since Mr. Warehouser knew both people, and recognized Columbus's signature, the exchange was made without any problem.

As more and more people engaged in this activity, the backs of certificates were lined so that Larios could pay it over to Vendrell who could pay it over to

[1] It also includes shares in money market mutual funds and certain other accounts that businesses keep with banks.

Zoro, and so forth. When the lines were all used up, the last man would go to the warehouse and ask for a new certificate. The gold gathered dust in the back room. Seldom, if ever, did people want the gold.

Now assume that Don Quixote, that crazy tilter at windmills, married Mr. Warehouser's daughter. The father felt a responsibility to help his son-in-law get started in a career. Since he did not have any gold of his own he simply wrote out a certificate of deposit of gold and gave it to him. Thus, Mr. Warehouser became a banker just like bankers today. What he banked on was that not all the depositors would come and want their gold at once. He had to count on this because there was not enough gold in the vaults to pay everyone who had outstanding claims on it at one time.

As Quixote prospered along with others to whom certificates were lent, the warehouse-become-bank also prospered. But the bank always kept just enough gold around as reserves to meet the occasional withdrawal that certificate holders made on it. So it is today. No commercial bank has enough cash in its vaults and reserves that can be turned to cash immediately to pay all the people who hold deposits with it on any one day. Given sufficient time, a bank could sell its assets and get the cash needed to pay all its depositors, but it could not be done in a single day or even over several weeks.

After a time, the bank accepted deposits but did not bother to give a depositor a certificate with the depositor's name printed on it. It just kept a record of the deposit. Then, when the depositor wanted to withdraw some money the bank simply printed up a note with the bank's name on it, saying that the bank "guaranteed to pay the holder X amount in gold on demand." This bank note was said to be guaranteed by the bank and carry the bank's credit. Bank notes circulated as money, and when a borrower came in to ask for a loan, the bank would issue the borrower its own notes to use to make the purchase that the borrower wanted to make. Today, in the U.S., the Federal Reserve Bank issues the bank notes (dollars) that circulate as money. Commercial banks no longer issue their own notes. But as we shall soon see, they do create deposit money.

COMMERCIAL BANKS

Unlike other countries that have a few banks with many branches located throughout the land, in the U.S. we have over 14,000 different banks altogether. The extent of branching by banks is regulated by the laws of the fifty states. In some states very limited branching is allowed—Illinois and Texas for example. In California, on the other hand, statewide branching is allowed, and a few very large banks there have many branches. Bank of America headquartered in San Francisco is the largest bank in the world if size is measured by financial assets owned or managed.

States can charter and regulate banks, but so can the Comptroller of the Currency of the U.S. Treasury Department, who is responsible for regulating and issuing charters to national banks. Thus national and state banks compete with each other in providing services to depositors and loans to businesses.

Our central bank, the Federal Reserve System, plays the role of banker to those banks that are members of the system. In other words, a commercial bank that is a member of the Fed system keeps deposits at the Fed and can borrow from the Fed just as individuals keep deposits and borrow from banks. The Fed is a banker's bank. All national banks that are chartered by the federal government are required to hold membership in the Fed. State banks can choose to be members of the Fed if they like, but it is not required.

The breakdown of types of banks, whether state or national, and whether Fed member or nonmember, is provided in Table 25-2. An additional classification is insured or noninsured. This refers to whether or not the bank has its deposits insured by the Federal Deposit Insurance Corporation. The FDIC insures each depositor, up to a $100,000 limit, against loss in case the bank should fail as a business—literally, in this case, go bankrupt. In some but not all states, banking law may require that state banks join the FDIC. All members of the Fed and all national banks must join the FDIC. Thus, the only banks that are not insured are a few hundred small state commercial banks.

As you can see from the table, the majority of banks are not members of the Fed. Nontheless most of the larger banks are members, and member banks hold about 70 percent of bank demand deposits, down from 85 percent in 1947. Nonmember banks are usually the smaller rural banks that cannot or will not meet the requirements to become members of the Fed or the FDIC. But this has been changing in recent years. In the 1960's and 1970's many banks abandoned their national charter and took out state charters so they could leave the Fed. They found that costs associated with membership were greater than the benefits received from membership. But this attrition of membership was halted by legislation in 1980.

BANKING BALANCE SHEETS

A bank's *net worth* equals the difference between its assets (vault cash, balances with correspondent banks, securities, loans, reserves) and its liabilities (borrowings and time and demand deposits).

All banks and businesses compute balance sheets. These balance sheet accounts itemize the assets, liabilities, and **net worth** (capital account) of the firm. A composite balance sheet for all banks appears in Table 25-3. The technique of double entry accounting is used, wherein the total of the asset column on the top of the table must equal the total of the liability plus net worth column toward the bottom. Any change in an account must show twice—either as an equal change in the other side of the balance sheet, or as an offsetting change in some other item on the same side.

Before examining the details in Table 25-3 the reader may glance at the broad categories. Assets consist generally of cash plus all loans, investments, and the like, that are claims against others. When a bank makes a loan, the borrower signs a note promising to repay the bank. This note is a claim to that person's resources—a claim on income or assets. An investment by the bank is simply a special form of loan. Instead of creating the note itself as it does when a borrower comes into the bank, the bank purchases securities in the bond market. These securities may have been issued by the federal government, state goverments and municipalities, or by corporations. In essence, by purchasing a bond the bank has lent money to the bond's issuer.

TABLE 25-2
Commercial Banks in the U.S. and Possessions.

Type of bank	Number of banks		
	1947	1972	1978
Member banks			
National	5,005	4,696	4,616
State	1,918	1,018	1,005
Total	6,923	5,714	5,621
Nonmember	7,261	8,161	9,007
Total commercial banks	14,184	13,875	14,628

Source: *Federal Reserve Bulletin.*

Toward the bottom of the table we see the bank's liabilities listed. They consist principally of the deposits that individuals, businesses, and governments have made. Liabilities are claims against the bank. They represent what the bank owes to its customers.

Also, lower down, there is listed the net worth, or as it is sometimes called, the capital accounts. When a bank is started, investors put up some money and take ownership of shares of stock in the company. As the bank

TABLE 25-3
Assets and Liabilities of Commercial Banking Institutions, December 1980 (billions of dollars)

Cash assets, total	218.6
Currency and coin	20.7
Reserves with Federal Reserve Banks	28.2
Balances with depository institutions	84.9
Cash items in process of collection	84.7
Loans and investments, excluding interbank	1,262.3
Loans, excluding interbank	932.5
Commercial and industrial	330.6
Other	601.9
U.S. Treasury securities	113.7
Other securities	216.3
Other assets[2]	221.7
Total assets/total liabilities and capital	**1,702.7**
Deposits	1,239.9
Demand	453.6
Savings	201.6
Time	584.7
Borrowings	211.5
Other liabilities	135.5
Net worth	115.8

Commercial banking institutions include domestically chartered commercial banks, branches and agencies of foreign banks, Edge Act and Agreement corporations, and New York State foreign investment corporations. Source: *Fed. Res. Bulletin,* March 1981.

grows, the authorities require that some earnings be placed in reserve funds and undivided dividends. These items also represent claims that the owners of the banks have on their banks. If the banks were to stop and pay off all claims on them, and have all borrowers repay all loans, that is, collect on all its assets, then since assets are greater than liabilities the difference is net worth—the amount the bank would owe to its owners, or the value of the owner's claims on the bank's assets. The basic relation is assets = liabilities + net worth (capital). This equality is found in the middle of the table. Items above it sum to 1,702.7, and so do items below.

To understand how banks play a role in creating the nation's money supply, we need to examine some of the specific items in the balance sheet so we will understand just where they originate. We begin with assets.

Assets

Currency and coin This is vault cash. It is the money in the bank's vault and the drawers the tellers use. It is used to pay depositors when they come to request cash. Vault cash is also counted as part of the legal reserve that banks are required by law to maintain.

Reserves with Federal Reserve Banks This item represents the deposits that member banks keep in the Federal Reserve. All banks are now required by law to keep some deposits in the Fed as reserves. Nonmember banks are also required to keep reserves under state laws.

Balances with domestic banks Banks do a lot of business with each other. Small banks keep deposits in large banks and these deposits are counted as legal reserves when the bank is a state bank and not a member of the Fed. But big banks keep deposits with each other, too. Bankers speak of their *correspondent* banks. If you travel from one city to another and wish to do business there, your local banker will give you a check on his correspondent bank in the other city.

Loans These may be classified in many different ways, but most loans that commercial banks make are for business purposes. The typical business will borrow the money it needs to purchase its inventory of merchandise. Then, as it sells its product, it repays the loan. Banks lend to farmers and to consumers to buy consumer durables such as cars and washing machines. Banks will lend money to homeowners and businesses so they can buy properties. The bank will take a mortgage on the property in these cases.

Investments The principal securities in a commercial bank's portfolio of assets are securities issued by government, either federal or state or local. The U.S. Treasury bills and bonds that banks hold are part of the national debt. The state and municipal securities that banks hold have been issued to finance special projects such as school construction or putting in a sewage system. As you can see, money is only one kind of asset.

Liabilities

Demand deposits Banks accept deposits from individuals and businesses and agree to repay the depositor whenever the depositor chooses to request, or to demand, repayment. An individual or business can spend these deposits by writing a check. Looking carefully at a check one will see that it says "Pay to the order of." So, by signing a check an individual directs the bank to pay money to the designated person. Since people will nearly always accept checks for sizable purchases, these demand deposits are spendable money.

Time deposits and savings accounts When a bank accepts money for deposit for a specific period of time, it is called a time deposit. In the case of a savings deposit the time period is not specified. Banks pay interest on time and savings deposits. The distinction between demand and time deposits is rapidly disappearing. In the 1980 legislation described on p. 627 Congress allowed banks, savings and loan associations, and credit unions to structure savings accounts so that checks can be written against them. In effect this turned some savings accounts into demand deposits.

Borrowings Banks sometimes need to borrow money from other banks or from the Federal Reserve. Of course, in essence, when someone deposits money in an account at the bank, it amounts to a loan to the bank. So, to have a liability account that we label borrowing is simply to call attention to the special nature of the borrowing when the bank negotiates a loan from the Fed or from another bank.

BANK DEPOSITS AND MONEY CREATION

The *fractional reserve* process allows banks to create money because reserves held in excess of the required level are excess revenues and can be loaned at a rate of interest.

The purpose of this section is to describe the process of money creation by commercial banks under what is called a **fractional reserve** banking system. It is called a fractional reserve system because banks are required by law to hold some fraction of the money deposited with them in the reserve accounts. Since most large banks in the U.S. are members of the Federal Reserve System we shall simply assume that banks are members in the following examples and speak of the reserve requirements imposed by the Fed, and not attempt to discuss the various reserve requirements imposed by the fifty states on state chartered nonmember banks.

To describe the deposit creation process we shall use just a few items from the balance sheet of Table 25-3 and show how changes in these items lead to changes in the volume of deposits and therefore changes in the money supply. These abbreviated balance sheets are sometimes called T accounts even though they are not what accountants call T accounts. Although cash inflow is not the principal source of bank reserves, we begin with a simple example of money created on the basis of a flow of cash that is taken out of circulation and deposited in a bank. Later we shall explain about the primary source of bank reserves.

Bank #1

Assets		Liabilities	
Reserves on deposit with the Fed plus vault cash	+$1000	Demand deposits	+$1000
Total	+$1000	Total	+$1000

Assume that Bank 1 has reached a point that it has no extra money to lend. At that time Mr. A enters with $1,000 in cash and opens a checking account with Bank 1. The bank now has a liability of $1,000 and its cash reserves are correspondingly increased by $1,000. We have placed plus signs before the amounts entered in order to indicate that we are speaking of a positive change in the account, and not the size of the account. Double entry accounting guarantees that changes in each side tallies to $1,000.

Assume the Federal Reserve imposes a reserve requirement of 15 percent, that is, required reserves are 15 percent of demand deposits.[2] Let *RR* stand for required reserves, *DD* stand for demand deposits, and r stand for the required reserve ratio, so r = 15 percent. Then the law setting the ratio at 15 percent requires that

$RR = 15\%$ of DD
or $RR = r \times DD$.

There is a certain minimum value that required reserves can assume given the level of demand deposits that a bank has. Since Bank 1 now has $1,000 more demand deposit liability than it had earlier, 15 percent of that or $150 must be held in the reserve account. This leaves $850 that the bank can lend. As indicated in the T account, we can call these *excess reserves* or *ER* for short. In formula form, where *TR* is total reserves, $ER = TR - rDD = \$850$.

Bank #1

Assets		Liabilities	
Reserves	+$1,000	Demand deposits	+$1,000
Req. res. + 150			
Excess res. + 850			

[2] Reserve requirements established December 30, 1976 and in effect in August 1980 were 7 percent on deposits up to $2 million, 9-1/2 percent on deposits from $2 million to $10 million, 11-3/4 percent on deposits from $10 million to $100 million, 12-3/4 percent on deposits from $100 to $400 million, and 16-1/4 percent on deposits over $400 million.

However, the Depository Institutions Deregulation and Monetary Control Act of 1980 specifies that by 1986 these requirements be set uniformly at 3 percent on deposits up to $25 million and, initially, 12 percent on deposits over $25 million. The Federal Reserve was given power to change reserve requirements within a range of 8 to 14 percent.

Bank 1 in our example now has $850 in excess reserves. Suppose that Mr. B walks into the bank and just happens to want to borrow $850. Then take total reserves and subtract required reserves to arrive at excess reserves that the bank can lend. The T account of Bank 1 after the loan to Mr. B is

Bank #1

Assets		Liabilities	
Reserves	+$1,000	DDs	$1,000 (Mr. A)
Loan	+850		+850 (Mr. B)
Total	$1,850	Total	$1,850

The process does not stop here. Mr. B did not borrow that money just to let it sit in the bank. He wants to buy something with it. So Mr. B writes a check to Mr. C for $850 and Mr. C deposits the check in his bank, Bank 2. Now Bank 2 has reserves of $850. The check clears through to Bank 1 and it loses $850 of its reserves. The accounts of Banks 1 and 2 read

Bank #1

Assets			Liabilities	
Reserves	+$1,000 −850	+$150	DDs	+$1,000 (Mr. A)
				+850 (Mr. B)
Loan		+850		−850
Total		$1,000	Total	$1,000

Bank #2

Assets			Liabilities	
Reserves		+$850	DDs	+$850 (Mr. C)
Req. res.	+$127.50			
Excess res.	+722.50			
Total		$850	Total	$850

At this point we can emphasize that the supply of money has been increased by $850. Mr. A still has his $1,000 deposit, but Mr. B got $850 and spent it so that now Mr. C has this $850. Both Mr. A and Mr. C can write checks against their deposits. But again the process does not stop. Assume Mr. D comes into the lobby of Bank 2 and asks for a loan. How much can Bank 2 lend to Mr. D? Since it must keep 15 percent in reserve it can lend the remaining 85 percent of the deposit.

$$RR = (.15)(\$850) = \$127.50$$

$$\text{New } ER = (.85)(\$850) = \$722.50$$

So Mr. D can borrow $722.50 and Bank 2 must keep $127.50 against the new deposit of $850.[3] The T account for Bank 2 is now

Bank #2

Assets		Liabilities	
Reserves	+$850	DDs	+$850 (Mr. C)
Loan	+722		+722 (Mr. D)
Total	+$1,572	Total	+$1,572

Mr. D in turn writes a check to Mr. E for $722.50. Mr. E goes to his bank, call it Bank 3, and deposits the check. The check eventually clears through Bank 2. The T accounts for Banks 2 and 3 read as follows:

Bank #2

Assets			Liabilities	
Reserves	+$850 − 722	+$128	DDs	$850 (Mr. C)
				+722 (Mr. D)
Loan		+722		−722
Total		+$850	Total	+$850

Bank #3

Assets		Liabilities	
Reserves	+$722	DDs	+$722 (Mr. E)
Total	+$722	Total	+$722

[3] In general, the level of excess reserves = total reserves − required reserves or $ER = TR - r\,DD$. Thus if $TR = \$1000$, then $ER = 850 - .15(850) = \$722.50$.

Mr. F now comes into Bank 3 for a loan. The amount he can borrow is the amount of excess reserves in Bank 3, or $614. Mr. F gets his loan from Bank 3, and writes a check to Mr. G who deposits it in Bank 4. After the checks clear, the accounts are as follows:

Bank #3

Assets			Liabilities	
Reserves	+$722 − 614	+$108	DDs	+$722 (Mr. E)
Loan		+614		+614 (Mr. F) −614
Total		$722	Total	$722

Bank #4

Assets		Liabilities	
Reserves	+$614	DDs	+$614 (Mr. G)
Total	+$614	Total	+$614

In principle, the process can continue down to the last penny. At each stage the residual reserve and the amount of the loan get smaller. Table 25-4 summarizes the activity using rounded numbers.

When there are no leakages, the whole banking system can magnify an initial deposit by a *multiplier* equal to one over the reserve ratio.

The initial deposit of $1,000 has been expanded by the banking system into total deposits of $6,667 or by a multiple of 6-2/3. We have assumed there are no leakages; that is to say, we assumed that all money withdrawn as loans will end up returning to the system as the borrower spends the money and the person who receives the check deposits it to his or her own account. The **multiplier** associated with deposit creation, 6 2/3, is uniquely related to the legal reserve ratio, 15 percent; it is simply the reciprocal of the ratio. If $RR = rDD$, then dividing both sides by r gives

$$DD = 1/r \times RR$$

$$DD = 1/.15 \times RR = 6.67\ RR.$$

So, if the legal reserve ratio were 10 percent, the multiplier 1/r would be 1/.10 or 10. This would mean that *DD* could expand tenfold in response to an initial deposit when there are no leakages in the system. If the reserve ratio were 20 percent, the multiplier would be 5; if it were 30 percent the multiplier would be 3-1/3; if it were 50 percent the multiplier would be 2, and so forth.

TABLE 25-4
Deposit Creation Process

Bank	Reserves	Loans	Deposits
1	150	850	1,000
2	128	722	850
3	108	614	722
4	92	522	614
5	78	444	522
6	67	377	444
⋮	⋮	⋮	⋮
All other banks	377	2138	2515
Total	1,000	5,667	6,667

The Money Supply

If we define money to include just currency in circulation (C) (in circulation means in the pockets of the public and outside of the banks—it can be spent) and demand deposits (*DD*), then

$$M = C + DD.$$

Potential new money equals excess reserves divided by the reserve ratio.

In the process we have described we began with Mr. A making a deposit of $1,000 in cash. Suppose he took the cash out of his mattress and brought it to the bank because he was not sleeping well on his lumpy mattress. Thus, cash is reduced by 1,000 and deposits expanded by $6,667, so the net increase in *M* is only 5,667. Demand deposits increased by a multiple of 6-2/3 but money only increased by a multiple of 5-2/3. The amount of new money created can be calculated by

$$\text{New money} = \frac{\text{excess reserves}}{\text{reserve ratio}} = \frac{850}{.15} = \$5{,}667.$$

Leakages

All this is descriptive of the multiplier effect on deposits and money if there are no leakages, but of course in the real banking system there are several important leakages that prevent the multipliers from working to their fullest extent. For example, a leakage can occur if one of the borrowers along the line did not want his loan in the form of a checking account but wanted to hold cash instead. Perhaps Mr. F borrowed the $614 and took cash out of the bank and sewed it in his mattress because he believes banks cannot be trusted. Thus, he just reverses what Mr. A had done in the first place. When Mr. F does this, the deposit expansion process abruptly halts. If we look at the net result we see that Mr. A deposited $1,000 but Mr. F withdrew $614, thus the net amount of increase in currency held in the banks is only $386. If we apply the multiplier of 6.67 to this amount we get $2,572 in demand deposits, or the sum of the first three rounds of 1,000 plus 850 plus 722. Thus, the multiplier applies to whatever amount of cash remains in the banks. When some cash is withdrawn and is not returned to circulation we say a leakage occurs, so that the full demand deposit creation process is not realized.

In reality, the full multiplier effect is not realized because of *leakages* such as undeposited cash; also, banks may choose to hold more reserves than required.

Other leakages that are important to recognize should be mentioned. Managers of one of the banks may, for some reason, decide to hold onto some of its excess reserves and simply not lend them out. In the U.S. today banks in general try to hold as little in excess reserves as they can because they want to keep as fully lent or invested as possible so they will earn as much income as possible. In other countries where markets for lending and borrowing are not as well developed as in the U.S., there may be many situations in which banks will hold a significant amount of excess reserves and hence reduce the extent of deposit creation. So, we say there can be a leakage into excess reserves just as we said there could be a leakage into currency in circulation.

A Single Bank

We have described how flows of money in a system of numerous banks allow the commercial banking system to create deposit money. If there had been only one bank in the system which everyone used—the only bank in a small country—the multiplier process of deposit creation would still apply as we described it. The single bank, Bank 1, in this situation is the banking system. All those demand deposits of Mr. A, B, C, and so on would simply have been listed under Bank 1.

When there are many banks in a system, the manager of a single bank does not have the impression that a single bank creates money. As more money is deposited in the single bank, the bank can make more loans. Thus, the bank manager has the impression that he is only lending out that money that has been deposited in his bank, and not creating new money. But as we saw, a group of banks in a system creates money just as would be the case if there were only a single bank in the economy.

DEPOSIT CONTRACTION

The banking system can *contract* the nation's money supply by recalling loans or selling off some of its securities.

For an exercise to enhance our understanding of the relation of bank activities to money creation, let us follow through what happens if money is destroyed by banks. Suppose a bank has no excess reserves (loaned up) and cannot lend out one penny more. A depositor bounces up to the teller's window and says, "Hi there, I want to withdraw $1,000." As a consequence the bank's balance sheet is (showing changes only)

Bank #1

Assets		Liabilities	
Reserves	−$1,000	DDs	−$1,000

Assume the bank owns some short-term Treasury bonds like those defined earlier. Its reserve requirement against the $1,000 deposit was $150. It loses $1,000 in reserves as the result of the withdrawal, leaving the bank $850 deficient in reserves against the remaining deposits. What can it do? It can sell $850 worth of securities. It does so to a person who writes a check against his account in Bank 2 to pay for the bond. Assume Bank 1 takes the check over to Bank 2 and gets cash and brings it back to its own vaults. Now the net result is shown in the T account. Bank 1's deposits have fallen by $1,000, its reserves by $150 and its loans and/or investments by $850.

Prior to this Bank 2 was also fully loaned. But now Bank 2 is deficient in reserves by $850. So it must sell $722 of its bonds. It can afford to lose $128 in legal reserves because its demand deposits are now lower by $850, but it has to replenish $722 of its reserve position. Bank 2 therefore sells off $722 in bonds

Bank #1

Assets		Liabilities	
Reserves	−150	DDs	−1,000
Bonds	−850		

Bank #2

Assets		Liabilities	
Reserves	−$850	DDs	−$850

to a person who draws down his account at Bank 3 by $722. Now, if Bank 2 takes the cash, the accounts of bank 2 are straightened out, but Bank 3 is in trouble. Assuming Bank 3 was fully loaned up at the outset, Bank 3 is now short of reserves against its remaining deposits of $722 − 108 = $614. And so it goes. The whole process continues to operate in reverse until the overall decline in demand deposits reaches $6,667. The multiplier of 6-2/3 operates in *both* directions.

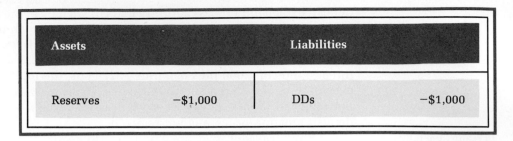

Bank #2

Assets		Liabilities	
Reserves	−128	DDs	−850
Bonds	−722		

Bank #3

Assets		Liabilities	
Reserves	−722	DDs	−722

Banks are simultaneously private and public enterprises; they earn a profit while creating money by government charter.

We shall see in the following chapter that the monetary authorities can control to a great extent the amount of reserves the banks have available. They can add to bank reserves and allow commercial banks to expand the money supply, or they can subtract bank reserves and cause banks to contract the money supply. Thus, money is created and destroyed by commercial banks with the blessing of the nation's central bank and Treasury officials.

BANK INCOME

The U.S. Constitution gives Congress authority over the U.S. money supply. Congress, in turn, delegates its authority to the executive branch through the offices of the Secretary of the Treasury. It has also delegated its authority by establishing the Federal Reserve System. But commercial banks are thought of as private profit-making institutions. They are corporations chartered by states, or by the Comptroller of the Currency. Private individuals make investments in, and hold ownership of, commercial banks. Although commercial banks are highly regulated, they nevertheless operate with a view toward earning income and profit for their owners just like any other business. One could say they are literally and figuratively in the business of making money.

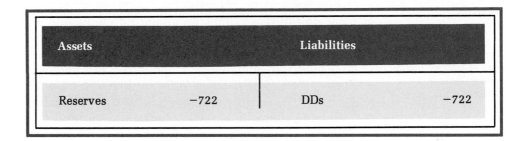

Under the Constitution, Congress could simply have government take over and operate all commercial banks, because banks create money. It would not do this, of course, but it has the full constitutional authority to do so. Thus, banks are placed in a unique position in our society because they perform as the principal creators of the nation's money supply on the one hand, which is Congress's duty, but are private profit-making institutions on the other hand. If they did not earn enough income to operate profitably, banks would go out of business, and Congress would be forced to replace them somehow. So banks are simultaneously private and public institutions.

Bank Income and the Prime Rate

Banks earn revenues by *loaning*, earning income on *securities* they purchase, and charging for *services*.

Just how do banks go about earning income? They do it by charging interest on the **loans** they create, by earning interest on **securities** they purchase, by collecting service charges for the checking account facilities they provide to their customers, and by charging for various other **services** they provide such as managing trust accounts, arranging for credit, and so forth.

The *prime rate* is the rate of interest banks charge their best customers.

Interest rates rise and fall over time, and bank profits respond in concert. One interest rate that is widely reported in newspapers is the **prime rate**. A large bank will announce changes in this rate and other banks will follow suit. This is the rate that banks offer to their most credit-worthy customers for a short-term loan. Big corporations like General Motors and AT&T have prime borrowing status. If you ask a treasurer in a local corporation what his firm's borrowing status is, he may say, "We can get our money at 1/2 or 1/4 percent above prime." Such a borrower has a very good credit rating. Most businesses, then, measure their credit position using the prime rate as a base.

How Banks Earn Profits for Their Owners: Leverage

If a bank borrows money from its customers by giving them time deposits and paying them 6 percent interest, how does the bank make any money? Of course, the answer is that it lends the money out at 10 percent. In this way the bank only makes 4 percent net on its loan. Does this mean, then, that the bank only makes a return of 4 percent, and if so is not this an unprofitable business to be in when you can make anywhere between 6 and 10 percent by putting your money in a bank or lending it to a business?

The answer is no. The 4 percent is *not* the return made by the *owners* of the bank. The bank's owners are using other people's money, not their own money.

Assume owners put up $1 million and build a bank. Then assume that people deposit $10 million on which the bank pays 6 percent and the bank then lends out $10 million at 10 percent. Thus, the earnings per year will be $400,000, reflecting the 4 percent differential between what was borrowed and what was lent. This $400,000 return to those who invested in the original bank is a 40 percent return! Earning a little bit of money on a lot of other people's money is the name of the game in banking, as it is in other businesses.

The example, of course, is exaggerated. Out of the 4 percent differential must also come all of the expenses associated with the bank's operations. Real life owners of banks do not generally receive more than 10 or 12 percent, or so, on their investments. This is the same kind of return that businesses in general can be expected to pay to investors.

Nevertheless the idea of using other people's money along with only a little of your own means that you are leveraged up. A small profit over all means a large percentage profit on your share. By the same token, a small loss over all may wipe out your share altogether. Hence, the greater the leverage, the greater risk of loss and the greater the possibility of gain.

Interest

Nearly everyone is both a borrower and a lender. However, banks pursue borrowing and lending with a vengeance. They borrow huge amounts of money from their depositors. They do not have to pay interest on those demand deposit checking accounts that most of us hold, but they often charge low fees for checking account services or reduce the service charges if the customer holds a minimum balance in the account. On time and savings deposits, of course, banks do have to pay their customers some interest. Banks profit, therefore, from the *difference* between what they must pay to some people who lend to them and what they earn on the loans they, in turn, make to other people. Essentially, bankers are middlemen who produce services for the public.

Thus, if the demand for commercial loans is high, the prime rate is high, then the difference between what banks receive in interest and what they must pay in interest may also be large. Under these circumstances, bank profits rise.

While any one commercial bank has to compete for business with all the other commercial banks, the banking system as a whole is heavily subsidized by its money-creating power. Because banks, as a group, create money, they can also earn interest on it. In theory banks as a group are subsidized through this earning power provided to them as a result of their money-creating power.

HISTORIC LEGISLATION

In March of 1980 President Carter signed into law the Depository Institutions Deregulation and Monetary Control Act. This legislation provided for sweeping changes in the structure of financial institutions. It authorized savings and loan associations, mutual savings banks, and credit unions to offer checking accounts to their depositors. It also authorized these thrift institutions to offer credit card services and to make some consumer loans of the sort that commercial banks routinely make. In our description of the money creation process, we focused on commercial banks and not thrift institutions. But it is clear that this legislation will allow the thrifts to become more like commercial banks. Indeed, inasmuch as they now offer checking accounts they too create money that people can use to pay bills. The measure of money M1-B includes these checking deposits in thrift institutions.

The 1980 law also provides that commercial banks that are not members of the Federal Reserve and thrift institutions all begin holding legal reserves against checking deposits after a phase-in period. Reserve requirements will eventually be made uniform for all financial institutions that offer checking accounts.

Among its many provisions, the law established a Depository Institutions Deregulation Committee and gave it authority to implement the law's other provisions by 1986. It will also phase out interest rate ceilings on saving accounts thereby introducing competitive interest rates.

While it provides for deregulation of interest rates on savings, at the same time this law brought about 9,000 nonmember banks and about 28,000 thrift institutions under federal regulations. Therefore, to call it a deregulation law is, to an extent, misleading. But whatever its name, it will make U.S. banking much more competitive. At the same time it will bring all those institutions that create checking account money under the fractional reserve system within the Fed's control.

CHAPTER SUMMARY

In general, money is whatever is accepted as payment for goods and services, and as settlement of debts. A barter system exists when goods and services are directly traded for other goods and services. You might say that money is defined by what money does. Money has three functions:

1. It serves as a medium of exchange to facilitate trade. It avoids the problems of a large scale barter system and permits economic activities to be specialized, resulting in increased efficiency and productivity.
2. It serves as a store of value. It is an asset that can be set aside and used later while retaining its value. Since money has the property of liquidity, it can be used to buy all other assets, whereas nonmoney assets cannot easily be used to trade for other nonmoney assets unless they have been converted into money first. The ease with which an asset can be converted to money increases its degree of liquidity.
3. It serves as a unit of account because the relative market value of commodities is denominated in money prices, so that money functions as the single standard for making comparisons of worth. It also serves as an accounting unit for deferred payments.

To have value, money must be scarce. Gold is naturally scarce, but the printing of paper money must be under the monopoly control of the government to ensure its scarcity. Indeed, gold is too scarce, and there is additional problem that it is costly to use and heavy to ship.

There are several official measures of money in the U.S. M1-A consists of cash held by the public plus demand deposits—checkable accounts—at commercial banks. M1-B consists of cash held by the public plus checkable accounts at all financial institutions such as credit unions, savings banks, and savings and loans institutions as well as banks. Eventually M1-A will be dropped and M1-B will simply become M1. M2 includes everything in M1-B plus some other highly liquid accounts that businesses keep with banks. Two other broader measures of money are M3 and L, consisting of M2 plus still other highly liquid assets.

There are over 14,000 banks in the U.S., with less than half being members of the Federal Reserve System, the national U.S. banking system. Member banks account for about 70 percent of all demand deposits of U.S. commercial banks, down from 85 percent in 1947. Because the Federal Reserve does not pay interest on member bank reserves which it holds, many commercial banks have left the Federal system in the last decade.

Banks compute balance sheets listing their assets, liabilities and net worth. Assets are claims the bank has against others; among these assets are securities, loans, and reserves. Liabilities are claims against banks, consisting of things like borrowings and time and demand deposits. The difference between assets and liabilities is net worth or equity, or what the bank owes to its owners: bank assets of owners against which there are no liabilities.

Commercial banks that are members keep their reserves with the Federal Reserve

System. However, a small part of reserves consists of cash held on the premises for making cash transactions like cashing checks. This is vault cash. Banks use double entry bookkeeping, so that by definition assets = liabilities + net worth. Thus, a new deposit by a customer is a liability but is also entered as reserves in the asset column. Banks are required by law to hold a certain fraction of these reserves against deposits. This fractional reserve process allows banks to create money, because reserves held in excess of the required level are excess reserves and can be loaned at a rate of interest. The amount of excess reserves equals total reserves minus required reserves—where required reserves are equal to the fractional reserve requirement or reserve ratio—times the level of demand deposits. In shorthand, the formula is $ER = TR - (r \cdot DD)$. The whole banking system can magnify an initial deposit by a multiplier equal to 1 over the reserve ratio; that is by $1/r$. The difference between total deposits created and the initial deposit equals new money and is equal to excess reserves divided by the reserve ratio, or potential new money $= ER/r$.

In reality, the full multiplier effect is not realized because of leakages from the banking system, as when people do not deposit cash into accounts but hold the cash instead. Banks may also choose to hold more reserves than required.

The banking system can also contract the nation's money supply by recalling loans or selling off some of its securities. When the purchaser writes a check to pay for the security, the bank it is written against loses that much in reserves. If it then falls short of its reserve requirement it must call in some loans or sell off some of its securities, and the process ripples through the system.

Commercial banks are chartered either by the state or the federal government. New legislation requires that various thrift institutions hold reserves against checking accounts. Bank are in business to earn a profit as does any business. They earn revenues by lending, by earning interest on securities they purchase, and by charging for a variety of services. The prime rate is the rate of interest banks charge their best customers. Banks earn profit on loans because of leverage. Though they may pay 6 percent to a depositer and lend out at 9 percent to a borrower, they are earning more than 3 percent on the negotiation because they are lending depositors' money, not their own. They can do this because of the money creating power the government charter gives them.

QUESTIONS

1. Which of your assets is more liquid; your diamond ring or your waterbed? Explain.
2. In 1980 the Canadian dollar was worth about 85 cents in U.S. money. Which is more liquid in Seattle, Washington, a bus token or a Canadian quarter? Why?
3. Using money reduces costs. What costs? Or is this double-talk?
4. If most money is bank debt, then why can your debt not be money? You accept checks from others, do you not? So, what is the problem?
5. Commercial banks can make loans but they do not create money since they cannot print it. Do you agree? Comment.
6. If you go to the bank and take out a loan of $1,000 in *cash*, in itself, does this increase the money supply? Explain. Do banks normally lend in cash? Comment.
7. Under Regulation Q, there is a limit of 5-1/4 percent interest that banks and thrift institutions can pay customers on their savings accounts. When price (interest) competition among banks is thus constrained, competition is likely to be expressed in other forms. One is free checking accounts. It cost at least 30 cents in 1979 for a bank to clear a check, whereas it is often free to the customer.

a. Do you think the average consumer would be better off in a system in which he is paid a market rate of interest on his deposit but is charged a market fee for writing checks?
b. What other forms of nonprice competition have you observed that banks engage in?
c. Is the interest rate limit discriminatory? If so, against whom?

8. Beginning in November 1978 banks were permitted to begin automatic transfer service. Funds in savings accounts (interest bearing) could be automatically transferred by the banks to checking accounts (noninterest bearing) when the money was needed to cover checks. What can you say about the distinction between M1-A and M1-B money? Would automatic transfers likely have a temporary positive or negative effect on the *growth* of M1-A during the transition period? Why?
9. Suppose banks expect hard times ahead. How might their ensuing behavior be self-fulfilling?
10. Why is the actual money multiplier less than the theoretical money multiplier?
11. Is money an asset? Are all assets therefore money? If Mr. Fat Cat is a millionaire, does that necessarily mean he has $1 million in cash, including his checking account? Therefore, is net worth different from money? (Hint: check Table 25-3.)
12. It is pay day. Each worker deposits his pay check and writes no checks for the next two weeks. Can the banking system nevertheless increase the money supply during that time if the banks were fully loaned up when the checks were deposited, and if no added reserves are made available by the Fed?
13. Which of the following would officially be included as part of the M1-A money supply in the U.S.? M1-B? M2?
   a. Gold in Fort Knox.
   b. A $2 bill in your wallet.
   c. A $5 bill in your bank's vault.
   d. A Treasury bond you own.
   e. A check.
   f. A checking account.
   g. A Canadian dollar in your pocket.
   h. A credit card you make a purchase with.
   i. $200 in your savings account in a commercial bank.
   j. $200 in your checkable savings account at a savings and loan.
   k. A 1-ounce gold piece in your pocket.
14. Indicate whether the following transaction in itself results in an increase, a decrease, or no change in the M1-A money supply:
   a. You find $100 on the street and deposit it in your checking account.
   b. You buy a $1,000 government bond that you pay for with a check.
   c. You receive a cash loan of $200 from a friend.
   d. You receive a loan of $200 from a friend in the form of a check with which you pay your landlord, who deposits $100 in his checking account and spends $80 for a wool sweater at Sears and $20 to pay off parking tickets.
   e. You pay $400 rent to your landlord, who turns around and buys $400 worth of city bonds.
   f. You give $20 to your nephew for Christmas in the form of two tens. One falls out of his pocket while he is walking down the street.
   g. You take out a loan from your bank for $100, write a check to your friend for the same amount to pay off an old debt. He deposits it in the very same bank.
   h. A commercial bank increases its vault cash inventory by $10,000 by drawing down its account at the Fed.
   i. An uninsured bank is robbed of $20,000. Does the answer change if the bank was already fully loaned up?
   j. You deposit $150 in currency in a noncheckable savings account at the bank.

15. A banking system has a 20 percent reserve requirement. If a bank is fully loaned up, and a $5,000 cash deposit is made, how much can it lend? By how much can the banking system increase the money stock?
16. Palm Tree Bank is the only bank on the island. It has a reserve requirement of 20 percent. A deposit of $5,000 is made; how much are its added reserves after all lending?
17. A banking system has a 20 percent reserve requirement. The public decides it wants to carry $100,000 more in currency. Will the money stock rise or fall? By how much?
18. You are shown the following balance sheet of a bank.

Assets		**Liabilities**	
Vault cash	$ 2,000	Demand deposits	$110,000
Reserves with		Time deposits	30,000
Federal bank	25,000	Net worth	20,000
Loans	50,000		
Securities	83,000		

Assume the reserve requirement is 20 percent. Calculate
a. The bank's assets.
b. Its reserves.
c. Its required reserves against demand deposits.
d. Its excess reserves.
e. The maximum amount of new loans it can make initially.
f. The maximum increase in the money supply the banking system can make if all other banks are fully loaned up.

Chapter 26

The Federal Reserve System

PROGRESS REPORT

A. In Chapter 25 we discussed what money is, what money does, and how we measure it. We also examined the commercial banking system and the role it plays in creating money. Governments produce money, but acting together the commercial banks produce even more money than the government does in the form of demand deposits. The Federal Reserve System was briefly described.

B. The government and its agents can and do limit the extent of money creation. The Federal Reserve System is the principal agent involved in controlling the money supply in the U.S. This chapter is devoted to a fuller description of "the Fed" and its functions. We begin the chapter with a brief history of banking in the U.S.

C. In Chapter 27 we shall shift our attention away from the supply of money and how it is controlled, to the demand for money and its integration into the macroeconomic model.

A BRIEF HISTORY OF BANKING IN THE U.S.[1]

The erratic growth of U.S. banking was marked by several major recessions caused by panics and bank failures stemming from overissuing paper money.

The early development of monetary and banking institutions in colonial America was erratic. Very little money circulated. Barter, the direct exchange of goods, was common. What was called *country pay* was used for money. In the Virginia colony in 1618 an official value for tobacco was specified so that it could be used as a means of payment. In Massachusetts barter was not efficient, coins were scarce, and experiments with paper money took place in 1690. Bills of credit were issued by the state. On the face of a bill was a statement of its value in metallic money and its acceptability as payment for taxes to the treasurer. Eventually, due to the ease with which it could be printed, paper money was overissued and redemption in coin was halted.

In June 1775, the Continental Congress authorized an issue of $82 million in bills of credit; but pressure for war funds quickly depreciated subsequent issues and by 1780 $1 in coins was worth $80 in Continental currency. This gave rise to the expression "not worth a Continental."

The First and Second Banks of the U.S.

Alexander Hamilton pushed hard and got Congress to establish a national bank in 1791. States also chartered private banks. The First Bank of the U.S. exerted a stabilizing influence on state banks. Notes issued by state banks circulated as money, and by presenting notes of state banks for redemption in coin (gold and silver), the First Bank inhibited overissues of these notes by state or "country" banks. After twenty years of operation, when its charter was up for renewal, Congress by a single vote defeated the proposal to renew the First Bank's charter.

In the void left by the absence of a national bank, states granted more bank charters. These banks often overissued their notes, so that inflation, runs on banks, and fraud followed. To avoid the chaos caused by overissue of paper money by banks, Congress established the Second Bank of the U.S. in 1816. As creditor of state banks it could at its discretion reduce the amount of money in circulation by increasing the redemption of state bank notes. The Second Bank also issued its own notes, and these provided a uniform currency throughout the country since traders across the country did not have to rely on notes of various state banks. It competed with state banks, and its loans were important for agriculture and commerce on the western frontier. Yet the bank fell into disfavor. It was doomed with the election of Andrew Jackson in 1828, who favored the state banks. Even before the bank's charter ran out, the Treasury stopped making deposits in the Bank of the U.S. and transferred funds to designated state banks instead. Without the leverage of the Treasury, banks could neither exert much influence on the country's financial markets nor control

[1] To provide the reader with this brief section on banking history we have summarized an excellent article by Edward E. Veazey, "Evolution of Money and Banking in the U.S.," *Business Review*, Federal Reserve Bank of Dallas, Dec. 1975, pp. 1–12.

issues of state banks. By 1837 the volume of state bank notes doubled and a rapid inflation resulted. As bank notes lost value, people turned them in for gold and silver, and a wave of bank failures led to a severe depression because there was not enough metallic money to back all of the bank notes.

National Banking Act

In 1846, the Independent Treasury Act was passed, which instructed the Treasury Department to keep all the money it collected. All bank settlements with the Treasury were to be settled in specie or Treasury notes. But the act was ignored when Civil War funds were badly needed. The war brought on inflation, and the outflow of gold from its coffers forced the Treasury to stop redeeming notes in gold or silver. Then Congress authorized the Treasury to issue demand notes to pay for its purchases. This amounted to the out-and-out printing of paper money. The new notes were called greenbacks because the green ink on the back side of the dollar bill was all that backed the money since it was no longer backed by gold. The law also made these notes "legal tender for all debts, public and private."

But greenbacks proved inadequate for financing the war, and in 1863 the National Banking Act was passed. It established provisions for chartering national banks to which the Treasury could sell its bonds. A 10-cent tax on all state bank notes was passed, forcing many state banks to join the national system. Banks in the system had to buy government bonds equal to one third of their invested capital. National banks issued notes in amounts tied to their ownership of government bonds. A uniform paper currency was established. Dollar bills were all printed by the federal government and looked very much the same as they do today, and each bill had printed on its face the name of the national bank that had issued it. Thus, for the first time a uniform national currency emerged in the U.S.

There was a serious defect in this system. In the summer and winter when loan demand was slack, country banks deposited their reserves in New York City banks. Considering them as reserves, the New York banks expanded their loans. However, in the spring and fall when money was needed for growing crops and harvesting, the country banks withdrew their deposits, leaving the city banks short on liquidity. This led to panic and recession several times.

The controversy over gold and silver money—bimetallism—raged for thirty years. After yet another financial panic and the depression of 1893, brought on by the pubic's desire to redeem its paper notes for Treasury gold, President McKinley signed the Gold Standard Act of 1900. Unfortunately, in 1907 the failure of the Knickerbocker Trust Company initiated another bank crisis.

Federal Reserve System

In December 1913, Woodrow Wilson signed into law the Federal Reserve Act. The country was divided into 12 districts, each with its own regional Federal Reserve Bank. All national banks had to be members. State banks were given the option to join the system or not. Member banks were required to maintain

The current Federal Reserve System was established in 1913 to control the nation's money supply and regulate credit.

reserves as a percentage of their deposit liabilities. Their reserves were held as deposits in their district Federal Reserve Bank, not with other commercial banks. Thus, the Federal Reserve Banks became banker's banks. They are also called central banks. The gold standard was kept as backing for paper currency and gold coins circulated. The supply of currency was to be made flexible to keep pace with the public's demand for the form in which it chooses to hold its money. Flexibility was to be accomplished by allowing member banks to borrow from the Fed when they needed extra cash. The Fed performed the central banking function, to be lender of last resort. Also the Federal Reserve was made fiscal agent of the Treasury and became the Treasury's bank.

In the late 1920s problems emerged. The Fed in 1928 and 1929 tried to curb a stock market boom by discouraging loans for security speculation. It also wanted to keep alive the economic expansion. It tried to achieve both objectives at the same time. However, although economic expansion was curtailed, speculation was not deterred. As the situation deteriorated, panic erupted in the stock market and it crashed in October 1929.

Depression

Within a year after the crash many banks had shut down. Some 256 banks failed in November 1930, and another 352 in December. To achieve the liquidity needed to protect themselves from failure, banks sold bonds at lower and lower prices and interest rates rose. Banks held more excess reserves and deposits contracted. The money supply fell and the economy spiraled into depression.

The problem was seriously compounded when Britain abandoned the gold standard in 1931, no longer issuing gold for redeemed pounds from foreign countries. Since the U.S. still redeemed in gold, these countries sought out the U.S. The gold outflow meant a smaller domestic money supply and less lending for investments. With the country already in the midst of a depression, this aggravated the economic downturn.

A third banking panic hit the country in 1933. In 1934 the Gold Reserve Act placed all gold under government control. Gold coins that formerly circulated as part of the currency supply were withdrawn from circulation.

In response to the disastrous economic and financial scene, Congress passed important laws to regulate banking. These enabled the Fed to refuse bank loans for speculative purposes. They also prohibited the payment of interest on demand deposits. Such interest paid by city banks had attracted large seasonal flows of funds out of the country banks to New York City for investment in stockbroker loans. This sometimes led to the failure of a country bank. Banking legislation strengthened the Fed's authority to regulate reserve requirements and allowed it to set maximum interest payable on savings and time deposits. It also removed the Comptroller of the Currency and the Secretary of the Treasury from membership on the Federal Reserve Board in order to reduce the Treasury's influence on the Board and strengthen the Fed's independence. Further legislation established the Federal Deposit Insurance Corporation (FDIC), which now insures every depositor's account up to $100,000 in FDIC member institutions.

There were six mild recessions between 1950 and 1980, but none produced panics in the nation's banking and financial markets.

STRUCTURE OF THE FEDERAL RESERVE

The Federal Reserve System consists of 12 district banks with 24 branches and is headed by a 7-member Board of Governors appointed by the President.

The Federal Reserve is comprised of 12 districts with a main bank in each district and 24 branch banks throughout the system, as shown in Figure 26-1. The branch banks are not evenly distributed geographically. The area of District 6 has 5 branch banks, Districts 1 and 3 have none. Each Reserve bank is supposed to give emphasis to the particular problems of the region wherein it resides, supervising member banks. At the same time it helps to administer nationwide monetary and credit policies. Each of the Federal Reserve district banks is therefore operated for public service and benefit.

Each of the 12 Federal Reserve banks has 9 directors. (Refer to Figure

Figure 26-1

The Federal Reserve System
Boundaries of Federal Reserve districts and their branch territories

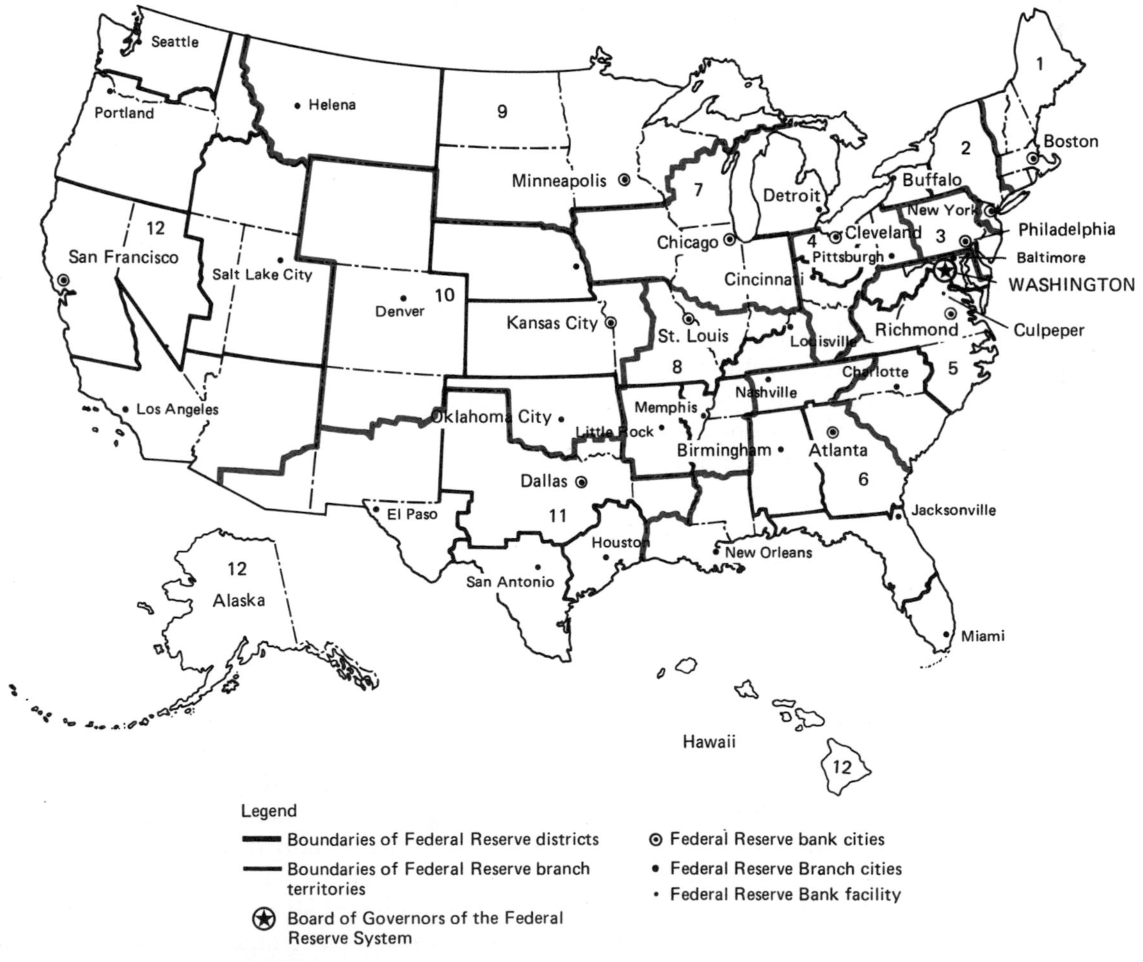

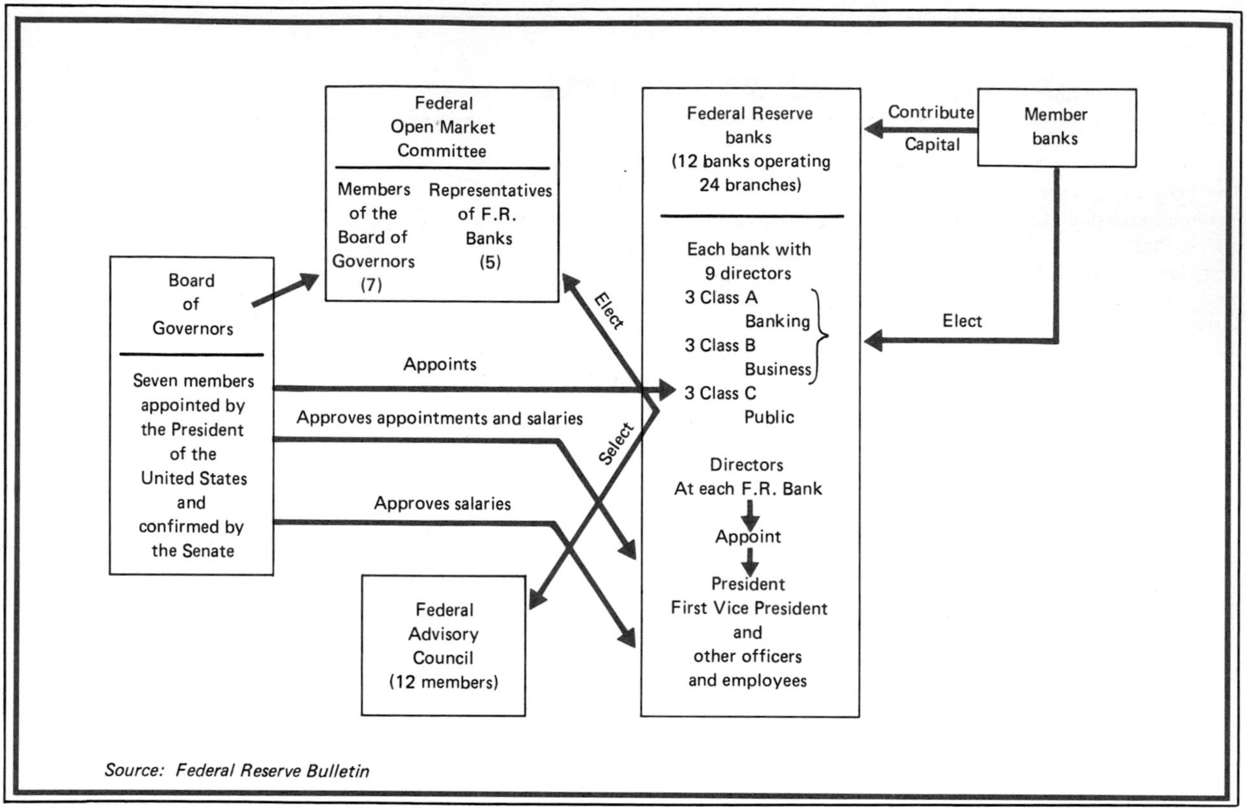

Figure 26-2

26-2.) The 3 Class A directors may be bankers and must represent the member banks. The 3 Class B directors cannot be officers or employees of the bank but must be employed in their districts in business, agriculture, or other industrial activities. Both Class A and Class B directors are elected by votes of member commercial banks. The 3 Class C directors are appointed by the Fed's Board of Governors from the public at large. Thus, bankers do not constitute a majority of the directors of each district Federal Reserve Banks.

Board of Governors

The Board of Governors of the Federal Reserve System consists of 7 members appointed by the President of the U.S. and confirmed by the Senate for a term of 14 years with a rotation occurring every 2 years. No 2 members can come from the same Federal Reserve district. One of the 7 Board members is appointed by the President to serve as chairman for a 4-year term, and may be reappointed.

The Board supervises the Federal Reserve System. It issues regulations and conducts bank examinations through its field examiners. It also authorizes bank ventures such as mergers and branching, and it decides what business activities member banks are allowed to engage in. The Board must report to Congress frequently. All 7 members of the board sit on the 12-member Federal Open Market Committee (FOMC), where monetary and credit policy is determined and carried out. More on this shortly.

Functions of the Fed

The Fed also handles member banks' reserve accounts, clears their checks, and assists the Treasury.

Aside from the important monetary and credit stabilizing activities, the Fed handles member bank reserve accounts; it also distributes coin and paper currency to the community through member banks. As a bank it issues Federal Reserve notes just like state and national banks once did in earlier days.

The Fed provides check-clearing services for its members and requires that all banks using its facilities clear its checks at par. Years ago, if you traveled to another town and wrote a check on your home town bank for $100, the local bank would only give you, say, $98 for it. Only a handful of banks still do this and no bank using the Fed's clearing services are allowed to do it.

Check Clearing

One of the services of the Federal Reserve is to act as a clearing house for checks written against the deposits of member banks and nonmember par banks. The enclosed chart traces a check as it is cleared from one Federal Reserve district to another. Let us start in Seattle, located in the 12th district. Mr. Swim mails a check for $10 to Macmillan Publishing Company in New York City, located in the 2nd district.

When Macmillan receives the check, it deposits the check in its account at Chase-Manhattan Bank of New York City, which credits the Macmillan account to the amount of $10. The reserves of Chase-Manhattan are also increased $10 when the check proceeds to the Federal Reserve Bank of New York, which credits the reserves of Chase-Manhattan by $10. Federal Reserve district banks do not have accounts with one another. The Federal Bank in New York sends the check to the Federal Reserve Bank in San Francisco (actually it would go to the branch bank in Seattle). Then the Federal Reserve Bank of New York sends a wire to the Interdistrict Settlement Fund in Washington, D.C. They proceed to debit $10 on the account of the Federal Reserve Bank in the 12th district and credit $10 to the account of the New York Federal Reserve Bank, located in the 2nd district.

The Reserve Bank in San Francisco (the branch bank in Seattle) deducts $10 from the reserves of the First National Bank in Seattle. It then

Interdistrict Settlement Fund

A	L
	Reserve Bank of New York +$10
	Reserve Bank of San Francisco −$10

sends the check to the First National Bank in Seattle, which proceeds to reduce Mr. Swim's account by $10 and to return his canceled check to him.

Check Clearing Operations of the Federal Reserve

Note:
Those banks which are *not* members of the Federal Reserve System will keep an account with a member bank in order to clear any checks they receive.

A wire is sent to the *Interdistrict Settlement Fund* in Washington D.C. They transfer $10 from the account of the 12th District Federal Reserve Bank to the 2nd Federal Reserve Bank District Account.

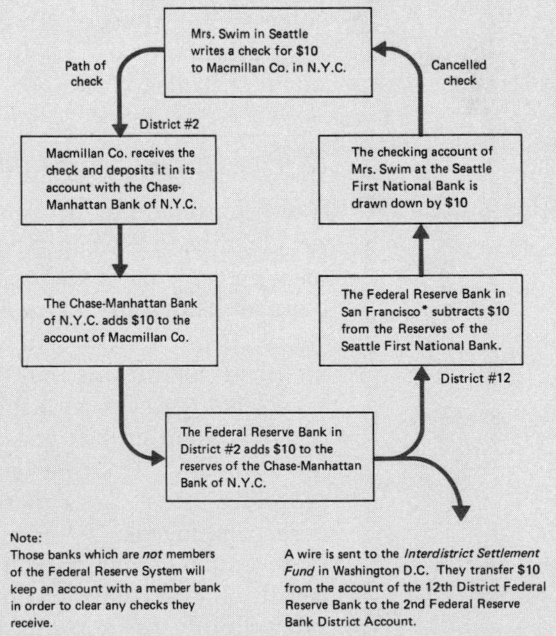

Other functions of the Fed involve its services to the Treasury. The Treasury uses the Fed as its bank by keeping checking accounts at the Fed and paying bills by writing checks against its account. The Fed assists the Treasury by handling the Social Security payments by employees, and helps the Treasury in its debt sales and redemptions as well.

Fed Ownership and Profits

When the Fed was established, all national banks were required to become members and were required to purchase shares of its stock. The Fed pays dividends to its member bank shareholders. It would be a mistake, however, to consider the Fed as an institution owned by the member banks, except in an irrelevant technical sense.

The resources invested in shares of Fed stock by member banks were used to get the Fed established as an independent agency. Since then, the Fed has operated and paid its expenses out of its own earnings. It does not require appropriations from Congress for its expenses. Since the Fed can literally create money whenever it wishes, it never runs short. When it wishes to purchase something it gives the seller a check on itself. It does not have to have money in some account to do this because its check is money.

From its holdings of government securities, the Fed earns huge amounts of interest income from the Treasury. So great is its income that after paying all of the expenses of monitoring and operating 12 Federal Reserve banks around the country and the Board of Governors offices in Washington, D.C., it uses only about 5 percent of its earnings and has 95 percent of them left over. Nearly all its earnings come from interest on Treasury debt. So, the Treasury is the principal source of the earnings. And at the end of the year the Fed simply gives back to the Treasury some 95 percent of what it took in. Thus, while in some technical accounting sense one could say the Fed is a highly profitable institution, the term profit hardly applies. The Fed, *de facto*, is not owned by member banks. It is a government agency responsible to Congress.

The Fed is primarily responsible to Congress.

Requirements of Membership

Once chartered by the Comptroller of the Currency, a member bank is required to subscribe to the capital account of its district reserve bank an amount equal to 3 percent of its own capital, and another 3 percent is subject to call. A member bank must maintain legally required reserves either as cash in its own vaults or as deposits with a district Federal Reserve Bank. Other nonmember financial institutions that offer checking account services are also required to hold legal reserves with the Fed. Member banks must cash without exacting a penalty (remit at par) checks drawn against them when presented by the Fed for payment. Also, they must comply with the Clayton Antitrust Act, which prohibits interlocking directorates—the sharing of bank officers and certain other employees. To ensure that member banks are meeting their reserve requirements, each bank is required to keep a ledger showing its financial condition every day. To do so would impose unreasonable bookkeeping costs. They simply cannot control things that quickly or precisely. Currently the requirements are that they must maintain reserves on a daily average basis this week sufficient to cover the daily average level of deposits they held during the week two weeks prior to this week. As much as a 2 percent deficiency in holdings of required reserves is allowed so long as any deficiency is made up the next week. On the other hand, if the bank finds it has excess reserves of more than 2 percent above its requirements, it may apply these to next week's requirements. Deficiencies in excess of 2 percent are penalized, and if they consistently occur a bank can be fined or lose its charter. If a bank consistently does not meet its legal requirements, the Fed closes it down.

Independence of the Federal Reserve

Although created by Congress in 1913, the Fed has been given substantial independence from government. Since each member of the Board is appointed for a term of 14 years, with a rotation of 1 of the 7 members every 2 years, no President can pack the board with his own appointees and gain control, although he can appoint the chairman for a 4-year period. In the short run the Fed is protected from daily political pressures, although Presidents do sometimes lean on the Board. Congress created the Fed and it could also destroy it if intense public pressure were to be applied.

INSTRUMENTS OF MONETARY POLICY

The Federal Reserve System is charged with forming and implementing monetary policy. It accomplishes its objectives principally by controlling the reserves of member banks. Through such control the Fed can regulate the volume of credit. The Fed can also vary the volume of reserves available to the banks. It can encourage member banks to speed up or slow down their creation of money and bank credit. It has at its disposal three major and three minor tools to achieve its purposes. The three major tools are (1) setting the fractional reserve requirements for member banks, (2) raising or lowering the discount rate, and (3) engaging in open market operations that affect the volume of reserves available to banks. To put it differently, through these tools the Fed can (1) adjust legal requirement on the amount of reserves banks must hold, (2) adjust the cost to the banks of borrowing reserves, and (3) adjust the volume of reserves available to the banking system. Thus, all three tools are directly related to control over some aspect of bank reserves.

The three major instruments of monetary policy available to the Fed are *setting the fractional reserve requirement, adjusting the discount rate,* and, most importantly, *engaging in open market operations.*

The three minor instruments are (4) Regulation Q, (5) margin regulations and selective credit controls, and (6) moral suasion. Each of the six tools deserves attention.

Fractional Reserve Requirement

The Fed *reduces* money supply growth by raising the reserve ratio and discount rate and selling Treasury securities; it *increases* money growth by the opposite actions.

In discussing the money-creating power of banks in the previous chapter we outlined the nature of reserve requirements. When the legal reserve ratio is lowered, member banks can expand loans and create more deposit money. Conversely, if the reserve ratio is raised, banks will contract the volume of deposits and loans. As a matter of practice the Fed changes the legal reserve

Paper Money

Have you ever wondered what the markings on paper money mean? These Federal Reserve Notes are issued in denominations of $1, $2, $5, $10, $20, $50 and $100. At one time $500, $1,000, $5,000 and $10,000 denominations were printed. Printing of these sizes was discontinued by the Federal Reserve on December 27, 1945, but remaining supplies of them were issued until July 14, 1969. Each Federal Reserve Bank issues (not prints) its own notes in relation to the needs of its own area for liquidity. The notes themselves are printed by the Bureau of Engraving and Printing – a branch of the Treasury – on orders placed with the Treasury by the Federal Reserve districts. Specially trained Treasury engravers cut the individual designs for paper currency into steel dies. Rolls are made of the individual features and used to make a composite design. The master die is then used in a series of operations leading to the manufacture of the press plates. For reasons of security each feature, for example the portrait or the lettering on the ornamentation, is done by a separate engraver. Special paper is used and the Bureau manufactures its own inks following secret formulas. Commercially produced paper is used. It is illegal for anyone to manufacture or use a similar type, except by special permission.

Until July 1929, U.S. currency was 7.42 inches by 3.13 inches. Since then the size is 6.14 by 2.61 inches. The Serial number appears in two places on the face of all U.S. currency now in use and always has 8 digits. It has a prefix letter (F in the example), and a suffix letter (A in the example) unless they are star notes (see the paragraph below). The prefix letter is always the same letter as that in the bank seal. Thus, notes issued by the Federal Reserve Bank of Atlanta are Sixth District notes and the letter preceding the serial number is the sixth letter of the alphabet – F. The notes are numbered in lots of 100,000,000 and a star is substituted for the 100,000,000th note because the digits in the serial number are limited to eight. The suffix letter can vary from A to Z, except for O, because of its confusion with zero. Hence, the serial number of the first run of any denomination note for each series for the Atlanta bank will carry the letter combination F–A, the second F–B, and so on through F–Z. No two notes of the same kind, denomination, and series have the same serial number. Serial numbers colored red are notes that have been issued by the Treasury. These are few. Silver certificates have a blue seal.

Star notes are notes printed to replace those damaged during the printing process. These notes are made up with independent runs of serial numbers and are otherwise identical to the notes they

ratio very infrequently. It is considered to be a blunt policy tool. A change of 1 percent would have immense impact on monetary expansion or contraction if not offset by other Fed actions. Furthermore, managers of banks find changes disruptive and difficult to handle.

The Discount Rate

The discount rate is the rate of interest charged on loans made to member banks by the Fed. The loans are short term. Most are for a few days but some extend for as long as a few weeks. The process is referred to as borrowing at the discount window. The term discount refers to the deduction of interest costs from the face value of the loan. For example, the bank will sign an IOU for $1,000.

replace, except that a star is substituted for the suffix letter. Such a note would look like F 00000000*.

The series shows the year the design was first used on a note. If later only a slight change is made in the design, not requiring a new engraving plate, the series year remains the same. But a letter is added to indicate that the design differs slightly from the previous printing. An example would be, a change in the signature of the Secretary of the Treasury. The C in 1935C would signify that the particular design has been slightly modified on three occasions.

The note position letter is the small letter shown in the upper left and lower right hand corners – N in the example. If the note has been printed on one of the Bureau's newer presses that print 32 notes to the sheet, the letter in the upper left hand corner will be followed by a number – 3 in the example. This indicates the position of the note on the printing plate.

The plate serial number is the number to the right of the note position letter in the lower right hand corner. It identifies the plate from which this particular note was printed – 46 in the example. Thus, 46 indicates this was the 46th plate made for that type, denomination, and series of note. On the reverse side of the note there is a different plate serial number just inside the ornamental border on the lower right hand side. On the Great Seal the Latin phrase *annuit coeptis* stands for "He has favored our undertakings", *novus ordo seclorum* for "A new order of ages", and *e pluribus unum* for "out of many, one". On the pyramid is the date MDCCLXXVI or 1776.

Another branch of the Treasury is the Bureau of the Mint for coins. Congress established the mint in Philadelphia in 1792. Branch mints operate in Denver and San Francisco. The latter is now known as an assay Office, and it produces only proof sets for coin collectors.

The design of a coin cannot be changed inside of a 25-year period unless authorized by Congress. Selection of design for coins is made by the Director of the Mint under approval of the Secretary of the Treasury. Congress can also prescribe a design or coin change.

The penny is made of an alloy of 95 percent copper and 5 percent zinc. The nickel is 75 percent copper and 25 percent nickel. Since 1965 no silver has been used in dimes and quarters. Silver in half dollars amounted to 40 percent and was removed completely beginning in 1971. The Eisenhower silver dollar (1971) has only 40 percent silver in one issue and no silver in the others.

The dies in the presses in Philadelphia undergo 33 tons of pressure to stamp a penny or nickel and 125 tons for a silver dollar. During one day in the Denver mint operating with 54 presses, the mint stamped

17,200,000 pennies
720,000 nickels
1,200,000 dimes
960,000 quarters
160,000 half dollars
40,000 silver dollars.

P.S. Employees and visitors are allowed no samples.

Source: Federal Reserve Bank of Atlanta.

The Fed will discount it by $50 and give the bank $950. The bank pays back $1000 at the end of the period. It has borrowed $950 and paid interest of $50 on the loan.

Although the authority still exists for commercial banks to discount their notes at the Fed, for many years now the practice has been for the Fed to issue loans in the form of direct advances. The Fed simply accepts the bank's IOU if the IOU is backed by collateral. Collateral put up by banks is usually in the form of government securities, but other kinds of securities are also acceptable to the Fed. Thus, discounting as such is rarely if ever done, and using the term discount rate for the borrowing rate is, in a sense, inappropriate. The term is a holdover from earlier days when discounting rather than direct lending was the practice of the Fed.

Each of the 12 Federal Reserve banks is allowed to set its own discount rate, but all changes must be approved by the Board of Governors and as a practical matter the rates are the same around the country. If the discount rate is raised, the cost of borrowing to member banks rises and they have less inclination to borrow in order to make more loans. If it is lowered, banks have more incentive to borrow reserves and create new loans and deposits.

Since the 1920s the Fed has relied much less on the discount rate as a monetary tool than it did in previous years. These days it is used as a way to allow members to adjust their reserve positions to meet short-term liquidity needs in an orderly fashion. For example, country banks need more liquidity at harvest time as farms require more cash. They then use less reserves after the crops come in, are sold, and the farmers have repaid their loans at the bank. Because of the seasonality of this need for borrowing, the Fed has established a program where banks with special seasonal needs for reserves can count on accommodation from the Fed.

After being dormant as a policy tool for decades—dormant in the sense that changes in the discount rate merely followed other interest rates and were never used to set policy—in 1978 the Fed changed this policy and began active use of the discount rate again. In particular, in November 1978 when the dollar was falling in value on the foreign exchange markets, one means of supporting the dollar was to have tighter money and higher interest rates at home. The Fed announced an unprecedented one percentage increase in the discount rate from 8.5 to 9.5. Continuing through 1979 and up until the recession began in 1980, the Fed used the discount rate actively to signal to the public that rates are going up. But as rates fell in the spring of 1980 again, the discount rate merely followed the market down. Thus, the discount rate as a tool of policy is sometimes used actively and sometimes neglected.

Open Market Operations (OMO)

When the Fed enters the market to buy or sell U.S. government securities for the purpose of changing the volume of reserves of member banks, it is said to be engaging in open market operations. This tool is considered to be the principal tool the Fed has to control the money supply. Every working day of the week the Fed engages in open market trades to bring the reserves of the banking system into line with policy objectives. Central banks in smaller countries rely more extensively on required reserve ratios and discount rate changes than on open market operations, because they do not have the large well-developed market for government securities that the U.S. has.

Let us trace how OMO works to reduce the money supply. If an individual buys a government security he or she writes a check against a bank account and gives it to the Fed. The Fed collects this check from the bank on which it was drawn by reducing the bank's account at the Fed. Since the bank's deposits in the Fed are part of the bank's legal reserves, the bank's reserves are reduced by the amount of the check.

Consider a simple example. Suppose the Fed sells $50 million worth of securities to an individual who pays for it with a check against his account in Commercial Bank 1.

Fed		Commercial bank	
A	L	A	L
Gov't bonds—$50	Member bank reserves—$50	Reserve—$50 deposits at Fed	Demand deposit—$50

If the legal reserve ratio were 20 percent then the deposit multiplier would be 1/.2 = 5. A reduction of $50 million in reserves would force a contraction of $250 million in demand deposits inclusive of the initial decline caused by the depositor's purchase of the Fed's offering.

In the T accounts we see that the Fed has $50 million less in government bond holdings. Also, the Fed observes that the check is drawn on Bank 1. So, it reduces that bank's account and forwards the check to the bank. When Bank 1 receives the check, it sees its account at the Fed is down, and it collects from the individual who wrote the check by reducing the demand deposit account. These entries are shown in the bank's T account. The transaction is then complete. Bank reserves, and lending power, have been contracted. If the bank were fully loaned prior to the Fed's action, it would have to contract its loans and deposits and the money supply would fall.

Buying Treasury Bills

Treasury bills are offered with maturities of 3, 6, and 12 months. They are sold in minimum amounts of $10,000 and multiples of $5,000 above the minimum. They can be bought through either competitive or noncompetitive bids. A competitive bid means the bidder must specify the price he or she is willing to pay. The largest competitive bids are tendered by dealers, banks, insurance companies, corporations; relatively minor amounts are tendered by individuals. There is a risk; if the bid is too low the Treasury may reject the offer. A noncompetitive bid or tender does not require the buyer to specify a price but agrees to pay the average price of the competitive tenders accepted by the Treasury. The Treasury normally does not reject noncompetitive tenders, but they are limited to a maximum of $500,000 for each new offering.

A noncompetitive tender can be submitted in person between 9 a.m. and 3 p.m. at Federal Reserve banks or their branches, or by mail any day of the week before the auction. Auctions on 3- and 6-month bills are held every Monday (or the previous Friday if Monday is a holiday). Auctions on 12-month bills are held approximately every four weeks. Treasury bills are only issued in book entry form. When purchased, the buyer receives a receipt instead of an engraved certificate. This is to protect the public from loss, theft, and counterfeiting. Ownership is recorded in an account set up for the owner at the Treasury. Redemption of bills is made automatically at maturity and the Treasury will mail the owner a check. The income from Treasury bills is exempt from state and local taxes but not from the federal income tax.

It is clear that the entire process would be reversed if the Fed bought government securities instead of sellng them. The same T accounts would be changed except all entries would be positive instead of negative. The individual who sold the bonds would be given a check by the Fed drawn on itself. To collect this money the individual takes it to his bank and deposits it. The depositor's account is increased. The bank reads the check, and seeing that it is drawn on the Fed credits its reserve account and sends it to the Fed for collection. The bank's reserve account is up on its own books, and when the Fed receives the check the Fed in turn increases the bank's account on its books. This balances out against the increase in the Fed's holdings of government securities, since it now owns more bonds than before.

Thus, *all* the signs are *positive* when the Fed buys securities, and they are *all negative* when it sells. When the Fed wants to *expand* bank reserves and the money supply it *buys* government securities. When it wants to *contract* reserves and the money supply, it *sells* government securities. No one is forced to buy the securities. The government simply enters the market and offers competitive bond yields.

The Monetary Base as High-Powered Money

The Fed controls a *monetary base* (or high-powered money) that includes member bank reserves plus currency held by the public.

In our description of the Fed's control over the money supply with open market operations, we have referred to its control over the volume of bank *reserves*. Bank reserves are not monies that people can spend, but banks can use reserves to create lots of demand deposit money. In a sense, then, bank reserves are high-powered monies because on the base of a dollar of reserves banks can create several dollars of regular spending money. This presumes that banks *want* to create money. They may choose to hold some reserves idle, that is, they may choose to hold reserves in excess of their legal requirements. If they do hold some excess reserves, the supply of spending money will not expand as much as it would if they held no excess reserves. Therefore, the Fed's control over reserves (high-powered money) is quite great—much greater than its control of the public's spending money.

If we ask ourselves, therefore, just exactly what it is that is under the control of the Fed and the Treasury—the two monetary authorities in the U.S.—the answer is the monetary base. The base is made up of bank reserves and the currency in circulation. Bank reserves consist, for the most part, of member bank deposits in the Fed and currency in bank vaults. Add to this the currency that the people hold and you have the base of the money supply. In this way the monetary base is controlled by the Fed and the Treasury combined.

Regulation Q

The Fed has regulations running from A to Z, but Regulation Q is of special significance. You have been to the bank and been told how much interest the bank is willing to pay on savings that you deposit with it. It is similar at a savings and loan—usually 1/4 of 1 percent higher than the commercial bank pays at the time of this writing. In their advertising, banks sometimes announce

"The maximum allowed by law." The law in question is the Fed's Regulation Q. Under Regulation Q the Fed sets a ceiling on the interest rates that banks can pay to its depositors. In the case of savings and loan associations, the Federal Home Loan Bank Board sets the ceilings.

From time to time the ceiling rates are changed by the authorities. Ceiling rates are like usury laws. They tell the depositor that he is not allowed to charge the bank more than a certain rate of interest for his loan to the bank. The Depository Institutions Deregulation and Monetary Control Act of 1980 directs that the Depository Institutions Deregulation Committee abolish Regulation Q by 1986. Thus, in future years Regulation Q will no longer be available to the Fed as a policy instrument as it has been on occasion in the past several years. It works as a policy tool by inducing what we call disintermediation.

***Disintermediation* occurs when market interest rates exceed the interest limits set by Regulation Q for the Fed's member banks.**

Disintermediation is a term used to describe what sometimes happens because of Regulation Q. First, what is intermediation? It occurs when one decides not to buy securities or property directly, but to deposit money with a bank and let the bank lend it out. Banks are intermediaries between a lender and a borrower. One can either lend to a business directly or choose to use an intermediary. Thus, financial intermediaries are useful in channeling savings into investment. They reduce search costs as savers seek a productive use for their savings. Disintermediation takes place when people withdraw funds from banks and purchase securities issued by corporations and governments or other assets directly. Deposits at banks and thrift institutions decline.

Thus, when interest rates in the marketplace rise above what Regulation Q allows banks to pay, many savers will take their money out of the bank and put it into securities issued by business and government. This means that, in the absence of offsetting actions by the Fed, banks cannot lend as much as before, and may not be able to create as much money as before.

On occasion, therefore, the Fed has allowed Regulation Q to remain below other market interest rates for the explicit purpose of cutting off the ability of banks to attract funds and expand deposits. Hence, this regulation is sometimes viewed as an instrument or tool that the Fed can use to restrict the expansion of money credit.

Unfortunately for the citizens, however, Regulation Q has many adverse side effects. Small savers who rely on savings accounts and deposits in savings banks to store their wealth are essentially discriminated against by this regulation. They have not the expertise or the resources to purchase securities on the open market as wealthier investors do, so their return to saving is kept below what wealthy people can earn.

Furthermore, one particular industry, the housing construction industry, is badly served by this regulation. This industry has suffered extreme ups and downs from monetary policy. When interest rates rise, lenders cannot attract funds from savers because of Regulation Q, and they cut off funds to people who want to build or buy a home. A recession in construction follows. Thus, in their efforts to dampen economic activity, the Fed's managers have subjected the housing construction industry to periodic recessions. Tight monetary policy hurts some people more than others.[2] For these reasons, among others, the Congress has ordered that Regulation Q, first introduced to reduce competition

[2] For fuller details on the market distortions caused by Regulation Q see Wesley Lindow, *Inside the Money Market* (New York: Random House, 1972), Chapter 13.

between banks after the wave of bank failures in early 1930s, be phased out by 1986.

Margin Requirements

The Fed sets *margin requirements*—the minimum downpayment on stocks and investment loans.

When an investor buys stocks on the stock market he is allowed to borrow the money and put up the stocks that he buys as collateral against the loan. Banks handle lines of credit for stockbrokers, who arrange for sales of stocks to their customers. If the margin requirement is 60 percent, say, these brokers can buy $1,000 worth of AT&T stock and bill the customer for $600, having arranged for an automatic loan from the bank for another $400 to cover this $1,000 purchase.

If the price on the stock exchange falls, the bank will make a margin call on the owner. It will say, "Pay us another $40 because your stock is now worth only $900 and we cannot lend you more than 40 percent of this amount, or $360. You must pay us another $40 and reduce your loan from us down to $360 from $400. That way we will still be lending you only 40 percent of the market value of the securities we are holding as collateral." Such margin calls as these are common during periods when the stock market is falling.[3]

Stock margins were first imposed in the wake of the panic in New York in October 1929. Prices fell and people sold stock to meet their loans—often worth over 90 percent of the stock's value when it was purchased. The wholesale sale of stock to meet call loans contributed to the declining prices and the crash that followed. It was felt that by prohibiting people from borrowing too much against their stock collateral, a panic of 1929 proportions could be avoided.

Under the Credit Control Act of 1969, the President has the power to install certain selective credit controls. These are controls over such things as the minimum down payment on installment loans and the maximum length of time for repayments. In 1980 such controls were imposed briefly by the Carter administration. The President authorized the Federal Reserve to determine and administer these for him. Thus, while the Fed does not itself have power to install these direct controls over credit terms, it will doubtless serve as the principal administrator of such controls as it did when extensive use was made of them during World War II.

Moral Suasion

Central banks often use *moral suasion,* verbal suggestions to member banks to slow down or expand loans by a suggested amount.

The Bank of England used moral suasion extensively for hundreds of years. The bank's authorities were aware of the role they played as regulators of the supply of money and credit and simply wrote letters to the presidents of the handful of commercial banks in England telling them, "We think it would be appropriate to allow loans to expand about 8 to 10 percent over the coming year." Such letters were treated as orders in the degree of compliance, because everyone knew that the economy's stability depended upon it. The Bank of England began operations in 1694 as a private bank and was nationalized in 1946. Only after that did it begin to use open market operations.

[3] Actually the margin requirement is 50 percent.

Of course, it is easier to use moral suasion to control the money supply if you have only a dozen banks to deal with. It is a different matter in an economy with 14,000 banks. Nevertheless, our Federal Reserve authorities do exercise pressure from time to time by requesting voluntary compliance with suggested lending guidelines.

FEDERAL FUNDS AND THE FED FUNDS RATE

The *Federal Funds rate* is the interest rate banks charge one another for lending their excess reserves, usually for quite short periods of time; it sets the trend for other interest rates.

Federal Funds are not funds that the Fed owns, or funds that the Treasury owns. Rather they are, for the most part, funds that commercial banks own but keep on deposit at the Fed. If one commercial bank owes some money to another commercial bank, it may pay its debt by writing a check on its account at the Fed. Thus, the other bank deposits its check in its account at the Fed. The debt was paid in Fed funds. Usually, of course, the bank does not actually write checks, rather it tells the Fed by wire or telephone or messenger to transfer funds from its account to the other bank's account.

A practice that grew in the late 1950s has now become commonplace among all banks of any significant size; the practice of borrowing or lending Fed Funds. Let us say that a bank has more reserves than it needs, with these reserves held in the form of a deposit at the Fed. The bank's manager will call around the country to ask other banks if they need more reserves. Perhaps a bank in New Orleans could use more reserves, so a loan is made to that bank—that is, one bank lends Federal Funds to the other bank. The lending bank's account at the Fed is transferred to the other bank's account. The New Orleans bank will keep the funds overnight, or for a few days at most, and then pay back the principal and interest. This is a loan in a market—the Fed Funds market. And the interest rate paid for the loan is called the Fed Funds rate. It is the rate of interest charged by banks when they lend to each other. It goes up and down during the day just as other interest rates do.

When the Fed drains reserves from the banking system, many banks will find themselves short of reserves and will be bidding for funds in the market. This will drive up the Fed Funds rate. Similarly, if the Fed supplies reserves to the system, the banks will have more reserves than they need. Then they will offer Fed Funds into the market and the Fed Funds rate will begin to fall. Thus, by adding or withdrawing the reserves of the banks the Fed can push interest rates on Fed Funds either down or up. Movements in the Fed Funds rate tend to push other interest rates in the same direction.

For many years the Fed announced target ranges for the Fed Funds interest rate, and most securities dealers would watch that rate as an indicator of whether or not the Fed was adding or withdrawing reserves in carrying out an easier or tighter monetary policy stance. In 1979 the Fed relaxed its control over the Fed Funds rate to a considerable extent, and began to watch bank reserves more closely and the Fed Funds interest rate less closely. Nevertheless, the Fed is always committed to a policy of stabilizing interest rates should the market become disorderly.

FOMC AND MONETARY POLICY

How exactly does the Fed carry out its open market operations? The 12-member Federal Reserve Open Market Committee (FOMC) is composed of the 7 members of the Board of Governors, 4 district Federal Reserve Bank presidents who serve on a 1-year rotating basis, and the president of the New York district Federal Reserve Bank, who is permanently appointed to the committee. The reason for this permanent membership is that open market operations are carried out by the Federal Reserve Bank of New York because of its proximity to the nation's principal financial markets. The other 8 district presidents are free to attend the FOMC meetings as observers.

The Board usually meets on the third Tuesday of every month in Washington, D.C., around a 30-foot long oval Honduras mahogany table. The major purpose of the Board members in these meetings is to decide, in their role as monetary managers, whether to buy or sell government securities. Their decision depends upon their assessment of the economy's stabilization needs—whether to pick it up, slow it down, or maintain a steady course. After reports are heard from the System Open Market Account managers for Domestic Operations and for Foreign Operations and from senior economists reporting on domestic and financial developments and their significance for the long-term outlook, the formation of monetary policy is the next item of business. Proposals are considered and a course of action is decided.

Officers of the trading desk at the Federal Reserve Bank in New York are instructed by the manager of the Open Market Account to contact the 36 licensed primary government securities dealers with whom the Fed does business, and either buy or sell securities according to instructions. These trading operations are performed in New York City day by day.

Suppose it is decided that a $250 million purchase of Treasury bills would provide the needed reserves to the banking system—not an overly large amount in the dealer's market. When the bills are purchased they are paid for with checks drawn on the Federal Reserve. When the dealers deposit the checks in their banks, these banks clear them with the Fed, which credits the reserves of the member banks. Actually, checks as such are seldom if ever used. Transfers can be made by memo and by wire, but it is useful to think of checks clearing the system.

There are about 36 dealers who guarantee to create a market for government securities and other money instruments. This means they are ready to buy and sell any security issue just as a stockbroker does for stocks. There are about 12 commercial banks who act as dealers; the remainder are nonbank dealers, but they obtain financing from banks to hold their inventories of securities. Dealers must confer daily with the open market officers of the Federal Reserve Bank of New York.

The dealer structure grew naturally as the public debt became larger and open market operations began to replace the discount window as the major monetary tool. The profit potential for offering this service to the government materialized, and a rapid growth began in the 1930s. In order to perform their financial middleman function, dealers require larger inventories of money instruments on which they can make money as security prices fluctuate. They can instantly get in touch with corporations, state and local governments, small and large banks, and private investors all around the country to arbitrate prices and yields in order to round up required funds. They issue daily quotation sheets listing the price at which they are willing to buy or sell or on which to begin negotiations. Thus, they do not operate through a centrally organized exchange like the stock market, where there are official public listings for everyone to see.

TREASURY DEPARTMENT

The Treasury Department was created by Congress on September 2, 1789. It formulates and recommends policy for fiscal, financial, and public debt activities, serving as overall financial agent for the U.S. government. It is involved in certain aspects of law enforcement and supervises the manufacture of coin and currency. The Secretary of the Treasury also serves as the U.S. Governor of the International Monetary Fund (IMF) and other international banks related to foreign economic development.

Treasury Balances in the Fed

The Treasury does its banking at the Fed, just as individuals bank at a local bank. If the Treasury needs to pay someone to fulfill its contractual obligations, it gives that person a check on its account at the Fed. Treasury payments include (1) wages for government employees, (2) purchases of materials and equipment such as nuclear submarines, (3) welfare, Social Security, and tax refunds, (4) interest on its debt and payments for bonds that are maturing, and (5) purchases of gold and silver.

Items 1 and 2 represent payments for the carrying out of the functions of government. Item 3 is sometimes called transfer payments because tax money from some is paid out to others. Item 4 arises because the federal government has a national debt of nearly a trillion dollars on which the Treasury pays interest of over $50 billion a year. During any one year over one third of the debt matures and must be refinanced. The amounts involved exceed $300 billion. Item 5, gold and silver purchases, used to be important. Nowadays the Treasury is selling gold, not buying it. Nevertheless, we need to list it because it may become important again in the future.

Looking at commercial bank and Fed balance sheets, let us see what happens when the Treasury buys something.

Fed		Commercial bank	
A	L	A	L
	Member bank reserves +$1,000 Treasury deposits −$1,000	Reserve deposit in Fed. +$1,000	Demand deposit +$1,000

The Treasury spends money to finance government activities like paying workers, military expenditures, tax refunds, welfare and Social Security, and interest on its debt.

The Treasury sends a Social Security check to your grandmother, and she takes it to the bank, or cashes it at the local grocery and the grocer takes it to the bank; commercial bank demand deposits increase by $1,000, shown on the liability side of the bank's T account.

Since the check is drawn on the U.S. Treasury to collect its money the bank sends it to the Fed for deposit, so the bank's deposits at the Fed go up and on the Fed's T account we see that member bank reserves are up. When the Fed sees the check was written by the Treasury, it collects from the Treasury by reducing its account.

The Treasury collects money by collecting taxes and selling securities, and occasionally by selling gold.

Although member bank reserves may increase, the money supply does not usually expand because of the payments the Treasury makes. The reason is that the Treasury must get some money from somewhere in order to be able to spend it. Taxation is the usual source. If the Treasury is short of funds, it will borrow them. So, the Treasury collects money whenever (1) it collects taxes, (2) it sells bonds to the public to borrow some spending money, or (3) it sells something, like gold or surplus materials. Let us assume Beth gets a paycheck. The employer withholds some of it to pay for taxes. Instead of giving this money to her the employer sends a check to the government. Now the entire process we went through with the T accounts is reversed. The Treasury deposits the check in its account at the Fed. The Fed sees that it is drawn on a commercial bank and reduces that bank's reserves. When the bank receives the check it sees that its reserve account is down, and it collects from Beth's employer by reducing the employer's demand deposit account.[4]

The Treasury's taxing, borrowing and spending do not change the net money supply.

We conclude that the Treasury does not tax people unless it needs money to spend. And it does not borrow money unless it needs it for spending. So, the Treasury takes money from the people when it taxes and/or borrows but it repays other people when it spends what it has collected. Therefore, the money supply in the hands of the public is *not affected* by a combination of Treasury taxing and spending. Government spending can go up and down, so can taxing, but if the Treasury's account at the Fed stays the same then there will be no change in the money supply or in the ability of commercial banks to expand or contract the money supply because of spending and taxing.

[4] The interested student can check the library or write a note addressed simply to the Federal Reserve Bank of Chicago, Chicago, Ill., and ask for a free copy of *Modern Money Mechanics*, a pamphlet that explains what we have done here in straightforward fashion but in greater detail.

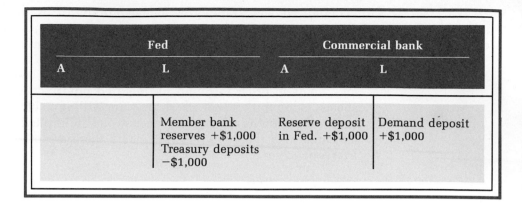

Gold sales and purchases by the Treasury involve additional consideration, because the Treasury can print and issue gold certificates to pay for new gold and/or destroy gold certificates when it sells gold. In this case, buying gold adds to bank reserves and selling gold reduces bank reserves. The Federal Reserve can take counteracting open market operation measures in these special cases, so the general conclusion is that control over the money supply is independent of government spending and taxing decisions as reflected in Treasury receipts and expenditures.

MONETIZING THE TREASURY'S DEBT

As we have seen, when the Treasury sells bonds to the public and spends the proceeds of that sale, there is no change in the money supply. However, if the Federal Reserve should buy those bonds instead of the public by writing a check to the Treasury for the bonds, then member bank reserves would increase when people deposit the Treasury checks they receive in their accounts at commercial banks. And the debt is said to have been monetized by the Fed. In a sense we could say that these combined actions of the Treasury and Fed amount to the printing of money by the government to pay for its purchases. Of course, *any* purchase of bonds by the Fed can be thought of as a monetization of debt. The Fed can buy old bonds or newly issued bonds. Thus, it is an oversimplification to say that when the Treasury indulges in deficit spending and must issue bonds the debt will be monetized. It is only monetized when and if the Fed decides that monetary expansion is appropriate for the economy and takes action to expand bank reserves by buying government securities.

The Fed may monetize a Treasury's issue of debt by purchasing it.

CHAPTER SUMMARY

Early banking in the U.S. developed erratically until the early part of the twentieth century. Before 1791, without a central bank to control the money supply, states chartered many private banks that tended to overissue paper money backed by insufficient amounts of gold and silver. As depositors lost confidence in the paper they panicked, and runs on the banks resulted in depleting the banks' gold and silver backing. When the banks collapsed the paper money became worthless. The abrupt decline in the money supply and credit led to a depression. Alexander Hamilton got Congress to establish the first national bank in the U.S. It worked well, but Congress let its charter lapse after twenty years. When the states chartered more banks to take its place, paper money was overissued, fraud and runs on the banks followed, causing chaos and depressions again. Hence the Second Bank of the U.S. was set up in 1816. But it was doomed by the election of Andrew Jackson in 1828, and state banks took up the slack. Overissues of paper money again led to an eventual depression after 1837. In 1863 the National Banking Act was passed that allowed for national banks to be chartered, to which the Treasury could sell its bonds. The national banks could issue bank notes in amounts tied to their ownership of Treasury bonds and payable with a uniform paper currency printed by the government. However, in the spring and fall country banks made heavy withdrawals leaving city banks short of cash. Again panic, bank failures, and recessions appeared. Another bank crisis in 1907 finally led to the formation of the current Federal Reserve System in 1913. However, for a variety of reasons, hundreds of banks experienced runs in 1930 and 1931 and collapsed. The economy went into a deep recession lasting through the 1930s. New bank regulations were passed, and there has been no repeat of the collapse of the U.S. banking system since despite six recessions since 1950.

It is the role of the Fed to control the nation's money supply and regulate credit. The Fed provides check clearing services to its members and financial advice, and assists the Treasury. The Fed is owned by its members but they have little power. The Fed is primarily responsible to the Congress that created it. About 95 percent of the Fed's earnings are turned over to the Treasury since profits are not the reason for the Fed's existence, although it earns some profit.

The Federal Reserve System consists of 12 districts with 24 branch banks headed by a 7-member Board of Governors selected for terms of 14 years, with one rotation every 2 years. From these, the chairman is designated by the President for a 4-year term.

The three major instruments of monetary policy available to the Fed are setting the fractional reserve requirement, adjusting the discount rate, and open market operations. Raising the reserve ratio and the discount rate reduce growth in the money supply. And the selling of Treasury securities also reduces the potential for money growth because it lowers member banks' levels of excess reserves. Conversely, reducing the reserve ratio and the discount rate and buying Treasury securities leads to a potential expansion of the money supply. The major tool is open-market operations. The Fed by changing the level of excess reserves through its open market operations alters the monetary base to which the creation of M1-A and M1-B monies is related. The monetary base (or high-powered money) includes member bank reserves plus currency held by the public.

There are three minor tools of monetary policy. One is the setting of margin requirements; that is, the minimum down payment required by purchasers of stocks, the minimum down payment on installment loans, and reserve requirements on issuers of credit cards. The second is Regulation Q, which limits the interest rate banks can pay savers. This leads to the phenomenon of disintermediation. When market rates of interest rise above the regulated rate, depositors withdraw deposits from banks and thrift institutions to put their funds into higher yielding securities offered by government and business. The third is moral suasion, verbal suggestions by the Fed to member banks to slow down or expand loans by a suggested amount.

The Federal Funds rate is the interest rate banks charge one another for lending their excess reserves, usually for quite short periods of time, like overnight. This rate sets the trend for other interest rates.

The Federal Open Market Committee consists of 12 members, including the 7 Board of Governors. They meet every 3 or 4 weeks to decide on policy. Directives are sent to the open-market trading desk in New York City. Officers there contact the licensed government dealers to begin implementation of monetary policy on a daily basis. For a fee and hoped-for capital gains, they create a market for government securities by negotiating with well-known buyers and sellers of securities over the prices of securities and other terms surrounding the sale.

The Treasury Department was created in 1789. It is the fiscal agency of the federal government, and its banker is the Fed. The Treasury collects taxes, sells gold, and sells securities when it wants to borrow money. The Treasury spends money to finance government activities like paying its workers, tax refunds, welfare, Social Security, interest payments on the debt, and military expenditures. When the Treasury taxes and borrows from the public there is no net change in the money supply. However, the money supply does increase if the Fed monetizes the Treasury's debt. That is, if the Fed steps in and buys the Treasury's securities by writing a check to the Treasury against the Fed's account. When the Treasury sends the check to a citizen, and the citizen deposits it in a bank or cashes it there, the money supply goes up. Treasury actions can create conflicts for the Fed in implementing the Fed's monetary policy goals, particularly when it finds it necessary to monetize Treasury debt when it desires to contract the money supply.

QUESTIONS

1. What is the federal funds rate? Why is it important?
2. The Fed rarely discounts member bank loans. Explain this.
3. A newspaper reports that "The Fed drained reserves from the banking network last Friday when the Federal funds were trading at 9 and 11/16 percent." Interpret this statement.
4. If you read in the papers that "Fed sales of securities take funds from the banking system because dealers draw on their commercial bank accounts to pay for their purchases," what is going on?
5. "While the Fed has control of the money supply, it does not, however, determine the quantity of currency in circulation." Can you make sense out of this?
6. What do you suppose would happen to the money supply M1-A if the service charge on checking accounts were increased?
7. How might each of the following affect the money supply?
   a. The Fed raises the discount rate.
   b. Reserve requirements of banks are reduced.
   c. The Fed engages in open market sales of securities.
   d. The public wishes to increase its ratio of currency to demand deposits.
   e. Electronic transfer of nonchecking time deposits to demand deposits is introduced.
   f. Bank service charges on checking accounts are raised.
   g. The Treasury borrows from the Fed but does not immediately spend the funds.
   h. The Treasury borrows from the Fed and spends the funds.
8. Excess reserves of the banking system are thought to rise when market interest rates rise and fall when the discount rate rises. Why might this be logically if not necessarily true?
9. Today the discount window of the Fed is essentially a safety valve for the banking system. Explain what this means. What other safety valves do member banks have?
10. Suppose the partial accounts of the Fed and the combined commerical member banks read as shown at the top of p. 656 (in billions). Assume the fractional reserve requirement is 10 percent and that the public holds $47 billion in coin and currency.
    a. How much M1-A money is there? M2 money?
    b. Are there excess reserves? If so, how much?

Federal Reserve bank

A		L	
Treasury currency	$4	Federal Reserve notes	$50
Securities	50	Treasury deposits	2
Loans to members	2	Member bank reserves	25
Gold certificates	24	Capital accounts	3

Commercial banks

A		L	
Reserves	$25	Demand deposits	$190
Loans	165	Time deposits	75
Securities	100	Treasury deposits	5
Buildings & equipment	10	Net worth	30

c. If free reserves equal excess reserves minus member bank borrowings from the Fed, how large are free reserves?
d. How large is the monetary base?
e. The Treasury sells $3 billion in securities to the Fed and then spends the money. What then are the final levels of excess reserves, free reserves, the monetary base M1-A money, and the balance sheets of the Fed and commercial banks, assuming no leakages and the commercial banks make no new loans?
f. Suppose, instead, the Fed sold $3 billion in securities directly to the commercial banks. What are the effects on the monetary base, free reserves, excess reserves, M1-A, and the balance sheet under the same assumptions?
g. Assume, instead, the Fed sold $3 billion in securities directly to the public. What are the effects on excess reserves, free reserves, the monetary base, M1-A, and the balance sheet under the same assumptions?
h. Suppose the public decides to reduce its holdings of currency by $3 billion. Trace the effects again under the same assumptions.

11. When the Treasury collects taxes, is the money supply affected? Why, or why not?

Chapter 27

The Demand for Money

I don't like money much actually, but it quiets my nerves.

—Joe Louis

PROGRESS REPORT

A. In Chapter 24 the simple Keynesian model of the economy was described without explicitly introducing money and the price level. Leaving out money amounts to a serious deficiency in our attempt to understand the complete Keynesian model. In Chapter 25, therefore, we began our introduction of money by examining the role of commercial banks in creating money. Chapter 26 continued on to an examination of the role of the Federal Reserve System — the nation's central bank — and how it influences the amount of money commercial banks can create.

B. The demand for money is explored in this chapter. It is a more complicated concept than the money supply, but crucially important to the understanding of current debates in macroeconomic stabilization policy. First, the classical notions of the demand for money — money as a medium of exchange — are examined. Then reasons for and explanations of Keynes's modifications of the demand for money are introduced. A direct link between the demand for money and GNP is provided by Keynesian theory that is vague in the simple classical model. The link is the rate of interest as it is determined by the supply and demand for money.

C. Chapter 28 examines the way an economy moves over time. The changes in its output, income, and employment. Economies reflect a process at work called business cycles or business fluctuations.

Our ultimate purpose is to explain how the demand and supply of money affects employment, interest rates, and output at the aggregate level of the economy. We begin with the accepted classical doctrine that prevailed before 1936.

THE EQUATION OF EXCHANGE

The *equation of exchange* says that by definition expenditures on final goods per period must equal dollar receipts; $MV_Y = PQ$ where M is the money supply, V_Y, is the income velocity of money, P is the price level, and Q is units of output.

The following discussion is based on a fundamental relation in economics known to the Scottish philosopher, David Hume (1711–1776). It is called the *equation of exchange.*

$$MV_Y = PQ$$

where

M = the stock of money. It is the supply of money at a given time. It is also the quantity of money held, since what people hold in cash balances at a given time must be equal to the supply of money. If you spend a dollar, you do not have it any longer, somebody else does. It stays in circulation. The amount being held at any given time is the amount the banks and the Fed and the Treasury have supplied. Therefore, M represents *both* money held and money supplied, and as we saw in Chapter 25 is often measured by M1-B—cash held by the public plus commercial bank demand deposits and other checking accounts in thrift institutions.

The *income velocity* of money is the average number of times each dollar is spent on the purchase of a final good or service during the year.

V_Y = the **income velocity** of money. This is simply the average number of times each of those dollars that make up M1-B changes hands during some time period when final goods and services are bought and sold. When people make exchanges with each other in a market economy they use dollars. How many times do these dollars change hands or become income, on the average, during a month or year? The answer is the value of V_Y.

P = the general price level. It is an average of prices of all those final goods and services provided and exchanged in the economy over the time period chosen for our observation.

Q = the total quantity of all final goods and services produced and sold during the year. The emphasis is on the exchange of *final* goods and services. We are not here concerned with all of the intermediate transactions associated with all of the intermediate stages that ultimately result in a finished good. Our interest is directed to the *income* received with the exchange of a final good.

The right hand side of the expression, PQ, must equal the dollar amount of all *receipts* from the sale of final goods and services over a period of time conventionally designated as one year. The left-hand side, MV_Y, is therefore the total dollar *expenditures* made in purchasing final goods and services in the current period.

As it stands, this equation is an identity. This means that it is true by definition that

$$MV_Y \equiv PQ$$

Dollar expenditures per period ≡ Dollar value of output per period

because we have defined the four terms in the equation in such a way that the equation must hold. The two sides of the equation are simply two sides of the same coin—six of one and half dozen of the other. Breaking out the left and right sides in more detail gives

MV_Y = Number of dollars
× Average number of times each dollar changes hands
= Dollar expenditure per period

PQ = Average price of goods and services
× Number of exchanges of final products per period
= Dollar receipts or value of output per period.

Identities, Equations and the Quantity Theory

Since the expression $MV_Y \equiv PQ$ is an identity, in and of itself it does not explain or predict anything. It is reminiscent of the distinction between an identity and an equation in the Keynesian income-expenditure model where $Y \equiv C + I_A + G$ is an identity, which of itself does not predict anything; compared to $AD = C + I_p + G$ which is an equation predicting the level of spending out of national income Y. Any three of the terms M, P, and Q can be assigned any values whatsoever, and a value of V_Y can be found to make the left hand side equal to the right hand side. For example, take any three numbers $M = 10$, $P = 2$ and $Q = 25$. We can always find a value of V_Y to make $MV_Y \equiv PQ$. All that is necessary is to solve for V_Y. Divide each side by M to get

$$V_Y \equiv \frac{PQ}{M} \equiv \frac{2 \times 25}{10} \equiv \frac{50}{10} \equiv 5.$$

Thus, V must equal 5 in this case because this is true by our definition of V. However, this identity can be converted into a conditional equation by assuming that the velocity of money V is a behavioral constant.[1] Classical economists held that its value was constant because society has certain buying habits and relatively consistent spending behavior. An economic equation expresses something about how people behave, in this case how fast society turns over money. The speed of transactions are constrained institutionally by society's mode of communications and transportation—computers, telephone, cable, letters, planes; and by its institutions—banks, mutual funds, clearing houses for checks. Suppose for these reasons V were always equal to 5, then

[1] A conditional equation is one that holds for only some of the values of its variables, unlike the identity, which holds for all possible values of its variables.

you can see that not just any arbitrary assignment of numerical values to M, P, and Q will necessarily yield $V = 5$. Only certain values will. This converts the identity into a conditional equation and leads to a theory expressing the relation between the supply of money and the general level of prices called the **quantity theory of money**

THE INCOME APPROACH TO THE QUANTITY THEORY

In the early classical tradition, all intermediate transactions involving money were accounted for in the equation of exchange. But most people are concerned about the level of income that an economy generates, because it is income that determines the standard of living that a people can enjoy. Lots of transactions are made that amount to spinning your wheels and not getting anywhere. A house is sold from one person to another, but there is still just one house available for living. There is no net gain in income to the people collectively as a result of this exchange, except for the minor amount of benefit because after the trade the home ownership is better allocated than it was before. However, this is only a tiny portion of the value of the house itself. Hence, we are more interested in the relation between money and income than between money and transactions.

To focus our attention on income we have written the equation of exchange to read

$$MV_Y \equiv PQ \equiv Y$$

where Y is measured by GNP, and

V_Y = average number of times each dollar is spent *on a final good* during the year.

(The reader should recall that $MV = Y = C + I_A + G$ is also identically true.) To obtain a ball park estimate of the income velocity of money for the U.S. economy, put the money supply at \$500 billion and money GNP at \$2.5 trillion so that[2]

$$V_Y = \frac{GNP}{M} = \frac{\$2.5 \times 10^{12}}{\$5 \times 10^{11}} = 5.$$

You have all heard the refrain, "too much money chasing too few goods—that's why we have inflation." This is a statement from the quantity theory. It appeals to common sense. In the fully employed classical system there is a certain amount of goods out there in the economy to be exchanged at any given time. That is, Q is also relatively constant. Therefore both V_Y and Q are independent of M and P. Thus, in the quantity theory both V_Y and Q are

[2] 10^{11} is 1 with 11 zeros after it (one hundred billion) and 10^{12} is 1 followed by 12 zeros (one trillion).

assumed to be constant so that $M\overline{V}_Y = P\overline{Q}$ where the bar indicates a constant. Now we can say that if the Fed lets the money supply increase, then prices will increase—too much money with too few goods means prices rise. If we put the equation in the following form by dividing both sides by the quantity of goods (Q) we get

Because the classical theory assumed velocity was constant and the system produced full employment, the equation of exchange could be converted into the *quantity theory of money,* which predicts that the price level is directly related to the money supply.

$$P = \left(\frac{\overline{V}_Y}{Q}\right) M_S$$

where the expression V_Y/Q is constant since Q and V_Y themselves are constant. Since Q and V_Y are constant, this equation expresses a theoretical relation between M and P. It is not just an identity but a theory because it *predicts* what will happen to the price level if the money supply is increased. It is therefore in principle a testable hypothesis. An increase in money causes prices to rise directly. The equation can be used to express the level of prices. As we shall see, economists recognize that other forces affect prices, but all of them accept the proposition that if the Fed creates too much money, inflation results.

THE CASH BALANCES APPROACH TO THE EQUATION OF EXCHANGE

The *cash-balance* form focuses on the duration money is held; M_d = k′GNP where k′ is the reciprocal of the velocity of money indicating the fraction of income held in the form of money balances.

The terms of the expression can be rearranged and presented in different ways. In presenting the identity with the **cash balances** approach we simply move V_Y from the left hand side of the identity over to the right hand side by dividing both sides by V_Y. Thus, we write

$$M \equiv \frac{1}{V_Y} GNP.$$

To simplify we use the letter k' to represent the reciprocal of V_Y, that is we simply let $k' = 1/V_Y$ and now we write the identity as

$$M \equiv k'GNP.$$

In this analysis the k' is not the same k we used to designate as the multiplier in Chapter 24. To distinguish it from the Keynesian multiplier k we write it as k'.

When V_Y is 5, it follows that k' is 1/5 or .20. Substituting this in the identity we can write

$$M = 20\% \text{ of } GNP.$$

Again, over the year, if there is about $500 billion in money in the economy at all times, it will sustain a level of money GNP in the neighborhood of $2.5 trillion, and 20 percent of $2.5 trillion is $500 billion.

The difference between the income approach and the cash balances approach is one of form and not of substance; nevertheless, both approaches

The income form, $MV_Y \equiv GNP$, focuses on how fast people spend money.

have merit because of the way the numbers are interpreted in the two cases. In the income approach we look at $MV_Y \equiv GNP$ and think of people spending this money on the left side where velocity V_Y equals the speed of circulation of the average dollar. It represents the flow of money in the system and is equated with the money value of the society's output on the other side, *PQ* or *GNP*. When we look at it in this way we are led to examine money flows and ask the question, "Why do people spend the money they do?"

But when we put the expression into the form $M \equiv k'GNP$, the information is the same but this time we are led to ask the question "Why do people hold the money they are holding at any given time?" Our focus is on the demand for money to hold rather than on money flows, where k' is the fraction of money income held as money balances. In this way our attention is shifted toward concern for the stock of money and its importance to the general level of income in the society.

We can, therefore, use the income approach and the cash balances approach to the quantity theory more or less interchangeably inasmuch as they reflect the same phenomena.

THE QUANTITY THEORY OF THE DEMAND FOR MONEY

Desired Versus Actual Cash Balances

The equation of exchange is again converted from an identity into an equation and a theory by introducing the distinction between the actual balances people hold and balances people desire to hold—just as we discussed the actual level of investment compared to the desired or planned level of investment. What balances people actually hold may not be what they necessarily want to hold at a given time. Since $GNP = Y$, we can write the identity as

(1) $M \equiv k'Y$

and in equation form as

(2) $M_D = k'Y.$

What is the difference between equations 1 and 2? The k′ in 2 indicates what level of cash balances people desire to hold. For if income is $10,000 a year and k' is 1/4, then M_D is $2,500 or that fraction of income people choose to hold in cash balances on the average per year. The demand for money M_D now represents the desired level of cash balances. The desired balances may diverge from the amount of balances people actually hold. For instance, if the Federal Reserve increases the supply of money so that people find themselves holding more cash balances than they really want to hold, then the actual ratio of M_D/Y becomes a higher ratio than k', their desired ratio. In order to restore their desired k' ratio, people increase their spending in order to remove the extra cash balances. The induced spending causes aggregate demand to rise. If the economy is already fully employed, the result is "too many dollars chasing too few goods." Under these circumstances, prices rise. Since $PQ = Y$ and output Q is fixed at full employment, then P rises so that income Y must rise too. Income must also rise because as prices rise, what are higher prices to buyers reappear as higher incomes to sellers.

The increased spending continues until the rise in prices, hence the rise in income, is sufficient to restore the desired ratio k' of money to income. To emphasize the point; the M in $MV = Y$ is the money stock M_S. In a state of temporary disequilibrium M_S is not necessarily the same amount of money as now appears in the expression $M_D = k'Y$ because this M_D is the desired level of money balances. Only in equilibrium does $M = M_S = M_D$ where the actual and desired levels of cash balances equal the money stock in circulation. Of course, it must always be true that, in or out of equilibrium, what people actually hold in cash balances must equal the money supply, as in (1). However, expression (2) introduces a behavioral aspect that the old formulation did not.

VELOCITY OF MONEY AND K′

We have hinted that there is an inverse relationship between how long cash balances are held and how often they are spent. The longer the period of time dollars are held, the less frequently they are spent. Conversely, the shorter the period of time money is held, the more frequently money changes hands. How fast money circulates is called the velocity of money. If money is not spent as soon as it is acquired, then there is a period of time over which it is held. The longer it is held, the lower is the velocity of money. Hence, velocity is

$$V = \frac{\text{average number of times each dollar is spent}}{\text{time period}}.$$

Alternatively, since $k' = 1/V$,

$$k' = \frac{\text{time period}}{\text{average number of times each dollar is spent}}$$

$$= \text{time period that the average dollar is held between transactions.}$$

To be more concrete, suppose $V = 4$, signifying that our typical dollar is spent 4 times a year or once every 3 months. This can also be interpreted as signifying that the typical dollar is held, on the average, for a period of 1/4 of a year or 3 months. Thus, if $V = 4/1$ times a year, $k' = 1/4$ of a year $= 3$ months.

Consider the following example based on individual behavior. Private Lavish is a soldier who spends his monthly paycheck with abandon and ends up with no money to spend later in the month. Private Frugal, on the other hand, carefully spreads out his purchases over the month. Lavish's income velocity is much higher than Frugal's. Thus, the average holding of cash balances over the month by Frugal is greater than for Lavish.

Assume each of them receives $400 a month and that there are exactly 4 weeks to a month. They have the following spending patterns. Frugal spends $100 the first day. He, therefore, holds $300 in balances for a week, at the end of which time he spends another $100. He then holds $200 in balances for a week, after which time he spends $100 more. He holds the remaining $100 for a week and spends $50 to start the fourth week. He holds onto the $50 and spends it on the last day of the last week which we shall assume for convenience is the last day of the month. Private Lavish spends $200 on payday and holds $200 in balances for one week, after which time he spends $100 starting the second week. He has $100 in balances remaining, which he holds for a week and then spends $50 of it the first day of the third week. Starting the fourth week, he spends the last $50 and holds zero balances over the last week. Thus,

	Cash Balances Held During			
	1st week	2nd week	3rd week	4th week
Frugal	$300	$200	$100	$50
Lavish	$200	$100	$ 50	$ 0

Over the month, Frugal holds average cash balances amounting to

$$\frac{300 + 200 + 100 + 50}{4} = \frac{650}{4} = \$137.50.$$

Lavish, on the other hand, holds average cash balances over the month of

$$\frac{200 + 150 + 50 + 0}{4} = \frac{350}{4} = \$87.50.$$

Note that at no given time does Frugal actually hold exactly $137.50 or Lavish hold $87.50, though during the period each holds an average of the calculated amount of cash balances. We have seen thus far that the amount of cash balances held per period is a function of both the level of income and spending habits.

Constancy of Velocity and of k′

The classical economists held that the velocity of money was nearly constant in the short run. Since factors affecting velocity are institutional and technological, such as the state of banking techniques, the time between pay checks, and

Underground Liquidity

Professor Peter Guttman of the City College of New York contends that there has been a significant rise in the ratio of cash balances to demand deposits in the U.S. over the last three decades.

$$\text{Ratio} = \frac{\text{cash balances}}{\text{demand deposits}}.$$

His figures suggest that this ratio has been rising since the early 1950s, when it was about .21, to where it is once again approaching the 1945 high of .36. Why the increased demand for cash? Guttman believes it is due to the increased tax avoidance behavior that goes on in a growing underground economy. This underground economy produces income. It consists of the unrecorded income of moonlighters and single job holders who deal in cash only and file no income tax return on extra earned income. They might be waitresses understating tips, physicians who pressure patients to pay in cash, babysitters, home mechanics, teenagers who forsake the minimum wage in order to get a job, working illegal immigrants, farmers and other self-employed people who underreport, and all sorts of odd jobbers doing only sporadic part-time work. Still others are involved in illegal activities like gambling, prostitution, and narcotics, and obviously cannot report this income to the IRS or readily deposit it in checking accounts. Thus, this underground economy subsists through undocumented cash transactions and in some cases barter. It averages to about $600 an adult, more than is necessary for ordinary transactions purposes. Guttman believes it now amounts to about 10 percent of the GNP. He also argues that because this activity is unrecorded, unemployment and poverty figures are too high, including the data for the ghettos where many transactions are made in direct cash. As inflation progresses and the marginal tax bite grows (bracket creep), the amount of unrecorded income will rise.

Others disagree. While they do not deny the existence of this underground economy, they do not accept the conclusion there has been a substantial rise in the demand for cash relative to checking deposits. Gillian Garcia is one who dissents. She claims that there is an appearance of a rise in the demand for currency because of a decline in the measured amount of demand deposits — the denominator of the ratio. The explanation lies in the fact that a big bank often turns the large deposits made by corporations into Treasury bills for just one night. The next day, however, they are returned to the account at the banks under so-called repurchase agreements (RPs). Instead of converting the accounts into Treasury bills permanently, the bank only converts the deposits into Treasury bills overnight for borrowers of these funds such as other banks, government securities dealers, or pension funds, who may need funds right away. The sellers of these Treasury bills agree to buy back the bills (repurchase) them from the bank the very next day. Thus, at the close of the day, the Federal Reserve will not record the funds loaned out overnight as part of the bank's deposits. Instead, the Fed measures the deposits as being down and therefore the ratio of cash to deposits as being up.

There has been a vast increase in such repurchase activity since the 1960s. When the understated bank deposits are accounted for, the ratio is approximately the same in the 1970s as it was in the early 1950s. Garcia concludes that the underground economy has therefore stayed at about the same proportion of the GNP over the years, so there has been no significant percentage increase in the ratio of the demand for cash to demand deposits. Others claim growing amounts of U.S. currency held overseas is also being overlooked. Who is right?

---

the rapidity of communications and transportation. Such factors change slowly over the long run and change only imperceptibly in the short run. If velocity is nearly constant, then the demand for cash balances must also be nearly constant because the inverse of a constant is also a constant. Invariably, since $V = 1/k'$ is constant, then k' must also be constant.

Absolute and Relative Prices: Money as a Veil in the Classical System

Classical theory held that money is a veil that has no effect on relative prices, therefore no effect on resource allocation.

In the classical system economists assume full employment all the time. That is, the output of the economy is as great as it can be given the limited availability of resources. Of course, if Q is a maximum and therefore a constant and k' is a constant in the equation $M = k'PQ$, any change in M will lead to a proportional change in P. But P represents the average level of all prices. If M doubles, presumably P doubles, and *all* individual prices double, too. If all individual prices double, there is no change in any of the relative prices that affect the allocation of resources.

Therefore, money is sometimes said to be a veil through which one cannot see the real variables of the system—the relative prices that ration resources, output, and employment. Thus, a change in the money supply does not affect resource allocation. Money is neutral in its effect on the real sector.

A simple example makes the point. Assume the *absolute* prices of butter and oleomargarine are

$$\text{Butter} = \frac{\$1.00}{\text{lb}} \qquad \text{Oleo} = \frac{\$.60}{\text{lb}}.$$

The *relative* price of butter to oleo is 100/60 = 5/3.

Let the supply of money double. Because Q and k' are fixed, only the price level can change. It doubles too. The *absolute* prices of butter and oleo in money terms are now:

$$\text{Butter} = \frac{\$2.00}{\text{lb}} \qquad \text{Oleo} = \frac{\$1.20}{\text{lb}}.$$

The *relative* price of butter to oleo is 2.0/1.2 = 5/3, and it is unchanged.

Therefore, money is merely a medium of exchange that makes it easier for buyers and sellers to make their anticipated expenditures and acquire those desired goods and services that are the real source of their satisfaction. Changes in it have no effect on the pricing system and its rationing function of allocating scarce resources among competing ends.

Of course, this holds only under the classical view where full employment is assumed to exist all the time and therefore Q is a constant. If changes in M can lead to changes in Q, then money is no longer a veil. It does impact on the real sector of the economy.

Many of today's economists agree that money is not a veil in the short run—that it does affect relative prices and cause changes in resource allocation. However, many still believe that in the longer run, when prices have finally adjusted after a year or so, relative prices and real resource allocation remain unchanged. Money is still only a veil in the long run. Thus, it is important to keep M from changing too much because of adverse short-run effects, but it really does not matter much in affecting resource allocation over the long haul.

KEYNES REVISITED

During the Great Depression of the 1930s, the most influential economist of the twentieth century, John Maynard Keynes (1883–1946), came to believe that the massive unemployment of the time could not be adequately explained by classical theory. The expansion of member bank reserves by the Federal Reserve in order to stimulate the economy did not work (though there is a debate over whether they might have acted too late and improperly, otherwise monetary policy would have worked, according to others). With employment, output, and aggregate demand falling, prices and wages should also fall to return the system to a state of full employment. However, instead of lending the additional reserves in a period of deepening recession, banks simply accumulated excess reserves to provide enough liquidity for themselves as protection against runs on the banks by a public desiring to increase liquidity. Because of some bank failures, many depositors panicked into withdrawing their demand deposits. Banks also hesitated to make loans because of the high risk of borrowers defaulting on the loans at that time. Nor in such a climate of pessimism were firms about to borrow from banks for purposes of expanding plant capacity. With the occurrence of both the attempted expansionary monetary policies of the Fed and the severe decline in output and employment combined with low interest rates, Keynes concluded that the velocity of money was not stable—at least in the short run.

Consider again $MV_Y \equiv PQ$. During the Great Depression output and employment were falling while the Fed appeared to be increasing money supply M. The only way the right side of the equation could fall while M was being increased on the left side would be if velocity V were declining more than enough to offset the rise in the supply of money M. Keynes reasoned that wages and prices were flexible upward but sticky downward. That is, while workers and firms would go along with wages and prices rising, they were much less likely to accept money wages and prices falling.

THE DEMAND FOR MONEY

The Transactions Motive

In the classical scheme, people held cash balances only to coordinate anticipated *transactions*.

People desire to hold money—exercise a demand for money—principally for transactions purposes. Money balances function as a means to bridge the time gap between anticipated receipts and anticipated expenditures like payments of bills and purchases of groceries. Receipt of income and the spending of it do not occur continuously but intermittently. Receipts and expenditures occur in discrete time intervals—in lumps. These lumps are derived from the spending habits of individuals as well as the payment policies of businesses.

Transactions balances are held because people anticipate they will want to make certain expenditures. They know the paycheck will have to be used to pay the monthly rent or mortgage, to buy food supplies, to pay the insurance that is due on the car, to purchase gasoline for the car, to see the dentist for a periodic checkup. Money as a medium of exchange makes the process of payment more efficient and much less costly to negotiate. When people know the expenditures that have to be made, and when the next income will be received, they will hold certain amounts of money balances to smooth the process of payments and purchases.

Business firms also hold transactions balances. They must make weekly or monthly wage and salary disbursements and pay for shipments of materials they receive. Any extra cash firms might hold is often invested in Treasury bills or other near-money assets that yield a return while not tying up cash for too long as managers mull over investment decisions.

Keynes agreed with the classical economists that people demand money to hold for transactions purposes, but he also introduced two additional motives that make up the demand for money.

The Precautionary Motive

The *precautionary motive* for holding cash balances is a function of income like the transaction motive, but is based on uncertainty and contingency.

Empirically it is not possible to separate the precautionary from the transactions motive. The precautionary reason for holding cash balances is, essentially, related to the level of income just as the transactions demand is related to income. Whereas those balances that were held in order to satisfy transactions demands were balances held to make anticipated purchases, the precautionary motive said that cash balances were held to make unexpected or unanticipated purchases. In recognizing the precautionary demand, Keynes's theory introduces the element of uncertainty. You carry extra cash on a vacation, or for a long car trip should the car break down on the road and need repairs. Or you walk into a store and experience serendipity—you suddenly see something on sale you always wanted but did not expect to find. Thus, you carry cash as insurance for such contingencies. Since demand for precautionary balances is related to the level of income, the precautionary motive can simply be lumped in with the transactions motive.

The Speculative Motive

Keynes said people also hold cash balances for *speculation,* the buying and selling of bonds in response to anticipated changes in the direction of interest rates for anticipated capital gains.

More essential to the theory of the demand for money is the introduction by Keynes of the speculative motive for holding money. It arises from expectations about the behavior of prices in the bond market, or what is the same thing, the expected behavior of the rate of interest and its meaning for the yield on bonds. While people hold money, they also hold other assets such as bonds, because such assets provide yields or returns. Thus, bonds compete with money for a place in one's portfolio of assets.

We say that money is the ultimate in a liquid asset. It is as perfectly liquid as it seems to be when it slips through our fingers. In our meaning of liquid here, however, we refer not to the fact that it does flow, but that it *can* flow. Money can be spent here and now—it can be transformed into *any* other asset by its holder. For example you can buy a house with it. Other assets are not so liquid however. If you own bonds and want to buy a house you have to first sell the bonds, get the money, and then buy the house. Bonds are not perfectly liquid because you cannot simply spend them. If you own a boat and want to exchange it for a house you have even more problems. It is a lot easier to sell bonds than it is to sell a boat. So getting the money is not easy. Thus, the easier it is to change an asset into money, the more liquid we say the asset is. People have a preference for liquidity because liquidity provides more options and for those options to be acted on quickly; this is desirable when things can change suddenly in an uncertain world.

If you ask around you will find that most people are holding some money and also some bonds or savings accounts or some other type of financial security. So, at any particular time a representative person can sell a bond and get money or sell money and get a bond. A person can shift back and forth. But if the person wants to hold more cash, he or she must give up the interest that would otherwise be paid on the bond. Thus, the *opportunity cost of holding money is the interest given up from holding a bond.*

Keynes said that *liquidity preference* is a function of both interest rates and income.

If interest rates rise, we say the cost of money has gone up. And by cost we mean not only the cost to the borrower of money but also the opportunity cost to the holder of money whether he borrowed it or just owned it free and clear. When money is borrowed the lender is paid interest, and if the potential lender holds onto money, interest that could be earned is sacrificed. Either way, the holder of money is paying for the privilege of his **liquidity preference**.

If interest rates rise, the cost of holding money rises so less of it is held. If interest rates fall, the cost of holding money falls and the amount of money balances held increases. In this sense the interest rate is the cost or price paid for holding onto money over a period of time. Thus, the interest rate is related to the quantity of money demanded. That is, the quantity of money demanded is a function of the interest rate.

This demand function for liquid balances of money is shown in Figure 27-1. It is like any other demand function with the price of money, the interest rate, on the vertical axis, and the quantity of money measured along the horizontal axis.

At the current market rate of interest of i_a, desired aggregate holdings of cash balances are M_a. If the rate of interest (yield) rises to i_b, i.e., if the opportunity cost of holding money increases to i_b, the quantity demanded of liquidity or cash balances is M_b.

Because investors buy bonds to get a return, by its very nature the act of investment is also speculation, for after the bond is bought the value of the bond may go up or down. If the holder wants to sell it, he or she may gain or lose depending on which direction the bond's price changed. Now, for any individual speculator, the decision on whether to buy bonds or not depends on what he perceives to be the future direction of bond prices. There is an inverse relation between bond prices and the interest yield on bonds. If a bond sells for $100 and pays $10 interest, the rate is 10 percent. If the same bond sells for $50 a year later, and still pays $10 interest, then the interest yield to the investor is $10 on a $50 investment, or 20 percent. When the bond price falls the yield rises, and vice versa.

Keynes argued that each investor has his own subjective notion of what the usual or normal yield (interest rate) should be and about which rate the market rate of interest fluctuates. If the observed rate is above this investor's normal rate, he believes this current rate is only temporary, and expects the

Figure 27-1

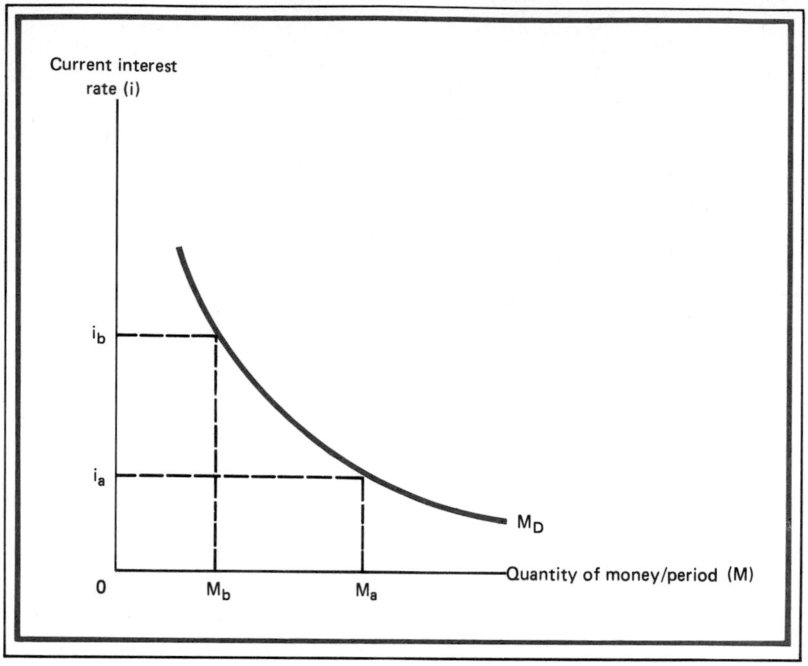

market rate of interest to fall eventually. Hence, if he buys the bonds now when the interest rate is high and above the normal rate, when the interest rate does fall bond prices will rise, and he will realize a profit called a capital gain. If, for instance, the normal rate is $i_a = 4\%$ and the market rate is $i_b = 6\%$, the individual would buy the bonds now before the yield falls back to 4 percent. And as the yield falls the price of the bond rises. By purchasing the bonds in order to obtain this speculative gain, he reduces his cash holdings from M_a to M_b.

Conversely, if the market rate of interest has temporarily fluctuated below 4 percent to 3 percent, he expects it will eventually return to 4 percent. He would, in this circumstance, not buy bonds but hold onto cash in anticipation that bond prices will fall in the future, in which case he will willingly purchase the cheaper bonds at that time. If he were to buy the bonds now he would realize a capital loss when the yield rises to 4 percent, since he would receive a lower price if he sold them then.

The curve drawn in the figure is sometimes called a liquidity preference curve or a curve showing the speculative demand for money. One observes that if there were no uncertainty about the future rates of interest, there would be no speculative demand for money, only transactions and precautionary demands. As it is, however, although each individual is certain about what he believes to be the normal rate of return, there is no guarantee he is indeed correct.

Calculating Bond Prices and Yields

The discussion on liquidity preference necessitates an understanding of the relation between the price of a bond—its value—and the bond's yield. The following table provides all the information we need.

Date	Par value	Coupon rate	Coupon payment	Market rate of interest	Market value of bond	Capital gain or loss
When issued	$1,000	4%	$40	4%	$100	$0
3 years later	1,000	4%	$40	5%	800	−200
5 years later	1,000	4%	$40	2%	2,000	+1,000

Numbers to the left of the vertical line never change.

Par value The initial value of the bond and what is repaid to the holder when the bond matures.

Coupon rate The annual interest rate the bond pays—its yield—stated in percentage terms.

Coupon payment The annual interest payments stated in dollars. It is fixed and never changes.

Market value Actually the present value of the bond. If we assume the bond never matures, then in perpetuity the market price or present value of the bond is $PV = R/i = 40/.04 =$ $1,000. Since the coupon rate R is fixed in money terms, PV varies inversely with the market rate of interest.

Capital gain or loss Net change in the value of the bond.

The table shows that when a $1,000 bond is issued paying a yield of 4 percent the coupon payment is $40 a year. The 4 percent yield on the bond when it is issued corresponds to the market rate of interest of 4 percent. The value of the bond were it to be resold would be $1,000. So there would be no capital gain or loss incurred if it were to be resold.

Assume that 3 years after the bond was issued, the market rate of interest has risen from 4 percent to 5 percent. At what price can the bondholder sell the bond? The capitalized value of the bond is now $PV = R/i = \$40/.05 = \$800$. Why has the bond's value fallen to $800? Because if someone were to invest $800 at the current market rate of interest of 5 percent, he or she could earn $.05 \times \$800 = \$40$ a year. This is the exact amount of the coupon payment yielded by the bond issued 3 years earlier. So why buy the bond at its original price? To do that means spending $1,000 for a bond yielding $40 a year, for a yield of only 4 percent. Why buy a bond yielding 4 percent if your money can now get you 5 percent. That is, if $1,000 were invested now at 5 percent, the return would be $50.

Consequently, the original buyer of the bond now holds a bond worth only $800. Selling it leads to a loss of $200, the capital loss—ignoring of course any effects of inflation on the value of the dollar. The table indicates that 5

Figure 27-2

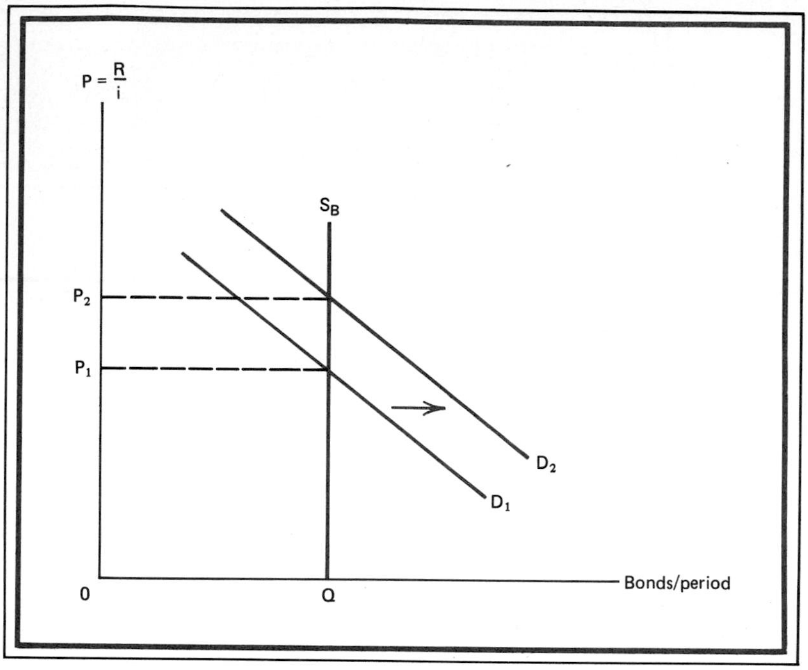

years later, the market rate of interest has fallen to 2 percent. The market value of the bond is therefore $PV = R/i = \$40/.02 = \$2{,}000$. The reason for the rise in the bond's value is that today you would have to invest $2,000 to earn $40 a year if the market rate of interest were 2 percent. However, the bondholder is earning $40 a year, having originally only paid $1,000 for the bond. A person who invested $1,000 today at 2 percent would earn only $20 a year. Therefore, since the bond pays $40 a year, then at the current rate of 2 percent the bond is worth $2,000. Thus, if the owner resells the bond for $2,000, he or she earns $1,000 over the original price—the capital gain. Figure 27-2 is a graph of the bond market. The supply of bonds is shown as vertical since we shall assume their number is fixed. The vertical axis shows the price of bonds and that it varies inversely with the rate of interest. If there is an increase in the demand for bonds from D_1 to D_2, the price of bonds rises from P_1 to P_2. Stated alternatively, since $P_1 = R/i_1$ and the coupon rate R is fixed, the rate of interest i_1 must fall to i_2.

Listed at the top of page 673 are the famous Moody's bond ratings. The Aaa bonds are the least risky municipal and corporation bonds, with risk increasing going down the column.

Liquidity Trap

Keynes believed the yield on bonds (the interest rate) fell so low during the Great Depression of the 1930s that the liquidity preference curve—the demand curve for cash balances—became perfectly elastic, that is to say, horizontal. Speculators held cash fully expecting that the current low rate of interest was considerably below what they considered to be the normal rate. Interest rates

Rating	Explanation
Aaa	Best quality
Aa	High quality
A	Upper medium grade
Baa	Medium grade
Ba	Speculative elements
B	Undesirable
Caa	Poor
Ca	Highly speculative
C	Extremely poor

could only go up. They could fall no further. Keynes called such a situation a liquidity trap, illustrated in Figure 27-3 where a hypothetical rate of interest of 1 percent is assumed. In such a situation, no matter how much the Federal Reserve attempted to expand the money supply from M_S to $M_S{}'$ to $M_S{}''$, speculators merely sat on the additional balances from M_a to M_b and up. Monetary policy was ineffective in a severely depressed economy, concluded Keynes, since it could not stimulate borrowing and investment by firms or stimulate the issuing of loans by banks, who preferred liquidity. Interest rates were simply too low to be pushed any lower by the Fed's expanding bank reserves M. The large holdings of cash balances amounted to a substantial leakage from the circular flow, seriously depressing aggregate demand. He believed that

Figure 27-3

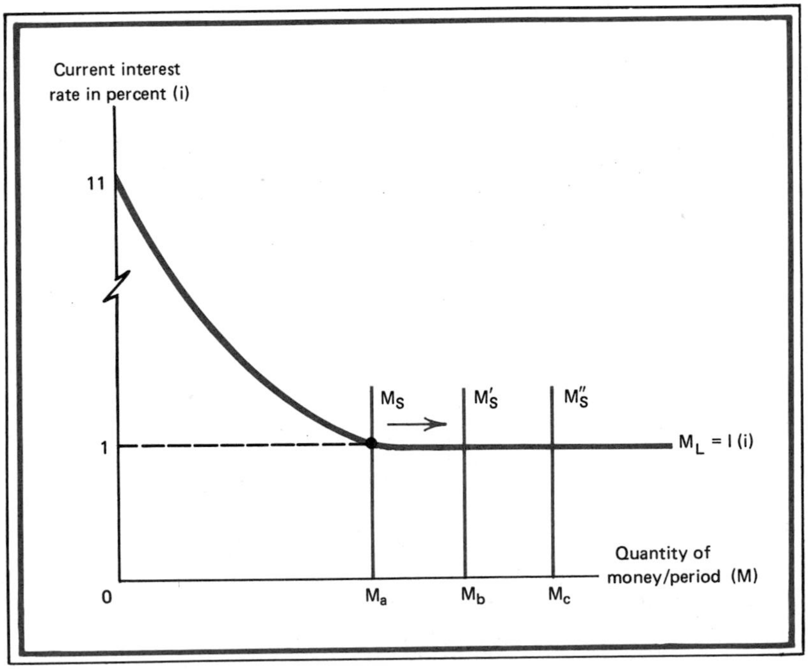

increasing the money supply to drive interest down in order to stimulate investment did not work. It was too much of a load for interest rates to pull. For this reason Keynes advocated direct government intervention to lift aggregate demand through the use of fiscal policy pump-priming by lowering taxes and enlarging government expenditures—deficit financing by design: a break with the traditional fiscal philosophy of balanced budgets.

In contrast, at $i = 11$ percent in the figure as drawn, the liquidity preference curve is vertical along the axis and no speculative cash balances are desired. We shall assume that this situation holds when speculators in the bond market *all* believe this interest rate to be above whatever is considered to be the normal yield. Everyone's expectations are that interest rates can go no higher, they can only fall. Given this assumption, the logical course of action would be not to hold any speculative money balances under the Keynesian prescription, but to put all speculative money into bonds.

Velocity of money If interest rates rise and speculators shift from money to bonds, then the velocity of money will rise as cash balances are reduced. As interest rates rise and velocity increases, k' will fall. Smaller amounts of cash balances will be held on the average during any given month. And, of course, if interest rates fall then the velocity of money falls too, ceteris paribus. When velocity falls, k' increases as people choose to hold on to larger amounts of money balances.

The conclusion of Keynes's analysis was that in a period of deep recession and low interest rates, when there is likely to be a liquidity trap, attempts by the Federal Reserve to stimulate aggregate demand by increasing the supply of money is offset by a substantial drop in the velocity of money, or, what is the same thing, a strong desire by economic units to increase their holdings of speculative cash balances and by the banks to increase reserves.

Thus, the Keynesian analysis broke with classical analysis, breaking the direct classical link between the money supply and prices in an underemployed economy. By introducing a liquidity and/or speculative demand for money, Keynes amended the equation of exchange and introduced interest rates into the demand function for money, as we now demonstrate.

MONETARY EQUILIBRIUM MECHANICS

In the Keynesian framework the total demand for money balances is equal to the sum of the transactions and precautionary and speculative demands. Since both the transactions and precautionary demands for money are related to income, we lump them together and simply let M_T represent the demand for money to be used to effect transactions and support a given level of income in the economy. Thus, again we write

$$M_T = k'Y$$

which is the familiar classical form of the equation of exchange. Then we define $M_L = l(i)$, which we have been talking about in reference to Figure 27-3. M_L is the demand for money for liquidity or speculative purposes and it is functionally related to the level of interest rates represented by i. This simply means that we are looking at the liquidity function as a function of the interest rate.

Letting the total demand for money M_D equal the summation of the transactions demand M_T and the speculative demand M_L at each rate of interest, we write

$$M_D = M_T + M_L$$

or in more general shorthand notation,

$$M_D = f(i, \overline{Y}).$$

We have finally brought the old fashioned equation of exchange around, added interest rates, and have formed the function that we call the demand function for money. The quantity of money demanded is a function of interest rates and income, and not just a function of income alone.

We can draw the function by looking at a family of curves as in Figure 27-4. What we do is select three different values for income Y, namely $\overline{Y}$, $\overline{\overline{Y}}$ and $\overline{\overline{\overline{Y}}}$ to illustrate shifts in the demand for money schedule using Y as the shift parameter. We draw three different curves showing the relation between M_D and i for three different income levels. As income rises, the curve shifts rightward. When income rises, people desire to hold more money balances for transactions purposes. Hence, the demand for money shifts to the right. More balances are held *at each rate* of interest. When the interest rate is i_a, for example, balances increase from M_a to M_b and on to M_c as income goes from $\overline{Y}$ to $\overline{\overline{Y}}$ to $\overline{\overline{\overline{Y}}}$.

Figure 27-4

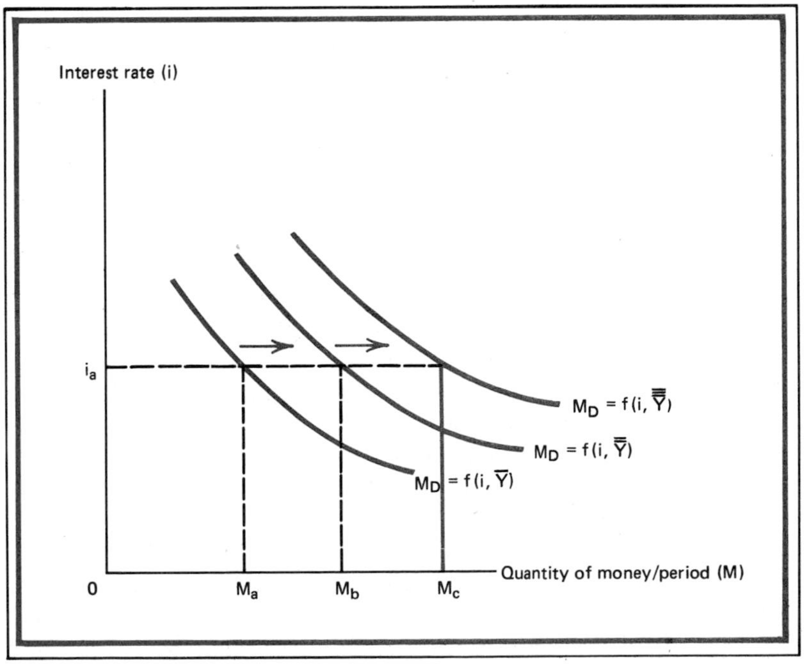

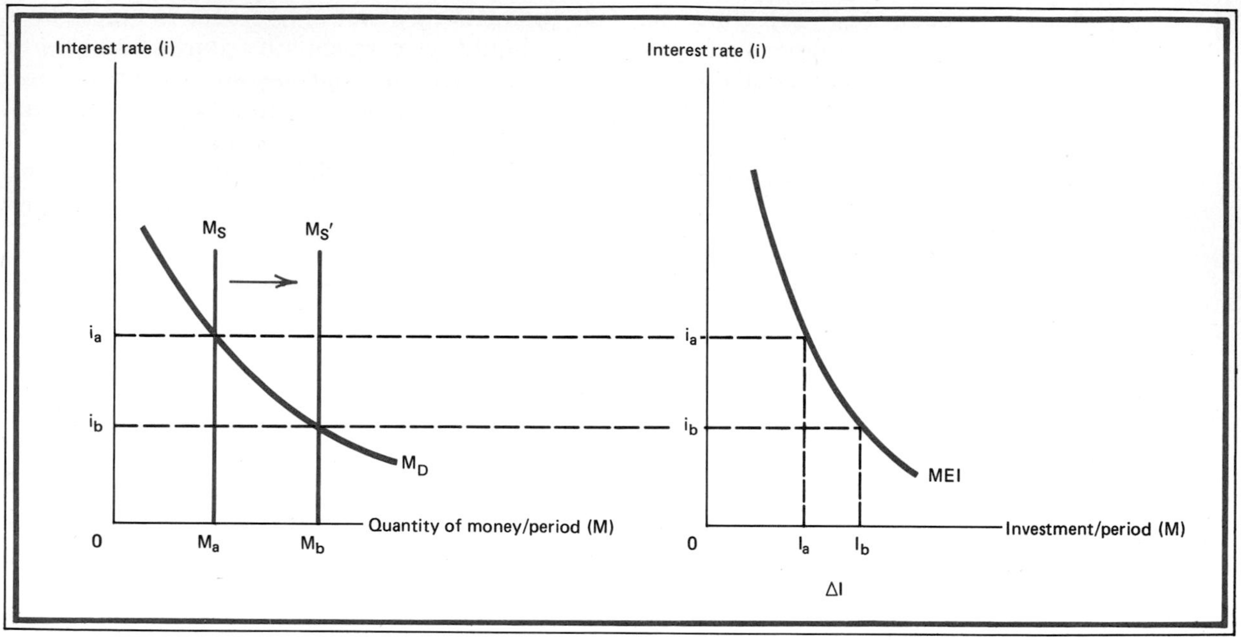

Figure 27-5

Figure 27-5 shows the money market in an initial state of equilibrium at i_a where $M_S = M_D$. The M_S curve is drawn as a vertical line because the money supply is presumed not to vary with the interest rate. If the Federal Reserve pursues expansionary policies by purchasing Treasury bonds from the non-bank public, the M_S curve shifts to $M_{S'}$. At the old rate of interest, i_a, the quantity supplied of money is now greater than the quantity of money people desire to hold. People adjust their holdings of assets by moving out of cash. They do this by purchasing bonds. But hold on—for every seller there must be a buyer, and in the aggregate not everybody can buy securities without somebody selling them at the same time. To resolve this question, keep in mind that the price of a security is inversely related to the market rate of interest. The intent of people to buy more bonds implies an increase in demand for bonds, driving up bond prices and lowering the interest rate. As the interest rate falls to i_b the opportunity cost of holding money is lower than before, and people become willing to hold more cash than before. The result is that, at an interest rate which has fallen to i_b, speculators are holding an amount of M_b of cash balances. Only at this interest rate are investors willing to hold the additional money created by the Fed's actions. At this point buyers and sellers in the aggregate have arbitrated to the new equilibrium where $M_D = M_{S'}$. The trade-off between cash and bonds is stabilized, with desired cash balances equal to actual cash balances.

In the same figure we have drawn a graph of an investment demand schedule, or what we have called the marginal efficiency of investment. At the new lower rate of interest, a reading of the *MEI* schedule indicates an increased amount of investment expenditures by firms. Aggregate demand is now higher, and the multiplier effect magnifies the initial effect of the increase in investment to create a multiple increase in nominal income.

The transmission mechanism We can now ask ourselves, how does money affect income in the Keynesian model? The transmission mechanism in the Keynesian model goes like this. The Fed takes action to increase the money supply. This lowers the rate of interest. The lower rate of interest stimulates investment expenditures by firms. The increased investment expenditures raise the level of aggregate demand. The higher aggregate demand via the multiplier magnifies the increase in national income. We can describe the process as follows:

For expansion: Fed action M_s up, i down implies I up, GNP up

For contraction: Fed action M_s down, i up implies I down, GNP down

COMPLETING THE MODEL

Only one final step is required to complete the model for our purposes. It is to recognize that as income increases from the expansion of investment, there will be an increase in the demand for money because the investment increases income and causes the demand for money curve to shift rightward, as illustrated in Figure 27-6. Since $M_D = f(i, \overline{Y})$ as Y increases, the quantity of money demanded will also increase. Here, however, because the demand for money function shifts rightward, the interest rate i_a does not fall to i_b because the new equilibrium between $M_{S'}$ and M_D occurs at point c not b. Nor does investment increase from I_a to I_b. Instead i_a falls only to i_c and I_a increases only to I_c.

Figure 27-6

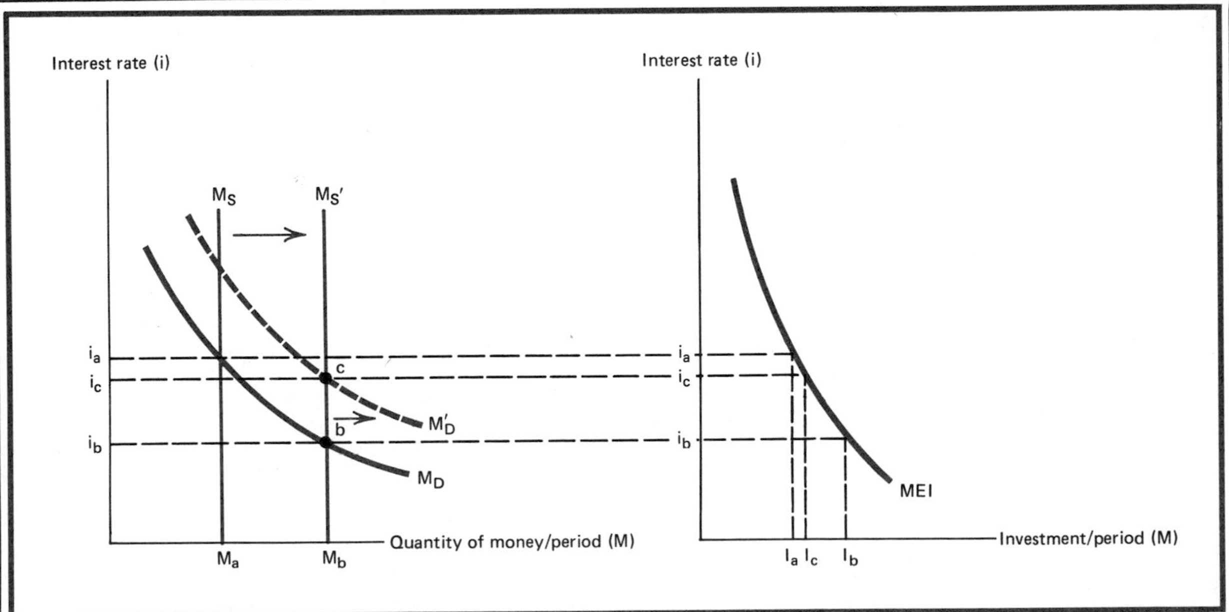

Keynesian Transmission Mechanism

The Fed's action to increase the money supply goes as follows:

M_s up, i down, I up, GNP up.

To complete the analysis we trace through the impact of the resulting increase in *GNP*.

GNP up, M_d up, i up, I down, GNP down some.

The effect of the money supply in the Keynesian system is *transmitted* through interest rates and investment to the real sector of the economy—employment, output, and relative prices.

The level of *GNP* is higher than before, but not as high as it would have been if the transactions demand for money had not increased in the process. Thus, as *M* increases, *i* falls and *I* increases, and so does *GNP*, but the increase in *GNP* is moderated somewhat, though not fully offset, by the increased demand for transactions balances.

This is the way monetary policy works in the Keynesian model. It is often referred to as the Keynesian transmission mechanism; namely, how money policy transmits its effect through the interest rate to the real sector of the economy—employment, output, and relative prices.

Using the Graphs

The sequence described in the preceeding section can be graphically reproduced by collecting the investment, aggregate expenditure, and money demand graphs into one graph as in Figure 27-7. We start out with the system in equilibrium. The money supply stock equals the demand for the stock of money indicated by M_a in panel (1) and determines the equilibrium rate of interest i_a. With the interest rate equal to i_a in panel (2), the level of investment

Figure 27-7

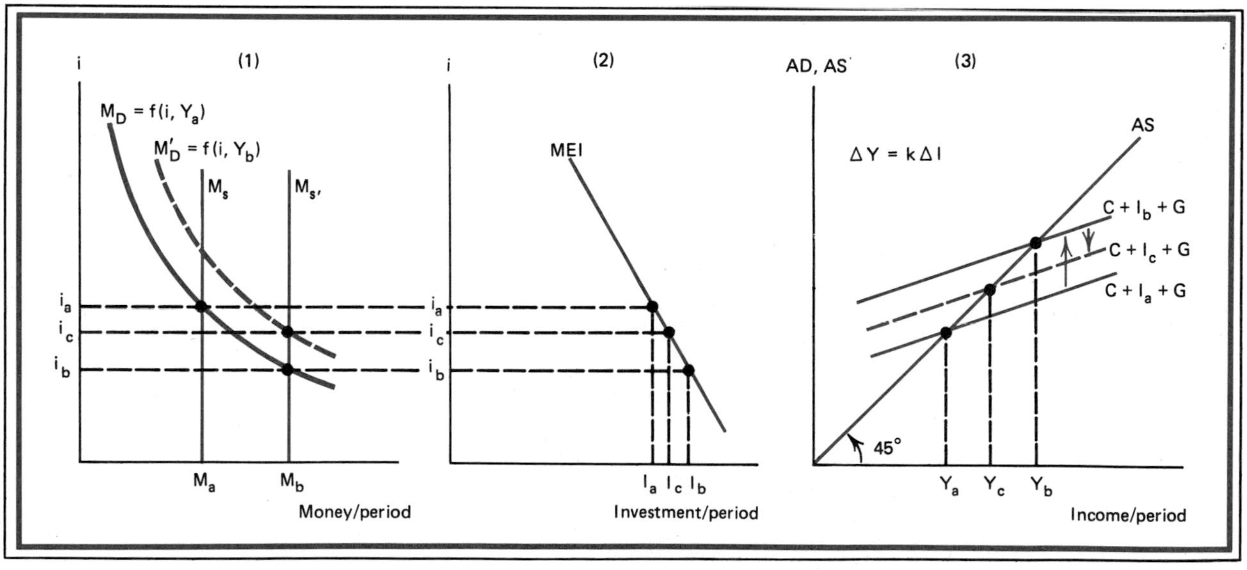

is I_a. When the level of investment I_a is added to $C + G$ in panel (3), the equilibrium level of GNP or aggregate income is $Y_a = C + I_a + G$.

Assume as before that the Fed increases the stock of money from M_a to M_b illustrated in panel (1) by the shift of the money supply curve from M_S to M_S'. The M_S and M_S' curve are shown as vertical because we assume that at any given time the supply of money (a stock) is fixed and does not vary with the interest rate. The initial effect is that the interest rate temporarily falls to i_b where the demand and supply of money are in a new equilibrium with $M_S' = M_D$.

Now let us show in detail how the adjustment to a new equilibrium in the money market takes place. When M_S increases to M_S', there occurs, at the initial interest rate i_a, an excess supply of money, i.e., $M_b > M_a$. People are now holding more money balances than they want to. They therefore desire to buy more bonds and reduce their cash balances in the process. But for every buyer there must be a seller. Therefore, it is impossible for everyone to buy bonds because there would be no sellers. For some people to be induced to hold more cash instead of buying bonds the interest rate must fall. This comes about because the desire for everyone to buy bonds increases the demand for bonds and drives up the price of bonds. When the bond price goes up interest rates must fall. As the interest rate falls some bond buyers for speculative reasons increase their cash balances; they can only do this by selling some bonds. The process continues, with the interest rate falling to i_b bringing the money balance market into equilibrium where the cash balances people desire to hold is the same as the actual money supply. The fall in the interest rate to i_b causes the level of investment to increase to I_b as illustrated in panel (2). It has become cheaper for firms to borrow money for investment purposes. Thus, the rate of return on additional projects becomes profitable. That is, for some projects on the boards, $r > i_b$ is anticipated whereas prior to this a projected $r < i_a$ made them unfeasible.

The Keynesian multiplier takes over and the change in investment acts through the multiplier to induce a magnified increase in income Y. But we don't stop here. We have a simple general equilibrium model: everything affects everything else. The initial change in the money supply ripples through the system. Because income has risen, people desire to increase their cash balances as they act to maintain a certain preferred ratio of balances to income M/Y. Since income is higher so too must the demand for money rise in order to maintain $M/Y = k'$ the same. (Remember, k' is not the multiplier k shown in panel (3)). Therefore, since the parameter Y_a in panel (1) has changed, there is a shift in the demand for money curve M_D to M_D'. Observe it does not shift to the right far enough to raise the rate of interest back up to i_a, but only to an intermediate level, say, to i_c. This second round of changes in the interest rate in panel (1) has repercussions on investment in panel (2). The initial impact of the fall in the interest to i_b is moderated by the subsequent rise in the interest rate to i_c. Thus investment increases to something less than I_b, to I_c. Predictably, the smaller change in investment, $\Delta I = I_c - I_a$ leads to a smaller change in aggregate demand, and through the multiplier, to a smaller increase in national income to only Y_c. The rounds of adjustment continue in smaller doses until the system finally settles in a final equilibrium. But in each panel the final resting point is somewhere between the initial values and the value resulting from the first shock to the system.

The analyses can be performed for other variables when the system is bumped off equilibrium and must find its way to a new equilibrium. Thus, one can trace the effects of an autonomous change in investment from the result of a technological innovation, or the effect of the public's spending habits slowing down or speeding up, or the consequences of a change in taxes or a decrease or increase in government expenditures. The initial shock displacing the system from equilibrium can begin in any one of the three panels.

MONEY EXPANSION AND INFLATION

Our description of the way economic activity expands when money is injected into the system needs one more comment. So far we have pointed out that increased money leads to increased gross national product. Gross national product is money income that we label Y. And it is equal to price times quantity produced, $Y = PQ$. What we wish to clarify here is that if gross national product, or Y, increases, this increase can either be the result of Q increasing or of P increasing, *or* of both P and Q increasing a little bit.

The world Keynes lived in when he wrote was full of unemployment. Perhaps monetary expansion and investment would put people back to work so that output would expand. That is, Q would expand a lot but P would not expand very much. Today, however, there is not a great deal of unemployment in most industrial economies. Therefore, when money expands and income expansion follows, the increase in income is mostly the result of increases in P and not so much the result of increases in Q. Price increases define inflation. If an economy is operating at or near capacity, then money expansion is inflationary. Finally, if they wish to avoid inflation, monetary authorities should not expand the money supply when the economy is fully employed. They should only expand the money supply by large amounts if the economy is plagued with considerable unemployment.

REAL MONEY BALANCES

Earlier in the chapter we learned about the cash balance version of the equation of exchange. We wrote the equation in this form as

$$M = k'PQ$$

where PQ also represents $GNP = GNY$ or simply Y. Dividing both sides of this equation by the general price index P gives

$$M/P = k'Q.$$

Of what significance is this form of the equation of exchange? On the left hand side there is M/P, and we call it the real balances of money or real money balances. However, the variable M under control of the Fed is expressed in nominal or money terms. It is, say, \$500 billion, meaning that out there in the economy there are this many dollars either in people's pockets or cash registers, or recorded in books in their bank accounts. Nothing about nominal M, in itself, tells us how much a person can buy with his or her holdings of M. However, the variable M/P is a different matter. The variable M/P is also nominal M multiplied by $1/P$. The value of $1/P$, where P is the general price level, indicates how big a batch of commodities can be bought with a dollar. It is a measure of the purchasing power of a dollar. Thus, if $P = 20$ cents, it is possible to buy 5 items for a dollar, or $1/.20 = 5$. If $P = 50$ cents, then you can buy $1/.5 = 2$ items for a dollar. If $P = \$2$, then $1/2 = 0.5$ items or half an item can be bought with a dollar. In general, $1/P$ indicates the purchasing power of a dollar. The higher the general price level, the less an individual dollar can buy of goods and services. It follows that M/P represents the purchasing power or the amount of goods and services the existing nominal money supply M can buy at the prevailing level of prices.

If the coefficient k' in the equation $M/P = k'Q$ is more or less stable, then an amount of real money M/P is demanded if an amount of real goods Q is to be purchased. That is, the amount of real balances people hold is directly related to the economy's output of real goods Q, if k' is essentially stable.

For example, if M in the economy is \$500 billion and $P = 1$, then M/P is also \$500 billion. Then assume that we have inflation and P increases to 1.25. Now the value of M/P is $\$500/1.25 = \$400$ billion. Consequently, a 25 percent increase in prices from 1 to 1.25 indicates a 20 percent *decrease* in real balances of money from \$500 to \$400 billion. The money that used to buy \$500 billion worth of goods will now buy only as much as \$400 billion used to buy. The nominal money supply remains the same at \$500 billion because there are still a total of \$500 billion in pocketbooks, in cash registers, and in deposit at banks. But these nominal balances of M will not buy as much as before, and are now only worth \$400 billion in purchasing power because P has risen.

As a variable, real balances of money play a role in economic analysis. An increase in the money supply created by the Fed will tend to increase the price level. However, as prices increase, the purchasing power of a given nominal amount of money will fall. Thus, real balances of money will fall until the inflation eventually stops. A single injection of nominal money will be expansionary and may lead to a higher price level. If no further injections of money occur, inflation will stop because the higher price level will reduce the real balances of money available to the spending public. Thus, knowing the concept of real balances of money helps us understand how an inflationary process is halted when the central bank stops creating new money.

CHAPTER SUMMARY

It is true by definition that expenditures per period must equal dollar receipts per period. The identity is formalized in the equation of exchange $MV = PQ$ where M is the money supply, V the income velocity of money, P is the price level, and Q is units of output. Given the arbitrary selection of values for any three variables, the fourth can be determined. However, if one of the variables is constrained to a certain value or values because it reflects human behavior, then arbitrary selection of values for the other variables will not necessarily yield the correct value for the behaviorally determined variable. The expression becomes an equation, since the value that some variables in the expression can take is conditioned by the variable whose value reflects something about human or societal behavior. Thus, the values the other variables can take is not arbitrary since they must fit with the value of the behaviorally determined variable or variables. In the classical system the velocity of money was a function of various institutional factors and was considered to be constant. The income velocity of money is the average number of times each dollar is spent on the purchase of a final good or service during the year. The dollar referred to here is an abstract dollar. There are 5 in a 5-dollar bill, 10 in a 10-dollar bill, and so on.

Because classical theory assumed velocity was constant and the system produced at full employment, then the equation of exchange could be converted into the quantity theory of money $P = \left(\frac{\overline{V}}{Q}\right)M$, which predicts that the price level is directly related to the money supply. Thus, money was a veil affecting only the level of prices and not relative prices and output in the real sector.

Another restatement of the equation of exchange is the cash-balance approach, stated as $M = k'GNP$. The income form $MV = GNP$ considers how *fast* people *spend* money, whereas the cash-balance approach considers how *long* people *hold* onto money. If V is the velocity of money, indicating how fast on average each dollar is spent per period, then $k' = 1/V$ indicates on average how long each dollar is held between receiving and spending it. If V is constant, then so is k', indicating what fraction of their income people want to hold in cash balances.

The cash-balance approach gives rise to the difference between the amount of desired balances held out of income and the actual amount of balances held similar to planned investment versus actual investment. If people hold more cash balances than they want to, then they are analogously holding unplanned inventories of cash balances. Thus, if the Fed increases the money supply so that the ratio of cash balances to income is greater than k', people spend the excess balances. This causes aggregate demand to rise. If the economy is already fully employed then the price level will rise. The actual money supply must by definition equal the amount of money people are holding. But it may not be the amount people desire to hold. Most important to remember is that in the classical scheme, the only reason for holding money was for transactions purposes; namely, to have cash handy to make anticipated purchases between receipts of income. It was a means of coordinating expenditures with income which was received in lumps.

Keynes challenged several aspects of classical monetary theory. First, he argued that in the short run the velocity of money was highly variable. Thus, if the money supply increased but velocity dropped sharply, then the price level would actually fall and unemployment would rise since the low velocity was indicative of a sluggish economy. In the short run, therefore, the price level and the money supply were not directly related. To explain this Keynes introduced two additional reasons that cash balances are demanded. One is to keep extra cash available to make expenditures that were not initially anticipated. This is the precautionary motive and it is mostly a function of the level of income. The second is the speculative motive. Cash balances are held in order to make and act on quick decisions about buying bonds in response to anticipated changes in the direction of interest rates for purposes of an anticipated capital gain. Since the price of a bond varies inversely with the interest rate, when interest rates are expected to fall, the prices of bonds are expected to go up. Thus, the purpose is to buy bonds at a low price and sell them at a higher price and earn a capital gain. Hence, because of changing expectations about future bond prices, speculators jump in and out of cash balances. Changing interest rates affect the velocity of money and break the direct link between money and the price level predicted by the quantity theory of money.

Together, the three demands for cash balance make up the total demand for liquidity preference. It is an inverse function of the interest rate, with income as the parameter shifting the demand-for-money schedule. When combined with the supply of money, it determines the market rate of interest. This affects the level of investment, which because of the multiplier has a magnified effect on income, output, and employment. Therefore money, according to Keynes, is not neutral since its supply and demand determine a rate of interest that transmits its effect to the real sector of the economy.

Real cash balances are money balances divided by the price level, hence this variable is a measure of the purchasing power of the existing money supply. In this form $M/P = k'Q$, so that, for example, if the economy is fully employed so that Q is fixed, and there is a rise in prices, the value of real balances falls, thus reducing purchasing power and thereby bringing a halt to the inflation. Or, if the Fed increases the money supply, raising the level of actual real balances above the desired level, the additional balances are spent, raising the price level until the desired real balance ratio is reached and spending stops, but the economy has undergone a rise in its price level at full employment. The new money has no more purchasing power, since inflation eroded it.

QUESTIONS

1. Private Jones receives his salary on payday and spends all of it immediately and is broke for the remainder of the month. Private Smith puts his in the battalion safe and spends nothing over the month, since he's stuck on an outpost in Anarctica. What is the velocity of money over the month in each situation? The cash balance to income ratio?
2. The equation of exchange is $MV = PQ$ and the quantity theory is $P = \left(\frac{V}{Q}\right)M$. Which is the identity and which is the conditional equation? Why the difference, since both expressions contain the same variables?
3. Why does holding money involve a cost, since none of it is spent? Is this merely economic gibberish?
4. Would we be better off without money since it seems to bring out the worst in people?
5. Which motive(s) for holding money is (are) emphasized in each of the following?
   a. Mary receives $20 a month as her allowance.
   b. Jane is boarding a plane for a two-week vacation in Mexico. Mom slips her $50 should she see the shawl that mom told her about.
   c. A broker sells off some of his stock because he expects stock prices to fall significantly.
   d. Peggy always carries extra change in order to be certain to have coins for parking meters, telephones, and cigarette machines.
   e. A man wins $30,000 in the Irish Sweepstakes, he puts it into a trust fund for his 10-year-old daughter.
   f. Firms build up cash balance just before the Christmas season.
   g. A bank sells off half of its U.S. security holdings for German marks because it anticipates the price of the mark will jump relative to the dollar.
6. One theory of the demand for money (cash balances) directs attention to the proper-

ties that make money a desirable object to *hold* as distinct from another theory that views money as an object to *spend*. Identify these theories. Which theory is really an identity? Other than income, what other factors affect the amount of income people choose to hold as cash balances?

7. The liquidity trap refers to excessive drinking when bond prices fall. True? Comment.
8. According to Keynes, what expectations concerning the interest rate would justify buying bonds in preference to holding cash?
9. If the amount of money the public desires to hold is less than the amount of money it actually holds, the public restores equilibrium by reducing the amount of money it actually holds. False? Explain.
10. As prices of securities fall, the quantity demanded of money also falls. True? Explain.
11. How could the money supply be $200 billion while nominal GNP is $800 billion? Does not the money supply place an upper limit on the size of nominal GNP? Explain.
12. Suppose in a two-good economy 6 units of good A are produced selling for $2 each and 8 units of good B are produced selling for $3 each. If the money supply is $9, what is the income velocity of money in this economy?
13. Only people who spend all of their income have a cash balance problem. Those who save some income will always have that much in balances ready to put to work. Criticize this statement.
14. According to Keynesian analysis, the level of interest rates plays an important role in determining the level of aggregate income; yet the rate of interest is influenced by the level of aggregate income. Is this a chicken-and-egg proposition which defies explanation? Explain this apparent circularity in reasoning.
15. Refer to the three-diagram general equilibrium model in the chapter to answer the following questions. Graph and explain the sequence of effects of:
    a. An improvement in technology and autonomous investment.
    b. A speed-up in spending habits.
    c. A tax cut.
    d. A recession is expected.
16. Refer to the three-diagram general equilibrium model below to answer the questions that follow it.

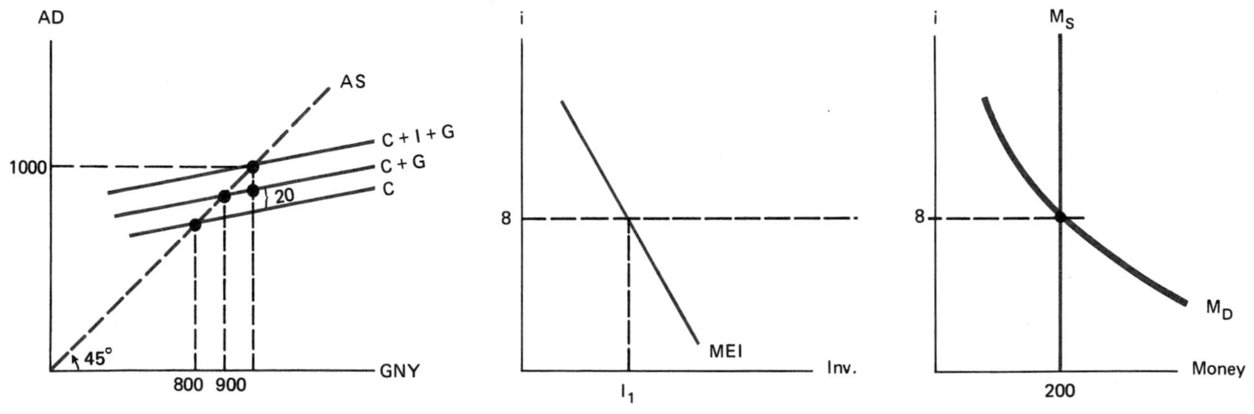

a. What is the level of the money supply? Of money demanded?
b. What is the rate of interest?
c. What is the level of aggregate demand? Of gross national income? The level of government expenditures?

d. What is the value of the *MPC*? What is the value of the *MPS*? The multiplier? The level of investment?
e. Using the equation of exchange, calculate the income velocity of money.
f. Suppose government expenditures increase by 10. What is the level of *GNY* after the first round of adjustment?
g. As a result, will the demand for cash balances go up or down? Will the quantity demanded of cash balances be higher or lower in the new equilibrium? Is the velocity of money now higher or lower than it was in e? Or is it unchanged? Explain.
h. If the money supply is unchanged, will the price of bonds go up or down? The interest rate? Why?
i. In the second round of adjustment, therefore, will the level of investment be greater or less than I_1 or remain at I_1, if the effect of the increase in *GNY* dominates the effect caused by a rise in the interest rate?
j. As a consequence, will *GNY* in the second round be greater or smaller than it was *after* the first round adjustment in f occurred?

17. Assume the economy is at full employment and the money supply is then increased by 10 percent, while the velocity of money falls by 20 percent. Will the price level go up or down? By what percentage?
18. You just bought a bond for $800. The face value of the bond indicates that when issued its value was $1,000 and it yielded 5 percent. Using the abbreviated formula for calculating the value of a bond, the yield on your investment of $800 is how much? Suppose two years later the market rate of interest falls to 4 percent. What is the value of the bond?

Chapter 28

Business Fluctuations

Business history repeats itself, but always with a difference.

— Wesley Mitchell

PROGRESS REPORT

A. In Chapter 27 we analyzed the demand for money and integrated it into the Keynesian macroeconomic model. The price level was then introduced by converting the demand for money balances into a demand for real balances.

B. Now we want to describe how a nation's economy can have its ups and downs over time. Analyzing such movements is usually called the study of business cycles. The term cycle connotes a certain regularity or repetitiveness that data do not support. So some economists prefer to refer to business fluctuations rather than business cycles. We will use the terms interchangeably.

C. After observing how business fluctuates from period to period we shall, in Chapter 29, look into the stabilization policies that governments undertake to smooth fluctuations in real gross national product.

Fluctuation in aggregate economic output, income, and employment continues to consume the attention of many economists employed by universities, by the Federal Reserve and commercial banks, by the Department of Commerce, and by the economic research divisions of large corporations. **Business cycles** can be intrinsically induced in a market economy by the economic decisions of households, businesses, and government policymakers in response to economic forces from both inside and outside the economy. Ups and downs in aggregate economic activity are a recurrent phenomenon. Aggregate output and income do not suddenly change in clearly observable discrete jumps from one level of economic activity to another. A cycle normally develops slowly as changes in economic conditions are gradually transmitted from one segment of the economy to another through many related processes. These processes are cumulative, each process or major variable in the system being individually observable and each one displaying its own particular fluctuation.

Business cycles are recurrent, nonperiodic variations in the economy's real GNP.

Although business fluctuations are recurrent, they are not periodic. That is to say, they do not appear with predictable frequency lasting for definite periods of time like a pendulum that traces its previous path in successive movements. Not every fluctuation in aggregate economics is considered a cycle. In order to be considered a cycle, fluctuations must last long enough to develop in both upward and downward directions over a period of time. The U.S. Department of Commerce qualifies a cycle as having a duration of at least 15 months, with any significant upward or downward phase of the cycle lasting for at least 5 months. Deviations shorter than this and also those too shallow in their change of direction are screened out and considered as only temporary aberrations.

Cycles under 15 months long and expected seasonal variations are not counted as cycles. A phase of a cycle must last at least 5 months.

Thus cycles should not be confused with seasonal variations. For example, heavy spending during the Christmas season and the subsequent decline in activity in January and February is not considered a business cycle. Nor are lower car sales during the winter months and the higher sales during the fall examples of a business cycle. The same holds for the higher sales of air conditioners between May and July. These are not examples of the business cycle because these seasonal fluctuations are short, periodic, and predictable. The statisticians who study cycles adjust and smooth out these seasonal variations. Thus, when you hear the words seasonally adjusted in the news, you have some notion of what it means.

Variations can also occur within cycles, since any aggregate is composed of subparts. Spending on consumer durables and capital equipment used in producing them tends to move in wide cycles, that is, from peak to peak or trough to trough on both the supply and demand sides. However, nondurable goods and perishable items like food are relatively noncyclical; expenditure on nondurables is rather consistent and stable. Subcycles occur at different times and with different intensities in such variables as bank deposits, wholesale and retail sales, layoffs, quit rates for jobs, interest rates, and others.

Spending on consumer durables and capital goods tends to vary over time, while purchases of perishable goods are relatively constant.

Figure 28-1 illustrates the **period** and **amplitude** (intensity) of a cycle and provides names for different phases of the cycle. The period of a business cycle is measured either from peak to peak or trough to trough. Troughs are the lower turning points where the cycle reaches the bottom of its contraction. Peaks are upper turning points where the cycle reaches the top of its expansion.

A cycle's length or _period_ is measured from peak to peak (upper turning points) or trough to trough (lower turning points).

Figure 28-1

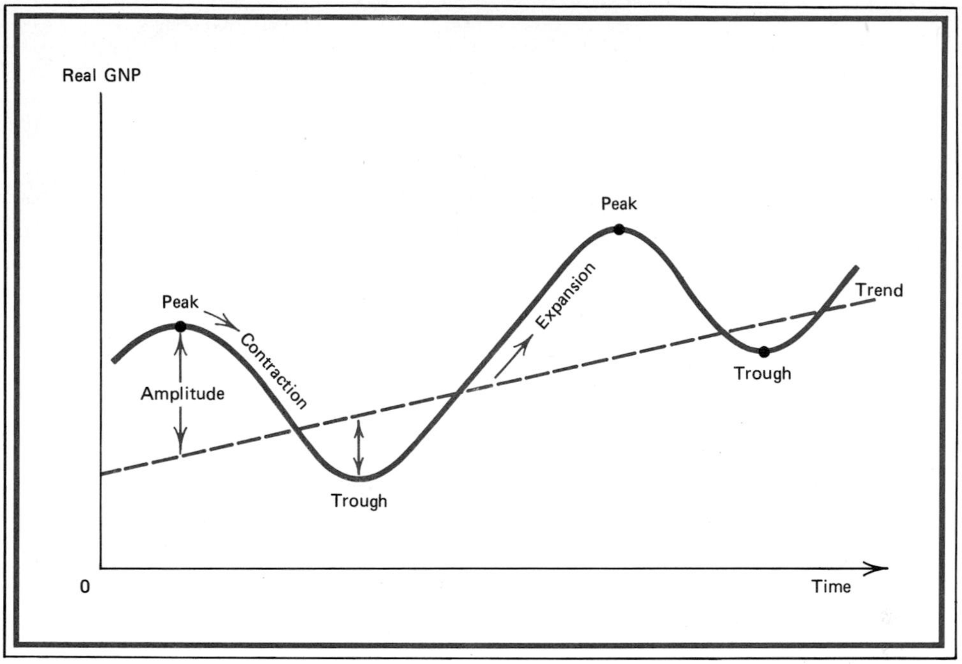

A cycle's depth or *amplitude* is measured vertically from an imaginary trend line.

The depth of the rise or fall, that is the intensity of the cycle, measures its deviation from an imaginary trend line about which the economy's real GNP supposedly oscillates. The trend line shown here is rising, indicating a growing economy over time. There is no reason for the amplitudes from cycle to cycle to be the same or for the amplitude of the expansion to equal the amplitude of the decline.

Table 28-1 is a history of U.S. business cycles covering the period 1854 to 1980. Notice the differing durations and amplitudes of the cycles. The longest contraction, lasting 65 months, began October 1873 and ended March 1879. The shortest phase began August 1918 and ended March 1919, a period of 7 months. The shortest post-World War II recession of August 1957 to April 1958 lasted just 8 months. Notice the long contraction of 43 months that occurred during the initial Depression years from August 1929 to March 1933. From December 1854 to January 1980 there have been 29 cycles, with the recessions lasting about 19 months and the expansions about 33 months.

Because one recession is long and another is short does not mean that the longer recession is the more severe one. The short 1957–1958 recession of 8 months was harsh. But the longer 10-month July 1953 to May 1954 recession was comparatively mild. The 1957–1958 downturn saw GNP fall by an average annual rate of about 6 percent, with unemployment reaching 7.4 percent of the labor force. The 1953–1954 slump in GNP only averaged about 3.3 percent and unemployment never went above 6 percent.

TABLE 28-1
Business Cycle Expansions and Contractions in the United States: 1854 to 1980

Business cycle reference dates		Duration in months			
				Cycle	
Trough	Peak	Contraction (trough from previous peak)	Expansion (trough to peak)	Trough from previous trough	Peak from previous peak
December 1854	June 1857	(x)	30	(x)	(x)
December 1858	October 1860	18	22	48	40
June 1861	April 1865	8	46	30	54
December 1867	June 1869	32	18	78	50
December 1870	October 1873	18	34	36	52
March 1879	March 1882	65	36	99	101
May 1885	March 1887	38	22	74	60
April 1888	July 1890	13	27	35	40
May 1891	January 1893	10	20	37	30
June 1894	December 1895	17	18	37	35
June 1897	June 1899	18	24	36	42
December 1900	September 1902	18	21	42	39
August 1904	May 1907	23	33	44	56
June 1908	January 1910	13	19	46	32
January 1912	January 1913	24	12	43	36
December 1914	August 1918	23	44	35	67
March 1919	January 1920	7	10	51	17
July 1921	May 1923	18	22	28	40
July 1924	October 1926	14	27	36	41
November 1927	August 1929	13	21	40	34
March 1933	May 1937	43	50	64	93
June 1938	February 1945	13	80	63	93
October 1945	November 1948	8	37	88	45
October 1949	July 1953	11	45	48	56
May 1954	August 1957	10	39	55	49
April 1958	April 1960	8	24	47	32
February 1961	December 1969	10	106	34	116
November 1970	November 1973	11	36	117	47
March 1975	January 1980	16	58	52	74
Average, all cycles:					
28 cycles, 1854–1980		19	[1]34	52	53
6 cycles, 1919–1945		18	35	53	53
6 cycles, 1945–1980		11	[2]49	59	[2]60
Average, peacetime cycles:					
23 cycles, 1854–1980		23	[3]28	46	47
5 cycles, 1919–1945		20	26	46	45
4 cycles, 1945–1980		11	[4]39	45	[4]49

Note: Underscored figures are the wartime expansions (Civil War, World Wars I and II, Korean War, and Vietnam War), the postwar contractions, and the full cycles that include the wartime expansions.

[1]29 cycles [2]7 cycles [3]24 cycles [4]5 cycles

Source: National Bureau of Economic Research, Inc. as compiled in Business Conditions Digest, Oct. 1980, U.S. Department of Commerce,: 105, and slightly modified here.

CAUSES OF CYCLES

Sunspots

Early economists attributed business cycles to sunspot activity, income maldistribution, random political shocks, and monetary disturbances.

English economist William Stanley Jevons (1835–1882) provocatively maintained that business cycles were the result of sunspots that somehow affected the weather, which in turn is critically important to farmers because weather affects their crops. Freezes, too much rain, too much sun—all these could reduce crop yields and drive up prices. At other times bumper crops would drive prices down. In the largely agrarian economies of the nineteenth century, crop yields were directly related to the use and need for railroads and the steel that built tracks and freight hauling cars. The jobs and income created by a good crop had effects throughout the economy. Also, lower food prices, the result of an abundant crop, meant that more nonfood goods could be purchased. Thus, aggregate demand was stimulated.

Before writing off Jevons as an eccentric, one should be reminded that subsequent scientific research by twentieth century astrophysicists have confirmed that magnetic and radioactive emissions intensify when sunspots appear. And they appear, on the average, about every 11 years. They affect, for example, radio and television satellite communications, both of which are a form of electromagnetic energy. It is not clear to scientists as yet what exact effect sunspots have on the frequency, intensity, and length of droughts, on causing destructive spells of heavy rain, and on geographical changes in weather patterns. The suspicion exists, however, that they do have an effect. Although in modern industrial economies the agricultural sector is no longer the major component of GNP, nevertheless severe fluctuations in farm production caused by abnormal weather conditions can significantly affect the general consumer price level and industries that purchase its output and sell inputs to it.

Income Maldistribution

This nineteenth-century theory of the cycle takes the position that wealthy people, who are a small minority of the population, do not spend proportionately as much out of their income on consumer goods as do society's poor. Today we would say that the average propensity to consume of the relatively rich falls as their income rises. Poor people, however, supposedly spend less in absolute dollars for consumer goods than the rich. During the upswing, income rises but the rich while spending more do not continue to spend at the same rate that income is rising. Eventually overproduction results and unsold goods remain. Prices and profits fall while unemployment goes up and production falters. This process continues until population growth causes demand to rise again.

There are some flaws in this theory. Although the average propensity to consume of richer people might be smaller than that of poorer people, there are a great many more poor people than rich people. Thus the major source of aggregate demand must come from the spending of the relatively poor, because there are too few rich to have a major effect on the aggregate. Also, how could population growth among people who are unemployed stimulate aggregate demand? When prices fall, it is true that any cash balances they hold are worth more. But are the cash balances worth so much more that they overcome the negative effect of a decline in wage income from falling prices and loss of jobs, as the classical model would suggest? Under conditions of job uncertainty, would not people be cautious about spending their money for anything other than basic consumer goods?

The economist Friedrich Hayek reports that in the booming decade before the crash of 1929 in the U.S., production rose by 30 percent while wages rose little. Consequently, profit returns to high income savers soared, and they invested in all kinds of fanciful and often foolish get-rich-quick schemes. However, the shift of profits toward big savers caused a major reshuffling in income shares among the population. People among the top 1 percent of the income distribution ladder raised their disposable income share from 12.2 to 18.9 percent, and people in the top 5 percent of the income distribution ladder raised their share from 24.3 percent to 33.5 percent of total national income. This left something like 60 percent of the 30 million remaining families in the U.S. with an average income of slightly less than $2,000 a year. The result was a substantial decline in aggregate demand. Today, however, a progressive tax structure and government transfer payments can act to reduce some of the income disparities across groups and boost aggregate demand.

Random Shocks

This theory, if you can call it that, states that business cycles are started by arbitrary wars and political events that display no consistent or predictable pattern to their occurrence. Thus, World War I was said to be partly, but significantly, caused by the June, 1914 assassination at Sarajevo, Austria of the Archduke Ferdinand, the heir to the Hapsburg empire. The severe inflation of the early 1970s was largely a result of stepped-up Vietnam military expenditures combined, many thought, with an erroneous tax policy—taxes should have been raised. The inflation of 1973 and thereafter and the downturns in 1974 and 1979 were directly related to the OPEC cartel's oil embargo of 1973 and the subsequent oil price increases through the remainder of the decade. The sharp rise in oil prices in 1979 were related to the overthrow of the Shah of Iran, since the revolution disrupted the commerce of the country, causing oil exports to the U.S. from Iran to drop substantially. Rising oil prices raise production costs that curtail production, then income, then aggregate demand.

Political events such as these can have far-reaching effects on economies. In response to outside shocks economic activity can be suddenly changed, driving nations into slumps or booms. In the end, the random shock hypothesis is simply an assumption about the initiating causes of cycles, and is not part of cycle theory itself.

Monetary Theories

Since the money supply has a great effect on economic activity, but with a lag and in ways not precisely understood, manipulation of the money supply and interest rates by the Federal Reserve is alleged to be as frequently on the wrong track as it is on the right track. The mistakes prove to be destabilizing to the economy. Thus, fiddling with the money supply is reputed to be a major reason for business cycles because it constantly alters expectations and economic behavior and prevents the economy from moving on a steady course of growth. Instead, in the monetary view, the economy follows an erratic course of stop and go related to the Federal Reserve's judgmental changes in the rate of growth of the money supply. Business cycles are, therefore, seen primarily as a money and banking problem.

INVESTMENT THEORIES

Changes in business investment spending have a major influence on aggregate economic performance.

Many economists hold the view that fluctuations in GNP stem from actions of decision makers who go through alternate moods of optimism and pessimism about the economy, which affect their investment decisions. Consumer spending and business investment behavior are thought to be subject to unpredictable whims in a complex relation between economic forces and the human psyche. However, psychological motives beg the question. Why do attitudes of consumers and investors change? Might not attitudes and expectations about the economy be simply the result of the economy's behavior—a symptom and not the cause? Negative attitudes might deepen the already existing downturn while positive attitudes might further encourage an already developing expansion, but it is difficult to know whether or not changing attitudes initiate the cyclical swings.

No doubt there are many forces at work in any business cycle, exerting pressure to a different degree in each cycle and making each cycle unique. If the explanations of the cycle were simple, there would be no problem. Nevertheless, there is general agreement that a major, if not the major, element that marks business cycles is changes in business investment spending.

Secular Stagnation

In the 1930s Alvin H. Hansen, a Harvard economist, proposed the theory that a maturing economy would reach a point of diminishing returns to growth as both geographical and investment frontiers dried up. *Secular* refers to cumulative effects leading to long-run trends. According to this theory, once the western United States was settled there was no more land to develop. Most of the railroads, dams, large electrical plants, and roads had been built. As affluence spread, additional demand for basic plant and equipment slowed down, so that capital growth wound down. To stimulate spending, it would be necessary for the government to prod the economy with fiscal stimulus, since returns to investment in the private sector were not now high enough to be a sufficient incentive. In the 1930s this argument had some appeal. It reappeared in the 1970s concerning the shortage of oil and energy in general. It seems to imply that there is a limit, an impassible frontier to human knowledge, imagination, and ingenuity beyond which there are no more useful ideas pointing to new ways to squeeze more output and profit from the earth's finite resources.

The Super Cycle?

Would you believe it if someone told you that capitalistic systems experience an overall supercycle lasting roughly half a century? In the mid-1920s the Russian economist Nikolai Kondratieff (Kahn-draht'-i-eff) said they do and went to jail for it. After studying historical economic data covering approximately 150 years, he hypothesized that capitalistic systems move in long waves or cycles lasting on the *average* a period of 50 years. If correct, the U.S. is due for its fourth Kondratieff cycle as illustrated in the graph. He gave no theory for the alleged phenomenon. It was merely an historical observation. The supercycle contains within it a number of the shorter, ordinary business cycles discussed in this chapter. However, the supercycle is purported to have three distinct phases: a long expansionary period of growth and rising prices, a relatively much shorter period when prices top off and settle down with economic activity flattening out, and a long period of falling output, employment, and prices. The downturn phase of the cycle is marked by an initial *primary recession*, then a plateau following a temporary cessation in the downturn, and finally a much deeper longer lasting *secondary slump*. An expansion beginning in the 1780s peaked about the year 1800, after which it began to fall gradually. About 1812 prices suddenly dropped, thus beginning the primary recession. The decline remained at a plateau lasting until about 1820. Then the secondary slump took over and terminated in approximately 1840. A new supercycle began its expansionary phase, reaching its peak roughly around 1855, after which the primary recession began, with the plateau lasting until about 1874. The secondary slump lasted until 1896, after which the expansionary phase of the third Kondratieff cycle began rising until early 1920. A short primary recession occurred from 1920 to mid 1921. The flattening out of the downturn persisted until 1929. Then the Great Depression continuing to 1941 signaled the secondary slump of the third wave.

Is the next supercycle upon us? Was the 1971–1973 recession a primary recession beginning the downturn of the fourth wave, and was 1973–1980 the plateau period before the secondary slump descends upon us? Or are we still in the plateau period? Though prices no longer seem to fall, the post-Vietnam inflation has resulted in smaller increases in real incomes and productivity, and profit rates since 1967 are below the rates of the 1945–1965 period. Is this sluggishness since 1967 evidence of the plateau period?

Kondratieff viewed the long cycle of capitalist economies of the West as a self-cleansing process — a retrenchment for future expansion. Since he did not say that capitalism would collapse after a series of these cycles according to Marxist doctrine, Stalin banished him to Siberia in 1930. He became mentally ill and ended up in solitary confinement and died there, a victim of ideological fanaticism.

Source: Alfred Malabre, Jr., *Wall Street Journal*, Oct. 12, 1979.

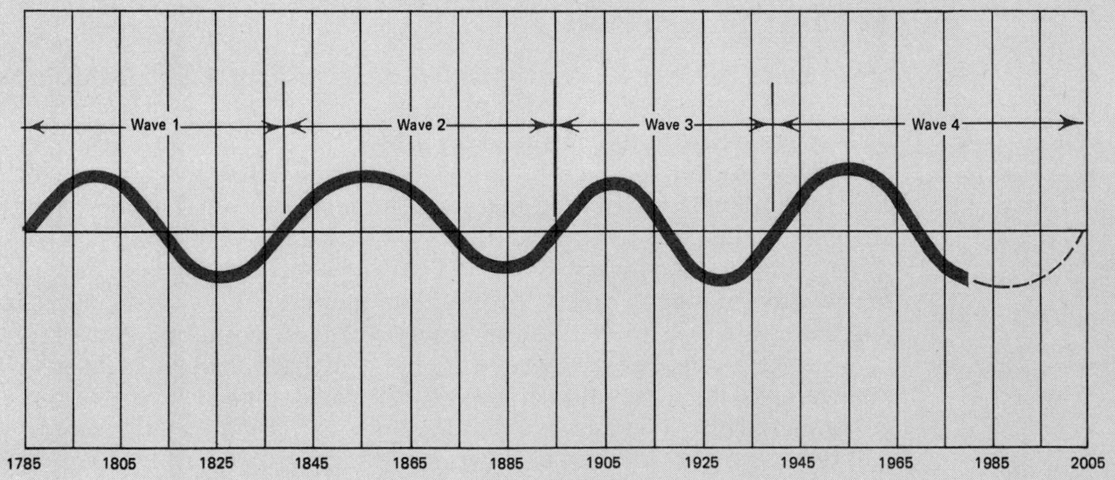

In the nineteenth century there was anxiety and pessimism about the emerging shortage of whale oil used as lubrication and as fuel for lamps. Prices were rising as demand increased relative to supply. Then Edison invented the incandescent lamp—the light bulb. There is no reason for assuming that there is only a certain, limited inventory of knowledge and ideas to pick from, like tomatoes in a box. New knowledge creates new questions and additional knowledge is gained in trying to answer them. Knowledge is an open ended, expanding adventure through history that makes it possible for mankind to extend from time to time the finite boundaries of resources.

Creative Destruction

***Creative destruction* is the process of replacing old with new technology. Introducing new methods causes business cycles that are a necessary ingredient of long–term economic growth.**

The vision of an unbounded frontier to human knowledge is expressed in the writings of the economist Joseph A. Schumpeter (Shum′-pay-ter), who put forth the hypothesis that the ups and downs of the business cycle were a necessary part of the capitalistic system, part of its growing pains in a process of creative destruction. In a system driven and nourished by profits, cycles lead to growth. In downturns inefficiency, deadwood, and even efficient machines are removed to clear the way for even more efficient machines, new growth, and a higher standard of living. According to Schumpeter, it is the inventor who creates new ideas and processes. But it is the innovator who puts the inventions to work for practical ends—and profit. Thus, the innovator—the entrepreneur—engages in implementing *autonomous* technological change as he pursues the dream of large profits. This kind of investment differs from *induced* investment, induced by a growth in aggregate demand. It was the innovators who built the railroads after the steam engine was invented and were the first to make the big profits. This activity causes an expansion in the economy. The profits then attract a host of imitators who, in their eagerness, overinvest and saturate the market. Many end up bankrupt, since the market is not big enough for all of them. Thus, the economy goes into a downturn, into a period of retrenchment as the imitators fall by the wayside. But the cycle turns up again as new innovators implementing new inventions get things moving again and push the economy to a new, higher standard of living until the next downturn and retrenchment. The business cycle is therefore a necessary evil. To smooth it out by taxing profits would be to remove the motivation provided by the possibility of large profits necessary for entrepreneurs to assume the large risks attendant to the implementation of new markets and technology. With no stimulus to innovation the standard of living would stagnate and the economic welfare of the people would decline.

Accelerator Theory

The *accelerator model* shows the impact of changes in consumer spending on investment spending.

Investment expenditures may be affected by random events or by government monetary and fiscal policies, the money supply, money demand, profits, contracting economic frontiers, and attitudes. The relation between investment by firms and spending on consumer durables by households is a strong one and can be traced in the data. It has given rise to the accelerator theory of business cycles. This is not a complete theory of investment, of course, but it does help explain the wide variation in the level of business investment over the cycle.

As you know, gross investment consists of investment spending by firms on plant and equipment, residential or nonresidential construction, and changes in inventories. The volume of investment spending is much less stable than either household consumption or government spending. The accelerator theory of business cycles accounts for this instability in investment spending by asserting that small changes in consumer purchases of durable goods give rise to much wider swings in investment. Consumer durables like cars, television sets, and washing machines are relatively expensive items that last for a long time. In a downturn, purchases of them can be postponed. But nondurables like food, clothing, and transportation to work on buses and trolleys cannot be postponed. Hence, their consumption varies little over the cycle. Thus a small increase in consumer demand for durables leads to a magnified change in purchases of capital equipment. Although the theory is able to predict wide fluctuations in investment, it has serious limitations as a theory of the business cycle. We shall discuss them after developing the model. We can formalize the acceleration effect with the formula

$$I = \Delta K = a\Delta Q$$

where K is the capital stock, I is investment and equals the change in the capital stock, ΔK, and ΔQ is the change in the output (sales) of consumer goods per period. When multiplied by a price index, the output is converted to money income. The letter a is a constant where $a = K/Q$, the capital/output ratio. For example when $a = 3$, its approximate aggregate historical value, it indicates that it requires $3 of capital investment to produce an output flow of $1 a year. Therefore, if the machine lasts for 6 years before it is fully depreciated, it produces a flow of $6 and more than pays for itself.

When $a = 3$, the change in consumer goods sold, ΔQ, produces a change in capital expenditures by 3 times the amount of the change in sales. Moreover, as we shall soon show, the level of investment spending depends not on the level of consumer goods sales but on the *rate of change* of consumer sales. Not only is the absolute change in the amount of sales important from period to period, but so also is the rate of change of the amount of sales. Do sales change by the same amount, or by increasing or decreasing amounts from period to period? The result of this relation is that the *rate of increase* of sales must not fall in order just to maintain the same level of investment expenditures. If the rate of sales falls, then it is multiplied by a, causing the change in investment to fall even farther. But if the rate of sales increases from one period to the next, the increase in investment expenditures is magnified and rises even faster.

ACCELERATOR CALCULATIONS

This section provides the round-by-round details of the accelerator in action. Take your ringside seat and observe fully. Knockout Company Inc. produces boxer trunks requiring the use of sewing machines costing $30,000 each. Individually the machines create $10,000 of output a year. The capital/output ratio is therefore equal to 3. Assume the firm currently owns 10 machines of different vintages such that one a year becomes worn out. Ten machines produce $100,000 worth of boxer trunks a year. Table 28-2 begins with year 1. Sales are $100,000 and 1 machine is replaced and no new machines are purchased. Gross investment is equal to the price of the replaced machine or $30,000. In year 2, sales increase by $10,000. One machine is replaced but 1 new one is added to provide for the increased $10,000 in sales. Thus, gross investment is 2 × $30,000 equals $60,000. Sales have increased 10 percent while investment has increased 100 percent. In dollars, gross investment has increased $30,000 when sales increased by $10,000. It is what one would expect with a capital/output ratio of 3. In year 3, sales again rise by $10,000 for a 9.1 percent increase. One machine is replaced and 1 new one added because of the induced investment created by the rise in sales. The total number of machines is increased to 12. This time investment is the same because, though sales increased absolutely, sales have not increased relative to the increase in second-year sales. The *rate* of sales must increase if the rate of investment is to rise. Instead, it fell from 10 percent to 9.1 percent. Assume that in year 4 sales increase by $20,000, for an increase of 16.7 percent over third-year sales. One machine is replaced but 2 new machines are required to provide for the extra $20,000 in sales. Gross investment is 3 × $30,000 equals $90,000, representing an increase of 50 percent over year-3 investment expenditures. In year 5 things slow down; there is no increase in sales over the previous year. Therefore, no new machine need be purchased, only the one replacement machine is needed. In this situation, a zero increase in sales over year 4 has resulted in a large decline in gross investment of 67 percent, from $90,000 to $30,000.

Suppose that in year 6 sales drop by $10,000 below fifth-year sales, for a decline of 7.1 percent. No new machine is purchased nor is the next worn-out machine replaced, so that gross investment falls by 100 percent. Therefore, the

TABLE 28-2

Year	Sales (dollars)	Percentage change in sales	Total machines operating	Replaced machines	New machines	Gross investment expenditures*	Percentage change in gross investment expenditures
1	$100,000	—	10	1	0	$30,000	—
2	110,000	10	11	1	1	60,000	100
3	120,000	9.1	12	1	1	60,000	0
4	140,000	16.7	14	1	2	90,000	50
5	140,000	0	14	1	0	30,000	−67
6	130,000	−7.1	13	0	0	0	−100
7	110,000	−15.4	11	0	−1	0	—
8	110,000	0	11	0	0	0	—
9	120,000	9.1	12	1	1	60,000	—

*Gross investment cannot be less than zero. It is impossible for negative net investment (disinvestment) to be greater than depreciation. Negative investment is at most equal to the depreciated machine that is not replaced (see chapter 23). The −1 in the New machine column refers to an idled machine, not a depreciated machine. This is another deficiency of the accelerator model.

levels of net investment and gross investment are zero. The total number of machines in use drops to 13. In year 7 things get worse as sales drop by $20,000 more. Another worn-out machine is not replaced. In addition, one working machine not yet ready for replacement is idled. The total number of machines in use is 11. Gross investment is already zero and cannot drop further. There is disinvestment, that is, net investment is negative since a machine is idled. In year 8 sales maintain the previous year's level of $110,000. Another machine wears out and is not replaced, but the idle machine is activated. Net investment and gross investment are again zero. Finally, suppose sales in year 9 jump up to $120,000. One machine is replaced but another one is added to produce the extra $10,000 worth of boxer trunks. Therefore, replacement is 1 machine and so is net investment; hence gross investment rebounds briskly to $60,000 with the number of machines increasing by 1 to a total of 12.

Except when gross investment hits zero, notice that the fluctuations in the percentage of investment expenditures are much greater than the percentage changes in consumer sales revenue.

ACCELERATOR-MULTIPLIER MODEL

The combination of *accelerator and multiplier models* predicts wide and amplified swings in GNP.

The accelerator and the Keynesian multiplier interact and reinforce the swings of the business cycle. We can trace the interaction between them. Since we have assumed that all output is sold, we can set $Q = C$. The accelerator relation now reads

$$I = a\Delta C.$$

The familiar relation expressing the effect on GNP of additional investment expenditures is

$$\Delta GNP = k_i \Delta I.$$

To get things going, suppose there is a tax increase that causes sales to decline. The result is a magnified decline in investment expenditures by firms. The drop in investment expenditures is transmitted through the Keynesian multiplier k_i to induce a magnified decline in GNP or GNY. Since consumption is a function of income, the decline in income causes sales to fall, which is once again transmitted through the accelerator to shock investment into a greater decline. Again, the fall in investment operates through the multiplier to further depress income. The sequence is illustrated by

> *C* down, *I* down more, *GNP* down more, *C* down, *I* down more, *GNP* down more, and so on.

where *down more* means the effect is magnified by either the multiplier or the accelerator as the case may be. The slump bottoms out when firms are finally forced to replace their fully depreciated equipment which they had stopped replacing because of idle capacity. The new investment expenditures stimulate employment and income in the capital goods sector, which through the mechanism of the multiplier spills over into the consumer good industries, lifting consumer spending. Consumer spending is accelerated and forces up investment spending again, and the cycle begins to enter into its recovery phase. When the recovery finally slows down as the economy approaches its upper capacity, the slowdown in sales again ripples through the system and creates a downward momentum once more.

DEFICIENCIES IN THE MODEL

Although the accelerator model explains why investment can change erratically in response to changes in consumer demand, it is only a partial explanation of investment behavior. There are a number of implicit assumptions in the model which greatly limit its acceptance as an adequate explanation of investment behavior.

1. The model assumes that capital equipment can be created almost instantaneously in response to a change in consumer sales. The gestation period for capital formation is relatively long. The lag in the production of capital is not accounted for.

2. The model assumes that all output is sold, which is not the case. Thus, inventory, a component of investment, is not treated in the model. Furthermore, in a period of recovery from a downturn in the economy, firms can increase sales without increasing the capital stock because of excess capacity—those idle machines can be reactivated.

3. Even if the firm were operating at full capacity, an increase in consumer demand in the short run can be handled by firms using existing capacity more intensely, for example, overtime work or second shifts. Thus, firms do not change the amount of their stock of capital when changes in demand are temporary or short-run. High sales of Christmas cards during the holiday are obviously only a temporary, seasonal, increase in sales. Increased plant capacity would not be the response to it.

4. As we learned in Chapter 23, there are several other important variables affecting the investment decision which are not included in the accelerator model; among them interest rates, expectations about future markets, and changes in technology. Thus, new technology can alter the capital/labor ratio as well as the capital/output ratio, since capital innovation may lower unit labor costs. That is, each worker using new equipment is more productive. It may take the shape of requiring less labor to produce the same amount of output or the same number of workers producing more output. At any rate, the relative price of the produced good may decline, thereby increasing the quantity of sales per unit of capital.

5. According to Chapter 23, gross investment cannot be less than zero. For it is impossible for negative investment (indicating a decline in the capital stock) to be greater than depreciation. But the table shows −1 under the new machine column for a machine that has not been depreciated but idled. This is

another deficiency in the model. Also, since gross investment cannot be less than zero, in a downturn the table shows that the percentage changes in gross investment expenditures are undefined. Thus, the model has little meaning in a downturn. Further, in a downturn, if a decline in consumer sales is particularly upsetting, the effect on businessmen's expectations could cause planned investment to decrease by more than the 3 times the decline in consumer sales.

FORECASTING

Economists, government officials, and businessmen are interested in changes in the level of business activity—in the changing levels of production, employment, and income. They would like to be able to forecast future activity in order to choose the appropriate policies that are to be pursued now. A firm wants to know if it should build another plant or step up production of heavy machinery. Since these things are not built and produced overnight, it wants to have some idea of economic conditions, say, 6 months or a year from now. The government would like to know if the economy is heading for a contraction or an expansion so it can head off a recession at the pass, or slow down a too-rapid expansion leading to a serious inflation. It can then use expenditures and taxes to counteract undesirable changes in the direction of the whole economy. When it does this, the government is engaging in stabilization policy. Thus the forecaster analyzes the past and current performance of certain business indicators that may shed light on future aggregate economic activity. To this purpose researchers have developed economic indicators. These are key statistical series providing the forecaster a clue to economic conditions. The forecaster must evaluate them and combine the information they yield with his own insights and judgments. Forecasting requires both analytical technique and art. For there exists no sure-fire method of calling all the turns in the business cycle. No two business cycles are identical; each has its own personality. This is not surprising, when one is reminded that they primarily stem from individual human choice and behavior in an environment of uncertainty about future events.

THE INDICATORS

No one variable can be the sole compass pointing the way for the whole economy. Therefore, statistical series measuring several economic activities are cumulated into a composite picture of the economy. The Department of Commerce analysts publish a list of primary indicators, each one in itself composed of a number of separate economic indices.

The original work on business indicators began in the deep recession of 1937, when the government requested the then National Bureau of Economic Research to put together a list of indicators that might be expected to signal a desperately hoped-for recovery. The work was begun by Wesley Mitchell and Arthur Burns, and extended in 1950 by Geoffrey Moore. The former two concluded that no single indicator existed, but they did come up with a list of some 21 indicators that appeared to be the most available, useful, and reliable within bounds.

Over time that list has changed and been revised so that today the list of composite indicators totals 22.[1] Of these, 12 are leading indicators, 4 are coincident indicators, and 6 are lagging indicators. They require some explanation.

***Leading indicators* precede and thus foretell the cycle.**

***Coincident indicators* coincide with and thus indicate the cycle.**

***Lagging indicators* follow and thus confirm the cycle.**

Leading indicators are indicators that turn down before the peak and up before the trough. In other words, they ideally anticipate impending changes in aggregate economic activity.

Coincident indicators coincide with turns in activity. They go down at the peak and up at the time of the trough. They verify that the turn is taking place.

Lagging indicators tend to confirm that the turn has taken place and to confirm movements in the coincident index. They go down after the peak and up after the trough.

There are six criteria used in determining which indicators will enter the list. They are as follows:

1. *Economic significance.* How well understood and how important for the business cycle are the variables.

2. *Statistical adequacy.* How good are the data and are there enough data based on monthly and quarterly time series.

3. *Timing at turns.* How consistently has the series led, lagged, or coincided with turns in the business cycle. This is the most important factor of the six.

4. *Conformity to historical cycles.* How regularly have the movements in a specific indicator reflected the expansions and contractions in the economy at large: that is, have not been thrown off or obscured by relatively large or random variations which have to be screened out.

5. *Smoothness.* How quickly can a real cyclical turn be identified and not confused with shorter and irregular movements not indicative of a major turn in economic activity at large. It is like tracking a missile with radar. If the missile changes direction, when does it become a turn? You do not want to project a turn when no turn is impending. Therefore, there is a time lapse from the turn to the recognition of the turn. The desire is to shorten that lag as much as possible and smooth transitions.

6. *Timeliness.* How promptly available are the data, and how frequently are they reported. This gets the least emphasis of the six.

Below is a list of the indicator groups with a brief explanation for each. Remember, these indicators do not predict correctly 100 percent of the time. In addition, there is not only the difficulty of predicting cyclical turns, but how long a recession or recovery will be, and what is the intensity, i.e., the amplitude of the cycle. Most of the time expansions endure longer than do contractions, as you can see by comparing the first two columns in Table 32-1.

[1] For full details and revisions see *Business Conditions Digest*, May 1975, Nov. 1975, and Nov. 1976 published by the Department of Commerce.

LEADING INDICATORS

1. *Average workweek.* A company tries to keep its skilled labor, so its first step toward expanding or curtailing production is to lengthen or shorten its workweek. This series measures the average number of hours per production worker per week. It includes levels up to that of foreman. Desk jobs are excluded.

2. *Net business formation.* Represents entries and departures of businesses from the total business population.

3. *Common stock prices.* Based on the Standard and Poors index of 500 common stocks.

4. *New building permits.* Authorized by local issuing departments on a month-to-month basis. Permits, of course, precede actual construction.

5. *Layoff rates in manufacturing.* Tends to lead more consistently at the troughs. Expressed as monthly rate per 100 employees. Includes employer-initiated suspensions from pay status which last, or are expected to last, more than 7 consecutive calendar days.

6. *Vendor performance.* Percentage of purchasing agents reporting slower monthly deliveries in the Greater Chicago area. Delivery slowdowns spread during expansions but begin to give way to speed-ups as the rate of growth and capacity utilization begin to fall, as often happens before a downturn.

7. *Contracts and orders for plant and equipment.* New contract awards to building, public works, and utilities contractors, including new orders received by manufacturers in the machinery and equipment industries. Specifically includes warehouses, garages, service stations, streets, highways, bridges, parks, sewage, electric and gas plants, shipbuilding, and railroads. Excludes farm machinery and machine shops, household appliances, communication equipment, and electrical components.

8. *Real money balances (in 1972 dollars).* M2 money deflated by the CPI. A reduction in real money balances normally anticipates a downturn and an increase anticipates an upturn.

9. *Percentage change in total liquid assets.* A weighted index consisting of holdings by the private domestic nonfinancial sector of currency, deposits at commercial banks and nonbank thrift institutions, savings bonds, credit union shares, short term marketable (resalable) Treasury securities, and commercial paper.

10. *Net change in inventories on hand and on order.* Consists of both manufacturing and trade inventories and unfilled orders (excluding unfilled orders for capital goods and defense products) received by manufacturers. If it increases, then sales are falling and a downturn follows.

11. *New orders for consumer goods and materials.* Includes new orders for durable goods (excluding capital and defense products) and for four nondurable goods industries which have unfilled orders: textile and mill products; paper and allied products; printing, publishing and allied products; leather and leather products.

12. *Percentage changes in sensitive prices.* The producer price index of

crude materials excluding foods and feeds. Crude materials consists of basic commodities entering the market for the first time at the production or assembling point. It does not include goods officially classified under manufacturing. It does include things like raw products of firms, fisheries, quarries, waste materials used in place of crude products, plant and animal fibers, oilseeds, sand and gravel, paper, iron, iron ore, leaf tobacco, steel scrap, coal, and crude petroleum.

COINCIDENT INDICATORS

1. *Number of employees on the nonagricultural payroll.* Includes government as well as part-time and temporary workers. Excluded are people on layoff, strike, the self-employed, military personnel, and domestics.

2. *Index of industrial production.* Is highly sensitive to fluctuations in demand and largely reflects manufacturing output.

3. *Personal income less transfer payments.* Excludes transfers since they are often countercyclical.

4. *Manufacturing and foreign trade sales.* Manufacturing sales is much better as a cyclical indicator than foreign trade sales, but the combination adds breadth and diversity.

LAGGING INDICATORS

1. *Labor cost per unit of output.* Measures the relationship between the volume of manufactured goods produced and the cost of labor related to their production; it also includes executive salaries, bonuses and tips, and fringe benefits. Unit labor costs rise after the peak and fall after the slump has bottomed out.

2. *Commercial and industrial loans outstanding.* Measures the average weekly dollar amount of business loans outstanding each month, including all loans for commercial and industrial purposes. Data come from 330 banks reporting to the Federal Reserve; normally increases after an expansion and declines after a contraction.

3. *Manufacturing and trade inventories.* Measures the end-of-month value in dollars of stocks on hand in manufacturing, retail, and merchant wholesalers establishments.

4. *Average duration of unemployment.* Measures length of time in weeks of the officially unemployed who have been continuously looking for work, or in cases of persons in layoffs, since the termination of most recent employment. A period of two weeks or more during which a person ceased looking for work is considered to break the continuity of the present period of seeking work.

5. *Ratio of consumer installment debt to personal income.* Measures the

The Great Depression

Do you know people over 50 years of age who turn the lights out when they leave a room or are inclined to store things instead of throwing them out? They were born or grew up during the Depression which spanned the years between 1929 and 1941. The Dow-Jones fell from an all-time high of 381 in September 1929 to an ultimate low of 41 in July 1932, a decline of 339 points. There is no single answer to this complex world-wide economic disaster, which saw GNP fall from $104.4 billion in 1929 to $72.7 billion in 1933 and rise again to only $100.5 billion by 1938 (in 1929 constant dollars). Unemployment was only 1,550,000 in 1929 (3.2 percent of the labor force) and increased to 12,830,000 in 1933 (24.9 percent of the labor force); it fell to 10,390,000 (19 percent) by 1938. When one adds the families of those unemployed, one can estimate perhaps over 40,000,000 people were affected in a population of less than 130,000,000. The CPI (1929 = 100) fell from 100 in 1929 to 75.2 in 1933 and by 1938 had risen to only 82.2. Per capita income fell nearly 30 percent between 1929 and 1933. However, for those with jobs the average decline in money wage rates was only 18 percent, hence their real incomes went up. Corporate profits in 1936 were one fifth below the 1926–1928 average. Farm income was down severely.

Some of the reasons offered for the Depression of the 1930s were:

1. Overexpansion of steel and durable goods production, particularly automobiles, in response to the booming prosperity of the 1920s, resulting in excessive inventories. Some one third of U.S. families had cars in 1920 and three fourths of them by 1929. There was also a surplus of residential housing and office buildings. Firms began to cut back production to reduce the excess inventories.
2. Credit overextension: Mortgages and consumer installment buying increased greatly by 1929 backed with little liquidity (hard cash) by consumers. When markets began to falter, calls on installment and other loans picked up, causing defaults and foreclosures to accelerate. The easy credit policy was abetted by the easy money policy of the Federal Reserve in the 1920s, which was passive about commercial banks expanding loans in expectation of larger profits in an environment of pervasive optimism in the nation. Often these loans were used for speculation. In 1928 the Fed did a turnabout; interest rates went up. Instead of borrowing more, firms resorted to issuing large amounts of common stock to raise capital. Margins on stocks in the 1920s were very low, 10 to 20 percent; that is, one could deposit 20 percent in cash against the stock's value and the brokerage firm would carry you by lending the difference. Once stock prices began to fall, investors did not have the liquidity or the collateral to pay off the difference; loans could not be repaid, firms went bankrupt, and the economy rapidly contracted as the pyramid of credit collapsed. With it went the great expectations of 1.5 million American stock-

dollar value of consumer installment debt outstanding at the end of each month per dollar of monthly personal income. Tends to fall after an expansion when employment goes up and rise when employment goes down.

6. *Average prime rate charged by banks.* The interest rate commercial banks charge most creditworthy customers on short-term loans. Its movements tend to greatly lag general business activity and open market money rates. It moves infrequently, although in recent years it has bounced around some.

Facts to Keep in Mind

There are five pieces of empirical information related to the business cycle that we will list here. Before their importance can be understood, it will be neces-

holders. The automobile and steel industries felt it first, then construction and farming.

3. Foreign markets: Another push toward collapse was related to the European monetary crisis of 1931. Whether the downturn started here or abroad is hard to say, but when the U.S. stubs its toe the world hurts. In May 1931, the Vienna Bank, Credit Anstalt, failed. Many Europeans had deposits there. They rushed to withdraw their funds. Eventually the panic spread to other European central banks finally reaching London, causing the Bank of England to cease converting the pound sterling into gold. Panicky holders of sterling then rushed to convert them into dollars to then exchange these dollars for U.S. held gold. Since our money stock was based on the amount of gold in U.S. coffers, the Fed, in order to prevent the outflow of gold, tried to stimulate investment by foreigners in the U.S. by inducing foreigners to use their dollars to buy U.S. securities instead of U.S. gold. So the Fed raised the discount rate from 1 percent to 3.5 percent. This action caused a serious contraction of U.S. bank reserves in an already ailing economy. Other nations tried to impede contractions in their economies by raising import taxes and setting up import quotas; foreign trade slowed greatly as other countries retaliated by setting up their own trade barriers. The U.S. increased tariffs on over 20,000 items with passage of The Smoot-Hawley Tariff Act on June 17, 1930.

4. As state revenues fell because of rising unemployment, following the balanced-budget mentality of the times, states raised taxes and reinforced the decline in aggregate demand and employment. In 1932 the federal income tax rate limit was pushed from 25 percent to 63 percent.

Postscript

Keynes and other contemporaries believed the free market system had serious shortcomings. It was not always self corrective. Monetary policy was felt to be ineffective in deep recessions. Attempted increases in the money supply only resulted in banks building up excess liquidity to protect themselves against runs and expected interest rate increases. Firms refused to borrow in a climate of pessimism. Monetary policy failed because one cannot force banks to lend or firms to borrow. Fiscal stimulation was the answer, said the Keynesians. Not so, said the monetarists: They allege that Fed policies turned a normal business downturn into an avalanche. The money supply fell by 33 percent form 1929 to 1933. By then, counteractive monetary policy was ineffective because it was too little, too late. Free markets were not the problem; foolish, late, feeble monetary policy was. The Fed failed to provide adequate liquidity to cover demand deposit withdrawals from member banks by the public. The public panicked, and runs on the bank occurred causing over 9,000 out of 24,700 banks to shut down by 1933. This controversy between the Keynesians and monetarists remains alive today.

See Lester Chandler, America's Greatest Depression, 1929–1941 (New York: Harper and Row, 1970).

Quit rates, labor productivity, real wages, prices, and profits behave predictably over a cycle.

sary to understand more about labor markets and inflation, to be discussed in upcoming chapters. Keep them in mind.

1. Quit rates are the rates at which people choose to leave their jobs. The quit rate falls during a recession and rises during an expansion in the economy over the course of the business cycle.

2. Labor productivity usually declines during a recession and rises during an expansion—or at least during the recovery phase of an expansion.

3. The real wage bill typically moves in the *same* direction as employment. When employment is rising during an expansion total real wages rise, and when employment is declining total real wages decline. Recall that the real wage bill equals the money wage bill divided by the price level.

4. During early phase of a downturn in the economy firms do not reduce the money wage rate paid to employees. They tend instead to retain them for a

while in anticipation that the downturn may be only temporary. But if the economic slowdown continues, workers are eventually laid off. Therefore, workers are not given the option of staying on at a lower wage rate. These workers then become involuntarily unemployed.

Also, during a downturn many companies, particularly the large ones, tend not to lower their prices. In fact, their prices may even rise despite a slowdown in the economy. During an upturn prices will rise, but not as rapidly for larger firms as for smaller ones.

5. Profits rise rapidly during booms because prices are flexible upward. During downturns, even if prices still rise unit labor costs rise faster so that profits do not rise proportionately with the price level.

CHAPTER SUMMARY

Business cycles or business fluctuations are recurrent, nonperiodic variations in the economy's real GNP. Although recurrent they are not periodic because they do not appear with predictable frequency and for predictable periods of time. Expected seasonal variations are not counted as cycles. To be officially counted as a business fluctuation a variation in real GNP must last at least 15 months, with an upward or downward phase lasting at least 5 months, according to definitions used by the U.S. Department of Commerce.

Consumer durables (goods defined as lasting a year or more) and capital goods tend to move in longer and deeper cycles, while purchases of perishable goods (defined as lasting less than a year) are relatively invariant.

The length of time of a cycle is called the period, and the depth of a cycle its amplitude. Amplitude is measured vertically from an imaginary trend line. The period can be measured from peak to peak or trough to trough. Peaks are upper turning points and troughs lower turning points.

Because one business fluctuation may be longer than another does not mean it was more severe. Cycles arise from many cumulative effects so that each one has unique characteristics.

In the nineteenth century, sunspots were offered as a cause of business cycles. Since economies were mostly agrarian, changes in weather caused by sunspots affected crop yield, which affected the use of transportation equipment and therefore steel production. Also, significant changes in income distribution were thought to cause business fluctuations. The average propensity to consume of the rich is lower than that for the poor. Hence, the greater is the income share going to the relatively few rich, the lower is total spending by the many more poor, causing a net decline in aggregate demand.

Another possible source of business cycles is the random shock theory. The sudden emergence of arbitrary political events and wars disrupts commerce, destabilizing the economy. Monetary theories connected business cycles to the banking system and unpredictable variations in the money supply caused by bank policies.

Economists agree that, however induced, changes in investment spending have a major influence on aggregate economic performance. The accelerator model shows how changes in consumer spending have an accelerated impact on investment spending wherein changes in sales generate even wider percentage changes in investment spending. When the accelerator model is combined with the multiplier model, wide swings in GNP are predicted to occur and to be amplified.

Deficiencies of the accelerator model are the implicit assumptions that capital is instantaneously created, all output is sold, there is no allowance for new technology that changes the capital/output and capital/labor ratios assumed fixed by the accelerator (a) of the model, and in downturns the model implies that gross investment could be less than zero, which it cannot.

The secular stagnation theory proposed first in the 1930s by Alvin Hansen depends on the notion that a mature economy reaches a frontier limit of investment possibilities where additional investments would yield smaller and smaller gains to productivity, hence declining profits, because of dwindling open land area and market saturation.

Joseph Schumpeter introduced the term creative destruction, contending that business cycles are a necessary ingredient of long-term economic growth. Entrepreneurs take inventors' ideas and market them for practical ends in the pursuit of profit. These profits attract new entrants and overload the market, eliminating the imitators and the deadwood. New growth is stimulated by the more imaginative high-risk rollers who gamble on putting to practical application yet newer techniques that move the economy out of the downturn and again raise its living standards.

In order to minimize the depth and duration of business cycles, forecasters attempt to understand them and smooth out the fluctuations in real GNP. The tracking and prediction of cycles is based on analyzing and interpreting the 12 leading indicators, the 4 coincident indicators, and the 6 lagging indicators, for a total of 22. Leading indicators are defined as those that turn down prior to the peak and up prior to the trough. Coincident indicators coincide with the cycle, peaking and troughing when the cycle does, indicating the cycle is in a turn. Lagging indicators turn down after the peak and up after the trough, confirming that the turn has indeed occurred. However, indicators are not foolproof and their successful interpretation also depends upon the particular insights and art of the forecaster. Studies of cycles have revealed that quit rates, labor productivity, real wages, prices, and profits tend to behave in a predictable and consistent way over the cycle.

QUESTIONS

1. The tendency of inflation to persist since World War II even during economic contractions has led economists to stress the study of real variables compared to nominal variables expressed in current prices. How is it possible that real declines in the economy may be obscured?
2. Business fluctuations are cycles but not periodic cycles. Explain. Does this sentence fit with cycle expert Wesley Mitchell's statement, "Business history repeats itself, but always with a difference."
3. What classification of indicator is it that keeps rising for a brief while after a recession sets in, and falls for some months after an economic recovery starts?
4. Suppose a businessman says, "More than anything else the shape of this recession from here on and the timing of the turnaround will be determined by what happens to inventories. Sometimes the lag involved in pulling inventories in line with sales produces a V-shaped recession. Production plunges, and until inventories are sold they shoot up again when new orders are placed." Is there a theory that can account for a V-shaped recession? Explain.
5. Refer to Table 28-1 to specify the following:
   a. The beginning and final months and years in which a contraction lasted 14 months.

b. The beginning and final months and years an expansion lasted for 39 months.
c. The dates the cycle lasted 117 months from trough to trough.
d. The length of the cycle from peak to peak from December 1969 to November 1973.

6. How do we immediately know when an economy has entered a recession?
7. Suppose the real GNP drops sharply for one quarter, climbs a very small amount the next quarter, and then drops sharply again in the next quarter. Would this 9-month pattern constitute a bona fide recession even though real GNP had not fallen for 2 consecutive months? What else would you need to know?
8. Suppose in the last recession overall real corporate profits after taxes dropped nearly 40 percent, consumer loan delinquencies increased 50 percent, factory capacity fell from 88 percent to 71 percent, the unemployment rate doubled to 9 percent, the money supply went up slightly, after tax income saved by consumers rose, and the number of new private housing starts went down. Does each situation fit a specific indicator? If not, to what broad indicator might it be related?
9. To what hypothesis would you attribute cycles caused by the following?
   a. Saudi Arabia undergoes a political coup and reduces oil exports to the U.S. by half.
   b. The rich get poorer and the poor get richer through new tax changes.
   c. Antarctica bursts with new U.S. settlements.
   d. All the carrier pigeons and starlings confused by strong magnetic disturbances around the earth descend on Iowa, destroying the corn crop used to feed livestock as well as humans.
   e. "Sales are down. We'll have to cut back operations."
   f. The Fed reduced the size of the monetary base.
10. Each one of the 20 lathes in a shop costing $20,000 apiece can be used to turn 10,000 funnels a year selling for $1 each. Beginning in the 7th year the shop begins to replace 1 lathe a year. Suppose sales from the 7th to the 11th year are respectively $200,000, $210,000, $230,000, $230,000, and $200,000. What is the capital/output ratio? The total number of lathes operating each year? How many lathes are replaced and added or idled each year? And what are gross investment expenditures each year? What is the percentage increase in sales in the 8th year? If the MPC equals 3/4, what is the effect on national income when sales increase in the eighth year?

Chapter 29

Stabilization Policy

PROGRESS REPORT

A. In Chapter 28 we learned something about the ups and downs of the aggregate economy over the years. Although with the policies in recent years we have been able to prevent the reoccurrence of deep depressions, we have not eliminated recurrent downturns in business activity.

B. This chapter provides us with a glance into the formulation and implementation of stabilization policies – policies designed to stabilize economic activity, that is, to prevent inflation and also to prevent unemployment and depression. Principal policies described are, of course, monetary and fiscal. The chapter ends with the debate between two schools of thought concerning the relative effectiveness of fiscal and monetary policy in regulating aggregate demand.

C. In Chapter 30 we shall take a closer look at the problem of unemployment and specific characteristics of labor markets and wages.

Stabilization policy employs *monetary* and *fiscal* tools.

To maintain economic stability, our government employs **monetary** and **fiscal** tools in an attempt to control business fluctuations. It is not desirable for the economy to experience either severe downturns in employment or output, or to undergo a too-rapid expansion that starts prices rising rapidly and steeply. The ideal is to have steady growth and maintain full employment while keeping prices steady—no easy task.

FISCAL POLICY

***Fiscal policy* is the automatic or discretionary use of government spending, taxes, and debt management to adjust employment, prices, and aggregate demand.**

Fiscal policy is the use of government spending, taxes, and debt management to adjust employment, prices, and aggregate demand. Increased government spending and/or lowering taxes will raise aggregate demand. Lower government expenditures and/or raising taxes will reduce the level of aggregate demand. Fiscal policy was sponsored by Keynes during the 1930s when he argued—rightly or wrongly—that the economy was too depressed for monetary policy to work.

Fiscal stabilizers are of two related kinds; automatic (or built-in) and discretionary. Discretion means exercising judgment, and discretionary policy reflects a deliberate act by Congress or the President that changes government expenditures or taxes and directs how those taxes and expenditures are to be structured. The effects of a single act of law may be long-lasting. For example, a tax may be set up in such a way that tax collections change automatically in the economy without Congress having to take any further deliberate action about them as the level of national income fluctuates over the business cycle. Thus, when the economy is in an upswing taxes will rise and operate to moderate the expansion so that the economy does not overheat as much as it otherwise would. Or, during a downswing in the cycle when household income is declining because of layoffs and fewer working hours, government expenditures that transfer income to households are automatically activated. For example, if you decide to install a thermostat in your house in order to conserve fuel, this is a judgment about energy control on your part—a discretionary act. However, once the thermostat is built into the house it operates automatically without any decision on your part other than setting its temperature level. It shuts off the burner when the temperature gets too high and turns it on when the temperature is too low, thus maintaining the house—or room—near a steady level without any interference on your part thereafter. In an analogous way built-in stabilizers, once implemented through discretionary action by Congress, help slow down a decline in GNP when GNP is falling, and also help slow down a rise in GNP when GNP is rising.

Examples of Discretionary Fiscal Policy

The first occasion on which the U.S. Congress cut taxes for the express purpose of stimulating a slow-moving economy was in 1964 under the leadership of President Johnson. The tax cut proposal had originally been put forward by

President Kennedy and the Chairman of the Council of Economic Advisors, Walter Heller. Unfortunately, the escalation of hostilities in Vietnam began in 1965, and many thought it was a poor time to have cut taxes. By contrast, Congress was in session in June of 1951 when the Korean War began, and it promptly raised taxes to insure that the military could make its expenditures out of tax revenues and without generating budget deficits. The effect was that we had little domestic inflation as a result of the Korean War. In this case the deliberate policy act was a discretionary stabilizer helping to moderate aggregate demand, whereas the idea behind the 1964 tax cut was to spur the economy on.

Since 1964 there have been occasions on which a surcharge has been placed on the income tax. There have also been tax credits that reduce the amount of taxes that some people must pay. Some policymaking authorities have suggested that the President be given discretionary authority to raise or lower taxes by as much as 5 percent if he feels that a tax change is warranted by economic conditions. However, Congress has, under the Constitution, the power to authorize taxes and spending, and this authority is jealously guarded.

Examples of Automatic Fiscal Stabilizers

The progressive income tax and unemployment benefits are examples of automatic *fiscal stabilizers.*

The principal example of an automatic fiscal stabilizer is the income tax. As the economy moves into a cyclical upswing, the amount of taxes collected under a given income tax rate structure will increase. This increase in taxes will act as a restraint on expansion. The increased amount of taxes collected cannot cause a downturn in the economy because taxes only increase if the economy is actually moving up.

Similarly, in the downswing of the economy the amount of taxes collected will decrease, leaving more relative income for families to spend. This spending means that the economy will not falter to the extent it otherwise might.

And, of course, the income tax in the U.S. is based on a graduated scale. Thus, not only do tax collections rise as income rises, but *average effective tax rates* also rise as individual incomes go into higher marginal tax brackets.

A second significant automatic stabilizer with important implications for the economy is unemployment compensation. When the economy moves into a downturn workers become unemployed, and this triggers the spending of reserve funds to provide the unemployed with purchasing power. With this purchasing power in hand, aggregate spending in the economy does not decline to the extent it otherwise would. The timing of compensatory spending is also more immediate in its effects than income tax changes, since some of the tax effects are only realized at the time of tax filing. The effects from spending have a quick impact.

Indexed Taxes

Some economists have argued that inflation puts people into higher tax brackets when it should not be allowed to do so. Let us say your wages go up by 50 percent, and the prices of everything you buy also go by 50 percent. If other things remain unchanged you are just as well off as before since you have the same purchasing power as before. Then the Internal Revenue Service gets into the act. Your marginal tax rate rises from 10 to 15 percent. Thus the Federal Government exacts 15 percent of your added income instead of 10 percent. So, because of graduated tax brackets you end up worse off. In Canada the tax rate is adjusted (indexed) to erase this effect of inflation on income taxes and proposals to do the same in the U.S. have been mentioned. But if one of the appropriate policies to combat inflation is to collect more taxes, then to erase the effect of inflation on tax collections will reduce the extent of the restraining effect of income taxes on the economy. It is uncertain, therefore, whether using indexed taxes as a built-in stabilizer is wise macroeconomic policy. Another view is that it is favorable because by indexing taxes no quiet tax increases from inflation or illusory tax decreases offset by inflation could be pulled off. Thus, if the government wanted to increase its spending it would have to openly raise taxes.

There are other fiscal programs that operate automatically to stabilize the economy, but the income tax and unemployment compensation are the two most important.

THE NATIONAL DEBT

Debt management is also a tool of fiscal policy. When the government spends more than it collects from taxes, it has to borrow money in order to finance its deficit. It could, of course, simply print more paper money as it did during the Revolutionary War and again during the Civil War. But this is frowned upon as not being an example of sound finance for it is likely to be very inflationary.

The national debt arouses the concern of many citizens both in and out of government. There are, however, several misconceptions about the national debt that compel people to cry out for a balanced budget to allay their anxieties. Upon clarification, the national debt is not nearly as bad as most people think.

The debt is a result of past and current fiscal policies. The idea is that when aggregate demand is slack with too much unemployment existing, government deficits would pump up the economy. And when aggregate demand is too strong, causing inflation, budget surpluses would suppress the excess demand. Federal deficits are neither necessarily a blessing nor a curse. It depends when they are used and to what extent.

Owed to Whom?

The federal government borrows to pay its debt by selling *bonds* to private citizens and institutions.

The national debt is owed to individuals and organizations who have purchased government **bonds** issued by the U.S. Treasury. This constitutes an act of borrowing from the public. Although some of the bonds are sold to foreigners, U.S. bonds are for the most part purchased internally. Therefore, the U.S. national debt is primarily owed by domestic taxpayers to domestic bond buyers.[1] When the bonds mature the government must pay back the principal (the original price of the bond) plus interest. Now suppose the bonds come due and the government still has not collected enough taxes to pay them all off. What does it do? The Treasury can sell more bonds to raise the money to pay off the original bondholders. This is called **rolling over** the debt. Sounds like some kind of a shell game, does it not? But it is a fact. And it works so long as the new bondholders are confident they will be paid when the bonds mature. They have this confidence for the simple reason that the government has a monopoly in the printing of money. As a last resort, it can always do this if it cannot sell enough new bonds. It can avoid default by running the printing press. On the other hand it can always raise interest rates (the yield on the bond) and be assured that it can sell more new bonds before resorting to printing more money.

Rolling over the debt is selling new securities to pay off matured securities.

Will not future generations have to pay the higher interest costs? Yes. But the payments will go primarily to other citizens who purchase the bonds. Thus, the national debt is essentially an internal one. It is owed by some U.S. citizens to other U.S. citizens. It stays in the family, except for the share of it that is owned by foreign bondholders.

So long as some U.S. citizens are repaying other U.S. citizens, the money stays and circulates within the economy and U.S. citizens in general do not have to give up real goods and services because of the debt. Viewed from this perspective, the economy need never go bankrupt in the same sense that a firm can go bankrupt. Furthermore, the government does not withhold the money from the circular flow, it injects it into the economy and stimulates aggregate demand. This creates income magnified by the multiplier, thereby creating more taxable income which helps pay off the bonds. When there is government debt, spending is taking place and aggregate demand is stimulated. When aggregate demand is depressed debt creation is a good thing for the economy.

Government Debt and Inflation

National debt financing need not be inflationary unless it is monetized by the Fed.

Do federal deficits cause inflation? Not necessarily. Whether deficits are inflationary or not depends on their size and how they are financed. If the deficit is financed by selling bonds to the public it is not inflationary. What the bondholders would otherwise spend is spent by the government. This principle also applies to corporations in the private sector, which borrow by selling bonds to the public, and to private sector individuals who borrow the savings of other individuals. None of these borrowings should significantly change aggregate demand. In government borrowing, interest payments simply transfer purchasing power from taxpayers to bondholders.

However, if aggregate demand is already near full employment, and the Treasury issues new securities which in large part are not bought by the public but by the Federal Reserve, the Fed's collaboration allows the government's borrowing to increase spending, bank reserves, and demand deposits, raising aggregate demand and prices. The Fed is said to monetize the debt. It is as if

[1]The size of the foreign debt is growing. It has gone from about 4 percent of federal government debt in the 1960s to about 14 percent by 1980.

new money is printed. The private sector does not have its debt monetized. Thus government deficits can be inflationary in a way that private deficits are not. The larger the monetized federal debt the greater is the potential for inflation, unless aggregate demand is significantly down. Uncontrolled inflation can destabilize the economy and throw it back into a recession, even a depression, because the inflation can instill a high degree of uncertainty into business decisions, thus causing investment expenditures to drop significantly.

Another problem with a large federal deficit is the negative effect it might have on private investment because of crowding out. We shall get to this soon.

The Debt Burden of Fiscal Policy

Although most of the national debt is owed by U.S. citizens to other U.S. citizens, there is still a question of which U.S. citizens bear the burden of the debt. Specifically, who will end up paying the taxes to pay off the interest on the bonds? There are two schools of opinion. The first is that the current generation will pay the debt. The second is that future generations will bear the tax burden.[2]

Suppose the government sells bonds to the public in order to generate funds to build a dam to produce electric power. The first group would claim that the burden is only borne by the current generation. Building the dam uses up labor and current materials that would otherwise have been used to produce something by the private sector. Therefore, the reduction of output in the private sector is replaced by the increase in output, the dam, in the public sector. This is true even if the debt is repaid 2, 3, 4 or more years from now when the government must repay the bondholders plus interest. The net effect is zero because the public who benefits from the dam pays for it with taxes. Future generations benefit by getting the dam financed by the debt they inherit. Like individuals, generations get what they pay for.

The majority view holds that the burden of the national debt is not passed on to *future generations,* except to a small extent.

However, the second group takes the position that **future generations** bear the burden of the debt and the current generation gets the dam free of charge. The argument goes that current generation bond buyers buy the bonds voluntarily. They willingly sacrifice some current consumption in order to consume more later because of the interest they earn. But bondholders do not gain or lose because they bought public bonds to build the dam rather than corporate private bonds to build something else. For the corporate bonds to be competitive, they would have to pay the same rate of interest as the government bonds. Therefore bondholders are indifferent between government and private bonds. Nonetheless, future taxpayers must still pay the interest on the government bonds. Hence, a big part of the tax burden is shifted to them. This position is only held by a small minority of economists. And most economists believe any burden on future generations is of a low magnitude. For it is the current generation that sacrifices the *real* resources (labor, materials). Furthermore, if the economy is not fully employed, the opportunity cost of those otherwise unemployed resources is zero.

[2]See Edgar and Jacquelene Browning, *Public Finance and the Price System* (New York: The Macmillan Co., 1979), pp. 391–395.

Crowding Out

Heavy government borrowing at high interest rates may *crowd* private investment *out* of the capital market.

One approach to the net burden versus net benefit effects from one generation to the next hinges on the amount of capital stock future generations inherit, how government expenditures are financed, and whether the economy was fully employed or not.

Suppose the economy is already fully employed and the government decides to build another dam which is completely financed by taxes paid by the current generation that must therefore reduce its current level of consumption. The government incurs no debt because it sells no bonds for the project. Hence, the government does not compete with the private sector for loanable funds by selling bonds to the public. And the current generation bears the tax burden. There is an inflationary bias because the balanced budget multiplier is expansionary.

However, suppose the government had financed the dam with borrowed money from selling bonds to the public. As we know, many of these bonds are purchased with the savings of households. These savings of households are a source of investment capital for firms. In order for the government to induce lenders to buy its bonds, it raises the yield on the bonds—the interest rate. This forces private corporations to raise their yield since they compete for funds by selling bonds too. The higher rate of interest forces firms to lower their investment expenditures as they reduce the amount of their bond issues. The government is said to crowd out the private sector from the financial capital market. Increased government expenditures on the dam simply reduce private investment expenditures by the same amount. Whereas in the previous example higher taxes lowered consumer spending, in this example social overhead capital (the dam) is created in the place of private capital (machines, factories). Future generations inherit the same amount of physical capital but of a different kind. Also, the stock of capital passed onto future generations may still be less if—as is argued by some—the government is not as efficient as the private sector. However, society will get a dam that it is unlikely any private firm would have built.

Crowding out may not occur if the economy is operating below full employment. If government spending on the dam occurred during a recession, then no net tax burden need be passed on to future generations. The government deficit stimulates aggregate demand and creates employment, income, and perhaps generates an equal amount of private savings that would not otherwise have occurred. Although taxpayers must pay the interest on the bonds, they also earn income they would not otherwise have earned. Again, future generations inherit a larger stock of capital than they otherwise would have since equivalent investment by the private sector would not have been made in a less than fully employed economy.

Distribution Effects

The prior discussion dealt primarily with the tax burden for either current or future generations. However, in either case, there are transfers of income *within* generations because of government created debt that must be repaid whether or not there are tax bearing effects *across* generations.

Too Much Debt?

The government can continue to pay off its old debts by creating new debt. So long as the government can find buyers for its new bond issues it can use the revenues to pay off interest on the old bonds. If necessary, it can always print more money. This is done by selling its bonds to the Federal Reserve System, which then creates a deposit account for the Treasury.[3] The Treasury can spend this money just as it could spend its tax collections. The money was created for the Treasury just as a commercial bank creates money for its depositors when it has excess reserves. Thus, the government's agencies, the Treasury and the Fed, can work together to, in effect, print money and pay off debts.

Can the federal debt held by the public become too large? What is too large, and what is the consequence of a large debt? The numbers below show the ratio of the federal debt to GNP in selected years.

End of Year	Federal debt as a percent of GNP
1945	122
1950	83
1955	60
1960	49
1965	40
1970	29
1975	27
1979	27
1980	28

Source: *U.S. Budget in Brief.*

Thus, even as the federal debt rises in absolute terms it steadily fell as a percentage of GNP since World War II. The economy has been growing faster than the federal debt. This signifies that the economy is better able to generate increased tax revenues to pay off the debt. Notice that in the 1970s while the ratio was falling, inflation skyrocketed. One cannot necessarily conclude, however, that the federal debt is not a major source of inflation, since the way that the debt is financed is important. Inflation in the 1970s was assisted by other factors, for example, the OPEC cartel's price fixing. In 1979, when the inflation rate was about 16 percent, it was estimated that about 7 or 8 percent of it was because of higher OPEC oil prices.

The 1945 figure above is high because of the heavy borrowing to finance World War II. However, debt size cannot be ignored. If spending raises the debt

[3] The Federal Reserve does not normally purchase debt directly from the Treasury. The Treasury sells to the public and then the Fed buys it back. The result is as if the Fed bought directly from the Treasury.

faster than the growth in GNP, more taxes have to be collected to finance the deficit. If taxes are not raised to cover the deficit and the government resorts to financing the deficit by creating more money by the Federal Reserve monetizing the Treasury's debt, then aggregate demand can rise faster than aggregate supply. This causes prices to rise. Rising prices to one become higher incomes to others and place these individuals into higher marginal tax brackets. In fact, peoples' real incomes may rise very little. Thus inflation acts as an implicit or hidden tax. The real debt of the government actually falls because it is repaying bondholders with cheaper money. Furthermore, the inflationary tax may seriously reduce incentives on the part of workers as they are pushed into higher marginal tax brackets. It is not clear what the effect would be on firms since their real debt, like the government's, becomes smaller as a result of inflation.

If the government decides to reduce the debt/GNP ratio by raising explicit taxes, it may also adversely affect aggregate supply because it may again lower incentives of people to produce. Moreover, if the Fed does not monetize the debt, aggregate demand is also affected, for the increased taxes reduce disposable income and therefore consumption. Business expectations are adversely affected by the increase in excess capacity because of cutbacks in production, further reducing consumption; then via the accelerator income drops further. Hence the economy could experience a serious contraction if the Treasury chooses to retire a substantial part of the federal debt by raising taxes.[4] It leaves the economy with less ability to generate taxable income.

During a recession, government deficit spending can stimulate aggregate demand and raise employment.

Properly managed debt can be a helpful tool of stabilization. If the government can borrow money from bondholders, then the additional government spending it makes possible may create jobs and raise national income that yields higher tax revenues. Ironically, therefore, the debt may actually be reduced because of an increase in the initial borrowing by the government. This has been the traditional Keynesian philosophy of fiscal policy in a less than fully employed economy.

The Balanced Budget ($\Delta G = \Delta T$)

An annually *balanced budget* can magnify cyclical swings in GNP.

With discussion of the national debt behind us, we offer a few parting words about the sentiment expressed by many for a balanced budget. To have a budget always balanced is *not* necessarily a desirable ambition. Assume aggregate demand falls for some reason and the economy is in a recession in the current period. Since income in the period is down so are tax revenues. The government finds itself running a deficit if it continues to maintain current expenditures. To remove the deficit might require reducing expenditures until they equalize with the now lower tax revenues so that $\Delta G = \Delta T$ over the period. But in a recession, reduced government expenditures mean that aggregate demand is reduced even more, hence a further decline in income takes place and reinforces the economy's recession.

[4]Contraction in the economy can also occur if suddenly, over a short period of time, households attempt to reduce their household debt or businesses to reduce their debt for capital expenditures. Thus, government debt is more similar to private debt in its effects than is commonly realized, except that the private debtor can default whereas the government does not. It can always print more money. The Treasury normally retires debt by issuing fewer new securities than the number of outstanding securities that mature in a week or month.

Conversely, if the economy is in an expansionary phase causing incomes, hence tax revenues, to rise, then in the current period tax receipts may rise above expenditures. To maintain a balanced budget with $\Delta G = \Delta T$ requires that government expenditures in the period be increased, which further intensifies the boom. Thus, from fluctuation to fluctuation the amplitude of the swing in the economy from period to period would be magnified by pursuing a balanced budget policy, and would therefore be a destabilizing policy.

MONETARY POLICY

Monetary policy **is the discretionary manipulation of the nation's money supply, interest rates, and some credit conditions to regulate private sector spending.**

Monetary policy is the manipulation of the nation's money supply and interest rates for the purpose of regulating the level of private sector spending. M1-A and M1-B, and on up to L, are the monetary aggregates continually scrutinized by the 7-member Board of Governors of the Federal Reserve System plus 5 others who comprise the Federal Open Market Committee (FOMC). When the Fed directs the dealers to sell Treasury bills, notes, and bonds, it reduces the level of bank reserves and consequently reduces the ability of the commercial banking system to create money.[5] When the dealers are instructed to buy Treasury securities, commercial bank reserves are expanded and the banks' ability to create money is made easier.

Also, when the Fed raises the discount rate, interest rates in general go up, borrowing becomes more expensive to member banks, firms, and households, thus reducing spending levels. When interest rates are lowered, the discount rate is lowered, then borrowing, and by implication private spending, are both stimulated.

Because monetary policy is carried out through the directives of the FOMC, monetary policy is discretionary. It is dependent upon the judgment of the 12-member committee and is therefore subject to human error.

Lags

The timing of stabilization policy is complicated by inside *lags* (recognition and decision), transition lags, and outside lags (spending, production).

As with any policy—fiscal or monetary—the timing of action, the degree of action taken, and the ultimate impact of the action taken are all important factors in regulating fluctuations in the economy. The problem of lags is a fundamental one in any discussion of policy. Figure 29-1 exhibits the general sequence associated with monetary and fiscal policy. Starting from the far left at time t_0, the direction from left to right measures the time period. The various lags are indicated.[6]

Forecasting is not a precise science, so it may take a while before economic activity changes to a degree that it is recognized as a more than tempo-

[5]Bills are usually issued with maturities of 3 months, 6 months, and 1 year. Notes are issued with maturities of 1 to 10 years, and bonds usually have a maturity of over 10 years.

[6]For a fuller discussion see Ronald Teigan and Warren Smith, "Readings in Money, National Income, and Stabilization Policy." 2d ed. (Homewood, Ill.: Richard D. Irwin, Inc., 1970).

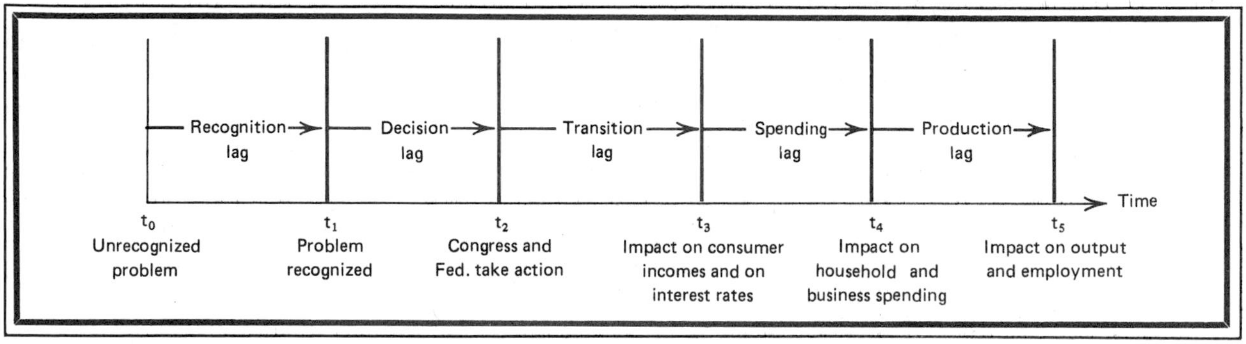

Figure 29-1

rary change. For example, how long do the economic indicators have to indicate a downturn before it is recognized there is a recession? This delay in recognizing that there is a problem is, not surprisingly, called the *recognition lag* and is indicated by the time period t_0 to t_1 in the graph.

Once the problem is recognized it takes time for bureaucrats to come to a decision. This is a *decision lag.* For monetary action this lag is short, since the FOMC meets about every three weeks and will promptly arrive at a decision about open market action. The open market desk will then buy or sell securities as directed. However, fiscal policy concerns taxes and budgeting, so that the decision lag represented by the time period from t_1 to t_2 can be very long. Political bickering that revolves around differing social philosophies, the proper role of government, and political tactics and strategy all contribute to the fiscal decision lag.

The overall lag from t_0 to t_2 is referred to as the *inside lag* where it refers to actions within the Federal Reserve System on monetary policy and to actions within Congress on fiscal policy.

Once the Fed decides on monetary action or Congress on fiscal action, there is a *transition lag,* designated by the period between t_2 and t_3, before which time any action taken actually begins to have an effect. Changes in the money supply eventually affect interest rates, and tax cuts or government expenditures affect consumers' income and business revenues. The period from t_3 to t_4 represents the *spending lag.* Once consumer incomes and corporate revenues are affected, it takes some time for them to assess and react to the changes by increasing their spending. The final lag from t_4 to t_5 is the *production lag,* sometimes called the *impact lag.* It is the time it takes for change in interest rates, credit, the money supply, taxes, or government expenditures that increased (or decreased) spending to actually have an impact on the economy's level of employment and output. The duration from t_3 to t_5 is also designated as the *outside lag* since it is characterized by economic activity that results outside of the Fed or Congress, caused by decisions made inside the Fed or Congress.

A comparison of lags between monetary and fiscal policy follows.

Inside lag The recognition lag is probably the same for monetary policy as for fiscal policy. The decision lag for the Fed is practically zero whereas for Congress, being the political body it is, the decision lag is much greater. Therefore, the inside lag is shorter for monetary policy.

Transition lag This lag is usually shorter for fiscal policy. Once a decision is made, tax changes can be felt in the next paycheck. Depending on the kind of expenditure, government agencies can act very quickly when it comes to spending the citizens' money. However, decisions to build a water project or design a new sophisticated weapon can involve a long period of survey, design, and planning, with little actual expenditures occurring in the short run.

Monetary policy definitely takes time to work through the financial institutions and to alter banks' reserve positions before it begins to have an effect on household and business spending decisions.

Outside lag This is made up of the spending and production lags. The spending lag associated with fiscal policy, particularly for tax changes, is shorter than for monetary policy. Depending on the type of expenditure, however, government expenditure lags are not always shorter than expenditures induced by monetary policy. As for the production lag, once spending is begun—whatever the policy that stimulated it—the production lag is the same. Thus, overall, the outside lag is usually shorter for fiscal than for monetary policy. The conclusions are hedged; the issues are complex and measurement is tricky.

It would be convenient briefly to summarize and compare the strengths and weaknesses of monetary and fiscal policy.

Monetary Policy – Strengths

Monetary policy has a shorter *inside lag* and usually longer *transition* and *outside lags* than fiscal policy.

1. The Fed is much more, but not completely, immune than Congress to political pressure in making monetary decisions. Its existence and popularity is not dependent directly on the voting citizen.

2. The Fed reaches decisions quickly. Therefore its decision lag is practically nonexistent.

3. Open market operations permit the Fed to manipulate the money supply in small, gradual doses, enabling it to make potentially smooth, nondisruptive changes in the economy.

4. The Fed tends to be more impartial since its policies influence total expenditures throughout the economy with no distinction made between regional and local areas. Nor is there direct intervention into the private and personal decision making of individuals and private businesses concerning economic matters.

5. Monetary policy seems to work faster in cooling down an overheated economy than it does in warming up a cold one.

Fiscal Policy – Strengths

1. Fiscal policy has a shorter outside lag than monetary policy for tax changes, but not necessarily for changes in government expenditures.

2. Because of the progressive structure of the income tax, where the size of the tax increases proportionately more than income increases and decreases proportionately less than income decreases, the size of the multiplier is reduced, causing the economy to fluctuate less in response to upswings and

downswings. Other aspects of fiscal policy, such as unemployment insurance, tend to dampen business cycles too.

3. Many government programs and their expenditures are inherently stable. Long-term projects continue to be funded despite changes in aggregate activity in the short term.

4. Government expenditures and taxes can be focused on specific geographical areas and economic activities without affecting the total economy in an unintended way. Examples are the Job Corps, student loans, tax credits, programs for the inner city, and disaster funds.

5. Fiscal policies can promote equity and efficiency. By government funding of education, job training, inner city rehabilitation, and changing taxes, society can achieve both improved productivity and income distribution.

6. Fiscal policy seems to work faster in stimulating a sluggish economy.

Monetary Policy – Weaknesses

1. Monetary policy involves human judgment, which can lead to errors. Historically the Fed has been more concerned with inflation than with unemployment when a choice between the two has to be made.

2. Monetary policy usually has a longer outside lag. Also, the effect and the length of these lags vary. Lags have varied from 6 to 24 months and more in their effects.

3. The Fed has tended to rely on achieving simultaneously both money supply targets and interest rate targets that are more often incompatible or otherwise simultaneously unattainable. We shall have more to say on this later in the chapter.

4. Because the velocity of money does vary in the short run, there is slippage between increases in the money stock and GNP. That is, there does not exist a direct short-run linkage between money and GNP. Therefore, monetary policy is sometimes ineffective in the short run. This too will be discussed later in the chapter.

5. Monetary policy is not impartial or equitable in its effects.

a. When money policy is tight, interest rates rise. Large companies have more resources than smaller ones and generate larger internal earnings that can be used for investment expenditures. Smaller companies are more dependent on commercial banks and must borrow proportionately more, and at higher rates since they have less collateral and are considered more risky.

b. Because of the differences in structure of industries, some markets are much more sensitive to changes in the interest rate—housing, for example, as compared to manufacturing and services. Nor are all regions equally sensitive to interest and loanable funds. The Pacific Northwest is hard hit when credit is tight because its lumber industry is directly dependent on the rate of housing construction. This has a strong regional impact.

Fiscal Policy – Weaknesses

1. Discretionary fiscal policy also involves human judgment. A policy may be inappropriate. The economics of fiscal policy is complicated. Some of

the technical information politicians receive comes from special-interest lobbies. Other information comes from polls, newspapers, and magazines. Lobbies are also a source of campaign funds. Thus fiscal legislation is often flavored with the spice of political expediency and fraught with political bickering. Nor are politicians always aware of the fuller implications of their fiscal policies on stabilizing the economy.

2. All of the above can make for very long decision lags with legislation bottled up in committees. By the time consent is reached it may be too late or be inappropriate because the conditions that motivated it have since passed. And to pass it might make the current situation worse. Thus, a tax cut is passed a year after the recession has passed and it now reinforces an inflationary expansion. This may then require that more severe, very unpopular countermeasures be taken later, and may not be adopted when desperately needed.

3. Public philosophy enters into fiscal policy, because it means government intervention. What should be its extent? How much should the government intervene into local levels and impose on private agreements? If, as many believe, free markets are a necessary condition for a free society, will the hand of government become too heavy and suffocate freedom?

4. Equity and efficiency are affected because fiscal policy, particularly government expenditures, may involve two conflicting goals—fairness and efficiency. What is mandated as fair to one group may be unfair to another. If standards are lowered to accommodate fairness in order for institutions and firms to qualify for government funds, productivity, hence living standards, may decline.

5. A democracy by its nature leads people to believe they have a key to the Treasury. Excess government expenditures can, if mismanaged, lead to excess aggregate demand and an inflated dollar that becomes weakened relative to foreign currencies. Because the dollar is the major world currency, an inflated dollar disrupts world financial markets and trade.

TO FINE-TUNE OR FOLLOW THE RULES?

We have seen in the paragraphs above that various lags and side effects accompany different stabilization policies. Because of these, some economists take the position that more emphasis should be placed on monetary policy while others favor balanced use of both fiscal and monetary policies depending on the circumstances. There is always a tendency to oversimplify the issues involved in a debate and to place people into camps—the intellectuals vs. the hard-hats, the conservatives vs. the liberals, the hawks vs. the doves, and so forth. In economics, unfortunately, we tend to do the same; thus, we classify the monetarists vs. the Keynesians.

The Keynesians tend to believe that the government has the duty to balance monetary and fiscal policies carefully so as to offset the effects of swings in private investment, consumption, and trade balances on the macroeconomy. If these swings are carefully offset, the economy can continue to develop and grow along relatively stable growth paths for the benefit of the people.

Keynesians advocate the *activist policy* of *fine-tuning the economy* to achieve the proper balance of monetary and fiscal policy.

Attempts to draw the right balance of monetary and fiscal policies is sometimes called **fine-tuning the economy** and is referred to as activist policy. It implies active manipulation of monetary and fiscal policies to ensure just the right amount of aggregate demand exists in the economy—an amount sufficient to keep the economy fully employed, but not enough to create inflation.

The monetarists, on the other hand, tend to reject the active use of fiscal policy for stabilization purposes. They agree that in theory fiscal policy has some impact but claim that it is of minor importance. With regard to monetary policy, they believe that instead of trying to fine-tune the economy by adjusting the money supply from month to month, it would be far better simply to keep the money supply growing at a steady rate—that is, follow a monetary growth rule whereby the money supply is allowed to grow at a rate approximately equal to the rate of growth of GNP. Historically, this rate has averaged about 3.2 percent per annum over the past century—sometimes called the near beer rate of growth because some states limit the sale of beer that is greater than 3.2 percent alcohol by volume. Some monetarists argue that the money supply rate of growth should, in the long run, be held to 3.2 percent.

To classify economists as monetarists and Keynesians may have its uses in news reporting, but it can cloud the underlying substance of the issues. Most of the debate is *not* over the theory, but over the shape and stability of the underlying curves that tell us the strength, degree, or the predictability of the economy's response to a particular policy action. In economics we would say that the issues are empirical. The issues concern how accurate our knowledge and understanding of the extent of the response to policy is, rather than whether a response of some extent does occur. To press home this thought it can be pointed out that when President Ford called a summit meeting and invited over 20 economists of all persuasions to advise him on the state of the economy, *all* the eminent and respected economists in attendance agreed that a tax cut would be appropriate at the time. But the newspaper headlines reported, "Economists Disagree on *Size* of Tax Cut" (italics added). It is all too clear that newspapers and other media forms rely on controversy to get attention. The *real* news was that 20 economists *actually agreed* about something—both Keynesians and monetarists.

We emphasize that putting people in camps of opinion often blurs the true image. In what follows we shall try to explain why different economists have different views about the way stabilization policies should be implemented. But in doing so we too fall briefly into the error of classifying people somewhat arbitrarily according to their opinions about stabilization policy actions.

Monetarists

Monetarists advocate stabilizing the economy by adhering to a constant rate of growth in the *money supply*.

Those economists who consider themselves monetarists believe that by far the major variable affecting the level of output and prices in the economy is the **money supply**. They also believe that the primary source of instability in the economy resides with discretionary monetary policy as exercised by the Federal Reserve System. An eminent monetarist in the 1960s and 1970s is Milton Friedman (Nobel prize 1976), now retired from the University of Chicago. He has hammered away at the Fed, arguing for replacing discretionary monetary policy and instituting in its place a monetary rule. The money supply growth rates during the 1970s varied from month to month and year to year in ranges as high as 10 percent. Friedman's recommendation would be to reduce this rate of growth slowly—8 percent next year, 7 percent the year following, 6 percent, 5 percent, and so forth, until a 4 percent rate is reached. In other words, the Fed would eventually arrive at a growth rate of money that would provide the economy with enough money balances to meet the steady growth in the volume of exchange in a steadily growing economy. Doing this, he argues, would remove much of the uncertainty in the economy about expected prices and interest rates caused by the Fed's patchwork manipulation of the money supply. Firms, households, and unions would be able to establish more consistent spending and investment patterns—patterns whose inconsistent behavior in the past has been so important in instigating business cycles.

In the past Professor Friedman has advocated that there be a 100 percent reserve requirement imposed on commercial banks.[7] The effect of this would be to remove the ability of commercial banks to manipulate the supply of money by making loans made possible by reserves acquired through holdings of demand deposits. Under these conditions only the Fed and the Treasury could create money. Commercial banks would no longer have the power to create money as they do under the fractional reserve system. Under 100 percent reserves the Fed and Treasury could exercise more direct control over money. One might think that having direct and certain control over the money supply would mean that Fed authorities could better use monetary policy in deliberate and specific amounts in order to regulate aggregate demand. Most monetarists, however, do not actively want to use monetary policy. They prefer direct control so that monetary policy will consist of keeping money growing at a constant rate. The reason, of course, is that monetarists claim that most of the instability in the economy has been the result, not of sudden changes in private investment and consumption, but of misguided and destabilizing changes in money brought about by inappropriate policies. There are several factors to the argument. One concerns lags.

Lags

As we mentioned earlier, it is difficult to know when an apparent change in output and employment is only temporary and when it is more long-lasting. It is the old recognition lag. The decision lag for the Fed is short, and changes in its policy are easy to make. The problem with monetary policy comes with the outside lag made up of the spending and production lags. The monetarists insist that monetary lags are long and variable in their effects. The lag in effect on output is about 9 months; effects on price levels occur 2 years later. The impacts of monetary policies are spread out over time. The repercussions are not felt immediately and fully at a given time, but gradually and cumulatively. Nor does each monetary action bring on identical, measurable results. The magnitude of effects varies as well as the length of the lags. Friedman believes

[7]Friedman suggests that commercial banks can make profits by (a) charging full costs for servicing checks, and (b) lending and investing their nondemand deposit holdings. The banks do not agree. They do very well lending out your money.

that sometimes it takes about two years for changes in the nominal money supply to affect the general level of prices. Nearly all economists agree that in the long run the rate of inflation is directly related to the growth rate of the money stock. Excessive growth in the money stock can cause inflation, or aggravate inflation originating from other causes. Permissive growth of the money supply can be used to accommodate inflation caused by measures taken to avoid unemployment. More on this topic will appear in the inflation chapter. However, in the short run there is not necessarily a direct link between the money supply and the price level because there are output effects before there are price effects.

If we look at our old friend, the equation of exchange, we see that $MV = PQ$, or $M = k'PQ$ since $k' = 1/V$, where PQ is the dollar value of income Y because $PQ = Y$. The monetarists believe that k' (or V) is relatively stable. Therefore if money, M, increases, according to this equation, either prices (P) or output (Q) can increase. In the long run all the change will be in the price level.

The argument is as follows. When the nominal stock of money is excessively boosted by Fed action, then real balances M/P go up initially because while the money supply is higher, prices in the system are still temporarily the same. Since the price level is the same, people hold more real balances than they want. They increase their expenditures in order to restore their desired level of real balances. The first effect is increased output because aggregate demand has gone up but there is a lag in the price adjustment. Thus, in the short run spending and output are up, but prices are sticky. It therefore appears in the short run that the direct link between the money supply and the price level is weak, and that velocity apparently increases (k' decreases) as people step up spending. But that is only because of the lag in the adjustment of prices to the increased money supply. In the long run output is limited by the resource base of the economy, so that the price level will by then have risen in response to the increase in money until M/P is again at the same ratio, though both M and P are now individually higher. Thus, in the long run, the relation between M_S and P that was obscured because of short-run price lags is borne out once the dust kicked up by the Fed has settled. That is to say, the velocity of money is not highly variable as the short run seems to indicate.

Of course, if there is a lot of unemployment and output is low, then an increase in money may cause little or no change in prices and a big increase in output. We do observe that in an expansionary phase of a cycle the velocity of money seems to speed up. However, averaged over the full cycle it really has not. Also, if output is high and there is little or no unemployment, then an increase in money will directly lead to an increase in price and little or no increase in output. Velocity would vary little since M and P rise together.

Money and Interest Rate Targets

In 1975, as part of its procedure for formulating its policies, the Fed began to announce its interest rate and money supply targets. The targets were set in the form of a range rather than a specific amount. For example, in 1976 the target range for the interest rate on Federal funds was 5 to 5.75 percent. As we learned when we studied the Fed's control over bank resources, federal funds are principally bank excess reserves on deposit at the Fed that banks lend and borrow from each other. If the Fed supplies additional resources by selling government securities (open market operations), these added reserves mean that more banks have deposits to lend to other banks, and interest rates on these loans will fall. Thus, by buying government securities, the Fed can push these short-term interest rates down, and by selling government securities they can push rates up for a temporary period. So if the rate climbed to a level above the 5.75 percent target lid, the manager of the Federal Open Market Account would order that government securities be purchased and this would push the rate back to within the target range. In general, Fed authorities find it relatively easy to manipulate this fundamental rate and keep it within the target range.

However, the Fed also sets target ranges for growth in both M1-A, M1-B and M2 as well. The target range for M1-B might be 5 to 9 percent, and for M2 6 to 11 percent. Unfortunately, the money supply is not as easy to control as the Federal funds rate. Money supply data must be revised frequently, and Federal Reserve officials simply do not know precisely what rate of growth in M1-B and M2 is occurring until several weeks after the fact. Current estimates of the money supply are published each week for the preceding week, but these are based on incomplete information. In 1979, for example, the Fed missed its target range for M1-B in 5 of the 12 monthly periods. So long as some of the misses are above the range and others are below the range, the average for the year can still come out within the range.

Whether or not the Fed can meet its targets over longer periods is not really the main concern, which is that the underlying economic situation may easily be such that the targets can turn out to be inconsistent with each other. A 5 percent rate of growth of M1-B may be consistent with a 10 percent federal funds rate if investment, consumer, and government demand is high, but consistent with only a 6 percent fed funds rate if demand is low.

Let us use the graph in Figure 29-2 to illustrate what we are talking about. The interest rate (federal funds rate) is on the vertical axis and the size of the money stock, both demand and supply, is measured on the horizontal axis.

Observe that the horizontal axis measures the stock (amount) of M1-B money and is not here measured in rates of change. Although when the stock of money is increased from M to M' the difference can be expressed as a percentage change.

Assume the demand for money schedule is $M_D = f(i, \overline{Y}_1)$, its position dictated by the public's behavior, that is, how much of its income it chooses to hold in M1-B balances. If the Fed targets the federal funds rate at i_1, it must target the money stock at M. It is easy for the Fed to hit its interest rate target by engaging in open market operations that adjust bank excess reserves. However, because of data lags and because of the ease with which M1-B and M2 are altered because depositors shift funds among different accounts sometimes caused by Fed operations, the Fed does not have immediate control of the money supply. It may not attain its money supply target of M; it may overshoot it and hit M'. If it does, the public will spend the excess balances and drive up the price level—not a desirable result if the Fed is trying to prevent rising prices.

The problem of hitting the two targets simultaneously is compounded because the Fed does not know the precise location of the demand for money schedule. It can shift. Suppose it shifts to $M_D' = f(i, \overline{Y}_2)$ in Figure 29-2. Based on the original schedule, the Fed believes it can reach its target of i_1 by adjusting the money stock to M. Instead, the interest rate rises to i_3 based on the new

Figure 29-2

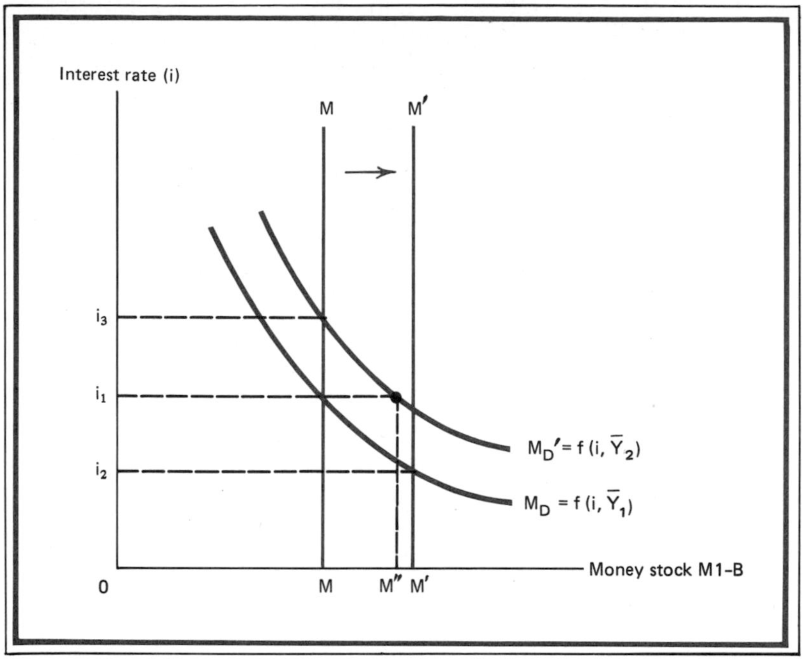

schedule, as yet unknown. Or if it hits i_1, it will find that it had to increase the money supply to M''.

Thus, we also see how money supply policy effects are intimately linked to the demand side for money. Because of this uncertainty, the Fed's attempt to engage in stabilizing action might further destabilize the economy. As a case in point, suppose the Fed picks an interest rate target of 8 percent, up from 7 percent. At the same time, unknown to the Fed—or anyone—the economy begins a downturn. This causes borrowing to decline, which prevents the interest rate from rising to 8 percent. To prevent the downturn, if it knew about it, the Fed could step up the growth in the money supply through open market purchases of securities. However, this also prevents the interest rate in the Federal funds market from reaching 8 percent. Unaware of the downturn in the economy, the Fed pursues its 8 percent interest rate target by being forced to contract the money supply growth below 5 percent. This also amplifies the downturn in the economy because bank reserves are reduced when the Fed sells off securities in open market operations. By adhering to an interest rate target, the money supply is inadvertently used to accentuate the decline in the economy. Conversely, suppose the Fed chooses to lower the interest rate target to 6 percent from 8 percent. In the meantime the economy moves into an upswing. This increases the demand for loans and prevents the interest rate from falling below 8 percent. To lower the interest rate the Fed reacts by buying bonds on the open market, and this causes bank reserves to increase and the money supply growth to exceed 7 percent. Not only is the target overshot, but the expansion has been fed more fuel and burns hotter.

Thus, the Fed finds it hard to match up its desired combination of interest rate and money supply targets simultaneously. If it gives priority to the interest rate target, it has to keep fudging the money supply to reach it. Fluctuations in the money supply introduce additional uncertainties and further fluctuations into the economy because they affect consumer and business expectations. The Fed can give priority to the money supply and let the interest rate float to find its own level consistent with the money supply. The Fed did this somewhat in October 1979. The result was that by early 1980 the interest rate rose from 12 to 20 percent, initiating the recession of 1980.

Therefore, monetarists argue that the Fed policy should be simply to keep the money supply target and abandon the interest rate target, so that interest rates simply seek their own levels—levels that reflect supply and demand conditions in the financial markets. It is the money supply that is the most significant policy variable.

There are other unfavorable side effects on the economy from interest rate gyrations. A spurt in short-run rates means that car dealers and clothing stores want to cut back their inventories because they normally borrow in order to purchase the inventories. Hence, they cancel long-term orders for new cars and clothing and the auto and clothes manufacturers start cutting back on production, laying off workers. Stopping an inflation in this way means paying the piper with unemployment.

THE TRANSMISSION MECHANISM

Monetarists and Keynesians disagree on how changes in the money supply are *transmitted* to the real sector because they disagree on the sensitivity of the demand for money and investment to changes in the interest rate.

As we saw earlier, the monetarists contend that changes in M lead to changes in P and Q more or less according to the formula $M = PQ/V$, which can also be written $M = k'Y$ since $PQ = Y$ and $k' = 1/V$. In today's more sophisticated monetarist formulation of the equation of exchange, k' is not a numerical constant but it is stable, that is, it does not bounce around unpredictably. Although it may change, its direction of change can be anticipated. For example, if a strong inflation occurs, people are likely to move out of holding cash and into buying things, thus lowering holdings of real cash balances. Things—physical assets—tend to increase in value relative to cash during an inflation, so that people substitute out of cash and into something they hope will maintain its value.

Therefore, with k' (or V) relatively stable, the transmission mechanism from the monetary sector to the real sector is relatively direct. That is, when the Fed increases the money supply the transmitted effect to the real sector is direct. There is little slack in the linkage from an increase in money to a rise in income. To put it vividly, the new money is mainlined directly into the circular flow of the economy with no significant leakage caused by a buildup in cash balances. Thus, in the monetarists' view the transmission mechanism is that changes in the money supply change income. In shorthand notation

$$\Delta M \xrightarrow{\text{direct}} \Delta Y$$

In this view, the **speculative** motive for holding cash balances is minor. The demand for cash is essentially a **transactions** demand. Thus the demand for cash balances is relatively insensitive to changes in the interest rate.

According to the Keynesians, the transmission mechanism from the

The heart of the Monetarist-Keynesian debate is whether the *speculative* or *transactional* motive for cash balances is more important.

monetary sector to the real sector is less direct since it must pass through the interest rate variable. Since velocity is considered as relatively less stable, particularly in the short run, changing the money supply may cause a substantial change in cash balances because the quantity of money demanded is relatively sensitive to changes in the interest rate. Increases in M may not directly affect prices or output because much of the additional money may be absorbed into cash balances. Therefore, there may be no direct link in the shortrun between M and Y because of slippage caused by counter variations in the velocity of money. M goes up, but V goes down (or k' up) so the net effect on Y is small. To the Keynesians what is more reliable and stable is not the velocity of money, but the effects of changes in taxes and government spending that when amplified by the multiplier provide a more direct, predictable transmitted effect on Y. Thus, to the Keynesians changes in the money supply affect interest rates (and cash balance holdings), which affect investment and via the multiplier change income, hence consumption. In shorthand language

$$\Delta M \rightarrow \Delta i \rightarrow \Delta I \xrightarrow{k} \Delta Y \text{ and } \Delta C.$$

This monetary process is valid, argue the Keynesians, but it is not as reliable as the process involving the multiplier k that connects changes in government expenditures and taxes to changes in income, hence to changes in consumption.

$$\Delta G \text{ and } \Delta T \xrightarrow{k \text{ direct}} \Delta Y \text{ and } \Delta C.$$

Therefore, the Keynesians stress that the Fed must use activist monetary policy. The Fed should use interest rate targets that can counteract undesirable accumulations or decumulations of cash balances, caused by volatile changes in the short-run velocity of money, in order to smooth out fluctuations in the economy. They maintain that as the Fed learns more it will learn to do a better job of short-run stabilization policy.

Posh, respond the monetarists. To adjust interest rates means changing the amount of money, and in the short run while the direct effects of changing the money supply exist, they are obscured because of adjustment lags, and are not fully clear in their effects until the lags work out. Because of this the Fed may speed up when it should slow down money growth. It is like driving a car with loose linkage from the gas pedal (money supply) to the carburetor (economic activity). You step on the gas but do not know when the car will accelerate or by how much. It may accelerate one half mile down the road when you may need to hit the brakes. But if a monetary rule is applied, all cars are run by a steady automatic gas pedal, and move ahead at the same speed.

Not necessarily, reply the Keynesians. Just because changes in the money supply correlate with changes in money income you should not always infer that changes in income are caused by changes in the money stock. The causation can also run in the reverse direction. For example, everyone knows that spending increases in April for spring buying and in August for vacations, and that spending is down in January and February after Christmas. And what about Christmas? At this time is the increased spending a result of an increase in the money supply or does an increase in spending trigger a response in the money stock? Does not the increase in buying over the holiday occur *independent* of changes in the money supply? Income rises during the season because of bonuses, overtime, and increased part-time employment. Spending spurts because of the nature of a holiday season. The Fed responds to the increased demand for liquidity over the holiday by increasing the money supply. Thus, for a variety of imperfectly understood behavioral and institutional reasons, the demand for money balances can shift causing velocity and k' (or V) to change sharply, thus breaking any tight or direct link between M_S and Y in the short run. The money supply M and income Y correlation can just as easily be explained by the Fed's increasing the money supply to meet the demand for greater transactions balances in an economy whose real sector is growing. A growing economy must be nourished with more money. The monetarists seem to view the short run as a black box inside of which the institutional and behavioral transmission mechanism is hidden. They argue, what does it matter what is inside the black box so long as we can predict accurately what will happen in the long run. The monetarists take an operational approach. If one observes that pushing down the money supply pedal of the car leads—with a lag—to a measurable change in the progress of the car, then we have a predictable, useful relation. The Keynesians reply that it is also important to understand the short-run relations, to know what is going on inside the box, for things do not always correlate the way the monetarists predict, at least in the short-run. Thus, putting money into a black transmission box is not enough. A mechanic is needed to explain how the gear box of monetary policy works; not just for the long haul, but for the short-run trips too when the monetary pedal seems to have little connection with the speed of the car.

Consequently, a monetary rule may also be destabilizing, say the Keynesians. For example, assume that the demand for real balances M/P is constant and that the nominal money supply is increased by 5 percent, with real income and the interest rate fixed. This causes the price level to go up by 5 percent as people spend the extra money to keep the level of real balances M/P the same. However, suppose the demand for real balances is not stable and increases by, say, 2 percent. The price level falls by 2 percent because spending declines as cash balances increase. In order to maintain both the price level and M/P constant when the demand for real balances rises by 2 percent, the nominal money supply should be decreased by 2 percent, implying that the next increase in the money supply should only be 3 percent to maintain price stability. If a monetary rule required that the stock of money be increased 5 percent, it would be inflationary and inappropriate for price stability. With discretionary monetary policy the Fed could avoid inflation. Judgment by the Fed and flexibility in the use of fiscal policy by the government are both necessary if stabilization policy is to succeed at all. Markets are not always as self-correcting as the monetarists seem to think, argue the Keynesians.

SENSITIVITY OF CASH BALANCES AND INVESTMENT

Why do the monetarists and Keynesians disagree about the sensitivity of the demand for cash balances to changes in the interest rate, which has important implications as to which transmission mechanism is more reliable for stabilization policy?

This is a tough subject and for our purposes it will necessarily be simplified. In Keynes's original formulation of the demand for money function, cash balances were a function of the interest rate and current income. But today some economists treat the demand for cash balances as a function of interest rates and wealth. Wealth is made up of a spectrum of both financial (bonds, stocks) and physical assets (houses, cars, stereos, washers). Wealth is a stock that yields either a flow of income over time, for example, a bond that provides an annual coupon payment or a stock that pays a yearly dividend; or wealth is a stock that yields a stream of services over time, e.g., the number of rides provided by your car or the number of washings from your washing machine year after year. Both the Keynesians and monetarists agree that spending on housing is indeed sensitive to interest rate (mortgage rate) changes. However, they part company when it comes to how sensitive firms' investment spending on plant and equipment, and household spending on consumer durables, are to changes in the interest rate. Household spending on durables concerns credit on cars and appliances. Consumer durables are those washing machines, dryers, toasters, and so on, lasting for a year or more. This constitutes a much larger market in dollar volume than the housing market and has a more dominant effect on GNP. According to the monetarists, the speculative demand for money is of relatively minor importance whereas the transactions demand is quite important. When the money supply, say, is increased, excess cash balances are created. They are largely spent in the durable goods market since more money means easier credit is available there. Thus, changing money changes interest rates but does not result in the additional money being absorbed into cash balances. It gets spent. Thus velocity is stable. There is little change in cash balances. The additional money is passed through. Therefore, the demand for money is relatively insensitive to changes in the interest rate whereas spending is sensitive to it. However, spending by firms is indeed sensitive to interest rate changes. Increasing money lowers the interest rate initially and reduces borrowing costs to firms, thus making capital spending projects more feasible as they move down the investment (MEI) schedule.

The monetarists give less play to the speculative motive for holding cash balances. For them, the demand for money is also a function of bonds, stocks, and other financial assets. When the yield or return on bonds falls relative to stocks, investors would not necessarily move out of bonds into cash. They would move into stocks or some other asset yielding a higher return. They juggle their portfolio. They do not jump into cash with each fall in the interest rate. The financial markets offer different kinds of bonds, each with its own interest rate. These yields frequently change relative to one another. Though the general interest rate may fall, the rate on one financial asset may fall less, thus increase relative to another, and would still be a better investment than simply holding more cash. Many of these assets are liquid, with short maturity periods, and switching is easy. Bonds with longer maturity can be traded in secondhand markets. Therefore, conclude the monetarists, the speculative motive for demanding money is unresponsive to changes in the interest rate compared to the response of consumers in the consumer durables market, which has a transactions motive. In the consumer durables market, lowering the interest rate does not increase money holdings, it stimulates household and investment spending, which dominates cash balance buildups for speculative purposes.

The Keynesians take a different approach. They argue that the speculative motive for holding cash balances has relatively more influence than the monetarists allow. Were the interest rate to fall, bond speculators would get out of bonds and into cash. The bond and stock markets are large markets. With the velocity of money variable, a decline in the interest rate does not have that much of an effect on household spending on durables. Moreover, investment decisions by firms are uneven and respond more to businessmen's expectations about the market and anticipated growth in GNP than they do to changes in the interest rate and borrowing costs. In other words, rightward shifts in the MEI curve are more important than movements down along the MEI curve in determining the amount of investment spending.

As you see, the differences are empirical, not theoretical, and are based on the sensitivity of the demand for money and investment expenditures to changes in the interest rate and expectations.

CROWDING OUT

The degree to which the Monetarist or Keynesian position is correct depends on the degree of *crowding out* asserted by the former, or of *crowding in* asserted by the latter.

The heart of the matter goes back to the familiar accounting identity, savings plus taxes equal planned investment plus government expenditures ($S + T = I_p + G$, or rewriting, $S = I_p + (G - T)$). Both business and government borrow for investment and spending reasons, respectively. Savings derive from households and the undistributed profits and depreciation allowances of firms. Assume that for a one year accounting period (in billions)

Business saving	+ household saving	=	planned investment	+ deficit.
\$135	\$71	=	\$200	\$6
(206)			(206)	

We ignore the foreign sector. Suppose the projections for the next period look like

$$S_B + S_H < I_p + (G - T).$$

$$\$160 + \$75 < \$204 + \$60$$

$$(235) \qquad (264)$$

Thus, the supply of funds is projected to be only \$235 billion and the demand \$264 billion. As we have learned, when disequilibrium exists, forces operate to restore equilibrium. The question is; Where will the adjustments take place? Or how will the deficit be financed? Well, the government (Treasury) can borrow.

The monetarists argue that when the government borrows to finance its deficits, firms in the private sector will be crowded out of the credit market by rising interest rates. When the government collects the money to spend, it reduces the private sector spending on investment goods. This lack of investment will impair future productivity and future economic growth. The Keynesians respond that deficit spending can succeed in activating cash balances as bond buyers buy government bonds. For when the government spends the borrowed balances, it will stimulate the economy. The growth in sales and profits will generate internal funds for capital improvement and growth. Also, as income rises so will saving, thus making loanable funds available to business. Tax revenues will also rise, implying that less borrowing will be necessary, so that interest rates will decline, inducing more private investment. This is *crowding in*.

The monetarists disagree. To them, the way fiscal policy works is like this. Competition between the government and the private sector for borrowed funds prevents the interest rate from falling. This is particularly undesirable during a contractionary phase of the economy. If the Treasury tries to prevent interest rates from rising by selling bonds and the Federal Reserve cooperates by buying them, the reserves of the Fed are increased when the Treasury spends the Fed's checks as it pays for various government expenditures. When individuals and firms in the private sector deposit them in their banks, this increases the reserves of those banks allowing them to increase loans. This is an indirect way of printing money, and the debt is monetized. The result is that the money supply is increased as well as the possibility of higher rates of inflation. As money income rises so do the income tax rates that drain the expansionary momentum generated by the additional government expenditures. This is called fiscal drag. In addition, the Fed may range beyond its money supply target.

Under a progressive income tax, fiscal drag is the automatic increase in marginal taxes as income rises.

Any residual expansion of GNP associated with the government spending is not really caused by fiscal policy, because the GNP expansion actually resulted from increasing the money supply to support the expenditures. By that very fact, fiscal policy becomes disguised monetary policy.

Fiscal policy is not really effective in raising real aggregate demand, and there is a by-product, namely inflationary price expectations. Therefore, the government expenditures multiplier is insignificant in increasing output. As government debt crowds out the private sector and fuels inflation, the private sector cannot sustain adequate improvements in productivity. Its profit rate falls, making it more difficult to obtain funds by selling stock, and it must depend more on borrowing (selling bonds) that becomes more costly as inflation drives up interest rates.

What other doomsday forecasts are implied here? As the economy's rate of productivity and growth slow down there is an additional upward push on prices because of inadequate boosts in aggregate supply. As employment declines, higher government spending is required to subsidize the unemployed. The productive are taxed more heavily to finance the transfer payments. The taxes could reach a point where those who produce are discouraged from producing more; they may work fewer hours, causing further declines in aggregate supply.

Thus, according to some monetarists, too much government spending, the impairment of private investment through higher interest, and the destruction of incentives through higher taxes make impossible the attainment of stable prices, full employment, and sufficient economic growth. Disenchantment with the government sets in. The government responds with more tampering, introduces more regulation and inefficiency. As the situation worsens, the media and politicians will blame it on the failure of private enterprise, the capitalistic system, and outdated notions of free markets. The government will further encroach upon the operation of free markets, destroying their vitality.

And capitalism will come to an end—only being a temporary respite from the world's long history of government totalitarianism. The U.S. will join history's normal mainstream of authoritarianism and tyranny, slowly, almost unnoticed, but inevitably.

Not necessarily so, reply the Keynesians. No doubt private investment will fall slightly at first because of the higher interest rates instigated by government borrowing. But the net effect will be an increase in investment because government spending will stimulate the economy. Income will rise; shifts in investment will more than compensate for the decline caused by higher interest rates. According to Keynesian theory the demand for money is relatively sensitive to interest rates. When the interest rate rises, speculators reduce their holdings of cash balances, speeding up the velocity of money. The spending stimulates aggregate demand. Thus, fiscal policy is expansionary. The money supply is increased to meet the transactions demand required to lubricate a growing GNP. So the government expenditure multiplier is significant. Tax receipts will rise and the economy's ability to pay off the debt is improved. Moreover, the monetarists' contention that capital growth will be stymied overlooks the excess capacity so common in the economy. Thus, with expansion of aggregate demand funded by government debt, the inflationary effect will be small.

Even then, some inflation is a lesser evil than too much unemployment. Much of the government transfer payments are made to train individuals to increase their skills and productivity in order to make them employable, bestowing greater net benefits to themselves and society in the long run. (The monetarists prefer that the private sector be stimulated through business tax cuts and less competitive government borrowing in order to create permanent jobs for people in slots where they are really needed.)

Finally, ask the Keynesians, why is there such a distrust of government? Cannot a democratic society be economically responsible and socially innovative without stifling incentives and initiative and without becoming a bully? Democracy is a government of the people. Its actions express the approval of the people. The message is that the people want more government services. If they want more, then they must pay. If there is an enemy in big government, "it is us!"

THE GRAPHS

Figures 29-3a and b neatly summarize and focus the monetarist-Keynesian debate. Money balances are used instead of real balances because they greatly reduce the analytical complexities while still illuminating the issues. Figure 29-3a describes the different results predicted by the monetarists and the Keynesians from adopting pure monetary policy (taxes and government expenditures held fixed). Figure 29-3b describes the different results predicted by pursuing pure fiscal policy (money supply fixed). The figures are not necessarily drawn to scale, for purposes of illustrating the concepts. An underemployed economy is assumed.

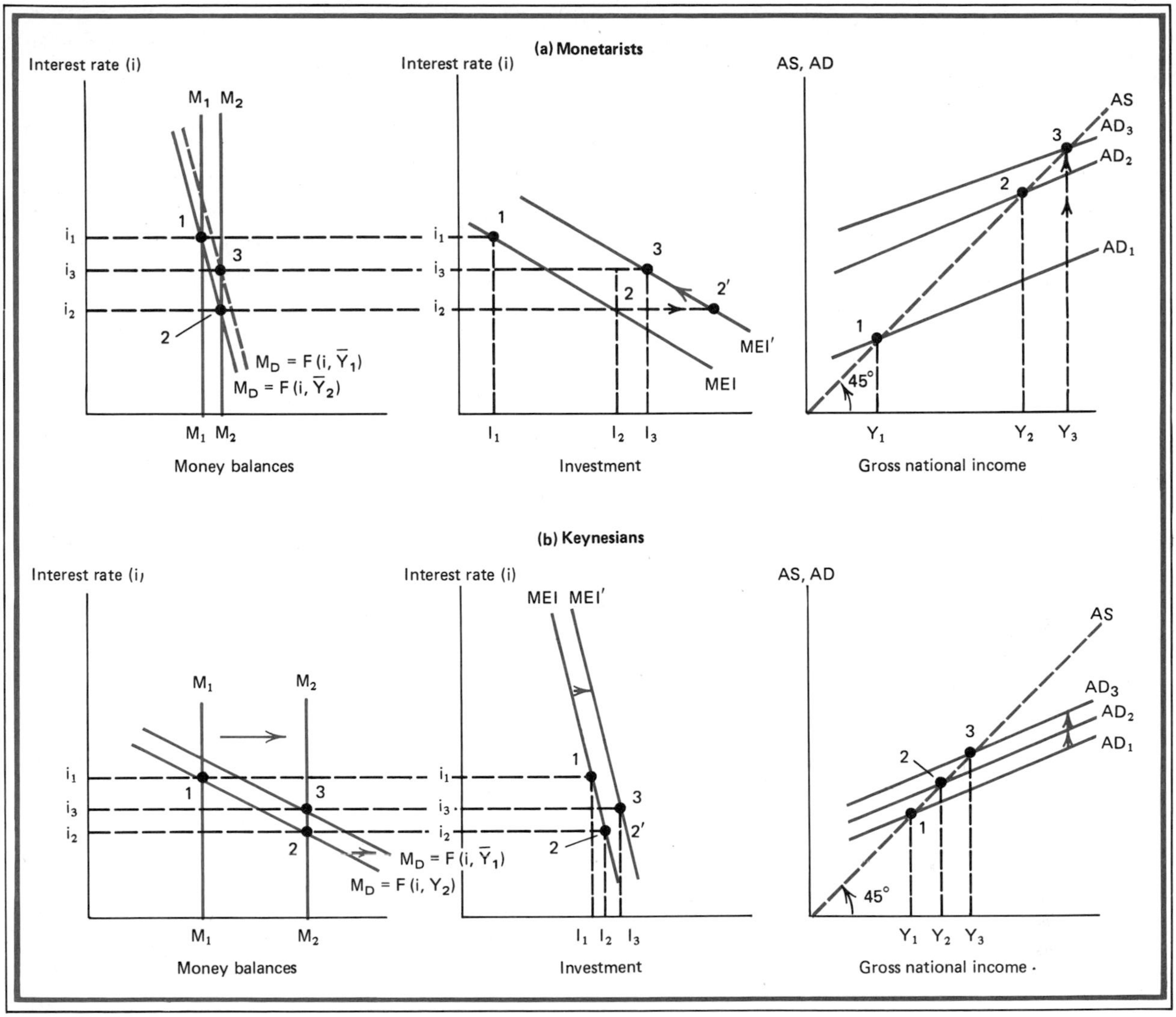

Figure 29-3

PURE MONETARY POLICY

Monetarists Begin with the upper graphs in Figure 29-3, starting from left to right. Assume the Fed increases the money supply (hence money balances) by buying open market securities. This shifts the money supply schedule rightward from M_1 to M_2. The money supply schedule is shown as vertical because the money stock is fixed at any given time, and because banks do not actually hold many excess reserves whose size fluctuates much with changes in the interest rate. Since the demand for money (liquidity preference) is relatively insensitive to changes in the interest rate, the interest rate declines from i_1 to i_2. There is also an increase in money balances from M_1 to M_2.

Equilibrium in the monetary sector moves from point *1* to point *2* (in each figure the sequence is *1*, *2*, *3*). There are repercussions in the investment sector, where investment is sensitive to changes in the interest rate. When the interest rate falls from i_1 to i_2, investment increases substantially from I_1 to I_2 for reasons described earlier. Thus the change in investment shifts aggregate demand upward from AD_1 to AD_2. The investment multiplier magnifies the change in income, so that income rises from Y_1 to Y_2. In a general equilibrium model, effects ripple through the system. The rise in income shifts the liquidity preference schedule from $M_D = f(i, \overline{Y}_1)$ to $M_D = f(i, \overline{Y}_2)$ and drives the interest rate back up some to i_3 and to equilibrium at point 3. Two things occur in the investment sector. Higher income Y_2 causes a rightward shift in the investment schedule from *MEI* to *MEI'*. And at the interest rate i_2, the amount of investment would be indicated by point *2'*. However, the effect of the new interest rate of i_3 moves decision-makers up along the new investment schedule *MEI'* to point *3* and a level of investment I_3. Therefore, aggregate demand is shifted upward again to AD_3 because of the additional net induced investment $I_3 - I_2$. The investment multiplier then operates to raise income to Y_3. A sequence of adjustments continues until permanent equilibrium is obtained. The result is that interest rates end up lower than i_1 but higher than i_2, with significant increases in both investment and income. Thus, monetary policy is quite effective in stimulating aggregate demand in a less than fully employed economy.

Keynesians The quantity of money demanded is sensitive to changes in the interest rate. To achieve an equivalent decline in the interest rate from i_1 to i_2 requires a much larger increase in the money supply, yielding also a much larger rise in money balance holdings as equilibrium in the monetary sector moves from point 1 to point 2. Moreover, investment is insensitive to changes in the interest rate. When the interest rate falls from i_1 to i_2, the increase in the amount of investment from I_1 to I_2 is small compared to what the monetarists predict. As a result, the small increase in investment causes only a small upward shift in aggregate demand from AD_1 to AD_2, hence only a small increase in income from Y_1 to Y_2. As before, the rise in income shifts the liquidity preference curve from $M_D = f(i, \overline{Y}_1)$ to $M_D = f(i, \overline{Y}_2)$, pushing the interest rate back up some to i_3. And, as before, the increase in income shifts the investment schedule *MEI* rightward to *MEI'* and to a temporary stopping place at point *2'*. However, the higher interest rate i_3 moves the system up along *MEI'* to point *3* and to a new level of investment I_3, a smaller secondary boost in investment. The multiplier operates to increase income from Y_2 to Y_3. The changes are small. Thus, a larger increase in the money supply leads to smaller effects on the real sector. Therefore, monetary policy is a relatively weak stimulant in an underemployed economy—in the short run.

PURE FISCAL POLICY

Monetarists Refer to Figure 29-4. With the money supply fixed, assume the government cuts taxes and/or increases government expenditures, causing aggregate demand to shift upward to AD_2 from AD_1. The related multiplier

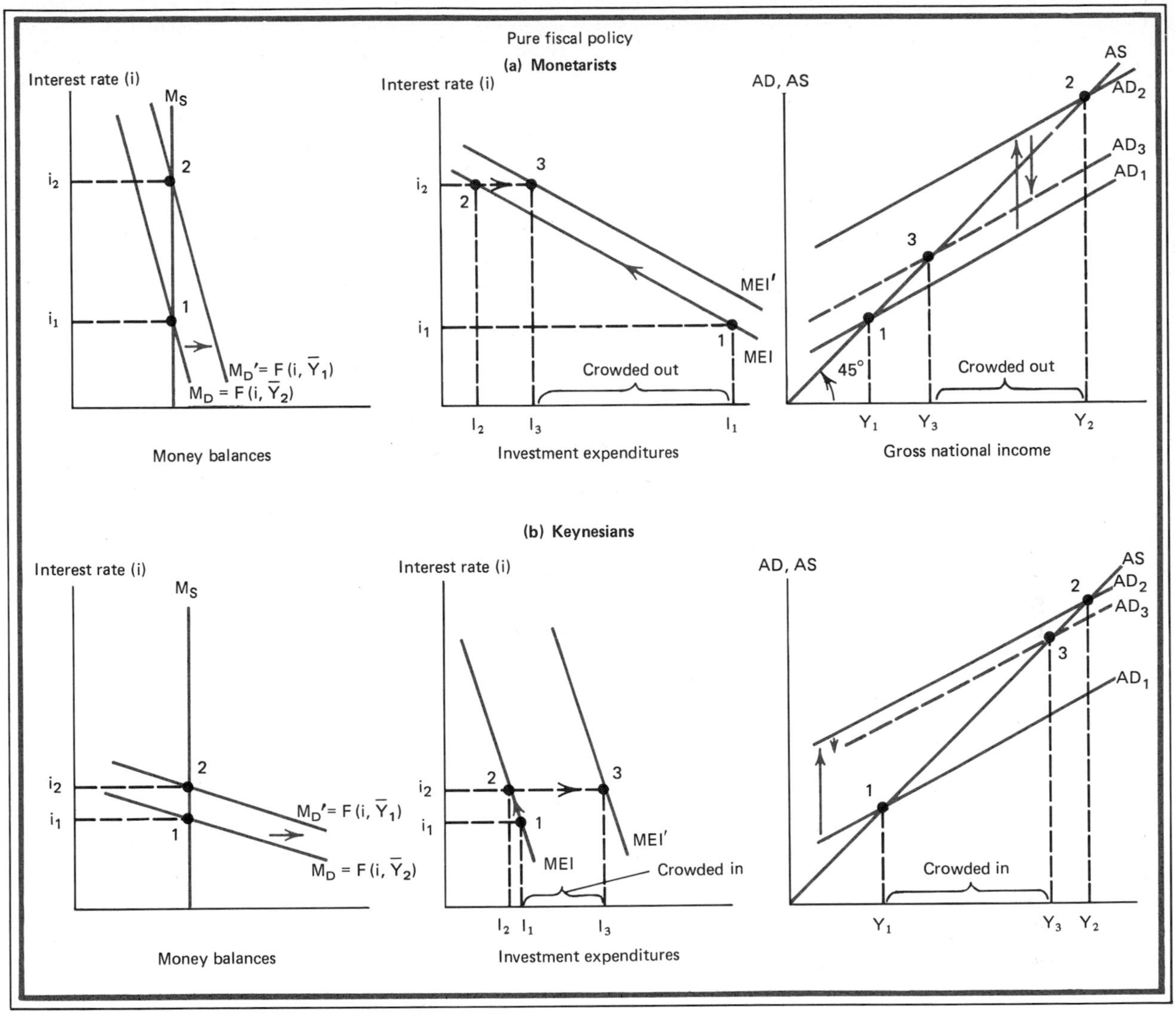

Figure 29-4

magnifies national income, raising it from Y_1 to Y_2. At the higher income, there is an increased demand for transactions balances so the demand curve M_D shifts to the right to M_D'. With M_S fixed, there is excess demand for cash balances at the interest rate i_1. This causes the interest rate to rise to i_2. The increase to i_2 is large because the M_D' curve is quite insensitive to interest rate changes since the speculative motive is weak. When the interest rate rises to i_2 there is movement up along the *MEI* curve from point 1 to 2, and interest-sensitive investment falls to I_2. But since income initially rose to Y_2, there was also a shift of the *MEI* curve to *MEI'* that raised I_2 to I_3. Thus, after the adjustments, potential investment equal to $I_1 - I_3$ is crowded out, thus shifting aggregate demand back down to AD_3 and income to Y_3. The net effect of pure fiscal policy leads to a significant crowding out of private sector investment expenditures. Therefore the effect of fiscal policy, in itself, is a minor one in a less than fully employed economy.

Keynesians Again, assume aggregate demand is shifted upward to AD_2 by government fiscal action. By reason of the multiplier effect, income expands to Y_2. As a result, the M_D curve shifts to the right, causing an excess demand for cash balances at i_1. This, however, leads to a smaller rise in the interest rate to i_2 because the M_D' curve is sensitive to changes in the interest rate. The quantity demanded of balances will fall faster than the monetarists think it will as i rises, since the speculative motive for holding cash balances is significant. The rise in the interest rate causes a decline in interest-insensitive investment from I_1 to I_2. But the initial rise in income Y_2, dominates and leads to a net increase in investment, thus shifting the investment schedule rightward to *MEI′*, thereby increasing the amount of investment to I_3. In conclusion, the crowding out of private sector investment is small and crowding in is much greater. Fiscal action has significant impact on investment, aggregate demand, and national income in a less than fully employed economy.

A FISCAL POLICY RULE

Having been exposed to arguments favoring a money supply rule—keep it growing at 3.2 percent or so come hell or high water—some members of Congress have also proposed a fixed fiscal policy rule. It takes the form of a suggested limit on growth in government spending. Pass a law that prohibits government spending from growing at more than 3.2 percent per year. After all, if money growth rates in excess of output growth can cause inflation, it is also true that increases in government spending at a rate in excess of output growth can also cause inflation. A comprehensive anti-inflationary policy would surely involve restraining both monetary and fiscal stimuli. Just what would happen to taxes and deficits or surpluses in the budget under such a rule is unclear. But its obvious intent is to limit expansion of government—a goal dear to the hearts of many Americans.

How effective such a rule would be is questionable, however, in a democracy where Congress passes a law to tell itself what to do. There is a tendency for it to tell itself to abandon its rule whenever it wants to. For example, in essence we already have a law that limits spending growth in the form of a law setting a ceiling on the national debt. It is a very old law and each year a temporary extension is made. If the national debt is limited to $900 billion, for example, and the Treasury needs more than this limit allows, it goes to the Congress and asks that the ceiling be lifted to $950 billion. What is the Congress going to do? Deny the Treasury's request? Not likely. To do so would mean the federal government would not be able to pay its bills. Failure to pay its bills is not going to instill confidence in government and there would be a big change in the list of names read off on the roll call of the Senate and House the next time the elections came around.

Thesis, Antithesis, and Synthesis

The philosopher G. W. F. Hegel pointed out that man's understanding of the world that surrounds him is improved by steps. In dialogue with colleagues, someone puts forward a thesis or theory such as Keynes did when he formulated the theory of income determination. After winning approval and acceptance among the group, further discussion leads opponents of the thesis to put forward alternative theories that seem to stand against the original thesis, such as the monetarists have brought in opposition to Keynesian theory. A debate rages. Finally, dialogue evolves that accepts the better parts of both the thesis and antithesis and forms these into a synthesis that becomes the new widely accepted thesis—sometimes called the conventional wisdom. Today the Keynesian and monetarist positions are in the synthesis stage of development. This process by which understanding develops is called the Hegelian dialectic. Already the conventional wisdom in macroeconomic theory accepts the better parts of both Keynesian and monetarists viewpoints. But while there is synthesis in theory, there is still disagreement over answers to the normative question, What should stabilization policy be like?

CHAPTER SUMMARY

Stabilization policy employs the tools of both monetary and fiscal policy. Fiscal tools are government spending, taxes, and debt management. Fiscal stabilizers are of the automatic and discretionary kind. Thus, to set up the income tax is a discretionary act. Once set up the progressive income tax is an automatic stabilizer, since it slows down the rise in GNP when GNP is rising and slows down the decline in GNP when GNP is falling. Unemployment benefits also operate automatically to reduce the degree of fluctuation in GNP below what fluctuations in GNP would be without them. Indexing taxes to the inflation involves letting the tax rate fall in proportion to the inflation rate in order to keep peoples' real income from falling. There is disagreement about the benefits of such indexing. Some believe it would impose no discipline on society to control inflation.

The federal government incurs a debt when tax revenues fall short of its spending and it must borrow the difference. Most of the national debt is internal, with one citizen owing it to another. The government borrows by selling securities that private citizens and institutions buy. When the securities mature, it can pay off the securities by selling new securities called rolling over the debt. It can do this so long as the public is willing to buy the securities. With the deficit financed in this way it need not be inflationary, for monies the public would spend is spent by the government instead. However, the deficit can be inflationary if the Fed buys the Treasury securities, for this injects new money into the system. It may buy too many. This action of the Fed is called monetizing the debt.

The majority view is that the national debt is not passed on to future generations. It is paid by the current generation, who sacrifice real resources of labor and materials when the government, say, builds a dam, since those resources could have been used to produce something else by the private sector. There is an income transfer, however, since future generations are taxed to pay interest to bondholders, but they inherit the services of the dam too.

It is possible for heavy government borrowing to cause crowding out. To get the funds it needs, the government must offer a competitive interest yield to attract buyers for its securities. This raises the borrowing costs to private investors, who may delay or cancel private capital formation. If the economy is in recession there may be no crowding out, since the private funds might not have been spent had the government not borrowed them. In this situation, the government deficit can stimulate aggregate demand and raise employment. The ratio of the federal debt to GNP has declined steadily since its high of 122 percent in 1945 to 27 percent in 1979. Nonetheless, too much federal debt is inflationary, and if monetized causes an inflation that often has undesirable income redistribution effects.

Because the government spending multiplier is larger than a tax multiplier, a balanced budget is expansionary when expenditures are raised equally with taxes, and contractionary when lowered equally with taxes. An annually balanced budget can be destabilizing since it can reinforce both downturns and upturns, leading to wider cyclical swings in GNP.

Monetary policy concerns the regulation of the nation's money supply, interest rates, and some credit conditions. Monetary policy is discretionary as prescribed by the Fed.

Effective stabilization policy requires taking the right action at the right time. This objective is complicated by lags. First there is the recognition lag—realizing there is a problem. Second is the decision lag—deciding what to do. These two make up the inside lag. Third is the transition lag or the time it takes before an action begins to take hold on the economy. Next is the spending lag, indicating the time it takes the public to respond to the policy that alters spending behavior. Finally comes the production lag, when public spending begins to impact on production. These last two comprise the outside lag.

The inside lag for monetary policy is shorter than for fiscal policy and in most cases longer for the transition and outside lags.

There are both comparative advantages and disadvantages to monetary and fiscal policies. For example, politics plays a bigger role in fiscal policy but can be focused on certain trouble spots of the economy. Monetary policy decisions are much less political but their impact is much more widespread.

Attempts by the authorities to achieve the proper balance of monetary and fiscal policy is known as fine tuning, and implies active, continuous judgments involving manipulation of economic variables. This *activist* policy is supported by Keynesian oriented economists.

Monetarists reject activist monetary policy and advocate a monetary rule as a better way to attain stability. They also believe fiscal policy is of minor importance for attaining stability, since it too may ultimately depend on monetary policy. Because lags are long and variable in their effects, the Fed is essentially guessing in its monetary policy adjustments, and is wrong as often as not. Hence, it is a source of instability, and it should announce and stick to a constant rate of growth in the money supply to stabilize the public's expectations about money growth and smooth the economy's fluctuations. Monetarists argue that the Fed should abandon its interest rate targets and stick to money supply targets, because it is nearly impossible to keep both money supply and interest rates within target ranges. Trying to do so leads to erratic changes in the money supply. However, the Keynesians can provide an example where a monetary rule is also destabilizing.

The difference between the two schools relates to the different views they hold regarding the transmission mechanism. The monetarists see the demand for money as primarily a demand for transactions balances, the quantity of money demanded is little affected by changes in the interest rate, since the public knows what level of real balances it wants to hold. Thus, if the Fed increases the money supply above what is desired, the extra money is directly spent and its effect directly transmitted to spending, mostly on consumer durables. Since the ratio of M/P remains essentially stable, so too is the velocity of money.

The Keynesians give much more importance to the speculative motive for holding cash balances. Even though the Fed increases the money supply, the public may choose to absorb the additional money for speculative reasons; hence, it is not directly spent in the real sector. The velocity of money can fall, canceling the Fed's action. That is, the velocity of money is highly variable—at least in the short run. Thus, the link between money and the price level and income is not direct or tight. Therefore, in a recession monetary policy could be weak, necessitating the use of fiscal policy that more quickly and directly impacts the real sector of the economy by raising aggregate demand. The monetarists contend that fiscal policy is a weak stimulus and is really disguised monetary policy when the debt is monetized by the Fed. The degree to which the monetarist or Keynesian position is correct depends on the degree of crowding out asserted by the former, or the degree of crowding in (the activation of idle balances) asserted by the Keynesians. These effects are related to the relative sensitivity of the demand for money and investment to changes in the rate of interest, and to whether the transactions motive or the speculative motive for holding money balances is the stronger one.

QUESTIONS

1. What is the difference between fiscal and monetary policy, and which institution implements which policy?
2. Taxation as a tool of fiscal policy is ineffective because of its long decision lag. Why is this lag long? How might it be shortened?
3. "The basic purpose of government taxation is to finance government spending. In a recession, tax revenue falls because income falls; therefore, either (1) government spending must be reduced, or (2) marginal and average tax rates must be raised to finance and same level of government spending."
   a. Do you agree with the first statement? Explain.
   b. With the second? Explain.
4. What arguments can you give against the idea of indexing the tax rate to cancel the effects of inflation? What argument for indexing taxes? Is the indexing an example of an automatic or discretionary stabilizer? Why?
5. Are the following examples of discretionary fiscal policy, automatic fiscal policy, or neither?
   a. Social Security payments indexed to the inflation.
   b. A national tax amendment that would generally limit the percentage increase in each year's federal spending to the percentage rise in the GNP. But the spending limit would go lower whenever the inflation rate exceeded 3 percent.
   c. Funds for floods and other natural disasters.
   d. Food stamps.
6. What does it mean to say that the Treasury can roll over the debt. Can private corporations do it? Are there therefore no differences between private and government debt? Explain.
7. A newspaper item says, "Inflation will help narrow the federal budget deficit this year." How is that possible?
8. Observed deficits during a recession are primarily due to the economy's effect on the budget, not the budget's influence on the economy. Interpret the statement.
9. Laurel and Hardy in a 1941 film, *A Haunting We Will Go* are conned by a bunco artist into believing a small portable device—an inflato—will convert $1 bills into $10 and $100 bills. They buy it. Oliver claims, "This machine could take the country out of bankruptcy." Suppose the device did reproduce $100 bills.
   a. The year 1941 was the last year of the Great Depression. Would the country have

been better off if the inflation had substantially raised the public's cash holdings?

b. If the economy had been fully employed instead, would the interest rate go up or down in the short run? Why? In the long run? Why?

10. In January 1976, Senator Harry F. Byrd was quoted as saying, "The debt by the end of fiscal year June 30, 1976 would be $620 billion. Some 35 percent of that debt was accumulated between fiscal 1971 to fiscal 1976. The other 65 percent was accumulated over a period of 150 years prior to 1971." Does the U.S. issue 150-year maturity bonds? To what extent, if at all, is he right in that we still owe debt incurred 150 years ago? To what extent is he wrong?
11. "If the federal deficit can be financed by selling bonds to you and me, then it really isn't inflationary." What is the reasoning behind this statement?
12. What are, if any, the benefits to you of the large national debt of 1942–1945 that actually exceeded the GNP and caused the severe inflation of 1946–1949?
13. Some politicians and laymen argue that government deficits are inflationary. Under what circumstances is this true? False?
14. What argument can you give that government debt caused by government financing the construction of a bridge does not impose a burden on future generations? What is meant by *burden*? Suppose the future generation must pay a substantial part of the taxes on the bridge. What argument can you make that the future generation nonetheless incurs no net loss?
15. If the Treasury in a given week issues fewer securities whose total value is less than what the Treasury pays out on matured securities, what is it actually doing?
16. In October 1979, Paul Volcker, chairman of the Board of Governors of the Federal Reserve, said, "Things will be different this time." He meant that though the Fed is not going to completely ignore the federal funds rate, the Fed will be much more willing to let the rate fluctuate more than in the past. In other words, the market will set the federal funds rate. "The system will add or drain reserves on the basis of reserve estimates." Why is this a significant change and one that pleased the monetarists?
17. The Fed says the money supply has been hard to control. If someone replies, "Yes, particularly when the Fed has been primarily trying to control something else." What is that something else, and why does it make M_S hard to control?
18. Assuming that fiscal policy is effective, how does private saving actually increase even though the federal government when it borrows competes with the private sector for funds? Crowding-out proponents argue that government competition for funds drives up interest rates that depress private business investment since the level of investment is a function of interest rates. Can you explain why private savings might still be able to increase and be available for private sector investment needed for economic growth?
19. "The evil of the federal deficit is that it creates costlier debt elsewhere in the economy." Explain this remark. Is this costlier debt necessarily bad? Explain.
20. Keynesians contend that federal borrowing would tap otherwise used speculative cash and be fed into the spending stream. A deficit operates to mop up balances and stimulate the economy. How? What is this called?
21. What effect would a serious inflation have on the velocity of money? The demand for real balances? Why?
22. The velocity of money varied slightly around 3-1/2 from 1910 to 1930, dropped to below 3 during the 1930s, and bottomed out to 2 around 1946 and thereafter continued to rise reaching about 6 in 1979. The upward trend has been attributed to the adoption by firms and banks of more efficient cash and payment techniques; for example, the use of computers to quickly adjust bank balances that keep excess reserves closed to reserve margins and the use of credit and banking cards by the

public. How did these innovations raise velocity? Why was velocity so low during World War II? Was not military spending very high then?

23. What is the concern by the business community, and others, about federal deficit financing? Do businesses not deficit-finance too? So what is the fuss?
24. What is meant by the statement that the primary differences between the Keynesians and monetarists is empirical?
25. "Monetarism is the nonmonetarist world in which lags disappear. When lags disappear then you are back in the classical world." Explain.
26. Milton Friedman would like to see discretionary monetary policy abandoned and a monetary rule substituted. Is it because monetary policy is not that important? Explain. What problems are associated with a monetary rule?
27. One group writes the basic relation between money and income as $Y = aM$ and the other by $M = aY$. What, if anything at all, is each equation predicting? Which equation is associated with the monetarists and which with the Keynesians?
28. (With reference to 27) Franco Modigliani of MIT says, "I wish the monetarists would understand that if you are dealing with a great depression, then the constancy of a is a luxury you cannot use." What does he mean?
29. Modigliani also said (refer to 28), "It is unfortunate but true that value judgments end up playing a major role in economists' assessments of parameters (such as a) and the evidence they consider." What bearing and implications does this have on the stabilization controversy?
30. Do you believe a depression like the one in the 1930s is much less likely today? Why? Would you say it is impossible? Why, or why not?

Chapter 30

Employment and Unemployment

PROGRESS REPORT

A. Chapter 29 discussed stabilization policy with full employment as one of the stabilization goals of policy.

B. In this chapter the nature of unemployment is examined. We explain why official estimates of unemployment must be interpreted carefully. Then several types of unemployment are discussed, followed by more recent hypotheses about causes of unemployment and possible remedies. Unemployment is seen as a complex interaction between economic and institutional influences. Several hypotheses are also offered to explain why money wages tend not to fall even when aggregate demand declines. The chapter ends with a discussion of job creating fallacies.

C. Chapter 31 introduces the dilemma proposed by trying to remove unemployment in the economy – the lower unemployment falls, the greater is the threat to price stability. The result of lower unemployment will surely be inflation. Various theories of inflation are discussed in some detail.

Along with inflation, unemployment is a major concern of macroeconomic analysis. But what exactly is unemployment? Does it signify the lack of a job, any job, or lack of a good job? What is, therefore, a good job? When is a wage too low or adequate? Is someone employed who only works 10 hours a week? 15? or 20? Suppose a person who works 20 hours a week makes twice as much in wages or salary as someone who works 40 hours a week. Is the part-time worker still only partially employed, hence partially unemployed? And who are the unemployed? Is it someone who does not have a job? Suppose they are not looking for one? Is someone who has quit looking really unemployed? Are underemployed people really unemployed? For example, is the engineer with a bachelor's degree who can only find a job as a taxi driver really unemployed, even though he has a job of sorts? What about people who do unpaid volunteer work? What about workers who are on strike and loggers who are idle because of the danger of fire in overly dry forests? How should they be classified? Or what about students who leave summer jobs to return to school and people in the military? What about people who are leaving one job to take another but will be idle 10 days during the switch?

THE LABOR FORCE

The total *labor force* includes people 16 or over actively looking for jobs plus military personnel. It excludes the institutionalized or disabled, students, housekeepers, and discouraged job-seekers.

Before discussing details about who is officially employed or unemployed, first we need to know who is in the labor force.

Total labor force: Those 16 and over who either have a job or are actively looking for a job plus those in the military.
Not in the labor force: Those who have no job nor are actively looking for a job. That includes

1. Those under 16 years of age.
2. Those who are inmates of institutions such as prisons and mental hospitals regardless of age.
3. Housekeepers, students, the disabled, and the retired.
4. Other: Those who do not fit into any of the above. They do not participate because (a) they want to work only at certain times of the year, (b) they are discouraged individuals who believe no jobs are available that fit their experience and training so they quit looking, or (c) they are financially independent and desire no job.

Civilian labor force: The total labor force minus people in the military.
Noninstitutional population: Civilians not in institutions.

The *participation rate* is the ratio of the labor force to the noninstitutional civilian population.

The size of the labor force is illustrated in Table 30-1 for the years 1929 to 1980. Those individuals who are considered to be in the labor force are called labor force participants. The **participation rate** is the ratio of participants to the total civilian noninstitutional population 16 and over. Rates for selected years appear in Table 30-2. Participation and unemployment rate calculations are depicted in Table 30-3.

TABLE 30-1 Employment Status of the Noninstitutional Population 16 Years and Over, Selected Years 1947 to 1980 (Numbers in Thousands)

		Total labor force		Civilian labor force							
					Fmployed			Unemployed			
Year	Total noninstitutional population	Number	Percent of population	Total	Total	Agriculture	Nonagricultural industries	Number	Percent of labor force	Not in labor force	Average weeks unemployed during year
1947	103,418	60,941	58.9	59,350	57,038	7,890	49,148	2,311	3.9	42,477	—
1950	106,645	63,858	59.9	62,208	58,918	7,160	51,758	3,288	5.3	42,787	12.1
1955	112,732	68,072	60.4	65,023	62,170	6,450	55,722	2,852	4.4	44,660	13.0
1960	119,759	72,142	60.2	69,628	65,778	5,458	60,318	3,852	5.5	47,617	12.8
1965	129,236	77,178	59.7	74,455	71,088	4,361	66,726	3,366	4.5	52,058	11.8
1970	140,182	85,903	61.3	82,715	78,627	3,462	75,165	4,088	4.9	54,280	8.8
1975	153,449	94,793	61.8	92,613	84,783	3,380	81,403	7,830	8.5	58,655	14.1
1979	163,620	104,996	64.2	102,908	96,945	3,297	93,648	5,963	5.8	58,623	10.8
1980	166,246	106,821	64.3	104,719	97,270	3,310	93,960	7,448	7.1	59,425	11.9

Source: Employment and Earnings, Nov. 1980. Monthly Labor Review, Feb. 1981, and Economic Report of The President, 1980.

TABLE 30-2 Participation Rates (Total Labor Force as a Percentage of Total Noninstitutional Population, Selected Years 1950 to 1980)

	1950	1955	1960	1965	1970	1975	1980
Total	59.2	59.3	59.4	58.9	60.4	61.2	63.8
Male	86.4	85.3	83.3	80.7	79.7	77.9	77.4
Female	33.9	35.7	37.7	39.3	43.3	46.3	51.6

Source: Economic Report of The President, 1981, Table B-27, p. 264.

TABLE 30-3 Participation and Unemployment Rates of Noninstitutional Population, Oct. 1980

Civilian noninstitutional population	167,005,000
Civilian labor force	105,415,000
Employed	97,933,000
Unemployed	7,482,000
Not in labor force	59,469,000

$$\text{Participation rate} = \frac{\text{labor force}}{\text{civilian population}} \times 100 = 63.1\%$$

$$\text{Unemployment rate} = \frac{\text{Unemployed}}{\text{labor force}} \times 100 = 7.1\%$$

Source: U.S. Dept. of Labor, Bureau of Labor Statistics.

Definitions and Data Collecting

In order to study the phenomenon of employment and unemployment, definitions and data collecting are necessary. Employment data are collected for the Bureau of Labor Statistics (BLS)[1] by the Bureau of the Census (since 1940), which also publishes them monthly in the *Current Population Survey* (CPS). The information is gathered from surveys of households and business establishments.

Once a month, during the week that includes the 19th of that month, the Bureau of the Census conducts its household survey for the BLS. The purpose is to estimate the employment status for the prior week containing the 12th of the month. Thus, there is a lag of a week. Since it is impractical and costly to interview every household, a sample from among the 3,100 counties in the U.S. is selected, comprising some 924 areas and covering some part of every state. Overall, some 70,000 households are interviewed. Military data are acquired from the Department of Defense (DOD). Each month about one fourth of the sample is replaced with other households. The people interviewed are not asked whether they consider themselves as employed or not. Their employment status is decided by standards set up by the Bureau of the Census when they examine and interpret the information on the questionnaires. Fourteen- and fifteen-year olds can be interviewed but have not been included in the official statistics since 1947.

The *unemployment rate* is the percentage of unemployed in the civilian labor force.

The **unemployment rate** is an estimated measure of the percentage of unemployed among the *civilian* labor force. It is the civilian population not in institutions that is of interest to us.

Counting the Employed

Civilians 16 and over are considered employed if, during the survey week, they were paid or worked for profit a minimum of one hour, or worked 15 hours or more without pay in a family operated enterprise. Also included are persons with jobs but who were not at work for a temporary period during the survey week because of illness, vacation, a labor dispute, bad weather, or personal problems.

Counting the Unemployed

Persons 16 and over and in the labor force are considered unemployed if they were not working during the survey week but were available for work (except for temporary illness) and made specific efforts to find a job within the past 4 weeks by either applying directly to an employer, checking with friends or relatives, registering with a private or public employment office, answering ads, or being on a union or professional register. Also included are those who were waiting for work and were waiting to be called back to a job from which they had been laid off, or were waiting to report to a new paying job within 30 days. Figure 30-1 displays the relationships, and Table 30-4 provides some numbers.

[1] The BLS publishes the *Monthly Labor Review* and the *Employment and Earnings Journals* under the auspices of the Department of Labor.

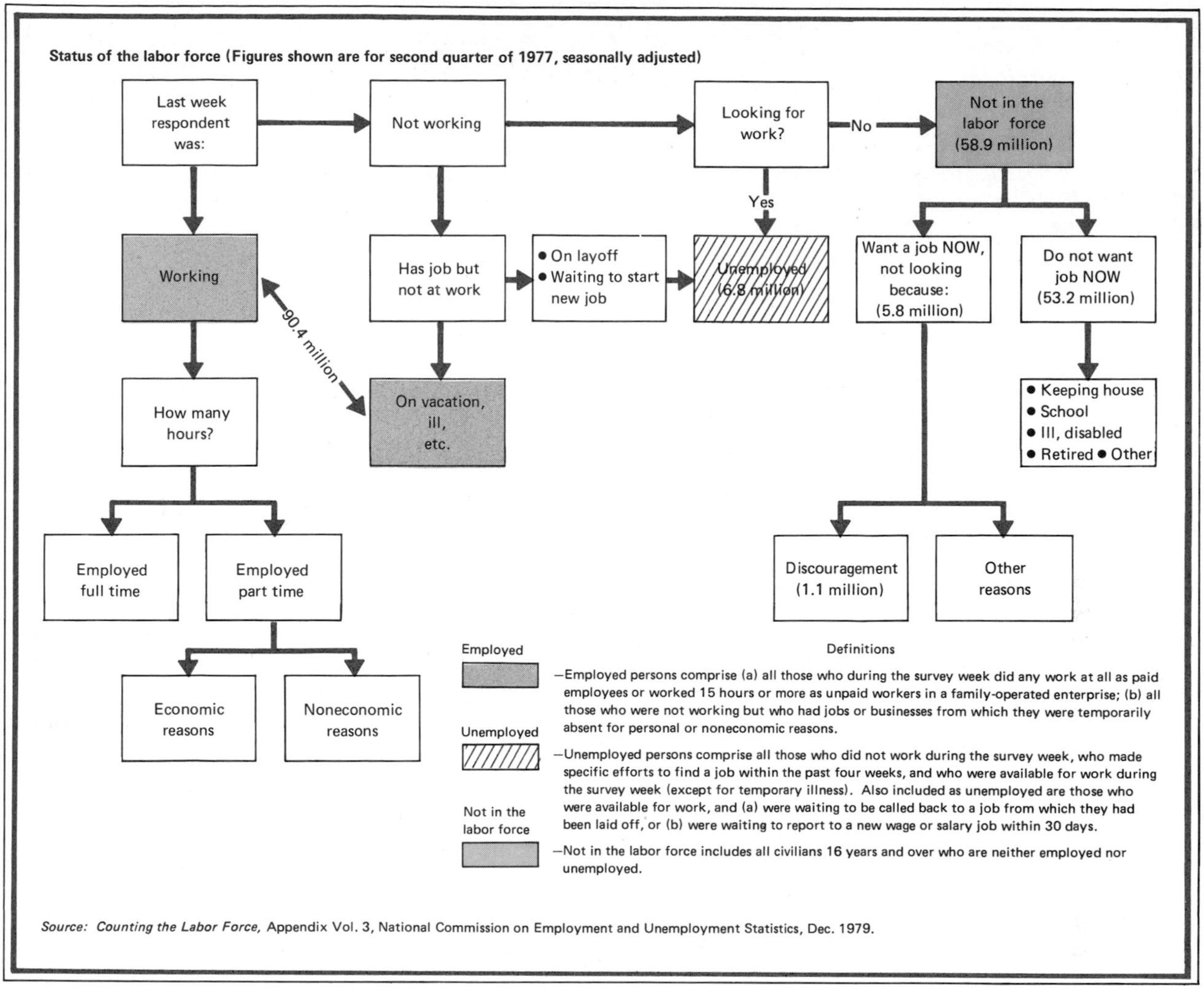

Figure 30-1

Full-time Employment

Counted as *full-time workers* are those working 35 or more hours weekly, those working 1 to 34 hours weekly for noneconomic reasons but normally working full time, and those working part time for economic reasons.

The definition of **full-time workers** used by the BLS includes:

1. Persons working 35 hours or more in the survey week.
2. Persons who work less than 35 hours for noneconomic reasons (bad weather, vacation, illness, labor dispute, school, want part time, full time only in peak season) but usually work full time.
3. Persons on part time for economic reasons (slack work at the firm, material shortages, repairs to plant and equipment, start or termination of a job during survey week, or cannot find full-time work) whether or not they usually work full time.

Some 40 percent of people defined to be full-time employees work less than 35 hours a week. Part-timers in the labor force are defined as those unemployed who seek only part-time work plus those working who only want to work part time and usually do so.

TABLE 30-4
Employment Status of the Civilian Noninstitutional Population, July 1977 (Thousands of Persons 16 Years of Age and Over)

Employment status	July
Total civilian noninstitutional population	156,547
Civilian labor force	99,314
Employed	92,372
At work	81,111
Full time	62,767
Part time	18,343
With a job but not at work	11,261
On strike	138
On vacation	8,933
Bad weather	48
Temporary illness	1,296
Other	846
Unemployed	6,941
Looking for full-time work	5,797
Looking for part-time work	1,144
Not in the labor force	57,234
Keeping house	34,740
In school	1,915
Unable to work	2,874
Other	17,706

Source: U.S. Dept. of Labor, *Employment and Earnings.*

In December 1979 the National Commission on Employment and Unemployment statistics published a report concluding that methods for measuring the unemployment rate were adequate nationally but poor for local areas.

Some New Definitions

Since 1969 the BLS has been publishing a new series that breaks down the unemployed into job losers and job leavers, something a little different from the quit and layoff series also compiled by the BLS.[2] Since February 1977 the BLS has also published data dividing job losers into those on layoff and those permanently separated from their jobs. The total number of unemployed now comprise the sum of job leavers, job losers, reentrants, and new entrants. The labor market flow is shown in Figure 30-2. The figure shows the older categories used by the BLS in parentheses. A breakdown of the data is provided in Table 30-5.

Unemployment statistics distinguish among *job losers, job leavers, reentrants,* and *new entrants.*

Job losers are persons on *temporary layoff* (of less than 30 days) or on *indefinite layoff* (of 30 days or more with no set recall date), plus persons who are *permanent job losers* who were fired or retired (involuntarily) and began immediately to look for work in the 4 weeks preceding the survey.

Job leavers are persons who quit their previous jobs and immediately began looking for work in the 4 weeks prior to the survey.

[2] Bureau of Labor Statistics, *Employment and Earnings,* Feb. 1972.

Figure 30-2

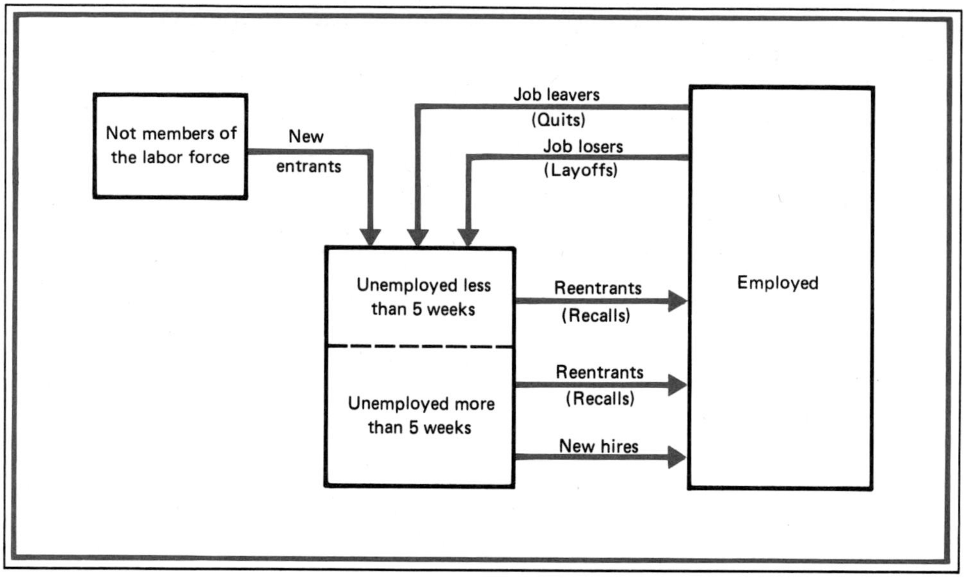

Reentrants are those who previously worked at a full-time job lasting 2 weeks or longer but who later dropped out of the labor force for a while before again looking for work.

TABLE 30-5
Unemployed Persons 16 Years and Over, by Reason and Sex; for Selected Years 1969 to 1980 (percentages)

	1969	1971	1973	1975	1978	1980[1]
Total						
Job losers	35.9	46.3	38.7	55.4	41.6	49.3
Job leavers	15.4	11.8	15.7	10.4	14.1	12.2
Reentrants	34.1	29.4	30.7	23.8	30.0	28.0
New entrants	14.6	12.5	14.9	10.4	14.3	10.5
	100.0	100.0	100.0	100.0	100.0	100.0
Male						
Job losers	45.5	55.5	48.2	65.6	51.5	60.6
Job leavers	15.7	11.0	14.9	8.4	13.3	10.7
Reentrants	26.7	23.1	23.6	17.5	22.6	19.6
New entrants	12.1	10.4	13.3	8.5	12.6	9.1
	100.0	100.0	100.0	100.0	100.0	100.0
Female						
Job losers	26.5	34.8	28.3	42.5	31.4	36.2
Job leavers	15.2	12.8	16.6	12.9	14.9	13.9
Reentrants	41.3	37.2	38.5	31.8	37.6	37.6
New entrants	17.0	15.2	16.6	12.8	16.1	12.3
	100.0	100.0	100.0	100.0	100.0	100.0

[1]Preliminary data.
Source: U.S. Dept. of Labor, *Employment and Earnings*.

New entrants are persons who never worked at a full-time job lasting 2 weeks or more.

In addition to these developments, the data collection has been expanded and more in-depth interviews implemented. More information is being obtained from and for persons not in the labor force, e.g., 14- and 15-year-olds and those who have given up looking for work and why they have given up looking. Prior to 1967 these details were not gathered by the survey.

Interpretation of Data

As you may have inferred by now, stated unemployment figures must be carefully interpreted to arrive at their real meaning. It is possible for the unemployment rate to be overstated or understated.

In 1979 economists John Barron of Purdue University and Wesley Mellow of the Labor Department published a study covering 3,188 unemployed persons, in which they concluded jobless insurance led to recipients spending 20 percent less time looking for work than those not drawing benefits. The average recipient remained unemployed almost eight weeks longer than a person not applying for benefits. This, of course, inflates the unemployment figures. Recorded unemployment is also higher because the definitions count as being unemployed those students looking for but not finding part-time work. If such students were not counted, the unemployment rate would drop by about one half percent. The lengthening of search time for people who are temporarily yet voluntarily unemployed because other members of the household are working, or do not want just any job, or are seeking a wage which is unrealistically high in the current job market for which their skills are inadequate to command the wage they seek, all tend to overstate the amount of real unemployment.

Conversely, the announced level of unemployment gleaned from the statistics may very well understate real unemployment. As we have noted, the official count considers many part-time workers as fully employed. Many of these prefer full-time work, i.e., work of 35 hours or more a week, but are not able to find it. They are partially unemployed. Consider the person who is fully employed performing tasks below his or her level of training and competence, for example, the unemployed teacher who is driving a taxi. These instances are forms of what is called disguised unemployment. Of course, one could counter that the teacher turned taxi driver simply means that the value society places on an additional teacher is less than the market value society places on an additional taxi driver. Therefore, from the overall viewpoint of the economy he is not underemployed. That is to say, the labor market is signaling that society does not need another teacher; it needs another taxi driver.

Finally, there are those persons who become discouraged and give up looking for work and are dropped from the official statistics. Several researchers concluded, however, that discouraged workers should not be included since few seek work even when demand is high.[3] Our discussion here is assuming a nearly fully employed economy and is not to be construed in the back-

[3] Rose McElhatten, "Should Discouraged Workers Be Counted in the Labor Force?—A Job Search Approach." The Federal Reserve Bank of San Francisco, *Economic Review*, Winter 1980. The 1979 study by the National Commission for Employment and Unemployment Statistics recommended that more information be gathered on the labor force attachment of discouraged workers.

drop of the tragic imagery of the 1930's depression where unemployed people would have happily taken any job offered.

Business cycle fluctuations can also provide misleading clues about economic health. During periods of contraction many firms, anticipating that the slowdown will only be temporary, react by retaining their workers—particularly skilled ones. Even though they are being underused, the administrative costs to the firm of processing layoffs and of rehiring as well as taking new people when the recovery occurs is more expensive than keeping already proven personnel on the payroll. They hoard or stockpile labor. Of course, once the decline is seen as more than temporary, layoffs will occur. But in the short run, economic decline is not immediately reflected in rising unemployment. There is a lag.

Likewise, in periods of recovery, when aggregate demand is rising the unemployed find jobs more rapidly. It might also engender optimism in those officially categorized as not being in the labor force to become participants. They are apt to be the lesser skilled. When they become actively involved in searching for jobs they suddenly show up in the unemployment statistics. In this case, the rising unemployment figures obscure the real improvement in the economy.

NORMAL UNEMPLOYMENT

Is there a normal rate of unemployment in industrialized economies? If so, what is it? Is it equal, perhaps, to the number of vacant jobs or to those who want jobs but cannot get the right one at the right wage? Is it equal to those who want jobs—any job—but cannot get them?

Table 30-1 indicates that in the period between World War II and 1958 the average rate of unemployment was around 4 percent, but after that it has averaged closer to 5 percent. From the years 1943 to 1945 unemployment was quite low. However, one must remember there were 11,000,000 people in the military during that period. Also, from 1966 to 1969 the rate was a little less than 4 percent. Again, the economy was supporting a war; government expenditures were higher without upward pressure on aggregate demand being eased by a sufficient tax increase. As a result, the price rises reflected the beginnings of a major increase in the rate of inflation which extended into the 1980s. From 1966 to 1970, during the Vietnam War, over 3 million people were members of the armed forces each year. Other thousands went underground or fled the country. Many others sought refuge from the draft by going to college, removing themselves as statistics in the noninstitutional civilian labor force.

For many years 4 percent was considered the normal unemployment rate. Today many economists argue that it is higher, perhaps 5 percent. There is speculation it may go higher because of inevitable structural changes in the economy as the nature of production and the labor force change.

Using historical data, Arthur Okun (pronounced O'-kun) derived Okun's law that related unemployment to GNP.[4] A prediction of Okun's law says that

[4] Arthur M. Okun, "Potential GNP: Its Measurement and Significance," *Proceedings of the Business and Economics Statistics Section of the American Statistical Association, 1962,* pp. 98–104.

GNP must grow by 3.3 percent to yield a 1 percentage point decline in unemployment. Why the sluggish response of employment to increases in GNP? Okun offered several reasons. One is that in bad times inexperienced adult women, the young, and other unskilled workers leave or are the first laid off from jobs. In good times they try to regain jobs. But leaving is easier than entering—first fired and last hired. Thus their rehiring lags the growth in GNP. Second, the nature of modern business reinforces the first explanation. Output is expanded initially in the recovery phase of a cycle by using the existing labor overtime. In an expansion a firm may hire one more machine operator who greatly increases output, but it need not hire more janitors, file clerks, and telephone operators to increase output at the start. Third, during slowdowns some part-time people are laid off. When or if they return to work during upswings many will want full-time jobs.

COSTS OF UNEMPLOYMENT

The economic *costs of unemployment* can be measured by the loss of production or income; there are also unrecorded emotional and psychological costs.

The economic cost of unemployment can be measured by considering either the loss of output to the economy or the loss of income to factors of production. Because of unemployment, actual GNP is less than the potential GNP that would be realized at full employment. The difference between the actual GNP and potential GNP is the GNP gap. It is usually positive, implying that potential GNP minus actual GNP is greater than zero. It is possible for the difference to be slightly negative because of overtime and firms running their plants at rates beyond the most efficient level of capacity. A rough estimate of the GNP gap is derived by multiplying average worker productivity times the number of unemployed. From the income side, the GNY gap would be determined by multiplying the average annual wage by the number of unemployed.

Aside from direct economic losses, there are social costs to unemployment that no doubt impact on the economic measurements. These social costs involve things like mental breakdowns, depression, the decay of unused skills, increases in crime (mostly among the young), as well as family disputes and broken marriages.

TYPES OF UNEMPLOYMENT

The labor market is in a constant state of flux. People periodically assess their job prospects, revise expectations, and refocus ambitions. At any one moment people are leaving jobs, entering new jobs, returning to old jobs, others are in that transitional period between leaving one job and heading to another. These labor flows occur under all market conditions, stable or unstable. Thus at all times there are some people who are classified as unemployed, many for periods of very short duration, others for longer periods of time.

We shall first briefly outline four traditional theories espoused as the cause of unemployment before proceeding to more recent theories.

Cyclical Unemployment

Cyclical unemployment **is caused by recurrent fluctuations in aggregate demand.**

Aside from seasonal variations, there is unemployment that is definitely tied to recurrent changes in aggregate demand. During a downswing in economic activity, the rate of those leaving jobs (but not quitting) rises while the rate of those entering employment declines. In downswings, therefore, the net effect is an increase in the unemployment rate.

Cycles obscure differences in the composition of the labor force, hiding details of the cycle's effect on component parts of the labor force. For example, the manufacturing sector may feel the effect of a downswing more quickly and intensely than elements of the service sector. The data reveal that when job losers are divided into job losers on layoff and those on permanent separation, those on layoff vary much more over the cycle than do permanent separations. That is, those on layoff are unemployed for shorter durations in the cycle.

Frictional Unemployment

Frictional unemployment **is the short-term, normal inactivity between jobs.**

Frictional unemployment is the rate of unemployment that results from the time it takes new entrants to go through the process of finding their first job, as well as those who are in the process of changing jobs and are necessarily unemployed even though their unemployment may be of short duration. The emphasis here is that frictional unemployment represents the time spent looking for a job. The BLS estimates that duration to be a period of less than 5 weeks. In fact, a majority of those unemployed are idle for less than 1 month. The BLS disaggregates unemployment data into groupings of 1–4 weeks, 5–14 weeks, and 15 weeks and over. Often they subdivide the 5–14 week period. It has been observed that the number of people unemployed for over 15 weeks rises dramatically over the year when unemployment is high. Since 1971 the average number of weeks of unemployment among the unemployed has been above 11-1/2 weeks. Given what was just said about the majority of unemployed being unemployed for less than 1 month, the implication is that there is a minority of unemployed who were without jobs for substantially longer than 15 weeks over the year. See Table 30-6.

Under the more recent BLS classifications, rising unemployment rates correlate with those who are classified as job losers even though job losers generally constitute less than half of those who are unemployed. Other unemployed include new entrants, reentrants, and job leavers. As unemployment has increased, job losers have increased disproportionately to those classified in these other three categories.

Structural Unemployment

Structural unemployment **is due to the mismatching of applicants' skills and the requirements of vacant jobs.**

Structural unemployment results from impersonal changes in the labor market arising from the emergence of new products and techniques and the need for new skills to provide them, while at the same time other products become obsolete and the demand for the accompanying skills declines. You might say it is long-run frictional unemployment. Supply and demand schedules respond to the reshuffling of resource use—human and nonhuman—that alters relative prices. Electronic pocket calculators replace slide rules; computers replace clerks; plastic pipes make metal ones unnecessary; children ride skate boards instead of playing marbles and stickball. Tennis becomes

TABLE 30-6
Unemployment by Duration, 1947–80 (Monthly Data Seasonally Adjusted; Thousands of Persons 16 Years of Age and Over)

Year	Total unemployment	Duration of unemployment: Less than 5 weeks	5–14 weeks	15–26 weeks	27 weeks and over	Average (mean) duration in weeks
1947	2,311	1,210	704	234	164	—
1948	2,276	1,300	669	193	116	8.6
1949	3,637	1,756	1,194	428	256	10.0
1950	3,288	1,450	1,055	425	357	12.1
1951	2,055	1,177	574	166	137	9.7
1952	1,883	1,135	516	148	84	8.4
1953	1,834	1,142	482	132	78	8.0
1954	3,532	1,605	1,116	495	317	11.8
1955	2,852	1,335	815	366	336	13.0
1956	2,750	1,412	805	301	232	11.3
1957	2,859	1,408	891	321	239	10.5
1958	4,602	1,753	1,396	785	667	13.9
1959	3,740	1,585	1,114	469	571	14.4
1960	3,852	1,719	1,176	503	454	12.8
1961	4,714	1,806	1,376	728	804	15.6
1962	3,911	1,663	1,134	534	585	14.7
1963	4,070	1,751	1,231	535	553	14.0
1964	3,786	1,697	1,117	491	482	13.3
1965	3,366	1,628	983	404	351	11.8
1966	2,875	1,573	779	287	239	10.4
1967	2,975	1,634	893	271	177	8.8
1968	2,817	1,594	810	256	156	8.4
1969	2,832	1,629	827	242	133	7.9
1970	4,088	2,137	1,289	427	235	8.7
1971	4,993	2,234	1,578	655	517	11.3
1972	4,840	2,223	1,459	597	562	12.0
1973	4,304	2,196	1,296	475	337	10.0
1974	5,076	2,567	1,572	563	373	9.7
1975	7,830	2,894	2,452	1,290	1,193	14.1
1976	7,288	2,790	2,159	1,003	1,336	15.8
1977	6,855	2,856	2,089	896	1,015	14.3
1978	6,047	2,793	1,875	746	633	11.9
1979	5,963	2,869	1,892	684	518	10.8
1980	7,448	3,208	2,411	1,028	802	11.9

Source: U.S. Dept. of Labor, Employment and Earnings.

fashionable, increasing the demand for tennis rackets, balls, and equipment with which to restring the rackets. Raw materials become scarce and synthetics take their place; factories move and demand for labor in a particular area falls, but sociological and psychological factors prevent the labor force from moving out of an area to other areas for jobs such as happened in Appalachia in the 1950s and 1960s when the demand for coal fell while that of oil and gas rose. Also, population growth changes the composition of the labor force. The high birth rate after World War II raised the proportion of teenagers in the population from 7 to 9.3 percent in the 1960s. The higher unemployment levels among blacks and Hispanics is related to the higher birth rates among them since their average age is lower, rendering them less employable. The women's movement is encouraging women to reenter the labor force after their childbearing years. Women are marrying later and having fewer children. All these factors affect the unemployment rates.

As the kind of work people do changes, where less muscle and more technique is required, structural unemployment results as skills are not matched to job openings. The proportion of service jobs (hotel attendants, restaurant help, repairmen) is increasing, whereas there is a relative decline in manufacturing and construction jobs.

With more women and teenagers entering the labor market, the participation rate rises and translates into higher unemployment statistics. Their job turnover rate and absentee rate on the average is higher.

Because of these mismatches of skills to job vacancies, a consistent unemployment level of less than 4 percent does not seem possible at this time. In fact 5 percent or more may now have to be accepted as the natural level of unemployment. But this seems a rather arbitrary way of defining away unemployment. The full employment level is lowered from 96 percent to 95 percent or less by merely redefining what is full employment or what constitutes natural unemployment.

Some economists, not many, believe an unemployment rate of 4 percent or less is achievable because the higher educational levels of today's population satisfy the increasing number of jobs that now require more education and training—the kinds of jobs in which there are less turnover and more stable work patterns. There is support among these economists for more government supported programs such as work study, student loans, manpower and training, and Job Corps. The Federal government spends over $10 billion a year on training and employment programs.

Keynesian Unemployment

Keynesian unemployment **stems from a persistent weakness in aggregate demand due to an inadequate stabilization policy.**

Improper monetary and fiscal management gives rise to deficient aggregate demand. The job lines appear and lengthen. If aggregate demand is strong enough, the job lines will dwindle and the unemployed will go to work. More government spending and tax cuts leading to growth is the fiscal path to job creation when there is slack in the private sector. The more ardent Keynesians tend to dismiss the structural explanations for unemployment and maintain that unemployment is an involuntary consequence of aggregate demand being too low. Critics contend that financing such an expansion would lead to large deficits and be inflationary. Not so, is the reply. In the short run there would be deficits, but more people working, even with lowered tax rates, would give rise to greater tax revenues because taxable income would be larger. Higher levels of aggregate demand would stimulate increased production. Supply would keep pace with demand, and inflation need not be a serious problem. Even then, some inflation is worth the price if the economy can operate more consistently at or near full employment. The human and economic cost of unemployment is greater than the burdens imposed by some inflation on some people. Some inflation is socially worth the reduction in unemployment.

Others respond that a policy that boosted aggregate demand cannot alter structural facts. Using inflation to increase employment will not reduce unemployment among the unemployable. It will only have serious long-term effects on prices. The result will be an increasing trade-off between inflation and unemployment. That is, higher prices and higher unemployment will occur simultaneously. An inflationary environment creates uncertainty among producers and higher wage expectations among workers. Producers delay expansion and workers hold out for higher wages. The result is that both prices and unemployment rise. This messy soup is called stagflation—the unskilled remain unemployed while still others are added to stew in the unemployment pot. Traditional fiscal policy in a modern, industrially sophisticated economy would increase the demand for those materials and human skills already employed, without reducing the number of jobless or increasing the short-run supply of resources. The result is that aggregate demand temporarily rises, but supply does not. This results in bottlenecks (shortages), causing production costs to rise, which creates uncertainty about investment expenditures by firms, eventually leading to layoffs and further declines in aggregate demand.

MORE RECENT THEORIES

In recent years some new theories about the labor market have appeared which incorporate some of the ideas embedded in the former theories and in some cases are extensions or refinements of them.

Job Search Theory

According to the *job search theory*, job search unemployment is voluntary unemployment related to the greater time taken to acquire more information about jobs.

According to job search theory, labor turnover and the duration of time between jobs is viewed as a logical extension of the maximization principle and an explanation for frictional unemployment. Job seekers do not necessarily take the first job offered nor do employers hire the first applicant interviewed. A person is acquiring information while searching for a job, and the longer the duration the more information he or she can obtain. The expectation is that the longer wait is rewarded by a better quality and a better paying job, such that the future psychic and monetary rewards will more than make up for the loss of income experienced in the longer search taken. The workers also have expectations about what pay their skills command. They may be in error about this. If so, it will take time for the person to realize this unpleasant fact.

According to the job search theory, the job searcher is investing in information. Hence, the major element in unemployment is not lack of jobs but frequent voluntary job turnover—short spells of unemployment. Search theorists contend that by reducing the frictions in acquiring information on which to realistically base expectations, the unemployment figures can be significantly reduced. Lower the information gap and reduce voluntary unemployment. Some analysts of the labor market do not accept this concept. Job search, they feel, cannot explain the higher unemployment rates among teenagers, blacks, and women, higher than can be accounted for by the normal process of job hopping. But job search proponents believe the unemployment rates can definitely be reduced through better and faster matchings of job seekers to job vacancies, through improved job counseling, skills being taught that supply the skills actually demanded, and transportation subsidies to the unemployed to interview for and take jobs in other areas. They would also attempt to remove restraints imposed by special interests' licensing requirements, and union rules and policies that tightly regulate entry in various kinds of employment and invariably increase the length, hence the cost of job search. Examples are laws that require the licensing of all kinds of repairmen, unions preventing high school age musicians from playing at school dances held off the school grounds, and the creation of tight entry regulations into apprenticeship programs. The programs themselves, often artificially lengthened, serve as an important device to discourage entry into skilled crafts.

Human Capital Theory

Human capital **consists of education, training, and experience which enhance prospects for employment.**

Developed initially by Theodore Schultz (Nobel Prize, 1979) and Gary Becker at the University of Chicago, human capital theory emphasizes a microeconomic approach to unemployment. The decision maker is rational and makes choices calculated to maximize his income and wealth by deciding whether or not to invest in himself and, if so, how much and for how long. Investment takes the form of education and training pursued formally in educational institutions or by private arrangement with an employer whereby the employee willingly accepts a lower pay, if any, in order to learn the business. This investment in oneself is to increase one's human capital, making one more efficient and productive. The higher the productivity the higher is one's earning power in a competitive system.

This theory, as with the job search model, places more emphasis on the supply side of the labor market and associates employment opportunities with free, personal investment choices by workers. The objective is to qualify oneself for a stable, well-paying job at which one is likely to stay. As you can see, the human capital theory model provides some justification for employment levels and the existing wage distribution. Thus, there is some connection to structural arguments. Work-study, manpower training, and polishing rusty skills are also viewed as a means of increasing one's human capital.

Critics claim this approach ignores the whole complex of cultural, institutional, and psychological factors explaining why some people do or do not have the motivation or perception to pursue the acquisition of human capital. Such factors must be better understood if the persistent problem of unemployment is to be solved. In this regard, argue the job-search critics, the problem is not a lack of jobs but the excessive turnover rate. To others, institutional discrimination is the primary cause of the lack of human capital among the chronically unemployable. But the human capital theory only says that low human capital is a cause of low earning power. It does not explain why some do not try to raise or cannot raise their human capital.

Voluntary and Temporary Unemployment

One controversial theory of *voluntary and temporary unemployment* is attributed to the high turnover in unskilled, secondary, dead end jobs and to the current structures of unemployment benefits and payroll taxes.

A rather controversial theory of voluntary and temporary unemployment has been put forth by Martin Feldstein.[5] He does not believe that the Keynesian policy of increasing aggregate demand will work effectively in today's labor market. Since a low of 2.9 percent in 1953, unemployment has been as low as 4 percent only four times. One of the reasons is the nature and composition of the labor force. It is not that the jobs do not exist; it is that they are highly unstable jobs with high turnover rates. These are jobs taken in greater proportion by women, teenagers, and minorities. For instance, in a high unemployment year like 1971 (5.9 percent), 45 percent of those unemployed had been out of work less than 5 weeks, whereas in 1969 it was 58 percent. Job losers account for less than half of total unemployment, leaving job leavers, new entrants, and reentrants to comprise the majority. Thus, the turnover rate is the highest among those in the work force who are the least employable. Teenagers are now getting more competition from adult women for these unstable jobs. Among the nonwhite population, quit rates exceed layoffs. As a group, women, nonwhites, and teenagers hold proportionately more of the menial, boring, dead end jobs at which they work briefly, then quit, soon to take up a similar type of employment. The jobs are low paying and unappealing with little or no opportunity for advancement.

The high voluntary turnover rate of these groups overstates the rate of unemployment. What is being measured is not lack of jobs but the volatility of employment in undesirable jobs. In Boston's Action for Boston Community Development (ABCD) program in 1966, approximately 15,000 low income people were referred to jobs. Of these, 70 percent were offered jobs. Some 45 percent rejected the offers. Of those who took jobs, less than one half stayed for one month. Lack of education and low paying dead-end jobs offering little possibility for advancement led to petty theft, lateness, and high absentee, quit, and layoff rates.

Feldstein strongly argues that the current structure of unemployment insurance (UI) has a serious disincentive effect on both employees and employers. It encourages both the frequency of turnovers and the length of unemployment between jobs. First designed in the 1930s, employment benefits are supported by a payroll tax paid by the employer. Firms pay into the fund based on the earnings of laid off employees.

Feldstein reasons that in its current form the UI system subsidizes both employers and employees in cyclical industries where production and employment is volatile and consists of unstable, temporary kinds of jobs. The subsidy results because there is a ceiling on the amount of the payroll tax any one firm has to pay, no matter how many workers it lays off.

Since the more stable industries do not experience major fluctuations in

[5] Martin Feldstein, "The Economics of the New Employment," *The Public Interest*, Fall 1973.

production, they end up subsidizing employers in cyclical industries. Employers gain who keep their operations more cyclical than need be. By hiring temporary workers they keep their payroll costs down while getting the more stable employers to pay a disproportionate share into the state unemployment fund. Associated unions often get workers to accept the layoffs by stressing the availability of the unemployment compensation. It is possible for the UI benefits to be greater than the taxes the employer had to pay into the fund.

Feldstein believes it would be better to introduce a system whereby each employer carried his own payroll tax load by removing the ceiling on the tax. Employers would then have cause to create more stable jobs by smoothing out production, which could be achieved by improved scheduling, greater inventory flexibility, better technology, and more off-season work.

Aside from rapid turnover, the greater the benefits the more time taken in searching for employment, since the cost of remaining unemployed is reduced. In 1975, a high unemployment year, Congress broadened the benefits, adding 13 weeks in the year to the covered unemployed (those registered at government employment offices as actively seeking work) who had already exhausted their benefits. For some states this meant that benefits covered a year or more. The sustained high level of unemployment may have been a result of this policy. One's hunch becomes stronger when it is realized that real income in 1973 rose by 6 percent and declined thereafter to rise again by 3 percent in 1977. Many people may have had unrealistic wage expectations after 1973, and the improved benefits lengthened their search times as they operated under unrealistic notions about wage expectations.

Supplemental food and welfare benefits may also extend the search period among those who work at the more menial jobs. This too causes the unemployment rate to be higher than otherwise. Apple growers in the Northwest often have a hard time in the fall getting pickers because the migrants move on to other areas at that time. Not enough of the locally unemployed want to perform these jobs since the pay is hardly better than UI benefits.

The unemployment benefits also induce a longer duration of unemployment because in most states UI income is not taxed while earned wages are. In Massachusetts, for instance, the UI benefits for a family of four at one time replaced more than 80 percent of the wages after taxes lost from an extra week of unemployment for some income groups; in particular cases it was over 100 percent. For other states it has varied from 60 to 80 percent. Not only that, but at times half the benefits have gone to families in the top half of the income distribution, while only 17 percent went to families making less than $5,000 a year. In general, the structure of UI benefits should be changed—not removed altogether—but set up to discourage voluntary, long-term unemployment.

THE DUAL LABOR MARKET THEORY

Some researchers feel that the previous hypotheses, notably the human capital and job search-labor turnover theories, place too much emphasis on the voluntary and personal choices of individuals supposedly operating in a flexible and competitive labor market, who can readily carry through intentions to increase their human capital or search efforts if they so choose. Though the human capital approach is useful, it is not enough. Why do some people not invest more in themselves? To answer this Doeringer and Piore[6] argue that labor market analyses must probe more deeply into the sociological and institutional patterns of labor market behavior. The voluntary unemployment approach has something most economists accept but does not provide an adequate explanation for unemployment behavior.

The *dual labor theory* distinguishes sharply between the voluntary unemployment of the primary sector and the involuntary unemployment of the secondary sector, and stresses the social and institutional barriers that poor ethnics face in seeking access to primary jobs.

The **dual labor theory** hypothesis is an attempt to incorporate and recast earlier theories into a broader, more comprehensive model. It stipulates that the labor market is divided into primary and secondary markets, the former reflecting stable employment and the latter unstable employment as proposed by Feldstein. The primary sector consists of the higher paying, higher skilled, and preferred jobs including better working conditions and chances for advancement. Such jobs provide stable employment and workers can identify with either the company, the union, or the craft. Unemployment in the primary sector is therefore involuntary in the Keynesian tradition. The employee is usually laid off and does not quit, and is waiting to be recalled, viewing his idleness as temporary until the economy picks up again. He may in the meantime take a lesser job.

The secondary market consists of the unskilled, lower paying, dead-end jobs with high turnover from layoffs, firings, and quits when unemployment benefits encourage longer job search.

Although education and vocational training are important, most skill acquisition is derived in the practical environment of the job itself. Thus, the main variable in obtaining primary sector skills is social acceptability. This cannot be bought as one buys education. For example, most poor ethnic groups form tight subcultures which may present a dilemma to the youth who wants to enter the job mainstream by acquiring socially acceptable values and work habits not shared by the boys on the corner or the gang at the pool hall. Also, jobs in the secondary market are not stable enough, nor do they pay enough for the group as a whole to change its routine and take jobs in which they could settle down. Instead, the period of alienation and adolescence is prolonged. The high unemployment rate among minorities is due not to lack of willingness to work but to the inability to obtain primary sector jobs.

To make matters worse, employers and unions in the primary sector often appear to favor temporary solutions in periods of labor shortage. Instead of creating more primary type jobs they employ secondary workers temporarily, without any view to upgrading them because of the risk and cost. Thus, even in full employment periods the duality persists. Unions are concentrated in the primary sector and do not seem too interested in moving more people into primary sector jobs, because this may introduce more competition for these jobs, preventing wages from rising as much as unions would like. It would also reduce the number of stable, permanent jobs available to current union members.

For institutional reasons, money wage rates quite often do not respond to supply and demand. The downward rigidity of money wages results in fewer

[6] Peter Doeringer and Michael Piore, "Unemployment and the Dual Labor Market," *The Public Interest*, Winter 1975.

workers being employed. Also, job structure is somewhat inflexible and unresponsive to changes in wages and productivity. This is not because firms are irrational about capital equipment decisions, but because of the size of the operation and nature of the work. Consider for example an assembly line where everyone is performing a repetitive task and making the same product. Changes in wages and productivity may not alter significantly the structure of the operation, i.e., the kinds of things workers are basically doing.

To rectify unemployment among youths and minorities, the dualists propose broad public policies to prevent discrimination in the primary market and policies which will create more primary jobs in order to permit secondary job workers to take on more primary market jobs. Their solution is therefore more political than economic. The approach should be, first, changing institutional structure by having the government become more active in pressing for compliance with affirmative action programs, expanding minimum wage coverage, and loosening restrictive union practices while encouraging further unionization; second, adopting a long-run, *stable* full employment policy. The first approach is designed to convert more secondary jobs into primary type jobs. This has already occurred somewhat in longshore work, unskilled construction, and office cleaning. By legislating higher wages, secondary jobs become more costly to employers and it becomes worthwhile to convert them into primary jobs. This may be possible with hospital and hotel jobs. The second approach requires a persistent and steady level of aggregate demand growth to open up more primary type jobs. As in the past, it will not work if policy retains its stop-and-go nature. With a commitment by the government to firm, steady full employment policies, employers and unions would be willing to provide more primary sector jobs so as to admit more secondary market workers to them. Then, employers and unions would be more willing to absorb the higher training, fringe benefit, pension, and unemployment insurance costs involved in accepting more secondary characteristic workers into the primary job sector.

Criticisms of Dual Theory

***Critics* of the dual labor market theory argue that the distinction between primary and secondary jobs is blurry and that many in the latter simply lack the desire to acquire the human capital required for primary jobs.**

Critics argue that creating more primary job openings for secondary type workers will not work because these workers do not have the necessary skills for primary type jobs. That is why they have secondary type jobs in the first place. Many of these people are also of an attitude that they will not undergo the necessary sacrifices in training and education in order to acquire the skills needed to qualify for primary type jobs.[7] Stimulating aggregate demand so the economy can absorb these unskilled workers into jobs may only seriously inflate the economy without increasing output and productivity proportionately. Productivity can be increased if there is an attempt to improve the human capital of secondary type workers and restructure unemployment benefits to minimize frequent job turnover and unemployment layover. All these are difficult to achieve.

Furthermore, the dualists' strict distinction between primary and second-

[7] See Michael Wachter, "Primary and Secondary Labor Markets: A Critique of the Dual Approach," *Brookings Papers on Economic Activity*, Vol. 3 (1974).

The Minimum Wage

The Fair Labor Standards Act of 1938 established the first legal minimum wage at 25 cents an hour with provisions to go to 40 cents an hour. The table shows the chronology.

Year	Minimum Wage/Hour
1938	.25
1956	1.00
1961	1.15
1963	1.25
1967	1.40
1968	1.60
1975	2.25
1978	2.65
1981	3.35

The minimum wage covers over 58 million workers, though over 53 million already earn more than the minimum. It is strongly supported by the AFL-CIO, and they seek to have it raised further. Congressmen from the northeastern part of the U.S. also support it as they see firms moving to the south and southwest parts of the U.S. where money wage rates have traditionally been lower.

It has been argued that the minimum wage seriously affects employment among teenagers and young adults because it prevents employers from hiring them at less than minimum wage during the period in which they can be trained, and once trained, receive a wage higher than the minimum that reflects their worth to the firm. The minimum wage, it is said, destroys opportunities for on-the-job training for the young. Others claim that young workers today will not willingly take jobs at less than the minimum wage rate so that it actually may increase the desire to work among the young.

But many economists disagree, claiming that there is still some negative effect. Unions seek a minimum wage rate in the range of about 70 percent of the lowest unionized wage in manufacturing. One reason is to protect older union workers from being replaced by younger workers who might work for less. The result is increased unemployment among the very young. Also, more of the lower paying jobs are now being taken by women who reenter the labor force. In other cases labor-saving devices are introduced when the minimum wage rises. Others counter that the minimum wage does not cause unemployment because inflation essentially neutralizes minimum wage increases.

Yet, in 1961, after the minimum wage was raised to $1.15 an hour, then to $1.25 in 1963, unemployment among white teenagers subsequently rose to over 14 percent, and for black teenagers over 30 percent. Rarely have these rates fallen below these figures as the economy entered the 1980s. This could be because of other institutional factors such as higher birth rates among minorities compared to nonminorities, and the changing nature of work that requires more education.

Thus while the minimum wage likely has some effect on teenage unemployment, the severity of its effect remains unresolved.

ary jobs is not supported by the data. People move easily among jobs. How does one separate a reasonably good secondary job from a typical primary job? Nor has there been enough attention paid by the dualists to the changing age-sex composition of the labor force. Because of this structural factor, employment is little affected by propping up aggregate demand. Teenagers and older returning women come into the job market with low levels of human capital. Furthermore, legislating minimum wage increases in these traditionally low paying jobs will only increase the wages of those already holding better paying primary jobs as the demand for these workers will increase relative to the unskilled. Nor will unions remove barriers to better paying jobs or alter cost-increasing work rules to let in more secondary type workers who can be used more flexibly and thereby endanger strictly defined and jealously guarded job jurisdictions—as, for example, on construction sites.

High wage jobs do not create high wage workers. Rather good workers generate good wages. In this connection, while discrimination has no doubt been a factor in wage differentials, the dualists have not examined whether discrimination has its effect for those working while *in* the job or whether its effect is felt *before* entering the work force. That is to say, to what extent does discrimination *before* the job affect the desire to acquire necessary skills and attitudes toward work as well as personal habits and self-esteem that are important to work performance and productivity when *in* the job?

STICKY MONEY WAGES

***Wages* are sticky downward because of worker resistance, job hoarding, explicit and implicit job contracts, the wage contour phenomenon, job competition replacing wage competition, and firms' long-run skill maintenance programs.**

Thus far we have offered several interpretations of employment data. We have seen that the source of unemployment is a combination of lack of human capital intricately related to social and institutional conditions, among them the rational process of being unemployed while gathering information about the job market—voluntary unemployment in an environment of welfare and unemployment insurance. Research in these areas has been intensive and continues. Some hypotheses emphasize the involuntary aspect of unemployment while others place more weight on the voluntary nature of unemployment and the institutional characteristics of labor markets.

We take a different tack now. We want to understand why, during a downturn in the economy, money wages and prices are both sticky downward. Wages will be discussed first. There is some irony here. Keynes's original work in macroeconomics stemmed from an apparent failure in microeconomic labor markets. Substantial declines in employment and aggregate demand were not corrected by falling wages that would otherwise induce firms to rehire workers and restore aggregate demand. Today the macroeconomic failure of aggregate demand management using fiscal policy to stop simultaneous inflation and unemployment has forced economists to reexamine the microeconomic foundations upon which macroeconomics is based. Therefore, incentive behavior in microeconomic labor markets have to be better understood.

At the end of Chapter 28 on business cycles we listed five pieces of empirical information. It was mentioned that we observe that quit rates fall (and layoffs rise) during a recession. Nonetheless, many firms try to resist layoffs, particularly if the downturn is seen as only temporary, as a short-run fluctuation in demand for its products that will shortly return to its normal level. Consequently, firms often hoard or stockpile labor when business is slow. This is in contrast to classical employment theory that states that during a downswing there results an excess supply of workers at the current real wage and some have to be laid off. Competition by the unemployed for jobs would bid down the real wage rate, leading firms to increase the quantity of workers employed, thereby restoring equilibrium in the labor market.

However, in modern markets this simply does not happen. Money wage rates do not fall in the short run. If the downturn persists, layoffs occur instead. But workers do not have the option of accepting a lower money wage. They remain employed at the same wage or are laid off. There are two things implied here: (1) firms retain workers during a slowdown, and (2) when the choice has to be made, firms do not lower money wage offers but lay off some workers instead.

One hypothesis to explain the first implication is that in today's job market workers' skills are very specialized, and represent considerable investment by a company in on-the-job training to perform tasks specific to the company. Therefore training and rehiring is costly. When layoffs occur, workers often do not have the skills for other jobs with other firms. Thus, if laid-off workers anticipate eventually returning to the same job with the same firm, they get by on unemployment insurance during the interim and do not necessarily look for other jobs. This is consistent with the data that show that when older adult workers are laid off they are unemployed on the average for longer periods of time in the primary job market than are unskilled, younger workers in the secondary job market. Of course, the younger workers are unemployed much more frequently.

Hoarding labor also explains why, during a recession, labor productivity declines. During a downturn, as workers are not immediately laid off, unit labor costs rise because with production down the worker's hourly productivity declines. Since money wages do not fall but output does, costs per unit of output go up. However, real wages, equal to money wages/price level, fall because as we shall see in Chapter 31 prices may continue to rise.

Job search theory predicts that in a slack economy there are fewer job opportunities; this explains the decline in quit rates at such times. Searching for another job therefore involves higher information costs—meaning that search time would be longer and the opportunity cost of looking for a new job would be higher. Obviously, during upswings search costs are lower; hence quits are higher because individuals have a better chance of finding another job—and sooner. Thus, one would also expect layoffs to rise during an upturn.

This now takes us to the second implication, namely, that firms prefer to lay off workers instead of lowering the money wage rate.

Explicit contracts Many workers engage in wage agreements with employers that apply over some time period, for example, civil servants and college professors. And, of course, unions do it. Unions do not accept money wage cuts when demand for products is slack. Why not? One explanation is that union leaders want job security too and want to be reelected. Agreeing to a wage cut, particularly when prices are still rising, will only make *all* of the union members unhappy even though no one might be laid off. Thus, if wages are not cut, or even raised, so that some workers are laid off but most are not, then the job-keeping workers are not unhappy, only the relatively few laid off are. In addition, the union has flexed its muscle and also saved face. It has delivered a good contract to the membership. Therefore money wages remain fixed despite fluctuations in demand for services and products.

You might respond that nearly 80 percent of the labor force is nonunionized and many other workers such as salesmen, migrant workers, and bank clerks make short-term arrangements. Yet their money wage rates do not fall and they are laid off instead or have their hours reduced. Nonetheless, labor arrangements differ across industries because the product markets in which these industries do business differ greatly. Consumer tastes and behavior vary in different product markets. Manufacturing is heavily unionized while services and white collar unionization in relative percentages is much less. Furthermore, if nonunionized firms were to cut money wages, there is a strong likelihood that workers will choose to unionize. Firms want to avoid this if possible.

Money wage rates did not fall that much even before industrial unions were legalized in 1935. When money wages were cut at times prior to 1935, there were strikes, vandalism, and killings. The benefits of labor peace were purchased at the expense of not cutting money wages. Instead, layoffs were the more common technique. By taking this approach the firms could argue that it was not their fault, rather it was the result of general economic conditions over which the company had no control. But wages, it was assumed, they could control. So cutting wages was an act of bad faith that generated hostility and retaliation.

Implicit contracts and job rationing This theme states that workers and firms are risk-averse. Workers desire job security and firms need a readily available, skilled, dependable work force. Therefore, they reach an implicit agreement to average workers' income over time. At the same time firms are guaranteed availability of workers with the specific skills the firm requires in a very segmented, nonhomogeneous labor market. Firms therefore engage in good will and offer job security to workers even though there will occur short-run variations in their sales. Firms ration jobs at a given wage rate. That is, they have a pretty good idea as to the size of their market—the amount of their sales given their plant capacity. And they know about how many workers they will need and what special skills they should have in this limited product market. The firm therefore averages the workers' income by keeping them on even during bad times at the current wage. Most workers are not competing for the same jobs as was the case with classical theory where workers were considered homogeneous—more or less interchangeable. There are instead limited pools of workers with different specialized skills. Firms cannot get other workers to take their place by offering lower money wages, because they will not be able to obtain qualified workers with the appropriate skills, and it would be too costly to train them compared to keeping the current workers on at the same wage. Furthermore, to bid the right kind of workers from other companies will raise wage rates to all companies in the industry. In order to keep their specialized workers, the companies choose not to earn a bad reputation by either cutting wages too readily or laying workers off. For when the upturn comes workers would be reluctant to return, preferring to stay with the firms that stood by them during bad times. Thus, when firms retain workers it is understood that workers will be carried during slack periods but that they will work harder during upswings in the economy.

Wage contours There is a definite pattern of wage differentials that has existed over the decades across different types of jobs. Even as all wages rise, relative wages across job classifications persist. This pattern is called the wage contour. As a result, there have been no large changes in income distribution related to incomes earned from occupations. The thesis is that wage differentials across jobs are related to self-esteem; it is as much a prestige contour as it is a wage contour. Workers compete for incomes. Thus, firemen want the same pay as policemen. Government workers the same pay as workers in the same job categories in the private sector. Doctors and professionals in general think they should earn more than nonprofessionals. Individuals believe they are entitled to fairness in terms of wages. And those who invest heavily in their human capital feel they should earn more than those who do not, since they have spent so much more time and sacrifice acquiring that human capital.

Job competition Companies want to hire people who will benefit them the most at the least training cost. Thus, while college may not train many people for a specific job, it does prepare them to be trained more cheaply for specific tasks within the firm in a learn-by-doing process. So the labor market is a process of matching potentially trainable personnel with job vacancies. People compete for jobs by being better prepared to be trained for jobs once they are hired and not by bidding the wage down. In this regard the job competition model is a variation of human capital theory and fits well with job rationing and segmentation of skills in the labor market. But there is more. In a dynamic technological society, informed updating of skills while on the job is important to the firm. The modern firm is interested in long-run efficiency and growth. The firm achieves this best not by trying to make short-run adjustments in money wages in response to short-run fluctuations in aggregate demand over the cycle. Instead, it keeps the most trainable workers on the job and avoids layoffs when possible in order to improve the skills of its core workers. Call it skill maintenance. A worker, like an engine, is kept tuned and management keeps modifying and retooling the individual on the job as it tries to improve his efficiency—and his wages—for purposes of making him more productive. For a laid-off worker to try to come back at a lower wage would disrupt the firm's worker maintenance program over the long run. Aside from union resistance where that applies, for the firm to accede to a wage cut would also threaten the wage differential and contour of workers in job categories, reduce self-esteem, cause disturbances, and create a negative image of the company. It would become more difficult in the future to hire the type of workers it wants. The firm maximizes growth in the long run by absorbing higher unit wage costs in a current downturn, in order to increase the productivity of its retained workers over the long run.[8]

[8] Students who have studied microeconomics first might conclude that wages are not determined by marginal productivity theory. Instead it would appear that wage rates are institutionally determined with the number of workers hired being adjusted so that a kind of average productivity of the group equals the given wage rate. Thus, marginal productivity theory becomes a theory of determining how many workers to employ rather than determining the wage rate, at least over the short run. In addition, because of labor stockpiling, the marginal productivity of retained workers during an economic downturn is temporarily lower than their wage rate, and is temporarily higher than their wage rate during an economic upturn when production accelerates. At these times the wage rate is off the demand curve for labor which supposedly derives from marginal productivity theory. Thus, the labor market does not clear with the quantity supplied equal to the quantity demanded in equilibrium, and a nonmarket clearing condition exists. For a fuller discussion see Lester Thurow, *Generating Inequality*, (Basic Books, Inc., 1975), chapter 4.

Sticky Prices

Prices are sticky downward because of long-term contracts with buyers, transaction costs, and, in concentrated industries, the desire to avoid destabilizing price competition.

Prices too tend to be sticky downward. Why do firms not lower prices in a downswing? First of all as we said, firms often hoard skilled labor in downturns because of the specialized nature of jobs and the training costs involved. Much of a firm's labor is in some sense a fixed factor. Like a machine or building that a firm purchases, it is not sold off because the firm experiences a temporary decline in sales. Therefore, when demand fluctuates downward in the short run, the firm still carries the fixed cost of both machines and its skilled labor. Therefore unit costs rise when there is idle capacity—human and nonhuman. In a system where there are a few large firms in an industry, the firm is to a degree insulated from price competition. It is large enough to exercise market power and influence price. It is a price-searcher instead of a price-taker as a very small, intensely competitive firm would be that is one among many sellers. Thus in the short run when output falls because of a decline in aggregate demand, unit costs rise. Some of these firms choose to exercise their pricing power and raise prices so as to maintain a price-to-cost differential, a fixed markup above average costs. This is particularly true where a firm desires a certain profit target. When costs rise, the price is raised to maintain the same profit per unit of product produced. In the short run most firms do not raise prices by the full markup.

Price rigidity can also be explained by prices being rigid even in the short run, because firms want to maintain a profit target over the long run. In order to sustain good customer relations with large volume buyers, the firm does not change its price with every fluctuation in the market. Furthermore, many of its contracts are long term and the price is fixed. It is cheaper and also better public relations to keep the price fixed, based on what it considers to be its normal production level averaged over the year. It is cheaper because the transactions costs of advertising price changes and pacifying—and losing—steady customers can be high. Search costs related to information about constantly changing prices in an industry are significantly lowered to both buyer and seller from contracting for a steady price for stated time periods. Finally, sticky downward prices result from government-imposed support quotas and tariffs (trigger prices on steel); price-fixing schemes such as floor prices on sugar and milk; and entry restrictions such as ICC regulations on trucks. Studies indicate that prices are not very sensitive to short-run changes in demand. Costs have a much greater effect on prices. In the short run, before prices are changed, output is adjusted instead.

In summary, what we have said about rigid wages and prices applies in an economy where aggregate demand is below a full employment level. When aggregate demand is near full employment, then the theory has to change. It is not alone explainable by institutional constraints in the labor market. One approach is to bring *price expectations* into the model. It provides some insight into the events of an expanding economy; a time when there is not a serious deficiency of aggregate demand, but where both inflation and unemployment occur simultaneously. This inflation—and stagflation—are the subjects of Chapter 31. Price expectations link up with job search and the attempt to acquire information about expected prices so as to estimate one's real wage.

AUTOMATION

Automation, **while labor saving, creates a demand for different skills and jobs in the long run.**

The Industrial Revolution has produced, since its inception in the 1700s, much anger, misunderstanding, and fear. Unions representing workers on the docks, in printing, and in construction have consistently fought against the inroads of new labor-saving technology, reluctantly yielding as more generous contracts eased their fears of job insecurity. In England from 1811 to 1816 a group of workers smashed new labor-saving textile machinery in protest against unemployment. They were called Luddites, supposedly named after a feebleminded man, Ned Ludd, who in 1779 smashed two pieces of equipment belonging to his employer. If automation replaces jobs for people, how has it been possible to absorb the ever growing population into the labor force?

Labor Saving Innovations

Labor saving innovations increase the productivity of the worker. Innovation can proceed in two ways. The firm can turn out the same output with less labor, or it can produce more output with the same amount of labor. For example, one pile driver can replace a number of men using sledge hammers to secure a beam into the ground. Or the same person in the large meat section of a retail grocery chain can weigh, wrap, and stamp much more meat using the sophisticated electromechanical machinery now available. On the docks, containerization has made it possible for a much smaller longshore crew to unload a ship.

The higher productivity of these workers is reflected in their higher wages but it can reduce the amount of labor hired in these particular uses. However, the increased productivity and efficiency of operations can lower product prices, thereby increasing the quantity demanded, which stimulates further investment and increased hiring. It follows that there may be a drop in demand for workers in a particular use, but technological innovation increases the demand for more workers in a new activity. For instance, in the short run, office computers replaced many clerks who formerly worked with desk calculators. However, the computer also created new demands for design engineers, programmers, maintenance technicians, and key punch operators. The former clerk must acquire the new skills for the new market, and in the process raise his or her productivity and income. Therefore, labor saving innovations may temporarily replace workers, but in the longer run create a new demand for people with skills to serve the new markets. In an ever changing industrialized economy, education and retraining is a continuous process.

So long as wages rise in response to the increased productivity of each worker, the increased output can be absorbed by the higher demand that rising wages create. Thereby a growing labor force can be absorbed as well. The nation's wealth expands. The greatest increases in productivity in the U.S. economy have occurred in agriculture and manufacturing, much less so in services (auto repairs, haircuts, taxi rides).

If it should happen that the income distribution effects of the productivity gains be such that sufficient aggregate demand resulting directly from that income does not absorb the increased output, then it is necessary to pursue appropriate fiscal and monetary policies to redistribute some of the income in order to prop up aggregate demand.

Share-the-Work Fallacy

***Share-the-work schemes* are inefficient and inflationary since they may cause skyrocketing production costs.**

A popular notion is to spread the available work among more people: two 4-hour shifts using two people instead of one 8-hour shift using one person. But Labor is not homogeneous. One worker is not a module exactly equal to the other. One skilled worker over 8 hours is more productive than one skilled worker performing 4 hours and an unskilled one the other 4 hours. Also, those on 4-hour shifts would want higher wage rates to maintain income. Thus, for administrative and production reasons, the marginal costs of operating could rise significantly, producing serious bottlenecks and inflation. There is a fallacy here—the available work is like a pie so there is only so much of it that can and must be shared. Not so—the greater the number of skilled employees working in the labor force and the greater the capital expansion, the larger the output so that the income pie grows and more workers are potentially employable.

JOB CREATION FALLACY

A job is *created* if its addition increases total productivity and is not simply an income transfer derived from increasing the taxes on productive workers.

Another fallacy is attempting to justify projects because they create jobs when in fact they do not or do not increase social benefits. There are many proposals that claim to expand jobs by building a road, or a dam, or restoring an old building, a museum, or public grounds. The projects are said to be good ones because the benefits are greater than the costs, the jobs created being part of the benefits. The Army Corps of Engineers, for example, calculate just such benefit-cost ratios, which when greater than one, provide the economic rationale for a dam or canal. But labor is an input, just as are materials, and it should be valued on the cost side of the ratio at its opportunity cost, not on the benefit side. If the opportunity cost of the labor used is zero, the job creation argument may hold up. However, if the labor used has positive opportunity costs, this signifies it has value in alternative uses to alternative employers. Therefore, given scarcity, these resources to be acquired must be bid away from being used elsewhere. When many of the pipe welders left the Far Western U.S. to work on the Alaskan pipeline, this did not create jobs for otherwise unemployed pipe welders; it bid up the cost of getting pipe welders in Washington, Oregon, and California. If the pipeline put an unemployed teenager to work whose opportunity cost was zero, the pipeline in this sense was job creating—but, and a big but, the project must be socially useful. It must create capital growth *and* better efficiency, that is, create more output per dollar of investment than before and free costly labor resources for new productive activities.

True, a good capital project or a capital invention is job destroying in the immediate sense, but such an innovation releases—frees—more resources to the economy. As an example, the building of the Panama Canal meant using less resources—ships and seamen—going from the same origin to the same destination. This kind of resource saving is the basis for economic growth and development. It reduces the price of shipped goods, increasing the amount demanded of them and other goods, induces more investment, thereby increasing the demand for labor in shipping and in other uses. Through labor saving inventions—automation—labor becomes more productive with the result of higher wages and real income.[9]

Be wary of arguments which are justified on the dubious point of being job creating. What is created must be socially useful in that scarcity is grudgingly compelled to yield more. Putting the unemployed to work building an island airport that will not be used is wasteful. Many make-work public programs do not teach skills conducive to permanent employment. They are simply income transfer schemes and not job creating programs. They do not free up otherwise costly labor resources for other uses. They may increase employment but not create new jobs. There is a difference. Nonetheless, increasing such employment can help social stability.

CHAPTER SUMMARY

Determining the accurate level of unemployment is not straightforward. Quoted employment and unemployment figures can be misleading by either overstating or understating the real hardship or well-being of the labor force.

The total labor force includes those participants 16 or over actively looking for jobs, plus those in the military. The civilian labor force includes those 16 years or over actively looking for jobs who are not in the military or institutionalized. Others not included are housekeepers, students, the disabled, and the discouraged job seekers. The participation rate is the percentage of labor force participants in the civilian noninstitutional population. Employment data are provided by the Census Bureau to the Bureau of Labor Statistics, gathered from monthly surveys. The unemployment rate is the ratio of unemployed to the civilian labor force. Counted as full-time workers are those who work 35 hours or more during the survey week, persons who work 1 to 34 hours for noneconomic reasons but who usually work full-time, plus those who work part-time for economic reasons whether or not they usually work 35 hours or more. Since 1969 the BLS has used new definitions besides quits and layoffs. They are job losers, job leavers, reentrants, and new entrants.

Official statistics are often misleading because many part-time workers are counted as fully employed when they are not; some people are counted who are really underemployed because they are overqualified for jobs they hold. Unemployment and welfare benefits increase search time, raising unemployment figures above what they would otherwise be. Also, the behavior of firms over the business cycle distorts employment figures, keeping many workers on when aggregate demand is in decline.

The economic costs of unemployment can be measured by the loss of production

[9] Capital-saving innovations involve replacing one type of capital input with another. For example, the steamship replaced the sailing vessels, jet planes replaced propeller planes, and transistors replaced tubes in televisions and radios. They may or may not be job creating.

or by the loss of income. There are also additional unrecorded emotional and psychological costs.

Four traditional sources of unemployment are cyclical, frictional, structural, and Keynesian. They are overlapping, however. Cyclical unemployment is caused by recurrent fluctuations in aggregate demand. Frictional unemployment is related to job inactivity resulting from the normal process of changing jobs, and is a short-term phenomenon. Structural unemployment might be considered as long-run frictional unemployment. It results because of changes in production techniques, rendering some skills obsolete. Thus skills are mismatched with job vacancies. Also, changes in the age and sex composition of the labor force create mismatchings between unqualified applicants and the more sophisticated skills required in the newly emerging kinds of jobs. Because of these causes, the economy is considered fully employed if unemployment is 4 or 5 percent.

Keynesian unemployment is related to a persistent weakness in aggregate demand unrelated to cyclical and structural influences. It is blamed on inadequate stabilization policy.

Two more relatively recent approaches to explain unemployment are the job search and human capital theories. Job search focuses on the voluntary nature of unemployment. The unemployed are engaging in information gathering. And it would not be maximizing behavior to take the first available job. The longer search may be worth the higher costs of wages lost while looking. Human capital theory stresses the investment in themselves by individuals who seek out schooling and training in order to improve and attain marketable skills. It predicts a connection between education and the raising of productivity and earning power. It does not delve into psychological or cultural reasons why some individuals choose not to improve the level of their human capital.

Much unemployment is temporary, arising from the high turnover rate in secondary type (unskilled) jobs. These are low skilled jobs where periods of employment are punctuated by frequent and voluntary lapses of unemployment. Reasons lie in the dead-end nature of the jobs and the disincentives created by the current structure of unemployment benefits; and also the payroll tax, which encourages cyclical industries not to create primary (skilled) type jobs but to stay with the secondary kind.

The dual labor market theory views unemployment as involuntary. It exists because of social and institutional patterns that make it difficult for poor ethnics to gain access to primary jobs. Their backgrounds leave them with socially unacceptable characteristics which make it difficult to gain employment in better jobs. And to acquire these characteristics alienates them from their peer group. The secondary jobs do not pay enough for them to be able to settle down. The government should move to remove the various social and institutional barriers put up by both employers and unions. Critics of the dual theory respond that many of these workers are simply not productive enough to be employed in primary jobs, and that the line of distinction between primary and secondary jobs is blurred. The age-sex composition of the labor force tends to channel many workers into lower paying jobs since they lack sufficient human capital. Nor will craft unions readily remove entry restrictions to accommodate them.

Keynes pointed out that money wages are sticky downward. In recent years several theories have appeared to explain this. Among them are job hoarding in downturns by companies, explicit and implicit contracts between workers and employers, the wage contour phenomenon, job competition replacing wage competition, and firms' long-run skill maintenance programs.

Job hoarding occurs because skilled personnel represent a large investment by the firm, often to perform tasks specialized to the firm. Laying them off, and possibly losing them permanently, is costly and to be avoided. Many workers make formal contracts with employers something like a no-cut clause an athlete signs. Examples are civil servants, tenured college faculty, and to some extent, union seniority clauses. Implicit contracts exist in that there is an understanding that workers will be carried during slack periods and work harder during peak periods. It is as if income is averaged over employed plus unemployed periods. Thus, the company is engaging in goodwill by not reducing wages. It also avoids conflicts that attempting to lower money wages would cause. This is because of the wage contour effect. Workers compete for income so that patterns of wage differentials across occupations exist.

Given the higher degree of specialization in today's job market, one worker is not interchangeable with another. Workers do not compete by offering to work for less but by being better qualified. A firm knows the size of its market and rations the jobs among applicants not by letting wages be bid down, but by letting qualifications be bid up. Such workers are much cheaper to train.

This also fits with the hypothesis that highly skilled workers are a scarce resource and firms want to maximize long-run profits and growth. They do this by constantly upgrading their best workers through keeping them employed, not by forcing them to strike or leave by attempting to reduce their wages to achieve short-term profit gains. To do so would disrupt their on-the-job training progress.

Prices, too, tend to be sticky downwards. One reason is that firms sign long-term contracts with buyers. Hence, sellers wish to keep their best customers and do not change prices with each fluctuation in the market. Further, the transactions cost of frequent price changes can be more costly than price rises would be worth. Another reason is that firms in concentrated industries possess some price setting power. To avoid destabilizing price competition, such firms prefer to cost compete rather than price compete.

Automation, while labor saving, creates jobs in the long run, though these are often different jobs from the ones that were lost. Share-the-work schemes are inefficient and inflationary, since they would cause production costs to skyrocket.

Jobs are created only when a new operation or technique increases output per worker and releases skilled labor for other uses. Skilled workers have opportunity costs; they are inputs and therefore are costs of production. They must be bid away from other uses. However, if a person whose opportunity cost is zero becomes productively employed, then a job is created. Make-work projects while increasing employment are not necessarily job creating if total product and efficiency is not increased. They are simply income transfers paid with the taxes of productive workers. However, such schemes can have social benefits by reducing political disturbances and social offenses.

QUESTIONS

1. You are given the following information:

Total civilian noninstitutional population 16 and over	79,954,000
Total labor force	37,087,000
Civilian labor force	36,998,000
Employed civilians	33,553,000

   a. How many employed people are not in the civilian labor force? Where are they?
   b. How many unemployed are there?
   c. What is the unemployment rate?
   d. What is the participation rate?
2. Which of the following are not considered part of the civilian labor force during the survey week?

   a. Housekeepers.
   b. Loggers idled by tinder dry forests.
   c. The daughter who works less than 15 hours in the family business for nothing.
   d. Apple pickers in Washington State in February after the fall harvest.
   e. A paper boy who spends 10 hours delivering papers.
3. Which of the following are officially considered as part-time workers during the survey week?
   a. A construction worker on the site only 5 hours because of bad weather, who usually works full time.
   b. A person working 20 hours at a gasoline station who is looking for a full-time job.
   c. A person who only works in the morning while the kids are in school.
   d. A fisherman who only works on the boats all day during the fishing season from May to October.
   e. The auto plant worker who is on a half-time schedule for 2 months because inventories of car dealers are high.
4. Which of the following would be counted as officially unemployed?
   a. A person who is employed on the 22nd of the month which falls in the week including the 19th of the month, but was unemployed on the 10th day of the month which fell in the week including the 12th of the month.
   b. A 13-year-old held in a juvenile center.
   c. A 22-year-old in prison.
   d. A 67-year-old taxicab driver.
   e. A 55-year-old in a tuberculosis sanitorium.
   f. A 35-year-old out two weeks with the flu.
   g. Someone laid off and sitting around expecting to return to the job in 2 weeks.
   h. A grocery store owner who shuts down to visit his mother in Canada for 2 weeks.
   i. A steelworker on strike for 3 weeks.
5. State whether the following situations would tend to understate or overstate real unemployment:
   a. Part timers who want to work full time.
   b. An aircraft engineer who is forced to work as a draftsman since engineering jobs are scarce.
   c. Firms which stockpile skilled labor during a downturn.
   d. Teenagers and the unskilled who frequently change jobs.
   e. Students who are unemployed and looking for part-time work.
   f. People who are laid off but expect to be rehired by their old employer.
   g. Those who are not working but are to begin a new job within the next 30 days.
6. The unemployment rate in 1950 was comprised primarily of male heads of households. There were no food stamps or extended welfare programs. Would you say the unemployment rate was more or less reliable in 1980 than in 1950? Why? Also, does the fact that welfare and food stamp recipients have to register for work make a difference in your answer? Explain.
7. In January 1980 there was a conflict between the Actors Guild (the actor's union) and actors working without compensation in the approximately 200 off-off Broadway theaters in New York City. These theaters could not survive if they had to pay the actors. The guild wanted to stop this practice and was putting pressure on the city to shut the theaters down.
   a. If the guild succeeded in requiring these theaters to pay at least a percentage of the actors' equity pay scales, and the theaters did not survive, what type of unemployment would this be?
   b. Is this unemployment explained by Feldstein's hypothesis? Why are the actors willing to work for free? Are they being ripped off?
   c. Why is the guild so insistent despite the actors' willingness to work for nothing?

8. A slowdown in the growth of the money supply causes a moderate recession. What type of unemployment is this?
9. What labor market hypothesis accounts for corporate profits declining during a downturn in the business cycle? Does this hypothesis also explain why profits rise during the initial phase of a recovery but level off after that?
10. Sandy is idled between jobs. She will be going to Los Angeles in two weeks to take up a new job. Mary is a computer programmer, but at the moment there are only a few openings—and they do not pay enough. Are they both unemployed? Voluntarily or involuntarily? Does your answer depend on which theory about the labor market your answer is based? Explain.
11. As greater numbers of older women and teenagers enter the labor force and get jobs, would you expect the productivity of the economy to go slightly up or down? Why? What labor market theory justifies your answer?
12. Under the dual labor theory, why is schooling that increases human capital not likely to be effective in opening up primary jobs to the poor?
13. The unemployed are an ever changing mass, on a kind of shuttle moving between working and waiting, never fitting comfortably into one job but usually able to find another soon. What labor market hypothesis fits this description?
14. "Many minorities seem at a disadvantage during job interviews. The schools don't teach these kids how to handle themselves and give a good appearance." Which labor market hypothesis supports this view?
15. To qualify for unemployment benefits the unemployed must have worked in jobs covered by unemployment insurance (UI). To earn the highest allowable benefits one must have earned enough for the maximum length of time, and must have been involuntarily terminated. The UI system is intended to redistribute income. Whom do you think receives the greater share of UI benefits, those in the second fifth of the income distribution or in the bottom fifth? Why?
16. An official of the Socialist Workers Party was quoted as saying, "The government spends millions of dollars on the military. Why don't they spend it on jobs."
    a. Does military spending have no impact on the labor market?
    b. In what sense might military spending be job creating? Not be job creating?
17. "The decision to put people on the public payroll has nothing to do with public need. The real question is whether the hiree produces output equal to the cost of hiring him." If it does not, has the government created a job or not? Explain.
18. A patio can be constructed by either one skilled cement worker or 3 unskilled teenagers in the same amount of time. Suppose the wage of the cement worker is $120 a day and that of each teenager is $42 a day. Would the contractor, if given the option, hire the skilled worker or the 3 teenagers? Why? Suppose the union pushes for a minimum wage of $45 a day. Approximately what daily wage could the union negotiate for the cement worker? Does the minimum wage decrease the probability of the cement worker being hired instead of the teenagers? Does it raise the standard of living of the teenagers and prevent their exploitation? Comment.
19. How have some businesses reduced the effect of higher minimum wage legislation?
20. Are each of the following labor saving or capital saving?
    a. Computerized typesetting is forcing sharp reductions in the typesetters' union membership.
    b. Bessemer ovens for making steel replace the open hearth ovens.
    c. The total number of jobs in the textile mills expands after the cotton gin and wipes out the jobs of those manually separating the fiber from the seeds.
    d. D-2 the talking robot, learns to walk the dog. Marge has more time for grocery shopping.
    e. D-3 replaces D-2 on the assembly line.

Chapter 31

Inflation

Everyone has won, and all shall have prizes.

—Alice in Wonderland

PROGRESS REPORT

A. In Chapter 29 we examined various approaches to policies we might use to stabilize economic activity. The principal goals of stabilization policies concern unemployment and inflation. In Chapter 30 we examined in some detail the nature of the problem of unemployment and some proposals for dealing with it directly.

B. In this chapter we concentrate on inflation. We have discussed it before, but the nature of the inflationary process is complex and it is such an important problem in today's world that the further attention paid to it here is necessary.

C. In Chapter 32 our attention shifts away from the domestic economy and its problems to the international economy and the study of economic relations that cross political boundaries.

Inflation and unemployment are like inseparable twins abandoned on the doorstep of modern economies. They are unwanted but cannot be ignored. In the decade of the 1970s it was inflation that presented the larger problem, crying out for attention, whereas in previous decades it was unemployment. Our analysis of inflation will include discussion of several related causes. As we shall see, they will turn out to be variations on a major theme, the harmonic counterpoint in the symphony of inflation. Like violins mixed with cellos and cellos with oboes, so do expectations cue prices and prices march in time with costs.

***Inflation* is a sustained increase in the level of prices.**

First, we must ask ourselves, what is inflation? *Inflation is a sustained increase in the general level of prices,* measured by the Consumer Price Index. By contrast, a one-time jump in the level of prices, say of 10 percent, does not itself signify that the economy is in an inflationary state if prices thereafter remain stabilized at the higher level. To be *sustained* suggests that the inflation will continue in a self-perpetuating process, like cells dividing into more cells. However, when the price level increases by, say, 1 percent a year, there is no great concern since it is nearly imperceptible. Yet the level of prices is rising and by definition it is inflation. But when prices rise consistently by 5, 10, or 15 percent a year people become aware that the dollar buys less. The expectation is created that it is going to buy even less in the future and the economy seems to be under siege.

EFFECTS OF INFLATION

Inflation makes people nervous but is it necessarily a bad thing? Yes, if increasing prices causes the economy to wind down and stall in a deep recession, creating political and social chaos. This can be the effect of hyperinflation—runaway inflation. It can wipe out savings and seriously cramp new capital expenditures if it causes more resources to be devoted to speculation and less to production. Output and employment will fall. Speculators will try to profit by guessing where changes in relative price differences will occur most rapidly, putting more financial resources into existing goods whose prices they believe will inflate the fastest instead of creating new goods.

With ordinary inflation, however, the problem is not so much that of a recession but of income redistribution effects. There are gainers and losers. During an inflation, the nation as a whole does not experience a loss in total income. A higher price to one becomes a higher income to another. The problem is that the income redistribution is uneven. The pie does not get smaller, it gets cut up in different sizes. We should modify this last statement slightly. If the inflation is caused by higher oil prices, for example, real income is being transferred abroad, and the economy as a whole loses. The domestic pie in this case can get smaller.

The essential point is that inflation causes real income transfers because some groups anticipate the inflation and take corrective action to negate inflation's adverse effect. Those who do not correctly anticipate inflation will lose out. But even here, it frequently happens that some people cannot take corrective action even if they have good information. In the past, regulations prohibited a small saver with less than $5,000 from converting savings deposits paying 5 percent to bankers' acceptances that might have paid 12 percent.[1] Retired people on a relatively fixed income cannot keep up with tax assessments on the increasing value of their property even though their houses are worth more; they can only convert the house into cash and rent a cheaper apartment. But they lose the benefits they enjoy from owning their own home that they worked for all their lives, despite the fact that Social Security payments are indexed to the inflation.

INFLATION REDISTRIBUTES WEALTH

Individuals and households hold monetary and real assets as well as monetary and real liabilities. When an unanticipated inflation occurs, those who are net monetary debtors benefit from the inflation and those who are net monetary creditors lose. Some definitions are needed.

Real assets **are claims on specific items whose dollar value changes with the price level; *monetary assets* are claims on current or future fixed numbers of dollars.**

Real assets are claims on specific items whose dollar value changes with the price level. Examples are houses, stocks, real estate, cars, and other kinds of durable goods. These assets usually rise in value in rough proportion or better to rises in the price index. We shall ignore changes in relative prices among real assets in the example below.

Monetary assets are claims on current or future fixed numbers of dollars, things like Treasury bills and bonds, savings and checking accounts, or mortgage money owed. When the price level rises, the real value of these nominal dollars received in fixed amounts falls.

Real liabilities **are obligations to deliver a given quantity of goods or services now or in the future even if their dollar value changes; *money liabilities* are debts to be paid now or in the future in a fixed number of dollars.**

Real liabilities are obligations to deliver a given quantity of goods or services now and in the future even if their dollar value changes. Examples are a contract to provide a certain number of labor hours or a promise to deliver a certain amount of oil at a prearranged price. If the price level rises, the dollar value of the liabilities in real terms rises because the same good or service is now obtained with cheaper dollars.

Money liabilities are debts that are to be paid now or in the future in a fixed number of dollars. Examples are mortgages, bank loans, and credit card debts. When the price level rises, the dollar value of the debt remains unchanged but the real value of the debt falls.

We can now list situations where gains and losses accrue under inflation.

Those Who Are Better Off

Net monetary *debtors gain* real wealth from unanticipated inflation; net monetary *creditors lose.*

1. *Owners of real assets.* They do not lose and often gain. However, in the 1970s dividend payments to stockholders did not keep pace with the inflation rate.

[1]Nonbank financial institutions created mutual funds shares allowing small savers to earn much higher rates of interest than 5 1/4 percent. Banks are trying to get restrictions imposed on nonbank financial institutions because of the heavy withdrawal of savings deposits from banks by the public.

2. *Borrowers*. Debtors gain since they repay their debts with cheaper dollars. This includes corporations if they are net debtors.

3. *Those with political clout*. Federal retirees and Social Security recipients gain because their retirement payments are indexed to the inflation with the increases at least as large as the cost of living. Gains also accrue to those with GI mortgages and student loans as well as those who borrow in states where usury laws exist, if the interest rate is below the market rate. Banks gained in the past since they lent at high rates on short-term loans while legally forbidden to pay interest on deposits above a mandated maximum level, which can be far below their lending rate. If wage and price controls exist, those exempt from the controls also gain.

4. *The government*. Since the income tax is a progressive tax, the government collects proportionately more taxes as inflation pushes people into higher money income brackets. Furthermore, the government is a net debtor and it gains when it pays bondholders interest on its debt with cheaper dollars.

5. *Others*. Those gain—or do not lose—who correctly anticipate the rate of inflation and are able to speculate and correct for it.

Those Who Are Worse Off

1. *Holders of money assets*. Since payments are fixed in money terms, when the price level rises the real return falls. Thus holders of cash and pensioners receiving fixed incomes lose.

2. *Lenders*. Creditors, to whom money is owed, lose. They are repaid with cheaper dollars.

3. *Those without political clout*. Among the losers are low wage workers and low income families who do not qualify for food stamps and other kinds of government transfers such as education loans; workers whose wages are not indexed to the inflation; lenders who are subject to usury laws and those who cannot get dispensations from wage and price controls.

4. *Taxpayers*. Higher rates of inflation increase money income, pushing people into higher marginal tax brackets.

5. *Others*. Those lose who are adversely affected by changes in relative prices because different goods change prices at different rates; for example, coffee prices may rise faster than the price of tea; and those who do not anticipate the inflation, or anticipate it incorrectly by underestimating its rate of change, or anticipate it but are not able to correct for it. Utilities lose because they mostly borrow by selling long-term bonds. Inflation raises interest rates, increasing their borrowing costs, which hinders capital formation. Those lose for whom the price of physical assets they own declines relative to the prices of other kinds of physical assets which appreciate more.

In reality, most individuals fit into more than one of these situations. What matters is the net position of the individual or group. If people, on net, are borrowers of money, they will gain from an inflation. If on net they are lenders of money they will be worse off. We examine the details.

AN EXAMPLE

Examine the account of a net monetary debtor before an inflation takes place.

Net Monetary Debtor Year 1 Before Inflation

Assets		Liabilities and net worth	
Real		Monetary	
House	$50,000	Mortgage outstanding	$40,000
Monetary			
Savings bonds	10,000	Net wealth (worth)	20,000
Total	$60,000	Total	$60,000

This account shows a net monetary debtor. The monetary assets are $10,000 while the monetary liabilities are $40,000. This is a *net monetary debt position* of $30,000. (We shall ignore interest rate payments and real liabilities in this example.) The debtor has borrowed $40,000 from the bank to finance a house valued at $50,000. Total assets are $60,000 and net worth is $20,000. Assume after a period of time prices rise by 100 percent. Assume also that all real assets appreciate by the same amount. The debtor's balance sheet changes as a result of the doubling of prices and the changes are noted on the next balance sheet.

Net Monetary Debtor Year 2 After Inflation

Assets		Liabilities and net worth	
Real		Monetary	
House	$100,000	Mortgage outstanding	$40,000
Monetary			
Savings bonds	10,000	Net wealth (worth)	70,000
Total	$110,000	Total	$110,000

Now total assets are $110,000. The value of the house has increased by $50,000 but the money value of the bonds is still only $10,000. The mortgage liability is still only $40,000. (We ignore mortgage payments here.) Net worth has increased from \$20,000 to \$70,000 in monetary terms, but is this person actually \$50,000 better off? The answer is that this person is better off but only \$15,000 better off in real terms. Let us see why.

The real value of the house, its monetary value deflated by the price rise, is back to \$50,000. Now the real value of the savings bonds is only \$5,000 rather than its face value of \$10,000, because dollars will only buy half as much as they formerly did. Similarly, the mortgage is now less in real terms. Its monetary value is \$40,000, but since it can be paid off with dollars that have only half of the purchasing power they used to have, the mortgage is only \$20,000 in real terms. These changes in the accounts leave net worth equal to \$35,000. It has increased from its original value of \$20,000 by \$15,000. Thus, the individual has gained \$15,000 in real terms from the inflation.

Notice that the real value of the house has not changed from its original value. However, the \$40,000 mortgage is only a \$20,000 burden in real dollars. Thus, there is a gain to the debtor of \$20,000 on this account. But the debtor has lost \$5,000 in purchasing power on the savings bonds. Thus, a loss of \$5,000 on the bond coupled with a gain of \$20,000 on the mortgage results in a net gain of \$15,000 in net worth. This inflation has made the net monetary debtor better off.

The basic relations used above are:

Net wealth = assets − liabilities.

But assets and liabilities are composites of real and monetary parts. Hence

Net wealth = (real assets + monetary assets) − (real liabilities + monetary liabilities)

Collecting real and monetary parts we get

Net wealth = (real assets − real liabilities) + (monetary assets − monetary liabilities).

Therefore,

Nominal net wealth = net real assets + net monetary assets.

Initial values were \$20,000 = \$50,000 + (\$10,000 − \$40,000). If the price index (P) doubles from 1 to 2, then the value of real assets rises but the money value of the monetary assets remains unchanged. The \$50,000 real asset is the house and its money value doubles to \$100,000. Thus

Nominal net wealth in year 2 = P (net real assets) + (net monetary assets).

\$70,000 = 2(50,000) − 30,000.

Recall that monetary assets are fixed in dollar terms. Dividing each term by P yields real net worth in year 2. Thus one can go directly to the answer by dividing the \$70,000 in the table by 2:

real net wealth = nominal net wealth/P = \$70,000/2 = \$35,000 in year 2

Deflated Values for Net Monetary Debtor Year 2

Assets		Liabilities and net worth	
Real		Monetary	
House	$50,000	Mortgage outstanding	$20,000
Monetary		Net wealth (worth)	
Savings bond	5,000	Total	35,000
Total	$55,000		$55,000

A net monetary creditor would be made worse off with inflation. If the individual in the example were in a reverse position and had only $10,000 remaining on his mortgage and $40,000 in savings bonds, he would be a net monetary *creditor* to the tune of $30,000. His assets would be the house plus the bonds or $90,000, and liabilities would only be $10,000, so net worth would be $80,000. From the inflation he would lose $20,000 as his bond-holdings were cut in real value and would only gain $5,000 from the reduced real burden of his mortgage. Thus, in real terms his net worth would decline by $15,000 from $80,000 to $65,000. In this example we are ignoring the effects of adjustments that changes in interest rates will bring about as people generally anticipate the inflation.

MODIFYING THE MODEL

Since inflation signifies a rising price level, it only seems logical to incorporate the price level explicitly in the model. Panel A of Figure 31-1 depicts the standard Keynesian cross where the implicit assumption is that the price level is constant below the full employment level of national income Y_f denominated in money terms. Thus, for income levels Y_1 through Y_f the price level is constant at P_1 as output increases from Q_1 to Q_f. However, beyond full employment, output cannot exceed Q_f so that national income now rises because the price level increases to P_2. The sequence of changes corresponds to increases in aggregate demand shifting upward from AD_1 through AD_4 and equilibrium positions *a*, *b*, *c*, and *d*. These points correspond to the same points in panel B. There the price level is indicated on the vertical axis, and output, or real income, is measured on the horizontal axis. Real income equals money income divided by the price level. Money income, Y_1, for instance, is represented by the shaded area in panel B. If we assume for the moment that the amount of labor hours is fixed, then output Q_f can be treated as a proxy for a fully employed economy. The economy cannot produce more output than Q_f because everyone in the labor force is fully employed. Thus, when aggregate demand is increased to AD_4 (and point *d* in panel B) output cannot increase, hence the

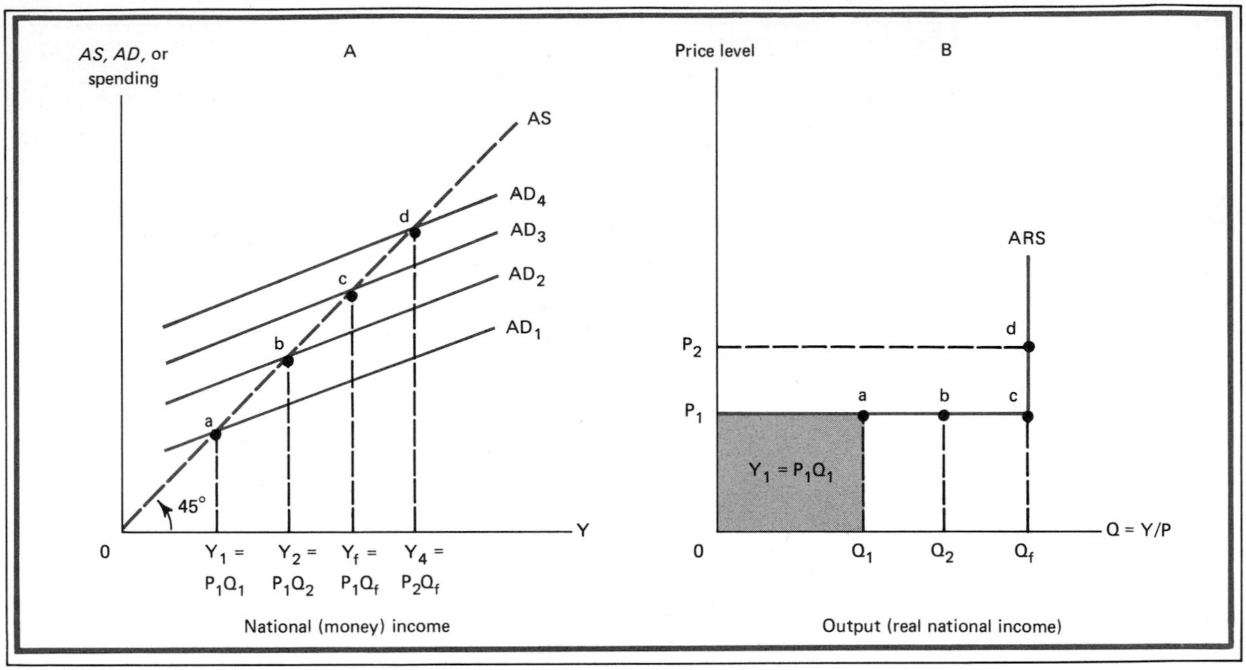

Figure 31-1

The *aggregate real supply* curve is derived from the Keynesian cross. It is a schedule of how much output the economy will produce at different price levels.

price level absorbs the impact of higher spending and rises to P_2. Real income is the same at points *c* and *d* in panel B and equals Q_f or Y_f/P. The curve *ARS* is called the **aggregate real supply** schedule.

Figure 31-2 introduces another slight modification. Below output Q_1 the economy is seriously underemployed, so there is no upward pressure on the price level. Because, however, prices are sticky downward (at least in the short run) the *ARS* schedule is horizontal up to Q_1. When output is above Q_1 the price level begins to rise. As output approaches Q_f, the price level begins to rise more steeply. It rises more sharply as it passes through point *b* and eventually becomes vertical at output Q_g. "Normal" full employment output Q_f can be exceeded in the short run, if we relax the assumption that each worker in the current labor force works only a fixed number of hours. Or we can assume that new workers can be attracted into the labor force during a temporary expansion in the economy related to a business upswing. In the short run, before plant capacity can be expanded, existing facilities can be used more intensively, thus allowing output to expand beyond Q_f. Of course, even in the short run current capacity limitations of the economy are ultimately reached and the *ARS* curve becomes vertical at Q_g. However, the *ARS* curve rises rapidly when Q_f is exceeded, because efficiency falls off as the additional costs of producing additional output rises sharply. Furthermore, as the economy nears full employment because of expanding aggregate demand, those workers not normally included as permanent members of the labor force who enter to take jobs are apt to be among the least skilled and are therefore least efficient. Hence, additional costs increase in greater proportion than additional output. To compensate for this, firms may raise prices to cover higher costs per unit of output produced, forcing the *ARS* curve to become more steep.

Figure 31-2

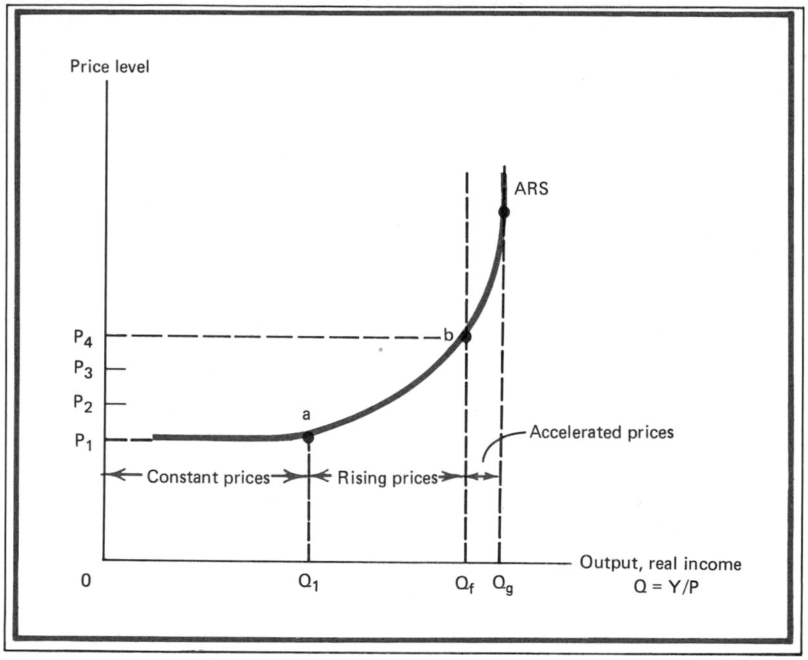

Shifts in ARS

The *ARS schedule* can *shift* because of changes in technology, taxes, input costs, capacity, labor force size and skill, and government regulations.

It must be said that while economists' understanding of aggregate demand needs improvement, it is still better understood than aggregate supply. In the long run the relation of aggregate output to the price level is influenced by many interrelated variables that can cause the aggregate supply curve to shift. Among them are technology, taxes, input costs, capacity, labor force size and skill, and government regulations.

Technology. This is a repeat of material on investment in Chapter 23. Technological innovations improve production efficiency and alter (raise) the capital-labor ratio. New technology offsets the diminishing returns to capital experienced by adding more of the same kind of capital. The downward shift in the ARS_1 to ARS_2 in Figure 31-3 reduces upward pressures on the price level. Thus point *c* indicates that output Q_f can be supplied with the price level at P_1 instead of at P_4.

Taxes. Lowering taxes on workers' incomes may provide further incentives for workers to work more hours. Some taxes and subsidies can also stimulate new capital formation by business. Additional capital will shift the ARS schedule downward. But it should be noted that the increased investment spending that is required to form new capital will stimulate demand. Thus, the initial effects of tax breaks on investment are inflationary, but after the new capital comes on line it is deflationary.

Input costs. Decreasing prices for labor and materials reduce production costs, thus shifting the aggregate supply curve downward. Rising oil prices in the 1970s are indicated by an upward shift in the ARS schedule and a higher index of prices.

Figure 31-3

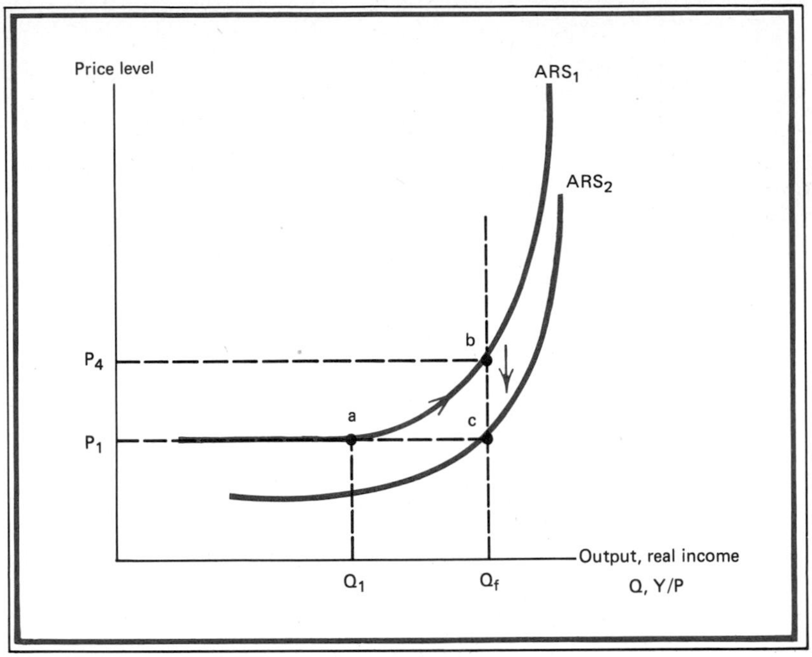

Capacity. The nation's production-possibility frontier can be expanded because the ARS schedule is shifted downward as a result of expansion of investment in physical facilities such as plant, equipment, and tools, and in the expansion of distribution outlets. Obviously the influence of technology, where capacity can be improved within the same physical plant, is important.

Labor force size and skill. The greater the participation rate of those in the labor force, the greater the potential output of the economy. Moreover, the better equipment available to workers the more productive they will be. It is as if the labor force has been increased in size. In addition, investment by workers into developing their human capital—their skills, training, and experience—will increase labor productivity, shifting the ARS curve downward.

Government regulations. Regulations which improve the health, safety, and morale of workers can shift the ARS schedule downward. However, where regulations are intrusive and burdensome, costs imposed by regulations may outweigh benefits, thus shifting the aggregate supply curve upward indicating decreased efficiency.

What are the effects on the economy's *productivity*? Increased productivity shifts the aggregate supply curve downward, retarding inflation, while decreased productivity shifts it upward, generating inflation.

CAUSES OF INFLATION

We shall take a step-by-step approach to explain the source of an inflationary bias in modern economies. We start out with traditional hypotheses, then work up to more recent hypotheses. The more recent theories will incorporate the contents of earlier theories, for as we said, the inflationary apparatus contains parts within parts. It is impossible to pick out a single cause and effect on which all economists would agree. They acknowledge the diverse sources of inflation but often differ regarding the degree of pressure exerted by the different sources. Also, both supply and demand sides must be included in the analysis of inflation.

Demand-Pull

Demand-pull **inflation is caused by aggregate demand growing faster than aggregate supply.**

Inflation is characterized by aggregate demand outpacing aggregate supply. Because of limitations in adjusting both the size of the plant and the amount of machinery in the short run, and because it is harder to hire more skilled workers as the economy approaches full employment Q_f in Figure 31-3, the additional output must be squeezed from the economy's existing capacity shown by the movement from *a* to *b* on ARS_1. The price level approaches P_4 with prices also tending to lead wages in an expansion. But in the long run wages catch up. Since money wages are sticky downward, higher wages are not offset by increased productivity in the long run if there is no compensating downward shift in aggregate real supply to equilibrium such as point *c* and to the original price level P_1, because of inadequate expansion of capacity and other productivity increasing measures. It then behooves policymakers to destimulate aggregate demand by implementing appropriate monetary and fiscal policies, if possible.

Cost-Push

Cost-push **inflation is caused by increases in input costs independent of changes in aggregate demand.**

According to some, inflation is characterized by a rise in the price level that is not initially fired up by an increase in aggregate demand. Inflation is considered to be independent of aggregate demand pressures. Inflation is attributed instead to the influence wielded by big business and strong labor unions in the product and labor markets respectively. Both big corporations and unions in basic industries are insulated to a major degree from price and wage competition. The sequence is that prices are first pushed up by rising labor costs because of generous contract agreements negotiated by labor unions with monopoly power in the labor market. This is true, it is argued by cost-push proponents, even though union membership is less than 25 percent of the U.S. labor force. Unions are concentrated in the basic manufacturing and transportation sectors, and are moving rapidly in organizing the government sector at the local, state, and national levels. Thus, union influence looms large in the auto, steel, rubber, and oil industries; on the docks, with the railroad and trucking industries; and among postal workers and teachers. They are able to gain wage increases larger than any improvements in productivity, thus forcing up unit production costs. For example, the UAW contract in 1979 with the deeply financially troubled Chrysler Corporation contained agreements for wage increases of 33 percent over a three-year period.

Figure 31-4

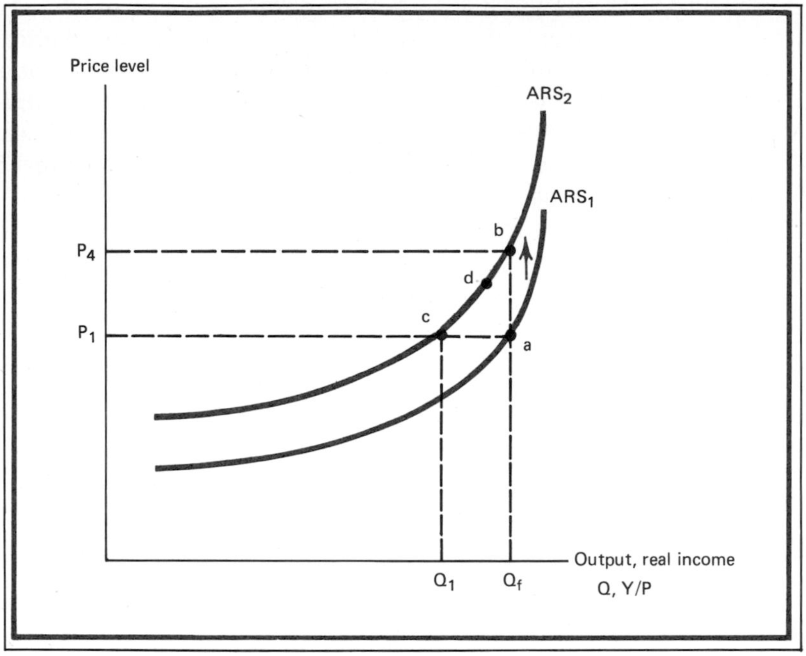

Figure 31-4 illustrates the situation. Forces of cost-push shift the ARS_1 up to ARS_2. There are several possibilities. If the economy started at point *a* and there is no reduction in output (employment), then the cost impact is absorbed only by a rise in prices from P_1 to P_4 with the system moving to a new equilibrium at point *b*. Or if the unlikely effect is that the full impact is absorbed by a reduction in output (employment) with no rise in the price level, then new equilibrium occurs at point *c*. More likely, there will be some reduction in output with the price level rising but not reaching P_4, with the system attaining a new intermediate equilibrium at point *d*. Monetary and fiscal policy cannot be used to manipulate aggregate demand to control pure cost-push, because cost-push operates on the supply side independently of the demand side. Implementation of wage-price guidelines have been tried to prevent costs pushing upward while they at the same time operate to try to minimize the pulling effect of aggregate demand.

The power of large corporations is the other side to cost-push inflation. Some economists believe that firms with market power easily pass on higher input costs by raising prices. The argument is that powerful corporations have a target rate of profit as their objective. When costs rise, prices are marked up to maintain the designated profit margin above average cost. Since much of manufacturing is concentrated, with a handful of firms accounting for a large majority of industry output, price competition that could lead to devastating price wars and endanger profits and threaten survival is carefully avoided. These firms prefer to cost compete. They try to reduce costs by being more efficient through introducing better technology and organizational improvements, instead of competing by offering lower relative retail prices than their rivals. Only firms with sufficient market power can behave by substituting cost competition for price competition.

Structural Inflation

Structural inflation **is caused by resource immobility and lags as the economy reacts to changing supply and demand.**

This kind of inflation is related to cost-push inflation, but some economists make the following distinction. With cost-push, prices rise even when there is no increase in aggregate demand. But with structural inflation price rises can derive initially from increases in aggregate demand that feed back through the system, activating cost-push forces.

Structural inflation results from resource immobility and lags. Resources cannot quickly adjust to changing supply and demand conditions. There are frictions in the institutions and economic sectors of society that deliberately or unavoidably prevent resources from being transferred or adapted to changing market conditions. The rigidity of certain market structures and institutions prevents prices, wages, and human and nonhuman resources from readily bending and accommodating a changing market environment. What are some of these rigidities?

Bottlenecks and capacity limits Assume an economy is operating near full employment. Suppose there is an increase in demand for coal and a decrease in demand for oil in an energy conscious economy. Even though there may be no net increase in aggregate demand, the price level may rise. The increased demand experienced by the coal industry requires bidding away labor and capital resources from the oil industry that are not specialized in coal producing activities, hence are less efficient there. Thus shortages of skills and special materials appear in the short run. This is compounded by the geographic immobility of resources, further driving up costs of production to the coal industry. If the coal industry can pass on higher costs via a price increase, then the price level rises. It rises because the reduced demand for oil does not result in a decline in money wages for oil workers, but leads to some layoffs instead. Nor does reduced demand for oil lead to a commensurate fall in sticky prices. The higher coal prices are then passed through to other firms which may not have undergone an increase in demand for their products. Thus, a cost-push effect can result in one sector of the economy from an increase in demand initiated in another sector of the economy because of structural bottlenecks.

Capacity constraints also play a role. Suppose the Fed stimulates the demand for housing and factories by pursuing low interest rate targets. If the lumber industry is operating near full capacity, short-run lumber prices are forced up because of the lag in capacity expansion. The supply side cannot adjust quickly enough to sudden, major changes in demand.

Public sector The costs of running the government have grown proportionately faster than costs in the private sector over the last 20 years. State and local government expenditures have grown relative to the private sector. Expenditures by all governments have leveled off to about 23 percent of GNP. The power, size, and militancy of public unions increased greatly in the 1970s. They represent large, well-organized, and well-funded voter blocs. They support active political lobbies. Creation of the new Department of Education in 1979 owes much to pressure from the National Education Association (NEA), a large teachers' union.

It is one thing for a union to strike a private firm, since the effect on the public is small or nonexistent. But a strike by a public union against the government is potentially much more disruptive—and even dangerous for public health and safety. A private company must compete with other companies in the marketplace. Therefore, the consumer can choose among substitute products and alternative producers. However, the government is the sole supplier of many kinds of services—police protection, fire control, garbage collection. What does this all have to do with inflation? The government is administered by politicians with one eye on the budget and the other eye on the next election. The incentive for the politician is to settle a public strike as quickly as possible because a disgruntled, inconvenienced public may throw him out of office. Better to settle a strike soon and let the public bear the cost with higher taxes later. This reaction is unlike that of the private entrepreneur, who must keep a bigger eye on costs and profits and will tend to resist union demands more strongly. The firm seeks an economic solution, the politician emphasizes the political. They are maximizing different things. As the demand for government services continues to grow so will the costs of providing them—and because the politician is not spending his own money he will more readily grant inflationary wage and pension benefits to employees for purposes of political survival.

What makes the problem worse is that it is harder to achieve cost efficiencies in the service sector than in the manufacturing and farming sectors, and the service sector is growing in size relative to both of them. Wages of public employees rise but their productivity gains lag behind the other two sectors.

Sector problems Certain fundamental sectors of the economy have been a persistent source of inflation in the economy. We have already mentioned the public sector. In the private sector the construction industry has not been a brick of price stability. Nor has the medical care industry kept the economy's price pulse in check. In November of 1979 Congress rejected the President's bill to impose price controls on hospital costs that have consistently outpaced the price index.

At times in the 1970s the unemployment rate in the construction industry reached 20 percent. Nonetheless wages increased anywhere from 9 to 18 percent. Higher labor costs and housing prices can be explained by the unique structure of the industry. The price of basic lumber can change suddenly and boldly in reaction to the government deciding to reduce or increase cutting on public lands.

Moreover, the construction industry consists of many local firms operating alongside a few very large national companies. Most of the industry is composed of many small contractors confronting an array of craft unions. During labor-management conflicts, the few large national contractors may sign contracts with unions that set a pattern throughout the country that conflict with what local contractors can afford and would otherwise agree to, thus undermining local builders' resistance to strikes by the local branches of the union. The locals working for the small contractors want what other members are earning who work for the national contractors—the wage-contour phenomenon. Thus, excessive wage increases spread like grass fire, causing inflation throughout the industry despite major productivity increases.

Also, through the application of political pressure, unions sometimes manage to get restrictive building codes passed. These laws often prevent the use of newer, cheaper materials, particularly prefabricated items. Standardized building materials frequently cannot be used in every area. This prevents builders from obtaining potential price discounts on large purchases of standardized materials.

Medical expenditures amount to about 10 percent of GNP. Some believe it will reach 20 percent. Hospital stays are very expensive. There are several causes. One is the Medicaid and Medicare programs that stimulate demand for services but ignore the supply side. Most researchers familiar with the problem also attribute high hospital costs to a combination of higher malpractice insurance; redundant technology among hospitals—where one sophisticated machine could serve an area, all hospitals in the area have one; rising labor costs; overbedding; increasing government regulations; the nonprofit nature of many hospitals leading to less concern with cost efficiencies; and the lack of price competition in the health care market.

Cash flow hypothesis[2] Labor costs are a major cost to most firms. Thus, firms are constantly on the lookout for ways to save on labor costs and raise output by increasing capital relative to labor. But the new capital must also be more efficient. To do this firms have to increase their cash flow (depreciation and those profits not distributed to stockholders as dividends) to be invested into research and development (R&D) in order to discover labor-saving, hence cost-saving, technology. This goal necessitates generating higher retail earnings. This is done in three ways. First, these large industrial firms do not operate at full capacity with the existing technology because extra costs rise rapidly the closer they operate near full capacity. Second, possessing market power, they are insulated from rigorous price competition and are able to produce less than their potential output yet mark up their prices. Third, the fixed capital costs are quite high because the existing plant, though not fully used, is nevertheless costly to let stand idle. Consequently, they settle strikes quickly, offering little resistence to excess wage demands because they are in a position to pass the labor costs on as higher prices. When the new technology comes on line they can cut their wage bill (not wage rates) because they need fewer workers to run the more productive newer capital equipment, and without having to raise prices (until the next labor contract is negotiated), which means higher profits and retained earnings to be put into more R&D that will further reduce the wage bill.

Supply Shocks

Supply shocks (such as sharp decrease in the availability of a basic raw material) can cause inflation.

Imagine that the U.S. has a falling out with Saudi Arabia, a country which exports more oil to the U.S. than any other OPEC member. The drastic reduction in oil supplies would cause an oil shortage and energy prices would rise sharply. This is a supply shock—in this case an abrupt disruption in supply from outside the economy.

The U.S. imports nearly half of its oil. The cost of a barrel of crude oil in 1972 was about $2.50. Eight years later it was over $30. This causes the price index to rise. In itself, a jump in oil prices should not cause a *sustained* rise in

[2]Charles Levinson, *Capital, Inflation, and Multinationals* (New York: The Macmillan Co., 1971).

the price levels, though the inflation rate may rise over a finite period of adjustment in response to it. Prices should stabilize once the economy has adjusted to and absorbed the rise in the price of oil. However, if every year or two the price of oil is raised by OPEC, then oil price increases will sustain an inflation, with prices never reaching a resting place.

Other supply shocks have occurred from time to time in some basic raw materials such as magnesium, chrome, and uranium. As world demand for these resources increases, the rising price to U.S. importers will also have an inflationary impact on the economy. Given the increasing economic interdependence of the modern world, shortages in one part of the world inflict price increases on everyone. It would not be surprising to see cartel arrangements emerge in other raw material markets.

TOO MUCH MONEY

Monetarists believe the primary cause of inflation is *excessive increase in the money supply.*

All economists recognize that if the Federal Reserve policies lead to the creation of too much money, particularly if the economy is at or near full employment, inflation will be the direct result. The majority also recognize the upward effect on prices of cost-push, demand-pull, and structural influences aside from the purely monetary sources of inflation. But the monetarists argue that inflation—by which is meant a *sustained* increase in prices—is primarily caused by too much money creation and that other causes of inflation are of minor importance. They also contend that obtrusive interference by the government creates serious disincentive effects in both the labor and product markets. Thus, they argue that too much aggregate demand from excessive money creation and obstacles to aggregate supply from government interference have combined to stick the U.S. economy with the inflation experienced in the decade of the 1970s. The monetarists do not deny that cost-push structural impediments to mobility of resources exist in the economy. What they do deny is that these alone can *sustain* an inflation. Cost-push by itself cannot cause inflation unless it is consistently encouraged by the Fed's permissive expansion of the money supply. This causes aggregate demand to outpace aggregate supply. To the monetarists, inflation is not a complex symphony, it is an old familiar tune, "too much money chasing too few goods."

There Is No Inflation in a Barter Economy

Envision an island on which live a baker, and a farmer who grows peaches. It is a simple barter economy that does not use money to carry out exchange. Suppose the baker will exchange 1 loaf of bread for 4 peaches. Conversely, the farmer must be willing to trade 4 peaches for 1 loaf of bread. The opportunity cost (price) of 1 loaf of bread is therefore 4 peaches, and the cost of one peach is 1/4 a loaf of bread.

Now suppose there is a change in tastes and the farmer wants more bread. With the increased demand for bread the baker raises the price of bread to 8

Going, Going, . . . , Gone

In the years of 1922 and 1923 a defeated Germany experienced an extraordinary hyperinflation. It began during the years of World War I, 1914–1918, when the German government issued increasing amounts of paper money to finance its war expenditures. It became worse after the Versailles peace treaty agreements required that Germany make reparations to France, Belgium, and other countries. An agreement of 1921 called for Germany to pay 132 billion in gold marks in yearly installments of 2 billion marks plus 26 percent taken from Germany's export receipts.

Capital fled Germany to other countries. When Germany defaulted in 1923, French and Belgium troops occupied the Rhineland. The German workers resisted with work slowdowns in the mines and factories as well as some sabotage. These acts made the inflation worse because of supply shortages they created. From a 1914 prewar rate of 4.20 marks to 1 dollar, the mark fell in 1922 from 162 marks down to 7,000 marks to 1 dollar. By July 1, 1923 the exchange was at 160,000 marks to 1 dollar. On October 1 it fell to 242,000,000 marks to 1 dollar; by November 20, 1923 it fell to the unbelievable level of 4,200,000,000 marks to 1 dollar. By November 27 domestic German prices stood at 1,422,900,000,000 times the 1913 level. Incredibly, on July 22 of the same year, a ham sandwich cost 24,000 marks. By November a newspaper cost 200,000,000 marks. The money supply increased by about 50% in 1921, to about 1,000% in 1922, and grew to 25,000,000,000% in 1923. It was difficult to get a check cashed. People who allocated money for trips found they ran out of it on the way. Money had to be carried in a bag to make small purchases at a grocery. Public servants were paid once a week, then once a day. On November 20, 1923 the existing reichsmark was declared by the government to be money no longer. A new currency was introduced, the rentenmark, one of which was equivalent to 1 trillion of the old reichsmarks. It was backed by a mortgage to foreign lenders on government land and other physical assets. It worked. Foreign investment picked up, the currency stabilized, and the budget began to balance. The stability lasted until the U.S. stock market crash of 1929, which led to heavy U.S. capital withdrawals in 1931–1932 and economic disaster for Germany, opening the way for Hitler's rise to power.

peaches a loaf to the peach farmer. Hence, the price of bread has doubled (from 4/1 to 8/1). But the other side of the coin is that the price of peaches has been cut in half, from 1/4 to 1/8. The general price level remains unchanged. Bread doubled in price but peaches were halved in price, so there is no change in the average price of both goods. In a barter economy it is impossible for the general price level to rise.

However, suppose the economy had been using paper money as a medium of exchange. An eccentric old man arrives on the island with a yen for the island's superior bread and peaches at prices he likes. He also arrives with a sack of cash so the island's money supply goes up. As he spends the additional cash, both the price of bread and the price of peaches will rise in money terms. The old man, by increasing the money supply, has caused the general price level to rise without necessarily altering the price of bread relative to the price of peaches.

The Real World

Cost-push and structural factors may cause prices to rise. Monetarists argue, however, that they cannot keep an inflation going. Once the economy experiences a short-run rise in prices and is able to adjust and absorb the higher prices, the inflation should stop. But if monetary policy is passive, if it does not discourage rises in prices and wages, inflation does not stop.

A specific example is the cost of crude oil that has raised production costs to oil-using companies—the airlines, fertilizer producers, bus companies, electric utilities, and many others. The affected industries pass on these costs to others by raising prices on goods and services. Those firms and industries who can do so raise their product prices since they desire to maintain their profit margins. However, wages and prices do not fall on products not dependent on oil as an input. As consumers pay more for oil-based products they would reduce their demand for non-oil-based goods. By the normal process of demand and supply, the prices and wages should not rise in these industries. More of the economy's income would be spent on oil-based goods, reducing the level of expenditures on non-oil-based goods. Prices and wages would be rising in one sector and falling in the other. The end result would be a stable overall price level. The change in prices would average to zero—but this is not what happens. Workers do not readily accept money wage cuts, so they end up unemployed instead. The Fed, fearing a serious recession, increases the rate of growth of the money stock. Wages, prices, hence demand do not fall in non-oil-based industries. Prices in oil-dependent industries are up, and they do not fall in non-oil-dependent industries. So, the average level of prices must rise.

For example, suppose a firm raises its prices but other firms in the industry expect the Fed to stick to a restrictive monetary policy. Thus, other firms would not be inclined to raise their prices too. Nor would they easily grant substantial wage increases to workers. In these circumstances, the price-raising firm would not trigger a Pied Piper price effect with other companies following. The price-raising firm would find it is now in a noncompetitive position and lose sales to other firms; workers would have to be laid off, forcing the union to be more moderate in its wage demands in order to protect jobs. But if firms and unions expect the Fed to increase the money supply growth rate to accommodate the wage and price increases, then the price-raising firm need not worry about loss of sales to competitors because they too will raise prices and offer less resistance to wage demands. Inflation is the price that has to be paid if a passive monetary policy is used to keep unemployment down.

A NEW BALL GAME

The *Phillips curve* suggested an inverse trade-off between unemployment and inflation rates.

In 1958 A. W. Phillips pointed out that for nearly a century in England a stable relationship had existed between the rate of inflation (Phillips actually used the rate of change in money wage rates) and the unemployment rate.[3] He showed that the unemployment rate and the inflation rate moved in opposite direction by specific amounts. In the U.S., **Phillips curve** estimates also indicated a stable, historical relation—a trade-off—between the inflation and

[3] A. W. Phillips, "The Relation Between Unemployment and the Rate of Change of Money Wage Rates in the United Kingdom 1861–1957," *Economica*, 25, No. 100 (Nov. 1958): 283–299.

Figure 31-5

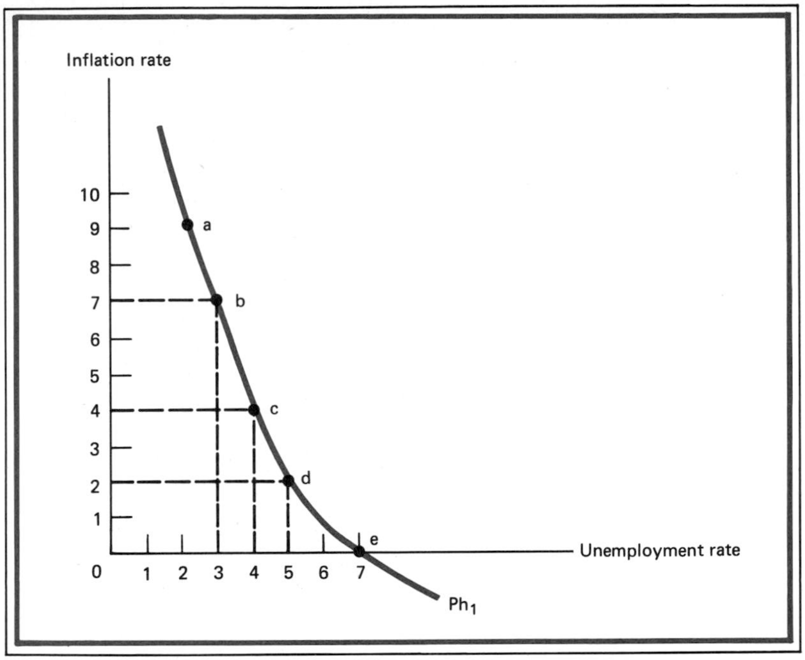

unemployment rates illustrated by curve Ph_1 in Figure 31-5. It immediately caught the fancy of economists who saw it as a new tool for stabilization, and policymakers in government eagerly latched on to it. For example, point *c* on the curve suggests that the U.S. economy could maintain an inflation rate of 4 percent per year if it tolerated a 4 percent unemployment rate. Using hypothetical numbers, if the authorities wanted to reduce the rate of inflation to 2 percent, they would have to engage policies that allow the unemployment rate to rise to 5 percent. The trade-off point is *d*. To achieve a zero rate of inflation, or constant prices, would necessitate forcing the economy to point *e*, to an unemployment rate of 7 percent of the labor force. In essence, in order to reduce the unemployment rate by moving along curve Ph_1 from *d* to *c*, the government could make use of fiscal policy by reducing taxes or increasing government expenditures or both. The Fed could also expand the money supply by buying securities.

Beginning in 1970 and continuing into the 1980s, it became increasingly and distressingly clear that the trade-offs embodied in the curve Ph_1 no longer applied. The trade-off became worse in that *both* the unemployment rate *and* the inflation rate were moving in the same direction—up! Between the years 1979 to 1980, unemployment increased from about 5.8 percent to 7.1 percent, while the rate of inflation increased from 8.5 to about 9.0 percent. In other words, the economy moved from a trade-off indicated by point g to the trade-off at point *h* shown in Figure 31-6. It is not possible for both the inflation rate and the unemployment rate to go up on a given Phillips curve like Ph_1.

Both going up together was something new—stagflation. How can this happen? One explanation is that the Phillips curve simply shifted from Ph_1 to Ph_2. Given the curve Ph_2, for the economy to reduce the inflation rate to 8.5 percent requires accepting an unemployment rate of over 7.1 percent, indicat-

Figure 31-6

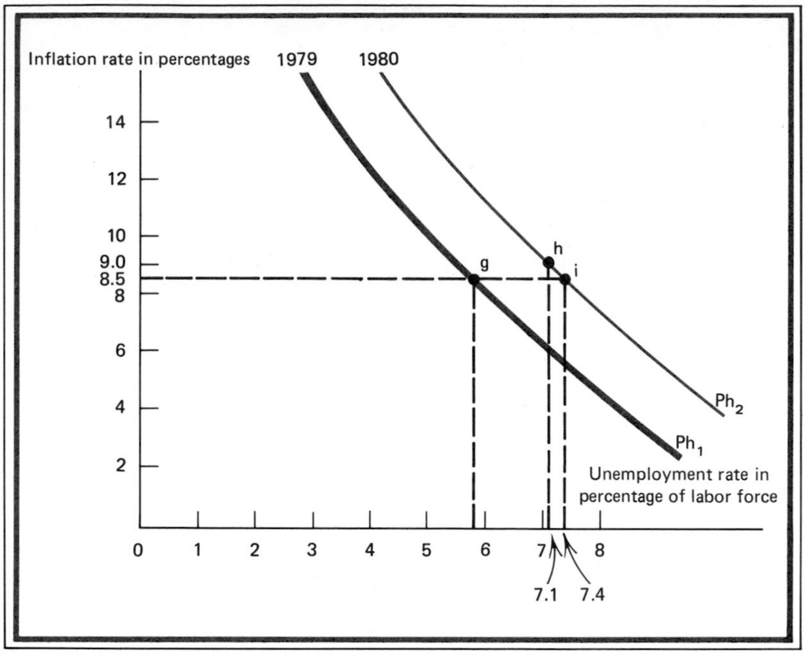

ing the trade-off is now at point *i* on curve Ph_2. To attain the same rate of inflation of 8.5 percent now requires tolerating an unemployment rate of over 7.4 percent.

Natural Rate Hypothesis and the Importance of Expectations

The *Friedman-Phelps hypothesis* holds that the Phillips curve trade-off is a short-run phenomenon arising from misconceptions of the actual inflation rate, resulting in a temporary effect on the real sector.

In 1968, working independently, Milton **Friedman** and Edmund **Phelps** developed a new hypothesis about unemployment and inflation. It denied the existence of the traditional Phillips curve trade-off between employment and inflation in the long run. To them, the Phillips curve was only a short-run phenomenon that exists temporarily because people have limited information and are uncertain about future changes in the economy. Thus, there is a timing lag between what they perceive as the situation until they learn the true situation. It causes producers and workers to increase or decrease temporarily normal supplies of their resources. After people have time to correct their mistakes, their expectations about prices will coincide with the actual behavior of price movements.

Therefore, in the long run the Phillips curve is not sloped downward, instead it is vertical and is vertical at the economy's "natural" level of unemployment of 4 or 5 percent of the labor force. This natural rate was explained earlier as deriving from frictional and structural unemployment. Figure 31-7 illustrates the hypothesis and the relation between the short-run and long-run Phillips curves. Observe that the actual rate of inflation is measured on the vertical axis and the unemployment rate on the horizontal axis. The long-run natural unemployment rate is taken to be 4 percent. Each short-run Phillips

Figure 31-7

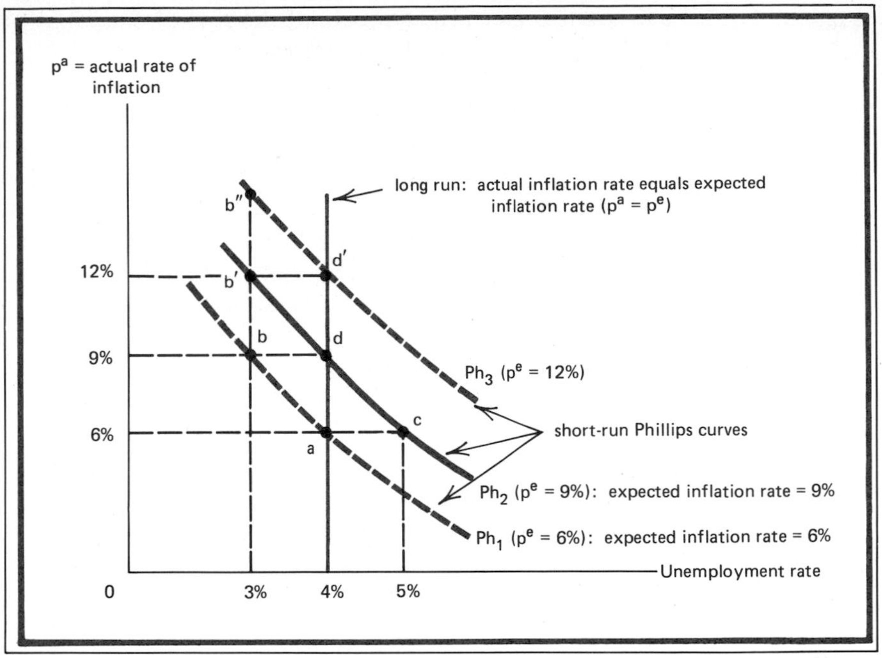

schedule represents the trade-off between the actual rate of inflation and the unemployment rate for a given expected rate of inflation. Notice, the higher is the anticipated rate of inflation, the further outward is the short-run schedule shifted. Assume the economy is at point *a* where the expected and actual rates of inflation are both 6 percent. Suppose the authorities seek a goal of only a 3 percent unemployment rate. Expansionary policy increases aggregate demand and reduces the unemployment rate to 3 percent. Although prices—with some delay—rise faster than money wages and cause real wages to fall, workers do not initially recognize this. In response to the rise in aggregate demand individual producers step up production and hire more workers. New entrants into the labor force reduce their search time. Moreover, already employed workers may work overtime. Initially, workers interpret an increase in money wage offers as a rise in their real wage because they incorrectly believe that the expected inflation rate is 6 percent. As a result, the system moves to point *b* on the Ph_1 curve drawn under the condition that the expected rate is 6 percent, whereas it is now actually 9 percent as measured on the vertical axis. Eventually workers realize that the actual rate of inflation is 9 percent. They therefore increase their search time in order to seek out increases in money wage offers that do not represent a reduction in real wages. Unions bargain harder and may strike for longer periods, the economy returns to its natural unemployment rate of 4 percent—but at point *d* where the inflation rate is 9 percent. At point *d*, however, the actual and expected rates are the same. The short-run Phillips curve has shifted to Ph_2, reflecting an expected inflation rate now adjusted to 9 percent. Thus point *d* lies on the vertical long-run Phillips curve. The vertical line is generated by points like points *a* and *d*, at the 4 percent natural unemployment rate. One point is taken from each of the shifted short-run curves. There is no long-run inflation-unemployment tradeoff possible unless people are consistently mistaken about the rate of expected price increases compared to the actual rate of price increases.

However, if the Fed chooses to keep unemployment at 3 percent, and increases the money supply to achieve it, the actual rate of inflation would rise to 12 percent. Once again such a policy causes the actual rate of inflation to lead the expected rate of inflation that was anticipated to be 9 percent. Thus, sustained deviations below the natural unemployment rate are purchased at the price of an explosive, accelerating inflation; this prediction of the Friedman-Phelps hypothesis is shown by the path *b* to *b*″. If money growth is slowed and the public revises its expectations, the economy operates on the long-run vertical line at points like d and d′. At these points, the inflation *rate* (not the *level* of prices) is stabilized in an inflationary equilibrium.

Start with point *a* again, only this time suppose workers believe that the inflation rate is 9 percent when it is actually only 6 percent. Thus money wage offers are seen as reductions in their real wage, so search time lengthens and resistance to contract agreements by unions stiffens. Consequently, the unemployment rate rises to 5 percent and the economy is at point *c* on the Ph_2 curve, reflecting the expected inflation rate of 9 percent. Workers eventually learn that the inflation rate is only 6 percent, so they shorten search time and unions ease their demands when current contracts expire. The system moves back to point *a* on the long-run vertical line, where both the expected and actual inflation rates are 6 percent with the economy returning to its **natural unemployment rate** of 4 percent.

Monetarists say that on the long-run vertical Phillips line, expected and actual inflation rates are equal and the economy is at its *natural rate of unemployment*.

According to the Friedman-Phelps model, neither businesses nor unions can start an inflation. That is, sustain a continuous rise in prices. Even large firms with market power face price competition. They are not monopolists, although they are able to pass on higher costs by charging higher prices. Hence, they can *prolong* an inflation. Nor can all unions increase real wages in the long-run (except through productivity improvements), because higher wages are passed through as higher prices leaving real income unchanged. Although some unions can increase members' real incomes, members of weaker unions often experience a fall in real income. However, by striving to keep pace with or surpass price increases, strong unions, too, can prolong an inflation.

Relative Price Information

Suppose the demand for blue jeans falls. Is this because blue jeans are suddenly not fashionable, or is it because of an overall decline in the economy's aggregate demand related to changes in monetary or fiscal policy? If it is the result of changes in public tastes, then the blue jeans industry responds by reducing output and employment. But if blue jeans sales are down because of an overall decline in the economy's spending, there is downward pressure on all prices and on all wage increases, but with no change in output or employment in the long run. Real variables—output and employment—are unaffected once buyers and sellers adjust their price expectations to the actual behavior of prices. If sellers learn the drop in sales is because people demand fewer blue jeans, the company is forced to cut back production. But a general decline in aggregate spending that leaves *relative* prices unchanged will not alter decisions about buying or selling *this* good or *that* good. Hence, changes in the rate of inflation will not lead to significant variations in output and employment. The conclusion is that the natural unemployment rate is essentially vertical when *relative* prices, determined by supply and demand, do not change; only the *absolute* price level changes. It is relative prices upon which daily decisions are made. In the short run, however, the initial effect will be on output and employment, not on prices, no matter what the cause of the decline in blue jean demand. In the long run, however, blue jean output will fall if the decline is the result of a change in tastes. Blue jean prices will also fall if the decline in demand is because of a decline in aggregate spending.

Adaptive Expectations

The Friedman-Phelps natural rate hypothesis (hereafter F-P) is based on the notion of *adaptive expectations.* Expectations about the future behavior of prices are formed by observing the behavior of prices over the past. Consequently, today's monetary and fiscal policy would have little or no influence on peoples' expectations about the movement in future prices. There would be a lag in the effect of current policy in forming peoples' expectations about tomorrow. Tomorrow's expectations are, instead, formed by past price experiences associated with prior monetary and fiscal policies only.

If prices have risen by 10 percent each year over the past 2 years, people come to expect that prices will increase 10 percent next year regardless of policymakers' decisions this year. Were aggregate demand to decline next year because of policy adopted this year, people would nevertheless expect prices to rise by at least 10 percent next year, and they will continue to do so until they perceive that the actual rate of inflation has fallen below 10 percent. A union, for instance, will include in its next contract wage increases of at least 20 percent over the next 2 years in anticipation of a 10 percent a year rate of inflation. An employer will estimate the future price at which he can expect to sell his product and compare it to what he expects to have to pay his workers in order to help him decide whether to hire or lay off someone. Workers, too, will compare the money wage offers they receive with the real wage offer they anticipate earning based on the worker's expectation of how future prices will behave—and that is based on past price behavior. Banks will build in the anticipated inflation rate to calculate the money rate of interest at which they will make loans.

THE ROLE OF MONEY

The F-P hypothesis argues that the anticipated higher incomes and the resultant increases in spending derive from increases in the money supply. Producers may be willing to produce more, workers to work more, and lenders to lend more. They view themselves as holding more cash balances than they desire to hold. If the money stock had not been increased, the stepped up spending would drive up prices and lower real balance holdings below the desired level.

Spending would slow down as people rebuild their balances, leading to a halt in inflation growth.

Assume, however, that the money supply continues to grow. The heavier spending will initially cause an increase in output and a reduction in business inventories. Firms, at first, do not know the source of the increased spending, whether it is occurring in just their industry or throughout the economy, and whether it is simply a temporary aberration or a permanent change in demand. Prices do not immediately go up and the economy dips below its natural unemployment rate. There is a price-adjustment lag in the early phase. If the spending continues, however, prices will begin to catch up, and then some.

Furthermore, when spending begins to slacken, prices will lag in the adjustment downward as well. Once people adjust their expectations upward, then when demand declines, expectations—and actual prices—are slower to adjust downward even when unemployment rises above its natural rate as plants operate with greater excess capacity. If people believe that the rate of inflation will be 9 percent next year too, but the actual rate has fallen to 6 percent, they still believe their money income represents a decline in their real income. Producers and workers begin to withhold some resources from the market. Workers take longer to search for new jobs while unemployed, or offer to work less hours, or unions threaten to strike, and remain out for longer periods of time. Thus, *stagflation* makes its appearance—prices and unemployment rise together, contrary to their opposite movements along the short-run downward sloping Phillips curve.

Bargaining for wage increases greater than price increases only leads to a temporary reduction in the level of employment. Sustained price rises—inflation—can only be the result of an accommodating money supply policy.

The Adjustment Process

We are ready to trace a fuller sequence of interactions when aggregate demand is altered. Suppose the policy makers adopt expansionary monetary and fiscal policy, causing aggregate demand to shift upward. Prices are sticky at first so that firms step up output and draw down their inventories. Increased spending and contracting inventories require more inputs to expand production—labor and raw materials like iron ore to make steel. Prices in basic raw materials are sensitive to demand changes, so prices go up initially there. Also the more competitive, less concentrated industries and nonunionized industries tend to respond sooner with price and wage increases and earn temporary extra profits. They increase production, while those with long-term contracts do not lift prices. However costs begin to creep up through the markets from the basic sectors. Eventually big firms mark up the price to cover the higher costs and maintain the profit margin. When new contract time arrives, unions and independent workers seek higher wages to cover the rise in the cost of living and to get a share of the greater profits. However, one firm's higher prices are another's higher costs. So the process builds as the chain, once disturbed, transmits its energy to all the links. It takes time for price and cost increases to flow in sequence through the system and affect all product prices. It takes time for people with limited information to realize that the change is pervasive, and not simply a change in their industry and in their segment of the job market. When the inflation is sustained, people then begin to revise expectations about prices. Thus, there is an *expectations lag* between the time product prices rise, and keep on rising, and before people revise their expectations. Until then, actual prices run ahead of expected prices. These expectations are then built into new price and wage contracts by firms and workers. If aggregate demand and the actual inflation rate slacken, the built-in price expectations will overshoot the inflation rate. And, on the downside, it takes much longer for the expected inflation rate to catch up to the actual downward inflation rate. While this is going on firms are charging prices that have become too high, and workers want real income that is also too high—unemployment creeps upward and inventories slowly build. If policymakers react to the downturn and the unemployment too soon by prematurely stimulating aggregate demand, it will only lead to a temporary reduction in unemployment and a permanent increase in inflation—the state of stagflation again. The unfortunate result of this sympathy shift in aggregate demand by the government is to keep the unemployment rate below the natural rate because people continue to think that rises in their own money incomes is really a rise in their real incomes even as they experience a higher and higher rate of inflation. People have to run faster and faster to stay at the same real income place on the treadmill of accelerating money income.

The upshot is that output and employment are usually more flexible over

Figure 31-8

The inflationary transmission mechanism

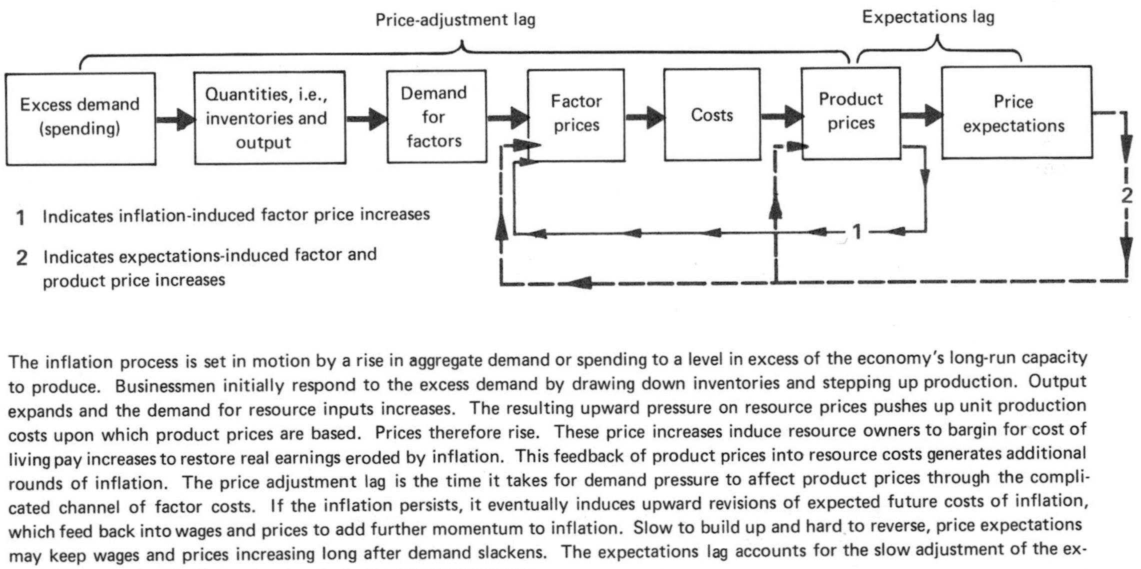

The inflation process is set in motion by a rise in aggregate demand or spending to a level in excess of the economy's long-run capacity to produce. Businessmen initially respond to the excess demand by drawing down inventories and stepping up production. Output expands and the demand for resource inputs increases. The resulting upward pressure on resource prices pushes up unit production costs upon which product prices are based. Prices therefore rise. These price increases induce resource owners to bargin for cost of living pay increases to restore real earnings eroded by inflation. This feedback of product prices into resource costs generates additional rounds of inflation. The price adjustment lag is the time it takes for demand pressure to affect product prices through the complicated channel of factor costs. If the inflation persists, it eventually induces upward revisions of expected future costs of inflation, which feed back into wages and prices to add further momentum to inflation. Slow to build up and hard to reverse, price expectations may keep wages and prices increasing long after demand slackens. The expectations lag accounts for the slow adjustment of the expected future rate of inflation to changes in the actual current rate.

Source: Thomas M. Humphrey, *The Persistence of Inflation.* Federal Reserve Bank of Richmond 1975 Annual Report. Reprinted in Michael P. Dooley et al., eds.: *The Political Economy of Decision Making.* Beverly Hills and London: Sage Publications, Inc., 1979, pp. 89-113.

Figure 31-9

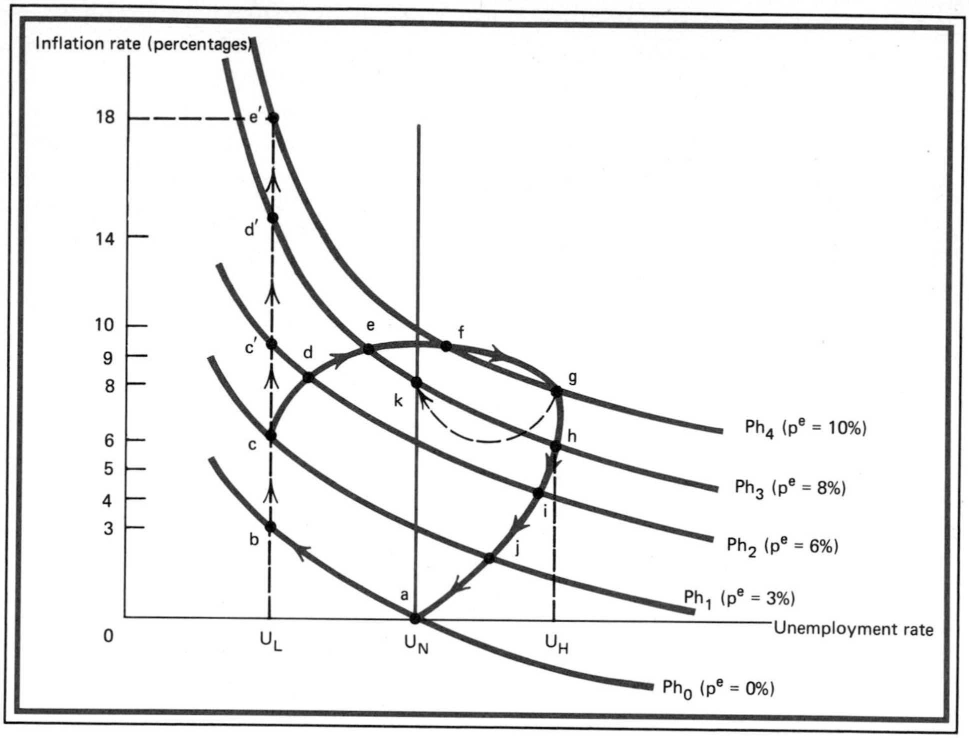

short periods than prices and wages, and less flexible than prices over the long period. A capsule summary of the inflationary transmission mechanism is illustrated in Figure 31-8.[4] Notice that price expectations funnel back to impact on both input costs and product prices. The actual rise in product prices also feeds back on input costs lower down in the chain.

TRACKING A STABILIZATION CYCLE

In order to track a stabilization cycle, refer to Figure 31-9. Assume the economy is in long-run equilibrium at point *a*, the expected inflation rate p^e is zero. At point *a*, since it lies on the long-run vertical Phillips curve, the expected and actual inflation rates are equal. Again the actual rate of inflation is calculated along the vertical axis, while the expected inflation rates are expressed by the relative positions of the short-run Phillips curves.

For whatever reason, suppose the policy makers move to reduce the rate of unemployment below U_N by stimulating aggregate demand, say, by monetary expansion that activates demand-pull forces. As a consequence, suppose

[4]For more details see Thomas M. Humphrey, "The Persistence of Inflation," in *The Political Economy of Policy-Making*, Michael P. Dooley et. al., eds. (Beverly Hills, London: Sage Publications, Inc., 1979), pp. 89–113. First printed in the 1975 *Annual Report* and then reprinted in *Economic Review*, Federal Reserve Bank of Richmond, Sept./Oct. 1979.

the actual rate of inflation rises to 3 percent and unemployment declines to U_L, indicated by point *b* on curve Ph_0.

However, workers eventually learn that the actual rate of inflation is 3 percent and modify their expectations, taking into account that higher money incomes nonetheless represent a reduction in their real income.

Expectations are that prices will rise by 3 percent in the next period, hence the Phillips curve shifts to Ph_1 reflecting those new expectations as workers begin to play catch-up. Because of demand-pull, the actual rate of inflation is 3 percent and further creates an anticipated inflation rate of 3 percent, so that the actual inflation rate jumps to 6 percent in the next period. However, producers and workers had expected only a 3 percent rise. Being mistaken, people reduce search time believing their real incomes have risen, which keeps the unemployment rate at U_L below the economy's natural rate. Furthermore, producers, anticipating higher demand, prices, and profits, step up production, raise their money wage offers, and hire more workers. At this point if the Fed does not act to reduce aggregate demand, then once people learn that the actual rate of inflation is 6 percent, they expect it will be 6 percent in the next period. Thus, again, the Phillips curve shifts right to Ph_2 as people revise their expectations. The economy is in danger of an accelerated inflation, as shown by points *c′* and *d′*.

If the Fed now becomes concerned when the economy is at point *c* and decides instead upon slower money growth to reduce aggregate demand, unemployment will creep above U_L toward U_N. Assume that because of the reduction in aggregate demand, the actual rate of 6 percent inflation rises to 8 percent, for a 2 percent rise, when people expected a 3 percent rise from 3 to 6 percent. The economy moves to point *d*. However, people are as yet unaware that the inflation rate has risen to 8 percent, and do not revise their expectations downward.

When they learn that the rate of increase in the inflation rate is an additional 2 percent, to 8 percent, they revise their expectations to 8 percent. The Phillips curve shifts to Ph_3. The Fed continues to slow money growth, reducing aggregate demand further such that the economy's inflation rate peaks at about 9-1/2 percent as the economy reaches its natural unemployment rate U_N. But because the inflation rate increase was 2 percent in the previous period, people figure it will increase by 2 percent more to 10 percent in the next period. The curve shifts to Ph_4. At this point the deflationary effects of declining aggregate demand finally cause the actual rate to fall below the expected rate of inflation as the economy proceeds through point *f* then to g. Money wage offers are now interpreted as a reduction in real wages, search time lengthens, and unemployment rises above U_N to U_H. At point g the actual inflation rate is 8 percent, while expectations are that it is 10 percent. But the revision of expectations continues to lag changes in the actual rate, this time on the downward side. Notice that even at point g, though the actual rate of inflation is starting down, the *absolute* price level continues to rise simultaneously with an increase in unemployment—a state of *stagflation* exists. Actually stagflation began to appear just beyond point *c*.

Meanwhile with aggregate demand going down and unemployment going up, prices belatedly begin not to fall but to rise slower at only an 8 percent rate while the expected rate is 10 percent. Workers view money wage increases below a rate of 10 percent as a decline in their real wages, since their reactions are still conditioned by the previous inflation rate expectation of 10 percent per year. The demand for at least 10 percent wage increases with the actual rate of inflation at 8 percent would appear to make inflation cost-push in nature at this point. It is, however, really because of a delayed demand response to previous demand-pull forces that are still seen to be unchanged. The economy therefore moves from point g to point *h*. However, the authorities persist and do not stimulate aggregate demand, forcing the actual rate of inflation to 6 percent. The short-run Phillips curve shifts to Ph_2 and the system moves to point *i* and an actual inflation rate of 4 percent.

Eventually, as aggregate demand declines and its effect is felt throughout the system, people begin to realize that the actual *rate* of inflation is going down and begin to revise their expectations, although they have still not completely caught up to the decline in the actual rate. They realize that a decline in money wage rate increases is not as much of a decline in real wage rates as they initially thought. Moreover, some have been unemployed for quite a while now, and things do not look as though they are going to get better, so they reduce their search time and unemployment starts to fall. Those still employed are less likely to quit under the circumstances. In fact, quit rates do decrease during a recessionary phase in the cycle. Thus, as the expected and actual inflation rates come closer together, the economy moves to *j* then to *a* with the system returning to its normal long-run unemployment rate of U_N and a zero inflation rate, hence to a constant absolute price level.

Stop-and-Go Policy

Because of substantial wage and price stickiness in the downward direction, it is much more difficult to decelerate an inflation than it is to accelerate one. It is harder to convince people that the inflation rate is slowing down instead of continuing upward. The downward adjustment just detailed might take two, three, or more years. The recession must persist and hurt if wage and price expectations are to moderate substantially. And there's the rub.

Because of the unpopularity of unemployment and its political implications for an administration in office, a tug of war between inflation and unemployment has often led to a stop-and-go stabilization policy with a built-in tendency toward an inflationary bias. Wages and prices go up faster than they go down (if at all) and also stay up longer than they stay down.

If the policymakers turn timid after their efforts cause the system to move from *f* to g because unemployment increases to U_H despite their success in reducing the actual rate of inflation from 10 to 8 percent, they might again resort to expanding aggregate demand. Hence, the system would not move on to *i* as before, but move on to *k* as the authorities restimulate aggregate demand and, with lags, redirect downward price expectations into rising ones.

Unfortunately it takes much longer for the economy to go from g to *i*, than for it to move along from g to *k* because of the greater resistance of prices and wages to slowing down than to speeding up. The net effect is stop-and-go policies that involve asymmetrical adjustments upward as compared to downward leading to an inflationary spiral depicted in Figure 31-10. There are temporary pauses in an upward trend. Notice that in the upward trend unemployment falls a little below the natural rate, and at the resting periods for inflation unemployment rises above the natural unemployment rate. For this reason the

Figure 31-10

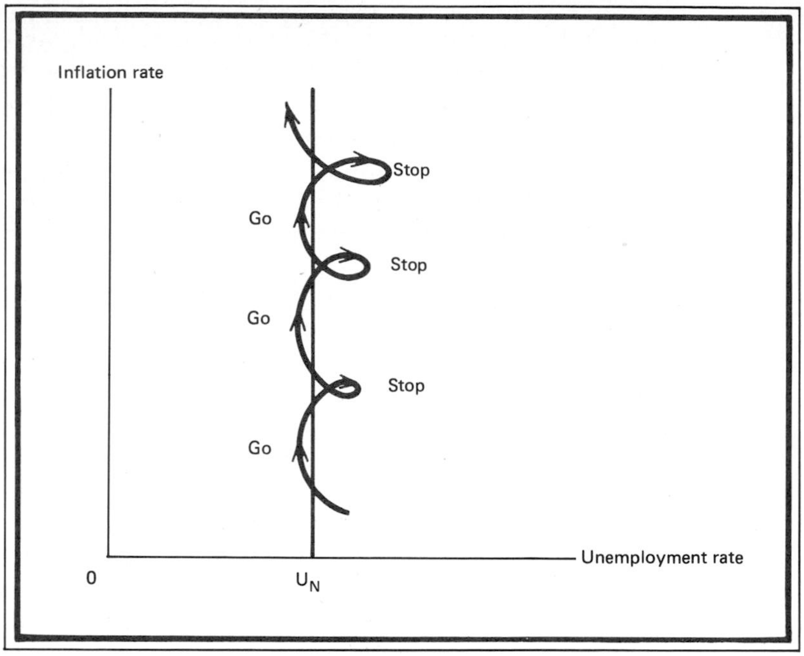

monetarists argue for a monetary rule that would increase the money supply by a fixed percentage a year in order to stabilize price expectations, keep the economy on the vertical long-run curve, and prevent a rising rate of inflation.

As you can see, the F-P hypothesis has returned in a much more sophisticated fashion to the "old time religion" of excess aggregate demand or demand-pull inflation. In the long run too much money only affects the price level and not output or employment if the economy is operating at or near its natural rate of unemployment. Money expansion only causes temporary short-run increases, because people have not sorted out what is happening to their real incomes since they are unaware of the immediate changes on the actual inflation rate. Once the adjustment lags have been brought up to date, money does not affect the real sector of the economy, namely, output and employment. The real sector is self-regulating and will find its way home to its natural long-run equilibrium by following the paths of supply, demand, and relative prices. In the long run money will only determine at what price level inflationary equilibrium will occur once people have figured out the actual behavior of prices.

RATIONAL EXPECTATIONS

The hottest issue in macroeconomics in years is the rational expectations hypothesis (hereafter REH). It includes and extends the notion of adaptive expectations indigenous to the F-P hypothesis. Under the F-P hypothesis a

The *rational expectations* hypothesis says the Friedman-Phelps hypothesis is deficient because there is no systematic misunderstanding by the public of the actual inflation rate.

little extra employment and output can be squeezed from the economy by consistently staying one step ahead of people's expectations, by keeping them temporarily ignorant of the actual rate of inflation. The F-P hypothesis intimates that people do not catch on to the *systematic* policy changes instigated by the policy makers. Pubic information lags, since the public's expectations are caught off guard by policy, particularly by discretionary monetary policy of the Federal Reserve System.

The F-P hypothesis predicts that changes in money growth will influence output and employment in the short run only if changes in the inflation rate and changes in policy are unanticipated, and in the longer period only if these changes are consistently unanticipated by the public, as described by the sloping, short-run Phillips curve. This occurs because the public cannot be instantaneously aware of the short-run price and wage implications of every fiscal or monetary shock to the economy. It takes the long-run period for the public to perceive permanent changes in aggregate demand and relative prices.

Under the REH hypothesis, the public cannot be systematically misled about the short-run implication of policies and their predictable effect on the economy. Policies that have been consistently applied come to be detected as patterns by the public, so that the public can revise its expectations instantaneously and even take counteraction prior to expected policy changes, or before another policy change can otherwise take effect. Because the public knows the likely course of monetary and fiscal policy, policy changes come as no surprise, and consequently have no impact even in the short run. Given certain assumptions about how expectations are formed, traditional fiscal and monetary policies will fail. They will have no effect on the real sector—output, employment, and real income—even in the short run. Thus, there is no short-run Phillips curve offering a menu of possible trade-offs between inflation and unemployment. Given a decade or two of exposure to systematic judgments by the authorities, the effects of traditional monetary and fiscal policy become predictable. The public now has this information even before there is any policy change. When policy does change, or is expected to change, its information is not just past information; there is also current information. The public does not have to wait to react to effects. It can react immediately because it knows what the effects will be. Hence it can nullify what would have otherwise been the effects of traditional policy because it will not systematically underpredict policy effects. Thus, traditional policy cannot reduce unemployment; it only yields more inflation. The system simply moves from one point of inflationary equilibrium to another on the vertical, long-run line. There is no temporary, short-run Phillips curve, because information is current—it comes with no lags. The public does learn from economic history, so traditional policy now condemns the economy to a permanent, inflationary bias.

Let us look at a fiscal policy example. REH says that short-run trade-offs in inflation and unemployment cannot be exploited by the policy authorities.

For example, whenever the economy experiences an unemployment rate of 6 percent, the government always launches a program to try to lower unemployment to 5 percent by increasing spending. Before the unemployment rate drops below 6 percent, the public anticipates that the inflation rate will, therefore, increase from 7 percent to say 9 percent. Unions, banks, and employers will immediately incorporate the 9 percent inflation rate into their decisions; they will *not* behave as if the inflation rate will remain at 7 percent. The public will adjust its portfolios by transferring to bonds and other assets that return higher yields and it will spend less. The result is that the expansion in the economy will be slowed even more. Anticipated rising prices signify that real balances will decline below desired levels. The public will, therefore, also spend less in order to rebuild its real balances. Nor will producers be misled. They react by slowing down production, which also helps to nullify the policy goal of lowering unemployment.

To keep ahead of the public's revised expectations, the Fed has to keep changing policy. REH advocates say that that is not policy, it is a dice game and "not everyone will win, nor will everyone get a prize." Once the game is up it becomes harder for anticipated and actual inflation rates to diverge and monetary policy will be neutralized, affecting the price level and not the real sector. Only if the policy makers can succeed in changing the actual rate of inflation without causing the same change in the expected inflation rate can real variables be changed because people are fooled. New information will be quickly absorbed and expectations soon adjusted. Thus, several years ago when New York City was verging on financial collapse because it could not pay off its bonds, the immediate response in the bond market was a sudden substantial rise in bond yields to account for the new element of risk in the bond markets. This, of course, meant that bond prices fell. They were much cheaper. Thus, expectation of default by New York City was quickly incorporated into peoples' expectations. We say that the bonds were discounted to include the possibility of New York defaulting on the bonds. Or suppose the Fed boosts the money supply in the economy, hoping to reduce interest rates and perk up investment spending. Because the public fears a higher inflation rate, the money rate of interest rises by the expected rate of inflation. Consumers may reduce their real balance holdings, but firms may not spend the additional balances on direct capital formation. Thus the hoped-for investment spending may not occur.

With the REH, we are back into the classical model. Markets will clear and people will maximize, basing their supply and demand decisions on real variables and on perceived changes in relative prices, not on the absolute price level. Though people do not have perfect information, they cannot be *systematically* fooled. Using all available information, they make the best possible estimate of all the *relative* prices that influence their decisions. As their expectations change, they do not all invest in the same way, work in the same way, or spend in the same way. For this reason some economists argue for a monetary rule. Increasing the money supply by X percent a year will stabilize expectations. Buyers and sellers would then reduce the resources they devote trying to keep ahead of the policy makers; instead, they could use these resources to create more output in preference to speculating and adjusting their portfolios to protect themselves from inflation.

The REH does not claim that everyone makes the right correction in forming his or her expectations. Rather, people participating in the markets on *average* are correct about assessing past and current information about the future where systematic policy has been in effect. Only nonsystematic (random or erratic) shocks like floods, freezes, or wars can throw off people's expectations on the average.

Advocates of REH believe that macropolicies of the past decade have not worked well because they were not adequately founded on microeconomic behavior. Greater attention must be devoted to how people form their expectations in the product, labor, and financial markets, and how that affects their decisions as they act in their own best interest in response to changes in relative prices.

Criticisms of REH

Dissenters from the rational expectations hypothesis acknowledge that alerting the discipline to the importance of price expectations has raised some serious questions about the effectiveness of traditional stabilization actions. However, they contend that REH has some serious weaknesses. For REH is really a resurrected though much more sophisticated classical theory, and some of the limitations of the original classical theory still haunt its relevance.

First, it is not realistic to presume that the public has the understanding and all the current information it needs about something as large and complex as the U.S. economy. Its information is limited. The average citizen does not read the Federal Reserve Bulletin to monitor each monetary maneuver of the Fed, or understand what it means or how every change in fiscal policy affects him or her. Although some markets like bonds, stocks, and commodities are highly organized, centralized, and quickly disseminate information about current prices, local labor and product markets have regional characteristics that are not uniformly affected by monetary and fiscal policy at the national level.

Second, inputs are not homogeneous in their use in the production of all goods. Thus, factors of production specialized in one use cannot be easily and costlessly shifted to another use or area in a speedy response to changes in relative prices caused by shifts in demand, even if expectations are revised instantaneously. The transactions costs of shuffling real resources is not negligible. Supply cannot immediately respond. Some people who want to respond, and know how to respond, cannot do so right away. Activist fiscal policy can speed up the transition and affect output and employment.

Third, many labor and product markets are locked into fixed long-term contracts, both of the implicit and explicit kind. Unless contracts can be immediately renegotiated or contain escalator clauses adjusted for falling as well as rising prices, there is no adjustment for changes in relative prices induced by changes in demand or supply during the contract period.[5]

REH advocates respond that such shifts in demand and supply do catch some people off guard, but on the average the public will predict correctly. That is, when people revise their expectations about inflation, as many are as likely to overcorrect as to undercorrect so that policy will have no net effect on the real variables, or the real effect may not be in the direction intended. Also, when there are sudden supply or demand shocks which may cause short-run

[5]For more details see Kenneth Arrow, "The Future and the Present in Economic Life," *Economic Inquiry*, April 1978, pp. 157–173; and Neil G. Berkman, "A Rational View of Rational Expectations," *New England Economic Review*, Jan./Feb. 1980: 18–29.

unemployment in affected sectors, the expected habit of employing monetary and fiscal policy to prevent money incomes from falling in these subsectors is precisely the policy that gets the economy into an inflationary psychology initially. These markets will adjust faster than in the past if the authorities indicate ahead of time that they will not accommodate rising money wages when unemployment is rising in these afflicted parts of the economy, because expectations will be changed by the announcement of such a policy. Thus inflation can be reduced, and faster than it has been thought possible.

Conclusion

Perhaps we can invoke the Hegelian synthesis once again. As the Keynesians believe, adjustments in the real sector of the economy—output and employment—cannot happen quickly, so traditional, activist policy can have some affect on the real sector in the short run. From the REH supporters' side, it must be recognized that intelligent humans are constantly learning, and can begin to react to frustrate traditional policy when it is consistently and systematically repeated, by revising their expectations and behavior much more quickly than ever before.

SUPPLY SIDE ECONOMICS

***Supply side* economists say inflation can be best curbed by stimulating productivity growth on the supply side by lowering business and consumer taxes to stimulate saving and work effort, reducing government spending deficits, and removing the counterproductive government regulations.**

The other counterattack on Keynesian aggregate demand management is directed toward the microeconomics of the supply side of the economy implied earlier in the discussions on investment and the ARS (aggregate real supply) curve. Since World War II, economists concentrated on aggregate demand management with emphasis on government expenditures and deficits embodied in activist, fiscal, and monetary policy to stimulate spending and encourage production. Critics, as far back as F. Hayek in the 1930s, said Keynesian style demand management must end in the economy being mired in inflation and declining productivity. The Keynesian legacy is that pumping up demand raises prices, and restraining spending creates unemployment. However, what fine-tuning overlooked was how relative prices affect individual behavior. How do costly regulations and high marginal tax rates affect the trade-off between leisure and work, spending, and saving? That is, what actually drives an economy? What are the effects on incentives? Have we been unwittingly subsidizing consumption and taxing production? As money income rises, people are thrown into higher marginal tax brackets. Is the additional real income worth the additional effort? Or is the result only a small increase in real income because of inflated prices and taxes? In the 1970's Keynesian policies were designed to offset temporary swings in the economy by adjusting aggregate demand instead of pursuing long term growth in aggregate supply.

For example, we discussed the balanced budget multiplier earlier. Raising taxes and government expenditures by the same amount ($\Delta G = \Delta T$) was said to be expansionary, and was offered as a justification for government expenditures. As G rises so does T equally. Yet what are the effects of an *absolute* rise in taxes on work and production incentives? Incentives are dampened. It is taking *proportionately* more government spending these days for government to produce equivalent growth in real GNP.

The basic thrust of supply side economics is to stop rising inflation that results from an excess of aggregate demand over aggregate supply. Since reducing aggregate demand to slow inflation causes painful unemployment, it is preferable to stimulate the supply side that will result in lower costs of production and lower product prices. Lower prices and improved productivity will encourage more output while solving unemployment and inflation. It is a return to supply creating demand.

Supply side economics proposes to achieve these goals by (1) designing tax cuts to encourage more household saving, which is a major source of funds for business investment, (2) lowering the level of taxes and marginal tax rates on income in order to encourage individuals to work additional hours because the marginal income will not be so heavily taxed that workers choose additional leisure instead, (3) enlarging business savings through lower operating taxes, faster depreciation write-offs, and higher investment tax credits to stimulate new capital investment, (4) reducing the number of regulations, and (5) cutting the level of government deficit spending. These five means can raise productivity.

For example, Social Security is a tax on employment. The employer hires the additional worker based on all the costs, not just wages but fringe payments for medical care and the like as well as the payroll tax. If demand curves mean anything, the higher the price the lower the quantity of workers demanded. The increased Social Security payroll tax to both employers and workers reduces jobs, and incentives to produce for producers and to work for workers. Supply-siders believe taxes can be cut if government deficits are reduced. But government deficits cannot be cut, and a balanced budget reached if high tax rates stifle economic growth.

Suppose an automobile mechanic is taxed in the 25 percent marginal income tax bracket. For every additional $100 he earns, the tax is $25. His wife wants him to fix the roof. He can either pay a roofer (also in the 25 percent bracket) $80 a day or do it himself. His opportunity cost is $100, namely, what he can earn fixing cars in a day if he chooses not to fix the roof. Assume that after taxes he earns $75. By fixing the roof himself, he will save $5. Thus, he chooses to fix the roof. The government's tax take shrinks by $45 ($25 lost from the mechanic plus $20 lost from the roofer).

Assume, instead, the tax rate is 15 percent. After-tax earnings of the mechanic are now $85. He can hire the roofer for $80, and come out $5 ahead. But the roofer gets to work and the government collects $15 + $12 = $27 in taxes. Even if money wages do not stop rising, improved productivity will nevertheless lower unit labor costs, while market competition will force firms to keep prices as low as possible. With production up and prices slowed, the velocity of money would go up and support more transactions, so that the Fed need not increase the rate of money growth. With income up, the demand for cash balances would also rise and absorb the excess money balances that, when spent previously, had pushed prices upward. In addition, increased saving combined with reduced government spending will lower interest rates and reduce crowding out. This will stimulate private capital formation, and raise aggregate income and tax revenues, making balanced federal budgets a greater possibility. Both inflation and unemployment could be substantially reduced through constancy in money supply growth and by lower competitive prices. Thus, aggregate real supply can be shifted downward, or analogously the short run Phillips curve can be shifted inward, reducing the trade-off.

Criticisms

Many economists who support supply side concepts in principle believe its successes would be modest. Aggregate demand has been growing at about 12 percent a year in recent years while real GNP has been growing about 2 percent a year, yielding a net inflation rate of approximately 10 percent. An increase of real GNP from 2 to 4 percent is extremely difficult to achieve and would still leave a residual 8 percent inflation rate. Thus, they conclude that excess aggregate demand is the main problem. Unfortunately, many economists believe it would require 4 or 5 years of substantial unemployment to eliminate inflation by lowering aggregate demand. If, however, there is any truth in the rational expectations theory, the speed of adjustment to stable prices and full employment can be much faster than traditionally thought if explicitly consistent policy is adopted.

But skepticism remains. The effects of policy cannot be predicted accurately, for the problem is staggeringly complex. Instead of stimulating work effort, lowering taxes may have the opposite effect. Go-getters will work harder to gain bigger after-tax rewards, but lazier people left with more after-tax income may choose to work less. Also, because tax cuts act faster in stimulating spending than in increasing supply—which is a long run phenomenon—inflation may become worse. Furthermore, balancing tax cuts with reduced government spending means reductions in public services. They will be strongly resisted by consumer and labor groups and by politicians who represent them. Supply-side policies will initially cause more unemployment, particularly since stimulating supply is a long run phenomenon. Thus results will be slow, whereas public patience in a democracy is notoriously short.

Incomes Policy

There is another small but growing minority of economists who feel that traditional monetary and fiscal policies are inadequate to achieve price stability with full employment. For reasons already discussed, a voluntary approach on the part of all economic agents is not workable. The solution, it is believed, is to attain full employment and then implement an incomes policy. It is a scheme involving mandated directives on wages, incomes, and prices. These controls could either be permanent or temporary. They could take the form of guidelines, that is, monitored adjustments, or an outright freeze on wages and prices. It is felt the virtue of an incomes policy would be to lower drastically the amount of speculation that diverts resources away from production and would break the inflationary psychology. If outright freezes are not acceptable, then incomes policy takes on the mantle of wage-price guideposts.

Guideposts work in the following manner. Average labor force productivity for the economy is calculated by dividing the size of the labor force into the GNP.

$$\text{Average productivity} = \frac{\text{GNP}}{\text{labor force}}.$$

Assume for argument's sake that average productivity for the economy is 3 percent. For industries whose productivity is greater than 3 percent over the period, let wages go up by 3 percent and lower product prices. For those industries whose productivity is less than 3 percent, let wages increase by less than 3 percent and raise prices slightly. The result would be that on the *average* the general price level will stay approximately constant.

There are other possibilities. If increased productivity in the private sector can be passed off as lower prices, this would remove pressure on the public service sector to raise wages, since real incomes there would not fall if the general price index stayed the same.

If wage-price guidelines sound idealistic, they are. Many economists do not believe they would suffice and find them unnecessary, unworkable, and contrary to principles of free market efficiency. Others argue that guidelines simply would not correct for the root causes, namely the institutional rigidities and improper fiscal and monetary policy. Whatever is said against wage-price controls applies more forcefully to a wage-price freeze. Weaknesses of wage-price guidelines are itemized as follows:

1. Many costly hours in industry and government are wasted in administering and enforcing the unenforceable. Many unions and firms would not fully cooperate.

2. If kept on for too long, serious misallocation results. Commodities under strong controls become relatively cheaper than commodities under weaker controls. Consequently, capital begins to move from strongly controlled to weakly controlled industries, causing shortages in the strongly controlled sectors.

3. Resource misallocation also occurs when the mandated rigidities do not allow prices to respond to changes in demand and supply conditions which would normally change relative prices and redirect resource use and rewards.

4. Higher than normal profits to businesses could appear because firms could become more cost efficient without lowering their prices in order to be more competitive.

5. Under profit control margins, businesses could deliberately become lax about efficiency, raising their costs and justifying requests for price increases by the wage-price board.

6. Controls create uncertainty among producers with regard to when controls will be lifted and what is legal and illegal, and whether prices can be raised to cover costs. Wholesalers may build up inventories waiting for controls to be lifted, causing shortages at the retail level. The uncertainty also gives rise to reduction in capital spending, which adds to unemployment and future product shortages.

7. Wage controls reduce worker productivity by removing incentives.

8. In reality, measuring productivity increases is a difficult task and

would lead to conflicts between management, unions, and the government authorities concerning what the wage increases should be.

9. Wage drift cannot be controlled. Earnings as compared to regulated hourly wage rates can differ because of overtime payments, bonuses, and job reclassifications.

10. With prices controlled, product debasement can occur either by lowering the quality of the inputs or lowering the quality without lowering the price.

11. Controls are inequitable because requests submitted to the wage-price board are often judged by political interests and by the political clout of the petitioner.

12. Controls do not get at the cause of inflation and once lifted the pent-up economy would experience a burst of rapid inflation. Or, if controls are permanent resource misallocation would amplify. Controls applied for a long time have never worked.

CHAPTER SUMMARY

Inflation is a sustained increase in the level of prices. Since higher costs to one represent higher incomes to another, inflation results in some redistribution of income. People who anticipate the inflation can often take action to nullify losses in their real income. In general, those gain from an inflation who are net monetary debtors; those lose real wealth who are net monetary creditors, or are on fixed incomes.

The macromodel can be modified to take into explicit account the change in the price level which was assumed constant in the Keynesian cross model up to the full employment level. This modification results in the aggregate real supply curve (ARS). The ARS schedule can shift because of changes in technology, taxes, input costs, capacity, labor force size and skill, and government regulations.

Traditional sources of inflation are ascribed to *demand-pull,* where aggregate demand grows faster than aggregate supply; *cost-push,* where prices rise independently of aggregate demand because of increases in input costs alone; *structural factors* where prices rise because of the immobility of both human and nonhuman resources that cannot be readapted soon enough to changing market conditions, so that bottlenecks and capacity limitations arise, driving up costs. Structural inflation may be triggered by aggregate demand forces that activate lagged cost-push responses. Structural inflation also rises from institutional arrangements such as the rising influence of public sector unions, noncompetitive pricing in the medical health industry, and the price-setting power of capital-intensive large corporations in concentrated industries desiring to generate large research revenues to create new labor-saving technology.

Supply shocks are another inflationary source. They may consist of higher prices for imported oil, raising domestic production costs, a sharp decrease in the availability of a basic, scarce, raw material, or a severe reduction in food production because of adverse weather.

The monetarists claim that all of the above may cause a rise in prices in particular parts of the economy. There may also be a one-time increase in the price level because of one of these supply effects. But they do not continue to be a source of persistent rising prices unless the nation's money supply is increased and accommodates all individuals and groups trying to maintain their relative income positions. In a barter economy a decrease in the supply of one commodity raises its cost, because it takes more of other commodities to acquire it, thus rendering these other commodities cheaper. Thus if the cost of one commodity rises, the others must fall. However, in a money-using economy when the cost of one commodity increases, more income would be spent on it and less on other goods, reducing the demand for them and thus lowering their price so that the average price level would be unchanged—and real income too. Moreover, because money wages and prices are sticky downward, then when more income must be spent for one basic good, for example, oil, so that less income would be available to spend on non-oil goods, the price of non-oil goods do not fall nor do money wages. Instead it is output, hence employment that is reduced. Thus the price level rises along with unemployment. To prevent this, if the money supply is expanded so that the higher priced oil can be bought but without causing demand to decline for non-oil goods, then unemployment does not increase; however, prices must increase, and they must continue to increase, because money supply expansion must grow at a faster rate than the public's expectations about the inflation rate. For this leads the public to believe rising money wages signify rising real wages. The monetarists contend that industrial economies have a natural rate of unemployment. Unemployment can only fall below this level if the public's expectations about future prices is lower than the actual rate. Once the public brings its expectations in line with the actual rate of inflation, then the economy will remain at the natural rate of unemployment but in a state of inflationary equilibrium.

Between 1958 and 1970, the generally accepted stabilization doctrine was based on the Phillips curve. It suggested there was an inverse trade-off between the unemployment rate and the inflation rate. Thus, to reduce the unemployment rate required raising the inflation rate. And to reduce the inflation rate required raising the unemployment rate. It became apparent that the trade-off was becoming worse, that the Phillips curve was shifting outward. The Friedman-Phelps (F-P) hypothesis explained this by explicitly introducing price expectations. It argues that the Phillips curve trade-off is a short-run phenomenon arising from the disparity between the expected inflation rate and the actual inflation rate. This misconception temporarily causes impacts on the real sector, that is, on employment, output, and relative prices, and also causes shifts in the short-run Phillips curve since each curve exists for a different expected inflation rate. But in the long run the misconception can be removed. There is one point on each Phillips curve where the expected and actual inflation rates are equal. The sequence of these points, one from each short-run curve, generates the long-run vertical line that must exist at the economy's natural rate of unemployment.

In the long run, therefore, say the monetarists, the money supply only determines prices and the rate of inflation, and does not affect the real sector of the economy as described by the natural rate of unemployment reflected in the vertical line.

It is only because people are temporarily fooled by monetary or fiscal policy (financed by money creation) that real effects are observed. Once the public catches on, prices, not output, are affected by policies that create excess demand.

The reason the real sector is affected in the short run as reflected by the sloping Phillips curve is that output decisions are made before price and wage decisions. If new money creation increases demand for an industry's product, at first it cannot tell if the increase is temporary or if it is widespread and permanent, or confined solely to the industry. Hence output and inventories adjust before prices are altered, since many price and wages are locked into contracts for some period. However, if the rise in demand operates throughout the economy, costs begin to rise, putting pressure on prices. Higher prices to one intermediate producer become higher costs to another until higher prices are transmitted throughout the economy. The public develops new expectations about future prices, and when contracts expire, prices and wage rates incorporate these expectations. If the Fed pursues a permissive monetary policy, expectations are realized or even revised upward and renegotiated in new contracts. When these revised expectations overshoot actual inflation rates, it appears to be a cost-push effect, when it is really a delayed response to excess aggregate demand combined with accelerated price expectations. Thus, in the long run money creation will directly affect prices, leaving relative prices unchanged and the economy producing at its natural level on the vertical Phillips line.

The F-P hypothesis is based on adaptive price expectations. Namely, past price behavior is extrapolated into the future. Some monetarists have added a new twist to price formation behavior expressed in the rational expectations hypothesis (REH). Here, there is no short-run Phillips curve; misinformation about the actual inflation rate cannot cause short-term real effects and a trade-off between inflation and employment because, except for purely random events, there is no misinformation. For the public uses not only past price information, but all available information. It therefore includes perceived, systematic response patterns in monetary and fiscal policy by the Fed and Congress to certain economic circumstances even before the authorities react to those circumstances. If so, the public is not, on the average, misled by the effects of potentially certain policies, and corrects beforehand. Hence, there are no short-term effects on output and employment and on the real sector. Thus anticipated monetary growth affects only absolute prices, not relative prices. So the economy is always more or less on the vertical long-run curve, thereby invalidating traditional policies. To stop inflation means slowing monetary growth and letting price and wage increases subside. Keynesians, in particular, respond that to depress aggregate demand to stop inflation is too painful a solution because it takes too long for wage rates to fall and labor markets to adjust. The result would be a deep, long, socially destabilizing recession. Stimulating reasonable aggregate demand combined with job training programs and wage-price guidelines would be a better approach. The monetarists respond that rising inflation is destabilizing and demoralizing too. And wage-price controls simply do not work in the long run because the basic root of inflation is excess money creation, triggering accelerated price expectations that cannot be stopped by stop-and-go policies, which come to be expected and therefore unbelieved as serious policies to control inflation.

An adjunct to the attack on traditional Keynesian aggregate demand management is *supply side* economics. Control demand by reducing government spending and stimulate supply by reducing regulations and lowering taxes in order to raise productivity, reduce inflation, raise profits and real take-home wages to stimulate business and individual incentives. Skeptics believe improved supply side productivity can help slow inflation, but excess aggregate demand, because of excessive government spending and passive monetary policy of the Federal Reserve, is the main problem.

QUESTIONS

1. In a barter economy inflation just cannot happen. Do you agree or disagree? Explain.
2. Indicate which type or types of inflation—demand-pull, cost-push, supply shock, or structural—is associated with each one of the following cases. Also, if structural, which aspect of structural is in evidence—sector, capacity effects, government, or other.

a. The economy has become less flexible over the years.
b. The government did not raise taxes in the late 1960s when it should have.
c. The OPEC oil cartel raised prices half a dozen times during the 1970s.
d. If an industry is concentrated, price increases in the midst of a recession are no surprise.
e. In an economy where individual products and the labor skills to produce them are highly specialized, sudden and severe changes in demand for specific products cannot be quickly met, and costs rise.
f. Capacity and labor shortages across a broad spectrum of industries occur because of vigorous monetary and fiscal policy.
g. An increase in Social Security payroll taxes is levied on employers.
h. The incentives to strike are strengthened if the cost can be buried in the overall budget and deferred to the future.
i. A foreign war cuts off major supplies of imported, basic raw materials.
j. Chrysler Corporation got into deep financial trouble when it did not have the cash to convert its plant to build more compact cars to meet both government mileage targets and sudden consumer demand for smaller cars.
k. Wages rise faster than productivity irrespective of decreases in aggregate demand.

3. "You would not be wrong to regard the green pieces of paper in your wallet as receipts for taxes paid." What is implied in this facetious comment about inflation?
4. The yield on a government savings bond is:
   4% after 6 months
   6 1/2% after 5 years
   7% after 11 years (maturity).
   This prompted an economist to say, "The government's advertising of savings bonds (called war bonds in 1942 and energy bonds in the 1970s) would cause a car dealer to be arrested for fraud." Why? A government official responded that "a 7 percent return after 11 years is a good return, because by the time the bond matures the yield on other kinds of bonds will be down, and at 7 percent they'll be a bargain." Do you agree? Explain.
5. Set up the account and calculate the real net wealth of the creditor discussed early in the chapter (on page 783 below the table).
6. What arguments can you give to support the notion that the costs of creeping inflation are much less than the costs of trying to avoid it? What arguments against? Why is a "sympathy demand" shift not necessarily an act of policy kindness?
7. With more spending on energy required there should be less spending for other products. Why isn't there?
8. Prices and costs used to decline during a recession. Now they do not. How come?
9. A spokesman for an electrical products company said, "Despite the recession, the competitive situation does not require that we move prices back. We raised a number of prices recently and publicized the increases to inform competitors as well as our customers. Our competitors generally follow suit rather quickly, and we follow them pretty quickly when they do it." Is there any theory to explain this? Is the law of supply and demand being violated? Comment.
10. Prices rise because the cost of production rises and the cost of production is primarily the cost of labor, whether directly or indirectly in the costs of materials. Since prices cannot fall below costs for long, and so long as labor does not cost less, prices will not fall significantly regardless of the level of demand. Tax increases do not stop this process because people simply recircuit demand into a demand for higher gross income to maintain after-tax income." How is this possible according to the monetarists?

11. A lagged feedback of price expectations on future wages and prices is often identified with what type of inflation? What other hypothesis could explain the situation? Explain.
12. What is a Phillips Curve? List at least three forces that might push the curve away from the origin.
13. Although the Phillips curve hypothesis was once useful for stabilization policy, it contained a flaw. What flaw apparently invalidated it during the 1970s?
14. If inflation is perfectly anticipated, what is the shape of the Phillips curve? Why?
15. Many market characteristics that determine the natural level of unemployment are man made and policy made. Can you give a few examples? Do you therefore believe Congress should rigidly target a minimum unemployment rate by law?
16. Firms tend to respond to a change in demand by attempting to adjust output and employment initially, without major changes in relative prices and wages. Explain.
17. Suppose that the government had instituted an investment tax credit early in previous recessions in order to stimulate investment. However, this time firms wait for the recession to end before investing, causing a decline in current demand. Henceforth would this tax policy practically ensure continuance of the recession? Why? Is this an example of adaptive or rational expectations?
18. The price level expected for next period will be higher than the price level that was previously expected to prevail in the current period. This is an example of what kind of expectation?
19. Mary is looking for an apartment. She checks the newspaper ads and calls only to find that the apartment has been taken. Next time she gets the Sunday paper on Saturday the moment it is available in order to get an earlier peek at the ads. She calls and finds the apartment has been rented. What hypothesis seems to fit this situation? Explain.
20. One argument against the quick adjustments seemingly implied in the rational expectations hypothesis is that long-term contracts fix prices and wages for too long a period. Can you think of two ways of getting around long-term contract constraints?
21. In the long run, after the economy has fully adjusted to some steady rate of inflation, what can you say about the relation between actual prices experienced, price expectations, and adaptive versus rational expectations based on price determinations?
22. How does supply-side economics differ from traditional Keynesian stabilization policy? Why do many economists believe it alone cannot eliminate inflation? And what do these economists believe is still necessary to do in order to control inflation?
23. Use the graph on page 818 to answer the questions:

    Assume the economy is at point *a*.

    a. Will people on the average be experiencing rising, falling, or the same money wages at *a* as compared to *b*?
    b. Is the expected rate of inflation at *a* more, less, or the same as the actual rate of inflation?
    c. Is unemployment at *a* more, less, or the same as the natural rate?
    d. Is the expected rate of inflation for curve III 8 percent, 12 percent, 4 percent, or unknown?
    e. If money supply growth is reduced in this period, will the expected rate of inflation next period be 8 percent, 4 percent, below 8 percent, or 12 percent? Explain.
    f. If money supply growth is reduced in this period, will the actual inflation rate next period be below 4 percent, 8 percent, 12 percent, between 4 percent and 8 percent or between 8 percent and 12 percent? Explain your answer.

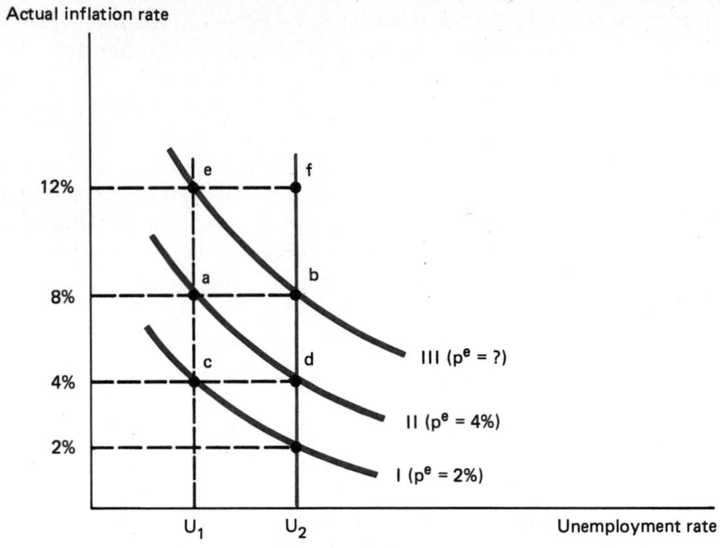
Actual inflation rate
12%
8%
4%
2%
e
f
a
b
c
d
III (pᵉ = ?)
II (pᵉ = 4%)
I (pᵉ = 2%)
U1
U2
Unemployment rate

Chapter 32

International Trade and Exchange Rates

PROGRESS REPORT

A. In recent chapters we finished our study of macroeconomics in a closed economy after having built an economic model, suggested how it could guide us in implementing stabilization policies, and then examined the problems of employment and inflation in some detail.

B. Now we move on to consider the foreign sector of our economy and its relation with other economies of the world. International trade is much more important to a small country than it is to a large country, which is more likely to be relatively self-sufficient in producing goods for its own consumption. When goods are exchanged across national boundaries we have international trade. Because of this, international politics cannot be ignored when considering international trade realistically. It is one thing to buy a foreign product; it is another to figure out how to pay for it since it must be bought with foreign currency. Thus, we proceed to examine how exchange rates are determined.

C. In Chapter 33 we shift our gears once again and move on to a new topic, economic growth. Trading nations and less well developed economies are progressing and in most parts of the world the standard of living is rising. We shall examine what economists can say about growth.

World trade has grown immensely since the end of World War II. Except for a very few isolated communities, no country is independent of the economic forces operating in the larger world. Domestic economies of Europe, the Americas, Asia, and Africa, are all integral parts of the global economy.

In 1980 the U.S. imported nearly half of its crude oil. Textiles and tools are imported from Taiwan and India, shoes from Italy, television sets from Japan. As a percentage of gross national product U.S. merchandise exports increased from 3.6 percent in 1955 to 7.7 percent in 1980. World trade has grown more rapidly than U.S. domestic trade. International investment has grown too.

Countries trade for their *mutual benefit*.

Why do countries trade? They trade for the same reason that individuals do—for **mutual benefit**. Nations gain from trade, total production increases, and the world income becomes bigger. Everybody can get into the act and benefit. Just as the U.S. economy has grown partly because of free trade among its states, so can the world economy progress by free trade among its nations. Even if a country had no *absolute* advantage over any other country, it and its trade partners could mutually benefit. Economist David Ricardo (1772–1823) was the first one to prove this proposition about mutual benefit, even for the least advantageous. Its proof hinges on the concept of *comparative advantage*, which in essence is just another view of the fruits of specialization.

COMPARATIVE ADVANTAGE

***Comparative advantage* arises from the maximization of gains that results when nations specialize in producing and trading only those goods which they can produce at the lowest opportunity cost.**

Countries can benefit from trade whenever one country has a comparative advantage in the production of a commodity. The reason they can benefit is that world production increases if each country specializes and produces that particular product for which it has a comparative advantage, and then trades with the other countries. The following example will clarify this point.

Let us assume that the linear production possibility curves of Figure 32-1 represent the potential output of logs and bricks by U.S. and Canadian producers. Loads of logs are measured on the horizontal axis and batches of bricks are measured on the vertical axis. Looking at the figure for the U.S. on the left side we see on the horizontal axis that when U.S. producers devote their efforts entirely to the production of logs they can produce 30 loads per period. Alternatively, if they devoted their efforts to producing only bricks they could produce 50 batches. The numbers 30 and 50 represent the intercepts of the production possibility curve with the respective axes. It is also possible for U.S. producers to divide their efforts and produce 30 batches of bricks along with 12 loads of logs. This combined output for each period is designated by point A in the figure.

Glancing at the Canadian graph in the figure we observe that Canadian producers can produce either 24 batches of bricks or 24 loads of logs or some linear combination of the two such as at point B where 14 bricks and 10 logs are produced.

The numbers of this hypothetical example suggest that the U.S. has what

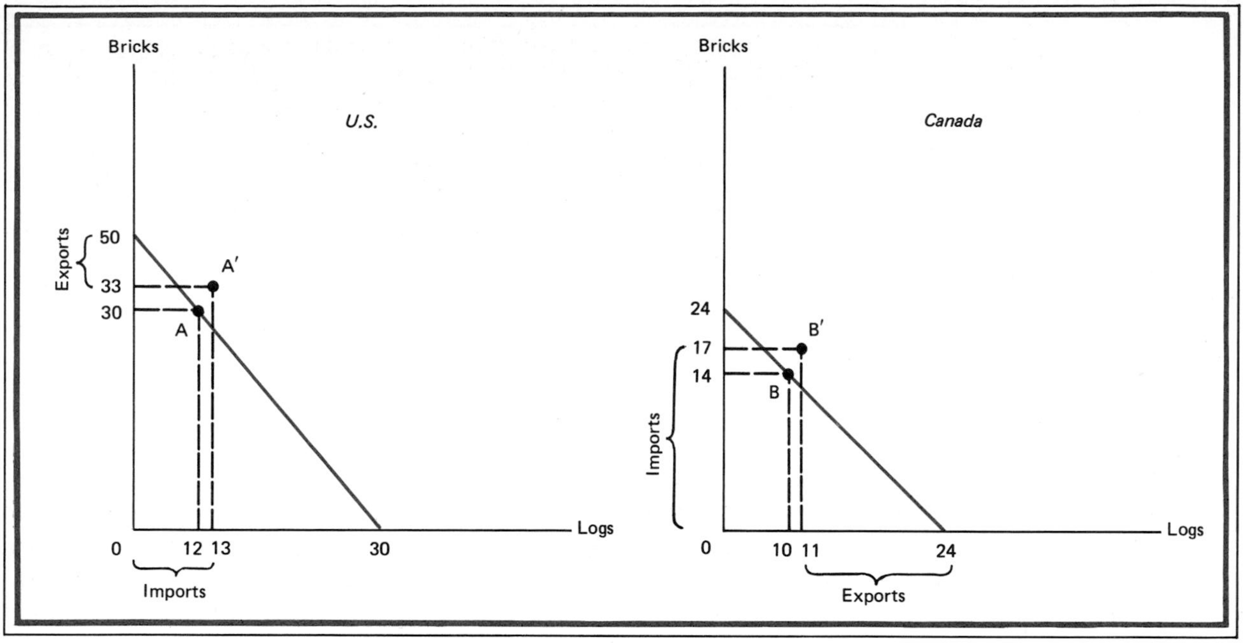

Figure 32-1

is called an absolute advantage in the production of both logs and bricks. It simply means that U.S. producers can, if they wish, produce more logs or more bricks or more of any combination than Canadian producers can. If the two production possibility curves were drawn on the same graph, the U.S. curve would lie to the right of the Canadian curve. The U.S. could outproduce Canada. Whatever package of logs and bricks Canada produced, the U.S. could produce a larger package. This is what absolute advantage means.

One would think that if the U.S. can outproduce Canada there would be no reason for the two countries to trade with each other. But this is not the case. Trade gives benefits if one country has a comparative advantage in production of one of the two goods. To see why refer to the graphs again.

If the U.S. only produces bricks, it can produce 50 of them. It therefore sacrifices 30 logs it could produce if it only produced logs. Hence the ratio is 50 bricks to 30 logs. If the ratio is divided through by 50 it reads 1 brick to 3/5 of a log. Or in shorthand 1B:3/5L. This says that the opportunity cost of the U.S. to produce 1 brick is the sacrifice of 3/5 of a log. Alternatively, if the ratio is divided through by 30, it reads 1 log to 5/3 brick or 1L:5/3B. The opportunity cost to the U.S. of producing 1 log is 5/3 bricks sacrificed in production. This is also the slope of the U.S. production possibility curve (without a minus sign). For Canada the ratio is 24 logs to 24 bricks. Dividing through by 24 yields 1 log to 1 brick or 1L:1B or conversely 1B:1L.

Assume there is no trade and that the U.S. is producing 30 bricks at point *A*, then it must have sacrificed producing $30 \times 3/5 = 18$ logs. Hence it is consuming $30 - 18 = 12$ bricks at point *A*. Similarly if Canada produces 14 bricks, then it must sacrifice producing 14 logs since 1L:1B. Hence it is consuming only $24 - 14 = 10$ bricks at point *B*. These numbers appear under the heading "without trade" in the table.

	Without trade		With specialization in production	
	Bricks	Logs	Bricks	Logs
U.S.	30	12	50	0
Canada	14	10	0	24
Total	44	22	50	24

Now let us assume that each country specializes in the production of the good in which it has a comparative advantage. The U.S. producers have a comparative advantage in brick production and the Canadians have a comparative advantage in log production. That is to say, the opportunity cost for the U.S. to produce 1 brick is the sacrifice of 3/5 of a log. The opportunity cost for Canada to produce 1 brick is the sacrifice of 1 log, which is a greater sacrifice. On the other hand, the opportunity cost for the U.S. to produce 1 log is 1-2/3 bricks, whereas for Canada it is 1 brick. Thus, it costs more for the U.S. to produce logs than for Canada; the slopes of the production possibility curves indicate the opportunity costs for each country to produce bricks and logs. The table shows that with specialization in production the total production of both bricks and logs is up. Brick output rose from 44 to 50 and log output rose from 22 to 24.

The next step is to divide this higher level of world output by letting the two countries trade with each other. One possible outcome could be:

	With specialization and trade	
	Bricks	Logs
U.S.	33	13
Canada	17	11
Total	50	24

U.S. consumption of bricks is up from 30 to 33 and Canadian consumption is up from 14 to 17. Similarly, in Canada, log consumption is increased from 10 to 11 and in the U.S. from 12 to 13. The points showing these consumption levels after trading are A' and B' in the graphs.

It is clear that if each country specializes in the production of those goods in which it has a comparative advantage, then total output will increase and consumption in both countries can increase. Thus, trade allows for efficiency in the use of scarce economic resources.

One thing to notice is that if the *slopes* of the production possibility curves of the two countries were the *same*, there could be no gain in total world output from specialization and trade. It is only when the opportunity costs (slopes) of the two countries differ that we say one country has a comparative advantage over the other in the production of a good. Thus, comparative advantage depends on the *relative* costs of production of the two goods in the two countries. Furthermore, for both countries to gain from trade, they must exchange at a trade-off intermediate **between the domestic exchange ratios**.

For both nations to benefit from trade they must exchange at a ratio *between their different domestic exchange rates*.

For, if the U.S. trades at Canada's domestic exchange rate (1 brick for 1 log), the U.S. gains all the benefits and Canada none. Conversely, if Canada trades at the U.S.'s domestic exchange rate (1 brick to 3/5 of a log), then Canada gains all the benefits and the U.S. none. Both gain if the U.S. trades with Canada at an intermediate rate, for example, 1 U.S. brick per 13/17 of a Canadian log, where 13/17 (.764) is larger than 3/5 (.600) and smaller than 1. The table showing specialization and trade indicates this. The U.S. produces 50 bricks and exports 17 of them in order to import 13 logs (17 × 13/17). Canada exports 13 logs and imports 17 bricks (13 × 17/13), as Fig. 32-1 shows.

Restraints on freedom of trade prevent these beneficial effects of trade from coming about. Nevertheless, countries continue to restrain trade. Let us now turn, therefore, to examine the arguments that surround the debate over whether or not countries should impose **tariffs**, **quotas**, and other restraints on free trade.

***Tariffs* are taxes on imported goods and import *quotas* are limits on the quantities of imported goods.**

ARGUMENTS AGAINST FREE TRADE

Ever since Ricardo worked out the principles of comparative advantage, well-known arguments against it are repeated endlessly. They persist because of their emotional appeal and because there is some partial truth to them that obscures the whole truth.

Nations of the world have imposed and removed tariffs (a tax on foreign imports) over the years in response to changing conditions. Today in the U.S. there is increasing pressure from some industries and unions to "protect" domestic jobs either by increasing tariffs or imposing physical quotas. These critics of free trade argue that what is true in theory is not always true in practice. A particular U.S. industry being priced out of business by foreign imports certainly does not gain from free trade. But overall more industries gain than do not gain.

Arguments *supporting* trade protectionism include cheap foreign labor, infant industries, and national defense.

Let us examine some of the arguments the protectionists offer in their support of tariffs and quotas. They concern such things as cheap foreign labor, infant industries, and national defense.

Low Foreign Wages

This argument assumes that because foreign labor is abundant and cheap, foreign goods can be produced at lower prices than U.S. goods where labor costs are higher. The result is a loss of jobs to foreigners "who work for nothing." But the U.S. does with regularity export commodities—things like airplanes, electrical machinery, pocket calculators, wheat, coal, and computers. Wages paid to workers in these industries in the U.S. are much *higher* than they are in most of the countries to which the U.S. exports these goods. High wages reflect the high productivity of the workers in these industries. On the other hand, in those industries where U.S. producers are weakly competitive or noncompetitive such as cotton textiles, shoes, gloves, television parts, and rugs, U.S. imports are large. Yet wages in these import-competing industries are *low* relative to wages paid to other U.S. workers in strong exporting industries. Low wages reflect low productivity. Countries will export goods produced in industries where productivity and wages are *high*, causing cost per unit of output to be relatively low.

In spite of the tariffs and quota restrictions already existing to protect many noncompetitive U.S. industries, these tend to be inefficient industries in which the U.S. does not have a comparative advantage. Tariffs, therefore, encourage the use of too many resources in such activities when the U.S. should be devoting more resources to industries where comparative advantage prevails.

It is true that foreign competition can cause a particular unprotected industry to lose profits, sales, and jobs, and that in the short run the benefits to that particular industry from retaining protection are sizable. Every producer, in search of his own private interest, will ask for protection. But the benefits are to those protected and *not* to the rest of us who have to pay more for the more expensive domestic goods.

Thus, to sew up the tattered sleeve of job-loss logic, consider that when Datsuns are imported into the U.S. fewer U.S. cars may be sold. Nonetheless, Datsun imports require employment of dealers, mechanics, and parts clerks in the U.S. distribution outlets. Conversely, the export of Northwest logs may reduce jobs in local mills, but it increases employment among longshoremen on the docks. Finally, if the U.S. did not import, other nations could not acquire U.S. dollars to buy U.S. exports, and this would reduce the number of potential domestic jobs.

Infant Industries

The infant industry proposal revolves about the inability of a small, new, domestic industry to get on its feet and to survive long enough to be able to compete vigorously with larger, already established competitors. This particularly applies to the less developed countries vis-à-vis the developed industrialized countries. The idea is that eventually these countries will be able to establish a comparative advantage provided these industries can survive long enough. In terms of the production possibility curves of Figure 32-1, what is being argued is that a given country's curve can move outward if a particular industry is protected and given adequate time to develop. Once developed, tariffs and other protective barriers can be removed.

Another aspect of the infant industry argument is that by protecting several industries for a time, a less developed country is able to diversify its industrial base. This may be important because it is often the case that a poor country's trade depends almost exclusively on one item—say coffee. If a crop fails it has a devastating effect on the country's income. To diversify the industrial base would help.

The infant industry argument for protection has a kernel of truth to it. As a practical matter, however, it fails for one principal reason. There never arises a good time to remove the barriers. Under protection the industry expands. Therefore, no matter when it is decided that protection should be removed the industry would be hurt and suffer unemployment. The removal of protection would force the industry to contract. Private interests in the industry would argue convincingly that protection should continue and that it would be premature to remove it now. The inefficiencies that accompany trade restriction continue to harm the consuming public. They pay more for these higher priced goods produced domestically and consequently have less income remaining to buy other things. And because domestic prices are higher, trade protection may not raise real wages in the long run.

National Defense

The more a country specializes, the less diversified its economy and the greater its dependence on, and vulnerability to, others. Tariff barriers therefore can soothe the national psyche. The U.S. for example would no doubt sleep better if it could attain its desired goal of energy independence. Self-sufficiency is a broader issue than that of national defense itself. The U.S. is very inefficient at shipbuilding, for example. Ship construction in the U.S. is subsidized by over 70 percent, yet the U.S. insists on building many of its own ships. For reasons of national security it wishes to maintain its shipbuilding capacity should a war emergency occur. Special interests such as the shipbuilding firms and the associated unions keep reminding us of the danger of depending on foreign made ships, even though foreign ships can often be obtained for lower prices than U.S. ships.

The national defense argument is weak on both political and economic grounds. Countries that trade extensively with each other have reason to prevent war. Politicians with warlike intent will think twice if they know that significant trading interests will oppose them. Trade, if free, tends to make friends because both parties to trade stand to benefit.

Second, if the resources that are wasted by inefficient production caused by high tariffs were to be spent directly to build and maintain an arsenal and an army, more real spending would go toward defense and the likelihood of war would again be reduced. Thus, not only is it economically costly to protect industries for national defense purposes, but it is counterproductive in that it reduces an important restraint on warlike actions—free trade.

It appears that none of the protectionist arguments has great merit when it is analyzed carefully. Most economists agree that a policy of gradual removal of trade restraints would be good economics.

WHY COMPARATIVE ADVANTAGE?

A *comparative advantage* may stem from natural resources, geography, or even the culture of a country.

There are several reasons that make free trade desirable for countries having a comparative advantage in producing one good or the other. Countries vary in their human and physical resources. Even weather serves as a basis for comparative advantage. Oranges grow in warm climates. Most coal deposits seem to lie in the Northern Hemisphere. Some countries have coal, oil, and water; others have none. Some countries are landlocked; others have access to the sea. There seem to be differences in national character and culture that result in advantages in some activities rather than in others. Some countries with large populations are labor-abundant.

The U.S. is usually cited as an example of a country with relatively abundant capital and scarce labor. That is, the *ratio* of capital to labor, the K/L ratio, in the U.S. is much higher than in, say, India or Peru. Japan has a scarce land supply whereas Canada and Australia are land-abundant and labor-scarce.

Figure 32-2

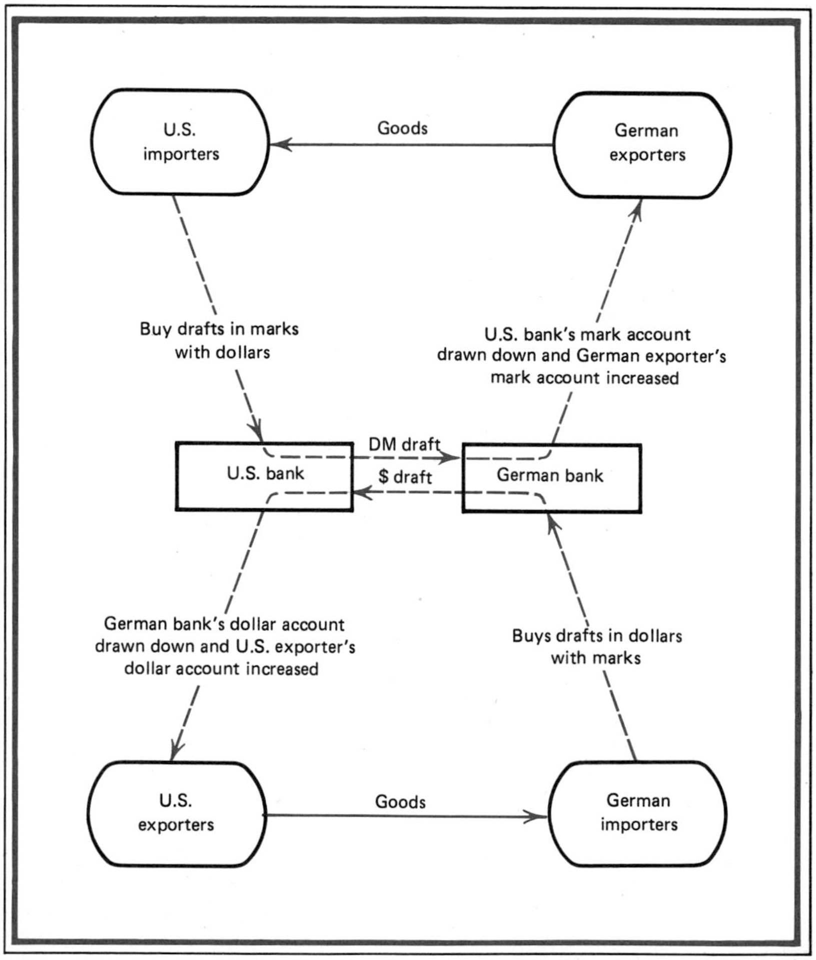

Thus, Canada exports logs and Australia mutton. The production of both logs and mutton requires large land areas. Countries that have abundant labor will produce certain labor-intensive goods such as textiles relatively more cheaply than others. Therefore it is not surprising to find Hong Kong, Korea, and Taiwan efficient at producing them. But computers and heavy machinery require lots of capital and capital in the U.S. is, relatively speaking, much cheaper than in Hong Kong. It follows that the U.S. is inefficient in the production of textiles but efficient in the production of items like computers. Trade is based on such comparative advantages.

PAYING FOR YOUR IMPORTS

Having discussed the benefits of trade, let us now examine briefly some aspects of international payments. For example, how does the German exporter get paid if he sells a Volkswagen to a U.S. importer? If you are a tourist in Germany, it is quite simple to trudge into a German bank and exchange your dollars into deutschemarks. If the German shopkeepers are willing to accept your dollars, as many are willing to do, they can negotiate the conversions themselves at their banks. But what if you go to your local Volkswagen dealer in the U.S. to purchase a VW Rabbit. How does the German car exporter get paid in marks? The usual process is rather simple to understand. There are U.S. banks that have correspondent banks in Germany where the U.S. bank keeps an account in marks. Likewise, the German bank has a correspondent bank in the U.S. where it maintains an account in dollars. The banks act as middlemen for international traders. You pay dollars to your bank and your bank uses its marks to pay the German exporter.

Figure 32-2 illustrates the sequence. If a U.S. resident buys a Volkswagen for $6,000 on a check drawn on his account at a U.S. bank, the car importer would buy a bank draft (a special kind of check) denominated in the appropriate number of marks (say 13,600) at the correspondent bank. Start at the upper left corner of the figure. The U.S. bank then notifies the German bank to draw down its account in marks by 13,600 marks and the German exporter is notified that a bank draft awaits him. When the German exporter deposits it at his bank his account is credited by 13,600 marks. Conversely, the bottom half of the figure shows that when a German importer buys an IBM computer from a U.S. exporter, the German importer uses his check denominated in marks to purchase a bank draft denominated in dollars. The German bank draws down its account in the U.S. in dollars and the U.S. exporter's balance in dollars at his bank is increased by the amount of the draft he deposits there.

EXCHANGE RATES

We now turn the discussion to an understanding of how much one currency is worth in terms of another currency. The price of currency is now the issue.

Figure 32-3

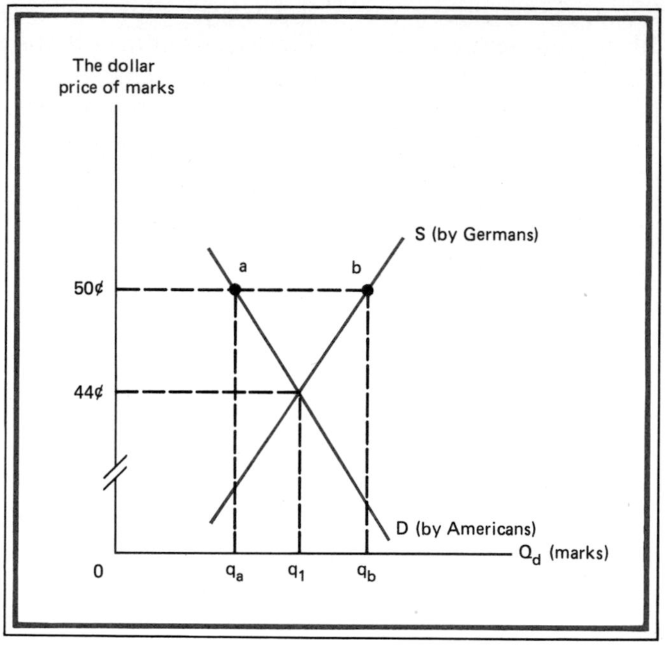

Flexible Rates

Flexible exchange rates **are determined by the world supply and demand for the various currencies.**

Freely fluctuating exchange rates are determined by supply and demand for the various national currencies. The markets for currencies operate in the same way that freely competitive markets for goods operate. A demand for, say, German deutschemarks (DM) reflects the demand for German goods. German demand for dollars is the result of a demand for U.S. produced goods. The two currencies act as mediums of exchange.

Figure 32-3 is a graph of the market for German marks. On the vertical axis the dollar price of marks is measured, and the quantity of marks exchanged each period is measured on the horizontal axis. The supply curves of marks offered by German holders reflects their demand for U.S. goods. The demand curve for marks reflects the demand in the U.S. for German goods.

The supply curve of marks slopes upward to the right, implying that the quantity of marks Germans would be willing to provide increases as the dollar price of the mark rises. The Germans get more for their marks and find U.S. goods becoming cheaper. They increase the quantity of marks supplied to acquire more U.S. goods.

Conversely, the demand curve for marks slopes downward to the right. As the price of the mark in dollar terms falls, it requires fewer dollars to buy the same number of marks. In effect German goods would become cheaper in the U.S. and the quantity of German goods demanded in the U.S. would rise. (Notice, we said quantity supplied and quantity demanded and not supply and demand increased, since the curves have not shifted.) In equilibrium where 1 mark is priced at 44 cents, the quantity of marks exchanged in the market is q_1.

As an example of exchange rate calculations suppose a U.S. resident buys a VW for $6,000. In Figure 32-3 the mark is priced at 44 cents; what does the car cost in marks? To obtain how marks trade for a dollar, do the following:

$$\frac{1 \text{ mark}}{.44 \text{ dollars}} = 2.27 \text{ marks/dollar.}$$

Then,

$$\frac{6{,}000 \text{ \sout{dollars}}}{1 \text{ VW}} \times \frac{2.27 \text{ marks}}{\text{\sout{dollar}}} = 13{,}620 \text{ marks per VW.}$$

Another example: Suppose a U.S. importer buys a television set from Japan. If the exchange rate is 1 yen = .0041 dollars and the price of the set equal to 97,600 yen, then

$$\frac{1 \text{ yen}}{.0041 \text{ dollars}} = 244 \text{ yen/dollar.}$$

Hence,

$$\frac{1 \text{ dollar}}{244 \text{ \sout{Yen}}} \times \frac{97{,}600 \text{ \sout{Yen}}}{1 \text{ TV}} = 400 \text{ dollars per TV.}$$

Referring again to the figure, assume a temporary disequilibrium occurs when the dollar price of the mark rises to 50 cents. There exists an excess supply of marks at this price by the amount $ab = q_b - q_a$. In a freely fluctuating system the market will respond to remove the excess supply by adjusting the price back to equilibrium. With marks in excess supply, people can succeed in converting marks into dollars by asking a lower dollar price for their marks. As the price of marks falls, people will increase the quantity demanded of marks until quantity demanded and supplied are equal at 44 cents to the mark.

Through trade, currencies accumulate in the foreign exchange departments of major banks that can buy or sell them through the foreign exchange houses in New York, London, and Tokyo. It takes about eight seconds to negotiate a trade price with a broker on the phone.

SHIFTS IN SUPPLY AND DEMAND

The supply and demand curves for currencies can *shift* due to changes in national income, tastes, expectations about currency values, interest rates, and inflation rates.

Several factors can cause the supply and demand curves for foreign exchange to shift. For example, when the U.S. undergoes a rise in its general price level the dollar price of U.S. goods is higher. At the *existing rate* of exchange more U.S. dollars are required to buy U.S. goods; also, more German marks are required to purchase U.S. goods. U.S. goods are now more expensive to Germans. At the same stroke the U.S. finds German goods relatively cheaper at the current exchange rate. This leads to an increase in demand for German marks (goods) in the U.S. at each exchange rate. The result is that the demand curve

Figure 32-4

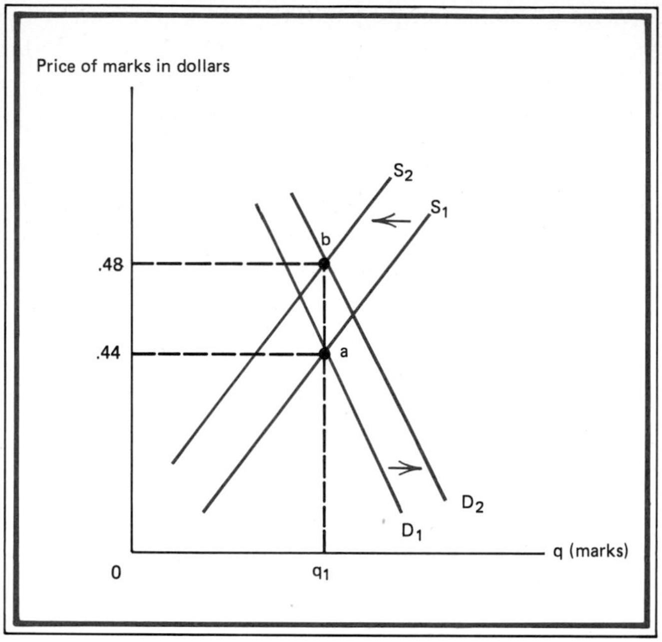

for marks shifts to the right in Figure 32-4. But there is also a decreased supply of marks provided at each exchange rate by Germans (less demand for U.S. goods, hence dollars), and the supply curve shifts to the left. The dollar price of the mark rises to 48 cents at the new equilibrium. The mark appreciates in value relative to the dollar since it now takes more dollars to buy marks as the market moves from *a* to *b*. Note that the price of the mark rises. The volume of marks traded can remain unchanged at q_1 at the new exchange rate as shown in the figure. Of course the shifts of the two curves do not necessarily balance each other and there could result a change in quantity traded as well. The curves shift in the opposite directions if the U.S. experiences a deflation.

The conclusion is that, with inflation, the dollar buys fewer goods at home, and it buys fewer goods abroad as well because foreign currencies become more expensive in the foreign exchange market. We say that the value of the dollar depreciates with inflation.

Other factors besides inflation cause shifts in the demand and supply for foreign exchange. For example, when national income rises there is typically a significant increase in imports. Greater production all around requires more materials, so more imported materials are required. As income and purchasing power are up, consumers will buy more foreign goods as well. Thus, imports of all kinds rise when an economy expands. And this leads to an increase in the demand for foreign exchange. The demand curve shifts rightward. If exchange rates are free to move with the market, the value of foreign currencies will rise to some extent. This rise tends to put the brake on imports, to slow the rise in imports but not to stop the rise.

Of course, many other factors may shift the demand and supply curves. Tastes for imports may change, political disruptions may reduce supply and alter currency values, and so forth.

Foreign Investments

One final factor that affects demand and supply is important to mention. People in different countries not only buy and sell goods and services, they also invest in each other's plant and equipment, farm lands, and businesses, among other things. If a U.S. investor wishes to invest in a German vineyard, there will be a demand for marks. And if a German investor wishes to purchase stock in an Alaskan cannery, there will be a supply of marks.

Because investments affect demand and supply it is also the case that relative interest rates in the trading countries will alter the amounts of marks demanded and supplied. This will, in turn, affect the exchange rates. For example, if interest rates rise is Germany, it will make investments relatively attractive. Thus the U.S. will increase its demand for marks to buy German securities. The demand curve will shift to the right and the value of marks will rise. And, of course, the process works in reverse as well.

The entire analysis of demand and supply for foreign exchange could have been done in terms of the demand for dollars instead of the demand for marks. Indeed, a graph with the price of dollars in terms of marks (instead of the price of marks in dollars) and dollars traded on the horizontal axis (instead of marks) would have given exactly the same information as the curves shown. This is because a demand curve for dollars is exactly the same as the supply curve of marks. The two curves tell the same story. A German demands dollars and offers to supply marks to get them. Similarly a supply curve for dollars tells the same story as a demand curve for marks. The only difference is in the way we label the two axes, that is, in the graph we choose to use.

BALANCE OF PAYMENTS

A country's *balance of payments* is a record of all its economic transactions with the rest of the world.

A country's balance of payments is a record of transactions between its residents and foreign residents over a specified period. The presentation of the accounts may take many forms. The *Survey of Current Business* published by the U.S. Department of Commerce regularly contains a table of estimates of international transactions with 81 different accounts and memoranda. This is far more detail than is required for our purposes. The Survey also publishes a summary version of its large table, and Table 32-1 is adapted from that summary.

If all of the accounting is recorded accurately, then the balance of payments should always balance. This is because double entry accounting methods require that the value of every transaction be recorded twice. This is the same accounting method that a business firm uses in preparing its balance sheet. For example, if a firm uses cash to buy a machine its asset account called *cash* is reduced and its asset account called *machinery* is increased. The total of all assets has not changed. If, on the other hand, the firm borrows cash from someone, the asset account *cash* is increased and the liability account *borrowings* is also increased by the same amount. Thus, both assets and liabilities have increased by the same amount and the balance between the two is maintained. Broadly speaking, every firm has two kinds of liabilities; first are those due to creditors, and second are those due to stockholders or owners. The latter are distinguished from other liabilities by calling them owners' equity. By carefully maintaining records using two entries for each transaction, the assets will always equal the liabilities plus equity. With assets on one side of a table and liabilities plus equity on the other side, the two sides should always have identical totals. That is, the double entry accounting method ensures that balance sheets always balance. So it is with the balance of payments.

For example, if a U.S. resident exports a good to a foreigner, the account called exports is increased, but if the foreigner has agreed to pay the exporter in six months' time, the account called financial claims on foreigners is also increased. In this way balance is always maintained in the accounts.

It is clear, of course, that the keeping of current records on *all* international transactions would be an impossible task. Thus, the authorities who keep the books must often rely on samples of information about transactions. And samples always involve some error of estimation. Furthermore, discrepancies can arise when the value reported on an export is not the same as the payment actually received. For these reasons a sizeable statistical discrepancy is usually

TABLE 32-1
U.S. International Transactions, 1979 (Billions of Dollars)

Sources of foreign exchange		Uses of foreign exchange		Sources − uses	
I. Current account					
A. Exports of merchandise (visibles)	182.1	Imports of merchandise	211.5	Balance of trade	−29.4
B. Military sales abroad	7.2	Military spending abroad	8.4		
C. Income from foreign investments	65.9	Foreign income from investments in U.S.	33.5		
D. Services sold by U.S.	31.1	Services purchased by U.S.	27.6		
E. Net unilateral transfers	—		5.6		
F. Exports of goods an services by U.S.	286.3	Imports of goods and services by U.S.	286.6	Balance on current account	−0.3
II. Capital account					
G. Change in foreign direct investment in U.S.	7.7	Change in U.S. direct investment abroad	24.8		
H. Change in unofficial private loans by foreigners	41.4	Change in unofficial private loans by U.S.	37.5		
I. Change in official loans by foreign governments and central banks	−15.2	Change in official U.S. reserves	1.1		
J. Change in loans and investments by foreigners (or net capital inflows)	33.9	Change in loans and investment by U.S. (or net capital outflows)	63.4	Unadjusted balance on capital account	−29.5
K. Allocation of Special Drawing Rights	1.1				1.1
L. Errors and omissions	28.7				28.7
	63.7		63.4	Balance on capital account	0.3
Total	350.0		350.0	Balance of payments	0

Source: U.S. Dept. of Commerce, *Survey of Current Business*, March 1980, Preliminary data.

found and is reported as a separate account in order to get the numbers to add up.

Transactions are commonly grouped into major categories. However, while overall the balance of payments must balance, there is no particular reason that various subcategories of the accounts must equal each other. Thus, the terms *surplus* and *deficit* that are frequently used in reporting on the state of our international transactions should be interpreted with respect to the relation between specific subcategories of the balance of payments and not of the balance of payments itself.

Let us turn now to Table 32-1 and examine the items shown there. There are three columns of numbers, one of which records those transactions that can be thought of as sources of foreign exchange, the other as uses of foreign exchange. The third column shows the difference between them.

A balance of payments account has two broad, inclusive categories—the *current* and *capital accounts* that together should balance to zero.

The balance of payments account is divided into two broad categories; the **current account** and the **capital account**

Line A records exports and imports of merchandise. Since line A refers exclusively to physical goods, these exports and imports are sometimes called *visibles*. There were $182.1 billion worth of such exports by the U.S. in 1979. When a foreigner buys U.S. corn there is an export of a good and this is a source of foreign exchange to the U.S. Imports of visibles were $211.5 in 1979. When a U.S. citizen purchases a Sony television set, this represents a drain of foreign exchange held by the U.S. In 1979 the U.S. imported $29.4 billion more in goods than it exported. Thus, in that year there was a deficit in the balance of trade. However, this is not necessarily a bad thing. On net, U.S. citizens exported more in U.S. dollars than the country earned in foreign currency, and therefore on net consumed more goods. Thus the trade deficit raised the U.S. standard of living. Would you prefer instead not to trade your paper assets for imported physical assets when it is much cheaper to produce paper money?

Line B is straightforward. The U.S. sells weapons and other military goods to foreign countries, hence these are sources of foreign reserves. The U.S. also has military bases overseas and spends abroad, using up foreign currencies.

Line C shows income from foreign investments. U.S. holders of foreign stocks earn dividends, and holders of foreign bonds and other financial assets earn interest. These income flows are sources of foreign currency. Trading in the assets themselves, the stocks or bonds, are recorded in the capital account, not in the current account. In analogous fashion, the income earned by foreign investments in the U.S. uses up U.S. reserve assets.

Line D refers to exports and imports of services. Service exports include such things as a foreigner traveling on a U.S. airline, shipping freight on a U.S. ship, renting a hotel room in the U.S. as a tourist, or buying insurance from a U.S. company. Foreigners therefore supply their currencies and demand dollars. In similar fashion, when a U.S. tourist rents a room in Paris, U.S. reserves of foreign francs are used up. U.S. citizens use francs obtained by supplying dollars.

Line E in the table shows grants, remittances, and other transfers. These unilateral transfers are payments that do not involve an exchange of goods or services. For example, the government may grant some aid to a less developed country. Or, the children of foreigners living in Chicago may send money home to their parents. These kinds of remittances can be substantial items for some countries. In 1979 these transfers amounted to $5.6 billion dollars. In order to make them, U.S. residents used this amount of foreign exchange.

When these unilateral transfer payments are pooled with exports and imports, another balance can be struck. It is called the balance on current account. In 1979 the U.S. had a deficit in this balance of $0.3 billion dollars. This balance is of some interest because it is the balance on all accounts *other than* the financial claims, or capital accounts. All items in the current account, except for line A, are sometimes called *invisibles* since many of them are not tangible goods, although some are—for example, sales of military equipment.

Look at the capital accounts recorded on lines G to L. Line G under the sources column indicates that foreigners increased direct investment in the U.S. by $7.7 billion. They may have purchased a factory or office building. In doing so they supplied pounds. Conversely, a U.S. purchase of property in Britain uses up foreign exchange held by U.S. residents.

Line H under sources indicates that foreigners increased loans to private U.S. citizens by $41.4 billion in the form of, for instance, the purchase of corporate securities and privately owned secondhand Treasury securities from private U.S. citizens and commercial banks. These securities are either short term that mature in less than a year, or long term, maturing in a year or more and actively resold for speculative purposes. They change hands rapidly in response to changing interest rates among countries. Alternatively, U.S. residents in 1979 increased lending to foreigners by buying foreign private securities that used up $37.5 billion in foreign reserves held by U.S. residents.

Line I is complicated and we shall simplify it. This entry covers official reserve asset settlements between governments conducted by their central banks and treasuries. The official reserve assets are gold, foreign currencies, Special Drawing Rights (SDRs), and a country's reserve position with the International Monetary Fund (IMF; see box).

The $1.1 billion entry under the uses column indicates that the U.S. used foreign exchange to add to its reserves. In 1979 it increased its reserve inventories by accepting allocations of SDRs from the IMF of $1.1 billion. Under the sources column the entry is −$15.2 billion. This tells us that foreigners reduced their holdings of U.S. Treasury securities, which, of course, implies a reduction in sources of foreign currency to the U.S. government. Row I therefore indicates that U.S. official reserve assets have risen by less ($1.1 billion) than foreign official claims on the U.S. government and central banks reserve assets have increased ($15.2 billion). Hence, the U.S. must have increased its payout of dollars to foreigners when foreigners reduced their holdings of Treasury securities. It is in this vague sense that a balance of payments deficit may be said to exist. However, because foreign governments and central banks chose to hold dollars, this did not require a net outflow of U.S. reserve assets. There are at least three reasons foreign treasuries and central banks may choose to hold dollars. (1) Many foreign countries consider the dollar an important reserve currency. (2) In the long run foreign governments may believe the dollar will become a stronger currency and they will be able to buy more other foreign currencies with it later. (3) A country might not cash in dollars for reserves because in today's system of flexible exchange rates cashing in dollars at the world's currency exchanges for one's own reserve currency would depreciate the value of the dollar and appreciate a country's own currency. This would make U.S. goods cheaper and imports to them more expensive. A strong exporting nation like Japan wants to prevent this. It would support the price of the dollar by not converting dollars into other reserves or even by deliberately entering the market and buying more dollars.[1]

Under the abandoned fixed exchange system, imbalances among countries were cleared by transferring official reserves such as gold. Under today's flexible exchange rates gold does not have to be exchanged, so that imbalances can be removed by the adjustment of currency exchange prices to a new market clearing equilibrium price for currencies. Therefore, a balance of payments deficit has lost its meaning.

Line J indicates that the unadjusted capital account is in deficit. Now it must be true if the current account is in deficit, the capital account should be in surplus and vice versa, because the total account must balance. To remedy this, allocations of special drawing rights and errors and omissions are entered in the capital account. Recorded in line K under sources we see that the U.S. received an additional allocation of Special Drawing Rights worth $1.1 billion, also recorded under the uses column. This item will be described in greater detail a few pages below. The overriding adjustment is found in the statistical discrepancy of $28.7 billion. This figure is an arbitrary entry that brings the sources and uses into balance. However, most all of the errors and omissions are considered to be in the capital account. When included it brings the capital account to $0.3 billion and cancels the deficit of $0.3 billion in the current account. If the account had been in surplus to this point, errors and omissions would have been negative by the residual amount.

THE BALANCE OF TRADE AND NATIONAL INCOME

The *foreign trade multiplier* shows the magnified effect of net exports on national income.

Net exports (exports minus imports) are part of a country's *aggregate demand*.

Earlier the balance of trade was defined as exports less imports. The balance of trade may be in surplus or deficit, or it may be in balance. In the macroeconomic model developed earlier it was pointed out that increases in consumption spending, increases in investment spending, and increases in government spending all serve to generate increases in national income. It is also the case that increases in exports and a surplus in the balance of trade will cause magnified increases in income via the **foreign trade multiplier**. If foreigners decide to buy more U.S. products, then the production and sale of goods to them has the same effect on their income as it has on income of domestic consumers, investors, and government. Net exports are part of **aggregate demand**. For example, in Figure 32-5 income is measured on the horizontal axis, and all forms of spending including spending by foreigners for exports are measured on the vertical axis. The aggregate demand curve is drawn for a given level of net exports, and a resulting equilibrium level of income. Let X stand for exports and M for imports. Then $(X - M)$ stands for net exports and is positive if X is greater than M and negative if smaller than M. If net exports of goods and

[1] By this act, however, Japan absorbs some of the U.S. federal budget deficit, resulting in an increase in Japan's money supply, since reserves are the basis for domestic money creation. Thus in its role as issuer of a reserve currency the U.S. has been a source of world-wide inflation.

Figure 32-5

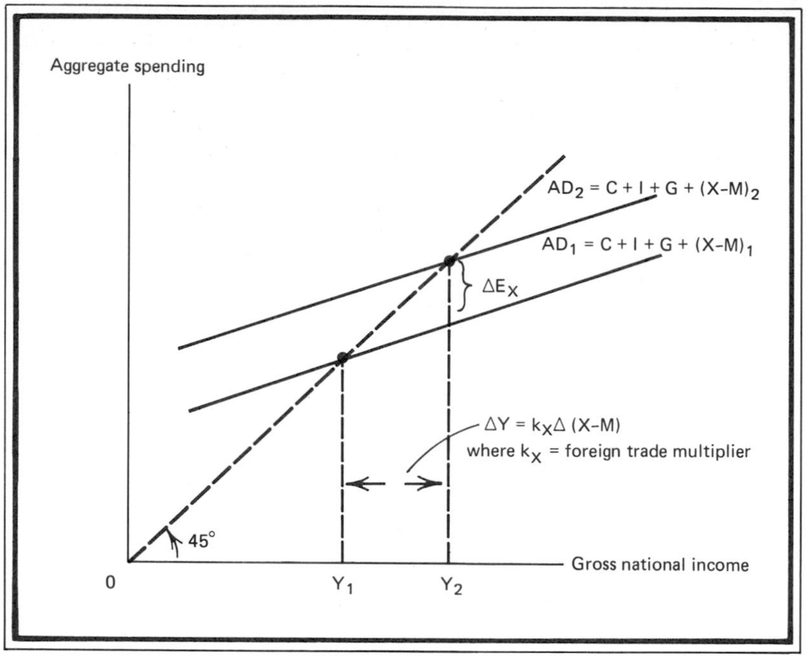

services should increase for some reason, say from $(X - M)_1$ to $(X - M)_2$ then income would increase, via the foreign trade multiplier, to Y_2. Therefore, if an economy is plagued with a recession one way to stimulate economic activity would be to subsidize export activities. Many countries of the world have strong and highly subsidized programs to promote exports. These include programs designed to attract tourists so that more tourist services are sold.

One problem with export subsidies is that if government taxes must be increased to pay for the subsidies then consumer spending by local people is reduced, and to this extent the effect on income is partially offset. Another problem is that if subsidies are used, the gains from trade that result from the existence of comparative advantage are partially undone. Therefore, although it is recognized that national income can be pushed up or down by changes in exports, economists usually recommend that monetary and fiscal policies be used to accomplish national income goals rather than adjustments in the levels of exports.

A country's export position is better improved by using *stabilization* policy to achieve national income goals than by tampering with export levels.

In many countries, however, exports and imports are a big part of national income. Dependency on exports can be very great for some less developed countries. Sometimes the world market for an important export item is unstable, and when the price of the item swings high and low a nation's income is subject to wide swings up and down. In these cases it may be desirable to promote **stability** somehow.

If exports expand when there is widespread unemployment, income can expand without inflation. But if they expand when employment is full, then the expansion will lead to inflation. When inflation occurs at home, the foreigners who are buying the exports now find them to be more expensive. Therefore, exports are likely to stop growing or even decline until their volume no longer acts as a stimulus to economic activity.

***Fluctuating* exchange rates help adjust foreign trade imbalances in the current account.**

Another way that a return to balance in the balance of trade can come about is found in the free **fluctuation of exchange rates**. As exports expand, the buyers of the goods will want more dollars. Bidding for the dollars will bid up their price in terms of foreign currency. Therefore, even if the dollar price of an item for export does not go up, since foreigners must pay more of their own money to get dollars, it costs them more to buy the good. Again, this will lead foreigners to cut back on their spending in the U.S. and will help remove the surplus in the balance of trade and push the balance of trade back into a balanced position.

The reverse is also true, of course. If exports should fall off for some reason, the decline in income and employment would tend to hold down prices and make U.S. goods cheaper so that foreigners would again be induced to buy them. Also the value of the dollar might fall as foreigners want fewer dollars to buy the reduced amount of goods. The reduced demand for dollars would lower the price of dollars and again U.S. goods would become cheaper.

INTEREST RATE LEVELS, INFLATION RATES, INCOME, AND THE RATE OF EXCHANGE

In the section on the balance of payments we also noted the balance on capital accounts. The capital accounts will be in deficit if the U.S. adds to its investments abroad more than foreigners add to their investments in the U.S. That is, it will be in deficit if capital outflows exceed capital inflows. Foreigners will be induced to invest more of their funds in U.S. investments when **interest rates** in the U.S. rise relative to interest rates in other countries. Higher interest rates in the U.S. will lead to an increase in the demand for dollars and an increase in the exchange value of the dollar. This will make U.S. goods more expensive to buy and will lead to a cutback in U.S. exports to foreigners. This cutback in the balance of trade will put the balance of trade into deficit. The deficit, in turn, will then act to offset the surplus in the balance on capital accounts, and this will tend to push the payments balance toward equilibrium. Thus, changes in interest rates will then affect the value of the dollar in the markets for foreign exchange.

Fluctuating *interest rates* regulate the capital flow across borders.

Inflation Rates

Differences in inflation rates in two countries will also affect the values of the currencies. If the U.S. has a high inflation rate relative to that of Germany, then U.S. goods become more expensive and Germans want fewer dollars. The reduced demand for dollars will then reduce the dollar's value on the foreign exchange markets until U.S. goods become attractive in price again because German marks can now buy more dollars.

Income and the Rate of Exchange

Changes in national income will also affect the value of the dollar on world exchange markets. This is because changes in income will cause changes in the level of imports. It has been estimated that an increase in income of $1 billion will result in an increase in imports of about 10 percent of this amount or about a $100 million. Thus, as U.S. income grows relative to income in England there will be an increase in the demand for English goods and for pounds to use to buy them. This will push the pound up in value and the dollar down in value. It will tend to make English goods more expensive to the U.S. and U.S. goods cheaper to the English, so that there will be a return to balance in the balance of trade.

The upshot is that those who wish to predict changes in rates of exchange must watch differentials in interest rates, inflation rates, and rates of growth in income. Sorting out the net effect of all three is, to say the least, extremely difficult.

Since monetary and fiscal policies have important effects on interest rates, inflation, and economic activity, these policies also affect exchange rates and the balance in the current and capital accounts. On some occasions what is good policy for the domestic economy may be bad for the economy's international position. If the value of the dollar is weak and if the domestic economy needs stimulus, a lowering of interest rates to stimulate spending will have adverse effects on the balance of payments. Lower interest rates will push the capital accounts into deficit as capital outflows occur. A higher income at home will push the balance of trade into deficit as increased income causes imports to expand. These pressures combine to weaken the value of the dollar even further. And if the expansion causes inflation to accelerate too, the situation is even worse.

In conclusion, it is clear that the more open an economy is, the more difficult it is to implement effective macroeconomic stabilization policies without disturbing the balance of trade, the balance of payments, and the international value of the dollar.

INTERNATIONAL PAYMENTS MECHANISMS – SOME HISTORY

At one time the world operated on the automatic or pure gold standard, then on the gold-pound-sterling standard, and then on the dollar-gold standard. Today the world operates under flexible exchange rates.

We described earlier how exchange rates move up and down in response to supply and demand forces. But it was not always that way. Nations have frequently instituted rules designed to keep exchange rates stable between countries. One set of rules is widely known as the gold standard.

The Automatic Gold Standard

Gold has long been used as a medium of exchange, and during the seventeenth and eighteenth centuries gold minted into coins was the universal international currency. There were several reasons for gold's popularity. It was scarce since its amount is controlled by nature. It was durable as well as malleable and possessed psychological appeal, leaving people with a secure feeling of owning something permanent and real. Most importantly, people were confident it would be generally accepted as payment. Under the automatic or gold specie arrangement, all legal money was gold coin and the value of gold in coins or in

Gold

Gold bullion used by central banks in their transactions is usually the standard 400-troy ounce (about 27.4 lbs) bar. For private holders there is a kilo bar small enough to fit into a coat pocket. A popular size in India is the 10-tola bar. There is also the South African 1-ounce krugerrand. Bar sizes go on down to as low as 5 grams. Gold does not tarnish or corrode and is used in electronics, dentistry, artistic crafts, and for medallions. The largest producer of gold is South Africa (50 percent) followed by Russia, Canada, and the U.S.

Gold bars usually have different shapes depending where they are cast. Bars in the U.S. are rectangular bricks 7″ by 3-5/8″ by 1-1/8″ to 1-3/4″ thick. Those gold bars cast in Denver, Colorado, have rounded corners. Those cast in New York and San Francisco have pointed corners. Most bars cast outside the U.S. are trapezoidal.

There are some gold bars that are less than 1-5/8″ thick, called Hershey bars. It seems at the end of a casting process there may not be enough melted gold remaining in the crucible to make a standard bar. The gold varies in purity between different pourings, so this remaining gold cannot be added to other pourings.

Each bar bears a stamped seal and an identification number. The seal indicates when and where the bar was cast, the identification number its purity. Gold bars must be at least 99.5 percent pure gold and weigh between 350 to 430 troy ounces to qualify as good delivery. The impurities (0.5 percent) usually consist of copper, silver, and other materials either too difficult or too expensive to remove. Colors are revealing too. Butter-yellow bars are nearly 100 percent pure from usually newly mined gold, whereas reddish bars contain copper. Other impurities result from remelting gold coins and jewelry.

On occasion a bar has a notched edge made by an assayer to sample the gold's purity. Assay chips are kept to be added when melted to another bar in process.

From 1933 to January 1, 1975 U.S. citizens could not hold gold legally or trade gold bullion, certificates, or coins within the U.S. without a Treasury license. Now they can. There has been no great rush by U.S. citizens to do so.

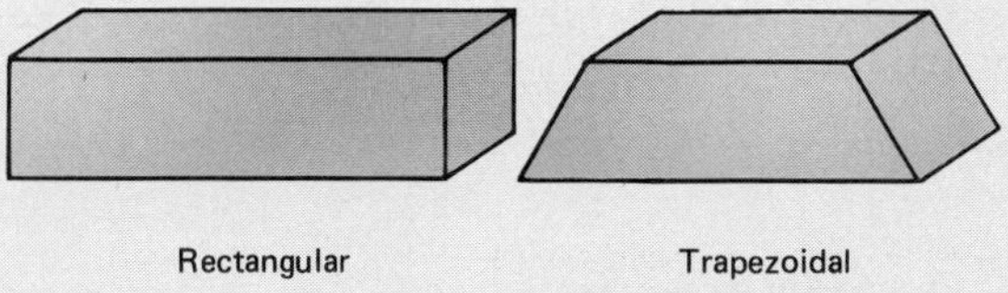

Source: *Delaware Valley Industry*, March 1975.

some other form was the same since any ornament could be easily melted down. Private individuals could hold and ship gold in and out of the country.

For most international transactions gold bullion was used—400 troy ounce bars of gold (about 27.4 pounds). In this way gold served as international money and there was enough gold to satisfy international liquidity to support world transactions. The domestic money supply in each country was tied to gold and was automatically adjusted by gold flows. For instance, if Spain acquired more gold wealth from its South American excursions, its ships brought more gold home and its money supply increased. The money supply directly affected the level of absolute prices. In Spain the gold inflow caused a rise in its absolute price level, making its exports more expensive and its imports cheaper. As a result of the changes in the price levels in Spain, the Spaniards would begin to import more French goods and export less goods to France, causing some of the gold to flow to France. Then the French would have some inflation, but Spain's inflation would stop or be reversed. Then, trade between the two countries would return to balance. Imbalances in trade would automatically be corrected by movements of gold from Spain to France, since those movements altered their domestic money supplies. Money supply changes caused relative prices between the two countries to change and restore the balance of trade.

By the 1880s countries were defining their paper currency units in terms of gold, and each of them agreed to convert its paper currency, held by other nations, into gold upon request. Thus, the U.S. defined the dollar as containing 23.22 fine grains of gold, which is to say, one ounce of gold traded for $20.67. This was referred to as the par value of the dollar. For Britain, the par value of the pound equaled 113.0016 grains of pure gold. This made the par value of the dollar in pounds obtainable by dividing 113.0016/23.22 = 4.8665 pounds to the dollar.

Under these definitions of the dollar and the pound in terms of gold, assume that Britain exports more to the U.S. than it imports. In the process Britain acquires a surplus of dollars while the U.S. runs a deficit in that it owes Britain either pounds or gold, since Britain could request either in exchange for the dollars it holds.

By the *implicit* international rules, when Britain turns in its dollars for U.S. gold, the U.S. should reduce its supply of domestic money to maintain its ratio of money to gold. When the money supply is reduced, prices should decline in the U.S. With lower prices at home, people in the U.S. would stop importing from Britain and the gold outflow would come to a stop. This mechanism would ensure that the fixed rate of exchange between the dollar and the pound is sustained.

Figure 32-6 is a graphical example of how fixed exchange rates work. If the U.S. experiences an inflation there is an increase in demand for pounds by the U.S., the demand curve shifts from D_1 to D_2, moving the equilibrium from *a* to *b*. The exchange rate is $2.4 to 1 pound. If rates were flexible the supply

Figure 32-6

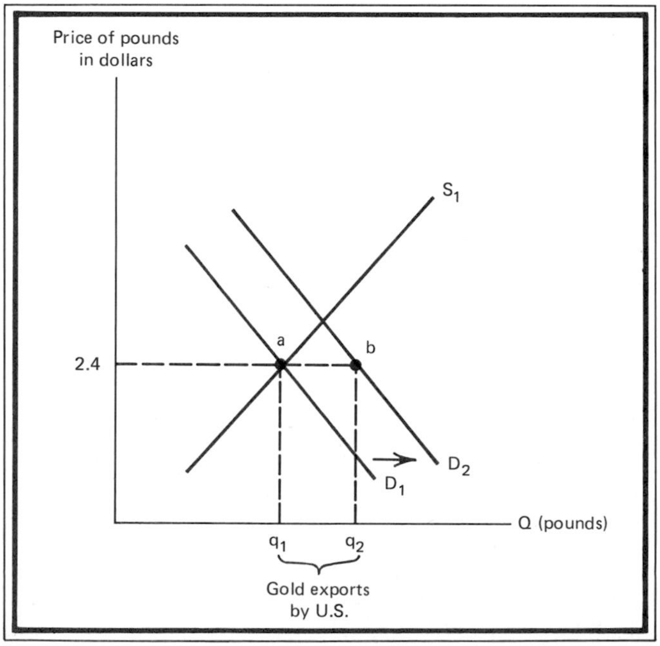

curve of pounds S_1 would shift left, because pounds now buy fewer U.S. goods, establishing a new higher price of the pound in dollar terms. However, because exchange rates are fixed under the gold exchange standard, the supply curve S_1 does not shift left. Instead the exchange rate remains at $2.4 to the pound. At the original exchange rate the U.S. wants q_2 pounds. Since it only has q_1 it must pay out gold. The gold outflow should cause the money supply to fall in the U.S. This will stop the inflation and reverse the shift in the demand curve. So the exchange rate remains stable.

The Decline of the Gold Standard

When World War I (1914–1918) broke out, the gold standard disintegrated. Hostile submarines made shipping gold highly risky. The ships were also needed for wartime operations. By 1922 the implicit understanding to convert domestic currencies into gold on request was largely abandoned. With international gold liquidity seriously impaired, a patchwork of controls emerged to regulate international transactions. The patchwork nature of these controls hampered world trade.

The ensuing chaos aroused the desire for some order. Around 1926 the gold exchange standard was reinstated, with one important difference since the world's gold supply was becoming increasingly inadequate to handle the volume of international transactions. Namely, the dollar and the pound sterling were introduced as reserve currencies. All trading countries could use these as well as gold to settle their international debts with each other. But the waters of international trade did not stay calm for long. The gold standard soon became a source of instability.

When the Depression of the 1930s descended upon the industrialized world, countries became more and more reluctant to play by the rules. Deficit countries did not contract their money supplies when they experienced loss of gold reserves. Prices and wages were sticky downward; when aggregate demand declined, it was employment that bore the brunt of the adjustment if the money supply decreased. As confidence weakened, cental banks rushed to convert their dollar and pound sterling reserves into gold, causing worsening downswings in those countries losing gold. Lack of gold liquidity again became a problem. The various governments broke the fixed exchange rate rules and offset the deflationary effect of gold outflows by expanding their money supplies through central bank actions.

Dollar-Gold Standard

With the advent of World War II (1939–1945) world trade stopped for the most part. Nonetheless, the desire for some form of stable exchange rates lingered on like memories of happy, youthful days. In Bretton Woods, New Hampshire, in 1944 representatives of major countries of the world met to restore the international monetary system to a workable reality. The intent was to modify the gold exchange standard while avoiding the chaos that followed from the devaluation wars of the 1930s. One innovation was the adaptation of the moving or adjustable peg principle. This concept circumvented the problems of strictly fixed exchange rates yet prevented frequent lapses into floating exchange rates. The moving peg was supposed to allow for orderly variations in exchange rates, not sudden, unexpected jumps in currency values in the short run. When surpluses or deficits persisted, the par values could be adjusted either through depreciations or appreciations of domestic currencies. This somewhat removed the tyrannical role of gold on domestic money supplies.

There was now room for some slack between gold and domestic currencies. The International Monetary Fund (IMF) was created to provide temporary reserves to deficit nations so as to support the existing exchange rates among them, and if at all possible avoid adjustments in them, at least in the shorter period. Temporary deficits could be easily carried and tolerated by IMF intervention. Each country was allowed to revalue its currency one time by as much as 10 percent without IMF permission and beyond 10 percent if a "fundamental disequilibrium" existed. But there was no precise definition of this concept or any procedure for changing exchange rates beyond 10 percent. Because the U.S. economy emerged from the war as the strongest by far, the U.S. dollar was eagerly sought and held by other countries as a reserve currency, satisfying the need for international liquidity since the gold supply was inadequate to fulfill this function completely.

So strong was the demand for U.S. dollars after the war, there was said to be a dollar shortage. The pound sterling continued to play a reduced role as a medium of exchange, but most countries pegged their currency to the dollar. The dollar in turn was pegged to gold at $35 an ounce. The dollar operated as the *de facto* world currency, a reserve currency behaving as the store of value and unit of account providing the solution to the ever present world liquidity problem. The role of the dollar was an unexpected aftermath of the Bretton Woods agreement.

The agreement worked reasonably well until about 1958, when the U.S. began to experience deficits. After several years of deficits, the dollar shortage threatened to become a dollar glut. Foreign countries were then holding dollars beyond what they considered to be comfortable and necessary amounts. Confidence was the major element involved. Was the dollar as good as gold after all? The mighty dollar might have to be devalued. If that were to happen those countries holding large dollar reserves would realize a substantial capital loss, since those dollars would buy less gold and their exports would be more expensive relative to U.S. currency. Countries desisted from using the movable peg mechanism to adjust the trade imbalances to compensate for the overvalued dollar.

Because they were uncertain about effects on trade and patriotic pride, other countries refused to appreciate their currencies against the dollar, thus preventing timely and orderly adjustments. The U.S. felt it could not devalue the dollar because it would cause world-wide disturbance in economies, perhaps creating a chain of devaluations as countries would attempt to maintain their relative currency positions.

There are several conflicting problems simultaneously confronting a reserve currency nation like the U.S.—a veritable monetary Catch 22. Since there does not exist enough gold to satisfy liquidity, the dollar is used to provide it. But it only serves this purpose if the U.S. runs deficits because this is how others acquire dollars. If the U.S. deficits become too large, countries begin to lose confidence in the weakening dollar and pressure for its devaluation builds. The U.S. could have stopped its loss of gold by monetary contraction, hoping thereby to lower domestic prices relative to foreign prices. This would raise its exports while lowering its imports and the U.S. would reacquire foreign-held dollars and gold. But employment would fall before prices would, and a domestic recession would be bad for politicians.

The surplus countries could have acted, too. They could have either chosen to let their domestic price levels rise or they could have appreciated their own currency against the dollar. But foreign exporters pressured their governments not to appreciate their currencies because their competitive positions and profit margins would erode. The surplus countries failed to act.

Several approaches were taken to relieve the balance of payments problem. The U.S. entered into swap agreements with eleven major countries. The Federal Reserve and central banks of these countries traded their currencies with each other at some specified spot rate. This allowed the U.S. temporarily to increase its holdings of foreign currencies without having to redeem dollars for gold.

Nonetheless, pressure on the dollar continued through the 1960s, leading to a serious run on U.S. gold in 1968. Other countries would not appreciate their currencies. The U.S. could not unilaterally depreciate without disrupting world economies and trade. On August 15, 1971 President Nixon stopped the Treasury from converting foreign held dollars into gold on demand. Gold no longer backed the dollar.

The world temporarily embarked on a system of managed float, also called *dirty float,* where central banks of major countries intervened in the market to buy and sell currencies so as to keep exchange rates within a gliding band varying from one to two percent per year. This was supposed to permit gradual changes to take place over much longer periods. Still, things were unstable. Germany was forced to appreciate the mark beyond the band limit while the U.S. deficit stubbornly persisted. The dollar was still overvalued. In February 1973 the U.S. again devalued the dollar, this time to $42.22 for an ounce of gold. This seemed to work for a while. Despite all, the U.S. deficits continued. Shortly thereafter the OPEC oil embargo and the ensuing 500 percent rise in crude oil prices caused a large volume of dollars to accumulate among the OPEC members, causing the dollar to continue to weaken throughout the 1970s.

Jamaica Accord

In January 1976 some 128 nations met to attempt once again a reform of the international monetary system and its three chronic problems of (1) liquidity, (2) confidence, and (3) orderly currency adjustment. The hope was to reduce the importance of gold. The IMF was instructed to dispose of one third of its gold holdings. It did this by refunding one sixth to member countries, most of them the less developed countries, on the basis of their quotas; and by selling off another one sixth with the profits also going to the poorer countries. Nor would the IMF any longer accept gold in transactions, demanding instead domestic currencies.

The 10 largest industrial countries agreed that they would not increase their gold stocks before January 1978. Nor would they take action to fix the

IMF and the World Bank

An outcome of the Bretton Woods meeting of 1944 was the creation of the International Monetary Fund (IMF) and the World Bank. The purpose of the IMF was to promote exchange rate stability in its status as a permanent world institution to help finance nations' temporary balance of payments deficits in a system of fixed exchange rates in order to lessen the degree of disequilibrium. It also worked toward the progressive elimination of trade restrictions and to support the observance of accepted rules of international financial conduct while pursuing the orderly growth of world trade. A further intent was to engineer confidence in member countries by making IMF resources available to them.

In 1945 the IMF started with 30 members; it now has over 125 members. In fact, most countries outside the Communist bloc belong to it. Initially the IMF was financed by participants paying membership fees or quotas composed of 3/4 of their own currency and 1/4 in gold. The size of these quotas varied in proportion to a country's trade volume. Since the advent of floating exchange rates in the early 1970s, there is less emphasis on gold and more use of foreign currencies and Special Drawing Rights (SDRs). Members can vote to change another country's quota as the situation requires.

Countries that are running a deficit in a particular currency can buy the currency they need by offering more of its own currency (now SDRs too) beyond its quota. Such borrowings of foreign currencies are called *tranches.* A country can borrow 4 tranches with no single tranche exceeding 25 percent of its initial subscription. Thus, if a country pays in 100 dollars, it can borrow 100 dollars. Thereafter it can borrow 4 more times in quantities up to 25 dollars. A country can therefore borrow as much as 200 percent of its subscription quota.

Loans must be repaid within 3 to 5 years. So-called temporary loans are due to be repaid from 6 to 12 months. When borrowing, a country must submit a letter of intent and prescribe the policies it will undertake to correct its economic problems that are causing its serious deficits. The IMF continues to push for a SDR standard, hoping eventually to have all nations accept it alone as international currency.

The World Bank is a world intergovernmental organization with all stocks owned by member nations. It sells bonds and bank notes to private investors to gather its financial resources. After World War II it helped finance the reconstruction and development of countries whose economies were destroyed by the war. Today it primarily assists the less developed countries. Only members of the IMF can be World Bank members.

price of gold. This meant that gold was not to be used as a unit of account. Managed float was kept as the mechanism of exchange adjustments by central banks. About 59 countries chose to fix their currencies against the dollar while some 37 fixed their exchange rates against other currencies or against a bloc of currencies made up of several currencies like those of the Common Market countries. Some 30 countries including the U.S. did not fix their currencies but agreed to intervene if their exchange rates varied too much. Although they arrived at no format or formula for settling disputes about currency movements, there was an understanding that things should proceed in an orderly fashion for the good of all. There would be cooperation with the IMF.

Although currency alignments to gold were officially ended and exchange rate flexibility was accepted, it was expected that countries would operate their floating currencies in a responsible manner, keeping within defined ranges. Thus, the diversity of the international monetary system of the late 1970s was tailored to each country's own political and economic structure. Gold played a less significant role, with the dollar still serving its liquidity function. Domestic monetary policy has been cut free of the dictates of gold and the fixed exchange rates associated with it. The world is now functioning under floating or flexible exchange rates. It remains to be seen how well this will continue to work and whether the underlying desire for stability in exchange rates will create a movement once again to reinstate some type of gold exchange standard.

SPECIAL DRAWING RIGHTS

In a move to settle the international reserve problem and the plague of an unstable reserve currency (the dollar) and the shortage of another (gold), the IMF in a 1967 meeting proposed a new world reserve currency called SDRs—

Eurodollars

The Eurodollar (E$) market is a well organized, internationally established money market for U.S. dollars held in time deposits by foreign banks, foreign branches of U.S. banks, or by other types of financial institutions. A Eurodollar is a deposit denominated in U.S. dollars at any bank outside of the U.S. The depositor may be a foreigner, e.g., a London shopkeeper, who deposits dollars into an interest bearing account that is denominated in dollars in his London bank. Bank deposits denominated in currencies other than that of the bank's country are Eurocurrencies. Dollars make up about 85 percent of Eurocurrencies. Eurodollars while used earlier only became significant around 1958. They were started by the Russians, who wanted dollars but were afraid to put them in U.S. banks. A Eurodollar *operation,* however, only happens when Eurodollars are lent by the foreign banks holding them. Most E$ deposits are made when commercial banks shift their dollar holdings across borders in response to small changes in interest rate differentials. The E$ market has its own internal interest rate structure independent of national counterparts. Yet banks dealing in E$ often charge lower rates on loans too. It is a wholesale money market operating on a narrow profit margin made viable by the volume of the transactions. Deposits vary from $1 to $50 million. When banks do make loans to nonbank private borrowers, multiple expansion of E$ can occur. Private owners of E$ deposits are international corporations (multinationals) and OPEC oil sheiks. As with domestic commercial banks deposits of E$ are not physical paper money but bank liabilities.

Increasingly E$ have emerged as an important source of international reserve currency, replacing gold while impeding the desired development of Special Drawing Rights usage. Eurodollar transactions have increased world currency reserves. They have been progressively substituted for the U.S. balance of payments deficit as a source of world currency liquidity.* Eurodollars are *not* an *official* U.S. liability to foreign governments. They therefore muddy the evidence concerning the U.S. balance of payments deficit.

U.S. banking authorities do not allow U.S. banks in the U.S. to accept deposits denominated in other currencies. Thus, the U.S. itself has no Eurocurrency market as such. However, subject to some limits, U.S. banks may borrow and lend *dollars* in the Eurodollar market, and many have established branches in foreign countries where they are allowed to enter the market along with other foreign banks.

*For more details see Jane S. Little, *New England Economic Review,* May/June 1977, Federal Reserve Bank of Boston, pp. 11–17.

Special Drawing Rights—also referred to as paper gold. They represented an effort to create a new reserve asset to replace gold, to ensure adequate international liquidity, and to help deficit countries ride out payments imbalances without serious shocks to their import-export transactions. SDRs are not convertible to gold but they are backed by a full gold guarantee in order to be acceptable on a par with gold reserves. They are intended to be a source of owned, not borrowed, reserves. They were activated in September of 1969.

The SDRs' value was originally tied to the par value of the dollar ($35 to 1 ounce of gold). But after July 1, 1974, because currencies floated in value, a different valuation was used. A standard basket of 16 currencies was used to calculate the SDRs' value. After January 1, 1981 the number of currencies was reduced to five. In percents they are U.S. dollar, 42; deutschemark, 19; pound sterling, 13; French franc, 13; Japanese yen, 13. By proper weighting the purchasing power of SDRs remains independent of exchange rate movements. The SDRs can be added to a country's reserves for exchange purposes; central banks can use them to settle debts directly and can have the IMF submit them to another country in exchange for that country's currency. Thus, a country wanting to use SDRs must convert them to another country's currency.[2] Not all major countries have fully utilized SDRs. Some, like France, lack complete confidence in SDRs and cling to gold reserves. If allowed to work, the IMF could truly become a world bank and SDRs could become the single reserve currency for the world. Unlike the dollar, SDRs do not depend for their availability on a major currency country running a deficit in its official reserve account, and they are virtually costless to create.

FIXED VS. FLEXIBLE EXCHANGE RATES

Let us summarize the advantages and disadvantages of fixed versus freely fluctuating foreign exchange rates.

Fixed Rates The advantage of fixed exchange rates is found in the security and certainty they provide to international traders. Buyers and sellers can compare prices immediately and arrange by contract for goods to be delivered months ahead, secure that prices and costs will not vary. Trade flourishes best where uncertainty is least. If used, properly fixed rates can provide a self-correcting mechanism to keep trade in balance because they force discipline on domestic monetary policy.

A chronic disadvantage of fixed rates has been that governments chafe under the discipline that fixed rates impose on domestic stabilization policy, particularly when the domestic economy is undergoing rising unemployment. Conversely, when a country is experiencing inflation concurrent with long-term deficits indicative of a fundamental disequilibrium, its currency becomes inflated and pressure builds for the exchange value of its currency to fall, that

[2] For more details see George Halm, *A Guide to International Money Reform* (Lexington, Mass.: D. C. Heath and Co., 1975), pp. 41–45.

is, to depreciate and/or to be devalued if it is a reserve currency. Under a system of fixed exchange rates, particularly for a reserve currency, exchange rates are difficult to change smoothly. When rates do change, they jump. Instead of gentle ripples, there is a splash that disrupts the whole international environment. Because national pride is involved, countries hold off devaluation as long as possible; but once done the accumulated pressure of the ever enlarging deficits bursts loose. Hence the transition is neither smooth, gradual, nor easily absorbed without serious repercussions to national economies and international contracts. Fixed rates, therefore, work better in dealing with short-term imbalances, not long-standing ones. The price paid for certainty in the international markets is the uncertainty and constraint it imposes on internal monetary policy and employment. These of course can be and often are subject to the sometimes erratic, deliberate decisions of national governments themselves.

Flexible exchange rates The appeal and advantage of freely fluctuating rates is their apparent simplicity. The cumbersome apparatus of fixed exchange rates is removed, worries about liquidity, i.e., runs on gold, disappear. The national ego, so worrisome during reluctant yet necessary devaluation of currencies, is automatically soothed, or at least not threatened. The free operation of supply and demand in the market makes these determinations without official interference or haggling. The necessity to carry large volumes of reserve gold and key currencies is removed. Deficits are temporary, with the adjustments to equilibrium orderly and gradual. Flexible exchange rates need not infringe on the autonomy of domestic monetary and fiscal policy. Given the downward inflexibility of domestic prices and wages, floating or freely fluctuating rates may be the only practical structure for a country to clear away a chronic deficit and realign its price and cost structure.

The disadvantages of fluctuating rates are several. Certainty and stability are of primary importance to make world trade viable, and the market variations in currency values make it difficult to know what an import costs or an export will bring. When a currency is weakened and depreciation looms as a real possibility, deliberate excess speculation may be engendered. Speculators may sell that currency, increasing its supply and forcing its price lower than basic factors could justify. Once it falls, they will buy back the depreciated currency with the now stronger currency they acquired in the process, and possibly realize a substantial capital gain.[3]

If a government does not want to be blamed for the falling standard of living when imports become more expensive as its currency depreciates, it may pursue further monetary expansion. Wages and incomes rise to accommodate the higher import prices. The result is a worsening inflation and further currency depreciation. Its own currency could eventually become worthless and it would be left with no foreign held currencies to carry on further trade. Its economy could collapse and social instability erupt as austere economic discipline—or none at all—was imposed. Freely fluctuating exchange rates do

[3] For the most part speculators serve to moderate exchange rate fluctuations rather than accentuate them. When speculators anticipate that a currency will appreciate they buy that currency. They will move out of overappreciated currencies and into the overly depreciated currencies whenever they can take advantage of the expected capital gains. By doing so they bring relative values into line. However, it is also possible for speculation to force currencies out of line. Central banks often counter excessive fluctuations in the value of a currency that speculators might cause by entering the market and either buying or selling large amounts of the currency as the situation requires.

not engender the domestic monetary discipline that a system of fixed rates tends to do.

Flexible exchange rates **free the domestic money supply but create uncertainties for traders; however, these uncertainties can largely be removed by forward contracts.**

As for **flexible exchange rate** instability obstructing trade, the use of forward exchange contracts can remove part of the uncertainty by providing for a hedge against rate changes. For instance, suppose an importer contracts for a Volkswagen in January that is to be delivered in April when he must pay the price of 12,000 marks. Assuming the exchange is 1 mark to 40 cents, the importer would have to pay out $4,800. But when April arrives suppose the exchange rate is 1 mark to 50 cents. Under these circumstances the importer would have to pay $6,000 for the car. To avoid this risk, for a fee the importer buys a futures contract from an exchange dealer or broker who agrees to sell the importer 12,000 marks in April, but at a price agreed upon in January. An exporter can also buy forward. It is the dealer, however, who assumes the risk. Actually, if the dealer also wants to avoid speculative risks and is only interested in earning commissions, he too can make a deal to buy 12,000 marks forward. Thus, by buying and selling forward he avoids any large capital gain or loss. Or he could buy at the spot price in January, hold the marks, and deliver them in April. The result is that importers and exporters can, to a considerable extent, avoid having to take risks by using the futures market for foreign exchange.

CHAPTER SUMMARY

World trade continues to grow, and intereconomic penetration by nations grows deeper. Countries trade for the same reason that individuals do—because both gain. The underlying rationale behind the mutual benefit from trade lies in the concept of comparative advantage, defined as the maximization of gains that results when nations specialize in producing and trading only those goods which they can produce at the lowest opportunity cost. Comparative advantage exists even for a country that has no absolute advantage in the production of any good. It is still more efficient in the production of some goods than other goods. If the opportunity costs are the same for two nations producing two identical goods, there is no gain from either one specializing in producing just one of the commodities and then trading. For nations to benefit from trade they must exchange at a ratio in between the two differing domestic exchange ratios. For if country A traded at B's domestic exchange ratio then A would receive all the benefits. And, conversely, if B traded at A's domestic exchange ratio, then B would receive all the gains.

Barriers to restrict the amount of trade consist of tariffs and import quotas. Tariffs are usually in the form of a percentage of the total price of the item. Import quotas are limits set on the number of goods that can be imported. Among the arguments justifying trade restrictions are cheap foreign wages, infant industries, and national defense. The view of protectionists is that foreign wages are lower than U.S. wages, so foreign goods can be produced more cheaply. However, this argument overlooks the other side of the coin, namely productivity. The U.S. exports many goods produced by workers earning higher wages than foreign workers, yet the U.S. produces these exported goods more cheaply because worker productivity is high and consequently per unit costs of production are lower than foreign per unit costs. Wages are lower in U.S. industries where productivity is lower than in other U.S. industries.

The infant industry argument insists that beginning industries be protected when they are small and noncompetitive. Trade protection gives them time to grow larger, hence to become more competitive, at which time trade barriers can be removed.

The national defense argument centers on maintaining productive flexibility, keeping some operations going despite their being economically inefficient and noncompetitive, as is shipbuilding in the U.S.

A country may possess a comparative advantage due to relatively abundant labor, capital, land, or natural resources.

Since nations use different currencies, in order to trade they must establish the relative value of one currency to another. These are called foreign exchange rates. In the early 1970s the world adopted flexible exchange rates, with relative currency prices determined by the world supply and demand for the various currencies as recorded daily in the major exchange centers of the world located in London, New York, and other cities. The actual process of negotiating payments with bank drafts between importers and exporters in their respective currencies is handled by banks in one country that have correspondent banks in other countries where they keep accounts denominated in the foreign countries' currency.

The supply and demand curves for foreign currency are conceptually no different from other kinds of supply and demand curves, where there is movement along them as the price of a currency in terms of another currency changes. These curves can also shift because of changes in national income, tastes, expectations about currency values, interest rates, and inflation rates.

A country's balance of payments is a record of all its economic transactions with the rest of the world. The balance of payments account must always balance because of the method of double entry booking. Each transaction is recorded as both an asset and a liability. Of course, subcategories of the account may not balance. The account has two broad and inclusive categories—the current and capital accounts that should balance to zero. When they do not a statistical discrepancy—mostly errors and omissions in the capital account—is either added or subtracted to balance the overall account.

Net exports equal to exports minus imports is the fourth element in aggregate demand. Associated with it is the foreign trade multiplier that causes a magnified effect on national income.

Many countries subsidize their export industries to strengthen domestic employment, but these subsidies are supported with taxes that reduce the expansionary impact on national income the subsidies generate. Export subsidization may also undo some of the gains from trade derived from comparative advantage. Economists recommend that instead of tampering with export levels, stabilization policy be used to achieve national income goals.

Under a flexible exchange rate system, fluctuating currency values will adjust foreign trade imbalances in the current account. A country that imports more than it exports will likely cause the value of its currency to fall. Its currency now buys less abroad and its goods become cheaper to foreigners. This acts to redress the trade imbalance.

In the capital account, fluctuating interest rates regulate the capital flows across borders. In particular, short-term securities purchases and sales respond quickly to changes in interest rate differentials. High interest rates attract foreign currencies and low rates chase currencies away.

Because so many variables affect the value of a country's currency, they complicate stabilization policy. Policies that strengthen the currency may simultaneously adversely affect domestic employment. The more open an economy is to foreign trade the more difficult is stabilization policy.

During the nineteenth and part of the twentieth century, trade imbalances between nations were corrected by gold payments. Gold, being scarce and desirable, served as the basis for a world currency, that is, as a universal medium of exchange.

However, as world trade expanded, there was too little gold to completely satisfy this function. Hence other paper currencies emerged as the reserve currency, the dollar being the major one. After World War II the dollar was pegged to gold, and other currencies were pegged to the dollar, hence indirectly to gold. Trade deficits were then payable in either dollars or gold under a fixed exchange rate system. This worked so long as dollars were as "good as gold." However, as war-torn economies redeveloped and these countries acquired large dollar holdings, and as the U.S. economy inflated, lack of confidence that the dollar would keep its value grew, and dollar surplus countries began to want either gold or stronger currencies in exchange for the excess dollars. The U.S., lacking adequate gold reserves and experiencing rising domestic inflation, was forced to devalue the dollar. This still did not correct the imbalance. Ultimately the U.S. ceased paying in gold, thus violating the fixed exchange rate conditions and forcing the world to adopt flexible exchange rates.

SDRs—Special Drawing Rights—were introduced in 1967 in the hope that they would serve as the universal reserve currency and solve the world liquidity problem, with the International Monetary Fund functioning as the world's banker. However, SDRs have not been completely accepted.

The advantage of a fixed exchange rate is the certainty about currency values it provides to importers and exporters. However, it ties down a country's monetary policy because the money supply might have to be trimmed in order to maintain the fixed exchange rate. This can lead to domestic recessions. Under flexible exchange rates the domestic money supply is freed of the fixed exchange rate discipline. Downward adjustments in the value of the currency then act as the buffer against excess money expansion. However, flexible rates create uncertainties for traders. The uncertainty can be removed largely by the traders buying forward contracts. Thus an importer can buy a futures contract from a broker who agrees to sell the importer foreign exchange, say, four months from now, but at a price agreed upon today, even if the price of the foreign currency rises over the next four months.

QUESTIONS

1. Assume Argentina and Chile are two-good economies. If Argentina devoted all its resources per period raising beef it could produce 48 units per period per man hour. If it only grew lemons it could grow 24 units. Chile could grow either all of 20 units of lemon or all of 20 units of beef per period per man hour.
   a. Which country produces lemons the cheaper and which one beef? Draw the production possibility curve for each country, assuming constant costs.
   b. What are the domestic exchange ratios? Is there a basis for trade?
   c. Suppose there is no trade and Argentina produces 36 units of beef and 6 units of lemon while Chile is producing 6 units of beef and 14 units of lemon. Show these combinations on a graph. Pick a foreign exchange ratio halfway between the two domestic ratios. What did you pick?
   d. Let each country specialize, with Argentina exporting 8 beef units to Chile. How many beef and lemon units does each end up consuming? Show this on the graphs.
   e. Suppose Argentina traded at Chile's domestic exchange rate. Who benefits and who gains? Show your calculations.

2. Many ships belonging to the U.S. and Canada fly under "foreign flags of convenience" employing only foreign seamen, who are paid lower wages than U.S. and Canadian merchant seamen. A maritime union spokesman said, "Those ships hurt our (Canadian) economy and deprive Canadians of jobs. We say it's time our government found the guts to tell those fat corporate welfare bums that there will be no more free lunches at the expense of Canadian voters and taxpayers." Who is better off and worse off here? Is the Canadian economy hurt by ships flying under foreign flags? Why? Will Canadian seamen who are laid off necessarily be permanently unemployed? Explain.
3. Interpret this statement of Milton Friedman: "U.S. workers who produce goods sold to Japan earning yen used to buy Japanese steel, are producing steel for the U.S. just as much as the men who tend the steel furnaces in Gary, Indiana."
4. Does the U.S. gain from exports or from imports? Before answering, what on net has been exported and imported when the U.S. "balance of trade is in deficit"?
5. What are the predictable results of significantly protective tariffs? If the U.S. does not import from Japan, how can the U.S. export to Japan? What must Japan have to buy U.S. products? How does Japan get it?
6. If 2.2 U.S. dollars exchange for 1 English pound and 1.7 German marks exchange for one U.S. dollar, for how many pounds does one German mark exchange? If a Rolls-Royce sells for $60,000, how many English pounds will the U.S. purchaser need in order to buy the car?
7. When the prime interest rate rose above 21 percent in December 1980, what would you predict happened on the average to the exchange rate of the dollar relative to other currencies? Why? Also, what effect would U.S. excess money supply growth likely have on the value of the dollar relative to other currencies? Explain. How could the reverse effect come about?
8. Assuming flexible exchange rates, which one of the following shifts the demand curve for a foreign currency by the U.S.? In which direction is the shift?
   a. The Federal Reserve sharply cuts the money supply.
   b. Japan buys a seafood processing plant in Seattle.
   c. West Germany enters the market to support the price of the dollar.
   d. The U.S. experiences an inflation relative to the rest of the world.
   e. Interest rates rise in Europe relative to the U.S.
9. Are the following uses or sources of foreign currencies to the U.S.?
   a. A U.S. citizen buys a Datsun.
   b. A foreign government reduces its holding of U.S. securities.
   c. The IMF allocates SDRs to the U.S. government.
   d. The U.S. Treasury sells off some gold.
   e. A U.S. resident buys insurance from Lloyd's of London.
   f. Renault purchases 46 percent of American Motor Company's stock.
10. Which of the following are visibles and which invisibles in the balance of payments account?
    a. Royalties received from abroad by a U.S. playwright.
    b. Purchases of a U.S. bond by a foreign resident.
    c. A stock sold to a foreign resident.
    d. A government pension paid abroad.
    e. A U.S. factory abroad.
    f. Earnings from a U.S. factory abroad.
    g. Interest paid to a U.S. holder of a foreign security.
    h. A U.S. fighter plane sold to Turkey.
11. In 1976 an advisory committee suggested that since the world is on a system of flexible exchange rates the words surplus and deficit should be avoided as much as possible since they imply notions of good and bad, and this interpretation is often

incorrect. For example in 1977 OPEC members on net bought $7.5 billion in U.S. corporate and government securities. Explain the significance of this for U.S. payments deficits.

12. Under a system of fixed exchange rates, if the U.S. were in deficit how would the debt be adjusted? Suppose the deficit persisted; how would it be dealt with?
13. In 1977 foreign central banks spent about $28 billion trying to support the dollar, equal to half the U.S. federal budget deficit. Interpret this statement. What happens to Germany's money supply when its central bank buys dollars with marks? Does the U.S. inflation have any connection to prices in Germany?
14. Suppose the Federal Reserve expands the money supply significantly raising the dollar price of the mark. Explain this sentence. In response, the German central bank can either (a) let its assets dwindle or (b) enter the market and buy dollars. Would it likely choose course a or b? Why? Does your answer in any way relate to question 13?

Chapter 33

Economic Growth

What we call progress is the exchange of one nuisance for another.

— Havelock Ellis

PROGRESS REPORT

A. International trade was the subject of the preceding chapter. In it the importance of free trade to the consuming public was emphasized.

B. In this final chapter aspects of economic growth are examined. Growth is important to consumer well-being. It is especially important to less developed countries. Principal factors that give rise to economic growth are increases in the capital stock and improvements in technology. But economic growth and development also require the existence of a political and social climate conducive to progress. Growth rates in the U.S. have faltered in recent years, and a brief review of some proposed causes of the slow growth problem concludes this study.

In addition to full employment, stable prices, and balanced trade, is the goal of balanced economic growth. Growth is a process underdeveloped countries wish to accelerate and the already industrialized countries wish to sustain. Growth involves more jobs, more purchasing power, more goods, and more leisure—in common language, a higher standard of living. An additional benefit is a more equitable distribution of income. Despite inflation it is still possible for the living standard to rise so long as the economy's productivity can be improved.

Measuring Growth and Productivity

The preferred measurement of *economic growth* is the change in real GNP per capita. Growth is realized by increasing per capita productivity.

There are several criteria for measuring economic growth. It can be measured by the increase in GNP in constant dollars—real GNP growth. Many economists, however, prefer to measure growth as the increase in real GNP per capita. This is the increase in the material standard of living per person. In order to raise per capita GNP and per capita consumption it is necessary to improve productivity. Improved productivity means that more output is produced per unit of input.

Economic Growth and Economic Development

The study of *economic growth* concentrates on measurable variables, while the study of *economic development* also includes intangible social, legal, and political influences.

Many economists choose to make a distinction between **growth** and **development**. Economic growth analysis concentrates on variables that are identifiable and, most importantly, quantifiable, such as aggregate measures of output, income, productivity, and the allocative efficiency of resources, whether an economy is mature or underdeveloped. The variables promoting growth are often embedded in formal mathematical models from which growth paths traced through time can be derived and analyzed. The study of growth is undertaken in the hope that some new and incisive analytical generalization can be found that might help transform economic midgets into potent industrial giants.

Economic development, on the other hand, incorporates analysis of many influences that are noneconomic but nonetheless impact on economic performance—legal, cultural, and institutional factors. Unfortunately, these cannot be easily introduced as measurable variables into formal models. The total social environment that conditions the nature and direction of economic decisions is too complex.

Economists know more about economic growth than they do about economic development, since the focus of growth is narrower and less ambitious than it is for development. To have economic development there must be economic growth. But economic growth is, in principle, possible without the concurrent experience of economic development. For example, suppose a foreign based firm sends skilled personnel abroad and invests capital in an underdeveloped country to operate a tin mine. The host country collects taxes from the foreign run company, raising per capita income of the host population. However, there is no other effect on the structure of the host country outside the tin mining sector. The economic structure and relations in the nonmining sectors remain unaffected. The kind of work that is done, the way it is done, the institutional environment, property rights, and land distribution are unchanged. Moreover the additional government revenues may not trickle down to the average citizen and alter income distribution. One should, of course, realize that the distinction between growth and development is a loose and overlapping one. There is no formal, universally acceptable theory of economic development, no formalized model that can predict the optimal mix of social and institutional arrangements and values that would serve as the assured catalyst for underdeveloped economies.

CLASSICAL GROWTH THEORY

***Classical economists* were more concerned with growth and income distribution than with allocative efficiency.**

The **classical economists** of the eighteenth and nineteenth centuries isolated the basic variables of economic growth that are just as important today as they were then. The classical economists were more interested in analyzing what causes growth and its effect on income distribution, and were less concerned with the conditions for attaining resource efficiency than economists are today. Land, labor, and capital were recognized as the three major inputs in an economy's production processes. They also acknowledged the importance of technological change and the impact of the social environment. However, these were of interest insofar as they affected the use of the three classes of inputs.

Adam Smith (1723–1790) held a somewhat optimistic view of the possibilities for long-term growth. Gains in productivity (output per worker) could be realized both through the greater specialization of labor tasks and through the use of machinery. These gains follow from the application of comparative advantage in production. So long as there exist no institutional restraints on either domestic or foreign trade, the size of the market could expand. A larger market would confer lower production costs per unit of output. For example, as the number of customers expanded, a delivery truck could serve more customers, thus lowering the average cost per unit of output allocated to the truck. Two trucks could serve more than double the number of customers. A second machine could more than double output, lowering the average cost per unit of production allocated to the machines. This phenomenon of lower unit cost from expanding the size of operations—increasing all inputs together—is known as *economies of scale.*

However, in the classical system it is primarily *capital accumulation* that is the source of growth, for it allows labor to specialize. It also raises the capital-labor ratio, letting each worker use more machinery and equipment. This makes the worker more productive. Higher productivity translates into higher real income per person, and higher income encourages population growth. The goal of capital formation is profit through increased productivity, and the rate of capital formation depends upon the rate of saving. The higher the demand for capital, the higher the rate of interest. The higher the rate of interest, the greater the willingness of people to save and more capital is created.

Diminishing Returns and the Stationary State

If wage rates are very low, at a subsistence level, neither the population nor the labor force can grow. There is simply not enough food to support more life. But if there is saving and capital accumulation then labor productivity will rise and wages will rise above the subsistence level. This means that population and the labor force can and will grow in a developing community.

However, as capital accumulates its marginal productivity may fall, according to the law of diminishing returns. This states that as successive amounts of one resource (e.g. capital) are added to fixed amounts of other resources (e.g. labor or land), beyond some point the marginal or extra output will decline. Then the wage rate will stop growing, and so will population. Growth will eventually come to a slow halt with the economy phasing into a long-run stationary state. There will be no new investment but only expenditures for replacement capital. Profit, output per worker, and income per capita will remain constant. The economy will have attained and will henceforth sustain its maximum long-run standard of living, having reached the limit of its long-run productivity.

Figure 33-1 measures real income per person on the vertical axis and time on the horizontal axis. Real income and wages rise as capital accumulates and the labor force expands. At point *p*, productivity peaks and diminishing returns to capital accumulation set in. Over a long period of time productivity and profit decline with the wage rate converging to its subsistence rate. From time t_1 on, the economy remains in the stationary no-growth state. However, the subsistence level itself has risen over time since socioeconomic attitudes of what is considered to be the minimum level of well-being changed while the economy experienced its expansionary phase of progress. So the stationary state in developed economies is not one of dire poverty or of opulence. The stationary state may lie far into the future, but it is not a doomsday vision. This is not so for underdeveloped economies. For a variety of reasons their maximum potential growth consistent with their natural resource limits is not attained. Maximum growth is aborted and the stationary state is reached much

Figure 33-1

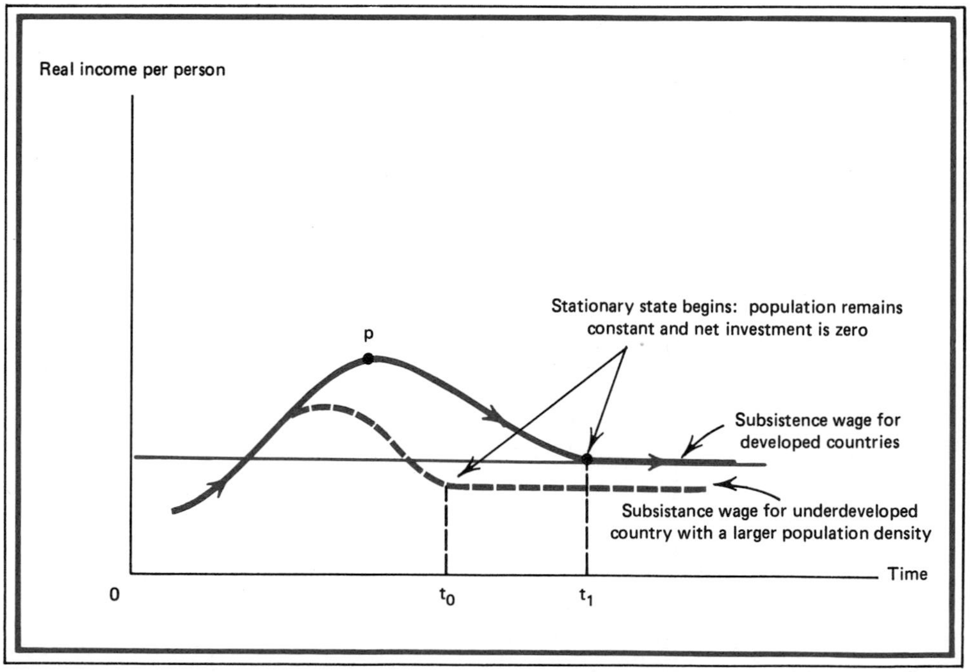

sooner while still at a hardship subsistence level. The dashed line at time t_0 indicates this.

Thomas Malthus (1766–1834) is the source of the gloomy prediction that an exploding population working with a fixed supply of food-producing land will lead to world-wide starvation. According to Malthus, diminishing marginal productivity of labor must occur as the labor-land ratio rises. That is, output per worker will decline. The rate of increased food production cannot keep up with the birth rate, falling further behind over time. For a while capital accumulation and new technology will keep the wolf from the door. However, in the long run diminishing returns to labor will occur as birth rates exceed food propagation. Using deficient U.S. data, Malthus concluded that the population would double every 25 years given a growth rate of slightly under 3 percent a year.

The spirit of Malthus still haunts some modern thinking (see box in Chapter 1). Figure 33-2 illustrates the concepts. As population increases over time and more land is worked to produce food, output per worker rises. Eventually further increases in population given limited arable land result in diminishing returns of labor. Wages decline and the subsistence level is reached at p_{t_1} where population growth is finally stopped. New technology will shift the solid real income curve to the right and extend the level of bare survival to point p_{t_2}. But beyond this point the human race cannot survive without a better balance between population growth and living standards.

David Ricardo (1772–1823) developed a growth model similar to Smith's in many of its aspects, while stressing a slightly different approach to the population versus land relation from that of Malthus. With Malthus, the fixed supply of land becomes too crowded. With Ricardo, as population grows it becomes necessary to cultivate more land of poorer and poorer quality. This

Figure 33-2

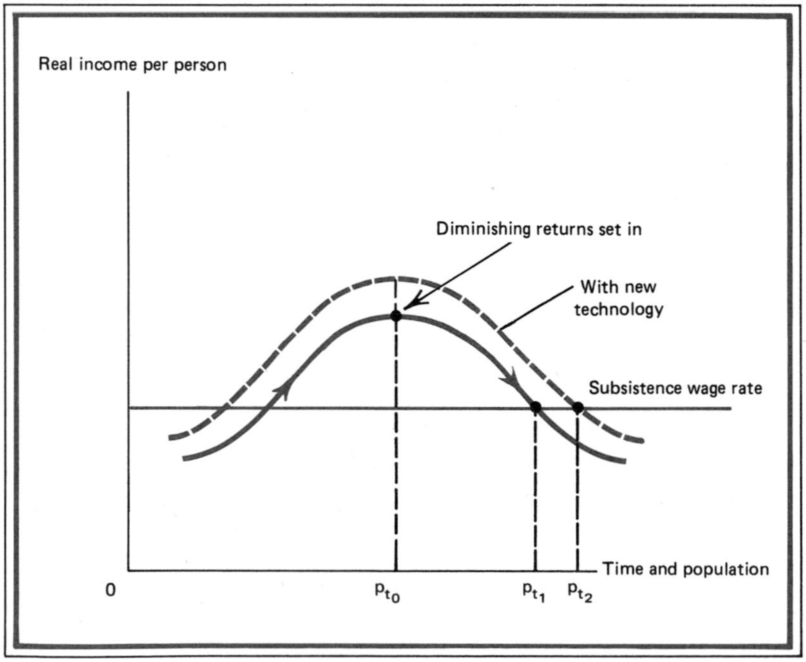

land will yield less food per acre using the same amount of capital and labor. Increased usage of inferior land, even as technology is still yielding increased returns to capital, will come to dominate the increased productivity provided by new technology, so overall productivity will begin to decline. As with Smith, Ricardo's model predicts that the economy must, like water seeking its own level, follow its path to its long-run stationary equilibrium state of stagnation similar to Figure 33-1.

However, the early stages of growth for Ricardo are much slower than for Smith, with the subsistence level variable and historically determined. Hence, the higher the subsistence wage level, the sooner is capital accumulation stopped because profits are pinched sooner.

Long-run income distribution predicted by Ricardo's model is not a happy one. The revenue dividend is divided among rent to land, wages to labor, and profit to owners of capital. In the early stages of growth land is abundant so rents are cheap. There are increasing returns to capital so profits are high and the rising demand for labor drives up the wage rates substantially above the bare subsistence level. However, as capital accumulates and the labor force expands and both work more of the inferior land, diminishing productivity of capital and labor occurs and the profit rate begins to decline. Land rents rise and the share of total revenue going to capital and labor falls. With labor and capital productivity declining further and land revenues rising, capital accumulation slows but continues until profits disappear and wages bottom out. The small minority of the population who own land end up rich, while the majority of the population, being nonlandowners, end up poor. The economy stagnates into the long-run stationary state of no growth and bare subsistence for most people—at least by prevailing socioeconomic standards.

John Mill (1806–1873) was more optimistic than Malthus and Ricardo. There need not be diminishing returns to new knowledge, so the economy need not converge to a stationary state of subsistence. With new technology and increasing economies of scale from larger markets the economy can reach its peak level of real wages before diminishing productivity becomes irreversible. Perhaps the birth rate will decline as real income increases because life styles will change. Fewer children and more education will make people more aware of alternative social horizons and will change their behavior. Hence, income per person can be maximized with the population stabilizing at point p_{t_0} in Figure 33-2. Thus the economy can enter a stationary state with living standards permanently above bare subsistence, shown by the solid line in Figure 33-3. Or new technology might allow for increases in real income per person for a fixed population, so that the living standard can continue to rise as indicated by the dashed line. Human knowledge, not just land, is also a resource base that can continue to expand and overcome diminishing returns to capital accumulation. (The earliest view of technology offsetting the limited nourishing power of the earth was espoused in 1589 by Giovanni Botero.[1])

Mill's insight has thus far proved to be correct. To the greatest extent it would appear to be new knowledge that has made it possible for real income to rise as population continued to expand. The tired economy stagnating into the stationary state has not yet appeared in the industrialized economies. It will come eventually, some warn. But a theory to be useful must be testable in a

[1] Delle cause della grandezza e magnificenza delle citta. 1589.

Figure 33-3

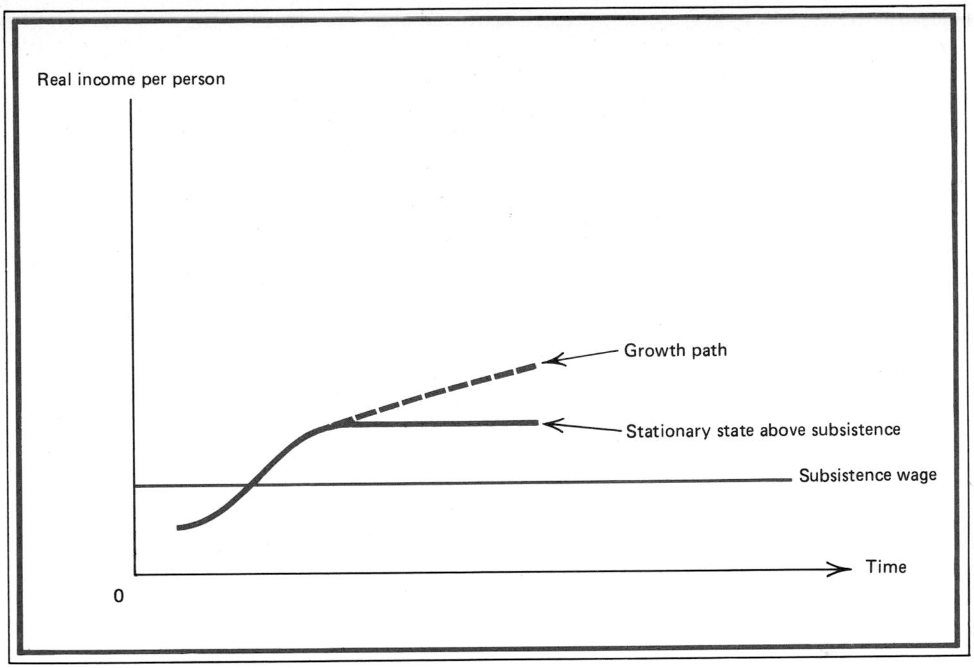

finite time period. To frame a theory in the context of an indefinite time period is to have no meaningful theory at all. A theory can never be refuted if there is no time limit on checking its predictions.

Sources of Growth

We wish now to delve further into some of the details of the sources of modern growth. There is no single input that can account for all of the increase in productivity. Land taken alone is not productive, nor is capital, nor labor in any significant degree. Although rough estimates of the contribution rendered by each input can be made, these contributions can only exist in the context of the output of the total producing unit.

Natural resources Land and the minerals contained in it are certainly important to growth. Do you think the history of the Western world would have been different if the land of Southern Europe had held the large deposits of iron or coal instead of Northern Europe? But geography alone does not explain economic growth. Israel has little water, Japan and Hong Kong have few natural resources, and Holland has a limited amount of land along with one of the world's highest population densities. Yet all of these geographic areas have growing industrialized economies. It is conceivable that in the austere environment of the Antarctic a thriving industry will some day exist, just as Holland pushed back the sea, Israel made the desert bloom, Hong Kong made the textile machines hum, and Japan produced steel from iron ore imports. It is possible that the bleak land of one of the world's ice caps could be given industrial life. Perhaps it will happen first on Alaska's North Shore. Therefore, we turn to more significant causes of growth than that attributable solely to natural resource location.

Capital accumulation Capital accumulation can make land more productive and create land where it did not exist before. Offshore wells can drill oil from the bottom of the sea, flood control can permanently reclaim lost land, and land fill can create new land.

One principal way to increase labor productivity is to have the capital stock grow faster than the labor force. That is to say, productivity will increase if the capital/labor ratio (K/L) rises (capital deepening). Building a makeshift elevator on a construction site is more productive than hiring many more workers to carry bricks up ladders. Of course, as some workers build the elevator they cannot at the same time be transporting bricks up ladders. Therefore capital formation is the process of sacrificing something now to realize greater benefits later. Moreover, capital formation releases scarce labor resources to be used elsewhere, thus increasing total output while using the same number of workers.

To raise living standards through capital creation consumers must be willing to sacrifice some current consumption—to save. Saving is a function of both economic and noneconomic variables. Capital accumulation depends principally on society's marginal propensity to save out of income. Saving is also affected by the people's willingness to bear risk, the government's tax structure, and cultural attitudes and beliefs as they relate to incentives to capture the rewards of risk and effort. Income distribution may also affect it. An economy with a few rich and the remainder poor will not be likely to see much investment.

The process of capital accumulation is self-perpetuating. The greater the capital stock, the greater the wherewithal to increase the capital stock. The process of new capital formation will shift the economy's production possibility curve outward. In Figure 33-4 the solid line shows the various packages of goods 1 and 2 that can be produced with a given resource base. But if this resource base is increased as it is if new raw material deposits are discovered, or if land is reclaimed, or if machinery is constructed, then the capacity to produce is increased. The production possibility curve will shift outward and is represented by the dashed curve in the figure. Production can then increase from point *a* to point *b* and the people can consume more of both goods. The curve will also shift out if the labor force is increased. But if this means more people to provide for, although it means more output, it may not mean more output per capita. The standard of living may or may not rise when output is increased because of a labor force that grows too fast.

Technological Change If there is an improvement in technology the production possibility curve will shift out, offsetting diminishing returns from using more capital embodying the now older technology. In this case more can be produced with *existing* resources and standards of living will rise. The rate of capital formation is often tied to technological change. There is more to growth than simply replacing old capital and building more of the same. New capital will usually incorporate new knowledge and not merely raise the K/L ratio but lower the capital/output ratio. Using more of the same kind of capital will eventually lead to diminishing returns to capital, causing the capital/output

Figure 33-4

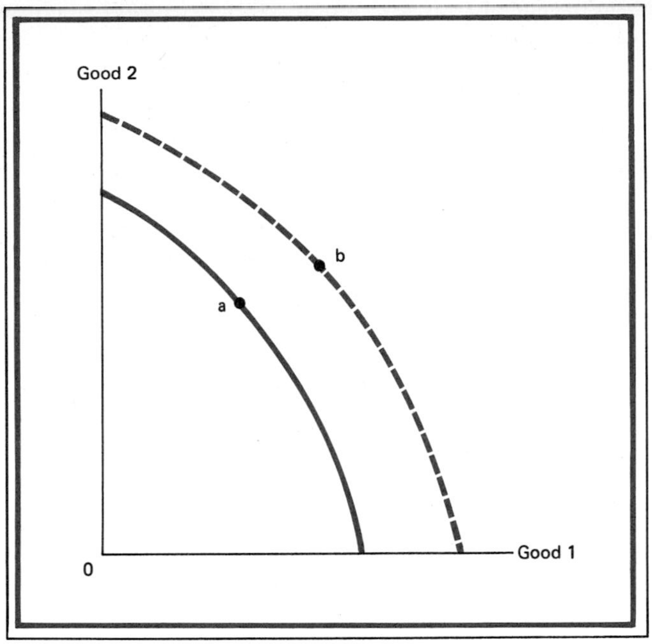

ratio to rise, since it now takes proportionately more capital to produce another unit of output. The introduction of new technology as capital accumulation occurs can offset diminishing returns and lead to a decline in the capital/output ratio, or at least prevent it from rising.

The spring of innovation flows from research and development (R&D). The larger are business profits and savings the larger the expenditures on R&D will usually be. Examples of innovation in recent years are robots on auto assembly lines, electron beams that etch complete circuits on tiny silicon chips capable of performing the data processing function of 5,000 transistors, and glass fibers that carry laser impulses containing coded telephone voice information where 25 of them take up the space of one copper cable and at half the cost, and new computers that can electronically file and recall more information using fewer workers per unit of information at a lower unit cost than manual filing and older vintage computers. It took 146 labor hours to produce a car in 1946 in Detroit; by 1990 it is estimated it will take 103 hours.

Organizational and Managerial Knowledge

Technology includes not only improvements in machinery and inventions but also improvements in organizational skills. Henry Ford did not invent the gasoline engine, nor did J. D. Rockefeller discover oil, but Ford knew how to put a car in every garage and Rockefeller how to fill the tank. Ford found ways to build cars faster and cheaper. Innovative managers and entrepreneurs (owners) find ways to reorganize production methods, cut production costs, create efficient networks of distribution outlets to expand the market, and realize economies of scale. Ways are found to upgrade workers' skills, to create subdepartments specializing in certain functions, adopt new cost-cutting techniques of inventory control, implement statistical quality control programs, and introduce time study techniques, all of which improve productivity and shift the production possibility curve outward.

Human Capital

Just as investment in new technology improves the performance of physical capital, so can human skills and knowledge—human capital—be enhanced by formal training and education in vocational and academic programs. It is no mere accident that productivity of the U.S. economy has for so long correlated so well with the increase in the average number of years of schooling of the population. The colleges and universities may have been among the most productive institutions in Western culture. More and better information is being imparted as each generation inherits the accumulated human capital of the preceding generations. Better educated people possessing a more general background of knowledge are more easily and quickly trained to perform new duties. They are more flexible in adapting to and finding different ways to solve problems by nontraditional means.

Government

Many government expenditures go toward creating social overhead capital such as roads, bridges, dams, canals, and harbors that reduce transportation costs to private firms. This confers scale economies upon them by vastly increasing the potential size of their markets. Also, to the degree that government prevents monopolies and encourages business entry and price competition, the potential for increased efficiency, output, and innovation is amplified.

Moreover, since the government is the final arbiter of property rights, the establishment of more liberal private property rights allows individuals and businesses to capture potentially larger monetary rewards crucial to both workers and entrepreneurial incentives. The government, by granting legal identity to corporations and rights of limited liability to stockholders, opens the way for corporations to play a major role in economic growth. Regulations relating to public health and safety may also bring about long-term productivity gains because a healthier worker in a more contented environment will be more productive. To the degree that government is free of corruption and the more efficient it is at crime enforcement and prevention, production and service costs to business are lower and the higher is productivity. Government reduces the business and individual uncertainties from both loss of property and personal injury. Hence, it can help attain full and efficient resource use.

Allocative Efficiency

The more flexible and mobile are resources, the more quickly can they be reallocated to more efficient uses as market conditions change. Once they are slotted, they must be able to perform to their maximum efficiency in those slots. In this regard, financial institutions have to provide huge loans to capital markets where they are most needed. Banks and other money institutions have to provide avenues to efficiency and quickly channel funds to the highest bidder and—one therefore supposes—to their best use since that is where demand is the highest. This mobility of funds and resources is the greatest when impeded least by social and religious customs, special interest power blocs, and their self-serving regulations and restrictions. Change must be permitted if there is to be progress even if that change is sometimes personally unpleasant and threatening. Thus grossly inefficient industries that cannot survive world competition should not be salvaged and subsidized unless some short-term help will yield long-term gains in allocative efficiency and productivity.

THE U.S. EXPERIENCE: PARADISE LOST?

The U.S. economy has experienced remarkable growth in this century. However since about 1967 there has been a slowdown in the growth rate, and since 1974 the growth rate has been low. During the 1950s growth averaged about 3.9 percent a year and rose to an average of 4.1 percent during the decade of the 1960s. It slowed to an annual average increase of under 2.9 percent during the 1970s and to 2.1 percent for the 1973 to 1979 years. Table 33-1 is compiled from a study by Edward F. Denison. It indicates the actual percentage growth in national income for four selected periods as well as the percentage growth attributable to the components.

TABLE 33-1
Sources of Growth in Real National Income for Selected Periods 1929–1976, in Percentages at Average Annual Rates

	1929–76	1948–73	1969–73	1973–76
National income	2.98	3.65	2.91	0.58
A. Total factor input	1.82	2.13	1.78	1.23
1. Labor: Accounting for the level of employment hours worked, and age-sex composition (excluding education)	0.95	1.01	0.64	0.10
2. Education	0.41	0.41	0.50	0.67
3. Capital accumulation	0.46	0.71	0.64	0.46
4. Land	0.00	0.00	0.00	0.00
B. Output per unit of input	1.16	1.52	1.13	−0.65
5. Advances in knowledge (N.E.C.)[1]	0.73	1.10	1.22	−0.58
6. Economies of scale	0.27	0.32	0.32	0.19
7. Improved resource allocation	0.26	0.29	0.11	−0.01
8. Irregular factors	−0.07	−0.14	−0.39	0.07
9. Other	−0.03	−0.05	−0.13	−0.32

[1]N.E.C. not elsewhere classified.
Source: Modified from Edward F. Denison, *Accounting for Slower Economic Growth: The United States in The 1970s* (Washington, D.C.: The Brookings Institution, 1979), Table 8-1, p. 104.

National income is the sum of two aggregated components. First, total factor inputs, namely the contribution to the growth in real income from the increase in the number of inputs, labor and capital, plus the adjustment for labor quality because of education. The second component is the increase in output per unit of input, or the growth in real national income from improvements in efficiency, assuming the number of inputs remains constant.

Most U.S. economic growth has derived from advances in *knowledge*, including education, scale economies, and new technology.

From 1929 to 1976, Denison's figures show that advances in **knowledge** (entry 5), if included in knowledge are the contributions to education (entry 2) as well as managerial and organizational skills that lead to scale economies (entry 6), accounted for 47.3 percent of the increase in national income. When capital accumulation is added, total contribution to growth in national income from these categories equals 62.8 percent.

Entries 1 and 2, a measure of more work done, indicate the effects on growth in real national income from changes in the number of employed people, changes in the labor participation rate, and the changing age and sex mix of the labor force, adjusted for education. Entry 3 covers inventories, nonresidential structures and equipment, and residential dwellings. Entry 4 shows that changes in land available per worker has averaged to zero. What this means is that as the labor force grows, capital improvements can operate as if to create more land by improving the quality of the land so that the yield of the land can rise. Hence the land–labor ratio can rise, or at least not decline. Thus, more crop per acre can be grown per worker or more ore mined per acre. Of course, land productivity will decline as natural resources disappear in one area and equally rich sources are not found elsewhere. Entry 6, economies of scale, refers to the rise in output per unit of input made possible by changes in the size of the market as mentioned earlier. Under entry 7, resource allocation, Denison measured the effects on efficiency of changes in resource mobility mostly related to the decline of surplus farm labor, including inefficient nonfarm self-employment and unpaid labor in small, inefficient family businesses. Item 8, irregular factors, measures the impact of random or unsystematic changes from weather, labor strikes, lockouts, and from changes in demand over the business cycle, for example the tendency of firms to stockpile skilled workers during downturns in the economy, which causes wide fluctuations in the measurement of labor productivity over the cycle. The last category, *other*, consists for the most part of adjustments in productivity for pollution abatement, worker safety and health, dishonesty and crime, and the minor effect of the changing ratio of occupied to vacant dwellings, a kind of idle capacity measure of housing capital.

Some Observations

The data for 1973–1976 are disturbing. From 1929 to 1976 average annual growth in real income was 2.98 percent, of which 1.16 was attributable to productivity increases. Growth in real income was only 0.58 percent in the 1973–1976 period, with a decline of −0.65 percent in productivity (category B). Advances in knowledge and scale economies, accounted for 1.00 of the annual percentage increase of 2.98 in growth from 1929 to 1976, whereas in 1973–1976 their contributions were a negative share (−.39) of total income. The large drop in advances from knowledge (new technology and R&D) of

−0.58 was overcome by the large increase in the impact of education of 0.67 with some help from capital accumulation of 0.46. The increase in work done, netting out education, was quite small. When work done is combined with advances in knowledge the decline in the 1973–1976 period was substantial. It continued into 1981 though data are not available in the table.

WHY THE DECLINE?

Declining U.S. productivity since 1973 has been attributed to inflation, declining basic research, taxes, inappropriate stabilizing policies, the changing age-sex mix of the labor force, overregulation by the government, and short-sighted corporate management and labor unions.

If the U.S. is phasing into Kondratieff's downturn described in Chapter 28, thus beginning the next 50-to-60-year-long cycle, what has been the cause of the 1973–1980 sluggishness in growth and productivity? Has the U.S. economy reached the peak of its maturity to enter its long-term glide path before being grounded in the stagnation of the stationary state predicted by most of the classical economists? Denison cannot pinpoint the decline to a single source, and attributes it to the cumulative effects of several things much as the nickel and dime repairs on an ailing auto create a large total repair bill. Different writers emphasize different sources with, however, overlapping in a few categories—slowness in creating new technology that lengthens the average age of the use of existing capital, taxes, increasing government regulations, inappropriate stabilization policies, energy prices, a falling export share, sagging profit rates, and the changing age-sex composition of the work force with more untrained young people and older women entering the labor market.

Research and development (R&D) in the U.S. as a percentage of GNP has dropped from about 2.91 percent in 1965 to an estimated low of 2.3 percent in 1980. The decline has been greatest in basic research. When the U.S. space program ended in the late 1960s after the successful moon shots, federal money for basic research going to industry and the universities dropped sharply, despite a small increase in expenditures by the private sector, as more funds were shifted into welfare programs. Foreigners are applying for an increasing share of U.S. patent rights. Some economists such as Denison believe the R&D argument is overplayed, maintaining that the possibility for new technological discoveries is drying up. Major breakthroughs in knowledge are in a holding pattern, at least for the time being. There has also been a relative decline in the brightest students majoring in engineering and the sciences, and in engineering relative to science. The largest increase in enrollments are occurring in business, law, and vocational skills consistent with the slowness in growth of technical manpower.

Table 33-1 shows lower rates of *capital accumulation since 1973*. This is consistent with the data on the U.S. saving rate. *Personal saving* in the U.S. hovered around 6 percent until 1975 and declined to around 3.4 percent in 1980. This contrasts to average household saving of about 20 percent in Japan and 14 percent in West Germany, both strong growth economies. By comparison, investment in the U.S. in plant and equipment as a percentage of GNP has fallen from about 10 percent in 1970 to less than 8 percent in 1979, in Japan from 21 percent to 15 percent, and West Germany from about 10 to 9 percent.

A justifiable concern for the environment, health and safety standards, and affirmative action has brought with it an avalanche of new *government regulations* that have raised production and legal costs, increased employment for attorneys and bureaucrats, and lowered productivity. Most economists believe these things have been a factor, particularly where additional costs are less than the additional benefits to society. Duplication of rules and agency overlaps have resulted, where rules of one agency contradict or are otherwise incompatible with rules of another agency. Thus the Environmental Protection Agency (EPA) pushes for cleaner air while the Department of Energy encourages firms to switch from clean oil to dirtier coal. Or, cars have to be safer but lighter to be more fuel efficient. The effect is to impede resource efficiency by preventing companies from substituting one input or process for another without costly compliance and legal actions. Overall, the major effect of the newer regulations, often appearing suddenly and unpredictably, is to greatly increase business uncertainty, which results in costly delays in starting up new capital formation.

Furthermore, the impact of *government policies* such as price controls, taxation, depreciation, welfare, defense, and reduction in research support have discouraged saving and investment and encouraged consumption. Budget deficits rise to cure unemployment and stagnation, causing *inflation* that is then followed by tight monetary policy that drives up the interest rate. The higher inflation rate combines with higher marginal tax rates to encourage consumption and reduce the incentive to save because inflation erodes the value of savings, imparting some accidental truth to the pitches of television hucksters "to buy now at reduced prices and save." The lower savings combined with higher interest rates and heavier government borrowing may have discouraged private capital formation. And what of rapid *inflation* and its negative influence on investment? Is it due mostly to oil prices? For sure, the devastating decline in U.S. growth and productivity from 1973 to 1980 correlates with the oil embargo of 1973, the recession of 1973–1975, and the periodic surge in crude oil prices since. But is it the major cause of productivity decline? There is no unanimous agreement here. Denison believes the effect is small, arguing that the major impact comes from the lag in substituting less-energy-using capital equipment and in converting to cheaper energy sources. Others believe the effect of OPEC oil prices is a major and permanent cause in productivity decline since 1973, that it has reduced potential national income by 5 or 6 percent. However, the decline in productivity for all other major industrialized nations has also dropped substantially since 1973, except for West Germany, as shown in Table 33-2. And yet West Germany has had the lowest inflation rate among the free industrialized countries, and imports a much larger percentage of its oil than does the U.S. Thus, many economists contend that government fiscal, monetary, and regulatory policies are a greater factor than rising OPEC oil prices in both declining real income per capita and labor productivity.

Another sector that has been partly blamed for the disappointing decline in advances in knowledge and its importance for declining productivity of the U.S. economy is *corporate management*. The criticism is that corporate managers have been short-sighted—more concerned with quarterly profit targets and fast payoffs rather than long-term maximization and larger but delayed returns from greater expenditures in basic research. Hyping new products before they are commercially ready results in long-term losses because of defects, break-

TABLE 33-2
Percent Annual Change in Productivity for Selected Periods and Countries

	1960–1966	1967–73	1973–1979
Japan	8.5	10.0	4.2
Italy	7.3	6.6	3.3
West Germany	5.8	5.0	5.0
France	5.4	5.7	5.1
Canada	4.3	4.9	2.8
U.S.	4.2	2.9	2.1
United Kingdom	4.1	3.8	0.6

Source: U.S. Dept. of Labor, Bureau of Labor Statistics.

downs, costly recalls, and sales without stamina. Some experienced executives contend that many of the new MBAs major mostly in marketing and finance, since these have been the two fastest tracks to the top. They are not independent entrepreneurs but team players more interested in security than in dreams that challenge the spirit and the imagination, and that call forth the sacrifices that some day could make dreams real.

Managers often join with security-minded unions in supporting government subsidization of business losers because they are not competitive enough to survive on their own. The economies of England and Sweden have already been hurt by these policies in the last decade, and insofar as unions prevent efficient resource reallocation and input flexibility they too must share some of the blame for the decline of U.S. productivity.

Growth: Possible? Desirable?

The debate over economic growth and the ecology sometimes seems more popular than Monday Night Football and weekend rock telecasts. Do the dire conclusions of the classical economists and the doomsday predictions of some modern computer-simulated models indicate that we have finally come to the end of the line with economic growth? And if not, is it in our interest to continue to grow? The prediction is that natural resources will be depleted—oil early in the twenty-first century, coal 200 years or so later, and with the population bomb someday land itself. Doomsdayers argue that improved technology and input substitutes cannot stave off the inevitable much longer. The result will be chaos as a grasping population competes for diminishing resources.

Suppose continued growth is possible. Is it a possibility devoutly to be wished? Some say no because GNP does not accurately reflect, if at all, the quality of life. In the past it did. But the economy has now matured and further growth threatens the quality of life. As income per person rises and population grows, the result is more goods and more congestion that will create more regulation, more alienation and the loss of the sense of community as individuals and special interests fight harder for their preferences both private and social. Maximizing the consumption of goods ignores, it is argued, the intangibles of life: what the economist Mishan calls "the inevitable loss of authentic human experience."[2]

Is the authentic life diminished by an environment where advertising creates a new level of wants for supposedly unnecessary things when more has to be done to meet existing needs? Economic growth is based on improving efficiency, and according to critics in order to satisfy the artificially created demands of the compulsive consumer who can buy everything but contentment while overloading his psyche and the environment. The irony may be that the overindulged consumer may generate equally compulsive antisocial behavior inappropriate to sustaining an efficient system that allowed for that higher consumption.

The economist Kenneth Boulding likens the view that more consumption and more production are by definition good to the "cowboy economy"—those untamed societies of romantic, exploitive recklessness, where the modern industrial cowboy consumers and producers ride off into the next resource sunset once the current resource site has been wasted.[3] Mishan agrees and argues that continued growth in the West can no longer bring the good life. "The flame is not worth the candle."

As Dostoevski once said "Man is an ungrateful biped." In this vein, economist Robert Solow of MIT takes a more orthodox, less pessimistic attitude. Solow's response to the doomsdayers notes that there are chronic complainers now as in the past, and they will exist in the future. If growth continues, how can we know if people were happier yesteryear when per capita consumption was lower than 30 or 50 years from now when income per capita will be higher? They will simply be dissatisfied about new things. Furthermore, the problem of growth and the problem of the environment are separate issues. Solow says, "One gets the notion that you favor growth if you are the sort of person whose idea of heaven is to drive 90 miles an hour down a six-lane highway reading billboards, in order to pollute the air over some crowded lake with the exhaust from twin 100-horsepowered outboards, and whose idea of food is Cocoa Krispies. On the other hand, to be against growth is to be a granola-eating, backpacking, transcendental-meditating canoe freak."[4] However, pollution would occur even without growth. It is really a matter of redefining property rights so that the full costs of pollution are paid, thus removing the gains garnered from producing at less than full social cost. Specifically, the smoke-producing factory either pays to install antipollution equipment, or is fined. Similarly, drivers pay more for cars with antipollution filtering systems.

In a world of scarcity there are always tradeoffs. We want hospitals, universities, and wilderness areas for backpacking. But hospitals are heavy users of fuel and electricity. And their sophisticated equipment contains rare metals that require energy-intensive processes to convert the ores into finished products. Universities are heavy consumers of paper which requires the cutting of

[2]E. J. Mishan, "Growth and Antigrowth: What Are the Issues?" *Challenge*, Nov./Dec. 1974.
[3]Kenneth E. Boulding, "The Economics of the Coming Spaceship Earth," from Henry Jarrett, ed., *Environmental Quality in a Growing Economy* (Baltimore: Johns Hopkins Press, for Resources of the Future, Inc., 1966).
[4]Robert M. Solow, "Is the End of the World at Hand? What the Growth vs. No-Growth Business is Really All About," *Challenge*, March/April 1973.

forests. Backpackers also require equipment that uses light metals such as aluminum, a high energy using industry. Over the last two decades in the U.S. estimates are that only 10 percent of the increase in energy consumption is the result of population growth. The other 90 percent is attributed to the larger per capita consumption of energy deriving from the greater use of electric hair-dryers, microwave ovens, air conditioners, dish washers, clothes dryers, and so on—so much a part of a better material standard of living.

Zero Economic Growth

While some people have championed a policy of zero economic growth (ZEG), most economists hold that ZEG is not the best of all possible solutions. ZEG has undesirable income distribution effects. Economic growth has been the route for the poor to raise their living standards and to attain, if not income parity, at least a position of less inequality. Nor can the U.S. help underdeveloped countries of the world by producing and consuming less, but through helping those countries to produce by improving its own productivity. The world pie is not fixed; it can grow. Poorer countries cannot be helped by the U.S. adopting a goal of ZEG and asking its people to share more of their existing wealth. How can people be made to agree to that? Who is more dangerous to social and political stability—a person with nothing to lose or one with everything to lose? As more people desire to enter the labor force under a policy of ZEG, where will the new jobs come from? Job sharing will cause a decline in efficiency. Who will make the sacrifice, and will it create a less competitive society?

If acceptable living standards are to survive with ZEG then the logical conclusion is that zero population growth (ZPG) is the adjunct to ZEG. How is a ZPG policy to be enforced in a free society?

ZEG would require rationing goods just as ZPG requires rationing children. Individual desires would clash with government regulations, respect for the law would falter, and its proscriptions violated. ZEG is a dismal blueprint for the future, one of class warfare and overall despair, a world without hope. There should be growth, but we should balance social benefits against social costs when considering new technologies and new policies.

CHAPTER SUMMARY

Among the goals of stabilization policy is economic growth. One measure of growth is the increase in real GNP per period. A better measurement is real GNP per capita. Production growth can be achieved by simply using more inputs. It can also be realized by increasing per capita productivity, that is, more output per unit of input.

Economists often distinguish between economic development and economic growth. The study of growth concentrates on changes in measurable variables like employment, output, and productivity. Development, however, also includes the analysis of nonquantifiable factors, the intangible influences of social, legal, and political forces on the quantifiable growth variables. Growth variables are often embedded in formal, mathematical models. Thus the focus of growth is narrower than for development. To have development there must be growth, but growth is possible without development because even though total income may go up, no institutional changes may follow from it.

The classical economists from Adam Smith to John Mill isolated the important variables of economic growth that still apply today. They were more concerned with growth and income distribution than with analyzing the nature of allocative efficiency.

The essential ingredients in the growth recipe they stressed were capital formation, new technology, population growth, the division or specialization of labor, and the concept of diminishing returns to capital, labor, and land.

They understood that capital was productive and that raising the capital-labor ratio increased labor productivity, leading to both rising profits and wages. However, as more capital was employed per worker, diminishing returns to capital would eventually occur. Namely, the additional capital would lead to successively smaller and smaller improvements in productivity, eventually slowing profit and wage growth. New technology would for a long time offset, even dominate, diminishing returns, but a point would be reached where diminishing returns would eventually prevail. The economy would cease to grow and would gradually slide into a no-growth long-run stationary state where of necessity population growth would cease. The stationary state would end up with wages at the subsistence level. This level is determined by prevailing socioeconomic standards. That is, population growth by choice will stop at a minimum living standard in line with socially determined preferences. However, for underdeveloped economies, the subsistence wage would be one of stark, bare subsistence.

According to Malthus, all societies face bitter poverty if they do not curb their sexual appetites. Population growth proceeds much faster than new technology can make the limited land yield more food. Given limited land, there will be diminishing returns to labor in food production as the work force grows. Only starvation will stop the population expansion.

The predictions of both Ricardo and Smith are less gloomy than Malthus, with Smith more optimistic than Ricardo. Ricardo believed that the early stages of growth will occur more slowly than Smith thought, and that undesirable extremes in income distribution will result in the long run.

Ricardo said that as incomes rise population is encouraged to grow, and increasing amounts of inferior land have to be cultivated. Total income is distributed among labor wages, profit to owners of capital, and rent to landowners. As more inferior land is tilled, land rents rise but labor and capital productivity declines, causing a relative decline in wages and profits. The result is that rents of landowners will come to represent an ever increasing share of total national income.

John Mill was the most optimistic. People, by using foresight and intelligence, and in response to rising income during the expansionary phase of growth, could change their life styles and choose to reduce population growth before diminishing returns set in. They could therefore attain a long-run steady state at a level considerably above the subsistence level, or—by halting population growth early enough and continuing to discover new technologies—actually sustain long-term rising real incomes.

Economic growth in the U.S. began to slow significantly in the latter 1960s, and has worsened since 1973. Edward Denison's massive study measured the change in real income and productivity for the U.S. covering 1929 to 1976. He divided the sources of U.S. economic growth into two broad categories—growth in the amount of total factor inputs and growth derived from improvements in productivity of those inputs. The first category measures the increase in the amount of capital, of workers and hours worked, and the work force age-sex mix. Adjustments for worker education were included. The second category, the increase in output per unit of input, includes advances in knowledge or technology; economies of scale, i.e., the influence of managerial and organization knowledge; more efficient resource allocation; and the impact of pollution abatement, regulations, crime, and dishonesty.

The major part of U.S. economic growth has derived from a combination of education and scale economies with new technology. Since 1973, except for education, growth derived from economies of scale and new technology has dropped sharply. The more narrowly defined entry, advances in knowledge, actually indicates a negative rate.

Denison believes the decline in the growth rate cannot be traced to one cause alone; it is an accumulation of many small effects. Others disagree, arguing that rising energy prices and the inflation they helped to accelerate play a big part. Most economists believe there has been too little spending on basic research and too much growth in government regulations, often of the wrong kind. Others trace much of the productivity decline to the changing age-sex mix, with more less skilled and less trained teenagers and women entering the labor force; they see this effect as only temporary until these workers acquire more experience and skills.

Criticism has been aimed at short-sighted corporate managers who seek fleeting profits—and quick promotions—and neglect to build solidly for long-run growth and profits. Also at fault are security obsessed labor unions with their inflexible and costly work rules that reduce efficiency and make U.S. products less competitive in world markets.

Some people question the benefits of any further growth. Their position is that potential resource depletion is now a reality. Also, the quality of life will no longer be improved by growth as it was in the past. To increase consumption of what are now in many cases unnecessary goods is to overload both the environment and the human psyche, thus diminishing authentic human experience.

Others respond that it is not possible to compare the levels of human happiness across generations. More importantly, growth and pollution are really different issues. Pollution existed before massive technology and has always arisen because of improperly defined property rights. To seek zero growth is to shut off opportunities for the poor, since economic growth has been the major path to their upward mobility. And if zero economic growth is to be reached by zero population growth, who will enforce it and how will it be done without driving citizens to reject and rebel against government infringements on their personal lives and choices?

QUESTIONS

1. Why the dismal conclusions in the writings of the classical economists? How is the law of diminishing returns to be overcome? Can it be, if it is a law? Reread the definition recalling that scientific predictions are conditional statements based on given assumptions. What are the assumptions?
2. A quotation from the *International Teamster*, March 1979, page 17 reads, "While it is true that technology spurs productivity, it is equally true that the progress of such change eventually goes full circle and begins to retard productivity." Can you state in economic terms what the quotation concludes? Does it follow that economic growth must eventually stop?
3. The quotation in Question 2 continues, "When the product becomes standardized, as to production lines, unskilled labor replaces masterly hands. From then on it's simply a matter of business management as to whether or not a manufacturing enterprise continues to improve its productivity." In what line in Table 33-1 does this statement imply lies the major source of further productivity? Is one to con-

clude that in an advanced technological system there is no place for "masterly hands"? Explain.

4. After the deaths of Elvis Presley and John Lennon the news media rhapsodized about their influence on changing peoples' lives. Do you believe they had more impact on your life than Thomas Edison's invention of the moving picture, Henry Ford's introduction of the moving assembly line, Enrico Fermi's construction of the first controlled nuclear chain reaction, the medical scientists' development of the birth control pill, and the invention of the wheel? That is, do you think social change precedes or follows from technological change? If you are not sure, read question 5.
5. So-called primitive societies have also created music and complex social structures, as have industrialized societies like the U.S. Yet the former are static and the latter dynamic. What single factor clearly distinguishes these societies (aside from the one having and the other not having a written language). What relationship do you think literacy has to the economic growth that can be located in Table 33-1?
6. Consider the following example by Geoffrey Moore. Assume that in year 1 the population of a town is 100 and that 50 people are employed producing 500 widgets a year. Suppose that in year 2 the town's 10 high school graduates take jobs in the widget factory for the first time, but the 10 new workers only produce 7 widgets each a year.
   a. What is the town's per capita widget production in year 1? In year 2? Productivity per worker in years 1 and 2?
   b. Has the town's productivity declined? Is this a bad thing? Why not? Would you predict that if employment were to stay at 60 in year 3, per worker productivity would remain the same? Why not?
   c. To what lines in Table 33-1 does this problem best apply?
7. The U.S. population is expected to continue to grow more slowly over the next 30 years, hence growth in the size of the market will likely also slow down. What specific entry in Table 33-1 will be affected by this prediction, if true?
8. Labor union officials have been known to laud the union contribution to U.S. economic growth since World War II. Yet since that time nonfarm labor union membership has declined from about 37 percent to under 23 percent. Nonunion wages in the U.S. are higher than union wages in many other industrialized countries. Employment and production in U.S. unionized industries such as steel and autos continue to decline. If the union claims are correct, what line(s) in Table 33-1 might support these claims? What lines would suggest other causes? Does it follow that if poor countries were to unionize their work forces prosperity would follow?
9. What implication does a policy of zero economic growth have for the young?
10. Robert Solow says economic growth and pollution are two separate issues. This seems to defy everything we have heard about the pollution problem. Why does he conclude this?

Index

G

H

I

J

K

L

Q

R

S